D1756742

Séfer haḤinnuch סֵפֶר הַחִנּוּךְ

THE BOOK OF [MITZVAH] EDUCATION

סֵפֶר הַחִנּוּךְ

כנראה מאת רבנו פנחס
(אחיו של רבנו אהרן) הלוי
איש ברצלונה

מהדורה מנוקדת, מבוססת על
ההוצאה הראשונה (וונציה רפ״ג)
בהשוואה עם ארבעה כתבי־יד עתיקים,
עם תרגום והערות באנגלית, מאת
אלחנן וונגרוב

כרך רביעי: ספר במדבר, וספר דברים חלק ראשון

הוצאת ספרים פלדהיים
ירושלים / ניו יורק / תשמ״ח

Séfer haḤinnuch

꧁꧁꧁꧁꧁꧁꧁ THE BOOK OF [MITZVAH] EDUCATION ꧁꧁꧁꧁꧁

evidently by Rabbi Pinḥas
(brother of Rabbi Aaron) haLévi
of Barcelona

the Hebrew text (with *n'kudoth*)
based on the first edition (Venice 1523)
compared with four old manuscripts,
with a translation and notes, by
Charles Wengrov

VOLUME IV: NUMBERS, & DEUTERONOMY, PART 1

꧁꧁꧁꧁꧁꧁꧁꧁꧁꧁꧁꧁꧁꧁꧁꧁꧁꧁꧁꧁꧁

FELDHEIM PUBLISHERS
Jerusalem / New York / 5748 (1988)

כל הזכויות שמורות
למוציאים לאור
הוצאת ספרים פלדהיים בע״מ
ירושלים

First published 1988
ISBN 0-87306-457-7
(The set: ISBN 0-87306-145-4)

Philipp Feldheim Inc.
200 Airport Executive Park
Spring Valley, NY 10977

Feldheim Publishers Ltd
POB 6525 / Jerusalem, Israel

Printed in Israel

contents

מכתב ברכה

ממרן הגאון ר׳ מרדכי גיפטר שליט״א

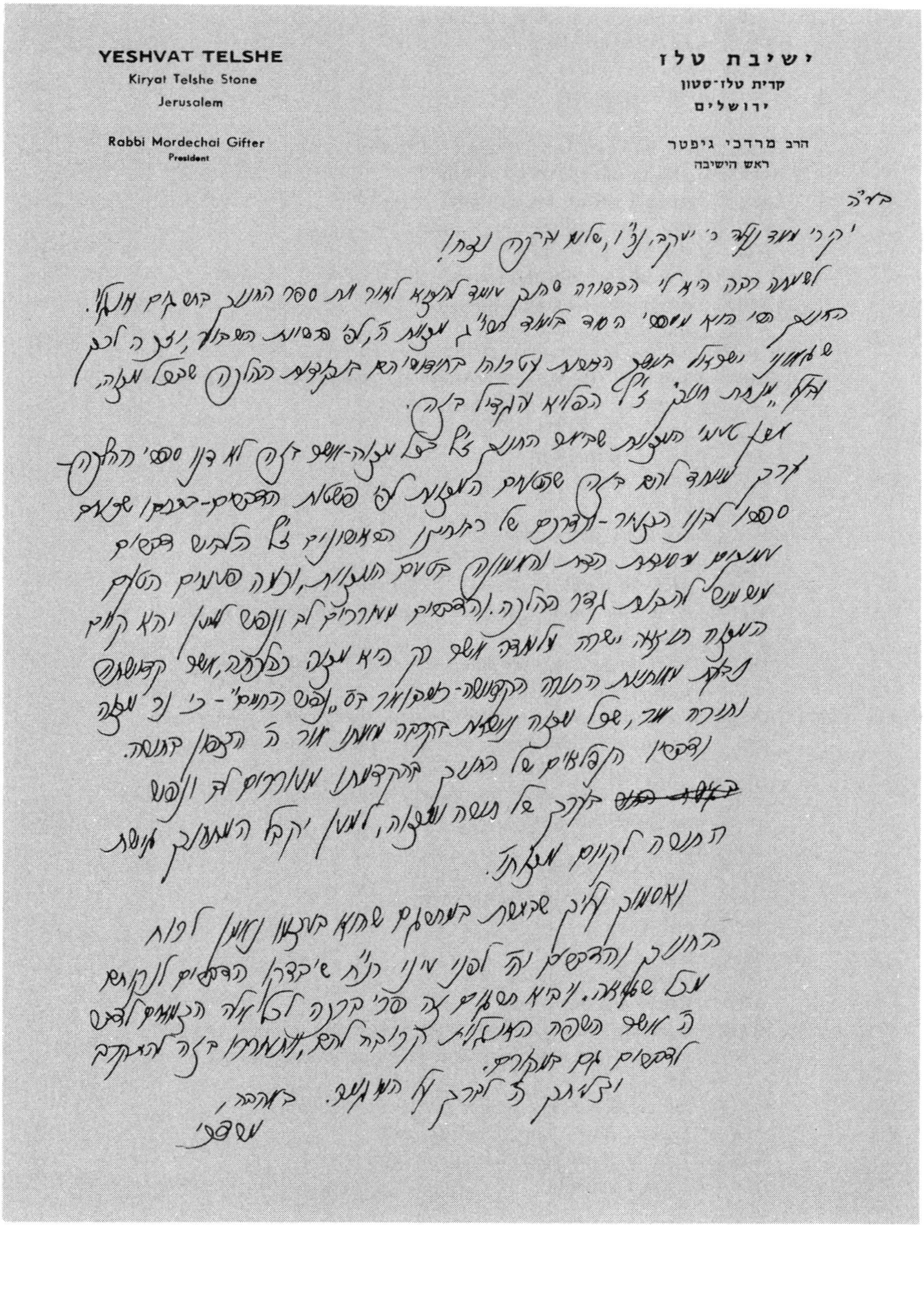

YESHVAT TELSHE
Kiryat Telshe Stone
Jerusalem

Rabbi Mordechai Gifter
President

ישיבת טלז
קרית טלז-סטון
ירושלים

הרב מרדכי גיפטר
ראש הישיבה

ב"ה

ידידי מאד נעלה ר' יעקב, נ"י, שלום וברכה נצח!

לשמחה רבה היא לי הבשורה שכת"ר עומד להוציא לאור את ספר החינוך בתרגום אנגלי.
החינוך הרי הוא מספרי היסוד בלמוד תרי"ג מצות ה', לפי פשטות המקרא, וזכה לכך
שגאוני ישראל הגדולים עטרוהו בחידושיהם בקביעות ההלכה שבכל מצוה,
ובפרט "מנחת חינוך" זצ"ל הפליא להגדיל בזה.

ואף טעמי המצוות שביאר החינוך ז"ל בכל מצוה - אשר בזה לא דנו ספרי ההלכה -
דרכו שעמד לרוב בזה שפירש טעמי המצוות לפי פשטות הכתובים - כדרכו שכתב
ספרו לבני הנעורים - כדרכם של רבותינו הראשונים ז"ל לבאר הכתובים
מתוך עומק דברי הדת והאמונה בטעם המצוות, ורבה פעמים הטעם
משמש להבנת גדר ההלכה. והדברים מעוררים לב ונפש למען יהא קיום
המצוה בשמחה ושירה עלמודה אשר רק היא מצוה כהלכה, אשר קדושתה
כלולה בתורתה התורה הקדושה - כמבואר בס' "נפש החיים" - כי כל מצוה
נרתקת אור, שכל מצוה נושאת בקרבה מעתה אור ה' הצפון בתורה.

ודברי הקדמות של החינוך בהקדמתו מעוררים לב ונפש
~~[illegible]~~ בדרך של תשובה ושמחה, למען יקבל המעיין מושג
התורה לקיום מצותיה.

ואסיים ברכה שבעזרת המתפלל שהוא ברצון נאמן לשפוך
החינוך והדברים גם לבני עמנו ר"ח שיבדקו הדברים לנקודת
עם שלמה. ויביא תשועה [illegible] ברכה לגאולה הגמורה
ה' אשר השפה האנגלית קרובה להם, ומאורו יבא להתקרב
לדברים גם המקרא.

ויזכנו ה' לברך את העולם. באהבה,
מרדכי

List of abbreviations, etc.

§   numbered section or *mitzvah*
ad loc.   *ad locum*, at the place
b.   *ben*, the son of
cf.   *confer*, compare
col.   column
Deut.   the Book of Deuteronomy (*d'varim*)
ed.   edition of; edited by; editor
e.g.   *exempli gratia*, for example
et al.   *et alii*, and others (i.e. people)
etc.   *et cetera*, and others
et seq.   *et sequentes*, and the following
Ex., Exod. the Book of Exodus (*sh'moth*)
ff.   and pages following
Gen.   the Book of Genesis (*b'réshith*)
Guide   Rambam (R. Moshe b. Maimon, Maimonides), *Guide of the Perplexed* (*Moreh N'vuchim*)
ibid.   *ibidem*, at the (same) place
idem   the same (person)
i.e.   *id est*, that is
l.   line
Lev.   the Book of Leviticus (*va-yikra*)
loc. cit. *loco citato*, in the place cited
MdRSbY   *Midrash d'Rabbi Shimon b. Yoḥai* (ed. Epstein-Melamed)
MH   R. Joseph Babad, *Minḥath Ḥinnuch* (commentary on the *Ḥinnuch*)
MhG   *Midrash haGadol*, anthology of Midrash, etc. compiled in Yemen, 14th century
MS (plural, MSS) *manuscriptum*, manuscript (plural, *manuscripta*, manuscripts)
MT   Rambam (R. Moshe b. Maimon, Maimonides), *Mishneh Torah* (also known as *Yad Ḥazakah*)
MY   R. Yitzḥak *ha-kohén* Aronovsky, *Minḥath Yitzḥak* (commentary on the *Ḥinnuch*)
n.s.   new series
Num.   the Book of Numbers (*ba-midbar*)
op. cit. *opera citato*, in the work cited
o.s.   old series
p. / pp.   page / pages
q.v.   *quod vide*, which see
R.   Rabbi, Rabbénu, Rav
ShM   Rambam (Maimonides), *Séfer haMitzvoth*
sic   so, thus (i.e. something that looks peculiar is so in the source cited)
s.v.   *sub verbo*, *sub voce*, under the word (or words)
TB   *Talmud Bavli*, Babylonian Talmud
TJ   *Talmud Yerushalmi*, Jerusalem Talmud
viz.   *videlicet*, namely

Séfer haḤinnuch סֵפֶר הַחִנּוּךְ

THE BOOK OF [MITZVAH] EDUCATION

ספר במדבר

ספר דברים

סדרות דברים — ראה

NUMBERS

DEUTERONOMY

SIDROTH D'VARIM – RE'ÉH

סֵפֶר בְּמִדְבַּר סִינַי

🕎 🕎 🕎 🕎 🕎 🕎 🕎

סֵדֶר רִאשׁוֹן אֵין בּוֹ מִצְוָה לְחֶשְׁבּוֹנֵנוּ

🕎 נָשֹׂא

יֵשׁ בָּהּ ז׳ מִצְווֹת עֲשֵׂה וִי״א מִצְווֹת לֹא־תַעֲשֶׂה

[מִצְוַת שַׁלּוֹחַ טְמֵאִים חוּץ לְמַחֲנֵה־שְׁכִינָה]

שסב לְשַׁלֵּחַ הַטְּמֵאִים חוּץ לְמַחֲנֵה־שְׁכִינָה, שֶׁנֶּאֱמַר: צַו אֶת בְּנֵי יִשְׂרָאֵל וִישַׁלְּחוּ מִן הַמַּחֲנֶה כָּל צָרוּעַ וְכָל זָב וְכֹל טָמֵא לָנָפֶשׁ; וְיָדוּעַ הָיָה לָהֶם בַּמִּדְבָּר עַד

* As MH notes, however, *Halachoth G'doloth* posits one negative precept as derived from the first *sidrah*: Prefacing its main text is a listing of passages in the Pentateuch that are to be considered the sources of the 613 *mitzvoth* which, by Rabbinic tradition, were given at Sinai. Among the prohibitions punishable by whiplashes (*malkoth*) we find (ed. Warsaw 1875, 3a col. 2) *they shall not go in to see as are swallowed* (Numbers 4:20, literal translation), which is in the first *sidrah*. Similarly, a few lines below this we read, "a Levite *shall not serve any more*" (Numbers 8:25), which is in the third *sidrah*.

In ShM however (third root principle), Rambam states that the 613 must be *mitzvoth* which apply for all time, and not for one period of our history alone (ed. Heller, p. 9 col. 1; voweled ed. Kafeḥ, p. 14): For the phrase of the Talmudic Sages about the 613, "given at Sinai," means that they were given for all time, even though temporary commandments were also given there to Moses our Master. And Rambam continues (ed. Heller, 9a2–9b1; ed. Kafeḥ, p. 15): "Yet someone else erred about this main principle too, and he listed, when pressed by the need [to find all 613], *and they shall not go in to see when the holy objects are swallowed* (literal translation); and he also listed [the passage] *shall not serve any more*, concerning the Levites. Yet these too apply not for all generations but only [of old] in the wilderness. Although they [the Sages] said that 'it alludes to one who steals a *kasvah*,' it is clear enough that they said 'it is a hint' [to tell us] that the plain meaning of the verse is not about this matter. Nor is it in the category of

NUMBERS

༚ ༚ ༚ ༚ ༚ ༚ ༚ ༚

In the first *sidrah* there is no precept by our reckoning.*

sidrah naso
(Numbers 4:21–7:89)

There are seven positive and eleven negative precepts in it.

[THE PRECEPT OF SENDING THE RITUALLY
UNCLEAN OUTSIDE THE CAMP OF THE SHECHINAH]

362 to send the ritually unclean out of the camp of the *shechinah* (Divine Presence): as it is stated, *Command the Israelites that they shall put out of the camp everyone afflicted with* tzara'ath, *and everyone with a discharge, and everyone unclean through the dead* (Numbers 5:2). It was known to them in the wilderness where the boundary of the camp of

transgressions that incur death at Heaven's hands, as it is made clear in the Tosefta (see K'réthoth i and Z'vaḥim xii) and in Sanhedrin (TB 81b)."

In the Mishnah (Sanhedrin ix 6) we read, "If someone steals a *kasvah* (or *kisvah*), zealots may strike him down." The *g'mara* (TB 81b) explains that *kasvah* (a vessel of libation, per Numbers 4:7) denotes any holy vessel of the Temple service; and it asks, "Where is this hinted at [in Scripture]?" The reply is Numbers 4:20, *and they shall not go in to see when the holy objects are swallowed, and* [thus] *die*.

Hence the plain meaning of this verse is that when the *mishkan* (Tabernacle) had to be moved in the Israelites' journey through the wilderness, the Levites of the branch of Kohath were not to come and take the holy objects and vessels, to transport them, until the *kohanim* had completely covered and wrapped them ("swallowed" them in the wrapping cloths): for a violation of this injunction would incur death at Heaven's hands. But the Talmudic Sages also find in this passage a hint of another meaning: If someone steals ("swallows"—palms, spirits away) a holy vessel of the Temple service, he too is punishable. As the Oral Tradition teaches, if zealots catch him in the act, they may strike him down then.

Consequently Rambam refutes *Halachoth G'doloth*: In its plain meaning the verse gives an instruction for the wilderness only (and so too Numbers 8:25, setting an

הֵיכָן גְּבוּל מַחֲנֵה־שְׁכִינָה; וּכְמוֹ־כֵן לְדוֹרוֹת תִּקָּרֵא מַחֲנֵה־שְׁכִינָה — וְהִיא בִכְלַל מִצְוָה זוֹ — בֵּית־הַמִּקְדָּשׁ וְכָל הָעֲזָרָה שֶׁהִיא לְפָנֶיהָ.

וְאָמְרוּ בְּסִפְרִי: "וִישַׁלְּחוּ מִן הַמַּחֲנֶה" — אַזְהָרָה לַטְּמֵאִים שֶׁלֹּא יִכָּנְסוּ לַמִּקְדָּשׁ; וְאָמְרוּ בִּפְסָחִים: "וְיָצָא אֶל מִחוּץ לַמַּחֲנֶה" — מִצְוַת עֲשֵׂה.

וְנִכְפְּלָה מִצְוָה זוֹ בְּמָקוֹם אַחֵר, שֶׁנֶּאֱמַר: כִּי יִהְיֶה בְךָ אִישׁ אֲשֶׁר לֹא יִהְיֶה טָהוֹר מִקְּרֵה לָיְלָה וְיָצָא אֶל מִחוּץ לַמַּחֲנֶה, וּפֵרוּשׁוֹ מִחוּץ לְמַחֲנֵה־שְׁכִינָה. וּכְמוֹ־ כֵן נִכְפְּלָה בְּמָקוֹם זֶה בְּעַצְמוֹ, שֶׁחָזַר וְאָמַר פַּעַם שְׁנִית: אֶל מִחוּץ לַמַּחֲנֶה תְּשַׁלְּחוּם.

וּכְבָר כָּתַבְתִּי כִּי בְהִכָּפֵל הָאַזְהָרוֹת בְּמִצְוֹת, הוֹרָאָה קְצָת בְּחֹמֶר הַמִּצְוָה, שֶׁהַשֵּׁם חָפֵץ בְּטוֹבַת בְּרִיּוֹתָיו, וְהִזְהִירָם וְחָזַר וְהִזְהִירָם עָלֶיהָ, כְּדֶרֶךְ בְּנֵי־אָדָם יַזְהִירוּ זֶה אֶת זֶה הַרְבֵּה פְעָמִים בְּכָל דָּבָר הַצָּרִיךְ לָהֶם צֹרֶךְ רַב. וְאִם אָמְנָם שֶׁמָּצִינוּ גוּפֵי תּוֹרָה נֶאֶמְרוּ בְּרֶמֶז, הַכֹּל בְּטַעַם נָכוֹן.

מִשָּׁרְשֵׁי הַמִּצְוָה, לְפִי שֶׁעִנְיַן הַטֻּמְאָה יָדוּעַ לַחֲכָמִים שֶׁיַּחֲלִישׁ כֹּחַ הַנֶּפֶשׁ הַשִּׂכְלִית וִיעַרְבֵּב אוֹתָהּ וְיַפְרִיד בֵּינָהּ וְהַשֵּׂכֶל עֶלְיוֹנֵי הַשָּׁלֵם, וּתְהִי נִפְרֶדֶת עַד אֲשֶׁר תִּטְהָר, וּכְמוֹ שֶׁכָּתוּב בְּעִנְיַן הַטֻּמְאָה: וְלֹא תִטַּמְּאוּ בָּהֶם וְנִטְמֵתֶם בָּם, וְדָרְשׁוּ זִכְרוֹנָם לִבְרָכָה: וְנִטַּמְתֶם בָּם, כְּלוֹמַר שֶׁעֲוֹנוֹת הַשֵּׂכֶל מְטַמְטְמִים בְּטֻמְאָה. עַל־

age limit till when Levites might carry the objects and parts of the *mishkan* in the wilderness). And it only hints or alludes to the ban on stealing a holy vessel of the Temple service; it is thus not a Scriptural *source* for the precept. Moreover, such a theft evidently incurs no punishment after the act.

Ramban, however (*hassagoth* on ShM, *ad loc.*) fully upholds *Halachoth G'doloth*: The verse cited (Numbers 4:20) more than "hints" at the theft of a Temple service vessel. It applies by indirect interpretation to such an act; and as we find in other instances, by such interpretation a Scriptural passage which the Sages call a hint can serve as the source of a Torah law. Moreover, such a theft certainly incurs death at Heaven's hands; if it did not, zealots could not possibly have the right to strike the thief down during the act if they catch him at it. It is, further, an injunction for all time, as it applies whenever a man may find a holy Temple vessel and decide to make off with it. Similarly, the injunction in Numbers 8:25 applies for all time: for whenever holy objects, of the *mishkan* or the Temple, would (or will) have to be the moved, the task would be the Levites', and with it goes this injunction. (For a full discussion see ShM with the *hassagoth* of Ramban, ed. Chavel, pp. 52 ff.)

In his *Séfer Mitzvoth Gadol*, R. Moses of Couçy mentions theft of a holy Temple vessel, but only in passing, in his discussion of punishment by whiplashes (positive precept § 105); he does not list it as one of the 613.

As MH notes, however, our author remains faithful to the listing of Rambam, and simply states that in the first *sidrah* there are no *mitzvoth*.

⟨4⟩

the *shechinah* was. And so for all generations it would be called the camp of the *shechinah*, i.e. the area to which this precept applies— the Sanctuary and the entire forecourt that faced it.[1]

Now, it was taught in the Midrash *Sifra:*[2] "that they shall put out of the camp"— this is an admonition to the ritually unclean that they should not enter the Sanctuary [area].[3] But it was said in the Talmud tractate *P'saḥim* (68a): "then he shall go outside the camp" (Deuteronomy 23:11)— this is a positive precept.

This precept was repeated elsewhere, for it is stated, *If there shall be among you any man who is not clean through an occurrence of night, then he shall go outside the camp (ibid.),* which means outside the camp of the *shechinah*. So was it also reiterated in this very place, for it is stated again, a second time, *outside the camp shall you send them* (Numbers 5:3).[4]

I have written previously (§336)[5] that when admonitions are repeated among the precepts, it is some indication of the seriousness of the [particular] precept: For the Eternal Lord desires good for His human beings; so He adjured them, then again adjured them about it, in the way that people will caution one another many times about anything that is very necessary for them. And if, on the other hand, we find main laws of the Torah conveyed by intimation, all is for a proper reason.

At the root of the precept lies the reason that the nature of ritual uncleanness was known to the Sages, that it weakens the strength of the intelligent spirit and muddles it, separating it from the perfect supernal [Divine] Intelligence; and so it remains separated until it becomes ritually purified— as it is written regarding ritual impurity, *and you shall not defile yourselves with them,* v'nitméthem bam, *that you should become unclean by them* (Leviticus 11:43), which our Sages of blessed memory interpreted[6] as *v'nitamtem bam,* "that you should

§362   1. From the Gate of Nicanor, where the Israelites' court began, and within; TB Z'vaḥim 116b.

2. Sifre, Numbers §1.

3. I.e. the admonition lies in the continuation in verse 3, *that they shall not defile their camp.*

4. The first three paragraphs are based to some extent on ShM positive precept §31.

5. Second paragraph; so also §228, paragraphs 4–5.

⟨5⟩   6. TB Yoma 39a.

כֵּן בַּמָּקוֹם הַקָּדוֹשׁ וְהַטָּהוֹר אֲשֶׁר רוּחַ אֱלֹהִים שָׁם אֵין רָאוּי לִהְיוֹת בּוֹ הָאִישׁ הַמְלַכְלָךְ בְּטֻמְאָה.

וְהָעִנְיָן הַזֶּה יֵשׁ לְדַמּוֹתוֹ עַל דֶּרֶךְ מָשָׁל לְפַלְטְרִין שֶׁל מֶלֶךְ, שֶׁמַּרְחִיקִין מִמֶּנּוּ כָל אִישׁ צָרוּעַ וְנִמְאָס בְּגוּפוֹ אוֹ אֲפִלּוּ בְּמַלְבּוּשָׁיו, וּכְעִנְיַן מַה שֶּׁכָּתוּב: כִּי אֵין לָבוֹא אֶל שַׁעַר הַמֶּלֶךְ בִּלְבוּשׁ שָׂק.

מִדִּינֵי הַמִּצְוָה, מַה שֶּׁאָמְרוּ זִכְרוֹנָם לִבְרָכָה שֶׁהַמְצֹרָע, שֶׁהוּא חָמוּר בְּטֻמְאָתוֹ, שֶׁמְּטַמֵּא בְאֹהֶל, חָמוּר גַּם-כֵּן בְּשִׁלּוּחוֹ, וְהוּא מִשְׁתַּלֵּחַ חוּץ לִשְׁלֹשָׁה מַחֲנוֹת, דְּהַיְנוּ חוּץ לִירוּשָׁלַיִם; הַזָּבִין וְזָבוֹת וְנִדּוֹת וְיוֹלְדוֹת, שֶׁאֵין טֻמְאָתָם חֲמוּרָה כָל-כָּךְ, שִׁלּוּחָם חוּץ לִשְׁתֵּי מַחֲנוֹת, שֶׁהֵן מַחֲנוֹת כֹּהֲנִים וּלְוִיִּם, וְזֶהוּ חוּץ לְהַר-הַבַּיִת; וּטְמֵא-מֵת, שֶׁאֵין טֻמְאָתוֹ חֲמוּרָה כָל-כָּךְ, אֵינוֹ מִשְׁתַּלֵּחַ אֶלָּא חוּץ לְמַחֲנֶה אַחַת, לְפִיכָךְ מֻתָּר לְהִכָּנֵס בְּהַר-הַבַּיִת.

וּמַה הִיא חֻמְרָא בְזָבִין יוֹתֵר מִטְּמֵא-מֵת, שֶׁהַזָּב מְטַמֵּא מִשְׁכָּב וּמוֹשָׁב וַאֲפִלּוּ מִתַּחַת הָאֶבֶן, מַה שֶּׁאֵין הַמֵּת מְטַמֵּא כֵן. וּטְמֵא-מֵת וּבוֹעֲלֵי נִדּוֹת וְכָל הַגּוֹיִם דֶּרֶךְ כְּלָל מְשַׁלְּחִין אוֹתָם מִן הַחֵיל, אֲבָל טְבוּל-יוֹם נִכְנָס לְשָׁם. עֶזְרַת נָשִׁים מְשַׁלְּחִין מִמֶּנָּה טְבוּל-יוֹם אֲבָל לֹא מְחֻסַּר כִּפּוּרִים, וּמֵעֶזְרַת יִשְׂרָאֵל וְלִפְנִים אֲפִלּוּ מְחֻסַּר כִּפּוּרִים אֵינוֹ נִכְנָס שָׁם; וְיֶתֶר פְּרָטֶיהָ, מְבֹאָרִים בְּפֶרֶק אָבוֹת הַטֻּמְאָה, שֶׁהוּא פֶּרֶק רִאשׁוֹן מִסֵּדֶר טָהֳרוֹת.

וְנוֹהֶגֶת מִצְוָה זוֹ בַּזְּכָרִים וּנְקֵבוֹת בְּכָל זְמַן, שֶׁאֲפִלּוּ בַּזְּמַן הַזֶּה, שֶׁהַמִּקְדָּשׁ שֵׁמֵם

---

7. TB P'saḥim 67a.

8. If he entered a tent or house, etc. everything in it became ritually unclean, although he touched nothing. (That this is the severe aspect of his defilement is taught in Sifre, Numbers § 1.)

9. The camp of the Israelites was from the gate of Jerusalem to the Temple Mount; the camp of the Levites was from the entrance to the Temple Mount till the Gate of Nicanor; and the camp of the *shechinah* (called also the camp of the *kohanim*) extended from the Gate of Nicanor to include the holy of holies.

10. Mishnah, Kélim i 8; TB P'saḥim 68a.

11. I.e. if he lies on a stone slab which is on a bed, even though his weight makes no significant impression on the bed, it is nevertheless defiled (Mishnah *ibid*. MT *hilchoth m'tam'é mishkav* vi 5).

12. Mishnah *ibid*.

13. Within the wall of the Temple Mount was another wall, ten handbreadths high; within that was a strip of land ten cubits wide, called the *ḥél*.

14. See § 176; Mishnah, Kélim i 8.

become occluded, obtuse by them." In other words, the wellsprings of the intelligence become blocked up by ritual uncleanness. Therefore, in the place of holiness and purity, where the spirit of God is, it is not fitting that a man sullied by ritual defilement should be present.

This matter can be likened, by way of parable, to the royal palace of a king, from which every man who is ill with *tzara'ath* or loathsome in his body, or even in his clothes, is kept well removed. It is in keeping with the verse, *for no one might enter the king's gate clothed with sackcloth* (Esther 4:2).

Among the laws of the precept, there is what the Sages of blessed memory taught:[7] that a man infected with *tzara'ath*, having a severe form of ritual uncleanness, since he causes uncleanness through a tent,[8] is likewise treated severely in his removal, being put out of the three camps,[9] which means outside Jerusalem. As to men and women with a discharge, women defiled by the menses, and women who gave birth, whose ritual impurity is not so severe, their removal is out of two camps, i.e. the camps of the *kohanim* and the Levites, which means beyond the Temple Mount.[10] As to one defiled by the dead, whose uncleanness is not even that severe, he is put out of no more than one camp; hence he is permitted to enter the Temple Mount.

Now, in what way is the defilement of those with a discharge more severe than the uncleanness of one defiled by the dead? A man with a discharge causes defilement through couch or seat [anything on which he sits or lies]—even from under a stone;[11] whereas someone defiled by the dead does not impose impurity thus.[12] As to anyone defiled by the dead, those who were conjugally intimate with women defiled by the menses, and all heathen in general, they would be sent out of the *ḥel* [a strip of land within the Temple Mount's inner wall];[13] a *t'vul yom*, however [who underwent ritual immersion and would be ritually clean at nightfall], might enter there. From the men's and women's forecourts [at the Sanctuary] a *t'vul yom* was sent out, but not someone lacking atonement.[14] As to the area further within the Israelite's forecourt, even one lacking atonement would not enter there.[12] The rest of its details are explained in the first chapter of the Mishnah tractate *Kélim*, which begins the order of *Tohoroth*.

This precept applies to both man and woman at all times. For even at the present time, when for our sins, the Sanctuary is devastated, it is

בַּעֲווֹנוֹתֵינוּ, אָסוּר לְהִכָּנֵס בּוֹ טָמֵא. וְעוֹבֵר עַל זֶה וְנִכְנָס בְּמָקוֹם שֶׁאֵינוֹ רַשַּׁאי בְּעוֹדוֹ טָמֵא בַּצְּדָדִים שֶׁפֵּרַשְׁנוּ, בִּטֵּל עֲשֵׂה, מִלְּבַד שֶׁעָבַר עַל לָאו, כְּמוֹ שֶׁנִּפְרֵשׁ בְּסֵדֶר זֶה [סִי׳ שס״ג] בְּעֶזְרַת הַשֵּׁם.

[שֶׁלֹּא יִכָּנֵס טָמֵא בְּכָל הַמִּקְדָּשׁ]

שסג שֶׁנִּמְנַע כָּל טָמֵא מֵהִכָּנֵס בְּכָל הַמִּקְדָּשׁ, שֶׁדִּמְיוֹנוֹ לְדוֹרוֹת כָּל הָעֲזָרָה מִשַּׁעַר נִיקָנוֹר וְלִפְנִים, שֶׁהוּא תְחִלַּת עֶזְרַת יִשְׂרָאֵל, שֶׁנֶּאֱמַר "וְלֹא יְטַמְּאוּ אֶת מַחֲנֵיהֶם", כְּלוֹמַר מַחֲנֵה שְׁכִינָה. וְהָרְאָיָה מִהְיוֹת זֶה מִכְּלַל הַלָּאוִין, מַה שֶּׁאָמְרוּ זִכְרוֹנָם לִבְרָכָה בִּגְמָרָא מַכּוֹת: הַבָּא אֶל הַמִּקְדָּשׁ טָמֵא, חַיָּב כָּרֵת; כְּתִיב עֹנֶשׁ וּכְתִיב אַזְהָרָה: כְּתִיב עֹנֶשׁ, "אֶת (מקדש) [מִשְׁכַּן] יי טִמֵּא וְנִכְרְתָה"; אַזְהָרָה, "וְלֹא יְטַמְּאוּ אֶת מַחֲנֵיהֶם". וְאָמְרוּ בְמִכְלָתָּא נַם־כֵּן: "צַו אֶת בְּנֵי יִשְׂרָאֵל וִישַׁלְּחוּ [מִן הַמַּחֲנֶה]", בַּעֲשֵׂה; מִנַּיִן בְּלֹא־תַעֲשֶׂה—דִּכְתִיב: וְלֹא יְטַמְּאוּ אֶת מַחֲנֵיהֶם.

וְנִכְפְּלָה הַמְּנִיעָה בְּמִלָּה אַחֶרֶת, דִּכְתִיב: וְאֶל הַמִּקְדָּשׁ לֹא תָבֹא. וְאָמְרוּ בְסִפְרָא: לְפִי שֶׁנֶּאֱמַר "וְהִזַּרְתֶּם אֶת בְּנֵי יִשְׂרָאֵל מִטֻּמְאָתָם", שׁוֹמֵעַ אֲנִי בֵּין מִתּוֹכוֹ בֵּין מֵאַחֲרָיו, כְּלוֹמַר שֶׁמִּי שֶׁקָּרֵב לַמִּקְדָּשׁ מֵאֲחוֹרָיו וְהוּא טָמֵא שֶׁיְּהֵא חַיָּב כָּרֵת—תַּלְמוּד לוֹמַר "בְּיוֹלֶדֶת וְאֶל הַמִּקְדָּשׁ לֹא תָבֹא", כְּלוֹמַר שֶׁאֵין לְשׁוֹן בִּיאָה אֶלָּא בְּנִכְנָס לְפָנִים. וְשָׁם נִתְבָּאֵר שֶׁדִּין יוֹלֶדֶת וְדִין שְׁאָר טְמֵאִים שָׁוִין בָּזֶה. מִשָּׁרְשֵׁי הַמִּצְוָה, בְּעִנְיַן הֶרְחֵק הַטֻּמְאָה מִמְּקוֹם הַקֹּדֶשׁ כָּתַבְתִּי לְמַעְלָה בְּסֵדֶר

---

15. See § 184, last paragraph.

§363 1. I.e. the *mishkan* (Tabernacle), the portable temporary Sanctuary built in the wilderness, on the journey to the holy land. The verse cited below refers initially to this.

2. This is the Midrash known to us as *Sifre Zuta*, which Rambam likewise calls Mechilta. While the original is not extant, passages were gathered from Yalkut Shim'oni, Be-Midbar Rabbah, and (principally) Midrash haGadol, by H. S. Horovitz (Leipzig 1917). References will be by page numbers and lines in this edition. The present passage is on p. 227, lines 12–13.

3. Sifra, *thazri'a, parashah* 1, 1.

4. The first two paragraphs are based on ShM negative precept § 77.

forbidden to enter there while ritually unclean.[15] If someone transgressed this and entered a location where he was not permitted while ritually impure, under the conditions that we explained, he would disobey a positive precept, apart from violating a negative precept, as we will explain in this *sidrah* (§ 363), with the Lord's help.

[THAT A RITUALLY DEFILED PERSON SHOULD NOT ENTER ANYWHERE IN THE SANCTUARY

363 that we should restrict everyone ritually unclean from entering anywhere in the [original] Sanctuary,[1] whose counterpart for later generations was the entire forecourt, from within the Gate of Nicanor, which is the beginning of the Israelites' court; for it is stated, *that they shall not defile their camp* (Numbers 5:3), which means the camp of the *shechinah* (Divine Presence). And the proof that this is in the category of negative precepts lies in what the Sages of blessed memory said in the Talmud tractate *Makkoth* (14b): If anyone enters the Sanctuary while ritually unclean, he is punishable by *karéth* [Divine severance of existence]; the penalty is written, and the injunction is written; the penalty is written — *he has defiled the tabernacle of the Lord* [*and that soul shall be cut off*] (Numbers 19:13); the injunction — *that they shall not defile their camp*. It was likewise taught in the Midrash *Mechilta*:[2] "Command the Israelites that they shall put out of the camp" (Numbers 5:2) — it is a positive precept; how do we know it involves a negative precept? — because it is written, *that they shall not defile their camp*.

Now, this restriction was reiterated in other words: for it is written, *nor shall she come into the Sanctuary* (Leviticus 12:4), and it was stated in the Midrash *Sifra*:[3] Since it is stated, *Thus shall you separate the Israelites from their uncleanness, that they should not die in their uncleanness by defiling My tabernacle that is in their midst* (Leviticus 15:31), I might infer [that it means] whether within it or round about it — in other words, that if anyone comes close to the Sanctuary from its back side while ritually unclean, he incurs the penalty of *karéth*? Hence Scripture states regarding a woman who gave birth, *nor shall she come into the Sanctuary*. In other words, the term "coming" denotes nothing but entering within. And it is elucidated there that the law for a woman who gave birth and the law for other ritually impure persons are alike in this respect.[4]

⟨9⟩   As to the root reason concerning the removal of ritual impurity far

זֶה מִצְוָה רִאשׁוֹנָה [סִי׳ שס״ב] מַה שֶּׁיָּדַעְתִּי, וְגַם מִדְּרִיגֵי הַמִּצְוָה כָּתַבְתִּי קְצָת, וְעוֹד אוֹדִיעֲךָ כְּלָל בְּעִנְיָן זֶה, שֶׁכָּל הַטָּעוּן בִּיאַת מַיִם מִן הַתּוֹרָה, וְהִיא הַטֻּמְאָה שֶׁהַנָּזִיר שֶׁל תּוֹרָה מְגַלֵּחַ עָלֶיהָ, חַיָּב כָּרֵת עַל בִּיאַת מִקְדָּשׁ אִם נִכְנַס לְשָׁם קֹדֶם טְבִילָה וְהֶעֱרֵב שֶׁמֶשׁ; אֲבָל הַטָּמֵא בְּטֻמְאַת מֵת שֶׁאֵין הַנָּזִיר מְגַלֵּחַ עֲלֵיהֶן, אַף־עַל־פִּי שֶׁהוּא טָמֵא טֻמְאַת שִׁבְעָה, הֲרֵי זֶה פָּטוּר עַל בִּיאַת מִקְדָּשׁ.

וְכֵן הַנּוֹגֵעַ בְּכֵלִים שֶׁנָּגְעוּ בְּאָדָם שֶׁנָּגַע בְּמֵת, אוֹ שֶׁנָּגַע בְּאָדָם בְּכֵלִים הַנּוֹגְעִים בְּמֵת, אַף־עַל־פִּי שֶׁהוּא טָמֵא רִאשׁוֹן לְעִנְיָן הַטֻּמְאָה וּלְטַמֵּא בְּשַׂר הַקֳּדָשִׁים, הֲרֵי זֶה פָּטוּר עַל בִּיאַת מִקְדָּשׁ, וּדְבָרִים אֵלּוּ הֲלָכָה. וְאַף־עַל־פִּי שֶׁהוּא פָּטוּר, מַכִּין אוֹתוֹ מַכַּת מַרְדּוּת. וְהַטֻּמְאוֹת שֶׁהַנָּזִיר מְגַלֵּחַ עֲלֵיהֶן אוֹ שֶׁאֵינוֹ מְגַלֵּחַ, בְּמַסֶּכֶת נָזִיר יִתְבָּאֵר הַכֹּל.

וְהַזּוֹרֵק כֵּלִים טְמֵאִים לַמִּקְדָּשׁ, אֲפִלּוּ הָיוּ כֵלִים טְמֵאִים שֶׁנָּגְעוּ בְּמֵת, פָּטוּר מִן הַכָּרֵת אֲבָל חַיָּב מַלְקוֹת, שֶׁנֶּאֱמַר: וְאִם לֹא יְכַבֵּס וּבְשָׂרוֹ לֹא יִרְחָץ; וְלָמַדְנוּ מִפִּי הַשְּׁמוּעָה שֶׁעַל רְחִיצַת גּוּפוֹ עָנוּשׁ כָּרֵת, וְעַל כִּבּוּס בְּגָדִים לוֹקֶה אַרְבָּעִים; וְיֶתֶר פְּרָטֶיהָ, נִתְבָּאֲרוּ בְּפֶרֶק רִאשׁוֹן מִשְּׁבוּעוֹת וּבְהוֹרָיוֹת וּבִכְרֵתוֹת וּבִמְקוֹמוֹת מִזְּבָחִים.

וְנוֹהֶגֶת מִצְוָה זוֹ בִּזְכָרִים וּנְקֵבוֹת; וַאֲפִלּוּ בַּזְּמַן הַזֶּה יִתְחַיֵּב כָּרֵת הַנִּכְנָס לְשָׁם וְהוּא טָמֵא בַּצְּדָדִין שֶׁכָּתַבְנוּ, שֶׁקְּדֻשַּׁת הַמָּקוֹם עָלָיו אֲפִלּוּ הַיּוֹם שֶׁהוּא שָׁמֵם,

5. Explained among the laws of precept § 376.

6. So MT *hilchoth bi'ath ha-mikdash* iii 13–14.

7. In MT *ibid.* we find that "these words are definitive law by statement of the Oral Tradition"; standard editions of *Séfer haHinnuch* have "and these words are definitive law [given] to Moses [orally] from Sinai." While our brief version may possibly be an early scribal error, the purport of the three versions is essentially the same, and the text has consequently not been emended.

The point here is that ordinarily, when *tum'ah* (ritual uncleanness) is transmitted from one entity to another, the *tum'ah* decreases in severity by one degree. Thus, if the first entity is *ta-mé* (ritually unclean) in the first degree, the second becomes *ta-mé* only in the second degree. Utensils that touch a corpse, however, are an exception to the rule: They become a source of *tum'ah* in the same degree (to the same extent) as the corpse. Yet as our author notes, this holds true only for further transmission of ritual uncleanness to meat from holy sacrifices, and not in regard to entering the *béth ha-mikdash* (the Sanctuary). And this is a law by Oral Tradition only, with no basis in Scripture.

8. MT *ibid.* 15.

9. Sifra, *aharé moth, perek* 11, 13.

10. I.e. if he underwent ritual immersion but did not subject his (defiled) clothes

from the site of holiness, I wrote above, in the first precept of this *sidrah* (§ 362) what I know; and also of the laws of the precept I wrote a few. But in addition, let me tell you a rule in this subject: that whoever requires ritual immersion in water [for his purification] by the law of the Torah, having a defilement on whose account a *nazir* would shave his hair,[5] incurs *karéth* for coming into the Sanctuary if he enters it before ritual immersion and the setting of the sun. But if someone becomes defiled by an uncleanness from the dead on whose account he does not shave his hair,[5] even though he is defiled for seven days, he is free of penalty for entering the Sanctuary.[6]

So too, if someone touches utensils that have been touched by a man who had contact with a corpse, or if he touches a man who has touched utensils that had been in contact with a corpse, even though he is defiled in the first degree as regards ritual uncleanness, and can transmit defilement to the flesh of holy sacrifices, he is free of punishment for entering the Sanctuary; and these words are definitive law.[7] Yet even though he is free of punishment, he is given chastisement for disobedience.[8] As to those defilements on whose account a *nazir* would shave his hair and those for which he would not, it is all explained in the Talmud tractate *Nazir*.

If someone throws ritually unclean objects into the Sanctuary, even if they are defiled objects that had touched a dead person, he is not punishable by *karéth*, but he does incur whiplashes: For it is stated, *But if he does not wash them* [his clothes] *or bathe his flesh* (Leviticus 17:16), and we learned through the Oral Tradition[9] that regarding the bathing of his body [ritual immersion] he is punishable by *karéth*, but concerning the washing of the clothes, he would be whipped with forty lashes.[10] The rest of its details are clarified in the first chapter of the Talmud tractate *Sh'vu'oth*, in *Horayoth* and *K'réthoth*, and in certain places in the tractate *Z'vaḥim*.

This precept applies to both man and woman; and even at the present time one would be punishable by *karéth* if he entered there while ritually unclean, under the conditions that we wrote. For the sanctity of the site[11] rests upon it even today, when it is desolate, as

to ritual immersion, and thus entered the Sanctuary; hence this is the punishment for introducing any defiled objects into the Sanctuary by any direct means; MT *ibid.* 16.

11. MS Vatican and the first edition have *ha-shem* instead of *ha-makom*; i.e. the holiness of the Eternal Lord.

וּכְמוֹ שֶׁדָּרְשׁוּ זִכְרוֹנָם לִבְרָכָה מִדִּכְתִיב "וַהֲשִׁמּוֹתִי אֶת מִקְדְּשֵׁיכֶם", כְּמוֹ שֶׁכָּתַבְתִּי לְמַעְלָה בְּאַחֲרֵי־מוֹת לֹא־תַעֲשֶׂה א' [סִי' קפ"ד].

[מִצְוַת וִדּוּי עַל הַחֵטְא]

שסד שֶׁנִּצְטַוֵּינוּ לְהִתְוַדּוֹת לִפְנֵי הַשֵּׁם עַל כָּל הַחֲטָאִים שֶׁחָטָאנוּ בְּעֵת שֶׁנִּתְנַחֵם עֲלֵיהֶן, וְזֶהוּ עִנְיַן הַוִּדּוּי: שֶׁיֹּאמַר הָאָדָם בְּעֵת הַתְּשׁוּבָה "אָנָּא הַשֵּׁם פָּשַׁעְתִּי וְעָוִיתִי כֵּן וְכֵן", כְּלוֹמַר שֶׁיַּזְכִּיר הַחֵטְא שֶׁעָשָׂה בְּפֵרוּשׁ בְּפִיו וִיבַקֵּשׁ כַּפָּרָה עָלָיו, וְיַאֲרִיךְ בַּדָּבָר כְּפִי מַה שֶׁיִּהְיֶה צַחוּת לְשׁוֹנוֹ.

וְאָמְרוּ זִכְרוֹנָם לִבְרָכָה שֶׁאֲפִלּוּ הַחֲטָאִים שֶׁחִיְּבָה הַתּוֹרָה קָרְבָּן עֲלֵיהֶם צָרִיךְ הָאָדָם אֶל הַוִּדּוּי עִם הַקָּרְבָּן; וְעַל זֶה נֶאֱמַר: דַּבֵּר אֶל בְּנֵי יִשְׂרָאֵל אִישׁ אוֹ אִשָּׁה כִּי יַעֲשׂוּ מִכָּל חַטֹּאת הָאָדָם לִמְעֹל מַעַל בַּיי וְאָשְׁמָה הַנֶּפֶשׁ הַהִיא וְהִתְוַדּוּ אֶת חַטָּאתָם אֲשֶׁר עָשׂוּ. וְאָמְרוּ בְּמִכְלְתָא: לְפִי שֶׁנֶּאֱמַר "וְהִתְוַדָּה אֲשֶׁר חָטָא", יִתְוַדֶּה עַל חֵטְא שֶׁחָטָא; "עָלֶיהָ", (עַל חַטָּאת) כְּשֶׁהִיא קַיֶּמֶת, לֹא מִשֶּׁנִּשְׁחֲטָה; כְּלוֹמַר בְּעוֹד שֶׁבְּהֵמַת הַקָּרְבָּן חַיָּה וְלֹא מִשֶּׁנִּשְׁחֲטָה.

וְעוֹד אָמְרוּ שָׁם: לָמַדְנוּ חִיּוּב הַוִּדּוּי לִמְטַמֵּא מִקְדָּשׁ וְקָדָשָׁיו; מִנַּיִן אַתָּה מְרַבֶּה שְׁאָר כָּל הַמִּצְוֹת; כְּלוֹמַר שֶׁהַמִּקְרָא הַזֶּה בָּא בְּפָרָשַׁת וַיִּקְרָא בִּמְטַמֵּא מִקְדָּשׁ וְקָדָשָׁיו, מִנַּיִן אַתָּה מְרַבֶּה שְׁאָר כָּל הַמִּצְוֹת; דִּכְתִיב: דַּבֵּר־אֶל בְּנֵי יִשְׂרָאֵל וְגוֹמֵר שֶׁנִּדְרַשׁ הַכָּתוּב כְּאִלּוּ לֹא נִכְתַּב עַל דָּבָר מְיֻחָד. וּמִנַּיִן שֶׁיֵּשׁ בַּמַּשְׁמָע הַזֶּה אַף מִיתוֹת וּכְרֵתוֹת—שֶׁנֶּאֱמַר גַּבֵּי וִדּוּי אַהֲרֹן בְּאַחֲרֵי־מוֹת "לְכָל

---

12. TB M'gillah 28a.

13. Last paragraph.

§364   1. (Literally, with his mouth.) So R. Judah b. Bava in TB Yoma 86b. The text of the confession directly above, "…I sinned rebelliously" etc. (פשעתי ועויתי) follows the reading of the three oldest manuscripts and the first edition. The fourth manuscript and all later editions read חטאתי עויתי ופשעתי "I have sinned inadvertently, committed iniquity deliberately, and done wrong rebelliously" — in harmony with what our author writes in the last paragraph of this section. Putatively, this earlier reading derives from the first version of ShM, which our author had in Hebrew translation — a loose, imprecise general confession, which Rambam presumably corrected in his later version, in keeping with TB Yoma 36b.

2. So ShM positive precept §87, apparently derived from TB Yoma 36b (see MY).

3. Sifre Zuta 229–30.

4. Our author now adds: in other words, while the animal for the offering is alive, and not after it has been ritually slain. With our text (from the first edition, and so in Sifre Zuta ed. Horovitz) this seems superfluous. However, in MS Vatican 163/1 the words 'al ḥattath ("over the ḥattath") are absent, and this might have been

our Sages of blessed memory interpreted,[12] since it is written, *and I will make desolate your sanctuaries* (Leviticus 26:31)—as I wrote above, in the first negative precept of *sidrah aḥaré moth* (§ 184).[13]

[THE PRECEPT OF CONFESSION OVER SINS]

364 that we were commanded to confess before the Lord to all the sins we committed, at the time we are remorseful over them. This is the substance of the confession that a man should say at the time of repentance: "I pray Thee, O Eternal Lord: I sinned rebelliously and committed iniquity deliberately, thus and so"; in other words, he should mention the sin he did explicitly, in words,[1] and beseech forgiveness for it; and let him continue at length about the matter, according to the eloquence of his tongue.[2]

Now, our Sages of blessed memory said that even for those sins over which the Torah imposed the obligation of an offering, a man needs to make confession with the offering. About this it was stated, *Speak to the Israelites: When a man or woman shall commit any of the sins that men do, to commit a breach of faith against the Lord, whereupon that soul will be guilty, they shall then confess their sin which they have done* (Numbers 5:6–7). And it was taught in the Midrash *Mechilta*:[3] Since it is stated, *he shall confess what he sinned* (Leviticus 5:5), he is to confess to the sin he committed; *over it* (*ibid.*)—over the *ḥattath* (sin-offering) while it is alive, not after it has been ritually slain.[4]

Our Sages stated further there:[5] We have thus learned the duty of confession for one who brought defilement to the Sanctuary and its holy objects; from where do you learn to extend this to all other precepts? In other words, this verse (Leviticus 5:5) occurs in *sidrah vayikra* about one who brings defilement to the Sanctuary and its holy objects; then how do you know to add on all other precepts?—because it is written, *Speak to the Israelies...they shall then confess* (Numbers 5:6–7). This means that we interpret the verse as though it were not written about anything in particular. And how do we know that this meaning [of the verse] extends also to sins incurring death sentences and *karéth*?—because it is stated about the confession of Aaron in *sidra aḥaré moth, for all their sins* (Leviticus 16:16), which the

our author's original version, thus requiring the addition. (The other three manuscripts read instead, *'al ḥét*, "over the sin"—the result of a scribal error.)

5. *Ibid.* 230, l. 1–4.

חַטֹּאתָם", וְדָרְשׁוּ זִכְרוֹנָם לִבְרָכָה: לְרַבּוֹת מִצְוַת לֹא־תַעֲשֶׂה; וְ"כִי יַעֲשׂוּ" דִּכְתִיב כָּאן, לְרַבּוֹת מִצְוַת עֲשֵׂה; כְּלוֹמַר אִם בִּטֵּל מִצְוַת עֲשֵׂה שֶׁהָיָה יָכוֹל לַעֲשׂוֹת, שֶׁחַיָּב לְהִתְוַדּוֹת עָלֶיהָ.

וְעוֹד דָּרְשׁוּ (זִכְרוֹנָם לִבְרָכָה) שָׁם בִּמְכִלְתָּא: "מִכָּל חַטֹּאת הָאָדָם", מִמַּה שֶּׁבֵּינוֹ לְבֵין חֲבֵרוֹ: עַל הַגְּנֵבוֹת וְעַל הַגְּזֵלוֹת וְעַל לָשׁוֹן הָרָע. וְזֶה הַוִּדּוּי, צָרִיךְ בֶּאֱמֶת שֶׁיָּשִׁיב הֶחָמָס אֲשֶׁר בְּכַפָּיו, שֶׁאִם לֹא־כֵן, מוּטָב שֶׁלֹּא יִתְוַדֶּה עַל זֶה. "לִמְעוֹל מַעַל", לְרַבּוֹת כָּל חַיָּבֵי מִיתוֹת, שֶׁיִּתְוַדּוּ. יָכוֹל אַף הַנֶּהֱרָגִין עַל־פִּי זוֹמְמִין, כְּלוֹמַר אַף־עַל־פִּי שֶׁהוּא יוֹדֵעַ שֶׁלֹּא חָטָא, אֶלָּא שֶׁהוּעַד עָלָיו עֵדוּת שֶׁקֶר, שֶׁיְּהֵא חַיָּב לְהִתְוַדּוֹת עַל זֶה — תַּלְמוּד לוֹמַר "וְאָשְׁמָה הַנֶּפֶשׁ": לֹא אָמַרְתִּי אֶלָּא כְּשֶׁיִּהְיֶה שָׁם אַשְׁמָה, אֲבָל לֹא כְּשֶׁיָּדַע שֶׁאֵין לוֹ חֵטְא אֶלָּא שֶׁהוּעַד שֶׁקֶר עָלָיו. הִנֵּה הִתְבָּאֵר שֶׁכָּל מִינֵי הָעֲוֹנוֹת הַגְּדוֹלִים וְהַקְּטַנִּים וַאֲפִלּוּ מִצְוֹת עֲשֵׂה, חַיָּב הָאָדָם עֲלֵיהֶם הַוִּדּוּי.

וּלְפִי שֶׁבָּאָה מִצְוָה זוֹ שֶׁל וִדּוּי עִם חִיּוּב הַקָּרְבָּן, כְּמוֹ שֶׁכָּתוּב בְּפָרָשַׁת וַיִּקְרָא, דִּכְתִיב שָׁם "וְהֵבִיא אֶת אֲשָׁמוֹ" וְגוֹמֵר, שֶׁמָּא יַעֲלֶה בַּמַּחֲשָׁבָה שֶׁאֵין הַוִּדּוּי לְבַדּוֹ מִצְוָה בִּפְנֵי עַצְמָהּ אֶלָּא מֵהַדְּבָרִים הַנִּגְרָרִים אַחַר הַקָּרְבָּן — עַל־כֵּן הָיוּ צְרִיכִים לְבָאֵר בִּמְכִלְתָּא שֶׁאֵינוֹ כֵן, אֶלָּא מִצְוָה בִּפְנֵי עַצְמָהּ הִיא. וְכֵן אָמְרוּ שָׁם: יָכוֹל בִּזְמַן שֶׁהֵם מְבִיאִין מִתְוַדִּין, וּמִנַּיִן אַף בִּזְמַן שֶׁאֵינָן מְבִיאִין — שֶׁנֶּאֱמַר: בְּנֵי יִשְׂרָאֵל ... וְהִתְוַדּוּ, כְּלוֹמַר שֶׁהַקַּבָּלָה בָּאָה לִדְרֹשׁ כֵּן.

וַעֲדַיִן הָיִיתִי אוֹמֵר שֶׁאֵין הַוִּדּוּי אֶלָּא בָאָרֶץ, כְּלוֹמַר אַף־עַל־פִּי שֶׁמִּתְוַדִּין בְּלֹא קָרְבָּן, מִכָּל־מָקוֹם שֶׁלֹּא יְהֵא חִיּוּב הַוִּדּוּי אֶלָּא בָאָרֶץ, כִּי שָׁם עִקַּר הַכַּפָּרָה וְשָׁם הַקָּרְבָּנוֹת וְעִקַּר הַכֹּל בָּהּ; מִנַּיִן אַף בַּגָּלֻיּוֹת — דִּכְתִיב: וְהִתְוַדּוּ אֶת עֲוֹנָם וְאֶת עֲוֹן

6. *Ibid.* l. 9–17.
7. *Ibid.* l. 4–5.

Sages of blessed memory interpreted to extend it to negative precepts; while the words "shall commit" written here (Numbers 5:6) extend it to positive precepts; in other words, if someone failed to keep a positive precept that he was able to observe, he is obligated to confess to it.

Our Sages of blessed memory further expounded there in the Midrash *Mechilta*:[6] "any of the sins that men do" (Numbers 5:6) — of those that are between a man and his fellow-man: about theft, robbery, and evil gossip. But this confession really requires that he should return the seized property that is in his hands (possession); for otherwise, it were better that he does not confess about it. "To commit a breach of faith" — this is to include all those punishable by death sentences, that they should confess. I might think this includes also those sentenced to death by scheming witnesses? — in other words, even though one knows he did not sin, but false testimony was given against him, he should be obligated to confess to it? Hence Scripture states, *whereupon that soul will be guilty*: I do not apply this unless there is guilt there, but not when a person knows he has no guilt but that falsehood was testified against him. It has thus been clarified that over all sorts of iniquities, great and small, and even over positive precepts [not done] a man has an obligation of confession.

Now, because this precept of confession was given with the obligation of an offering, as written in *sidrah va-yikra* — for it is written there, *he shall bring his guilt-offering*, etc. (Leviticus 5:15) — it might perhaps occur to one to think that confession by itself is not a precept in its own right, but one of the things that follow in the wake of an offering. Hence it was necessary to make it clear in the Midrash *Mechilta* that it is not so, but it is a *mitzvah* by itself. And so it was stated there:[7] I might think that [only] at the time [an offering] is brought, confession is made; how do we know it means [even] at a time when one is not brought? — because it is stated, *to the Israelites... they shall then confess* (Numbers 5:6–7). In other words, it is in the Oral Tradition to interpret it so.

Yet I might still say that confession is to be observed only in the land [of Israel]? In other words, although confession should be made when there is no offering, the obligation to confess should prevail nowhere but in the land, since there the main essence of atonement prevails, there the offerings exist, and the essence of everything is there. How do we know it applies also in the exile? — because it is

אֲבוֹתָם, כְּלוֹמַר עֲוֹן אֲבוֹתָם שֶׁחָטְאוּ וְגֹרְשׁוּ מִן הָאָרֶץ. וְכֵן אָמַר דָּנִיֵּאל בְּחוּצָה
לָאָרֶץ: לְךָ יי הַצְּדָקָה וְלָנוּ בֹּשֶׁת הַפָּנִים, וְגוֹמֵר. הִנֵּה הִתְבָּאֵר שֶׁהַוִּדּוּי מִצְוָה בִּפְנֵי
עַצְמָהּ, וְנוֹהֵג בְּכָל מָקוֹם. וְאָמְרוּ בְּסִפְרָא גַּם־כֵּן: "וְהִתְוַדָּה", זֶה וִדּוּי דְּבָרִים.

מִשָּׁרְשֵׁי הַמִּצְוָה, לְפִי שֶׁבְּהוֹדָאַת הֶעָוֹן בַּפֶּה תִּתְגַּלֶּה מַחֲשֶׁבֶת הַחוֹטֵא וְדַעְתּוֹ,
שֶׁהוּא מַאֲמִין בֶּאֱמֶת כִּי גָּלוּי וְיָדוּעַ לִפְנֵי הָאֵל בָּרוּךְ הוּא כָּל מַעֲשֵׂהוּ, וְלֹא יַעֲשֶׂה
עַיִן רוֹאָה כְּאֵינָהּ רוֹאָה. גַּם מִתּוֹךְ הַזְכָּרַת הַחֵטְא בִּפְרָט וּבְהִתְנַחֲמוֹ עָלָיו יִזָּהֵר
מִמֶּנּוּ יוֹתֵר פַּעַם אַחֶרֶת לְבַל יְהִי נִכְשָׁל בּוֹ; אַחַר שֶׁיֹּאמַר בְּפִיו "כָּזוֹ וְכָזוֹ עָשִׂיתִי
וְנִסְכַּלְתִּי בְמַעֲשַׂי", יִהְיֶה נִגְדָּר שֶׁלֹּא יָשׁוּב לַעֲשׂוֹת כֵּן; וּמִתּוֹךְ כָּךְ יֵרָצֶה לִפְנֵי
בּוֹרְאוֹ, וְהָאֵל הַטּוֹב הֶחָפֵץ בְּטוֹבַת בְּרִיּוֹתָיו הִדְרִיכָם בְּדֶרֶךְ זוֹ יִזְכּוּ בָהּ.

מִדִּינֵי הַמִּצְוָה, מַה שֶּׁאָמְרוּ זִכְרוֹנָם לִבְרָכָה שֶׁהַתְּשׁוּבָה הִיא שֶׁיַּעֲזֹב הַחוֹטֵא
חֶטְאוֹ וִיסִירֶנּוּ מִלִּבּוֹ וּמִמַּחְשַׁבְתּוֹ וְיִגְמֹר בְּלִבּוֹ שֶׁלֹּא יַעֲשֵׂהוּ עוֹד, כְּדִכְתִיב: יַעֲזֹב
רָשָׁע דַּרְכּוֹ וְאִישׁ אָוֶן מַחְשְׁבֹתָיו, וְאַחַר־כָּךְ יִתְוַדֶּה עָלָיו, כְּלוֹמַר שֶׁיֹּאמַר דִּבְרֵי
הַתְּשׁוּבָה בְּפִיו, שֶׁנֶּאֱמַר: וַיַּעֲשׂוּ לָהֶם אֱלֹהֵי זָהָב. וְגַם־כֵּן צָרִיךְ לְהַזְכִּיר בְּפֵרוּשׁ
שֶׁלֹּא יָשׁוּב לַעֲשׂוֹת הַחֵטְא עוֹד, שֶׁנֶּאֱמַר: וְלֹא נֹאמַר עוֹד אֱלֹהֵינוּ לְמַעֲשֵׂה יָדֵינוּ
וְגוֹמֵר.

וְאָמְרוּ זִכְרוֹנָם לִבְרָכָה שֶׁשָּׂעִיר הַמִּשְׁתַּלֵּחַ הָיָה מְכַפֵּר, בְּשֶׁעָשָׂה תְּשׁוּבָה, עַל
כָּל עֲבֵרוֹת שֶׁבַּתּוֹרָה, הַקַּלּוֹת וְהַחֲמוּרוֹת, בֵּין שֶׁעָבַר עֲלֵיהֶן בְּזָדוֹן אוֹ בִשְׁגָגָה, בֵּין
שֶׁהוֹדַע לוֹ אוֹ לֹא הוֹדַע לוֹ; אֲבָל אִם לֹא עָשָׂה תְּשׁוּבָה אֵין שָׂעִיר מְכַפֵּר אֶלָּא עַל
הַקַּלּוֹת. וּמַה הֵן הַקַּלּוֹת, וּמַה הֵן הַחֲמוּרוֹת: עֲבֵרוֹת שֶׁחַיָּבִין עֲלֵיהֶן מִיתוֹת בֵּית־

8. *Ibid.* l. 7–9.

9. Sifra, *aḥaré moth, parashah* 4, 6.

10. MT *hilchoth t'shuvah* ii 2–3, based on TB Ta'anith 16a.

11. I.e. Moses thus confessed explicitly the sin of the Israelites (making the golden calf) when he prayed for their forgiveness; TB Yoma 86b.

12. MT *ibid.* 2.

13. TB Sh'vu'oth 2a, 12b; MT *ibid.* i 2 (see *Kessef Mishneh, Leḥem Mishneh*).

⟨16⟩

written, *they shall confess their iniquity and the iniquity of their fathers* (Leviticus 26:40), *To Thee, O Lord, belongs righteousness, and to us shamefacedness*, etc. (Daniel 9:7).[8] It is thus clear that confession is a precept in its own right. And so it is in force everywhere. It was likewise stated in the Midrash *Sifra*:[9] "and he shall confess" (Leviticus 16:21) — this means a confession in words.

At the root of the precept lies the reason that by the avowal of sin by one's own mouth, the thought and perception of the sinner is revealed — that in truth he believes that his every action is known and revealed before God, blessed is He; and [thus] he does not assume the [supernal] Eye that sees to be as though unseeing. Moreover, by mentioning the sin in detail and expressing remorse over it, he will be more careful another time that it should not bring him to grief. After saying with his mouth, "Thus and thus did I do, and I was foolish in my actions," he will be restrained not to go back and do so again; and as a result, he will be acceptable before his Creator. The good God, who desires the good reward of His human beings, has guided them in this way to become virtuous in it.

Among the laws of the precept, there is what the Sages of blessed memory taught:[10] that repentance means that the sinner should abandon his sin and remove it from his heart and his thoughts, and resolve in his heart that he will not do so again — as it is written, *let the wicked forsake his way, and the man of iniquity his thoughts* (Isaiah 55:7); and after that he should confess it, i.e. he should say the words of the repentance with his mouth — as it is stated, *and they have made them a god of gold* (Exodus 32:31).[11] Then he must likewise mention explicitly that he will not go back and do this sin any more: as it is stated, *and we will say no more, "Our god,"* to the work of our hands, etc. (Hosea 14:4).[12]

Our Sages of blessed memory taught too[13] that the goat despatched [into the wilderness on the Day of Atonement] brought atonement when one repented of any and every sin in the Torah [that he may have done], the minor and the serious ones, whether he committed them deliberately or unwittingly, whether they became known to him or not. But if one did not repent, the goat sent away [into the wilderness] would bring atonement for none but minor transgressions. Now, which are the minor ones and which the major, serious ones? Sins that are punishable by death sentences of the *beth din* (court) or by *kareth* [Divine severance of existence], and so too a vain

דִּין אוֹ כָרֵת, וְכֵן שְׁבוּעַת שָׁוְא וָשֶׁקֶר אַף־עַל־פִּי שֶׁאֵין בָּהֶן כָּרֵת, מִן הַחֲמוּרוֹת הֵן; וּשְׁאָר מִצְוֹת עֲשֵׂה וְלֹא־תַעֲשֶׂה שֶׁאֵין בָּהֶן כָּרֵת נִקְרָאוֹת קַלּוֹת כְּנֶגֶד הָאֲחֵרוֹת.

וְעַכְשָׁו בַּעֲוֹנוֹתֵינוּ שֶׁאֵין לָנוּ מִקְדָּשׁ וְלֹא מִזְבַּח כַּפָּרָה, אֵין לָנוּ אֶלָּא תְשׁוּבָה. וְהַתְּשׁוּבָה מְכַפֶּרֶת עַל כָּל הָעֲבֵרוֹת; אֲפִלּוּ רָשָׁע גָּמוּר כָּל יָמָיו וְעָשָׂה תְשׁוּבָה שְׁלֵמָה בָּאַחֲרוֹנָה, אֵין מַזְכִּירִין לוֹ שׁוּם רִשְׁעוֹ, שֶׁנֶּאֱמַר: וְרִשְׁעַת הָרָשָׁע לֹא יִכָּשֶׁל בָּהּ בְּיוֹם שׁוּבוֹ מֵרִשְׁעוֹ.

בַּמֶּה דְבָרִים אֲמוּרִים שֶׁהַתְּשׁוּבָה לְבַדָּהּ מַסְפֶּקֶת, בִּדְבָרִים שֶׁבֵּין אָדָם לַמָּקוֹם, כְּגוֹן הָאוֹכֵל דְּבַר אִסּוּר אוֹ בּוֹעֵל בְּעִילָה אֲסוּרָה, וְכֵן הַמְבַטֵּל אַחַת מִמִּצְוֹת עֲשֵׂה וְכַיּוֹצֵא בָזֶה; אֲבָל עֲבֵרוֹת שֶׁבֵּין אָדָם לַחֲבֵרוֹ, כְּגוֹן הַחוֹבֵל בַּחֲבֵרוֹ אוֹ הַגּוֹזֵל מָמוֹנוֹ, אוֹ בְכָל דָּבָר אַחֵר שֶׁהֵזִיקוֹ שֶׁלֹּא כַדִּין, בֵּין בְּמַעֲשֶׂה בֵּין בְּדִבּוּר, אֵין נִמְחָל לוֹ לְעוֹלָם בִּתְשׁוּבָה בִּלְבָד עַד שֶׁיִּתֵּן לַחֲבֵרוֹ מַה שֶׁהוּא חַיָּב לוֹ וְעַד שֶׁיְרַצֵּהוּ; וְאִם לֹא רָצָה חֲבֵרוֹ לְהִתְרַצּוֹת לוֹ, כְּבָר אָמְרוּ זִכְרוֹנָם לִבְרָכָה מַה תַּקָּנָתוֹ.

וּמֵעִנְיַן הַמִּצְוָה כְּמוֹ־כֵן מַה שֶׁאָמְרוּ בְתוֹסֶפְתָּא, שֶׁעֶשְׂרִים וְאַרְבָּעָה דְבָרִים הֵם שֶׁמְּעַכְּבִין אֶת הַתְּשׁוּבָה, וְשָׁם מָנוּ אוֹתָן חֲכָמִים. וְיֶתֶר פְּרָטֵי הַמִּצְוָה, יִתְבָּאֲרוּ בְּפֶרֶק אַחֲרוֹן מִיּוֹמָא.

וְנוֹהֶגֶת מִצְוָה זוֹ בְּכָל מָקוֹם וּבְכָל זְמַן, בִּזְכָרִים וּנְקֵבוֹת. וְעוֹבֵר עַל זֶה וְלֹא הִתְוַדָּה עַל חֲטָאָיו בְּיוֹם הַכִּפּוּרִים, שֶׁהוּא יוֹם קָבוּעַ מֵעוֹלָם לִסְלִיחָה וְכַפָּרָה, בִּטֵּל עֲשֵׂה זֶה; וְאוֹי לוֹ לְאָדָם אִם יָמוּת בְּלֹא וִדּוּי וְנָשָׂא עֲווֹנוֹ. וְעִקַּר הַוִּדּוּי שֶׁקִּבְּלָנוּ מֵרַבּוֹתֵינוּ, וְנָהֲגוּ בָהּ כָּל יִשְׂרָאֵל בִּימֵי הַתְּשׁוּבָה, הוּא "אֲבָל חָטָאנוּ אָשַׁמְנוּ" וְכוּלֵי.

וְאָמְרוּ זִכְרוֹנָם לִבְרָכָה בְּשַׁבַּת פֶּרֶק בַּמֶּה מַדְלִיקִין: מִי שֶׁחָלָה וְנָטָה לָמוּת, אוֹמְרִין לוֹ: הִתְוַדֵּה, שֶׁכֵּן דֶּרֶךְ כָּל הַמּוּמָתִין מִתְוַדִּין. וְכֵן בְּמַסֶּכֶת שְׂמָחוֹת תַּנְיָא:

---

14. I.e. though we now have no Temple service of sacrifices on *Yom Kippur*, repentance alone is quite enough, if it is sincere. MT *ibid.* 3, based on TB Kiddushin 40b.

15. So TB Yoma 85b; Bava Kamma 92a; MT *ibid.* ii 9.

16. TB Yoma 86a; MT *ibid.*

17. Not found in our editions, but in the small (minor) tractates (R. Nissim, cited in *Kessef Mishneh* to MT *hilchoth t'shuvah* iv 4).

18. TB Yoma 87b; MT *ibid.* ii 8.

or false oath even though these do not entail *karéth*, are among the serious, major ones. Other positive and negative precepts, which do not involve *karéth*, are called minor ones, in comparison with the others.[13]

Now, however, when for our sins we have neither Sanctuary nor altar for atonement, we have nothing [to turn to] but repentance. Even if a person was utterly wicked all his days and then achieved complete repentance at the last, nothing of his wickedness is to be mentioned to him: for it is stated, *and as for the wickedness of the wicked, he shall not stumble over it on the day when he turns from his wickedness* (Ezekiel 33:12).[14]

Yet where does this rule hold, that repentance alone is enough?—in matters between man and the omnipresent God: for example, if one ate something forbidden or had forbidden conjugal relations, or if he ignored one of the positive precepts, and so forth. But as for transgressions between man and his fellow-man—for instance, if someone wounds another or seizes his goods in robbery, or if through some other means he causes him damage unjustly, whether by action or by speech—these are never forgiven him through repentance alone, until he gives his fellow-man what he owes him, and until he pacifies him.[15] And if the other does not wish to become amiable toward him, long ago the Sages of blessed memory said what the remedy is for it.[16]

In the subject-matter of the precept there is likewise what was stated in the Tosefta:[17] that there are twenty-four things which can prevent repentance; and there the Sages listed them. The remaining details of the precept are clarified in the last chapter of the tractate *Yoma*.

This precept is in effect everywhere, at every time, for both man and woman. If a person transgresses this and does not confess his sins on the Day of Atonement, which is the day set from time immemorial for forgiveness and atonement, he disobeys this positive precept. And woe to a man if he should die without confession, bearing his sin. The main text of confession that we have received from our sages, and which all Jews have the practice of saying in the days of penitence, is "Yet we have sinned, become guilty," etc.[18]

Then the Sages of blessed memory taught in the second chapter of the Talmud tractate *Shabbath* (32a): If someone falls ill and seems likely to die, he is told, "Confess, for so is it the way for all who

נָטָה לָמוּת, אוֹמְרִין לוֹ: הִתְוַדֵּה עַד שֶׁלֹּא תָמוּת, הַרְבֵּה שֶׁנִּתְוַדּוּ וְלֹא מֵתוּ וְהַרְבֵּה
שֶׁלֹּא נִתְוַדּוּ וָמֵתוּ, וְהַרְבֵּה שֶׁמְּהַלְכִין בַּשּׁוּק וּמִתְוַדִּין, שֶׁבִּזְכוּת שֶׁאַתָּה מִתְוַדֶּה
אַתָּה חַי. אִם יָכוֹל לְהִתְוַדּוֹת בְּפִיו, יִתְוַדֶּה; וְאִם לֹא, יִתְוַדֶּה בְּלִבּוֹ.

וְכָתַב הָרַב מֹשֶׁה בֶּן נַחְמָן זִכְרוֹנוֹ לִבְרָכָה שֶׁכָּךְ קִבֵּל מֵחֲסִידִים וְאַנְשֵׁי מַעֲשֶׂה,
שֶׁסֵּדֶר וִדּוּי שֶׁל שְׁכִיב־מְרַע כָּךְ הוּא: מוֹדֶה אֲנִי לְפָנֶיךָ ה' אֱלֹהַי וֵאלֹהֵי אֲבוֹתַי
שֶׁרְפוּאָתִי בְיָדֶיךָ וּמִיתָתִי בְּיָדֶיךָ. יְהִי רָצוֹן מִלְּפָנֶיךָ שֶׁתִּרְפָּאֵנִי רְפוּאָה שְׁלֵמָה;
וְאִם אָמוּת, תְּהֵא מִיתָתִי כַפָּרָה עַל כָּל הַחֲטָאִים עֲווֹנוֹת וּפְשָׁעִים שֶׁחָטָאתִי
וְשֶׁעָוִיתִי וְשֶׁפָּשַׁעְתִּי לְפָנֶיךָ, וְתֵן חֶלְקִי בְּגַן־עֵדֶן וְזַכֵּנִי לָעוֹלָם הַבָּא הַצָּפוּ
לַצַּדִּיקִים.

וְתִזְכֹּר הַסֵּדֶר הַזֶּה לוֹמַר חֲטָאִים תְּחִלָּה וְאַחַר־כָּךְ עֲווֹנוֹת וְאַחַר־כָּךְ פְּשָׁעִים,
כְּמוֹ שֶׁזָּכַרְנוּ "חָטָאתִי עָוִיתִי פָּשַׁעְתִּי", לְפִי שֶׁכְּבָר חָלְקוּ בָזֶה בַּגְּמָרָא רַבִּי מֵאִיר
וַחֲכָמִים, וְרַבִּי מֵאִיר סָבַר דְּאִפְּכָא הוּא דְאָמְרִינַן, וּכְמוֹ שֶׁאָמַר מֹשֶׁה: נֹשֵׂא עָוֹן
וָפֶשַׁע וְחַטָּאָה; וַהֲלָכָה כַּחֲכָמִים דְּסָבְרֵי שֶׁהַחֲטָאִים מַזְכִּיר תְּחִלָּה, וְטַעַם הָעִנְיָן
מְפֹרָשׁ בַּגְּמָרָא.

[מִצְוַת סוֹטָה שֶׁיְּבִיאָהּ הַבַּעַל אֶל הַכֹּהֵן וְיַעֲשֶׂה לָהּ כַּמִּשְׁפָּט הַכָּתוּב]

שסה לְהָבִיא הָאִשָּׁה הַשּׁוֹטָה אֶל הַכֹּהֵן, שֶׁיַּעֲשֶׂה לָהּ כַּמִּשְׁפָּט הַכָּתוּב עָלֶיהָ
בַּפָּרָשָׁה; וְעִנְיַן הַסּוֹטָה מְפֹרָשׁ הוּא בַכָּתוּב שֶׁהִיא הָאִשָּׁה שֶׁקִּנֵּא בָהּ בַּעֲלָהּ, וּכְבָר
פֵּרְשׁוּ זִכְרוֹנָם לִבְרָכָה: מַאי לְשׁוֹן שׁוֹטֶה? — כְּלוֹמַר סָטַת מִבַּעֲלָהּ, כִּי רֹב הַקִּנְאוֹת
יָבוֹאוּ בִּסְבַת פְּרִיצוּת הָאִשָּׁה, וְלָכֵן תִּקָּרֵא שׁוֹטָה מִבַּעֲלָהּ, מִכֵּיוָן שֶׁקִּנֵּא בָהּ.

19. Not found in our editions, but thus cited in Ramban, *Torath ha'Adam, sha'ar
ha-sof,* and R.'Ashér, Mo'éd Katan iii §76. It is found, however, in *S'maḥoth d'R.
Ḥiyya* (*S'maḥoth Zutrathi*) I 2 (*Massecheth S'maḥoth,* ed. Higger, pp. 211–12).
   20. Ramban *ibid.* toward the end.
   21. TB Yoma 36b.

§365   1. Numbers 5:11–13.
   2. To the extent that he cautioned her not to be alone in secret with another
man; *ibid.* 14.
   3. Rashi to *ibid.* 12.

approach death to confess." So too in the tractate *S'maḥoth* we learn:[19] If he is approaching death, he is told, "Confess before you die. There are many who confessed and did not die, and many who did not confess and did die; and there are many who walk about in the marketplace who have had confession. For by the merit of your confessing you will live." If he can avow [his sins] with his mouth, let him do so; and if not, let him confess in his heart.

Now, Ramban of blessed memory wrote[20] that so he received the tradition from men of kindly piety and scrupulous observance, that the order of confession for a dangerously ill bed-ridden person is this: "I acknowledge before Thee, Lord My God and God of my fathers, that my cure lies in Thy hands, and my death lies in Thy hands. May it be Thy will that Thou shalt cure me with a perfect healing. And if I die, may my death be a price of atonement for all the sins, iniquities and deliberate wrongs that I sinned, committed and deliberately did before Thee. Grant my portion in the Garden of Eden, and grant me the merit to attain life in the world-to-come, which awaits the righteous."

Remember this order of service, to say "inadvertent sins" first, then "deliberate iniquities," and afterward "rebellious wrongs," as we cited it: "I sinned inadvertently, committed deliberate iniquity, acted rebelliously." For long ago, R. Me'ir and the Sages differed about this in the Talmud,[21] and R. Me'ir held that we should say it in a different order, as Moses said: *forgiving deliberate iniquity, rebellious wrong and unintentional sin* (Exodus 34:7). But the definitive law follows the Sages, who hold that inadvertent sins are to be mentioned first; and the reason for the matter is explained in the Talmud.[21]

[THE PRECEPT OF SOTAH, A STRAYING WOMAN
SUSPECTED OF INFIDELITY]

365 to bring an aberrant, straying wife to the *kohen*, that he should carry out for her the regulation written about her in the *sidrah*.[1] The meaning of "a straying wife" is explained in the Writ: that it is a woman whose husband was jealous about her;[2] and long ago the Sages of blessed memory explained[3] what the term *sotah* (straying woman) means: i.e. she strayed away from her husband. For most instances of jealousy occur on account of unchastity of the woman; hence she is called *sotah*, a woman straying, from her husband, since he was jealous about her. The verse that conveys this precept is, *If any*

וְהַכָּתוּב הַמּוֹרֶה עַל מִצְוָה זוֹ הוּא: אִישׁ אִישׁ כִּי־תִשְׂטֶה אִשְׁתּוֹ וְגוֹמֵר וְהֵבִיא הָאִישׁ אֶת־אִשְׁתּוֹ אֶל הַכֹּהֵן.

שֹׁרֶשׁ מִצְוָה זוֹ נִגְלֶה לְכָל רוֹאֵי הַשֶּׁמֶשׁ, שֶׁהוּא שֶׁבַח גָּדוֹל בָּאֻמָּה לִהְיוֹת לָנוּ תַחְבּוּלָה לְהוֹצִיא הַחֲשָׁד מִתּוֹךְ לְבָבֵנוּ בְּנָשׁוֹתֵינוּ וְלָדַעַת בֶּאֱמֶת אִם זִנְּתָה הָאִשָּׁה תַּחַת בַּעְלָהּ אוֹ לֹא זִנְּתָה—מַה שֶׁאִי־אֶפְשָׁר לְכָל גּוֹי וּמַמְלָכָה לִהְיוֹת בֵּינֵיהֶם כֵּן, וְעַל אוֹתָן נֶאֱמַר "אָכְלָה וּמָחֲתָה פִיהָ וְאָמְרָה לֹא פָעַלְתִּי אָוֶן", כִּי מִי יִגַּלֶּה עַל בְּנוֹתֵיהֶם כִּי תִזְנֶינָה וְעַל כַּלּוֹתֵיהֶם כִּי תְנָאַפְנָה.

וְעַמֵּנוּ נִתְקַדֵּשׁ בְּכָל דָּבָר שֶׁבִּקְדֻשָּׁה, וְנָתַן לָנוּ הָאֵל מוֹפֵת לָדַעַת עִנְיָן זֶה הַנֶּעֱלָם מִשְּׁאָר הָעַמִּים, וּמִתּוֹךְ כָּךְ תִּתְרַבֶּה בֵּין אִישׁ לְאִשְׁתּוֹ אַהֲבָה וְשָׁלוֹם שָׁלֵם וְזַרְעֵנוּ יִהְיֶה קָדוֹשׁ. וּמָה אַאֲרִיךְ עוֹד בִּפְרָטֵי עִנְיָנִים אֵלֶּה וְהַכֹּל נִגְלֶה בְּלֵב כָּל מֵבִין. וְלָכֵן בִּהְיוֹת טַעַם הָעִנְיָן נֵס בְּאֻמָּתֵנוּ וְכָבוֹד גָּדוֹל לָהֶם, פָּסַק מִשָּׁעָה שֶׁנִּתְקַלְקְלוּ בַּעֲבֵרוֹת, כְּמוֹ שֶׁאָמְרוּ זִכְרוֹנָם לִבְרָכָה: מִשֶּׁרַבּוּ הַנּוֹאֲפִים פָּסְקוּ מֵי סוֹטָה, שֶׁנֶּאֱמַר "לֹא אֶפְקוֹד עַל בְּנוֹתֵיכֶם כִּי תִזְנֶינָה" וְגוֹמֵר, וּפֵרוּשׁ הַכָּתוּב לוֹמַר שֶׁלֹּא יֵעָשֶׂה לָהֶם הַנֵּס הַגָּדוֹל הַזֶּה לִהְיוֹת הַמַּיִם בּוֹדְקִין אֶת הָאִשָּׁה אִם זִנְּתָה.

מִדִּינֵי הַמִּצְוָה, מַה שֶׁאָמְרוּ זִכְרוֹנָם לִבְרָכָה שֶׁעִנְיַן הַקִּנּוּי הוּא כְּגוֹן שֶׁאָמַר לְאִשְׁתּוֹ בִּפְנֵי עֵדִים "אַל תִּסָּתְרִי עִם פְּלוֹנִי"; וַאֲפִלּוּ הָיָה אָבִיהָ אוֹ אָחִיהָ אוֹ גּוֹי אִם עֶבֶד אוֹ שָׁחוּף, וְהוּא הָאִישׁ שֶׁאֵינוֹ מוֹלִיד, וְנִסְתְּרָה עִם אֶחָד מֵהֶם בִּפְנֵי עֵדִים, אוֹ שֶׁשָּׁהֲתָה עִמּוֹ כְּדֵי טֻמְאָה, שֶׁהִיא כְּדֵי לִצְלוֹת בֵּיצָה וּלְגָמְעָהּ, הֲרֵי זוֹ אֲסוּרָה עָלָיו בַּעְלָהּ עַד שֶׁתִּשְׁתֶּה מֵי הַמָּרִים וְיִבָּדֵק הַדָּבָר. וּבִזְמַן שֶׁאֵין שָׁם מֵי סוֹטָה תֵּאָסֵר עָלָיו לְעוֹלָם וְתֵצֵא בְּלֹא כְתֻבָּה.

4. Expression based on Hosea 4:14. The root reason is based on Ramban to Numbers 5:20.

5. I.e. the water that she was to be made to drink at the Sanctuary (Numbers 5:24) was no longer given her; TB Sotah 47a.

6. Cf. Ramban to Numbers 5:20: Scripture does not convey here that adulterous women will be free of guilt because their husbands are adulterous, but merely that this great miracle would not be wrought for them for their honor and for their being a holy people, since they do not appreciate this favor and do not desire it [i.e. the favor of having the means to remain a chaste, holy people, since the men act immorally]....This is why it is stated, *and the man shall be free from iniquity* (ibid. 31): when the man is free of iniquity, the water will probe his wife...

7. TB Sotah 2a: MT *hilchoth sotah* i 1.

8. TB Sotah 24a.

9. *Ibid.* 26b.

10. *Ibid.* 2a.

11. *Ibid.* 4a.

12. MT *ibid.* 2.

man's wife goes astray, etc. *then the man shall bring his wife to the* kohen (Numbers 5:12, 15).

The root reason for this precept is clear to all who see sunlight. For it is most praiseworthy for our nation that we should have a method for removing from the midst of our heart any suspicion of our wives, and to know for certain if a woman committed immorality while under her husband's authority or did not — whereas it is impossible for any other nation or kingdom to have anything like this among them. To them the verse applies, *she ate and wiped her mouth, and said, "I have done no wrong"* (Proverbs 30:20). For who is to reveal about their daughters when they play the harlot, or about their daughters-in-law when they commit adultery?[4]

Our people, though, was hallowed by every kind of holiness. So God granted us a paranormal sign to know this matter which is hidden from other peoples. And as a result, love and perfect peace would increase and grow between a man and his wife, and our progeny would be hallowed. Why should I continue further at length about details of these matters, when all is obvious in the heart of everyone with understanding? But therefore, since the matter was in essence a miracle in our nation and a mark of great honor for them, it ceased from the time they degenerated through transgressions. As the Sages of blessed memory said, once the licentious multiplied, the water of the straying wife ceased:[5] for it is stated, *I will not punish your daughters when they play the harlot*, etc. (Hosea 4:14). The meaning of the verse is to convey that this great miracle would not be wrought for them, that the water should probe the woman if she committed an immoral act.[6]

Among the laws of the precept there is what the Sages of blessed memory said:[7] that in substance jealousy [here] means, for example, if one told his wife before witnesses, "Do not closet yourself with so-and-so." Then even if it was her father, her brother,[8] a heathen, a slave, or an impotent man,[9] and she secreted herself with one of them before witnesses,[10] if she stayed with him long enough to become defiled, which is the time it takes to roast an egg and eat it,[11] she is forbidden to her husband until she will drink the water and the matter will thus be probed.[12] At a time when there is no [ritual of] water for the straying wife, she becomes forbidden to him forever, and is to leave [be divorced] without payment of the *k'thubah*

⟨23⟩ (marriage contract).[13]

אֲבָל אָמַר לָהּ "אַל תְּדַבְּרִי עִם אִישׁ פְּלוֹנִי", אֵין זֶה קִנּוּי, וְלֹא תֵאָסֵר עָלָיו
בְּקִנּוּי זֶה אַף־עַל־פִּי שֶׁנִּסְתְּרָה עִמּוֹ. קִנֵּא לָהּ בִּפְנֵי שְׁנַיִם וְרָאָה אוֹתָהּ הוּא בְּלֹא
עֵדִים שֶׁנִּסְתְּרָה עִם אוֹתוֹ שֶׁקִּנֵּא לָהּ, הֲרֵי זוֹ אֲסוּרָה עָלָיו וְיוֹצֵיא וְיִתֵּן כְּתֻבָּה,
שֶׁאֵין יָכוֹל לְהַשְׁקוֹתָהּ עַל־פִּי עַצְמוֹ. וְכֵן אִם שָׁמַע הָעָם מְרַנְּנִים אַחֲרֶיהָ שֶׁזִּנְּתָה
עִם הָאִישׁ שֶׁקִּנֵּא לָהּ, עַד שֶׁהַנָּשִׁים הַטֹּווֹת לְאוֹר הַלְּבָנָה מְדַבְּרוֹת עָלֶיהָ, יוֹצֵיא
וְיִתֵּן כְּתֻבָּה.

וּמַה שֶּׁאָמְרוּ זִכְרוֹנָם לִבְרָכָה גַּם־כֵּן, שֶׁיֵּשׁ נָשִׁים שֶׁבֵּית־דִּין מְקַנְּאִין עֲלֵיהֶן,
וְהֵן: מִי שֶׁנִּתְחָרֵשׁ בַּעֲלָהּ אוֹ נִשְׁתַּטָּה אוֹ שֶׁהָיָה בִּמְדִינָה אַחֶרֶת אוֹ שֶׁהָיָה חָבוּשׁ
בְּבֵית־הָאֲסוּרִים; וְלֹא לְהַשְׁקוֹתָהּ אֶלָּא לְפָסְלָהּ מִכְּתֻבָּתָהּ. וְזֶה הָעִנְיָן הוּא
כְּשֶׁשָּׁמְעוּ בֵית־דִּין שֶׁהָעָם מְרַנְּנִים אַחֲרֶיהָ מֵאָדָם אַחֵר, שֶׁקּוֹרְאִין לָהּ וְאוֹמְרִים
לָהּ "אַל תִּסְתַּתְּרִי עִמּוֹ"; וְאִם נִסְתְּרָה עִמּוֹ אַחַר־כֵּן, בֵּית־דִּין אוֹסְרִין אוֹתָהּ עַל
בַּעֲלָהּ לְעוֹלָם וְקוֹרְעִין כְּתֻבָּתָהּ, וּכְשֶׁיָּבוֹא בַעֲלָהּ נוֹתֵן לָהּ גֵּט.

וּמַה שֶּׁאָמְרוּ, שֶׁאִם שָׁתַת מֵי הַמָּרִים פַּעַם אַחַת עַל אִישׁ אֶחָד וְנִקְתָה מֵהֶם,
וְחָזַר וְקִנֵּא לָהּ עָלָיו וְנִסְתְּרָה עִמּוֹ, אֵינָהּ שׁוֹתָה עַל־יָדוֹ פַּעַם אַחֶרֶת לְעוֹלָם, אֶלָּא
תֵאָסֵר עַל בַּעֲלָהּ וְתֵצֵא בְּלֹא כְתֻבָּה; אֲבָל אִם קִנֵּא לָהּ בַּאֲנָשִׁים חֲלוּקִים, אֲפִלּוּ
מֵאָה פְעָמִים הִיא שׁוֹתָה.

וּלְעוֹלָם אֵין כּוֹפִין אוֹתָהּ לִשְׁתּוֹת, בֵּין שֶׁאָמְרָה "נִטְמֵאתִי" אוֹ שֶׁאָמְרָה "אֵינִי
טְמֵאָה וְאֵינִי שׁוֹתָה", אֶלָּא תֵצֵא בְּלֹא כְתֻבָּה וְתֵאָסֵר לְבַעֲלָהּ לְעוֹלָם. וְאִם בַּעֲלָהּ
הוּא שֶׁאָמַר "אֵינִי רוֹצֶה לְהַשְׁקוֹתָהּ", תֵּצֵא וְתִטֹּל כְּתֻבָּה.

---

13. TB Sotah 2b; TJ i 1.

14. TB Sotah 6b.

15. MT *hilchoth sotah* i 8, based on TB Kiddushin 66a.

16. TB Sotah 31a. Women knitting by moonlight in Talmudic times would
gather for companionship, and would naturally fall to talking.

17. *Ibid.* 24a, 27a.

18. MT *hilchoth sotah* i 11; see also Rashi, TB Sotah 24a, s.v. *v'elu*.

19. TB Sotah 18b, 18b–19a.

20. MT *ibid.* 12.

21. TB Sotah 24a; MT *ibid.* ii 1.

If, however, he [the husband merely] told her, "Do not speak with so-and-so," this does not constitute jealousy, and she does not become forbidden to him through this [expression of] jealousy even if she closeted herself with that person.[14] If he expressed his jealousy to her before two [witnesses] and he then saw her, without witnesses, secreting herself with the one about whom he expressed his jealousy to her, she would thus become forbidden to him, and he is to divorce her, paying the amount of the k'thubah—for he cannot make her drink [the bitter water] by his own evidence.[15] So too, if he heard people gossiping about her that she acted immorally with the man about whom he had expressed his jealousy to her, to such an extent that even women knitting by moonlight were talking about her, he should grant a divorce, paying the amount of the marriage contract.[16]

There is, likewise, what the Sages of blessed memory taught:[17] that there are women to whom the *beth din* (court) is to express the jealousy, these being one whose husband became a deaf-mute or lost his reason, or if he was in another land, or confined in prison. But this does not serve to have her drink [the bitter water], but only to disqualify her from [receiving payment of] her marriage contract. This course is taken when the *beth din* judges hear people gossiping about her in regard to another man; then they call her and tell her, "Do not conceal yourself with him." And if she did closet herself with him after that, the *beth din* is to declare her forbidden to her husband and tear up her k'thubah (marriage contract); and when her husband comes, he is to give her a divorce.[18]

There is, further, what the Sages taught: that if a woman drank the bitter water once over a certain man and was absolved by it, and then [her husband] expressed jealousy to her again about him, and she secreted herself with him, she is not ever to drink [the bitter water] on his account another time, but rather becomes forbidden to her husband, and is to leave [divorced] without payment of the k'thubah.[19] If, however, he expressed jealousy to her about different men, even a hundred times she is to drink [the bitter water].[20]

She is never compelled to drink it if she says, "I was defiled," or, "I was not defiled, yet I will not drink it," but she rather leaves [divorced] without payment of the k'thubah, and remains forbidden to her husband for all time. If, however, it is the husband who says, "I do not wish to make her drink it," she is to leave [with a divorce] and receive the payment of the marriage contract.[21]

וְיֵשׁ נָשִׁים שֶׁאֵינָן שׁוֹתוֹת אַף־עַל־פִּי שֶׁרָצוּ הֵן וּבַעֲלֵיהֶן, וַחֲמֵשׁ־עֶשְׂרֵה נָשִׁים הֵן, וְאֵלּוּ הֵן: אֲרוּסָה וְשׁוֹמֶרֶת יָבָם, דִּכְתִיב: תַּחַת אִישָׁהּ, וְאֵלּוּ אֵינָן עֲדַיִן תַּחַת אִישׁ; וּקְטַנָּה אֵשֶׁת גָּדוֹל, דִּכְתִיב: אֲשֶׁר תִּשְׂטֶה אִשָּׁה, וְזוֹ אֵינָהּ אִשָּׁה עֲדַיִן; וּגְדוֹלָה אֵשֶׁת קָטָן, דִּכְתִיב: תַּחַת אִישָׁהּ, וְזֶה אֵינוֹ עֲדַיִן אִישׁ; וְאֵשֶׁת אַנְדְּרוֹגִינוֹס, דִּכְתִיב: אִישָׁהּ, וְזֶה אֵינוֹ אִישׁ גָּמוּר; וְאֵשֶׁת סוּמָא, דִּכְתִיב: וְנֶעְלַם מֵעֵינֵי אִישָׁהּ, וְזֶה אֵין לוֹ עֵינַיִם, וְהַחִגֶּרֶת, דִּכְתִיב: וְהֶעֱמִיד הַכֹּהֵן אֶת הָאִשָּׁה, וְזוֹ אֵינָהּ יְכוֹלָה לַעֲמֹד; וּמִי שֶׁאֵין לָהּ כַּף־יָד, דִּכְתִיב: וְנָתַן עַל כַּפֶּיהָ, וְזוֹ אֵין לָהּ כַּף; וְכֵן אִם הָיְתָה יָדָהּ עֲקֻמָּה אוֹ יְבֵשָׁה, שֶׁאֵינָהּ יְכוֹלָה לִקַּח בָּהּ, הֲרֵי זֶה כְּמִי שֶׁאֵין לָהּ; וַאֲפִלּוּ הָיְתָה יְכוֹלָה לִקַּח בְּאַחַת לְבַד אֵינָהּ שׁוֹתָה—דִּכְתִיב: כַּפֶּיהָ, וְהָאִלֶּמֶת, דִּכְתִיב: וְאָמְרָה הָאִשָּׁה; וּמִי שֶׁאֵינָהּ שׁוֹמַעַת, דִּכְתִיב: וְאָמַר אֶל הָאִשָּׁה; וְכֵן הוּא שֶׁהָיָה חִגֵּר אוֹ קָטוּעַ אוֹ אִלֵּם אוֹ חֵרֵשׁ, וְכֵן הִיא שֶׁהָיְתָה סוּמָא, דִּכְתִיב: אִשָּׁה תַּחַת אִישָׁהּ, עַד שֶׁתִּהְיֶה הִיא שְׁלֵמָה כָּמוֹהוּ וְהוּא כְּמוֹתָהּ.

וְיֶתֶר פְּרָטֶיהָ, וְסֵדֶר הַשְׁקָאַת הַסּוֹטָה, וּבְאֵי זֶה צַד בּוֹדְקִין הַמַּיִם אוֹתָהּ וּבְאֵי זֶה צַד אֵין בּוֹדְקִין אוֹתָהּ, הַכֹּל מְתְבָּאֵר יָפֶה בַּמַּסֶּכְתָּא הַבְּנוּיָה עַל זֶה, וְהִיא מַסֶּכֶת סוֹטָה.

וְנוֹהֶגֶת מִצְוָה זוֹ בִּזְמַן הַבַּיִת בִּזְכָרִים, לְפִי שֶׁעֲלֵיהֶם מֻטָּל שֶׁיַּעֲשׂוּ לַנָּשִׁים הַמַּעֲשֶׂה הַזֶּה כְּדֵי לִבְדֹּק אוֹתָן, אִם רָאוּ שֶׁצְּרִיכוֹת הֵן לְכָךְ; וְדַוְקָא כְשֶׁיֵּשׁ שָׁם בֵּית־דִּין שֶׁל שִׁבְעִים וְאֶחָד, שֶׁכָּךְ קִבַּלְנוּ שֶׁאֵין מַשְׁקִין הַסּוֹטָה אֶלָּא בְּבֵית־דִּין שֶׁל שִׁבְעִים זְקֵנִים בַּמִּקְדָּשׁ. וְעוֹבֵר עַל זֶה וְקִנֵּא לְאִשְׁתּוֹ וְנִסְתְּרָה וְלֹא הֱבִיאָהּ אֶל הַכֹּהֵן לַעֲשׂוֹת לָהּ הַמַּעֲשֶׂה הַכָּתוּב בַּפָּרָשָׁה, בִּטֵּל עֲשֵׂה זֶה.

22. See § 35, note 8.

23. I.e. she is not yet married to her brother-in-law, but is forbidden to marry anyone else while waiting for him.

24. This is generally rendered, "when a wife goes astray," but the Hebrew for wife, 'ishah, also bears the meaning of woman.

25. Similarly, this is generally rendered, "under her husband's authority," but 'ish, husband, also bears the meaning of man.

26. This follows a reading found only in the oldest manuscript. In the next three manuscripts the reading is שאינה יכולה ליקח באחת לבד by a scribal oversight between the identical terms יכולה ליקח. In an attempt to make sense of it, this was later amended to שאינה יכולה ליקח כי אם ביד אחת (!) בלבד.

27. Literally, when a woman under her husband; but the Hebrew for "under" can also mean "in place of," suggesting that the two should be equal, interchangeable as it were, in their lack of physical handicaps.

28. MT hilchoth sotah ii 2–3 (sources in Kessef Mishneh).

29. TB Sotah 7a.

There are women, though, who are not to drink [the bitter water] even if both they and their husbands wish it. These are fifteen women, namely: one who was betrothed;[22] one waiting for levirate marriage (§598), for it is written, *being under her husband's authority* (Numbers 5:29), and she is not yet under her husband's authority;[23] a minor who is the wife of an adult, for it is written, *when a woman goes astray* (Numbers 5:29),[24] and she is not a woman yet; a grown woman who is the wife of a minor, for it is written, *while under her man's authority* (ibid.),[25] and he is not yet a man; the wife of a hermaphrodite, since it is written, *her man's authority*, and this is not a complete man; the wife of a blind man, since it is written, *and it is hidden from the eyes of her husband* (ibid. 13); a lamed woman, for it is written, *And the* kohen *shall have the woman stand* (ibid. 18), and she cannot stand; one who has no hand, since it is written, *and he shall place on her hands* (ibid.), and this one lacks a hand; so also if her hand was twisted or withered, so that she could not take anything with it: it is thus as if it were missing; and even if she could [merely] take things with only one [hand][26] she does not drink [the bitter water], since it is written, *her hands*; a mute woman, as it is written, *and the woman shall say* (ibid. 22); one who does not hear, as it is written, *and he shall say to the woman* (ibid. 19); so likewise if he [the husband] was lamed or one-handed, mute or deaf; and so too if she was blind — for it is written, *when a woman under her husband's authority*[27] (ibid. 29): [the law does not apply] until she is as whole [in body] as he, and he as she.[28]

The rest of its details, the procedure of giving a straying wife [the bitter water] to drink, and under which conditions the water probes her [to determine her innocence or guilt] and under which conditions it does not so probe her — all is well explained in the Talmud tractate built about this, i.e. the tractate *Sotah*.

This precept applies at the time the Temple exists, for males, since the obligation lies on them to carry out this procedure for women, to examine them, if they should see that they require this. But this means specifically when there is a *beth din* (court) of seventy-one [justices]; for so we received the Oral tradition,[29] that a straying wife is to be given [the bitter water] to drink only at the *beth din* of seventy elders at the Sanctuary. If a person transgressed this, expressing jealousy of his wife whereupon she concealed herself [with the other man] and he then did not bring her to the *kohen* to carry out for her the procedure

〈27〉

[שֶׁלֹּא לָתֵן שֶׁמֶן בְּקָרְבַּן סוֹטָה]

שסו שֶׁלֹּא נִתֵּן שֶׁמֶן בְּקָרְבַּן סוֹטָה, שֶׁנֶּאֱמַר: וְהֵבִיא אֶת קָרְבָּנָהּ וְגוֹמֵר לֹא יִצֹק עָלָיו שֶׁמֶן.

מִשָּׁרְשֵׁי הַמִּצְוָה, אָמְרוּ רַבּוֹתֵינוּ זִכְרוֹנָם לִבְרָכָה: כְּדֵי שֶׁלֹּא יִהְיֶה קָרְבָּנָהּ מְהֻדָּר, שֶׁהַשֶּׁמֶן קָרוּי אוֹר וְהִיא עָשְׂתָה בַחֹשֶׁךְ, וְעָשְׂתָה מַעֲשֶׂה בְּהֵמָה שֶׁנִּרְבַּעַת לַכֹּל, לְפִיכָךְ מִנְחָתָהּ גְּרוּעָה לִהְיוֹת שְׂעוֹרִים.

וְהָרַב מֹשֶׁה בֶּן נַחְמָן זִכְרוֹנוֹ לִבְרָכָה כָּתַב בְּעִנְיַן קָרְבָּנָהּ שֶׁל שׁוֹטָה עַל צַד הַפְּשָׁט גַּם־כֵּן, כִּי הַקָּרְבָּן הַזֶּה, הַבַּעַל מֵבִיא אוֹתוֹ מִשֶּׁלּוֹ עַל קִנְאָתוֹ שֶׁקִּנֵּא בָהּ, כְּדֵי שֶׁיִּנָּקֵם יי נִקְמָתוֹ מִמֶּנָּה. וְטַעַם הַשְּׂעוֹרִים, שֶׁתִּהְיֶה שַׂעֲרַת חֲמַת יי חֵמָה יוֹצֵאָה וְסַעַר מִתְחוֹלֵל עַל רֹאשׁ הָרְשָׁעָה הַזּוֹנָה יָחוּל, וּכְעִנְיַן צְלִיל שְׂעוֹרִים הָאָמוּר בְּגִדְעוֹן, שֶׁפָּתְרוּ אוֹתוֹ לְסַעַר וּמְהוּמָה רַבָּה; וְכֵן בִּכְלִי חֶרֶשׂ סִימָן שֶׁתִּשָּׁבֵר כִּכְלִי יוֹצֵר, וְכֵן הֶעָפָר סִימָן שֶׁתָּמוּת וְתָשׁוּב אֶל עָפָר.

וּבְעִנְיַן הַשֶּׁמֶן לֹא דִבֵּר מְאוּמָה, וְאַעֲנֶה בּוֹ אֲנִי חֶלְקִי: כִּי הַשֶּׁמֶן עֶלְיוֹן עַל כָּל הַמַּשְׁקִין, שֶׁהוּא צָף עַל כֻּלָּן; וְעַתָּה הַשּׁוֹטָה שֶׁקִּלְקְלָה מַעֲשֶׂיהָ, וַיְסִירָהּ בַּעֲלָהּ מִגְּבִירָה, וּנְתָנָהּ לְמַטָּה בְּשֵׁפֶל וּבְבִזָּיוֹן, אֵין רָאוּי לְהָבִיא בְּקָרְבָּנָהּ הַשֶּׁמֶן הַנִּכְבָּד, שֶׁהוּא נָכוֹן לְאוֹרָה וְלִגְדֻלָּה, לְמָשְׁחָה בּוֹ הַמְּלָכִים וְהַכֹּהֲנִים הַגְּדוֹלִים; וּכְלָל הָעִנְיָנִים שֶׁנִּצְטַוֵּינוּ בָהֶם, לְתַקֵּן מַחֲשֶׁבֶת הָעוֹשִׂים בַּמְּלָאכָה וְלָתֵת אֶל לִבָּם כִּי הַמְקֻלְקָל בְּמַעֲשָׂיו, כָּל דְּרָכָיו יָבוֹאוּ בְחֶרְפָּה וּבְבֹשֶׁת, וּכְדֵי בִזָּיוֹן וָקֶלֶס; וְלַטּוֹבִים

§366   1. TB Sotah 15a, M'nahoth 6a; Rashi to Numbers 5:15.

2. Since it is burned for illumination.

3. Rashi *ibid.* based on Tanhuma, *naso* 3 (ed. Buber, 5): Oil is light... and this one loved the darkness; therefore let there be no light in her *minhah*.

4. I.e. fodder; TB Sotah 14a; Sifre, Numbers §8; Tanhuma *ibid.* Rashi *ibid.*

5. Ramban, commentary, Numbers 5:15.

6. Adaptation of Jeremiah 23:19.

7. Cf. Jeremiah 19:1, *Thus said the Lord: Go and get a potter's earthen bottle...*and *ibid.* 10–11, *Then you shall break the bottle...and you shall say to them: Thus says the Lord of hosts: Even so will I break this people and this city, as one breaks a potter's vessel, that cannot be made whole again...*Cf. also Psalms 2:9, *Thou shalt dash them in pieces like a potter's vessel.*

8. Echoing Genesis 3:19, *for dust (earth) you are, and to dust (earth) you shall return.*

9. Expression based on Esther 1:18, end.

written in the Scriptural section, he would [thus] disobey this positive precept.

[TO PUT NO OIL IN THE MEAL-OFFERING
OF A SOTAH]

366 that we should not put oil in the offering of a straying wife, as it is written, *and he shall bring her offering*, etc. *he shall pour no oil on it* (Numbers 5:15).

As to the root purposes of the precept, our Sages of blessed memory said[1] it is in order that her offering should not have distinction: for oil is called light,[2] and she acted in the dark.[3] And she committed the deed of an animal, that allows all to mate with it; therefore her *minḥah* (meal-offering) is an inferior, debased one, being of barley.[4]

Now, R. Moses b. Naḥman (Ramban) of blessed memory likewise wrote[5] in regard to the offering of the stray wife, from the aspect of the plain meaning, that the husband brings this offering out of his own means on account of the jealousy that he felt toward her, so that the Lord will take His revenge from her. The reason for the barley, *se'orim*, is that there should be a storm, *sa'arah*, of the Lord's anger: A fury should go forth, and a whirling storm should burst upon the head of the wicked wanton woman.[6] This is similar to the term, *a cake of barley bread* (Judges 7:13), stated in connection with Gideon, which was interpreted as symbolizing storm and great tumult. So too was [the bitter water taken] in an earthen vessel (Numbers 5:17), as a sign that she would be broken like a potter's vessel.[7] And so was the earth (*ibid.*) a sign that she would die and return to the earth.[8]

Regarding the oil, however, he [Ramban] said nothing. Then let me respond with my share about that. For oil is above all other liquids, since it floats above them all. Now that this fool corrupted her ways of action, her husband removed her from her status of ladyship and reduced her to the lowest level, in debasement and disgrace. Hence it is not fitting to bring in her offering the distinguished ingredient of oil, which is intended for light and grandeur, to anoint kings and every *kohen gadol* with it. The general purpose of these matters about which we were bidden is to rectify the thought of those who carry out the tasks involved, and to make them aware that if someone becomes corrupt in his deeds, all his ways will lead to

disgrace and shame, and enough contempt and contumely.[9] For those

יֵיטִיב יי וְשִׂמְחָה וְשָׂשׂוֹן וִיקָר יַשִּׂיגֵם.

מִצְוָה זוֹ עִם דִּינֶיהָ מְבֹאֶרֶת בַּכָּתוּב, אֵין לְהַאֲרִיךְ בָּהּ.

וְנוֹהֶגֶת בִּזְמַן הַבַּיִת, וּכְמוֹ שֶׁכָּתַבְנוּ לְמַעְלָה בְּסֵדֶר זֶה בְּמִצְוַת שׁוֹטָה עֲשֵׂה ג' [סי' שס"ה], שֶׁאֵין מַשְׁקִין הַשּׁוֹטָה אֶלָּא בְּבֵית-דִּין שֶׁל שִׁבְעִים וְאֶחָד בַּמִּקְדָּשׁ. וְכֹהֵן הָעוֹבֵר עַל זֶה וְיָצַק שֶׁמֶן בְּמִנְחַת שׁוֹטָה, עָבַר עַל לָאו, וְלוֹקֶה.

[שֶׁלֹּא לָשִׂים לְבוֹנָה בְּקָרְבַּן סוֹטָה]

שסז שֶׁלֹּא (להשים) [לָשִׂים] לְבוֹנָה בְּקָרְבַּן שׁוֹטָה, שֶׁנֶּאֱמַר: וְלֹא יִתֵּן עָלָיו לְבֹנָה.

מִשָּׁרְשֵׁי הַמִּצְוָה, כָּעִנְיָן מַה שֶּׁכָּתַבְתִּי בַשֶּׁמֶן, כִּי הַלְּבוֹנָה הֲדוּרָה בְּקָרְבָּן וְרֵיחָהּ טוֹב, וְלָכֵן אֵין רָאוּי לְאִשָּׁה הַחוֹטֵאת לְהַדֵּר קָרְבָּנָהּ. וְעוֹד אָמְרוּ זִכְרוֹנָם לִבְרָכָה עַל זֶה, שֶׁהָאִמָּהוֹת הַכְּשֵׁרוֹת וְהַצְּנוּעוֹת קְרוּיוֹת לְבוֹנָה, שֶׁנֶּאֱמַר "וְאֶל גִּבְעַת הַלְּבוֹנָה", וְזוֹ פֵּרְשָׁה מִדַּרְכֵיהֶן.

וּמִצְוָה זוֹ גַם-כֵּן מְבֹאֶרֶת בַּכָּתוּב, וְעִנְיָנָהּ כָּתוּב בַּחֲבֶרְתָּהּ, אֵין לְהַאֲרִיךְ בָּהּ.

[שֶׁלֹּא יִשְׁתֶּה הַנָּזִיר יַיִן אוֹ כָּל מִינֵי שֵׁכָר]

שסח שֶׁלֹּא יִשְׁתֶּה הַנָּזִיר יַיִן, אוֹ כָּל שֵׁכָר שֶׁעִקַּר עֵרוּבוֹ יִהְיֶה יַיִן, שֶׁהוּא מֹהַל הָעֲנָבִים; דְּאִלּוּ מֹהַל שְׁאָר הַפֵּרוֹת, אַף-עַל-פִּי שֶׁנִּקְרָא שֵׁכָר, לֹא נֶאֱסַר עַל הַנָּזִיר, אֶלָּא בְּתַעֲרֹבֶת הַיּוֹצֵא מִן הַגֶּפֶן; וְעַל זֶה נֶאֱמַר: מִיַּיִן וְשֵׁכָר יַזִּיר וְגוֹמֵר וְכָל מִשְׁרַת עֲנָבִים לֹא יִשְׁתֶּה, כְּלוֹמַר שֶׁכָּל תַּעֲרֹבֶת שֶׁיֵּשׁ בּוֹ עֲנָבִים בִּכְלָל הָאָסוּר; וְהִפְלִיג בְּמִנְיָנָהּ וְאָמַר שֶׁאֲפִלּוּ נִתְחַמֵּץ הַיַּיִן אוֹ הַשֵּׁכָר שֶׁנִּתְעָרֵב עִמּוֹ אָסוּר לִשְׁתּוֹתוֹ,

---

10. Literally, will overtake them.

§367   1. Tanḥuma, *naso* 3 (ed. Buber, 5); Rashi to Numbers 5:15.

§368   1. I.e. one who took a vow to be a *nazir* (which has the general sense of being apart, abstinent, ascetic), and thus assumed certain obligations and restrictions; Numbers 6:1–21.

2. I.e. alcoholic beverage.

3. So Rambam understands the term *shéchar* in Numbers 6:3 (MT *hilchoth n'ziruth* iii 1); Rashi on the verse, though, explains it as old wine (and it is generally translated as strong drink).

4. I.e. even if it fermented and became alcoholic.

who are good, however, the Lord will do good, and gladness, joy and honor (Esther 8:16) will be their lot.[10]

This precept, with its laws, is clarified in the Writ, and there is no need to be lengthy about it.

It is in effect when the Temple is extant, as we wrote above in this *sidrah*, in the third positive precept about the straying wife (§ 365) — that the straying wife is made to drink [the bitter water] nowhere but at the great *beth din* of seventy-one [justices] at the Sanctuary. If a *kohen* transgressed this and poured oil on the *minḥah* (meal-offering) of the straying wife, he would violate a negative precept, and should receive whiplashes.

[TO PUT NO FRANKINCENSE IN THE
MEAL-OFFERING OF A SOTAH]

367 not to put frankincense in the offering of a straying wife: as it is written, *nor shall he put frankincense on it* (Numbers 5:15).

The root purpose of the precept is like the point we wrote about oil. For frankincense adds distinction to an offering, and its savor is good. It is therefore not suitable for a sinful woman, to adorn her offering. Moreover, our Sages of blessed memory said[1] that the worthy and modest Matriarchs are called [symbolically] frankincense, as it is stated, *and to the hill of frankincense* (Song of Songs 4:6) — and she departed from their ways.

This precept too is elucidated in the Writ; and its subject-matter is written in its companion [precept, § 366]; there is no need to continue at length about it.

[THAT A NAZIR IS FORBIDDEN TO DRINK WINE
OR ANY STRONG WINE DRINK]

368 that a *nazir*[1] should not drink wine or any liquor[2] whose main ingredient is wine,[3] which means a liquid from grapes; for as to liquid from other fruits, even if it is called liquor,[4] nothing was forbidden a *nazir* but a liquid deriving from the grapevine. Hence it was stated, *from wine and liquor shall he abstain*, etc. *neither shall he drink any liquid of grapes* (Numbers 6:3); in other words, any [liquid] mixture containing [a derivative or flavoring of] grapes is included under the prohibition. But [the Torah] made the restriction quite far-reaching, and stated that even if the wine or the strong drink in which wine was mixed turned to vinegar, it is forbidden to drink it. Hence Scripture

וְעַל זֶה אָמַר הַכָּתוּב: חֹמֶץ יַיִן וְחֹמֶץ שֵׁכָר לֹא יִשְׁתֶּה. וְאֵין אֵלּוּ שְׁנֵי לָאוין,
כְּלוֹמַר לָאו בְּיַיִן וְלָאו אַחֵר בְּחֹמֶץ, שֶׁהֲרֵי לֹא אָמַר יַיִן וְחֹמֶץ יַיִן לֹא
יִשְׁתֶּה. וְלָמַדְנוּ מֵעַתָּה כִּי הַשּׁוֹתֶה הַיַּיִן וְהַחֹמֶץ אֵינוֹ לוֹקֶה (אֶלָּא עַל אַחַת).

מִשָּׁרְשֵׁי עִנְיַן הַנְּזִירוּת, כָּתַבְתִּי בְּמִצְוַת עֲשֵׂה בְּסֵדֶר ד' [סִי' שֵׁע"ד] מַה
שֶּׁיָּדַעְתִּי; וְגֹדֶל הַרְחָקַת הַנָּזִיר מִכָּל תַּעֲרֹבֶת הַיַּיִן, הַכֹּל מִן הַטַּעַם הַכָּתוּב שָׁם.

מִדִּינֵי הַמִּצְוָה, מַה שֶּׁאָמְרוּ זִכְרוֹנָם לִבְרָכָה שֶׁכָּל הַיּוֹצֵא מִן הַגֶּפֶן, בֵּין פְּרִי בֵּין
פְּסֹלֶת, כְּלוֹמַר הַזָּג שֶׁהִיא הַקְּלִפָּה, וְהַחַרְצָן שֶׁהוּא הַזֶּרַע שֶׁבְּתוֹכוֹ, אָסוּר לַנָּזִיר,
וּכְמוֹ שֶׁמְּפֹרָשׁ בַּכָּתוּב; אֲבָל הֶעָלִין וְהַלּוּלְבִּין וְהַגְּפָנִים וְהַסְּמָדַר, הֲרֵי אֵלּוּ מֻתָּרִין,
שֶׁאֵינָן לֹא פְרִי וְלֹא פְסֹלֶת אֶלָּא כְּמוֹ עֵץ הֵם נֶחֱשָׁבִים, וְיֶתֶר רֻבֵּי פְּרָטֵי הַמִּצְוָה,
מְבֹאָרִין בְּמַסֶּכְתָּא הַבְּנוּיָה עַל זֶה, וְהִיא מַסֶּכֶת נָזִיר.

וְנוֹהֵג אִסּוּר זֶה בִּזְכָרִים וּנְקֵבוֹת, בְּכָל מָקוֹם וּבְכָל זְמָן, שֶׁכָּל מִי שֶׁנָּדַר נְזִירוּת
חַיָּב לְהִזָּהֵר מִיַּיִן וְשֵׁכָר וְחֹמֶץ יַיִן וְחֹמֶץ שֵׁכָר וּמִכָּל מִשְׁרַת עֲנָבִים. וְעוֹבֵר עַל זֶה
וְשָׁתָה רְבִיעִית לֹג יַיִן אוֹ אָכַל כַּזַּיִת עֲנָבִים לַחִים אוֹ יְבֵשִׁים אוֹ מִפְּסֹלֶת שֶׁלָּהֶם
שֶׁהוּא הַחַרְצַנִּים וְהַזַּגִּין, חַיָּב מַלְקוֹת; וַאֲפִלּוּ אָכַל כַּזַּיִת בֵּין הַכֹּל, כְּלוֹמַר שֶׁלָּקַח
מְעַט מְעַט מִכָּל אֶחָד מֵאֵלּוּ שֶׁזָּכַרְנוּ עַד שֶׁהָיוּ בֵּין כֻּלָּם שִׁעוּר כַּזַּיִת וַאֲכָלוֹ, לוֹקֶה,
שֶׁכָּל אִסּוּרֵי נָזִיר מִצְטָרְפִין זֶה עִם זֶה לַכַּזַּיִת לְהַלְקוֹת עֲלֵיהֶן.

אֲבָל שְׁאָר אִסּוּרִין שֶׁבַּתּוֹרָה אֵין מִצְטָרְפִין זֶה עִם זֶה, חוּץ מִבְּשַׂר נְבֵלָה עִם

5. The paragraph is based on ShM negative precept §202. The last three
Hebrew words, 'e-la 'al 'ahath, are absent in the oldest manuscripts, leaving the
sentence incomplete, by an apparent scribal error. Judging from ShM, though,
perhaps it should be completed with the word sh'ta-yim: i.e. "he is not given two
floggings."

The point here is that Numbers 6:3 apparently has three injunctions: *From wine
and liquor he shall abstain; no vinegar of wine or liquor shall he drink; neither shall he drink
any liquid of grapes*; and we might take the first two parts to denote two separate
negative precepts. Were this so, however, Scripture would have used the verb
"drink" in both instances. The change of verb indicates that the second part of the
verse merely extends the meaning or scope of the first part.

6. In its original form, this work presents all the positive precepts of a *sidrah* first,
and then the negative; hence "I wrote"; here, however (as in most editions), all the
precepts follow the order of their bases in Scripture, and this is therefore found later
on.

7. TB Nazir 34b; MT *hilchoth n'ziruth* v 1.

8. Mishnah, 'Orlah i 7; MT *ibid.* 2.

9. See §31, note 2. The phrase "liquid derived from grapes" (*mishra·th 'anavim*)
should read more correctly "any suffusion, or liquid from steeping, of grapes"; it
might be best understood as any liquid with a flavoring derived directly from
grapes.

states, *no vinegar of wine and no vinegar of liquor shall he drink (ibid.)*; but these are not two negative precepts — i.e. one negative precept about wine, and another about vinegar, since it does not say, "he shall not drink wine, nor vinegar of wine shall he drink." Hence we have learned that if someone drinks wine and vinegar, he is not given whiplashes for any but one [transgression].[5]

About the root purpose of the theme of the *nazir*, I wrote in the fourth positive precept of this *sidrah* (§ 374)[6] what I know; and the great degree to which a *nazir* is removed from any mixture of wine is all for the reason written there.

Among the laws of the precept there is what the Sages of blessed memory taught:[7] that anything derived from the grape, whether fruit or waste product — meaning the skin and the seeds within — is forbidden a *nazir*, as is explained in the Writ (Numbers 6:4); but as for leaves, sprouts, sap of the vines, and budding berries, these are permitted, since they are neither fruit nor waste product, but are reckoned like [part of] a tree.[8] The rest of the numerous details of the precept are explained in the Talmud tractate built about this [subject], namely, the tractate *Nazir*.

This prohibition applies to both man and woman, everywhere, at every time. For whoever takes a vow to be a *nazir* is duty-bound to abstain from wine, liquor, vinegar of wine, vinegar of liquor, and from liquid derived from grapes. If anyone violated this and drank a fourth of a *log*[9] of wine, or ate an olive's amount of fresh or dry grapes, or of their waste products, meaning the seeds and the skins, he would incur the punishment of whiplashes.[10] Even if he ate an olive's amount of everything together, i.e. if he took a bit of every one of those items that we mentioned, until among them all [together] there was the measure of an olive's amount, and he ate this, he should receive a whipping.[11] For all items forbidden a *nazir* are reckoned together to add up to an olive's worth, to impose a flogging of whiplashes for them.

Other forbidden foods of the Torah, however, are not reckoned together, one with another, except flesh of a carcass[12] with flesh of a

---

10. MT *ibid.*
11. TB Nazir 34a; MT *ibid.* 3.
12. I.e. an animal that died without being properly ritually slain.

בְּשַׂר טְרֵפָה, וּפִגּוּל עִם נוֹתָר, שֶׁמִּצְטָרְפִין. וְשִׁשָּׁה דְבָרִים שֶׁבְּקָרְבַּן תּוֹדָה, שֶׁהֵן חֵלֶב וּבָשָׂר וְסֹלֶת וְשֶׁמֶן וְיַיִן וְלֶחֶם, גַּם־כֵּן מִצְטָרְפִין; וְאֵין צֹרֶךְ לוֹמַר שֶׁכָּל דָּבָר שֶׁהוּא מִשֵּׁם אֶחָד שֶׁמִּצְטָרֵף, כְּגוֹן נִבְלַת שׁוֹר וְנִבְלַת שֶׂה וְנִבְלַת צְבִי וְכָל כַּיּוֹצֵא־ בָזֶה.

וְלִמְּדוּנוּ זִכְרוֹנָם לִבְרָכָה שֶׁאֵסוּר הוּא שֶׁמִּצְטָרֵף לִכְזַיִת, כְּאִלּוּ שֶׁזָּכַרְנוּ, אֲבָל הֶתֵּר אֵינוֹ מִצְטָרֵף לְאִסּוּר בְּכָל הָאֲסוּרִין שֶׁבַּתּוֹרָה, כְּלוֹמַר שֶׁמִּי שֶׁאָכַל חֲצִי זַיִת אִסּוּר וַחֲצִי זַיִת הֶתֵּר מְעֹרָבִין בְּיַחַד לֹא יִתְחַיֵּב מַלְקוֹת, בֵּין בְּאִסּוּרֵי נָזִיר בֵּין בְּכָל שְׁאָר הָאֲסוּרִין; וַאֲפִלּוּ בְּקָדָשִׁים וּבָשָׂר בְּחָלָב וְגֵעוּלֵי גוֹיִם, שֶׁיֵּשׁ בָּהֶן קְצָת חִדּוּשׁ, כְּמוֹ שֶׁמְּפֹרָשׁ בִּפְסָחִים וּבְנָזִיר, גַּם־כֵּן מִכֵּינָן שֶׁלֹּא אָכַל כְּזַיִת מִן הָאִסּוּר, אֵין חִיּוּב מַלְקוֹת בַּדָּבָר לְעוֹלָם; שֶׁאֵין הֲלָכָה כְּרַבִּי עֲקִיבָה דִּסְבִירָא לֵיהּ הָכִי בְּמַסֶּכֶת נָזִיר פֶּרֶק שְׁלֹשָׁה מִינִין, וְיַלִּיף לַהּ מִקְּרָא דִ"וְכָל מִשְׁרַת", אֶלָּא הֲלָכָה כְּרַבָּנָן, דִּפְלִיגֵי עֲלֵיהּ, וּמוֹקְמֵי הַאי קְרָא הָתָם, וְכֵן בְּמַסֶּכֶת פְּסָחִים, לִלְמֹד מִמֶּנּוּ שֶׁטַּעַם הָאֲסוּר אָסוּר כְּמוֹ עִקָּרוֹ, בֵּין בְּנָזִיר בֵּין בְּכָל אֲסוּרִים שֶׁבַּתּוֹרָה.

וְכֵן נֶאֱמַר שָׁם: וְהַאי "וְכָל מִשְׁרַת" לְהָכִי הוּא דְאָתָא, הַהוּא מִבָּעֵי לֵיהּ לְכִדְתַנְיָא: "מִשְׁרַת"—לִתֵּן טַעַם כְּעִקָּר, שֶׁאִם שָׁרָה עֲנָבִים בְּמַיִם וְיֵשׁ בָּהֶן טַעַם יַיִן, אָסוּר; מִכָּאן אַתָּה דָן לְכָל אֲסוּרִים שֶׁבַּתּוֹרָה: וּמַה נָזִיר וְכוּלֵי, עַד הָא מַנֵּי, רַבָּנָן, וְאִכָּא דְאָמְרֵי כְּרַבִּי עֲקִיבָה.

13. For all are forbidden by one and the same prohibition. MT *hilchoth ma'achaloth 'asuroth* iv 16–17, based on TB Me'ilah 15b, 16a, 17b.

14. About which the law is generally severe.

15. Meat with milk becomes forbidden (by Torah law) only if they were cooked together, but not if the meat was, for example, steeped in the milk for a long time (see TB P'sahim 44b, and Rashi there s.v. *tari lêh*). Food cooked in a heathen's vessel becomes forbidden because the vessel contains in its walls the flavor of the heathen's food cooked in it previously, which it now adds to what the Jew cooks—even though this flavor that the pot adds does not improve the food (even if freshly added) but tends to spoil it. Ordinarily, though, a forbidden flavor (not from the walls of a pot) added to permitted food can make it prohibited only if it improves it.

16. The word *mishrah* denotes a steeping in liquid; hence R. 'Akiva rules that if a *nazir* steeped an olive's amount of bread in wine and ate it, he is to be given a whipping, although he did not consume a fourth of a *log* of wine, the minimal amount punishable.

17. A teaching by the Sages of the Mishnah that was not included in the Mishnah.

18. It would depend on whether the *baraitha* meant that the grapes contributed a punishable minimal amount of wine to the water (so the Sages) or even if not (so R. 'Akiva). "Those who say" actually denotes R. Yohanan, according to the Talmud;

fatally ill or wounded animal, and *piggul* (§ 144) with *nothar* (§ 143), which are considered together. So too the six items in a *todah* (thanks) offering, namely: forbidden fat, meat, fine flour, oil, wine and bread; they are likewise reckoned together. And there is no need to say that everything ranked under one name is considered together: for example, the carcass of an ox, the carcass of a lamb, and the carcass of a deer; and so anything like that.[13]

Now, our Sages of blessed memory taught us that it is only one forbidden food with another that can be reckoned together [at times] to total an olive's amount. But permissible food cannot be considered together with any forbidden food among all the prohibitions in the Torah. In other words, if someone ate half an olive's amount of forbidden food and half an olive's amount of permissible food mixed together, he would not be punishable by whiplashes, whether it involved what is forbidden a *nazir* or any other prohibited foods. This likewise applies even to holy offerings,[14] meat with milk, and food contaminated [through cooking in pots] of heathens, which contain some new, unusual element [in their law],[15] as explained in the tractates *P'saḥim* (44b) and *Nazir* (37b). As long as an olive's amount of the forbidden food was not eaten, there is never a punishment of whiplashes. For the definitive law does not follow R. 'Akiva, who so rules in the sixth chapter of the tractate *Nazir* (37b), deriving his view from the verse, *neither shall he drink any* mishrah *(liquid) of grapes* (Numbers 6:3).[16] Rather, the definitive law follows the Sages who differ with him, and interpret this verse there, and likewise in the tractate *P'saḥim* (44b), to infer from it that the flavor of the forbidden food is as prohibited as the food itself, both in regard to a *nazir* and with all other forbidden food in the Torah.

So was it stated there: Was this verse about "any *mishrah* (liquid) of grapes" then given for this purpose? It is needed for the purpose taught in a *baraitha*:[17] "any *mishrah*"—this is to make the flavor [as forbidden] as the original food: that if one steeped grapes in water and it has a flavor of wine, it is prohibited. From here you have the law for all forbidden foods in the Torah: If for a *nazir*, etc. till [the Talmud concludes:] Whose view is this?—that of the Sages; and there are those who say, that of R. 'Akiva.[18]

MY would therefore so emend this, considering the original a scribal error. It may be, however, merely our author's paraphrase.

וּבְפֵרוּשׁ טַעַם כְּעִקָּר, הַרְבֵּה פֵרוּשִׁים נֶאֶמְרוּ בוֹ, וְאֶחָד מֵהֶם, וְהוּא הַטּוֹב לְפִי הַדּוֹמֶה, שֶׁכָּל אִסּוּר שֶׁאֵינוֹ בְעֵינוֹ אֶלָּא שֶׁנִּתְעָרֵב בְּתוֹךְ הֶתֵּר וְנָתַן טַעַם בּוֹ — לְאַפּוֹקֵי אִם נִתְעָרֵב בְּמִינוֹ, שֶׁאֵין כָּאן נְתִינַת טַעַם — עַל זֶה יֵאָמְרוּ זִכְרוֹנָם לִבְרָכָה שֶׁטַּעַם הָאִסּוּר אָסוּר כְּמוֹ עִקָּרוֹ, וְלָזֶה הֻצְרַךְ מִקְרָא זֶה ד"וְכָל מִשְׁרַת": שֶׁאִם לֹא שֶׁלִּמְּדָנוּ דָבָר זֶה מִן הַמִּקְרָא הַזֶּה, הָיִיתִי דָן, שֶׁכָּל שֶׁנִּתְעָרֵב בְּהֶתֵּר אָסוּר בְּמִינוֹ אוֹ אֲפִלּוּ בְּשֶׁאֵינוֹ מִינוֹ, שֶׁיִּבָּטֵל בְּרֹב, מִן הַכְּלָל הַיָּדוּעַ לָנוּ מִדִּין הַתּוֹרָה דְּחַד בִּתְרֵי בָּטֵל, כְּלוֹמַר בְּרֻבָּא, דְּלִשּׁוֹן "תְּרֵי" לָאו דַּוְקָא.

וְאַחַר שֶׁיָּדַעְנוּ זֶה, יֵשׁ לָנוּ לָדוּן הַטַּעַם כְּמוֹ הַמַּמָּשׁ. וּמַהוּ הַדִּין הַיָּדוּעַ לָנוּ בְּמַמָּשׁוֹ מִבְּלִי תַעֲרֹבֶת — שֶׁמִּי שֶׁאָכַל כְּזַיִת אִסּוּר מִבְּלִי שֶׁהָיַת שִׁעוּר אֲכִילַת פְּרָס, שֶׁלּוֹקֶה עָלָיו; אֲבָל שָׁהָה יוֹתֵר מִזֶּה, פָּטוּר. וְזֶה הַדִּין בְּעַצְמוֹ הוּא שֶׁנֶּאֱמַר בְּטַעֲמוֹ, שֶׁאִם נִתְעָרֵב מִן הָאִסּוּר בְּהֶתֵּר כְּזַיִת בִּכְדֵי אֲכִילַת פְּרָס, וְאָכַל מִמֶּנּוּ שִׁעוּר אֲכִילַת פְּרָס מִבְּלִי שֶׁהָיָה שְׁהִיָּה הַנִּזְכֶּרֶת, לוֹקֶה עָלָיו; אֲבָל אָכַל מִמֶּנּוּ פָּחוֹת מִכֵּן, אוֹ שֶׁנִּתְעָרֵב בּוֹ מִן הָאִסּוּר פָּחוֹת מִשִּׁעוּר זֶה, אֵינוֹ לוֹקֶה עָלָיו.

וּכְמוֹ־כֵן אָמְרוּ קְצָת הַמְפָרְשִׁים שֶׁבִּכְלַל אִסּוּר טַעֲמוֹ וְלֹא מַמָּשׁוֹ לְהַלְקוֹת עָלָיו, הוּא כָל זְמַן שֶׁנָּתַן הָאִסּוּר טַעַם בַּהֶתֵּר כָּל־כָּךְ, כְּאִלּוּ נִתְעָרֵב בּוֹ אִסּוּר כְּזַיִת בִּכְדֵי אֲכִילַת פְּרָס, וְאַף־עַל־פִּי שֶׁלֹּא יָדַעְנוּ כַּמָּה שִׁעוּר נִכְנַס בּוֹ מִמַּמָּשׁוּת הָאִסּוּר.

וְלֹא כֵן דַּעַת הָרַב מֹשֶׁה בֶּן מַיְמוֹן זִכְרוֹנוֹ לִבְרָכָה, לְפִי הַנִּרְאֶה מִדְּבָרָיו

19. Given in *tosafoth*, TB Ḥullin 98b, s.v. *Rava*.
20. TB Gittin 54b.
21. So TB Ḥullin 98b.
22. TB K'rithoth 12b. For if he made a sufficiently long pause between bites (the time needed to eat four eggs) it is as though he ate two amounts at different occasions, neither of which was large enough to warrant lashes.
23. The time needed to eat four eggs (according to Rambam, three eggs).
24. MT *hilchoth ma'achaloth 'asuroth* xv 3.
25. Rabad (R. Abraham b. David), gloss to MT *hilchoth n'ziruth* v. 7.

As to the meaning of "the flavor [forbidden] as the original," many explanations were said about it. One of them,[19] and it is the best as it seems, is that any forbidden food that does not exist in its original state but became merged or blended with permissible food, imparting its flavor to it—to exclude a case where it became blended with its own kind [of food, that was permissible], where there is no imparting of flavor—about this the Sages of blessed memory ruled that the flavor of forbidden food is as prohibited as the actual food; and for this the passage about "any *mishrah* (liquid) of grapes" is needed. For if we did not derive this rule from this verse, I would have decided that whatever forbidden matter became blended into permissible food, whether it was of its own kind or even of a different kind, it should become nullified by a majority—by the rule known to us from the law of the Torah, that one [forbidden amount] in two permissible ones is nullified[20]—i.e. by a majority,[21] because two is not meant strictly.

Now that we know this, it is for us to rule about flavor as if it were the actual food. And what is the law known to us about actual forbidden food without anything mixed with it?—that if a person ate an olive's amount of forbidden food without a lapse of time [from start to end of the eating] long enough to eat a *p'ras* (half a loaf) of bread, he is given lashes (a whipping) for it;[22] but if he tarried longer than that, he is free of penalty. Then this law about [forbidden food] by itself is what we will apply about its flavor: that if of the forbidden food, an olive's amount was mixed into a quantity of permissible food that can be eaten in the time it takes to consume a *p'ras* of bread,[23] and someone ate of it as much as can be consumed in this period of time, without the above-mentioned lapse, he would receive whiplashes for it. If he ate of it less than that, or if less than that amount of forbidden food was blended into it, he would not receive a whipping for it.[24]

Some authorities[25] likewise said that in general, the rule that over the prohibition against the flavor of forbidden food without its substance, a whipping should be given over it—this [applies] as long as the forbidden element imparts as much flavor to the permissible food as if an olive's amount of the forbidden ingredient had been blended into a quantity of permissible food that could be eaten in the same time as a *p'ras* (half a loaf) of bread—even if we do not know what quantity of the substance of the forbidden food merged with it.

⟨37⟩   This, however, is not the view of R. Moses b. Maimon [Rambam]

בְּהַפְלָאָה וּקְדָשָׁה, אֶלָּא דְּלָא לָקֵי לְעוֹלָם, לְדַעְתּוֹ, עַד דַּעְתֵּנוּ שֶׁאֹכַל מִמַּמָּשׁוּת הָאָסוּר כְּזַיִת, אוֹ בִּפְנֵי עַצְמוֹ אוֹ בְּתַעֲרֹבֶת כְּזַיִת בִּכְדֵי אֲכִילַת פְּרָס. וּלְפִי סְבָרָתוֹ זֹאת, מַה שֶּׁאָמְרוּ שָׁם "מִשְׁרַת" לִתֵּן טַעַם כְּעִקָּר, כְּגוֹן שֶׁשָּׁרָה עֲנָבִים בְּמַיִם, לְעִנְיָן אִסּוּרָא הוּא שֶׁאָמְרוּ כֵן, וְלֹא לְמַלְקוֹת.

[שֶׁלֹּא יֹאכַל הַנָּזִיר עֲנָבִים לַחִים]

שסט שֶׁלֹּא יֹאכַל הַנָּזִיר עֲנָבִים לַחִים, שֶׁנֶּאֱמַר: וַעֲנָבִים לַחִים ... לֹא יֹאכֵל. וְאָמְרוּ זִכְרוֹנָם לִבְרָכָה בְּמַסֶּכֶת נָזִיר: "וַעֲנָבִים לַחִים ... לֹא יֹאכֵל", לְהָבִיא אֶת הַבֹּסֶר.

כָּל עִנְיַן מִצְוָה זוֹ כַּמִּצְוָה הַקּוֹדֶמֶת לָהּ. וּמִשָּׁרְשֵׁי עִנְיַן הַנְּזִירוּת, כָּתַבְתִּי לְמַעְלָה עֲשֵׂה ד' [סי' שע"ד]; אֵין צֹרֶךְ לְהַחֲזִירוֹ.

[שֶׁלֹּא יֹאכַל הַנָּזִיר צִמּוּקִים]

שע שֶׁלֹּא יֹאכַל הַנָּזִיר צִמּוּקִים, שֶׁנֶּאֱמַר: וַעֲנָבִים לַחִים וִיבֵשִׁים לֹא יֹאכֵל — שֶׁלֹּא תֹאמַר: הוֹאִיל וְנִשְׁתַּנָּה שָׁמָם שֶׁנִּקְרָאִין צִמּוּקִים וְלֹא עֲנָבִים, הֻתְּרוּ, לְפִיכָךְ בֵּאֵר הַכָּתוּב הָאָסוּר גַּם בָּהֶם.

וְכָל עִנְיָנָהּ כַּמִּצְווֹת הַקּוֹדְמוֹת; וּמִי שֶׁאָכַל כְּזַיִת מֵהֶם, לוֹקֶה.

[שֶׁלֹּא יֹאכַל הַנָּזִיר זֶרַע הָעֲנָבִים]

שעא שֶׁלֹּא יֹאכַל הַנָּזִיר זֶרַע הָעֲנָבִים, שֶׁנֶּאֱמַר: מֵחַרְצַנִּים ... לֹא יֹאכֵל. כָּל עִנְיָנָהּ כַּמִּצְווֹת הַקּוֹדְמוֹת; וְאִם אָכַל מֵהֶן כְּזַיִת, לוֹקֶה.

---

26. MT *hilchoth n'ziruth* v 7; *hilchoth ma'achaloth 'asuroth* xv 3.

27. I.e. it is always forbidden, but a whipping is only given as stated above.

§369   1. Here, as in most editions, the precept is found below; in the original, however, the author gave all the positive precepts first, and then all the negative.

of blessed memory, as it appears from his words in the *Book of Solemn Utterance* and the *Book of Holiness*.[26] Rather, in his view, a person is never given whiplashes until we know that he ate either an olive's amount of the forbidden food's substance by itself or an olive's amount mixed into as much [of permissible food] as can be eaten in the same time as a *p'ras*. Then according to this opinion of his, when the Sages stated there that the term *mishrah* [in the verse] is meant to make the flavor the same as the actual [forbidden element under the law]—for instance, if someone steeped grapes in water—it is only in regard to the prohibition that they said this, but not in regard to whiplashes.[27]

[THAT A NAZIR IS PROHIBITED FROM EATING
FRESH GRAPES]

369 that a *nazir* should not eat fresh grapes, as it is stated, *nor shall he eat fresh grapes* (Numbers 6:3); and our Sages of blessed memory taught in the Talmud tractate *Nazir* (TJ vi 2): "nor shall he eat fresh grapes"— this is to include unripe grapes.

The entire subject-matter of this precept is like that of the preceding precept (§ 368). And some of the root purpose of the rules about a *nazir*, I have written above in the fourth positive precept (§ 374);[1] there is no need to repeat it.

[THAT A NAZIR IS PROHIBITED FROM EATING
DRIED GRAPES]

370 that a *nazir* should not eat raisins, as it is stated, *nor shall he eat fresh grapes or dried* (Numbers 6:3); for you should not say, "Since their name was changed, as they are called raisins and not grapes, they have become permissible"; hence the Writ made the prohibition clear about them too.

Its entire subject-matter is like that of the earlier precepts. If any [*nazir*] ate an olive's amount of them, he should be given whiplashes.

[THAT A NAZIR IS PROHIBITED FROM EATING
GRAPE SEEDS]

371 that a *nazir* should not eat the seeds of grapes, as it is stated, *he shall eat nothing...from the seeds* (Numbers 6:4). Its entire subject matter is like that of the previous precepts. If [a *nazir*] ate an olive's amount of them, he should be given lashes of the whip.

[שֶׁלֹּא יֹאכַל הַנָּזִיר קְלִפַּת הָעֲנָבִים]

שעב שֶׁלֹּא יֹאכַל הַנָּזִיר קְלִפַּת הָעֲנָבִים, שֶׁנֶּאֱמַר: וְעַד זָג לֹא יֹאכֵל, וּפֵרוּשׁ זָג הִיא הַקְּלִפָּה. כָּל עִנְיָנָהּ כַּמִּצְוֹת הַקּוֹדְמוֹת.

וְנִתְרַבּוּ הָאַזְהָרוֹת בְּהַרְחָקַת הַיַּיִן וּבְכָל הַיּוֹצֵא מִן הַגֶּפֶן, לְפִי הַדּוֹמֶה, מִפְּנֵי שֶׁיֵּשׁ בְּכָל הַיּוֹצֵא מִמֶּנָּה כֹּחַ רַב לְהַגְדִּיל הַיֵּצֶר, וְזֶה יָדוּעַ לְחַכְמֵי הַטֶּבַע.

וּכְשֶׁרָצוּ שָׁם לְקַיֵּם שֶׁזֶּה הַתַּנָּא דְּתָנֵי מַלְקֻיּוֹת תְּנָא וְשַׁיַּר, וְשֶׁיִּתְחַיֵּב הַנָּזִיר יוֹתֵר מֵחָמֵשׁ מַלְקֻיּוֹת, שֶׁאָמְרוּ: וְהָא שַׁיַּר לַאו דְּ״לֹא יַחֵל״, וְלֹא אָמְרוּ ״וְהָא שַׁיַּר לַאו דְּחֹמֶץ״—וְהַטַּעַם, לְפִי שֶׁלֹּא יִתְחַיֵּב עַל הַיַּיִן וְעַל הַחֹמֶץ שְׁתַּיִם, כְּמוֹ שֶׁאָמַרְנוּ, מִפְּנֵי שֶׁהַחֹמֶץ נֶאֱסָר מֵחֲמַת עִקָּרוֹ שֶׁהוּא יַיִן, וְעִנְיַן הַכָּתוּב כְּאִלּוּ אָמַר שֶׁעִקַּר אִסּוּרוֹ שֶׁל יַיִן לֹא סָר מִמֶּנּוּ בְּהַפְסִדוֹ, כְּמוֹ שֶׁזָּכַרְנוּ לְמַעְלָה בִּמְקוֹמוֹ. וּמִמַּה שֶׁרָאוּי שֶׁתֵּדָעֵהוּ שֶׁאֵלֶּה אִסּוּרֵי נָזִיר מִצְטָרְפִין כֻּלָּן לִכְזַיִת, וְלוֹקִין עַל כְּזַיִת. עַד כָּאן.

וְכָתַב הָרַב מֹשֶׁה בֶּן מַיְמוֹן זִכְרוֹנוֹ לִבְרָכָה: וְהָרְאָיָה עַל הֱיוֹת אֵלֶּה הַחָמֵשׁ, כְּלוֹמַר הַיַּיִן וְהָעֲנָבִים וְהַצִּמּוּקִין וְהַחַרְצָן וְהַזָּג, כָּל אֶחָד וְאֶחָד מִצְוָה בִּפְנֵי עַצְמָהּ, שֶׁהֲרֵי מִתְחַיֵּב אָדָם מַלְקוּת אַחַת עַל כָּל אֶחָד וְאֶחָד, וּכְמוֹ שֶׁאָמְרוּ זִכְרוֹנָם לִבְרָכָה בַּמִּשְׁנָה: וְחַיָּב עַל הַיַּיִן בִּפְנֵי עַצְמוֹ וְעַל הָעֲנָבִים בִּפְנֵי עַצְמָן וְעַל הַחַרְצַנִּים בִּפְנֵי עַצְמָן וְעַל הַזַּגִּין בִּפְנֵי עַצְמָן; וְאָמְרוּ כְּמוֹ־כֵן בְּמַסֶּכֶת נָזִיר: אָכַל עֲנָבִים לַחִים וִיבֵשִׁים, חַרְצַנִּים וְזַגִּים, וְסָחַט אֶשְׁכּוֹל שֶׁל עֲנָבִים וְשָׁתָה, לוֹקֶה חָמֵשׁ.

[שֶׁלֹּא יְגַלַּח הַנָּזִיר שְׂעָרוֹ כָּל יְמֵי נִזְרוֹ]

שעג שֶׁלֹּא יְגַלַּח הַנָּזִיר שְׂעָרוֹ כָּל יְמֵי נְזִירוּתוֹ, שֶׁנֶּאֱמַר: תַּעַר לֹא יַעֲבֹר עַל רֹאשׁוֹ. מִשָּׁרְשֵׁי הַמִּצְוָה, כָּתַבְתִּי לְמַעְלָה מַעֲלָה ד' [סִי' שע״ד].

---

§372   1. So TB Nazir 34b.

    2. ShM negative precept § 206.

    3. Mishnah, Nazir vi 2 (TB 34b).

    4. I.e. he did not exhaust all the possibilities for a *nazir* to incur many sets of whiplashes through one activity.

    5. Equally prohibited in Numbers 6:3.

[THAT A NAZIR IS FORBIDDEN TO EAT
GRAPE SKINS]

372 that a *nazir* should not eat the skin of grapes, for it is stated, *even to* zag *he shall not eat* (Numbers 6:4), and the meaning of *zag* is the skin.[1] All its subject-matter is like that of the earlier precepts.

Now, the injunctions to keep far from wine and anything that comes from the grape were multiplied, as it would seem, because in everything that derives from it there is a great force to increase the inclination; and this is known to those learned about nature.

Well, Rambam of blessed memory wrote:[2] The proof that these five — meaning wine, grapes, raisins, seeds and skin — are each and every one a precept by itself is that here a man is punishable by a whipping of one set of lashes for each and every one [of the five]. As the Sages of blessed memory said in the Mishnah:[3] he is punishable for wine separately, for grapes separately, for the seeds separately, and for the skin separately. So did they likewise teach in the Talmud tractate *Nazir* (38b): If someone ate both fresh and dried grapes, and seeds and skin, then squeezed out [the juice of] a bunch of grapes and drank it, he is to be whipped with five sets of lashes.

Now, [Rambam continues] when the Sages there wished to conclude that this Sage of the Mishnah who taught about the separate punishments of lashes "taught and left over,"[4] and that a *nazir* can incur more than five floggings, they said, "But he left aside the injunction not to break one's word" (§ 407), and they did not say, "But he left over the injunction against vinegar."[5] The reason is that a person would not be punishable twice for wine and vinegar, as we stated (§ 368), because vinegar was forbidden on account of its main element, which is wine. The sense of the verse is as though it said that the essential ban on the wine does not leave it when it becomes spoiled, as we mentioned above, in its proper place (§ 368). Another thing fitting for you to know is that these items forbidden to a *nazir* can be reckoned as combined together, all of them, to total an olive's amount; and one is flogged with whiplashes for an olive's amount. Thus far [Rambam's words].

[THAT A NAZIR IS PROHIBITED FROM SHAVING
HIS HAIR ALL HIS DAYS AS A NAZIR]

373 that a *nazir* is not to shave his hair all the days that he is a *nazir*, as it is written, *no razor shall come upon his head* (Numbers 6:5). About

מִדִּינֵי הַמִּצְוָה, מַה שֶּׁאָמְרוּ זִכְרוֹנָם לִבְרָכָה שֶׁאֶחָד הַמְגַלֵּחַ בְּתַעַר אוֹ
בְּמִסְפָּרַיִם כְּעֵין תַּעַר, אוֹ שֶׁתָּלַשׁ הַשֵּׂעָר בְּיָדוֹ, כָּל זְמַן שֶׁקְּצָצָה מֵעִקָּרָהּ, לוֹקֶה;
אֲבָל כָּל זְמַן שֶׁהִנִּיחַ מִמֶּנּוּ כְּדֵי לָכֹף רֹאשׁוֹ לְעִקָּרוֹ אֵינוֹ לוֹקֶה, שֶׁאֵין זֶה כְּעֵין
תַּעַר. הֶעֱבִיר עַל רֹאשׁוֹ סַם שֶׁמַּשִּׁיר אֶת הַשֵּׂעָר וְהִשִּׁיר אֶת שְׂעָרוֹ, אֵינוֹ לוֹקֶה
[אֶלָּא בִּטֵּל מִצְוַת עֲשֵׂה]. נָזִיר שֶׁגִּלַּח כָּל רֹאשׁוֹ אֵינוֹ לוֹקֶה] מִשּׁוּם הַתִּגְלַחַת אֶלָּא
אַחַת. וְאִם הִתְרוּ בוֹ עַל כָּל שֵׂעָר וְשֵׂעָר וְאָמְרוּ לוֹ "אַל תְּגַלַּח", וְהוּא מְגַלֵּחַ,
לוֹקֶה עַל כָּל אַחַת וְאַחַת.

וְכֵן מֵעִנְיַן הַמִּצְוָה מַה שֶּׁאָמְרוּ בְּמַסֶּכֶת שַׁבָּת: נָזִיר חוֹפֵף וּמְפַסְפֵּס, אֲבָל לֹא
שׁוֹרֵק, כְּלוֹמַר שֶׁחוֹפֵף שְׂעָרוֹ בְּיָדָיו וְחוֹכֵךְ בְּצִפָּרְנָיו, וְאִם נָפְלוּ שְׂעָרוֹת מִתּוֹךְ
הַחֲפִיפָה וְהַפִּסְפּוּס אֵינוֹ חוֹשֵׁשׁ, אַחַר שֶׁאֵין כַּוָּנָתוֹ לְהַשִּׁירוֹ, וְאֶפְשָׁר גַּם־כֵּן שֶׁלֹּא
יְהֵא נָשָׁר מִפְּנֵי זֶה; אֲבָל לֹא סוֹרֵק בְּמַסְרֵק, לְפִי שֶׁהַמַּסְרֵק מַפִּיל וּמַשִּׁיר הַשֵּׂעָר
בְּלִי סָפֵק. וְכֵן לֹא יָחֹף בַּאֲדָמָה, מִפְּנֵי שֶׁמַּשֶּׁרֶת הַשֵּׂעָר וַדַּאי; אֲבָל אִם עָשָׂה כֵן,
אֵינוֹ לוֹקֶה. וְיֶתֶר פְּרָטֶיהָ, בְּמַסֶּכֶת נָזִיר.

וּלְעִנְיַן בְּמִי נוֹהֶגֶת וּבְאֵי זֶה זְמַן, וְעֹנֶשׁ הָעוֹבֵר עָלֶיהָ, הַכֹּל כְּדִין שְׁאָר מִצְוֹת
הַנָּזִיר שֶׁכְּתַבְנוּ. וּמִכָּל־מָקוֹם יֵשׁ לְבָרֵר כָּאן שֶׁאִם גִּלַּח אֲפִלּוּ שַׂעֲרָה אַחַת יִתְחַיֵּב
מַלְקוֹת עָלֶיהָ, וּכְמוֹ שֶׁאָמְרוּ בְּנָזִיר פֶּרֶק שְׁלֹשָׁה מִינִין: אָמַר רַב חִסְדָּא: לִלְקוֹת
בְּאַחַת, לְעַכֵּב בִּשְׁתַּיִם—כְּלוֹמַר שֶׁלֹּא קִיֵּם מִצְוַת עֲשֵׂה דְגִלּוּחַ כָּל זְמַן שֶׁנִּשְׁתַּיְּרוּ
בְּרֹאשׁוֹ שְׁתֵּי שְׂעָרוֹת; לִסְתֹּר אֵינוֹ סוֹתֵר אֶלָּא בְּרֹב רֹאשׁוֹ—כְּלוֹמַר אֵינוֹ סוֹתֵר

---

§373   1. See § 369 note 1.

2. TB Nazir 39a, 40a; MT *hilchoth n'ziruth* v 11.

3. MT *ibid.* 12, based on Sifre Zuta, 241 l. 24. The bracketed addition follows an
emendation by R. Isaiah Pik, based on MT *ibid.* It was evidently omitted by a
scribal oversight between the identical terms אינו לוקה.

4. Originally in Mishnah, Nazir vi 3 (hence MY suggests that *Shabbath* here
may be a scribal error for *Nazir*).

5. I.e. which has a depilatory effect—even if he does not intend to use it as a
depilatory; TB Nazir 42a.

6. MT *hilchoth n'ziruth* v 14, based on Sifre Zuta (see note 3).

7. Numbers 6 : 18; § 377.

8. And start counting them anew.

the root reason for the precept I have written above, in the fourth positive precept (§ 374).[1]

Among the laws of the precept, there is what the Sages of blessed memory taught:[2] that whether [a *nazir*] shaved [his hair] with a razor or scissors in the manner of a razor, or he plucked the hair out with his hand, as long as he detached it at the roots, he is to receive whip-lashes. But as long as he left enough of it to be able to bend the tip back to the root, he does not receive a whipping, for this is not "in the manner of a razor." If a person spread an ointment on his head that removes the hair [a depilatory] and he thus removed his hair, [he would not incur a whipping but would disobey a positive precept. If a *nazir* shaved his entire head] he would be punished for the shaving with no more than one whipping.[3] But if he was warned over each and every hair [separately, the witnesses] telling him, "Do not shave," and he did shave it, he would receive a flogging for each and every one.

So is it also of the subject-matter of the precept what the Sages taught in the Talmud tractate *Shabbath* (50b):[4] A *nazir* may wash or rub and part [his hair] but not comb it. In other words, he may wash or rub his hair with his hands and scratch with his fingernails, and if hairs fall out as a result of this washing or rubbing and parting, he need not be concerned, since it is not his intention to make them fall out, and it is equally possible that they will not fall out on account of this. But he may not arrange and smooth it with a comb, because a comb makes hair fall out and be removed beyond any doubt. So should he also not rub it with earth,[5] because it certainly makes hair fall out; but if he did so, he would not receive whiplashes.[6] The rest of its details are in the Talmud tractate *Nazir*.

Now, to whom it applies and at which time, and the punishment for one who violates it — the law on all this is the same as for the other precepts about the *nazir* that we have written. However, it remains to be clarified here that if he shaved even one hair, he would be punishable by whiplashes for it, as stated in the sixth chapter of the tractate *Nazir* (40a): Said R. Ḥisda: To receive a flogging one is enough; to deter, two. In other words, he has not fulfilled the positive precept of shaving [when his period as a *nazir* ends][7] as long as two hairs remain on his head. As for cancelling [the period of a *nazir*, said R. Ḥisda] nothing but [shaving] most of the head cancels it. In other words, he does not void the reckoning of his days as a *nazir*[8] unless he

חֶשְׁבּוֹן יְמֵי נְזִירוֹ אֶלָּא אִם־כֵּן גִּלַּח רֹב רֹאשׁוֹ; אֲבָל גִּלַּח מְעוּטוֹ, אַף־עַל־פִּי שֶׁעָבַר
עַל לָאו דְּ"תַעַר לֹא יַעֲבֹר עַל רֹאשׁוֹ", אֵינוֹ סוֹתֵר חֶשְׁבּוֹן הַיָּמִים בְּכָךְ.

וְנוֹהֵג אִסּוּר זֶה בְּכָל מָקוֹם וּבְכָל זְמָן, בִּזְכָרִים וּנְקֵבוֹת: שֶׁכָּל מִי שֶׁקִּבֵּל עָלָיו
נְזִירוּת, וַאֲפִלּוּ בַּזְּמָן הַזֶּה, אָסוּר לְגַלֵּחַ אֲפִלּוּ שַׂעֲרָה אֶחָת. וְעוֹבֵר עַל זֶה וְגִלַּח
אֲפִלּוּ שַׂעֲרָה אַחַת, חַיָּב מַלְקוֹת.

[מִצְוַת גִּדּוּל שְׂעַר נָזִיר]

שעד שֶׁנִּצְטַוָּה הַנָּזִיר, וְהוּא הָאָדָם שֶׁהִפְרִישׁ עַצְמוֹ מִן הַיַּיִן, לְגַדֵּל שְׂעַר
רֹאשׁוֹ כָּל יְמֵי הַזִּירוֹ לַיָי, שֶׁנֶּאֱמַר: גַּדֵּל פֶּרַע שְׂעַר רֹאשׁוֹ. וּלְשׁוֹן מְכִלְתָּא: "גַּדֵּל
פֶּרַע" — מִצְוַת עֲשֵׂה; וּמִנַּיִן בְּלֹא־תַעֲשֶׂה — תַּלְמוּד לוֹמַר: תַּעַר לֹא יַעֲבֹר עַל רֹאשׁוֹ.

מִשָּׁרְשֵׁי הַמִּצְוָה, הַקְדָּמָה: כְּבָר כָּתַבְתִּי בִּפְתִיחַת הַסֵּפֶר כִּי הֱיוֹת בְּעוֹלָמוֹ שֶׁל
הַקָּדוֹשׁ־בָּרוּךְ־הוּא בְּרִיָּה מְשֻׁתֶּפֶת מֵחֹמֶר וְשֵׂכֶל, וְזֶהוּ הָאָדָם, הָיָה דָבָר רָאוּי
וּמְחֻיָּב כְּדֵי לִהְיוֹת קִלּוּסוֹ, בָּרוּךְ הוּא, עוֹלֶה יָפֶה מִבְּרִיּוֹתָיו, שֶׁעִם בְּרִיָּה זוֹ לֹא
יֶחְסַר מֵעוֹלָמוֹ כָּל הָאֶפְשָׁרוּת שֶׁיֵּשׁ בְּדַעְתֵּנוּ לְהַשִּׂיג וְכוּלִי, כְּמוֹ שֶׁכָּתַבְתִּי שָׁם.

וְאֵין סָפֵק כִּי לוּלֵא מִן הַטַּעַם הַזֶּה, שֶׁנִּתְחַיֵּב שֶׁכְּלֵנוּ לִשְׁכֹּן בְּתוֹךְ חֹמֶר בַּעַל
הַתַּאֲווֹת וְהַחֲטָאִים, רָאוּי הָיָה שֶׁכְּלֵנוּ לַעֲמֹד לְשָׁרֵת לִפְנֵי בּוֹרְאוֹ וּלְהַכִּיר כְּבוֹדוֹ
כְּאֶחָד מִבְּנֵי־אֱלֹהִים הַנִּצָּבִים עָלָיו. וְאָמְנָם מִפְּנֵי הַחִיּוּב הַזֶּה נִשְׁתַּעְבֵּד לִשְׁכֹּן בָּתֵּי
חֹמֶר, וְאַחַר שֶׁנִּשְׁתַּעְבֵּד לָזֶה מֻכְרָח עַל־כָּל־פָּנִים לִנְטוֹת מֵעֲבוֹדַת בּוֹרְאוֹ לִפְעָמִים
וּלְהִשְׁתַּדֵּל בְּצָרְכֵי הַבַּיִת אֲשֶׁר יָדוּר שָׁם, כִּי לֹא יִתְקַיֵּם בִּנְיַן הַבַּיִת, עֵצָיו וַאֲבָנָיו
וִיסוֹדוֹתָיו, מִבִּלְתִּי שֶׁיַּשְׁגִּיחַ הָאָדָם עָלָיו.

וְאִם־כֵּן, אַחֲרֵי הֱיוֹת כַּוָּנַת הָאָדָם בִּיצִירָתוֹ עַל מַה שֶּׁאָמַרְנוּ, בְּכָל עֵת שֶׁיּוּכַל
שִׂכְלוֹ לְמַעֵט בַּעֲבוֹדַת הַחֹמֶר וְיָשִׂים מְגַמָּתוֹ לַעֲבוֹדַת קוֹנוֹ, אָז טוֹב לוֹ, וּבִלְבַד

---

§374   1. Sifre Zuta, 241 l. 24; so cited also in ShM positive precept §92, but the printed edition has only the first part.

1a. The Hebrew, he-yoth, is the reading of the four manuscripts. The editions have the more normal form bihyoth, evidently by a scribal emendation.

2. Literally, one of the sons of God; the expression is based on Job 1:6, 2:1.

has shaved the greater part of his head; but if he shaved a smaller part of it, even though he transgressed the negative precept, *no razor shall come upon his head*, he does not thereby void the reckoning of the days.

This prohibition applies in every place and time, for both man and woman. For whoever places himself under a vow to be a *nazir*, even at the present time, is forbidden to shave even one hair. If someone violates this and shaves even one hair, he is punishable by whiplashes.

[THE PRECEPT OF LETTING A NAZIR'S HAIR
GROW LONG]

374 that a *nazir*, who is a man who has imposed abstinence from wine on himself, was commanded to let his hair grow all the days that he has made himself a *nazir* to the Lord: for it is stated, *letting the hair of his head grow long* (Numbers 6:5). In the language of the Midrash *Mechilta*:[1] "letting the hair ... grow long" — this is a positive precept; how do we learn that it also involves a negative precept? — Scripture states, *no razor shall come upon his head* (ibid.).

As for the root reason for the precept, [let me begin with] a preface. I wrote previously, at the opening of the work, that since there is[1a] in the world of the Holy One, blessed is He, a creature composed of both physical matter and intelligence, namely man, it should be a fitting and necessary thing, in order that His praise should ascend well from His humans, that with this human creature no possibility [for perfection] which it is in our power to grasp should be lacking from His world, and so forth, as I wrote there.

Now, there is no doubt that if not for this reason, that our intelligence was compelled to dwell within physical matter given to cravings and sins, our intelligence would have been fit to stand and minister before its Creator, and to recognize His glory, like one of the Divine angels[2] that are ranged about Him. However, because of this ordained necessity, it was subjugated and constrained to live in physical "dwellings"; and having been subjugated to this, it is compelled in any event to turn aside from the service of its Creator at times and to exert effort for the needs of the "dwelling" [the body] in which it lodges. For the structure of a house — its timber, stones and foundations — will not endure without man giving it watchful care.

Since it is so, inasmuch as the purpose set for man in his formation was what we have stated, at any time that his intelligence can lessen

its service for the physical matter [of his body] and set its aim toward

שֶׁלֹּא יִטֹּשׁ מְלֶאכֶת הַבַּיִת לְגַמְרֵי וְיַחֲרִיבֶהוּ, כִּי גַם זֶה יֵחָשֵׁב לוֹ עָוֹן שֶׁהַמֶּלֶךְ
חָפֵץ לִהְיוֹת לוֹ בְּרָיָה כָזוֹ; וְכִדְאָמַר רַבִּי יוֹסֵי בְּמַסֶּכֶת תַּעֲנִית פֶּרֶק שְׁלִישִׁי, שֶׁאֵין
הַיָּחִיד רַשַּׁאי לְסַגֵּף עַצְמוֹ בְּתַעֲנִית; וּפָרִישׁ רַב יְהוּדָה בְּשֵׁם רַב טַעְמֵיהּ דְּרַבִּי יוֹסֵי
מִשּׁוּם דִּכְתִיב "וַיְהִי הָאָדָם לְנֶפֶשׁ חַיָּה" — אָמְרָה תוֹרָה: נְשָׁמָה שֶׁנָּתַתִּי בָךְ הַחֲיֵה;
וְעַל זֶה אָמַר הַמֶּלֶךְ הֶחָכָם: אַל תְּהִי צַדִּיק הַרְבֵּה וְאַל תִּתְחַכַּם יוֹתֵר לָמָּה תִּשּׁוֹמֵם.

וְזוּ הִיא קְדֻשַּׁת הַנָּזִיר וּמַעֲלָתוֹ, בְּהַנִּיחוֹ מְלֶאכֶת הַחֹמֶר, וְיִשָּׁבֵר תַּאֲווֹתָיו בְּמַה
שֶׁאֵינוֹ חֻרְבָּן גָּמוּר אֶל הַבַּיִת, כְּגוֹן מְנִיעַת שְׁתִיַּת הַיַּיִן וְגִדּוּל הַשֵּׂעָר; כִּי בָזֶה יִכָּנַע
הַיֵּצֶר וְלֹא יִדְלֹף הַבַּיִת בַּעֲבוּרוֹ וְלֹא יֵהָרְסוּ פִּנּוֹתָיו, אֲבָל תִּתְחַזֵּק בּוֹ עֲבוֹדַת הַשֵּׂכֶל
וְיֵאוֹרוּ מַהֲלָכָיו וּכְבוֹד יי תִּשְׁכֹּן עָלָיו, וְיִתְקַיֵּם בָּאִישׁ הַזֶּה כַּוָּנַת הַבְּרִיאָה, מִבְּלִי
הִתְמַעֵט עֲבוֹדַת שִׂכְלוֹ שֶׁכְּלוֹ אֶל בּוֹרְאוֹ מִפְּנֵי שִׁתּוּף הַחֹמֶר שֶׁבּוֹ.

וְהָרְאָיָה שֶׁעִנְיַן גִּדּוּל הַשֵּׂעָר הוּא כְּמוֹ־כֵן מִפְּנֵי הַכְנָעַת הַיֵּצֶר כְּמוֹ שֶׁאָמַרְנוּ,
מַה שֶּׁאָמְרוּ זִכְרוֹנָם לִבְרָכָה בְּנָזִיר רֵישׁ פֶּרֶק קַמָּא: אָמַר רַבִּי שִׁמְעוֹן הַצַּדִּיק:
מִיָּמַי לֹא אָכַלְתִּי אֲשַׁם נָזִיר־טָמֵא, אֶלָּא פַּעַם אַחַת, בָּא אָדָם אֶחָד לְפָנַי מִן
הַדָּרוֹם, רְאִיתִיו יְפֵה־עֵינַיִם וְטוֹב־רֹאִי וּקְוֻצּוֹתָיו סְדוּרוֹת לוֹ תַלְתַּלִּים. אָמַרְתִּי לוֹ:
מָה רָאִיתָ לְהַשְׁחִית שֵׂעָרְךָ זֶה נָאֶה? אָמַר לִי: רוֹעֶה הָיִיתִי לְאַבָּא בְּעִירִי, וְהָלַכְתִּי
לְמַלֹּאות מַיִם מִן הַמַּעְיָן, וְנִסְתַּכַּלְתִּי בִּבְבוּאָה שֶׁלִּי, וּפָחַז יִצְרִי עָלַי וּבִקֵּשׁ לְטָרְדֵנִי
מִן הָעוֹלָם. אָמַרְתִּי לוֹ: רָשָׁע, לָמָּה אַתָּה מִתְגָּאֶה בְּעוֹלָם שֶׁאֵינוֹ שֶׁלְּךָ, בְּמִי שֶׁהוּא
עָתִיד לִהְיוֹת רִמָּה וְתוֹלֵעָה, הָעֲבוֹדָה שֶׁאֲגַלְּחָךְ לַשָּׁמַיִם. מִיָּד עָמַדְתִּי, חֲמַדְתִּיו

---

3. Literally, will not leak.

4. If a *nazir* became ritually unclean during his period of consecration and
abstention, he had to bring a lamb for an *'asham* (Numbers 6:9–12); but in addition,
the days he had spent as a *nazir* till then became void (they did not count) and he
had to consecrate a new period of time (thirty days as a rule) to spend as a *nazir*. As
the Talmud explains (TB N'darim 9b), people who took the vow initially to be a
nazir generally did so under emotional stress (fear, rage, or remorse over sins,
according to the early commentaries). When they became defiled and had to begin
the period as a *nazir* all over again, there was a good chance that they would regret
their original vow, since it had not been purely "to the Lord." This would cast a
tinge of doubt over the validity of their original vow (for if a person expresses his
regret of a vow to a learned scholar he can possibly have it annulled), which in turn
would cast a tinge of doubt over the validity of the *'asham*. Hence R. Shim'on the
tzaddik generally refused to eat the meat of such an offering (although he was a
kohen gadol and the meat had to be eaten by *kohanim*—Leviticus 7:6).

5. For if he became ritually unclean during his days as a *nazir*, or else when the
period ended, the hair had to be shaved off completely; Numbers 6:18 (§377).

the service of its Maker, it is good for it then, provided it does not abandon the chores of the "dwelling" [its physical abode] completely and wreck it. For this would also be considered a sin for him, since the King desires to have a human being like that. As R. Yosé said in chapter 3 of the Talmud tractate *Ta'anith* (22b), an individual does not have the right to afflict himself by fasting; and R. Judah in the name of Rav explained R. Yosé's reason: It is because it is written, *and man became a living soul* (Genesis 2:7); the Torah said [thus, in effect], "The soul that I set in you, do you keep alive." In this vein the wise king [Solomon] said, *Do not be righteous overmuch, and do not make yourself overwise; why should you destroy yourself?* (Ecclesiastes 7:16).

This, then, is the holiness of the *nazir* and his exalted level, when he leaves [his] labor for the physical matter and breaks his cravings where it will not mean a total wreckage for the "dwelling" [the body]: for example, abstention from drinking wine, and letting the hair grow. For thus the evil inclination will be subdued, yet the "dwelling" will not cease to be intact[3] because of that, nor will its corners be demolished. Rather, the service of the intelligence will be strengthened within him; its routes will be illuminated, and the glory of the Lord will dwell upon him. In this man the purpose of creation will be realized, as the service of his intelligence on behalf of his Creator will not be diminished because physical matter was made an integral part of him.

Now, the proof that the reason for letting the hair grow is likewise for the sake of subduing the evil inclination lies in what the Sages of blessed memory related in the tractate *Nazir* (4b) at the beginning of the first chapter: R. Shim'on the *tzaddik* (righteous) said: In all my days I did not eat of the *'asham* (guilt-offering) of a defiled *nazir*,[4] except once. A certain man came before me from the south. I saw that he had beautiful eyes and was good-looking, and his locks of hair were arranged for him in ringlets. I asked him, "Why did you see fit to destroy this handsome hair of yours?"[5] He answered me, "I was a shepherd for my father in my town. I went to draw water from the wellspring, and I gazed at my reflection [in the water]. My evil impulse hastened upon me and wished to drive me out of the world. Then I said to it; "O wicked one, why do you grow proud in a world that is not yours, over one who is destined to become [food for] maggots and worms? By the Temple service, I swear I will shave you for the sake of Heaven." I stood up at once, embraced him[5a] and kissed

⟨47⟩

וְנִשְׁקַתִּיו עַל רֹאשׁוֹ וְאָמַרְתִּי לוֹ: בְּנִי, כְּמוֹתְךָ יִרְבּוּ נוֹדְרֵי נְזִירוּת; עָלֶיךָ הַכָּתוּב
אוֹמֵר: אִישׁ...כִּי יַפְלִא לִנְדֹּר נֶדֶר נָזִיר לְהַזִּיר לַיָי.

וְעַל-כֵּן, כְּדֵי לְהַכְנִיעַ הַיֵּצֶר, גַּם-כֵּן נִצְטַוָּה לְגַלֵּחַ כָּל שְׂעָרוֹ בִּמְלֹאת יְמֵי נִזְרוֹ
וְלֹא הֻרְשָׁה לְתַקֵּן אוֹתָם וְלִטֹּל מֵהֶם קְצָת, כְּדֵי שֶׁלֹּא יָשׁוּב יִצְרוֹ עָלָיו כַּאֲשֶׁר
בַּתְּחִלָּה, אֲבָל נִתְחַיֵּב לְגַלְּחָם מִכֹּל [וָכֹל], כִּי אֵין סָפֵק שֶׁהַשֵּׂעָר הַגָּדוֹל בְּיוֹתֵר אוֹ
הַגִּלּוּחַ הַגָּמוּר יַפְסִיד תֹּאַר הָאָדָם.

וְאַל תִּתְפַּשֵּׁנִי בְּטַעַם זֶה שֶׁכָּתַבְתִּי מִמַּה שֶׁאָמְרוּ זִכְרוֹנָם לִבְרָכָה "יָבִיא כַּפָּרָה
עַל עַצְמוֹ שֶׁצִּעֵר עַצְמוֹ מִן הַיַּיִן", כִּי גַם זֶה יִתָּכֵן עַל טַעֲמֵנוּ: כִּי אַחַר שֶׁאָמַרְתִּי
שֶׁאֵין רְשׁוּת נְתוּנָה לְאָדָם לְהַשְׁחִית בֵּיתוֹ וּלְקַלְקֵל דָּבָר בַּבִּנְיָן אֲשֶׁר בָּנָה הַבּוֹנֶה
הָרִאשׁוֹן, רָאוּי לוֹ לְהָבִיא כַּפָּרָה עַל נַפְשׁוֹ, כִּי אוּלַי נָטָה מִן הַגֶּדֶר הַמְחֻיָּב עָלָיו
בְּעִנְיַן גּוּפוֹ וְנִשְׁמָתוֹ, כִּי שֶׁמָּא טָבְעוֹ וּבִנְיָנוֹ נָכוֹן עַל צַד שֶׁהַנְּזִירוּת עִנּוּי יָתֵר מִדַּי
עַל נַפְשׁוֹ; וְכָל דַּרְכֵי יְיָ יְשָׁרִים וְצַדִּיקִים יֵלְכוּ בָם.

וְהָרַב מֹשֶׁה בֶּן נַחְמָן זִכְרוֹנוֹ לִבְרָכָה כָּתַב בְּפֵרוּשָׁיו עַל דֶּרֶךְ הַפְּשָׁט, בְּטַעַם
הַחַטָּאת שֶׁמֵּבִיא הַנָּזִיר לְכַפָּרָה, כִּי הָעִנְיָן הוּא שֶׁצָּרִיךְ כַּפָּרָה בְּשׁוּבוֹ לְהִטַּמֵּא
בְּתַאֲווֹת הָעוֹלָם, דְּמִכֵּיוָן שֶׁהָיְתָה עָלָיו רוּחַ יְיָ וְהִתְחִיל לִהְיוֹת נָזוּר לַיָי, רָאוּי הָיָה
לַעֲמֹד כֵּן כָּל יָמָיו. וְשִׁבְעִים פָּנִים יֵשׁ לַתּוֹרָה.

מִדִּינֵי הַמִּצְוָה, מַה שֶׁאָמְרוּ זִכְרוֹנָם לִבְרָכָה שֶׁאִם נִתְגַּלַּח הַנָּזִיר, בֵּין בְּזָדוֹן בֵּין
בִּשְׁגָגָה וַאֲפִלּוּ בְּאֹנֶס, הֲרֵי זֶה סוֹתֵר מִנְיָנוֹ וּמַתְחִיל לִמְנוֹת שְׁלֹשִׁים יוֹם, דְּקַיְמָא
לָן, סְתַם נְזִירוּת שְׁלֹשִׁים יוֹם, כְּדֵי שֶׁיִּהְיֶה לוֹ "פֶּרַע". וּבַמֶּה דְבָרִים אֲמוּרִים,
כְּשֶׁנִּתְגַּלַּח בְּרֹב רֹאשׁוֹ בֵּין בְּתַעַר בֵּין בְּמִין תַּעַר וְלֹא נִשְׁאַר כְּדֵי לָכֹף רֹאשָׁן
לְעִקָּרָן; אֲבָל גִּלַּח מְעוּט שְׂעַר רֹאשׁוֹ, אֵינוֹ סוֹתֵר מִנְיָנוֹ מִפְּנֵי-כֵן. וּכְמוֹ-כֵן אֵינוֹ

5a. This term (חמדתיו) is found only in the oldest of the four MSS, and in the
first edition.   In all other copies of the *Ḥinnuch* (to my knowledge) it is absent,
in keeping with our Talmud texts in both Nazir 4b and N'darim 9b. It is also
found, however, in certain early MSS of TB N'darim, in *Yalkut Shim'oni* §710
(1st ed., Salonica 5287/1527, p. 220b; standard ed., Warsaw 5636/1876, p. 454a),
and in *Halachoth G'doloth*, 2nd ed. Hildesheimer, II p. 305. In general, the text of
the incident as given here is far closer to the wording in TB N'darim 9b, with
variants recorded in ed. Hershler, than to the text we have in Nazir 4b.

6. Since his intention was truly "to the Lord," for the sake of Heaven.

7. I.e. trim it.

8. TB Nazir 19a; hence perhaps any ascetic practice may be sinful.

9. The sentence is based on Hosea 14:10.

10. Ramban to Numbers 6:14.

11. That a *nazir* was to bring at the conclusion of his period of abstention.

12. TB Nazir 39a.

13. *Ibid.* 39b–40a.

him on the head, and I said to him, "My son, may there be many like you vowing to be a *nazir*. About you does Scripture state, *When a man... shall speak clearly to take the vow of a* nazir, *to become consecrated to the Lord*[6] (Numbers 6:2)."

Hence, in order to subdue the evil impulse, one was likewise commanded to shave all his hair at the completion of his days as a *nazir*. Nor was he permitted to fix his hair or to take some off from it,[7] so that his impulse should not return upon him as at the beginning. He was rather given the duty to shave it off entirely. For past any doubt, unusually long hair or its total shaving spoils the appearance of a man.

Now, do not seize hold of me to question this reason I have written, because of what the Sages of blessed memory said: Let him bring an atonement for himself for having afflicted himself [by abstention] from wine.[8] This too is in accord with our reason. For since I said that a man was not given permission to destroy his [bodily] "dwelling" or to spoil anything in the [bodily] structure which the first Builder constructed, it is right for him to bring an atonement for himself; for perhaps he swerved past the proper boundary that he is obligated to observe regarding his body and his soul. Perhaps his nature and constitution are balanced in such a way that the life of a *nazir* is too much of an affliction for his spirit. But all the ways of the Eternal Lord are right, and the righteous shall walk in them.[9]

However, R. Moses b. Naḥman [Ramban] of blessed memory wrote in his commentary[10] by way of the plain meaning, as an explanation for the *ḥattah* (sin-offering),[11] that the reason is that he needs atonement as he returns to become defiled by the cravings of the world. For since the spirit of the Lord was upon him and he began to be a *nazir* to the Lord, it would have been fitting for him to remain so all his days. Well, there are seventy facets [of meaning] to the Torah.

Among the laws of the precept, there is what the Sages of blessed memory taught:[12] that if a *nazir* had his hair shaved, whether deliberately or unwittingly, or even under duress, it cancels his reckoning [of his time as a *nazir*] and he is to begin counting thirty days [anew]. For we have a standing rule: the general, unspecified period of a *nazir* is thirty days,[12] so that he can acquire a large growth of hair. Now, when does this rule hold?—if he shaved the greater part of his head, whether with a razor or anything like a razor, and not enough remained so that the tip of a hair could be bent back to its root.[13] But if he shaved a small part of his head, his reckoning [of days] is not

סוֹתֵר מִנְיָנוֹ מִפְּנֵי שֶׁתִיַּת הַיַּיִן, וַאֲפִלּוּ שָׁתָה מִמֶּנּוּ יָמִים רַבִּים; אֲבָל סוֹתֵר הוּא מִנְיָנוֹ מִפְּנֵי הַטֻּמְאָה, כְּמוֹ שֶׁמְּפֹרָשׁ בַּכָּתוּב.

וּמַה שֶּׁאָמְרוּ זְכָרוֹנָם לִבְרָכָה גַּם־כֵּן בְּעִנְיַן נְזִירוּת, דְּכָל כִּנּוּיֵי נְזִירוּת כִּנְזִירוּת, כְּלוֹמַר מִי שֶׁהָיָה עִלֵּג (אוֹ) [בְּ]מְקוֹמוֹת שֶׁהַכֹּל עִלְּגִין עֲלֵיהֶן וְדַרְכָּן לוֹמַר בִּמְקוֹם נָזִיר "נָזִיק" אוֹ "נָזִיחַ" אוֹ "פָּזִיחַ", וְאָמַר אֶחָד מִלְּשׁוֹנוֹת אֵלּוּ עַל עַצְמוֹ—כְּגוֹן שֶׁאָמַר "אֱהֵא נָזִיק" אוֹ "נָזִיחַ" אוֹ "פָּזִיחַ", הֲרֵי זֶה נָזִיר; [וְ]שֶׁאֵין אוֹמְרִים בִּנְזִירוּת שֶׁיִּהְיוּ דִּבְרֵי פִיו בְּכִוּוּן כִּלְבָבוֹ כְּמוֹ בִשְׁבוּעָה, אֶלָּא מִכֵּיוָן שֶׁבִּלְבָבוֹ לְהִנָּזֵר וְאָמַר דְּבָרִים שֶׁיֵּשׁ לְהָבִין בָּהֶן שֶׁיִּהְיֶה נָזִיר, אַף־עַל־פִּי שֶׁהֵן מִלּוֹת שֶׁאֵין עִנְיַן הַנְּזִירוּת מוּבָן מִתּוֹכָן יָפֶה, הֲרֵי זֶה נָזִיר.

וְכֵן מַה שֶּׁאָמְרוּ שֶׁיָּדוֹת נְזִירוּת כִּנְזִירוּת; וּמַה הֵן הַיָּדוֹת, כְּגוֹן שֶׁאָמַר "אֱהֵא" וְהָיָה נָזִיר עוֹבֵר לְפָנָיו, הֲרֵי זֶה נָזִיר; אוֹ שֶׁאָמַר "אֱהֵא נָאֶה" וְתָפַס בִּשְׂעָרוֹ, הֲרֵי זֶה נָזִיר; וְכֵן הָאוֹמֵר "הֲרֵינִי נָזִיר מִן הַחַרְצַנִּים בִּלְבָד" אוֹ "מִן הַתִּגְלַחַת" אוֹ "מִן הַטֻּמְאָה בִּלְבָד"—הֲרֵי זֶה נָזִיר גָּמוּר.

וְהָאוֹמֵר "הֲרֵינִי נָזִיר עַל־מְנָת שֶׁאֶשְׁתֶּה יַיִן" אוֹ "אֶטַּמֵּא לְמֵתִים" אוֹ "אֲגַלַּח", הֲרֵי זֶה נָזִיר וְאָסוּר בְּכֻלָּם, מִפְּנֵי שֶׁהִתְנָה עַל מַה שֶּׁכָּתוּב בַּתּוֹרָה, וּתְנָאוֹ בָּטֵל. וְנִשְׁאָלִים עַל הַנְּזִירוּת כְּדֶרֶךְ שֶׁנִּשְׁאָלִין עַל שְׁאָר הַנְּדָרִים. וְהָאָב מַדִּיר בְּנוֹ קָטָן עַד י״ג שָׁנָה וְיוֹם אֶחָד בְּנָזִיר, אֲבָל לֹא הָאֵם, וְדָבָר זֶה קַבָּלָה. וְהַגּוֹיִים אֵין

---

14. *Ibid.* 44a.

15. Numbers 6:8, 12.

16. TB Nazir 2a.

17. The original reads, "if someone had a distorted or stammering speech, or it was in regions where all spoke peculiarly." At first glance this might denote two separate cases: (1) if an individual spoke strangely but was still understandable; (2) if everyone in the region spoke a strange dialect or whatever, although the individual by himself might not be very understandable. Yet in our author's sources (see note 19 and MT *hilchoth n'darim* i 16) we find nothing of the kind. The original has therefore been emended in accord with the sources. For the point of the law, as found both there and in later halachic works, is that though the man by himself might not be understood, in his locale he is, because everyone there speaks as he does. Hence his vow in his locale takes effect.

18. The original reads, "For the rule is not applied to a *nazir*," etc. It has been emended in accord with MY note 12, q.v. This also obviates the difficulty noted by R. Judah Rosanes (author of *Mishneh l'Melech*), q.v.

19. TB Nazir 2b; MT *hilchoth n'ziruth* i 8.

20. Since they reveal the intention as well as substitute expressions.

21. Because he thus obliquely expresses a vow that will obligate him to let his hair grow.

22. TB Nazir 3b.

cancelled on account of this. So too does he not cancel his reckoning on account of drinking wine, even if he should drink it many days.[14] But he does interrupt his reckoning on account of ritual uncleanness, as stated clearly in the Writ.[15]

Then there is what the Sages likewise said regarding the *nazir*,[16] that all substitute expressions for the *nazir*'s vow are the same [in law] as the vow itself. In other words, if someone had a distorted or stammering speech in regions where all spoke thus peculiarly,[17] and it was their way to say *nazik* instead of *nazir*, or *nazi-aḥ* or *pazi-aḥ* and he applied one of these words to himself—for instance, if he said, "I shall be a *nazik*," or "a *nazi-aḥ*," or "a *pazi-aḥ*"—he thus becomes a *nazir*. And also, the rule is not applied to a *nazir*[18] that the words of his mouth must precisely express his heart's wish, as it is in the case of an oath. Rather, since [the intention] in his heart was to become a *nazir*, and he said words which could be understood to mean that he was to be a *nazir*, even if they are words from which the subject of the *nazir* cannot be understood so well, he becomes a *nazir*.[19]

There is, too, what the Sages said:[16] that "handles" [intimations, incomplete statements] about the vows of a *nazir* are like the vows themselves.[20] Now, what are these "handles"?—for instance, if one said, "I shall be," and a *nazir* was passing by before him, he becomes a *nazir*; or if he said, "I shall be handsome" while he held his hair, he becomes a *nazir*.[21] So too, if someone said, "I shall be a *nazir* only to abstain from grape seeds," or "from shaving," or "from ritual un-cleanness alone," he becomes a complete *nazir*.[22]

If a person says, "I shall be a *nazir* on condition that I may drink wine," or "that I may be defiled by the dead," or "that I may shave my hair," he becomes a *nazir* and is forbidden all of them, because he made a condition about something written in the Torah,[23] and his condition has no validity.[24] Requests may be made for release from the *nazir*'s vow, as they may be made about other vows.[25] A father may vow his small son, till the age of thirteen years and a day, to be a *nazir*, but not a mother; this is an Oral Tradition.[26] To non-Jews the

23. Which thus imposes a prior obligation on him.

24. *Ibid.* 11a.

25. *Ibid.* 20b, etc. About requests for release from a vow, see § 30, paragraphs 17–20.

26. TB Nazir 28b, 29b.

לָהֶם נְזִירוּת, אֲבָל יֵשׁ נְזִירוּת בַּעֲבָדִים וּבְנָשִׁים. וְהַבַּעַל וְהָאָב מֵפֵר לָאִשָּׁה נֶדֶר
נְזִירוּת כְּמוֹ שְׁאָר נְדָרִים; וְכֵן הָאָדוֹן, אִם יִרְצֶה, כּוֹפֶה לָעֶבֶד לִשְׁתּוֹת יַיִן וּלְהִטַּמֵּא.

וְנוֹהֶגֶת מִצְוָה זוֹ, שֶׁחַיָּב בִּגְדוּל הַשֵּׂעָר כָּל מִי שֶׁנָּדַר בְּנָזִיר, בְּכָל מָקוֹם וּבְכָל
זְמַן, בַּזְּכָרִים וּבַנְּקֵבוֹת; שֶׁאַף־עַל־פִּי שֶׁלִּמְּדוּנוּ זִכְרוֹנָם לִבְרָכָה שֶׁהַנְּזִירוּת נוֹהֶגֶת
בְּאֶרֶץ־יִשְׂרָאֵל, כְּלוֹמַר שֶׁחַיָּב כָּל אָדָם לִהְיוֹת נוֹהֵג נְזִירוּתוֹ בְּאֶרֶץ־יִשְׂרָאֵל כְּמִנְיַן
הַיָּמִים שֶׁנָּדַר, וְשֶׁאֵין עוֹלִין לוֹ הַיָּמִים לִימֵי נֶדֶר נִזְרוֹ אֶלָּא שָׁם, בְּחוּצָה לָאָרֶץ גַּם־
כֵּן כָּל דִּקְדּוּקֵי נְזִירוּת עָלָיו. לְפִיכָךְ מִי שֶׁנָּדַר בְּנָזִיר בַּזְּמַן הַזֶּה הֲרֵי זֶה נָזִיר
לְעוֹלָם, לְפִי שֶׁעַכְשָׁו, בַּעֲוֹנוֹת, אֵין לָנוּ בֵּית שֶׁיָּבִיא קָרְבְּנוֹתָיו בִּמְלֹאת יְמֵי
נִזְרוֹ. וְעוֹד אָמְרוּ זִכְרוֹנָם לִבְרָכָה שֶׁכּוֹפִין אוֹתוֹ, אִם יֵשׁ בָּנוּ כֹחַ לְכוֹפוֹ, לַעֲלוֹת
בָּאָרֶץ וְלִנְהֹג נְזִירוּתוֹ שָׁם עַד שֶׁיָּמוּת, אוֹ עַד שֶׁיִּבָּנֶה בֵּית־הַמִּקְדָּשׁ וְיַשְׁלִים
קָרְבְּנוֹתָיו.

[שֶׁלֹּא יִכָּנֵס הַנָּזִיר לְאֹהֶל הַמֵּת]

שעה שֶׁלֹּא יִכָּנֵס הַנָּזִיר לְאֹהֶל הַמֵּת, שֶׁנֶּאֱמַר: עַל נֶפֶשׁ מֵת לֹא יָבֹא.

מִשָּׁרְשֵׁי הַרְחָקַת הַטֻּמְאָה מִמְּקוֹם הַקָּדוֹשׁ, כָּתַבְתִּי בְּסֵדֶר זֶה בְּמִצְוָה רִאשׁוֹנָה
[סִי' שס"ב] מַה שֶּׁיָּדַעְתִּי וְהוּא הַדִּין וְהוּא הַטַּעַם לְהַרְחִיק הָאִישׁ הַקָּדוֹשׁ מִמֶּנָּה;
וּבְטַעַם טֻמְאַת גּוּף הָאָדָם הַמֵּת, כָּתַבְתִּי גַּם־כֵּן מַה שֶׁהִשַּׂגְתִּי, בְּסֵדֶר אֱמֹר אֶל
הַכֹּהֲנִים, לֹא־תַעֲשֶׂה א' [סִי' רס"ג].

מִדִּינֵי הַמִּצְוָה, מַה שֶּׁאָמְרוּ זִכְרוֹנָם לִבְרָכָה שֶׁאֵין הַנָּזִיר חַיָּב מִשּׁוּם בִּיאָה
בְּאֹהֶל הַמֵּת עַד שֶׁיִּכָּנֵס שָׁם כֻּלּוֹ; וְאַף־עַל־פִּי שֶׁמֵּעֵת שֶׁיַּכְנִיס שָׁם חָטְמוֹ אוֹ
אֶצְבְּעוֹת רַגְלָיו נִטְמָא, מִכָּל־מָקוֹם אֵין נִקְרָא בִּיאָה עַד שֶׁיִּכָּנֵס כֻּלּוֹ. לְפִיכָךְ נָזִיר
שֶׁנִּכְנַס לְבַיִת שֶׁהַמֵּת בְּתוֹכָהּ בְּשָׂדֶה, תֵּבָה וּמִגְדָּל, וּבָא חֲבֵרוֹ וּפָרַע גַּג הַתֵּבָה

27. *Ibid.* 61a.

28. I.e. the husband when she is married, and the father before her maturity; *ibid.* 20b, 23a, etc. and see Numbers 30 : 4-7.

29. I.e. if the slave vowed to be a *nazir*; TB Nazir 62b.

30. While by Torah law, all rules and requirements of being a *nazir* apply equally in and outside the land of Israel, by decree of the Sages all territories other than the holy land are considered in the same state of *tum'ah* (ritual uncleanness) as a corpse; consequently, any days observed by a *nazir* outside the holy land cannot count toward the fulfillment of his vow; see *ibid.* 19b-20a.

31. I.e. since, as stated in the paragraph's first sentence, the precept of *nazir* is in effect everywhere, at all times.

32. The paragraph is based on MT *hilchoth n'ziruth* ii 20-21.

§375   1. I.e. any house or structure that would contain or cover over both the *nazir* and the dead body.

law of the *nazir* does not apply; but the state of a *nazir* can be borne by slaves and women.[27] A husband and a father can make null and void a woman's vow to be a *nazir*, just like other vows.[28] Likewise, if a master wishes, he can force his slave to drink wine and become defiled.[29]

This precept, that whoever vows to be a *nazir*, is duty-bound to let his hair grow, is in force everywhere at every time, for both man and woman. For though the Sages of blessed memory instructed us that the process of being a *nazir* is in force in the land of Israel — which is to say that every man is required to observe his time as a *nazir* in the land of Israel, according to the number of days that he vowed, and no days count for him as days of his vow other than there — outside the land all the detailed restrictions of a *nazir* also lie upon him.[30] Therefore,[31] if anyone vows to be a *nazir* at the present time, he remains a *nazir* for all time, because now, for our sins, we have no Temple so that he could bring his offerings at the completion of his days as a *nazir*. And our Sages of blessed memory said further that he is to be compelled, if we have the power to coerce him, to go up to the land [of Israel] and to conduct himself there as a *nazir* till he dies, or until the Sanctuary is rebuilt and he will fulfill the obligation of his offerings.[32]

[THAT A NAZIR SHOULD NOT ENTER A DEAD MAN'S TENT]

375 that a *nazir* should not enter the tent of a dead person,[1] as it is stated, *he shall not come into the aura of a dead body* (Numbers 6:6).

Regarding a root reason for keeping ritual uncleanness far from a location of sanctity, I wrote in the first precept of this *sidrah* (§ 362) what I knew; and for the same consideration and the same reason a sanctified man is to be kept removed from it. About the reason for the ritual uncleanness of the body of a dead person, I likewise wrote what I have understood, in the first negative precept of *sidrah 'emor* (§ 263).

Among the laws of the precept, there is what the Sages of blessed memory taught: that a *nazir* is not punishable for entering the "tent" of a dead person unless he enters it completely.[2] Even though, from the time he puts his nose or fingers into it, he becomes defiled, it is

2. TB Nazir 43a. He is punishable, however, for having made himself defiled, *ta-mé* (§376).

מֵעָלָיו מִדַּעְתּוֹ, לוֹקֶה שְׁתַּיִם: אַחַת מִשּׁוּם ״לֹא יָבֹא״ וְאַחַת מִשּׁוּם ״לֹא יִטַּמָּא״, שֶׁהֲרֵי עַכְשָׁו טֻמְאָה וּבִיאָה בָּאִין כְּאַחַת. וְנָזִיר שֶׁנִּכְנַס בְּאֹהֶל הַמֵּת אוֹ בְּבֵית הַקְּבָרוֹת בִּשְׁגָגָה, וְאַחַר שֶׁנּוֹדַע לוֹ שָׁהָה לְשָׁם כְּדֵי הִשְׁתַּחֲוָיָה בַּמִּקְדָּשׁ, חַיָּב מַלְקוֹת. וְיֶתֶר פְּרָטֶיהָ, מְבֹאָרִים בְּמַסֶּכֶת נָזִיר.

וְנוֹהֵג אִסּוּר זֶה בְּכָל מָקוֹם וּבְכָל זְמַן, בַּזְּכָרִים וּנְקֵבוֹת. וְעוֹבֵר עָלָיו וְנִטְמָא בְּצַדָּדִין שֶׁאָמַרְנוּ, חַיָּב מַלְקוֹת.

[שֶׁלֹּא יִטַּמָּא הַנָּזִיר בְּמֵת וּבִשְׁאָר טֻמְאוֹת]

שע"ו שֶׁלֹּא יִטַּמָּא הַנָּזִיר בְּמֵת, שֶׁנֶּאֱמַר: לְאָבִיו וּלְאִמּוֹ ... לֹא יִטַּמָּא וְגוֹמֵר. אַף־עַל־פִּי שֶׁכְּבָר כָּתַבְתִּי בְּמִצְוָה רִאשׁוֹנָה זֶה טַעַם בְּהַרְחָקַת הַטֻּמְאָה מִן הַקֹּדֶשׁ, עוֹד אַגִּיד הָעוֹלֶה עַל רוּחִי בְּטַעַם הַחֹמֶר הַגָּדוֹל שֶׁבְּנָזִיר, שֶׁנִּצְטַוָּה שֶׁלֹּא יִטַּמָּא גַּם לְאָבִיו וּלְאִמּוֹ, וְאֵין צָרִיךְ לוֹמַר בִּשְׁאָר קְרוֹבִים, וַהֲרֵי הַכֹּהֵן הֶדְיוֹט, שֶׁגַּם הוּא קָדוֹשׁ, מִטַּמֵּא בָּהֶן.

וְהָעִנְיָן הוּא, לְפִי הַדּוֹמֶה, כִּי קְדֻשַּׁת הַכֹּהֵן חָלָה עָלָיו מִמֵּילָא, לֹא הֻסְכַּם הוּא עָלֶיהָ וּמִדַּעְתּוֹ לֹא נִהְיְתָה, כִּי־אִם מִלֵּדָה וּמִבֶּטֶן נִתְקַדֵּשׁ בְּכֹח שִׁבְטוֹ שֶׁכֻּלּוֹ קֹדֶשׁ, וְהַנְהָגָתוֹ עִם קְרוֹבָיו כְּכָל שְׁאָר בְּנֵי הָעוֹלָם, כִּי אֵין חִלּוּק בֵּין הָאִישׁ הַכֹּהֵן לִשְׁאָר הָעָם, זוּלָתִי כִּי לְעִתִּים יַעֲבֹד בֵּית אֱלֹהָיו, וְאָמְנָם לְעִתִּים גַּם־כֵּן יִשְׁכֹּן בְּהֵיכָלָיו

---

3. In ordinary entry, part of the *nazir*'s body (e.g. his nose or hand) is inserted first in the tent, making him defiled, but not punishable for it. Only by such an entry does his entire body become defiled at once, and he is punishable for the violation of the two prohibitions — for only thus has he — all of him at once — "come into the aura of a dead body."

4. I.e. he was made aware of the situation and was warned to leave.

5. MT *ibid.* 19, based on TB Nazir 17a; and see *tosafoth*, TB Sh'vu'oth 17a, s.v. 'o'én.

6. I.e. in which his body enters enclosed in a container and is then exposed all at once to the defiling atmosphere.

§376　　1. I.e. one week in twenty-four, when his "watch" or family group would be on duty at the Sanctuary.

nevertheless not called "entering" [to be punishable for this] unless he goes inside entirely. Therefore, if a *nazir* entered a house containing a dead man [while enclosed] in a palanquin, a box or a portable turret, and his fellow-man came and opened the roof of the container above him by his knowledge and will, he would be whipped with two sets of lashes: one on account of [this precept] "he shall not come [into the aura," etc.], and one on account of "he shall not defile himself" (Numbers 6:7, § 376); for here defilement and entering occur at once, together.[3] If a *nazir* entered the tent of a dead person or a graveyard unwittingly, and after it was told him[4] he remained there long enough for a person to prostrate himself [in worship] at the Sanctuary, he would be punishable by whiplashes.[5] The rest of its details are explained in the Talmud tractate *Nazir*.

This prohibition is in effect everywhere, at every time, for both man and woman. If [a *nazir*] violates it and becomes defiled under the circumstances that we mentioned,[6] he is punishable by whiplashes.

[THAT A NAZIR SHOULD NOT BECOME
DEFILED BY A DEAD PERSON OR ANY OTHER
UNCLEANNESS]

376 that a *nazir* should not be defiled by the dead, as it is stated, *Neither for his father nor for his mother ... shall he make himself unclean*, etc. (Numbers 6:7).

Although I wrote previously, in the first precept of this *sidrah* (§ 362), a reason for keeping ritual uncleanness well away from the sacred, I will relate further what comes to my mind regarding the great severity imposed on a *nazir*, i.e. that he was commanded not to defile himself even for his father or mother, and needless to say, for other kin — and yet an ordinary *kohen*, who was also hallowed, should defile himself for them (§ 264).

The reason, as it would seem, is that the sanctity of the *kohen* attaches to him automatically, of itself. He did not consent to it, and it did not come about through his conscious choice; rather, from birth, from the womb he was sanctified by virtue of his tribe, which is altogether hallowed. In his behavior toward his close kin he is then like all other people in the world; for there is no [real, essential] difference between a man who is a *kohen* and the rest of the people, except that at times he serves at the House of God.[1] But indeed, at times he will equally dwell in his quarters and will be happy with his

וְיָגֵל עִם אוֹהֲבָיו, וּלְשִׂמְחָה וּלְמִשְׁתֶּה יִקְרָא רֵעָיו וּקְרוֹבָיו, עַל־כֵּן יֵחַם לְבָבוֹ
עֲלֵיהֶם וְגַם הֵם עָלָיו, וּמִפְּנֵי זֶה הָרְשָׁה לְהִטַּמֵּא לָהֶם, כִּי כָל דַּרְכֵי הַתּוֹרָה נֹעַם וְכָל
נְתִיבוֹתֶיהָ שָׁלוֹם.

אָכֵן הָאִישׁ הַנָּזוּר לַיְיָ, כָּל יְמֵי נִזְרוֹ קָדוֹשׁ הוּא לַיְיָ, וּכְמוֹ שֶׁהֵעִיד עָלָיו הַכָּתוּב
"כִּי נֵזֶר אֱלֹהָיו עַל רֹאשׁוֹ", לֹא יִטַּמֵּא בְּתַאֲווֹת הָעוֹלָם, וְלֹא יִמָּצֵא בֵית מִשְׁתָּאוֹת
וּבִסְעֻדַּת רֵעִים, כִּי הַפְּרָשָׁתוֹ מִן הַיַּיִן מוֹכַחַת עָלָיו שֶׁנָּתַן לִבּוֹ לְהָבִין וּלְהִתְעַנּוֹת
לִפְנֵי יְיָ וּלְתַקֵּן דַּרְכֵי נַפְשׁוֹ וּלְהַנִּיחַ תַּעֲנוּגֵי הַגּוּף הֶחָשׁוּךְ; וְאַחֲרֵי שׂוֹמוֹ כָל לִבּוֹ
וְכָל מַחְשְׁבוֹתָיו אַחֲרֵי נַפְשׁוֹ הַיְקָרָה, וְצָרְכֵי עַצְמוֹ וּבְשָׂרוֹ נָטַשׁ—מַה חֶפְצוֹ
בְּקִרְבַת רֵעָיו וְאוֹהֲבָיו עוֹד, זוּלָתִי לְמִצְוָה.

אֵין סָפֵק כִּי בְּהִתְעַלּוֹת הַנֶּפֶשׁ יֵקַל מְאֹד בְּעֵינֶיהָ הֲנָאַת הַגּוּף וְכָל עִנְיָנוֹ; כָּל־
שֶׁכֵּן שֶׁלֹּא תִפְנֶה אַחַר חֶבְרַת הַגּוּפִים אֲחֵרִים, וְאִם קְרוֹבִים הֵמָּה אוֹ רְחוֹקִים, וְלֹא
תִמְצָא תַעֲנוּג בְּכָל דָּבָר מֵהַדְּבָרִים זוּלָתִי בַּעֲבוֹדָה הַקְּדוֹשָׁה אֲשֶׁר נִתְקַשְּׁרָה בָהּ,
וְעֵינֶיהָ אֵלֶיהָ תָּמִיד.

וְעַל־כֵּן, לְרֹב קְדֻשָּׁתוֹ וּמַעֲלָתוֹ וּפְרִישׁוּתוֹ מֵאֶחָיו, תִּמְנָעֵנּוּ הַתּוֹרָה מֵהִטַּמֵּא
לָהֶן, וּכְעִנְיַן הַכֹּהֵן הַגָּדוֹל, כִּי מִהְיוֹתוֹ מַעְלָה מְאֹד בְּעִנְיָנֵנוּ וְנִפְרָשׁ מֵחֶבְרַת
הָאוֹהֲבִים וְאֵין כָּל עֲסָקָיו וּמַחְשְׁבוֹתָיו זוּלָתִי בַּעֲבוֹדַת אֱלֹהָיו יִתְבָּרַךְ, תִּמְנָעֵנּוּ
הַתּוֹרָה גַם־כֵּן מֵהִטַּמֵּא לְאֶחָד מִכָּל קְרוֹבָיו; וְטַעַם הַנֶּאֱמָר עָלָיו בַּכָּתוּב בְּהַרְחָקַת
הַטֻּמְאָה נֶאֱמָר גַּם עַל הַנָּזִיר, זוּלָתִי שֶׁבַּכֹּהֵן הִזְכִּיר שֶׁמֶן, מִפְּנֵי שֶׁהוּא מָשׁוּחַ בּוֹ,
וּבְנָזִיר לֹא הִזְכִּיר שֶׁמֶן, שֶׁבְּכֹהֵן נֶאֱמַר: כִּי נֵזֶר שֶׁמֶן מִשְׁחַת אֱלֹהָיו עָלָיו, וּבְנָזִיר
נֶאֱמַר: כִּי נֵזֶר אֱלֹהָיו עַל רֹאשׁוֹ.

וְאוּלַי תַּחְשֹׁב לְהָשִׁיב עָלַי כִּי הַנָּזִיר לִזְמַן, בְּהַשְׁלִים זְמַנּוּ יָשׁוּב לִימֵי עֲלוּמָיו.

---

2. I.e. at their death, to attend at their burial.
3. Literally, has given his heart; expression based on Daniel 10:12.
4. Literally, and all his thoughts after his precious spirit (soul).

good friends; and for an occasion of rejoicing and a feast he will call his friends and his kin. Therefore his heart will grow warm [with affection] toward them, and so they toward him. For this reason he was permitted to defile himself for them[2]—for all the ways of the Torah are *pleasantness, and all its paths are peace* (Proverbs 3:17).

However, if a man has vowed to be a *nazir* to the Lord, then all the days of his vow to be a *nazir* he is consecrated to the Lord as Scripture attests about him, *because his separation to God is upon his head* (Numbers 6:7). Then he is not to become defiled through worldly cravings, and is not to be found in any house of feasting or a banquet of friends. For his separation from wine attests about him that he has set his heart[3] to understand and practice abstinence before the Lord, and to repair the ways of his spirit, leaving aside the pleasures of the benighted body. Then having set his whole heart and all his thoughts on the good of his precious spirit,[4] and having cast off the needs of his self and his flesh, why should he desire the company of his companions and friends any longer, except for some *mitzvah*?

There is no doubt that as the spirit is raised to a higher level, the pleasure of the body, with all that concerns it, becomes very insignificant in its eyes. Then all the more certainly will it not go after the company of other persons, whether they are near or far; and it will find pleasure in nothing whatever except in the hallowed [Divine] service to which it has become attached, and to which it constantly looks.

Therefore, on account of his great holiness, his exalted level, and his separation from his brothers, the Torah restrains him from becoming defiled for them—as the rule is for a *kohen gadol*: that since he is very exalted in his position and separated from the company of his friends, and all his affairs and thoughts are on nothing but the service of his God (be He blessed), the Torah restricts him likewise from defiling himself for anyone among all his close kin. And the reason stated about him in the Writ, for keeping ritual uncleanness away, is stated also about a *nazir*, except that about the *kohen*, oil is mentioned, because he was anointed with it, while about a *nazir*, oil is not mentioned. For regarding a *kohen* it is stated, *for the consecration of the anointing oil of his God is upon him* (Leviticus 21:12), while of the *nazir* it is stated, *because his consecration to God is upon his head* (Numbers 6:7).

Now, you might think to raise the objection against me that a ⟨57⟩ *nazir* is [thus only] for a set time; when his time is completed, he will

וְיִרְדֹּף תַּאֲווֹתָיו, וְאִם־כֵּן לָמָּה יִהְיֶה חָמוּר יוֹתֵר מִכֹּהֵן הֶדְיוֹט—הַתְּשׁוּבָה כִּי הָאָדָם אַחַר הַזִּירוֹ לַה' פַּעַם אַחַת, תִּקְנָה יֵשׁ בּוֹ לְקַדֵּשׁ עַצְמוֹ וּלְהוֹסִיף יוֹם יוֹם בְּטוּבוֹ, וּמִן הַשָּׁמַיִם מַסְכִּימִין עַל יָדוֹ, וּכְעִנְיָן שֶׁאָמְרוּ זִכְרוֹנָם לִבְרָכָה: בָּא לְטַהֵר מְסַיְּעִין אוֹתוֹ; וְאַחַר שֶׁהִזִּיר אֲפִלּוּ יוֹם אֶחָד, יִסְתַּיַּע וְיַשְׁלִים כָּל יָמָיו בְּטָהֳרָה.

מִדִּינֵי הַמִּצְוָה, מַה שֶּׁאָמְרוּ זִכְרוֹנָם לִבְרָכָה שֶׁיֵּשׁ טֻמְאַת מֵת שֶׁאִם נִטְמָא הַנָּזִיר בָּהּ, מְגַלֵּחַ וְסוֹתֵר הַיָּמִים הַקּוֹדְמִין וּמַתְחִיל לִמְנוֹת יְמֵי נְזִירוּתוֹ אַחַר כֵּן, וְיֵשׁ טֻמְאַת מֵת שֶׁאֵין מְגַלֵּחַ בַּעֲבוּרָהּ וְלֹא סוֹתֵר הַיָּמִים הַקּוֹדְמִים, וְאַף־עַל־פִּי שֶׁהִיא טֻמְאַת שִׁבְעָה, לְפִי שֶׁלֹּא נֶאֱמַר בּוֹ "וְכִי יִטְמָא לְנֶפֶשׁ" אֶלָּא "וְכִי יָמוּת מֵת עָלָיו", דְּמַשְׁמָע עַד שֶׁיִּטַּמֵּא בְּטֻמְאוֹת שֶׁהֵן בְּעַצְמוֹ שֶׁל מֵת.

וְאֵלּוּ הֵן הַטֻּמְאוֹת שֶׁהַנָּזִיר מְגַלֵּחַ עֲלֵיהֶן: עַל הַנֵּפֶל, וַאֲפִלּוּ לֹא נִתְקַשְׁרוּ אֵיבָרָיו בְּגִידִין; וְעַל כְּזַיִת מִן הַמֵּת, וְעַל כְּזַיִת נֶצֶל; וְעַל עֲצָמוֹת שֶׁהֵן רֹב מִנְיַן הָעֲצָמוֹת, אַף־עַל־פִּי שֶׁאֵין בָּהֶן רֹבַע הַקַּב; וְעַל עֲצָמוֹת שֶׁהֵן בִּנְיָנוֹ שֶׁל מֵת, אַף־עַל־פִּי שֶׁאֵין בָּהֶן רֹבַע הַקַּב; וְעַל חֲצִי קַב עֲצָמוֹת, אַף־עַל־פִּי שֶׁאֵין בָּהֶן רֹב בִּנְיָנוֹ וְלֹא רֹב מִנְיָנוֹ, וּבִלְבַד שֶׁכָּל הָעֲצָמוֹת יִהְיוּ מִשֶּׁל מֵת אֶחָד וְלֹא מִשְּׁנֵי מֵתִים; וְעַל שִׁדְרָה הַבָּאָה מִן הַמֵּת, וְעַל הַגֻּלְגֹּלֶת שֶׁל מֵת אֶחָד, וְעַל אֵבֶר מִן הַמֵּת, וְעַל אֵבֶר מִן הַחַי מֵאָדָם שֶׁיֵּשׁ עֲלֵיהֶן בָּשָׂר שֶׁרָאוּי לַעֲלוֹת בּוֹ אֲרוּכָה כַּחַי; וְעַל חֲצִי לֹג דָּם הַבָּא מִמֵּת אֶחָד, וְעַל מְלֹא חָפְנַיִם רֶקֶב הַמֵּת.

וְאֵי זֶהוּ נֶצֶל — זֶה בְּשַׂר הַמֵּת שֶׁנִּמּוֹחַ וְנַעֲשָׂה לֵחָה סְרוּחָה; וְאֵין רֶקֶב הַמֵּת מְטַמֵּא עַד שֶׁיִּקָּבֵר עֵרֹם בְּאָרוֹן שֶׁל שַׁיִשׁ וְיִהְיֶה כֻלּוֹ שָׁלֵם; חָסֵר מִמֶּנּוּ אֵבֶר אוֹ

5. TB Shabbath 104a.

6. I.e. from Heaven.

7. Rambam, commentary to Mishnah, Nazir vii 3, and MT hilchoth n'ziruth vii 1; and see tosafoth, TB Nazir 54a, s.v. kélim.

8. TB Nazir 50a.

9. Ibid. 49b.

10. Ibid. The term is explained in the next paragraph.

11. I.e. of a corpse.

12. TB Nazir 50a (and see tosafoth, s.v. Rava 'omér).

13. Mishnah, 'Oholoth ii 6.

14. I.e. were it now attached to the body (tosafoth s.v. v'al 'éver); TB Nazir 49b.

15. Ibid. The paragraph is based on MT hilchoth n'ziruth vii 2.

return to his days of youthful activity and will pursue his desires. Then if that is so, why should he be treated more stringently than an ordinary *kohen*? The answer is that after a man has consecrated himself to the Lord once, there is hope for him that he will hallow himself and add day by day to his goodness, and from Heaven his activity will be approved—in keeping with what the Sages of blessed memory said:[5] If one comes to be purified, he is given aid.[6] Then after he has vowed to be a *nazir* even one day, he will be given aid, and he can complete all his days [on earth] in purity.

Among the laws of the precept, there is what the Sages of blessed memory taught:[7] that there is a ritual uncleanness of the dead on account of which, if a *nazir* became defiled by it, he is to shave his hair and consider the preceding days void, and he begins to count his days as a *nazir* [anew] thenceforward; but there is [also] a ritual uncleanness of the dead on account of which he does not shave his hair and does not void the previous days, even though it is a defilement for seven days. For it is not stated about him, "And if he shall be unclean through a dead body," but rather, *And if any man should die beside him* (Numbers 6:9), which signifies that this applies only if he becomes defiled by uncleannesses that are in the dead person himself.

Now, these are the sources of uncleanness over which a *nazir* is to shave his hair: over a stillborn child, even if its limbs did not yet become joined and bound with sinews;[8] over an olive's amount from a corpse;[9] over an olive's amount of *nétzel*;[10] over bones which constitute a majority of the number of bones,[11] even though they do not measure a quarter of a *kav*;[12] over bones that form [most of] the structure of a corpse, even if they do not make up a quarter of a *kav*;[12] over half a *kav* of bones even if they do not comprise the majority of its [the corpse's] structure or the majority of its number [of bones],[9] provided all the bones are from one corpse and not from two bodies;[13] so too over a spinal column that comes from a corpse, and over the skull of any one body;[9] over an organ or limb from a corpse, and over an organ or limb from a living person, containing flesh that would be capable of growing new, healing tissue as a live, viable limb;[14] over half a *log* of blood that derives from one corpse; and over full handfuls of earth with decaying flesh of a corpse.[15]

What is *nétzel*?—it is the flesh of a corpse that is dissolving and turning into a fetid liquid.[8] The earth in which a corpse is decomposing does not cause defilement unless it was buried unclothed in a

שֶׁנִּקְבַּר בִּכְסוּתוֹ אוֹ בְאָרוֹן שֶׁל עֵץ אוֹ שֶׁל מַתֶּכֶת, אֵין לוֹ רָקָב; וְלֹא אָמְרוּ רָקָב אֶלָּא לְמֵת בִּלְבַד, לְהוֹצִיא הָרוּג, שֶׁהֲרֵי חָסֵר דָּמוֹ.

קָבְרוּ שְׁנֵי מֵתִים כְּאַחַת, אוֹ שֶׁגָּזְזוּ שְׂעָרוֹ אוֹ צִפָּרְנָיו וְקָבְרוּם עִמּוֹ, אוֹ אִשָּׁה עֻבָּרָה שֶׁמֵּתָה וְנִקְבְּרָה וְעֻבָּרָהּ בְּמֵעֶיהָ, אֵין הָרָקָב שֶׁלָּהֶם מְטַמֵּא; וְכֵן אִם טָחַן הַמֵּת עַד שֶׁנַּעֲשָׂה רָקָב, אֵינוֹ מְטַמֵּא, עַד שֶׁיֵּרָקֵב מֵאֵלָיו. וְכֵן אִם נִטְמָא בְרֹבַע הָעֲצָמוֹת הַבָּאִים מִשִּׁדְרָה אוֹ מִן הַגֻּלְגֹּלֶת בְּאֹהֶל, הֲרֵי זֶה סָפֵק טָמֵא.

כָּל אֵלּוּ שְׁתֵּים־עֶשְׂרֵה טֻמְאוֹת שֶׁמָּנִינוּ, אִם נָגַע נָזִיר בְּאַחַת מֵהֶן אוֹ אִם נְשָׂאָהּ, אוֹ הֶאֱהִיל הַנָּזִיר עָלֶיהָ אוֹ הֶאֱהִילָה הַטֻּמְאָה עַל הַנָּזִיר, (אִם) [אוֹ] הָיָה הַנָּזִיר וְאַחַת מִטֻּמְאוֹת אֵלּוּ בְּאֹהֶל, הֲרֵי זֶה מְגַלֵּחַ תִּגְלַחַת טֻמְאָה וּמֵבִיא קָרְבַּן טֻמְאָה וְסוֹתֵר אֶת הַכֹּל — חוּץ מִן הָרָקָב שֶׁאֵינוֹ מְטַמֵּא בְמַגָּע, שֶׁאִי־אֶפְשָׁר שֶׁיִּגַּע בְּכֻלּוֹ, שֶׁהֲרֵי אֵינוֹ גוּף אֶחָד; אֲבָל אִם נְשָׂאוֹ אוֹ נִטְמָא בְאָהֳלוֹ, מְגַלֵּחַ.

וְכֵן נָזִיר שֶׁנָּגַע בְּעֶצֶם הַמֵּת, אֲפִלּוּ בְעֶצֶם כִּשְׂעוֹרָה, אוֹ נְשָׂאוֹ, הֲרֵי זֶה מְגַלֵּחַ עָלָיו וּמֵבִיא קָרְבַּן טֻמְאָה וְסוֹתֵר אֶת הַקּוֹדְמִין; וְאֵין עֶצֶם אֶחָד מְטַמֵּא אָהֳלוֹ. אֲבָל אִם נִטְמָא בְגוּשׁ אֶרֶץ הָעַמִּים אוֹ בִשְׂדֵה שֶׁנֶּחֱרַשׁ קֶבֶר בְּתוֹכָהּ, (שֶׁאֵין) [שֶׁהֵן] מְטַמְּאִין בְּמַגָּע וּבְמַשָּׂא; אוֹ שֶׁהֶאֱהִילוּ עָלָיו וְעַל אַחַת מִן הַשְּׁתֵּים־עֶשְׂרֵה טֻמְאוֹת הַנִּזְכָּרוֹת שָׂרִיגִים הַיּוֹצְאִים מִן הָאִילָנוֹת, אוֹ הַפְּרָעוֹת הַיּוֹצְאוֹת מִן הַגָּדֵר, אוֹ מַטָּה אוֹ גָמָל וְכַיּוֹצֵא בוֹ, וְנִטְמָא בְאָהֳלָן; אוֹ בְרֹבַע עֲצָמוֹת שֶׁאֵין בָּהֶן לֹא רֹב מִנְיָן וְלֹא רֹב בִּנְיָן; אוֹ שֶׁנִּטְמָא בִרְבִיעִית דָּם, וְאַף־עַל־פִּי שֶׁהוּא מְטַמֵּא בְמַגָּע וּבְמַשָּׂא

---

16. TB Nazir 51a–b.

17. Having been shed when he was killed; TB Niddah 27b. The paragraph is based on MT *ibid*. 2–3.

18. TB Nazir 51a.

19. *Ibid*. 51b.

20. *Ibid*. 52b. The paragraph is based on MT *ibid*. 4.

21. I.e. even without touching it.

22. With his body, etc.

23. So TB Ḥullin 126b. The paragraph is taken from MT *hilchoth n'ziruth* vii 5.

24. Any clod of earth brought into the land of Israel from beyond its borders is considered a source of defilement if it is touched or carried.

25. TB Nazir 54a.

coffin of marble, and it was whole. If any limb was missing from it, or if it was buried in its garment, or in a casket of wood or metal, the law of the earth of decomposition does not apply to it.[16] Moreover, the law about earth of decomposition was postulated only about an ordinary corpse, excluding someone put to death, since his blood would be lacking.[17]

If two bodies were buried together, or if the hair or nails of one were cut and buried with it, or if a pregnant woman died and was buried with her embryo in her womb, their earth of decomposition does not cause defilement.[18] So too if a corpse was ground up until it became like earth of decomposition, it does not cause defilement[19] — not unless it decomposes of itself. Again, if [a nazir] was defiled by a quarter [of a kav] of bones deriving from a spinal column or from a skull in their tent, it is a matter of doubt if he is ritually unclean.[20]

Now, regarding all these twelve sources of defilement that we listed, if a nazir touched one of them or carried it,[21] or if a nazir covered it[22] like a tent, or if the source of uncleanness formed a tent-like covering over the nazir, [or] if the nazir and one of these sources of uncleanness were [together] in a tent—he is to shave his hair on account of defilement and bring an offering over defilement, reckoning everything null and void—except in the case of earth with decaying flesh: it does not defile upon being touched, because it is impossible to touch it all, since it is not one compact entity. But if one carried it or became defiled in its tent, he would shave his hair.[23]

So too, if a nazir touched a bone of a corpse, even a bone the size of a kernel of barley, or if he carried it, he is to shave his hair because of it and bring an offering over defilement, considering the preceding [days] nullified; but one bone would not make his tent defiled.[9] If, however, he was made ritually impure by a lump of earth from the nations,[24] or by a field in which a grave was plowed up—which cause defilement through touch or carrying; or if a tent-like covering was formed over him and one of the twelve sources of defilement mentioned [above], by boughs growing out of trees or by pieces [twigs or stones] protruding from a fence or hedge,[25] or by a bed or a camel[26] or anything like that, and he became defiled by their tent [which they formed]; or by a quarter [of a kav] of bones which constitute a majority of neither the number nor the structure [of a corpse's bones]; or if he was defiled by a quarter [of a log] of blood

⟨61⟩

וּבְאֹהֶל, אוֹ שֶׁנִּטְמָא בְגוֹלָל אוֹ בְדֹפֶק, שֶׁהֵן מְטַמְּאִין בְּמַגָּע וּבְמַשָּׂא; אוֹ שֶׁנִּטְמָא בְּאֵבֶר מִן הַחַי אוֹ בְאֵבֶר מִן הַמֵּת שֶׁאֵין עֲלֵיהֶן בָּשָׂר כָּרָאוּי לְפִי הָעִנְיָן שֶׁזָּכַרְנוּ — הֲרֵי זֶה אֵינוֹ סוֹתֵר.

אַף־עַל־פִּי שֶׁבְּכָל אֵלֶּה הוּא טָמֵא טֻמְאַת שִׁבְעָה וּמַזֶּה בַּשְּׁלִישִׁי וּבַשְּׁבִיעִי, אֵינוֹ מְגַלֵּחַ תִּגְלַחַת טֻמְאָה וְלֹא מֵבִיא קָרְבָּנוֹת וְלֹא סוֹתֵר אֶת הַקּוֹדְמִין; אֲבָל כָּל יְמֵי הַטֻּמְאָה אֵין עוֹלִין לוֹ לְמִנְיָן יְמֵי נְזִירוּתוֹ.

וְכֵן מֵעִנְיַן הַמִּצְוָה, מַה שֶּׁאָמְרוּ שֶׁהַמִּטַּמֵּא הַנָּזִיר, אִם הָיָה הַנָּזִיר מֵזִיד לוֹקֶה, וְזֶה שֶׁטִּמְּאוֹ עוֹבֵר מִשּׁוּם "וְלִפְנֵי עִוֵּר" וְגוֹמֵר; וְאִם הַנָּזִיר שׁוֹגֵג וְזֶה שֶׁטִּמְּאוֹ מֵזִיד, אֵין אֶחָד מֵהֶן לוֹקֶה, וְלָמָּה אֵינוֹ לוֹקֶה הַמְּטַמֵּא הַנָּזִיר — לְפִי שֶׁנֶּאֱמַר בְּנָזִיר "וְטִמֵּא רֹאשׁ נִזְרוֹ", כְּלוֹמַר שֶׁאֵין חַיָּב מַלְקוֹת אֶלָּא בוֹ כְּשֶׁהוּא מְטַמֵּא מִדַּעְתּוֹ. וְיֶתֶר פְּרָטֶיהָ, בְּמַסֶּכֶת נָזִיר.

וְנוֹהֵג אִסּוּר זֶה בְּכָל מָקוֹם וּבְכָל זְמַן, בַּזְּכָרִים וּנְקֵבוֹת. וְעוֹבֵר עַל זֶה וְטִמֵּא עַצְמוֹ בְּמֵזִיד בַּצְּדָדִין שֶׁבֵּאַרְנוּ, לוֹקֶה. וְכָתַב הָרַב מֹשֶׁה בֶּן מַיְמוֹן זִכְרוֹנוֹ לִבְרָכָה שֶׁהַנָּזִיר שֶׁטִּמֵּא עַצְמוֹ בְּמֵזִיד יִתְחַיֵּב ד' מַלְקִיּוֹת: מִשּׁוּם "לֹא יִטַּמָּא" וּמִשּׁוּם "לֹא יָחֵל דְּבָרוֹ" וּמִשּׁוּם "לֹא תְאַחֵר לְשַׁלְּמוֹ" וּמִשּׁוּם "לֹא יָבֹא", אִם הָיְתָה בִּיאָה וְטֻמְאָה כְּאֶחָת.

[מִצְוַת גִּלּוּחַ הַנָּזִיר וַהֲבָאַת קָרְבְּנוֹתָיו]

שעז שֶׁיְּגַלַּח הַנָּזִיר שְׂעָרוֹ וְיָבִיא קָרְבָּנוֹת כְּשֶׁיַּשְׁלִים נְזִירוּתוֹ, וְכֵן כְּשֶׁיִּטַּמֵּא,

26. TJ Nazir vii 3; Tosefta, 'Oholoth ix, beginning.

27. On which the top-stone would rest.

28. Four paragraphs above.

29. The paragraph is based on MT *hilchoth n'ziruth* vii 6.

30. MT *ibid.* 7, based on TB Nazir 54b.

31. MT *ibid.* v 20, based on TB Nazir 44a.

32. MT *ibid.* 21.

—even though this causes defilement through touch, carrying, and a tent; or if he became defiled by the top-stone of a tomb, or by the frame about a tomb,[27] which cause impurity on being touched or carried; or if he became defiled by a limb from a live person or a limb from a corpse which do not contain the proper, required kind of flesh in accord with the condition we mentioned[28]—he does not make [his preceding days as a *nazir*] void.[29]

Even though, in all these instances, he becomes ritually unclean for seven days, and must be sprinkled [with lustral water for uncleanness] on the third and seventh days, he does not remove his hair by a shaving over defilement, nor does he bring offerings, and he does not void the preceding days [of his time as a *nazir*]. However, all the days of ritual impurity are not included in the reckoning of his days as a *nazir*.[30]

Likewise, in the subject-matter of the precept, there is what the Sages said:[31] that if someone defiles a *nazir*, the *nazir* having managed this deliberately, he is to be given whiplashes, while the one who defiled him has transgressed the injunction, *you shall not put a stumbling-block before the blind*, etc. (Leviticus 19:14, §232). If the *nazir* acted unwittingly, while the one who defiled him acted deliberately, neither of them is given whiplashes. Why does the one who defiled the *nazir* not receive a whipping?—because it is stated about the *nazir*, *and he defiles his consecrated head* (Numbers 6:9), which is to denote that the punishment of lashes applies only to him, when he defiles himself knowingly.[31] The rest of its details are in the Talmud tractate *Nazir*.

This prohibition is in effect everywhere, at every time, for both man and woman. If [a *nazir*] transgressed this and defiled himself deliberately in any of the ways that we explained, he should be given whiplashes. And Rambam of blessed memory wrote[32] that if a *nazir* willfully made himself ritually unclean, he is punishable by four sets of lashes: on account of the injunctions, *He shall not make himself unclean* (Numbers 6:7, §376), *he shall not break his word* (ibid. 30:3, §407), *you shall not be slack to pay it* (Deuteronomy 23:22, §574), and *he shall not come near a dead body* (Numbers 6:6), if the "coming near" and the defilement occur at once.

[THE PRECEPT OF SHAVING A NAZIR'S HAIR
AND BRINGING HIS OFFERINGS]

〈63〉 **377** that a *nazir* should shave his hair and bring offerings when he

שֶׁנֶּאֱמַר: (וביום) [בְּיוֹם] מְלֹאת יְמֵי נִזְרוֹ, וְכֵן: וְכִי יָמוּת מֵת עָלָיו וְגוֹמֵר. וְאָמְרוּ בְּסִפְרָא: שְׁלֹשָׁה מְגַלְּחִין וְתִגְלַחְתָּן מִצְוָה: הַנָּזִיר וְהַמְצֹרָע וְהַלְוִיִּים. אוּלָם שְׁלֹשָׁה אֵלֶּה אֵינָם שָׁוִים לְכָל דִּבְרֵיהֶם, שֶׁגִּלּוּחַ הַלְוִיִּים הָיָה לְשָׁעָה בַּמִּדְבָּר וּבַשְּׁנַיִם הָאֲחֵרִים מִצְוָה נוֹהֶגֶת לְדוֹרוֹת.

וְכָתַב הָרַב מֹשֶׁה בֶּן מַיְמוֹן זִכְרוֹנוֹ לִבְרָכָה שֶׁשְּׁנֵי גִלּוּחִים אֵלוּ שֶׁל נָזִיר, שֶׁהֵן גִּלּוּחַ טֻמְאָה וְגִלּוּחַ טָהֳרָה, אֵין רָאוּי לִמְנוֹתָן כִּי-אִם מִצְוָה אַחַת, לְפִי שֶׁעִנְיָן גִּלּוּחַ הַטֻּמְאָה אֵינוֹ מִצְוָה בִּפְנֵי עַצְמָהּ כְּלָל אֶלָּא דִין מִדִּינֵי מִצְוַת הַנְּזִירוּת הוּא, שֶׁבֵּאֵר הַכָּתוּב שֶׁאִם נִטְמָא הַנָּזִיר בִּימֵי הַנְּזִירוּת, שֶׁיִּגַּלַּח וְיָבִיא קָרְבָּן וְאָז יָשׁוּב וִיגַדֵּל פֶּרַע בִּקְדֻשָּׁה כְּבַתְּחִלָּה, כָּל יְמֵי הַנְּזִירוּת שֶׁאָסַר עַל נַפְשׁוֹ—כְּמוֹ שֶׁיֵּשׁ לַמְצֹרָע גַּם-כֵּן שְׁתֵּי תִגְלָחוֹת וְהֵן מִצְוָה אַחַת. וְאַחַר שֶׁאֵין זֶה עִקַּר הַמִּצְוָה אֶלָּא דִין מִדִּינֶיהָ, אֵין רָאוּי לִמְנוֹתוֹ לְמִצְוָה בִּפְנֵי עַצְמָהּ, וּכְמוֹ שֶׁבֵּאֵר הָרַב זִכְרוֹנוֹ לִבְרָכָה בְּסֵפֶר הַמִּצְוֹת שֶׁלּוֹ בָּעִקָּר הַשְּׁבִיעִי.

וּבְסֵדֶר "זֹאת תִּהְיֶה", מִצְוַת עֲשֵׂה בּ' [סִי' קעד] כָּתַבְתִּי גַּם-כֵּן בְּשֵׁם הָרַב זִכְרוֹנוֹ לִבְרָכָה מַה הִיא הַסִּבָּה בְּמִנּוּתֵנוּ תִגְלַחַת נָזִיר וְקָרְבְּנוֹתָיו מִצְוָה אַחַת, וְתִגְלַחַת מְצֹרָע וְקָרְבְּנוֹתָיו שְׁתֵּי מִצְוֹת, וְשָׁם תִּרְאֶנּוּ מְבֹאָר אִם תִּרְצֶה לִלְמֹד.

מִשָּׁרְשֵׁי מִצְוָה זוֹ שֶׁל גִּלּוּחַ כָּל הַשֵּׂעָר בִּמְלֹאת יְמֵי הַנְּזִירוּת וַהֲבָאַת הַקָּרְבָּנוֹת, כָּתַבְתִּי בִּכְלָל שֹׁרֶשׁ (מצוה) [מִצְוַת עֲשֵׂה] הַקּוֹדֶמֶת [סִי' שע"ד] מַה שֶׁיָּדַעְתִּי.

מִדִּינֵי הַמִּצְוָה, מַה שֶׁאָמְרוּ זִכְרוֹנָם לִבְרָכָה: הֵיכָן מְגַלֵּחַ שְׂעָרוֹ—בְּעֶזְרַת נָשִׁים; וְלִשְׁכַּת נְזִירִים הָיְתָה שָׁם בְּקֶרֶן דְּרוֹמִית-מִזְרָחִית, וְשָׁם מְבַשְּׁלִים שַׁלְמֵיהֶן

§377 1. Sifra, m'tzora, perek 2, 6; so also Mishnah, N'ga'im xiv 4.
2. Numbers 8 : 7.
3. ShM positive precept § 93.
4. Once when he is healed, and again seven days afterward.
5. Mishnah, Middoth ii 5.

completes his period as a *nazir*, and so too if he becomes defiled: for it is stated, *when the days of his consecration are fulfilled*, etc. (Numbers 6:13), and again, *if any man should die beside him*, etc. (ibid. 9). Now, it was taught in the Midrash *Sifra*:[1] Three were to shave their hair, their shaving being a religious duty: a *nazir*, a man suffering *tzara'ath*, and the Levites. However, the cases of the three are not the same in all respects: for the shaving of the Levites was at one particular time in the wilderness,[2] while for the other two, the religious duty remains in force for all generations.

Well, Rambam of blessed memory wrote[3] regarding these two duties of shaving the hair for the *nazir*, namely, the shaving in defilement and the shaving in ritual purity, that it is not proper to reckon them as anything but one precept: because the subject of shaving the hair in defilement is not a precept by itself at all, but rather one law among the laws of the precept of the *nazir*'s period, which the Writ explains: that if a *nazir* became defiled during the days of consecration and abstinence, he is to shave his hair and bring an offering; and then he is again to grow his hair long in sanctity, as at the beginning, all the days of consecration that he imposed on himself—just as there are, equally, two instances of shaving the hair for a man ill with *tzara'ath*,[4] and they are one precept. And since this is not the main part of the precept but only one of its laws, it is not right to list it as a precept by itself—as the master scholar [Rambam] of blessed memory explained in his *Book of Precepts*, in the seventh root principle.

In the second positive precept of *sidrah m'tzorah* (§174) I wrote too, in the name of the master scholar of blessed memory, what the reason is for our listing the shaving of the *nazir* and his offerings as one precept, whereas the shaving of the [cured] *m'tzora* and his offerings are reckoned as two. There you will see it explained, if you wish to learn.

As to the root reasons for this precept of shaving all the hair at the completion of one's period as a *nazir*, and bringing the offerings, I wrote in the general consideration of the root reason for the previous [positive] precept (§374) what I knew.

Among the laws of the precept, there is what the Sages of blessed memory taught:[5] Where does he shave his hair?—in the Temple forecourt of the women; there was a chamber for the *nazir* there, in the southeast corner; there they would cook [the meat of] their *sh'lamim* (peace-offerings), and would throw their hair into the fire.

וּמַשְׁלִיכִין שְׂעָרָן לָאֵשׁ; וְאִם גִּלַּח בַּמְּדִינָה יָצָא; וּבְכָל מָקוֹם שֶׁמְּגַלֵּחַ, תַּחַת הַדּוּד מַשְׁלִיךְ שְׂעָרוֹ, וְאֵינוֹ מְגַלֵּחַ עַד שֶׁיְּהֵא פֶתַח הָעֲזָרָה פָתוּחַ, שֶׁנֶּאֱמַר "פֶּתַח אֹהֶל מוֹעֵד", וְאֵין פֵּרוּשׁ הַכָּתוּב שֶׁיְּגַלַּח כְּנֶגֶד הַפֶּתַח, שֶׁבִּזְיוֹן מִקְדָּשׁ יִהְיֶה בָזֶה.

וְכֵן מַה שֶּׁאָמְרוּ זִכְרוֹנָם לִבְרָכָה בְּמִצְוָה זוֹ: נָזִיר מְמֹרָט אֵינוֹ צָרִיךְ לְהַעֲבִיר תַּעַר, וְאַף־עַל־פִּי שֶׁאֵין לוֹ שֵׂעָר, וְכֵן אִם אֵין לוֹ כַּפַּיִם, הֲרֵי זֶה מַקְרִיב קָרְבְּנוֹתָיו וְשׁוֹתֶה יַיִן אַחַר־כֵּן וּמִטַּמֵּא; וַאֲפִלּוּ יֵשׁ לוֹ שֵׂעָר, מִכֵּיוָן שֶׁהֵבִיא קָרְבְּנוֹתָיו, אַף־עַל־פִּי שֶׁלֹּא גִלַּח, אֵין הַתִּגְלַחַת מְעַכֶּבֶת וְשׁוֹתֶה וּמִטַּמֵּא לָעֶרֶב, דְּמִשֶּׁנִּזְרַק עָלָיו אֶחָד מִן הַדָּמִים מִקָּרְבְּנוֹתָיו הֻתַּר אַף־עַל־פִּי שֶׁלֹּא נָתַן עַל כַּפָּיו וְלֹא הֵנִיף, שֶׁכָּל הַדְּבָרִים הָאֵלֶּה לְמִצְוָה וְלֹא לְעִכּוּב. וְאַף־עַל־פִּי שֶׁאֵין הַתִּגְלַחַת מְעַכֶּבֶת, מִצְוָה לְגַלֵּחַ אֲפִלּוּ לְאַחַר זְמַן מְרֻבֶּה.

וְנָזִיר שֶׁגִּלַּח בְּלֹא תַעַר אוֹ שֶׁגִּלַּח בְּתַעַר וְשִׁיֵּר שְׁתֵּי שְׂעָרוֹת, לֹא עָשָׂה וְלֹא כְלוּם, וְלֹא קִיֵּם מִצְוַת גִּלּוּחַ, בֵּין נָזִיר טָהוֹר בֵּין נָזִיר טָמֵא. גִּלַּח עַל הַשְּׁלָמִים וְנִמְצָא פָסוּל, תִּגְלַחְתּוֹ פְסוּלָה וּזְבָחָיו לֹא עָלוּ לוֹ. גִּלַּח עַל שְׁלֹשֶׁת הַבְּהֵמוֹת שֶׁהוּא מַקְרִיב וְנִמְצֵאת אַחַת מֵהֶן כְּשֵׁרָה, תִּגְלַחְתּוֹ כְּשֵׁרָה וְיָבִיא שְׁאָר הַזְּבָחִים וְיִקָּרְבוּ כְהִלְכָתָן.

שָׁלֹשׁ בְּהֵמוֹת אֵלּוּ שֶׁאָמַרְנוּ, הֵם כֶּבֶשׂ לְעוֹלָה וְכִבְשָׂה לְחַטָּאת וְאַיִל לִשְׁלָמִים; וּמֵבִיא עִם הָאַיִל שִׁשָּׁה עֶשְׂרוֹנוֹת וּשְׁנֵי שְׁלִישִׁית עִשָּׂרוֹן סֹלֶת, וְאוֹפֶה מֵהֶן עֶשְׂרִים חַלּוֹת. וְיֶתֶר פְּרָטֶיהָ, בְּמַסֶּכֶת נָזִיר.

וְנוֹהֶגֶת בִּזְמַן הַבַּיִת, בִּזְכָרִים וּנְקֵבוֹת. וְעוֹבֵר עַל זֶה וְלֹא גִלַּח, אוֹ שֶׁגִּלַּח בְּלֹא תַעַר, אוֹ שֶׁגִּלַּח וְשִׁיֵּר שְׁתֵּי שְׂעָרוֹת, בִּטֵּל עֲשֵׂה. אֲבָל שִׁיֵּר אַחַת לְבַדָּהּ, אֵין הַמִּצְוָה

---

6. Literally, in the province; i.e. anywhere in the land of Israel outside the area of the Temple.

7. MT hilchoth n'ziruth viii 3, based on his reading in TB Nazir 45b, as found in TJ (Radbaz).

8. I.e. into the fire beneath it, where he was cooking the meat of his sh'lamim (Numbers 6:18); source in note 7.

9. TB Nazir 45a. The paragraph is based on TB ibid.

10. MT hilchoth n'ziruth viii 5, based on TB Yoma 61b and Tosefta, Nazir i.

11. To receive what the kohen should give him (Numbers 6:19).

12. TB Nazir 46b.

13. I.e. if he failed to do the shaving.

14. MT ibid. based on TB Nazir 45b–46a.

15. MT ibid. 6.

16. Mishnah, N'ga'im xiv 4. (This paragraph is based on MT ibid. 6, 8, 10.)

17. Numbers 6:14.

18. See §136, note 3.

19. TB M'nahoth 76a, 78a.

But if he shaved his hair in the country,[6] he would [also] acquit himself of his obligation.[7] Wherever he did the shaving, though, he would throw the hair under the cauldron.[8] He would not do the shaving until the entrance to the Temple court was open, for it is stated, *at the entrance of the tent of meeting* (Numbers 6:18), and the meaning of the verse is not that he should do the shaving directly opposite the entrance, as this would constitute a disgrace for the Sanctuary.[9]

There is, too, what the Sages of blessed memory said regarding this precept:[10] A bald-headed *nazir* need not wield the razor. But even if he has no hair, and likewise if he has no hands,[11] he brings his offerings, drinks wine afterward, and may then become defiled.[12] And even if he has hair, once he has brought his offerings, then even if he has not shaved his hair, the shaving does not constrain him:[13] He may drink [wine] and become defiled in the evening. For once blood from one of his offerings is sprinkled on him, he is released, even if it was not put on his hands and he did not lift up and wave [the boiled shoulder of the ram, etc.]—for all these things are religious duties, but are not to hold back [his release].[14] Yet even though the shaving of the hair is not a matter that can prevent [his release],[13] it is a religious duty to do the shaving, even if after a great length of time.[15]

If a *nazir* shaved his hair without a razor, or if he shaved with a razor but left over two hairs, he accomplished nothing at all; he did not fulfill the precept of shaving the hair, whether he was a ritually clean *nazir* or a defiled one.[16] If he did the shaving upon the ritual slaying of the *sh'lamim* (peace-offering), and it turned out to be disqualified, his shaving is disqualified, and his sacrifices are not accredited to him.[12] If he shaved his hair upon the ritual slaying of the three animals that he offers up, and one of them was found to be acceptable, then his shaving is acceptable, and he is to bring the other sacrifices [anew], to be offered up according to their law.[12]

These three animals that we mentioned are a male lamb for an 'olah (burnt-offering), a female lamb for a *ḥattath* (sin-offering), and a ram for a *sh'lamim* (peace-offering).[17] With the ram he would bring six and two thirds measures called *'issaron*[18] of fine flour, and bake from it twenty loaves.[19] The rest of its details are in the tractate *Nazir*.

It is in effect when the Temple exists, for both man and woman. If [a *nazir*] violated it and did not shave his hair, or he shaved it without a razor, or he shaved it and let two hairs remain, he would [thus]

מִתְבַּטֶּלֶת בִּשְׁבִיל שֵׂעָר אֶחָת, וַאֲפִלּוּ גִּלַּח וְשִׁיֵּר שְׁתֵּי שְׂעָרוֹת וְאַחַר־כָּךְ נָשְׁרָה
אַחַת מֵהֶן מֵעַצְמָהּ, אִם גִּלַּח הָאַחֶרֶת, אַף־עַל־פִּי שֶׁשֵּׂעָר אֵין כָּאן, שֶׁהֲרֵי שַׂעֲרָה
אַחַת אֵינָהּ חֲשׁוּבָה שֵׂעָר כְּמוֹ שֶׁאָמַרְנוּ, מִצְוַת גִּלּוּחַ יֵשׁ כָּאן, לְפִי שֶׁכְּבָר גִּלַּח כָּל
רֹאשׁוֹ חוּץ מִן הַשְּׁתַּיִם וּנְפִילַת הָאַחַת אֵינָהּ כְּלוּם שֶׁשַּׂעֲרָה אַחַת אֵינָהּ חֲשׁוּבָה
לִכְלוּם, וּכְשֶׁיְּגַלַּח הָאַחֶרֶת הֲרֵי הַשְּׁלִים גִּלּוּחוֹ לְגַמְרֵי וְקִיֵּם מִצְוַת גִּלּוּחַ.

וְאַף־עַל־פִּי שֶׁהִתְגַּלַּחַת אֵינָהּ מְעַכֶּבֶת מִשְּׁתוֹת הַיַּיִן וּמֵהִטַּמֵּא, כְּמוֹ שֶׁאָמַרְנוּ,
הֲבָאַת הַקָּרְבָּנוֹת מְעַכֶּבֶת הַכֹּל, וְאִם לֹא הֵבִיאָן בִּטֵּל עֲשֵׂה זֶה וְהוּא אָסוּר לִשְׁתּוֹת
יַיִן וּלְהִטַּמֵּא עַד שֶׁיְּבִיאֵם; שֶׁאַף־עַל־פִּי שֶׁגִּלַּח, לֹא נִשְׁלְמָה הַמִּצְוָה עַד שֶׁהֵבִיא
הַקָּרְבָּנוֹת.

[מִצְוַת בִּרְכַּת כֹּהֲנִים בְּכָל יוֹם]

שעח שֶׁנִּצְטַוּוּ הַכֹּהֲנִים שֶׁיְּבָרְכוּ יִשְׂרָאֵל בְּכָל יוֹם, שֶׁנֶּאֱמַר: כֹּה תְבָרְכוּ אֶת
בְּנֵי יִשְׂרָאֵל אָמוֹר לָהֶם.

מִשָּׁרְשֵׁי הַמִּצְוָה, שֶׁחָפֵץ הַשֵּׁם בְּטוּבוֹ הַגָּדוֹל לְבָרֵךְ עַמּוֹ עַל־יַד הַמְּשָׁרְתִים
הַחוֹנִים תָּמִיד בֵּית יי וְכָל מַחְשַׁבְתָּם דְּבֵקָה בַּעֲבוֹדָתוֹ וְנַפְשָׁם קְשׁוּרָה בְּיִרְאָתוֹ כָּל
הַיּוֹם, וּבִזְכוּתָם תָּחוּל הַבְּרָכָה עֲלֵיהֶם וְיִתְבָּרְכוּ כָּל מַעֲשֵׂיהֶם, וִיהִי נֹעַם הַשֵּׁם
עֲלֵיהֶם.

וְאַל תִּתְמַהּ לֵאמֹר: וְלוּ חָפֵץ הַשֵּׁם בְּבִרְכָתָם, יְצַו אֹתָם אֶת הַבְּרָכָה וְאֵין צֹרֶךְ
בְּבִרְכַּת הַכֹּהֲנִים—כִּי כְבָר הִקְדַּמְתִּי לְךָ פְּעָמִים רַבּוֹת כִּי בְּכֹחַ הֶכְשֵׁר מַעֲשֵׂינוּ
תָּחוּל הַבְּרָכָה עָלֵינוּ, כִּי יָדוֹ הוּא בָּרוּךְ הוּא פְּתוּחָה לְכָל שׁוֹאֵל בִּהְיוֹתוֹ מֻכְשָׁר וּמוּכָן
לְקַבָּלַת הַטּוֹב.

וְעַל כֵּן, כִּי בָחַר בָּנוּ מִכָּל הָעַמִּים וְרָצָה שֶׁנִּזְכֶּה בְּטוּבוֹ, הִזְהִירָנוּ וְצִוָּנוּ לְהָכִין

20. By shaving the last hair he completed the performance of the
commandment, despite the interruption when he left over the two hairs. This is
evidently based on another version of TB Nazir 42a (MH).

§378   1. This is the original practice, found in the Talmud (TB Ta'anith 26b) and set
down in Rambam's code of Jewish law (MT *hilchoth t'fillah* xiv 1); and it is so
observed in the land of Israel to this day. However, as R. Moses Isserles (Rama)
notes in Shulḥan 'Aruch 'Oraḥ Ḥayyim, § 128, 44, the custom among Ashkenazic
Jewry in the Diaspora is for the *kohanim* to give the blessing only at the *musaf* service
on festival days, because they are then in a happy mood, free of the troubles and
worries of life in the exile.

2. I.e. in the merit of the *kohanim*, the blessing would be effective for the
Israelites.

⟨68⟩

disobey a positive precept. But if he left only one, the precept has not been disobeyed on account of one hair. Now, even if he did the shaving and left over two hairs, and afterward one of them fell out by itself, if he shaved the other, then even though there was no hair here, for one hair is not considered hair, as we said, there was yet a commandment of shaving here: For he had previously shaved his entire head except for the two, and one falling out is of no matter, since one hair is considered inconsequential. Then when he shaved the other one, he thus completed his shaving entirely and fulfilled the commandment of shaving.[20]

Now, although the shaving would not hold him back from drinking wine and becoming defiled,[13] as we said, the bringing of the offerings does hold everything back; if he did not bring them, he would disobey a positive precept, and would be forbidden to drink wine or become defiled until he brought them. For even if he shaved his hair, the commandment would not be fulfilled until he brought the offerings.

[THE PRECEPT OF THE BLESSING OF THE
KOHANIM EVERY DAY]

378 that the *kohanim* were commanded to bless the Israelites (Jewry) every day:[1] for it is stated, *Thus shall you bless the Israelites, saying to them*, etc. (Numbers 6:23).

At the root of the precept lies the reason that in His great goodness, the Eternal Lord desires to bless His people through the ministering servants who stay constantly in the Temple of the Lord, whose every thought is attached to His service, and whose spirit is bound to reverent fear for Him the entire day. In their merit, the blessing would take effect for them;[2] all their deeds would be blessed, and the pleasant goodness of the Eternal Lord would be with them.

Now, do not wonder and ask: If the Eternal Lord desires that they be blessed, let Him command His blessing [to abide] with them, and there is no need for the benediction of the *kohanim*. For I have already told you beforehand, many times, that by the force of the worthiness of our acts, blessing will be bestowed upon us. For His hand (blessed is He) is open to every person who asks, as he is worthy and readied for the reception of good reward.

Therefore, because He chose us out of all the nations and wished that we should merit to attain His good reward, He adjured us and

מַעֲשֵׂינוּ וּלְהַכְשִׁיר גּוּפֵנוּ בְּמִצְוָותָיו לִהְיוֹתֵנוּ רְאוּיִים אֶל הַטּוֹב; גַּם צַנְּנוּ בְטוּבוֹ
הַגָּדוֹל לְבַקֵּשׁ מִמֶּנּוּ הַבְּרָכָה, וְשֶׁנִּשָּׂא אוֹתָהּ עַל־יַד הַמְשָׁרְתִים הַטְּהוֹרִים, כִּי כָל
זֶה יִהְיֶה זְכוּת לְנַפְשֵׁנוּ, וּמִתּוֹךְ כָּךְ נִזְכֶּה בְטוּבוֹ.

מִדִּינֵי הַמִּצְוָה, מַה שֶׁאָמְרוּ זִכְרוֹנָם לִבְרָכָה, שֶׁאֵין הַכֹּהֲנִים נוֹשְׂאִים כַּפֵּיהֶם
אֶלָּא בַעֲשָׂרָה, וְהַכֹּהֲנִים מִן הַמִּנְיָן. וְכֵיצַד הִיא נְשִׂיאוּת כַּפַּיִם: בְּשָׁעָה שֶׁיַּגִּיעַ
שְׁלִיחַ־צִבּוּר לָעֲבוֹדָה, כְּלוֹמַר כְּשֶׁיִּרְצֶה לְהַתְחִיל בְּבִרְכַּת "רְצֵה", כָּל הַכֹּהֲנִים
הָעוֹמְדִים בְּבֵית־הַכְּנֶסֶת עוֹלִין לַדּוּכָן, וּפְנֵיהֶן לְמוּל הַהֵיכָל וַאֲחוֹרֵיהֶם כְּלַפֵּי הָעָם,
וְאֶצְבְּעוֹתֵיהֶם כְּפוּפוֹת עַל כַּפֵּיהֶם, עַד שֶׁיַּשְׁלִים שְׁלִיחַ־צִבּוּר בְּרִכַּת הֹודָאָה.

וְאַחַר־כָּךְ מַחֲזִירִין פְּנֵיהֶן כְּלַפֵּי הָעָם וּפוֹשְׁטִין אֶצְבְּעוֹתֵיהֶם וּמַגְבִּיהִין יְדֵיהֶן
כְּנֶגֶד כִּתְפֵיהֶם, וּמַתְחִילִין "יְבָרֶכְךָ", וּשְׁלִיחַ־צִבּוּר מַקְרֵא אוֹתָן מִלָּה מִלָּה,
שֶׁנֶּאֱמַר "אָמוֹר לָהֶם", וְהֵם עוֹנִים אַחֲרָיו בְּקוֹל נָאֶה; וּכְשֶׁמַּשְׁלִימִין פָּסוּק
רִאשׁוֹן, כָּל הָעָם עוֹנִין אָמֵן, וְכֵן בְּפָסוּק שֵׁנִי וּשְׁלִישִׁי; וּכְשֶׁיַּשְׁלִימוּ הַג' פְּסוּקִים
מַתְחִיל שְׁלִיחַ־צִבּוּר בְּ"שִׂים שָׁלוֹם" וְגוֹמֵר, וְהַכֹּהֲנִים מַחֲזִירִין פְּנֵיהֶם כְּלַפֵּי
הַקֹּדֶשׁ וְכוֹפְפִין אֶצְבְּעוֹתֵיהֶן וְעוֹמְדִין שָׁם בַּדּוּכָן עַד שֶׁיִּגְמֹר בְּרָכַת "שִׂים שָׁלוֹם",
וְחוֹזְרִין לִמְקוֹמָן.

וּמִנְהָגֵנוּ הַיּוֹם שֶׁהַכֹּהֲנִים אֵינָן עוֹלִין בַּדּוּכָן אֶלָּא עוֹמְדִין לִפְנֵי הָאָרוֹן וְעוֹשִׂין
כַּסֵּדֶר שֶׁכָּתַבְנוּ; וְקֹדֶם שֶׁיַּחֲזִירוּ פְנֵיהֶם לְבָרֵךְ הָעָם מְבָרְכִים: בָּרוּךְ אַתָּה ה'
אֱלֹהֵינוּ מֶלֶךְ הָעוֹלָם אֲשֶׁר קִדְּשָׁנוּ בְּמִצְוֹתָיו וְצִוָּנוּ בִּקְדֻשָׁתוֹ שֶׁל אַהֲרֹן וְצִוָּנוּ

    3. Our author echoes here the Talmudic teaching, "The Holy One, blessed is
He, yearns for the prayer of the righteous" (TB Yevamoth 64a).

    4. TB M'gillah 23b.

    5. The minimum required for congregational prayer.

    6. MT hilchoth t'fillah viii 5, based on TB Sotah 38b.

    7. Hebrew, duchan, a stage or platform in the court of the kohanim at the
Sanctuary, where they stood to give the blessing (see three paragraphs below about
the practice in latter times); TB Sotah 38b.

    8. The most holy part of the Temple; see §95, twenty-third paragraph.

    9. Derived from TB Sotah 38a.

    10. Derived from Tanḥuma, naso 8; ed. Buber, 15.

    11. TB Sotah 38a.

    12. The first word of the blessing: [The Lord] bless you (Numbers 6 : 24).

    13. Midrash cited in tosafoth, TB B'rachoth 34a, s.v. lo ya'aneh.

    14. TB Sotah 37b (see Rashi s.v. ba-m'dinah). The two paragraphs are based on
MT hilchoth t'fillah xiv 3.

    15. I.e. the héchal; see note 8.

    16. TB Sotah 39b. The paragraph is based on MT ibid. 4.

    17. TB Sotah 39a; MT ibid. 12. The long form of the benediction given here is

commanded us to arrange our activities and make ourselves worthy through His *mitzvoth*, to be deserving of the good reward. Moreover, in His great goodness, He commanded us that we should entreat Him for blessing,[3] and we should beseech it through the pure ministering servants. For all this will bring merit to our spirits, and as a result we will be worthy to attain His goodness.

Among the laws of the precept, there is what the Sages of blessed memory taught:[4] that the *kohanim* are not to raise their hands [and give the blessing] unless there are ten present,[5] the *kohanim* being counted in the number.[6] And how is the raising of the hands done? When the reader of the congregation reaches the benediction of the Temple service, i.e. when he wishes to start the benediction, *r'tzéh* ["Accept with favor, Lord our God, Thy people Israel and their prayer"] all the *kohanim* attending in the synagogue go up to the platform,[7] their faces turned toward the *héchal*[8] and their backs toward the people,[9] and with their fingers bent over on their palms — thus until the reader leading the service completes the benediction of giving thanks.[10]

After this they turn their faces toward the people[9] and spread out their fingers, raising their hands directly opposite their shoulders;[11] and they begin [with the word] *y'varech'cha*,[12] the reader of the congregation leading them in the utterance, word by word; for it is stated, *saying to them* (Numbers 6:23);[13] and they respond after him in a fair voice.[11] When they complete the first verse, the entire congregation responds with *amen*. And so the second verse, and the third.[14]

When they have finished the three verses, the reader of the congregation begins the benediction *sim shalom* ["Grant peace, goodness and blessing," etc.] and the *kohanim* turn their faces back toward the holy area,[15] bending their fingers in, and remaining there on the platform until he completes the benediction of *sim shalom*, when they return to their places.[16]

Today it is our custom that the *kohanim* do not go up on a platform but rather stand before the holy ark and follow the order that we have written. Before they turn around to bless the people, they say the benediction, "Blessed art Thou, Lord our God, King of the world, who has sanctified us with His commandments and commanded us about the holiness of Aaron and commanded us to bless His people Israel with love."[17] Every time they would turn around,

לְבָרֵךְ אֶת עַמּוֹ יִשְׂרָאֵל בְּאַהֲבָה. וְכָל פָּנוֹת שֶׁיִּהְיוּ פוֹנִין, כְּגוֹן חֲזָרַת פְּנֵיהֶם לַצִּבּוּר
אוֹ לַהֵיכָל, יִהְיוּ לְעוֹלָם דֶּרֶךְ יָמִין.

וְשִׁשָּׁה דְבָרִים מוֹנְעִין מִן הַכֹּהֲנִים נְשִׂיאוּת־כַּפַּיִם: הַלָּשׁוֹן וְהַמּוּמִין וְהָעֲבֵרָה
וְטֻמְאַת הַיָּדַיִם וְהַשָּׁנִים וְהַיַּיִן. וּבֵאוּר דְּבָרִים אֵלֶּה, עִם יֶתֶר פְּרָטֵי הַמִּצְוָה, הַכֹּל
מְבֹאָר בְּפֶרֶק אַחֲרוֹן מִמְּגִלָּה וְתַעֲנִית וּבַשְּׁבִיעִי מִמַּסֶּכֶת סוֹטָה.

וְנוֹהֶגֶת מִצְוָה זוֹ בְּכָל מָקוֹם וּבְכָל זְמַן בַּכֹּהֲנִים, כִּי עֲלֵיהֶם מִצְוָה זוֹ לְבָרֵךְ אֶת
יִשְׂרָאֵל. וּבְשַׁחֲרִית וּבְמוּסָף וּבִנְעִילָה חַיָּבִין לְבָרְכָם, אֲבָל בְּמִנְחָה שֶׁל כָּל יוֹם אֵין
שָׁם נְשִׂיאוּת־כַּפַּיִם, מִפְּנֵי שֶׁבְּמִנְחָה כְּבָר סָעֲדוּ כָל אָדָם וְיֵשׁ שָׁם חֲשַׁשׁ יַיִן, וְשִׁכּוֹר
אָסוּר בִּנְשִׂיאוּת־כַּפַּיִם; אֲפִלּוּ בְמִנְחַת תַּעֲנִית גָּזְרוּ זִכְרוֹנָם לִבְרָכָה אָטוּ מִנְחָה שֶׁל
כָּל יוֹם, וּכְדִפְסַק רַב נַחְמָן בְּפֶרֶק בַּתְרָא דְתַעֲנִית; אֲבָל אָמְרוּ שָׁם: אֶלָּא הָאִידָנָא
מַאי טַעְמָא פָּרְסֵי יָדַיְהוּ כָהֲנֵי בְמִנְחָתָא דְתַעֲנִיתָא, הוֹאִיל וְסָמוּךְ לִשְׁקִיעַת הַחַמָּה
מַצְלוּ לַהּ כִּתְפִלַּת נְעִילָה דַּמְיָא.

[מִצְוַת מַשָּׂא הָאָרוֹן בַּכָּתֵף]

שׁעט שֶׁנִּצְטַוּוּ הַכֹּהֲנִים שֶׁיִּשְׂאוּ הָאָרוֹן עַל הַכָּתֵף כְּשֶׁמּוֹלִיכִין אוֹתוֹ יִשְׂרָאֵל
מִמָּקוֹם לְמָקוֹם, שֶׁנֶּאֱמַר: כִּי־עֲבוֹדַת הַקֹּדֶשׁ עֲלֵהֶם בַּכָּתֵף יִשָּׂאוּ.

found also in *Halachoth G'doloth*, 1st ed. Hildesheimer, p. 222; 2nd ed. Hildesheimer,
I p. 466; H. Aaron of Lunel, *'Orḥoth Ḥayyim*, I (Jerusalem 1956), p. 242a; R.
Abraham of Narbonne, *Séfer ha'Eshkol*, ed. Albeck (Jerusalem 1935–38), p. 47 (but
with one word supplied as a correction). Apparently it was, too, the version known
to Rashi: see Rashi to TB M'gillah 27b, s.v. *v'lo nasa'thi*, and *Maḥzor Vitry* (by a
disciple of his), p. 100 (but cf. also *Dikduké Sof'rim* on Rashi *loc. cit.*). A shorter
version (without "and commanded us about the holiness of Aaron") is found in
Séder R. 'Amram Ga'on, ed. Goldschmidt, p. 35. Our standard version (merely "who
has hallowed us with the holiness of Aaron and commanded us to bless" etc.)
derives from R. Isaac 'Alfasi, M'gillah iv (ed. Jerusalem 1969, I p. 313b); MT *ibid.*;
etc.

18. TB Yoma 17b, etc. MT *ibid.* 13.

19. Lack of clear speech.

20. In MT *hilchoth t'fillah* xv 3 this is defined to denote a *kohen* who killed a
human being, served or worshipped in idolatry, or converted to an idolatrous
religion (i.e. even if he did not serve or worship in it, but declared himself its
faithful devotee). According to Rambam, repentance is of no avail, but other
authorities differ (see *Shulḥan 'Aruch 'Oraḥ Ḥayyim* §128, 35 and 37, with *Mishnah
B'rurah*).

21. I.e. if they are not washed before.

22. In MT *ibid.* 4 this is defined to denote a youngster until his beard has grown
in. See, however, *tosafoth* to TB Ḥullin 24b, s.v. *nithmalé z'kano* (and R. David ibn
Zimra, *Lilshonoth haRambam*, p. 16 §38: in MT ed. Shulsinger, appendix to vol. 1)

for example, in turning their faces to the people, or toward the *héchal*, it should always be by way of the right side.[18]

Six things can constrain the *kohanim* from lifting the hands [and giving the blessing]: the tongue,[19] blemishes and disfigurements, transgression,[20] ritual uncleanness of the hands,[21] years (age),[22] and wine.[23] The explanation of these terms, along with the remaining details of the precept, are all elucidated in the last chapter of the Talmud tractate *M'gillah*, in *Ta'anith*, and in the seventh chapter of the tractate *Sotah*.

This precept is in force everywhere, at every time, for the *kohanim*; for on them lies this religious duty, to bless the Jewish people. At *shaharith* (the morning prayers), *musaf* (the additional service), and *ne'ilah* (the closing service)[24] they are obligated to give the blessing; but at *minhah* (the afternoon prayers) of every day, there is no lifting of the hands [to give the blessing], for at [the time of] *minhah* every man has already eaten, and there is reason to fear that wine was taken,[25] and an inebriated person is forbidden to lift the hands [and give the blessing]. Even at *minhah* of a day of fasting, the Sages of blessed memory decreed against it [as a protective measure] for the sake of the daily *minhah*,[26] as R. Naḥman ruled in the last chapter of the tractate *Ta'anith* (26b). However, they said there: But then, at the present time, for what reason do the *kohanim* spread their hands [to give the blessing] at *minhah* on a day of fasting? — Because it is close to sunset when they say the prayers, it resembles the prayer-service of *ne'ilah*.[27]

[THE PRECEPT OF CARRYING THE HOLY ARK
ON THE SHOULDERS]

379 that the *kohanim* were commanded that they should carry the Ark[1] on the shoulders when the Israelites would take it from place to

that this refers only to the youngster's going up to give the blessing on his own; with elders he may go up when they think him ready for it. For the law as observed today, see further *Shulḥan 'Aruch ibid.* 34, with *Mishnah B'rurah*.

23. If a *kohen* drank a quarter of a *log* of wine at once; MT *hilchoth t'fillah* xv 1.

24. Said on *Yom Kippur* (the Day of Atonement) toward sunset.

25. Literally, and there is a suspicion of wine. On this law in general, see note 1.

26. To make certain that *kohanim* should not err and give the blessing at the afternoon prayers of an ordinary day.

27. Hence it is distinctive, and the error indicated in note 26 will not occur.

וְכָתַב הָרַב מֹשֶׁה בֶּן מַיְמוֹן זִכְרוֹנוֹ לִבְרָכָה: אַף־עַל־פִּי שֶׁמִּצְוָה זוֹ בָּאָה לַלְוִיִּם, בָּעֵת הַהִיא הָיָה, כְּלוֹמַר בַּמִּדְבָּר, לְמִעוּט מִסְפַּר הַכֹּהֲנִים בַּיָּמִים הָהֵם; וְאוּלָם לְדוֹרוֹת, הַכֹּהֲנִים חַיָּבִין בְּמִצְוָה זוֹ וְהֵם יִשָּׂאוּהוּ, כְּמוֹ שֶׁהִתְבָּאֵר בְּסֵפֶר יְהוֹשֻׁעַ וְסֵפֶר שְׁמוּאֵל.

וְהָרַב מֹשֶׁה בֶּן נַחְמָן זִכְרוֹנוֹ לִבְרָכָה כָּתַב: זֶה שֶׁאָמַר הָרַב שֶׁנֶּעְתְּקָה הַמִּצְוָה לַכֹּהֲנִים אֵינוֹ אֱמֶת; חָלִילָה לָּנוּ שֶׁנֹּאמַר שֶׁנִּשְׁתַּנָּה שׁוּם מִצְוָה בַּתּוֹרָה, שֶׁיִּהְיוּ נִפְסָלִים הַלְוִיִּם מִמַּשָּׂא הָאָרוֹן לְעוֹלָם. וְיָפֶה פֵּרַשׁ, וְהַלְוִיִּם נְשָׂאוּהוּ בִּימֵי דָוִד, שֶׁנֶּאֱמַר "וַיְהִי בֶּעְזֹר הָאֱלֹהִים אֶת הַלְוִיִּם נֹשְׂאֵי אֲרוֹן בְּרִית יי", וְכָתוּב "וְכָל הַלְוִיִּם הַנֹּשְׂאִים אֶת הָאָרוֹן" וְגוֹמֵר. אֲבָל בֶּאֱמֶת כִּי הַכֹּהֲנִים וְהַלְוִיִּם כֻּלָּן כְּשֵׁרִין בְּמַשָּׂא הָאָרוֹן מִן הַתּוֹרָה, שֶׁכֻּלָּן נִקְרְאוּ לְוִיִּם, וּכְמוֹ שֶׁכָּתוּב, "וְהַכֹּהֲנִים הַלְוִיִּם", וְכֵן כָּתוּב "וַיִּתְקַדְּשׁוּ הַכֹּהֲנִים וְהַלְוִיִּם לְהַעֲלוֹת אֶת אֲרוֹן יי אֱלֹהֵי יִשְׂרָאֵל ... כַּאֲשֶׁר צִוָּה מֹשֶׁה כִּדְבַר יי בִּכְתָבָם בַּמֹּטוֹת עֲלֵיהֶם". וְאָמְרוּ בְּסִפְרִי: וְהֵיכָן צִוָּה —"וְלִבְנֵי קְהָת לֹא נָתָן" וְגוֹמֵר, כִּי כֻלָּם נִקְרְאוּ בְּנֵי קְהָת.

וְעוֹד כָּתַב כִּי מַה שֶּׁאָמַר הָרַב מֹשֶׁה בֶּן מַיְמוֹן זִכְרוֹנוֹ לִבְרָכָה שֶׁהִתְבָּאֵר זֶה בְּסֵפֶר יְהוֹשֻׁעַ וּשְׁמוּאֵל, לֹא מָצָא הוּא הַבֵּאוּר הַזֶּה אֲבָל מָצָא מָצָא בְּהֶפֶךְ, שֶׁהֲרֵי נֶאֱמַר שָׁם: וַיְצַוּוּ אֶת הָעָם לֵאמֹר כִּרְאוֹתְכֶם אֵת אֲרוֹן בְּרִית יי אֱלֹהֵיכֶם וְהַכֹּהֲנִים הַלְוִיִּם נֹשְׂאִים אֹתוֹ.

אֲבָל הָאֱמֶת כְּמוֹ שֶׁאָמַרְנוּ, שֶׁכָּל הַשֵּׁבֶט כָּשֵׁר לְמַשָּׂא הָאָרוֹן; וְעוֹד שֶׁמְּפֹרָשׁ הוּא הַדָּבָר בִּגְמָרָא סוֹטָה, שֶׁאָמְרוּ זִכְרוֹנָם לִבְרָכָה: כֵּיצַד עָבְרוּ יִשְׂרָאֵל אֶת הַיַּרְדֵּן—בְּכָל יוֹם לְוִיִּם נוֹשְׂאִים אֶת הָאָרוֹן וְהַיּוֹם נְשָׂאוּהוּ כֹהֲנִים; כְּלוֹמַר בְּיוֹם

---

§379   1. I.e. the Ark made in the wilderness (Exodus 37:1–9), kept in the holy of the holies in the *mishkan* (Tabernacle) and later in the Sanctuary, which contained the tables of stone with the Ten Commandments, and the Torah scroll which Moses wrote; cf. Rashi to TB Sotah 33b, bottom, s.v. *uch'sheheheziruhu limkomo*.

2. ShM positive precept §34. (Our author evidently cites from the first version of ShM, and similarly Ramban — see note 4. In our editions of ShM, Rambam writes a bit more at length.)

3. The only *kohanim* then were Aaron and his sons El'azar and 'Ithamar.

4. Ramban, commentary (*hassagoth*) to ShM, root principle 3, s.v. *v'ra'ithi l'ha-rav* (ed. Chavel, pp. 56 ff.).

5. Sifre, Numbers §46. (Aaron, from whom all *kohanim* were descended, was a grandson of Kohath: Exodus 6:18, 20).

6. As Rambam cites it, the verse reads, *with the* kohanim *the Levites bearing it*: i.e. the *kohanim* alone, who are so designated at times in Scripture, since as descendants of Aaron all *kohanim* are members of the tribe of Lévi. Ramban, however, reads "with the *kohanim and* the Levites bearing it" — at variance with the massoretic text

place: for it is stated, *because the service of the holy things belonged to them: they carried them on the shoulder* (Numbers 7:9).

Now, R. Moses b. Maimon [Rambam] of blessed memory wrote:[2] Although this precept was given the Levites at that time, i.e. in the wilderness, on account of the small number of *kohanim*,[3] for future generations, however, the *kohanim* bear the obligation of this precept, and they must carry it—as it is made clear in the *Book of Joshua* and the *Book of Samuel*.

However, R. Moses b. Naḥman [Ramban] of blessed memory wrote:[4] "As to what the master stated, that the precept was transferred to the *kohanim*, it is not true. Far be it from us to say that any precept whatever in the Torah was altered, that the Levites were forever disqualified from carrying the Ark." He elucidated well; indeed, the Levites carried it in the days of David: For it is stated, *And it was when God helped the Levites carrying the ark*, etc. (I Chronicles 15:26); then it is written, *and all the Levites who were carrying the ark*, etc. (*ibid.* 27). "But in truth [Ramban continued] the *kohanim* and the Levites were all acceptable for carrying the Ark, by the law of the Torah—for they are all called Levites: as it is written, *But the* kohanim *the Levites* (Ezekiel 44:15); and so is it written, *So the* kohanim *and the Levites sanctified themselves to bring up the ark of the Lord, the God of Israel...as Moses had commanded according to the word of the Lord, on their shoulder with the poles upon them* (I Chronicles 15:14–15); and it was taught in the Midrash *Sifre*:[5] Where had he commanded [this]?—*But to the sons of Kohath he gave none*, etc. (Numbers 7:9), for they all were ranked as the sons [descendants] of Kohath."

He [Ramban] wrote further that regarding what R. Moses b. Maimon of blessed memory said, that this was made clear in the *Book of Joshua* and the *Book of Samuel*, he did not find this clarification, but rather found the opposite: For it is stated there, *and they commanded the people, saying: When you see the ark of the covenant of the Lord your God, with the* kohanim *and the Levites bearing it* (Joshua 3:3).[6]

The truth, though [he continued], is as we said—that the entire tribe was qualified for bearing the Ark. Moreover, the matter was explicitly stated in the Talmud tractate *Sotah* (33b): for the Sages of blessed memory described how the Israelites crossed the Jordan: Every day the Levites would carry the Ark, but that day the *kohanim* bore

it—i.e. on the day they crossed the Jordan, *kohanim* alone carried it.

עָבְרָם הַיַּרְדֵּן וּנְשָׂאוּהוּ כֹּהֲנִים לְבַדָּם, כִּי כֵן כָּתוּב: וַיֹּאמֶר יְהוֹשֻׁעַ אֶל הַכֹּהֲנִים
לֵאמֹר שְׂאוּ אֶת אֲרוֹן הַבְּרִית—כְּדֵי לְהֵעָשׂוֹת הַנֵּס עַל־יְדֵי כֹהֲנִים, שֶׁהֵם קֹדֶשׁ
קָדָשִׁים בַּשֵּׁבֶט.

וּלְפִי הַדּוֹמֶה, מַה שֶּׁאָמַר הָרַב מֹשֶׁה בֶּן מַיְמוֹן זִכְרוֹנוֹ לִבְרָכָה שֶׁמְּבֹאָר הוּא
בִּיהוֹשֻׁעַ, מִזֶּה הַמִּקְרָא הוּא, וְאֵינֶנּוּ בֵּאוּר הֶכְרֵחִי כְּלָל, כְּמוֹ שֶׁבֵּאַרְנוּ; וְזֶה שֶׁנֶּאֱמַר
בְּסֵפֶר מְלָכִים: וַיָּבִיאוּ הַכֹּהֲנִים אֶת אֲרוֹן בְּרִית יי אֶל מְקוֹמוֹ אֶל דְּבִיר הַבַּיִת אֶל
קֹדֶשׁ הַקֳּדָשִׁים, גַּם זֶה אַל אַל יְקֻשֶּׁה עָלֶיךָ, כִּי מִפְּנֵי שֶׁהַלְוִיִּים אֵינָם נִכְנָסִים לְבֵית
קֹדֶשׁ הַקֳּדָשִׁים הִכְנִיסוּהוּ הַכֹּהֲנִים לְבַדָּם.

וְהָעִקָּר, לְפִי הַדּוֹמֶה, כְּדִבְרֵי הָרַב מֹשֶׁה בֶּן נַחְמָן זִכְרוֹנוֹ לִבְרָכָה, שֶׁכָּל הַשֵּׁבֶט
כָּשֵׁר לְמַשָּׂא הָאָרוֹן; וּמַה שֶּׁכָּתוּב ”וַיֹּאמֶר לַלְוִיִּם” וְגוֹמֵר ”תְּנוּ אֶת אֲרוֹן הַקֹּדֶשׁ
בַּבַּיִת אֲשֶׁר בָּנָה שְׁלֹמֹה בֶן דָּוִיד מֶלֶךְ יִשְׂרָאֵל אֵין לָכֶם מַשָּׂא בַּכָּתֵף”, עוֹד עִנְיָנֵנוּ
שֶׁלֹּא יִצְטָרְכוּ יִשְׂרָאֵל עוֹד לָשֵׂא הָאָרוֹן מִמָּקוֹם לְמָקוֹם, אֲבָל אֵין הָעִנְיָן שֶׁאִם
יִצְטָרְכוּ לָשֵׂאת אוֹתוֹ שֶׁלֹּא יִשָּׂאוּהוּ הַלְוִיִּים; וְזֶה דָבָר בָּרוּר וְנִגְלֶה לַכֹּל.

וּמַה שֶּׁאָמְרוּ זִכְרוֹנָם לִבְרָכָה, מוּמִין פּוֹסְלִין בְּכֹהֲנִים וְאֵין שָׁנִים פּוֹסְלִין
בְּכֹהֲנִים, לֹא אָמְרוּ כֵן אֶלָּא בַּעֲבוֹדַת הַכְּהֻנָּה, שֶׁאֵין פּוֹסְלִין בְּאוֹתָהּ עֲבוֹדָה, אֲבָל
בַּעֲבוֹדַת הַמַּשָּׂא גַּם בְּכֹהֲנִים פּוֹסְלִין שָׁנִים כְּמוֹ בַלְוִיִּים.

מְשָׁרְשֵׁי הַמִּצְוָה, לְפִי שֶׁכָּל עִקַּר כְּבוֹדָן שֶׁל יִשְׂרָאֵל הוּא הַתּוֹרָה, שֶׁבָּהּ נִבְדְּלוּ
מִשְּׁאָר הָעַמִּים וְנַעֲשׂוּ חֵלֶק יי; עַל־כֵּן רָאוּי וְכָשֵׁר לָשֵׂאת אוֹתָהּ בְּכִתְפֵי הָאֲנָשִׁים
הַנִּכְבָּדִים וְהַמְּקֻדָּשִׁים שֶׁבָּנוּ, וְאֵין צֹרֶךְ לְהַאֲרִיךְ בְּמוּבָן לְתִינוֹקוֹת שֶׁל בֵּית רַבָּן.

כָּל עִנְיַן מִצְוָה זוֹ מְבֹאָר בַּכָּתוּב, וְהוּא שֶׁיִּשְׂאוּ הַכֹּהֲנִים וְהַלְוִיִּים הָאָרוֹן בַּכָּתֵף
בְּעֵת שֶׁיִּצְטָרְכוּ לְנָשְׂאוֹ מִמָּקוֹם לְמָקוֹם, כְּגוֹן בְּעֵת מִלְחָמָה אוֹ לְשׁוּם דָּבָר אַחֵר,

---

— evidently from a manuscript or scroll of the Book of Joshua that he had. Nor can
this be dismissed as a scribal error, for Ramban repeats it shortly afterward. And the
reading is apparently reflected in three early editions of Targum Jonathan (see
Sperber, *The Bible in Aramaic*, II p. 4) as well as the Septuagint and Peshitta.
Commenting on this, however, both R. Isaac de Leon (*M'gillath Esther* on ShM) and
R. Chavel (ed. ShM with Ramban's *hassagoth*, p. 58) simply note that the verse is
not as Ramban cites it, and can thus furnish no proof for him. Hence, continues R.
Chavel, Ramban must have meant the proof to derive mainly from the Talmud (see
the passage from TB Sotah 33b in the next paragraph): Thence we learn that every
day the Levites carried the ark; therefore Joshua had to alert the Israelites that on
this day the *kohanim* alone would carry it, *as an exception to the rule.*

7. This paragraph too is from Ramban (note 4; ed. Chavel, p. 58).

8. TB Ḥullin 24a.

9. There is no age of compulsory retirement.

10. I.e. the age of fifty (Numbers 8:25).

For it is so written: *And Joshua spoke to the* kohanim *saying; Take up the ark of the covenant* (Joshua 3:6) — so that the miracle should be wrought through the *kohanim,* who were the very holiest part of the tribe.

Now, as it would seem, the statement of R. Moses b. Maimon of blessed memory that it is made clear in the *Book of Joshua,* would mean by this verse (Joshua 3:6). Yet it is not an incontrovertible clarification at all, as we said. As for the verse in the *Book of Kings, And the* kohanim *brought in the ark of the covenant of the Lord to its place, to the sanctuary of the house, to the most holy place* (I Kings 8:6) — this too should not present any difficulty for you. For since the Levites might not enter the chamber of the holy of holies, the *kohanim* alone took it in.[7]

The crux of the matter, as it would seem, is as R. Moses b. Naḥman of blessed memory said: that the entire tribe was qualified to carry the Ark. As to the verse, *And he said to the Levites... Put the holy ark in the house which Solomon the son of David, king of Israel, built; you have no more carrying on the shoulders [to do]* (II Chronicles 35:3) — its meaning is but that the Israelites would have no further need to carry the Ark from place to place. But the sense is not that should they have need of carrying it, the Levites should not transport it. This is something clear and obvious to all.

As for what the Sages of blessed memory said:[8] Blemishes are a cause of disqualification among *kohanim,* but years (age) are not a cause of disqualification among *kohanim*[9] — they said this in regard to nothing but the Temple service of the *kohen,* that [age] does not bring disqualification to that service; but in the service of carrying, years bring disqualification for *kohanim* too, as for Levites.[10]

At the root of the precept lies the reason that the entire main glory of the Israelites is the Torah; for by it were they separated from the other nations, and became the portion of the Lord. It is therefore fitting and eminently suitable to carry it on the shoulders of the honorable and worthy men among us. There is no need to go on at length about something understandable to school-children.

The entire subject-matter of this precept is explained in the Writ: namely, that the *kohanim* and Levites were to bear the Ark on the shoulder at any time that they needed to carry it from one place to another— for example, at a time of war, or for any other purpose; and they were not to carry it by a wagon or on the back of an animal.

⟨77⟩

וְלֹא יִשָּׂאוּהוּ בַּעֲגָלָה אוֹ עַל־גַּבֵּי בְהֵמָה; וּכְבָר שָׂמוּ חֲכָמִים לְדָוִד טוֹעֶה בְדָבָר שֶׁהַתִּינוֹקוֹת קוֹרִין אוֹתוֹ, בְּנָשְׂאוּ הָאָרוֹן עַל הָעֲגָלָה.

וְנוֹהֶגֶת מִצְוָה זוֹ בִּזְמַן שֶׁיִּשְׂרָאֵל עַל אַדְמָתָן, כִּי אָז הָיוּ צְרִיכִין לָשֵׂאת אֲרוֹן בְּרִית יי מִפְּנֵי מִלְחָמָה אוֹ בַאֲשֶׁר יְצַוֶּה מַלְכָּם; אֲבָל עַכְשָׁו, בַּעֲווֹנוֹתֵינוּ, אֵין לָנוּ מֶלֶךְ וְלֹא אֲרוֹן לָשֵׂאת בְּשׁוּם מָקוֹם. וּמִצְוָה זוֹ מֻטֶּלֶת עַל שֵׁבֶט לֵוִי, וְעַל שְׁאָר יִשְׂרָאֵל שֶׁיַּסְכִּימוּ עַל יָדָם. וְזֶה שֶׁנָּהֲגוּ בַּגָּלִיּוֹת הַיּוֹם לְהוֹצִיא סֵפֶר תּוֹרָה לִקְרֹאת מַלְכֵי הָאֻמּוֹת, אֵין זֶה בְחִיּוּב מִצְוָה זוֹ כְּלָל, שֶׁכָּל בְּנֵי־יִשְׂרָאֵל רַשָּׁאִין לָשֵׂא אוֹתוֹ; וְאִם מִדֶּרֶךְ כְּבוֹד הַתּוֹרָה יִבְחֲרוּ גַם הַיּוֹם שֶׁיִּשָּׂאוּהוּ מִבְּנֵי לֵוִי, תָּבוֹא עֲלֵיהֶם בְּרָכָה.

☙ בְּהַעֲלֹתְךָ אֶת הַנֵּרוֹת

שָׁלֹשׁ מִצְווֹת עֲשֵׂה, וּשְׁתַּיִם מִצְווֹת לֹא־תַעֲשֶׂה

[מִצְוַת פֶּסַח שֵׁנִי בְּאַרְבָּעָה־עָשָׂר בְּאִיָּר]

שפ שֶׁיֵּעָשֶׂה פֶּסַח שֵׁנִי בְּאַרְבָּעָה־עָשָׂר בְּאִיָּר כָּל מִי שֶׁלֹּא יָכֹל לַעֲשׂוֹת פֶּסַח רִאשׁוֹן בְּאַרְבָּעָה־עָשָׂר בְּנִיסָן, כְּגוֹן מֵחֲמַת טֻמְאָה אוֹ שֶׁהָיָה בְדֶרֶךְ רְחוֹקָה, שֶׁנֶּאֱמַר: בַּחֹדֶשׁ הַשֵּׁנִי בְּאַרְבָּעָה־עָשָׂר יוֹם (לחדש) [בֵּין הָעַרְבַּיִם] יַעֲשׂוּ אֹתוֹ. וְעוֹד הוֹרוּנוּ חֲכָמִים זִכְרוֹנָם לִבְרָכָה דְּלָאו דַּוְקָא טֻמְאָה וְרָחוֹק הַדֶּרֶךְ לְבָד, אֶלָּא כָּל שֶׁשָּׁגַג אוֹ נֶאֱנַס, אוֹ אֲפִלּוּ הֵזִיד, וְלֹא הִקְרִיב בָּרִאשׁוֹן, מַקְרִיב בַּשֵּׁנִי.

מִשָּׁרְשֵׁי הַמִּצְוָה, לְפִי שֶׁמִּצְוַת הַפֶּסַח הוּא אוֹת חָזָק וּבָרוּר לְכָל רוֹאֵי הַשֶּׁמֶשׁ בְּחִדּוּשׁ הָעוֹלָם, כִּי אָז בָּעֵת הַהִיא עָשָׂה עִמָּנוּ הָאֵל בָּרוּךְ הוּא נִסִּים וְנִפְלָאוֹת

Long ago the Sages regarded David as making an error about something that children would read [in the Hebrew Scripture], when he transported the Ark on a wagon.[11]

This precept is in effect at the time that the Israelites are [settled] on their land, for then they would need to transport the Ark of the covenant of the Lord on account of war, or as their king would command them. Now, however, for our sins we have neither a king nor an Ark to transport anywhere. This precept is an obligation imposed on the tribe of Lévi, and on the rest of the Israelite people to agree about them. As for the custom observed in the exile today, to bring out a Torah scroll in formally greeting kings of the nations, that is not part of the obligation of this precept at all; for all Israelites (Jews) are permitted to carry it. And if, by way of honoring the Torah, they would decide today too that descendants of Lévi should [then] carry it, may blessing be bestowed upon them.

sidrah b'ha aloth'cha
(Numbers 8–12)

[It contains] three positive and two negative precepts.

[THE PRECEPT OF THE "SECOND PASSOVER" OFFERING ON THE 14TH OF IYAR]

380 that whoever is unable to bring through the first Passover offering, on the fourteenth of Nissan — for instance, on account of ritual uncleanness, or being on a distant journey — is to bring through a second Passover offering on the fourteenth of Iyar: for it is stated, *in the second month, on the fourteenth day at dusk, they shall bring it through* (Numbers 9:11). And our Sages of blessed memory taught us further[1] that it does not apply particularly in cases of ritual uncleanness and distant travel alone, but rather anyone who unwittingly, under coercion or by accident, or even deliberately, did not bring [the Passover offering] at the first occasion, is to bring it at the second.

At the root of the precept lies the reason that the precept of Passover is a powerful, clear sign [attesting] for all who see the sun, to the creation of the world out of nothing. For then, at that time, God (blessed is He) wrought for us great miracles and wonders, and

גְּדוֹלוֹת וְשִׁנָּה טֶבַע הָעוֹלָם לְעֵינֵי עַמִּים רַבִּים, וְרָאוּ כָל עַמֵּי הָאָרֶץ כִּי הַשְׁגָּחָתוֹ וִיכָלְתּוֹ בַּתַּחְתּוֹנִים; וְאָז בָּעֵת הַהִיא הֶאֱמִינוּ הַכֹּל וְיַאֲמִינוּ כָּל הַבָּאִים אַחֲרֵיהֶם לְעוֹלָם בֶּאֱמֶת שֶׁהוּא בָּרוּךְ הוּא בָּרָא הָעוֹלָם יֵשׁ מֵאַיִן בְּעֵת שֶׁרָצָה, וְהוּא הָעֵת הַיָּדוּעַ; וְאַף־עַל־פִּי שֶׁבְּרִיאַת הַיֵּשׁ מִן הָאַיִן הוּא דָבָר נִמְנָע מִדֶּרֶךְ הַטֶּבַע, כִּי כְּמוֹ־ כֵן נִמְנָע לְבְקֹעַ מְצוּלוֹת יָם עַד עֲבֹר בְּתוֹכוֹ עַם כָּבֵד בַּיַּבָּשָׁה וְיָשׁוּבוּ לִמְקוֹמָן, וּלְהַחֲיוֹת עַם גָּדוֹל וָרַב אַרְבָּעִים שָׁנָה מִלֶּחֶם הַיּוֹרֵד מִן הַשָּׁמַיִם יוֹם יוֹם, וְיֶתֶר הָאוֹתוֹת וְהַמּוֹפְתִים שֶׁעָשָׂה לָנוּ בָּעֵת הַהִיא, שֶׁכֻּלָּן נִתְחַדְּשׁוּ בְּהֶפֶךְ הַטְּבָעִים.

וְעִנְיַן חִדּוּשׁ הָעוֹלָם הוּא הָעַמּוּד הֶחָזָק בֶּאֱמוּנָתֵנוּ וּבְתוֹרָתֵנוּ, כִּי לְמַאֲמִינֵי הַקַּדְמוּת אֵין תּוֹרָה וְחֵלֶק לְעוֹלָם הַבָּא עִם יִשְׂרָאֵל, יָדוּעַ הַדָּבָר, אֵין לְהַאֲרִיךְ בִּמְפָרְסָם.

עַל־כֵּן הָיָה מֵרְצוֹנוֹ בָּרוּךְ הוּא לְזַכּוֹת בְּמִצְוָה זוֹ הַנִּכְבֶּדֶת כָּל אִישׁ יִשְׂרָאֵל, וְאַל יְעַכְּבֵהוּ אֹנֶס וְרָחוּק מָקוֹם מֵעֲשׂוֹתָהּ, כִּי־אִם יְקָרֵהוּ עָוֹן שֶׁנֶּאֱנַס בַּחֹדֶשׁ הָרִאשׁוֹן וְלֹא זָכָה בָהּ עִם הַקּוֹדְמִין, יַעֲשֶׂה אוֹתָהּ בַּחֹדֶשׁ הַשֵּׁנִי. וּלְפִי שֶׁהוּא יְסוֹד גָּדוֹל בַּדָּת, הִגִּיעַ הַחִיּוּב גַּם־כֵּן אַף עַל הַגֵּר שֶׁנִּתְגַּיֵּר בֵּין פֶּסַח רִאשׁוֹן לַשֵּׁנִי, וְכֵן קָטָן שֶׁהִגְדִּיל בֵּין שְׁנֵי הַפְּסָחִים, שֶׁחַיָּבִין לַעֲשׂוֹת פֶּסַח שֵׁנִי.

מִדִּינֵי הַמִּצְוָה, מַה שֶּׁאָמְרוּ זִכְרוֹנָם לִבְרָכָה בִּפְסָחִים פֶּרֶק מִי שֶׁהָיָה טָמֵא: מַה בֵּין רִאשׁוֹן לַשֵּׁנִי—הָרִאשׁוֹן חָמֵץ אָסוּר בְּ"בַל יֵרָאֶה" וּ"בַל יִמָּצֵא", וְהַשֵּׁנִי חָמֵץ וּמַצָּה עִמּוֹ בַּבַּיִת; וְהַשֵּׁנִי אֵינוֹ נוֹהֵג אֶלָּא יוֹם אֶחָד, וְאֵין שָׁם יוֹם־טוֹב וְאָסוּר

---

2. Cf. generally, Ramban, Commentary, Exodus 20:2.
3. TB P'saḥim 93a.

changed the [workings of] nature in the world before the eyes of many peoples. Then all the peoples of the earth saw that His watchful regulation and His power extend to the lower [terrestrial] realms. Then, at that time, all believed—and so would all who came into the world after them believe—in truth, that He (blessed is He) created the world out of nothing at a time that He desired, this being the time known [by the Jewish calendar]—even though the creation of something out of nothing is an impossible matter by the way of nature. For it is likewise impossible to divide the depths of the sea until a massive people crosses through it on dry land, whereupon they return to their place; and so to sustain a large, numerous people forty years by food that descends from heaven day by day; and so the rest of the miracles and wonders that He wrought for us at that time. For all were new manifestations, in opposition to the natural order.[2]

Now, the concept of the creation of the world as a new entity [not pre-existing] is a mighty pillar in our faith and our Torah. For those who believe in its [eternal] pre-existence have no Torah and no share in the world-to-come with the Israelites. It is a known thing; one should not continue at length about a matter of common knowledge.

It was therefore His desire (blessed is He) to make every Israelite meritorious by this estimable precept [of bringing the Passover offering], and to let no accident or distance of location restrain him from observing it. Hence if some trouble befalls him and he is forcibly restrained in the first month, so that he cannot observe it meritoriously with those who precede him, let him observe it in the second month. And because it is a great fundamental in the religion, the obligation extends also to a proselyte who becomes converted between the first Passover and the second; and so too if a child has grown [to his age of obligation] between the two Passovers—these have the duty to present the second Passover offering.[3]

Among the laws of the precept, there is what the Sages of blessed memory said in the ninth chapter of the Talmud tractate *P'sahim* (95a): What difference [in law] is there between the first [Passover] and the second? At the first, *hamétz* (leavened food) is forbidden by the injunctions that it should not be seen (Exodus 13:7, §20) and should not be found (*ibid*. 12:19, §11); at the second, both *hamétz* and *matzah* may be with him in the house. The second is observed for only one day; it is not a proper festival day, nor is there any ban on work.

מְלָאכָה; וְהָרִאשׁוֹן טָעוּן הַלֵּל בַּאֲכִילָתוֹ, וְהַשֵּׁנִי אֵין טָעוּן הַלֵּל בַּאֲכִילָתוֹ, וְזֶה וְזֶה
טְעוּנִין הַלֵּל בַּעֲשִׂיָּתוֹ; וּשְׁנֵיהֶם נֶאֱכָלִין צָלִי עַל מַצּוֹת וּמְרוֹרִים, שֶׁבְּפֵרוּשׁ נֶאֱמַר
בַּכָּתוּב כֵּן; וּשְׁנֵיהֶם דּוֹחִין אֶת הַשַּׁבָּת, וּבִשְׁנֵיהֶם אֵין מוֹתִירִין וְלֹא שׁוֹבְרִין עֶצֶם,
שֶׁבְּפֵרוּשׁ הִזְהִיר הַכָּתוּב גַּם בָּזֶה בְּ"לֹא תוֹתִירוּ", "וְעֶצֶם לֹא יִשְׁבְּרוּ בוֹ".

וְאִם תִּשְׁאַל, בְּנִי: וְלָמָּה לֹא יִשְׁווּ שְׁנֵיהֶם לְכָל דָּבָר, שֶׁהֲרֵי בְּפֵרוּשׁ נֶאֱמַר כָּאן
בְּפֶסַח שֵׁנִי "כְּכָל חֻקַּת הַפֶּסַח יַעֲשׂוּ אֹתוֹ"—דַּע כִּי כְבָר עוֹרְרוּ אוֹתָנוּ חֲכָמִים
זִכְרוֹנָם לִבְרָכָה בָּזֶה, וּבֵאֲרוּ בְּפֶרֶק מִי שֶׁהָיָה טָמֵא שֶׁבְּמִצְווֹת שֶׁבְּגוּפוֹ שֶׁל פֶּסַח
הַכָּתוּב מְדַבֵּר, כְּגוֹן לְאָכְלוֹ עַל מַצּוֹת וּמְרוֹרִים וְשֶׁלֹּא לְהַשְׁאִיר מִמֶּנּוּ וְשֶׁלֹּא
לִשְׁבֹּר בּוֹ עֶצֶם, וּכְמוֹ שֶׁפֵּרַשְׁנוּ; וְלִמְּדוּנוּ לוֹמַר כֵּן מֵאֲשֶׁר פֵּרַשׁ הַכָּתוּב כָּאן בְּפֶסַח
שֵׁנִי קְצָת מִדִּינָיו, וְאִלּוּ הָיָה שָׁוֶה לְגַמְרֵי עִם הָרִאשׁוֹן יֹאמַר "כְּכָל חֻקַּת" וְגוֹמֵר,
וְדַיּוֹ; וְכֵן אָמְרוּ שָׁם: מָה עֶצֶם מְיֻחָד שֶׁבְּגוּפוֹ, אַף כֹּל וְכוּלֵי.

וְכֵן מֵעִנְיַן הַמִּצְוָה מַה שֶּׁאָמְרוּ גַּם־כֵּן שֶׁהַטָּמֵא שֶׁנִּדְחָה לְפֶסַח שֵׁנִי הוּא מִי
שֶׁנִּטְמָא בְּטֻמְאָה חֲמוּרָה הַמְעַכַּבְתּוֹ מִלֶּאֱכֹל הַפֶּסַח, כְּגוֹן זָבִים וְזָבוֹת נִדּוֹת
וְיוֹלְדוֹת וּבוֹעֲלֵי נִדּוֹת, וְכֵן טְמֵא מֵת שֶׁנִּטְמָא בְּטֻמְאָה מִן הַמֵּת שֶׁהַנָּזִיר מְגַלֵּחַ
עָלֶיהָ, וּכְמוֹ שֶׁפֵּרַשְׁנוּ בְּסֵדֶר נָשֹׂא; אֲבָל אִם הָיָה טָמֵא בִּשְׁאָר טֻמְאוֹת מִן הַמֵּת
שֶׁאֵין הַנָּזִיר מְגַלֵּחַ עָלֶיהָ, וְכֵן אִם נָגַע בְּנִבְלָה וּבְשֶׁרֶץ וְכַיּוֹצֵא בָּהֶן, וַאֲפִלּוּ בְּיוֹם
אַרְבָּעָה־עָשָׂר, הֲרֵי זֶה טוֹבֵל, וְשׁוֹחֲטִין עָלָיו אַחַר טְבִילָה, וְלָעֶרֶב כְּשֶׁיַּעֲרִיב
שִׁמְשׁוֹ אוֹכֵל פִּסְחוֹ.

3a. The psalms of praise and thanksgiving: Psalms 113–118.

4. Exodus 12:9–10, Numbers 9:11–12.

5. They may be offered up even on the Sabbath if it is the proper time, although
it would ordinarily constitute a violation of the Sabbath.

6. TB P'saḥim 95a.

7. E.g. that it should be a male lamb, whole (unblemished), in its first year of
life; how is it offered up; and that it is to be eaten roasted.

8. See Leviticus 11:29–30.

9. TB P'saḥim 90b; MT *hilchoth korban pesaḥ* vi 2.

The first requires *hallél*[3a] [to be said] when it [the Passover offering] is eaten, while the second does not require *hallél* [to be said] when it is eaten; but both require *hallél* when they are being offered up; and both [offerings] are eaten roasted, with *matzoth* and bitter herbs — for it is distinctly stated so in the Writ.[4] Both thrust aside the Sabbath;[5] and with both, nothing is to be left over, and no bone is to be broken: for Scripture distinctly adjured about this [offering] too that *they shall leave none of it till the morning, nor break a bone of it* (Numbers 9:12).

Now, you might ask, my son: But why are the two not regarded as equal in every respect, since it is explicitly stated here, about the second Passover offering, *according to the entire statute of the passover shall they keep it* (Numbers 9:12)? Know that the Sages of blessed memory alerted us to this [question] long ago, and they explained in the ninth chapter of the tractate *P'saḥim* (95a) that this verse applies to the precepts about the actual Passover offering itself: for instance, to eat it with *matzoth* and bitter herbs, not to leave any of it over, and not to break any bone of it — as we explained. They taught us to accept this because Scripture specifies here, about the second Passover, some of its laws. Were it completely equivalent to the first, Scripture should have stated, *according to the entire statute* [*of the passover*] etc. and no more. They stated there likewise:[6] Just as the essential characteristic of a bone is that it is of its body, so does every precept about its body apply,[7] etc.

There is also in the subject-matter of the precept what the Sages likewise said:[2] that a ritually unclean person who is deferred to the second Passover is one who became defiled by a severe uncleanness that prevents him from eating the Passover offering: for instance, men and women with irregular discharges, women defiled by the menses and those who gave birth, and persons who were conjugally intimate with women defiled by the menses. And so too one who was defiled through the dead in a way that would make a *nazir* shave his hair because of it, as we explained in *sidrah naso* (§ 376). But if he became defiled through any other uncleanness from the dead, over which a *nazir* would not shave his hair, and so too if he touched a carcass or a [dead] creeping animal,[8] and so forth, even on the fourteenth day [of Nissan], he merely undergoes ritual immersion, [the Passover offering] is ritually slain for him after the immersion, and in the evening, when the sun has set, he eats his Passover offering.[9]

Similarly, in the subject-matter of the precept there is what the

וְכֵן מֵעִנְיַן הַמִּצְוָה מַה שֶּׁאָמְרוּ זִכְרוֹנָם לִבְרָכָה שָׁם בְּפֶרֶק מִי שֶׁהָיָה טָמֵא, עַל
דֶּרֶךְ הַהֲלָכָה הַמְקֻיֶּמֶת, שֶׁדֶּרֶךְ רְחוֹקָה תִּקָּרֵא כָּל שֶׁהוּא רָחוֹק מְחוֹמוֹת יְרוּשָׁלַיִם
חֲמִשָּׁה-עָשָׂר מִילִין, אֲבָל פָּחוֹת מִכֵּן אֵין נִקְרָא דֶּרֶךְ רְחוֹקָה. וְיֶתֶר פְּרָטֶיהָ,
בְּמַסֶּכֶת פְּסָחִים.

וְנוֹהֶגֶת מִצְוָה זוֹ בִּזְמַן הַבַּיִת, בִּזְכָרִים בְּתוֹרַת חִיּוּב, וּבִנְקֵבוֹת בְּתוֹרַת
רְשׁוּת—שֶׁכֵּן הוֹרוּנוּ זִכְרוֹנָם לִבְרָכָה, שֶׁנָּשִׁים שֶׁנִּדְחוּ לְפֶסַח שֵׁנִי מִפְּנֵי טֻמְאָה אוֹ
מִפְּנֵי אֶחָד מֵהַדְּבָרִים שֶׁנִּזְכָּרְנוּ, שֶׁעֲשִׂיַּת הַפֶּסַח שֵׁנִי לָהֶם רְשׁוּת: רָצוּ שׁוֹחֲטִין רָצוּ
אֵין שׁוֹחֲטִין; וּמִן הַטַּעַם הַזֶּה אֵין שׁוֹחֲטִין עֲלֵיהֶם בִּפְנֵי עַצְמָן בְּשַׁבָּת.

וְהָאִישׁ הָעוֹבֵר עַל זֶה וְהֵזִיד וּבִטֵּל עֲשֵׂה זֶה וְלֹא הִקְרִיב פֶּסַח שֵׁנִי, כְּשֶׁנֶּאֱנַס
וְלֹא יָכֹל לְהַקְרִיב פֶּסַח רִאשׁוֹן, חַיָּב כָּרֵת; זֶהוּ דַעַת רַבִּי בַּמִּשְׁנָה. אֲבָל רַבִּי נָתָן
וְרַבִּי חֲנִינָא וְרַבִּי עֲקִיבָה פּוֹטְרִין אוֹתוֹ מִן הַכָּרֵת, מִכֵּיוָן שֶׁלֹּא הֵזִיד בָּרִאשׁוֹן; וְאֵין
צָרִיךְ לוֹמַר שֶׁאִם הֵזִיד וּבִטֵּל הָרִאשׁוֹן, וּבִטֵּל גַּם הַשֵּׁנִי, בֵּין בְּזָדוֹן בֵּין בִּשְׁגָגָה,
שֶׁחַיָּב כָּרֵת לְדִבְרֵי הַכֹּל, מִכֵּיוָן שֶׁהֵזִיד וְלֹא הִקְרִיב קָרְבַּן יְיָ בְּמוֹעֲדוֹ.

וְזֹאת הִיא אַחַת מִשְּׁתֵּי מִצְווֹת עֲשֵׂה שֶׁבַּתּוֹרָה שֶׁמִּתְחַיְּבִין עָלֶיהָ כָּרֵת, כְּמוֹ
שֶׁאָמַרְנוּ בְּסֵדֶר בֹּא אֶל פַּרְעֹה.

[מִצְוַת פֶּסַח שֵׁנִי שֶׁיֵּאָכֵל עַל מַצּוֹת וּמְרוֹרִים]

שפא שֶׁכָּל הַמְּחֻיָּב בְּפֶסַח שֵׁנִי שֶׁיֹּאכַל בְּשַׂר הַפֶּסַח עַל מַצּוֹת וּמְרוֹרִים,
שֶׁנֶּאֱמַר: עַל מַצּוֹת וּמְרֹרִים יֹאכְלֻהוּ.

מִשָּׁרְשֵׁי מִצְוַת כָּל עִנְיַן הַפֶּסַח כָּתַבְתִּי בְּסֵדֶר בֹּא אֶל פַּרְעֹה, וְאֵין סָפֵק כִּי כָל

10. On the fourteenth of Nissan at sunrise; if the distance is less, a person could comfortably reach Jerusalem in the afternoon, in time.

11. TB P'saḥim 91b.

12. Being a voluntary matter, it could not thrust aside the prohibition of the Sabbath. But they might share in a Passover offering sacrificed for men.

13. TB P'saḥim 93b.

14. I.e. the views of everyone mentioned above: but R. Ḥananya b. 'Akavya acquits him of the punishment. See MT hilchoth korban pesaḥ v 2.

15. The reference is apparently to §5, but actually our author wrote this explicitly in §2.

§381   1. See §§ 5–8, 11.   ⟨84⟩

Sages of blessed memory said there in the ninth chapter of the tractate *P'saḥim* (93b) as the established normative law, that it is considered a distant journey when anyone is fifteen *mils* away from the walls of Jerusalem;[10] but if it is less than that, it is not called a distant journey. The rest of its details are in the Talmud tractate *P'saḥim*.

This precept is in effect at the time the Temple exists, for men in the nature of an obligation, and for women in the nature of a permitted, voluntary matter. For so the Sages of blessed memory instructed us:[11] that if women were deferred to the second Passover on account of ritual uncleanness or one of the [other] matters that we mentioned, keeping the second Passover would be voluntary, optional for them: If they wished, they could have [a Passover offering] ritually slain [for them], and if they wished, they would not have it ritually slain. And for this reason, it was not to be ritually slain for them alone on the Sabbath.[12]

If a man transgressed this and deliberately disobeyed this positive precept by not bringing an offering at the second Passover, having been unable by accident or compulsion to bring the offering at the first Passover, he would incur the punishment of *karéth* [Divine severance of existence]. This is the view of Rabbi [Judah haNassi] in the Mishnah.[3] However, R. Nathan, R. Ḥanina and R. 'Akiva consider him free of the penalty of *karéth*, since he did not act deliberately [to fail to bring the offering] at the first [Passover].[13] But needless to say, if someone deliberately failed to bring the first one, and then failed to bring the second, whether willfully or inadvertently, he would deserve *karéth* according to everyone's view,[14] since he was willful and did not bring the offering of the Lord in its appointed time.

This is one of two positive precepts in the Torah over which the punishment is *karéth*, as we stated in *sidrah bo*.[15]

[THAT THE "SECOND PASSOVER" OFFERING IS TO
BE EATEN WITH MATZAH AND BITTER HERBS]

381 that everyone obligated to observe the second Passover should eat the meat of the Passover offering with *matzoth* and bitter herbs: as it is stated, *they shall eat it with unleavened bread and bitter herbs* (Numbers 9:11).

About the root reasons for the precept of the entire subject of the Passover offering, I wrote in *sidrah bo*;[1] and there is no doubt that the

עִנְיַן פֶּסַח שֵׁנִי אֵינוֹ כִּי־אִם מִיסוֹדוֹ שֶׁל רִאשׁוֹן; יָדוּעַ הַדָּבָר.

מִדִּינֵי הַמִּצְוָה, מַה שֶּׁאָמְרוּ זִכְרוֹנָם לִבְרָכָה שֶׁהַמַּצּוֹת צְרִיכוֹת שְׁמּוּר גָּדוֹל שֶׁלֹּא יָבוֹאוּ לִידֵי חִמּוּץ, עַד שֶׁחִיְּבוּנוּ זִכְרוֹנָם לִבְרָכָה לְהִזָּהֵר בָּהֶם אֲפִלּוּ מֵעִדָּן קְצִירָה שֶׁלֹּא יָבוֹאוּ עֲלֵיהֶן מַיִם, פֶּן יָבוֹאוּ לִידֵי חִמּוּץ; וְיֶתֶר רִבּוּי פְּרָטֵיהֶן בְּעִנְיַן הַלִּישָׁה וְהָאֲפִיָּה, בְּפֶסַח רִאשׁוֹן; וּכְלַל הַכֹּל הוּא שֶׁנַּעֲשֶׂה בָּהֶן שְׁמִירָה גְדוֹלָה מֵחִמּוּץ.

וְכֵן מַה שֶּׁפֵּרְשׁוּ בִמְרוֹרִים שֶׁכָּל עֵשֶׂב מַר הוּא בִכְלַל מְרוֹרִים שֶׁהִזְכִּיר הַכָּתוּב, וְשֶׁאָדָם יוֹצֵא יְדֵי חוֹבָתוֹ (בְּפֶסַח) בְּכֻלָּן, לְפִי שֶׁהַצַּנָּאָה לָנוּ בְּמָרוֹר זֵכֶר לְ"וַיְמָרְרוּ אֶת חַיֵּיהֶם", וּבְכָל עֵשֶׂב מַר יָזְכֹּר הַדָּבָר; אֲבָל מִכָּל־מָקוֹם בֵּרְרוּ לָנוּ חֲכָמֵינוּ זִכְרוֹנָם לִבְרָכָה לֶאֱכֹל הַחֲזֶרֶת, כִּי בָהּ זֵכֶר הַתַּמְרוּר מִצַּד הַקֶּלַח, שֶׁטַּעֲמוֹ מַר קְצָת, וְגַם יֵשׁ בָּהּ הִדּוּר לַמִּצְוָה יוֹתֵר מִבִּשְׁאָר עֲשָׂבִים מָרִים, גַּם כִּי שְׁמָהּ הָדוּר, שֶׁנִּקְרֵאת חָסָא, וְרֶמֶז בִּרְכָה בּוֹ שֶׁחָס רַחֲמָנָא עָלֵינוּ וּפְדָאָנוּ מִיַּד הַמִּצְרִיִּים הַקָּשִׁים. וּמִכָּל אֵלֶּה יֵשׁ הִתְעוֹרְרוּת וְזֵכֶר אֶל לֵב בְּנֵי־אָדָם בְּעִנְיָן (הַנִּסִּים שֶׁנַּעֲשׂוּ לָנוּ בְמִצְרַיִם), וּלְפִיכָךְ הַקְּבִיעָה הַהֲלָכָה שֶׁרָאוּי לָנוּ לַחֲזֵר אַחַר הַחֲזֶרֶת.

פְּרָטֶיהָ גַּם־כֵּן בְּמַסֶּכֶת פְּסָחִים.

וְנוֹהֶגֶת בִּזְמַן הַבַּיִת, בַּזְּכָרִים וְלֹא בַנְּקֵבוֹת, כִּי כְמוֹ שֶׁאֵין שְׁחִיטַת פֶּסַח שֵׁנִי חוֹבָה לָהֶן אֶלָּא רְשׁוּת, כְּמוֹ שֶׁאָמַרְנוּ בַּמִּצְוָה הַקּוֹדֶמֶת, כֵּן אֲכִילַת מַצָּה וּמָרוֹר

---

2. TB P'saḥim 40a; MT *hilchoth ḥamétz u-matzah* v 9.

3. The Mishnah, P'saḥim ii 6 (TB 39a), reads, "Now, these are the green leafy vegetables with which one can fulfill his obligation [to eat *maror*, bitter herbs] on Passover: Romaine lettuce, endives, picridium, eringium, and *maror*." Here, states R. Aaron haLévi, the word *maror* "is a general term for any bitter vegetable like these [four preceding ones], which are somewhat fit [not too bitter] to be eaten..." (cited *ad loc.* in *Ritba*). Similarly Me'iri: "It means any bitter herbs." This is evidently the basis of our author's view here. However, Rashi and Rambam *ad loc.* explain this *maror* as one specific vegetable (Rashi: *amerfoil* in old French); hence the Mishnah lists only five specific kinds as acceptable, Romaine lettuce being the first; and so Rambam rules in MT *hilchoth ḥamétz umatzah* vii 13 (and so other authorities).

4. Literally, any bitter grass.

5. So TB P'saḥim 116b.

6. TB P'saḥim 39a; TJ ii 5: Just as its beginning [before the stalk hardens] is sweet, and its end [when the stalk hardens] is bitter, so did the Egyptians treat our ancestors in Egypt; at first, *in the land have your father and your brothers dwell* (Genesis 47:6), and afterward, *they embittered their lives with hard labor, in mortar and in brick* (Exodus 1:14).

⟨86⟩

entire subject-matter of the "second Passover" stems from nothing
but the basis of the first. The point is evident.

Among the laws of the precept, there is what the Sages of blessed
memory said:[2] that the *matzoth* need great watchful care that they
should not become leavened, so much so that they (of blessed
memory) obligated us to take precautions with them even from the
time of the cutting [of the wheat], that no water should get to it, for
fear that they might become leavened. The rest of their multitude of
details in regard to kneading and baking [are to be found] in connection with the first Passover. The crux of the whole matter is that great
precautions were taken with them against leavening.

There is, too, what the Sages explained about the bitter herbs:[3]
that any bitter green leafy vegetable[4] can be included under the term
"bitter herbs" that Scripture mentions, and a man can acquit himself
of his obligation on Passover with any of them. For the commandment given us about the bitter herbs is [that they should be] a remembrance that *they made their lives bitter* (Exodus 1:14);[5] and the matter
can be commemorated with any bitter leafy vegetable. Yet, nevertheless, the Sages of blessed memory singled out for us [as best] to eat
Romaine lettuce.[6] For with it the remembrance of the bitterness is by
way of the stalk, whose taste is slightly bitter, and with it there is also
more of an enhancement of the precept than with other bitter green
leafy vegetables[7] — especially as its name conveys enhancement: For
its Hebrew name is *ḥasah*, in which there is the hint of a blessing, that
the merciful God *ḥas*, had compassion on us and redeemed us from the
hand of the harsh Egyptians.[8] Well, through all these [points] there is
an arousal and remembrance for the heart of people about the matter
(of the miracles that were wrought for us in Egypt).[9] Therefore the
definitive law was set that it is proper for us to seek after lettuce.

Its details are also [found] in the Talmud tractate *P'saḥim*.

It is in effect at the time of the Temple, for men, but not for
women: because just as the ritual slaying of the offering at the second
Passover is not an obligatory matter in their behalf, but only a
voluntary one, as we said in the previous precept, so is the eating of

7. Perhaps because its leaves and stem are handsomer than those of other green
leafy vegetables (MY).

8. So TB P'saḥim 39a.

9. The part in parentheses is not in the oldest manuscripts, and is thus evidently a
later interpolation.

עִמּוֹ אֵינָהּ חוֹבָה לָהֶן; וּמְבֹאָר גַּם זֶה שָׁם בְּמַסֶּכֶת פְּסָחִים. וְעוֹבֵר עַל זֶה וְאָכַל פֶּסַח שֵׁנִי מִבְּלִי מַצָּה וּמָרוֹר, בִּטֵּל עֲשֵׂה זֶה.

[שֶׁלֹּא לְהוֹתִיר כְּלוּם מִבְּשַׂר פֶּסַח שֵׁנִי לְמָחֳרָתוֹ]

שפב שֶׁלֹּא לְהוֹתִיר כְּלוּם מִבְּשַׂר הַפֶּסַח שֵׁנִי לְמָחֳרָתוֹ, שֶׁהוּא יוֹם חֲמִשָּׁה־עָשָׂר בְּאִיָּר, שֶׁנֶּאֱמַר: לֹא יַשְׁאִירוּ מִמֶּנּוּ עַד בֹּקֶר. כָּל עִנְיָנָהּ בַּלָּאו הַבָּא עַל זֶה בְּפֶסַח רִאשׁוֹן, הַכָּתוּב בְּסֵדֶר בֹּא אֶל פַּרְעֹה, וְהוּא שָׁם שֵׁנִי לָאו שֵׁנִי [סִי׳ ח].

[שֶׁלֹּא לִשְׁבֹּר עֶצֶם מֵעַצְמוֹת פֶּסַח שֵׁנִי]

שפג שֶׁלֹּא לִשְׁבֹּר עֲצָמוֹת מִכָּל עַצְמוֹת הַפֶּסַח, שֶׁנֶּאֱמַר: וְעֶצֶם לֹא יִשְׁבְּרוּ בוֹ. כָּל עִנְיַן לָאו זֶה מְכֻנָּן בַּלָּאו הַבָּא עַל זֶה גַּם־כֵּן בְּפֶסַח רִאשׁוֹן, בְּסֵדֶר בֹּא אֶל פַּרְעֹה, וְהוּא שָׁם לָאו ח׳ [סִי׳ ט״ז], תִּרְאֵנּוּ מִשָּׁם אִם רְצוֹנְךָ לָדַעַת.

[מִצְוַת תְּקִיעַת חֲצוֹצְרוֹת בַּמִּקְדָּשׁ וּבְמִלְחָמָה]

שפד לִתְקֹעַ בַּחֲצוֹצְרוֹת בַּמִּקְדָּשׁ בְּכָל יוֹם בְּהַקְרִיב כָּל קָרְבָּן, וּכְמוֹ־כֵן בִּשְׁעַת הַצָּרוֹת, שֶׁנֶּאֱמַר "וְכִי תָבֹאוּ מִלְחָמָה" וְכוּלִי, וְכָתוּב אַחֲרָיו גַּ־ס־כֵּן: וּבְיוֹם שִׂמְחַתְכֶם וּבְמוֹעֲדֵיכֶם וּבְרָאשֵׁי חָדְשֵׁכֶם וּתְקַעְתֶּם בַּחֲצֹצְרֹת עַל עֹלֹתֵיכֶם וְעַל זִבְחֵי שַׁלְמֵיכֶם וְגוֹמֵר. וְאַף־עַל־פִּי שֶׁהִזְהִיר הַכָּתוּב בְּיוֹם שִׂמְחָה וּמוֹעֵד וְרֹאשׁ חֹדֶשׁ, לָאו דַּוְקָא, דִּבְכָל יוֹם הָיוּ תוֹקְעִין בַּמִּקְדָּשׁ בַּחֲצוֹצְרוֹת עַל הַקָּרְבָּן.

וְכֵן מְבֹאָר בְּרֹאשׁ הַשָּׁנָה, פֶּרֶק רָאוּהוּ בֵּית־דִּין, שֶׁאָמְרוּ שָׁם: הַכֹּל חַיָּבִין

---

10. In TB P'saḥim 120a there are differing views whether *matzah* must be eaten the first evening of Passover by the law of the Torah when there is no Passover offering; then evidently at the second Passover the obligation to eat *matzah* and bitter herbs is only in conjunction with the offering, and hence it could not be more obligatory than the offering itself (MY).

§384   1. More specifically, at every daily *'olah* (burnt-offering), in the morning and again toward evening, and at every *musaf* (additional) offering: TB Sukkah 53b.

   2. I.e. mass trouble (community-wide): TB Ta'anith 19a; MT *hilchoth ta'anith* i 1.   〈88〉

matzah and bitter herbs with it not obligatory for them. This too is explained there, in the tractate *P'saḥim*.[10] If someone transgressed this and ate of the second Passover without *matzah* and bitter herbs, he would disobey this positive precept.

[TO LEAVE OVER NOTHING OF THE SECOND
PASSOVER OFFERING UNTIL THE NEXT DAY]

382 not to leave anything over from the meat of an offering at the second Passover until the next day, which is the fifteenth day of Iyar: for it is stated, *they shall leave none of it until the morning* (Numbers 9:12). All its subject-matter is [to be found] in the negative precept given about this at the first Passover, written in *sidrah bo* as the second negative precept there (§8).

[THE PROHIBITION AGAINST BREAKING ANY
OF THE BONES OF THE SECOND PASSOVER
OFFERING]

383 not to break any bones among all those of the offering of the second Passover: as it is stated, *nor shall they break a bone of it* (Numbers 9:12). The entire subject-matter of the injunction is identical with that of the negative precept given also about this at the first Passover, in *sidrah bo*, where it is the eighth negative precept (§16). You can see it there, if it is your desire to know [it].

[THE PRECEPT OF SOUNDING TRUMPETS
AT THE SANCTUARY AND IN BATTLE]

384 to sound trumpets in the Sanctuary every day when every offering was sacrificed,[1] and so likewise in time of troubles:[2] for it is stated, *And when you go to war*, etc. *you shall sound an alarm with the trumpets* (Numbers 10:9), and it is written afterward, as well, *Also on the day of your gladness and at your appointed seasons, and at the beginnings of your months, you shall blow the trumpets over your burnt-offerings and over the sacrifices of your peace-offerings*, etc. (*ibid.* 10). Now, although Scripture gave instructions about a day of gladness, an appointed festive season, and the beginning of a month, these are not meant particularly. For every day they would sound the trumpets at the Sanctuary over an offering.[1]

So it was explained in the third chapter of the Talmud tractate *Rosh haShanah* (29a). For it was stated there: All have the obligation

בִּתְקִיעַת שׁוֹפָר: כֹּהֲנִים לְוִיִּם וְיִשְׂרָאֵלִים; וּמִתָּמַהּ תַּלְמוּדָא עָלָהּ בַּגְּמָרָא:
פְּשִׁיטָא, אִי הַנֵּי לָא מְחַיְּבֵי (מַאי) [מַאן] מְחַיֵּב? וּמְהַדַּר לֵיהּ: כֹּהֲנִים אִצְטְרִיכָא לֵיהּ,
סַלְקָא דַעְתָּךְ אָמֵינָא הוֹאִיל וּכְתִיב "יוֹם תְּרוּעָה" וְגוֹמֵר, וְהַנֵּי כֹהֲנֵי הוֹאִיל
וְאִיתַנְהוּ בִּתְקִיעָה דְכָל הַשָּׁנָה כֻּלָּהּ, דִּכְתִיב "וּתְקַעְתֶּם בַּחֲצֹצְרֹת עַל עֹלֹתֵיכֶם"
וְגוֹמֵר; וּמְהַדַּר לֵיהּ: מִי דָמֵי, הָתָם חֲצוֹצְרוֹת, הָכָא שׁוֹפָר. לָמַדְנוּ מִכָּל־מָקוֹם
דִּבְכָל הַשָּׁנָה כֻּלָּהּ, כְּלוֹמַר בְּכָל יוֹם וָיוֹם, אִכָּא חֲצוֹצְרוֹת בַּמִּקְדָּשׁ. וְאָמְרוּ בְּמַסֶּכֶת
עֲרָכִין פֶּרֶק שֵׁנִי: אֵין פּוֹחֲתִין מֵעֶשְׂרִים וְאַחַת תְּקִיעָה בַּמִּקְדָּשׁ, וְלֹא מוֹסִיפִין עַל
אַרְבָּעִים וּשְׁמֹנֶה.

מִשָּׁרְשֵׁי הַמִּצְוָה, לְפִי שֶׁבִּשְׁעַת הַקָּרְבָּן הָיוּ צְרִיכִין לְכַוֵּן דַּעְתָּם יָפֶה בְּעִנְיָנוֹ,
כְּמוֹ שֶׁיָּדוּעַ, שֶׁהוּא נִפְסָל בְּמַחֲשָׁבוֹת יְדוּעוֹת, וְגַם־כֵּן צָרִיךְ הַקָּרְבָּן כַּוָּנָה שְׁלֵמָה
לִפְנֵי אֲדוֹן הַכֹּל שֶׁצִּוָּנוּ עָלָיו; וְגַם־כֵּן בְּעֵת הַצָּרָה צָרִיךְ הָאָדָם כִּוּוּן גָּדוֹל בְּהִתְחַנְּנוֹ
לִפְנֵי בוֹרְאוֹ שֶׁיְּרַחֵם עָלָיו וְיַצִּילֵהוּ מִצָּרָתוֹ. וְלָכֵן נִצְטַוּוּ בִּתְקִיעַת הַחֲצוֹצְרוֹת
בְּעֵתִּים אֵלֶּה: לְפִי שֶׁהָאָדָם, מֵהֱיוֹתוֹ בַּעַל חֹמֶר, צָרִיךְ הִתְעוֹרְרוּת גָּדוֹל אֶל
הַדְּבָרִים, כִּי הַטֶּבַע מִבְּלִי מֵעִיר יַעֲמֹד כְּיָשֵׁן, וְאֵין דָּבָר יְעוֹרְרֵהוּ כְּמוֹ קוֹלוֹת הַנִּגּוּן,
יָדוּעַ הַדָּבָר, וְכָל־שֶׁכֵּן קוֹל הַחֲצוֹצְרוֹת, שֶׁהוּא הַקּוֹל הַגָּדוֹל שֶׁבְּכָל כְּלֵי הַנִּגּוּן.

וְעוֹד יֵשׁ תּוֹעֶלֶת נִמְצָא בְּקוֹל הַחֲצוֹצְרוֹת לְפִי הַדּוֹמֶה, מִלְּבַד הַהִתְעוֹרְרוּת אֶל
הַכַּוָּנָה, כִּי בְכֹחַ קוֹלוֹת יָסִיר הָאָדָם מִלִּבּוֹ מַחֲשֶׁבֶת שְׁאָר עִסְקֵי הָעוֹלָם, וְלֹא יִתֵּן
לֵב בְּאוֹתָהּ שָׁעָה כִּי־אִם בְּדָבָר הַקָּרְבָּן; וּמָה אַאֲרִיךְ וְיָדוּעַ זֶה לְכָל אֲשֶׁר הִטָּה אֹזֶן
לִשְׁמֹעַ חֲצוֹצְרוֹת וְקוֹל שׁוֹפָר בְּכַוָּנָה.

3. Cf. Ibn Ezra to Numbers 10:9.

of [hearing] the sounding of the *shofar* [the ram's horn, on *Rosh
haShanah*] — *kohanim*, Levites and Israelites. The Talmud wonders
about this in the *g'mara*: This is obvious; if these would not be
obligated, who would be obligated about it? The answer is then
given: "It was necessary to mention the *kohanim*. It might have
occurred to your mind to think: Inasmuch as it is written, *it is a day of
blowing the horn* (Numbers 29:1) etc. and these *kohanim* are involved
with sounding the horn the entire year, as it is written, *you shall blow
the trumpets over your burnt-offerings*, I might have said they are not
obligated [to hear the *shofar* on *Rosh haShanah*]." But this is
countered: "Are they then alike? there it is trumpets; here it is a
shofar."

Then in any event, we have learned that the entire year, i.e. every
single day, there were trumpets [sounded] at the Sanctuary. And it
was stated in the second chapter of the Talmud tractate *'Eruvin* (10a):
They never sounded less than twenty-one trumpet-blasts at the
Sanctuary, nor more than forty-eight.

At the root of the precept lies the reason that at the time of an offering they had to focus their thoughts well about its purpose. As is
known, it could become disqualified through certain specific thoughts
(§ 144). Moreover, an offering required perfect concentration of intention before the Sovereign Master of all who commanded us about
it. So also at a time of trouble, a man needs great concentration when
he pleads before his Creator that He should have pity on him and
rescue him from his misfortune. Therefore they were commanded
about sounding the trumpets at these times. For man, being possessed
of physical matter [the body], requires a great arousal to matters. For
human nature, with nothing to arouse it, will remain asleep. And
nothing will stir him like sounds of melody — it is a known matter — and all the more certainly trumpets, the blast of which is the
strongest sound among all musical instruments.[3]

And there is another benefit to be found in the blast of the trumpets, as it would seem, apart from the arousal to proper intention. For
by the force of the sounds, a man will remove from his heart the
thought of other affairs of the world, and will pay attention at that
time to nothing but the matter of the offering. But why should I go
on at length, when this is known (evident) to anyone who gives ear
to hear trumpets and the peal of the *shofar* with proper intention?

〈91〉   Among the laws of the precept, there is what the Sages of blessed

מִדִּינֵי הַמִּצְוָה, מַה שֶּׁאָמְרוּ זִכְרוֹנָם לִבְרָכָה בְּמַסֶּכֶת מְנָחוֹת, שֶׁהַחֲצוֹצְרָה הָיְתָה בָּאָה מִן הָעֶשֶׁת שֶׁל כֶּסֶף, כְּמוֹ שֶׁבָּא בַּכָּתוּב; מִשְּׁאָר מִינֵי מַתָּכוֹת, פְּסוּלָה; וּמַה שֶּׁאָמְרוּ זִכְרוֹנָם לִבְרָכָה, שֶׁאֵין פּוֹחֲתִין לְעוֹלָם בַּמִּקְדָּשׁ מִשְּׁתֵּי חֲצוֹצְרוֹת וְלֹא מוֹסִיפִין עַל מֵאָה וְעֶשְׂרִים; וְיֶתֶר פְּרָטֶיהָ, מְבֹאָרִין בְּסִפְרֵי וְרֹאשׁ הַשָּׁנָה; וְגַם־כֵּן בְּמַסֶּכֶת תַּעֲנִית בֵּאֲרוּ שֶׁאָנוּ מְצֻוִּין בִּתְקִיעַת הַחֲצוֹצְרוֹת בְּעֵת הַצָּרָה.

וְנוֹהֶגֶת מִצְוָה זוֹ בִּזְמַן הַבַּיִת בְּכֹהֲנִים, שֶׁעֲלֵיהֶם הַמִּצְוָה לִתְקֹעַ בַּחֲצוֹצְרוֹת, וּכְעִנְיָן שֶׁכָּתוּב בָּהֶן בְּמַסַּע הַמַּחֲנוֹת: וּבְנֵי אַהֲרֹן הַכֹּהֲנִים יִתְקְעוּ בַּחֲצֹצְרוֹת. וְשֶׁמָּא תֹאמַר: לֹא הָיוּ תוֹקְעִין הֵם עַל הַקָּרְבָּן אֶלָּא הַלְוִיִּם —אֵינוֹ כֵן, שֶׁהֲרֵי בְּפֵרוּשׁ אָמְרוּ בְּמַסֶּכֶת (מִדּוֹת פֶּרֶק שִׁשִּׁי) [תָּמִיד פֶּרֶק שְׁבִיעִי]: נָתְנוּ לוֹ יַיִן לְנַסֵּךְ, הַסְּגָן עוֹמֵד עַל הַקֶּרֶן וְהַסּוּדָרִין בְּיָדוֹ, וּשְׁנֵי כֹהֲנִים עוֹמְדִים עַל שֻׁלְחַן הַחֲלָבִים, וּשְׁתֵּי חֲצוֹצְרוֹת בְּיָדָם; תָּקְעוּ וְהֵרִיעוּ וְתָקְעוּ. הֲרֵי נִתְבָּאֵר שֶׁעַל־יְדֵי כֹהֲנִים נַעֲשֵׂית מִצְוָה זוֹ, וְשֶׁהִיא מִצְוָה תְּמִידִית לָהֶן, כְּלוֹמַר שֶׁבְּכָל יוֹם הָיוּ תוֹקְעִין, וְלֹא בְּיוֹם מוֹעֵד וְרֹאשׁ חֹדֶשׁ בִּלְבָד.

אֲבָל רָאִיתִי לְהָרַב מֹשֶׁה בֶּן מַיְמוֹן זִכְרוֹנוֹ לִבְרָכָה שֶׁכָּתַב: בִּימֵי הַמּוֹעֵד כֻּלָּן וּבְרָאשֵׁי חֳדָשִׁים הָיוּ הַכֹּהֲנִים תּוֹקְעִין בַּחֲצוֹצְרוֹת וְהַלְוִיִּים אוֹמְרִים שִׁירָה. נִרְאֶה מִדְּבָרָיו שֶׁדַּעְתּוֹ שֶׁבִּשְׁאָר הַיָּמִים אַף הַלְוִיִּים תּוֹקְעִין בַּחֲצוֹצְרוֹת.

וְאִם עָבְרוּ עַל זֶה הַכֹּהֲנִים וְלֹא תָקְעוּ בִּשְׁעַת הַקָּרְבָּן, וְכֵן אִם לֹא תָקְעוּ בְּעֵת הַצָּרָה, בִּטְּלוּ עֲשֵׂה זֶה.

---

4. TB ʿArachin 13a.

5. I.e. generally, not merely when the Israelites in the wilderness had to move one from one resting-place to another, as the plain meaning indicates; TB Sukkah 54a.

6. To raise as a signal, when the libation (drink-offering) was poured, so that the *kohanim* at the table (see directly below) would sound the trumpets.

7. MT *hilchoth k'lé ha-mikdash* iii 5.

memory said in the Talmud tractate *M'nahoth* (28a), that a trumpet was made from a bar of silver, as it is conveyed in Scripture (Numbers 10:2); but from any other kinds of metal, it was unacceptable. Then there is what the Sages of blessed memory said:[4] that there were never to be fewer than two trumpets at the Sanctuary, and never more than 120. The rest of its details are explained in the Midrash *Sifre* and the tractate *Rosh haShanah*; in the tractate *Ta'anith* (15b) it was also elucidated that we are commanded to have the trumpets sounded at a time of trouble.

This precept is in effect at the time the Temple exists, for the *kohanim*, since the religious duty lies on them to sound the trumpets, in accord with what is written of them at the journeying of the camps [of Israelites in the wilderness], *And the sons of Aaron, the* kohanim, *shall blow the trumpets* (Numbers 10:8).[5] Yet you might think that they did not give the sounds over an offering, but rather the Levites? It was not so: for you see, it was distinctly taught in the seventh chapter of the Mishnah tractate *Tamid* (vii 3): He [the *kohen gadol*] was given the wine for the libation, and the *s'gan* (assistant) stood at the corner [of the altar] with scarves in his hands,[6] while two *kohanim* stood at the table of the fat pieces, with two trumpets in their hands; they blew a clear, a broken, and a clear blast. So it was made plain that this religious duty was carried out by the *kohanim*, and it was a regular religious obligation for them; in other words, every day they would sound [the trumpets] and not merely on a day of a festive season and the beginning of a month.

Yet I saw that R. Moses b. Maimon of blessed memory wrote:[7] On all the days of the festive seasons and the beginnings of the months, the *kohanim* would sound the trumpets and the Levites uttered song. It appears from his words that his view is that on other days, the Levites also blew the trumpets.

If the *kohanim* transgressed this and did not blow [the trumpets] at the time of an offering, and so if they did not sound them at a time of trouble, they would disobey this positive precept.

שְׁלַח לְךָ אֲנָשִׁים

שְׁתֵּי מִצְוֹות עֲשֵׂה וְאַחַת מִצְוַת לֹא־תַעֲשֶׂה

[מִצְוַת חַלָּה]

שפה לְהַפְרִישׁ חַלָּה מִכָּל עֲרִיסָה וְלִתֵּן אוֹתָהּ לַכֹּהֵן, שֶׁנֶּאֱמַר: רֵאשִׁית עֲרִסֹתֵכֶם חַלָּה תָּרִימוּ תְרוּמָה. וְדָרְשׁוּ זִכְרוֹנָם לִבְרָכָה: "רֵאשִׁית עֲרִסֹתֵכֶם" — כְּדֵי עִסַּתְכֶם; וְעִסַּת הַמִּדְבָּר הָיְתָה עֹמֶר, וְהָעֹמֶר עֲשִׂירִית הָאֵיפָה הוּא, וְהָאֵיפָה שָׁלֹשׁ סְאִין, וְהַסְּאָה שִׁשָּׁה קַבִּין, וְקַב אַרְבַּעַת לֻגִּין, וְלֹג שִׁשָּׁה בֵיצִים; נִמְצֵאת הָאֵיפָה תל"ב בֵּיצִים, עֲשִׂירִיתָהּ מ"ג בֵּיצִים וְחֹמֶשׁ בֵּיצָה, וְזֶהוּ שִׁעוּר עִסָּה הַמְחֻיֶּבֶת בְּחַלָּה.

מִשָּׁרְשֵׁי הַמִּצְוָה, לְפִי שֶׁחִיּוּתוֹ שֶׁל אָדָם בִּמְזוֹנוֹת וְרֹב הָעוֹלָם יִחְיוּ בְּלֶחֶם, רָצָה הַמָּקוֹם לְזַכּוֹתֵנוּ בְּמִצְוָה תְּמִידִית בְּלַחְמֵנוּ כְּדֵי שֶׁתָּנוּחַ בְּרָכָה בּוֹ עַל־יְדֵי הַמִּצְוָה וּנְקַבֵּל בָּהּ זְכוּת בְּנַפְשֵׁנוּ, וְנִמְצֵאת הָעִסָּה מָזוֹן לַגּוּף וּמָזוֹן לַנֶּפֶשׁ; גַּם לְמַעַן יִחְיוּ בוֹ מְשָׁרְתֵי הַשֵּׁם הָעוֹסְקִין תָּמִיד בַּעֲבוֹדָתוֹ, וְהֵם הַכֹּהֲנִים, מִבְּלִי יְגִיעָה כְּלָל; שֶׁאִלּוּ בִתְרוּמַת הַגֹּרֶן יֵשׁ לָהֶם עָמָל לְהַעֲבִיר הַתְּבוּאָה בִכְבָרָה וְלִטְחָן אוֹתָהּ, אֲבָל כָּאן יָבוֹא חֻקָּם לָהֶם מִבְּלִי צַעַר שֶׁל כְּלוּם.

מִדִּינֵי הַמִּצְוָה, מַה שֶּׁאָמְרוּ זִכְרוֹנָם לִבְרָכָה שֶׁאֵין חִיּוּב הָעִסָּה מִשֶּׁנָּתַן הַקֶּמַח בָּעֲרִיסָה, אֶלָּא הַחִיּוּב הוּא מִשְׁעַת גִּלְגּוּל, כְּלוֹמַר מִשֶּׁיְּעָרֵב הַקֶּמַח וְהַמַּיִם, מִיָּד חִיּוּב הַחַלָּה חָל.

וַחֲמֵשֶׁת הַמִּינִין הֵם שֶׁחַיָּבִין בְּחַלָּה: הַחִטִּים וְהַשְּׂעוֹרִים וְכֻסְמִין וְשִׁבֹּלֶת שׁוּעָל וְשִׁיפוֹן, שֶׁנֶּאֱמַר "וְהָיָה בַּאֲכָלְכֶם מִלֶּחֶם הָאָרֶץ", וְאֵין קָרוּי לֶחֶם אֶלָּא פַּת

---

1. TB 'Eruvin 83a; and see Rashi, TB P'sahim 48b, s.v. *hamésheth r'va'im*.

2. Hence the amount generally kneaded at any one time in the wilderness.

3. Derived from Exodus 16:16, *Gather of it every man according to his eating, an omer a head.*

4. So Exodus 16:36.

5. So MT *hilchoth bikkurim* vi 15, based on TB 'Eruvin 83a (*Kessef Mishneh*).

6. I.e. they receive a loaf already baked or dough ready for baking.

7. Mishnah, Hallah iii 1.

8. *Ibid.* i 1.

sidrah sh'laḥ
(Numbers 13–15)

[It contains] two positive precepts, and one negative.

[THE PRECEPT OF ḤALLAH, A PORTION OF
DOUGH SET ASIDE FOR THE KOHEN]

385 to separate *ḥallah* [the *kohen*'s share] from every batch of dough
and give it to a *kohen*: for it is stated, *Of the first of your dough you shall
set apart* ḥallah (*a cake*) *for a gift* (Numbers 15:20); and our Sages of
blessed memory interpreted:[1] "Of the first of your dough"—out of a
quantity sufficient for your dough.[2] A batch of dough in the
wilderness was [in the quantity] of an 'omer;[3] an 'omer was a tenth of
an 'éphah;[4] an 'éphah contained three *se'ah*; a *se'ah* was the equal of six
kav; a *kav* was four *log*; and a *log* was the measure of six eggs. Consequently, an 'éphah was the measure of 432 eggs, a tenth part of it being
forty-three and one-fifth eggs. This is the quantity of dough that entails the obligation of *ḥallah*.[5]

At the root of the precept lies the reason that man's sustenance is
by food, and most of the world lives on bread. The omnipresent God
wished to make us meritorious by a constant *mitzvah* with our bread,
so that blessing will dwell on it through the religious good deed, and
we shall earn merit for ourselves. As a result, the dough provides food
for the body and food for the spirit. [Moreover] it is also in order that
the ministering servants of the Eternal Lord should live (be sustained)
by it—those who are constantly engaged in His service, namely, the
kohanim—without any toil at all. For with the *t'rumah* [*kohen*'s por-
tion] from the granary there is toil for them, to pass the grain through
a sieve and to grind it. Here, though, their allotted portion comes to
them without any difficulty at all.[6]

Among the laws of the precept, there is what the Sages of blessed
memory taught:[7] that the obligation [to give] of the dough is not as
soon as the flour is put in the kneading-trough; rather, the obligation
comes from the time of the kneading. In other words, as soon as the
flour and water are mixed together, the obligation of *ḥallah* takes
effect at once.

There are five species [of grain] that entail the obligation of *ḥallah*:
wheat, barley, spelt, oats and rye.[8] For it is stated, *then it shall be that*

when you eat of the bread of the land (Numbers 15:19), and nothing is

הַנַּעֲשֵׂית מֵאֵלּוּ; וְכֻלָּן מִצְטָרְפִין לְשִׁעוּר חַלָּה. וּמִי שֶׁלֹּא הִפְרִישׁ חַלָּה בָּעִסָּה, מַפְרִישָׁהּ מִן הַלֶּחֶם, שֶׁנֶּאֱמַר "בַּאֲכָלְכֶם מִלֶּחֶם"—מְלַמֵּד שֶׁהַחִיּוּב גַּם בְּלֶחֶם. וַאֲפִלּוּ הַלָּשׁ פָּחוֹת מִכְּשִׁעוּר, שֶׁהוּא פָּטוּר מֵחַלָּה, אִם אַחַר־כָּךְ לָשׁ פַּעַם אַחֶרֶת וְהִשְׁלִים הַשִּׁעוּר, וְנִתְעָרֵב כָּל הַפַּת בִּכְלִי אֶחָד שֶׁיֵּשׁ לוֹ תּוֹךְ, הַכְּלִי מְצָרְפָן לְחַלָּה.

וְשָׁמַעְתִּי מִפִּי מוֹרִי יִשְׁמְרוֹ אֵל, דְּדַוְקָא בְּשֶׁנָּתַן הַפַּת מִן הַתַּנּוּר לִכְלִי שֶׁיֵּשׁ לוֹ בֵּית קִבּוּל דַּוְקָא; אֲבָל הִנִּיחַ אוֹתוֹ כְּשֶׁהוֹצִיאוֹ מִן הַתַּנּוּר עַל־גַּבֵּי לוּחַ אוֹ עַל הַקַּרְקַע, וּבְכָל מָקוֹם שֶׁאֵין לוֹ תּוֹךְ, אַף־עַל־פִּי שֶׁנְּתָנוֹ אַחַר־כֵּן בְּסַל, כְּבָר נִפְטַר מֵחַלָּה; וְזֶהוּ שֶׁאָמְרוּ "הָרוֹדֶה וְנוֹתֵן לַסַּל", דְּדַוְקָא לַסַּל בְּשָׁעַת רְדִיָּה מִן הַתַּנּוּר, וְאֵין צָרִיךְ לוֹמַר שֶׁהַתַּנּוּר אֵינוֹ עוֹשֶׂה צָרוּף לְחַלָּה. הַסֻּבִּין שֶׁבַּקֶּמַח, קֹדֶם שֶׁרְקָדוֹ מַשְׁלִים לַשִּׁעוּר; אֲבָל אַחַר שֶׁרְקָדוֹ, אִם חָזַר וְעֵרְבוֹ, אֵינוֹ מַשְׁלִים לַשִּׁעוּר.

הַחַלָּה אֵין לָהּ שִׁעוּר יָדוּעַ מִן הַתּוֹרָה; אֲפִלּוּ לֹא הִפְרִישׁ אֶלָּא כִּשְׂעוֹרָה מִן הָעִסָּה, פָּטַר כָּל עִסָּה שֶׁבָּעֲרִיסָה מִדִּין חַלָּה; שֶׁלֹּא נֶאֱמַר בַּתּוֹרָה אֶלָּא "רֵאשִׁית עֲרִסֹתֵכֶם חַלָּה תָּרִימוּ", וְכָל שֶׁהוּא מֵרִים מִמֶּנָּה פָּטוּר הוּא בְּכָךְ. אֲבָל חֲכָמִים חִיְּבוּנוּ לְהַפְרִישׁ חֵלֶק אֶחָד מִן הָעִסָּה מֵעֶשְׂרִים וְאַרְבָּעָה, וְסָמְכוּ הַדָּבָר בְּמַה שֶּׁאָמַר הַכָּתוּב בְּמִצְוָה זוֹ "תִּתְּנוּ לַיָי", כְּלוֹמַר תֵּן לַכֹּהֵן מַתָּנָה רְאוּיָה, וְשִׁעֲרוּ הֵם שֶׁהִיא כֵן.

וְהַנַּחְתּוֹם, שֶׁהוּא עוֹשֶׂה עִסָּתוֹ לִמְכֹּר בַּשּׁוּק וְהִיא מְרֻבָּה, וְגַם צָרִיךְ לְרֶוַח, לֹא חִיְּבוּהוּ לָתֵת אֶלָּא אַחַת מֵאַרְבָּעִים וּשְׁמֹנָה; וּבֵין שֶׁהִרְבָּה בַעַל הַבַּיִת בְּעִסָּה, וּבֵין שֶׁמִּעֵט נַחְתּוֹם, דִּינָם כְּמוֹ שֶׁאָמַרְנוּ לְמַעְלָה.

עִסָּה שֶׁנִּלּוֹשָׁה בִּשְׁתֵּי קְצָווֹת הָעֲרִיסָה וְאֵין בְּאֶחָד מִן הַחֲלָקִים שִׁעוּר חַלָּה,

9. TB M'naḥoth 70b.

10. Sifre, Numbers §110.

11. Mishnah, Ḥallah ii 4; TB P'saḥim 48b. The paragraph is based on MT hilchoth bikkurim vi 2, 16, vii 3, viii 3.

12. Mishnah, Ḥallah ii 4. Neither the view in the preceding sentence nor this adduction of proof from the Mishnah is known to us from any other source. Cf. e.g. MT ibid. vi 16; Tur Yoreh Dé'ah §325.

13. MT hilchoth bikkurim vi 16, based on TB P'saḥim 48b.

14. Mishnah, Ḥallah ii 6; MT ibid. 18.

15. Sifre, Numbers §110; MT ibid. v 1.

16. Mishnah, Ḥallah ii 7; MT ibid. 2.

17. Mishnah ibid. MT ibid. 3.

called bread but a loaf made from [one of] these.⁹ All of them can be joined and considered together to form the minimal amount for *hallah*.⁸ If someone did not separate *hallah* from the dough, he is to separate it from the [baked] bread: for it is stated, *when you eat of the bread (ibid.)*, which teaches that the obligation applies also to the bread.¹⁰ Even if a person has kneaded less than the minimal amount, so that he is free of the obligation of *hallah*, if afterward he does kneading at another time, completing the minimal amount, and all the bread is placed together in a utensil that is a receptacle, the vessel joins them [into one amount to impose the duty] of *hallah*.¹¹

Now I heard directly from my master teacher, God protect him, that this rule applies specifically when the bread was put from the oven into a utensil that is definitely a receptacle; but if one placed it, when he took it out of the oven, on a tablet, on the ground, or in anything that is not a container, even if he put it afterward in a basket, he was already freed of the obligation of *hallah*. This is why the Sages taught,¹² "if one takes loaves from the oven and puts them in a basket"—specifically in a basket at the time they are taken from the oven. And needless to say, the oven does not make its contents be considered joined together to impose the obligation of *hallah*.¹³ Bran in the flour before it is sifted out, can help make up the minimal amount; but after it is sifted out, if it is mixed back in, it cannot help make up the minimal amount.¹⁴

There is no specific measure of *hallah* [to be given] by the law of the Torah; even if one separated no more than as much as a kernel of barley from a batch of dough, he acquitted all the dough in the kneading-trough from the obligation of *hallah*. For in the Torah nothing is stated but, *Of the first of your dough you shall set apart a cake* (Numbers 15:20); then whatever one separates from it, he is quit of the duty by that.¹⁵ The Sages, however, obligated us to separate one twenty-fourth part of the dough. They based the rate on what Scripture states about this precept: *you shall give to the Lord (ibid. 21)*—i.e. give the *kohen* a suitable gift—which they estimated to be that.¹⁶

As for a baker, who makes his dough to sell [the loaves] in the market, and it is of large quantity, and in addition he needs a profit—they obligated him to give no more than one forty-eighth.¹⁶ But whether a householder made a large batch of dough or a baker made a small one, the law for them is as we have stated above.¹⁷

⟨97⟩ If dough was kneaded at the two ends of the kneading-trough [in

אֵינָהּ מִתְחַיֶּבֶת בְּחַלָּה, אֶלָּא־אִם־כֵּן נָשְׁכוּ זֶה אֶת זֶה וְהֵן מֵאִישׁ אֶחָד. עִסָּה שֶׁנִּלּוֹשָׁה בֵּין בְּמַיִם בֵּין בְּכָל שְׁאָר מַשְׁקִין, וּבֵין שֶׁאֲפָאָהּ בְּתַנּוּר אוֹ בַקַּרְקַע אוֹ בְמַחֲבַת וּמַרְחֶשֶׁת, בֵּין שֶׁהִדְבִּיק הַפַּת תְּחִלָּה בָהֶן וְלִבְסוֹף הִרְתִּיחַ, כְּלוֹמַר שֶׁהִדְלִיק הָאֵשׁ תַּחְתֶּיהָ אוֹ הִרְתִּיחַ וְלִבְסוֹף הִדְבִּיק, בְּכָל עִנְיָנִים אֵלּוּ יֵשׁ חִיּוּב חַלָּה, שֶׁבְּכָל עִנְיָנִים אֵלּוּ לֶחֶם נִקְרָא; שֶׁאֵין הֲלָכָה כְמַאן דְּאָמַר אֵין לֶחֶם אֶלָּא הָאָפוּי בְתַנּוּר בִּלְבָד. אֲבָל הָעוֹשֶׂה עִסָּה לְיַבְּשָׁהּ בַּחַמָּה אוֹ לְבַשְּׁלָהּ בִּקְדֵרָה, אֵין בָּהּ חִיּוּב חַלָּה.

וְעִסַּת אַרְנוֹנָא, כְּלוֹמַר מְשֻׁתֶּפֶת בֵּין יִשְׂרָאֵל וְגוֹי, חַיֶּבֶת בְּחַלָּה, אִם יֵשׁ בְּחֵלֶק הַיִּשְׂרָאֵל שִׁעוּר חַלָּה. עִסָּה הַנַּעֲשֵׂית בִּשְׁבִיל בְּהֵמוֹת פְּטוּרָה מִן הַחַלָּה; וְאִם בִּשְׁבִיל בְּהֵמוֹת וְאָדָם, חַיֶּבֶת בְּחַלָּה. עִסָּה מְתֻקֶּנֶת, כְּלוֹמַר שֶׁהוּרְמָה מִמֶּנָּה חַלָּה, וְנִתְעָרְבָה בָהּ עִסָּה אַחֶרֶת שֶׁלֹּא הוּרְמָה מִמֶּנָּה חַלָּה, כֵּיצַד עוֹשֶׂה: מֵבִיא עִסָּה אַחֶרֶת וְסוֹמְכָהּ עָלֶיהָ, וְנוֹטֵל חַלָּה עַל הַכֹּל; וְאִם אֵין לוֹ עִסָּה אַחֶרֶת, נוֹטֵל מִמֶּנָּה חַלָּה בְּלֹא בְרָכָה, לְפִי הַדּוֹמֶה, לְפִי שֶׁנַּעֲשֵׂית כֻּלָּהּ טֶבֶל; וַאֲפִלּוּ מְעַט טוֹבֶלֶת כַּמָּה עִסָּה מְתֻקֶּנֶת, שֶׁהַטֶּבֶל אָסוּר בְּכָל־שֶׁהוּא, כְּמוֹ שֶׁכָּתַבְתִּי בְסֵדֶר אֱמֹר אֶל הַכֹּהֲנִים, לָאו י"ט [סִי רפ"ד]; וְיֵתֶר פְּרָטֶיהָ, מְבֹאָרִין בְּמַסֶּכֶת חַלָּה, וְכֵן בְּמַסֶּכֶת עָרְלָה.

וְנוֹהֶגֶת בִּזְכָרִים וּנְקֵבוֹת, בְּאֶרֶץ־יִשְׂרָאֵל בִּלְבָד מִדְּאוֹרַיְתָא, שֶׁנֶּאֱמַר: בַּאֲכָלְכֶם מִלֶּחֶם הָאָרֶץ. וְדַוְקָא בִזְמַן שֶׁכָּל יִשְׂרָאֵל שָׁם, כְּלוֹמַר רֻבָּם, שֶׁנֶּאֱמַר "בְּבוֹאֲכֶם", וּבָא הַפֵּרוּשׁ עַל זֶה: בְּבִיאַת כֻּלְּכֶם וְלֹא בְּבִיאַת מִקְצָתְכֶם. וּמִדִּבְרֵי סוֹפְרִים לְהַפְרִישׁ חַלָּה בְּחוּצָה לָאָרֶץ, כְּדֵי שֶׁלֹּא תִשְׁתַּכַּח תּוֹרַת חַלָּה מִיִּשְׂרָאֵל; וּמִפְּנֵי שֶׁאֵין הַחִיּוּב בָּהּ אֶלָּא שֶׁלֹּא תִשְׁתַּכַּח מִיִּשְׂרָאֵל, נָהֲגוּ לְהָקֵל בָּהּ בְּעִנְיָן שֶׁאֵין

18. Literally, unless they bit one another; i.e. they became so attached that they cannot be separated without each retaining some of the other.

19. Mishnah, Ḥallah ii 4, iv 1; MT *hilchoth bikkurim* vi 7.

20. Mishnah, *ibid.* 2.

21. TB B'rachoth 37b.

22. TB P'saḥim 37a.

23. MT *ibid.* 12.

24. TJ Ḥallah i 3; MT *ibid.*

25. I.e. part of it belonged to a non-Jew as a tax to sustain soldiers garrisoned there, etc.

26. Mishnah, Ḥallah iii 5.

27. *Ibid.* i 8; TJ i 6; Sifre Zuta p. 284, l. 5–9.

28. Mishnah, Ḥallah iii 8; MT *hilchoth bikkurim* vii 11.

29. I.e. produce, etc. from which the required parts were not separated; MT *ibid.* MY notes that here evidently the dough from which *ḥallah* was taken was larger in quantity than the other dough, which became merged with it; hence *ḥallah* must be separated from the whole only by Rabbinic law (for by Torah law, the

two batches] and neither of the batches has the required amount for the obligation of *hallah*, it entails no duty of *hallah* unless they became attached to one another[18] and they belong to one man.[19] Whether dough was kneaded with water or with any other liquid;[20] whether it was baked in an oven or on the ground,[21] in a pan or a deep dish;[22] whether one attached (set) the loaf within them first and applied the heat afterward—in other words, he lit the fire under it, or he applied the heat and attached the loaf afterward[22]—in all these circumstances there is the obligation of *hallah*, since in all these circumstances it is called bread.[23] For the definitive law does not follow the view of the one who ruled[22] that nothing is called bread but only what is baked in an oven. However, if a person makes a batch of dough to dry it in the sun[22] or to cook it in a pot, it entails no duty of *hallah*.[24]

A batch of dough for taxing,[25] i.e. which belongs jointly to an Israelite and a non-Jew, entails the obligation of *hallah* if in the Israelite's share there is the minimal amount for *hallah*.[26] Dough made for animals is free of the obligation of *hallah*; but if it is for both animals and people, it bears the obligation.[27] If dough was taken care of, i.e. *hallah* was separated from it, and other dough, from which *hallah* was not separated, became merged with it, what is to be done?—Another batch of dough is brought, and placed on the first, and *hallah* is taken off for the whole.[28] If one has no other dough, he is to take off *hallah* from it, without a benediction as it seems, because it all became *tevel*;[29] and even a small quantity can transform into *tevel* any amount of dough that was taken care of, since *tevel* is forbidden in any quantity at all, as I wrote in the nineteenth negative precept of *sidrah 'emor* (§ 284). The rest of its details are explained in the Mishnah tractate *Ḥallah*, and so too in the tractate *'Orlah*.

It applies to both man and woman in the land of Israel alone, by the law of the Torah: for it is stated, *when you eat of the bread of the land* (Numbers 15:19)—and this specifically means when the whole Israelite [Jewish] people is there, i.e. the greater part: for it is stated, *When you come into the land* (ibid. 18), about which the interpretation was given [in the Oral Tradition]:[30] when all come, and not some of them. It is a ruling of the Scribes, though, to separate *hallah* outside the land, so that the law of *hallah* should not become forgotten by Jewry;[31] but since its obligation is only in order that it should not be forgotten by the Jewish people, it was their practice to be lenient about it, so that from a large batch of dough no more than an olive's

⟨99⟩

מַפְרִישִׁין מֵעִסָּה גְדוֹלָה אֶלָּא כַזַּיִת, וּמַשְׁלִיכִין אוֹתָהּ בָּאֵשׁ, וְאֵינָהּ נֶאֱכֶלֶת לְשׁוּם
כֹּהֵן, קָטָן אוֹ גָדוֹל.

וְשָׁמַעְתִּי שֶׁיֵּשׁ מְקוֹמוֹת שֶׁנָּהֲגוּ לְהַפְרִישׁ חַלָּה גְדוֹלָה כְּשִׁעוּר שֶׁנָּתְנוּ לָנוּ בָהּ
חֲכָמִים. וְנוֹתְנִין אוֹתָהּ לְכֹהֵן קָטָן, שֶׁאֵין טֻמְאָה יוֹצֵאת עָלָיו מִגּוּפוֹ, אוֹ לְכֹהֶנֶת
קְטַנָּה שֶׁעֲדַיִן לֹא רָאֲתָה; אֲפִלּוּ לְכֹהֵן גָּדוֹל שֶׁטָּבַל לְקִרְיוֹ אוֹ לְזִיבָתוֹ נוֹתְנִין
אוֹתָהּ, וְאַף־עַל־פִּי שֶׁהוּא טָמֵא־מֵת נָהֲגוּ לְהַאֲכִילָהּ לוֹ בְּאוֹתָן מְקוֹמוֹת.

וְעוֹד נִרְאֶה שֶׁיֵּשׁ לְהָקֵל בָּהּ עוֹד בְּחַלַּת חוּצָה לָאָרֶץ, שֶׁאָדָם יָכוֹל לְבַטְּלָהּ
לְכַתְּחִלָּה בְרֹב, כְּמוֹ שֶׁבָּא בְמַסֶּכֶת (יְבָמוֹת) [בְּכוֹרוֹת] וּבִמְקוֹמוֹת אֲחֵרִים בַּגְּמָרָא.
וְאֵין בְּכָל הָאִסּוּרִין שֶׁבַּתּוֹרָה כֵּן, לְפִי יְדִיעָתִי, זוּלָתִי בְעֵצִים שֶׁנָּשְׁרוּ מִן הַדֶּקֶל
בְּיוֹם־טוֹב לְתוֹךְ הַתַּנּוּר, שֶׁמְּבַטְּלִין אוֹתָן גַּם־כֵּן לְכַתְּחִלָּה, וְכִדְאָמְרִינָן בְּיוֹם־טוֹב:
אָדָם מַרְבֶּה עָלֵיהֶם עֵצִים וּמַתִּירָן; וְאָמְרוּ בְטַעַם הַדָּבָר: מִשּׁוּם דְּמִקְלָא קָלֵי
אִסּוּרַיְהוּ, כְּלוֹמַר שֶׁהוּא דָבָר שֶׁכָּלָה בָאֵשׁ, וְלָכֵן הֵקֵלּוּ בַדָּבָר.

וְהָרַב מֹשֶׁה בֶּן מַיְמוֹן זִכְרוֹנוֹ לִבְרָכָה כָּתַב בְּסֵפֶר זְרָעִים הִלְכוֹת (תְּרוּמָה
ו)בִּכּוּרִים פֶּרֶק חֲמִישִׁי: וּבַזְּמָן הַזֶּה, שֶׁאֵין שָׁם עִסָּה טְהוֹרָה מִפְּנֵי טֻמְאַת מֵת,
מַפְרִישִׁין חַלָּה אַחַת בְּכָל אֶרֶץ יִשְׂרָאֵל, אֶחָד מֵאַרְבָּעִים וּשְׁמֹנָה, וְשׂוֹרֵף אוֹתָהּ
מִפְּנֵי שֶׁהִיא טְמֵאָה, וְיֵשׁ לָהּ שֵׁם עִקָּר מִן הַתּוֹרָה. וּמִכְּזַיִב עַד אֲמָנָה מַפְרִישִׁין
חַלָּה שְׁנִיָּה לְכֹהֵן לַאֲכִילָה, וְאֵין לָהּ שִׁעוּר, כְּמוֹ שֶׁהָיָה הַדָּבָר מְקֹדֶם. חַלַּת חוּצָה
לָאָרֶץ, אַף־עַל־פִּי שֶׁהִיא טְמֵאָה, הוֹאִיל וְעִקַּר חִיּוּבָהּ מִדִּבְרֵיהֶם אֵינָהּ אֲסוּרָה
בַּאֲכִילָה אֶלָּא עַל כֹּהֵן שֶׁטֻּמְאָה יוֹצְאָה עָלָיו מִגּוּפוֹ. וְכֵן בַּעֲלֵי קְרָיִין וְזָבִין וְזָבוֹת

---

larger quantity should make the smaller quantity insignificant, *ba-tél b'rov*); and
therefore, if there is no other dough, it is separated without a benediction.

30. TB K'thuboth 25a.

31. TB B'choroth 27a.

32. I.e. a twenty-fourth part (see five paragraphs above).

33. I.e. when mixed with a larger quantity of permissible food, it is regarded as
nullified and non-existent.

34. This is also the reading of R. Isaac 'Alfasi, MS: *'issuraihu* (*Dikduké Sof'rim*
II 4); our Talmud editions have *'issura* (i.e. "the forbidden matter was burnt up").

35. I.e. benefit is derived from them only when they are burnt and no longer
exist in substance.

36. This part of the land of Israel was inhabited by the original settlers under
Joshua, but not by those who returned from Babylonia under Ezra. As it was
considered ritually unclean like foreign lands, the true *hallah* could not be eaten by a
kohen and had to be burned, since it too was considered ritually unclean; but since
people ought not to think that it was undefiled *hallah*, fit for a *kohen*, which was thus
burned, a second portion had to be given a *kohen* (Mishnah, Ḥallah iv 4).

37. Adjacent to the land of Israel; see §84, tenth paragraph.

amount is to be separated, and it is thrown into the fire, not to be eaten by any *kohen*, young or adult.

I heard, however, that there are regions where it has been the custom to set apart a large amount of *ḥallah*, in the measure that the Sages gave for it,[32] and it would be given a young *kohen* [a child], from whose body no source of defilement would issue, or to a young female *kohen* who has not yet seen [any menstrual flow]. And even to an adult *kohen* who underwent ritual immersion on account of his nocturnal emission or his discharge, they would give it; even if he was defiled by the dead, it would be the custom to give it him to eat in those regions.

Moreover, it would seem right to be further lenient with *ḥallah* outside the land [of Israel], so that a man could nullify it from the start in a larger amount [of permitted food],[33] as we find in the tractate *B'choroth* (27a) and elsewhere in the Talmud. Such a rule is not found among any forbidden things in the Torah, to my knowledge, except in regard to branches that dropped from a palm-tree into a stove on a festival day: they too may be nullified from the start. As it was taught in the tractate *Bétzah* (4b): a man may add on wood over them and make them permissible; and the reason was given for the matter: because their forbidden part is burnt up.[34] In other words, it is something consumed by the fire;[35] therefore they were lenient in the matter.

Now, R. Moses b. Maimon [Rambam] of blessed memory wrote in the *Books of Seeds, hilchoth* (laws of) *bikkurim*, chapter 5 (v 9–10): At the present time, since there is no ritually clean dough, on account of defilement by the dead, one portion of *ḥallah* is separated [from a batch of dough] in all the land of Israel — one forty-eighth part — and it is burned, because it is ritually unclean and it bears the actual name [of *ḥallah*] by the law of the Torah. From Cheziv to Amanah, a second portion of *ḥallah* would be separated for the *kohen*, to be eaten;[36] and there is no fixed measure for this, as the rule was of yore. As for *ḥallah* outside the land [of Israel], even though it is ritually unclean, since its obligation is essentially by the ruling of the Sages it is only forbidden to be eaten by a *kohen* whose source of defilement emerges from his body — hence those with nocturnal emissions, men and women with discharges, women unclean from the menses and those who gave birth, and people with *tzara'ath* disease. But others

⟨101⟩

וְנִדּוֹת וְיוֹלְדוֹת וּמְצֹרָעִין; אֲבָל שְׁאָר הַטְּמֵאִין בְּמַגַּע הַטֻּמְאוֹת, אֲפִלּוּ טְמֵאֵי מֵת, מֻתָּרִים לְאָכְלָהּ.

לְפִיכָךְ, אִם הָיָה שָׁם כֹּהֵן קָטָן בְּחוּצָה לָאָרֶץ, בֵּין בְּסוּרְיָא בֵּין בִּשְׁאָר אֲרָצוֹת, רָצָה לְהַפְרִישׁ חַלָּה אַחַת, מַפְרִישׁ אֶחָד מֵאַרְבָּעִים וּשְׁמֹנָה, וְהִיא נֶאֱכֶלֶת לְקָטָן שֶׁעֲדַיִן לֹא רָאָה קֶרִי, וְלִקְטַנָּה שֶׁלֹּא רָאֲתָה נִדָּה, וְאֵין צָרִיךְ לְהַפְרִישׁ שְׁנִיָּה לָאֵשׁ. וְכֵן אִם הָיָה שָׁם כֹּהֵן גָּדוֹל שֶׁטָּבַל מִשִּׁכְבַת־זֶרַע אוֹ מִזִּיבָתוֹ, אַף־עַל־פִּי שֶׁלֹּא הֶעֱרִיב שִׁמְשׁוֹ, וְאַף־עַל־פִּי שֶׁהוּא טָמֵא מֵת, הֲרֵי זֶה מֻתָּר לֶאֱכֹל הַחַלָּה הָרִאשׁוֹנָה, וְאֵינוֹ צָרִיךְ לְהַפְרִישׁ שְׁנִיָּה בְּחוּצָה לָאָרֶץ. עַד כָּאן.

[מִצְוַת צִיצִית]

שפו לְהָטִיל צִיצִית בְּבֶגֶד שֶׁנִּתְכַּסֶּה בּוֹ, שֶׁנֶּאֱמַר ״וְעָשׂוּ לָהֶם צִיצִת״ וְגוֹמֵר. וְזֶה הַחִיּוּב הוּא כְּשֶׁיִּהְיֶה לַבֶּגֶד אַרְבַּע כְּנָפַיִם אוֹ יוֹתֵר, דִּכְתִיב ״עַל אַרְבַּע כַּנְפוֹת כְּסוּתְךָ״, וְיֵשׁ בִּכְלָל חָמֵשׁ אוֹ יוֹתֵר, אַרְבַּע; וְיִהְיֶה שִׁעוּרוֹ גָּדוֹל כְּדֵי שֶׁיּוּכַל לְהִתְכַּסּוֹת בּוֹ רֹאשׁוֹ וְרֹב גּוּפוֹ שֶׁל קָטָן הַמִּתְהַלֵּךְ לְבַדּוֹ בַּשּׁוּק מִבְּלִי שׁוֹמֵר, וּלְפִי הַדּוֹמֶה שֶׁזְּמַן זֶה הוּא כְּבַר־שִׁית כְּבַר־שֶׁבַע; וְשֶׁיִּהְיֶה הַטַּלִּית מִצֶּמֶר אוֹ מִפִּשְׁתִּים; זֶהוּ הַבֶּגֶד שֶׁאָנוּ חַיָּבִין לְהָטִיל בָּהּ צִיצִית כְּשֶׁנִּתְכַּסֶּה בּוֹ. הָיָה חָסֵר דָּבָר אֶחָד מִכָּל אֵלֶּה, כְּגוֹן שֶׁיֵּשׁ לוֹ פָּחוֹת מֵאַרְבַּע כְּנָפַיִם, אוֹ שִׁעוּר גָּדְלוֹ פָּחוֹת מִזֶּה שֶׁאָמַרְנוּ, אוֹ שֶׁהוּא מִשְּׁאָר הַמִּינִין, פָּטוּר מִן הַצִּיצִית מִן הַתּוֹרָה: כְּגוֹן בִּגְדֵי מֶשִׁי אוֹ אֲפִלּוּ שֶׁל צֶמֶר גְּמַלִּים אוֹ אַרְנָבִים אוֹ מְנוֹצָה שֶׁל עִזִּים, כָּל אֵלּוּ פְּטוּרִין מִן הַצִּיצִית מִן הַתּוֹרָה, שֶׁאֵין נִקְרָא בֶּגֶד סְתָם אֶלָּא בֶּגֶד שֶׁל צֶמֶר רְחֵלִים וּכְבָשִׂים אוֹ בֶּגֶד פִּשְׁתִּים; וְכֵן לְעִנְיַן צָרַעַת הַבֶּגֶד, כְּמוֹ שֶׁכָּתַבְתִּי בִּמְקוֹמוֹ [סִי׳ קע״ב].

38. Literally, if *his* sun, etc. — the idiom of the Talmud (TB P'saḥim 35a, Yevamoth 74b). Ordinarily, if a *kohen* became ritually defiled, he would have to undergo immersion and wait for sunset and nightfall before being permitted to eat holy food once more (per Leviticus 22:7).

§386　　1. So TB M'naḥoth 43b.

2. So *ibid.* 40b.

3. So *ibid.* 39b, etc. From the beginning to here is based on MT *hilchoth tzitzith* iii 1–2.

who are unclean through contact with sources of defilement—even those defiled by the dead — are allowed to eat it.

Therefore [Rambam continues] if there was a young *kohen* [a child] there, outside the land [of Israel], whether in Syria[37] or in other lands, if a person wished to separate one portion of *ḥallah*, he should separate one forty-eighth part, and it might be eaten by the child who has not yet seen any nocturnal emission or by a young girl [*kohen*] who has never experienced any menses. And there is no need to separate a second portion for the fire. So too, if there was an adult *kohen* there who underwent ritual immersion on account of seminal emission or on acount of his discharge, then even if the sun has not set as yet,[38] and even if he was defiled by the dead, he is permitted to eat the first *ḥallah* portion, and there is no need to set apart a second portion outside the land [of Israel]. Thus far [Rambam].

[THE PRECEPT OF TZITZITH, TASSELS ON A
FOUR-CORNERED GARMENT]

386 to insert *tzitzith* (tassels) in a garment with which one clothes himself: as it is stated, *that they shall make themselves fringes*, etc. (Numbers 15:38). This obligation applies when the garment has four corners or more:[1] for it is written, *on the four corners of your cloak* (Deuteronomy 22:12), and this includes [clothing with] five, or more than four, whose measure is large enough so that a child who can walk about in the market-place without a guardian can cover his head and most of his body with it.[2] This age would seem to be about six or seven. And the garment must be of wool or linen. This is the article of apparel in which we are duty-bound to insert *tzitzith* when we would clothe ourselves in it. If any one of all these features was lacking in it—for instance, if it had fewer than four corners, or if the measure of its size was less than the one we stated, or if it was of other kinds [of cloth], it is free of the obligation of *tzitzith* by the law of the Torah. For example, garments of silk, or even of the wool of camels or rabbits, or from the down of goats—all these are free of the duty of *tzitzith* by the law of the Torah. For generally, without specification, nothing is called a garment but an article of clothing made of the wool of lambs or sheep, or a garment of linen.[3] And the same rule holds in regard to *tzaraʿath* infection of clothing, as I wrote in its proper place (§ 172).

שֹׁרֶשׁ הַמִּצְוָה נִגְלֶה בַּכָּתוּב, שֶׁהִיא לְמַעַן נִזְכֹּר כָּל מִצְוֹת הַשֵּׁם תָּמִיד, וְאֵין דָּבָר בָּעוֹלָם יוֹתֵר טוֹב לְזִכָּרוֹן כְּמוֹ נוֹשֵׂא חוֹתַם אֲדוֹנָיו קָבוּעַ בִּכְסוּתוֹ אֲשֶׁר יְכַסֶּה בּוֹ תָמִיד, וְעֵינָיו וְלִבּוֹ עָלָיו כָּל הַיּוֹם. וְזֶהוּ שֶׁנֶּאֱמַר בּוֹ בַּכָּתוּב: וּזְכַרְתֶּם אֶת כָּל מִצְוֹת יי.

וְאָמְרוּ זִכְרוֹנָם לִבְרָכָה כִּי מִלַּת צִיצִית תִּרְמֹז לְתרי"ג מִצְוֹת, עִם צֵרוּף שְׁמֹנָה חוּטִין שֶׁבַּצִּיצִית וַחֲמִשָּׁה קְשָׁרִין שֶׁבּוֹ. וְעוֹד אוֹמֵר לִי לְבִּי שֶׁיֵּשׁ בּוֹ רֶמֶז וְזִכָּרוֹן שֶׁגּוּפוֹ שֶׁל אָדָם וְנַפְשׁוֹ, הַכֹּל לַה' בָּרוּךְ הוּא: כִּי הַלָּבָן רֶמֶז לַגּוּף, שֶׁהוּא מִן הָאָרֶץ, שֶׁנִּבְרֵאת מִן הַשֶּׁלֶג שֶׁהוּא לָבָן, כִּדְאַשְׁכְּחָן בְּפִרְקֵי רַבִּי אֱלִיעֶזֶר: הָאָרֶץ מֵהֵיכָן נִבְרֵאת, מִשֶּׁלֶג שֶׁתַּחַת כִּסֵּא הַכָּבוֹד; וְחוּטִין רֶמֶז אֶל הַגּוּף, כְּעִנְיָן אָמְרָם כִּי תְחִלַּת בְּרִיאַת הַגּוּף הוּא כְּעֵין חוּטִין, וּכְמוֹ שֶׁאָמְרוּ זִכְרוֹנָם לִבְרָכָה פֶּרֶק הַמַּפֶּלֶת: אָמַר רַב עַמְרָם: תָּנָא, שְׁתֵּי יַרְכוֹתָיו כִּשְׁנֵי חוּטִין שֶׁל זְהוֹרִית, שְׁנֵי זְרוֹעוֹתָיו כִּשְׁנֵי חוּטִין שֶׁל זְהוֹרִית.

וְהַתְּכֵלֶת, אֲשֶׁר עֵינוֹ כְּעֵין הָרָקִיעַ, יִרְמֹז לַנֶּפֶשׁ, שֶׁהִיא מִן הָעֶלְיוֹנִים; וְלָזֶה רָמְזוּ בְּאָמְרָם: מַה נִּשְׁתַּנָּה תְּכֵלֶת מִכָּל מִינֵי צִבְעוֹנִין, מִפְּנֵי שֶׁהַתְּכֵלֶת דּוֹמֶה לַיָּם, וְהַיָּם דּוֹמֶה לָרָקִיעַ, וְהָרָקִיעַ דּוֹמֶה לְכִסֵּא הַכָּבוֹד, שֶׁנֶּאֱמַר "וַיִּרְאוּ אֶת אֱלֹהֵי יִשְׂרָאֵל" וְגוֹמֵר; וְאוֹמֵר "כְּמַרְאֵה אֶבֶן סַפִּיר דְּמוּת כִּסֵּא", וְתַחַת כִּסֵּא הַכָּבוֹד מָקוֹם שֶׁנַּפְשׁוֹת הַצַּדִּיקִים גְּנוּזוֹת שָׁם; וּמִפְּנֵי־כֵן אָמְרוּ שֶׁכּוֹרְכִין חוּט הַתְּכֵלֶת עַל הַלָּבָן, שֶׁהַנֶּפֶשׁ הִיא הָעֶלְיוֹנִית, וְהַגּוּף תַּחְתּוֹן.

וְאָמְרוּ שֶׁעוֹשִׂין מִמֶּנּוּ ז' כְּרִיכוֹת אוֹ י"ג, לָרֶמֶז הָרְקִיעִים וְהָאֲוִירִים שֶׁבֵּינֵיהֶם,

---

4. Numbers 15 : 39.

5. Tanḥuma, koraḥ 12; Bamidbar Rabbah 18, 21; Midrash 'Aggadah II 113; Rashi to Numbers 15 : 39; Rashi, TB M'naḥoth 43b, s.v. sh'kulah.

6. Hebrew letters also serve as numbers; in the word tzitzith, tzadi = 90, yod = 10, tzadi = 90, yod = 10, tav = 400; hence the total value of the letters in the words is 600. But as the passage continues, in each tassel or fringe there are eight threads tied with five knots. Hence the total of 613.

7. I.e. the white threads.

8. I.e. of the embryo, as it begins to develop limbs.

9. I.e. to color one of the threads in the tzitzith.

10. Hence the blue thread should be over (around) the white.

11. TB M'naḥoth 39a.

The root purpose of the *mitzvah* is revealed in Scripture[4]— that it is in order that we should remember all the *mitzvoth* of the Eternal Lord constantly. Now, there is nothing in the world so good (efficacious) for remembering as carrying the seal of one's master affixed to the garment in which one clothes himself constantly, so that his eyes and his heart are on it all the day. In this sense it is stated about it in the Writ, *and you shall remember all the commandments of the Lord* (Numbers 15:39).

The Sages of blessed memory said further[5] that the word *tzitzith* hints at the 613 precepts in conjunction with the eight threads in the tassel and the five knots in it.[6] Moreover, my heart tells me that in it lies an implication and a reminder that a man's body and spirit are all for the Lord, blessed is He. For the white [in the tassels][7] alludes to the body, that is of the earth, which was created of the snow, which is white—as we find in *Pirké d'R. 'Eli'ezer* (iii): "From what was the earth created?—from the snow that is beneath the Throne of Glory." The threads also allude to the body in keeping with the statement of the Sages that at the beginning of the creation of the body, it resembles threads—as they (of blessed memory) stated in the third chapter of the tractate *Niddah* (25b): Said R. 'Amram: It was taught: His two thighs[8] are as two threads of crimson silk; his two arms are as two threads of crimson silk."

The *t'chéleth* [blue dye that colored one of the threads] whose appearance [color] is as the complexion of the [heavenly] firmament, alludes to the spirit, which is of the upper realms. Our Sages hinted at this when they said,[1] "Why was *t'chéleth* differentiated [singled out] from all kinds of dyes?[9]—because *t'chéleth* resembles the sea, the sea resembles the sky, and the sky resembles the Throne of Glory; as it is stated, *they saw the God of Israel; and there was under His feet as it were a pavement of sapphire stone, and like the very heaven for clearness* (Exodus 24:10); and it is stated too, *as the appearance of sapphire stone, there was the likeness of a throne* (Ezekiel 1:26)." Now, beneath the Throne of Glory is the place where the spirits of the righteous remain hidden. For this reason the Sages said that a thread of *t'chéleth* [i.e. dyed blue] is wound about the white [threads], for the spirit is upper [in origin] and the body is of the lower realm.[10]

And the Sages taught further that seven or thirteen windings were made with it, to allude to the firmaments [the heavens] and the spaces between them. As we read:[11] It was taught: "One who would make

‏וּכְמוֹ שֶׁאָמְרוּ: תָּנָא, הַפּוֹחֵת לֹא יִפְחֹת מִשֶּׁבַע, וְהַמּוֹסִיף לֹא יוֹסִיף עַל י״ג; לֹא‏
‏יִפְחֹת מִשֶּׁבַע, כְּנֶגֶד ז׳ רְקִיעִים, וְלֹא יוֹסִיף עַל י״ג, כְּנֶגֶד ז׳ רְקִיעִים וְשִׁשָּׁה‏
‏אֲוִירִים בֵּינֵיהֶם.‏

‏מִדִּינֵי הַמִּצְוָה, מַה שֶּׁאָמְרוּ זִכְרוֹנָם לִבְרָכָה שֶׁהַכְּסוּת שֶׁל חָמֵשׁ כְּנָפַיִם אוֹ שֵׁשׁ‏
‏אוֹ יוֹתֵר, אֵין מְטִילִין בּוֹ צִיצִית אֶלָּא בְּאַרְבַּע כְּנָפַיִם מִמֶּנּוּ הַמְרֻחָקוֹת; וּמַה‏
‏שֶּׁאָמְרוּ שֶׁאַרְבַּע צִיצִיּוֹת מְעַכְּבוֹת זוֹ אֶת זוֹ, שֶׁאַרְבַּעְתָּן מִצְוָה אַחַת; וּמַה שֶּׁאָמְרוּ‏
‏שֶׁהַתְּכֵלֶת אֵינוֹ מְעַכֵּב אֶת הַלָּבָן, וְהַלָּבָן אֵינוֹ מְעַכֵּב אֶת הַתְּכֵלֶת; אֵין הָעִנְיָן לוֹמַר‏
‏שֶׁהֵן שְׁתֵּי מִצְווֹת, שֶׁהַכֹּל מִצְוָה אַחַת הִיא, אֶלָּא לוֹמַר שֶׁאֵין מְעַכְּבִין זֶה אֶת זֶה —‏
‏כְּגוֹן אָנוּ הַיּוֹם, שֶׁאֵין אָנוּ מוֹצְאִין תְּכֵלֶת, שֶׁלֹּא נִמָּנַע מִפְּנֵי זֶה מֵהָטִיל חוּטִין‏
‏לְבָנִים מִבְּלִי תְכֵלֶת בְּטַלִּית, וּנְבָרֵךְ עֲלֵיהֶן כְּאִלּוּ הוּא בִּשְׁלֵמוּתוֹ עִם הַתְּכֵלֶת. וְכֵן‏
‏בִּזְמַן שֶׁהַתְּכֵלֶת נִמְצָא, מִי שֶׁלֹּא הָיוּ לוֹ חוּטִין לְבָנִים יָכוֹל לְהָטִיל תְּכֵלֶת בְּסָדִינוֹ,‏
‏וּמִתְעַטֵּף בּוֹ וּמְבָרֵךְ עָלָיו.‏

‏וְצֶבַע הַתְּכֵלֶת הַזֶּה שֶׁנִּצְטַוִּינוּ בּוֹ דּוֹמֶה לְעֵין הָרָקִיעַ בְּטָהֳרוֹ, וְהוּא נַעֲשָׂה בְדַם‏
‏דָּג אֶחָד שֶׁנִּקְרָא חִלָּזוֹן, שֶׁעֵינוֹ דוֹמֶה לְעֵין הַיָּם, וּבְיָם הַמֶּלַח הוּא מָצוּי, וְצוֹבְעִין‏
‏בּוֹ פְּתִיל שֶׁל צֶמֶר; וְזֶה יָמִים רַבִּים לְיִשְׂרָאֵל לֹא שָׁמַעְנוּ מִי שֶׁזָּכָה לִתְכֵלֶת‏
‏בְּטַלִּיתוֹ.‏

‏וְצָרִיךְ צְבִיעָה לְשֵׁם מִצְוָתוֹ, וְהַחוּטִין הַלְּבָנִים גַּם־כֵּן צְרִיכִין טְוִיָּה לְשֵׁם‏

---

12. I.e. of the blue thread about the white ones, before making a knot.

13. Midrash Tanna'im (from Midrash haGadol), Deuteronomy 22:12; MT *hilchoth tzitzith* iii 3.

14. TB M'naḥoth 28a.

15. If one does not meet the requirements of the law, it is as though none do.

16. TB M'naḥoth 38a.

17. I.e. one to put white threads at the corners, another to put blue. Rather, as our author continues, we have one precept to put four threads at each corner (which, when folded in half and knotted together, form eight threads). Originally some threads should be white and some blue (according to Rashi to TB M'naḥoth 38a, s.v. *ha-t'cheleth*, two out of the four; according to MT *hilchoth tzitzith* i 6, half of one thread, to become one of eight when the four are folded and knotted); but if only one color is available, all the threads may be of that color.

18. See three pragraphs above.

19. TB M'naḥoth 44a.

20. This is from MT *hilchoth tzitzith* ii 2. Rambam generally uses *yam ha-melaḥ* (literally, Sea of Salt, but commonly the name of the Dead Sea) to designate the Mediterranean, which is given in TB Shabbath 26a as the source of *ḥilazon*. (See on our text, ed. Chavel p. 770; on MT *loc. cit.* note in vocalized ed. Mosad haRav Kook.)

less should not make fewer [windings][12] than seven, and one who would add on should not increase them beyond thirteen. He should not make fewer than seven, corresponding to the seven firmaments [heavens]; he should not increase the number beyond thirteen, corresponding to the seven firmaments and the six spaces between them.''

Among the laws of the precept, there is what the Sages of blessed memory said:[13] that with a cloak with five corners, or six, or more, the *tzitzith* are inserted in none but the four corners furthest apart from one another. Then there is what they taught:[14] that the four tassels of *tzitzith* can prevent one another [from being acceptable][15] since the four comprise one *mitzvah*. There is, too, what they said:[16] that the *t'chéleth* [blue-dyed thread] does not restrain the white [threads from being acceptable] nor does the white restrain the *t'chéleth*. This is not meant to convey that they are two *mitzvoth*,[17] for it is all one precept; but it rather means that they do not prevent one another [from being acceptable in fulfilling it]. For example, when we today do not find *t'chéleth* [the proper blue dye] we should not refrain on that account from putting white threads without *t'chéleth* into the *tallith* [the four-cornered garment worn for prayer] and saying the benediction over them, as though it were complete with *t'chéleth*. So too, at a time that *t'chéleth* is available, if someone does not have white threads, he can insert *t'chéleth* [blue-dyed threads] in his tunic, wrap himself in it, and say the benediction over it.

Now, this dye of *t'chéleth* about which we were commanded, resembles the appearance of the sky in its [unclouded] clear state.[18] It is made from the blood of a certain water-creature called *hilazon*, whose look resembles the appearance of the sea.[19] It is found in the Sea of Salt [the Mediterranean];[20] and with it the thread of wool was dyed.[19] Yet it has been these many days for the people Israel that we have not heard of anyone who attained *t'chéleth* for his garment.[21]

It requires to be dyed for the purpose of its precept; and the white threads likewise need to be spun for the [direct] purpose of the *mitz-*

21. I.e. an accurate knowledge of the *hilazon* and the dye was lost to Jewry long ago, and it became the practice to wear *tzitzith* without the blue thread. It is so noted in Bemidbar Rabbah 17, 5: "but now we have nothing but the white [threads], for the *t'chéleth* was hidden." This echoes an earlier passage in Sifre, Deuteronomy § 354, that "it is hidden for the righteous in the world-to-come."

הַמִּצְוָה; וְאֵין טוֹוִין אוֹתָם מִצֶּמֶר הַנֶּאֱחָז בְּקוֹצִין כְּשֶׁהַצֹּאן רוֹבְצִין, וְלֹא מִן הַנִּימִין
הַנִּתְלָשִׁין מִן הַבְּהֵמָה, וְלֹא מִשִּׁיּוּרֵי שְׁתִי שֶׁהָאוֹרֵג מְשַׁיֵּר בְּסוֹף הַבֶּגֶד; וְאֵין עוֹשִׂין
אוֹתָן מִצֶּמֶר הַגָּזוּל, וְלֹא מִשֶּׁל עִיר הַנִּדַּחַת, וְלֹא מִשֶּׁל קָדָשִׁים; וְאִם עָשָׂה, פָּסוּל.

צִיצִית (שטוה) [שֶׁעָשָׂה] אוֹתָהּ גּוֹי פְּסוּלָה, שֶׁנֶּאֱמַר: דַּבֵּר אֶל בְּנֵי יִשְׂרָאֵל ...
וְעָשׂוּ; אֲבָל עֲשָׂאָהּ יִשְׂרָאֵל בְּלֹא כַוָּנָה, דִּיעֲבַד כְּשֵׁרָה. (וְשָׁמַעְתִּי מִגְּדוֹלִים
שֶׁהָעֲשִׂיָּה אֵינָהּ כְּשֵׁרָה בְּנָשִׁים.)

כֵּיצַד עוֹשִׂין הַצִּיצִית: מַעֲבִירִין אַרְבָּעָה חוּטִין בְּכַנְפֵי הַבֶּגֶד, שֶׁהֵן שְׁמֹנָה רָאשֵׁי
חוּטִין כְּשֶׁהֵן תְּלוּיִין בַּכָּנָף; וְאֵין תּוֹלֶה אוֹתָן סָמוּךְ מַמָּשׁ לִשְׂפַת הַבֶּגֶד, וְלֹא רָחוֹק,
אֶלָּא סָמוּךְ כְּשִׁעוּר גּוּדָל מֵרֹאשׁוֹ עַד הַפֶּרֶק רִאשׁוֹן, כִּדְאָמַר רַבִּי יַעֲקֹב אָמַר רַבִּי
יוֹחָנָן בַּגְּמָרָא: וְצָרִיךְ לְהַרְחִיק כִּמְלֹא קֶשֶׁר גּוּדָל, וְעוֹשֶׂה אֶחָד מֵהֶן גָּדוֹל כְּדֵי
שֶׁיִּכְרֹךְ בּוֹ הָאֲחֵרִים, וְקוֹשְׁרָן בַּחֲמִשָּׁה מְקוֹמוֹת קֶשֶׁר כָּפוּל, וּבֵין קֶשֶׁר וְקֶשֶׁר
עוֹשֶׂה ג׳ חֻלְיוֹת, וּבְאֶמְצָעוּת הַקֶּשֶׁר הָאַחֲרוֹן עוֹשֶׂה ד׳ חֻלְיוֹת, שֶׁנִּמְצְאוּ בֵּין כֻּלָּם
י״ג חֻלְיוֹת.

וְעוֹשֶׂה הַחוּטִין אֲרֻכִּים בִּכְדֵי שֶׁיַּסְפִּיקוּ שֶׁיִּהְיֶה בָּהֶן שְׁנֵי חֲלָקִים עָנָף, כְּלוֹמַר
בְּלֹא קְשָׁרִים וְחֻלְיוֹת, מִלְּבַד הַקְּשָׁרִים וְהַחֻלְיוֹת; זֶהוּ עִקַּר מִצְוָתוֹ לְכַתְּחִלָּה, אֲבָל
דִּיעֲבַד אֲפִלּוּ בְּחֻלְיָה אַחַת יָצָא. וְכֵן בְּדִיעֲבַד, אִם נִתְמַעֲטוּ חוּטֵי הַצִּיצִית, אֲפִלּוּ

22. I.e. with this holy intent; TB M'naḥoth 42b.

23. *Ibid.* MT *hilchoth tzitzith* i 11.

24. TB Sukkah 9a.

25. I.e. into idolatry, whereupon all the town's possessions were to be destroyed (Deuteronomy 13:16–17); MT *ibid.* based on TB M'naḥoth 38b–39a, 41a (*Kessef Mishneh*).

26. MT *ibid.* based on TB Sukkah 27b.

27. MT *ibid.*

28. TB M'naḥoth 42a. The original Hebrew text begins, "*Tzitzith* spun by a non-Jew"; but MH (288b, col. 1) curtly dismisses it as a scribal error and emends it. This is evidently just, since the proof text and the sentence that follows deal with "making the fringes" or tassels, i.e. tying the strings at the corners. Moreover, in the previous paragraph we read that the white threads must be spun for the direct purpose of the fulfillment of the precept, and a non-Jew cannot do that, since its obligation does not lie upon him. Hence the original text here would be superfluous.

29. MT *hilchoth tzitzith* i 12, based on the fact that the Talmud requires the proper intention in spinning the thread, without mentioning making the tassel.

30. Based on TB Gittin 45b (MY). This sentence is not in the manuscripts, however, and is thus apparently an interpolated later marginal note. (See further: *tosafoth* to TB M'naḥoth 42a, s.v. *mina-yin*; and *Shulḥan 'Aruch 'Oraḥ Ḥayyim*, § 14, 1.)

31. I.e. passed through a hole near the corner of the garment, they hang from their midpoint, and the four are thus doubled; TB M'naḥoth 41b (and Rashi s.v. *'amar R. Huna*), 42a (and Rashi s.v. *k'didan*).

vah.[22] They are not to be spun from wool that was caught on thorns when the sheep were lying, nor from tufts plucked from an animal, nor from remnants of the warp that the weaver leaves at the end of a garment.[23] They are not to be made of wool seized in robbery,[24] taken from a town led astray,[25] or from consecrated property;[26] and if one did so, they are disqualified.[27]

Tzitzith made by a non-Jew is unacceptable: for it is stated, *Speak to the Israelites...that they shall make themselves fringes* (Numbers 15:38).[28] But if a Jew made it without the proper intention [for the sake or purpose of the *mitzvah*], after the fact, having been done, it is acceptable.[29] And I have heard from great authorities that its implementation by women is not acceptable.[30]

Now, how are the *tzitzith* (tassels) made? Four threads are passed through the corner of the garment, which then form eight ends of the threads when they hang from the corner.[31] They are not hung actually close to the edge of the garment, nor far away, but as close as a thumb's length from its beginning to the first juncture. As R. Ya'akov said in R. Yoḥanan's name in the Talmud: one must leave a distance of the full first part of the thumb.[32] One of them [the threads] is made longer, so that it can be wound about the others, and they are tied in five places with a double knot.[33] Between each and every knotting, three windings[34] should be made, and before the last knot, four windings are made, so that among all there are thirteen windings.[35]

The threads are to be made long, in order that they should suffice so that two parts [two-thirds] of them should be the fringe [strings of the tassel] — in other words, apart from the knots and the wound section.[11] This is the basic, essential precept initially. After the fact, though, having being done, even with one section of winding the obligation is fulfilled.[36] So too, after the fact, if the threads of the *tzitzith* became shortened, even until nothing remained of them but

32. I.e. from the hole through which the threads are put, to the first knotting of the threads, at the very edge of the garment; *ibid.* 42a.

33. So Rashi, TB M'naḥoth 43b. s.v. *sh'kulah*; *tosafoth, ibid.* 39a, s.v. *lo yif-ḥoth*; and sources in note 5.

34. I.e. of one thread about the others.

35. See five paragraphs above, and MT *hilchoth tzitzith* i 7.

36. TB M'naḥoth 39a; this means that the long thread is wound (at least) three

times around the bunch, between two knottings (Rashi s.v. *'ela ḥulya 'eḥad*).

לֹא נִשְׁאַר בָּהֶן אֶלָּא כְדֵי עֲנִיבָה—כָּשֵׁר; אֲבָל נִפְסַק אֲפִלּוּ חוּט אֶחָד מֵהֶן מֵעִקָרוֹ—פָּסוּל.

וּמִי שֶׁיֵּשׁ לוֹ כְסוּת ד׳ כְּנָפַיִם, כָּל זְמַן שֶׁאֵינוֹ מִתְכַּסֶּה בָּהּ, אֵין חַיָּב לְהָטִיל בָּהּ צִיצִית, שֶׁהֲלָכָה כְּרַב דַּאֲמַר ”צִיצִית חוֹבַת גַּבְרָא”, כְּלוֹמַר חִיּוּב הָאִישׁ הוּא לַעֲשׂוֹת צִיצִית בְּבֶגֶד כְּשֶׁהוּא מִתְכַּסֶּה בוֹ, אֲבָל בְּבֶגֶד הַמֻּנָּח בְּקֻפְסָא אֵינוֹ חַיָּב לְהָטִיל בָּהּ צִיצִית; שֶׁאֵין הֲלָכָה כְמַאן דְּאָמַר חוֹבַת מָנָא הוּא, כְּלוֹמַר שֶׁאִם הָיוּ לוֹ לְאָדָם כַּמָּה טַלִּיתוֹת שֶׁל ד׳ כְּנָפַיִם בְּבֵיתוֹ, אֲפִלּוּ לֹא יִתְכַּסֶּה בָּהֶן לְעוֹלָם חַיָּב לְהַנִּיחַ בְּכֻלָּן צִיצִיּוֹת; זֶה אֵינוֹ, אֶלָּא הֲלָכָה כְּרַב, כִּדְאָמְרָן.

וּמִי שֶׁיֵּשׁ לוֹ טַלִּית שֶׁל פִּשְׁתָּן מֵטִיל בּוֹ צִיצִיּוֹת שֶׁל פִּשְׁתָּן; דְּלֵית הִלְכְתָא כְּבֵית שַׁמַּאי דְּאָמְרֵי סָדִין בְּצִיצִית פְּטוּרָה, כְּלוֹמַר דְּטַלִּית שֶׁל פִּשְׁתָּן, מִכֵּיוָן שֶׁאִי־אֶפְשָׁר לְהָטִיל בּוֹ תְכֵלֶת לְעוֹלָם מִשּׁוּם כִּלְאַיִם, כִּי הַתְּכֵלֶת וַדַּאי עַמְרָא הוּא, שֶׁצֶּבַע הַתְּכֵלֶת לֹא יִהְיֶה יָפֶה בְּפִשְׁתָּן לְעוֹלָם אֶלָּא בְּצֶמֶר, וְהַתּוֹרָה חִיְּבָה אוֹתָנוּ בִּתְכֵלֶת גְּמוּר; וּמִכֵּיוָן שֶׁאִי־אֶפְשָׁר לְהָטִיל חוּט צֶמֶר בְּפִשְׁתָּן לְעוֹלָם מִשּׁוּם כִּלְאַיִם, אַף חוּטִין שֶׁל לָבָן, כְּלוֹמַר שֶׁל פִּשְׁתָּן, אֵין מַנִּיחִין בּוֹ.

וְזֶהוּ שֶׁאָמְרוּ: סָדִין בְּצִיצִית—בֵּית שַׁמַּאי פּוֹטְרִין, וְאֵין הֲלָכָה כְּמוֹתָם; דְּטַעְמָא דִּידְהוּ מִשּׁוּם דְּלָא דָרְשֵׁי סְמוּכִין, וַהֲלָכָה כְּבֵית הִלֵּל דְּדָרְשֵׁי סְמוּכִין, דְּסָבְרֵי דְּלָאו דְכִלְאַיִם אֵינוֹ בְצִיצִית, שֶׁהַתּוֹרָה אָמְרָה: ”לֹא תִלְבַּשׁ שַׁעַטְנֵז ... גְּדִלִים תַּעֲשֶׂה”, כְּלוֹמַר אֲבָל ”גְּדִלִים תַּעֲשֶׂה לָךְ” מִשַּׁעַטְנֵז, וּמִשּׁוּם הָכִי קָא סָבְרֵי בֵּית הִלֵּל דְּסָדִין בְּצִיצִית חַיֶּבֶת, כְּלוֹמַר דְּמַנִּיחִין צִיצִית שֶׁל פִּשְׁתָּן בְּטַלִּית שֶׁל פִּשְׁתָּן, וַהֲלָכָה כְּמוֹתָם.

37. I.e. a bowknot; *ibid.* 38b.

38. At its beginning, where it is attached to the garment (Rashi); *ibid.* 39a.

39. *Ibid.* 42a.

40. *Ibid.* 40a.

41. It would never dye it properly.

42. TB M'naḥoth 40a. (Rashi and *tosafoth* understand this topic differently, to which fact our author alludes four paragraphs below.)

43. When one section of Scripture follows another directly, they do not regard it of any special significance, to be interpreted. Those who interpret it do so because the verses in question seem superfluous otherwise. Thus an injunction against a mixed cloth (see below in the text) is already given in Leviticus 19:19, and the precept of *tzitzith* in Numbers 15:37–41 (see TB Yevamoth 4a–b).

enough to make a loop,[37] it is acceptable. But if even one thread of them was severed at its point of origin,[38] entirely, it is disqualified.

When a person has a cloak with four corners, as long as he does not cover himself with it, he has no duty to attach *tzitzith* to it; for the definitive law follows Rav, who said that *tzitzith* is an obligation pertaining to the man.[39] In other words, it is the duty of the man to put *tzitzith* in a garment when he clothes himself with it; but for a garment left lying in a chest, he has no obligation to attach *tzitzith* to it. For the definitive law does not follow the one who ruled that it is an obligation pertaining to the article of clothing — which would mean that if a man has many four-cornered tunics in his house, even if he should never clothe himself in them he is duty-bound to put *tzitzith* in them all. This is not so, however, as the definitive law rather follows Rav, as we said.

A person who has a *tallith* (cloak) of linen is to insert in it tassels of linen: for the definitive law does not follow the School of Shammai who ruled[40] that a *sadin* (a garment of fine cloth) is free of the obligation of *tzitzith* — which means a linen tunic, in which it is never possible to insert *t'chéleth* [the blue-dyed thread], because of *kil'ayim* [the forbidden mixture of species]; for the *t'chéleth* [the blue thread] is certainly wool, because the dye of the *t'chéleth* would never turn out well in linen,[41] but only in wool, and the Torah gave us the obligation of absolute *t'chéleth*; and since it is impossible ever to insert a woolen thread in linen on account of *kil'ayim*, even [such] white threads, i.e. of linen, are not put in it.

Then this is why it was taught:[42] A linen tunic (*sadin*) in regard to *tzitzith* — the School of Shammai rule it free of the obligation, but the definitive law does not follow them. For their reason is that they do not interpret the proximity [of sections of Scripture],[43] while the definitive law follows the School of Hillel, that does interpret proximity, which thus holds that the injunction against *kil'ayim* does not apply to *tzitzith*: For the Torah said, *You shall not wear a mixed cloth, wool and linen together. You shall make yourself tassels on the four corners of your cloak* (Deuteronomy 22:11–12) — which denotes that the tassels may be made of mixed cloth. For this reason the School of Hillel holds that a linen tunic entails the obligation of *tzitzith*; in other words, tassels of linen are to be inserted in a linen *tallith*; and the definitive law is as they ruled.

However, *t'chéleth* [the blue-dyed thread] is not to be inserted in

אֲבָל אֵין מַנִּיחִין בּוֹ תְּכֵלֶת, גְּזֵרָה מִשּׁוּם קָלָא אִילָן, כְּלוֹמַר גְּזֵרָה שֶׁמָּא יִצְבְּעוּ אוֹתוֹ בְּצֶבַע אַחֵר שֶׁאֵינוֹ תְּכֵלֶת, וְיִהְיֶה כִּלְאַיִם שֶׁלֹּא בִּמְקוֹם מִצְוָה.

וְהִקְשׁוּ בַּגְּמָרָא בִּמְנָחוֹת עַל דָּבָר זֶה: לָא יְהֵא אֶלָּא לָבָן — כְּלוֹמַר לְבֵית הַלֵּל דְּדָרְשֵׁי סְמוּכִין, לָמָּה נִגְזֹר בָּזֶה — שֶׁאֲפִילוּ יִהְיֶה קָלָא אִילָן מַה בְּכָךְ, הֲרֵי אָמַרְנוּ דְּכִלְאַיִם הֻתְּרוּ בְּצִיצִית, כְּלוֹמַר אֲפִילוּ בְּלָבָן, כְּלוֹמַר אֲפִילוּ לְהַנִּיחַ בְּטַלִּית שֶׁל פִּשְׁתָּן צִיצִיּוֹת שֶׁל צֶמֶר לָבָן, וְאֵין צָרִיךְ לוֹמַר שֶׁל צֶמֶר צָבוּעַ בִּתְכֵלֶת כְּמִצְוָתוֹ.

וּפָרִיק: הַנֵּי מִלֵּי דְּאָמְרֵי בֵּית הַלֵּל דְּכִלְאַיִם הֻתְּרוּ בְּצִיצִית מִדְּרָשָׁא דִּסְמוּכִין, הֵיכָא דְּלֵכָּא מִינֵיהּ, כְּלוֹמַר הֵיכָא דְּלָא אֶפְשָׁר לָן בְּמִינֵיהּ, כְּגוֹן טַלִּית שֶׁהוּא שֶׁל פִּשְׁתָּן, שֶׁאִם אַתָּה רוֹצֶה לְהָטִיל בּוֹ תְּכֵלֶת, עַל־כָּל־פָּנִים אַתָּה צָרִיךְ צֶמֶר, שֶׁאִי־אֶפְשָׁר לִתְכֵלֶת אֶלָּא מִצֶּמֶר; בְּעִנְיָן זֶה סַמְכֵי בֵּית הַלֵּל אַדְּרָשָׁא דִּסְמוּכִין, וּמְחַיְּבֵי לְהָטִיל תְּכֵלֶת בְּסָדִין. אֲבָל הֵיכָא דְּאִכָּא מִינֵיהּ, כְּלוֹמַר הֵיכָא שֶׁאַתָּה רוֹצֶה לְהַנִּיחַ חוּטִין לְבָנִים בְּלֹא תְּכֵלֶת בְּטַלִּית שֶׁל פִּשְׁתָּן, אִי־אֶפְשָׁר לְךָ לְהַנִּיחַ בּוֹ שֶׁל צֶמֶר מִכֹּחַ אוֹתָהּ דְּרָשָׁא דִּסְמוּכִין, שֶׁהֲרֵי חוּטִין לְבָנִים מִפִּשְׁתָּן אֶפְשָׁר לְךָ לַעֲשׂוֹתָם.

וְהַיְנוּ דְּרַבִּי שִׁמְעוֹן בֶּן לָקִישׁ, דְּאָמַר רַבִּי שִׁמְעוֹן בֶּן לָקִישׁ: כָּל מָקוֹם שֶׁאַתָּה מוֹצֵא עֲשֵׂה וְלֹא־תַעֲשֶׂה, אִם אַתָּה יָכוֹל לְקַיֵּם אֶת שְׁנֵיהֶם, מוּטָב, וְאִם לָאו, יָבוֹא עֲשֵׂה וְיִדְחֶה אֶת לֹא־תַעֲשֶׂה; וְעַכְשָׁיו יָכוֹל אַתָּה לְקַיֵּם שְׁנֵיהֶם, דְּכֵיוָן שֶׁאִי־אַתָּה רוֹצֶה לְהַנִּיחַ בּוֹ תְּכֵלֶת, לְגַבֵּי לָבָן הֲרֵי בְּפִשְׁתִּים אֶפְשָׁר לְךָ, וְכֵיוָן שֶׁכֵּן, אִם תַּעֲשֵׂם מִצֶּמֶר, הֲווּ לְהוּ כִּלְאַיִם וְאָסוּר, וְתוּ לָא מִידֵּי.

וּמִפְּנֵי שֶׁיֵּשׁ בְּעִנְיָנִים אֵלֶּה הַרְבֵּה פֵּרוּשִׁים, הֶאֱרַכְתִּי לְךָ מְעַט בְּכָאן, וּבְכַמָּה שֶׁעָלָה בִּמְצוּדָתִי עָרַכְתִּי לְפָנֶיךָ שֻׁלְחָן, וְאִם תִּזְכֶּה בְּנִי הָאֱמֶת תִּבְחַן. וְאִם אוּלַי מִדֶּרֶךְ הַיָּשָׁר יַרְאֶה לְךָ לִסְתֹּר דַּרְכִּי בְּמָקוֹם זֶה אוֹ בְּאַחֵר, לֹא תִשָּׂא פְּנֵי אָב וָרַבָּן, וְהִנְנִי קוֹרֵא מֵעַתָּה סְתִירָתְךָ בִּנְיָן.

---

44. Hence unjustified and prohibited.

45. I.e. even if the colored thread was dyed with indigo, why should it be any more forbidden than white threads?

46. TB Shabbath 133a.

it, as a protective measure on account of indigo: In other words, it is a protective decree for fear that it might be colored by another dye which is not *t'chéleth*, and then it would be *kil'ayim* [forbidden] where it is not in the observance of a *mitzvah*.[44]

Yet the question was raised in the Talmud tractate *M'naḥoth* (40a) about this: Then let it be [regarded as] no more than white?[45] In other words, in the view of the School of Hillel, who interpret proximity, why should we make a protective decree about this? Even if it is [dyed] indigo, what of it? Here we said that *kil'ayim* was permitted for *tzitzith* — in other words, even with white [threads], i.e. even to insert threads of white wool in a *tallith* of linen, and so needless to say, [threads of] wool dyed in *t'chéleth*, as its religious duty requires.

The answer was given: In which instance did the School of Hillel say that *kil'ayim* was permitted for *tzitzith* by the interpretation of proximity? — where there is none of its own kind; in other words, where we cannot use its own kind: for example, with a *tallith* made of linen, where, if you wish to insert *t'chéleth* in it, you need wool at all events, since *t'chéleth* cannot possibly be of anything but wool. In that case the School of Hillel relied on the interpretation of proximity and made it obligatory to insert *t'chéleth* in a linen tunic. Where there is of its own kind, however — in other words, where you wish to put white threads without *t'chéleth* in a *tallith* of linen — you cannot possibly put woolen threads into it on the strength of the interpretation of proximity. For here you can make the white threads of linen.

And this follows the rule of R. Shim'on b. Lakish. For R. Shim'on b. Lakish said:[46] Wherever you find both a positive and a negative precept, if you can fulfill both, well and good; if not, let the positive precept come and thrust aside the negative one. Now, however, you are able to fulfill both. For since you do not wish to put *t'chéleth* in it, for the white [threads] linen is available to you. And since it is so, if you make them [the threads] of wool, it will be *kil'ayim*, which is forbidden, and nothing more than that.

Because there are many [differing] explanations in these topics, I have been a bit lengthy for you here, and with what came up in my net, I have set the table for you; and if you will merit, my son, you will discern the truth. And if perhaps from the perspective of honesty it will seem right to you to refute my approach in this or another instance, do not defer in homage to a father and master teacher, for thenceforth I would call your demolition (refutation) a construction.

וְדַע, שֶׁאַף־עַל־פִּי שֶׁאֵין חִיּוּב מִצְוָה זוֹ מִן הַתּוֹרָה אֶלָּא כְּשֶׁיֵּשׁ לוֹ לְאָדָם כְּסוּת
ד' כְּנָפַיִם, כְּמוֹ שֶׁאֵין חִיּוּב מִצְוַת מַעֲקֶה אֶלָּא בְּמִי שֶׁיֵּשׁ לוֹ גַג, אַף־עַל־פִּי־כֵן
הִזְהִירוּנוּ חֲכָמִים בְּמִצְוָה זוֹ הַרְבֵּה, וְאָמְרוּ שֶׁרָאוּי לְחַזֵּר עָלֶיהָ, וְאָמְרוּ שֶׁהַזָּהִיר
בָּהּ זוֹכֶה וּמְשַׁמְּשִׁין אוֹתוֹ עֲבָדִים רַבִּים, שֶׁהֲרֵי הַכָּתוּב שְׁקָלָהּ וְתָלָה בָהּ כָּל
הַמִּצְוֹת, שֶׁנֶּאֱמַר: וּרְאִיתֶם אֹתוֹ וּזְכַרְתֶּם אֶת כָּל מִצְוֹת יי. וְאָמַר רַבִּי אֶלְעָזָר
שֶׁהַזָּהִיר בָּהּ וּבִתְפִלִּין וּבִמְזוּזָה, מֻבְטָח הוּא שֶׁלֹּא יֶחֱטָא לְעוֹלָם, שֶׁנֶּאֱמַר: וְהַחוּט
הַמְשֻׁלָּשׁ לֹא בִמְהֵרָה יִנָּתֵק.

וְדִינֵי מִצְוָה זוֹ, בְּמַסֶּכֶת מְנָחוֹת פֶּרֶק רְבִיעִי תִּמְצָא אוֹתָן.

וְנוֹהֶגֶת מִצְוָה זוֹ בִּזְכָרִים בְּכָל מָקוֹם וּבְכָל זְמַן, אֲבָל לֹא בִּנְקֵבוֹת; וְאִם רָצוּ
הַנְּקֵבוֹת לְהִתְעַטֵּף, מִתְעַטְּפוֹת בְּלֹא בְּרָכָה כְּדַעַת קְצָת הַמְפָרְשִׁים, וּקְצָתָם אָמְרוּ
אֲפִלּוּ בִּבְרָכָה. וְעוֹבֵר עַל זֶה, וְלָבַשׁ בֶּגֶד צֶמֶר אוֹ פִשְׁתִּים גָּדוֹל כַּשִּׁעוּר שֶׁאָמַרְנוּ,
וְהוּא שֶׁלּוֹ, וְלֹא הֵטִיל בּוֹ צִיצִית, בִּטֵּל עֲשֵׂה זֶה; וְאִם הוּא שֶׁל שְׁאָר מִינִין, בִּטֵּל
מִצְוָה מִדְּרַבָּנָן. וְאִם אֵינוֹ שֶׁלּוֹ אֶלָּא שֶׁשָּׁאַל אוֹתוֹ, כָּל שְׁלֹשִׁים יוֹם, כְּלוֹמַר מִיּוֹם
שֶׁשְּׁאָלָהּ עַד תַּשְׁלוּם שְׁלֹשִׁים יוֹם, פְּטוּרָה מִן הַצִּיצִית; מִכַּאן וְאֵילָךְ חַיָּב לְהָטִיל בּוֹ
צִיצִית.

[שֶׁלֹּא לָתוּר אַחַר מַחֲשֶׁבֶת הַלֵּב וּרְאִיַּת הָעֵינַיִם]

שפז שֶׁלֹּא נָתוּר אַחַר מַחֲשֶׁבֶת הַלֵּב וּרְאִיַּת הָעֵינַיִם, שֶׁנֶּאֱמַר: וְלֹא תָתוּרוּ
אַחֲרֵי לְבַבְכֶם וְאַחֲרֵי עֵינֵיכֶם אֲשֶׁר אַתֶּם זֹנִים אַחֲרֵיהֶם.

עִנְיַן לָאו זֶה, שֶׁנִּמְנַעְנוּ שֶׁלֹּא לְיַחֵד מַחְשְׁבוֹתֵינוּ לַחְשֹׁב בְּדֵעוֹת שֶׁהֵם הֶפֶךְ
הַדַּעַת שֶׁהַתּוֹרָה בְּנוּיָה עָלָיו, לְפִי שֶׁאֶפְשָׁר לָבוֹא מִתּוֹךְ כָּךְ לְמִינוּת; אֶלָּא אִם
יַעֲלֶה עַל לִבּוֹ רוּחַ לַחְשֹׁב בְּאוֹתָן דֵּעוֹת הָרָעִים יְקַצֵּר מַחֲשַׁבְתּוֹ בָּהֶם, וִישַׁנֶּה
לַחְשֹׁב בְּדַרְכֵי הַתּוֹרָה הָאֲמִתִּיִּים וְהַטּוֹבִים; וּכְמוֹ־כֵן שֶׁלֹּא יִרְדֹּף הָאָדָם אַחַר

---

47. So MT *hilchoth tzitzith* iii 13; *tosafoth*, TB M'nahoth 41a, s.v. *'anshitho*, and
TB 'Arachin 2b s.v. *ha-kol*.

48. *Ibid.* 32b.

49. MT *ibid.* 9.

50. So Rabbénu Tam in *tosafoth*, TB Rosh haShanah 33a, s.v. *ha R.Yehudah*.

51. After MT *hilchoth tzitzith* iii 2 (based on TB M'nahoth 39b).

Now know that although, by the law of the Torah, the obligation of this precept applies only when a man has a four-cornered cloak,[47] just as there is no obligation of the precept of a parapet (§ 546) for anyone but a person who has a roof—nevertheless, the Sages cautioned us greatly about this *mitzvah*, saying that it is worth striving after it. And they said[48] that if one takes care to observe it, he will merit to have many servants attending upon him: for you see, Scripture made it the equal of all the precepts, which it connected with it: as it is stated, *and you shall look upon it and remember all the commandments of the Lord* (Numbers 15:39). And R. 'El'azar taught[1] that whoever is careful to observe it and the precepts of *t'fillin* (§§ 421–22) and *m'zuzah* (§ 423), is assured that he will never sin; for it is stated, *and a threefold cord is not quickly broken* (Ecclesiastes 4:12).

As to the laws of this precept, in chapter 4 of the Talmud tractate *M'nahoth* you will find them.

This precept applies to the males in every place and every time, but not to women. Yet if women want to clothe themselves [in a garment with *tzitzith*], they may so clothe themselves without saying a benediction, in the view of some authorities,[49] while some said [they may do so] even with the utterance of a benediction.[50] If someone violates this by putting on a [four-cornered] garment of wool or linen, large as the size we stated, which is his, not having inserted *tzitzith* in it, he disobeys this positive precept. If it is of other kinds [of cloth] he disobeys a precept of the Sages.[51] If it is not his own but he borrowed it, then all thirty days—i.e. from the day he borrowed it till the completion of thirty days—it is free of the duty of *tzitzith*. From then on, he is obligated to insert *tzitzith* in it.[19]

[NOT TO GO STRAYING AFTER ONE'S HEART
AND EYES]

387 that we should not stray after the thinking of the heart and the sight of the eyes: as it is stated, *and you shall not go about after your own heart and your own eyes, after which you go wantonly* (Numbers 15:39).

The substance of this injunction is that we were restricted not to devote our thoughts to entertain views that are opposed to the system of thought on which the Torah is constructed, since it is possible, as a result, to arrive at heresy. Rather, if a whim arises in one's heart to entertain those evil views, let him cut short his thinking about them and change course to ponder on the true, good ways of the Torah. So

מַרְאֵה עֵינָיו, וּבִכְלָל זֶה שֶׁלֹּא לִרְדֹּף אַחַר תַּאֲוֹת הָעוֹלָם הַזֶּה, כִּי אַחֲרִיתָם רָעָה,
וּכְדַי בִּזָּיוֹן וָקָצֶף; וְזֶהוּ שֶׁאָמְרוּ זִכְרוֹנָם לִבְרָכָה: וְלֹא תָתוּרוּ אַחֲרֵי לְבַבְכֶם—זוֹ
מִינוּת, וְאַחֲרֵי עֵינֵיכֶם—זוֹ זְנוּת, שֶׁנֶּאֱמַר: וַיֹּאמֶר שִׁמְשׁוֹן אֶל אָבִיו אוֹתָהּ קַח לִי
כִּי הִיא יָשְׁרָה בְעֵינָי.

שֹׁרֶשׁ מִצְוָה זוֹ נִגְלֶה, כִּי בָזֶה יִשָּׁמֵר הָאָדָם מֵחֲטֹא לַיי כָּל יָמָיו; וְהַמִּצְוָה הַזֹּאת
בֶּאֱמֶת יְסוֹד גָּדוֹל בַּדָּת, כִּי הַמַּחֲשָׁבוֹת הָרָעוֹת אֲבוֹת טֻמְאוֹת, וְהַמַּעֲשִׂים יַלְדֵיהֶן.
וְאִם יָמוּת הָאָדָם טֶרֶם יוֹלִיד, אֵין זֵכֶר לְבָנִים; נִמְצֵאת זֹאת הַמְּנִיעָה שֹׁרֶשׁ שֶׁכָּל
הַטּוֹבוֹת יוֹצְאוֹת מִמֶּנָּה.

וְדַע בְּנִי, וּתְהִי נָא מַרְגְּלָא בְּפוּמָךְ, מַה שֶּׁאָמְרוּ זִכְרוֹנָם לִבְרָכָה: עֲבֵרָה גּוֹרֶרֶת
עֲבֵרָה וּמִצְוָה גּוֹרֶרֶת מִצְוָה; שֶׁאִם תַּעֲשֶׂה תַּאֲוָתְךָ לְמַלֹּאת דַּעְתְּךָ הָרָעָה פַּעַם אַחַת,
תִּמְשֹׁךְ אַחֲרֶיהָ כַּמָּה פְעָמִים, וְאִם תִּתְחַזֶּה לִהְיוֹת גִּבּוֹר בָּאָרֶץ לִכְבֹּשׁ יִצְרְךָ וְלַעֲצֹם
עֵינֶיךָ מֵרְאוֹת בְּרַע פַּעַם אַחַת, יֵקַל בְּעֵינֶיךָ לַעֲשׂוֹת כֵּן כַּמָּה פְעָמִים; כִּי הַתַּאֲוָה
תִּמְשֹׁךְ הַבָּשָׂר כְּמִשֹׁךְ הַיַּיִן אֶל שׁוֹתָיו, כִּי הַסּוֹבְאִים לֹא תִשְׂבַּע נַפְשָׁם לְעוֹלָם בַּיַּיִן,
אֲבָל יִתְאַוּוּ אֵלָיו תַּאֲוָה גְדוֹלָה, וּלְפִי הַרְגִּילָם בּוֹ תֶּחֱזַק עֲלֵיהֶם תַּאֲוָתוֹ; וְלוּ
יִשְׁתּוּ כּוֹס מַיִם, יָפוּג יְקַד אֵשׁ תַּאֲוַת הַיַּיִן וְיֶעֱרַב לָהֶם.

כֵּן הַדָּבָר הַזֶּה: כָּל אִישׁ כְּהַרְגִּילוֹ בְּתַאֲוֹת וּבְהַתְמִידוֹ בָּהֶן, יֶחֱזַק עָלָיו יִצְרוֹ
הָרַע יוֹם יוֹם; וּבְהִמָּנְעוֹ מֵהֶם, יִשְׂמַח בְּחֶלְקוֹ תָּמִיד כָּל הַיּוֹם, וְיִרְאֶה כִּי הָאֱלֹהִים
עָשָׂה אֶת הָאָדָם יָשָׁר, וְהֵמָּה בִקְשׁוּ חֶשְׁבֹּנוֹת רַבִּים לְלֹא תוֹעֶלֶת שֶׁל כְּלוּם.

דִּינֵי הַמִּצְוָה זוֹ קְצָרִים, הֲרֵי בֵאַרְנוּ בָזֶה רֹב עִקָּרָן.

וְנוֹהֶגֶת מִצְוָה זוֹ בְּכָל מָקוֹם וּבְכָל זְמַן, בִּזְכָרִים וּנְקֵבוֹת. וְעוֹבֵר עַל זֶה וְיִחֵד
מַחְשַׁבְתּוֹ בָּעִנְיָנִים אֵלּוּ שֶׁזָּכַרְנוּ, שֶׁמְּבִיאִין הָאָדָם לָצֵאת מִדֶּרֶךְ דֵּעוֹת תּוֹרָתֵנוּ
הַשְּׁלֵמָה וְהַנְּקִיָּה וּלְהִכָּנֵס בְּדַעַת הַמַּהְבִּילִים הַכּוֹפְרִים, רַע נָמָר; וְכֵן מִי שֶׁהוּא תָר

---

§387   1. Expression taken from Esther 1:18, end.
2. TB B'rachoth 12b.
3. The paragraph is based on ShM negative precept §47.
4. That you should be given to recalling and quoting.
5. Mishnah, 'Avoth iv 2.
6. It will draw you to indulge the craving many times.
7. Expression based on Isaiah 33:15.

too [is it part of the precept] that a man should not chase after the sight of his eyes, which includes not pursuing the cravings of this world, for their end is evil, with enough disgrace and wrath.[1] In this respect our Sages of blessed memory said:[2] "and you shall not go about after your own heart" — this means heresy; "and after your own eyes" — this means immorality, as it is stated: *And Samson said to his father: Get her for me, for she is right good in my eyes* (Judges 14:3).[3]

The root purpose of this precept is evident: for by it a man will be guarded from sinning to the Lord all his days. This precept is truly a great foundation of the religion, since evil thoughts are the "fathers" of defilement and uncleanness, and the [resulting] actions are their "children"; and if a man should die before begetting any progeny, there will be no remembrance (no trace) of children. Consequently, this restriction is a root from which all good things can sprout.

Then know, my son, and pray let it be a precious adage in your mouth,[4] what the Sages of blessed memory said:[5] A transgression brings a transgression in its wake, and a *mitzvah* brings a *mitzvah* in its wake. For if you set your mind to fulfill your evil craving once, it will pull many other times after it.[6] But if you succeed in being "mighty in the land" (Psalms 112:2) to overcome your inclination and shut your eyes from looking on evil[7] but once, it will seem easy to you to do so many times. For desire draws the flesh as wine draws its drinkers, since the spirit of guzzlers is never satisfied with wine, so that they [ever] desire it with a great craving; and as they habituate their spirit to it, their craving grows the stronger. Yet if they were only to drink a cup of water [instead], the burning conflagration of desire for wine would cool, and life would be sweet to them.

So is this matter: As any man becomes accustomed to desires and persists in them, his evil inclination will overpower him day by day. But if he refrains from them, he will be happy with his lot constantly, all the day, and he will see *that God made man upright, but they have sought out many devices* (Ecclesiastes 7:29) to no avail whatever.

The laws of this precept are short; here we have thus explained most of the principal ones.

This precept is in force everywhere, at every time, for both man and woman. If a person violates this and devotes his mind to these matters that we mentioned, that lead a man to leave the way of the concepts of our perfect, pure Torah and to entertain the evil, bitter thought of the vain, confusing heretics; and so too if someone goes

⟨117⟩

אַחַר עֵינָיו, כְּלוֹמַר שֶׁהוּא רוֹדֵף אַחַר תַּאֲווֹת הָעוֹלָם, כְּגוֹן שֶׁהָיָה מֵשִׂים לְבוֹ תָּמִיד לְהַרְבּוֹת תַּעֲנוּגִים גְּדוֹלִים לְנַפְשׁוֹ מִבְּלִי שֶׁיְּכַוֵּן בָּהֶן כְּלָל לְכַוָּנָה טוֹבָה, כְּלוֹמַר שֶׁלֹּא יַעֲשֵׂם כְּדֵי שֶׁיַּעֲמֹד בָּרִיא וְיוּכַל לְהִשְׁתַּדֵּל בַּעֲבוֹדַת בּוֹרְאוֹ, רַק לְהַשְׁלִים חֶפְצוֹ בְּתַעֲנוּגִים—כָּל מִי שֶׁהוֹלֵךְ בְּדֶרֶךְ זֶה עוֹבֵר עַל לָאו זֶה תָּמִיד, בְּכָל עֵת עָסְקוֹ בְּמַה שֶּׁאָמַרְנוּ.

וְאֵין לוֹקִין עַל לָאו זֶה, לְפִי שֶׁאֵין מַעֲשֶׂה שֶׁנּוּכַל לְהַתְרוֹת בּוֹ הָעוֹבֵר עָלָיו, כִּי מִהְיוֹת הָאָדָם בָּנוּי בְּעִנְיָן שֶׁאִי-אֶפְשָׁר לוֹ שֶׁלֹּא יִרְאֶה בְּעֵינָיו לִפְעָמִים יוֹתֵר מִמַּה שֶּׁרָאוּי, וּכְמוֹ-כֵן אִי-אֶפְשָׁר לוֹ שֶׁלֹּא תִתְפַּשֵּׁט הַמַּחֲשָׁבָה לִפְעָמִים יוֹתֵר מִן הָרָאוּי, עַל-כֵּן אִי-אֶפְשָׁר לְהַגְבִּיל הָאָדָם בָּזֶה בִּגְבוּל יָדוּעַ; גַּם כִּי פְעָמִים אֶפְשָׁר לַעֲבֹר עַל לָאו זֶה מִבְּלִי שׁוּם מַעֲשֶׂה, וּכְבָר כָּתַבְתִּי לְמַעְלָה שֶׁכָּל לָאו שֶׁאֶפְשָׁר לַעֲבֹר עָלָיו מִבְּלִי מַעֲשֶׂה, אַף-עַל-פִּי שֶׁעָשָׂה בּוֹ מַעֲשֶׂה אֵין לוֹקִין עָלָיו, לְפִי הַדּוֹמֶה.

🔯   וַיִּקַּח קֹרַח

חָמֵשׁ מִצְווֹת עֲשֵׂה וְאַרְבָּעָה מִצְווֹת לֹא-תַעֲשֶׂה

[מִצְוַת שְׁמִירַת הַמִּקְדָּשׁ]

שפח שֶׁנִּצְטַוּוּ הַכֹּהֲנִים וְהַלְוִיִּים לִשְׁמֹר הַמִּקְדָּשׁ וְלָלֶכֶת סְבִיבוֹ תָּמִיד בְּכָל לַיְלָה וָלַיְלָה, כָּל הַלַּיְלָה. וּשְׁמִירָה זוֹ הִיא כְּדֵי לְכַבְּדוֹ וּלְרוֹמְמוֹ וּלְפָאֲרוֹ, לֹא מֵהְיוֹת שׁוּם פַּחַד מֵאוֹיֵב חָלִילָה, שֶׁנֶּאֱמַר: וְשָׁמְרוּ אֶת מִשְׁמֶרֶת אֹהֶל מוֹעֵד. וּלְשׁוֹן סִפְרֵי: "וְאַתָּה וּבָנֶיךָ אִתָּךְ לִפְנֵי אֹהֶל הָעֵדוּת", הַכֹּהֲנִים מִבִּפְנִים, וְהַלְוִיִּים אַף מִבַּחוּץ, כְּלוֹמַר לִשְׁמֹר אוֹתוֹ וְלָלֶכֶת סְבִיבָיו. וּבִמְכִלְתָּא אָמְרוּ: "וְשָׁמְרוּ אֶת

---

8. E.g. §§ 94, 113, 241.

§388   1. Sifre, Numbers § 116.

2. Sifre Zuta (see § 363, note 1) 292 l. 8–9; but our author's version is found in Midrash haGadol, Numbers 18 : 4 (290), and ShM positive precept § 22 and negative precept § 67.

straying after his own eyes—in other words, he pursues the desires of the world: for instance, if he should set his heart always to have ever more great pleasures for his spirit, without having any good intention thereby, which is to say that he does not so act in order to remain strong and be able to strive for the service of his Creator, but only to fulfill his desire for pleasures—whoever follows such a path violates this negative precept constantly, all the time that he occupies himself in what we have mentioned.

However, no flogging of whiplashes is suffered over this negative precept, since this is not a set, specific matter about which we could caution a person who transgresses it. Since a man is constructed in such a manner that it is impossible for him not to see at times more than is suitable, and so too it is impossible for him that sometimes the mind should not go further than is proper, it is therefore not possible to limit a man about this to a known (specific) boundary. Moreover, at times it is possible to transgress this injunction without any physical action at all; and I wrote previously, above,[8] that over any negative precept that one is able to transgress without any physical act, even if one did some deed about it, no whiplashes would be suffered, as it would seem.

sidrah korah
(Numbers 16–18)

[It contains] five positive precepts and four negative ones.

[THE PRECEPT OF GUARDING THE SANCTUARY]

388 that the *kohanim* and Levites were commanded to guard the Sanctuary and walk about it continually, every single night, the entire night, this watching being in order to honor, exalt and distinguish it [the Sanctuary], not because there was any fear of an enemy, perish the thought—for it is stated, *and they shall keep the watch of the tent of meeting* (Numbers 18:4). In the language of the Midrash *Sifre*:[1] *and you and your sons with you before the tent of the testimony* (ibid. 2)—the *kohanim* within, and the Levites also without; in other words, to guard it and walk about it. And in the Midrash *Mechilta* it was taught:[2] "they shall keep the watch of the tent of the meeting"

⟨119⟩

מִשְׁמֶרֶת אֹהֶל מוֹעֵד״, אֵין לִי אֶלָּא בַעֲשֵׂה, וְגוֹמֵר. הִנֵּה הִתְבָּאֵר שֶׁשְּׁמִירָתוֹ מִצְוַת עֲשֵׂה הִיא. וְשָׁם נֶאֱמַר עוֹד: גְּדֻלָּה לַמִּקְדָּשׁ שֶׁיֵּשׁ עָלָיו שׁוֹמְרִין; אֵינוֹ דוֹמֶה פַּלְטְרִין שֶׁיֵּשׁ עָלֶיהָ שׁוֹמְרִין, לְפַלְטְרִין שֶׁאֵין עָלֶיהָ שׁוֹמְרִין. וְיָדוּעַ שֶׁפַּלְטְרִין שָׁם הַהֵיכָל.

מִשָּׁרְשֵׁי הַמִּצְוָה, מַה שֶּׁכָּבַר כָּתַבְתִּי כַמָּה פְעָמִים, כִּי בִכְבוֹד הַבַּיִת סִבָּה לָתֵת מוֹרָאוֹ אֶל לֵב בְּנֵי־אָדָם, וּבְבוֹאֵנוּ שָׁם לְבַקֵּשׁ תְּחִנָּה וּסְלִיחָה מֵאֵת אֲדוֹן הַכֹּל, יִתְרַכְּכוּ הַלְּבָבוֹת אֶל הַתְּשׁוּבָה בִּמְהֵרָה, וְכָעִנְיָן שֶׁאָמַרְנוּ בָּאֲרֻכָּה בְּסֵדֶר וְאַתָּה תְּצַוֶּה [סִי׳ צ״ח]. וּמִכְּבוֹדוֹ שֶׁל בַּיִת הוּא לְמַנּוֹת עָלָיו שׁוֹמְרִין, כְּדֶרֶךְ הַמְּלָכִים הַגְּדוֹלִים אֲשֶׁר בָּאָרֶץ שֶׁיַּעֲשׂוּ כֵן, וּכְמוֹ שֶׁבָּא בִּמְכִלְתָּא, ״אֵינוֹ דוֹמֶה״ וְכוּלֵי, כְּמוֹ שֶׁכָּתוּב סָמוּךְ.

דִּינֵי הַמִּצְוָה, כְּגוֹן מַה שֶּׁאָמְרוּ זִכְרוֹנָם לִבְרָכָה, שֶׁאַרְבַּע וְעֶשְׂרִים עֵדָה שׁוֹמְרִים אוֹתוֹ בְּכָל לַיְלָה בְּאַרְבָּעָה וְעֶשְׂרִים מְקוֹמוֹת; הַכֹּהֲנִים שׁוֹמְרִים בְּג׳ מְקוֹמוֹת מִבִּפְנִים, וְהַלְוִיִּים בְּכ״א מְקוֹמוֹת מִבַּחוּץ. וּמַעֲמִידִין אֶחָד שֶׁהָיָה מְחַזֵּר עַל הַמִּשְׁמָרוֹת כָּל הַלַּיְלָה וַאֲבוּקוֹת דּוֹלְקוֹת לְפָנָיו, וְאִישׁ הַר־הַבַּיִת נִקְרָא; וְכָל מִשְׁמָר שֶׁאֵינוֹ עוֹמֵד וְאוֹמֵר לוֹ ״אִישׁ הַר־הַבַּיִת שָׁלוֹם עָלֶיךָ״, נִכָּר שֶׁהוּא יָשֵׁן, וְחוֹבְטוֹ בְּמַקְלוֹ; וּרְשׁוּת הָיָה לוֹ לִשְׂרֹף אֶת כְּסוּתוֹ, עַד שֶׁהָיוּ אוֹמְרִים בִּירוּשָׁלַיִם: מַה קּוֹל בָּעֲזָרָה—קוֹל בֶּן לֵוִי לוֹקֶה וּבְגָדָיו נִשְׂרָפִין, שֶׁיָּשֵׁן עַל מִשְׁמָרוֹ.

וְיֶתֶר פְּרָטֶיהָ, כְּגוֹן הֵיכָן הָיוּ הַלְוִיִּים וְהַכֹּהֲנִים שׁוֹמְרִים, וְאִם אֵרַע קֶרִי לְאֶחָד מֵהֶם כֵּיצַד הוּא עוֹשֶׂה, וְכֵיצַד סִדְרָן וּמַעֲשֵׂיהֶן סָמוּךְ לַשַּׁחַר, הַכֹּל מְתְבָּאֵר יָפֶה בְּפֶרֶק רִאשׁוֹן מִמַּסֶּכֶת תָּמִיד וּמַסֶּכֶת מִדּוֹת.

וְנוֹהֶגֶת בְּכֹהֲנִים וּלְוִיִּים בִּזְכָרִים, בִּזְמַן הַבַּיִת, כִּי הֵם נִתְיַחֲדוּ בְּצַנֶּאת שְׁמִירַת הַמִּקְדָּשׁ וְלֹא הַיִּשְׂרְאֵלִים. וְאִם עָבְרוּ עַל זֶה וּבִטְּלוּ שְׁמִירָה זוֹ, בִּטְּלוּ עֲשֵׂה, מִלְּבַד שֶׁעָבְרוּ עַל לֹא־תַעֲשֶׂה, כְּמוֹ שֶׁנִּכְתּוֹב בְּסֵדֶר זֶה [סִי׳ שצ״א] בְּעֶזְרַת הַשֵּׁם.

3. Sifre Zuta 292 l. 10–11.

4. Our author defined the *héchal* in §95, paragraph 22. The paragraph is based on ShM positive precept §22.

5. Mishnah, Middoth i 1–2.

—hence I know only that a positive precept is involved, etc. It is thus made clear that guarding it is a positive precept. And it was further stated there:[3] It is a matter of distincton for the Sanctuary that it has sentries; there is no comparison between a palace which has sentries about it and a palace without sentries. And it is known that "palace" is a name used for the *héchal* (the focal part of the Sanctuary).[4]

At the root of the precept lies the point I have written previously many times: that in the glorification of the Temple lies a purpose of instilling a reverent awe toward it in the heart of people, and as we come there to entreat grace and forgiveness from the Sovereign Master of all, [our] hearts will be softened toward speedy repentance — in keeping with what we said at length in *sidrah tetzavveh* (§ 98). Well, it is to the glory of the Temple to appoint sentries for it, in the manner of the great kings on the earth, who do so — as it is expressed in the Midrash *Mechilta*, "There is no comparison," etc. as written directly above.

The laws of the precept are, for example, what the Sages of blessed memory taught:[5] that a staff of twenty-four guarded it every night in twenty-four places; the *kohanim* kept watch at three places within, and the Levites at twenty-one locations outside. And one was appointed to make the rounds of the watches the entire night, with burning torches before him. He was called the man of the Temple Mount. If any sentry failed to stand and greet him, "Man of the Temple Mount, peace abide with you," it was evident that he was sleeping. He would strike him with his staff, and he had the right to set fire to his cloak, until it would be said in Jerusalem, "What is the sound in the Temple court?" "It is the sound of a Levite being beaten and his clothing burned because he slept at his watch."

The rest of its details — for instance, where the Levites and the *kohanim* kept watch; if one of them had a nocturnal emission, what he was to do; what their arrangement and actions should be close to dawn — these are all well explained in the first chapter of the tractate *Tamid* and the tractate *Middoth*.

It applies to the male *kohanim* and Levites at the time the Temple exists; for they were singled out in the commandment of guarding the Sanctuary, and not the Israelites. If they transgressed it and failed to keep this watch, they would thus disobey a positive precept, apart from the fact that they would violate a negative precept, as we will write in this *sidrah* (§ 391), with the Eternal Lord's help.

[שֶׁלֹּא יִתְעַסְּקוּ הַכֹּהֲנִים בַּעֲבוֹדַת הַלְוִיִּים וְלֹא הַלְוִיִּים בַּעֲבוֹדַת הַכֹּהֲנִים]

שפט שֶׁלֹּא יִתְעַסְּקוּ הַלְוִיִּים בַּעֲבוֹדַת הַכֹּהֲנִים, וְלֹא הַכֹּהֲנִים בְּעֵסֶק הַלְוִיִּים, אֶלָּא כָּל אֶחָד יַעֲשֶׂה מְלַאכְתּוֹ הַמְיֻחֶדֶת לוֹ, מִדִּכְתִיב: אִישׁ אִישׁ עַל עֲבֹדָתוֹ וְאֶל מַשָּׂאוֹ. וּבִלְשׁוֹן הַמְנִיעָה שֶׁבָּאָה בָּזֶה הוּא שֶׁנֶּאֱמַר בַּלְוִיִּים "אַךְ אֶל כְּלֵי הַקֹּדֶשׁ וְאֶל הַמִּזְבֵּחַ לֹא (יגשו) [יִקְרָבוּ]", וְאַחַר־כֵּן שָׁב הַכָּתוּב וְדִבֵּר אֶל הַכֹּהֲנִים וְאָמַר "וְלֹא יָמֻתוּ גַם הֵם גַם אַתֶּם", יִרְצֶה לוֹמַר בָּזֶה שֶׁ"אַתֶּם" כְּמוֹ־כֵן יִכְלָל אֶתְכֶם לָאו זֶה, כִּי כְּמוֹ שֶׁהַלְוִיִּים נִמְנָעִים מִמְּלַאכְתְּכֶם, כָּךְ אַתֶּם מִמְּלַאכְתָּם.

וּבִלְשׁוֹן סִפְרֵי: "אֶל כְּלֵי הַקֹּדֶשׁ וְ[אֶל] הַמִּזְבֵּחַ" — אַזְהָרָה; "וְלֹא יָמֻתוּ" — עֹנֶשׁ. אֵין לִי אֶלָּא הַלְוִיִּים שֶׁנֶּעֱנָשִׁין וּמֻזְהָרִין עַל עֲבוֹדַת הַכֹּהֲנִים; כֹּהֲנִים עַל עֲבוֹדַת הַלְוִיִּים מִנַּיִן, תַּלְמוּד לוֹמַר "גַם הֵם"; וּמֵעֲבוֹדָה לַחֲבֶרְתָּהּ מִנַּיִן, תַּלְמוּד לוֹמַר "גַם־אַתֶּם". וּמָצָאנוּ שֶׁבִּקֵּשׁ רַבִּי יְהוֹשֻׁעַ בֶּן חֲנַנְיָא לְסַיֵּעַ אֶת רַבִּי יוֹחָנָן בֶּן גֻּדְגְּדָה בַּהֲגָפַת דְּלָתוֹת — אָמַר לוֹ: חֲזֹר לַאֲחוֹרֶיךָ, שֶׁכְּבָר אַתָּה מִתְחַיֵּב בְּנַפְשֶׁךָ, שֶׁאֲנִי מִן הַשּׁוֹעֲרִים וְאַתָּה מִן הַמְשׁוֹרְרִים.

הִנֵּה הִתְבָּאֵר שֶׁכָּל לֵוִי שֶׁיַּעֲשֶׂה בַּמִּקְדָּשׁ אֶלָּא מְלַאכְתּוֹ הַמְיֻחֶדֶת לוֹ חַיָּב מִיתָה בִּידֵי שָׁמַיִם, וּכְמוֹ־כֵן הַכֹּהֲנִים הֻזְהֲרוּ שֶׁלֹּא יִקְרְבוּ בִּמְלֶאכֶת הַלְוִיִּים; וְאוּלָם אִם עָבְרוּ בָּזֶה אֵינָם בְּמִיתָה אֶלָּא בְּמַלְקוֹת.

וְאָמְרוּ בְמִכְלְתָּא: "אֶל כְּלֵי הַקֹּדֶשׁ וְאֶל הַמִּזְבֵּחַ לֹא (יגשו) [יִקְרָבוּ]", יָכוֹל אִם נָגְעוּ יְהוּ חַיָּבִין, תַּלְמוּד לוֹמַר "אַךְ", מִשּׁוּם עֲבוֹדָה הֵם חַיָּבִים, וְלֹא מִשּׁוּם נְגִיעָה; אֵין לִי אֶלָּא הַלְוִיִּים עַל־יְדֵי כֹהֲנִים, הַכֹּהֲנִים עַל־יְדֵי הַלְוִיִּים מִנַּיִן, תַּלְמוּד לוֹמַר "גַם אַתֶּם". וְשָׁם נֶאֱמַר: הַלְוִיִּים עַל שֶׁל כֹּהֲנִים בְּמִיתָה, וְאֵין הַכֹּהֲנִים עַל שֶׁל לְוִיִּם אֶלָּא בְּלֹא־תַעֲשֶׂה.

---

§389   1. Sifre, Numbers § 116.

2. The Hebrew for "neither" and "nor" is *gam*, literally "also"; this word is generally regarded, in the interpretation of the Sages, as superfluous, added only to extend the meaning or scope of a law in the Torah. However, *Kessef Mishneh* to MT *hilchoth k'lé ha-mikdash* iii 9, and R. Elijah Ga'on of Vilna on Sifre logically emend this to read first "neither you" (addressed to the *kohanim*) as the source of the law that a *kohen* is forbidden to do a Levite's work, and later "neither they" (referring to the Levites) as the source of the rule that one Levite is forbidden to do another's work.

3. TB 'Arachin 11b.

4. Sifre Zuta (see § 363, note 1) 291 l. 14–17.

5. Just as *gam* (also) is interpreted as an extension or amplification (note 2), so the Sages generally interpret *'ach* ("only") as a limitation.

6. See note 2; our Sifre Zuta reads, "neither they nor you."

389 that the Levites should not engage in the Divine labor of the *kohanim*, nor the *kohanim* in the tasks of the Levites, but each should rather do his work that is particularly for him: since it is written, *every man to his task and to his burden* (Numbers 4:19); the expression of restriction (prohibition) given for it is in the verse stated about the Levites, *but they shall not come close to the vessels of holiness or to the altar* (Numbers 18:3), while afterward the Writ returns to speak to the *kohanim*, saying, *that they shall not die, neither they nor you* (ibid.), meaning to convey by this that this negative precept is to include you [the *kohanim*] as well: For just as the Levites are excluded from your work, so you from their work.

In the language of the Midrash *Sifre*:[1] "to the vessels of holiness or to the altar"—this is the admonition; "that they shall not die"— this is the punishment. Now I know only that the Levites are punishable and admonished about the labor of the *kohanim*; how do I learn about the *kohanim* in regard to the labor of the Levites?—Scripture states "neither they."[2] And how do I learn about [transferring] from one labor to another?—Scripture states "nor you."[2] And so we find[3] that R. Joshua b. Ḥananya wished to help R. Yoḥanan b. Gudgada in locking the [Temple] doors. Said he to him, "Go back, for you are on the verge of becoming guilty to pay with your life: for I am among the gatekeepers, and you are one of the singers."

It has thus been made clear that any Levite who does at the Sanctuary anything but his work that is particularly for him [to do], is punishable by death at Heaven's hands. And so were the *kohanim* similarly adjured not to come close [and engage in] the work of the Levites. However, if they transgressed this, they are liable not to death but to whiplashes.

Now, it was taught in the Midrash *Mechilta*:[4] "[but] they shall not come close to the vessels of holiness or to the altar"—I might think that if they touched [any of these objects] they should be punishable?—Scripture states "only":[5] on account of doing work they incur penalty, but not on account of touching [them]. Now, I know this only about Levites in regard to *kohanim*; how do I learn this about *kohanim* in relation to Levites?—Scripture states, "nor you."[6] And it was stated there:[7] Levites who engage in the work of *kohanim*

מְשָׁרְשֵׁי הַמִּצְוָה, לְפִי שֶׁעֲבוֹדַת שְׁתֵּי כִתּוֹת אֵלֶּה הִיא עֲבוֹדָה יְקָרָה וּמְקֻדֶּשֶׁת, עַל־כֵּן צְרִיכָה הַמְּלָאכָה לְהִשָּׁמֵר מְאֹד מִן הַיֵּאוּשׁ וְהָעַצְלָה וְהַשִּׁכְחָה; וְאֵין סָפֵק כִּי כָל מְלֶאכֶת הַמֻּטֶּלֶת עַל שְׁנֵי אֲנָשִׁים אוֹ יוֹתֵר, הַפְּשִׁיעָה מְצוּיָה בּוֹ יוֹתֵר מִמְּלָאכָה הַמֻּטֶּלֶת עַל הָאֶחָד לְבַדּוֹ, כִּי הַרְבֵּה פְעָמִים יִסְמְכוּ שְׁנֵיהֶם כָּל אֶחָד עַל חֲבֵרוֹ וְתִתְבַּטֵּל הַמְּלָאכָה מִבֵּינֵיהֶם; זֶה דָבָר בָּרוּר לְכָל אָדָם. וְדֶרֶךְ מָשָׁל אָמְרוּ זִכְרוֹנָם לִבְרָכָה עַל כַּיּוֹצֵא בָזֶה: קְדֵרָה דְּבֵי שֻׁתְּפֵי לָא חֲמִימָא וְלָא קְרִירָא.

מִדִּינֵי הַמִּצְוָה, מַה שֶּׁאָמְרוּ זִכְרוֹנָם לִבְרָכָה: חֲמִשָּׁה־עָשָׂר מְמֻנִּים הָיוּ בַּמִּקְדָּשׁ, אֶחָד עַל הַזְּמַנִּים, כְּלוֹמַר לְכַוֵּן עֵת הַקָּרְבָּן, וּמִיָּד מְזָרֵז אוֹתָם וְאוֹמֵר "עִמְדוּ כֹהֲנִים לַעֲבֹד וּלְוִיִּים לַדּוּכָן וְיִשְׂרָאֵל לַמַּעֲמָד", וְכֵיוָן שֶׁשּׁוֹמְעִין קוֹלוֹ בָּאִין כָּל אֶחָד לִמְלַאכְתּוֹ. וְכֹהֲנִים וּלְוִיִּים יְדוּעִים הָיוּ עוֹבְדִים שָׁם, וּכְמוֹ שֶׁאָמְרוּ זִכְרוֹנָם לִבְרָכָה, כִּי מֹשֶׁה וּשְׁמוּאֵל הָרוֹאֶה וְדָוִד הַמֶּלֶךְ חִלְּקוּם לְאַרְבָּעָה וְעֶשְׂרִים מִשְׁמָרוֹת, כִּדְאִיתָא בְּמַעֲנִית; וְעוֹבֵד כָּל מִשְׁמָר שַׁבָּת אַחַת וְחוֹזְרִין חֲלִילָה. וְכָל אַנְשֵׁי הַמִּשְׁמָר מְחַלֵּק אוֹתָם רֹאשׁ הַמִּשְׁמָר לְבָתֵּי־אָבוֹת, וְכָל יוֹם מִימֵי הַשַּׁבָּת עוֹבְדִין בּוֹ אֲנָשִׁים יְדוּעִים, וְרָאשֵׁי הָאָבוֹת מְחַלְּקִין לָהֶם אֲנָשִׁים יְדוּעִים אִישׁ אִישׁ עַל עֲבוֹדָתוֹ, וְלֹא הָיוּ רַשָּׁאִין לְסַיֵּעַ זֶה אֶת זֶה. וְכֵן הַלְוִיִּים, לֹא הָיָה רַשַּׁאי לְסַיֵּעַ הַמְשׁוֹרֵר לַשּׁוֹעֵר, וְלֹא הַשּׁוֹעֵר לַמְשׁוֹרֵר.

וּמֵאֵלּוּ הַט"ו מְמֻנִּים שֶׁזָּכַרְנוּ, הָאֶחָד כְּבָר אָמַרְנוּ שֶׁהָיָה מְמֻנֶּה עַל הַזְּמַנִּים, וְהַשֵּׁנִי הָיָה מְמֻנֶּה עַל נְעִילַת שְׁעָרִים, שְׁלִישִׁי עַל הַשּׁוֹמְרִים, רְבִיעִי עַל הַמְשׁוֹרְרִים וְכוּלֵי, כְּמוֹ שֶׁבָּא בַּמִּשְׁנָה. וְיֶתֶר פְּרָטֶיהָ, בִּמְקוֹמוֹת בְּסֵדֶר קָדָשִׁים וּבְסִפְרֵי וּבְמִכְלְתָּא, כְּמוֹ שֶׁאָמַרְנוּ לְמַעְלָה.

וְנוֹהֶגֶת בִּזְמַן הַבַּיִת בְּכֹהֲנִים וּלְוִיִּים. וְלֵוִי הָעוֹבֵר עַל זֶה וְעָשָׂה בַּמִּקְדָּשׁ בִּמְלֶאכֶת כֹּהֵן, אוֹ אֲפִלּוּ בִּמְלֶאכֶת חֲבֵרוֹ הַלֵּוִי, חַיָּב מִיתָה בִּידֵי שָׁמָיִם. וְכֵן כֹּהֵן

---

7. Sifre Zuta 292 l. 4, reading of Midrash haGadol.

8. From the beginning to here is based on ShM negative precept §72.

9. Literally, hopelessness; i.e. abandonment of a duty, as one might act in despair.

10. TB 'Eruvin 3a; Bava Bathra 24b.

11. Mishnah, Sh'kalim v 1; TJ v 5.

12. I.e. to the platform (duchan) on which they stood to utter song.

13. Virtuous, worthy Israelites who avoided sin in their reverent fear were stationed regularly at the Sanctuary as representatives of all Israel, when the public animal offerings, sacrificed in behalf of the entire people, were offered up.

14. More specifically, Moses established eight watches, four by 'El'azar and four by 'Ithamar; Samuel established sixteen, and David, twenty-four.

15. I.e. each served one week in twenty-four, in a regular order which was then repeated.

incur death, but *kohanim* who engage in that of the Levites infringe
only a negative precept.[8]

At the root of the precept lies the reason that the service of these
two groups is precious, consecrated service; therefore this work must
be strongly guarded from abdication,[9] laziness and forgetfulness.
Now, there is no doubt that with any work imposed on two people
or more, forgetfulness happens more frequently than with a task
imposed on one alone. For many times, the two of them will rely
each on the other, and the work will be left undone between them.
This is something clear to every man. By way of illustration, the
Sages of blessed memory said about something like this:[10] The
contents of a pot belonging to partners are neither hot nor cold.

Among the laws of the precept, there is what the Sages of blessed
memory taught:[11] There were fifteen appointed men in the Sanctuary: one over the times, i.e. to determine the proper time of the
offering; and he would then alert them at once, saying, "Arise,
kohanim, to serve; Levites, to the platform;[12] and Israelites, to the
post."[13] And once they heard his voice, every one would come to his
task. Now, certain known *kohanim* and Levites would serve there; as
the Sages of blessed memory said, Moses, Samuel the seer and David
the king divided them into twenty-four "watches,"[14] as we find in
the Talmud tractate *Ta'anith* (27a). Every watch would serve a week,
and then the cycle would be repeated.[15] As for the members of the
watch, the head of the watch would divide them into "fathers'
houses";[16] every day of the week, certain people [of a "father's
house"] would serve, the heads of the "fathers' houses" apportioning
these certain people, every man to his task; and they were [then] not
permitted to help one another. So too the Levites: a singer was not
allowed to help a gatekeeper, nor a gatekeeper a singer.

Of the fifteen appointed men that we mentioned, to one we have
already referred, that he was assigned over the appointed times. The
second was assigned to the locking of the gates; the third, over the
sentries; the fourth, over the singers; and so on, as it appears in the
Mishnah.[17] The rest of its details are in various places in the Mishnah
order of *Kodashim* and the Midrashim *Sifre* and *Mechilta*, as we stated
above.

It is in effect when the Temple is extant, for the *kohanim* and the
Levites. If a Levite transgressed it and worked at the Sanctuary at the
task of a *kohen*, or even at the task of his fellow-Levite, he would

שֶׁעָבַר וְעָשָׂה בִּמְלֶאכֶת הַלֵּוִי, עָבַר עַל לָאו, אֲבָל אֵינוֹ חַיָּב מִיתָה, כְּמוֹ שֶׁאָמַרְנוּ
לְמַעְלָה. וּמִן הַדּוֹמֶה, כִּי הַכֹּהֵן שֶׁסִּיַּע בִּמְלֶאכֶת חֲבֵרוֹ הַכֹּהֵן, גַּם־כֵּן בְּמִיתָה.

[שֶׁלֹּא יַעֲבֹד זָר בַּמִּקְדָּשׁ]

שצ שֶׁלֹּא יַעֲבֹד זָר בַּמִּקְדָּשׁ, כְּלוֹמַר כָּל מִי שֶׁאֵינוֹ מִזֶּרַע אַהֲרֹן, שֶׁנֶּאֱמַר "וְזָר
לֹא יִקְרַב אֲלֵיכֶם"; וְנִכְפְּלָה הַמְּנִיעָה בָּזֶה בְּלָשׁוֹן אַחֵר בַּכָּתוּב, וְהוּא שֶׁנֶּאֱמַר: וְלֹא
יִקְרְבוּ עוֹד בְּנֵי יִשְׂרָאֵל אֶל אֹהֶל מוֹעֵד לָשֵׂאת חֵטְא לָמוּת.

מִשָּׁרְשֵׁי הַמִּצְוָה, כָּתַבְתִּי לְמַעְלָה בְּסֵדֶר זֶה עֲשֵׂה ג' [סִי' שצ"ד].

מִדִּינֵי הַמִּצְוָה, מַה שֶּׁאָמְרוּ זִכְרוֹנָם לִבְרָכָה שֶׁאֵין חִיּוּב קְרִיבָה זוֹ אֶלָּא
הַקָּרֵב לַעֲבוֹדָה מִכָּל הָעֲבוֹדוֹת שֶׁהֵן מְיֻחָדוֹת בְּכֹהֵן, וּכְמוֹ שֶׁאָמְרוּ זִכְרוֹנָם לִבְרָכָה:
מְקַבֵּלַת הַדָּם וָאֵילָךְ מִצְוַת כְּהֻנָּה — כְּגוֹן יְצִיקוֹת, בְּלִילוֹת, תְּנוּפוֹת, הַגָּשׁוֹת
וְהַרְבֵּה עֲבוֹדוֹת כָּאֵלּוּ מְפֹרָשׁוֹת בַּגְּמָרָא שֶׁמִּצְוָתָן בְּכֹהֵן — הֲרֵי אֵלּוּ כֻּלָּן בָּאַזְהָרָה
לְזָר, וְהַקָּרְבָּן פָּסוּל.

אֲבָל יֵשׁ שָׁם עֲבוֹדוֹת שֶׁאֵינָן בִּכְלַל אַזְהָרָה זוֹ, כְּגוֹן שְׁחִיטָה, שֶׁכְּשֵׁרָה אֲפִלּוּ
לְכַתְּחִלָּה בְּזָרִים, וַאֲפִלּוּ בְּקָדְשֵׁי קָדָשִׁים; וְכֵן הוֹלָכַת הָעֵצִים, וְכֵן הַדְלָקַת הַנֵּרוֹת,
שֶׁאִם הוֹצִיאָן הַכֹּהֵן לַחוּץ אַחַר שֶׁהֵיטִיב אוֹתָן, שֶׁמֻּתָּר לְזָר לְהַדְלִיקָן.

וְיֵשׁ מֵהֶן אַרְבַּע עֲבוֹדוֹת לְבַד מְיֻחָדוֹת שֶׁהֵן חֲמוּרוֹת, שֶׁיֵּשׁ בָּהֶן חִיּוּב מִיתָה,
וְהֵן זְרִיקָה, הַקְטָרָה, (הקרבה) נִסּוּךְ [הַמַּיִם, נִסּוּךְ הַיַּיִן], וַעֲלֵיהֶן נֶאֱמַר "וְהַזָּר

---

16. TB Ta'anith 15b.

17. Mishnah, Sh'kalim v 1.

18. So Sifre Zuta 291 l. 16 to 292 l. 2.

19. So *ibid.* 292 l. 2–3. This view of our author is discussed by R. Yeruḥam Fishel Perla in his notes to *Séfer haMitzvoth l'Rasag* (II, Warsaw 1916, pp. 422b–423a). As he indicates, Ramban likewise gives this view (Commentary, *hassagoth,* to ShM, positive precept §36; ed. Chavel, p. 173, last line). Not Ramban, however, but *Sifre Zuta loc. cit.* is evidently its source.

§390   1. As our author wrote first, in each *sidrah,* on its positive precepts, in the original this is found earlier. Here, as in most of the editions, the precepts are arranged in the order of their Scriptural verses; hence this comes below.

2. TB B'rachoth 31b, etc.

3. From an animal offering that was ritually slain.

4. While these two tasks might generally be done by an outsider (a non-*kohen*; TB P'saḥim 36a), for the meal-offering of a *kohen* they may not be done by an outsider, according to R. Naḥman (TB M'naḥoth 18b).

5. See e.g. Leviticus 14 : 22, 24.

6. So TB Yoma 27a.

7. So *ibid.* 24b.

incur death at Heaven's hands.[18] If a *kohen* likewise transgressed and did the work of a Levite, he would violate a negative precept, but would not deserve death, as we stated above.[7] It would seem, too, that if a *kohen* assisted in the work of his fellow-*kohen*, he would likewise incur the penalty of death.[19]

[THAT ONE WHO IS NOT A KOHEN SHOULD NOT WORK AT THE SANCTUARY]

390 that an outsider [a non-*kohen*] should not serve at the Sanctuary — in other words, whoever is not of Aaron's descendants: for it is stated, *but an outsider shall not come near to you* (Numbers 18:4). The restriction about this was repeated in another way in Scripture, when it was stated, *And henceforth the Israelites shall not draw near the tent of meeting, to bear sin and die* (ibid. 22).

About the root reason for the precept I have written above,[1] in the third positive precept in the *sidrah* (§ 394).

Among the laws of the precept, there is what the Sages of blessed memory said: that punishment over the injunction against coming near is incurred only by a person who approaches [to do] one of the tasks of service that are specifically for a *kohen*. As they (of blessed memory) taught:[2] from the collection of the blood[3] and onward it is the religious duty of the *kohanim*: for example, pouring [the oil into a dish], mixing [oil and flour],[4] lifting and waving,[5] bringing [a *minhah*, a meal-offering, to the southwest corner of the altar], and many tasks of service like these, explained in the Talmud, which are the religious duty of the *kohen*. All these are included in the admonition to the outsider, and [if he did any of them] the offering is disqualified.

However, there were tasks of service there which are not included in this admonition: for instance, ritual slaying, which is acceptable even initially, from the start, if done by outsiders — even with most holy offerings.[2] So too, bringing the wood [for the altar fire],[6] and likewise kindling the lights [of the *menorah*]:[7] if a *kohen* took them outside after trimming them, it is permissible for an outsider to light them.[8]

Among them though, there are only four particular tasks of service which are serious matters, involving a penalty of death [at Heaven's hand]. These are: sprinkling [the blood], burning [parts of offerings on the altar], pouring libations (drink-offerings) of water[9]

הַקְרֵב יוּמָת", וּכְמוֹ שֶׁנִּתְבָּאֵר בְּמַסֶּכֶת יוֹמָא בְּפֶרֶק "בָּרִאשׁוֹנָה כָּל מִי שֶׁהוּא
רוֹצֶה לִתְרֹם". וְיֵתֵר פְּרָטֶיהָ, מְבֹאָרִים שָׁם בְּיוֹמָא, וּבְפֶרֶק בַּתְרָא מִמַּסֶּכֶת זְבָחִים.

וְנוֹהֵג אִסּוּר זֶה בִּזְכָרִים וּנְקֵבוֹת בִּזְמַן הַבַּיִת, וְאַף בַּזְּמַן הַזֶּה, אַף־עַל־פִּי שֶׁהוּא
שְׁמֵם בַּעֲוֹנוֹתֵינוּ. וְעוֹבֵר עַל זֶה וְעָשָׂה בַמִּקְדָּשׁ אֲפִלּוּ הַיּוֹם אַחַת מִכָּל הָעֲבוֹדוֹת
שֶׁהֵם בַּכֹּהֲנִים, עוֹבֵר עַל לָאו, כְּמוֹ שֶׁכָּתַבְנוּ; וְאִם עָשָׂה אַחַת מֵאַרְבַּע עֲבוֹדוֹת
שֶׁזָּכַרְנוּ, חַיָּב מִיתָה בִּידֵי שָׁמָיִם.

[שֶׁלֹּא לְבַטֵּל שְׁמִירַת הַמִּקְדָּשׁ]

שצא שֶׁלֹּא לְבַטֵּל שְׁמִירַת הַמִּקְדָּשׁ, לָלֶכֶת סְבִיבוֹ תָּמִיד בְּכָל לַיְלָה, שֶׁנֶּאֱמַר
"וּשְׁמַרְתֶּם אֶת מִשְׁמֶרֶת הַקֹּדֶשׁ", וְיָדוּעַ שֶׁלְּשׁוֹן שְׁמִירָה עוֹמֵד בְּמָקוֹם לָאו —
וּכְמוֹ שֶׁאָמְרוּ זִכְרוֹנָם לִבְרָכָה: כָּל מָקוֹם שֶׁנֶּאֱמַר "הִשָּׁמֶר" "פֶּן" וְ"אַל" אֵינוֹ
אֶלָּא לֹא־תַעֲשֶׂה. וְאָמְרוּ בִמְכִלְתָּא: "וְשָׁמְרוּ אֶת מִשְׁמֶרֶת אֹהֶל מוֹעֵד", אֵין לִי
אֶלָּא בַעֲשֵׂה; וּמִנַּיִן בְּלֹא־תַעֲשֶׂה, תַּלְמוּד לוֹמַר "וּשְׁמַרְתֶּם אֶת מִשְׁמֶרֶת הַקֹּדֶשׁ".
עַד כָּאן. (וְאוּלַי דָּרְשׁוּ עֲשֵׂה וְלָאו כְּשֶׁיִּמָּצְאוּ שְׁנֵי הַמִּקְרָאוֹת מוֹרִים עַל דָּבָר אֶחָד,
וּמֵאוֹתוֹ שֶׁבָּא דֶרֶךְ צִוּוּי לִנוֹכֵחַ לָמְדוּ הָעֲשֵׂה, וְהַצִּוּוּי הַנִּסְתָּר שֶׁהוּא קַל מִמֶּנּוּ דָּרְשׁוּ
בַעֲשֵׂה, וְכָל שׁוֹקֵל הַדְּבָרִים בְּמֹאזְנֵי צֶדֶק יוֹדֶה בָּזֶה שֶׁהַנִּסְתָּר קַל מִצִּוּוּי שֶׁהוּא
לִנוֹכֵחַ.)

מִשָּׁרְשֵׁי הַמִּצְוָה עִם קְצָת דִּינֶיהָ כְּמִשְׁפַּט הַסֵּפֶר, כָּתוּב בְּסֵדֶר זֶה בְּמִצְוָה
רִאשׁוֹנָה [סִי' שפ"ח].

---

8. MT *hilchoth bi'ath ha-mikdash* ix 6–7.

9. At the festivities of *Sukkoth*, in the celebration of *simḥath béth ha-sho'évah* (TB Sukkah 51a–b).

10. In conjunction with offerings every day. The original reads, "These are: sprinkling, burning, offering up, [and] pouring libations." This must be, however, the result of a misunderstanding. In Talmudic usage, both *haktarah* (burning) and *hakravah* (offering up) denote making parts (or all) of an offering burn on the altar; hence the original gives only three forms of service. The text has therefore been emended in accord with the sources (TB Yoma 24b, MT *ibid.* 2). Quite possibly an early scribe understood *haktarah* to refer to *k'toreth*, incense, and thus found strangely missing the burning of parts of offerings on the altar; whereupon he added it by the term *hakravah* and condensed the last two (both the pouring of libations) into one. Surprisingly, the point seems to have escaped attention in both MH and MY.

11. See §184, where our author wrote similarly.

§391   1. TB 'Eruvin 96a, etc.

2. Sifre Zuta 292 l. 9; this version is found in Midrash haGadol, Numbers 18:4 (290) and ShM positive precept §22, negative precept §67.

3. From the beginning to here is based on ShM negative precept §67.

[and] of wine.[10] About them it was stated, *and the outsider that draws near shall be put to death* (Numbers 18:7), as it is clarified in the second chapter of the Talmud tractate *Yoma* (24a). The rest of its details are explained there in *Yoma*, and in the last chapter of tractate *Z'vaḥim*.

This prohibition applies to both man and woman at the time the Temple exists, and even at the present time, although it is desolate for our sins.[11] If someone transgresses this and does at [the site of] the Sanctuary, even today, one of the tasks of service that are to be done by *kohanim*, he violates a negative precept, as we have written. And if he does one of the four labors that we mentioned, he is punishable by death at Heaven's hand.

[NOT TO PUT AN END TO THE GUARDING OF THE SANCTUARY]

391 not to stop the guarding of the Sanctuary by walking about every night: for it is written, *And you shall keep the watch of the holy things* (Numbers 18:5), and it is known that the expression of "keeping, watching" occurs in place of an injunction. As the Sages of blessed memory taught:[1] wherever it says, "watch out," "lest" or "do not," it is nothing else but a negative precept. Then it was taught in the Midrash *Mechilta*:[2] *and they shall keep the watch of the tent of meeting* (ibid. 4)—hence I know only that a positive precept is involved; how do we learn of a negative precept?—Scripture states, *And you shall keep watch of the holy things.* Thus far [*Mechilta*].[3] (Now, perhaps they interpreted it as a positive and a negative precept when they found two verses instructing one thing; and from the one given as a command directly [to "you"] they derived the negative precept, whereas the indirect command [to "them"], which is less emphatic, they interpreted as the positive one.[4] Whoever weighs the words on scales of righteousness will acknowledge this, that the indirect expression is less emphatic than the direct command.)

As to the root reason for the precept, along with some of its laws, according to the system of this work, this is written in the first precept in this *sidrah* (§ 388).

4. Essentially (as Horovitz justly notes in his ed. *Sifre Zuta*) the text that the Midrash cites as a negative precept is puzzling, for it seems just as much a positive precept as the first text. And if (as our author writes above) we take it as a negative precept because its verb, *ush'martem* (And you shall keep watch) can be linked to *hishamer* (watch out), which by the rule of the Sages always denotes a negative

[מִצְוַת פִּדְיוֹן בְּכוֹר אָדָם]

שצב לִפְדּוֹת בְּכוֹר אָדָם, כְּלוֹמַר שֶׁמִּצְוָה עַל כָּל אִישׁ מִיִּשְׂרָאֵל שֶׁיִּפְדֶּה מִן הַכֹּהֵן בְּנוֹ שֶׁהוּא בְּכוֹר לְאִמּוֹ הַיִּשְׂרְאֵלִית, שֶׁנֶּאֱמַר: אַךְ פָּדֹה תִפְדֶּה אֵת בְּכוֹר הָאָדָם. וּמְצָאנוּ בְּמָקוֹם אַחֵר שֶׁתָּלָה הַכָּתוּב הַבְּכוֹרָה בְּפֶטֶר רֶחֶם, שֶׁנֶּאֱמַר בְּסֵדֶר בֹּא אֶל פַּרְעֹה: כָּל בְּכוֹר פֶּטֶר כָּל רֶחֶם בִּבְנֵי יִשְׂרָאֵל בָּאָדָם וּבַבְּהֵמָה לִי הוּא; וּפֵרוּשׁ פֶּטֶר רֶחֶם—פְּתִיחַת רֶחֶם, כְּלוֹמַר שֶׁהָיָה רִאשׁוֹן לִפְתֹּחַ רֶחֶם אִמּוֹ; וּמִפְּנֵי־ כֵן אָמְרוּ זִכְרוֹנָם לִבְרָכָה שֶׁהַבָּא אַחַר הַנְּפָלִים, כָּל נֵפֶל שֶׁאִמּוֹ טְמֵאָה לֵדָה מֵחֲמָתוֹ, הַבָּא אַחֲרָיו אֵינוֹ בְכוֹר לַכֹּהֵן, מִפְּנֵי שֶׁלֹּא פָתַח זֶה רֶחֶם אִמּוֹ, שֶׁהַנֵּפֶל פְּתָחוֹ, שֶׁקָּדַם לוֹ; אֲבָל כָּל נֵפֶל שֶׁאֵין אִמּוֹ טְמֵאָה לֵדָה בִּשְׁבִילוֹ, הַבָּא אַחֲרָיו בְּכוֹר לַכֹּהֵן. וּבְמַסֶּכֶת נִדָּה יִתְבָּאֵר חִלּוּק זֶה.

וּבְמַסֶּכֶת בְּכוֹרוֹת יִתְבָּאֵר כְּמוֹ־כֵן אֵיזֶהוּ בְכוֹר לַכֹּהֵן וְלֹא לְנַחֲלָה, אוֹ בְכוֹר לְנַחֲלָה וְלֹא לַכֹּהֵן; גַּם אָמְרוּ שָׁם שֶׁיֵּשׁ בְּכוֹר לַכֹּל, וְיֵשׁ שֶׁאֵינוֹ בְכוֹר לְאֶחָד מֵהֶם.

מִשָּׁרְשֵׁי הַמִּצְוָה, כָּתַבְתִּי מַה שֶּׁיָּדַעְתִּי בְּסֵדֶר בֹּא אֶל פַּרְעֹה, עֲשֵׂה ו׳ [סי׳ י״ח].

מִדִּינֵי הַמִּצְוָה, מַה שֶּׁאָמְרוּ זִכְרוֹנָם לִבְרָכָה שֶׁמִּצְוַת הַפִּדְיוֹן הוּא מְשֶׁיֵּשׁ לוֹ שְׁלֹשִׁים יוֹם וָמַעְלָה, שֶׁיֵּצֵא מִכְּלָל נֵפֶל, שֶׁנֶּאֱמַר: וּפְדוּיָו מִבֶּן חֹדֶשׁ תִּפְדֶּה. וּמִצְוָה זוֹ מֻשֶּׁלֶת עַל הָאָב; עָבַר הָאָב וְלֹא רָצָה לִפְדּוֹתוֹ, מִצְוָה עַל הַבֵּן לִפְדּוֹת עַצְמוֹ

---

precept, so can the verb in the first text, *v'sham'ru* (and they shall keep watch). Hence the explanation that the first text, an indirect command, is taken "at its face value": as a positive precept; while the second text, a direct command, is more emphatic and stern, and is therefore understood as a negative precept, by linking the verb to *hishamer* in the rule of the Sages.

This entire part in parentheses, however, is not in the oldest manuscripts or in any but the first edition. Although the sentence that follows does seem in the author's style, it may therefore yet be doubted if this came from his pen rather than from a later interpolation.

§392   1. I.e. a Jewish woman whose father is neither a *kohen* nor a Levite.

2. To clarify the uncommon Hebrew term, our author adds: The meaning of *petter rehem* is the opening of the womb, i.e. that he was the first to open his mother's womb [on being born].

3. TB B'choroth 46a, 47b; and see TB Niddah 21a, 24b.

4. I.e. between delivered fetuses and emissions in miscarriage which would render a woman ritually unclean, and those which would not.

5. I.e. to receive two shares of the father's legacy, as though he were two sons, which is generally the firstborn son's birthright.

6. TB B'choroth 48a, etc.

392 to redeem a human firstborn; in other words, it is a religious duty for every man among the Jewish people to redeem from the *kohen* his son who is the firstborn of his Israelite mother:[1] as it is stated, *but you shall redeem surely the firstborn of man* (Numbers 18:15). We find in another instance that Scripture expressed being firstborn as being the first to leave a womb: for it is stated in *sidrah bo, every firstborn, whatever opens the womb among the Israelites, both of man and of beast, is Mine* (Exodus 13:2).[2] For this reason, the Sages of blessed memory taught[3] that anyone that comes after stillborn infants—anything stillborn or aborted because of which its mother is ritually unclean on account of birth—is not a firstborn for a *kohen* [to be redeemed by him], because this one did not open his mother's womb, since the stillborn infant opened it, having come before him. But anything aborted because of which the mother is not ritually unclean on account of birth—whoever comes after it is a firstborn to [be redeemed by] a *kohen*. In the Talmud tractate *Niddah* (21a) this differentiation[4] is clarified.

In the tractate *B'choroth* (46a, 47b) it is likewise explained who is a firstborn in regard to a *kohen* but not for inheritance,[5] or for inheritance but not in regard to a *kohen*. It was further stated there that there is one who is a firstborn in both respects, and one who is a firstborn in neither of these respects.

As to the root reason for the precept, I wrote what I knew in *sidrah bo*, in the sixth positive precept (§ 18).

Among the laws of the precept, there is what the Sages of blessed memory taught:[6] that the religious duty of redemption applies from the time he is thirty days old and onward, since he has left the category of those [possibly] stillborn[7]—as it is stated, *As for their redemption, from the age of a month you shall redeem them* (Numbers 18:16). This religious duty lies on the father to fulfill.[8] If the father transgressed and did not wish to redeem him, the obligation lies on the son to redeem himself from [the time] that he grows up.[8] The

7. If a child dies within its first thirty days, it is regarded as though stillborn, i.e. as having come into the world without the ability to survive.

8. TB Kiddushin 29a.

מִשֶּׁיַּגְדִּיל. וְהַפִּדְיוֹן הוּא בֵּין בְּכֶסֶף הַשָּׁוֶה חָמֵשׁ סְלָעִים, בֵּין בְּשָׁוֶה־כֶסֶף מִן הַמִּטַּלְטְלִין, שֶׁגּוּפָן מָמוֹן; יָצְאוּ עֲבָדִים וְקַרְקָעוֹת וּשְׁטָרוֹת, שֶׁאִם פָּדָהוּ בָהֶן אֵינוֹ פָּדוּי.

חָמֵשׁ סְלָעִים שֶׁל פִּדְיוֹן הָאָב, יָכוֹל לִתְּנָם לְכֹהֵן אֶחָד אוֹ לְכֹהֲנִים הַרְבֵּה; וְהֶחָיּוּב לִתְּנוֹ לְכֹהֵן זָכָר וְלֹא לְכֹהֶנֶת, דְּ"אַהֲרֹן וּבָנָיו" כְּתִיב בְּכֶסֶף פִּדְיוֹן בְּכוֹר; וְאִם רָצָה הַכֹּהֵן לְהַחֲזִיר לוֹ הַפִּדְיוֹן אַחַר שֶׁנְּתָנוֹ לוֹ, יָצָא יְדֵי חוֹבָה, וּבִלְבָד שֶׁלֹּא יִתְּנֶנּוּ הוּא לוֹ עַל־מְנָת כֵּן; וְאִם נְתָנוֹ לוֹ עַל־מְנָת כֵּן אֵין בְּנוֹ פָּדוּי, עַד שֶׁיִּגְמֹר בְּלִבּוֹ לִתְּנוֹ לוֹ מַתָּנָה גְמוּרָה; וְאִם פֵּרֵשׁ וְנָתַן לוֹ עַל־מְנָת לְהַחֲזִיר, וְנִתְפַּיֵּס הַכֹּהֵן בְּכָךְ, בְּנוֹ פָּדוּי.

וְכֵן לְמָדוּנוּ רַבּוֹתֵינוּ שֶׁבְּזְמַנֵּנוּ, שֶׁבְּסֵדֶר כָּזֶה עוֹשִׂין פִּדְיוֹן הַבֵּן: מְבִיאִין כּוֹס יַיִן וַהֲדַס לְבֵית אֲבִי הַבֵּן אוֹ לְמָקוֹם אַחֵר, וְהַכֹּהֵן שֶׁיִּבְחַר בּוֹ הָאָב לָתֵת לוֹ פִּדְיוֹן בְּנוֹ, מְבָרֵךְ תְּחִלָּה עַל הַיַּיִן וְעַל הַהֲדַס, וְאַחַר־כָּךְ מְבָרֵךְ בְּרָכָה זוֹ: בָּרוּךְ אַתָּה יי אֱלֹהֵינוּ מֶלֶךְ הָעוֹלָם אֲשֶׁר קִדֵּשׁ עֻבָּר בִּמְעֵי אִמּוֹ, וּלְאַרְבָּעִים יוֹם חִלֵּק אֶת אֵיבָרָיו רמ"ח אֵיבָרִים, וְאַחַר־כָּךְ נָפַח בּוֹ נְשָׁמָה, כְּדִכְתִיב: "וַיִּפַּח בְּאַפָּיו" וְגוֹמֵר, עוֹר וּבָשָׂר הִלְבִּישׁוֹ וּבַעֲצָמוֹת וְגִידִים סְכָכוֹ, כְּדִכְתִיב: "עוֹר וּבָשָׂר תַּלְבִּישֵׁנִי וּבַעֲצָמוֹת וְגִידִים תְּשֹׂכְכֵנִי", וְצִוָּה לוֹ מַאֲכָל וּמִשְׁתֶּה דְּבַשׁ וְחָלָב לְהִתְעַנֵּג בּוֹ, וְזִמֵּן לוֹ שְׁנֵי מַלְאֲכֵי הַשָּׁרֵת לְשָׁמְרוֹ בְתוֹךְ מְעֵי אִמּוֹ, כְּדִכְתִיב "חַיִּים וָחֶסֶד" וְגוֹמֵר. אִמּוֹ אוֹמֶרֶת: זֶה בְּנִי בְכוֹרִי שֶׁבּוֹ פָּתַח הַקָּדוֹשׁ בָּרוּךְ הוּא דַלְתֵי בִטְנִי. אָבִיו אוֹמֵר: זֶה בְּנִי בְכוֹרִי הוּא וַאֲנִי מֻזְהָר לִפְדוֹתוֹ, שֶׁנֶּאֱמַר: "וְכֹל בְּכוֹר אָדָם בְּבָנֶיךָ תִּפְדֶּה"; יְהִי

9. TB B'choroth 49b.

10. Deeds are excluded because they are valued not for what they are but for what they can yield; slaves and land are excluded by the interpretation of Scriptural texts.

11. *Ibid.* 51a.

12. *Ibid.* 51b.

13. Numbers 18:8, 16; so MT *hilchoth bikkurim* i 10; *tosafoth,* TB P'saḥim 49b, s.v. *'amar,* differs.

14. TB Kiddushin 6b.

15. Derived from Ramban, *hilchoth b'choroth* v, who cites it as "an olden usage of the *ge'onim*"; and R. 'Ashér (Rosh), *hilchoth pidyon b'chor* §1, also cites this. The authoritative practice observed today differs.

16. On the wine: "Blessed art Thou…who created the fruit of the vine"; on the myrtle branch: "Blessed art Thou…who created branches of fragrance."

redemption may be either for money in 'the amount of five *s'la'im* [shekels] or for the equivalent of money[9] in movable goods which have inherent value, so that slaves, landed property and deeds are excluded:[10] If one was redeemed for them, he is not redeemed [it is not valid].[11]

As to the five *s'la'im* [shekels] for the redemption, the father may give them to one *kohen* or to many *kohanim*.[12] But the obligation is to give it to a male *kohen*, and not to a female: for Aaron and his sons are mentioned in connection with the money for the redemption of a firstborn.[13] If the *kohen* wishes to return him the redemption money after he gave it to him, he has [nevertheless] acquitted himself of his obligation;[11] only, he should not give it him [to the *kohen*, originally] on this condition. If he did give it him on this condition [that the *kohen* should return the money] his son is not redeemed[12]—not until he resolves in his heart to give it him [the *kohen*] as a complete gift. However, if he was explicit and did give it him on condition that it be given back, and the *kohen* was amenable to it, his son is redeemed.[14]

Now, so our sages of our time taught us, that by this procedure the redemption of a son is carried out:[15] A cup of wine and a myrtle branch are brought to the house of the son's father or to some other place. The *kohen* whom the father has chosen to give him the redemption fee for his son then recites the first benedictions on the wine and the myrtle branch.[16] After that he says this benediction: "Blessed art Thou, Lord our God, king of the world, who sanctified the embryo in his mother's womb and at forty days articulated its limbs, 248 organs and limbs, and afterward breathed a soul-spirit into it—as it is written, *and He breathed into his nostrils a living spirit* (Genesis 2:7). In skin and flesh did He array it, and with bones and sinews did He knit it together, as it is written, *Thou didst clothe me with skin and flesh, and knit me together with bones and sinews* (Job 10:11). And He ordained food and drink for him, honey and milk to delight in, and did assign him two ministering angels to protect him within his mother's womb, as it is written, *Thou hast granted me life and loving-kindness, and Thy providence has preserved my spirit* (ibid. 12). Now, his mother says, 'This is my firstborn son, with whom the Holy One, blessed is He, opened the doors of my womb.' His father says, 'This is my firstborn son, and I am adjured to redeem him, as it is stated, *and every firstborn of man among your sons you shall redeem* (Exodus 13:13).' May it be Thy will,

רָצוֹן מִלְּפָנֶיךָ יי אֱלֹהַי שֶׁכְּשֵׁם שֶׁזִּכִּיתָ אָבִיו לִפְדּוֹתוֹ, כֵּן תְּזַכֵּהוּ לְתוֹרָה חֻפָּה וּמַעֲשִׂים טוֹבִים. בָּרוּךְ אַתָּה יי מְקַדֵּשׁ בְּכוֹרֵי יִשְׂרָאֵל לְפִדְיוֹנָם.

וַאֲבִי הַבֵּן מְבָרֵךְ שְׁתַּיִם: "עַל פִּדְיוֹן הַבֵּן" וְ"שֶׁהֶחֱיָנוּ"; וְנוֹתֵן לַכֹּהֵן הַפִּדְיוֹן הַיָּדוּעַ, שֶׁהוּא חָמֵשׁ סְלָעִים כְּמוֹ שֶׁקָּצוּב בַּתּוֹרָה, וְהֵם שִׁשִּׁים (ארגיר"ץ) [ארגינ"ץ] שֶׁל כֶּסֶף צָרוּף בְּמִשְׁקַל אַרְצֵנוּ. וְאַחַר הַפִּדְיוֹן מְבָרֵךְ הַכֹּהֵן שְׁלֹשָׁה בְּרָכוֹת אֵלּוּ שֶׁכָּתַבְנוּ. עוֹד כָּתַב הָרַב מֹשֶׁה בֶּן נַחְמָן זִכְרוֹנוֹ לִבְרָכָה, שֶׁבְּשָׁעָה שֶׁנּוֹתֵן הָאָב כֶּסֶף פִּדְיוֹנוֹ לַכֹּהֵן, שֶׁנּוֹתֵן בְּנוֹ בְּיַד הַכֹּהֵן, וְאוֹמֵר לוֹ הַכֹּהֵן: "אִי זֶה חָבִיב עָלֶיךָ יוֹתֵר: בִּנְךָ אוֹ חָמֵשׁ סְלָעִים הַלָּלוּ", וְהָאָב מֵשִׁיב: "בְּנִי חָבִיב עָלַי". מִיָּד נוֹטֵל הַכֹּהֵן הַדִּינָרִין וּמוֹלִיכָן בְּיָדוֹ עַל רֹאשׁ הַבֵּן, וְאוֹמֵר: "זֶה תַּחַת זֶה, זֶה חִלּוּף זֶה, זֶה מָחוּל עַל זֶה, יֵצֵא זֶה לַכֹּהֵן וְיִכָּנֵס זֶה הַבֵּן לְחַיִּים וּלְתוֹרָה וּלְיִרְאַת שָׁמַיִם. יְהִי רָצוֹן שֶׁכְּשֵׁם שֶׁנִּכְנַס לְפִדְיוֹן, כֵּן יִכָּנֵס לְתוֹרָה, חֻפָּה וּמַעֲשִׂים טוֹבִים, וְנֹאמַר אָמֵן".

וְנוֹתֵן הַכֹּהֵן אֶת יָדָיו עַל רֹאשׁ הַבֵּן, וּמְבָרְכוֹ כְּפִי שֶׁיּוֹדֵעַ לְבָרְכוֹ, כְּגוֹן "הַשֵּׁם שֶׁמְּרֶךָ" וְגוֹמֵר, "כִּי אֹרֶךְ יָמִים וּשְׁנוֹת חַיִּים" וְגוֹמֵר, "הַשֵּׁם יִשְׁמָרְךָ מִכָּל רַע יִשְׁמֹר אֶת נַפְשֶׁךָ" וְגוֹמֵר; וְנוֹטֵל הַכֹּהֵן הַכֶּסֶף, וּמוֹצִיאוֹ לְכָל חֶפְצוֹ. וְיֶתֶר פְּרָטֶיהָ, בְּמַסֶּכֶת בְּכוֹרוֹת.

וְנוֹהֶגֶת מִצְוָה זוֹ בְּכָל מָקוֹם וּבְכָל זְמַן, בְּיִשְׂרְאֵלִים הַזְּכָרִים, אֲבָל לֹא בַּנְּקֵבוֹת;

17. I.e. it begins, "Blessed art Thou, Lord our God, king of the world, who hallowed us with His *mitzvoth* and commanded us."

18. It begins, "Blessed art Thou, Lord our God, king of the world"; TB P'saḥim 121b.

19. See §313, note 11. Earlier, Ramban likewise gives the value of a *sela'* (=the sacred *shekel*) as 12 *argents*, "according to the local currency" (Ramban, *hilchoth b'choroth* viii; in TB ed. Vilna, p. 63a); and he thus gives the amount for *pidyon ha-ben*, redeeming the firstborn, as 60 *argents* (Commentary on TB K'thuboth, end,. cited in R. Shim'on b. Tzemaḥ Duran, *Tashbétz*, III §226). Similarly Rashba, "in the currency of Barcelona": *Responsa*, I §200, §758. King Pedro III, ruler of Aragon and Catalonia from 1276 to 1285, issued a coin known as *denarius argenti*, "silver dinar" (personal communication by Yom Tov Assis, a research scholar on money among Jewry of old). This may have been the minting, or at least one minting, of a silver coin of standard weight and value, known in Jewish sources, in the plural, as ארגינץ. From these sources it seems to have been current in Aragon and Catalonia from the 12th to the 15th century, known perhaps in Aragon as *argent* and in Catalonia as *arienço* (see Zunz, JGL, pp. 554–56) or in the more hispanic form of *arienzo*, which the dictionaries define as "an old Catalonian coin." (Early in the 14th century a silver coin called *argento* was minted in Carpentras near Avignon, in southeast France: W. Carew Hazlitt, *The Coinage of the European Continent*, London 1893, p. 182.)

Lord my God, that even as Thou has granted his father the merit to redeem him, so shalt Thou grant him to merit attaining to the Torah, to the wedding canopy, and to good deeds. Blessed art Thou, Lord, who hallows the firstborn of Israel for their redemption."

The son's father [first] recites two benedictions: "about the redemption of a son,"[17] and "who has granted us life, sustained us, and granted us to reach this season."[18] He gives the *kohen* the known redemption-price, which is five *s'la'im* [shekels] as determined in the Torah, this being sixty *argents*[19] of refined silver in the value of our country. After the redemption, the *kohen* recites these three benedictions that we have written.[20]

Now, R. Moses b. Naḥman [Ramban] of blessed memory wrote further that at the time the father gives the money of his redemption to the *kohen*,[21] he puts his son in the hand of the *kohen*, and the *kohen* says to him, "Which is more dear to you: your son, or these five *s'la'im*?" The father replies, "My son is more dear to me." At once the *kohen* takes the coins and moves them in his hand over the head of the son, as he says, "This instead of that, this in exchange for that, this is given up for that. This shall go to the *kohen*, and that son shall enter into life, Torah, and a reverent fear of Heaven. May it be His will that even as he has been brought to redemption, so may he enter upon Torah study, the wedding canopy, and good deeds; and let us say *Amen*."

The *kohen* then places his hands on the child's head and blesses it as he knows how to bless it: for example, *The Lord be your protector, the Lord be your shade on your right hand* (Psalms 121:5); *for length of days and years of life and peace will they* [the commandments] *add to you* (Proverbs 3:2); *The Lord will keep you from all evil, He will protect your life* (Psalms 121:7), etc. The *kohen* then takes the money, and he may spend it for anything he desires. The rest of its details are in the Talmud tractate *B'choroth*.

This precept is in force everywhere, at every time, for male Israelites (Jews) but not for women. For so we learned in the Oral

20. I.e. on the wine and the myrtle branch, and the long benediction given two paragraphs above.

21. What follows is not found in our editions of Ramban, *hilchoth b'choroth*; cf. sources given in R. Israel al-Nakawa, *Menorath haMa'or* III 488, note to line 6. Cf. also R. 'Ashér, *hilchoth b'choroth* § 1, and *idem* on TB Rosh haShanah, I § 41.

שֶׁכָּךְ קִבַּלְנוּ: שֶׁהָאִישׁ, שֶׁהוּא בְּחִיּוּב לִפְדּוֹת עַצְמוֹ, הוּא חַיָּב לִפְדּוֹת בְּנוֹ, אֲבָל לֹא הָאִשָּׁה, שֶׁהִיא אֵינָהּ בַּת פְּדִיָּה. וְכֵן אֵינָהּ נוֹהֶגֶת בְּכֹהֲנִים וּלְוִיִּים, מִקַּל־וָחֹמֶר: אִם הֵם פָּטְרוּ יִשְׂרָאֵל בַּמִּדְבָּר מִפִּדְיוֹן בְּכוֹרוֹת, דִּין הוּא שֶׁיִּפְטְרוּ אֶת עַצְמָן.

וְעוֹד אָמְרוּ זִכְרוֹנָם לִבְרָכָה, שֶׁאֲפִלּוּ בֶן יִשְׂרָאֵל הַבָּא מִן הַכֹּהֶנֶת אוֹ הַלְּוִיָּה, בְּנוֹ מִמֶּנָּה פָּטוּר מִפִּדְיוֹן, לְפִי שֶׁהַדָּבָר תָּלוּי בָּאֵם, שֶׁבְּפֶטֶר רֶחֶם תָּלָה הַכָּתוּב.

וְעוֹבֵר עַל זֶה וְלֹא פָדָה בְנוֹ מִשֶּׁהוּא רָאוּי, כְּלוֹמַר מִשֶּׁעָבְרוּ עָלָיו שְׁלֹשִׁים יוֹם, אִם מֵת קֹדֶם שֶׁיִּפְדֶּנּוּ, בִּטֵּל עֲשֵׂה זֶה, וְאוֹי לוֹ שֶׁנָּשָׂא עֲוֹנוֹ עַל נַפְשׁוֹ. וְאַף־עַל־פִּי שֶׁאֵין לַמִּצְוָה זוֹ זְמַן קָבוּעַ, דְּבָכָל שַׁעְתָּא וְשַׁעְתָּא אַחַר שְׁלֹשִׁים יוֹם זְמַנָּהּ הִיא, אַף־עַל־פִּי־כֵן "חֲכַם לֵב יִקַּח מִצְוֹת", וִיקַדֵּם וְיַעֲשֶׂה מִיָּד שֶׁאֶפְשָׁר לוֹ, "וְחֵפֶץ ה' בְּיָדוֹ יִצְלָח".

וּלְפִי הַדּוֹמֶה, שֶׁהָאָב חַיָּב לְעוֹלָם לִפְדּוֹת בְּנוֹ, וַאֲפִלּוּ אַחַר שֶׁהִגְדִּיל הַבֵּן הַמִּצְוָה מֻטֶּלֶת עַל הָאָב, וּכְמוֹ שֶׁאָמַר הַכָּתוּב: וְכָל בְּכוֹר אָדָם בְּבָנֶיךָ תִּפְדֶּה; הֲרֵי שֶׁהִטִּיל הַמִּצְוָה עַל הָאָב; וְכֵן נִרְאֶה בְקִדּוּשִׁין.

[שֶׁלֹּא לִפְדּוֹת בְּכוֹר בְּהֵמָה טְהוֹרָה]

שצג שֶׁלֹּא נִפְדֶּה בְכוֹר בְּהֵמָה טְהוֹרָה. מִפְּנֵי שֶׁהַתּוֹרָה צִוְּתָה לִפְדּוֹת פֶּטֶר חֲמוֹר, אוּלַי יַעֲלֶה עַל דַּעְתֵּנוּ לִפְדּוֹת גַּם־כֵּן בְּכוֹר בְּהֵמָה טְהוֹרָה בִּבְהֵמָה אַחֶרֶת, עַל־כֵּן בָּאַתְנוּ הַמְּנִיעָה בָזֶה שֶׁלֹּא נִפְדֶּה אוֹתוֹ לְעוֹלָם; וַאֲפִלּוּ עָבַר וּפְדָהוּ אֵינוֹ פָּדוּי, וְעַל זֶה נֶאֱמַר "אַךְ בְּכוֹר שׁוֹר אוֹ בְכוֹר כֶּשֶׂב אוֹ בְכוֹר עֵז לֹא תִפְדֶּה קֹדֶשׁ הֵם"; בֵּאֵר הַכָּתוּב שָׁלֹשׁ הַבְּהֵמוֹת הַטְּהוֹרוֹת שֶׁהֵן בְּחִיּוּב מִצְוַת בְּכוֹר, כִּי מִינֵי

22. See Numbers 8:16–18 that the Levites replaced the firstborn as those consecrated to the Lord; thus they freed the firstborn from their hallowed state.

23. Since by being members of the tribe of Lévi, they had a holiness that absorbed and superseded the consecration of the firstborn; TB B'choroth 3b.

24. *Ibid.* 4a.

25. Perhaps from R. Judah's teaching that if a man has the duty of redeeming both himself and his son, his son takes precedence, because the obligation to redeem him is his father's (MY); or perhaps because the Talmud (Kiddushin 29a) lists this among other obligations that a father has toward his son, and the others clearly remain in effect when the son is grown—although the obligation lies on the son as well (MH).

§393   1. His action has no validity.

Tradition:[8] that a man, having the obligation to redeem himself, has the obligation to redeem his son; but not a woman, since she is not capable of being redeemed. So does it also not apply to *kohanim* and Levites, by *kal va-ḥomer* [reasoning from the less to the more]: If they freed the Israelites in the wilderness from redeeming the firstborn,[22] it is certainly just that they should free themselves.[23]

Our Sages of blessed memory taught further[24] that even an Israelite born to a female *kohen* or Levite—any son from her—is free of the duty of redemption, since the matter derives from the mother, as the Writ made it depend on being the first from the womb.

If a person transgressed this and did not redeem his son from the time he was fit for it, i.e. since he reached the age of thirty days, if he should die before redeeming him, he would have disobeyed this positive precept. Then woe to him that he bore his sin on his spirit. Hence, even though there is no fixed period for this precept, since every single hour after thirty days is its proper time, nevertheless, *the wise in heart will take precepts* (proverbs 10:8), and he will act early to observe it as soon as he is able to, *and the desire of the Lord will succeed in his hand* (Isaiah 53:10).

Now, as it seems, the father is always obligated to redeem his son; even after the son grows up, the religious duty lies on the father. As Scripture states, *every firstborn of man among your sons* you *shall redeem* (Exodus 13:13); thus it imposed the duty on the father; and so it also appears in the Talmud tractate *Kiddushin* (29a).[25]

[NOT TO REDEEM THE FIRSTLING OF A KOSHER DOMESTIC ANIMAL]

393 that we should not redeem the firstling of a pure (kosher) domestic animal; since the Torah ordained that the firstling of a donkey should be redeemed (§ 22), it might perhaps occur to us to redeem likewise the firstling of a pure animal [exchanging it] for another animal; therefore this restriction was given us, that we should never redeem it; and even if one transgressed and did redeem it, it is not redeemed.[1] Hence it is stated, *But the firstling of an ox, or the firstling of a sheep, or the firstling of a goat, you shall not redeem: they are holy* (Numbers 18:17). Scripture made it clear that it is the three kinds of pure domestic animals which are under the obligation of the precept of the firstborn animal; for the kinds of wild [kosher] animal, which

הַחַיָּה, שֶׁהֵן שִׁבְעָה, אֵינָם בְּתוֹרַת בְּכוֹרוֹת, וּכְמוֹ שֶׁכָּתַבְתִּי בְּסֵדֶר בֹּא עֲשֵׂה ו' סִימָן
(ט') [י"ח].

מִשָּׁרְשֵׁי מִצְוַת הַבְּכוֹר לְתִתּוֹ לַכֹּהֵן, כָּתַבְתִּי שָׁם, וְעִנְיַן הָאַזְהָרָה שֶׁלֹּא לִפְדּוֹתוֹ
נִקְשָׁר עִמּוֹ, וְקָחֶנּוּ מִשָּׁם.

דִּינֵי הַמִּצְוָה, כָּתַב הָרַב מֹשֶׁה בֶּן מַיְמוֹן זִכְרוֹנוֹ לִבְרָכָה: הַבְּכוֹר, כְּמוֹ שֶׁאֵין
פּוֹדִין אוֹתוֹ, כָּךְ אֵין הַכֹּהֵן יָכוֹל לְמָכְרוֹ בְּעוֹדוֹ תָם, דְּכֵיוָן שֶׁהוּא עוֹמֵד לְקָרְבָּן, אֵין
לַכֹּהֵן זְכוּת בּוֹ לְמָכְרוֹ. וּבַזְּמַן הַזֶּה שֶׁאֵין בַּיִת, הוֹאִיל וְלַאֲכִילָה עוֹמֵד הֲרֵי זֶה מֻתָּר
לְמָכְרוֹ וְאַף־עַל־פִּי שֶׁהוּא תָּמִים, בֵּין לְכֹהֵן בֵּין לְיִשְׂרָאֵל. עַד כָּאן.

וַדַּאי שֶׁזֶּה שֶׁאָמַר רַבֵּנוּ זִכְרוֹנוֹ לִבְרָכָה "הוֹאִיל וְלַאֲכִילָה עוֹמֵד",
כַּוָּנָתוֹ לוֹמַר
לִכְשֶׁיִּפּוֹל בּוֹ מוּם; וּבְכוֹר בַּעַל מוּם יֵשׁ לַכֹּהֵן לְמָכְרוֹ בְּכָל זְמַן, בֵּין בִּפְנֵי הַבַּיִת
וְשֶׁלֹּא בִּפְנֵי הַבַּיִת, בֵּין חַי בֵּין שָׁחוּט, לְכָל אָדָם וַאֲפִלּוּ לְגוֹי, דְּכָחֳלִין גְּמוּרִין הוּא,
וּכְמוֹ שֶׁכָּתוּב: הַטָּמֵא וְהַטָּהוֹר יֹאכְלֶנּוּ כַּצְּבִי וְכָאַיָּל. וּמִכָּל־מָקוֹם הִזְהִירוּ חֲכָמִים
שֶׁלֹּא לְמָכְרוֹ בַּשּׁוּק דֶּרֶךְ פַּרְהֶסְיָא, אֶלָּא בַּבַּיִת. וְיֶתֶר פְּרָטֶיהָ, מְבֹאָרִים בְּמַסֶּכֶת
בְּכוֹרוֹת.

וְנוֹהֶגֶת מִצְוָה זוֹ בְּאֶרֶץ־יִשְׂרָאֵל, כְּמוֹ מִצְוַת קִדּוּשׁ בְּכוֹר בְּהֵמָה טְהוֹרָה, שֶׁהוּא
נוֹהֵג בָּאָרֶץ בִּלְבַד כְּדַעַת קְצָת הַמְּפָרְשִׁים, בֵּין בִּפְנֵי הַבַּיִת וְשֶׁלֹּא בִּפְנֵי הַבַּיִת,
שֶׁנֶּאֱמַר "וְאָכַלְתָּ לִפְנֵי יי אֱלֹהֶיךָ ... מַעְשַׂר דְּגָנְךָ וְכֹּלֹי וּבְכֹרֹת בְּקָרְךָ וְצֹאנֶךָ",
וְדָרְשׁוּ זִכְרוֹנָם לִבְרָכָה: מִמָּקוֹם שֶׁאַתָּה מֵבִיא מַעֲשֵׂר, דְּהַיְנוּ אֶרֶץ־יִשְׂרָאֵל, אַתָּה
מֵבִיא בְּכוֹר צֹאן וּבָקָר. וּמִי שֶׁהֵבִיא מֵחוּצָה לָאָרֶץ בְּכוֹר לָאָרֶץ אֵין מְקַבְּלִין
הֵימֶנּוּ, וְלֹא יִקְרַב, דְּחֻלִּין גְּמוּרִין הוּא.

וְהַכֹּל חַיָּבִין בְּמִצְוָה זוֹ, כֹּהֲנִים לְוִיִּם וְיִשְׂרְאֵלִים, שֶׁנֶּאֱמַר: כָּל הַבְּכוֹר אֲשֶׁר
יִוָּלֵד וְגוֹמֵר. וְאַף־עַל־פִּי שֶׁנִּפְטְרוּ כֹהֲנִים וּלְוִיִּם מִפִּדְיוֹן בְּכוֹר אָדָם וּפֶטֶר חֲמוֹר,

2. So TB B'choroth 6a; the seven are listed in Deuteronomy 14:5.
3. MT *hilchoth b'choroth* i 17.
4. Derived from Mishnah, Ma'asér Shéni i 2, TB Bava Kamma 12b, T'murah 7b.
5. Derived from TB B'choroth 32b, 33a. MT *hilchoth b'choroth* i 3.
6. *Ibid.* 31a.
7. TB T'murah 21b.
8. Cf. MT *ibid.* 5.

are seven, are not included in the teaching about firstlings,[2] as I wrote in the sixth positive precept of *sidrah bo* (§ 18).

About the root reasons for the precept of the firstborn animal, to give it to a *kohen*, I wrote there (§ 18); and the significance of the admonition not to redeem it is connected with that; then gather it from there.

As to the laws of the precept, R. Moses b. Maimon [Rambam] of blessed memory wrote:[3] Just as one is not to redeem a firstling, so can a *kohen* not sell it while it is whole, unblemished; for since it is due to be an offering, the *kohen* has no right in it to sell it. At the present time, though, when there is no Temple, since it is due to be eaten, it is permissible to sell it even if it is whole, unblemished, either to a *kohen* or to an Israelite. Thus far his words.

Now, certainly, when our master sage of blessed memory said, "since it is due to be eaten," he meant to convey, when it would acquire a disfiguring blemish. A blemished firstling may be sold by a *kohen* at any time, both when the Temple exists and when it does not, whether it is alive or ritually slain,[4] [and he may thus sell it] to any man, even to a non-Jew;[5] for it is as a completely non-holy animal; as it is written, *the unclean and the clean alike may eat it, like the gazelle and like the hart* (Deuteronomy 15:22). Nevertheless, the Sages adjured us not to sell it in the market, publicly, but only in the house [privately].[6] The rest of its details are explained in the Talmud tractate *B'choroth.*

This precept is in effect in the land of Israel, like the precept of consecrating the firstling of a pure [kosher] domestic animal (§ 18), which is in force in that land alone, in the view of some authorities, both when the Temple exists and when it does not. For it is stated, *And you shall eat before the Lord your God... the tithe of your grain... and the firstlings of your herd and flock* (Deuteronomy 14:23); and our Sages of blessed memory interpreted:[7] From the place whence you bring the tithe, i.e. the land of Israel, you are to bring the firstlings of your flock and herd. If anyone brings a firstborn animal to the land [of Israel] from another country, it is not accepted from him, and is not to be offered up, since it is completely non-holy.[8]

All are obligated to observe this precept: *kohanim*, Levites and Israelites; for it is stated, *Every firstling that is born*, etc. (Deuteronomy 15:19). Although *kohanim* and Levites were freed from the obligation of redeeming a human firstborn and the firstling of a donkey, as we

כְּמוֹ שֶׁכָּתַבְנוּ בְּכָל אֶחָד מֵהֶם בְּסֵדֶר זֶה וּבְסֵדֶר בֹּא אֶל פַּרְעֹה, חַיָּבִין הֵם בָּזוֹ.

וְעוֹבֵר עַל זֶה וּפָדָה בְכוֹר בְּהֵמָה טְהוֹרָה, אַף־עַל־פִּי שֶׁלֹּא הוֹעִילוּ מַעֲשָׂיו וְאֵינוֹ פָדוּי, אֶלָּא בִּקְדֻשָּׁתוֹ הוּא כְּמוֹ שֶׁהָיָה, עָבַר עַל לָאו; שֶׁלְּעִנְיַן הַעֲבָרַת הַלָּאו לֹא אִכְפַּת לָן אִי אַהֲנוּ מַעֲשָׂיו אוֹ לָא, וְכִדְאִיתָא בִּתְמוּרָה פֶּרֶק רִאשׁוֹן בְּמַחֲלֹקֶת אַבַּיֵּי וְרָבָא. אֲבָל אֵינוּ לוֹקֶה, לְפִי שֶׁאֶפְשָׁר לַעֲבֹר עָלָיו מִבְּלִי מַעֲשֶׂה.

[מִצְוַת עֲבוֹדַת הַלֵּוִי בַּמִּקְדָּשׁ]

שצד לִהְיוֹת הַלְוִיִּים עוֹבְדִים בַּמִּקְדָּשׁ, לִהְיוֹת שׁוֹעֲרִים וּמְשׁוֹרְרִים בְּכָל יוֹם עַל הַקָּרְבָּן, שֶׁנֶּאֱמַר "וְעָבַד הַלֵּוִי הוּא" וְגוֹמֵר; וּלְשׁוֹן סִפְרִי: שׁוֹמֵעַ אֲנִי אִם רָצָה יַעֲבֹד וְאִם לֹא רָצָה לֹא יַעֲבֹד, תַּלְמוּד לוֹמַר "וְעָבַד הַלֵּוִי הוּא"—עַל כָּרְחוֹ; כְּלוֹמַר שֶׁהַדָּבָר הַהוּא חוֹבָה וְעִנְיָן מֻטָּל עָלָיו בְּהֶכְרֵחַ.

וְנִתְבָּאֵר כְּמוֹ־כֵן בְּפֶרֶק שֵׁנִי מֵעֲרָכִין, שֶׁהַשִּׁיר בַּפֶּה לֹא יֹאמַר אוֹתוֹ לְעוֹלָם אֶלָּא הַלֵּוִי. וְנִכְפְּלָה מִצְוָה זוֹ בְּלָשׁוֹן אַחֵר בַּתּוֹרָה, שֶׁנֶּאֱמַר: וְשֵׁרֵת בְּשֵׁם יְיָ אֱלֹהָיו; וְאָמְרוּ שָׁם בַּעֲרָכִין: אֵי זֶהוּ שֵׁרוּת שֶׁהוּא בְּשֵׁם יְיָ, הֱוֵי אוֹמֵר זוֹ שִׁירָה.

מִשָּׁרְשֵׁי הַמִּצְוָה, לְפִי שֶׁכְּבוֹד הַמֶּלֶךְ וְהַמָּקוֹם הוּא לִהְיוֹת שָׁם אֲנָשִׁים יְדוּעִים מִשֵּׁבֶט יָדוּעַ קְבוּעִים לְשֵׁרוּת, וְלֹא יִכָּנֵס זָר בֵּינֵיהֶם לַעֲבוֹדָה, כְּעֵין מַלְכוּתָא דְאַרְעָא: יְמַנּוּ לָהֶם אֲנָשִׁים יְדוּעִים נִכְבָּדִים לִהְיוֹת כָּל מְלֶאכֶת הַהֵיכָל נַעֲשִׂית עַל־יָדָם, כִּי לֹא רָאוּי לְמֶלֶךְ שֶׁיְּשַׁנֶּה בְּכָל יוֹם מְשָׁרְתִים לְפָנָיו, וְיִהְיוּ הַכֹּל מִשְׁתַּמְּשִׁים בְּכֶתֶר שֵׁרוּת הַמֶּלֶךְ; זֶה דָבָר בָּרוּר הוּא.

---

9. TB B'choroth 13a; MT *ibid.* 7.

§394   1. Sifre, Numbers § 119.

2. Because the verse means more literally, "*with* the name of the Lord," and in their singing the Levites pronounced His holy name (Rashi, TB 'Arachin 11a, s.v. *b'shém*). From the beginning to here is based on ShM positive precept § 23.

wrote about each in its proper place, in this *sidrah* (§ 392) and in *sidrah bo* (§ 18), they are obligated to observe this.[9]

If someone transgressed this and redeemed the firstling of a pure (kosher) domestic animal, even though his action availed nothing and it is not redeemed, but rather remains in its consecration as it was, he violated a negative precept. For in regard to violating an injunction, it is of no concern to us whether his actions were effective or not, as we read in the first chapter of the tractate *T'murah* (4b), in the controversy between Abbaye and Rava. But he would not receive whiplashes, since it is possible to transgress it without any physical action.

[THE PRECEPT OF THE LEVITE'S SERVICE AT THE SANCTUARY]

394 that the Levites should serve at the Sanctuary, to be gatekeepers and singers over the offerings every day: for it is stated, *And the Levite, he shall do the service of the tent of meeting* (Numbers 18:23). In the language of the Midrash *Sifre*:[1] I might understand that if he wished he might serve, and if he did not wish to, he need not serve; hence Scripture states, *And the Levite, he shall do the service* —even against his will. In other words, this matter is obligatory, something imposed on him as compulsory.

So was it likewise explained in chapter 2 of the tractate *'Arachin* (11a) that oral music was never to be uttered by anyone other than a Levite. This precept was reiterated in different phrasing in the Torah: for it is stated, *then he shall minister in the name of the Lord his God* (Deuteronomy 18:7). And it was stated there in the tractate *'Arachin* (11a): What is a ministry that is in the name of the Lord?— we can but say: it is song.[2]

At the root of the precept lies the reason that it is to the glory of the [Divine] King and the place that there should be certain people there from the certain, known tribe, permanently appointed to minister, and an outsider should not enter among them for the service —in keeping with [the practice of] royalty on earth: They appoint known honorable men, that all the work of the palace should be done by them. For it is not fitting for a king that he should change the ministering servants before him every day, and that all should thus make use of the crown of ministry to the king. This is something quite clear.

מִדִּינֵי הַמִּצְוָה, מַה שֶּׁאָמְרוּ זִכְרוֹנָם לִבְרָכָה שֶׁבֶּן לֵוִי שֶׁקִּבֵּל עָלָיו כָּל מִצְוַת
לְוִיָּה חוּץ מִדָּבָר אֶחָד, אֵין מְקַבְּלִין אוֹתוֹ עַד שֶׁיְּקַבֵּל אֶת כֻּלָּם. וַעֲבוֹדָה שֶׁלָּהֶן
הָיְתָה שֶׁהָיוּ שׁוֹמְרִים אֶת הַמִּקְדָּשׁ, כְּמוֹ שֶׁכָּתַבְנוּ בְּסֵדֶר זֶה, וְהָיוּ מֵהֶן שׁוֹעֲרִים
לִפְתֹּחַ וְלִסְגֹּר שַׁעֲרֵי הַמִּקְדָּשׁ; וְעִקַּר עֲבוֹדָתָם לְשׁוֹרֵר עַל הַקָּרְבָּן, וְלֹא הָיוּ אוֹמְרִים
שִׁירָה אֶלָּא בְּעוֹלוֹת צִבּוּר שֶׁהֵן חוֹבָה, וְעַל שַׁלְמֵי עֲצֶרֶת בְּעֵת נִסּוּךְ הַיַּיִן; אֲבָל עַל
עוֹלוֹת נְדָבָה שֶׁעוֹשִׂין הַצִּבּוּר לְקָיִץ הַמִּזְבֵּחַ, וְכֵן בִּנְסָכִים הַבָּאִין בִּפְנֵי עַצְמָן, אֵין
אוֹמְרִים עֲלֵיהֶם שִׁירָה.

לֵוִי הָאוֹנֵן מֻתָּר לַעֲבֹד וּלְשׁוֹרֵר. וְאֵין פּוֹחֲתִין לְעוֹלָם מִשְּׁנֵים־עָשָׂר לְוִיִּים
שֶׁעוֹמְדִין עַל הַדּוּכָן לוֹמַר שִׁירָה עַל הַקָּרְבָּן, וּמוֹסִיפִין עַד לְעוֹלָם. וְהַשִּׁירָה
שֶׁאוֹמְרִים הַלְוִיִּים הִיא בַּפֶּה, שֶׁעִקַּר שִׁירָה בַּפֶּה הִיא; וַאֲחֵרִים הָיוּ עוֹמְדִים שָׁם
שֶׁמְּנַגְּנִין בִּכְלֵי שִׁיר, מֵהֶם לְוִיִּים, וּמֵהֶם יִשְׂרְאֵלִים מְיֻחָסִין שֶׁמַּשִּׂיאִין אוֹתָם
לִכְהֻנָּה, שֶׁאֵין עוֹלֶה עַל הַדּוּכָן לְעוֹלָם אֶלָּא מְיֻחָס.

וְאֵין פּוֹחֲתִין לְעוֹלָם מִתִּשְׁעָה כִנּוֹרוֹת, וּמוֹסִיפִין עַד לְעוֹלָם. וְהַצַּלְצָלִים, הָיָה
אֶחָד בִּלְבָד. וּמִן הַדּוֹמֶה, כִּי הַטַּעַם לְפִי שְׁקוּל הַמְּצַלְצְתַּיִם גָּדוֹל וּמַבְעִית קְצָת,
וְאִלּוּ הָיוּ שָׁם הַרְבֵּה לֹא הָיוּ נִשְׁמָעִין יֶתֶר כְּלֵי הַנִּגּוּן שֶׁשָּׁם, וְכָל־שֶׁכֵּן שִׁירַת הַפֶּה.
וְהַחֲלִילִין שֶׁהָיוּ מְנַגְּנִין בָּהֶם, הָיָה אַבּוּב שֶׁלָּהֶם שֶׁל קָנֶה, מִפְּנֵי שֶׁקּוֹלוֹ עָרֵב.
וּשְׁנֵים־עָשָׂר יוֹם בַּשָּׁנָה הֶחָלִיל מַכֶּה לִפְנֵי הַמִּזְבֵּחַ; וְהוּא דּוֹחֶה שַׁבָּת, לְפִי שֶׁהוּא
מֵעֲבוֹדַת הַקָּרְבָּן, וְקָרְבָּן דּוֹחֶה הוּא אֶת הַשַּׁבָּת.

וְאֵין בֶּן לֵוִי נִכְנָס לַעֲבוֹדָה עַד שֶׁיְּלַמְּדוּהוּ חָמֵשׁ שָׁנִים, וּכְמוֹ שֶׁלָּמְדוּ זִכְרוֹנָם

3. TB B'choroth 30b.

4. I.e. while certain offerings (detailed below) were being sacrificed and
brought to the altar.

5. TB 'Arachin 11a–b.

6. Ibid. 12a; MT hilchoth k'lé ha-mikdash iii 2. The Hebrew for "summer-fruit
offerings", ka-yitz, means literally "summer"; it is understood here, however, as the
sweet fruits that ripen in the summer, as in II Samuel 16 : 1–2. By association it takes
on the sense of dessert, sweet food after the main course; and by further association
it denotes here voluntary offerings brought on the altar when it would otherwise be
idle (sacrifices being regarded symbolically as Divine "food" consumed by the
altar); see e.g. Rashi, TB Sh'vu'oth 12b top, s.v. ka-yitz.

7. Over the death of a near kin, before the burial.

8. Sifra, sh'mini, perek 2, 9.

9. TB 'Arachin 13b.

10. Ibid. 11a. (The paragraph is based on MT ibid. 3.)

11. TB 'Arachin 13a.

12. Ibid. 10a.

13. Although playing an instrument on the Sabbath is generally forbidden by a
rule of the Sages.

Among the laws of the precept there is what the Sages of blessed memory taught:[3] that if a Levite accepted every religious duty of the Levites except for one thing, he is not accepted until he adopts them all. Their service was that they would guard the Sanctuary, as we wrote in this *sidrah* (§ 388). Some of them were gatekeepers, to open and close the gates of the Sanctuary. But their principal service was to chant over offerings.[4] Now, they would utter song over none but the *'olah* (burnt) offerings of the whole community which were obligatory, and over the *sh'lamim* (peace-offerings) of *Shavu'oth* during the pouring of the wine.[5] But for voluntary *'olah* offerings that the whole community would present as the altar's "summer fruit offerings," and so when libations (drink-offerings) [of wine] were brought by themselves, song would not be uttered over them.[6]

A Levite in grief[7] was permitted to serve and chant.[8] There would never be fewer than twelve Levites standing on the platform to utter song over an offering; and more could be added without limit.[9] The song that the Levites would utter was by mouth; for principally, song is by mouth.[10] But others would be standing there, who played on musical instruments: some were Levites, and some were Israelites of distinguished lineage who were acceptable to intermarry with the *kohanim*. For none might ever go up on the platform but a person of distinguished descent.[10]

There were never fewer than nine lutes, and more might be added without limit. Of cymbals, though, there was but one [set].[11] It would seem that the reason is that the sound of cymbals is loud, and somewhat agitating; if there were many, the other musical instruments that were there would not be heard, and certainly not the chant of the mouth. As for the flutes on which they played, theirs was a reed flute, because its sound is sweet.[12] On twelve days of the year, the flute would play before the altar;[12] and it could thrust aside the Sabbath,[13] because it was part of the service of the offering, and the offering could thrust aside the Sabbath.[14]

A Levite would not enter to serve until he had been taught for five years, as the Sages of blessed memory inferred from Scripture;[15] and

14. The paragraph is based on MT *hilchoth k'lé ha-mikdash* iii 4–6.

15. Because Numbers 4:3 states that a Levite began his service at thirty, while Numbers 8:24 states that they were to enter for service at twenty-five; hence a five-year training period is inferred; TB Ḥullin 24a.

לִבְרָכָה מִן הַכָּתוּב. וּמִכָּאן אָמְרוּ זִכְרוֹנָם לִבְרָכָה, שֶׁתַּלְמִיד שֶׁלֹּא רָאָה סִימָן יָפֶה בְּתַלְמוּדוֹ חָמֵשׁ שָׁנִים, שׁוּב אֵינוֹ רוֹאֶה. וְאֵין נִכְנָס לַעֲבֹד לְעוֹלָם עַד שֶׁיְּהֵא גָדוֹל, שֶׁנֶּאֱמַר: אִישׁ אִישׁ עַל עֲבֹדָתוֹ. וְאֵין הַלֵּוִי נִפְסָל לַעֲבוֹדָה בְּשָׁנִים, וְלֹא בְּמוּמִין, אֶלָּא בְּקִלְקוּל הַקּוֹל, כְּגוֹן הַזְּקֵנִים שֶׁמִּתְקַלְקֵל קוֹלָם לְעֵת זִקְנָה. וְזֶה שֶׁנֶּאֱמַר בַּתּוֹרָה "וּמִבֶּן חֲמִשִּׁים שָׁנָה יָשׁוּב מִצְּבָא הָעֲבֹדָה", אֵינוֹ אֶלָּא בִּזְמַן שֶׁהָיוּ נוֹשְׂאִין הַמִּשְׁכָּן מִמָּקוֹם לְמָקוֹם; וַאֲפִלּוּ בְּעֵת זִקְנָה שֶׁנִּתְקַלְקֵל קוֹלוֹ, אֵינוֹ נִפְסָל לִשְׁמִירַת הַמִּקְדָּשׁ וְלַהֲגָפַת דְּלָתוֹת.

וְכָל זֶה עִם יֶתֶר פְּרָטֶיהָ יִתְבָּאֵר יָפֶה בִּמְקוֹמוֹת מִתָּמִיד וּמִדּוֹת; גַּם בְּפֶרֶק שֵׁנִי מֵעֲרָכִין מְבֹאָר קְצָת מֵעִנְיָן זֶה. וְהֶאֱרַכְתִּי לְךָ בְּנִי מְעַט בָּזֶה, כִּי מְהֵרָה יִבָּנֶה בֵּית־הַמִּקְדָּשׁ, וְתִצְטָרֵךְ לוֹ—אָמֵן, כֵּן יַעֲשֶׂה הַשֵּׁם.

וְנוֹהֶגֶת בִּזְמַן הַבַּיִת בַּלְוִיִּים. וְלֵוִי הָעוֹבֵר עַל זֶה, וְלֹא שָׁר עַל הַקָּרְבָּן בְּיוֹמוֹ הַקָּבוּעַ לוֹ, כִּי יָמִים קְבוּעִים לָהֶם לְפִי חִלּוּק הַמִּשְׁמָרוֹת, אֶלָּא שֶׁשָּׁתַק—בִּטֵּל עֲשֵׂה זֶה, וְעָנְשׁוֹ גָדוֹל מְאֹד, שֶׁנִּרְאָה כְּמִי שֶׁאֵינוֹ חָפֵץ בִּכְבוֹד עֲבוֹדַת הַשֵּׁם, וְעַל־כֵּן יִמְנָעֵהוּ הָאֵל מִכְּבוֹדוֹ. וַאֲשֶׁר יַחְפֹּץ מִן הַלְוִיִּים בַּעֲבוֹדַת בּוֹרְאוֹ, הַחַיִּים וְהַשָּׁלוֹם וְהַבְּרָכָה וְהַכָּבוֹד יִהְיוּ אִתּוֹ.

[מִצְוַת מַעֲשֵׂר רִאשׁוֹן]

שצה שֶׁנִּתְחַיְּבוּ בְּנֵי־יִשְׂרָאֵל לָתֵת חֵלֶק אֶחָד מֵעֲשָׂרָה חֲלָקִים מִזֶּרַע הָאָרֶץ לַלְוִיִּים, שֶׁנֶּאֱמַר "כִּי אֶת מַעֲשַׂר בְּנֵי יִשְׂרָאֵל אֲשֶׁר יָרִימוּ לַיי תְּרוּמָה נָתַתִּי לַלְוִיִּם", וְנֶאֱמַר בְּסֵדֶר אִם בְּחֻקֹּתַי: "וְכָל מַעְשַׂר הָאָרֶץ ... לַיי הוּא", וְזֶהוּ הַנִּקְרָא מַעֲשֵׂר רִאשׁוֹן.

מִשָּׁרְשֵׁי הַמִּצְוָה, לְפִי שֶׁשֵּׁבֶט הַלֵּוִי בָּחַר הַשֵּׁם בְּתוֹךְ אֶחָיו לַעֲבוֹדָתוֹ תָּמִיד בַּמִּקְדָּשׁ, וְעַל־כֵּן הָיָה מֵחַסְדּוֹ עֲלֵיהֶם לָתֵת לָהֶם מִחְיָתָם דֶּרֶךְ כָּבוֹד, כִּי כֵן יָאוֹת

16. Because he forgets what he has learned (Rashi *ibid.* s.v. *shelo' ra'ah*).
17. Since this is all the time Scripture allotted a Levite for training; TB *ibid.*
18. TB Ḥullin 24a. (The paragraph is based on MT *ibid.* 7–8.)
19. CF MT *ibid.* 9.

hence they (of blessed memory) said that if a student sees no good sign [of progress and success] in his study for five years,[16] he will never see any.[17] He was never to enter to serve until he was an adult:[9] for it is stated, *every man to his service* (Numbers 4:49). A Levite would not be disqualified to serve by years (age) or by disfiguring blemishes, but only by the deterioration of the voice—for instance, the old, whose voice becomes spoiled with age.[18] As for the verse in the Torah, *and from the age of fifty years he shall return from the service of the work* (Numbers 8:25), this applied only at the time that they would carry the *mishkan* (Tabernacle) from place to place. Yet even in the older years, when one's voice was deteriorated, he was not disqualified from guarding the Sanctuary and locking doors.[18]

All this, with the rest of its details, is explained well in various places in the tractates *Tamid* and *Middoth*; also in chapter 2 of *'Arachin* some of this subject is clarified. I have been a bit lengthy about this for you, my son, for the Sanctuary will soon be rebuilt, and you will need it—*amen*, may the Eternal Lord so accomplish it.

It applies at the time the Temple exists, for the Levites. If a Levite transgressed this and did not chant over an offering on his day that was set for him—for days were determined for them according to the division of the watches[19]—but rather kept silent, he would thus disobey this positive precept, and his punishment would be very great, for he would seem like one who does not desire the honor of service to the Eternal Lord. Therefore God would deprive him of honor. But as for anyone of the Levites who delighted in the service of his Creator, life, peace, blessing and honor would be with him.

[THE PRECEPT OF THE FIRST TITHE, FOR
THE LEVITES]

395 that the Israelites were commanded to give one part in ten of the grain of the land to the Levites: for it is stated, *For the tithe of the Israelites, which they set apart as a gift to the Lord, I have given to the Levites* (Numbers 18:24); and it is stated in *sidrah b'ḥukothai, And all the tithe of the land... is the Lord's* (Leviticus 27:30). This is what was called the First Tithe.

At the root of the precept lies the reason that the Eternal Lord chose the tribe of Lévi from among their brethren for His constant, regular service at His Sanctuary. It was therefore His loving-kindness toward them to give them their sustenance in an honorable way. For

לִמְשָׁרְתֵי הַמֶּלֶךְ, שֶׁתִּהְיֶה אֲרוּחָתָם מְזֻמֶּנֶת לָהֶם עַל־יְדֵי אֲחֵרִים שֶׁיְּכִינוּהָ לָהֶם,
וְלֹא יִצְטָרְכוּ הֵם לִיגַּע בְּדָבָר, זוּלָתִי בַּעֲבוֹדַת הַמֶּלֶךְ הַיְקָרָה. וְאַף־עַל־פִּי שֶׁהֵם הָיוּ
שְׁנֵים־עָשָׂר שְׁבָטִים, וּלְפִי חֶלְקַה שָׁנָה הָיָה רָאוּי שֶׁיִּטְּלוּ חֵלֶק אֶחָד מִשְּׁנֵים־עָשָׂר,
גַּם זֶה הַיִּתְרוֹן לָהֶם לִכְבוֹדָם, כִּי מִהְיוֹתָם מִבֵּית הַמֶּלֶךְ רָאוּי שֶׁתִּהְיֶה חֶלְקָם יְתֵרָה
עַל כֻּלָּם, וְיִתְרוֹן גָּדוֹל הוּא שֶׁיָּבוֹא לָהֶם חֵלֶק הָעֲשִׂירִי נָקִי מִכָּל הוֹצָאַת הַקַּרְקַע.

וְהַמְחַיֶּה הָאֵל בְּמָמוֹנוֹ, בִּרְכַּת הַשֵּׁם יִתְבָּרַךְ תָּנוּחַ עָלָיו בְּכָל אֲשֶׁר יֵשׁ
לוֹ, וְזֶהוּ אָמְרָם זִכְרוֹנָם לִבְרָכָה "מַעַשְׂרוֹת סְיָג לָעֹשֶׁר". גַּם אָמְרוּ זִכְרוֹנָם לִבְרָכָה
שֶׁאָסוּר לְאָדָם לַחְשֹׁב בְּלִבָּבוֹ וְלוֹמַר "אֲנַסֶּה אִם יֵיטִיב הַשֵּׁם לִי בְּהִתְעַסְּקִי
בְּמִצְווֹתָיו", וְעַל כַּיּוֹצֵא בָזֶה נֶאֱמַר "לֹא תְנַסּוּ אֶת יי אֱלֹהֵיכֶם" — זוּלָתִי בְּמִצְוָה
זוֹ, שֶׁהֻתַּר לַנְסוֹת אִם יְבָרְכֵהוּ הָאֵל בַּעֲשׂוֹתוֹ אוֹתָהּ וּבִהְיוֹתוֹ זָרִיז עָלֶיהָ; וּמְפֹרָשׁ
הוּא עַל־יְדֵי הַנְּבִיאִים, שֶׁנֶּאֱמַר: הָבִיאוּ אֶת כָּל הַמַּעֲשֵׂר אֶל בֵּית הָאוֹצָר ...
וּבְחָנוּנִי נָא בָּזֹאת אָמַר יי.

מִדִּינֵי הַמִּצְוָה, מַה שֶּׁאָמְרוּ זִכְרוֹנָם לִבְרָכָה שֶׁהַמַּעֲשֵׂר הַזֶּה אֲשֶׁר לַלְוִיִּם הוּא
חֻלִּין גְּמוּרִים, וּמֻתָּר לְאָכְלוֹ לְכָל אָדָם, בֵּין לֵוִי בֵּין יִשְׂרָאֵל, וַאֲפִלּוּ בְּטֻמְאָה,
שֶׁנֶּאֱמַר "וְנֶחְשַׁב לָכֶם תְּרוּמַתְכֶם", כְּלוֹמַר הַמַּעֲשֵׂר שֶׁהוּא מוֹרֶם מִתְּבוּאַת
הַיִּשְׂרָאֵל שֶׁהוּא לָכֶם, "כַּדָּגָן מִן הַגֹּרֶן וְכַמְלֵאָה מִן הַיָּקֶב". וְדָרְשׁוּ זִכְרוֹנָם
לִבְרָכָה: מַה גֹּרֶן וָיֶקֶב חֻלִּין לְכָל דָּבָר, אַף מַעֲשֵׂר רִאשׁוֹן שֶׁנִּטְּלָה תְּרוּמָתוֹ חֻלִּין
לְכָל דָּבָר. פֵּרוּשׁ שֶׁנִּטְּלָה תְּרוּמָתוֹ, כְּלוֹמַר אַחַר שֶׁהֵרִימוּ הַלְוִיִּם מַעֲשֵׂר מִן
הַמַּעֲשֵׂר שֶׁלָּהֶם וּנְתָנוּהוּ לַכֹּהֲנִים; זֶהוּ הַנִּקְרָא תְּרוּמָתוֹ. וְכָל מָקוֹם שֶׁנֶּאֱמַר
בְּמַעֲשֵׂר קֹדֶשׁ אוֹ פְּדִיָּה אֵינוֹ אֶלָּא בְּמַעֲשֵׂר שֵׁנִי.

§395   1. And not one part in ten (a tithe), which is a larger share.

2. I.e. a protective way of harboring and retaining it; Mishnah, 'Avoth iii 13.

3. TB Ta'anith 9a.

4. Literally: except with this *mitzvah*.

5. TB Yevamoth 85b (see also Rashi s.v. *mi lo*); MT *hilchoth ma'asér* i 2; and see note 6.

6. Sifre Zuta 298 l. 22–23; similarly Sifre, Numbers §122.

7. I.e. exchanging for money food that is a tithe, to render it non-holy.

so it befits the ministering servants of a king, that their provisions should be set for them by others, who would prepare it for them, and they should have no need to exert effort about anything other than the precious service of the king. Now, although there were twelve tribes, and by an equal division it would have been right for them to take [only] one part in twelve,[1] this increment was also for their honor. For since they were of the [Divine] King's house [the Temple], it was fitting that their share should be greater than that of all others; and it was a great added advantage that the one-tenth share should come to them clear, free of all the expense of [working farm] land.

Now, whoever sustains the ministering servants of God with his wealth, the blessing of the Eternal Lord (be He blessed) will abide with him, over all that is his. This is why the Sages of blessed memory taught: The tithes are a "fence" for wealth.[2] They (of blessed memory) also taught[3] that it is forbidden for a man to reckon in his heart and say, "I will make a test [to see] if the Eternal Lord will grant me good fortune when I attend to His *mitzvoth*." About something like that it was stated, *You shall not put the Lord your God to the test* (Deteronomy 6:16). Yet this *mitzvah* is an exception:[4] for it was permitted a person to test if God will bless him when he observes it and is alert about it. This was explicitly said by the prophets: for it is stated, *Bring the whole tithe into the storehouse... and test Me now by this, says the Lord* (Malachi 3:10).

Among the laws of the precept, there is what the Sages of blessed memory said:[5] that this tithe which is for the Levites is completely non-holy, and any man is permitted to eat it, whether a Levite or an ordinary Israelite, and even in ritual impurity: For it is stated, *And your separated gift*—i.e. the tithe, separated from the grain of the Israelites, which is yours—*shall be reckoned to you like the grain from the threshing-floor and like the fullness of the winepress* (Numbers 18:27); and our Sages of blessed memory interpreted:[6] Just as [the produce of] the threshing-floor and the winepress is non-holy in every respect, so is the First Tithe whose *t'rumah* [kohen's portion] was taken off, non-holy in every respect. The meaning of "whose *t'rumah* was taken off" is to signify after the Levites lifted off a tithe (tenth part) from their tithe and gave it to the *kohanim*; this is what is called "its *t'rumah*." And wherever sanctity or redemption[7] is mentioned about a tithe, it refers to nothing but the Second Tithe.

וְאָמְרוּ בְסִפְרֵי שֶׁכָּל שֶׁהוּא אֹכֶל־אָדָם, וְנִשְׁמָר, וְגִדּוּלוֹ מִן הָאָרֶץ, חַיָּב בְּמַעֲשֵׂר
וּבִתְרוּמָה; וּמַיְתֵי לַהּ מִדִּכְתִיב בַּתְּרוּמָה "רֵאשִׁית דְּגָנְךָ" וְגוֹמֵר, שֶׁדָּרְשׁוּ זִכְרוֹנָם
לִבְרָכָה: מַה דָּגָן וְתִירוֹשׁ וְיִצְהָר מַאֲכַל אָדָם וְגִדּוּלוֹ מִן הָאָרֶץ וְיֵשׁ לוֹ בְעָלִים,
שֶׁנֶּאֱמַר "דְּגָנְךָ", אַף כָּל כַּיּוֹצֵא בָהֶם חַיָּב בִּתְרוּמָה וּמַעֲשֵׂרוֹת. אֲבָל הַיְרָקוֹת,
אַף־עַל־פִּי שֶׁהֵן מַאֲכַל אָדָם, אֵין בָּהֶם חִיּוּב מַעֲשֵׂר אֶלָּא מִדְּרַבָּנָן, לְפִי שֶׁנֶּאֱמַר
בְּמַעֲשֵׂר "כָּל תְּבוּאַת זַרְעֶךָ", וְיָרָק אֵינוֹ נִקְרָא תְבוּאָה.

וּמִדִּבְרֵי הַגְּמָרָא, שֶׁאָנוּ סוֹמְכִין בָּהּ יוֹתֵר, נִרְאֶה שֶׁגַּם שָׁם בְּכָל הַפֵּרוֹת, חוּץ מִדָּגָן
תִּירוֹשׁ וְיִצְהָר, אֵין חִיּוּב הַמַּעֲשֵׂר בָּהֶן אֶלָּא מִדְּרַבָּנָן, וּקְרָא דְּמַיְתוּ בְּסִפְרֵי
אַסְמַכְתָּא בְּעָלְמָא הוּא; הָכִי אַסִּיקְנָא בְּרֵישׁ פֶּרֶק הַשּׂוֹכֵר אֶת הַפּוֹעֲלִים גַּבֵּי הַהִיא
דְּפָרִיק רַב פַּפָּא בִּתְאֵנָה עוֹמֶדֶת בַּגִּנָּה וְנוֹפָהּ נוֹטֶה לֶחָצֵר; וְאָמְנָם הָרַב מֹשֶׁה בֶּן
מַיְמוֹן זִכְרוֹנוֹ לִבְרָכָה כָּתַב הַפֵּךְ מִזֶּה, וּכְמוֹ שֶׁמָּצָא בְסִפְרֵי.

וְכֵן מֵעִנְיָנֵי הַמִּצְוָה מַה שֶּׁאָמְרוּ שֶׁאֵין מְעַשְּׂרִין מִן הֶחָדָשׁ עַל הַיָּשָׁן, וְלֹא מִן
הַיָּשָׁן עַל הֶחָדָשׁ, וְלֹא מִמִּין עַל שֶׁאֵינוֹ מִינוֹ, וְלֹא מִן הַחַיָּב עַל הַפָּטוּר וְלֹא מִן
הַפָּטוּר עַל הַחַיָּב, וְאִם עִשֵּׂר עֹשֶׂר אֵינוֹ מְעַשֵּׂר; אֲבָל מְעַשְּׂרִין שֶׁלֹּא מִן הַמֻּקָּף, אַף־
עַל־פִּי שֶׁבַּתְּרוּמָה אֵינוֹ כֵן, שֶׁאֵין תּוֹרְמִין אֶלָּא מִן הַמֻּקָּף. וּמִכָּל־מָקוֹם בִּשְׁאָר
דְּבָרִים שָׁוִים הֵן תְּרוּמָה וּמַעֲשֵׂרוֹת, דְּכָל שֶׁאָנוּ אוֹמְרִים בַּתְּרוּמָה "אֵין תּוֹרְמִין,
וְאִם תָּרַם—תְּרוּמָתוֹ תְּרוּמָה", כָּךְ בְּמַעֲשֵׂר: אִם הִפְרִישׁ, מַעְשְׂרוֹתָיו מַעֲשֵׂרוֹת;
וְכָל שֶׁהוּא פָטוּר מִן הַתְּרוּמָה פָּטוּר מִן הַמַּעֲשֵׂר. וּבְסֵדֶר שׁוֹפְטִים עָשֵׂה ו' [סִי'
תק"ז] נַאֲרִיךְ בַּדְּבָרִים בְּעֶזְרַת הַשֵּׁם, וְתִרְאֵנוּ מִשָּׁם.

8. Not found in our Sifre, but in Midrash Tanna'im, Deuteronomy 18:4.

9. MT *hilchoth t'rumah* ii 6, based on Midrash Tanna'im, Deuteronomy 14:22 and TJ Ma'as'roth i 1.

10. See *tosafoth* there, s.v. *hacha*.

11. MT *ibid.* 1; see note 8; but Rashba, cited in *Shittah M'kubetzeth* to TB Bava M'tzi'a 88a, s.v. *'amar R. Yannai*, also mentions it as from Sifre.

12. MT *hilchoth ma'asér* i 7, based on Mishnah, T'rumoth i 5, ii 4; TB Rosh ha-Shanah 12b, B'rachoth 54b, Ḥullin 26a.

13. E.g. some of this year's crop should not be given as the tithe to free last year's crop of the obligation.

14. E.g. grain at hand may be given as the tithe for grain stored some distance away; MT *ibid.* 6, based on Mishnah, Bikkurim ii 5.

15. MT *ibid.* 7.

Now, it was taught in the Midrash *Sifre*[8] that whatever is food for humans and is guarded, having grown from the earth, bears the obligation of the tithe and *t'rumah* [the *kohen*'s portion]. It derives this from the verse written about *t'rumah*: *The first-fruits of your grain*, etc. (Deuteronomy 18:4); for the Sages of blessed memory interpreted:[8] Just as grain, wine and oil are food for humans, are grown from the earth, and have owners, for it is stated, "your grain," so anything thus like them bears the obligation of *t'rumah* and the tithes. Vegetables, however, even though they are human food, do not entail an obligation of the tithe, except by the ruling of the Sages: for it is stated about the tithe, *all the grain from your seed* (Deuteronomy 14:22), and vegetables are not called grain.[9]

However, from the words of the Talmud, on which we rely the more, it appears that with all produce as well, except for grain, wine and oil, there is no obligation of the tithe except by the ruling of the Sages; and the verse quoted in the Midrash *Sifre* is merely to add an overtone of Scriptural support. This is the conclusion reached at the beginning of the seventh chapter of the tractate *Bava M'tzi'a* (88a), in connection with the reply of R. Papa about a fig tree standing in a garden whose trunk bends out into the courtyard.[10] However, R. Moses b. Maimon [Rambam] of blessed memory wrote the opposite of this, as he found in *Sifre*.[11]

So is it part of the subject-matter of the precept what the Sages taught:[12] that the tithe should not be separated from new produce for old,[13] nor from old produce for new; nor from one kind for a different kind [of produce]; neither from what has the requirement [of the tithe] for produce that is free of the requirement, nor from what is free of the obligation for produce that bears it; and if one did give the tithe thus, the produce is not tithed. However, produce that is not near at hand may be tithed,[14] although this is not the case with *t'rumah*: for *t'rumah* may be separated from nothing but what is near at hand. In other respects, however, *t'rumah* and the tithe are alike. For wherever we rule about *t'rumah* that it is not to be separated, but if it was, it is valid *t'rumah*, the same holds true for the tithes: If they were separated, they are valid tithes. And whatever is free of the obligation of *t'rumah* is equally free of the requirement of tithes.[15] In the sixth positive precept of *sidrah shof'tim* (§507) we will write at length of these matters, with the Eternal Lord's help. You can read it there.

⟨149⟩   So does the subject-matter of the precept contain what the Sages

וְכֵן מֵעִנְיַן הַמִּצְוָה, מַה שֶּׁאָמְרוּ (זִכְרוֹנָם לִבְרָכָה) שֶׁאֵין אָדָם חַיָּב לְהַפְרִישׁ
מַעֲשֵׂר מִן הַתּוֹרָה אֶלָּא הַגּוֹמֵר פֵּרוֹתָיו לְאָכְלָן לְעַצְמוֹ, אֲבָל הַגּוֹמְרָן לְמָכְרָן בַּשּׁוּק
פָּטוּר מִן הַתּוֹרָה, שֶׁנֶּאֱמַר "עַשֵּׂר תְּעַשֵּׂר" וְגוֹמֵר "וְאָכַלְתָּ"; וְכֵן הַלּוֹקֵחַ אַחַר
שֶׁנִּגְמְרָה מְלַאכְתָּן, כְּלוֹמַר שֶׁנִּמְרְחוּ בְּיַד מוֹכֵר, פָּטוּר מִן הַתּוֹרָה וְחַיָּב מִדִּבְרֵיהֶם,
שֶׁנֶּאֱמַר "תְּבוּאַת זַרְעֶךָ", כְּלוֹמַר שֶׁנִּגְמְרָה מְלַאכְתָּן בִּרְשׁוּתְךָ.

וְאֵין חִיּוּב מַעֲשֵׂר חָל בַּפֵּרוֹת עַד שֶׁיַּגִּיעוּ לְעוֹנַת מַעֲשֵׂר, שֶׁנֶּאֱמַר "מִזֶּרַע
הָאָרֶץ מִפְּרִי הָעֵץ", כְּלוֹמַר עַד שֶׁיֵּעָשֶׂה פְּרִי, וְכֵן הַתְּבוּאָה עַד שֶׁתְּהֵא תְבוּאָה,
שֶׁנֶּאֱמַר "תְּבוּאַת זַרְעֶךָ". וּמִכָּאן לָמְדוּ זִכְרוֹנָם לִבְרָכָה עוֹנַת הַפֵּרוֹת שֶׁהִיא
מִשֶּׁיַּגִּיעוּ הַפֵּרוֹת לְהַזְרִיעַ וְלִצְמֹחַ, הַכֹּל לְפִי מַה שֶׁהוּא. כֵּיצַד, הַתְּאֵנִים מִשֶּׁיֵּעָשׂוּ
רַכִּין שֶׁרְאוּיִין לֶאֱכֹל, הַתַּפּוּחִים וְהָאֶתְרוֹגִים מִשֶּׁיִּתְעַגְּלוּ, וְכֵן לְכָל פְּרִי וּפְרִי קָבְעוּ
עוֹנָתוֹ לַמַּעֲשֵׂר, כְּלוֹמַר שֶׁקֹּדֶם זְמַן זֶה הַקָּבוּעַ לָהֶם אוֹכְלִין מֵהֶן כָּל הַצָּרִיךְ, לְפִי
שֶׁאֵינָם בְּתוֹרַת מַעֲשֵׂר כְּלָל.

אֲבָל אַחַר זְמַן זֶה אֵין אוֹכְלִין מֵהֶן אֶלָּא עֲרַאי, עַד שֶׁיִּקָּבְעוּ לָהֶם גֹּרֶן
לְמַעֲשֵׂר. וְאַחַר שֶׁנִּקְבְּעָן קָבוּעַ לְמַעֲשֵׂר, אָסוּר לֶאֱכֹל מֵהֶם אֲפִלּוּ אֲכִילַת עֲרַאי. וְאֵי
זֶהוּ גָּרְנָן לְמַעֲשֵׂר: הַתְּבוּאָה מִשֶּׁיְּמָרַח, כְּלוֹמַר שֶׁיְּמָרַח פָּנֶיהָ בְּרַחַת כְּדֶרֶךְ שֶׁעוֹשִׂין
בְּנֵי־אָדָם אַחַר שֶׁעוֹשִׂין מִמֶּנָּה כְּרִי. וּבִירוּשַׁלְמִי מָצִינוּ עוֹד, שֶׁאִם אֵין דַּעְתּוֹ
לְמָרֵחַ, מִשֶּׁיַּעֲמִיד עֲרֵמָה מִתְּבוּאָתוֹ הֲרֵי גָּרְנוֹ לַמַּעֲשֵׂר, דִּבְגֹרֶן תָּלָה הַכָּתוּב, וַאֲפִלּוּ
בְּלֹא מֵרוּחַ, כֵּיוָן שֶׁאֵין דַּעְתּוֹ לְמָרֵחַ. וַאֲפִלּוּ עָשָׂה מִמֶּנָּה גֹּרֶן בְּתוֹךְ בֵּיתוֹ, גַּם שָׁם
עוֹשֶׂה הַגֹּרֶן קְבִיעוּת לְמַעֲשֵׂר.

וְהָא דְּאָמַר רַבִּי הוֹשַׁעְיָא: מַעֲרִים אָדָם עַל תְּבוּאָתוֹ וּמַכְנִיסָהּ בְּמוֹץ שֶׁלָּהּ כְּדֵי

---

16. TB Bava M'tzi'a 88a; MT *hilchoth ma'asér* ii 1–2.

17. See two paragraphs below.

18. So Midrash haGadol, Leviticus 27 : 30 (697); cf. MT *ibid.* 3.

19. TJ Ma'as'roth i 2.

20. Mishnah, Ma'as'roth i 2, 4; TJ i 3; MT *ibid.* 5.

21. MT *ibid.* 3.

22. This evidently denotes food taken casually, at random, one piece or one fruit
at a time, by hand: On "one at a time" see "one by one" in Mishnah, Ma'asroth iii
2, on which R. 'Ovadya Bertinoro comments that "this is not *keva*," i.e. a set meal,
and hence only *'achilath 'ara'i*, casual, random eating; see further "and if he
combined" in *ibid.* 3, on which Bertinoro notes that two units of food together
would be *keva*'. On "by hand" see "but not from a basket" etc. in *ibid.* 2, on which
R. Yehosef states in *M'lecheth Sh'lomoh ad loc.* that a basket (or any container) would
combine the units of food into a matter of *'achilath keva'*. Cf. also Abbaye's statement
in TB Sukkah 26a, and *tosafoth* s.v. *tarté*; and MT *hilchoth sukkah* vi 6.

23. So TJ Ma'as'roth i 4.

of blessed memory said:[16] that by the law of the Torah no man is duty-bound to separate the tithe except one who completes [the growth and preparation] of his produce to eat it himself. But if one completes its preparation in order to sell it in the market, he is free of the duty by the Torah's law: For it is stated, *You shall surely tithe*, etc. *And you shall eat* (Deuteronomy 14:22–23). So also the person who buys it after its work is completed, i.e. when it was smoothed over by the vendor[17]—he is free by the Torah's law, but obligated by the Sages' decree. For it is stated, *the produce from your grain* (*ibid.* 22): in other words, whose work was completed in your domain.

The obligation of the tithe does not take effect for produce until the season of the tithe is reached: for it is stated, *of the seed of the land, of the fruit of the tree* (Leviticus 27:30)—which is to say, not until fruit is grown; and so too grain: not until it is grain, since Scripture states, *the grain from your seed* (Deuteronomy 14:22).[18] From this our Sages of blessed memory inferred the season of the tithes: that it is from the time the produce is able to grow seeds and bloom, each according to what [its nature] is.[19] How [for example]?—figs, from the time they grow soft and fit to eat; apples and citrons (*'ethrogim*), from the time they grow rounded.[20] And so for each and every fruit they set the season of the tithe. This is to say that before this time which is set for them, one may eat of them whatever is needed, since they are not subject at all to the duty of the tithe.[21]

After this time, however, one is not to eat of them except as casual food, until their harvesting sets the obligation of the tithe for them; and after their harvesting makes the duty of tithing set for them, it is forbidden to eat of them even as casual food.[22] Now, what constitutes their "harvesting" for the tithe obligation?—grain, from when it is smoothed over; i.e. when its surface is made smooth and even with a winnowing-shovel, as people do after they make a pile of it.[23] In the Jerusalem Talmud we find further[23] that if a person does not intend to smooth it over, then from the time he makes a stack of his grain, that is its "harvesting" in regard to the tithe. For Scripture made it depend on the harvesting, even without smoothing it over, since he does not intend to smooth it down. Even if he made a stored pile of it within his house, there too the harvesting determines the obligation for the tithe.

Now, R. Hoshaya said: A man may use a stratagem with his grain and bring it in while still with its chaff, in order to free it from the

לְפָטְרָהּ מִמַּעֲשֵׂר, וְהִיא הֲלָכָה פְּסוּקָה כְּדְאַמְרִינָן בְּמַסֶּכֶת בְּרָכוֹת, הַהִיא מַיְרֵי
בְּשֶׁלֹּא הֶעֱמִיד מִמֶּנָּה עֲרֵמָה בְּתוֹךְ בֵּיתוֹ, וְכֵן שֶׁלֹּא מֵרְחָהּ, אֶלָּא דָּשׁ וְזָרָה מְעַט
מְעַט בְּלֹא מֵרוּחַ, וְנָתַן לָאוֹצָר מְעַט מְעַט. זֶהוּ הַנִּרְאֶה בְּעִנְיָן זֶה, וּבְזֶה הַדֶּרֶךְ כָּל
הַשְּׁמוּעוֹת עוֹלוֹת בְּקָנֶה אֶחָד בְּרִיאוֹת וְטוֹבוֹת.

וְאָמְרוּ זִכְרוֹנָם לִבְרָכָה שֶׁעוֹנַת הַקִּשּׁוּאִין וְהָאֲבַטִּיחִין וְהַדְּלוּעִין מִשֶּׁיְּשַׁפְשֵׁף,
כְּלוֹמַר שֶׁיָּסִיר אוֹתוֹ הַשֵּׂעָר דַּק שֶׁעֲלֵיהֶן; וְעוֹנַת כַּלְכָּלָה שֶׁל פֵּרוֹת מִשֶּׁיְּחַפֶּה
הַפֵּרוֹת שֶׁבָּהּ בְּעָלִין וּבְהוּצִין; וְכֵן לְכָל פְּרִי וּפְרִי קָבְעוּ זְמַן גָּרְנוֹ לְפִי מַה שֶׁהוּא,
הַכֹּל כְּמוֹ שֶׁבָּא בְּמַסֶּכֶת מַעֲשֵׂר.

וְעוֹד רָאִיתִי בְּעִנְיָן קְבִיעוּת הַמַּעֲשֵׂר מִן הַתּוֹרָה, שֶׁדַּעַת קְצָת מִן הַמְּפָרְשִׁים
שֶׁאֵין קְבִיעוּת מַעֲשֵׂר לְעוֹלָם בְּשׁוּם צַד עַד רְאִיַּת פְּנֵי הַבַּיִת, וְגַם שֶׁיִּהְיֶא בַּיִת
הָרָאוּי לְךָ, שֶׁנֶּאֱמַר: בְּעַרְתִּי הַקֹּדֶשׁ מִן הַבַּיִת; וְהוּא שֶׁיַּכְנִיסֵם לַפֵּרוֹת דֶּרֶךְ
הַשַּׁעַר, שֶׁנֶּאֱמַר "וְאָכְלוּ בִשְׁעָרֶיךָ וְשָׂבֵעוּ"; אֲבָל הַכְנִיסָן דֶּרֶךְ גַּגִּין וְקַרְפִּיפוֹת
פְּטוּרִין מִן הַמַּעֲשֵׂר וְהַתְּרוּמָה. וְכֵן כָּתַב הָרַב מֹשֶׁה בֶּן מַיְמוֹן זִכְרוֹנוֹ לִבְרָכָה:
נִרְאֶה לִי שֶׁאֵין לוֹקִין מִן הַתּוֹרָה עַל אֲכִילַת הַטֶּבֶל עַד שֶׁיִּקָּבַע בִּכְנִיסָתוֹ לְבֵיתוֹ,
אֲבָל בִּשְׁאָר דְּבָרִים הַקּוֹבְעִין לְמַעֲשֵׂר אֵין לוֹקִין עָלָיו אֶלָּא מַכַּת מַרְדּוּת.
וְיֶתֶר פְּרָטֶיהָ, מְבֹאָרִים בְּמַסֶּכֶת מַעֲשֵׂרוֹת.

וְנוֹהֶגֶת בִּזְכָרִים וּנְקֵבוֹת, בְּיִשְׂרְאֵלִים וּבַכֹּהֲנִים וּבַלְוִיִּים, שֶׁאַף־עַל־פִּי שֶׁכֹּהֲנִים
וּלְוִיִּם נוֹטְלִין הַמַּעֲשֵׂר מִיִּשְׂרָאֵל, חַיָּבִים הֵם לְעַשֵּׂר הַפֵּרוֹת שֶׁלָּהֶם בְּקַרְקְעוֹתֵיהֶם,
וּבְאִסּוּר טֶבֶל הֵם עֲלֵיהֶם עַד שֶׁיְּעַשְּׂרוּ אוֹתָן, שֶׁנֶּאֱמַר "כֵּן תָּרִימוּ גַם אַתֶּם", וּבָא

---

24. So, further, MT *hilchoth ma‘asér* iii 6. On the Talmudic citation see Rashi *ad loc.* s.v. *umachnissah* and s.v. *b’motz.* (Our Talmud editions, there, have R. ’Oshaya, but the early editions, etc. have R. Hoshaya — *Dikduké Sof’rim.*)

25. I.e. they harmonize or dovetail without contradiction. MY discusses this and finds that our author differs here with Rashi, TB P’saḥim 9a, s.v. *v’i ba’ith éma,* and follows MT *hilchoth ma‘asér* iii 6, as understood by Ramban, cited in *Shittah M’kubetzeth* to TB Bava M’tzi‘a 88b.

26. Mishnah, Ma‘as’roth i 5.

27. MT *hilchoth ma‘asér* iv 2; and see *tosafoth,* TB Bava M’tzi‘a 88a, s.v. *’ad sheyir’eh.* (What follows is meant by the law of the Torah, as opposed to the Rabbinic law of the Sages.)

28. E.g. it should not be too small for a proper house (cf. *tosafoth,* Sukkah 3a, s.v. *ba-yith*); see MT *ibid.* iv 3–4. (On the meaning of *p’né ha-ba-yith* see Rashi, TB Bava M’tzi‘a 88a, beginning.)

29. Hebrew, *karpifoth*; singular, *karpéf*: an enclosed unroofed space for storage, generally behind the house. E.g. it should not be too small for a proper house; see MT *ibid.* iv 3–4. (On the meaning of *p’né ha-ba-yith* see Rashi, TB Bava M’tzi‘a 88a, beginning.)

obligation of the tithe.[24] And this is a decisive ruling in law, as taught in the Talmud tractate *B'rachoth* (31a). But that means where the man does not make a stack of it within his house, and likewise he does not smooth it over, but rather that he threshes and winnows bit by bit without smoothing it over, and puts it into the granary bit by bit. This is what appears [to be the correct meaning] in this topic; and with this approach, all the traditional teachings *come up on one stalk, sound and fine* (Genesis 41:5).[25]

Our Sages of blessed memory taught further[26] that the season [of the tithe] for squash (marrows), melons and gourds (pumpkins) is from the time they are rubbed—i.e. the fine hair on them is removed. The season for a basket of fruit is from the time the fruit in it is covered with leaves and palm branches.[26] And so for every single fruit they determined the time of its "threshing" [completion of harvesting], according to what it is—all as conveyed in the Mishnah tractate *Ma'as'roth*.

Now, I have seen further on the subject of determining the time for the tithe by the law of the Torah, that the view of some authorities[27] is that there is no season set for the tithe ever, in any way, until [the produce is brought into] the sight of the face [interior] of the house, and moreover, it must be a house suitable for it:[28] for it is stated, *I have removed the sacred portions from the house* (Deuteronomy 26:13). But this means only if he brings the produce in by way of the gate, for it is stated, *that they may eat within your gates and be satisfied* (*ibid.* 12); but if he brought it in by way of the roofs or yards,[29] [the produce] is free of the obligation of *t'rumah* and the tithes. And so R. Moses b. Maimon [Rambam] of blessed memory wrote:[30] It seems to me that a flogging of whiplashes is not suffered by the law of the Torah for eating *tevel*[31] until [the duty of the tithe] is brought into effect by bringing it into one's house. But if [the duty was set] by other means which determine the obligation of the tithe, whiplashes are not suffered for it, but only punishment for disobedience. The rest of its details are explained in the Mishnah tractate *Ma'as'roth*.

It applies to both man and woman, whether Israelites, *kohanim* or Levites. For although the *kohanim* and Levites take the tithe from the Israelites, they have the duty of separating a tithe of their own produce on their own land; and it is forbidden to them as *tevel* until they separate the tithe from it: For it is stated, *So shall you also set apart* ⟨153⟩ *a gift* (Numbers 18:28), for which the interpretation was given:[32]

הַפֵּרוּשׁ עָלָיו: "אַתֶּם"—הַלְוִיִּים, "גַּם אַתֶּם"—לְרַבּוֹת הַכֹּהֲנִים. אֲבָל אַחַר שֶׁיַּעַשְׂרוּ אוֹתָן, אִם רָצוּ אוֹכְלִין הֵם בְּעַצְמָם הַמַּעֲשֵׂר, אוֹ יִתְּנוּ אוֹתוֹ לְכֹהֵן אַחֵר.

וּמִצְוָה זוֹ שֶׁל מַעֲשֵׂר, וְגַם מִצְוַת הַתְּרוּמָה, אֵינָהּ נוֹהֶגֶת מִן הַתּוֹרָה אֶלָּא בְּאֶרֶץ־יִשְׂרָאֵל לְבַדָּהּ, וּבִזְמַן שֶׁיִּהְיוּ שָׁם כָּל יִשְׂרָאֵל; כֵּן פָּסַק הָרַב מֹשֶׁה בֶּן מַיְמוֹן זִכְרוֹנוֹ לִבְרָכָה. וּבְסֵדֶר שׁוֹפְטִים בְּמִצְוַת תְּרוּמָה עֲשֵׂה ו' סִימָן (תצ״ו) [תק״ז] נְבָאֵר עוֹד בְּעֶזְרַת הַשֵּׁם הַחִלּוּקִין שֶׁיֵּשׁ בַּמַּעֲשֵׂר וּתְרוּמָה בֵּין אֶרֶץ־יִשְׂרָאֵל לְסוּרְיָא וְחוּצָה לָאָרֶץ; וְאִם חֲפָצְךָ בְּנִי לָדַעַת, גְּמֹר אוֹתוֹ מִשָּׁם.

[מִצְוַת הַלְוִיִּם לָתֵת מַעֲשֵׂר מִן הַמַּעֲשֵׂר]

שצו שֶׁנִּצְטַוּוּ הַלְוִיִּם לְהַפְרִישׁ מַעֲשֵׂר מִן הַמַּעֲשֵׂר שֶׁהֵם נוֹטְלִים מִיִּשְׂרָאֵל, וְשֶׁיִּתְּנוּ אוֹתוֹ לַכֹּהֲנִים, שֶׁנֶּאֱמַר: וְאֶל הַלְוִיִּם תְּדַבֵּר וְגוֹמֵר, וַהֲרֵמֹתֶם מִמֶּנּוּ תְּרוּמַת יי מַעֲשֵׂר מִן הַמַּעֲשֵׂר; וְזֶהוּ נִקְרָא בְּכָל מָקוֹם בַּגְּמָרָא תְּרוּמַת מַעֲשֵׂר. וְכִנּוּ לָשׁוֹן זֶה עַל דֶּרֶךְ הַכָּתוּב, שֶׁאָמַר "תְּרוּמַת יי", וּבֵאֵר הַכָּתוּב שֶׁהוּא נִתָּן לַכֹּהֲנִים, וּכְמוֹ שֶׁנֶּאֱמַר: וּנְתַתֶּם מִמֶּנּוּ אֶת תְּרוּמַת יי לְאַהֲרֹן הַכֹּהֵן.

וְהִזְהִיר הַכָּתוּב לְהַפְרִישׁ זֶה הַמַּעֲשֵׂר מִן הַטּוֹב וְהַנִּבְחָר, שֶׁנֶּאֱמַר "מִכָּל חֶלְבּוֹ אֶת מִקְדְּשׁוֹ מִמֶּנּוּ"; וְעוֹד נֶאֱמַר עַל זֶה "וְלֹא תִשְׂאוּ עָלָיו חֵטְא בַּהֲרִימְכֶם אֶת חֶלְבּוֹ מִמֶּנּוּ"—יוֹרֶה שֶׁאִם יוֹצִיאוּהוּ מִן הָרַע יִהְיֶה עֲלֵיהֶם חֵטְא; וְזֶה עִנְיָנוֹ כְּעִנְיַן לָאו הַבָּא מִכְּלַל עֲשֵׂה, וְלָכֵן אֵין לִמְנוֹת אוֹתוֹ מִן הַלָּאוִין.

מִשָּׁרְשֵׁי הַמִּצְוָה, הַקְדָּמָה: אֵין סָפֵק כִּי כָל שֵׁבֶט הַלֵּוִי הִבְדִּיל יי מֵעֲדַת יִשְׂרָאֵל לַעֲבוֹדָתוֹ תָּמִיד, וְאָמְנָם בְּשֵׁבֶט בְּעַצְמוֹ נִבְחַר בָּהֶם אֶחָד לִהְיוֹת לְכֻלָּם לְרֹאשׁ וּלְקָצִין וּלְיֹשֵׁר, הוּא וְזַרְעוֹ לְעוֹלָם, וְהוּא קֹדֶשׁ מְקֻדָּשׁ בַּשֵּׁבֶט לַעֲמֹד וּלְשָׁרֵת פְּנֵי יי

30. See note 27.

31. Produce from which the proper parts, e.g. *t'rumah* and the tithes, were not separated.

32. Midrash haGadol, Numbers 18:28 (311); MT *hilchoth ma'aser* i 3; similarly Sifre, Numbers § 121.

33. See § 389, note 2.

34. MT *ibid.* 4.

35. MT *ibid.* i 26.

§396   1. Not to give the "*t'rumah* of the tithe" from a poor (inferior) part.

2. Since an injunction or negative commandment that we learn from a positive precept is reckoned and treated as a positive one. The first two paragraphs are based on ShM positive precept § 129.

"you" — the Levites; "you also"³³ — to add the *kohanim*; but after they take the tithe from it, if they wish they may eat the tithe themselves,³⁴ or they may give it to another *kohen*.

Now, this precept of the tithe, as well as the precept of *t'rumah* (§ 496), is in effect by the law of the Torah nowhere but in the land of Israel alone, at the time that all Israelites are [settled] there. So R. Moses b. Maimon of blessed memory ruled.³⁵ In *sidrah shof'tim*, in the sixth positive precept, about *t'rumah* (§ 507), we will clarify further, with the Eternal Lord's help, the differences that there are for the tithe and *t'rumah* between the land of Israel and Syria or another foreign land. If it is your desire, my son, to know it, learn it from there.

[THE OBLIGATION OF THE LEVITES TO GIVE
A TITHE OF THE TITHE]

396 that the Levites were commanded to separate a tithe from the tithe that they take from the Israelites, and they are to give it to the *kohanim*: as it is stated, *Moreover, you shall speak to the Levites, etc. then you shall set apart from it a gift to the Lord, a tithe of the tithe* (Numbers 18:26). This is what is called everywhere in the Talmud, "*t'rumah* of tithe," which term was coined for it in accord with the phrase, "*t'rumah* (gift) to the Lord." Well, Scripture explains that it is to be given to the *kohanim*, as it is stated, *and you shall give from it the gift* (t'rumah) *for the Lord, to Aaron the* kohen (*ibid.* 28).

Now, Scripture gave an admonition to separate this tithe from the best and the choicest: as it is stated, *of all its best, its hallowed part from it* (Numbers 18:29). Then it was further stated about this, *And you shall bear no sin because of it, when you set apart its best part from it* (*ibid.* 32), which indicates that if they take it from a poor part, it will be a sin for them. Thus its nature is as the substance of an injunction¹ derived from a positive precept, and it is therefore not to be listed among the negative precepts.²

As to the root reason for the precept, [let me begin with] a preface: Past any doubt, the Lord set the entire tribe of Lévi apart from the Israelite community for His continual service. However, within the tribe itself, one of them was chosen to be the head, the chief officer, and prince—he and his descendants for all time. He was holy, consecrated within the tribe, to stand and minister in the Lord's presence continually, while the rest of the tribe was made subordinate

תָּמִיד, וּשְׁאָר כָּל הַשֵּׁבֶט נָתַן תַּחְתָּיו לְסַיֵּעַ בָּעֲבוֹדָה, וּכְמוֹ שֶׁכָּתוּב "וַיֹּאמֶר יי אֶל אַהֲרֹן אַתָּה וּבָנֶיךָ וּבֵית אָבִיךָ אִתָּךְ תִּשְׂאוּ אֶת עֲוֹן הַמִּקְדָּשׁ", כְּלוֹמַר כִּי כָל הַשֵּׁבֶט יְקַבֵּל שְׁמִירַת הַמִּקְדָּשׁ, "[וְאַתָּה] וּבָנֶיךָ אִתָּךְ תִּשְׂאוּ אֶת עֲוֹן כְּהֻנַּתְכֶם", כְּלוֹמַר שֶׁעִקַּר הָעֲבוֹדָה דְהַיְנוּ הַכְּהֻנָּה עֲלֵיכֶם הִיא; וּכְתִיב בַּתְרֵיהּ "וְגַם אֶת אַחֶיךָ מַטֵּה לֵוִי שֵׁבֶט אָבִיךָ הַקְרֵב אִתָּךְ וְיִלָּווּ עָלֶיךָ וִישָׁרְתוּךָ", כְּלוֹמַר שֶׁאַתָּה הָעִקָּר וְלֹא הֵם. וְכֵן כָּתוּב בְּמָקוֹם אַחֵר: וְנָתַתָּה אֶת הַלְוִיִּם לְאַהֲרֹן וּלְבָנָיו נְתוּנִם נְתוּנִם הֵמָּה לוֹ.

וְעַל־כֵּן, בִּהְיוֹת הַכֹּהֲנִים עִקַּר הַבַּיִת בַּעֲבוֹדַת אֱלֹהֵינוּ, זָכוּ בְכ"ד מַתָּנוֹת שֶׁנִּתְּנוּ לָהֶם הַמְפֹרָשׁוֹת בַּכָּתוּב, וּכְמוֹ שֶׁמְּנוּ אוֹתָם חֲכָמִים זִכְרוֹנָם לִבְרָכָה: עֶשֶׂר בַּמִּקְדָּשׁ וְאַרְבַּע בִּירוּשָׁלַיִם וְעֶשֶׂר בַּגְּבוּלִין; וּשְׁאָר שִׁבְטוֹ, שֶׁהוּא נִבְחַר עִמּוֹ לְסַיֵּעַ עַל־יָדוֹ, זָכוּ גַם־כֵּן לִחְיוֹת בְּטוֹבָה מִבְּלִי יְגִיעָה, עִם מַעֲשֵׂר הַפֵּרוֹת שֶׁנּוֹטְלִין מִכָּל יִשְׂרָאֵל.

וּלְמַעַן יֵדְעוּ וְיִתְבּוֹנְנוּ כִּי כָל חֶלְקָם בַּטּוֹבָה וְחֵלֶק אֲחֵיהֶם הִיא סִבַּת הָעֲבוֹדָה לַיי, נִצְטַוּוּ לָתֵת מִכָּל אֲשֶׁר יִטְּלוּ מִבְּנֵי־יִשְׂרָאֵל חֵלֶק הָעֲשִׂירִי לַמְשָׁרְתִים הַגְּדוֹלִים, וּבְכֵן יִתְּנוּ אֶל לִבָּם כִּי יֵשׁ גְּבוֹהִים עֲלֵיהֶם, וְגָבֹהַּ מֵעַל לְכֻלָּם, הוּא שׁוֹמֵר הַכֹּל יִתְעַלֶּה; גַּם כִּי יֵשׁ בָּזֶה זְכוּת וְכָבוֹד וּמַעֲלָה לַלְוִיִּם לְבִלְתִּי יִגְרַע שָׁמָם מִמִּצְוַת מַעֲשֵׂר בְּחֶלְקָם בַּתְּבוּאוֹת, וְאַל יֹאמְרוּ בְנֵיהֶם לִבְנֵיהֶם "זְכִיתֶם בַּתְּבוּאָה וַאֲנַחְנוּ בַּמִּצְוָה", וְעַכְשָׁיו יִהְיֶה הַמַּעֲנֶה "יֵשׁ תּוֹרָה וְיֵשׁ קֶמַח".

מִדִּינֵי הַמִּצְוָה, מַה שֶּׁאָמְרוּ זִכְרוֹנָם לִבְרָכָה שֶׁבֶּן לֵוִי שֶׁלָּקַח הַמַּעֲשֵׂר שִׁבָּלִים, (לֹא יִתֵּן תְּרוּמָתוֹ שִׁבָּלִים, אֶלָּא קוֹנְסִין אוֹתוֹ לָדוּשׁ וְלִזְרוֹת וְלִתֵּן לוֹ מַעֲשֵׂר מִן הַמַּעֲשֵׂר מַעֲשֵׂר דָּגָן, וְ)אֵינוֹ חַיָּב לָתֵת מַעֲשֵׂר הַתֶּבֶן אַחַר שֶׁיָּדוּשׁ הַכֹּל וְיִזְרֶה, אֲבָל

3. TB Bava Kamma 110a, Ḥullin 113b.

4. I.e. they were to be eaten, respectively, within the boundaries of the Sanctuary, within the city of Jerusalem, and anywhere in Israel.

5. I.e. they had both the *mitzvah* of the Torah to give a tithe and the flour they received as the tithe of the Israelites. This is by way of a playful reversal of a saying in Mishnah, 'Avoth iii 17: If there is no Torah, there is no flour.

6. Mishnah, T'rumoth x 6 and TB Bétzah 13a.

7. He is thus "penalized" for having gone and taken his tithe prematurely, before the owner made grain of the ears and gave *t'rumah* to a *kohen*. For now, when the owner does separate *t'rumah*, he will do so from a somewhat smaller amount of produce, and the amount of *t'rumah* will be proportionately smaller. For this the Levite must compensate by giving his "tithe of a tithe" to a *kohen* as a tenth of the grain (MY).

8. This part in parentheses is not in the oldest manuscripts, and thus must be a later interpolation, taken directly from MT (note 9).

to him to assist in the service; as it is written, *And the Lord said to Aaron: You and your sons and your father's house with you shall bear the iniquity of the sanctuary* — which is to say that the whole tribe is to accept the task of guarding the sanctuary; *and you and your sons with you shall bear the iniquity of your function as* kohanim (Numbers 18:1): in other words, the principal service, which is the function of the *kohanim*, is imposed on [all of] you. But it is written afterward, *And also your brethren the tribe of Lévi, the tribe of your father, bring near with you, that they may be joined to you and minister to you* (ibid. 2): which is to say that you are the main element, and not they. And so is it written in another instance: *And you shall give the Levites to Aaron and to his sons; they are wholly given to him* (Numbers 3:9).

Therefore, since the *kohanim* are the principal element at the Temple in the service of our God, they merited to receive twenty-four gifts, which were explicitly granted them in Scripture. As our Sages of blessed memory listed them,[3] there were ten at the Sanctuary, four in Jerusalem, and ten within Israel's borders.[4] And the rest of his tribe, which was chosen with him to assist him, likewise merited to live in goodness without toil, with the tithe from produce that they would take from all Israelites.

Yet in order that they [the Levites] might know and realize that all their share of good fortune, and the share of their brethren, was by virtue of the service to the Lord, they were commanded to give from all that they would take from the Israelites, a tenth part to the great ministering servants [the *kohanim*]. Thus they would realize in their heart that there are those superior to them, while the One superior to them all is the [Divine] Guardian of all (be He exalted). Moreover, in this lies merit, honor and elevation for the Levites, that their names might not be lacking from [the list of those who observed] the *mitzvah* of the tithe when they shared in the crops of grain; and let their [the Israelites'] sons not say to their sons, "You attained grain, but we, a *mitzvah*." Now the reply would be, "There is Torah, and there is flour."[5]

Among the laws of the precept, there is what the Sages of blessed memory taught:[6] that if a Levite took a tithe [in the form of] ears of grain, (he is not to give his *t'rumah* as ears, but he is rather penalized to thresh and winnow, and to give him [the kohen] the tithe of the tithe as a tenth of the grain;[7] but)[8] he is not obligated to give a tithe of the straw after threshing it all and winnowing it. But if he separated the

אִם תְּחִלָּה הִפְרִישׁ הַמַּעֲשֵׂר שֶׁבְּלֵים וְדָשׁ וְזָרָה, נוֹתֵן לוֹ חֶלְקוֹ מִן הַכֹּל.

וּמַה שֶּׁאָמְרוּ שֶׁתְּרוּמַת מַעֲשֵׂר שֶׁהָיָה בָהּ אֶחָד מִשְּׁמוֹנָה בַּשְּׁמִינִית מוֹלִיכָהּ לַכֹּהֵן, וּבִלְבַד שֶׁתְּהֵא תְּרוּמַת מַעֲשֵׂר וַדָּאִית וּטְהוֹרָה. (פָּחוֹת מִכֵּן אֵינוֹ מְטֻפֵּל לְהוֹלִיכָהּ, אֶלָּא מַשְׁלִיכָהּ בָּאוּר וְשׂוֹרְפָהּ.) וּמַה שֶּׁאָמְרוּ שֶׁתְּרוּמַת מַעֲשֵׂר מַפְרִישִׁין אוֹתָהּ שֶׁלֹּא מִן הַמֻּקָּף, שֶׁנֶּאֱמַר "מִכֹּל מַעְשְׂרֹתֵיכֶם תָּרִימוּ", כְּלוֹמַר אֲפִלּוּ יֵשׁ לְךָ מַעֲשֵׂר אֶחָד בִּמְדִינָה זוֹ וְאֶחָד בִּמְדִינָה אַחֶרֶת, אַתָּה מַפְרִישׁ תְּרוּמָה אַחַת עַל הַכֹּל. וּמִכָּל-מָקוֹם אָמְרוּ זִכְרוֹנָם לִבְרָכָה, שֶׁתַּלְמִידֵי חֲכָמִים אֵין תּוֹרְמִין אוֹתָהּ אֶלָּא מִן הַמֻּקָּף. וְיֶתֶר פְּרָטֶיהָ, מְבֹאָרִים בְּמַסֶּכֶת תְּרוּמוֹת וּמַעֲשֵׂרוֹת, וּבִמְקוֹמוֹת מִמַּסֶּכֶת דְּמַאי.

וְנוֹהֶגֶת מִצְוָה זוֹ בְּמָקוֹם שֶׁתְּרוּמָה וּמַעֲשֵׂר נוֹהֲגִין שָׁם; וּבְסִימָן (תצ״ו) [תק״ז] בְּסֵדֶר שׁוֹפְטִים נְבָאֵר הַכֹּל בְּעֶזְרַת הַשֵּׁם.

✡ זֹאת חֻקַּת

שָׁלֹשׁ מִצְוֹת עֲשֵׂה

[מִצְוַת פָּרָה אֲדֻמָּה]

שצז שֶׁנִּצְטַוּוּ יִשְׂרָאֵל לִשְׂרֹף פָּרָה אֲדֻמָּה, לִהְיוֹת אֶפְרָהּ מוּכָן לְמִי שֶׁיִּצְטָרֵךְ אֵלֶיהָ, מִטַּהֲרָה מִטֻּמְאַת מֵת, שֶׁנֶּאֱמַר: דַּבֵּר אֶל בְּנֵי יִשְׂרָאֵל וְיִקְחוּ אֵלֶיךָ פָרָה אֲדֻמָּה וְגוֹמֵר, וּכְתִיב לְמַטָּה מִזֶּה: וְהָיְתָה לַעֲדַת בְּנֵי-יִשְׂרָאֵל לְמִשְׁמֶרֶת וְגוֹמֵר.

אַף-עַל-פִּי שֶׁמִּלְּאַנִי לְבָבִי לִכְתֹּב רְמָזִים מִטַּעֲמֵי הַמִּצְוֹת שֶׁקָּדְמוּ עַל צַד הַפְּשָׁט, עִם הַהִתְנַצְּלוּת שֶׁהַמְּלָאכָה שֶׁהֵחַגִּוּ בָּהּ בְּנֵי וְהַנְּעָרִים חֲבֵרָיו, בְּמִצְוָה זוֹ רָפוּ יָדַי, וָאִירָא לִפְצוֹת פִּי עָלֶיהָ כְּלָל גַּם בַּפְּשָׁט: כִּי רָאִיתִי לְרַבּוֹתֵינוּ זִכְרוֹנָם לִבְרָכָה,

---

9. MT *hilchoth t'rumoth* iii 14.

10. MT *ibid*. 16, based on Mishnah, *T'rumoth* xi 8.

11. Mishnah, *Bikkurim* ii 5.

12. The word "all," regarded as otherwise superfluous, is interpreted as extending the meaning or scope of the precept.

13. TJ *Bikkurim* ii 1.

14. TB *Gittin* 30b.

§397   1. The Hebrew is מטהרה, which seems awkward, and may well be an early scribal error. In the Hebrew versions of ShM positive precept §113, R. Samuel ibn Tibbon has לטהרה, while R. Yosef Kafeḥ gives בטהרה.

tithe first, as ears, and then did the threshing and winnowing, he is to give him his share from everything.⁹

Then there is what the Sages said:¹⁰ that if the *t'rumah* of the tithe comprised an eighth of an eighth [a sixty-fourth, of a *log*] it is to be brought to the *kohen*—but only if it is *t'rumah* of a tithe for certain, and ritually pure. (If it was less than that, one need not bother to bring it [to a *kohen*] but he may rather throw it in the fire and burn it.)⁸ There is, further, what the Sages said:¹¹ that *t'rumah* of a tithe may be set apart from what is not next to it, for it is stated, *Out of all your tithes you shall set apart* t'rumah (Numbers 18:29)¹²—which is to say that even if you have one tithe in this country and one in another country, you may set apart one portion of *t'rumah* for it all.¹³ However, the Sages of blessed memory said¹⁴ that Torah scholars give the *t'rumah* only from what is directly nearby. The rest of its details are explained in the Mishnah tractates *T'rumah* and *Ma'asér*, and in certain places of the tractate *D'mai*.

This precept is in force in [every] place where *t'rumah* and the tithe are in force. At precept §507 in *sidrah shof'tim* we will clarify everything, with the Eternal Lord's help.

sidrah ḥukath
(Numbers 19–22:1)

[It contains] three positive precepts.

[THE PRECEPT OF THE RED HEIFER]

397 that the Israelites were commanded to burn a red heifer, so that its ash should be ready for anyone who would need it, for purification¹ from defilement by the dead: as it is stated, *Speak to the Israelites that they shall bring you a red heifer*, etc. (Numbers 19:2), and it is written further on, *and it shall be for the community of the Israelites for a safekeeping, for lustral water for impurity*, etc. (*ibid.* 9).

Although my heart emboldened me to write hints of the reasons for the preceding *mitzvoth* from the aspect of the plain meaning with the explanation that the task was to educate thereby my son and the lads [who are] his friends, at this precept my hands grow feeble, and I fear to open my mouth about it at all, even with the plain meaning.

הֶאֱרִיכוּ הַדִּבּוּר בְּעֹמֶק סוֹדָהּ וְגֹדֶל עִנְיָנָהּ, עַד שֶׁאָמְרוּ שֶׁהַמֶּלֶךְ שְׁלֹמֹה הִשִּׂיג לָדַעַת
בְּרֻבֵּי חָכְמָתוֹ כָּל טַעֲמֵי הַתּוֹרָה חוּץ מִזּוֹ, שֶׁאָמַר עָלֶיהָ: אָמַרְתִּי אֶחְכָּמָה וְהִיא
רְחוֹקָה מִמֶּנִּי; גַּם אָמְרוּ בְמִדְרָשׁ רַבִּי תַּנְחוּמָא: רַבִּי יוֹסֵי בְּרַבִּי חֲנִינָא אוֹמֵר: אָמַר
לוֹ הַקָּדוֹשׁ בָּרוּךְ הוּא לְמֹשֶׁה: לְךָ אֲנִי מְגַלֶּה טַעַם פָּרָה וְלֹא לַאֲחֵרִים; וְכַיּוֹצֵא
בָאֵלּוּ הַדְּבָרִים רַבִּים.

וְעַתָּה אַל יַחְשֹׁב שׁוֹמֵעַ שֶׁעִנְיָנֵי סוֹדָהּ וְסֵדֶר חֻקָּהּ הוּא מֵהְיוֹתָהּ מְטַהֶרֶת בְּהַגִּיעַ
אֶפְרָהּ עַל גּוּף הַמְּטַהֵר: שֶׁהֲרֵי כְּעֵין דָּבָר זֶה יִמָּצֵא בִשְׁאָר הַקָּרְבָּנוֹת, כְּעִנְיַן הַזָּב
וְהַיּוֹלֶדֶת, שֶׁתַּשְׁלוּם טָהֳרָתָן בְּקָרְבָּנָן הִיא. אֲבָל עִקַּר הַפֶּלֶא לְפִי מַה שֶּׁשָּׁמַעְתִּי הוּא
עַל הֱיוֹתָהּ מְטַהֶרֶת הַטְּמֵאִים וּמְטַמְּאָה הָעֲסוּקִים בִּשְׂרֵפָתָהּ; וְאַף־עַל־פִּי שֶׁבְּכָל
הַחַטָּאוֹת הַנִּשְׂרָפוֹת מִן הַפָּרִים וּמִן הַשְּׂעִירִים הַדִּין כֵּן, שֶׁהַשּׂוֹרֵף אוֹתָם מְטַמֵּא
בְגָדִים בִּשְׁעַת שְׂרֵפָתָן עַד שֶׁיֵּעָשׂוּ אֵפֶר, מִכָּל־מָקוֹם אֵין אֶפְרָן מְטַהֵר.

וְגַם־כֵּן הַתְּמִהָה הַגָּדוֹל בָּהּ בִּהְיוֹתָהּ נַעֲשֵׂית מִחוּץ לַמַּחֲנֶה, שֶׁלֹּא כְדֶרֶךְ שְׁאָר
הַקָּרְבָּנוֹת; וְעַל דָּבָר זֶה מוֹנִין הָאֻמּוֹת אֶת יִשְׂרָאֵל עָלֶיהָ, כִּי יַחְשְׁבוּ שֶׁהִיא נִזְבַּחַת
לַשְּׂעִירִים עַל פְּנֵי הַשָּׂדֶה כְּמִנְהָגָם הֵם. וְאָמְנָם כַּמָּה תְרוּפוֹת בְּעֶשְׂבֵי הָאֲדָמָה
וּבָאִילָנוֹת, מִן הָאֵזֶר אֲשֶׁר בַּלְּבָנוֹן עַד הָאֵזוֹב אֲשֶׁר בַּקִּיר, מְלֵאִים סְגֻלּוֹת בַּהֲפָכִים,
יְקָרְרוּ הַחַמִּים וִיחַמְּמוּ הַקָּרִים. וְאִלּוּ יָדַעְנוּ מַהוּת הַנֶּפֶשׁ וְשָׁרְשָׁהּ וּמַחְלָתָהּ
וּבְרִיאוּתָהּ, נָבִין בְּאוּלַי כִּי סְגֻלַּת הַפָּרָה גַּם־כֵּן לְהַחֲלִיא הַנֶּפֶשׁ וּלְטַמְּאָהּ בְּעֵסֶק
הַשְּׂרֵפָה, וְאַחֲרֵי הֱיוֹתָהּ אֵפֶר תְּרַפֵּא מַחֲלַת הַטֻּמְאָה; וְזֶה אֵינֶנּוּ בָּרוּר לְהַשִּׂיג
בְּעִנְיָנָן כְּלוּם, אֶלָּא שֶׁחִבַּת הַקֹּדֶשׁ וְהַחֵשֶׁק לְהַשִּׂיג יְדִיעָה בַּנִּסְתָּר, יָנִיד הַקָּנֶה לִכְתֹּב.

2. P'sikta d'R. Kahana iv (ed. Buber, 36a); Tanḥuma, ḥukath 6 (ed. Buber, 15); Bamidbar Rabbah 19, 3; Koheleth Rabbah, Ecclesiastes 7:23.

3. Tanḥuma, ḥukath 8 (ed. Buber, 24); P'sikta d'R. Kahana iv (ed. Buber, 39a); Bamidbar Rabbah 19, 6.

4. Cf. Bamidbar Rabbah 19, 1: All who dealt with the red heifer [to prepare the ash from it] would [thus] make their clothes defiled, yet that itself would make clothes ritually clean.

5. So Rashi, Numbers 19:2, based on the words of our Sages, according to Ramban ibid. It was evidently in a Midrash lost to us; but cf. P'sikta d'R. Kahana iv (ed. Buber 38b), etc. that this is one of four things against which Satan retorts, etc.

6. Cf. Leviticus 17:5, 7; and see Ramban to Numbers 19:2, referring to his commentary of Leviticus 16:8, that on this assumption the nations would plague the Israelites about the goat despatched into the wilderness on the Day of Atonement.

7. So three of the oldest manuscripts; MS Vatican and the first edition read, k'minhagam ha-yom, "as their practice is today"(!); most editions substitute k'min-hagam ha-ra, "as their evil practice was."

8. Cf. R. Sa'adyah Ga'on, 'Emunoth v'Dé'oth, II x: it is by no means extraordinary that one and the same thing should produce two opposite effects, depending on

For I saw that our Sages of blessed memory spoke at length of the profundity of its mystery and the greatness of its theme, until they said[2] that King Solomon attained knowledge, in the immensity of his wisdom, of all the reasons of the Torah except for this; for he declared about it, *I said, "I will get wisdom," but it is far from me* (Ecclesiastes 7:23). Moreover, it was related in the Midrash of R. Tanḥuma:[3] R. Yosé b. R. Ḥanina said: The Holy One, blessed is He, told Moses, "To you I will reveal the reason for the heifer, but not to others." And there are so many other passages like these.

Now, let not any listener think that the problem of its mystery and the order of its statute is because it brings ritual purification when its ash touches the body of a person becoming ritually clean. For you see, one can find something like this with other offerings, in regard to a man with a discharge and a woman who gave birth; the completion of their purification is by offerings. Rather, the main wonder, according to what I heard, is that it would purify the defiled, but would defile the people engaged in its burning.[4] Even though with all the *ḥattath* (sin) offerings that were burned, of bullocks and goats, such was the law, that for the one who burned them, his clothing became ritually unclean at the time they were burned until they turned to ash, their ash, however, did not bring ritual purification.

The wonder about it is great also in that it [the precept of the red heifer] was carried out beyond the [Israelite] camp, not in the way of other offerings. And on this matter the nations of the world would plague the Israelites,[5] thinking that it was sacrificed to satyrs in the open field,[6] as their own practice was.[7]

Yet indeed, how many medicines there are in the leaves of the earth and the trees, *from the cedar that is in Lebanon to the hyssop that grows out of the wall* (I Kings 5:13), full of rare contrary powers: They can cool the hot and heat the cold. If we but knew the nature of the human spirit, its root origin, its illness and its health, we might perhaps understand that it was the rare, wondrous characteristic of the heifer likewise to sicken the spirit and defile it during the task of burning it, yet after it turned to ash it could cure the illness of ritual uncleanness.[8] This is not a clarification to provide any comprehension whatever of the matter. It is only the love of holiness and the eagerness to achieve a knowledge of the hidden that moves the quill to write.

⟨161⟩ Among the laws of the precept, there is what the Sages of blessed

מִדִּינֵי הַמִּצְוָה, מַה שֶּׁאָמְרוּ זִכְרוֹנָם לִבְרָכָה, שֶׁמִּצְוַת פָּרָה שֶׁתִּהְיֶה בַת אַרְבַּע שָׁנִים אוֹ בַת שָׁלֹשׁ, וְאִם הָיְתָה זְקֵנָה כְּשֵׁרָה. וְאֵין לוֹקְחִין עֶגְלָה וּמְגַדְּלִין אוֹתָהּ, אֶלָּא פָרָה, שֶׁנֶּאֱמַר "וְיִקְחוּ אֵלֶיךָ פָרָה" וְכוּלֵּי. וְזֶה שֶׁנֶּאֱמַר בָּהּ "תְּמִימָה", כְּלוֹמַר תְּמִימוּת שֶׁל אַדְמִימוּת, שֶׁשְּׁתֵּי שְׂעָרוֹת שְׁחוֹרוֹת אוֹ לְבָנוֹת פּוֹסְלוֹת בָּהּ. אֲפִלּוּ הָיְתָה נוֹסָה כְּשֵׁרָה, וּבִלְבַד שֶׁכָּלָהּ אֲדֻמָּה, שֶׁאֵינָהּ צְרִיכָה תְּמִימוּת יוֹתֵר מִשְּׁאָר הַקָּרְבָּנוֹת.

וְאִם הָיוּ בָהּ שְׂעָרוֹת שֶׁעִקָּרָן אָדֹם וְרֹאשָׁן מִצֶּבַע אַחֵר, הַכֹּל הוֹלֵךְ אַחַר הָעִקָּר, וְגוֹזֵז בְּמִסְפָּרַיִם אֶת רֹאשָׁן עַד הָאָדֹם. וְהָעֲבוֹדָה פּוֹסֶלֶת בָּהּ, שֶׁנֶּאֱמַר "אֲשֶׁר לֹא עָלָה עָלֶיהָ עֹל", וְכָל הָעֲבוֹדוֹת הֵן כְּעֹל; לְפִיכָךְ אָמְרוּ זִכְרוֹנָם לִבְרָכָה שֶׁאִם פָּלוּ נָתַן טַלִּיתוֹ עָלֶיהָ, פְּסוּלָה. אֲבָל הָיְתָה צְרִיכָה שְׁמִירָה וּקְשָׁרָהּ בְּמוֹסֵרָה, כְּשֵׁרָה; אֲבָל אִם לֹא הָיְתָה צְרִיכָה שְׁמִירָה, פְּסוּלָה, שֶׁכָּל שְׁמִירָה שֶׁאֵינָהּ צְרִיכָה, מַשּׂוֹי הוּא. וְהָיְתָה נִלְקַחַת מִמְּעוֹת תְּרוּמַת הַלִּשְׁכָּה; וּפָרָה שֶׁנּוֹלַד בָּהּ פְּסוּל, פּוֹדִין אוֹתָהּ וְיוֹצְאָה לְחֻלִּין.

וּמַה שֶּׁאָמְרוּ בְעִנְיָן זֶה שֶׁהַשּׂוֹרֵף אוֹתָהּ שֶׁהוּא טָמֵא, הוּא הַמַּסִּיעַ בַּשְּׂרֵפָה, כְּגוֹן הַמְּהַפֵּךְ בַּבָּשָׂר וְהַמַּשְׁלִיךְ עֵצִים וְהַמְּהַפֵּךְ בָּאֵשׁ וְהַמְּחַתֶּה בַּגֶּחָלִים כְּדֵי שֶׁתִּבְעַר הָאֵשׁ, וְכַיּוֹצֵא בָזֶה; אֲבָל הַמַּצִּית אֶת הָאוּר לַכִּבְשָׁן וְהַמְּסַדֵּר אֶת הַמַּעֲרָכָה, טָהוֹר; וְכֵן הַמִּתְעַסֵּק בָּהּ מִשֶּׁנַּעֲשֵׂית אֵפֶר.

וּמַעֲלוֹת גְּדוֹלוֹת עָשׂוּ חֲכָמִים בְּטַהֲרַת פָּרָה בִּשְׂרֵפָתָהּ; וּמֵהֶן, שֶׁהָיוּ מַפְרִישִׁין שִׁבְעַת יָמִים קֹדֶם שְׂרֵפַת הַפָּרָה, כֹּהֵן הַשּׂוֹרֵף אוֹתָהּ, מִבֵּיתוֹ וּמֵאִשְׁתּוֹ, כְּמוֹ שֶׁמַּפְרִישִׁין כֹּהֵן גָּדוֹל לַעֲבוֹדַת יוֹם הַכִּפּוּרִים; וְדָבָר זֶה קַבָּלָה; וּבְכָל יוֹם וָיוֹם

the nature of the object that encounters it. For we see that fire liquefies lead, yet solidifies milk... good food is beneficial to a hungry person but harmful to one who is sated; and choice medicine might be beneficial to the sick yet harmful to a person in good health (English translation, New Haven 1948, 177–78).

9. Mishnah, Parah i 1.

10. Sifre Zuta 300 l. 14.

11. Sifre, Numbers § 123; Mishnah, Parah ii 5.

12. Mishnah *ibid.* 2.

13. The paragraph is based on MT *hilchoth parah 'adumah* i 1–2.

14. Tosefta, Parah i toward the end.

15. Inferred in TB Sotah 46a, and Midrash haGadol, Numbers 19:2 (328–29).

16. Mishnah, Parah ii 3.

17. *Ibid.* 2.

18. I.e. if it was not unruly; TB Shabbath 52a.

19. MT *hilchoth parah 'adumah* i 7.

20. These funds were from the half-shekels collected thrice annually from every Israelite, as opposed to *bedek ha-ba-yith*, money given for Temple repairs. The *lishkah* funds were used for the purchase of *korb'noth tzibbur*, offerings on behalf of all the

memory said:[9] that the precept of the red heifer [requires initially] that it should be four or three years old; but if it is older, it is acceptable. A young calf is not to be bought and raised, but only a heifer, since it is stated, *that they shall bring you a red heifer*, etc. (Numbers 19:2).[10] As for the term "faultless" stated about it (*ibid.*), it is to denote a faultless perfection of redness: For two black or white hairs disqualify it.[11] Even if it was stunted in growth, it is acceptable, provided it is altogether red;[12] for it does not require more wholeness or perfection of body than the other offerings.[13]

If it had hairs that were red at the root and their upper part was of another color, it all depends on the root part, and the upper parts are to be cut with scissors until the red part.[14] Labor disqualifies it, for it is stated, *and upon which a yoke has never come* (Numbers 19:2), and all labors are like a yoke.[15] Therefore the Sages of blessed memory said[16] that even if a person spread his cloak over it, it is disqualified. However, if it needed guarding and he tied it by the reins, it is acceptable;[17] but if it did not need guarding [and he so tied it] it is disqualified;[18] for any form of safekeeping that is not necessary is [as] a burden [put on it].[19]

It was bought with money from the Temple *lishkah* funds.[20] A heifer in which a disqualifying feature developed was to be redeemed, and it was released to be non-holy.[21]

Then there is what the Sages said in this subject,[22] that the person burning it who is defiled [thereby] would be anyone helping in the burning: for instance, one who turns over the flesh, throws on wood, stirs up the fire, or rakes up the embers so that the fire should blaze; and so forth. However, one who kindles the flame in the furnace or arranges the pile of wood remains ritually pure; and so to anyone who handles it after it has turned to ash [and been collected].[23]

The Sages set very high requirements in regard to the ritual purity of the heifer at its burning. Some of these were: that seven days before the burning of the heifer, the *kohen* who was to burn it was separated from his home and his wife, just as the *kohen gadol* was separated for the service of the Day of Atonement — this being an Oral Tradition.[24]

Israelites; and the red heifer was thus considered in the same category. Mishnah, Sh'kalim iv 2.

21. TB Sh'vu'oth 11b.
22. MT *ibid.* v 4, based on TB Yoma 68b, Z'vaḥim 106a; Mishnah, Parah iv 4.
23. So R. Isaiah Pik emends, in accord with Numbers 19:10.

מִימֵי הַפְּרִישָׁה מַזִּין עָלָיו מֵאֵפֶר פָּרָה מִן הַפָּרוֹת שֶׁנִּשְׂרְפוּ כְבָר, וְאֵין מַזֶּה עָלָיו
אֶלָּא אָדָם שֶׁלֹּא נִטְמָא בְמֵת מֵעוֹלָם, שֶׁהַמַּזֶּה צָרִיךְ שֶׁיִּהְיֶה טָהוֹר.

וְאִם תֹּאמַר: אִם־כֵּן שֶׁאֵין הַצֹּרֶךְ אֶלָּא כְדֵי שֶׁיְּהֵא עָלָיו טָהוֹר, הָיָה אֶפְשָׁר
שֶׁיְּהֵא עָלָיו אִישׁ וְאַף־עַל־פִּי שֶׁנִּטְמָא, מִכֵּיוָן שֶׁהָיָה עָלָיו—אֵינוֹ כֵן, דְּחַיְישִׁינָן
שֶׁמָּא זֶה שֶׁהָיָה עָלָיו לֹא הָיָה טָהוֹר מִשְּׁמָא מֵת. וְכֵן כָּל הַכֵּלִים שֶׁמְּמַלְּאִין בָּהֶן
לְהַזּוֹת עַל הַכֹּהֵן הַשּׂוֹרֵף אוֹתָהּ, כֻּלָּם כְּלֵי אֲבָנִים הָיוּ, שֶׁאֵין מְקַבְּלִין טֻמְאָה.

וְאִם תִּשְׁאַל: כֵּיצַד יִמָּצֵא אִישׁ שֶׁלֹּא נִטְמָא בְטֻמְאַת מֵת מֵעוֹלָם—אָמְרוּ
חֲכָמִים שֶׁהָיוּ בִירוּשָׁלַיִם חֲצֵרוֹת בְּנוּיוֹת עַל גַּבֵּי סֶלַע וְתַחְתֵּיהֶן חָלוּל מִפְּנֵי קֶבֶר
הַתְּהוֹם, וּמְבִיאִים נָשִׁים עֻבָּרוֹת וְיוֹלְדוֹת שָׁם וּמְגַדְּלוֹת שָׁם אֶת בְּנֵיהֶן; וּכְשֶׁרוֹצִין
לְהַזּוֹת עַל הַכֹּהֵן הַשּׂוֹרֵף, מְבִיאִין שְׁוָרִין, מִפְּנֵי שֶׁכְּרֵסָן נָפוּחַ, וּמַנִּיחִין עַל גַּבֵּיהֶן
דְּלָתוֹת, וְיוֹשְׁבִין עֲלֵיהֶן הַתִּינוֹקוֹת עַל גַּבֵּי הַדְּלָתוֹת, כְּדֵי שֶׁיְּהֵא אֹהֶל מַבְדִּיל בֵּינָם
וּבֵין הָאָרֶץ, מִפְּנֵי חֲשַׁשׁ קֶבֶר הַתְּהוֹם.

וְכוֹסוֹת שֶׁל אֶבֶן בְּיַד הַתִּינוֹקוֹת, וְהוֹלְכִין עַד מֵי הַשִּׁלּוֹחַ שָׁם וְיוֹרְדִין שָׁם וּמְמַלְּאִין,
שֶׁאֵין לָחוּשׁ שָׁם מִפְּנֵי קֶבֶר הַתְּהוֹם, שֶׁאֵין דֶּרֶךְ בְּנֵי־אָדָם לְקָבֵר בַּנְּהָרוֹת; וְחוֹזְרִין
וְעוֹלִין עַל הַדְּלָתוֹת שֶׁעַל הַשְּׁוָרִים וְהוֹלְכִין לְהַר־הַבַּיִת, וְשָׁם יוֹרְדִין וְהוֹלְכִין
בְּרַגְלֵיהֶן, מִפְּנֵי שֶׁכָּל הַר־הַבַּיִת וְהָעֲזָרוֹת תַּחְתֵּיהֶן חָלוּל מִפְּנֵי חֲשַׁשׁ קֶבֶר הַתְּהוֹם,
וּמְהַלְּכִין עַד פֶּתַח הָעֲזָרָה וְנוֹטְלִין מִן הָאֵפֶר וְנוֹתְנִין בַּכּוֹסוֹת וּמַזִּין עַל הַכֹּהֵן
הַשּׂוֹרֵף; וּמַטְבִּילִין הָיוּ הַתִּינוֹקוֹת מִפְּנֵי חֲשַׁשׁ שֶׁמָּא נִטְמְאוּ בְטֻמְאָה אַחֶרֶת. וְכָל
הַדְּבָרִים הָאֵלּוּ מִן הַמַּעֲלוֹת יְתֵרוֹת שֶׁבַּפָּרָה; וּבְהַר הַמִּשְׁחָה הָיְתָה נִשְׂרֶפֶת.

24. Mishnah, Parah iii 1; TB Yoma 2a; MT *hilchoth parah 'adumah* ii 2.
25. Mishnah *ibid.*
26. *Ibid.* 2–3.
27. TB Yoma 2a. The paragraph is taken from MT *ibid.* 7.
28. I.e. if there is a grave deep in the earth below, the remains of the dead
ordinarily defile anyone above, on the earth's surface, unless there is a hollow space
over the grave, to form a "tent"; this would interrupt or contain the defilement.
29. I.e. the distended bellies of the oxen.
30. A stream near the Temple Mount.
31. Tosefta, Parah ii.

Every single day of these days of separation, [water with] some of the ash of one of the heifers burned in the past would be sprinkled on him.[25] No one was to sprinkle this on him but a person who had never been defiled by the dead; for the one doing the sprinkling needed to be ritually pure.[26]

Now, you might ask: If it is so, that no more is necessary than that the one who sprinkles it on him should be ritually pure, then it is possible that a man should sprinkle it on him even if he was defiled [in the past], since he had been sprinkled upon [afterward and was thus purified]? This is not so: For it is feared that perhaps the one who did the sprinkling on him was not ritually clean from defilement by the dead. So too, all the vessels with which water was gathered for sprinkling on the *kohen* who was to burn it were all of stone, which was not subject to defilement.[27]

But you might ask, "How was a man to be found who never became ritually unclean by defilement by the dead?" Our Sages said[25] that there were forecourts in Jerusalem built over rock, and underneath it was hollow, in case of a grave in the depth.[28] Pregnant women were brought [to live there] and there they would give birth, and raise their sons. When it was desired to sprinkle [the purifying water] on the *kohen* who was to do the burning, oxen would be brought, because their bellies are distended; doors would be placed on their backs, and the youngsters would be seated on the doors — so that there would be a "tent"[29] separating them from the ground, because of the suspected possibility of a grave in the depth.

There were cups of stone in the youngsters' hands. They would go on to the waters of the Shiloaḥ,[30] descend there, and fill [the cups], since there was no need to be fearful there about any grave in the depth, as it is not the way of the people to bury [anyone] in [the beds of] streams. They would go up [again] on the doors atop the oxen, and proceed to the Temple Mount. There they would descend and go on foot, because it was hollow underneath the entire Temple Mount and the Temple forecourts, on account of the fear of a grave in the depth. They would walk to the entrance of the Temple court, take some of the ashes and put it in the cups, and would sprinkle the *kohen* who was to do the burning. Yet the youngsters were [previously] subjected to ritual immersion, for fear that perhaps they were defiled by some other uncleanness.[31] All these matters were among the extra high requirements set [by the Sages] for the [red] heifer. On the

וְדִין כֵּיצַד שׂוֹרְפִין אוֹתָהּ, וּבְאֵי זֶה מְקוֹמוֹת מַנִּיחִין מַדְשַׁן אֶפְרָהּ, וְכֵיצַד מְקַדְּשִׁין אֶת הַמַּיִם בְּאֵפֶר הַפָּרָה, וְכֵיצַד מְטַהֲרִין טְמֵאֵי מֵתִים בְּמֵי נִדָּה, וְיֶתֶר רַבֵּי פְּרָטֶיהָ — בַּמַּסֶּכְתָּא הַמְחֻבֶּרֶת עַל זֶה, וְהִיא מַסֶּכֶת פָּרָה.

וְנוֹהֶגֶת בְּאֶרֶץ־יִשְׂרָאֵל בִּזְמַן הַבַּיִת, וְהִיא מִן הַמִּצְווֹת שֶׁאָמַרְנוּ בְּרֹאשׁ הַסֵּפֶר שֶׁהֵן מֻטָּלוֹת עַל הַצִּבּוּר כֻּלָּן. וְאָמְרוּ רַבּוֹתֵינוּ זִכְרוֹנָם לִבְרָכָה שֶׁתֵּשַׁע פָּרוֹת אֲדֻמּוֹת נַעֲשׂוּ מִשֶּׁנִּצְטַוּוּ בְּמִצְוָה זוֹ עַד שֶׁחָרַב הַבַּיִת בַּשְּׁנִיָּה: הָרִאשׁוֹנָה עָשָׂה מֹשֶׁה עָלָיו הַשָּׁלוֹם, שְׁנִיָּה עָשָׂה עֶזְרָא, וְשֶׁבַע מֵעֶזְרָא עַד חֻרְבַּן הַבַּיִת; וַעֲשִׂירִית יַעֲשֶׂה הַמֶּלֶךְ הַמָּשִׁיחַ, שֶׁיִּגָּלֶה בִּמְהֵרָה בְיָמֵינוּ.

וּמִפְּנֵי שֶׁעִנְיָן זֶה שֶׁל פָּרָה אֲדֻמָּה הוּא דָבָר גָּדוֹל בֶּאֱמָתֵנוּ, שֶׁהָיְתָה מְטַהֶרֶת מִידֵי טֻמְאָה חֲמוּרָה, וְזוּלָתָהּ אִי־אֶפְשָׁר לְטָמֵא־מֵת לַעֲשׂוֹת פֶּסַח, שֶׁהִיא מִצְוָה גְדוֹלָה מְאֹד, נָהֲגוּ כָל יִשְׂרָאֵל לִקְרוֹת פָּרָשָׁה זוֹ בְּכָל שָׁנָה וְשָׁנָה בַּשַּׁבָּת הַקּוֹדֶם לְפָרָשַׁת הַחֹדֶשׁ; וּלְעוֹלָם אֵין מַפְסִיקִין בֵּין פָּרָשַׁת פָּרָה לְפָרָשַׁת הַחֹדֶשׁ, וְהַשַּׁבָּת הַקָּבוּעַ לְפָרָשַׁת הַחֹדֶשׁ לְעוֹלָם הוּא שַׁבָּת קֹדֶם נִיסָן.

[מִצְוַת טֻמְאָה שֶׁל מֵת]

שצח שֶׁנִּצְטַוִּינוּ לְהִתְנַהֵג בְּעִנְיַן טֻמְאַת הַמֵּת כְּמוֹ שֶׁצִּוְּתָה אוֹתָנוּ הַתּוֹרָה עָלָיו, שֶׁנֶּאֱמַר: זֹאת הַתּוֹרָה אָדָם כִּי יָמוּת בְּאֹהֶל כָּל הַבָּא אֶל הָאֹהֶל וְכָל אֲשֶׁר בָּאֹהֶל יִטְמָא שִׁבְעַת יָמִים.

מִשָּׁרְשֵׁי עִנְיַן טֻמְאַת הַגּוּף, כָּתַבְתִּי בְּסֵדֶר אֱמֹר אֶל הַכֹּהֲנִים לֹא־תַעֲשֶׂה א' סִימָן (רפ״ז) [רס״ג] מַה שֶּׁיָּכֹלְתִּי, וּכְמוֹ־כֵן קְצָת הַדִּינִים כְּמִנְהָגִי, וְקַחֵנּוּ מִשָּׁם. וּבְמַסֶּכֶת אֳהָלוֹת יִתְבָּאֲרוּ כָל דִּינֵי טֻמְאַת מֵת, וּבְסֵדֶר וַיְהִי בַּיּוֹם הַשְּׁמִינִי עָשֶׂה ד' סִימָן (קנ״ב) [קנ״ט] תִּרְאֶה כָתוּב גַּם־כֵּן כִּי הָרַב מֹשֶׁה בֶּן נַחְמָן זִכְרוֹנוֹ לִבְרָכָה

---

32. Mishnah, Parah iii 6; the two paragraphs are based on MT *hilchoth parah 'adumah* ii 7.

33. Mishnah, Parah iii 5.

34. For the *maftir*, after the regular Scriptural portion (the *sidrah*) was read.

35. I.e. before the Sabbath on which the Scriptural section beginning "This month shall be for you" (Exodus 12:1–20) is read for the *maftir*; see TB M'gillah 29a.

36. So that we should learn about the purification the week before we learn about the Passover offering (as a spiritual preparation in place of the inaccessible physical preparation); R. Isaac 'Alfasi, TB *ibid.* on the authority of the Jerusalem Talmud.

37. TB M'gillah 30a.

mount of anointing [Mount of Olives] it was burnt.[32]

As for the law on how it was to be burned, in which places the ash was to be stored, how the water [for cleansing the defiled] was to be consecrated by the ash of the heifer, and how those defiled by the dead were to be ritually purified by the lustral water—and the rest of its many details—[these are] in the tractate composed about this, namely, the Mishnah tractate *Parah*.

It is in effect in the land of Israel at the time the Temple stands. It is one of the precepts which we said at the beginning of the work are imposed on the entire community. Our Sages of blessed memory said[33] that nine red heifers were [thus] treated from the time this precept was commanded until the second Temple was destroyed. The first, Moses (peace abide with him) prepared; the second, Ezra did; and there were seven from Ezra till the destruction of the Temple. And the tenth, the royal Messiah will prepare, may he be revealed soon in our days.

Now, because this subject of the red heifer is a great, important matter for our nation, since it would bring cleansing from severe defilement, and without it, it was impossible for anyone defiled by the dead to sacrifice a Passover offering, which is a very great *mitzvah*, all Jewry has made it a practice to read this section of Scripture[34] every year on the Sabbath before "the portion of the month";[35] and an interruption is never made between "the portion of the heifer" and "the portion of the month,"[36] while the Sabbath set for "the portion of the month" is always the Sabbath before Nissan.[37]

[THE PRECEPT OF THE RITUAL UNCLEANNESS OF THE DEAD]

398 that we were commanded to behave in regard to defilement by the dead as the Torah commanded us about it: as it is stated, *This is the law: when a man dies in a tent, every one who comes into the tent and every thing that is in the tent shall be unclean seven days* (Numbers 19:14).

Regarding the root reasons for the matter of the ritual uncleanness of a dead body, I wrote in the first negative precept of *sidrah 'emor* (§ 263) what I was able to; and so too a few of the laws, according to my custom. Gather it from there. In the Mishnah tractate *'Oholoth*, all the laws of the ritual uncleanness of the dead are clarified. And in the fourth positive precept of *sidrah sh'mini* (§ 159) you will find written likewise that R. Moses b. Naḥman [Ramban] of blessed memory dif-

יַחֲלֹק עַל הָרַב מֹשֶׁה בֶּן מַיְמוֹן זִכְרוֹנוֹ לִבְרָכָה שֶׁלֹּא לַחְשֹׁב כָּל דִּינֵי הַטֻּמְאוֹת
בְּחֶשְׁבּוֹן הַמִּצְוֹת, וְנָמוֹקוֹ עִמּוֹ.

[מִצְוַת מֵי נִדָּה שֶׁמְּטַמְּאִין אָדָם טָהוֹר וּמְטַהֲרִין אָדָם טָמֵא

מִטֻּמְאַת מֵת בִּלְבָד]

שצט שֶׁנִּצְטַוִּינוּ בְּדִינֵי מֵי נִדָּה, כְּלוֹמַר בְּדִינֵי מֵי הַנִּזֶה, דְּהַיְנוּ מַיִם חַיִּים
מְעֹרָבִין בְּאֵפֶר פָּרָה שֶׁמַּזִּין בָּהֶם עַל הַטְּמֵאִים. וּלְשׁוֹן נִדָּה כְּלוֹמַר הַנִּזֶה, מִלְּשׁוֹן
זְרִיקָה, כְּמוֹ "וַיַּדּוּ אֶבֶן בִּי".

וְנִצְטַוִּינוּ בְּדִינִים הַיְדוּעִים בַּכָּתוּב, שֶׁמְּטַהֲרִין הַטָּמֵא, כְּמוֹ שֶׁנֶּאֱמַר "וְהִזָּה
הַטָּהוֹר עַל הַטָּמֵא" וְגוֹמֵר, וּמְטַמְּאִין הַטָּהוֹר טֻמְאָה חֲמוּרָה, כְּמוֹ שֶׁכָּתוּב "וּמַזֵּה
מֵי הַנִּדָּה" וְגוֹמֵר.

וּמַה נֹּאמַר בְּמִצְוָה זוֹ, וְחֻקַּת הַפָּרָה פְּלִיאָה נִשְׂגָּבָה לֹא אוּכַל לָהּ.

מִדִּינֵי הַמִּצְוָה, מַה שֶּׁאָמְרוּ זִכְרוֹנָם לִבְרָכָה שֶׁהַמַּיִם שֶׁנּוֹתְנִין (עַל) [עָלָיו]
הָאֵפֶר, אֵין מְמַלְּאִין אוֹתָן אֶלָּא בִּכְלִי מִן הַמַּעְיָנוֹת הַנּוֹבְעִים וּמִן הַנְּהָרוֹת
הַמּוֹשְׁכִין; וּנְתִינַת הָאֵפֶר עַל הַמַּיִם הוּא הַנִּקְרָא לְרַבּוֹתֵינוּ קִדּוּשׁ מֵי חַטָּאת,
וְהַמַּיִם שֶׁהוּא נוֹתֵן עֲלֵיהֶם הָאֵפֶר הֵן נִקְרָאוֹת בַּכָּתוּב מֵי נִדָּה.

וְהַכֹּל כְּשֵׁרִין לְמַלֵּאות וּלְקַדֵּשׁ, חוּץ מֵחֵרֵשׁ שׁוֹטֶה וְקָטָן; וְהַמִּתְעַסֵּק בִּמְלָאכָה
אַחֶרֶת בִּשְׁעַת מִלּוּי הַמַּיִם וּבְהוֹלָכָתָן, פְּסָלָן; וְאַחַר שֶׁנָּתַן בָּהֶן הָאֵפֶר אֵין הַמְּלָאכָה
פּוֹסֶלֶת בָּהֶן — כֵּן קִבַּלְנוּ הַדָּבָר; וְהַשָּׂכָר גַּם־כֵּן פּוֹסֵל בְּקִדּוּשׁ וּבַהֲזָיָה; כֵּיצַד: הַנּוֹטֵל
שָׂכָר לְקַדֵּשׁ אוֹ לְהַזּוֹת, מֵימָיו כְּמֵי מְעָרָה וְאֶפְרוֹ כְּאֵפֶר מַקְלֶה, אֲבָל הַנּוֹטֵל שָׂכָר

---

§399

1. I.e. this verb is from the same root as the noun *niddah*; so Rashi, Numbers 19:9.

2. See MT *hilchoth parah 'adumah* xv 1.

3. See §397, paragraphs 2–3.

4. Mishnah, Parah vi 5, etc. The original reads, "the water which was put
[poured] over the ash" etc. — in keeping with the literal meaning of Numbers
19:17. The Talmud states explicitly, however, that if the ash is put in first, it is not
acceptable and may not be used (TB Sotah 16b, T'murah 12b); cf. Ramban on
Numbers 19:17. Hence the text has been emended per MT *hilchoth parah 'adumah* vi
1. As to the meaning of Numbers 19:17, in view of the Talmud's ruling, see Rashi to
TB Sotah 16b, s.v. *v'rabbanan* (followed by Ramban on the verse), and *tosafoth* to TB
Yoma 43a, second s.v. *ha-kol*.

5. Derived from Numbers 19:17 and Mishnah, Parah viii 10.

6. Evident from *ibid.* vi 2, etc.

7. Numbers 19:9, 13, 20. The paragraph is based on MT *hilchoth parah 'adumah* vi 1.

8. Mishnah, Parah v 4; and see TB Yoma 42b that the same laws applied to
filling the vessel as to adding the ash.

9. Mishnah, Parah iv 4.

fers with R. Moses b. Maimon [Rambam] of blessed memory, not reckoning any of the laws of ritual uncleanness in the calculation of the precepts; and he has his reason.

[THE PRECEPT OF THE LUSTRAL WATER,
THAT IT DEFILES A RITUALLY CLEAN MAN
AND PURIFIES ONLY ONE DEFILED BY THE DEAD]

399 that we were commanded about the laws of *mé niddah* (the lustral water), i.e. the water for sprinkling, which is spring water mixed with ash of the [red] heifer, that was sprinkled on the ritually unclean. Now, the term *niddah* means to denote sprinkling, from the general sense of throwing, as it is stated, *va-yaddu,*[1] *they threw stones upon me* (Lamentations 3:53).

Now, we were commanded about its known laws in the Writ: that it purifes the ritually unclean, as it is stated, *and the clean person shall sprinkle upon the unclean* (Numbers 19:19); but it defiles the ritually pure with a severe uncleanness,[2] as it is written, *and he that sprinkles the lustral water*, etc. (*ibid.* 21).

Now, what shall we say about this precept, when the statute of the [red] heifer is a wondrous mystery, *so high that I cannot attain it* (Psalms 139:6)?[3]

Among the laws of the precept there is what the Sages of blessed memory said: that the water over which the ash was put was to be gathered in nothing but a vessel,[4] from welling springs or running rivers [streams].[5] The placing of the ash on the water is what was called by our Sages the sanctification of the water for cleansing;[6] and the water on which the ash is placed is called in the Writ *mé niddah* (the lustral water).[7]

All were acceptable to fill [the vessel with water] and consecrate it except a deaf-mute, a witless fool, and a child.[8] If a person busied himself with another task while filling [the vessel with] water and bringing it, he would [thus] disqualify it; but after he put the ash into it, [other] work would not disqualify it. So we learned the matter in the Oral Tradition.[9] Remuneration would equally disqualify it at the sanctification and the sprinkling: how so?—if a person took payment for the sanctification or the sprinkling, his water would then be like cave water[10] and his ash like ashes from a roast [equally unacceptable]. But if one took payment for filling [the vessel with water] he

עַל הַמִּלּוּי, אֵינוֹ פּוֹסֵל; וְיֶתֶר רְבֵי פְרָטֶיהָ, מְבֹאָרִים בְּמַסֶּכֶת פָּרָה.

וְנוֹהֶגֶת בִּזְמַן הַבַּיִת בִּזְכָרִים וּנְקֵבוֹת, שֶׁכֻּלָּם צְרִיכִים הַזָּאָה אִם נִטְמְאוּ בְמֵת, קֹדֶם שֶׁיִּכָּנְסוּ לַמִּקְדָּשׁ אוֹ יֹאכְלוּ הַקֳּדָשִׁים. וּמִי שֶׁעָבַר עַל זֶה וְלֹא קִבֵּל הַזָּאָה אִם צָרִיךְ לָהּ, בִּטֵּל עֲשֵׂה זֶה. וּכְבָר כָּתַבְתִּי בַּמִּצְוָה הַקּוֹדֶמֶת כִּי הָרַב מֹשֶׁה בֶּן נַחְמָן זִכְרוֹנוֹ לִבְרָכָה לֹא יִמְנֶה בְּחֶשְׁבּוֹן הַמִּצְוֺת כָּל דִּינֵי הַטֻּמְאוֹת, וּרְאָיוֹתָיו הַחֲזָקוֹת בְּסֵפֶר הַמִּצְוֹת שֶׁלּוֹ בְּמִצְוַת (ט"ו) [צ"ו].

סֵדֶר וַיֵּרָא בָּלָק אֵין בּוֹ מִצְוָה

ᕽ פִּינְחָס

שֵׁשׁ מִצְוֺת עֲשֵׂה

[מִצְוַת דִּינֵי נְחָלוֹת]

ת שֶׁנִּצְטַוֵּינוּ בְּדִינֵי נְחָלוֹת, כְּלוֹמַר שֶׁמִּצְוָה עָלֵינוּ לַעֲשׂוֹת וְלָדוּן בְּעִנְיַן הַנַּחֲלָה כַּאֲשֶׁר דָּנָה הַתּוֹרָה עָלֶיהָ, שֶׁנֶּאֱמַר "אִישׁ כִּי יָמוּת וּבֵן אֵין לוֹ וְהַעֲבַרְתֶּם אֶת נַחֲלָתוֹ לְבִתּוֹ, וְאִם אֵין לוֹ בַּת" וְגוֹמֵר, וְסוֹף הַפָּרָשָׁה "וְהָיְתָה לִבְנֵי יִשְׂרָאֵל לְחֻקַּת מִשְׁפָּט כַּאֲשֶׁר צִוָּה יְיָ אֶת מֹשֶׁה".

וְאַל תַּחְשֹׁב שֶׁאָמְרִי בָּזֶה שֶׁהַמִּצְוָה הִיא שֶׁנַּעֲשֶׂה בְּעִנְיַן הַנַּחֲלָה כַּאֲשֶׁר דָּנָה הַתּוֹרָה עָלֶיהָ, שֶׁאֶרְצֶה לוֹמַר שֶׁיִּהְיֶה הָאָדָם מְצֻוֶּה מֵהָאֵל לָתֵת מַה שֶׁיֵּשׁ לוֹ לְיוֹרְשׁוֹ עַל-כָּל-פָּנִים, כִּי הָאֵל בָּרוּךְ הוּא לֹא רָצָה לְהוֹצִיא נִכְסֵי הָאָדָם מֵרְשׁוּתוֹ, שֶׁלֹּא לַעֲשׂוֹת מֵהֶם כָּל חֶפְצוֹ, בִּשְׁבִיל יוֹרְשׁוֹ, כָּל עוֹד נִשְׁמָתוֹ בוֹ, כְּמוֹ שֶׁיַּחְשְׁבוּ חַכְמֵי הָאֻמּוֹת; אֲבָל הוֹדִיעָנוּ שֶׁזְּכוּת הַיּוֹרֵשׁ קָשׁוּר בְּנִכְסֵי מוֹרִישׁוֹ, וּבְהִסְתַּלֵּק כֹּחַ הַמּוֹרִישׁ מִן הַנְּכָסִים בְּמוֹתוֹ, מִיָּד נוֹפֵל עֲלֵיהֶם זְכוּת הַיּוֹרֵשׁ, כְּעִנְיַן הִשְׁתַּלְשְׁלוּת

---

10. I.e. from a source of still, collected water, not a running source, as required.
11. TB B'choroth 29a.
12. I.e. his commentary (*hassagoth*) to ShM.

would not thus disqualify it.[11] The rest of its numerous details are explained in the Mishnah tractate *Parah*.

It is in effect at the time the Temple exists, for both man and woman, since all require the sprinkling if they were defiled by the dead, before they can enter the Sanctuary or eat holy offerings. If someone transgressed this and did not undergo the sprinkling if he needed it, he would thus disobey this positive precept. I wrote earlier, in the preceding precept, that R. Moses b. Naḥman [Ramban] of blessed memory does not list any of the laws of ritual uncleanness in the reckoning of the precepts. His strong proofs are in his *Book of Precepts*,[12] in the ninety-sixth [positive] precept.

In *sidrah balak* (Numbers 22:2–25:9) there is no precept.

sidrah pin'ḥas
(Numbers 25:10–30:1)

[It contains] six positive precepts.

[THE PRECEPT OF THE LAWS OF INHERITANCE]

400 that we were commanded about the laws of inheritance; in other words, it is a religious duty for us to act and render judgment regarding inheritance as the Torah ruled about it — as it is stated, *If a man dies and has no son, then you shall transfer his inheritance to his daughter. And if he has no daughter*, etc. (Numbers 27:8–9); and the end of the Scriptural portion is, *And it shall be to the Israelites a statute of judgment, as the Lord commanded Moses* (ibid. 11).

Now, do not think that in saying about this precept that we should act regarding inheritance as the Torah ruled about it, I mean to convey that a man is commanded by God to give what he owns to his heir under all conditions. For God (blessed is He) did not desire to extract a man's property from his possession, that he might not do with it as he wishes, on account of his heir, as long as his spirit yet lives within him, as the wise men of the nations think. It rather informs us that the rights of the heir are attached to the property of the one who leaves it to him, and as the power of the one who leaves the legacy is removed from the property, upon his death, the rights of the heir take

הַיְצִירוֹת שֶׁרָצָה הַיּוֹצֵר בָּרוּךְ הוּא זֶה אַחַר זֶה מִבְּלִי הֶפְסֵק.

וְרַבּוֹתֵינוּ זִכְרוֹנָם לִבְרָכָה יִקְרְאוּ לַזְּכוּת הֶחָזָק שֶׁיֵּשׁ לְיוֹרֵשׁ בְּנִכְסֵי מוֹרִישׁוֹ בִּלְשׁוֹן "מְשַׁמֵּשׁ", כִּלְשׁוֹן אָמְרָם בְּהַרְבֵּה מְקוֹמוֹת: "נַחֲלָה מְמַשְׁמֶשֶׁת וְהוֹלֶכֶת", כְּלוֹמַר שֶׁזְּכוּת הַיּוֹרֵשׁ בַּמּוֹרִישׁ כְּאִלּוּ הַגּוּפִים זֶה בָזֶה דְּבוּקִים, שֶׁכָּל הַיּוֹצֵא מִן הָאֶחָד נוֹפֵל עַל הַשֵּׁנִי.

וּמִפְּנֵי־כֵן אָמְרוּ זִכְרוֹנָם לִבְרָכָה שֶׁאִם צִוָּה וְאָמַר הַמּוֹרִישׁ "אַל יִירָשֵׁנִי בְּנִי", אוֹ "בְּנִי פְּלוֹנִי לֹא יִירַשׁ עִם אֶחָיו", אוֹ "בִּתִּי תִּירָשֵׁנִי" בְּמָקוֹם שֶׁיֵּשׁ בֵּן, וְכַיּוֹצֵא בָעִנְיָנִים אֵלֶּה, אֵין בִּדְבָרָיו מַמָּשׁ, שֶׁאֵין בְּיָדוֹ לַעֲקֹר דְּבַר הָאֵל שֶׁאָמַר: יִירַשׁ הַיּוֹרֵשׁ מוֹרִישׁוֹ.

וְאַף־עַל־פִּי שֶׁאָמַרְנוּ שֶׁנְּכָסָיו בְּיָדוֹ לְכָל חֲפָצָיו, הָעִנְיָן הוּא לוֹמַר שֶׁיָּכוֹל הָאָדָם לִתְּנָם לְכָל מִי שֶׁיִּרְצֶה וְלַעֲשׂוֹת בָּהֶם כָּל חֶפְצַת נַפְשׁוֹ, וַאֲפִלּוּ לְאַבְּדָם, בְּכָל לָשׁוֹן חוּץ מִזֶּה שֶׁל יְרוּשָּׁה, לְפִי שֶׁזֶּה הַדִּבּוּר הוּא כְּנֶגֶד דְּבָרוֹ שֶׁל מָקוֹם וּגְזֵרָתוֹ, כִּי הוּא אָמַר יִירַשׁ הַיּוֹרֵשׁ, וְעַל־כֵּן אֵין כֹּחַ בְּיַד אָדָם לוֹמַר לֹא יִירַשׁ.

וְהַיְנוּ מַתְנִיתִין דְּיֵשׁ נוֹחֲלִין: הָאוֹמֵר "אִישׁ פְּלוֹנִי לֹא יִירַשׁ עִם אֶחָיו" לֹא אָמַר כְּלוּם, שֶׁהִתְנָה עַל מַה שֶּׁכָּתוּב בַּתּוֹרָה; וְכֵן הָאוֹמֵר "אִישׁ פְּלוֹנִי יִירָשֵׁנִי" בְּמָקוֹם שֶׁיֵּשׁ בַּת, "בִּתִּי תִּירָשֵׁנִי" בְּמָקוֹם שֶׁיֵּשׁ בֵּן, לֹא אָמַר כְּלוּם, שֶׁהִתְנָה עַל מַה שֶּׁכָּתוּב בַּתּוֹרָה; רַבִּי יוֹחָנָן בֶּן בְּרוֹקָה אוֹמֵר: אִם אָמַר עַל מִי שֶׁרָאוּי לְיָרְשׁוֹ דְּבָרָיו קַיָּמִין, וְעַל מִי שֶׁאֵינוֹ רָאוּי לְיָרְשׁוֹ אֵין דְּבָרָיו קַיָּמִין; פֵּרוּשׁ, אִם אָמַר עַל בֵּן בֵּין הַבָּנִים אוֹ עַל בַּת בֵּין הַבָּנוֹת שֶׁיִּירָשֶׁנּוּ אֶחָד מֵהֶם לְבַדּוֹ, דְּבָרָיו קַיָּמִין; וְדָרֵישׁ לֵיהּ בַּגְּמָרָא מִדִּכְתִיב "וְהָיָה בְּיוֹם הַנְחִילוֹ אֶת בָּנָיו", שֶׁהַתּוֹרָה נָתְנָה רְשׁוּת

§400   1. I.e. it follows or parallels nature's cycle of birth, life and death, in which the young replace the old.
2. E.g. TB Bava Bathra 115b.
3. TB Bava Bathra 126b.
4. *Ibid.* 130a.

effect over it immediately, paralleling the continuing chain of created human beings that the Maker (blessed is He) desired, one after the other, without interruption.[1]

Our Sages of blessed memory called this strong right that an heir has in the property of the one from whom he inherits, by the term *mishmush*, "movement," as they expressed it in many instances,[2] "an inheritance moves and comes"; which is to say that the right of the heir in regard to the one who leaves the legacy is as though the bodies were attached to one another, so that whatever leaves the one falls to the other.

For this reason our Sages of blessed memory said[3] that if the one leaving the inheritance ordained and said, "Let my son not inherit from me," or "That particular son of mine should not inherit with his brothers," or "Let my daughter be my heir" in an instance where he has a son, and so anything like these thoughts, his words have no validity. For it is not in his power to uproot the word of God, who declared that an heir is to inherit from one who leaves him property.

Now, although we said that a person's property is in his hand [under his power] for all his desires, the meaning of that is to convey that a man can give it to anyone he wishes and can do with it all that his spirit wishes — even to destroy it — by any expression, except that of inheritance. That utterance is against the word of the omnipresent God and His decree. For He said the heir is to inherit, and therefore a man has no power to say he shall not inherit.

This is [the teaching of] the Mishnah in the eighth chapter of the tractate *Bava Bathra* (126b): If a person says, "That man [my son] shall not inherit with his brothers," he has [in effect] said nothing, since he imposed a condition on what is written in the Torah. And so, too, if one said, "That man shall be my heir" in an instance where there is a daughter, [or] "Let my daughter inherit from me" in an instance where there is a son, he said nothing [in effect],[4] since he imposed a condition against something written in the Torah. R. Yoḥanan b. B'rokah said: If he spoke about someone due to inherit from him, his words are valid; but if about someone not due to inherit from him, his words have no validity.[4] This means that if he said about a son among the sons or a daughter among the daughters that [the] one alone is to be his heir, his words have validity. He derives it in the Talmud[4] from the verse, *then it shall be, on the day that he causes his sons to inherit* (Deuteronomy 21:16): thus the Torah gave the father the right to

לָאָב לְהַנְחִיל מִי שֶׁיִּרְצֶה מִן הָרְאוּיִין לִירַשׁ.

וְנִפְסְקָה שָׁם הֲלָכָה כְּזֶה כְּרַבִּי יוֹחָנָן לְגַבֵּי פְּשׁוּטִין אֲבָל לֹא לְגַבֵּי בְכוֹר, שֶׁאֵין כֹּחַ בָּאָב לַעֲקֹר יְרֻשָּׁה מִן הַבְּכוֹר בְּעִנְיָן זֶה.

וְכֵן אָמְרוּ שָׁם: הַמְחַלֵּק נְכָסָיו, רִבָּה לְאֶחָד וּמִעֵט לְאֶחָד וְהִשְׁוָה לָהֶן אֶת הַבְּכוֹר, דְּבָרָיו קַיָּמִין; וְאִם אָמַר מִשּׁוּם יְרֻשָּׁה לֹא אָמַר כְּלוּם; כָּתַב בֵּין בִּתְחִלַּת דְּבָרָיו בֵּין בְּאֶמְצַע בֵּין בַּסּוֹף מִשּׁוּם מַתָּנָה, דְּבָרָיו קַיָּמִין.

וּלְפִי הַדּוֹמֶה, אַף־עַל־פִּי שֶׁאֵין מַמָּשׁ בְּדִבְרֵי הָאוֹמֵר לְשׁוֹן יְרֻשָּׁה וּמַעֲשָׂיו אֵינָם כְּלוּם, כִּדְמְפָרֵשׁ בְּמַתְנִיתִין, בְּצִוּוּתוֹ כֵן הוּא מְבַטֵּל מִצְוַת עֲשֵׂה זֶה שֶׁל יְרֻשָּׁה מִשּׁוּם דְּעָבַר אַהֶרְמָנָא דְמַלְכָּא; וְכֵן אִם שֶׁמָּא לְאַחַר מוֹתוֹ קַיְּמוּ בֵית־דִּין אֶת דְּבָרָיו אֵלֶּה, יֵשׁ עֲלֵיהֶן גַּם־כֵּן עֲוֹן בִּטּוּל מִצְוַת עֲשֵׂה זֶה, מִלְּבַד עֹנֶשׁ לָאו דְּ"לֹא תַטֶּה מִשְׁפָּט"; וּלְפִי הַנִּרְאֶה מִדִּבְרֵי הָרַב מֹשֶׁה בֶּן מַיְמוֹן זִכְרוֹנוֹ לִבְרָכָה, שֶׁכָּל עִקַּר הָאַזְהָרָה אֵינָהּ רַק עַל הַבֵּית־דִּין שֶׁדָּנוּ בְּעִנְיַן הַנַּחֲלָה כֵן, וְזֶהוּ לְשׁוֹנוֹ שֶׁכָּתַב הוּא: מִצְוָה לָדוּן בְּדִין הַנַּחֲלָה — וּכְמוֹ שֶׁבֵּאַר הָעִנְיָן בְּמִצְוַת הֲפָרַת נְדָרִים שֶׁלְּפָנֵינוּ.

מִשָּׁרְשֵׁי הַמִּצְוָה, כְּדֵי שֶׁיֵּדַע הָאָדָם וְיִתְבּוֹנֵן כִּי הָעוֹלָם בְּיַד אָדוֹן מַשְׁגִּיחַ עַל כָּל בְּרִיּוֹתָיו, וּבִרְצוֹנוֹ וְחֶפְצוֹ הַטּוֹב זוֹכֶה כָל אֶחָד וְאֶחָד מִבְּנֵי הָעוֹלָם בְּחֵלֶק הַנְּכָסִים שֶׁהוּא מַשִּׂיג בְּעוֹלָמוֹ, וּמַתְּנָתוֹ בָרוּךְ הוּא מְבֹרֶכֶת שֶׁתִּמָּשֵׁךְ לְעוֹלָם לַאֲשֶׁר יִתְּנֶנָּה לוֹ, אִם לֹא כִי מֵחֵטְא הַקַּדְמוֹנִי נִקְנְסָה מִיתָה בָעוֹלָם; וּמִפְּנֵי סִלּוּק גּוּפוֹ אֵינוֹ בְדִין לִהְיוֹת הֶפְסֵק לְמַתְּנַת הָאֵל הַמְבֹרֶכֶת, אֲבָל תִּתְפַּשֵּׁט מֵאֵלֶיהָ בַּגּוּף הַמִּשְׁתַּלְשֵׁל מִמֶּנּוּ, שֶׁזֶּהוּ בְּנוֹ אוֹ בִתּוֹ.

וְאִם הוּא בַעֲוֹנוֹ יָמוּת וּבָנִים לֹא יִהְיוּ לוֹ, רְאוּיָה בִּרְכַת הַשֵּׁם שֶׁתָּשׁוּב אֶל

---

5. *Ibid.* 130a–b.

6. In keeping with Deuteronomy 21 : 15–17.

7. That he should receive an equal share, not a double share.

8. Rather than as gifts.

9. In his short listing of the precepts after his preface to MT: positive precept § 248. (In the first sentence, above, the term כדמפרש "as it is explained," is the reading of the oldest manuscript alone; all other copies, manuscript and printed editions, have כך מפרש "thus it is explained.")

10. I.e. about this (his positive precept § 95) he uses the same expression in the short listing (note 9), "to render judgment," etc. and in writing of it in his *Sefer ha-Mitzvoth* (ShM, Book of Precepts) he makes it evident that it is mainly a religious duty of the *beth din*.

11. Our author seems to echo a Talmudic teaching here: "When the Holy One, blessed is He, ordains any greatness for a man, He ordains it for his sons and his grandsons [and so on] till the end of all the generations" (TB M'gillah 13b).

assign his property as an inheritance to anyone he wishes among those qualified to inherit.

Now, the definitive law was decided there[5] about this as R. Yoḥanan ruled, in regard to ordinary heirs, but not in regard to a firstborn son: for the father has no power to tear away the inheritance of a firstborn in this manner.[6]

The Sages taught there likewise:[3] If someone divided his property [among his heirs] giving one more and one less, or if he made the firstborn equal to them,[7] his words are valid; but if he spoke of it as inheritance,[8] he [as much as] said nothing. If he wrote, though, either at the beginning, the middle, or the end of his words, "by virtue of a gift," his words remain in force.

It would seem, however, that even though there is no valid substance in the words of one who speaks in terms of inheritance, and his actions amount to nothing — as it is explained in the Mishnah — when he so commands, he disobeys this positive precept about inheritance, since he has thus acted against the Royal decree. So likewise, if perhaps after his death the *beth din* (court) carried out these words of his, they too would bear the sin of disobeying the positive precept, apart from punishment over the injunction not to pervert justice (§ 233). Indeed, as it would appear from the words of R. Moses b. Maimon of blessed memory, the principal injunction applies only to a *beth din* that so ruled in regard to inheritance. This is his language, in which he wrote:[9] "It is a *mitzvah*, a religious duty, to render judgment about the law of inheritance," as he explained the matter in the precept of nullifying vows (§ 406),[10] which lies ahead of us.

At the root of the precept lies the aim that a man should know and consider that the world lies in the hand (power) of a [Divine] Master who watches over all His human beings; and by His good will and desire, each and every one in the world gains possession of the share of property that he attains in his world. Now, His gift (blessed is He) is blessed that it should continue forever for anyone to whom He gives it — were it not that because of the primal sin, the decree of death was imposed in the world. Yet [merely] because of the removal of one's body, it would not be just that there should be a cessation of God's blessed gift. Rather, it should extend further, of itself, to the body that developed in continuity from him, this being his son or his daughter.[11]

⟨175⟩ And if he should die for his inquity, having no sons, it is right for

הַקָּרוֹב אֵלָיו, כִּי זֹאת הַבְּרָכָה שֶׁזָּכָה בָהּ זֶה, אוֹ זְכוּתוֹ גָּרְמָה לוֹ אוֹ זְכוּת אֲבוֹתָיו, אוֹ עִם הַקְּרוֹבִים לוֹ יוֹתֵר לָמַד כְּשִׁרוֹן הַמַּעֲשֶׂה שֶׁזָּכָה עִמּוֹ לַנְּכָסִים; וְלָכֵן בְּהִסְתַּלֵּק הוּא וְזַרְעוֹ מֵהֶן בְּחֶטְאוֹ, רְאוּיִים הַקְּרוֹבִים שֶׁסִּיְּעוּ אוֹתוֹ לִזְכּוֹת לִהְיוֹת קוֹדְמִין בָּהֶם לְכָל אָדָם.

מִדִּינֵי הַמִּצְוָה, מַה שֶּׁאָמְרוּ זִכְרוֹנָם לִבְרָכָה בְּמַתְנִיתִין דְּיֵשׁ נוֹחֲלִין: סֵדֶר נַחֲלוֹת כָּךְ הוּא: "אִישׁ כִּי יָמוּת" וְגוֹמֵר, הַבֵּן קוֹדֵם לַבַּת, וְכָל יוֹצְאֵי יְרֵכוֹ שֶׁל בֵּן קוֹדְמִין לְבַת; הַבַּת קוֹדֶמֶת לָאַחִין, וְכָל יוֹצְאֵי יְרֵכָהּ שֶׁל בַּת קוֹדְמִין לָאַחִין, אוֹ הָאֲחָיוֹת בְּמָקוֹם שֶׁאֵין אַחִין, קוֹדְמִין לַאֲחֵי הָאָב, וְכָל יוֹצְאֵי יְרֵכָיו שֶׁל אַחִין אוֹ שֶׁל אֲחָיוֹת קוֹדְמִין לַאֲחֵי הָאָב; וַאֲחֵי אָבִיו, אוֹ אַחְיוֹת אָבִיו בְּמָקוֹם שֶׁאֵין אַחִין לָאָב, קוֹדְמִין לִשְׁאָר קְרוֹבִין. זֶה הַכְּלָל: כָּל הַקּוֹדֵם בְּנַחֲלָה—יוֹצְאֵי יְרֵכוֹ קוֹדְמִין, וְהָאָב קוֹדֵם לְכָל יוֹצְאֵי יְרֵכוֹ; וְעַל הַדֶּרֶךְ הַזֶּה שֶׁאָמַרְנוּ הוֹלֵךְ וְעוֹלֶה עַד רֹאשׁ הַדּוֹרוֹת. לְפִיכָךְ אֵין לְךָ אֶחָד מִיִּשְׂרָאֵל שֶׁאֵין לוֹ יוֹרֵשׁ.

וּמַה שֶּׁאָמְרוּ שָׁם שֶׁאֵין הָאֵם יוֹרֶשֶׁת בָּנֶיהָ, וְדָבָר זֶה קַבָּלָה; וְהָאַחִים מִן הָאֵם אֵינָם יוֹרְשִׁים זֶה אֶת זֶה, דְּמִשְׁפַּחַת אֵם אֵינָהּ קְרוּיָה מִשְׁפָּחָה; וּבֵן מַמְזֵר אוֹ אָח מַמְזֵר הֲרֵי זֶה יוֹרֵשׁ כִּשְׁאָר הַבָּנִים, וַאֲפִלּוּ בֶן מַמְזֵר שֶׁנִּשְׁתַּמֵּד יוֹרֵשׁ הוּא; אֲבָל בֶּן שִׁפְחָה וְנָכְרִית אֵינוֹ יוֹרֵשׁ וְאֵינוֹ כְבֵן לְשׁוּם דָּבָר; וַחֲכָמִים תִּקְּנוּ שֶׁיְּהֵא הָאָדָם יוֹרֵשׁ אֶת אִשְׁתּוֹ מִן הַנִּשּׂוּאִין, וְסָמְכוּ הַדָּבָר מִן הַכָּתוּב.

וְכָתַב הָרַב מֹשֶׁה בֶּן מַיְמוֹן זִכְרוֹנוֹ לִבְרָכָה: וּמִכְּלַל זֶה הַדִּין שֶׁל נַחֲלוֹת בְּלִי

12. I.e. if there are both a son and a daughter, he inherits, and not she; TB Bava Bathra 115a.

13. She inherits sooner than her father's brothers.

14. I.e. over a paternal uncle of the deceased.

15. I.e. if a man left no descendants at all, his property goes to a brother (or sister) or any descendant of his (or hers). If there are no brothers or sisters, or descendants of theirs, it goes to a paternal uncle or aunt, or a descendant of theirs. If no heir is thus found, we look further back at the family tree, on the male side of descent, seeking a great-uncle or great-aunt, or a descendant of theirs; then a great-great-uncle, and so on—so that eventually some cousin, however distant, must be found.

16. TB Bava Bathra 108a, etc.

17. Literally, for the family of a mother is not called a family; *ibid.* and 110b.

18. MT *hilchoth naḥaloth* i 7, based on TB Yevamoth 22a. (The term "bastard" means the offspring of adulterous or consanguineous parents whose conjugal intimacy is punishable by death.)

19. I.e. if he converted to another faith; apparently derived from TB Kiddushin 18a (MY).

20. As opposed to a wife by *'erusin* (betrothal) alone (see §35, note 8); TB Bava Bathra 108a, 111b, etc.

the blessing of the Eternal Lord to transfer to a close kin. For this which this person merited to attain—either his virtue earned it for him, or the virtue of his fathers, or that of his very close kin; [thereby] he learned [the value of] worthiness in deed, with which he merited [to attain] material possessions. Then when he and his progeny are removed from it for his sin, the near relatives who helped him acquire the merit deserve to be ahead of every other man [in having it].

Among the laws of the precept there is what the Sages of blessed memory said in the Mishnah, in the eighth chapter of the tractate *Bava Bathra* (viii 2): The order of inheritance is so: *If a man dies*, etc. (Numbers 27:8); [hence] a son takes precedence over a daughter,[12] and all those descended from a son take precedence over a daughter; a daughter comes before brothers,[13] and all those descended from a daughter take precedence over the brothers. The brothers [of the deceased], or sisters where there are no brothers, take precedence over the father's brother;[14] and all those descended from the brothers or from the sisters come before the father's brothers. One's father's brothers, though, or his father's sisters in an instance where the father had no brothers, come before other relatives. This is the rule: Whoever takes precedence in inheritance, those descended from him [equally] take precedence; but the father comes before all those descended from him. And with this approach that we have stated, we can continue going back to the beginning of the generations.[15] You will therefore find no one in Jewry who has no heir.

Then there is what the Sages said there,[16] that a mother does not inherit from her sons, this being a teaching of the Oral Tradition. Brothers from one mother do not inherit from each other: for kinship through the mother is not called (considered) kinship.[17] A bastard son or a bastard brother does inherit like the other sons.[18] Even if a bastard son turned apostate, he inherits.[19] However, a son by a female slave or non-Jewish woman does not inherit, and he is not [considered] a son in any respect.[18] The Sages enacted an amendment that a man should inherit from his wife by *nissu'in* (finalized marriage),[20] and they substantiated the matter by Scripture.[21]

Now, R. Moses b. Maimon of blessed memory wrote:[22] Included

21. TB K'thuboth 83b, Bava Bathra 111b.
22. Rambam ShM positive precept § 248.

סָפֵק, הֱיוֹת הַבְּכוֹר נוֹטֵל פִּי שְׁנַיִם, שֶׁזּוֹ הִיא מִכְּלַל מִצְוַת הַנַּחֲלוֹת. וּפִי שְׁנַיִם פֵּרוּשׁוֹ שְׁנֵי חֲלָקִים: כְּלוֹמַר שֶׁאִם הָיוּ שְׁנֵי אַחִין, עוֹשִׂין מִן הַמָּמוֹן שְׁלֹשָׁה חֲלָקִים וְהַבְּכוֹר נוֹטֵל הַשְּׁנַיִם, וְאִם הָיוּ שְׁלֹשָׁה, עוֹשִׂין מִמֶּנּוּ אַרְבָּעָה חֲלָקִים וְנוֹטֵל הַשְּׁנַיִם, וְאִם הֵם חֲמִשָּׁה עוֹשִׂין מִמֶּנּוּ שִׁשָּׁה, וְעַל הַדֶּרֶךְ הַזֶּה לְעוֹלָם.

וְאֵין הַבְּכוֹר נוֹטֵל פִּי שְׁנַיִם אֶלָּא בִנְכָסִים הַמֻּחְזָקִים לְאָבִיו, כְּלוֹמַר שֶׁבָּאוּ בִרְשׁוּת אָבִיו בְּחַיָּיו, אֲבָל לֹא בִרְאוּיִים לָבוֹא אֶל אָבִיו, שֶׁנֶּאֱמַר: בְּכֹל אֲשֶׁר יִמָּצֵא לוֹ: כֵּיצַד: אֶחָד מִמּוֹרִישֵׁי אָבִיו שֶׁמֵּת לְאַחַר מִיתַת אָבִיו, אֵין הַבְּכוֹר נוֹטֵל בְּאוֹתָהּ יְרֻשָּׁה פִּי שְׁנַיִם.

וְכֵן אִם הָיְתָה לַאֲבִיהֶם חוֹב שֶׁחַיָּבִים לוֹ, וַאֲפִלּוּ בִשְׁטָר, אוֹ אֲפִלּוּ הָיְתָה סְפִינָה בַיָּם, אֵין לַבְּכוֹר בָּזֶה פִּי שְׁנַיִם, שֶׁאֵין זֶה מָצוּי לְאָבִיו. וְכֵן מִשְּׁעַת זֶה אֵין הַבְּכוֹר נוֹטֵל בַּשֶּׁבַח שֶׁשָּׁבְחוּ נְכָסִים אַחַר מִיתַת אָבִיו, כְּגוֹן שַׁחַת שֶׁנַּעֲשָׂה דָגָן וְהָאִילָנוֹת שֶׁהוֹצִיאוּ פֵּרוֹתֵיהֶן, שֶׁכָּל זֶה לֹא הָיָה מָצוּי לְאָבִיו בְּיָמָיו; אֲבָל אִילָן קָטָן שֶׁנַּעֲשָׂה גָדוֹל שֶׁלֹּא מֵחֲמַת הוֹצָאָה אֶלָּא מֵעַצְמוֹ גָּדַל אַחַר מוֹת אָבִיו קֹדֶם חֲלוּקָה, הַבְּכוֹר נוֹטֵל בָּזֶה פִּי שְׁנַיִם, דְּמָצוּי לְאָבִיו נִקְרָא מִכֵּיוָן שֶׁלֹּא נִשְׁתַּנָּה עִנְיָנוֹ.

וְהָאָב נֶאֱמָן לוֹמַר "זֶה בְּנִי בְּכוֹרִי", וְנֶאֱמָן לוֹמַר "זֶהוּ בְּנִי" אוֹ "זֶה אֵינוֹ בְּנִי", שֶׁהַתּוֹרָה הֶאֱמִינַתּוּ בָזֶה, דִּכְתִיב "כִּי אֶת הַבְּכֹר" וְגוֹמֵר "יַכִּיר", וְדָרְשׁוּ זִכְרוֹנָם לִבְרָכָה: יַכִּירֶנּוּ לַאֲחֵרִים; וַאֲפִלּוּ אֶחָד הָיָה מֻחְזָק שֶׁהוּא בֶן רְאוּבֵן וְאָמַר רְאוּבֵן שֶׁאֵינוֹ בְנוֹ, נֶאֱמָן עָלָיו וְלֹא יִירָשֶׁנּוּ. וְכָתַב הָרַב מֹשֶׁה בֶּן מַיְמוֹן זִכְרוֹנוֹ לִבְרָכָה: וְיֵרָאֶה לִי שֶׁאֲפִלּוּ הָיוּ לַבֵּן בָּנִים, אַף-עַל-פִּי שֶׁאֵינוֹ נֶאֱמָן עָלָיו לוֹמַר

23. Based on Deuteronomy 21:17. Our author now adds that the Hebrew term *pi sh'na-yim* means a double share (as explained in TB Bava Bathra 122b).

24. TB B'choroth 51b, etc.

25. TB Bava Bathra 119b; MT *hilchoth naḥaloth* iii 1.

26. Since the debt was yet to be collected, and the ship had yet to reach shore safely; TB Bava Bathra 125b; MT *ibid.*

27. TB Bava Bathra 124a. Rudimentary stalks of wheat (*shaḥath*) are only a first stage of its growth, potentially substance of value, but not something of actual worth at present.

28. MT *ibid.* 4, based on TB *ibid.*

29. Midrash Tanna'im *ad loc.* TB Kiddushin 78b.

30. MT *hilchoth maḥaloth* iv 2.

in this law of inheritance, past any doubt, is that a firstborn son takes a double share; for this is part of the precept of inheritance.[23] This is to say that if there were two sons, the property is to be arranged in three parts, and the firstborn takes two; and if there were three [sons] it would be arranged in four shares, and he would take two; if there were five of them, it would be arranged in six parts; and so on in this way for any number.

However, a firstborn is to take a double share only of property that was firmly in his father's ownership—in other words, it came into his father's possession in his lifetime; but not of what is due to come into his father's possession: for it is stated, *of all that is found with him* (Deuteronomy 21:17).[24] How would this rule apply? If one of those people from whom his father should inherit died after his father's death, the firstborn son does not take a double share of that legacy.[25]

So too if their father had a debt [to collect] that was owed him, even if by a deed (promissory note); or even if there was a ship at sea, the firstborn does not claim a double share of this, for it is not something that was available, at hand for his father.[26] So too, for this reason, a firstborn son does not take [a double portion] of the increase in value that the property gained after his father's death:[24] for instance, if rudimentary stalks of wheat grew to full size, or trees grew their fruit[27]—for all this was not available to his father in his days. However, if a small tree grew large not on account of any expenditure but it rather matured by itself after his father's death, before the division [of the property], the firstborn son does take a double share of that [increase in value], as it is considered [to have been] available to his father, since its essential nature did not change.[28]

A father is believed when he says, "This is my firstborn son"; and he is believed to say, "This is my son," or "This is not my son." For the Torah granted him credibility about this, since it is written, *but he shall acknowledge the firstborn*, etc. (Deuteronomy 21:17), which our Sages of blessed memory interpreted:[29] he shall make him known to others. Even if someone was firmly assumed to be Reuben's son, and Reuben said he was not his son, he is believed about him, and the latter does not inherit from him.[29] And R. Moses b. Maimon of blessed memory wrote:[30] It seems to me that even if the son had sons [of his own], although he [the father] is not believed about him in regard to lineage if he says this is not his son, and he [the son] is not firmly held

אֵינוֹ בְנוֹ לְעִנְיַן יְחוּס, וְאֵין מַחֲזִיקִין אוֹתוֹ מַמְזֵר עַל פִּיו, נֶאֱמָן הוּא לְעִנְיַן יְרֻשָּׁה וְלֹא יִירָשֶׁנּוּ.

וּמַה שֶּׁאָמְרוּ זִכְרוֹנָם לִבְרָכָה גַּם־כֵּן בְּעִנְיָן זֶה שֶׁהָאוֹמֵר לְאֶחָד "נְכָסַי לְךָ וְאַחֲרֶיךָ לִפְלוֹנִי", אִם הָרִאשׁוֹן רָאוּי לְיָרְשׁוֹ אֵין לַשֵּׁנִי בִּמְקוֹם רִאשׁוֹן כְּלוּם, דְּמִכֵּיוָן שֶׁזָּכָה בַּנְּכָסִים וְהוּא הָרָאוּי לִירַשׁ אוֹתָם, אֵין לַיְרֻשָּׁה הֶפְסֵק עוֹד מִפְּנֵי תְּנָאוֹ שֶׁל מוֹרִישׁ. וְעִם הַפֵּרוּשִׁים הַטּוֹבִים וְהַסְּבָרָא הוֹגֶנֶת לָמַדְנוּ בְּפֶרֶק יֵשׁ נוֹחֲלִין, שֶׁאֲפִלּוּ אָמַר לוֹ בִּלְשׁוֹן "מֵעַכְשָׁיו", כְּגוֹן שֶׁאָמַר לוֹ "נְכָסַי לְךָ וּמֵעַכְשָׁיו אַחֲרֶיךָ לִפְלוֹנִי", אַף־עַל־פִּי־כֵן אֵין לַשֵּׁנִי בִּמְקוֹם רִאשׁוֹן כְּלוּם, מִכֵּיוָן שֶׁהָרִאשׁוֹן רָאוּי לְיָרְשׁוֹ.

אֲבָל אִם אֵין רִאשׁוֹן רָאוּי לְיָרְשׁוֹ וְאָמַר לוֹ "מֵעַכְשָׁיו אַחֲרֶיךָ לִפְלוֹנִי", זָכָה הַשֵּׁנִי בְּגוּף הַנְּכָסִים, וְהָרִאשׁוֹן יֹאכַל הַפֵּרוֹת לְבַד כָּל יְמֵי חַיָּיו. וְאִם לֹא אָמַר לוֹ "מֵעַכְשָׁיו" אֶלָּא "נְכָסַי לְךָ וְאַחֲרֶיךָ לִפְלוֹנִי", לֹא קָנָה שֵׁנִי אֶלָּא מַה שֶּׁיִּשָּׁאֵר לָרִאשׁוֹן, וְאִם מְכָרָן רִאשׁוֹן אֵין כֹּחַ בַּשֵּׁנִי לְהוֹצִיאוֹ מִיַּד לוֹקֵחַ לְעוֹלָם, שֶׁבְּחֶזְקַת הָרִאשׁוֹן עוֹמְדִין כָּל יְמֵי חַיָּיו לְכָל חֲפָצָיו, בֵּין לְמָכְרָם בֵּין לְתִתָּם בְּמַתָּנָה לְכָל מִי שֶׁיִּרְצֶה.

וְכָל כָּךְ הֵם נְכָסִים אֵלּוּ בְּחֶזְקָתוֹ שֶׁל רִאשׁוֹן, שֶׁאִם אָמַר הַנּוֹתֵן "נְכָסַי לְךָ וְאַחֲרֶיךָ לִפְלוֹנִי וְאַחֲרָיו לִפְלוֹנִי", אִם מֵת שֵׁנִי בְּחַיֵּי רִאשׁוֹן, אָמְרוּ זִכְרוֹנָם לִבְרָכָה בַּגְּמָרָא שֶׁיַּחְזְרוּ הַנְּכָסִים לְיוֹרְשֵׁי רִאשׁוֹן, לְפִי שֶׁהַנּוֹתֵן לֹא שִׁיֵּר כְּלוּם בְּמַתְּנָתוֹ שֶׁל רִאשׁוֹן, אֶלָּא שֶׁיִּתְּנוֹ הַנְּכָסִים אַחֲרָיו לַשֵּׁנִי, וּמִיַּד הַשֵּׁנִי וּמִכֹּחוֹ יָבוֹאוּ לַשְּׁלִישִׁי, וּמִכֵּיוָן שֶׁהַשֵּׁנִי מֵת וְאִי־אֶפְשָׁר לַשְּׁלִישִׁי עוֹד שֶׁיִּזְכֶּה בָּהֶם מִכֹּחַ הַשֵּׁנִי כְּמוֹ שֶׁאָמַר הַנּוֹתֵן, יִשָּׁאֲרוּ הַנְּכָסִים בְּיַד מִי שֶׁהֵן בִּרְשׁוּתוֹ, לוֹ וּלְיוֹרְשָׁיו לְעוֹלָם.

31. The reason for this is technical, and is given fully in *Maggid Mishneh* to MT *ibid*.

32. TB Bava Bathra 129b, 133a. It should be noted that from here to the end of the "laws of the precept" the donor in question is an ill man facing death (*sh'chiv mé-ra'*), who is thus presumed to wish his gift to be in the nature of a bequeathment (see Rashba, *Responsa* I §1031; *Responsa attributed to Ramban,* §45).

33. Or, is yours (literally, "My property to you").

34. So Rashba (R. Sh'lomoh ibn 'Adreth), cited in *Béth Yoséf* to Tur Ḥoshen Mishpat, § 248.

35. Hence he acquires the property as inheritance, not as a gift, on which the owner could impose conditions.

36. Literally, eats the fruits alone.

37. So R. Isaac 'Alfasi, TB Bava Bathra 125b; and MT *hilchoth z'chiah umattanah* xii 12 (see *Maggid Mishneh*).

38. So TB Bava Bathra 137a.

to be a bastard by his word—he is believed about him in regard to inheritance, and [the son] is not to be his heir.[31]

Then there is what the Sages of blessed memory likewise said in this topic:[32] that if someone tells a person, "My property goes to you,[33] and after you to so-and-so," if the first one is fit to be his heir, the second receives nothing at all in place of the first. For once he attains the property and he was someone fit to inherit it, there can be no future interruption in the line of inheritance because of the terms set by the one who left the legacy. And with the good commentaries[34] and proper reasoning we learn in the eighth chapter of the tractate *Bava Bathra* (125b, 133a) that even if he told him [this] with the expression, "from now"—for example, "My property goes to you, and from now, after you to so-and-so"—the second one nevertheless acquires nothing in place of the first, since the first is fit to be his heir.[35]

If, however, the first was not suited to be his heir and he told him, "From now, after you [it goes] to so-and-so," the second becomes the owner of the property itself while the first receives only the revenue (usufruct)[36] all the days of his life.[37] If, however, he did not tell him "from now," but merely, "My property goes to you, and after you to so-and-so," the second acquires no more than what the first leaves behind; and if the first one should sell it, the second does not have the [legal] power ever to extricate it from the possession of the purchaser. For it stands in the firm possession of the first one all the days of his life, for all his wishes and desires, whether to sell it or present it as a gift to anyone at all whom he pleases.[38]

Indeed, this property is so much in the firm possession of the first one that if the one who gave it [to him originally] said, "My property goes to you, and after you to so-and-so, and after him to thus-and-so," if the second one then died in the lifetime of the first, the Sages of blessed memory said in the Talmud[32] that the property should go in turn to the heirs of the first one. For the one who gave it away reserved nothing in the gift [that he granted] the first but [the stipulation] that the property should be given after him to the second one, and from the hand (possession) of the second and through his legal right, it should go on to the third man. Now, since the second man died, and the third one cannot possibly gain possession of it any more through the legal power of the second one, in keeping with what the donor said, the property is to remain in the possession of the one in whose domain it now is, for him and his heirs forever.

וְהוּא הַדִּין שֶׁיֵּשׁ לָנוּ לָדוּן עַל הַדֶּרֶךְ שֶׁאָמַרְנוּ הֵיכָא שֶׁאָמַר הַנּוֹתֵן מַתְּנָתוֹ
בִּלְשׁוֹן "אִם", כְּגוֹן שֶׁאָמַר "נְכָסַי לִפְלוֹנִי, וְאִם מֵת יִנָּתְנוּ לִפְלוֹנִי", שֶׁאֵין אָנוּ
בָּאִין לָדוּן כֵּן מִטַּעַם לְשׁוֹן "אַחֲרֶיךָ", אֶלָּא טַעַם הַדָּבָר מִפְּנֵי שֶׁאָנוּ אוֹמְרִים כִּי
הָרִאשׁוֹן זוֹכֶה בְּגוּפָן שֶׁל נְכָסִים וּבְפֵרוֹתֵיהֶן, וּלְעוֹלָם מֻחְזָקִין בְּיָדוֹ עַד שֶׁנּוּכַל
לְהוֹצִיאָן מִמֶּנּוּ בִּרְאָיָה חֲזָקָה.

אֲבָל הֵיכָא שֶׁכָּתַב נוֹתֵן "נְכָסַי לְךָ וְאַחֲרֶיךָ לִי אוֹ לְיוֹרְשַׁי", אַף־עַל־פִּי שֶׁלֹּא
הִזְכִּיר לְשׁוֹן "מֵעַכְשָׁיו" בְּשִׁעוּר זֶה, יֵשׁ לָנוּ לָדוּן שֶׁאִם מֵת מְקַבֵּל מַתָּנָה שֶׁיַּחְזְרוּ
נְכָסִים לַנּוֹתֵן אוֹ לְיוֹרְשָׁיו; וַאֲפִלּוּ יָרַד וּמָכַר מְקַבֵּל מַתָּנָה, הַנּוֹתֵן מוֹצִיאָן מִיַּד
לוֹקֵחַ לִכְשֶׁיָּמוּת מְקַבֵּל מַתָּנָה: שֶׁאָמְרוּ חֲכָמִים בָּזֶה, שֶׁכָּל שֶׁמְּשַׁיֵּר לְעַצְמוֹ אוֹ
לְיוֹרְשָׁיו אֵינוֹ אֶלָּא כִּמְפָרֵשׁ: "מַתָּנָה זוֹ תִהְיֶה לְךָ לַאֲכִילַת פֵּרוֹת כָּל יְמֵי חַיֶּיךָ".

וּכְלָל הַדְּבָרִים שֶׁעָלוּ בְּיָדֵינוּ בְּעִנְיָנֵנוּ זֶה אַחַר יְגִיעָה רַבָּה, שֶׁכָּל זְמַן שֶׁהָרִאשׁוֹן
רָאוּי לִירַשׁ, מִכֵּיוָן שֶׁאָמַר לוֹ הַמּוֹרִישׁ "נְכָסַי לְךָ", אֵין בְּיָדוֹ עוֹד לְהִתָּם לְאַחֵר
וַאֲפִלּוּ לְיוֹרְשׁוֹ, אַחַר שֶׁמִּיָּד נִכְנְסוּ הַנְּכָסִים בְּחֶזְקַת יוֹרֵשׁ, וְאֵינוֹ אֶלָּא כְּמַתְּנָה
תְנָאִים בְּנִכְסֵי אָדָם אַחֵר, וּכְעִנְיָן שֶׁנֶּאֱמַר בָּזֶה בַּגְּמָרָא: הוּא סָבַר יֵשׁ לָהּ הֶפְסֵק,
כְּלוֹמַר לַיְרוּשָׁה, וְרַחֲמָנָא אָמַר אֵין לָהּ הֶפְסֵק.

וּגְדוֹלָה מִזֹּאת לִמְּדוּנוּ מוֹרֵינוּ יִשְׁמְרֵם אֵל, בִּרְאָיוֹת חֲזָקוֹת וּבְרוּרוֹת, שֶׁאֲפִלּוּ
הָאוֹמֵר לְמִי שֶׁרָאוּי לְיָרְשׁוֹ "נְכָסַי לְךָ וְאַחֲרֶיךָ לַהֶקְדֵּשׁ", אוֹ אֲפִלּוּ אָמַר
"וּמֵעַכְשָׁיו אַחֲרֶיךָ לַהֶקְדֵּשׁ", שֶׁהַיּוֹרֵשׁ זוֹכֶה בַּנְּכָסִים וְיֵשׁ לוֹ לְמָכְרָן וְלַעֲשׂוֹת בָּהֶן
כָּל חֶפְצָה נַפְשׁוֹ, וְאֵין כֹּחַ בַּהֶקְדֵּשׁ לְעוֹלָם לְהוֹצִיאָן מִיַּד לוֹקֵחַ אוֹ מְקַבֵּל מַתָּנָה,
מִן הַטַּעַם שֶׁכָּתַבְנוּ: דְּמִכֵּיוָן שֶׁאָמַר הַמּוֹרִישׁ לְיוֹרְשׁוֹ "נְכָסַי לְךָ", זָכָה בַּנְּכָסִים,

39. So R. Yonah, cited in Tur Ḥoshen Mishpat, § 248.
40. I.e. took possession of the field.
41. R. Huna b. R. Joshua in TB Bava Bathra 137b, as explained by Rashbam, commentary.
42. Literally, to eat the fruit.
43. Literally, that have come up into our hands.
44. E.g. he is one of the man's sons.
45. TB Bava Bathra 133a.
46. So Rashba, *Responsa*, I § 704; similarly *ge'onim* cited in *Béth Yoséf* to Tur Ḥoshen Mishpat, § 248, (16) [5].

The same law holds, that we are to render judgment in the way that we said, where the one who granted his gift spoke using the term "if": for example, if he said, "My possessions go to so-and-so, and if he dies, they shall be given to so-and-so." Since we do not come to render the judgment according to the meaning of the term "after you," the sense of the matter is rather that we say that the first one attains both the property itself and its income, and it is forever firmly held in his possession until we can extricate it from him by strong evidence.[39]

However, where the donor wrote, "My possessions go to you, and after you to me or to my heirs," even though he did not mention the term "from now" in this [stipulated] reservation, we have to rule that if the one who received the gift died, the property is to revert to the donor or to his heirs. Even if the recipient of the gift went down[40] and sold it, the donor can take it out of the purchaser's possession when the recipient dies. For the Sages said about this[41] that whoever stipulates a reservation for himself or his heirs, is no more than as one who stipulates explicitly, "This gift shall be for you [merely] to enjoy its income[42] all the days of your life."

The summary rule for all the matters that have come into our ken[43] in this subject, after great toil, is that as long as the first one is fit to inherit,[44] once the one who will leave the inheritance told him, "My property goes to you," it is no longer in his power to give it to another, even to another heir of his; for the property entered at once into the hold of [this] heir, and after that he is as no more than one who makes stipulations about the property of another man — in keeping with what was said in this regard in the Talmud:[45] "He thought there could be a limit to it — i.e. the inheritance — but the merciful God said it has no limit."

However, our master instructors, God protect them, taught us something that goes further than this, with strong, clear proofs:[46] that even if someone said to a person fit to inherit from him, "My property goes to you, and after you to *hekdesh* (the treasury of the Sanctuary)"; or even if he said, "and from now, after you, to *hekdesh*" — the heir attains the property, and he can sell it or do with it whatever his spirit wishes; and the Sanctuary treasury never has the power to extract it from the hand of the purchaser or the recipient of the gift, for the reason we wrote: Once the one leaving the inheritance said to his heir, "My property goes to you," he gained the

וְאֵין בְּיָדוֹ לְהַקְדִּישׁ אוֹתָן עוֹד אֶלָּא הֲרֵי הוּא כְּמַקְדִּישׁ נִכְסֵי אֲחֵרִים.

וּמַה שֶּׁיֵּשׁ לָעַיֵּן בְּעִנְיָן זֶה, שֶׁנִּרְאֶה בִּתְחִלַּת הָעִיּוּן קַשְׁיָא, כְּגוֹן מַה שֶּׁאָמְרוּ זִכְרוֹנָם לִבְרָכָה "אֲמִירָתוֹ לַגָּבוֹהַּ כִּמְסִירָתוֹ לְהֶדְיוֹט", וְעוֹד דְּבָרִים אֲחֵרִים, כְּבָר נָשָׂאנוּ וְנָתַנּוּ בָהֶן וְדִקְדַּקְנוּ אֶת כֻּלָּן יָפֶה, וְעָלָה הָעִנְיָן מְבֹרָר כְּמוֹ שֶׁכָּתַבְנוּ; וְיֵאָרֵךְ הָעִנְיָן אִם בָּאתִי לִכְתֹּב הַכֹּל, וְלֹא מִמְּלֶאכֶת סְפָרַי הוּא. וְאִם תִּזְכֶּה, בְּנִי, וְתִפְרָשׁ מִכְמֹרֶת בְּיַם הַתַּלְמוּד, הִיא תַעֲלֶה לְךָ הַכֹּל.

וְיֶתֶר פְּרָטֵי הַמִּצְוָה, מְבֹאָרִים בְּבָבָא בַתְרָא פֶּרֶק יֵשׁ נוֹחֲלִין.

וְנוֹהֶגֶת בְּכָל מָקוֹם וּבְכָל זְמַן, בִּזְכָרִים וּנְקֵבוֹת. וְעוֹבֵר עַל זֶה וְצִוָּה, בֵּין בָּרִיא בֵּין שְׁכִיב־מְרַע, שֶׁלֹּא יִירָשֶׁנּוּ הָרָאוּי לְיָרְשׁוֹ, בִּטֵּל עֲשֵׂה זֶה—וְהוּא שֶׁצִּוָּה כֵן בִּלְשׁוֹן יְרֻשָּׁה כְּמוֹ שֶׁאָמַרְנוּ, וְאַף־עַל־פִּי שֶׁאֵין בִּדְבָרָיו מַמָּשׁ, כְּמוֹ שֶׁכָּתַבְנוּ לְמַעְלָה בִּתְחִלַּת הָעִנְיָן.

וְהָרַב מֹשֶׁה בֶּן נַחְמָן זִכְרוֹנוֹ לִבְרָכָה כָּתַב כִּי הָרַב מֹשֶׁה בֶּן מַיְמוֹן זִכְרוֹנוֹ לִבְרָכָה חִסֵּר בְּמָקוֹם זֶה שְׁתֵּי מִצְווֹת: אַחַת מִצְוַת עֲשֵׂה וְאַחַת לֹא־תַעֲשֶׂה, וּשְׁתֵּיהֶן בִּבְכוֹר: שֶׁהָאָדָם מְצֻוֶּה לְהַכִּיר הַבְּכוֹר בְּמַתַּת פִּי שְׁנַיִם לוֹ, וְזֹאת הִיא מִצְוַת עֲשֵׂה עַל הָאָב שֶׁלֹּא חָשַׁב אוֹתָהּ הָרַב מֹשֶׁה בֶּן מַיְמוֹן זִכְרוֹנוֹ לִבְרָכָה בְּמִנְיָנוֹ; וּכְמוֹ־כֵן מֻזְהָר עָלָיו מֵהַעֲבִיר הַבְּכוֹרָה מִמֶּנּוּ, וְעַל זֶה נֶאֱמַר "לֹא יוּכַל לְבַכֵּר אֶת בֶּן הָאֲהוּבָה" וְגוֹמֵר, וְזֹאת הָאַזְהָרָה גַּם־כֵּן לֹא חָשַׁב הָרַב הַנִּזְכָּר אֶלָּא שֶׁכָּלַל הַכֹּל בְּמִצְוַת דִּין הַנַּחֲלוֹת.

[מִצְוַת תְּמִידִין בְּכָל יוֹם]

תא שֶׁנִּצְטַוּוּ יִשְׂרָאֵל שֶׁיַּקְרִיבוּ עַל־יְדֵי מְשָׁרְתֵי הַשֵּׁם, שֶׁהֵם הַכֹּהֲנִים, שְׁנֵי כְבָשִׂים בְּנֵי שָׁנָה תְּמִימִים לְעוֹלָה בְּכָל יוֹם, הָאֶחָד בַּבֹּקֶר וְהַשֵּׁנִי בֵּין הָעַרְבַּיִם,

---

47. TB Kiddushin 28b, etc.

48. When one merely says, "Let this part of my wealth belong to *hekdesh*" (be consecrated for use by the Temple treasury), it is as if he gave it bodily to its proper recipient (the treasurer of the Temple funds). Hence, if, as in the previous paragraph, someone told a person fit to inherit from him, "These possessions of mine go to you, and after you to *hekdesh*," we might think that the Temple treasury acquires as of now a sufficient claim or hold on the property in question to take possession of it upon the death of this recipient. This is what might "appear at first glance to be a difficulty." Nevertheless, the ruling stands as given in the previous paragraph.

49. Ramban, commentary to ShM end section, listing "precepts omitted by Rambam," s.v. *v'attah 'im tavin*.

property, and it is not in his [the donor's] power any more to consecrate them; he rather becomes here as one who consecrates the property of others.

Now, there are matters to look into carefully in this subject, which appear at first glance to be a difficulty—for instance, what the Sages of blessed memory taught:[47] A person's statement to the One on high is like his physical transmission to an ordinary person,[48] and other matters as well. We have already discussed and considered them, and drawn conclusions well about them all; and the subject-matter has emerged elucidated as we have written. The theme would grow lengthy, however, if I came to write it all, and this is not the task of my volume. But if you merit, my son, and will spread a fisher's net in the Sea of the Talmud, it will bring up everything for you.

The remaining details of the precept are explained in the eighth chapter of the tractate *Bava Bathra*.

It applies in every place and time, for both man and woman. If a person transgresses this and orders, whether while healthy or seriously ill, that the one due to inherit from him should not be his heir, he has disobeyed this positive precept—but this, only if he so ordered using the expression of inheritance, as we stated—even though his words amount to nothing, as we wrote above, at the beginning of the topic.

Now, R. Moses b. Naḥman of blessed memory wrote[49] that R. Moses b. Maimon [Rambam] of blessed memory omitted two precepts at this point, one positive and one negative, and both about a firstborn son: that a man is commanded to acknowledge a firstborn by giving him a double share; this is a positive precept that R. Moses b. Maimon of blessed memory did not reckon in his listing; and he is likewise adjured about him [his firstborn] not to transfer the birthright from him; about this it was stated, *he may not treat as the firstborn the son of the beloved one*, etc. (Deuteronomy 21:16). This admonition the above-mentioned master likewise did not reckon [as a precept] but rather included it entirely in the law of inheritance.

[THE PRECEPT OF THE REGULAR 'OLAH
OFFERING, SACRIFICED EVERY DAY]

401 that the Israelites were commanded that they should offer up, through the ministering servants of the Eternal Lord, namely the *kohanim*, two lambs in their first year, without blemish, as '*olah*

שֶׁנֶּאֱמַר: צַו אֶת־בְּנֵי יִשְׂרָאֵל וְאָמַרְתָּ אֲלֵהֶם אֶת־קָרְבָּנִי לַחְמִי וְגוֹמֵר, שְׁנַיִם לַיוֹם
עֹלָה תָמִיד. וּמִכָּל־מָקוֹם עִקַּר הָאַזְהָרָה לְבֵית־דִּין, כְּלוֹמַר הַחֲכָמִים מוֹרֵי הַתּוֹרָה
שֶׁבְּיִשְׂרָאֵל, כִּי עֲלֵיהֶם מֻטֶּלֶת מְלֶאכֶת הַצִּבּוּר, וּכְמוֹ שֶׁדָּרְשׁוּ זִכְרוֹנָם לִבְרָכָה:
"וְאָמַרְתָּ אֲלֵהֶם", אַזְהָרָה לְבֵית־דִּין.

מִשָּׁרְשֵׁי מִצְוַת הַקָּרְבָּנוֹת, כָּתַבְתִּי בְמִצְוַת הַמִּקְדָּשׁ בְּסֵדֶר וְיִקְחוּ לִי תְרוּמָה
עֲשֵׂה א׳ [סִי׳ צ״ה] הָעוֹלָה עַל רוּחִי בִּפְשַׁט הָעִנְיָן, וְאַחַר אוֹתָם הַטְּעָמִים אֲנִי
מַמְשִׁיךְ גַּם־כֵּן טַעַם הַתְּמִידִין, לוֹמַר שֶׁנִּצְטַוֵּינוּ בַּעֲבוֹדָה זוֹ הַתְּמִידִית שֶׁהִיא
פַּעֲמַיִם בַּיּוֹם, בְּזְרִיחַת הַשֶּׁמֶשׁ וּבִנְטוֹתוֹ לָעֶרֶב, לְמַעַן נִתְעוֹרֵר מִתּוֹךְ הַמַּעֲשֶׂה הַזֶּה
וְנָשִׂים כָּל לִבֵּנוּ וְכָל מַחְשְׁבוֹתֵינוּ לְדָבְקָה בַשֵּׁם בָּרוּךְ הוּא, כְּאָמְרִי כַּמָּה פְעָמִים
שֶׁהָאָדָם נִפְעָל וְטִבְעוֹ מִתְעוֹרֵר לְפִי עֵסֶק מַעֲשֵׂהוּ; וְלָכֵן בִּהְיוֹת הָאָדָם נָכוֹן שֶׁצָּרִיךְ
לְתַקֵּן לוֹ מָזוֹן שְׁתֵּי פַעֲמִים, עֶרֶב וָבֹקֶר, נִצְטַוָּה שֶׁיָּשִׂים שְׂמַעֲתוֹ וְעִסְקוֹ בְּעֵסֶק עֲבוֹדַת
בּוֹרְאוֹ גַּם־כֵּן שְׁתֵּי פְעָמִים, לְבַל תִּהְיֶה עֲבוֹדַת הָעֶבֶד לְעַצְמוֹ יְתֵרָה עַל עֲבוֹדָתוֹ
לְרַבּוֹ; וְכָל זֶה לָמָּה—כְּדֵי לְעוֹרֵר רוּחוֹ וְחֶפְצוֹ תָּמִיד לִזְכּוֹר אֶת בּוֹרְאוֹ, וּבְכֵן
יַכְשִׁיר מַעֲשָׂיו וְיִתְבָּרֵךְ מִמֶּנּוּ, כִּי חָפֵץ חֶסֶד הוּא, וּכְמוֹ שֶׁדָּרְשׁוּ זִכְרוֹנָם לִבְרָכָה:
"אִשֵּׁה רֵיחַ נִיחֹחַ לַיי"—שֶׁאָמַרְתִּי וְנַעֲשָׂה רְצוֹנִי—כְּלוֹמַר שֶׁכָּל חֵלֶק גָּבוֹהַּ מִכָּל
קָרְבָּן אֵינוֹ רַק חֶפְצוֹ בָּרוּךְ הוּא, שֶׁעָשָׂה הָעֶבֶד מַה שֶׁצִּוָּהוּ לְמַעַן יִכְשַׁר לִזְכּוֹת
בְּטוּבוֹ בָּרוּךְ הוּא.

מִדִּינֵי הַמִּצְוָה, מַה שֶׁאָמְרוּ זִכְרוֹנָם לִבְרָכָה שֶׁזְּמַן שְׁחִיטָתָן שֶׁל תְּמִידִין הוּא:
הַכֶּבֶשׂ הָאֶחָד שֶׁל בֹּקֶר, קֹדֶם שֶׁתַּעֲלֶה חַמָּה, מִשֶּׁיֵּאוֹר כָּל פְּנֵי מִזְרָח; וּפַעַם אַחַת
דָּחֲקָה שָׁעָה אֶת הַצִּבּוּר בְּבַיִת שֵׁנִי וְהִקְרִיבוּ תָמִיד שֶׁל שַׁחַר בְּאַרְבַּע שָׁעוֹת בַּיּוֹם;

---

§401   1. Sifre, Numbers § 142.
2. Literally, what arises on my spirit.
3. Sifre, Numbers § 143.
4. TB Yoma 28a; Mishnah, Tamid iii 2.
5. Literally, the hour pressed the community.

(burnt) offerings every day: the first in the morning and the second toward evening—as it is stated, *Command the Israelites and say to them: My offering, My food,* etc. *two a day, a continual burnt-offering* (Numbers 28:2–3). However, the principal injunction is for the *beth din*—in other words, the scholars, instructors of Torah in Israel; for the tasks of the community are imposed on them. As the Sages of blessed memory interpreted:[1] "and say to them"—it is an injunction to the *beth din*.

Regarding the religious duty of animal offerings I wrote in the precept of the Sanctuary, the first positive precept in *sidrah t'rumah* (§ 95), what comes to my mind[2] about the plain meaning of the subject; and following those reasons, I continue likewise [onto] a reason for the daily offerings, to say that we were given the duty of this continual service, which was twice a day—at sunrise and when it turned toward evening—that we might be stirred by this activity and set all our heart and all our thoughts to cling to the Eternal Lord, blessed is He.

As I have said many times, a man is influenced and his nature stirred according to the occupation of his activity. Therefore, since a man is so constituted that he needs to prepare food for himself twice [a day], evening and morning, he was commanded to set his purpose and occupation about the business of the service of his Creator likewise two times [a day] so that the work of the servant for himself should not be greater than his service to his Master. And why all this?—in order to bestir his spirit and desire continually to remember his Creator; and thus he will make his actions worthy and will be blessed by Him—for He delights in loving-kindness. As our Sages of blessed memory interpreted:[3] *an offering by fire, a pleasing savor to the Lord* (Numbers 28:8)—it is a satisfaction of spirit for Me that I spoke and My will was done. In other words, the entire [Divine] supernal share of any offering is nothing more than His [fulfilled] desire: that the servant did what He commanded him, that he might become virtuous to attain His good reward (blessed is He).

Among the laws of the precept there is what the Sages of blessed memory taught:[4] that the time for the ritual slaying of the daily offerings was [for] the one lamb, of the morning, before the sun would rise, when the entire expanse of the east would be alight. Once, though, there was a distressing occasion for the community[5] at the
time of the second Temple, and the daily offering was brought at the

וְהַכֶּבֶשׂ הַשֵּׁנִי שֶׁל בֵּין הָעַרְבַּיִם, מֵשֵׁשׁ שָׁעוֹת וּמֶחֱצָה וּלְמַעְלָה עַד סוֹף הַיּוֹם, זֶהוּ
זְמַנּוֹ; אֲבָל הָיוּ שׁוֹחֲטִין אוֹתוֹ בִּשְׁמוֹנֶה שָׁעוֹת וּמֶחֱצָה וְקָרֵב בְּתֵשַׁע
וּמֶחֱצָה. וּשְׁתֵּי שָׁעוֹת אֵלּוּ שֶׁמְּאַחֲרִין אוֹתוֹ הָיָה כְּדֵי שֶׁיַּקְרִיבוּ קָרְבְּנוֹת הַיְחִידִים
אוֹ שֶׁל צִבּוּר בֵּינְתַיִם, לְפִי שֶׁאָסוּר לְהַקְרִיב קָרְבָּן אַחַר תָּמִיד שֶׁל בֵּין הָעַרְבַּיִם.

וּכְמַעֲשֵׂה תָּמִיד שֶׁל שַׁחַר הָיָה מַעֲשֵׂה תָּמִיד שֶׁל בֵּין הָעַרְבַּיִם, אֶלָּא שֶׁאוֹתוֹ
שֶׁל שַׁחַר נִשְׁחַט עַל קֶרֶן צְפוֹנִית־מַעֲרָבִית שֶׁל בֵּית הַמִּטְבָּחַיִם, עַל טַבַּעַת שְׁנִיָּה,
וְשֶׁל בֵּין הָעַרְבַּיִם, עַל קֶרֶן צְפוֹנִית־מִזְרָחִית עַל טַבַּעַת שְׁנִיָּה, כְּדֵי שֶׁיְּהֵא נֶגֶד
הַשֶּׁמֶשׁ. וְיֶתֶר פְּרָטֶיהָ, מְבֹאָרִים בְּמַסֶּכֶת תָּמִיד וּבְפֶרֶק שֵׁנִי מִיּוֹמָא.

וְנוֹהֶגֶת מִצְוָה זוֹ בִּזְמַן הַבַּיִת, וְהִיא מִן הַמִּצְווֹת שֶׁהֵן מֻטָּלוֹת עַל הַצִּבּוּר, וְיוֹתֵר
עַל הַכֹּהֲנִים; וְאִם שֶׁמָּא חַס וְשָׁלוֹם יִתְרַשְּׁלוּ בָהּ שֶׁלֹּא לְהַקְרִיבָם בְּכָל יוֹם, בִּטְּלוּ
עֲשֵׂה זֶה, וְהַשְּׁגָגָה נִתְלֵית עַל כָּל עֲדַת יִשְׂרָאֵל הַיּוֹדְעִים בַּדָּבָר, אִם יֵשׁ כֹּחַ בְּיָדָם
לְתַקֵּן בְּשׁוּם צַד.

וְהָרַב מֹשֶׁה בֶּן נַחְמָן זִכְרוֹנוֹ לִבְרָכָה חָשַׁב בְּחֶשְׁבּוֹן הַמִּצְווֹת שְׁנֵי תְּמִידִין לִשְׁתֵּי
מִצְווֹת עֲשֵׂה, לְפִי שֶׁהֵן מִצְווֹת שֶׁאֵין מְעַכְּבוֹת זוֹ אֶת זוֹ, וּזְמַנָּהּ שֶׁל זוֹ לֹא זְמַנָּהּ
שֶׁל זוֹ.

[מִצְוַת קָרְבַּן מוּסָף שֶׁל שַׁבָּת]

תב שֶׁנִּצְטַוּוּ יִשְׂרָאֵל לְהַקְרִיב שְׁנֵי כְבָשִׂים קָרְבָּן בְּכָל יוֹם שַׁבָּת, מוּסָף עַל קָרְבַּן
הַתָּמִיד שֶׁל כָּל יוֹם, וְהוּא הַנִּקְרָא מוּסַף שַׁבָּת—שֶׁנֶּאֱמַר: וּבְיוֹם הַשַּׁבָּת שְׁנֵי
כְבָשִׂים וְגוֹמֵר.

מִשָּׁרְשֵׁי מִצְוַת הַמּוּסָפִין שֶׁל יָמִים טוֹבִים, כְּבָר כָּתַבְתִּי בְּסֵדֶר אֱמֹר אֶל
הַכֹּהֲנִים בְּמוּסַף פֶּסַח, עֲשֵׂה ח' [סִי' רצ"ט], מַה שֶּׁנִּרְאָה לִי עַל צַד הַפְּשָׁט, וּמוּסַף

6. MT *hilchoth tʾmidin* i 2, based on Mishnah, ʿEduyoth vi 1, and TJ Bʾrachoth
iv 1, which tells that during a siege of Jerusalem by the empire of Greece, the
Israelites would lower two small chests of gold coins over the city wall, for which
the Greeks gave them two lambs to haul up for the daily offerings. Once, though,
they mockingly gave them goats to haul up; but "the Holy One gave light to their
eyes and they found two inspected lambs [i.e. approved as without blemish] in the
chamber of lambs"; and that day the morning offering was brought at the fourth
hour. (The term "hour" means one twelfth the period from sunrise to sunset; and
all "hours" are counted from sunrise.)

7. Literally, between the evenings; see § 5, note 1.

8. TB Pʾsaḥim 58a. The paragraph is based on MT *ibid.* 2–3.

9. Set in the floor of the Temple forecourt.

10. Mishnah, Tamid iv 1; Sifre, Numbers § 142; Rambam *ibid.* 11.

11. Source in § 400, note 49.

12. I.e. if only the morning offering could be brought but not the second one,
or vice-versa, it is acceptable by itself.

SIDRAH PIN'HAS

fourth hour of the day.[6] As for the second lamb, of the afternoon,[7] from six and a half hours onward, till the end of the day — this was its time. However, they would always ritually slay it at eight and a half hours, and it would be offered up at nine and a half. The postponement of these two hours was in order that offerings of individuals or the community could be presented in the meantime. For it was forbidden to present any offering after the daily offering of the afternoon.[8]

Like the procedure of the daily offering of the morning, so was the procedure of the daily offering of the afternoon — except that the one of the morning was ritually slain at the northwest corner of the slaying-place, at the second ring;[9] while the one of the afternoon [was ritually slain] at the northeast corner, at the second ring, so that it should be facing the sun.[10] The rest of its details are explained in the Mishnah tractate *Tamid* and in the second chapter of *Yoma*.

This precept is in effect at the time the Temple stands. It is one of the precepts imposed on the community, but more particularly on the *kohanim*. And if perhaps, Heaven forbid, they should be negligent about it not to offer them up every day, they would disobey this positive precept; but an inadvertent sin would be accredited to all [in] the community of Israel who knew of the matter, if the power lay in their hand to amend [the situation] in any way.

Now, R. Moses b. Naḥman of blessed memory considered the two daily offerings, in the reckoning of the *mitzvoth*, as two positive precepts,[11] because they are religious duties that do not prevent each other [from being acceptable],[12] and the time for one is not the time for the other.

[THE PRECEPT OF THE MUSAF OFFERING
OF THE SABBATH]

402 that the Israelites were commanded to bring an offering of two lambs every Sabbath day in addition to the regular offering of every day, this being called the *musaf* (additional offering) of the Sabbath: as it is stated, *And on the Sabbath day two lambs*, etc. (Numbers 28:9).

Regarding root reasons for the *musaf* (additional) offerings of the festivals, I wrote previously in *sidrah 'emor*, in the eighth positive precept (§ 299), of the *musaf* of Passover, what occurred to me from the aspect of the plain meaning; and the *musaf* of the Sabbath hangs in

שַׁבָּת בְּאֶשְׁכּוֹל יֶתֶר הַמּוּסָפִין תָּלוּי גַּם הוּא; וְהָעִנְיָן כְּדֵי שֶׁנִּקְבַּע בְּמַחֲשַׁבְתֵּנוּ עִם מַעֲשֵׂה הַקָּרְבָּן גֹּדֶל הַיּוֹם וְרֹב קְדֻשָּׁתוֹ, וְכִי שֵׁשֶׁת יָמִים עָשָׂה יי אֶת הַשָּׁמַיִם וְגוֹמֵר, כְּמוֹ שֶׁכָּתוּב שָׁם; וְשָׁם כָּתַבְתִּי גַּם־כֵּן מְעַט מִדִּינֵי הַמּוּסָפִין וּכְלַל הָעִנְיָן, כְּמִנְהָגִי.

[מִצְוַת קָרְבַּן מוּסָף בְּכָל רֹאשׁ־חֹדֶשׁ]

תג שֶׁנַּקְרִיב קָרְבָּן מוּסָף בְּכָל רֹאשׁ־חֹדֶשׁ עַל הַתָּמִיד שֶׁל כָּל יוֹם, שֶׁנֶּאֱמַר: וּבְרָאשֵׁי חָדְשֵׁיכֶם תַּקְרִיבוּ עֹלָה לַיי פָּרִים בְּנֵי בָקָר שְׁנַיִם וְאַיִל אֶחָד כְּבָשִׂים בְּנֵי שָׁנָה שִׁבְעָה תְּמִימִם (וּמִנְחָתָם) ... וְנִסְכֵּיהֶם וְגוֹמֵר, וּשְׂעִיר עִזִּים אֶחָד לְחַטָּאת לַיי.

מִשָּׁרְשֵׁי הַמִּצְוָה, הַקְדָּמָה: יָדוּעַ לְכָל חֲכַם־לֵב בִּבְנֵי־אָדָם כִּי גַלְגַּל הַשֶּׁמֶשׁ וְגַלְגַּל הַיָּרֵחַ פּוֹעֲלִים, בְּכֹחָם הַנֶּאֱצָל עֲלֵיהֶם מֵאֲדוֹן כָּל הַכֹּחוֹת, בָּעוֹלָם הַשָּׁפָל, פְּעֻלּוֹת גְּדוֹלוֹת בְּגוּפוֹת בְּנֵי־אָדָם וּבְכָל מִינֵי שְׁאָר בַּעֲלֵי חַיִּים, גַּם בְּכָל הַצּוֹמֵחַ בָּאָרֶץ, מִן הָאֲרָזִים הַגְּדוֹלִים עַד הָעֲשָׂבִים הַדַּקִּים, וְדֶרֶךְ כְּלָל בְּכָל שֶׁהוּא מֵאַרְבַּע הַיְסוֹדוֹת שֶׁהֵם לְמַטָּה מֵהֶם וְתַחַת מֶמְשַׁלְתָּם—וְכֵן כָּתוּב בְּסֵדֶר וְזֹאת הַבְּרָכָה: וּמִמֶּגֶד תְּבוּאֹת שָׁמֶשׁ וּמִמֶּגֶד גֶּרֶשׁ יְרָחִים.

וּמְפֻרְסָם בְּכָל הֲמוֹן הָעָם, נְעָרִים עִם זְקֵנִים, כִּי כֹחַ הַלְּבָנָה נִכָּר בְּכָל אֲשֶׁר נַעֲשֶׂה בָאָרֶץ, כְּיָדוּעַ בְּכֹרְתֵי הָאִילָנוֹת לְבִנְיָנוֹת כִּי לֹא יִכְרְתוּם בִּזְמַן שֶׁהַלְּבָנָה בְּחִדּוּשָׁהּ עַד עֲבֹר חֲמִשָּׁה יָמִים אוֹ יוֹתֵר, וְיוֹרְדֵי הַיָּם גַּם־כֵּן אֵין מַפְלִיגִין בָּהּ עַד אַחַר חֲמִשָּׁה יָמִים שֶׁל חִדּוּשׁ הַלְּבָנָה, וְכֵן נִזְהָרִים כָּל בְּנֵי־אָדָם מֵהַקִּיז דָּם סָמוּךְ לְחִדּוּשָׁהּ, וְכַמָּה מְלָאכוֹת אֲחֵרוֹת קְטַנּוֹת וּגְדוֹלוֹת צְרִיכוֹת שְׁמִירָה שֶׁלֹּא לַעֲשׂוֹתָם בְּעוֹד שֶׁהַלְּבָנָה מִתְחַדֶּשֶׁת—עַד שֶׁיֹּאמְרוּ שֶׁהַפִּשְׁפְּשִׁין שֶׁיִּמָּצֵא שֶׁיְּמַצֵּא בַּמִּשְׂרָה אוֹ בְּתוֹךְ

§402   1. I.e. it is to be included with them in one category.

§403   1. I.e. fire, wind, water and dust, of which, it was traditionally taught, everything in creation is composed.

     2. It was a common, accepted practice to have a certain amount of blood removed from the body periodically as a health measure.

the cluster of the other *musaf* (additional) offerings.¹ The purpose is
that we should form a firm concept in our mind, with the presenta-
tion of the offering, of the importance of the day and its great degree
of holiness—and that *in six days the Lord made heaven and earth*, etc.
(Exodus 31:17), as it is written there. And there I wrote as well a bit
of the laws of the *musaf* offerings, and the general subject-matter,
according to my custom.

[THE PRECEPT OF THE MUSAF OFFERING
EVERY NEW-MONTH-DAY]

403 that we should present a *musaf* (additional) offering every
beginning of the month, in addition to the regular offering of every
day, as it is stated, *And at the beginnings of your months you shall present a
burnt-offering to the Lord: two young bullocks and one ram, seven lambs of the
first year without blemish* (Numbers 28:11), then their *minhah* (meal) offerings and drink-offerings (libations), etc. [and finally] *one goat for a
sin-offering to the Lord* (ibid. 15).

As for the root reasons for the precept, [let me begin with] a
preface: It is known to everyone wise in heart among men that with
their power that is imparted to them by the [Divine] Master of all the
powers and forces in the lowly [earthly] world, the cycle of the sun
and the cycle of the moon exert great influences on the bodies of
human beings, on all the species of other living creatures, and also on
all that grows from the ground, from the great cedars to the thin
grasses. And it is a general rule about anything that is of the four
elements,¹ that it is under them and subject to their dominion. Thus it
is written in *sidrah v'zoth ha-b'rachah: and with the choice fruits of the sun,
and with the choice yield of the moons* (Deuteronomy 33:14).

Moreover, it is common knowledge among the entire population,
young and old, that the force of the moon is evident in all that occurs
on earth—as it is known about those who cut trees [timber] for construction, that they will not cut them at the time that the moon is in
its renewal, until five days or more have passed. Those who go down
to the sea will likewise not set out on it till after five days from the
renewal of the moon. So too, all people beware of letting blood²
close to its renewal. And with many other labors, small and large,
care is needed not to do them while the moon is yet renewing
itself—to the extent that it is said that flax found in a pond for
steeping or within a dyer's kettle for boiling, at the renewal of the

הַיּוֹרֶה לְבַשֵּׁל בְּחִדּוּשׁ הַלְּבָנָה, שֶׁהוּא לוֹקֶה וְלֹא יִצְלַח אַחַר־כֵּן לַכֹּל; וּכְלַל הָעִנְיָנִים אֵלֶּה גְּלוּיִים וְנוֹדָעִים לַכֹּל, הָאֲרִיכוּת בָּהֶן יַלְדוּת.

וְלָכֵן, כִּי בִּקְדוּשָׁה שֶׁל לְבָנָה, לִפְעָלוֹת אָדָם יִתְחַדֵּשׁ עִנְיָן, וְהַכֹּל בִּדְבָרוֹ שֶׁל מָקוֹם בָּרוּךְ הוּא וּבִגְזֵרָתוֹ, רָאוּי לָנוּ גַּם־כֵּן לְחַדֵּשׁ וּלְהַקְרִיב קָרְבָּן נוֹסָף עַל שְׁאָר הַיָּמִים לִשְׁמוֹ בָּרוּךְ הוּא, לְהָעִיר רוּחֵנוּ וְלִקְבֹּעַ בִּלְבָבֵנוּ כִּי כָל הַחִדּוּשִׁים הַהֹוִים בָּעוֹלָם מֵאִתּוֹ בָּרוּךְ הוּא, וְכָל כֹּחַם שֶׁל גַּלְגַּלִּים לֹא יִמָּצֵא רַק מֵי לְבַדּוֹ; וְעִם הַמַּחֲשָׁבָה הַזֹּאת הָאֲמִתִּית תִּתְעַלֶּה נַפְשֵׁנוּ, וּבִרְכַת יי תָּחוּל עַל רֹאשֵׁנוּ.

דִּינֵי הַמִּצְוָה בְּעִנְיַן הַמּוּסָפִין, וּכְלַל הָעִנְיָן, כְּמִנְהָגֵי, כָּתַבְתִּי בְּמוּסַף הַפֶּסַח בְּסֵדֶר אֱמֹר אֶל הַכֹּהֲנִים [סִי' רצ"ט]. וְעוֹד אוֹדִיעֲךָ כָּאן שֶׁרֹאשׁ־חֹדֶשׁ שֶׁחָל לִהְיוֹת בְּשַׁבָּת, שִׁיר שֶׁל מוּסָף רֹאשׁ־חֹדֶשׁ דּוֹחֶה שִׁיר שֶׁל מוּסַף שַׁבָּת, כְּדֵי לְפַרְסֵם שֶׁהַיּוֹם רֹאשׁ־חֹדֶשׁ. וְיָדוּעַ שֶׁשִּׁירַת מוּסָפֵי שַׁבָּת בַּמִּקְדָּשׁ הִיא שִׁירַת הַאֲזִינוּ, וְהָיוּ מְחַלְּקִין אוֹתָהּ לְשִׁשָּׁה פְרָקִים בְּשִׁשָּׁה שַׁבָּתוֹת, וְהַסִּימָן הֲזִי"ו ל"ךְ, כְּדֶרֶךְ שֶׁאָנוּ קוֹרִין אוֹתָהּ בְּבֵית־הַכְּנֶסֶת.

[מִצְוַת קָרְבַּן מוּסָף בְּיוֹם חַג הַשָּׁבוּעוֹת]

תד שֶׁנִּצְטַוּוּ יִשְׂרָאֵל לְהַקְרִיב לַהֲקָרִיב קָרְבָּן מוּסָף בְּיוֹם חַג הַשָּׁבוּעוֹת, שֶׁהוּא יוֹם שִׁשִּׁי בְּסִינַי, שֶׁנֶּאֱמַר: וּבְיוֹם הַבִּכּוּרִים בְּהַקְרִיבְכֶם מִנְחָה חֲדָשָׁה לַיי בְּשָׁבֻעֹתֵיכֶם וְגוֹמֵר. כְּבָר כָּתַבְתִּי פְּעָמִים כִּי בְסֵדֶר אֱמֹר אֶל הַכֹּהֲנִים בְּמוּסַף דְּפֶסַח, עֲשֵׂה ח' [סִי' רצ"ט], דִּבַּרְתִּי מֵעִנְיַן הַמּוּסָפִים.

[מִצְוַת שׁוֹפָר בְּרֹאשׁ הַשָּׁנָה]

תה שֶׁנִּצְטַוִּינוּ לִשְׁמֹעַ קוֹל שׁוֹפָר בְּיוֹם רִאשׁוֹן שֶׁל תִּשְׁרֵי, שֶׁהוּא רֹאשׁ הַשָּׁנָה,

---

3. In the Responsa of Rashba ascribed to Ramban, §483, a similar view is expressed about the serious extent of the moon's influence on human fortunes and activities.

4. So TB Sukkah 54b.

5. Deuteronomy 32:1–43.

6. Here our author adds two Hebrew words as a mnemonic device, which are an acrostic composed of the first Hebrew letter of each of the six sections.

7. I.e. in the way Deuteronomy 32:1–43 in *sidrah ha'azinu* is divided into sections to be read respectively for the first six called to the Torah when it is read in the synagogue on a Sabbath morning; TB Rosh haShanah 31a.

⟨192⟩

moon, will be spoiled and will never be good for anything afterward. These matters in general are obvious and known to all; it would be childish to go on at length about them.[3]

Well, therefore, since with the renewal of the moon something is renewed for the activities of man, and it is all by the word·of the omnipresent God, blessed is He, and by His decree, it is fitting for us likewise to bring a new offering, something more than on other days, for His sake (blessed is He), to arouse our spirits and set firmly in our hearts that all new phenomena and renewals that occur in the world are due to Him, blessed is He, and all the power of the celestial cycles exists solely through the Lord alone. With this pure and true thought our spirit will be elevated, and the blessing of the Eternal Lord will abide about our heads.

The laws of the religious duty regarding *musaf* (additional) offerings, and the general subject-matter, according to my custom, I wrote about the *musaf* of Passover in *sidrah 'emor* (§ 299). I will tell you further here that when the beginning of the month occurs on the Sabbath, the chant for the *musaf* of the new-month-day thrusts aside [supersedes] the chant for the *musaf* of Sabbath,[4] in order to proclaim that it is the first day of the new month. Now, it is known that the chant for the *musaf* of Sabbath at the Sanctuary was the song of *ha'azinu*;[5] it was divided into six sections for six Sabbaths,[6] in the way that we read it in the synagogue.[7]

[THE PRECEPT OF THE MUSAF OFFERING
ON THE SHAVU'OTH FESTIVAL]

404 that the Israelites were commanded to bring a *musaf* (additional) offering on the festival day of *Shavu'oth*, which is the sixth day of Sivan: as it is stated, *And on the day of the first-fruits, when you bring a new meal-offering to the Lord at your feast of weeks*, etc. (Numbers 28:26). I have already written twice that in *sidrah 'enor*, at the eighth positive precept, about the *musaf* of Passover (§ 299), I spoke on the subject of the *musaf* offerings.

[THE PRECEPT OF THE SHOFAR
ON ROSH HASHANAH]

405 that we were commanded to hear the sound of the *shofar* (animal horn) on the first day of Tishri, which is the beginning of the

וּכְדִתְנָן בְּמַסֶּכֶת רֹאשׁ הַשָּׁנָה: בְּאֶחָד בְּתִשְׁרֵי רֹאשׁ הַשָּׁנָה לְשָׁנִים, שֶׁנֶּאֱמַר: יוֹם
תְּרוּעָה יִהְיֶה לָכֶם. וְאַף־עַל־פִּי שֶׁאֵין כָּאן זֵכֶר לִתְרוּעָה זוֹ אִם בְּשׁוֹפָר אוֹ
בְּמִצְלְתַּיִם אוֹ בְּכָל שְׁאָר כְּלֵי נִגּוּן, מִפִּי הַשְּׁמוּעָה לָמְדוּ זִכְרוֹנָם לִבְרָכָה שֶׁהִיא
בְּשׁוֹפָר, שֶׁכְּמוֹ שֶׁמָּצִינוּ בַּיּוֹבֵל שֶׁנֶּאֱמַר בּוֹ שׁוֹפָר.

מִשָּׁרְשֵׁי הַמִּצְוָה, לְפִי שֶׁהָאָדָם בַּעַל חֹמֶר, לֹא יִתְעוֹרֵר לַדְּבָרִים כִּי אִם עַל־יַד
מְעוֹרֵר, כְּדֶרֶךְ בְּנֵי־אָדָם בְּעֵת מִלְחָמָה, יָרִיעוּ אַף יַצְרִיחוּ כְּדֵי שֶׁיִּתְעוֹרְרוּ יָפֶה
לַמִּלְחָמָה; וְגַם־כֵּן בְּיוֹם רֹאשׁ הַשָּׁנָה, שֶׁהוּא הַיּוֹם הַנּוֹעָד מִקֶּדֶם לָדוּן בּוֹ כָּל בָּאֵי
עוֹלָם, וּכְמוֹ שֶׁאָמְרוּ זִכְרוֹנָם לִבְרָכָה: בְּרֹאשׁ הַשָּׁנָה כָּל בָּאֵי הָעוֹלָם עוֹבְרִין לִפְנֵי
הַשֵּׁם כִּבְנֵי מָרוֹן, כְּלוֹמַר שֶׁהַשְׁגָּחָתוֹ עַל מַעֲשֵׂה כָּל אֶחָד וְאֶחָד בִּפְרָט, וְאִם
זְכִיּוֹתָיו מְרֻבִּין יֵצֵא זַכַּאי, וְאִם עֲוֹנוֹתָיו מְרֻבִּין בִּכְדֵי שֶׁרָאוּי לְחַיְּבוֹ, מְחַיְּבִין אוֹתוֹ
לָמוּת אוֹ לְאַחַת מִן הַגְּזֵרוֹת, כְּפִי מַה שֶׁהוּא חַיָּב.

עַל־כֵּן צָרִיךְ כָּל אֶחָד לְהָעִיר טִבְעוֹ לְבַקֵּשׁ רַחֲמִים עַל חֲטָאָיו מֵאֲדוֹן הָרַחֲמִים,
כִּי אֵל חַנּוּן וְרַחוּם הוּא, נוֹשֵׂא עָוֹן וָפֶשַׁע וְחַטָּאָה, וְנַקֵּה לַשָּׁבִים אֵלָיו בְּכָל לִבָּם;
וְקוֹל הַשּׁוֹפָר מְעוֹרֵר הַרְבֵּה לֵב כָּל שׁוֹמְעָיו, וְכָל־שֶׁכֵּן קוֹל הַתְּרוּעָה, כְּלוֹמַר הַקּוֹל
הַנִּשְׁבָּר.

וּמִלְּבַד הַהִתְעוֹרְרוּת שֶׁבּוֹ, יֵשׁ לוֹ לָאָדָם זֵכֶר בַּדָּבָר שֶׁיִּשָּׁבֵר יֵצֶר לִבּוֹ הָרַע
בְּתַאֲווֹת הָעוֹלָם וּבַחֲטָאִים, בְּשָׁמְעוֹ קוֹלוֹת נִשְׁבָּרִים, כִּי כָל אָדָם כְּפִי מַה שֶׁיִּרְאֶה
בְּעֵינָיו וּבְאָזְנָיו יִשְׁמַע, יָכִין לְבָבוֹ וְיָבִין בַּדְּבָרִים; וְהַיְנוּ דְּאָמַר רַבִּי יְהוּדָה: בְּרֹאשׁ
הַשָּׁנָה תּוֹקְעִין בְּשֶׁל זְכָרִים—כְּלוֹמַר בְּקֶרֶן הַכְּבָשִׂים הַכָּפוּף, כְּדֵי שֶׁיִּזְכֹּר הָאָדָם

§405   1. TB Rosh haShanah 33b.
2. Leviticus 25 : 9.
3. More literally, all those come into the world. The manuscripts have *kol b'né*
'olam (or *ha'olam*), "all the children (people) of the world"; but this is the reading of
the Talmud.
4. The expression of His attributes is based on Exodus 34 : 6–7.
5. TB Rosh haShanah 26b.

year — as we learned in the Mishnah in tractate *Rosh haShanah* (2a): The first of Tishri is the beginning of the year for [the numbering of] the years — for it is stated, *it is a day of* t'ru'ah (*sounding the horn*) *for you* (Numbers 29:1). Now, although there is no indication here in this word *t'ru'ah* if it is to be with a *shofar* or cymbals or some other musical instrument, through the Oral Tradition our Sages of blessed memory learned[1] that it means with a *shofar*, just as we find in regard to the jubilee, where *shofar* is stated.[2]

At the root of the precept lies the reason that since man is a creature of physical matter, he is not aroused to things except by something stirring, in the way that people at the time of battle will sound horns and even shriek, in order to be well aroused to war. Then so too on the day of *Rosh haShanah*, the beginning of the year, which is the day determined of old for all those who came into the world[3] to be judged on it. As the Sages of blessed memory said in the tractate *Rosh haShanah* (16a): At the beginning of the year, all those who came into the world[3] pass before the Eternal Lord like sheep through a narrow pass. In other words, His concerned watchfulness is over the activity of each and every one individually: If his merits are the more, he emerges [judged as] virtuous, innocent; if his iniquities are the more, to the extent that he deserves punishment, he is sentenced to death or to one of the [lesser] decrees, according to what he has incurred.

For this reason everyone needs to arouse his nature to entreat mercy for his sins from the [Divine] Master of mercies; for He is a gracious, compassionate God, who forgives iniquity, wrongdoing and sin, and absolves[4] those who turn back to Him with all their heart. Now, the sound of the *shofar* greatly stirs the heart of all who hear it, and all the more certainly the sound of the *t'ru'ah*, which means the broken (quavering) peal.

Apart from the arousal that is [inherent] in it, there is a reminder for a man in the matter that he should break the impulse of his heart that is evil with the cravings and sinful matters of the world, as he hears the broken (quavering) sounds. For every person, according to what he sees with his eyes and hears with his ears, he will prepare his heart, and will [then] understand these matters. This is why R. Judah said:[5] On *Rosh haShanah*, a *shofar* [horn] from male animals is to be blown — in other words, the bent (curved) horn of rams, so that a man should remember when he sees it that he is to bend his heart [in

⟨195⟩

בִּרְאוֹתוֹ אוֹתוֹ שֶׁיְּכַוֵּן לִבּוֹ לַשָּׁמַיִם, וְרַבִּי לֵוִי פָּסַק הֲלָכָה כְּמוֹתוֹ, וּמִנְהָגָן שֶׁל יִשְׂרָאֵל כֵּן.

מִדִּינֵי הַמִּצְוָה, מַה שֶּׁאָמְרוּ זִכְרוֹנָם לִבְרָכָה שֶׁשִּׁעוּר הַשּׁוֹפָר הוּא כְּדֵי שֶׁיֹּאחֲזֶנּוּ אָדָם בְּיָדוֹ וְיֵרָאֶה לְכָאן וּלְכָאן, מִפְּנֵי שֶׁהוּא קֶרֶן; פֵּרוּשׁ: כָּל מַה שֶּׁהוּא שׁוֹפָר, כְּלוֹמַר שֶׁהוּא חָלוּל, שֶׁלְּשׁוֹן הַשּׁוֹפָר הָכִי מַשְׁמַע לְעוֹלָם: דָּבָר שֶׁיֵּשׁ לוֹ חָלָל—כְּגוֹן הַשּׁוֹפָר שֶׁל כֶּבֶשׂ, שֶׁיֵּשׁ לוֹ חָלָל שֶׁהַזַּכְרוּת בְּתוֹכוֹ; וְכָל שׁוֹפָר בְּכָל הָעוֹלָם שֶׁיֵּשׁ לוֹ חָלָל כְּמוֹ שֶׁפֵּרַשְׁנוּ, כָּשֵׁר לִתְקֹעַ בּוֹ בְּרֹאשׁ הַשָּׁנָה —לְאַפּוּקֵי קַרְנֵי רְאֵם וּשְׁאָר חַיּוֹת שֶׁקַּרְנֵיהֶם אֵינָם נִכְלָלִין בִּלְשׁוֹן שׁוֹפָר כְּלָל, לְפִי שֶׁאֵין בָּהֶן דָּבָר חָלוּל אֶלָּא אֶת הַזַּכְרוּת לְבָד.

אֲבָל קֶרֶן הַפָּרָה, אַף־עַל־פִּי שֶׁהוּא בִּכְלַל שׁוֹפָר, שֶׁהֲרֵי יֵשׁ לוֹ נַקְבּוּת וְזַכְרוּת, אֵינוֹ כָשֵׁר, מִפְּנֵי שֶׁהַכָּתוּב כְּלָלוֹ עִם הַפְּסוּלִין, שֶׁקְּרָאוֹ קֶרֶן, וּכְדִכְתִיב: בְּכוֹר שׁוֹרוֹ וְגוֹמֵר וְקַרְנֵי רְאֵם קַרְנָיו.

נִמְצָא לְפִי פֵּרוּשֵׁנוּ זֶה, שֶׁכָּל הַקְּרָנוֹת שֶׁבָּעוֹלָם פְּסוּלִין לִתְקֹעַ בָּהֶן בְּרֹאשׁ הַשָּׁנָה, חוּץ מִקַּרְנֵי הַכְּבָשִׂים וְהָרְחֵלִים וְגַם תְּיָשִׁים וְעִזִּים, לְפִי שֶׁלֹּא מָצִינוּ בָּעוֹלָם קַרְנוֹת חֲלוּלִין חוּץ מֵאֵלּוּ וְשֶׁל פָּרָה, כִּי קַרְנֵי כָּל הַחַיּוֹת אֵינָן חֲלוּלִין, וְנִמְצָא שֶׁאֵינָם בִּכְלַל לְשׁוֹן שׁוֹפָר שֶׁצִּוַּתְנוּ הַתּוֹרָה לִתְקֹעַ; וְשֶׁל פָּרָה גַּם־כֵּן כְּבָר הוֹצִיאוֹ הַכָּתוּב מִכְּלַל הַכְּשֵׁרִים וְהִכְנִיסוֹ עִם כְּלַל הַפְּסוּלִים, מִפְּנֵי שֶׁקְּרָאוֹ בִשְׁמָם.

וְאַל יִקְשֶׁה בְעֵינֶיךָ לִדְבָרֵינוּ אֵלֶּה, שֶׁהֲרֵי הַכָּתוּב קוֹרֵא שׁוֹפָר הַתְּיָשִׁים בִּלְשׁוֹן הַפְּסוּלִין, כְּדִכְתִיב "וְהַצָּפִיר קֶרֶן חֲזוּת בֵּין עֵינָיו", שֶׁהָעִנְיָן הַהוּא הָיָה בְּמַרְאֵה הַנְּבוּאָה, וְהוֹדִיעַ הַכָּתוּב שֶׁהָיָה שֶׁהָיָה נִרְאֶה לַנָּבִיא, לְרֹב תֹּקֶף הַצָּפִיר, כְּאִלּוּ הָיָה לוֹ קֶרֶן הַפְּסוּלִין, כְּלוֹמַר שֶׁהָיָה חָזָק מִבְּלִי נַקְבּוּת, וְאֵין הָעִנְיָן שֶׁיַּכְנִיסֵנוּ הַכָּתוּב עִם

---

6. *Ibid.* 27b.

7. Explained in the next paragraph; *ibid.* 26a.

8. So Ramban, commentary to TB Rosh haShanah.

9. Growing thus from the animal's head, which when removed, leaves the hollow part.

subservience] to Heaven. R. Lévi set the definitive law according to him, and this is the practice of the Jewish people.

Among the laws of the precept there is what the Sages of blessed memory taught:[6] that the minimal size of a *shofar* is a length enough for a man to hold it in his hand and it should be seen (visible) at either side [of the hand]. All animal horns are acceptable except that of a cow, since that is a *keren*.[7] This means whatever is a *shofar*, i.e. it is hollow, for the term *shofar* always has this sense[8] — something with a hollow space within, such as the horn of a ram, that has a hollow area within it, in which there is a bony [inner] part.[9] So any animal horn in the whole world which is hollow, as we explained, is acceptable [for us] to sound it on *Rosh haShanah* — which excludes the horns of buffalo and other animals whose horns cannot be included under the name of *shofar* at all, because they have nothing hollow but only the bony protrusion.

As for the horn of a cow, however, even though it can be included in the category of the *shofar*, since it has both a hollow outer part and a bony inner part, it is not acceptable — because Scripture included it with the disqualified ones, since it called it *keren*: as it is written, *His firstling bull, majesty is his, and his horns* (karnav) *are the horns* (karné) *of a wild-ox* (Deuteronomy 33:17).

Consequently, according to our explanation, all animal horns in the world are unacceptable to sound them on *Rosh haShanah* except the horns of rams and sheep, as well as goats — since we have not found any hollow animal horns in the world except these and that of a cow. For the horns of all [other] animals are not hollow, and as a result they are not in the category of the *shofar*, which the Torah commanded us to sound; and that of the cow Scripture likewise excluded previously from the category of acceptable ones and included it in the category of the disqualified ones, as it called it by their name.

Now, let it not be a difficulty in your eyes, according to these words of ours, that Scripture clearly calls the horn of rams by the term for the disqualified ones: as it is written, *and the goat had a conspicuous* keren *(horn) between his eyes* (Daniel 8:5). For that occurrence was in a prophetic vision, and the Writ tells that it appeared to the prophet, because of the goat's immense might, as though it had a horn of the disqualified kind; in other words, that it was strong, without a hollow outer part. But the import is not at all that Scripture

⟨197⟩

הַפְּסוּלִין כְּלָל כִּי־אִם בְּהֶפֶךְ, לְכָל מֵבִין.

וְהָאֱרַכְתִּי לְךָ, בְּנִי, מְעַט בְּכָאן, לְפִי שֶׁהַפֵּרוּשׁ הַזֶּה נִתְחַדֵּשׁ בְּמִשְׁנָה זוֹ מִזְּמַן קָרוֹב, וַאֲשֶׁר הָיוּ לְפָנִים פֵּרְשׁוּהָ בְּעִנְיָן אַחֵר.

וְכֵן מֵעִנְיַן הַמִּצְוָה מַה שֶּׁאָמְרוּ זִכְרוֹנָם לִבְרָכָה שֶׁכָּל הַקּוֹלוֹת כְּשֵׁרִים בְּשׁוֹפָר; וְאָמְרוּ גַם־כֵּן שֶׁאִם גֵּרְדוֹ הַשּׁוֹפָר עַד שֶׁהֶעֱמִידוֹ עַל גִּלְדּוֹ, כָּשֵׁר, וּמַה שֶּׁאָמְרוּ זִכְרוֹנָם לִבְרָכָה שֶׁיּוֹם־טוֹב שֶׁל רֹאשׁ הַשָּׁנָה שֶׁחָל בְּשַׁבָּת אֵין תּוֹקְעִין בּוֹ שׁוֹפָר, גְּזֵרָה שֶׁמָּא יִטְּלֶנּוּ יִשְׂרָאֵל אֶחָד וְיַעֲבִירֶנּוּ אַרְבַּע אַמּוֹת בִּרְשׁוּת הָרַבִּים וְיָבוֹא לִידֵי אִסּוּר סְקִילָה; וְהַדָּבָר הַזֶּה לֹא גָזְרוּ אוֹתוֹ חֲכָמִים בְּמָקוֹם שֶׁיֵּשׁ שָׁם בֵּית־דִּין שֶׁהוּא גָדוֹל בְּחָכְמָה — וְדַוְקָא שֶׁתּוֹקְעִין אוֹתוֹ שָׁם בִּישִׁיבַת הַבֵּית־דִּין.

וְהָרַב מֹשֶׁה בֶּן מַיְמוֹן זִכְרוֹנוֹ לִבְרָכָה כָּתַב שֶׁצָּרִיךְ לִהְיוֹת הַבֵּית־דִּין סָמוּךְ בְּאֶרֶץ־יִשְׂרָאֵל, וְשֶׁיִּהְיֶה בֵית־דִּין מְעֻלֶּה, מֵאוֹתָן שֶׁקִּדְּשׁוּ אֶת הַחֹדֶשׁ. וַאֲנִי שָׁמַעְתִּי שֶׁהָרַב רַבִּי יִצְחָק אַלְפָסִי זִכְרוֹנוֹ לִבְרָכָה הָיָה תּוֹקֵעַ שׁוֹפָר בִּישִׁיבָתוֹ בְּשַׁבָּת. וְאַתָּה בְּנִי, אִם תִּזְכֶּה, תִּבְחַר לְךָ הַטּוֹב בְּעֵינֶיךָ.

וְכֵן מֵעִנְיַן הַמִּצְוָה, מַה שֶּׁאָמְרוּ זִכְרוֹנָם לִבְרָכָה שֶׁחַיָּב אָדָם לִתְקֹעַ בְּרֹאשׁ הַשָּׁנָה שָׁלֹשׁ תְּקִיעוֹת שֶׁל שָׁלֹשׁ שָׁלֹשׁ, כְּלוֹמַר שָׁלֹשׁ פְּעָמִים תְּקִיעָה וּתְרוּעָה וּתְקִיעָה, שֶׁנִּמְצָא שֶׁהֵן שֵׁשׁ תְּקִיעוֹת וְשָׁלֹשׁ תְּרוּעוֹת; וּפֵרוּשׁ תְּרוּעָה כְּתַרְגּוּמוֹ: יְבָבָא, וְעִנְיַן יְבָבָא הוּא קוֹל שָׁבוּר, כְּלוֹמַר קוֹל יְלָלָה.

נִמְצָא שֶׁהַתּוֹרָה צִוְּתָה אוֹתָנוּ לַעֲשׂוֹת בַּשּׁוֹפָר קוֹל הַדּוֹמֶה לִילָלָה. וּמִפְּנֵי שֶׁמְּקוֹמוֹת הָעוֹלָם חֲלוּקִים בְּעִנְיַן הַיְלָלָה, שֶׁבְּמָקוֹם אֶחָד מְיַלְּלִין בִּגְנִיחוֹת גַּסּוֹת וּבְמָקוֹם אַחֵר בְּדַקּוֹת, וּבְמָקוֹם אַחֵר עוֹשִׂין הַכֹּל, גַּסּוֹת וְדַקּוֹת, נָהֲגוּ בְּכָל מָקוֹם וּמָקוֹם לִהְיוֹת מַתְרִיעִין בְּרֹאשׁ הַשָּׁנָה עַל דֶּרֶךְ שֶׁהָיוּ מְיַלְּלִין אִישׁ אִישׁ בִּמְקוֹמוֹ, וּבְכֵן יוֹצְאִין יְדֵי חוֹבָתָם בַּמִּצְוָה (שֶׁהַתּוֹרָה צִוְּתָה בְּקוֹל יְלָלָה, וּבְאֵי זֶה שֶׁיִּהְיֶה

10. The paragraph is based on Ramban *ibid*, as given in Ritba, commentary to TB Rosh haShanah 26a.

11. See notes 9, 10; the explanation is also given by R. Nissim on Rif, Rosh haShanah iii (cited in *Tosafoth Yom Tov* on Mishnah *ad loc.*).

12. TB Rosh haShanah 29b.

13. According to the Talmud (*ibid.*), one who wishes to learn from an expert how to sound the *shofar*.

14. I.e. in the presence of members of the *beth din*.

15. MT *hilchoth shofar* ii 9.

16. I.e. they had such authority; hence there could not be any in post-Talmudic times.

17. So too *Maggid Mishneh* to MT *ibid*.

18. I.e. three times, a series of *t'ki'ah, t'ru'ah, t'ki'ah*.

would include it with the unacceptable ones, but rather the opposite, for everyone who understands.[10]

I have been a bit lengthy for you here, my son, because this explanation was newly given for this passage in the Mishnah[6] recently,[11] while those who were beforetime explained it in a different manner.

In the subject-matter of the precept there is likewise what the Sages of blessed memory said:[6] that all sounds are acceptable with a *shofar*. They said, too,[6] that if a *shofar* was scraped out until its outer layer was left, it is acceptable. Then there is what they (of blessed memory) taught:[12] that if the festival day of *Rosh haShanah* occurred on a Sabbath, the *shofar* is not sounded, as a protective decree for fear that one Jew[13] might take it and carry it four cubits in the public domain and thus come to incur guilt over a prohibition meriting stoning. However, the Sages did not decree this ruling in a place where there is a *beth din* (religions court) that is great in wisdom — but this specifically if it is sounded there, at the *beth din* in session.[14]

Now, R. Moses b. Maimon of blessed memory wrote[15] that the *beth din* must be one that was ordained in the land of Israel, and it must be a distinguished *beth din*, of those that sanctified the [new] month.[16] Yet I heard that R. Isaac 'Alfasi of blessed memory would sound the *shofar* in his academy on the Sabbath.[17] But you, my son, if you will merit, you will choose for yourself what appears good in your eyes.

So also, in the subject-matter of the precept, there is what the Sages of blessed memory said:[1] that a man is obligated to sound on *Rosh haShanah* three [sets of] peals, each of three parts: that is to say, three times *t'ki'ah* (a clear blast), *t'ru'ah* (a broken call), and *t'ki'ah*[18] — which are, consequently, six *t'ki'ah* blasts and three *t'ru'ah* peals. The meaning of *t'ru'ah* is as its Aramaic translation: *y'bava* (sobbing); and the sense of *y'bava* is a broken sound, which is to say, wailing.

Hence we find that the Torah commanded us to produce a sound with the *shofar* that resembles a lament. But because regions of the world differ in regard to lament, since in one region they wail with large moans, and in another with small ones, while in yet another location they utter both large and small, it was the practice in every locality to sound the *t'ru'ah* on *Rosh haShanah* in the way that they would lament, each one in his region; and so they could acquit themselves of their obligation of the precept (that the Torah commanded about the sound of wailing. Hence in whatever locality at all one

בְּשׁוּם מָקוֹם בְּכָךְ הָיָה יוֹצֵא יְדֵי תוֹרָה בְּכָל מָקוֹם, וְאַף־עַל־פִּי שֶׁבִּמְקוֹמוֹ אֵין מְיַלְּלִין כֵּן, שֶׁהֲרֵי קַיָּם קַנֶּנֶת הַכָּתוּב וְעָשָׂה בְיוֹם זֶה יְלָלָה בַּשּׁוֹפָר).

עַד שֶׁקָּם רַבִּי אַבָּהוּ, וְלֹא יָשַׁר בְּעֵינָיו לִהְיוֹת יִשְׂרָאֵל חֲלוּקִים בְּמִנְהַג הַתְּרוּעָה, זֶה בְּכֹה וְזֶה בְּכֹה, שֶׁנַּעֲשָׂה תוֹרָה כִּשְׁתֵּי תוֹרוֹת, וְקִבֵּץ כָּל הַמִּנְהָגִים, וְהִתְקִין שֶׁיִּהְיוּ תוֹקְעִין בְּכָל הַמְּקוֹמוֹת בְּשָׁוֶה. וְלָצֵאת יְדֵי חוֹבָה מִכָּל הַיְלָלוֹת שֶׁנַּעֲשׂוֹת בָּעוֹלָם, תִּקֵּן לַעֲשׂוֹת הַתְּרוּעָה בִּשְׁלֹשָׁה צְדָדִין: כְּעֵין גְּנִיחוֹת גַּסּוֹת, דְּהַיְנוּ שְׁבָרִים; וּכְעֵין גְּנִיחוֹת דַּקּוֹת, דְּהַיְנוּ שֶׁאָנוּ קוֹרִין תְּרוּעָה; וְעוֹד בְּצַד אַחֵר, גְּנִיחוֹת גַּסּוֹת וְדַקּוֹת, כְּמִנְהַג אֶחָד הַמְּקוֹמוֹת, שֶׁעוֹשִׂין הַכֹּל בִּילְלוֹתֵיהֶם. וְנִמְצָא לְפִי זֶה שֶׁאָנוּ צְרִיכִין לִתְקֹעַ שָׁלֹשׁ שֶׁל שָׁלֹשׁ שָׁלֹשׁ, שָׁלֹשׁ פְּעָמִים שָׁלֹשׁ.

וְדִין שׁוֹפָר שֶׁנִּסְדַּק לְאָרְכּוֹ אוֹ לְרָחְבּוֹ; וְנָקַב וּסְתָמוֹ בְמִינוֹ אוֹ שֶׁלֹּא בְמִינוֹ; וְדִין נוֹתֵן שׁוֹפָר בְּתוֹךְ שׁוֹפָר; וְדִין תּוֹקֵעַ לְתוֹךְ הַבּוֹר וְהַדּוּת; וְדִין שׁוֹפָר שֶׁל עֲבוֹדָה זָרָה וְעִיר הַנִּדַּחַת; וְהַמֻּדָּר הֲנָאָה מֵחֲבֵרוֹ; וְדִין נִתְכַּוֵּן שׁוֹמֵעַ וְלֹא מַשְׁמִיעַ; וְיֶתֶר פְּרָטֶיהָ, מְבֹאָרִים בְּמַסֶּכֶת רֹאשׁ הַשָּׁנָה.

וְנוֹהֶגֶת בְּכָל מָקוֹם וּבְכָל זְמַן, בִּזְכָרִים וְלֹא בִנְקֵבוֹת, לְפִי שֶׁהִיא מִכְּלַל הַמִּצְווֹת שֶׁהַזְּמַן גְּרָמָהּ, שֶׁהַנָּשִׁים פְּטוּרוֹת. וְעוֹבֵר עַל זֶה וְלֹא שָׁמַע קוֹל שׁוֹפָר בְּיוֹם רֹאשׁ הַשָּׁנָה כְּסֵדֶר תְּקִיעוֹת שֶׁאָמַרְנוּ, שָׁלֹשׁ שֶׁל שָׁלֹשׁ שָׁלֹשׁ לְכָל הַפָּחוֹת, בִּטֵּל עֲשֵׂה זֶה. וְאִם שְׁמָעָן בְּהֶפְסֵק, וַאֲפִלּוּ בְּכָל הַיּוֹם, יָצָא: וּכְמוֹ שֶׁאָמְרוּ זִכְרוֹנָם לִבְרָכָה שֶׁאִם שָׁמַע אָדָם תֵּשַׁע תְּקִיעוֹת הַמְחֻיָּבוֹת בְּתֵשַׁע שָׁעוֹת בַּיּוֹם, וַאֲפִלּוּ מִתִּשְׁעָה בְנֵי־אָדָם, יָצָא. וְלָמַדְתִּי מִן הַחֲכָמִים אַל, שֶׁצָּרִיךְ מִכָּל־מָקוֹם שֶׁלֹּא לִשְׁמֹעַ קוֹל פָּסוּל בָּאֶמְצַע.

19. The part in parentheses, beginning five lines above, is not in the oldest manuscripts. It is thus evidently a later interpolation.

20. TB Rosh haShanah 34a.

21. Thus three times, *t'ki'ah sh'varim-t'ru'ah t'ki'ah*; three times, *t'ki'ah sh'varim t'ki'ah*; and three times, *t'ki'ah t'ru'ah t'ki'ah*. These last two paragraphs give the conception of R. Hai Ga'on, cited by R. Nissim, Rosh haShanah iii.

22. I.e. any space within the ground enclosed by cemented walls; TB Rosh haShanah 27b.

23. I.e. it was generally blown in idol-worship; *ibid.* 28a.

24. *Ibid.* See § 386, note 24.

25. Whether the other may sound the *shofar* for him to hear and so fulfill his obligation; *ibid.*

26. TB Rosh haShanah 28b.

27. I.e. the obligation comes at a specific time.

28. TB Rosh haShanah 34b.

might be, he would acquit himself of the Torah's requirement anywhere, even if in his own locality people did not lament like that: For he fulfilled the intention of Scripture and produced on this day a lament on the *shofar*.)[19]

[This was the situation] until R. Abbahu arose,[20] and it was not right in his eyes that the Israelites should be divided in practice about the *t'ru'ah*, this one so and that one so; for the Torah thus became as two Torahs. So he gathered all the practices, and he enacted an amendment that the *shofar* should be sounded in all localities identically. Then in order that we should acquit ourselves of the obligation with all the kinds of lament uttered in the world, he enacted that the *t'ru'ah* should be produced in three ways: resembling large groans, which means the *sh'varim*; resembling small moans, this being what we call *t'ru'ah*; and in yet another way — large and small groans, in the manner of one of the regions, where both were uttered in their wailing. The result is, accordingly, that we need to sound three groups of three *shofar* blasts each, three times.[21]

Then there is the law about a *shofar* that was cracked along its length, or along its width;[6] if it developed a hole and one filled it with its own kind [of material] or with something not of its own kind;[6] and the law if a person placed one *shofar* inside another;[6] the law if one blew the *shofar* within a pit or cellar;[22] the law about a *shofar* of an idol[23] or a town gone astray;[24] if one was forbidden under a vow to have any benefit from his fellow-man;[25] and the law if the listener had the intention [to fulfill the *mitzvah*] but not the one producing the sounds.[26] [These and] the rest of its details are explained in the Talmud tractate *Rosh haShanah*.

It is in force everywhere and at every time, for men, but not for women, as it is of the category of *mitzvoth* that time causes,[27] by which women are not obligated. If a person transgresses this and does not hear the sound of the *shofar* on the day of *Rosh haShanah* in the order of blasts that we stated — three groups, each of three peals, at the very least — he has disobeyed this positive precept. If he heard them with interruption, even [at intervals] during the whole day, he has acquitted himself of the obligation; it is as the Sages of blessed memory said,[28] that if a man heard the nine obligatory *shofar* blasts in the course of nine hours during the day, even from nine [different] people, he has fulfilled his duty. But I learned from the wise scholars of Torah, God protect them, that in any event it is necessary

🕎 רָאשֵׁי הַמַּטּוֹת

יֵשׁ בָּהּ מִצְוַת עֲשֵׂה אַחַת, וּמִצְוַת לֹא־תַעֲשֶׂה אַחַת

[מִצְוַת דִּין הֲפָרַת נְדָרִים]

תו שֶׁנִּצְטַוֵּינוּ בְּמִצְוַת הֲפָרַת נְדָרִים, כְּלוֹמַר שֶׁנָּדוּן בְּמִי שֶׁנָּדַר כַּאֲשֶׁר תְּצַוֶּה הַתּוֹרָה, שֶׁנֶּאֱמַר ״אִישׁ כִּי יִדֹּר נֶדֶר״ וְגוֹמֵר, כְּמוֹ שֶׁבָּא מְבֹאָר בַּפָּרָשָׁה.

וְכָתַב הָרַב מֹשֶׁה בֶּן מַיְמוֹן זִכְרוֹנוֹ לִבְרָכָה בְּמִצְוָה זוֹ, וְזֶה לְשׁוֹנוֹ: וְאֵין הָעִנְיָן שֶׁנִּתְחַיֵּב לְהָפֵר עַל־כָּל־פָּנִים; וְזֶה הָעִנְיָן בְּעַצְמוֹ הַבֵּן מִמֶּנּוּ כָּל זְמַן שֶׁתִּשְׁמָעֵנִי מוֹנֶה דִּין אֶחָד מֵהַדִּינִין, שֶׁאֵין זוֹ מִצְוָה בִּפְעוּלָה מֵהַפְּעוּלוֹת בְּהֶכְרֵחַ, וְאוּלָם הַמִּצְוָה הִיא הֱיוֹתֵנוּ מְצֻוִּין (שנתן) [שֶׁנָּדוּן] בְּדִין זֶה בְּדָבָר זֶה; אוּלָם הֱיוֹת הַבַּעַל וְהָאָב מְפֵרִים, כְּבָר בֵּאֵר הַכָּתוּב זֶה וְדִקְדֵּק בּוֹ; וּבָאַתְנוּ הַקַּבָּלָה שֶׁהֶחָכָם יַתִּיר הַנֶּדֶר לַכֹּל, וּכְמוֹ־כֵן הַשְּׁבוּעָה, וְהַהֲעָרָה עַל זֶה מַאֲמָרָם ״לֹא יַחֵל דְּבָרוֹ״, וְדָרְשׁוּ זִכְרוֹנָם לִבְרָכָה: הוּא אֵינוֹ מֵחֵל, אֲבָל אֲחֵרִים מוֹחֲלִין לוֹ. וְהַכְּלָל, שֶׁאֵין רְאָיָה עַל זֶה מִן הַכָּתוּב; וְהֵם עֲלֵיהֶם הַשָּׁלוֹם כְּבָר אָמְרוּ: הֶתֵּר נְדָרִים פּוֹרְחִין בָּאֲוִיר, וְאֵין לָהֶם עַל מַה שֶּׁיִּסְמָכוּ אֶלָּא הַקַּבָּלָה הָאֲמִתִּית לְבַדָּהּ, עַד כָּאן.

וְהָעוֹלֶה מִכָּל זֶה לְדַעְתּוֹ, לְפִי הַדּוֹמֶה, כִּי בְּהַתִּיר הֶחָכָם אֶת הַנֶּדֶר בְּמִצְוַת הַתּוֹרָה, אוֹ שְׁלֹשָׁה הַדְיוֹטוֹת, וְיַעֲשׂוּ הָעִנְיָן כְּכָל אֲשֶׁר תְּצַוֶּה הַתּוֹרָה עָלָיו

---

29. I.e. a wrong blast that does not belong in a particular sequence (see note 20); so Ramban, cited in *Maggid Mishneh* to MT *hilchoth shofar* iii 2.

§406   1. ShM positive precept §95.
2. TB Ḥagigah 10a.
3. Since the verse, as it is interpreted, barely hints at it.

(essential) not to hear any wrong, unacceptable *shofar* sound in the middle.[29]

sidrah mattoth

(Numbers 30:2–32:42)

There are one positive and one negative precept in it.

[THE PRECEPT OF THE LAW OF
NULLIFYING VOWS]

406 that we were commanded about the precept of nullifying vows, which is to say that we should decide the law about someone who took a vow as the Torah commands: as it is stated, *When a man vows a vow*, etc. (Numbers 30:3), as it is found explained in the Scriptural section.

Now, R. Moses b. Maimon of blessed memory wrote of this precept,[1] in these words: Now, the substance [of the precept] is not that we should be obligated to nullify it under any circumstances. Understand this very point from me whenever you will hear me list one of [such] laws, that it is not a commandment of one of the obligatory activities. The precept is rather that we are commanded that we are to decide by this law in this matter. In any event, how the husband and the father can nullify [a woman's vow] the Writ already clarified, being precise about it. And the Oral Tradition has come down to us that a learned scholar can release anyone from a vow, and likewise from an oath. There is an intimation of this in Scripture's statement, *he shall not break his word* (Numbers 30:3), which our Sages of blessed memory interpreted:[2] he may not [simply] break it, but others may absolve him. But the nub of the matter is that there is no firm proof for this from Scripture.[3] In the past they (of blessed memory) said[2] that the release from vows [is a matter that] "flies about in the air"; they have nothing on which to base it except the true Oral Tradition alone. Thus far [Rambam's words].

What emerges from all this, by his view, as it would seem, is that when an expert learned scholar releases someone from a vow by the precept of the Torah, or three ordinary people [do it], and they carry out the matter according to all that the Torah commands about it, properly and rightly, they have then fulfilled a positive precept. But

כַּהֹגֶן וּבְיֹשֶׁר, אָז קִיְּמוּ עָשׂה; וְאִם הִתִּירוּ הַנֶּדֶר שֶׁלֹּא כְּמִצְוַת הַתּוֹרָה, כְּגוֹן שְׁנֵי הֶדְיוֹטוֹת אוֹ יָחִיד שֶׁאֵינוֹ מֻמְחֶה, אַף־עַל־פִּי שֶׁהֻתְּרוּ אֵינוֹ הֶתֵּר יֵשׁ עֲלֵיהֶם עֹנֶשׁ בִּטּוּל עֲשֵׂה זֶה, וּכְעִנְיָן שֶׁכָּתַבְתִּי לְמַעְלָה בְּעִנְיָן מִצְוַת הַנַּחֲלוֹת, שֶׁהַמִּצְוָה "אַל יִירָשֶׁנִי בְּנִי", אַף־עַל־פִּי שֶׁדְּבָרָיו בְּטֵלִים, יֵשׁ עָלָיו עֹנֶשׁ בִּטּוּל הַמִּצְוָה, דְּעָבַר אַהֲרַמְנָא דְּמַלְכָּא שֶׁצִּוָּה אוֹתָנוּ בְּדִין הַיְרֻשָּׁה.

וְאוּלָם הָרַב מֹשֶׁה בֶּן נַחְמָן זִכְרוֹנוֹ לִבְרָכָה כָּתַב שֶׁאֵין לִמְנוֹת דִּין זֶה כְּלָל מֵחֶשְׁבּוֹן הַמִּצְוֹת, וְזֶה לְשׁוֹנוֹ: וְכֵן יֵרָאֶה שֶׁהֲפָרַת נְדָרִים לֹא תִמָּנֶה, לְפִי שֶׁהִיא שְׁלִילוּת, שֶׁנִּצְטַוֵּינוּ לַעֲשׂוֹת כָּל הַיּוֹצֵא מִפִּינוּ וְשֶׁלֹּא נַחֵל דְּבָרֵינוּ, רַק עַל פִּי הָאָב אוֹ הַבַּעַל. עַד כָּאן. וְדִבְרֵי פִי חָכָם חֵן.

מִשָּׁרְשֵׁי עִנְיַן הַנֶּדֶר וְהַשְּׁבוּעָה וְהַהֶתֵּר שֶׁלָּהֶם, כְּבָר הִרְחַבְתִּי הַמַּאֲמָר בָּהֶן כַּאֲשֶׁר הִשִּׂיגָה יָדִי, בְּסֵדֶר וַיִּשְׁמַע יִתְרוֹ, בְּאַזְהָרַת לֹא תִשָּׂא, ה', סִימָן (ל"ב) [ל'].

מִדִּינֵי הַמִּצְוָה, מַה שֶּׁאָמְרוּ זִכְרוֹנָם לִבְרָכָה: כָּל כִּנּוּיֵי נְדָרִים כִּנְדָרִים, חֲרָמִים כַּחֲרָמִים, שְׁבוּעוֹת כִּשְׁבוּעוֹת, נְזִירוּת כִּנְזִירוּת; כְּגוֹן הָאוֹמֵר קוֹנָם, קוֹנָח, קוֹנָס — הֲרֵי אֵלּוּ כִּנּוּיִין לְקָרְבָּן; חֵרֶק, חֵרֶךְ, חֵרֶף — הֲרֵי אֵלּוּ כִּנּוּיִין לְחֵרֶם; נָזִיק, נָזִיחַ, פָּזִיחַ — הֲרֵי אֵלּוּ כִּנּוּיִין לִנְזִירוּת; שְׁבוּתָה, שְׁקוּקָה, נָדָר בְּמוֹתָא — הֲרֵי אֵלּוּ כִּנּוּיִין לִשְׁבוּעָה.

וְעִנְיַן לְשׁוֹנוֹת אֵלּוּ שֶׁאָמְרוּ חֲכָמִים, שֶׁהֵם נְדוֹנִין כְּאִלּוּ הוֹצִיא הָאָדָם בִּשְׂפָתָיו הַלָּשׁוֹן כְּתִקְנוֹ, וְלֹא נָחוּשׁ לְמָה שֶׁאָנוּ מַצְרִיכִין פִּיו וְלִבּוֹ שָׁוִין, וַהֲרֵי לֹא הוֹצִיא הַדָּבָר כְּתִקְנוֹ מִפִּיו — הַטַּעַם מִפְּנֵי שֶׁיֵּשׁ בִּלְשׁוֹנוֹת אֵלּוּ מַשְׁמָעוּת הָעִנְיָן, שֶׁכָּל הַשּׁוֹמֵעַ יִגְזֹר עָלָיו שֶׁזֹּאת כַּוָּנַת הַנִּשְׁבָּע אוֹ הַנּוֹדֵר; וְאַחַר שֶׁכֵּן הוּא, הֲרֵי הוּא

---

4. I.e. the vow remains in force.
5. Ramban, commentary to ShM positive precept §96.
6. TB N'darim 2a.
7. I.e. the vow to be a nazir (§368).
8. Understood as a distortion of "Moses."
9. TB N'darim 10a.
10. Equally clear and in agreement.

if they release someone from a vow not by the way of the Torah's commandment — for example, two laymen, or one who is not a learned expert — then even though their release is no release,[4] they incur penalty for disobeying this positive precept. It is alike in substance to what I wrote above (§ 400), regarding the precept of inheritance, that if someone orders, "Let my son not inherit from me," even though his words are to no effect, he is liable to punishment for disobeying the precept, since he went against the edict of the [Divine] King who commanded us about the law of inheritance.

However, R. Moses b. Naḥman of blessed memory wrote that this law is not to be listed at all in the reckoning of the precepts. These are his words:[5] And it likewise seems right that the nullification of vows should not be listed, since it is a negative matter. For we were commanded to do all that proceeds out of our mouth, and we should not break our word, except on the utterance of a father or husband [or the *beth din*]. Thus far [his words]; and *the words of a wise man's mouth are gracious* (Ecclesiastes 10:12).

Regarding root reasons for the subject of the vow and the oath and release from them, I previously dwelt at length about them as my hand was capable, in the fifth negative precept of *sidrah yithro* (§ 30).

Among the laws of the precept, there is what the Sages of blessed memory taught:[6] All substitute expressions for vows are as vows; for *ḥérem* [a proscriptive vow of devotement], are as a vow of *ḥérem*; for oaths, are as oaths; and for the vow of a *nazir*,[7] are as a *nazir*'s vow. For instance, if someone says, *konam koné-aḥ*, or *konas*, these are substitute expressions for *korban*, an offering; *ḥérek, ḥérech*, or *ḥéref* — these are substitute expressions for *ḥérem*; *nazik, nazi-aḥ*, or *pazi-aḥ* — these are substitute expressions for the vow to be a *nazir*; *sh'vuthah, sh'kukah*, or "the vow of Moha"[8] — these are substitute expressions for an oath.[9]

The significance of these expressions that our Sages listed is that they are regarded in law as though the man produced the utterance with his lips in its correct form, and we are not concerned that we [generally] require one's heart and mouth to be equal,[10] yet here he did not express the matter properly with his mouth. The reason is that there is in these expressions an indication of the subject, so that anyone hearing [any of them] would decide about it that such was the

intention of the one who swore or vowed; and since it is so, it is as if

כְּאִלּוּ אָמַר הַדָּבָר מְבֹאָר כְּתִקּוּנוֹ; שֶׁאִם לֹא תֹאמַר כֵּן, נִמְצָא שֶׁאֵין בְּעוֹלְגִים נֶדֶר וּשְׁבוּעָה לְעוֹלָם, וְזֶה אֵינוֹ בֶאֱמֶת.

וְכֵן מַה שֶּׁאָמְרוּ זִכְרוֹנָם לִבְרָכָה שֶׁאַרְבָּעָה נְדָרִים הֵן שֶׁהֵן מֻתָּרִין, כְּלוֹמַר מֻתָּרִין לְגַמְרֵי, שֶׁאֵין צְרִיכִין שְׁאֵלָה לְחָכָם, וּכְדַעַת שְׁמוּאֵל בְּפֶרֶק אַרְבָּעָה נְדָרִים, דְּהִלְכְתָא כְּוָתֵהּ, וְאֵלּוּ הֵן: נִדְרֵי זֵרוּזִין, נִדְרֵי הֲבַאי, נִדְרֵי שְׁגָגוֹת, נִדְרֵי אֳנָסִין; וְשָׁם בְּאוֹתוֹ הַפֶּרֶק מְבָרֵר כֵּיצַד בְּכָל אֶחָד וְאֶחָד.

וְגוֹרְסִין בִּירוּשַׁלְמִי גַּבֵּי נִדְרֵי זֵרוּזִין: אָמַר רַבִּי זְעֵירָא: הָדָא דְתֵימַר בְּשֶׁאֵין מַעֲמִידִין, אֲבָל אִם הָיוּ מַעֲמִידִין, צְרִיכִין הֶתֵּר חָכָם; כְּלוֹמַר אִם הָיוּ מַעֲמִידִין דִּבְרֵיהֶם, כְּלוֹמַר שֶׁלֹּא נָדְרוּ אוֹתוֹ גֶדֶר לְזָרֵז אֶלָּא בְּדַוְקָא נָדְרוּ אוֹתוֹ, צְרִיכִין שְׁאֵלָה לְחָכָם. וְהוּא הַדִּין בְּוַדַּאי לִשְׁאָר הַשְּׁלֹשָׁה הַשְּׁנוּיִּים בַּמִּשְׁנָה, שֶׁאִם הָיוּ מַעֲמִידִין דִּבְרֵיהֶם, שֶׁצְּרִיכִים שְׁאֵלָה לְחָכָם.

וּמִיהוּ בְּכָל עִנְיָן, הֶחָכָם מַתִּירָן כָּל זְמַן שֶׁיִּמְצָא פֶּתַח לְהַתִּיר, כְּלוֹמַר שֶׁיִּמְצָא שׁוּם עִנְיָן שֶׁיֹּאמַר עָלָיו הַנּוֹדֵר "אִלּוּ הָיִיתִי יוֹדֵעַ בִּשְׁעַת הַגֶּדֶר דָּבָר זֶה לֹא הָיִיתִי נוֹדֵר"; וַאֲפִלּוּ בְּנוֹלָד פּוֹתְחִין לְהַתִּיר, וּבִלְבַד שֶׁיְּהֵא הַנּוֹלָד מָצוּי, אֲבָל לֹא בְּנוֹלָד שֶׁאֵינוֹ מָצוּי; כֵּן הוּא מְפֹרָשׁ בַּגְּמָרָא בִּנְדָרִים.

וְכֵן נַמִּי פּוֹתְחִין בַּחֲרָטָה, וְכִדְפָסַק רָבָא מִשְּׁמָהּ דְּרַב נַחְמָן בִּנְדָרִים, דְּפוֹתְחִין בַּחֲרָטָה וְנִזְקָקִין לְהַתִּיר אֲפִלּוּ לְמִי שֶׁנִּשְׁבַּע בֵּאלֹהֵי יִשְׂרָאֵל, שֶׁהִיא שְׁבוּעָה חֲמוּרָה; וְדַוְקָא בַּחֲרָטָה דְּמֵעִקָּרָא, כְּגוֹן "לֵב זֶה עָלֶיךָ", כְּלוֹמַר שֶׁמִּתּוֹךְ הַכַּעַס נָדַר אוֹתוֹ הַגֶּדֶר וְאַחַר שֶׁנִּתְיַשְּׁבָה דַעְתּוֹ תּוֹהֶא בְּנִדְרוֹ לְגַמְרֵי וְאֵינוֹ רוֹצֶה בּוֹ כְּלָל;

---

11. *Ibid.* 20b.

12. TB N'darim 21b.

13. *Vows of pressing:* Bargaining over an item of sale, the seller says, "Be this forbidden to me if I lower the price for you beyond a *sela'*," whereupon the buyer retorts, "Be it forbidden to me if I give you more than a *shekel*" (half a *sela'*), both being quite willing to settle for three *denarii* (one and a half *sh'kalim*; three fourths of a *sela'*) (Mishnah, N'darim iii 1; TB 20b). *Vows of exaggeration:* "May that be forbidden to me if I did not see on this road [as many people] as those who went up from Egypt [at the Exodus] or" "if I did not see a snake like the beam of an olive-press" (*ibid.* 2; TB 24b). *Vows in error:* "Be this forbidden to me if I ate" or "if I drank," and the man then remembered that he had taken something to eat or drink (*ibid.* TB 25b). *Vows affected by duress:* A man tells a friend, "Be I forbidden to derive any benefit from you unless you come to dine with me," and the friend became ill (*ibid.* 3; TB 27a; for a different example see *ibid.* 4, TB 27b). In all these cases it is obvious that there was no serious intent of a proper vow.

14. TJ N'darim iii 1 (cited in R. Nissim, commentary to TB N'darim 21 b).

15. See the first illustrative example in note 13.

16. So TB N'darim 22b.

he said the word clearly, in its proper form. For if you will not say so, the result is that for those with difficult or distorted speech there can never be any vow or oath; and this is not so in truth.

There is, too, what the Sages of blessed memory taught:[11] that there are four vows from which a person is absolved, i.e. released completely, so that they have no need of asking a learned scholar [to release them], following the view of Sh'muel in the third chapter of the tractate N'darim,[12] since the definitive law is as he ruled. These are: vows of pressing, vows of exaggeration, vows in error, and vows affected by duress; and there, in that chapter, it is clarified how [such vows might be made] in each and every case.[13]

Now, we read in the Jerusalem Talmud[14] concerning vows of pressing: Said R. Ze'ira: When does this rule hold? — when they do not confirm [their words]; but if they do confirm, they need the release of a learned scholar. In other words, if they affirmed their words, saying in effect that they did not make that vow to press [one another to yield],[15] but rather vowed it literally, they need [to make] a request to a learned scholar [to release them]. And the same law quite certainly applies to the other three [kinds of vows] taught in the Mishnah: that if they confirm their words, they need [make] a request to a learned scholar.

In any event, though, a learned scholar can release them as long as an opening is found to give a release: in other words, where some point is found about which the one who vowed can say, "Had I known this thing at the time of the vow, I would not have made it." Even for something "born" [a new fact or situation that arose afterward] the subject is opened to grant a release, provided the "newborn" matter is a usual development, but not if the new situation is unusual. It was thus explained in the Talmud tractate N'darim (64a).

So too, an opening can be based on remorse, as Rava ruled in the name of R. Naḥman in the tractate N'darim (22b) that an opening can be developed in regard to regret, and one is thus impelled to grant a release even to a person who swore by the God of Israel — which is a severe oath. But this applies specifically to regret that is retroactive, as of the very beginning: for example, "Were you [then] of such a heart?"[16] — in other words, he took that vow out of anger, and now that his mind has settled, he regrets his vow completely and does not want it at all. If, however, he regrets it [only] now, because of some

אֲבָל אִם נִתְחָרֵט עַכְשָׁיו מֵחֲמַת עִנְיָן שֶׁנִּתְחַדֵּשׁ לְאַחַר שֶׁנָּדַר, וְחָפֵץ הוּא בְּנִדְרוֹ עַד
עַכְשָׁיו, זוֹ אֵינָהּ חֲרָטָה מַעַלְיָתָא וְאֵין פּוֹתְחִין בָּהּ כְּלָל, שֶׁהֲרֵי כָּל הַבָּא לִשְׁאֹל עַל
נִדְרוֹ וַדַּאי מִתְחָרֵט הוּא עַכְשָׁיו, וְאִם־כֵּן לֹא הָיִינוּ צְרִיכִין בַּגְּמָרָא לַחֲזֹר לִמְצֹא
פֶּתַח הֶתֵּר בְּנֶדֶר, וּמָצִינוּ בַּגְּמָרָא שֶׁהָיוּ מְחַזְּרִין לִמְצֹא פְּתָחִים לַנּוֹדְרִים.

אֶלָּא וַדַּאי הָאֱמֶת כְּמוֹ שֶׁכָּתַבְנוּ, דְּבָעֵינָן חֲרָטָה דְּמֵעִקָּרָא; וְעוֹד, שֶׁכָּל יְסוֹד
הֶתֵּר נְדָרִים הוּא טַעֲנַת שְׁגָגָה אוֹ אֹנֶס, שֶׁהַתּוֹרָה אָמְרָה "הָאָדָם בִּשְׁבוּעָה", פְּרָט
לְאָנוּס, וּכְמוֹ־כֵן בָּעֵינָן פִּיו וְלִבּוֹ שָׁוִין, וְאִם־כֵּן מִשּׁוּם חֲרָטָה דְּמֵעַכְשָׁו אִי־אֶפְשָׁר
לִתְלוֹת שְׁגָגָה אוֹ אֹנֶס בְּעֵת הַשְּׁבוּעָה כְּלָל, אֲבָל בַּחֲרָטָה דְּמֵעִקָּרָא יֵשׁ טַעֲנַת שְׁגָגָה
וְאֹנֶס, שֶׁהֲרֵי מוֹדֶה שֶׁלֹּא הָיָה עוֹשֶׂה הַנֶּדֶר מֵעִקָּרָא אִם הָיָה יוֹדֵעַ זֶה.

וְיֵשׁ מִגְּדוֹלֵי הַמְּפָרְשִׁים שֶׁכָּתַב דְּאַף־עַל־גַּב דְּפַסְקִינָן הֲלָכָה כְּרָבָא אָמַר רַב
נַחְמָן דְּפוֹתְחִין בַּחֲרָטָה וְנִזְקָקִין לְאֱלֹהֵי יִשְׂרָאֵל, עַכְשָׁו נָהֲגוּ לְהַחְמִיר וְלֹא
כַּהֲלָכָה, וְאֵין אָנוּ נִזְקָקִין לְמִי שֶׁנִּשְׁבַּע בֵּאלֹהֵי יִשְׂרָאֵל אֶלָּא בְּמַה שֶׁהוּא כְּעֵין
אַרְבָּעָה נְדָרִים הַשְּׁנוּיִין בַּמִּשְׁנָה; וְעוֹד, דְּלָא מִזְדַּקְּקִין לִשְׁבוּעוֹת אֶלָּא בְּמִלְתָא
דְּאִית בַּהּ מִצְוָה, כְּגוֹן עֲשִׂיַּת שָׁלוֹם בֵּין אִישׁ לְאִשְׁתּוֹ אוֹ בֵּין אָדָם לַחֲבֵרוֹ, וְכַיּוֹצֵא
בְּעִנְיָנִים אֵלּוּ.

וְכֵן אָמְרוּ זִכְרוֹנָם לִבְרָכָה בְּעִנְיָן זֶה שֶׁהֶתֵּר נְדָרִים בִּשְׁלֹשָׁה הֶדְיוֹטוֹת, וַאֲפִלּוּ
דְּלָא גְּמִירֵי וּסְבִירֵי, וְהוּא דְּאַסְבְּרִי לְהוּ וְסָבְרִי, וּבְשָׁחַד מִנַּיְהוּ גְּמִיר מִכָּל־מָקוֹם.
וּכְמוֹ־כֵן אָמְרוּ שֶׁהֶתֵּר נְדָרִים בְּיָחִיד אִם הוּא מֻמְחֶה, וְהוּא הַדִּין כָּל הֵיכָא שֶׁיֵּשׁ

17. I.e. such a way is not sought at all, by questioning him, to find grounds for
releasing him from the vow.

18. I.e. that when the man made the vow, he was either in error (he had wrong
information or was under a mistaken impression) or he was compelled by force.

19. Which indicates, of his own free will.

20. I.e. had he known correctly what he was mistaken about.

21. See five paragraphs above. This is the view of a *ga'on* cited in R. Nissim to
TB N'darim 22b, s.v. *'amar Rava*.

22. So R. Hai Ga'on, cited in *ibid*.

23. TB B'choroth 36b.

24. This is derived perhaps from the statement in TB Sanhedrin 3a that civil
cases may be tried by three laymen because it is impossible that one of them should
not have learned the subject-matter (MY).

25. TB Yevamoth 25b, etc.

new situation that has arisen after he took the vow, so that he wanted the vow until now—this is not adequate remorse, and no such opening can be developed with this at all:[17] For clearly, whoever comes to be questioned about his vow certainly regrets it now. Hence [if this were enough] there would have been no need in the Talmud to seek about in order to find an opening for release from a vow; and we find in the Talmud that they would seek about to find openings for those who vowed.

Certainly, then, the truth can be only as we have written: that remorse is required as of the very start. Moreover, the entire basis for release from a vow is the contention of error or compulsion;[18] for the Torah said, *whatever a man shall utter clearly with an oath* (Leviticus 5:4),[19] to exclude someone coerced. And it is likewise required that his mouth and heart should be equal [in agreement]. Then if so, on the strength of regret as of now, it is impossible to consider him to have been in error or under coercion at all. However, where there is remorse as of the very beginning, there is a contention of error and compulsion: for here he acknowledges now that he would not have made the vow originally had he known this.[20]

Now, there is one of the great authorities who wrote that although the definitive law was decided according to Rava in the name of R. Naḥman, that an opening can be based upon regret, and we are impelled to [grant release even from an oath by] the God of Israel, it is our practice today to be stringent, not in accord with the definitive law, and we are not obliged to [grant release to] one who swore by the God of Israel, but only for anything akin to the four vows considered in the Mishnah.[21] Moreover, we are not inclined to [grant release from] any oaths other than something which involves a *mitzvah*, such as making peace between a man and his wife, or between a man and his fellow-man, or anything similar to these matters.[22]

Our Sages of blessed memory likewise said on this subject[23] that a release from vows [may be granted] by three ordinary persons (laymen), even if they did not study and do not understand the subject—but this only if when it is explained them they understand, and when one of them has learned it in any case.[24] So too they taught that release from vows [may be granted] by an individual, if he is a learned expert;[25] and the same law applies wherever he has permission (authority) from someone ordained, to absolve people from

לוֹ רְשׁוּת לְהַתִּיר נְדָרִים מִמִּי שֶׁהוּא סָמוּךְ, שֶׁדִּינוֹ כְּמֻמְחֶה; וְיֵשׁ שֶׁפֵּרַשׁ שֶׁכָּל שֶׁהוּא חָכָם גָּדוֹל בְּיִשְׂרָאֵל, אֲפִלּוּ הַיּוֹם שֶׁאֵין לָנוּ סְמִיכָה, יִקָּרֵא מֻמְחֶה; וַחֲבֵרָיו חֲלוּקִין עָלָיו.

וְדִין הַחוֹזֵר תּוֹךְ כְּדֵי דִּבּוּר מִנְּדָרִים וּשְׁבוּעוֹת, שֶׁחֲזָרָתוֹ חֲזָרָה. וּמַה שֶּׁאָמְרוּ שֶׁהָאָב מֵפֵר כָּל נֶדֶר, וְהַבַּעַל נִדְרֵי עִנּוּי וּדְבָרִים שֶׁבֵּינוֹ לְבֵינָהּ.

וְדִין הָאוֹמֵר "כָּל נֶדֶר שֶׁאֶדֹּר כָּל שָׁנָה זוֹ" אוֹ "מִכָּאן עַד עֶשֶׂר שָׁנִים — הֲרֵי הֵן בְּטֵלִים"; וְדִין סְתַם נְדָרִים לְהַחְמִיר וּפֵרוּשָׁן לְהָקֵל, וְדִין שֶׁאֵין אָדָם אוֹסֵר דָּבָר שֶׁאֵינוֹ שֶׁלּוֹ, וְדִין הָאוֹמֵר לַחֲבֵרוֹ "כִּכָּרִי אָסוּר עָלֶיךָ" אוֹ "כִּכָּר זֶה", וְדִין הַמֻּדָּר הֲנָאָה מֵחֲבֵרוֹ שֶׁפּוֹרֵעַ לוֹ אֶת חוֹבוֹ; וְדִין הַנּוֹדֵר מִן הַבָּשָׂר, שֶׁמֻּתָּר בְּרֹטֶב, וְאִם אָמַר "בָּשָׂר זֶה", אָסוּר אַף בַּרֹטֶב.

וְדִין מִי שֶׁנֶּאֶסְרָה הֲנָאָתוֹ עָלָיו שֶׁמֻּתָּר לְלַמְּדוֹ תּוֹרָה שֶׁבְּעַל-פֶּה, אֲבָל לֹא שֶׁבִּכְתָב, לְפִי שֶׁנּוֹטְלִין עָלֶיהָ שָׂכָר; וְדִין מַה שֶּׁאָמְרוּ: בִּנְדָרִים הַלֵּךְ אַחַר לְשׁוֹן בְּנֵי-אָדָם בְּאוֹתוֹ מָקוֹם וּבְאוֹתוֹ לָשׁוֹן וּבְאוֹתוֹ זְמַן שֶׁנָּדַר אוֹ שֶׁנִּשְׁבַּע; וְדִין (הַתְרַת) [הֲפָרַת] נְדָרִים שֶׁהוּא כָּל הַיּוֹם, כְּלוֹמַר לַיְלָה וָיוֹם, לֹא מֵעֵת לְעֵת, שֶׁנֶּאֱמַר "בְּיוֹם

26. TJ N'darim x 8.

27. Rambam — MT *hilchoth n'darim* vi 5.

28. TB N'darim 87a. (This means within the time it takes to say, in Hebrew, "Peace be with you, my master.")

29. MT *ibid.* xii 1 (others differ). This sentence is not in the oldest manuscripts, and may thus be a later addition. Yet it is taken from MT and is in the author's style, and thus it could have been in the original and subsequently omitted in an early copy.

30. Cf. Sifre, Numbers §153, and Rashi, to Numbers 30:4; and TB K'thuboth 47a. The term *na'arah* is defined most clearly in Rambam, *Commentary on Mishnah*, K'thuboth iii 7: Here let me clarify for you these names, to what they refer, and we will not have to go over them again wherever [they occur]: Thus: A female, from the day of her birth till she has lived through twelve full years and a day, is called a *k'tanah*, whether or not she has developed two [pubic] hairs [as signs of maturation]. If she has developed these signs after this time, she is called a *na'arah* from the time they developed.... After the development of these signs she remains a *na'arah* for six months...and after the six months she is called a *bogereth* (translation per ed. Kafeḥ).

31. TB N'darim 23b.

32. I.e. if the one who made such a vow explains afterward how he meant it in a lenient sense, his explanation is accepted; *ibid.* 18b.

33. *Ibid.* 47a, Ḥullin 40b.

34. TB N'darim 46a.

35. Since he is not giving the other pleasure but only sparing him loss; *ibid.* 33a.

36. *Ibid.* 52a.

37. *Ibid.* 35b.

vows[26]—for then he is regarded in law as a learned expert. There is also one who taught[27] that whoever is a great learned scholar in Jewry even today, when we have no ordination, is to be called a learned expert; but his colleagues differ with him.

Then there is the law of one who repudiates, within the time it takes to say a few words, his vows or oaths—that his repudiation is effective.[28] There is, further, what they said,[29] that a father may nullify every vow [of an unmarried *na'arah*],[30] but a husband, [only his wife's] vows of self-affliction or regarding matters between him and her.

Then we have the law of one who says, "Any vow that I take this entire year—or, from now till [the end of] ten years—shall be null and void";[31] the law that unspecific [ambiguous] vows are understood stringently, but their explanations are accepted leniently;[32] the law that a man cannot make something forbidden that is not his;[33] the law if someone says to his fellow-man, "My loaf of bread shall be forbidden to you," or [if he said] "This loaf";[34] the law that if one is forbidden to let his fellow-man benefit from him, he may pay his debt for him;[35] and the law that if a person vows abstinence from meat, he is permitted the gravy, but if he said, "this meat," he is forbidden the gravy too.[36]

[Going further, we have] also the law that if one was forbidden to have benefit from another person, the other is allowed to teach him Oral Torah, but not the written one, because payment is [generally] taken for that.[37] And there is the law that the Sages taught:[38] In vows it all depends on the language used by the people in that locality, for that expression, at that time that one took the vow or the oath. In addition, we have the law about the nullification of vows, that it may be done the entire day[39]—in other words, the night and the day, but not within twenty-four hours[40]—for it is stated, *on the day that he hears*

38. *Ibid.* 49a.

39. On which a father heard his young daughter, or a husband his wife, make the vow.

40. I.e. not within twenty-four hours from the time the vow is heard, but only until the next evening, when in Jewish reckoning a new day begins; TB N'darim 76b; MT *hilchoth n'darim* xii 15. (The emendation in the Hebrew is of an evident scribal error, noted in MY. The entire sentence, however, is not in the oldest manuscripts. And yet, for the same reason as above—see note 29—it could have been in the original, and for some reason survived only in the manuscript from which the first edition was printed.)

שָׁמְעוּ" וְיֶתֶר רַבֵּי פְּרָטֶיהָ, יִתְבָּאֲרוּ בָּאֲרֻכָּה בַּמַּסֶּכְתָּא הַמְּחֻבֶּרֶת עַל זֶה, וְהִיא מַסֶּכֶת נְדָרִים.

וְנוֹהֶגֶת מִצְוָה זוֹ בְּכָל מָקוֹם וּבְכָל זְמַן בִּזְכָרִים, אֲבָל לֹא בִּנְקֵבוֹת, שֶׁאֵינָן רְאוּיוֹת לְהַתִּיר נְדָרִים. וְהָעוֹבֵר עַל זֶה וְהִתִּיר אֶת הַנֶּדֶר שֶׁלֹּא כְּמִצְוַת הַתּוֹרָה בַּצְּדָדִין שֶׁכָּתַבְנוּ, אַף־עַל־פִּי שֶׁאֵינוֹ הֶתֵּר, בִּטֵּל עָשָׂה זֶה, כְּמוֹ שֶׁכָּתַבְנוּ בְּרֹאשׁ הַמִּצְוָה.

[שֶׁלֹּא נַחֵל דְּבָרֵנוּ בִּנְדָרִים]

תז שֶׁנִּמְנַעְנוּ שֶׁלֹּא לְשַׁנּוֹת מַה שֶּׁנְּחַיֵּב בְּנַפְשׁוֹתֵינוּ בְּדִבּוּר וְאַף־עַל־פִּי שֶׁהוּא בְּלֹא שְׁבוּעָה, וְאֵלֶּה הֵם הַנְּדָרִים, כְּגוֹן שֶׁיֹּאמַר הָאָדָם פֵּרוֹת הָעוֹלָם אוֹ פֵּרוֹת מְדִינָה פְּלוֹנִית אוֹ מִין פְּלוֹנִי שֶׁל פֵּרוֹת אֲסוּרִין עָלַיו, וּכְמוֹ־כֵן שֶׁיֹּאמַר אִשְׁתּוֹ אֲסוּרָה עָלַיו, וְכַיּוֹצֵא בְּאֵלּוּ הָעִנְיָנִים, שֶׁחַיָּב לְקַיֵּם דְּבָרָיו—וְעַל זֶה נֶאֱמַר "לֹא יַחֵל דְּבָרוֹ", וּפֵרְשׁוּ זִכְרוֹנָם לִבְרָכָה: לֹא יַעֲשֶׂה דְּבָרָיו חֻלִּין, כְּלוֹמַר שֶׁיְּחַיֵּב עַל נַפְשׁוֹ דָּבָר וְלֹא יְקַיְּמֵהוּ.

וּלְשׁוֹן גְּמָרָא שְׁבוּעוֹת, אָמְרוּ זִכְרוֹנָם לִבְרָכָה: קוֹנָמוֹת עוֹבֵר מִשּׁוּם "לֹא יַחֵל דְּבָרוֹ". וְכֵן בְּכָל מַה שֶּׁיִּדֹּר הָאָדָם לַקָּרְבָּן אוֹ לְבֶדֶק הַבַּיִת אוֹ לִצְדָקָה אוֹ לְבֵית־הַכְּנֶסֶת וְכַיּוֹצֵא בָּהֶן, עוֹבֵר עֲלֵיהֶן מִשּׁוּם "לֹא יַחֵל".

אֲבָל בְּעִנְיָנִים אֲחֵרִים, כְּגוֹן הַנּוֹדֵר לַחֲבֵרוֹ דָּבָר, אוֹ הָאוֹמֵר "דָּבָר פְּלוֹנִי אֶעֱשֶׂה" אוֹ "לֹא אֶעֱשֶׂה" שֶׁלֹּא בִּלְשׁוֹן נֶדֶר וְאִסָּר וְקוֹנָמוֹת, אַף־עַל־פִּי שֶׁהוּא מְכֹעָר וְלֹא יַעֲשׂוּ כֵן רַק פְּחוּתֵי הַנֶּפֶשׁ בִּבְנֵי־אָדָם, אֵינוֹ עוֹבֵר בְּ"לֹא יַחֵל", אֶלָּא בְּעִנְיָן שֶׁכָּתַבְנוּ. וְאָמְנָם עַל הַכֹּל נֶאֱמַר בַּתּוֹרָה: מִדְּבַר שֶׁקֶר תִּרְחָק.

§407   1. Sifre, Numbers § 153.

2. *If he does not keep his word.* The point is that here he does not set a restriction of some kind on an object or entity in regard to himself, but merely makes a firm promise; and this is not within the category of a *neder* (a vow).

(Numbers 30:6). The rest of its numerous details are clarified at length in the tractate composed about this, which is the Talmud tractate *N'darim*.

This precept is in effect everywhere, at every time, for men but not for women, as they are not acceptable (authorized) to grant release from vows. If someone transgresses this and absolves a person from a vow not following the charge of the Torah, in [some of] the circumstances that we have written, even though it is no release, he has disobeyed this positive precept, as we wrote at the beginning of the precept.

[THAT WE SHOULD NOT BREAK OUR WORD IN VOWS THAT WE MAKE]

407 that we are constrained not to change any obligation that we impose on ourselves by speech, even if it is without an oath — which means vows in which, for example, a man says that the produce of the world, or the produce of that country, or that certain species of fruit, should be forbidden to him; and likewise if he says that his wife should be forbidden to him, or anything similar to these conditions — he is duty-bound to keep his word. About this it is stated, *lo yahél: he shall not break his word* (Numbers 30:3), which our Sages of blessed memory explained[1] to mean: he shall not make his word *hullin*, profaned or desecrated—i.e. by obligating himself about something and not fulfilling it.

As the Talmud tractate *Sh'vu'oth* (20b) phrases it, the Sages of blessed memory taught: Over [broken] vows with the expression of *konam*, one transgresses the injunction, *he shall not break his word*. And so too over anything that a man vows for an offering, for the funds to keep the Temple in repair, for charity or for the synagogue, or anything similar — for [ignoring] them one transgresses the injunction not to break his word.

In other circumstances, though — for instance, if someone vows something to his fellow-man, or if he says, "I will do — or not do — that particular thing," without the expression of a vow, prohibition or *konam*, then although it is repugnant,[2] and no one but lowly, inferior types among human beings would do so, he does not violate the injunction not to break one's word — but only under the circumstances that we have written. However, about everything it is indeed stated in the Torah, *From a false matter, keep far* (Exodus 23:7).

וְהָרַב מֹשֶׁה בֶּן נַחְמָן זִכְרוֹנוֹ לִבְרָכָה כָּתַב שֶׁשְּׁתֵּי מִצְווֹת חֲלוּקוֹת הֵן: נִדְרֵי גָבוֹהַ וְנִדְרֵי בִטּוּי, וּכְמוֹ שֶׁנִּכְתֹּב לְמַטָּה בְּסֵדֶר כִּי תֵצֵא עֲשֵׂה ט"ו בְּסִימָן (תקמ"ו) [תקע"ה].

שֹׁרֶשׁ הַמִּצְוָה בְּעִנְיַן הַנְּדָרִים וְהַשְּׁבוּעוֹת, לְקַיֵּם כָּל דָּבָר, כָּתַבְתִּי כְבָר בְּסֵדֶר וַיִּשְׁמַע יִתְרוֹ יְתֵרוֹ לֹא-תַעֲשֶׂה ה' [סִי' ל'].

מִדִּינֵי הַמִּצְוָה, מַה שֶּׁאָמְרוּ זִכְרוֹנָם לִבְרָכָה: הוּא אֵינוֹ מֵחֵל אֲבָל אֲחֵרִים מוֹחֲלִין לוֹ, כְּגוֹן שְׁלֹשָׁה הַדְּיוֹטוֹת אוֹ יָחִיד מֻמְחֶה, כְּמוֹ שֶׁכָּתַבְנוּ בַּמִּצְוָה הַקּוֹדֶמֶת; וְהוּא הַדִּין גַּם-כֵּן שֶׁנִּשְׁאָלִין עַל הַהֶקְדֵּשׁוֹת וְעַל הַצְּדָקוֹת כָּל זְמַן שֶׁלֹּא בָאוּ לְיָדֵי גַבַּאי; וַאֲפִלּוּ עַל הַתְּרוּמָה וְעַל הַחַלָּה אָמְרוּ זִכְרוֹנָם לִבְרָכָה שֶׁנִּשְׁאָלִין עֲלֵיהֶן עַד שֶׁלֹּא בָאוּ לְיַד כֹּהֵן; וְיֶתֶר פְּרָטֵי הַמִּצְוָה, מְבֹאָרִים בְּמַסֶּכֶת נְדָרִים.

וְנוֹהֶגֶת בְּכָל מָקוֹם וּבְכָל זְמַן, בִּזְכָרִים וּנְקֵבוֹת. וְעוֹבֵר עַל זֶה וְנָדַר אוֹ אָסַר אִסָּר עַל נַפְשׁוֹ בְּלֹא שְׁבוּעָה וְלֹא קִיְּמוֹ, עָבַר עַל לָאו זֶה, אֲבָל אֵינוֹ לוֹקֶה עָלָיו, לְפִי שֶׁאֵין בּוֹ מַעֲשֶׂה; וְזֶה שֶּׁאָמְרוּ זִכְרוֹנָם לִבְרָכָה שֶׁהַנִּשְׁבָּע וּמֵמֵר וּמְקַלֵּל חֲבֵרוֹ בַּשֵּׁם, לוֹקִין אַף-עַל-פִּי שֶׁאֵין שָׁם מַעֲשֶׂה—זֶהוּ נִשְׁבָּע, אֲבָל מִשּׁוּם לָאו דְּ"לֹא יַחֵל", בְּנֶדֶר אוֹ אִסָּר שֶׁלֹּא בִשְׁבוּעָה, אֵין בּוֹ מַלְקוֹת.

3. Ramban, commentary to ShM positive precept §94.

4. TB Ḥagigah 10a.

5. The one who consecrated something or pledged charity may be questioned by a learned expert or three laymen, so that a way can be found to release him from his word, by determining that under other circumstances, etc. he would not have made the vow.

6. TB 'Arachin 23a; about charity: Rashba, *Responsa*, cited in Shulḥan 'Aruch Yoreh Dé'ah, §228, 42.

7. TB N'darim 59a.

8. As R. Judah Rosanes (author of *Mishneh l'Melech*) and MH note, this is most puzzling: If someone takes a vow, e.g. that certain food be forbidden to him, and he violates his vow, he receives no whiplashes, because the violation has involved no physical action. Yet what more blatant action can there be than taking food after one has expressly vowed that it should be forbidden for him to eat it? Moreover, in ShM negative precept §157 Rambam writes on this very point, "and if one transgresses and does what he has forbidden himself to do, he is to suffer whiplashes"; and he confirms his ruling in MT *hilchoth n'darim* i 5 and *hilchoth sanhedrin* xix 4. MY discusses the matter at length in an attempt to resolve the difficulty.

9. TB Sh'vu'oth 21a, T'murah 3a.

Now, R. Moses b. Naḥman of blessed memory wrote[3] that there are two separate precepts: vows concerning the supernal [Divine] realm, and vows of expression [about ordinary, unimportant matters] — as we will write in the fifteenth positive precept of *sidrah r'eh* (§ 575).

The root reason for the precept regarding vows and oaths, to fulfill everything, I wrote previously in the fifth negative precept of *sidrah yithro* (§ 30).

Among the laws of the precept, there is what the Sages of blessed memory taught:[4] he may not break or desecrate [his word] but others may absolve him [of it]: for instance, three ordinary persons or an individual learned expert, as we wrote in the previous precept. So is it also the law that annulment after questioning may be done about consecrations and pledges of charity,[5] as long as they did not reach the hands of the collector.[6] Even regarding *t'rumah* (§ 507) and *hallah* (§ 385), our Sages of blessed memory said[7] that annulment after questioning might be granted for them as long as they did not reach the hand of the *kohen*. The remaining details of the precept are clarified in the Talmud tractate *N'darim*.

It is in force everywhere, at every time, for both man and woman. If someone transgresses this, taking a vow or making something prohibited to him without an oath, and then he does not observe it, he violates this negative precept; but he would not receive whiplashes for it, since it involves no physical action.[8] In this regard the Sages of blessed memory said[9] that if someone swears [in vain], exchanges [a consecrated animal], or curses his fellow-man with the Divine name, he receives a flogging of whiplashes even though no physical action was involved. Yet that is only if one swore; but on account of the injunction not to break one's word regarding a vow or a solemn acceptance of abstinence without an oath, no whiplashes are given.

אֵלֶּה מַסְעֵי

יֵשׁ בָּהּ שְׁתֵּי מִצְווֹת עֲשֵׂה וְאַרְבַּע מִצְווֹת לֹא-תַעֲשֶׂה

[מִצְוַת יִשְׂרָאֵל לָתֵת עָרִים לַלְוִיִּם לָשֶׁבֶת בָּהֶן, וְהֵן קוֹלְטוֹת]

תח שֶׁנִּצְטַוּוּ יִשְׂרָאֵל לָתֵת לְשֵׁבֶט לֵוִי עָרִים לָשֶׁבֶת בָּהֶן, אַחַר שֶׁאֵין לָהֶם חֵלֶק
בָּאָרֶץ, שֶׁנֶּאֱמַר: צַו אֶת בְּנֵי יִשְׂרָאֵל וְנָתְנוּ לַלְוִיִּם מִנַּחֲלַת אֲחֻזָּתָם עָרִים לָשָׁבֶת;
וְנֶאֱמַר בְּסוֹף הַפָּרָשָׁה: כָּל הֶעָרִים אֲשֶׁר תִּתְּנוּ לַלְוִיִּם אַרְבָּעִים וּשְׁמֹנֶה עִיר.
וּמֵאֵלֶּה הֶעָרִים שֶׁל לְוִיִּם הָיוּ מֵהֶם עָרִים מְיֻחָדוֹת לִהְיוֹת מִקְלָט הָרוֹצֵחַ, וְאוּלָם
בְּכֻלָּן הָיָה לוֹ מִקְלָט, וּבְסֵדֶר שׁוֹפְטִים בְּמִצְוַת עָרֵי מִקְלָט בְּסִימָן (ת"ק) [תק"ף]
נִכְתֹּב בְּעֶזְרַת הַשֵּׁם מַה בֵּין מְיֻחָדוֹת לְכָךְ לְאוֹתָן הָאֲחֵרוֹת; וְהָיוּ קוֹלְטוֹת אוֹתוֹ
בִּצְדָדִים יְדוּעִים, כְּמוֹ שֶׁמְּפֹרָשׁ בַּכָּתוּב וּמְבֹאָר בְּמַסֶּכֶת מַכּוֹת.

שֹׁרֶשׁ הַמִּצְוָה הַזֹּאת: יָדוּעַ הוּא כִּי שֵׁבֶט הַלֵּוִי מִבְחַר הַשְּׁבָטִים וְנָכוֹן לַעֲבוֹדַת
בֵּית יי, וְאֵין לוֹ חֵלֶק עִם יִשְׂרָאֵל בְּנַחֲלוֹת שָׂדוֹת וּכְרָמִים; אֲבָל עָרִים הָיוּ צְרִיכִים
לָהֶם עַל-כָּל-פָּנִים, לָשֶׁבֶת הֵם וּבְנֵיהֶם וְטַפָּם וְכָל חַיָּתָם; וּמִפְּנֵי גֹדֶל מַעֲלָתָם
וְכֹשֶׁר פָּעֳלָם וְחִין עֶרְכָּם, נִבְחֲרָה אַרְצָם לִקְלֹט כָּל הוֹרֵג נֶפֶשׁ בִּשְׁגָגָה יוֹתֵר
מֵאַרְצוֹת שְׁאָר הַשְּׁבָטִים: אוּלַי תְּכַפֵּר עָלָיו אַדְמָתָם הַמְקֻדֶּשֶׁת בִּקְדֻשָּׁתָם.

וְעוֹד טַעַם אַחֵר בַּדָּבָר, כִּי בִהְיוֹתָם אַנְשֵׁי לֵבָב יְדוּעִים בְּמַעֲלוֹת הַמִּדּוֹת
וְחָכְמוֹת נִכְבָּדוֹת, יָדוּעַ לַכֹּל שֶׁלֹּא יִשְׂטְמוּ הָרוֹצֵחַ שֶׁיִּנָּצֵל שֶׁיָּנֻסוּ אֲלֵיהֶם וְלֹא יִגְּעוּ בּוֹ,
וְאַף כִּי יַהֲרֹג אֶחָד מֵאוֹהֲבֵיהֶם אוֹ מִגּוֹאֲלֵיהֶם, אַחַר אֲשֶׁר בְּפֶתַע בְּלֹא אֵיבָה
יַהַרְגֶנּוּ. וְעַל הַשֵּׁבֶט הַזֶּה הַנִּבְחָר נֶאֱמַר "הָאֹמֵר לְאָבִיו וּלְאִמּוֹ לֹא רְאִיתִיו",

sidrah mas'é

(Numbers 33–36)

There are two positive and four negative precepts in it.

[TO GIVE THE LEVITES CITIES TO DWELL IN,
AND TO GIVE REFUGE TO THE
UNINTENTIONAL MANSLAYER]

408 that the Israelites were commanded to give the tribe of Lévi cities to dwell in them, since they have no share in the land [of Israel]: for it is stated, *Command the Israelites that they shall give to the Levites, from the inheritance of their possession, cities to dwell in* (Numbers 35:2); and it is stated at the end of the Scriptural section, *All the cities which you give to the Levites shall be forty-eight cities* (*ibid.* 7). Among these cities of the Levites, some of them were cities specifically designated to be [places of] refuge for an [inadvertent] killer, although he could find refuge in all of them. In *sidrah shof'tim*, in the precept of the cities of refuge (§520), we will write with the Eternal Lord's help, what difference there was between those especially designated and the other ones. They would provide refuge for him under certain known circumstances, as explained in Scripture[1] and clarified in the tractate *Makkoth* (10a).

As for the root reason for this precept, it is known that the tribe of Lévi was the chosen one of the tribes, prepared for service in the Temple of the Lord, and it had no share with the Israelites in the inheritances of fields and vineyards. But cities they needed in any event, to dwell in them — they, their sons and infants, and all their livestock. And because of the greatness of their nobility, the worthiness of their activity, and the grace of their distincton, their territory was chosen to give refuge to anyone who kills a living soul inadvertently, rather than the grounds of the other tribes. Perhaps their land, hallowed by their holiness, would effect atonement for him.

There is, moreover, another reason for the matter: Since they were men of [good] heart, renowned for the eminent worth of their qualities and their noble wisdom, it was known (evident) to all that they would not detest the slayer who took refuge with them, and would not harm him, even if he killed one of their good friends or avenging blood relations,[2] since he killed him suddenly [accidentally], without enmity. About this chosen tribe it is stated, *who said of*

⟨217⟩

כְּלוֹמַר שֶׁלֹּא יַעֲשׂוּ דָבָר בָּעוֹלָם זוּלָתִי מִדֶּרֶךְ הַיֹּשֶׁר וְעַל כַּוּוּן הָאֱמֶת, וְלֹא יַשֶּׂה לָהֶם אַהֲבַת אָדָם, וַאֲפִלּוּ אַהֲבַת אָב וָאֵם וְאַחִים וּבָנִים, שֶׁהַטֶּבַע תְּחַיֵּב אַהֲבָתָם וְתַכְרִיחֶהָ, וְכָל־שֶׁכֵּן אַהֲבַת שְׁאָר בְּנֵי־אָדָם. וְעוֹד כָּתַבְתִּי בָּעִנְיָן עוֹד טַעֲנָה אַחֶרֶת בְּסֵדֶר בְּהַר סִינַי מִצְוַת לֹא־תַעֲשֶׂה י״א בְּסִימָן (שמ״ג) [שמ״ב].

דִּינֵי מִצְוָה זוֹ קְצָרִים, וּבַמִּצְווֹת הַנִּסְמָכוֹת אֵלֶיהָ, כְּגוֹן אַזְהָרַת ״שְׂדֵה מִגְרַשׁ עָרֵיהֶם לֹא יִמָּכֵר״, שֶׁבְּסֵדֶר בְּהַר סִינַי לָאו י״א [סי׳ שמ״ב], כָּתַבְתִּי קְצָת מִן הַדִּינִים. וּכְמוֹ־כֵן בְּמִצְוַת לְהַבְדִּיל עָרֵי מִקְלָט, שֶׁבְּסֵדֶר שׁוֹפְטִים עֲשֵׂה י׳ בְּסִימָן (ת״ק) [תק״ן], נִכְתּוֹב מֵהֶן בְּעֶזְרַת הַשֵּׁם, שֶׁשְּׁלָשְׁתָּן מֵעִנְיָן אֶחָד הֵן; וְאִם נַפְשְׁךָ לָדַעַת, הֲפֹךְ וַהֲפֹךְ בָּהֶן.

וְנוֹהֶגֶת מִצְוָה זוֹ בִּזְמַן שֶׁיִּשְׂרָאֵל שְׁרוּיִין עַל אַדְמָתָן, וְהִיא מִן הַמִּצְווֹת הַמֻּטָּלוֹת עַל הַצִּבּוּר כֻּלָּם, וְיוֹתֵר עַל רָאשֵׁי הָעָם; וּלְעָתִיד לָבוֹא, אַחַר יְרֻשָּׁה וִישִׁיבָה, מִיָּד נְקַיֵּם מִצְוַת עֲשֵׂה זוֹ, בִּמְהֵרָה בְיָמֵינוּ, אָמֵן.

[שֶׁלֹּא לַהֲרֹג מְחֻיַּב קֹדֶם שֶׁיַּעֲמֹד בַּדִּין]

תט שֶׁנִּמְנַעְנוּ שֶׁלֹּא לַהֲרֹג הַחוֹטֵא כְּשֶׁנִּרְאֵהוּ עוֹשֶׂה מַעֲשֶׂה הַחֵטְא שֶׁיִּתְחַיֵּב עָלָיו מִיתָה, קֹדֶם שֶׁנְּבִיאֵהוּ לְבֵית־דִּין; אֲבָל נִתְחַיַּבְנוּ לַהֲבִיאוֹ לִפְנֵי בֵית־דִּין וְנָבִיא עָלָיו הָעֵדִים לִפְנֵיהֶם, וְהֵם יְדִינוּהוּ בַּמֶּה שֶׁהוּא חַיָּב מִיתָה — שֶׁנֶּאֱמַר: וְלֹא יָמוּת הָרֹצֵחַ עַד עָמְדוֹ לִפְנֵי הָעֵדָה לַמִּשְׁפָּט.

וּלְשׁוֹן מְכִלְתָּא: יָכוֹל שֶׁיַּהַרְגוּ אוֹתוֹ מִשֶּׁיֵּהָרֵג אוֹ שֶׁנָּאַף, תַּלְמוּד לוֹמַר ״וְלֹא יָמוּת הָרֹצֵחַ עַד עָמְדוֹ״ וְגוֹמֵר. וַאֲפִלּוּ רָאוּהוּ בֵית־דִּין הַגָּדוֹל שֶׁהָרַג, יִהְיוּ כֻלָּם עֵדִים וְיִשְׂאוּ עֵדוּתָן אֵצֶל בֵּית־דִּין אַחֵר שֶׁיְּדִינוּהוּ. וְעוֹד אָמְרוּ בִּמְכִלְתָּא: הֲרֵי עֵדָה שֶׁרָאוּ אֶחָד שֶׁהָרַג אֶת הַנֶּפֶשׁ, יָכוֹל יַהַרְגוּ אוֹתוֹ עַד שֶׁלֹּא יַעֲמֹד אֵצֶל בֵּית־

---

3. See § 330, third paragraph from end, and § 335, end.

§409   1. Sifre Zuta (see § 363, note 1) 332 l. 12.

2. This evidently derives from R. 'Akiva's teachings in Tosefta, Makkoth iii 7, TB Rosh haShanah 26a (+Bava Kamma 90b), and Makkoth 12a. In the second of these teachings he differs with R. Tarfon, who holds that if the justices of the Sanhedrin saw a murder done, some of them may sit as a *beth din* (hold court) and receive testimony from the others. Our author, however, clearly follows R. 'Akiva here, requiring all the justices to turn witness and testify before another *beth din*. In MT *hilchoth 'éduth* v 8, Rambam merely states that a witness who testifies in a murder trial is not to speak or act as a judge. From this, though, R. Joseph Caro (*Kessef Mishneh*) infers that Rambam has adopted R. Tarfon's view: Only if he chooses to testify may a justice not serve as judge; otherwise he may. And R. Joseph Caro repeats this in *Béth Yosef* to *Tur Ḥoshen Mishpat*, §7 (6).

Consequently MH finds it strange that our author gives R. 'Akiva's view here,

his father and his mother, I have not seen him (Deuteronomy 33:9): in other words, they would do nothing in the world that was not in accord with decency, attuned to the truth, and no affection for a man would sway their heart—not even love for a father and mother, brothers and sons, whom human nature obligates, nay, compels one to love—and all the more certainly not love for any other human beings. I wrote further about the subject, yet another point of reason, in the eleventh negative precept of *sidrah b'har* (§ 342).

The laws of this precept are brief. In the precepts related to it, such as the injunction that *the fields of the open land about their cities may not be sold* (Leviticus 25:34), the eleventh negative precept in *sidrah b'har* (§ 342), I wrote a few of the laws; so too in the precept to set apart cities of refuge—the tenth positive precept in *sidrah shof'tim* (§ 520), we will write some of them, with the Eternal Lord's help, for all three are of one subject. And if it is your spirit's desire to know [them], turn and turn again [delving] into them.

This precept is in effect at the time the Israelites are settled on their land. It is one of the precepts imposed on the entire community, but more particularly on the heads of the people. In time to come, after the inheritance and settlement [of all the tribes on their territories][3] we shall fulfill this positive precept at once—soon in our days, *Amen.*

[NOT TO EXECUTE A GUILTY PERSON WHO
DESERVES DEATH, BEFORE HE STANDS TRIAL]

409 that we are constrained not to put a sinner to death when we see him doing the sinful act for which he incurs the death penalty, before we bring him to the *beth din* (court); but we are rather obliged to bring him before the *beth din*, and to bring witnesses about him before them [the justices], whereupon they are to judge him for the guilt that is his: for it is stated, *and the manslayer shall not die until he stands before the congregation for judgment* (Numbers 35:12).

In the language of the Midrash *Mechilta:*[1] I might think that he should be killed once he has killed or committed adultery?—Scripture states, *and the manslayer shall not die until he stands*, etc. Even if the great *beth din* (Sanhedrin) saw him committing the murder, they should all be witnesses and present their testimony at another *beth din*, which will judge him.[2] It was taught further in the Midrash *Mechilta:*[3] If a

community saw a person killing someone, I might think they should

דִּין—תַּלְמוּד לוֹמַר: וְלֹא יָמוּת הָרֹצֵחַ עַד עָמְדוֹ.

מִשָּׁרְשֵׁי הַמִּצְוָה, לְפִי שֶׁעִנְיְנֵי דִינֵי נְפָשׁוֹת הוּא דָבָר קָשֶׁה מְאֹד, שֶׁצָּרִיךְ דְּקְדּוּק גָּדוֹל בְּיוֹתֵר, וְנִצְטַוּוּ הָעֵדָה לִהְיוֹת מַצֶּלֶת הַנִּדּוֹן בְּכָל דָּבָר הָרָאוּי לְהַצִּילוֹ בִּשְׁבִילוֹ, לֹא שֶׁיַּטּוּ הַדִּין כְּדֵי לְהַצִּילוֹ חָלִילָה; וּכְמוֹ שֶׁדָּרְשׁוּ זִכְרוֹנָם לִבְרָכָה: "וְשָׁפְטוּ הָעֵדָה ... וְהִצִּילוּ הָעֵדָה", כְּלוֹמַר שֶׁצָּרִיכִין לְהַפֵּךְ בִּזְכוּתוֹ, וְאִם יֵשׁ לוֹ זְכוּת, יַצִּילוּהוּ, וְאִם לֹא—יֵהָרֵג.

וְעַל־כֵּן הַזְהַרְנוּ שֶׁיָּבוֹא הַדִּין עַל־כָּל־פָּנִים לִפְנֵי בֵית־דִּין, וְלֹא יְדִינּוּהוּ הָעֵדִים שֶׁרָאוּ הַדָּבָר בְּעֵינֵיהֶם לְעוֹלָם, כִּי אוּלַי מִתּוֹךְ רְאוֹתָן הָעִנְיָן לֹא יוּכְלוּ לְהַפֵּךְ בִּזְכוּתוֹ, כִּי יִתְעוֹרֵר לְבָבָם בְּחִיּוּבוֹ עַל־כָּל־פָּנִים.

דִּינֵי הַמִּצְוָה, כְּגוֹן מַה שֶּׁאָמְרוּ זִכְרוֹנָם לִבְרָכָה, דְּבַמֶּה דְבָרִים אֲמוּרִים שֶׁלֹּא נֶהֱרָג הַחוֹטֵא עַד שֶׁנְּבִיאֵהוּ לְבֵית־דִּין, כְּשֶׁעָבַר וְעָשָׂה הַחֵטְא; אֲבָל מִי שֶׁהָיָה רוֹדֵף אַחַר חֲבֵרוֹ לְהָרְגוֹ, אוֹ אַחַר נַעֲרָה מְאֹרָשָׂה, וְהִזְהִירוּהוּ וְלֹא נִמְנַע מִלִּרְדֹּף, אַף־עַל־פִּי שֶׁלֹּא קִבֵּל הַתְרָאָה חַיָּבִין אָנוּ לְהָרְגוֹ וּמֻזְהָרִין עָלָיו, וּכְמוֹ שֶׁנִּכְתַּב בְּעֶזְרַת

though ordinarily he follows Rambam faithfully. As R. Chaim Heller points out, however (ed. ShM, p. 173 note 17), not our author is to be wondered at but Rambam himself: for our author took this statement directly, with slight paraphrase perhaps, from ShM negative precept §292. The proper question is, then: Why did Rambam write so clearly in ShM in the vein of R. 'Akiva's teachings, and then write a law in MT in such terms that R. Joseph Caro could firmly infer from it that Rambam decides for R. Tarfon?

In MT *hilchoth rotzé-aḥ* i 5, Rambam seems to have left us further traces of his thinking on the question. He writes, "If a murderer has killed with willful intent, the witnesses are not to put him to death, nor those who saw him, until he comes to a *beth din*, and they [its judges] sentence him to death...." As remarked *ad loc.* in voweled ed. Mosad R. Kook (p. 261 note 32), the words "nor those who saw him" would seem to mean even if they were members of the Sanhedrin — which accords with R. 'Akiva's view.

To my humble mind it would therefore seem that while in ShM Rambam showed his acceptance of R. 'Akiva's ruling, later in MT, writing a formal work of *halachah*, he chose to adopt explicitly neither R. 'Akiva's nor R. Tarfon's view: He would not follow R. Tarfon, because the Talmud gives a powerful reason for R. 'Akiva's ruling: "Once they have seen him kill a living person, they cannot see anything in his favor" (TB Rosh haShanah 26a). Moreover, in Tosefta and TB Makkoth, only R. 'Akiva's teachings are given, with no mention of R. Tarfon, which would seem to give R. 'Akiva's view a certain approval and authority. Yet neither would Rambam give R. 'Akiva's ruling explicitly as the *halachah*, because, as R. Joseph Caro notes, R. 'Akiva was a pupil of R. Tarfon in Torah study, and where a pupil differs with his master teacher, his view is generally not followed. Hence Rambam leaves the question without an explicit, clearcut decision. Me'iri,

kill him yet before he stands in court?[4] — Scripture states, *the manslayer shall not die until he stands.*

At the root of the precept lies the reason that the matter of capital cases is something very difficult, which requires extremely great accuracy; and the community was commanded to save the person to be judged, in every way on his behalf that is right and due him to save him, although they are not to pervert justice to rescue him, perish the thought. As the Sages of blessed memory interpreted:[5] *then the community shall judge... and the community shall rescue* (Numbers 35:24-25) — as much as to say that they need to cast about seeking his innocence, and if he has any merit for acquittal they should save him; but if not, let him be put to death.

For this reason we were adjured that the case must come, in any event, before the *beth din*, and the witnesses who saw the occurrence with their own eyes should never judge him. For perhaps as a result of seeing the matter they cannot cast about in search of his right to acquittal, because their hearts will be aroused over his guilt no matter what.

The laws of the precept are, for example, what the Sages of blessed memory taught:[6] that when does this rule apply, that we should not put the sinner to death until we bring him to the *beth din*? — when he already went and committed the sin; but if someone was chasing after his fellow-man to kill him, or after a betrothed (*me'orasah*) maiden,[7] and he was cautioned yet did not desist from his pursuit, then even if he did not accept the warning,[8] we are duty-

however, flatly gives R. 'Akiva's view as the law, for the reason in the Talmud cited above (Me'iri on Rosh haShanah, p.186; on K'thuboth, p.101; on Makkoth, p.59a); and so decides Ritba (to Rosh haShanah 25b: Tel Aviv 1958, p.47a).

3. Sifre Zuta 332 l. 13-15. (The first two paragraphs are based on ShM negative precept §292).

4. I.e. out of a vengeance for justice, much as zealots may strike a man down at the time he is cohabiting with a heathen woman if they catch him in the act (MY).

5. TB Rosh haShanah 26a, etc.

6. TB Sanhedrin 73a.

7. One who is legally married to a man but is not yet living with him. It was the practice in Talmudic times to become bound in marriage and then take a year to prepare for life together. The first ceremony of marriage was called *'érusin*; the second, before beginning life together, *nissu'in*. The later practice is for both ceremonies to take place together.

8. I.e. when cautioned that what he wished to do was punishable by death, he

הַשֵּׁם בְּסוֹף סֵדֶר כִּי תֵצֵא בָּאַזְהָרַת "וְקַצֹּתָה אֶת־כַּפָּהּ לֹא תָחוֹס עֵינֶךָ" [סִי־
תר"א]. וְיֵתֶר פְּרָטֶיהָ, בְּמַסֶּכֶת מַכּוֹת.

וְנוֹהֶגֶת מִצְוָה זוֹ בִּזְכָרִים וּנְקֵבוֹת בְּכָל זְמַן, שֶׁאָנוּ מֻזְהָרִין שֶׁלֹּא נַהֲרֹג שׁוּם
חוֹטֵא, וְאַף־עַל־פִּי שֶׁרְאִינוּהוּ שֶׁעָשָׂה מַעֲשֶׂה שֶׁיִּתְחַיֵּב מָוֶת בְּבֵית־דִּין. וּבִזְמַן
הַבַּיִת חַיָּבִין לַהֲבִיאוֹ לְבֵית־דִּין וְהֵם יְדִינוּהוּ. וְעוֹבֵר עַל זֶה וַהֲרָגוֹ לַחוֹטֵא קֹדֶם
שֶׁיָּבוֹא לְבֵית־דִּין, אֲפִלּוּ אִם הָיָה דִינוֹ שֶׁיִּתְחַיֵּב בְּבֵית־דִּין, דִּין הַהוֹרְגוֹ כְּדִין רוֹצֵחַ,
וְנֶהֱרַג עָלָיו בִּזְמַן הַבַּיִת אִם יֵשׁ עֵדִים.

[מִצְוָה עַל בֵּית־דִּין לְהַשְׁלִיךְ מַכֵּה נֶפֶשׁ בִּשְׁגָגָה מֵעִירוֹ לְעָרֵי מִקְלָט,
וְעַל הָרוֹצֵחַ בְּעַצְמוֹ לָלֶכֶת שָׁם]

תי שֶׁנִּצְטַוּוּ בֵּית־דִּין שֶׁל יִשְׂרָאֵל לְהַשְׁלִיךְ מַכֵּה נֶפֶשׁ בִּשְׁגָגָה מֵעִירוֹ וּלְהוֹשִׁיבוֹ
בְּעָרֵי מִקְלָט, שֶׁנֶּאֱמַר: וְהֵשִׁיבוּ אֹתוֹ הָעֵדָה אֶל עִיר מִקְלָטוֹ וְגוֹמֵר, וְיָשַׁב בָּהּ עַד
מוֹת הַכֹּהֵן הַגָּדֹל. וְגַם הַמַּכֵּה גַם הוּא בִכְלַל מִצְוַת עֲשֵׂה זוֹ, שֶׁנֶּאֱמַר עָלָיו: כִּי
בְעִיר מִקְלָטוֹ יֵשֵׁב עַד מוֹת הַכֹּהֵן הַגָּדֹל.

מִשָּׁרְשֵׁי הַמִּצְוָה, לְפִי שֶׁעֲוֹן הָרְצִיחָה חָמוּר עַד מְאֹד, שֶׁבָּהּ הַשְׁחָתַת הָעוֹלָם,
עַד שֶׁאָמְרוּ זִכְרוֹנָם לִבְרָכָה שֶׁהַהוֹרֵג נֶפֶשׁ מֵזִיד, אֲפִלּוּ עָשָׂה כָל הַמִּצְוֹת, אֵינוֹ
נִצָּל מִן הַדִּין, שֶׁנֶּאֱמַר: אָדָם עָשֻׁק בְּדַם נָפֶשׁ עַד בּוֹר יָנוּס אַל יִתְמְכוּ בוֹ.

וְלָכֵן רָאוּי לְמִי שֶׁהָרַג אֲפִלּוּ שׁוֹגֵג, מִכֵּיוָן שֶׁבָּאת תַּקָּלָה גְדוֹלָה כָּזוֹ עַל יָדוֹ,
שֶׁיִּצְטַעֵר עָלֶיהָ צַעַר גָּלוּת, שֶׁשָּׁקוּל כִּמְעַט כְּצַעַר מִיתָה, שֶׁנִּפְרָד הָאָדָם מֵאוֹהֲבָיו
וּמֵאֶרֶץ מוֹלַדְתּוֹ וְשׁוֹכֵן כָּל יָמָיו עִם זָרִים. וְעוֹד יֵשׁ תִּקּוּן הָעוֹלָם בַּמִּצְוָה, בְּמַה
שֶׁבֵּאֵר הַכָּתוּב שֶׁיִּנָּצֵל עִם זֶה מִיַּד גּוֹאֵל הַדָּם, לְבַל יַהַרְגֶנּוּ עַל לֹא חָמָס בְּכַפָּיו,

did not reply, "I know, yet I am going to do it" (he did not accept the caution);
ordinarily this is a necessary condition before a *beth din* may impose punishment for
a crime.

9. *Ibid.* 72b.

bound to kill him,[9] and are so adjured about him, as we will write with the Eternal Lord's help toward the end of *sidrah ki thétzé*, about the injunction, *then you shall cut off her hand, your eye shall have no pity* (Deuteronomy 25:12; §601). The rest of its details are in the Talmud tractate *Makkoth*.

This precept applies to both man and woman, everywhere. For we are adjured not to kill any sinner, even if we have seen him doing the act for which he will be sentenced to death at the *beth din*; and at the time the Temple exists, we are duty-bound to bring him to the *beth din*, and they [the justices] will try him. If a person transgresses this and kills a sinner before he comes to the *beth din*, even if the law is that he should be found guilty by the *beth din*, the law for his slayer is as the law for any killer, and he is to be put to death for it at the time the Temple stands, if there are witnesses.

[THE DUTY OF THE COURT TO MAKE AN
UNINTENTIONAL KILLER GO TO A CITY OF REFUGE.
AND HIS DUTY TO GO THERE]

410 that a *beth din* of Israelites was commanded to cast out of his city a person who struck someone down inadvertently, and place him in the cities of refuge: as it is stated, *and the community shall restore him to his city of refuge*, etc. *and he shall live in it until the death of the* kohen gadol (Numbers 35:25). And the manslayer is equally included in this positive precept: for it is stated about him, *because he must stay in his city of refuge until the death of the* kohen gadol (*ibid.* 28).

At the root of the precept lies the reason that the crime of killing is utmostly serious, for in it lies [the kernel of] the destruction of the world—so much so that the Sages of blessed memory taught[1] that if a person kills someone deliberately, even if has observed all the *mitzvoth* he is not saved [thereby] from judgment: for it is stated, *A man laden with any person's blood shall hasten his steps to the pit; none will support him* (Proverbs 28:17).

It is therefore proper for one who killed even unintentionally, since such a great misfortune occurred by his hand, that he should suffer for it the anguish of exile, which is almost equal to the anguish of death, since a man is then separated from his friends and his native ground, and he lives all his days with strangers. Moreover, there is a rectification in the community through this precept, in the sense that the Writ explains: for in this way he will be rescued from the hand of

שֶׁהֲרֵי שׁוֹגֵג הָיָה. וְעוֹד תּוֹעֶלֶת בַּדָּבָר, לְבַל יִרְאוּ קְרוֹבֵי הַמֻּכֶּה הָרוֹצֵחַ לְעֵינֵיהֶם
תָּמִיד בַּמָּקוֹם שֶׁנַּעֲשְׂתָה הָרָעָה; וְכָל דַּרְכֵי הַתּוֹרָה נֹעַם.

מִדִּינֵי הַמִּצְוָה, מַה שֶּׁאָמְרוּ זִכְרוֹנָם לִבְרָכָה שֶׁאֵין הָרוֹצֵחַ בִּשְׁגָגָה גוֹלֶה אֶלָא־
אִם־כֵּן מֵת הַנֶּהֱרָג לְשָׁעָה שֶׁהֲרָגוֹ; אֲבָל חָבַל בּוֹ, אַף־עַל־פִּי שֶׁאֲמָדוּהוּ לְמִיתָה
וְחָלָה וָמֵת, אֵין זֶה גוֹלֶה, שֶׁמָּא הוּא בְּעַצְמוֹ קֵרֵב מִיתָתוֹ, אוֹ
בַּחֲבוּרָה וַהֲרָגַתְהוּ; וַאֲפִלּוּ שָׁחַט בּוֹ שְׁנֵי סִימָנִין וְעָמַד מְעַט, אֵינוֹ

וּמַה שֶּׁאָמְרוּ שֶׁיִּשְׂרָאֵל גּוֹלֶה אִם רָצַח עֶבֶד אוֹ גֵר תּוֹשָׁב, וְכָל־שֶׁכֵּן עֶבֶד שֶׁהֲרַג
יִשְׂרָאֵל, וְכֵן עֶבֶד שֶׁהֲרַג עֶבֶד אוֹ גֵר תּוֹשָׁב — שֶׁנֶּאֱמַר: (וְהָיְתָה) לִבְנֵי יִשְׂרָאֵל
(לְחֻקַּת מִשְׁפָּט) וְלַגֵּר (הַגֵּר) [וְלַתּוֹשָׁב] בְּתוֹכָם [תִּהְיֶינָה] שֵׁשׁ הֶעָרִים הָאֵלֶּה
לְמִקְלָט]; אֲבָל גֵר תּוֹשָׁב שֶׁהֲרַג אֶת יִשְׂרָאֵל, בֵּין מֵזִיד בֵּין שׁוֹגֵג, נֶהֱרָג עָלָיו; וְגוֹי
שֶׁהֲרַג אֶת הַגּוֹי, אֵין עָרֵי מִקְלָט קוֹלְטִין אוֹתוֹ.

וּמַה שֶּׁאָמְרוּ שֶׁהַבֵּן גּוֹלֶה עַל רְצִיחַת אָבִיו וְהָאָב בִּרְצִיחַת הַבֵּן; וּבַמֶּה דְּבָרִים
אֲמוּרִים, שֶׁלֹּא בִּשְׁעַת לִמּוּד, אֲבָל בִּשְׁעַת לִמּוּד וְהוּא שׁוֹגֵג, שֶׁכַּוָּנָתוֹ הָיְתָה לְלַמְּדוֹ
וּלְהוֹעִיל לוֹ בְּחָכְמָה אוֹ בְּאֻמָּנוּת, פָּטוּר מִגָּלוּת; וְכֵן הָרַב אֶת תַּלְמִידוֹ כְּמוֹ־כֵן.
וּמַה שֶּׁאָמְרוּ שֶׁתַּלְמִיד שֶׁגָּלָה מַגְלִין רַבּוֹ עִמּוֹ, שֶׁנֶּאֱמַר "וְנָס אֶל אַחַת מִן

2. A relative of the victim who may kill the slayer with impunity on finding him, to avenge the spilled blood (murder) of his kin; see Numbers 35:19–20, 25–27.

3. Expression based on Job 16:17.

4. And but for this law, the kin would be constantly disturbed by a reminder of what needs to be forgotten. Cf. TB Sukkah 32b, that a *hirduf* cannot be used among the four species on *Sukkoth*, instead of a *hadas* (myrtle branch), because it stings the hands (so Rashi), and as Abbaye cites, *its* [the Torah's] *ways are ways of pleasantness* (Proverbs 3:17).

5. TB Gittin 70b.

6. TB Makkoth 8b; Midrash haGadol, Numbers 35:15 (577); MT *hilchoth rotzé-aḥ* v 3.

7. A "slave" is the non-Jewish manservant of a Jewish owner, who is obligated to observe *mitzvoth* to the same extent as a Jewish woman. A *gér toshav* is a non-Jew settled in Israel who has undertaken to observe the seven precepts imposed on the descendants of Noah—hence on all mankind—which includes the renunciation of idolatry.

8. The original proof-text is "and it shall be for the Israelites as a statute of judgment, and so for the stranger who sojourns among you." Ed. Eshkol indicates that it may be an amalgam of Numbers 35:29 and 15; but neither part of this proof-text can be found there very exactly. The first part can rather be found in Numbers 27:11, and the second part in Exodus 12:49, neither, however, having any relevance to this *mitzvah*. The verse has therefore been emended in accordance with MT and MhG (see note 6). MT cites only part of it, till "in their midst"; and MhG has the same part as the heading of this teaching; but one MS of MhG reads *ha-gar* (who

the blood-avenger,[2] that he should not kill him when there was no violence in his hands,[3] since he had done it unintentionally. There is, too, a further benefit in the matter: that the kin of the victim should not see the manslayer before their eyes constantly, at the place where the evil [accident] occurred; for the ways of the Torah are pleasantness.[4]

Among the laws of the precept there is what the Sages of blessed memory taught:[5] that a person who killed unintentionally is not to be exiled [to a city of refuge] unless the victim died at the time he struck him down. But if he [only] wounded him, even if he was adjudged certain to die, and he fell ill and died, he is not exiled: perhaps he [the victim] hastened his own death, or air penetrated the wound and brought on his death. Even if he [the manslayer] cut through the two organs [gullet and windpipe], and [the victim] stood for a bit, he is not exiled because of him.[5]

Then there is what the Sages said:[6] that an Israelite is exiled if he [inadvertently] killed a slave or *gér toshav*;[7] and all the more certainly if a slave killed an Israelite; and so too if a slave killed another slave or a *gér toshav* — since it is stated, *For the Israelites and for the stranger and for the settler in their midst* [*shall these six cities be for refuge*] (Numbers 35:15).[8] However, if a *gér toshav* killed an Israelite, whether deliberately or inadvertently, he is put to death for it.[9] And if one heathen killed another, the cities of refuge would not harbor him.[9]

We have, too, what the Sages said:[10] that a son is exiled for the [inadvertent] killing of his father, and a father for the manslaughter of the son. Yet when does this rule apply? — not during instruction; but during the time of instruction, if he killed his son inadvertently when it was his intention to teach him and help him gain knowledge or a skill, he is free of the sentence of exile. And so likewise an instructor with his pupil.

In addition, there is what the Sages said:[11] that if a student is exiled, his instructor of Torah is exiled with him: for it is stated, *that*

sojourns) instead of *v'la-toshav* (and for the settler): see ed. Fisch, Jerusalem 1963, II p. 356, note 112. Possibly this error existed in early copies of MT (seemingly the source of MhG), and was copied into our author's work, whereupon an early scribe, finding the verse strange, "emended" it to what we have in our original text.

9. TB Makkoth 9a; MT *ibid.* 4.

הֶעָרִים הָאֵל(ה) וָחָי", וְדָרְשׁוּ זִכְרוֹנָם לִבְרָכָה: עֲשׂוּ לוֹ כְּדֵי שֶׁיִּחְיֶה — וְהַחָכְמָה תְּחַיֶּה אֶת בְּעָלֶיהָ.

וְדִין אִשָּׁה אוֹ עֶבֶד וְשִׁפְחָה שֶׁגָּלוּ, אִם חַיָּב הַבַּעַל אוֹ הָרַב בִּמְזוֹנוֹתָם שָׁם; וְדִין רוֹצֵחַ שֶׁמֵּת קֹדֶם שֶׁיִּגָּלֶה, שֶׁמּוֹלִיכִין עַצְמוֹתָיו לְשָׁם; וְדִין רוֹצֵחַ שֶׁהָרַג בְּעִיר מִקְלָטוֹ, וְכֵן לֵוִי שֶׁהָרַג בִּמְדִינָתוֹ; וְדִין אֵי זֶהוּ שׂוֹנֵא שֶׁנֶּאֱמַר עָלָיו כִּי בְאֵיבָה הֲרָגוֹ; וְדִין מַה שֶּׁאָמְרוּ שֶׁכָּל שֶׁהָרַג בְּדֶרֶךְ יְרִידָה גּוֹלֶה, וַאֲפִלּוּ עָלֶיהָ שֶׁהִיא צֹרֶךְ יְרִידָה; וְכָל שֶׁבְּדֶרֶךְ עֲלִיָּה אֵינוֹ גוֹלֶה, וַאֲפִלּוּ בִירִידָה שֶׁהִיא צֹרֶךְ עֲלִיָּה.

וְדִין רוֹצֵחַ שֶׁרָצוּ בְּנֵי עִיר מִקְלָטוֹ לְכַבְּדוֹ, שֶׁחַיָּב לוֹמַר "רוֹצֵחַ אָנִי", וְאִם אָמְרוּ "אַף-עַל-פִּי-כֵן", מֻתָּר לְקַבֵּל; וְדִין מִזְבֵּחַ שֶׁקּוֹלֵט כְּמוֹ עִיר מִקְלָט רוֹצֵחַ בִּשְׁגָגָה, וְדָוְקָא גַגּוֹ וּבְמִזְבֵּחַ בֵּית עוֹלָמִים, וְדָוְקָא כֹהֵן וַעֲבוֹדָה בְּיָדוֹ, אֲבָל לֹא אַחֵר; וְלֹא הָיוּ מַנִּיחִין אוֹתוֹ שָׁם אֶלָּא לְשָׁעָה, וְאַחַר-כָּךְ מוֹסְרִין לוֹ שׁוֹמְרִין וּמוֹלִיכִין אוֹתוֹ לְעִיר מִקְלָטוֹ. וּבַמֶּה דְבָרִים אֲמוּרִים, בִּמְחֻיָּבֵי גָלוּת מִן הַדִּין; אֲבָל מִי שֶׁפָּחַד מִן הַמֶּלֶךְ שֶׁלֹּא יַהַרְגֶנּוּ בְּהוֹרָאַת שָׁעָה וּבָרַח לַמִּזְבֵּחַ וְנִסְמַךְ, וַאֲפִלּוּ הוּא זָר, הֲרֵי זֶה נִצָּל, וְאֵין לוֹקְחִין אוֹתוֹ מֵעַל הַמִּזְבֵּחַ לְעוֹלָם: כֵּן רָאִיתִי שֶׁכָּתַב הָרַב מֹשֶׁה בֶּן מַיְמוֹן זִכְרוֹנוֹ לִבְרָכָה. וְיֶתֶר פְּרָטֶיהָ, מְבֹאָרִים בְּמַסֶּכֶת מַכּוֹת.

10. *Ibid.* 8a–b; MT *ibid.* 5.
11. TB Makkoth 10a.
12. Understood to mean Torah, ultimately the only wisdom worthy the name.
13. TB Gittin 12a; MT *hilchoth rotzé-ah* vii 2.
14. TB Makkoth 11b.
15. *Ibid.* 12b.
16. Numbers 35:21; TB Sanhedrin 27b, 29a.
17. TB Makkoth 7b.
18. E.g. through the downstroke of an axe, or in lowering a heavy bucket.
19. I.e. while lifting or raising something in order to lower it properly. (This is all discussed at length in MY.)
20. Literally, a *kohen* with Temple service in his hand; TB Makkoth 12a; MT *hilchoth rotzé-ah* v 12–13.
21. MT *ibid.* 14. *Kessef Mishneh* (*ad loc.*) queries this, however: Fearing that King Solomon would order him killed, Joab (Yo'av) ran to the altar and seized hold of its horns for safety; and Solomon still had him put to death (I Kings 2:28–34). The Talmud (TB Makkoth 12a) explains that Joab erred in running to the altar: It could give safety only if one grasped its roof, and he grasped its horns (I Kings 2:28); it could give safety only to a *kohen* engaged in his Divine service, and Joab was an outsider (a non-*kohen*; and hence "the law of the altar" that our author cited above). Yet, asks *Kessef Mishneh*, by this ruling of Rambam Joab's errors should not have mattered: he clearly "feared the king, that he should not put him to death by a special decree" (see I Kings 1:7 and R. David Kimhi on *ibid* 2:28). The altar should

by fleeing to one of these cities he might live (Deuteronomy 4 : 42), which the Sages of blessed memory interpreted:[11] Arrange matters for him so that he shall live — and *wisdom* [12] *gives life to him who possesses it* (Ecclesiastes 7 : 12).

Then there is the law about a woman, or a male or female slave, who is exiled [to a city of refuge], if the husband or master is responsible for their sustenance there.[13] And we have the law about a manslayer who died before he was exiled, that his remains are taken there;[14] the law if a manslayer killed [someone] in his city of refuge, and so too if a Levite killed [someone inadvertently] on his territory.[15] Further, there is the law on who is an enemy about whom it is stated [in Scripture] that he killed him in enmity;[16] and the law that the Sages taught,[17] that whoever committed manslaughter in a downward way[18] goes into exile, and even if it was with an upward motion needed for a downward one;[19] but for whatever [was committed] with an upward motion, one is not exiled, and so even if it was with a downward motion needed for an upward one.

[Going further, we have] the law about a manslayer whom the inhabitants of a city of refuge wished to honor: that he is duty-bound to say, "I am a manslayer"; and if they reply, "Even so," he is permitted to accept [the honor].[15] Then we have the law of the altar, that it grants safety like a city of refuge, to one who has killed inadvertently — but this, specifically its roof, and the altar in the permanent Sanctuary, and specifically [to] a *kohen* engaged in the Temple service,[20] but no one else. And they would not leave him there for more than a brief while; then they would assign guards to him and take him to his city of refuge. Where does this rule hold, however? — for those who deserve exile by law; but if someone feared the king, that he should not put him to death by a special decree, and he fled to the altar and leaned on it, then even if he is an outsider (a non-*kohen*), he is safe, and is never taken away from the altar. So I saw that R. Moses b. Maimon of blessed memory wrote.[21] The rest of its details are explained in the Talmud tractate *Makkoth*.

have given him protection, and yet Solomon had him killed right there!

In answer, *Kessef Mishneh* postulates that perhaps even in such an instance, the altar would not grant sanctuary to a *moréd b'malchuth*, one who rebelled against the crown; and as *tosafoth* states (TB Sanhedrin 49a, s.v. *mai ta'ma*), Joab had acted as a rebel against the crown when he murdered Amasa (II Samuel 20 : 9–10). Maharsha

וְנוֹהֶגֶת מִצְוָה זוֹ בִּזְמַן שֶׁיִּשְׂרָאֵל עַל אַדְמָתָן, וְסַנְהֶדְרִין שֶׁל שִׁבְעִים וְאֶחָד יוֹשְׁבִין בִּמְקוֹמָן הַמּוּכָן לָהֶם בִּירוּשָׁלַיִם, לָדוּן דִּינֵי נְפָשׁוֹת. וְאִם עָבְרוּ עַל זֶה בֵּית־דִּין שֶׁבְּכָל מָקוֹם וּמָקוֹם וְלֹא הִגְלוּ הָרוֹצֵחַ בִּשְׁגָגָה, בִּטְּלוּ עֲשֵׂה זֶה, וְעָנְשָׁם גָּדוֹל מְאֹד, לְפִי שֶׁהוּא סִבָּה לִשְׁפִיכוּת דָּמִים.

[שֶׁלֹּא יוֹרֶה הָעֵד בְּדִין שֶׁהֵעִיד בּוֹ בְּדִינֵי נְפָשׁוֹת]

תיא שֶׁלֹּא יְדַבֵּר הָעֵד בְּדִין אֲשֶׁר יָעִיד עָלָיו בְּדִינֵי נְפָשׁוֹת, זוּלָתִי בְּהַגָּדַת עֵדוּתוֹ לְבַד, וְאַף־עַל־פִּי שֶׁהוּא מַשְׂכִּיל וְחָכָם—שֶׁהָעֵד אֵינוֹ נַעֲשֶׂה דַיָּן בְּדִינֵי נְפָשׁוֹת, שֶׁנֶּאֱמַר: וְעֵד אֶחָד לֹא יַעֲנֶה בְנֶפֶשׁ לָמוּת. וְכָתַב הָרַב מֹשֶׁה בֶּן מַימוֹן זִכְרוֹנוֹ לִבְרָכָה: וְנִכְפַּל הַלָּאו בְּזֶה הָעִנְיָן, שֶׁנֶּאֱמַר "לֹא יוּמַת עַל פִּי עֵד אֶחָד", כְּלוֹמַר לֹא יֵהָרֵג בְּמִשְׁפַּט הָעֵד; וְאָמְרוּ בְּסַנְהֶדְרִין: "וְעֵד אֶחָד לֹא יַעֲנֶה בְנֶפֶשׁ", בֵּין לִזְכוּת בֵּין לְחוֹבָה; וּבֵאֲרוּ שֶׁטַּעַם זֶה הוּא מִשּׁוּם דְּמֶחֱזֵי כְּנוֹגֵעַ בְּעֵדוּתוֹ. וּבְדִינֵי נְפָשׁוֹת בִּלְבַד הוּא עִנְיָן זֶה, שֶׁאֵינוֹ יָכוֹל לַעֲנוֹת בּוֹ בֵּין לִזְכוּת בֵּין לְחוֹבָה, כְּמוֹ שֶׁאָמַרְנוּ.

מִשָּׁרְשֵׁי הַמִּצְוָה, מַה שֶּׁכָּתוּב בַּמִּצְוָה הַקּוֹדֶמֶת לְזוֹ.

on TB *ibid.*, s.v. *'ela'*, writes that apparently the Talmud posits that Joab was killed because he had acted as a *moréd b'malchuth* in supporting Adonijah for the throne in defiance of David's known wishes; cf. R. David Kimḥi (Radak) on I Kings 2:28. (See also Malbim on Exodus 21:14, §60; and R. Meir Simḥah of Dvinsk, *'Or Samé-aḥ* on MT *ibid.*).

Yet this would seem to leave another problem unanswered: What is the origin or basis for this final law of Rambam that our author cites in his name? How do we know from Torah sources that if one "fears the king, that he should not put him to death by a special decree," ordinarily the altar will give him safety, even if he is an outsider and he runs and grasps its horns?

The answer lies apparently in I Kings 1:50, *And Adonijah was frightened of Solomon, and he rose and went and caught hold of the horns of the altar.* Thereupon he wanted Solomon's word that he would not harm him, and Solomon gave it, on condition that Adonijah would remain Godfearing and valiantly loyal in the future (*ibid.* 51–52, with Targum Jonathan, Radak, etc.). In his commentary, the elder R. Isaiah di Trani (author of *Tosafoth Rid*, a younger contemporary of Rambam) writes on I Kings 1:50: If someone sinned toward his fellow-man and he feared the other might kill him, he would grasp the horns of the altar, so that the other should forgive him for the sake of the love of God. On account of this it is written about a warned deliberate killer, *from My altar shall you take him to die* (Exodus 21:14), and you are not to save him because he took hold of the horns of the altar. From this you can learn that such was the way of one who sought sanctuary: to grasp the altar's horns.

On this the editor of the commentary, R. Abraham Joseph Wertheimer, notes: 〈228〉

This precept is in effect at the time the Israelites are settled on their land, and the Sanhedrin (supreme court) of seventy-one meet in session at the place prepared for them in Jerusalem, to judge capital cases. If a *beth din* (court) of any locality transgressed this and did not exile an inadvertent killer [to a city of refuge, the judges] would thus disobey this positive precept, and their punishment would be very great, since it is a [possible] cause of bloodshed.[22]

[THAT A WITNESS WHO TESTIFIES IN A TRIAL
FOR A CAPITAL CRIME SHOULD NOT SPEAK
IN JUDGMENT]

411 that a witness should not speak out in the judgment (trial) regarding which he gives testimony in a capital case, but only to give his evidence, even if he is perspicacious and wise; for a witness may not become a judge in a capital case: as it is stated, *but one witness shall not respond about a person that he should die* (Numbers 35:30). Now, R. Moses b. Maimon of blessed memory wrote:[1] The injunction about this subject was reiterated, for it is stated, *he shall not be put to death by the mouth of one witness* (Deuteronomy 17:6), i.e. he shall not be killed by the ssentence of the witness; and it was taught in the tractate *Sanhedrin* (33b): "but one witness shall not respond about a person"— either for acquittal or for condemnation; it was then explained that the reason for this is that he would thus appear to be personally concerned about his testimony.[2] It is only in capital cases, however, that this rule applies, that he cannot speak up about him for either acquittal or condemnation, as we stated.

At the root of this precept lies the reason that was written about a precept shortly above (§409).

...Rambam wrote, "...if one was afraid of the king, that he might put him to death by royal sentence...and he fled to the altar and held close to it, even if he is an outsider [not a *kohen*] he is saved, and he is never taken from the altar to die." It seems that Rambam derived this law from here...and it appears that this is also our master's [R. Isaiah di Trani's] view...

§411   1. ShM negative precept §291.
      2. I.e. afraid that if his testimony can be instrumental in sending the man on trial to his death, then should he be judged (through the testimony of others) to have been a lying, scheming witness, he will be sentenced to death; Rashi, TB Sanhedrin 34a, s.v. *v'rabbanan.*

מִדִּינֵי הַמִּצְוָה, מַה שֶּׁאָמְרוּ זִכְרוֹנָם לִבְרָכָה, שֶׁעֵד שֶׁהֵעִיד בְּדִינֵי נְפָשׁוֹת וְאָמַר אַחַר־כֵּן "יֶשׁ לִי לְלַמֵּד עָלָיו זְכוּת", מְשַׁתְּקִין אוֹתוֹ, שֶׁאֵין מְקַבְּלִין מִמֶּנּוּ לְהוֹרוֹת עָלָיו שׁוּם דָּבָר אַחַר שֶׁהוּא עֵד עָלָיו. וּבַמֶּה דְבָרִים אֲמוּרִים, בְּדִינֵי נְפָשׁוֹת; אֲבָל בְּדִינֵי מָמוֹנוֹת יֶשׁ לָעֵד לְלַמֵּד זְכוּת אוֹ חוֹבָה, אֲבָל לֹא יִמָּנֶה מִן הַדַּיָּנִין וְלֹא יַעֲשֶׂה דִין, שֶׁאֵין עֵד נַעֲשֶׂה דַיָּן אֲפִלּוּ בְּדִינֵי מָמוֹנוֹת. וּבַמֶּה דְבָרִים אֲמוּרִים, בְּדָבָר שֶׁצָּרִיךְ עֵדִים מִן הַתּוֹרָה, אֲבָל בְּשֶׁל דִּבְרֵיהֶם עֵד נַעֲשֶׂה דַיָּן. וּמִפְּנֵי־כֵן נַעֲשָׂה דַיָּן בְּקִיּוּם שְׁטָרוֹת, דְּקַיְמָא לָן קִיּוּם שְׁטָרוֹת דְּרַבָּנָן, דְּמִדְּאוֹרַיְתָא עֵדִים הַחֲתוּמִים עַל הַשְּׁטָר נַעֲשָׂה כְּמִי שֶׁנֶּחְקְרָה עֵדוּתָן בְּבֵית־דִּין. וְיֶתֶר פְּרָטֶיהָ, בְּסַנְהֶדְרִין וּמַכּוֹת.

וְנוֹהֶגֶת מִצְוָה זוֹ בִּזְכָרִים לְבַד, וּבִזְמַן הַבַּיִת וְסַנְהֶדְרִין בִּמְקוֹמָן, כִּי אָז נָדִין דִּינֵי נְפָשׁוֹת, לֹא בִזְמַן אַחֵר, וְאָז נִצְטָרֵךְ לְעֵדוּת אֲנָשִׁים עַל זֶה. וְעֵד שֶׁהֵעִיד וְעָבַר עַל זֶה וְדִבֵּר בְּדִין בֵּין לִזְכוּת בֵּין לְחוֹבָה, עָבַר עַל לָאו זֶה, אֲבָל אֵינוֹ לוֹקֶה עָלָיו, לְפִי שֶׁאֵין בּוֹ מַעֲשֶׂה.

וְהָרַב מֹשֶׁה בֶּן נַחְמָן זִכְרוֹנוֹ לִבְרָכָה פֵּרֵשׁ זֶה הַכָּתוּב שֶׁל "לֹא יוּמַת עַל פִּי עֵד אֶחָד" בְּלָאו אַחֵר, וְהוּא שֶׁלֹּא לְקַבֵּל עֵדוּת מְיֻחֶדֶת בְּדִינֵי נְפָשׁוֹת, וְזֶהוּ כְּגוֹן שֶׁיִּהְיוּ הָעֵדִים רוֹאִין אוֹתוֹ אֶחָד מֵחַלּוֹן זֶה וְאֶחָד מֵחַלּוֹן אַחֵר רָחוֹק מִן הָרִאשׁוֹן, עַד כְּדֵי שֶׁאֵין הָעוֹמְדִין בַּחַלּוֹנוֹת יְכוֹלִין לִרְאוֹת זֶה אֶת זֶה, אֲבָל כֻּלָּן רוֹאִין בְּבַעַל הָעֲבֵרָה; וְנִתְבָּאֵר זֶה בְּפֶרֶק זֶה כֵּיצַד הָעֵדִים בְּמַסֶּכֶת מַכּוֹת.

[שֶׁלֹּא לָקַח כֹּפֶר לְהַצִּיל מִמָּוֶת הָרוֹצֵחַ]

תיב שֶׁלֹּא נִקַּח כֹּפֶר, כְּלוֹמַר פִּדְיוֹן, וַאֲפִלּוּ כָּל מָמוֹן שֶׁבָּעוֹלָם, לְהַצִּיל נֶפֶשׁ

3. TB Sanhedrin 34a; MT *hilchoth ʿeduth* v 8.

4. TB Sanhedrin 34b, etc.

5. TB Kʾthuboth 21b, etc.

6. *Ibid.* 18b.

7. Ramban, commentary to ShM negative precept § 290.

Among the laws of the precept, there is what the Sages of blessed memory taught:[3] that if a witness testified in a capital case and said afterward, "I have something to say to show his right to acquittal," he is silenced; for he is not accepted to demonstrate anything at all about him [the man on trial] since he was a witness about him. However, where does this rule hold?—in capital cases; in civil cases, though, a witness may demonstrate that one deserves either acquittal or condemnation. Yet he should not be reckoned as one of the judges, nor should he be made a judge: for a witness is not to be made a judge even in civil cases.[4] Where does this rule hold, however?—in a matter requiring witnesses by the law of the Torah; but if [they are required] only by the ruling of the Sages, a witness may be made a judge.[5] And for this reason he may act as judge in confirming documents [of obligation—deeds]: for we have an established rule:[6] the validation of deeds is [required] by the ruling of the Sages, since by Torah law, when witnesses are signed on a deed, it is as though their testimony had been examined in the *beth din* (court). The rest of its details are in the Talmud tractates *Sanhedrin* and *Makkoth*.

This precept applies to men only, at the time the Temple stands and the Sanhedrin (supreme court justices) are in their place; for then we can try capital cases; but not at any other time—and then we need the testimony of men for this. If a witness gave testimony and then transgressed this and spoke out about the judgment, whether for acquittal or for punishment, he would violate this injunction; but he would receive no whiplashes, since it involved no physical action.

Now, R. Moses b. Naḥman of blessed memory explained that verse, *he shall not be put to death by the mouth of one witness* (Deuteronomy 17:6), as meaning another injunction, namely, not to accept singular testimony in a capital case.[7] This means, for example, if the witnesses saw [the crime] one from this window and one from another window, far enough from the first so that those standing at the windows could not see each other, although both saw the criminal. This is explained in the first chapter of the tractate *Makkoth* (6b).

[TO TAKE NO RANSOM TO SAVE A KILLER
FROM HIS DEATH SENTENCE]

412 that we should not take any ransom, i.e. redemption-money,
even all the wealth in the world, to save the life of a slayer, that he

הָרוֹצֵחַ שֶׁלֹּא לְהָרְגוֹ, שֶׁנֶּאֱמַר: וְלֹא תִקְחוּ כֹפֶר לְנֶפֶשׁ רֹצֵחַ אֲשֶׁר הוּא רָשָׁע לָמוּת.

שֹׁרֶשׁ מִצְוָה זוֹ יָדוּעַ, שֶׁאִם הֻרְשׁוּ אֲדוֹנֵי הָאָרֶץ לָקַחַת כֹּפֶר מִיַּד הָרוֹצֵחַ, נִמְצָא שֶׁכָּל הַגָּדוֹל מֵחֲבֵרוֹ וְעָשִׁיר מִמֶּנּוּ יַהַרְגֶנּוּ אִם יֶחֱרֶה אַפּוֹ עָלָיו, וְיִתֵּן כָּפְרוֹ, וְנִמְצָא חֶרֶב אִישׁ בְּאָחִיו, וְהַיִּשׁוּב בָּטֵל.

מִדִּינֵי הַמִּצְוָה, מַה שֶּׁאָמְרוּ זִכְרוֹנָם לִבְרָכָה שֶׁאֲפִלּוּ רָצָה גּוֹאֵל הַדָּם לְפָטְרוֹ, וְאָמַר לַדַּיָּן שֶׁהוּא מוֹחֵל עַל דָּמוֹ וְשֶׁיִּקְחוּ מִמֶּנּוּ כֹפֶר אִם יִרְצוּ, אֵינָן רַשָּׁאִין לָקַחַת הַכֹּפֶר וְלֹא לְפָטְרוֹ בְּכָל מָמוֹן שֶׁבָּעוֹלָם, אֶלָּא יוּמַת כְּמִצְוַת הָאֵל עָלֵינוּ; וְיֶתֶר פְּרָטֶיהָ, בְּמַסֶּכֶת מַכּוֹת.

וְנוֹהֶגֶת בִּזְמַן הַבַּיִת בִּזְכָרִים וּנְקֵבוֹת, שֶׁעַכְשָׁיו בַּזְּמַן הַזֶּה אֵין לָנוּ עֵסֶק בְּדִינֵי נְפָשׁוֹת. וְאָמְרוּ בְכָאן בְּמַה שֶּׁנּוֹהֵג זֶה בִּנְקֵבוֹת, וְאַף־עַל־פִּי שֶׁהֵן אֵינָן דָּנוֹת, הָעִנְיָן הוּא שֶׁאִם אוּלַי בַּזְּמַן הַהוּא, מֵחֲמַת מַלְכוּת אוֹ סִבָּה אַחֶרֶת, יָבוֹא בְּיַד אִשָּׁה עִנְיָן שֶׁיִּשְׁאָלוּ מִמֶּנָּה לְהַצִּיל נֶפֶשׁ רוֹצֵחַ בִּשְׁבִיל מָמוֹן, שֶׁהִיא מֻזְהֶרֶת מִשׁוּם לָאו זֶה שֶׁלֹּא (יִקַּח) [תִּקַּח] הַמָּמוֹן (וִיצִילֵנוּ) [וְתַצִּילֵנוּ].

וְעוֹבֵר עַל זֶה, בֵּין אִישׁ בֵּין אִשָּׁה, וְלָקַח כֹּפֶר לְהַצִּיל הָרוֹצֵחַ, עָבַר עַל לָאו זֶה; וְעָנְשׁוֹ גָּדוֹל מְאֹד, כִּי הוּא סִבָּה לְאַבּוּד כַּמָּה נְפָשׁוֹת מִיִּשְׂרָאֵל.

[שֶׁלֹּא לָקַחַת כֹּפֶר מִחֻיָּב גָּלוּת לְפָטְרוֹ מִן הַגָּלוּת]

תיג שֶׁלֹּא נִקַּח כֹּפֶר מִחֻיָּב גָּלוּת מֵחֲמַת שֶׁהָרַג שׁוֹגֵג, לְפָטְרוֹ מִן הַגָּלוּת, שֶׁנֶּאֱמַר: וְלֹא תִקְחוּ כֹפֶר לָנוּס אֶל עִיר מִקְלָטוֹ לָשׁוּב לָשֶׁבֶת בָּאָרֶץ. וּלְפִי

---

§412   1. TB K'tuboth 37b.
        2. See § 410, note 2.

should not be put to death: for it is stated, *And you shall take no ransom for the life of a murderer who is guilty to die* (Numbers 35:31).

The root reason for this precept is known (evident): for if the rulers of the land were permitted to take ransom from the hand of a killer, the result would be that whoever is bigger than his fellow-man and richer than he is, will kill him if his anger flares up toward him and he will give his ransom. In consequence, *every man's sword shall be against his brother* (Ezekiel 38:21), and the settled community will be reduced to nothing.

Among the laws of the precept there is what the Sages of blessed memory taught:[1] that even if the blood-avenger[2] wishes to let him off free and he tells the judge that he forgives him the bloodshed and that they [the justices of the *beth din*] may accept ransom from him if they wish, they are not allowed to take the ransom, nor to set him free for all the wealth in the world, but he must rather die in accord with God's commandment to us. The rest of its details are in the Talmud tractate *Makkoth*.

It is in force at the time the Temple stands, for both man and woman; for now, at the present time, we have nothing to do with capital cases. Now, when I say here that this prohibition applies to women even though they do not sit in judgment [at court], the meaning is that if perhaps at that time, on account of the government, or some other reason, a situation will arise for a woman where she will be asked to save a killer's life for money, she is adjured on the strength of this injunction that she should not take the money and save him.

If someone transgressed this, whether a man or a woman, and took a ransom to rescue a killer, he would violate this negative precept, and his punishment would be very great, since it could be the cause of the loss of many lives in Jewry.

[TO TAKE NO RANSOM FROM SOMEONE
SENTENCED TO BANISHMENT, TO FREE HIM
FROM IT]

413 that we should not take ransom from a person who has incurred exile [to a city of refuge] because he killed inadvertently, to free him from [the sentence of] exile: for it is stated, *And you shall take no ransom* la-nus (*for one fled*) *to his city of refuge, for him to return to dwell in the land* (Numbers 35:32). According to this meaning, the word *la-*

מַשְׁמָעוּת זֶה, לְפִי הַדּוֹמֶה, יִהְיֶה "לָנוּס" פָּעוּל, כְּלוֹמַר לֹא תִקְחוּ כֹפֶר עַל מִי שֶׁהוּא נוּס אֶל עִיר מִקְלָטוֹ, לָשׁוּב לָשֶׁבֶת בְּאֶרֶץ מְגוּרֵי אֲבוֹתָיו.

שֹׁרֶשׁ אִסוּר הַכֹּפֶר בְּהוֹרֵג שׁוֹגֵג וְכָל עִנְיָנוֹ כְּעִנְיָן הוֹרֵג מֵזִיד, אֵין צֹרֶךְ לְהַאֲרִיךְ בּוֹ הַדִּבּוּר.

נִשְׁלַם סֵפֶר בְּמִדְבַּר סִינַי
תְּהִלָּה לְמֵאִיר עֵינַי.

§413   1. Similarly Rashi on the verse.

    * While the first line of the Hebrew couplet (translated freely here, with "poetic license") is found in all four manuscripts and the first edition, the second occurs only in the second manuscript (MS Vatican). The third and fourth have only the first line, and the first (oldest) manuscript continues after it, *baruch 'adonai* (blessed be the Lord).

nus, as it seems, would be a verbal noun: in other words, you shall not take ransom from one who is a *nus* [who has taken flight] to his city of refuge, to have him return to live in the land (region) where his father lived.[1]

The root reason for the prohibition against ransom for an unintentional killer, and all its subject-matter, is as in the theme of the deliberate killer; there is no need to elaborate on the matter.

ENDED IS THE BOOK OF NUMBERS,
PRAISE GOD THE WISE
WHO HAS BESTOWED THE LIGHT OF WISDOM
UPON MY EYES *

סֵפֶר אֵלֶּה הַדְּבָרִים

🕎 🕎 🕎 🕎 🕎 🕎 🕎 🕎

כָּתַב הָרַב רַבֵּנוּ מֹשֶׁה בֶּן נַחְמָן זִכְרוֹנוֹ לִבְרָכָה: עִנְיַן הַסֵּפֶר הַזֶּה יָדוּעַ שֶׁהוּא מִשְׁנֵה הַתּוֹרָה, יַחֲזֹר בּוֹ מֹשֶׁה רַבֵּנוּ עָלָיו הַשָּׁלוֹם לַדּוֹר הַנִּכְנָס בָּאָרֶץ רֹב מִצְוֹת הַתּוֹרָה הַצְּרִיכוֹת לְיִשְׂרָאֵל, וְיַזְהִיר אוֹתָם עֲלֵיהֶם אַזְהָרוֹת מְרֻבּוֹת וְיָפְחִידֵם הַרְבֵּה בָּעֳנָשִׁים, וּפְעָמִים יוֹסִיף בָּהֶן בֵּאוּר בִּקְצָתָם; אֲבָל בְּכָל מִצְוֹת הַכֹּהֲנִים לֹא יְדַבֵּר וְלֹא יוֹסִיף אַזְהָרָה, שֶׁהַכֹּהֲנִים זְרִיזִין הֵם.

וְעוֹד יוֹסִיף בַּסֵּפֶר הַזֶּה קְצָת מִצְווֹת שֶׁלֹּא נִזְכְּרוּ כְלָל, כְּגוֹן הַיִּבּוּם, וְדִין מוֹצִיא שֵׁם רַע, וְדִין גֵּרוּשִׁין בְּאִשָּׁה, וְעֵדִים זוֹמְמִין, וְזוּלָתָם; וְאֵין סָפֵק כִּי כָאן נֶאֶמְרוּ לְמֹשֶׁה בְּסִינַי אוֹ בְאֹהֶל מוֹעֵד בַּשָּׁנָה הָרִאשׁוֹנָה, כִּי בְּעַרְבוֹת מוֹאָב לֹא נִתְחַדֵּשׁ לוֹ אֶלָּא דִבְרֵי הַבְּרִית, כַּאֲשֶׁר נִתְפָּרֵשׁ בּוֹ; וְעַל־כֵּן לֹא נֶאֱמַר בַּסֵּפֶר הַזֶּה "וַיְדַבֵּר יי אֶל מֹשֶׁה לֵּאמֹר", "צַו אֶת בְּנֵי יִשְׂרָאֵל", אוֹ "דַּבֵּר אֶל בְּנֵי יִשְׂרָאֵל וְאָמַרְתָּ אֲלֵיהֶם" מִצְוָה פְלוֹנִית. עַד כָּאן.

וְזֶה שֶׁלֹּא הֻזְכְּרוּ אֵלֶּה הַמִּצְווֹת בַּסְּפָרִים הָרִאשׁוֹנִים כְּמוֹ שְׁאָר הַמִּצְווֹת, אַל תִּתְמַהּ בַּדָּבָר, אַחַר אָמְרָם זִכְרוֹנָם לִבְרָכָה בְּכַמָּה מְקוֹמוֹת "אֵין מֻקְדָּם וּמְאֻחָר בַּתּוֹרָה".

וְשֹׁרֶשׁ עִנְיָן זֶה לְפִי הַדּוֹמֶה, כִּי הַתּוֹרָה תִּכְלֹל כָּל הַחָכְמוֹת, מִלְּבַד פְּשַׁט עִנְיָנֶיהָ

---

1. Ramban, commentary on Pentateuch, introduction to Deuteronomy. This is the reading of the oldest manuscript; all other sources have Rambam (R. Moses b. Maimon), evidently by a scribal error. (The citation that follows is somewhat paraphrased from Ramban's original.)

2. I.e. in knowledge and observance of their precepts. So TB Shabbath 20a, etc.

3. I.e. the *mishkan* (Tabernacle) in the wilderness, forerunner of the Sanctuary. Cf. Ramban, *op. cit.*, Introduction to Genesis (Hebrew ed. Chavel, pp. 2–3).

4. I.e. the first year after the erection of the *mishkan*. Ramban's original reads, "in the first year, before the spies": i.e. until the spies sent by Moses into Canaan returned with their evil report and brought the Israelites to grief (Numbers 13–14), so that all men of fighting age had to die before the people could enter the promised Land (*ibid.* 14:29); "for so we find, that in all the thirty-eight years when they [the Israelites] were as though excommunicated, He did not speak with Moses; as Scripture states, *And it was when all the men of war were dead and gone from among the people, that the Lord spoke to me*" (Deuteronomy 2:16–17; Sifra, *va-yikra, perek* 2). In *his* citation of Ramban, in his longer commentary, R. Jacob b. Asher (*ba'al ha-turim*) has "in the *second* year" —i.e. after the departure of the Israelites from Egypt, for the

DEUTERONOMY

ﬥﬥﬥﬥﬥﬥﬥﬥﬥﬥﬥﬥﬥ

R. Moses b. Naḥman of blessed memory wrote:[1] The nature of this Book [of Scripture] is known, that it is a restatement of the Torah. Moses our Master (peace abide with him) reviews in it, for the generation that is to enter the land [of Israel], most of the Torah's precepts that the Israelites need [to know]; he adjures them about them with a great many admonitions, and cautions them greatly about the punishments. At times he adds an explanation about some of them. Yet about all the religious duties of the *kohanim* he neither speaks nor adds any admonition: for the *kohanim* were alert. [2]

In addition, he adds in this Book a few precepts that were not mentioned [previously] at all, such as levirate marriage (§ 598), the law for one who gives [his bride] an evil name (§ 553), the law of divorcing a woman (§ 579), and scheming witnesses (§ 524), and others. There is no doubt that all were imparted to Moses on Sinai or in the Tent of Meeting[3] in the first year:[4] for on the plains of Moab nothing new was imparted to him other than the words of the covenant, as it is explained there.[5] For this reason it is not stated in this Book, *And the Lord spoke to Moses, saying: Command the Israelites*, or, *Speak to the Israelites and say to them* this-and-this precept. Thus far [his words].

As to the fact that these certain precepts were not mentioned in the first Books [of the Writ] like the other precepts, do not wonder about the matter, since the Sages of blessed memory said in many instances:[6] There is no earlier and later [no chronological order] in the Torah.

The root reason for this matter,[7] it would seem, is that the Torah embraces all the wisdoms, apart from the plain meaning of its sweet

---

mishkan was erected at the start of the second year (Exodus 40:17). Thus some two years elapsed from the Exodus to the affair of the spies; and the thirty-eight years mentioned in the Midrash were the balance of their forty years in the wilderness.

5. Ramban, commentary on Deuteronomy 28:69.

6. E.g. TB P'saḥim 6b.

7. I.e. the lack of chronological order in the Written Torah.

הַמְּתֻקִּים וִיסוֹדוֹת מִצְוֹתֶיהָ הַחֲזָקִים; וְאֶפְשָׁר כִּי מִפְּנֵי־כֵן צָרִיךְ לִהְיוֹת פָּרָשִׁיּוֹתֶיהָ וְאוֹתִיּוֹתֶיהָ בְּמָקוֹם שֶׁהֵם, וְהַכֹּל מְכֻנָּן מֵאֵת אֲדוֹן הַחָכְמָה בָּרוּךְ הוּא; וְזֶה טַעַם מַסְפִּיק.

✡ אֵלֶּה הַדְּבָרִים

יֵשׁ בָּהּ שְׁתֵּי מִצְוֹת לֹא־תַעֲשֶׂה

[שֶׁלֹּא לְמַנּוֹת דַּיָּן שֶׁאֵינוֹ חָכָם בְּדִינֵי תוֹרָה, אַף־עַל־פִּי
שֶׁהוּא חָכָם בְּחָכְמוֹת אֲחֵרוֹת]

תיד שֶׁנִּשְׁמַע בֵּית־דִּין הַגָּדוֹל אוֹ רֹאשׁ גָּלוּת שֶׁלֹּא יַעֲמִיד דַּיָּן לִשְׁפֹּט אֶת הָעָם שֶׁלֹּא לָמַד חָכְמַת הַתּוֹרָה וּבֵאוּר מִשְׁפָּטֶיהָ הַיְשָׁרִים וְהַצַּדִּיקִים; וַאֲפִלּוּ יִהְיוּ בוֹ כַּמָּה מִדּוֹת נִכְבָּדוֹת, אַחַר שֶׁאֵינוֹ יוֹדֵעַ וּבָקִי בְּחָכְמַת הַתּוֹרָה אֵין רָאוּי לְמַנּוֹתוֹ דַּיָּן; וְעַל זֶה נֶאֱמַר: לֹא תַכִּירוּ פָנִים בַּמִּשְׁפָּט. וְכֵן פֵּרְשׁוּ זִכְרוֹנָם לִבְרָכָה: "לֹא תַכִּירוּ פָנִים בַּמִּשְׁפָּט", זֶה הַמְמֻנֶּה לְהוֹשִׁיב דַּיָּנִים — כְּלוֹמַר שֶׁאֵלָיו בָּאָה אַזְהָרָה זוֹ.

וְאָמְרוּ זִכְרוֹנָם לִבְרָכָה: שֶׁמָּא תֹּאמַר: אִישׁ פְּלוֹנִי נָאֶה אוֹ גִבּוֹר אוֹ עָשִׁיר אוֹ שֶׁיּוֹדֵעַ בְּכָל לָשׁוֹן, אוֹשִׁיבֶנּוּ דַּיָּן — לְכָךְ נֶאֱמַר "לֹא תַכִּירוּ פָנִים" וְגוֹמֵר, לְפִי שֶׁנִּמְצָא מְזַכֶּה אֶת הַחַיָּב וּמְחַיֵּב אֶת הַזַּכַּאי, וְלֹא מִפְּנֵי שֶׁהוּא רָשָׁע, אֶלָּא מִפְּנֵי שֶׁאֵינוֹ יוֹדֵעַ.

שֹׁרֶשׁ מִצְוָה זוֹ נִגְלֶה הוּא לַכֹּל.

דִּינֶיהָ, כְּגוֹן מַה שֶׁאָמְרוּ זִכְרוֹנָם לִבְרָכָה, שֶׁכְּשֵׁם שֶׁצָּרִיךְ הָרָאוּי לִהְיוֹת דַּיָּן לִהְיוֹת יוֹדֵעַ דִּינֵי הַתּוֹרָה, כְּמוֹ־כֵן צָרִיךְ לִהְיוֹת בַּעַל מִדּוֹת וְאָדָם כָּשֵׁר, שֶׁלֹּא יֹאמַר לוֹ הַנִּדּוֹן "טֹל קוֹרָה מִבֵּין עֵינֶיךָ", כְּלוֹמַר קְשֹׁט עַצְמְךָ וְאַחַר־כָּךְ קְשֹׁט אֲחֵרִים. הֲרֵי הוּא אוֹמֵר בַּתּוֹרָה גַּבֵּי דַיָּנִים "אֲנָשִׁים חֲכָמִים", כְּלוֹמַר יוֹדְעֵי הַחָכְמָה לָדוּן

---

1. The head of exiled Jewry in Babylonia, in Talmudic times.

2. Sifre, Deuteronomy § 17.

3. MT *hilchoth sanhedrin* ii 7; cf. TB Sanhedrin 88b: Whoever is wise and humble of stature, and the spirit of people is pleased with him, let him be a judge in his city (and similarly Tosefta, Sanhedrin vii); see also sources cited in MY.

4. The expression is from a passage in TB Bava Bathra 15b, on Ruth I:I, understood literally to mean, *And it was in the days of judging the judges*: It was a generation that judged its justices. He [a judge] would say to him [a person on trial], "Take the splinter out from between your teeth," and the other would reply, "Take the beam out from between your eyes."

themes and the mighty foundations of its precepts. And perhaps on this account it is necessary that its sections and letters should be located where they are, all being precisely arranged by the [Divine] Master of wisdom, blessed is He. This is an adequate reason.

sidrah d'varim
(Deuteronomy 1-3:22)

It contains two negative precepts.

[NOT TO APPOINT ANY JUDGE WHO IS UNLEARNED IN THE TORAH, EVEN IF HE IS GENERALLY LEARNED]

414 that the great *beth din* (supreme court) or the exilarch[1] is constrained not to appoint a justice to judge the people who has not learned the wisdom of the Torah and the clarification of its fair and righteous ordinances. Even if he has many noble qualities, since he is not knowledgeable and expert in the wisdom of the Torah it is not right to appoint him a judge. About this it was stated, *You shall not respect persons in judgment* (Deuteronomy 1:17); and so our Sages of blessed memory interpreted it:[2] "You shall not respect persons in judgment"—this means the official appointed to assign judges; in other words, this injunction was given him.

Our Sages of blessed memory taught further:[2] Perhaps you would say, "That man is handsome, or strong, or wealthy, or he knows every language; I will appoint him judge"?—It is therefore stated, *You shall not respect persons.* etc.—for he will be found declaring the guilty innocent and the innocent guilty, not because he is wicked but because he does not know.

The root reason for this precept is obvious to all.

Its laws are, for example, what the Sages of blessed memory said:[3] that just as a person fit to be a judge needs to be knowledgeable in the laws of the Torah, so does he need to be possessed of fine qualities and to be an honest worthy man, so that the person being judged should not tell him, "Take out the beam from between your eyes"[4]—in other words: Correct yourself, and afterward correct others. It is patently stated in the Torah regarding judges, *wise men* (Deuteronomy 1:13)—in other words, those who know wisdom, to ren-

דִּין אֱמֶת; "וִידֻעִים לְשִׁבְטֵיכֶם", אֵלּוּ שֶׁרוּחַ הַבְּרִיּוֹת נוֹחָה מֵהֶם; "אַנְשֵׁי חַיִל",
שֶׁהֵם גִּבּוֹרִים בַּמִּצְוֹת וּמְדַקְדְּקִים עַל עַצְמָם וְכוֹבְשִׁים אֶת יִצְרָם, עַד שֶׁלֹּא יִהְיֶה
לָהֶם שׁוּם גְּנַאי וְשׁוּם כָּעוּר, וּפִרְקָם נָאֶה. וּבִכְלַל אַנְשֵׁי חַיִל, שֶׁיִּהְיֶה לָהֶם לֵב
אַמִּיץ לְהַצִּיל עָשׁוּק מִיַּד עוֹשֵׁק, כְּעִנְיָן שֶׁנֶּאֱמַר: וַיָּקָם מֹשֶׁה וַיּוֹשִׁעָן; וּמַה מֹּשֶׁה
רַבֵּנוּ עָלָיו הַשָּׁלוֹם עָנָו, אַף כָּל דַּיָּן צָרִיךְ לִהְיוֹת עָנָו. וְיֶתֶר פְּרָטֶיהָ, מְבֹאָרִין
בְּסַנְהֶדְרִין וּבִמְקוֹמוֹת אֲחֵרִים בְּפִזּוּר.

וְנוֹהֶגֶת מִצְוָה זוֹ בְּכָל מָקוֹם וּבְכָל זְמָן. וְעוֹבֵר עַל זֶה וּמִנָּה דַּיָּן שֶׁאֵינוֹ חָכָם,
מֵחֲמַת עָשְׁרוֹ אוֹ טוֹב מַדּוֹתָיו אוֹ מֵאַהֲבָתוֹ אוֹתוֹ אוֹ מֵחֲמַת כְּבוֹד קְרוֹבָיו (בטל
עשה זה) [עָבַר עַל לֹא־תַעֲשֶׂה זוֹ], וְעָנְשׁוֹ גָּדוֹל מְאֹד, שֶׁכָּל עֹנֶשׁ דִּינֵי שֶׁקֶר שֶׁיָּדִין
אוֹתוֹ דַּיָּן מֵחֲמַת יְדִיעָתוֹ תָּלוּי עָלָיו, כִּי הוּא הַגּוֹרֵם.

וּמִכְּלַל מִצְוָה זוֹ גַּם־כֵּן, לְפִי הַדּוֹמֶה, שֶׁכָּל מִי שֶׁבָּחֲרוּ אוֹתוֹ בְּנֵי הַקָּהָל לְמַנּוֹת
עֲלֵיהֶם מְמֻנִּים לְשׁוּם עִנְיָן, שֶׁיָּשִׂים כָּל הַשְׁגָּחָתוֹ וְכָל דַּעְתּוֹ לְמַנּוֹת מֵהֶם הָרְאוּיִין
וְהַטּוֹבִים עַל אוֹתוֹ מִנּוּי שֶׁהַקָּהָל צְרִיכִין אוֹתוֹ, וְלֹא יָגוּר מִפְּנֵי אִישׁ לְמַנּוֹת מִי
שֶׁאֵינוֹ רָאוּי.

אָמְרוּ חֲכָמִים עַל מִי שֶׁהוּא מַעֲמִיד דַּיָּן שֶׁאֵינוֹ הָגוּן, שֶׁהוּא כְּאִלּוּ הֵקִים
מַצֵּבָה, שֶׁנֶּאֱמַר: וְלֹא תָקִים לְךָ מַצֵּבָה; וְאִם הוּא מָקוֹם שֶׁיֵּשׁ בּוֹ תַּלְמִידֵי־חֲכָמִים,
אָמְרוּ שֶׁהוּא כְּאִלּוּ נָטַע אֲשֵׁרָה, שֶׁנֶּאֱמַר: לֹא תִטַּע לְךָ אֲשֵׁרָה כָּל עֵץ אֵצֶל מִזְבַּח
יי אֱלֹהֶיךָ. וְעוֹד אָמְרוּ שֶׁכָּל הַמְמַנֶּה דַיָּן מֵחֲמַת עָשְׁרוֹ, עַל זֶה נֶאֱמַר: לֹא תַעֲשׂוּן
אִתִּי אֱלֹהֵי כֶסֶף וֵאלֹהֵי זָהָב. וְעוֹד הֶאֱרִיכוּ בָעִנְיָן זֶה וְאָמְרוּ שֶׁדַּיָּן שֶׁנָּתַן מָמוֹן כְּדֵי
שֶׁיִּתְמַנֶּה דַיָּן, אָסוּר לַעֲמֹד מִפָּנָיו וּמְקִילִין הַרְבֵּה בִּכְבוֹדוֹ, וְאָמְרוּ עָלָיו שֶׁהַטַּלִּית
שֶׁמִּתְעַטֵּף בָּהּ תִּהְיֶה בְּעֵינֶיךָ כְּמַרְדַּעַת הַחֲמוֹר. דֶּרֶךְ הַחֲכָמִים הָרִאשׁוֹנִים

5. A Talmudic expression: TB Shabbath 19a.

6. So that they are above criticism for any youthful indiscretion.

7. So ibid. 8a.

8. This follows the just emendation of R. Jacob Joseph Kallenberg, Séder ha-
Mitzvoth (Warsaw 1861); the original reads, "he has disobeyed (more literally:
treated as nought) this positive precept"—evidently a slip of the pen.

9. Cited in MT hilchoth sanhedrin iii 8, either from a Midrash lost to us or from a
different version in TB Sanhedrin 7b, where a similar passage is found.

10. The Hebrew for gods also denotes judges (and according to TB Shabbath
10a, a judge who gives a true verdict is reckoned as a partner of the Almighty in the
work of Creation). TB Sanhedrin 19a; MT ibid.

11. TJ Bikkurim iii 3; MT ibid. 9.

der true judgment; *and known to your tribes (ibid.)*—those with whom the spirit of people is pleased; *men of valor* (Exodus 18:21)— who are mighty in *mitzvoth* and scrupulously strict with themselves, and who subdue their [evil] inclination until they are possessed of nothing shameful and nothing repugnant, and whose youth was fine.[6] Included in the description, "men of valor", is the requirement that they should have a fearless heart, to rescue an oppressed, wronged person from the oppressor, in keeping with what Scripture states: *but Moses stood up and helped them* (Exodus 2:17). And just as Moses our Master (peace abide with him) was humble, so is it necessary for every judge to be humble.[7] The rest of its details are clarified in the Talmud tractate *Sanhedrin*, and in other places, scattered about.

This precept applies in every place and every time. If someone transgressed this and appointed a judge who was not a wise scholar, because of his wealth or fine qualities, or out of his affection for him, or on account of the eminence of his relatives, he would violate this negative precept,[8] and his punishment would be very great: because every penalty for false judgments which that judge will give out of his lack of knowledge, will be due to him, since he is the cause.

It is part of this precept too, as it would seem, that whomever the members of the community choose that he should appoint officials over them for any purpose, he should give all his watchful concern and all his thought to appoint those among them who are fit and good for that position which the community needs; and he should quail before no man to appoint someone unfit.

The Sages said about someone who appoints a judge who is not suitable:[9] It is as though he erected a pillar [for idol-worship], of which it is stated, *you shall not set yourself up a pillar* (Deuteronomy 16:22). If it is a locality that contains Torah scholars, they said it is as if he planted an 'Ashérah [a tree to be worshipped], of which it is stated, *You shall not plant yourself an 'Ashérah of any kind of tree beside the altar of the Lord your God* (ibid. 21). And they said, furthermore, that whoever appoints a judge on account of his wealth, about this it is stated, *You shall not make [to be] with Me gods of silver or gods of gold* (Exodus 20:20).[10] They went on further at length about this theme, and said[11] that if a judge gave money in order to be appointed judge, it is forbidden to stand [in respect] before him, and his honor is to be greatly disparaged. And they said of him[11] that the tunic in which he robes himself should be in your eyes as the pack-saddle of a donkey.

שֶׁבּוֹרְחִין מִלְהִתְמַנּוֹת דַּיָּנִים, אֶלָּא בְּמָקוֹם שֶׁאֵין גָּדוֹל מֵהֶם.

[שֶׁלֹּא יִירָא הַדַּיָּן בַּדִּין מֵאָדָם רָע]

תטו שֶׁנִּמְנַע הַדַּיָּן מִלִּירָא מֵאִישׁ מִלְּדַיֵּן דִּין אֱמֶת, וַאֲפִלּוּ הוּא אִישׁ מַזִּיק עַז־
פָּנִים עֲבֵה־הַמֹּחַ, אֶלָּא יַחְתּוֹךְ אֶת הַדִּין וְלֹא יָשִׂים לִבּוֹ כְּלָל לְמַה שֶּׁיִּקְרֶה עָלָיו
מֵהַהֶזֵּק בִּשְׁבִיל דִּינוֹ; וְעַל זֶה נֶאֱמַר "לֹא תָגוּרוּ מִפְּנֵי אִישׁ". וּלְשׁוֹן סִפְרִי: שֶׁמָּא
תֹאמַר יָרֵא אֲנִי מֵאִישׁ פְּלוֹנִי שֶׁמָּא יַהַרְגֵנִי אוֹ יַהֲרֹג אֶחָד מִבָּנֵי בֵיתִי, שֶׁמָּא יַדְלִיק
אֶת גְּדִישִׁי אוֹ שֶׁמָּא יְקַצֵּץ אֶת נְטִיעוֹתַי, תַּלְמוּד לוֹמַר: לֹא תָגוּרוּ מִפְּנֵי אִישׁ.
שֹׁרֶשׁ מִצְוָה זוֹ, הַשֵּׂכֶל מֵעִיד עָלָיו.

דִּינֵי הַמִּצְוָה, כְּגוֹן מַה שֶּׁאָמְרוּ זִכְרוֹנָם לִבְרָכָה: שְׁנַיִם שֶׁבָּאוּ לְפָנֶיךָ לַדִּין, אֶחָד
רַךְ וְאֶחָד קָשֶׁה, עַד שֶׁלֹּא תִשְׁמַע אֶת דִּבְרֵיהֶם, אוֹ אֲפִלּוּ מִשֶּׁתִּשְׁמַע אֶת דִּבְרֵיהֶם
וְאִי אַתָּה יוֹדֵעַ לְהֵיכָן הַדִּין נוֹטֶה, אַתָּה רַשַּׁאי לוֹמַר לָהֶם "אֵינִי נִזְקָק לָכֶם",
שֶׁמָּא יִתְחַיֵּב, וְנִמְצָא רוֹדֵף אַחַר הַדַּיָּן לְהָרְגוֹ; אֲבָל מִשֶּׁתִּשְׁמַע אֶת דִּבְרֵיהֶן וְתֵדַע
לְהֵיכָן הַדִּין נוֹטֶה, אִי אַתָּה רַשַּׁאי לוֹמַר לָהֶם "אֵינִי נִזְקָק לָכֶם", שֶׁנֶּאֱמַר: לֹא
תָגוּרוּ מִפְּנֵי אִישׁ. וְכֵן תַּלְמִיד הַיּוֹשֵׁב לִפְנֵי רַבּוֹ וְרָאָה זְכוּת לֶעָנִי, חוֹבָה לֶעָשִׁיר,
אֵינוֹ רַשַּׁאי לִהְיוֹת שׁוֹתֵק, שֶׁנֶּאֱמַר: לֹא תָגוּרוּ מִפְּנֵי אִישׁ.

וְנוֹהֶגֶת מִצְוָה זוֹ בְּכָל מָקוֹם וּבְכָל זְמַן בַּזְּכָרִים, כִּי לָהֶם הַמִּשְׁפָּט. וְעוֹבֵר עַל זֶה
וְלֹא רָצָה לָדוּן מִשֶּׁיָּדַע לְהֵיכָן הַדִּין נוֹטֶה, כְּמוֹ שֶׁאָמַרְנוּ, מִיִּרְאַת הַנִּדּוֹן, עָבַר עַל
לָאו זֶה; וְאִם הִטָּה גַם־כֵּן מִיִּרְאָתוֹ, עָבַר עַל לָאו זֶה, מִלְּבַד שֶׁעָבַר עַל לָאו דְּ"לֹא
תַטֶּה מִשְׁפָּט".

---

12. MT *ibid.* 10, based on TB Sanhedrin 14a, Horayoth 10a, 'Avodah Zarah 19b.

§415   1. On the verse (§ 17).

2. Hebrew, *n'ti'othai*—literally, ''my plantings''; the oldest of the manuscripts
reads *n'ti'athi*, ''my planting'' (singular); see ShM negative precept § 276 (on which
this paragraph is based), ed. Heller, p.168 note 2.

3.· TB Sanhedrin 6b.

4. Literally, soft.

5. I.e. I am not obligated (or inclined) to judge your case.

6. While his teacher is adjudicating a case between a rich and a poor man.

7. The paragraph is based on MT *hilchoth sanhedrin* xxii 1–2.

8. I.e. render an unjust verdict.

Well, it was the way of the early Torah scholars that they would flee from any appointment as judges unless it was in an instance where there was none greater than they.[12]

415 that a judge was prohibited from fearing any man and thus failing to render a true judgment, even if he is a man who inflicts injury and damage, insolent and thick-witted; but he should rather decide the case correctly and not give heed at all to what may happen to him in the way of damage on account of his judgment. About this it was stated, *you shall not be afraid of the face of any man* (Deuteronomy 1:17). In the language of the Midrash *Sifre*:[1] Perhaps you might say, "I am frightened of that man; it may be he will kill me, or kill someone in my household (family); it may be he will set fire to my stack of grain or cut down what I planted"?[2]—hence Scripture states, *you shall not be afraid of the face of any man.*

As for the root reason for this precept, human intelligence bears witness to it.

The laws of the precept are, for example, what the Sages of blessed memory taught:[3] If two have come before you to be judged, one amiable[4] and the other hard (tough), as long as you have not listened to their words (arguments), or even after you have heard their words, but you do not know [as yet] which way the judgment will tend to go, you have the right to tell them, "I am not bound to you."[5] But from the time you shall have listened to their words and you know which way the judgment tends, you have no right to tell them, "I am not bound to you": for it is stated, *you shall not be afraid of the face of any man.*[3] So too, if a student is sitting before his master teacher[6] and he sees something in favor of the poor man which is to the disadvantage of the rich man, he does not have the right to remain silent:[3] for it is stated, *you shall not be afraid of the face of any man.*[7]

This precept applies in every place and time, for men, since judging cases is [a duty] for them. If someone transgressed this and did not wish to judge a case from the time he knew which way the judgment was tending, as we stated, out of fear of the person on trial, he would violate this negative precept. And should he pervert justice,[8] likewise because of his fear, he would [equally] violate this

וָאֶתְחַנַּן

יֵשׁ בָּהּ שְׁמוֹנֶה מִצְווֹת עֲשֵׂה, וְאַרְבַּע מִצְווֹת לֹא־תַעֲשֶׂה

[שֶׁלֹּא לְהִתְאַוּוֹת מַה שֶּׁבְּיַד אַחֵינוּ בְּנֵי־יִשְׂרָאֵל]

תטז שֶׁנִּמְנַעְנוּ לִקְבֹּעַ מַחֲשַׁבְתֵּנוּ לְהִתְאַוּוֹת מַה שֶּׁבְּיַד אֶחָד מֵאַחֵינוּ בְּנֵי־
יִשְׂרָאֵל, לְפִי שֶׁקְּבִיעוּת הַמַּחֲשָׁבָה בְּתַאֲוָה עַל אוֹתוֹ דָבָר יִהְיֶה סִבָּה לַעֲשׂוֹת
תַּחְבּוּלָה לָקַחַת אוֹתוֹ מִמֶּנּוּ וְאַף־עַל־פִּי שֶׁאֵין רְצוֹנוֹ לְמָכְרוֹ, אוֹ עַל יְדֵי מֶקַח אוֹ
חֲלִיפִין, אוֹ בְּחָזְקָה אִם לֹא נוּכַל בְּעִנְיָן אַחֵר.

וְעַל זֶה נֶאֱמַר "וְלֹא תִתְאַוֶּה בֵּית רֵעֶךָ" וְגוֹמֵר. וְכָתַב הָרַב רַבֵּנוּ מֹשֶׁה בֶּן
מַיְמוֹן זִכְרוֹנוֹ לִבְרָכָה שֶׁאֵין שְׁנֵי הַלָּאוִין, שֶׁהֵן "לֹא תַחְמֹד" שֶׁבְּסֵדֶר וַיִּשְׁמַע יִתְרוֹ
וְ"לֹא תִתְאַוֶּה" שֶׁבְּסֵדֶר זֶה, לָאוִין כְּפוּלִין בְּעִנְיָן אֶחָד, אֲבָל הֵם שְׁנֵי עִנְיָנִים:
שֶׁלָּאו דְּ"לֹא תַחְמֹד" יְמָנֵעֵנוּ מִלָּקַחַת בְּשׁוּם צַד, בֵּין בְּדָמִים בֵּין שֶׁלֹּא בְדָמִים,
מַה שֶּׁקָּנָה זוּלָתֵנוּ, אִם אֵינֶנּוּ חָפֵץ לִמְכֹּר אוֹתוֹ דָבָר; וְלָאו זֶה דְּ"לֹא תִתְאַוֶּה"
יְמָנֵעֵנוּ אֲפִלּוּ הַתַּאֲוָה בּוֹ בְּתוֹךְ לִבֵּנוּ, כִּי עִם הַתַּאֲוָה יָבוֹא לְהִתְחַנֵּן לוֹ וּלְהַכְבִּיד
עָלָיו לְמָכְרוֹ אוֹ לְהַחֲלִיפוֹ לוֹ בְּכְלִי אַחֵר עַל־כָּל־פָּנִים; וְאַף־עַל־פִּי שֶׁהָאֶחָד מֵאֵלּוּ
הַלָּאוִין מוֹשֵׁךְ אֶת חֲבֵרוֹ, שְׁנַיִם יֵחָשְׁבוּ מִכָּל־מָקוֹם. וַהֲרֵי אַתָּה רוֹאֶה הַחִלּוּק
שֶׁבֵּינֵיהֶם.

וְאַל תִּתְמַהּ לוֹמַר: וְאֵיךְ יִהְיֶה בְּיָדוֹ שֶׁל אָדָם לִמְנֹעַ לִבּוֹ מֵהִתְאַוּוֹת אֶל אוֹצַר
כָּל כְּלֵי חֶמְדָּה שֶׁיִּרְאֶה בִּרְשׁוּת חֲבֵרוֹ וְהוּא מְכֻלָּם רֵיק וְרֵיקָם, וְאֵיךְ תָּבוֹא מְנִיעָה
בַּתּוֹרָה בְּמַה שֶׁאִי־אֶפְשָׁר לוֹ לְאָדָם לַעֲמֹד עָלָיו.

שֶׁזֶּה הַדָּבָר אֵינוֹ כֵן, וְלֹא יֹאמְרוּ אוֹתוֹ זוּלָתֵי הַטִּפְּשִׁים הָרָעִים וְהַחַטָּאִים

---

1. ShM negative precept § 266.

2. The Hebrew verbs in the two verses are different, but have about the same meaning in their plain, literal sense.

3. I.e. the earlier verse is taken to refer to *acting* on the intense desire for someone else's possession; see § 38.

4. I.e. one either leads to or results from the other.

injunction, apart from his breaking the injunction, *You shall not pervert justice* (Deuteronomy 16:19).

sidrah va'eth-ḥanan
(Deuteronomy 3:23-7:11)

It contains eight positive and four negative precepts.

[NOT TO DESIRE WHAT BELONGS TO OUR FELLOW-JEWS]

416 that we were forbidden to set our mind to long for what belongs to one of our brother Jews, because fixing one's mind on a desire for that object will be a cause of carrying out a scheme to take it from him even though it is not his wish to sell it—either by purchase or exchange or brute force, if we cannot [do it] any other way.

About this it was stated, *neither shall you desire your neighbor's house*, etc. (Deuteronomy 5:18); and R. Moses b. Maimon of blessed memory wrote[1] that the two precepts—i.e. *You shall not covet your neighbor's house* (Exodus 20:14) in *sidrah yithro*, and *neither shall you desire*[2] in this *sidrah* — are not reiterated injunctions about one theme, but are rather two subjects: The first, *You shall not covet*, forbids us to take in any way, for money or without money, what someone else has acquired if he does not wish to sell that thing;[3] while this injunction, *neither shall you desire*, forbids us even the longing for it within our heart. For with the longing desire, he will come to beseech him and importune him to sell it, or give it him in exchange for another object, under all circumstances. Now, even though one of these injunctions draws the other along with it,[4] they are reckoned as two [negative precepts] nonetheless; and here you see the difference between them.

Now, do not wonder and ask: But how can it be in a man's power to restrain his heart from longing for the treasure of every precious vessel that he may see in his fellow-man's possession, when he is without and deprived of them all? How can a restriction be given in the Torah about something to which a man cannot measure up?

This matter is not so; none but wicked fools who are sinful [enough to pay] with their life would speak so. For it is indeed in a

בְּנַפְשׁוֹתָם: כִּי הָאֻמְנָם בְּיַד הָאָדָם לִמְנֹעַ עַצְמוֹ וּמַחְשְׁבוֹתָיו וְתַאֲוֹתָיו מִכָּל מַה
שֶׁיִּרְצֶה, וּבִרְשׁוּתוֹ וְדַעְתּוֹ לְהַרְחִיק וּלְקָרֵב חֶפְצוֹ בְּכָל הַדְּבָרִים כִּרְצוֹנוֹ, וְלִבּוֹ מָסוּר
בְּיָדוֹ, עַל כָּל אֲשֶׁר יַחְפֹּץ יַטֶּנּוּ, וְהַשֵּׁם, אֲשֶׁר לְפָנָיו נִגְלוּ כָל תַּעֲלוּמוֹת, חֹפֵשׂ כָּל
חַדְרֵי בָטֶן, רוֹאֶה כְלָיוֹת וָלֵב, אֵין אַחַת קְטַנָּה אוֹ גְדוֹלָה טוֹבָה אוֹ רָעָה מִכָּל
מַחְשְׁבוֹת הָאָדָם נֶעֱלֶמֶת מִמֶּנּוּ וְלֹא נִסְתֶּרֶת מִנֶּגֶד עֵינָיו, יָשִׁיב נָקָם לְעוֹבְרֵי רְצוֹנוֹ
בְּלִבָּם, וְנוֹצֵר חֶסֶד לַאֲלָפִים לְאוֹהֲבָיו הַפּוֹנִים לַעֲבוֹדָתוֹ מַחְשְׁבוֹתָם; שֶׁאֵין טוֹב
לָאָדָם כְּמוֹ הַמַּחֲשָׁבָה הַטּוֹבָה וְהַזַּכָּה, כִּי הִיא רֵאשִׁית כָּל הַמַּעֲשִׂים וְסוֹפָן, וְזֶהוּ
לְפִי הַדּוֹמֶה עִנְיַן לֵב טוֹב שֶׁיִּשַׁבְּחוּהוּ חֲכָמִים בְּמַסֶּכֶת אָבוֹת.

וְהָרְאָיָה שֶׁאֵלּוּ שְׁנֵי הַלָּאוִין שֶׁזָּכַרְנוּ חֲלוּקִים בְּעִנְיָנָם וְנֶחְשָׁבִין לִשְׁנַיִם, מַה
שֶׁאָמְרוּ בִמְכִלְתָּא: "לֹא תַחְמֹד בֵּית רֵעֶךָ", וּלְהַלָּן הוּא אוֹמֵר "וְלֹא תִתְאַוֶּה",
לְחַיֵּב עַל הַתַּאֲוָה בִּפְנֵי עַצְמָהּ וְעַל הַחִמּוּד בִּפְנֵי עַצְמוֹ; וְשָׁם נֶאֱמַר: מִנַּיִן שֶׁאִם
נִתְאַוָּה סוֹפוֹ לַחְמֹד — תַּלְמוּד לוֹמַר: לֹא תִתְאַוֶּה וְלֹא תַחְמֹד; מִנַּיִן שֶׁאִם חָמַד
אָדָם סוֹפוֹ לִגְזֹל — תַּלְמוּד לוֹמַר: וְחָמְדוּ שָׂדוֹת וְגָזָלוּ.

שֹׁרֶשׁ מִצְוָה זוֹ יָדוּעַ הוּא, כִּי הַרְחָקַת הַגֶּזֶל מִבֵּין בְּנֵי-אָדָם תּוֹעֶלֶת הַכֹּל הִיא,
וְהַשֵּׂכֶל עֵד נֶאֱמָן בַּדָּבָר. וְאֵין בָּה אֲרִיכוּת דִּינִין, שֶׁכָּל עִנְיָנָהּ מְבֹאָר בַּכָּתוּב.

וְנוֹהֶגֶת בְּכָל מָקוֹם וּבְכָל זְמַן, בִּזְכָרִים וּנְקֵבוֹת; גַּם כָּל בְּנֵי הָעוֹלָם מְחֻיָּבִין בָּהּ,
לְפִי שֶׁהִיא עָנָף לְמִצְוַת גֶּזֶל, שֶׁהִיא אַחַת מִן הַשֶּׁבַע מִצְוֹת שֶׁנִּצְטַוּוּ עֲלֵיהֶם כָּל בְּנֵי
הָעוֹלָם.

וְאַל תִּטְעֶה, בְּנִי, בְּזֶה הַחֶשְׁבּוֹן שֶׁל שֶׁבַע מִצְוֹת בְּנֵי נֹחַ הַיָּדוּעַ וְהַמֻּזְכָּר
בַּתַּלְמוּד, כִּי בֶאֱמֶת שֶׁאוֹתָן שֶׁבַע הֵן כְּעִין כְּלָלוֹת, אֲבָל יֵשׁ בָּהֶן פְּרָטִים הַרְבֵּה,

5. Expression based on Proverbs 21:1. (On this question and answer cf. Ibn
Ezra to Exodus 20:14).

6. Literally, the kidneys. Cf. TB B'rachoth 61a, end: There are two kidneys in a
person; one counsels him to good, and one to evil....The Sages taught: The
kidneys counsel (suggest, prompt), the heart discerns, the tongue articulates, the
mouth completes, etc. See also Jeremiah 11:20, 12:2, 20:12, etc.

7. I.e. He can discern that such an "uncontrollable" desire is controllable. The
two sentences are based on a paragraph in the confession on *Yom Kippur* (the Day of
Atonement): *maḥzor* ed. Birnbaum p. 511 paragraph 3.

8. Expression based on Exodus 20:6.

9. I.e. it is also the result of good deeds that good thoughts can be entertained
the better.

10. MdRSbY, Exodus 20:14 (153).

11. TB Sanhedrin 57a.

man's power to restrain himself, his thoughts and his longing desires, from whatever he wishes. It lies in his free choice and his decision to repel his desire or draw it near in regard to all matters, as he wishes; and his heart is given over into his control; however he pleases, he may swerve it.[5] The Eternal Lord, before whom all secrets are revealed, *searches all the chambers of the innards* (Proverbs 20:27), seeing the organs of understanding[6] and the heart. Not one, large or small, good or bad, out of all the thoughts of a man is hidden from him, or concealed from the range of His sight.[7] He requites with vengeance those who disobey His will in their heart, but He keeps loving-kindness for thousands of generations, for those that love Him[8] who turn their thoughts to His service. For there is nothing so good for a man as a good, pure thought, since that is the beginning of all the [good] deeds, and their end;[9] and this, as it seems, is the significance of the "good heart" which the Sages would praise in the Mishnah tractate *'Avoth* (ii 9).

Now, the proof that these two injunctions that we mentioned are different in their content and reckoned as two [negative precepts] is what was taught in the Midrash *Mechilta*:[10] "You shall not covet your neighbor's house" — and elsewhere it is stated, "neither shall you desire" — to impose punishment for longing desire by itself and for covetous action by itself. And it was also stated there:[10] How do we learn that if a person has formed a longing desire, in the end he will act covetously? — Scripture states, *neither shall you desire*, and also, *You shall not covet*. And how do we learn that if he acted covetously, in the end he will commit robbery? — Scripture states, *And they covet fields and seize them* (Micah 2:2).

The root reason for this precept is known (evident): for the far removal of robbery from among people is of benefit to all; and the human intelligence is a trustworthy witness to this. There is no great length of laws about it, as all its content is clarified in the Writ.

It is in force everywhere, at every time, for both man and woman. All humankind too is duty-bound by it, since it is a branch of the precept about robbery, which is one of the seven precepts that all in the world were commanded to keep.

Now, make no mistake, my son, in this reckoning of the seven precepts for the descendants of Noaḥ, which is known and is mentioned in the Talmud.[11] For in truth, those seven are in the nature of main categories, and they contain many details. Thus you will find

כְּמוֹ שֶׁאַתָּה מוֹצֵא שֶׁאִסּוּר הָעֲרָיוֹת נֶחְשָׁב לָהֶם דֶּרֶךְ כְּלָל לְמִצְוָה אַחַת, וְיֵשׁ בָּהּ פְּרָטִים, כְּגוֹן אִסּוּר אֵם וְאִסּוּר אָחוֹת מִן הָאֵם וְאִסּוּר אֵשֶׁת אִישׁ וְאֵשֶׁת אָב וְזָכָר וּבְהֵמָה. וְכֵן עִנְיַן עֲבוֹדָה זָרָה כֻּלּוֹ נֶחְשָׁב לָהֶם מִצְוָה אַחַת וְיֵשׁ בָּהּ כַּמָּה וְכַמָּה פְּרָטִים, שֶׁהֲרֵי הֵם שָׁוִים בָּהּ לְיִשְׂרָאֵל לְעִנְיָן שֶׁחַיָּבִין בְּכָל מַה שֶּׁבֵּית־דִּין שֶׁל יִשְׂרָאֵל מְמִיתִים עָלֶיהָ; וּכְמוֹ־כֵן נֹאמַר אַחַר שֶׁהִזְהַרְנוּ בְּעִנְיַן הַגֶּזֶל, שֶׁהִזְהֲרוּ גַם־כֵּן בְּכָל הַרְחָקוֹתָיו.

וְאֵין כַּוָּנָתִי לוֹמַר שֶׁיִּהְיוּ כָּמוֹנוּ מֻזְהָרִין עַל זֶה בִּכְלָאו, שֶׁהֵם לֹא נִזְהֲרוּ בִּפְרָטֵי הַלָּאוִין כְּמוֹ יִשְׂרָאֵל, אֲבָל נִזְהֲרוּ דֶּרֶךְ כְּלָל בְּאוֹתָן שֶׁבְּעָה, כְּאִלּוּ תֵּאָמֵר עַל דֶּרֶךְ מָשָׁל שֶׁהִזְהִירָם הַכָּתוּב "אִישׁ אִישׁ אֶל כָּל שְׁאֵר בְּשָׂרוֹ לֹא תִקְרְבוּ", אֶל הָאֵם וְהָאָחוֹת וְכָל הַשְּׁאָר; וּכְמוֹ־כֵן בַּעֲבוֹדָה זָרָה גַם־כֵּן דֶּרֶךְ כְּלָל, וְכֵן בַּגֶּזֶל כְּאִלּוּ נֶאֱמַר לָהֶם "אַל תִּגְזֹלוּ", אֲבָל תִּתְרַחֲקוּ מִמֶּנּוּ בְּתַכְלִית; וּבִכְלָל הַהַרְחָקָה שֶׁלֹּא לַחְמֹד.

אֲבָל בְּיִשְׂרָאֵל אֵין הָעִנְיָן כֵּן, שֶׁרָצָה הַמָּקוֹם לְזַכּוֹתָם וְהִרְבָּה לָהֶם מִצְווֹת יוֹתֵר מֵהֶן, וְגַם בְּאוֹתָן שֶׁנִּצְטַוִּינוּ אֲנַחְנוּ וָהֵן, זָכִינוּ אֲנַחְנוּ לִהְיוֹת צֻוּוּיֵינוּ עֲלֵיהֶן בְּמִצְווֹת עֲשֵׂה וְלָאוִין נִפְרָדִים; וְכָל זֶה זְכוּת וְטוֹבָה לְנַפְשֵׁנוּ, שֶׁכָּל הָעוֹשֶׂה מִצְוָה אַחַת קוֹנֶה לוֹ פְּרַקְלִיט אֶחָד.

וְעוֹבֵר עַל זֶה וְקוֹבֵעַ מַחְשַׁבְתּוֹ לְהִתְאַוּוֹת בְּמַה שֶּׁיֵּשׁ לְזוּלָתוֹ, עוֹבֵר עַל לָאו זֶה; וְאֵין בּוֹ מַלְקוֹת לְפִי שֶׁאֵין בּוֹ מַעֲשֶׂה, אֲבָל עָנְשׁוֹ גָּדוֹל מְאֹד, כִּי הוּא סִבָּה לְכַמָּה תַקָּלוֹת, כְּמוֹ שֶׁיָּדוּעַ בְּמַעֲשֵׂה אַחְאָב וְנָבוֹת.

[מִצְוַת אַחְדוּת הַשֵּׁם]

תיז שֶׁנִּצְטַוִּינוּ לְהַאֲמִין כִּי הַשֵּׁם (יִתְבָּרַךְ) שֶׁהוּא הַפּוֹעֵל כָּל הַמְּצִיאוּת, אָדוֹן

---

12. So *ibid.* 58a.

13. So *ibid.* 56b.

14. Three words in the Hebrew—הן, זכינו אנחנו—are present only in the very oldest of the four manuscripts. In all other copies, manuscript or print, they are missing (evidently by an early copyist's oversight between identical words), leaving the text veritably beyond decipherment.

15. So Mishnah, 'Avoth iv 11.

that the ban on consanguineous, forbidden conjugal relations is reckoned in a general way as one precept; yet there are quite many details in it: for instance, the ban on a mother, the ban on a sister from the same mother, and the ban on a married woman and a father's wife, and on a male and an animal.[12] So too, the entire matter of idol-worship is reckoned as one precept for them, yet there are many, many details in it—since they are equal to the Israelites about it, in regard to the fact that they are punishable for anything over which an Israelite *beth din* (court) would sentence to death.[13] Then we likewise say that since they were adjured about robbery, they were equally adjured about all decrees to keep a person far away from it.

It is not my intention, though, to say that like us, they are adjured about this by a negative precept. For they were not cautioned about details of injunctions like the Israelites, but were rather adjured in a general way about those seven—as you might say by way of illustration, that Scripture cautioned them, *No man shall come intimately close to anyone near of kin to him* (Leviticus 18:6), to a mother, sister, and all the rest; and so likewise about idol-worship, equally in a general way. Then so too about robbery: it is as though they were told, "Do not commit robbery—but get utterly far away from it"; and included in getting far from it is the rule not to act covetously.

For Israelites, though, the matter is not so: the omnipresent God wished to make them meritorious, and He increased the precepts for them far beyond the number for them [the other nations]; and even with those that [both] we and they were commanded, we merited[14] that our orders about them are [often] through separate positive and negative commandments. All this provides merit and good reward for our spirits, because anyone who does one *mitzvah* (observes one precept) gains one guardian angel.[15]

If someone transgresses this and sets his mind to long for something that another has, he violates this negative precept; but it entails no flogging of whiplashes, since it involves no physical action. Yet his punishment will be very great, since it is a cause of many misfortunes, as is evident in the incident of Aḥab and Naboth (I Kings 21).

[THE PRECEPT OF THE ONENESS OF THE
ETERNAL LORD]

417 that we were commanded to believe that the Eternal Lord (be He blessed), the One who has produced all existence, is the Ruler of

⟨249⟩

הַכֹּל, אֶחָד בְּלִי שׁוּם שִׁתּוּף, שֶׁנֶּאֱמַר: שְׁמַע יִשְׂרָאֵל יְיָ אֱלֹהֵינוּ יְיָ אֶחָד; וְזֶה מִצְוַת
עֲשֵׂה הוּא, אֵינוֹ הַגָּדָה, אֲבָל פֵּרוּשׁ "שְׁמַע", כְּלוֹמַר קַבֵּל מִמֶּנִּי דָּבָר זֶה וְתָדְעֵהוּ
וְהַאֲמֶן בּוֹ, כִּי יְיָ שֶׁהוּא אֱלֹהֵינוּ, אֶחָד הוּא. וְהָרְאָיָה שֶׁזּוֹ הִיא מִצְוַת עֲשֵׂה, אָמְרָם
זִכְרוֹנָם לִבְרָכָה תָּמִיד בְּמִדְרָשָׁם: "עַל־מְנָת לְיַחֵד שְׁמוֹ", "כְּדֵי לְקַבֵּל עָלָיו מַלְכוּת
שָׁמַיִם", כְּלוֹמַר הַהוֹדָאָה בַּיִּחוּד וְהָאֱמוּנָה.

שֹׁרֶשׁ מִצְוָה זוֹ יָדוּעַ, כִּי זֶה עִקַּר אֱמוּנַת כָּל בְּנֵי הָעוֹלָם, וְהוּא הָעַמּוּד הֶחָזָק
שֶׁלֵּב כָּל בֶּן־דַּעַת סָמוּךְ עָלָיו.

מִדִּינֵי הַמִּצְוָה, מַה שֶׁאָמְרוּ זִכְרוֹנָם לִבְרָכָה שֶׁחַיָּב כָּל אֶחָד מִיִּשְׂרָאֵל לֵהָרֵג עַל
מִצְוַת יִחוּד, לְפִי שֶׁכָּל שֶׁאֵינוֹ מוֹדֶה בְּיִחוּדוֹ בָּרוּךְ הוּא, כְּאִלּוּ כּוֹפֵר בָּעִקָּר, שֶׁאֵין
שְׁלֵמוּת הַמֶּמְשָׁלָה וְהַהוֹד אֶלָּא עִם הָאַחֲדוּת הַגָּמוּר, וְלֵב כָּל חֲכַם־לֵב יִבְחַן זֶה;
וְאִם־כֵּן הֲרֵי מִצְוָה זֶה מִכְּלַל אִסּוּר עֲבוֹדָה זָרָה, שֶׁאֲנַחְנוּ מְצֻוִּין לֵהָרֵג עָלָיו בְּכָל
מָקוֹם וּבְכָל שָׁעָה.

וְיֶתֶר פְּרָטֶיהָ, מְפֻזָּרִין בְּמִדְרָשׁוֹת וּבִמְקוֹמוֹת בַּתַּלְמוּד; וְשָׁם מַעֲשִׂים הַרְבֵּה
מִכַּמָּה בְּנֵי־יִשְׂרָאֵל גְּדוֹלִים וּקְטַנִּים שֶׁנֶּהֶרְגוּ עַל קְדֻשַּׁת יִחוּדוֹ בָּרוּךְ הוּא, זֵכֶר כֻּלָּם
לִבְרָכָה.

וְנוֹהֶגֶת מִצְוָה זוֹ בְּכָל מָקוֹם וּבְכָל זְמַן, בִּזְכָרִים וּנְקֵבוֹת. וְעוֹבֵר עַל זֶה וְאֵינוֹ
מַאֲמִין בְּיִחוּדוֹ בָּרוּךְ הוּא, בִּטֵּל עֲשֵׂה זֶה, וְגַם כָּל שְׁאָר מִצְוֹת הַתּוֹרָה, כִּי כֻלָּם
תְּלוּיוֹת בֶּאֱמוּנַת אֱלֹהוּתוֹ וְיִחוּדוֹ; וְנִקְרָא כּוֹפֵר בָּעִקָּר וְאֵינוֹ מִכְּלַל בְּנֵי־יִשְׂרָאֵל,
אֶלָּא מִכְּלַל הַמִּינִין, וְהִבְדִּילוֹ יְיָ לְרָעָה. וְהַמַּאֲמִין בַּיְיָ וּבוֹטֵחַ בּוֹ יִשְׂגָּב.

§417   1. I.e. from Moses, who proclaimed this to the Israelites in the wilderness. It was not a mere piece of information that he gave them, but a principle of faith for Jewry to believe throughout its existence.

2. I.e. in their exegetical interpretation and homiletic teaching.

3. In ShM positive precept §2 we read: "in order to declare Me one"—and many [statements] like this. Their meaning in this matter is that He took us out of slavery and performed for us the acts of kindness and good favor that He did, only on condition that we believe in His oneness—for we are duty-bound about this. (Our author's version may be from the lost first draft of ShM, which Rambam thus later rewrote.) Cf. Sh'moth Rabbah 29, 3: Said R. Toviah b. R. Yitzḥak: *I am the Lord your God [who took you out of the land of Egypt]* (Exodus 20:2)—for on this condition did I take you out of the land of Egypt: that you accept My divine sovereignty upon yourselves.

4. ShM *ibid.* reads: This precept is also called "the kingship of Heaven," for they would say, "in order to accept" etc. Cf. Mishnah, B'rachoth ii 2 (TB 13a): R. Joshua b. Korḥa said: Why does the section of *Sh'ma* (Deuteronomy 6:4–9) precede the section of *v'hayah 'im shamo'a* (ibid. 11:13–21)?—so that one should first accept upon himself [submit to] the yoke of the precepts.

all, one, without any partnership — as it is stated, *Hear, Israel: the Lord our God, the Lord is one* (Deuteronomy 6:4). For this is a positive precept, not an informative statement. The meaning is rather: "Hear" — i.e. accept this matter from me,[1] and know Him and believe in Him, that the Lord, who is our God, is one. The proof that this is a positive precept lies in what the Sages of blessed memory would constantly say in their *midrash*:[2] "in order [for us] to declare His name one";[3] "in order to accept on oneself the yoke of the kingship of Heaven"[4] — in other words, the acknowledgment of the oneness and the belief [in it].

The root purpose of this precept is known (evident), since this is the core element of the faith of all mankind, and it is the mighty pillar on which the heart of every intelligent being sets its reliance.

Among the laws of the precept, there is what the Sages of blessed memory taught:[5] that everyone in Jewry is duty-bound to let himself be killed [if necessary] over the precept of declaring Him one, because if anyone does not acknowledge His oneness (blessed is He), it is as though he denies the main principle [of His existence]. For there could be perfection of His dominion and majesty only with complete, utter oneness; the heart of every man of wise perception can discern this. This being so, this *mitzvah* is then in the same category as the ban on idolatry, over which we are commanded to undergo death [if necessary] at any place and any time.

The rest of its details are scattered in the Midrashim and in various places in the Talmud. There many incidents are told of a good number of Jews, great and lowly, who were put to death for the sanctification of His oneness (blessed is He); may the memory of them all be for blessing.

This precept applies in every place and time, for both man and woman. If a person violates this and does not believe in His oneness (blessed is He), he thus disobeys this positive precept, and so too all the other precepts of the Torah: for they all are founded on[6] faith in His divinity and oneness. He is then called a denier of the main principle, and is not included in the category of Jews, but is rather in the category of heretics; *and the Lord shall set him apart for evil* (Deuteronomy 29:20). But he who believes in the Lord and trusts in Him will be made safe on high.

5. TB B'rachoth 61b.

‏וְזֹאת אַחַת מִן הַמִּצְוֹת שֶׁאָמַרְנוּ בִּתְחִלַּת הַסֵּפֶר שֶׁהָאָדָם חַיָּב בָּהֶם בְּהַתְמָדָה,‏
‏כְּלוֹמַר שֶׁלֹּא יַפְסִיק חִיּוּבָן מֵעָלָיו לְעוֹלָם וַאֲפִלּוּ רֶגַע קָטָן.‏

‏[מִצְוַת אַהֲבַת הַשֵּׁם]‏

‏תיח‏ ‏שֶׁנִּצְטַוֵּינוּ לֶאֱהֹב אֶת הַמָּקוֹם בָּרוּךְ הוּא, שֶׁנֶּאֱמַר: וְאָהַבְתָּ אֵת יי אֱלֹהֶיךָ.‏
‏וְעִנְיַן הַמִּצְוָה, שֶׁנְּחַשֵּׁב וְנִתְבּוֹנֵן בְּפִקּוּדָיו וּפְעֻלּוֹתָיו עַד שֶׁנַּשִּׂיגֵהוּ כְּפִי יְכָלְתֵּנוּ‏
‏וְנִתְעַנֵּג בְּהַשָּׂגָתוֹ בְּתַכְלִית הָעֹנֶג, וְזֹאת הִיא הָאַהֲבָה הַמְחֻיֶּבֶת.‏

‏וּבִלְשׁוֹן סִפְרִי: לְפִי שֶׁנֶּאֱמַר "וְאָהַבְתָּ", אֵינִי יוֹדֵעַ כֵּיצַד אוֹהֵב אָדָם אֶת הַמָּקוֹם‏
‏— תַּלְמוּד לוֹמַר "וְהָיוּ הַדְּבָרִים הָאֵלֶּה אֲשֶׁר אָנֹכִי מְצַוְּךָ הַיּוֹם עַל לְבָבֶךָ",‏
‏שֶׁמִּתּוֹךְ כָּךְ אַתָּה מַכִּיר אֶת מִי שֶׁאָמַר וְהָיָה הָעוֹלָם — כְּלוֹמַר שֶׁעִם הַתְבּוֹנְנוּת‏
‏בַּתּוֹרָה תִּתְיַשֵּׁב הָאַהֲבָה בַּלֵּב בְּהֶכְרֵחַ; וְאָמְרוּ זִכְרוֹנָם לִבְרָכָה שֶׁזֹּאת הָאַהֲבָה‏
‏תְּחַיֵּב הָאָדָם לְעוֹרֵר בְּנֵי־אָדָם בְּאַהֲבָתוֹ לְעָבְדוֹ, כְּמוֹ שֶׁמָּצִינוּ בְּאַבְרָהָם.‏

‏שֹׁרֶשׁ מִצְוָה זוֹ יָדוּעַ, שֶׁלֹּא יְקַיֵּם הָאָדָם מִצְוֹת הַשֵּׁם בָּרוּךְ הוּא יָפֶה רַק‏
‏בְּאַהֲבָתוֹ אוֹתוֹ.‏

‏דִּינֵי הַמִּצְוָה, שֶׁרָאוּי לוֹ לָאָדָם שֶׁיָּשִׂים כָּל מַחֲשַׁבְתּוֹ וְכָל מְגַמָּתוֹ אַחַר אַהֲבַת‏
‏הַשֵּׁם, וְיַעֲרִיךְ בְּלִבּוֹ תָּמִיד כִּי כָל מַה שֶּׁהוּא בָעוֹלָם מֵעֹשֶׁר וּבָנִים וְכָבוֹד, הַכֹּל‏
‏כְּאַיִן וּכְאֶפֶס נָתֹהוּ כְּנֶגֶד אַהֲבָתוֹ בָּרוּךְ הוּא; וְיִגַּע תָּמִיד כָּל הַיּוֹם בְּבַקָּשַׁת הַחָכְמָה‏
‏לְמַעַן יַשִּׂיג יְדִיעָה בּוֹ. סוֹף דָּבָר, יַעֲשֶׂה כָּל יְכָלְתּוֹ לְהַרְגִּיל מַחֲשְׁבוֹת לִבּוֹ כָּל הַיּוֹם‏
‏בֶּאֱמוּנָתוֹ וְיִחוּדוֹ, עַד שֶׁלֹּא יְהִי רֶגַע בַּיּוֹם וּבַלַּיְלָה בַּהֲקִיצוֹ שֶׁלֹּא יְהֵא זוֹכֵר אַהֲבַת‏
‏אֲדוֹנָיו בְּתוֹךְ לִבּוֹ. וְהָעִנְיָן עַל דֶּרֶךְ מָשָׁל, שֶׁיְּהֵא נִזְכָּר בְּאַהֲבַת הַשֵּׁם תָּמִיד כְּזִכְרוֹן‏

---

6. Literally, they all depend on.

§418   1. This is the reading of the three oldest manuscripts and the first edition, in accord with ShM positive precept §3, on which the first two paragraphs are based. The fourth manuscript and later editions reverse it: His handiwork and His commandments.

2. This is the reading of the fourth manuscript and editions after the first, in accord with ShM *ibid.* The older manuscripts and the first edition have *b'hashgaḥatho,* "in His watchful care."

3. Sifre, Deuteronomy § 33.

4. Through the Torah, with persistence and time, one gains a conception or appreciation of the Creator who gave the Torah, His immanence and influence in this world; and this must inevitably inculcate love of Him.

5. Sifre, Deuteronomy § 32.

6. Later editions add *umemshalah,* "and dominion"; it is, however, neither in the manuscripts nor in the first editions.

This is one of the precepts which we said at the beginning of the work a man is obligated to observe constantly: in other words, their duty never ceases to be imposed on him, even for a small instant.

[THE PRECEPT OF LOVE FOR THE ETERNAL LORD]

418 that we were commanded to love the omnipresent God, blessed is He: as it is stated, *And you shall love the Lord your God* (Deuteronomy 6:5). The substance of the precept is that we should consider and reflect on His commandments and His handiwork,[1] until we attain a concept of Him according to our ability, and we can then feel joy in apperceiving Him,[2] with the utmost delight. This is the obligatory, essential love.

In the language of the Midrash *Sifre*:[3] While it is stated, *and you shall love,* I do not know how a man is to love the omnipresent God; hence Scripture states, *And these words which I command you this day shall be on your heart* (Deuteronomy 6:6): for as a result of this you will "recognize" the One who spoke and the world came into existence. In other words, with reflection-understanding in the Torah, the love [of God] settles perforce in the heart.[4] And the Sages of blessed memory said[5] that this love should impel a man to arouse people about love for Him, to serve and worship Him—as we find in the instance of Abraham.

The root reason for this precept is known (evident): for man will not fulfill well the precepts of the Eternal Lord, blessed is He, unless he loves Him.

The laws of the precept are that it is right for a man to set his whole mind and his whole aim toward love for the Eternal Lord. He should constantly appreciate in his heart that all there is in the world of wealth, sons, and honor[6]—all is as nought and nothing, an utter void compared to love for Him, blessed is He. Then let him toil all the day, constantly, in search of wisdom, in order that he might attain a conception of Him.[7] Over and above everything, let him do all he can to accustom the thoughts of his heart the entire day to His faith and His oneness, until there will not be one moment, day or night, when he is awake, that he does not recall his love for his [Divine] Master within his heart. The meaning is, by way of analogy, that he should bear in mind his love for the Eternal Lord as one who yearns

7. See note 4.

הַחוֹשֵׁק תַּכְלִית הַחֵשֶׁק בַּחֲשׁוּקָתוֹ כָּל הַיּוֹם, שֶׁיַּשִּׂיג לַהֲבִיאָהּ אֶל בֵּיתוֹ. וְיֶתֶר פְּרָטֶיהָ, מְבֹאָרִים בִּמְקוֹמוֹת בַּתַּלְמוּד בְּפִזּוּר וּבְמִדְרָשִׁים.

וְנוֹהֶגֶת בְּכָל מָקוֹם וּבְכָל זְמַן, בִּזְכָרִים וּנְקֵבוֹת. וְעוֹבֵר עַל זֶה וְקוֹבֵעַ מַחְשְׁבוֹתָיו בָּעִנְיָנִים הַשְּׁמֵימִיִּים וּבְהַבְלֵי הָעוֹלָם שֶׁלֹּא לְשֵׁם שָׁמַיִם, רַק לְהִתְעַנֵּג בָּהֶם לְבַד, אוֹ לְהַשִּׂיג כְּבוֹד הָעוֹלָם הַזֶּה הַכּוֹאֵב, לְהַגְדִּיל שְׁמוֹ, לֹא לְכַוָּנָה לְהֵיטִיב לַטּוֹבִים וּלְחַזֵּק יְדֵי הַיְשָׁרִים, בִּטֵּל עֲשֵׂה זֶה וְעָנְשׁוֹ גָּדוֹל. וְזֹאת מִן הַמִּצְוֹת הַתְּמִידִיּוֹת עַל הָאָדָם וּמֻטָּלוֹת עָלָיו לְעוֹלָם.

[מִצְוַת תַּלְמוּד תּוֹרָה]

תיט מִצְוַת עֲשֵׂה לִלְמֹד חָכְמַת הַתּוֹרָה וּלְלַמְּדָהּ, כְּלוֹמַר כֵּיצַד נַעֲשֶׂה הַמִּצְוֹת וְנִשָּׁמֵר מִמַּה שֶּׁמְּנָעָנוּ הָאֵל מִמֶּנּוּ, וְלָדַעַת גַּם־כֵּן מִשְׁפְּטֵי הַתּוֹרָה עַל כִּוּוּן הָאֱמֶת; וְעַל כָּל זֶה נֶאֱמַר "וְשִׁנַּנְתָּם לְבָנֶיךָ"; וְאָמְרוּ זִכְרוֹנָם לִבְרָכָה: "בָּנֶיךָ", אֵלּוּ תַלְמִידֶיךָ; וְכֵן אַתָּה מוֹצֵא שֶׁהַתַּלְמִידִים קְרוּיִין בָּנִים, שֶׁנֶּאֱמַר: וַיֵּצְאוּ בְנֵי הַנְּבִיאִים. וְשָׁם נֶאֱמַר "וְשִׁנַּנְתָּם", שֶׁיְּהוּ מְסֻדָּרִין בְּתוֹךְ פִּיךָ, כְּשֶׁאָדָם שׁוֹאֵלְךָ דָּבָר, אַל תְּהֵא מְגַמְגֵּם לוֹ, אֶלָּא תְּהֵא אוֹמֵר לוֹ מִיָּד.

וְנִכְפְּלָה מִצְוָה זוֹ בִּמְקוֹמוֹת רַבִּים, שֶׁנֶּאֱמַר: וּלְמַדְתֶּם (ועשיתם) [אֹתָם וּשְׁמַרְתֶּם לַעֲשׂוֹתָם], לְמַעַן יִלְמְדוּן, וְלִמַּדְתֶּם אֹתָם אֶת בְּנֵיכֶם.

שֹׁרֶשׁ מִצְוָה זוֹ יָדוּעַ, כִּי בְלִמּוּד יֵדַע הָאָדָם דַּרְכֵי הַשֵּׁם יִתְבָּרַךְ, וְזוּלָתוֹ לֹא יֵדַע וְלֹא יָבִין וְנֶחְשַׁב כִּבְהֵמָה.

מִדִּינֵי הַמִּצְוָה, מַה שֶּׁאָמְרוּ זִכְרוֹנָם לִבְרָכָה: מֵאֵימָתַי מַתְחִיל הָאָב לְלַמֵּד אֶת בְּנוֹ תוֹרָה — מִשֶּׁיַּתְחִיל לְדַבֵּר מְלַמְּדוֹ "תּוֹרָה צִוָּה לָנוּ מֹשֶׁה", וּפָסוּק רִאשׁוֹן

---

8. Similarly MT *hilchoth t'shuvah* x 3.

9. So read the old manuscripts and the first edition: *ha-ko'év*. Later editions have *ha-kozév*, "false, deceiving" — perhaps because it is apt for the esteem and prestige which this world can bestow.

§419   1. Sifre, Deuteronomy § 34.

2. The original reads, "and you shall learn and you shall do" — already cited as a Scriptural text in TB Yevamoth 109b, whence it is likewise given in ShM positive precept § 11 (the basis of these first two paragraphs). There is, however, no such verse in Scripture; and the emendation of R. 'El'azar Landa in his *haggahoth* to the Talmud (printed also in the margin of TB ed. Vilna, *ad loc.*) has consequently been adopted.

3. TB Sukkah 42a.

[for something] with an utter longing remembers it, in his yearning all day to succeed in bringing it to his house.[8] The rest of its details are explained in various places in the Talmud, scattered about, and in the Midrashim.

It applies in every place, at every time, for both man and woman. If a person transgresses this and fixes his thoughts on the material interests and vapid vanities of the world, not for the sake of Heaven but only to pleasure himself in them, or to attain the esteem of this painful[9] world, to make his name great, not with any intention to do good for good people and to strengthen the hands of the honest — he disobeys this positive precept, and his punishment will be great. This is one of the constant precepts for a man, forever imposed on him [to observe].

[THE PRECEPT OF TORAH STUDY]

419 It is a positive precept to learn the wisdom of the Torah and teach it: in other words, how we are to carry out the precepts and keep away from what God has forbidden us; and likewise to know the ordinances of the Torah in accord with the truth. About all this it was stated, *and you shall teach them diligently to your children* (Deuteronomy 6:7), on which our Sages of blessed memory taught:[1] "your children" means your pupils; and so you find that students are called sons: for it is stated, *And there came forth the sons of the prophets* (2 Kings 2: 3). It was further stated there:[1] "and you shall teach them diligently" — [the Hebrew means] that they [the words of Torah] should be arranged in order in your mouth; when a man asks you something, do not stammer hesitantly at him, but rather answer him directly.

This precept was reiterated in many instances: as it is stated, *and you shall learn them and take care to do them* (Deuteronomy 5:1);[2] *that they may learn* (Deuteronomy 31:12); *And you shall teach them to your children* (ibid. 11:19).

The root reason for this precept is known (obvious): for by learning, a man will know the ways of the Eternal Lord (be He blessed), while without it he will neither know nor understand, and will be reckoned as an animal.

Among the laws of the precept there is what the Sages of blessed memory said:[3] From what time is a father to start teaching his son Torah? — From the time he begins to speak, he is to teach him, *Moses*

מִקְרִיאַת שְׁמַע שֶׁהוּא "שְׁמַע יִשְׂרָאֵל", וְאַחַר־כָּךְ מְלַמְּדוֹ מְעַט מְעַט מִפְּסוּקֵי הַתּוֹרָה, עַד שֶׁיְּהֵא בֶּן שֵׁשׁ אוֹ בֶּן שֶׁבַע, שֶׁמּוֹלִיכוֹ אֵצֶל מְלַמְּדֵי תִינוֹקוֹת. וְרָאוּי לְכָל בֶּן־דַּעַת שֶׁיִּתֵּן לִבּוֹ שֶׁלֹּא לְהַכְבִּיד עַל הַיֶּלֶד בַּלִּמּוּד בְּעוֹדֶנּוּ רַךְ הָאֵיבָרִים וְרַךְ הַלֵּבָב, עַד שֶׁיִּגְדַּל וְיִתְחַזֵּק כֹּחַ לִבּוֹ וְתִתְקֵף אֵיבָרָיו, וְעַצְמוֹתָיו יְמָלְאוּ מֹחַ, וְיוּכַל לִסְבֹּל יְגִיעַת הַלִּמּוּד וְלֹא יִקְרְנוּ חֳלִי הַהִתְעַלְּפוּת בְּסִבַּת הַיְגִיעָה רַבָּה עָלָיו; וְאוּלָם אַחַר הִתְחַזֵּק כֹּחוֹ וְיֵאוֹרוּ עֵינָיו לְהָבִין לְקוֹל מוֹרָיו, אָז רָאוּי וְכָשֵׁר הַדָּבָר וּמְחֻיָּב לְהָבִיא צַנָּארוֹ בְּעֻלָּה שֶׁל תּוֹרָה, וְלֹא יַרְפּוּהוּ מִמֶּנָּה אֲפִלּוּ כְּחוּט הַשַּׂעֲרָה, יַשְׁקוּהוּ תָּמִיד מִיֵּין רִקְחָהּ וְיַאֲכִילוּהוּ מִדִּבְשָׁהּ.

וְכֵן מֵעִנְיַן הַמִּצְוָה מַה שֶּׁאָמְרוּ זִכְרוֹנָם לִבְרָכָה: עַד הֵיכָן חַיָּב אָדָם לְלַמֵּד אֶת בְּנוֹ תוֹרָה — אָמַר רַב יְהוּדָה אָמַר שְׁמוּאֵל: כְּגוֹן זְבוּלוּן בֶּן דָּן — פֵּרוּשׁ: אָדָם הָיָה בְדוֹרָם שֶׁשְּׁמוֹ כֵן, שֶׁלִּמְּדוֹ אֲבִי־אָבִיו מִקְרָא וּמִשְׁנָה, תַּלְמוּד, הֲלָכוֹת וְאַגָּדוֹת. וְהִקְשׁוּ עַל זֶה בַּגְּמָרָא מַה שֶּׁהִקְשׁוּ, וְהָיָה הַתֵּרוּץ שֶׁהֶחָיֵיב לְלַמְּדָם מִקְרָא דְּהַיְינוּ תוֹרָה, כְּמוֹ שֶׁעָשָׂה אֲבִי־אָבִיו שֶׁל זְבוּלוּן, וְאַף־עַל־פִּי שֶׁזְּבוּלוּן בֶּן דָּן לִמְּדוֹ אֲבִי־אָבִיו יוֹתֵר. וּמִי שֶׁהוֹסִיף עַל חִיּוּב הַמִּצְוָה כַּאֲבִי־אָבִיו שֶׁל זְבוּלוּן בֶּן דָּן, תָּבוֹא עָלָיו בְּרָכָה.

וּמִי שֶׁלֹּא לִמְּדוּ אוֹתוֹ אֲבוֹתָיו שֶׁהֵם חַיָּבִין בָּזֶה, כְּגוֹן אָבִיו וַאֲבִי־אָבִיו, חַיָּב לְלַמֵּד עַצְמוֹ כְּשֶׁיִּהְיֶה גָדוֹל וְיַכִּיר בַּדָּבָר, שֶׁנֶּאֱמַר: וּלְמַדְתֶּם... (וַעֲשִׂיתֶם אֹתָם) [וּשְׁמַרְתֶּם לַעֲשֹׂתָם]. וְאִם הָיוּ הָאָב וְהַבֵּן צְרִיכִין לִלְמֹד וְאֵין בְּיָדוֹ שֶׁל אָב שֶׁיּוּכְלוּ שְׁנֵיהֶן לִלְמֹד תָּמִיד הוּא קוֹדֵם לִבְנוֹ, וְאִם בְּנוֹ נָבוֹן מִמֶּנּוּ וְתַלְמוּדוֹ מִתְקַיֵּם בְּיָדוֹ יוֹתֵר מִמֶּנּוּ, בְּנוֹ קוֹדְמוֹ.

וְעַד אֵימָתַי חַיָּב כָּל אָדָם לִלְמֹד תּוֹרָה — עַד יוֹם מוֹתוֹ, שֶׁנֶּאֱמַר: וּפֶן יָסוּרוּ

---

4. TB Bava Bathra 21a; MT *hilchoth talmud torah* i 6.

5. TB Kiddushin 30a.

6. *Ibid.* 29b; MT *ibid.* 3–4. (The Scriptural source has been corrected in the Hebrew in accord with MT. The inaccurate reading may have been derived unwittingly from the *Sh'ma* recited daily: Deuteronomy 11:19 and Numbers 15:39.)

commanded us the Torah (Deuteronomy 33:4), and the first verse of *Sh'ma yisra'el*, which is: *Hear, Israel (ibid.* 6:4); then he teaches him, bit by bit, some of the verses of the Torah, till he is a lad of six or seven, when he is to take him to children's teachers.[4] It would be right for every person of sense to take heed not to overburden the child with study while he is yet tender of limb and tender of heart—until he grows and the strength of his heart and the energy of his limbs are increased, and his bones fill with marrow, and he will be able to bear the exertion of study without falling ill with the fainting disease on account of the great effort demanded of him. Rather, after his energy grows strong and his eyes are alight to hearken with understanding to the voice of his teacher, then it is a right, proper and essential thing to bring his neck within the yoke of the Torah, and let him not be released from it even a hairsbreadth; let him be given of its spiced wine to drink and of its honey to eat.

There is likewise in the subject-matter of the precept what the Sages of blessed memory said:[5] To what extent is a man obligated to teach his son Torah? Said R. Judah in the name of Sh'mu'él: Like Zebulun b. Dan, for example—meaning that a man lived in their generation, so named, whose father's father taught him Scripture, Mishnah, Talmud, definitive law, and homiletic interpretations and narratives. A certain difficulty was then raised about this in the Talmud; and the reply was that the obligation is to teach him Scripture, which is the [Written] Torah, as Zebulun's paternal grandfather did, although Zebulun b. Dan's grandfather [actually] taught him more. But if someone does go beyond the obligation of the precept, like Zebulun b. Dan's grandfather, blessing will be bestowed upon him.

If someone was not taught by his fathers who have this duty, such as his father and his father's father, he is obligated to teach himself when he is grown and becomes aware of the matter: for it is stated, *and you shall learn them and observe to do them* (Deuteronomy 5:1).[6] If a father and son need to learn [the Torah] and the father does not have the means to enable both of them to study regularly, he takes precedence over his son. If, however, his son has greater comprehension than he and his learning endures with him [the son] more so than with him, his son takes precedence over him.[6]

Until when is every man duty-bound to study Torah?—till the day of his death: for it is stated, *and lest they depart from your heart all the*

מִלְּבָבְךָ כֹּל יְמֵי חַיֶּיךָ. וְעוֹד הִפְלִיגוּ חֲכָמִים בַּדָּבָר עַל דֶּרֶךְ הַמּוּסָר וְלִלַמֵּד בְּנֵי־
אָדָם חֵפֶץ, וְאָמְרוּ שֶׁאֲפִלּוּ בִשְׁעַת מִיתָה חַיָּב לִלְמֹד תּוֹרָה, שֶׁנֶּאֱמַר: זֹאת הַתּוֹרָה,
אָדָם כִּי יָמוּת.

וְכָל אֶחָד מִיִּשְׂרָאֵל חַיָּב בְּתַלְמוּד תּוֹרָה, בֵּין עָנִי בֵּין עָשִׁיר בֵּין בָּרִיא בֵּין בַּעַל
יִסּוּרִין, וּכְבָר אָמְרוּ זִכְרוֹנָם לִבְרָכָה שֶׁבְּעֵסֶק הַתּוֹרָה יִתְרַפְּאוּ כָל הָאֵבָרִים; וַאֲפִלּוּ
עָנִי הַמְחַזֵּר עַל הַפְּתָחִים, וַאֲפִלּוּ בַּעַל אִשָּׁה וּבָנִים, הַכֹּל חַיָּבִים לִקְבֹּעַ עִתִּים
בַּתּוֹרָה בַּיּוֹם וּבַלַּיְלָה, שֶׁנֶּאֱמַר: וְהָגִיתָ בּוֹ יוֹמָם וָלָיְלָה.

וּתְחִלַּת דִּינוֹ שֶׁל אָדָם אַחַר הַמָּוֶת הוּא עַל שֶׁנִּתְבַּטֵּל מִן הַלִּמּוּד, וּכְמוֹ שֶׁדָּרְשׁוּ
זִכְרוֹנָם לִבְרָכָה מִדִּכְתִיב ״פּוֹטֵר מַיִם רֵאשִׁית מָדוֹן״, כְּלוֹמַר מִי שֶׁפּוֹטֵר עַצְמוֹ מִן
הַמַּיִם, רֵאשִׁית קְטָטָה הוּא לְנַפְשׁוֹ אַחַר שֶׁיָּמוּת, וְאֵין מַיִם אֶלָּא תוֹרָה, שֶׁנֶּאֱמַר:
הוֹי כָּל צָמֵא לְכוּ לַמַּיִם. וְנִמְשְׁלוּ דִבְרֵי תוֹרָה לְמַיִם לְפִי שֶׁאֵין הַתּוֹרָה מִתְקַיֶּמֶת
אֶלָּא בְּאִישׁ דַּכָּא וּשְׁפַל רוּחַ וְלֹא בִגְבַהּ לֵב, כְּמוֹ שֶׁהַמַּיִם גַּם־כֵּן אֵין עוֹמְדִין
בֶּהָרִים אֶלָּא בָּעֲמָקִים.

וְכֵן מַה שֶּׁאָמְרוּ זִכְרוֹנָם לִבְרָכָה שֶׁחַיָּב אָדָם לְחַלֵּק זְמַנּוֹ לִשְׁלֹשָׁה חֲלָקִים,
שְׁלִישׁ בְּעֵסֶק תּוֹרָה שֶׁבִּכְתָב, וּשְׁלִישׁ בְּעֵסֶק תּוֹרָה שֶׁבְּעַל־פֶּה, כְּלוֹמַר לְהַרְגִּיל
עַצְמוֹ לִהְיוֹת בָּקִי בְּגִרְסַת הַמִּשְׁנָיוֹת וְהַבָּרַיְתוֹת, שֶׁתִּהְיֶינָה שְׁגוּרוֹת בְּפִיו, וּשְׁלִישׁ
לְהָבִין הָעִנְיָנִים מְשֹׁרֶשׁ; וְלֹא יָשִׂית כָּל לִבּוֹ בְּאַחַת מֵהֶן, פֶּן יִשְׁכַּח הַשְּׁאָר;
וּשְׁלָשְׁתָּן הֵן עִקַּר הַתּוֹרָה, שֶׁאִי־אֶפְשָׁר לָדַעַת זוּלָתָם.

וְכֵן מַה שֶּׁאָמְרוּ שֶׁחַיָּב הַצִּבּוּר שֶׁבְּכָל מָקוֹם וּמָקוֹם לְהוֹשִׁיב מְלַמְּדֵי תִינוֹקוֹת,
וְעִיר שֶׁאֵין בָּהּ תִּינוֹקוֹת שֶׁל בֵּית רַבָּן תֶּחָרֵב, וְכֵ״ה תִּינוֹקוֹת מוֹשִׁיבִין אֵצֶל מְלַמֵּד
אֶחָד.

וּמַה שֶּׁאָמְרוּ שֶׁלֹּא יֹאמַר אָדָם ״לִכְשֶׁאֶפָּנֶה אֶשְׁנֶה״, שֶׁמָּא לֹא יִפָּנֶה

---

7. MT *ibid.* 10.
8. TB Shabbath 83b.
9. TB Yoma 35b, 'Eruvin 35b.
10. TB 'Eruvin 54a.
11. TB Shabbath 31a; MT *hilchoth talmud torah* i 8.
12. TB Kiddushin 40b.
13. Expression based on Isaiah 57 : 15.
14. So TB Ta'anith 7a.
15. Teachings by Sages of the Mishnah that were not included in the Mishnah.
16. Literally, he should not set all his heart in.
17. TB Bava Bathra 21a; MT *hilchoth talmud torah* ii 1, 5.
18. TB Shabbath 119b; MT *ibid.* 1.
19. Mishnah, 'Avoth ii 4.

days of your life (Deuteronomy 4:9).[7] Moreover, the Sages further emphasized the matter by way of moral instruction and to teach human beings what is desirable, and they said[8] that even at the time of death a man is obligated to study Torah: for it is stated, *This is the Torah when a man dies* (Numbers 19:14).

Every single Jew has the duty of Torah study, the poor as well as the rich,[9] the healthy as well as the man with afflictions.[10] And long ago the Sages of blessed memory taught[10] that through occupation with Torah study all the limbs and organs are healed. Even a poor man who makes the rounds of the doors [of houses], even a man with a wife and children[9] — all are obligated to set fixed times of Torah study during the day and at night: for it is stated, *and you shall meditate in it day and night* (Joshua 1:8).[11]

The very beginning of a man's sentence after death is because he desisted from Torah study: as the Sages of blessed memory interpreted,[12] since it is written, *Letting water flow free is the beginning of strife* (Proverbs 17:14), which is to say: whoever grants himself freedom from the water — this is the beginning of contention for his spirit after he dies; and water denotes nothing other than the Torah: as it is stated, *Ho, everyone who thirsts, come to the water* (Isaiah 55:1). The Torah's words were likened to water because the Torah will endure in no one but a contrite person, humble in spirit,[13] and not in someone proud-hearted — just as water will likewise not remain in the mountains but only in the valleys.[14]

There is likewise what the Sages of blessed memory taught:[5] that a man is duty-bound to divide his time into three parts: a third for busying himself with the Written Torah, a third for engaging in the study of the Oral Torah — in other words, to train himself to be versed in the text of the Mishnah and *baraithoth*,[15] so that they will come fluently to his mouth; and a third to understand the topics at their root. He should not devote all his attention to[16] one of them, for he may forget the rest. And all three are the main core of the Torah, without which [three] it is impossible to know it.

So too, there is what the Sages said:[17] that the community in every single locality is obligated to establish children's teachers. A town in which there are no school-children studying Torah is destined to be destroyed.[18] Twenty-five children are to be assigned to one teacher.[17]

There is, further, what the Sages taught:[19] that a man should not say, "When I will have leisure I will study"; perhaps he will never

לְעוֹלָם, כִּי לֹא יֵדַע הָאָדָם מַה יֵּלֶד יוֹם, שֶׁעֶסְקוֹ שֶׁל עוֹלָם מִתְחַדֵּשׁ יוֹם יוֹם
וּמַדִּיחַ אֶת הָאָדָם מִדְּבַר לְדָבָר וּמִטְּרָדָה לִטְרָדָה, וְנִמְצְאוּ כָל יָמָיו יוֹצְאִין בְּבֶהָלָה
אִם לֹא יִתֵּן פְּנֵי עַל־כָּל־פָּנִים וְיִדְחַק עַצְמוֹ לְעָסְקָהּ שֶׁל תּוֹרָה. וְכָל שֶׁעוֹשֶׂה כֵן
וְחָפֵץ בְּבִרְכָה, מִן הַשָּׁמַיִם מְסַיְּעִין אוֹתוֹ, וּמְקִלִּין מֵעָלָיו טְרָדוֹת הָעוֹלָם
הַמַּבְהִילוֹת, וּמַעֲבִירִין מִמֶּנּוּ עֹל שֶׁל בְּרִיּוֹת, וְשׁוֹכֵן בְּשִׂמְחָה כָל יָמָיו בָּעוֹלָם הַזֶּה
וְטוֹב לוֹ לָעוֹלָם הַבָּא; וְאַשְׁרֵי הַמְּדַבֵּר בְּאֹזֶן שׁוֹמָעַת. וְיֶתֶר פְּרָטֶיהָ, מְבֹאָרִין
בְּקִדּוּשִׁין פֶּרֶק רִאשׁוֹן וּבִמְקוֹמוֹת מְפֻזָּרִים בַּתַּלְמוּד.

וְנוֹהֶגֶת מִצְוָה זוֹ בְּכָל מָקוֹם וּבְכָל זְמַן, בִּזְכָרִים אֲבָל לֹא בִנְקֵבוֹת, שֶׁנֶּאֱמַר
"בְּנֵיכֶם", וְדָרְשׁוּ זִכְרוֹנָם לִבְרָכָה: וְלֹא בְּנוֹתֵיכֶם. וְכֵן [אִשָּׁה] אֵינָהּ חַיֶּבֶת לְלַמֵּד
בְּנָהּ, דְּכָל שֶׁאֵינוֹ בַחִיּוּב לִלְמֹד אֵינוֹ בַחִיּוּב לְלַמֵּד. אֲבָל מִכָּל־מָקוֹם רָאוּי לְכָל
אִשָּׁה לְהִשְׁתַּדֵּל שֶׁלֹּא יְהוּ בָנֶיהָ עַמֵּי־הָאָרֶץ, אַף־עַל־פִּי שֶׁאֵינָהּ מְצֻוָּה מִדִּין
הַתּוֹרָה, וְשָׂכָר טוֹב יֵשׁ לָהּ בַּעֲמָלָהּ; וְגַם הָאִשָּׁה שֶׁלָּמְדָה תּוֹרָה, שָׂכָר יֵשׁ לָהּ. וְאַף־
עַל־פִּי־כֵן צִוּוּ חֲכָמִים שֶׁלֹּא יְלַמֵּד אָדָם לְבִתּוֹ תּוֹרָה, לְפִי שֶׁדַּעַת הַנָּשִׁים קַלָּה,
וּמוֹצִיאִין דִּבְרֵי תּוֹרָה לְדִבְרֵי הֲבַאי בַּעֲנִיּוּת דַּעְתָּן.

וְעוֹבֵר עַל זֶה וְלֹא לִמֵּד אֶת בְּנוֹ תּוֹרָה עַד שֶׁיֵּדַע לִקְרוֹת בְּסֵפֶר תּוֹרָה וְיָבִין
פֵּרוּשׁ הַכְּתוּבִים כִּפְשָׁטָן, בִּטֵּל עֲשֵׂה זֶה; וְכֵן כָּל מִי שֶׁיֵּשׁ סִפֵּק בְּיָדוֹ לִלְמֹד בְּשׁוּם
צַד, הוּא בִכְלַל עֲשֵׂה זֶה, וְעָנְשׁוֹ גָּדוֹל מְאֹד אִם לֹא יְקַיְּמֶנּוּ, כִּי הַמִּצְוָה הַזֹּאת הִיא
אִם לְכֻלָּן.

[מִצְוַת קְרִיאַת שְׁמַע שַׁחֲרִית וְעַרְבִית]

תכ שֶׁנִּצְטַוֵּינוּ לִקְרוֹת בְּכָל יוֹם עַרְבִית וְשַׁחֲרִית פָּסוּק אֶחָד מִן הַתּוֹרָה שֶׁבְּסֵדֶר
זֶה, וְזֵהוּ "שְׁמַע יִשְׂרָאֵל יי אֱלֹהֵינוּ יי אֶחָד"; וְעַל פָּסוּק זֶה נֶאֱמַר "וְדִבַּרְתָּ בָּם

20. Expression based on Proverbs 27:1.

21. Based on TB Shabbath 104a etc. and Mishnah, 'Avoth iii 5.

22. This evidently conveys a hope that the author's son, and other readers, will heed what he has written. The expression seems to derive from *Séfer Ben Sira* 25:13, "Fortunate is he who has found a companion and who talks to a listening ear" (ed. Segal, p. 152; and see note on p. 154).

23. TB Kiddushin 29b.

24. TB Sotah 21a.

25. See Mishnah, Sotah iii 4 (TB 20a) and MT *hilchoth sotah* iii 20. (Unlike effort expended to have her sons study, for this she receives only "reward" but not "good reward," since she is not commanded to learn Torah; see TB Sotah 21a, and more specifically MT *hilchoth talmud torah* i 13.)

26. TB Sotah 20a, 21b.

§420   1. See the fifth paragraph of this section, that reciting the first verse is the requirement of Torah law — which is all our author wishes to convey here; but by

have leisure. For a man does not know what a day will bring forth,[20] since the business of the world becomes new every day, and it drives a man from one thing to another, from one worrying concern to another; and as a result, all his days are spent in turmoil — if he will not set aside free time under all circumstances and force himself into the occupation of Torah study. And whoever does so and desires blessing, from Heaven he is helped; the distracting worrying concerns of the world are eased for him; the yoke of people is removed from him;[21] he will live in happiness all his days in this world, and good fortune will be his in the world-to-come. And fortunate is he who speaks to a listening ear.[22] The rest of its details are explained in the first chapter of the tractate *Kiddushin* and in scattered places in the Talmud.

This precept is in force everywhere, at every time, for men but not for women—since "your sons" is stated (Deuteronomy 11:19), and our Sages of blessed memory interpreted:[22] but not your daughters. So too, a woman has no obligation to teach her son [Torah]: for whoever is not under the obligation to learn is not under the obligation to teach.[23] Yet in any case, it is right for every woman to endeavor that her sons should not be ignoramuses, even though she is not so commanded by the law of the Torah; and good reward will be hers for her effort.[24] So too, if a woman studied Torah, there is reward for her.[25] Nevertheless, the Sages ordained[26] that a man should not teach his daughter Torah: for women are light-minded, and they will apply the words of Torah to matters of nonsense in their paucity of understanding.

If a person transgresses this and does not teach his son Torah until he knows to read the Written Torah and understand the meaning of the verses in their plain sense, he disobeys this positive precept. So too, anyone who has the means to learn [Torah] under any circumstances whatever, is included in the scope of this positive precept; and his punishment will be very great if he does not fulfill it, because this precept is the matrix of them all.

[THE MITZVAH OF RECITING THE SH'MA
EVERY MORNING AND EVENING]

420 that we were commanded to recite every day, evening and morning, one verse of the Torah which is in this *sidrah*, namely, *Hear, Israel: the Lord our God the Lord is one* (Deuteronomy 6:4).[1] Regarding

בְּשִׁבְתְּךָ" וְגוֹמֵר, "וּבְשָׁכְבְּךָ וּבְקוּמֶךָ", וּבָא הַפֵּרוּשׁ עַל זֶה: בְּשָׁעָה שֶׁבְּנֵי־אָדָם
שׁוֹכְבִין וּבְשָׁעָה שֶׁבְּנֵי־אָדָם קָמִין. וְקָא מַשְׁמַע לְהוּ לְרַבָּנָן שֶׁבְּשָׁעָה שֶׁבְּנֵי־אָדָם
שׁוֹכְבִין תִּקְרָא כָּל הַלַּיְלָה עַד שֶׁיַּעֲלֶה עַמּוּד הַשַּׁחַר, וּכְעִנְיָן שֶׁכָּתוּב "וּשְׁכַבְתֶּם
וְאֵין מַחֲרִיד", וְכֵן "לֹא יִשְׁכַּב עַד יֹאכַל טֶרֶף", דְּמַשְׁמַע כָּל שְׁעַת שְׁכִיבָה; וְעוֹד
שֶׁבְּנֵי־אָדָם חֲלוּקִים הֵם בְּמִדּוֹתָם בְּעִנְיַן הַשְּׁכִיבָה, יֵשׁ מֵהֶן שֶׁאֵינָם שׁוֹכְבִין עַד
חֲצִי הַלַּיְלָה, וְיֵשׁ עַד סוֹפָהּ, וְיֵשׁ שֶׁשׁוֹכְבִין מִיָּד בִּתְחִלַּת הַלַּיְלָה.

וּמִפְּנֵי־כֵן אָמְרוּ שֶׁזְּמַן קְרִיאַת שְׁמַע בָּעֲרָבִין מִשָּׁעָה שֶׁהַכֹּהֲנִים נִכְנָסִין לֶאֱכֹל
בִּתְרוּמָתָן, דְּהַיְנוּ צֵאת הַכּוֹכָבִים, עַד שֶׁיַּעֲלֶה עַמּוּד הַשַּׁחַר. וְשָׁעָה שֶׁבְּנֵי־אָדָם
קָמִין מַשְׁמַע לְהוּ מִתְּחִלַּת הַיּוֹם, כְּלוֹמַר כְּשֶׁהַבֹּקֶר אוֹר, כְּשֶׁאָדָם מַכִּיר אֶת חֲבֵרוֹ
בְּרָחוֹק אַרְבַּע אַמּוֹת, עַד שָׁלֹשׁ שָׁעוֹת שְׁלֵמוֹת. וְלֹא מַשְׁמַע לְהוּ הַקִּימָה כָּל הַיּוֹם
כְּמוֹ הַשְּׁכִיבָה, שֶׁאֵין דֶּרֶךְ אֶחָד מִבְּנֵי־אָדָם שֶׁהוּא בָּרִיא שֶׁיָּקוּם מִמְּטָתוֹ בְּסוֹף
הַיּוֹם אוֹ אֲפִלּוּ בְּאֶמְצָעוֹ. וְאָמְרוּ זִכְרוֹנָם לִבְרָכָה בִּקְרִיאַת שְׁמַע דְּשַׁחֲרִין דְּמִכָּל־
מָקוֹם מִכָּאן וָאֵילָךְ, כְּלוֹמַר מִסּוֹף שָׁלֹשׁ שָׁעוֹת עַד סוֹף הַיּוֹם, מִי שֶׁלֹּא קָרָא לֹא
הִפְסִיד שֶׁלֹּא יוּכַל לִקְרוֹתָהּ עִם בִּרְכוֹתֶיהָ.

מִשָּׁרְשֵׁי הַמִּצְוָה, שֶׁרָצָה הַשֵּׁם לִזְכוּת עַמּוֹ שֶׁיְּקַבְּלוּ עֲלֵיהֶם מַלְכוּתוֹ וְיִחֲדוּ
בְּכָל יוֹם וָלַיְלָה כָּל הַיָּמִים כָּל הַיָּמִים שֶׁהֵם חַיִּים: כִּי בִּהְיוֹת הָאָדָם בַּעַל חֹמֶר, נִפְתָּה אַחַר
הַבְלֵי הָעוֹלָם וְנִמְשָׁךְ לְתַאֲוֹותָיו, צָרִיךְ עַל־כָּל־פָּנִים זִכָּרוֹן תְּמִידִי בְּמַלְכוּת שָׁמַיִם
לְשָׁמְרוֹ מִן הַחֵטְא; עַל־כֵּן הָיָה מֵחַסְדּוֹ לְזַכּוֹתֵנוּ, וְצִוָּנוּ לִזְכּוֹר שְׁנֵי הָעִתִּים הָאֵלֶּה
בְּקֶבַע וּבְכַוָּנָה גְּמוּרָה: אַחַת בַּיּוֹם, לְהוֹעִיל לְכָל מַעֲשֵׂינוּ שֶׁבַּיּוֹם, כִּי בִּהְיוֹת הָאָדָם
זוֹכֵר בַּבֹּקֶר אַחְדוּת הַשֵּׁם וּמַלְכוּתוֹ, וְכִי הַשְׁגָּחָתוֹ וִיכָלְתּוֹ עַל הַכֹּל, וְיִתֵּן אֶל לִבּוֹ כִּי

the law of the Sages, as he continues there, all three sections of the *Sh'ma* (as we
have them in the daily prayer book) are to be recited twice daily. The view that
only the first verse is required by Torah law is derived from TB B'rachoth 13b (this
was R. Judah the *nassi's* recital of the *Sh'ma*), and Sukkah 42a (What is the recital of
the *Sh'ma?* — the first verse).

2. TB B'rachoth 10b.

3. Hence "lying down" evidently denotes the entire normal time of sleep.

4. *Ibid.* 2a.

5. I.e. *kohanim* who underwent ritual immersion during the day and wait for
nightfall to attain full ritual purity.

6. The term "hour" in Talmudic law, as in antiquity, means one twelfth the
period between the start and end of the day (the Ga'on of Vilna and *Magén Avraham*
differ on the determination of the start and end): see Isaiah 38:8, with Targum
Jonathan and Rashi; Mishnah, 'Eduyoth iii 8, with Rambam's commentary; and the
use of the term in TB B'rachoth 27a (by R. 'Aḥa' b. Ya'akov), B'réshith Rabba 10,
8 (ed. Theodor-Albeck I p. 85), etc.

7. So Ramban, commentary to TB B'rachoth, beginning.

this verse it was stated, *and you shall talk of them when you sit…and when you lie down and when you rise up (ibid.* 7); and the interpretation of this was given [in the Oral Tradition]:[2] at the time people lie down, and at the time people get up. Now, the Sages understood that "at the time people lie down" designates the entire night, until dawn comes up—in keeping with the verse, *and you shall lie down, and none shall make you afraid* (Leviticus 26:6),[3] and likewise, *he shall not lie down until he eats of the prey* (Numbers 23:24), which implies the entire time of lying down [lying in bed to sleep]. Moreover, people differ in their ways of behavior in regard to lying down [going to sleep]: There are those among them who do not lie down [to sleep] till midnight, and some not till its end, while some lie down at once at the beginning of the night.

For this reason the Sages said[4] that the period for reciting the *Sh'ma* in the evening is from the time the *kohanim* go in to eat their *t'rumah*,[5] which means at the appearance of the stars, until the dawn comes up. "The time that the people rise," they understand to mean from the beginning of the day, i.e. when the morning is light enough for a man to recognize his fellow-man at a distance of four cubits, until [the end of] three complete hours.[6] But rising does not signify for them the entire day, in parallel to lying down, since it is not the way of any person who is healthy that he should get up from his bed at the end of the day, or even in the middle of it.[7] However, the Sages of blessed memory said about the recital of *Sh'ma* in the morning[8] that in any event, from then on, i.e. from the end of three hours till the end of the day, whoever did not recite it has not lost out to be unable to say it with its benedictions.

At the root of the precept lies the reason that the Eternal Lord wished to make His people meritorious, that they should accept upon themselves His kingship and His oneness every day and night, all the days that they are alive. For since man is a physical entity that is enticed by the vapidities of the world and is drawn toward his desires, he needs, under any circumstances, a constant reminder of the kingship of Heaven to guard him from sin. It was therefore of His kindness to make us virtuous; and He commanded us to remember Him at these two times regularly, with utter concentration: once during the day, that it should be of benefit for all our actions during the day—for when a man remembers in the morning the oneness of the Eternal Lord and His sovereignty, and that His watchful concern

⟨263⟩

עֵינָיו פְּקוּחוֹת עַל כָּל דְּרָכָיו וְכָל צְעָדָיו יִסְפּוֹר, לֹא יִתְעַלֵּם מִמֶּנּוּ דָּבָר מִכָּל דְּבָרָיו,
וְלֹא יוּכַל מִמֶּנּוּ לְהַחְבִּיא אַחַת מִכָּל מַחְשְׁבוֹתָיו, הֲלֹא יִהְיֶה לוֹ לְמִשְׁמֶרֶת
מַחֲשַׁבְתּוֹ זֹאת וְהוֹדָעַת פִּיו בַּדָּבָר הַזֶּה כָּל הַיּוֹם הַהוּא; וְיִהְיֶה לוֹ הוֹדָעַת הַלַּיְלָה
בָּזֶה גַּם־כֵּן לְמִשְׁמָר כָּל הַלָּיְלָה.

וּמִפְּנֵי שֶׁיְּסוֹד הַמִּצְוָה מַה שֶׁנִּזְכָּרְנוּ, חִיְּבוּנוּ זִכְרוֹנָם לִבְרָכָה בָּהּ בְּכַוָּנַת הַלֵּב,
וְאָמְרוּ שֶׁאִם לֹא כִוֵּן לִבּוֹ בָּהּ לֹא יָצָא יְדֵי חוֹבָתוֹ, שֶׁאֵין אָדָם נִזְכָּר בְּשׁוּם דָּבָר
אֶלָּא־אִם־כֵּן יָשִׂים כַּוָּנָתוֹ בּוֹ; וְזֶהוּ שֶׁאָמְרוּ זִכְרוֹנָם לִבְרָכָה בְּבִרְכוֹת פֶּרֶק הָיָה
קוֹרֵא, תָּנוּ רַבָּנָן: "שְׁמַע יִשְׂרָאֵל יי אֱלֹהֵינוּ יי אֶחָד", עַד כָּאן צְרִיכָה כַּוָּנַת הַלֵּב.
וְהִצְרִיכוּנוּ לְהַאֲרִיךְ בְּ"אֶחָד", וְכִדְתַנְיָא הָתָם: (ספקוס) [סוּמְכוֹס] בֶּן יוֹסֵף אוֹמֵר:
כָּל הַמַּאֲרִיךְ בְּ"אֶחָד" מַאֲרִיכִין לוֹ יָמָיו וּשְׁנוֹתָיו; וְאָמַר רַב אַחָא בַּר יַעֲקֹב:
וּבְדָּל"ת; אָמַר רַב אַשִׁי; וּבִלְבַד שֶׁלֹּא יַחֲטוֹף בַּחֵי"ת. וְאָמְרוּ שָׁם: עַד כַּמָּה יִהְיֶה
אֲרִיכוּת זֶה, וְהָיְתָה הַתְּשׁוּבָה: עַד כְּדֵי שֶׁתַּמְלִיכֵהוּ בַּשָּׁמַיִם וּבָאָרֶץ וּבְאַרְבַּע
רוּחוֹת הָעוֹלָם, כְּלוֹמַר שֶׁתְּכַוֵּן שֶׁמְּמַשְׁלַתּוֹ בַּכֹּל הִיא וְאֵין כָּל דָּבָר נֶעְלָם מִמֶּנּוּ,
וּבְחֶפְצוֹ קִיּוּם כָּל הַדְּבָרִים.

מִדִּינֵי הַמִּצְוָה, מַה שֶׁאָמְרוּ זִכְרוֹנָם לִבְרָכָה שֶׁחַיָּב לְבָרֵךְ פָּסוּק רִאשׁוֹן הוּא מִן
הַתּוֹרָה, כְּמוֹ שֶׁאָמַרְנוּ, אֲבָל חֲכָמִים חִיְּבוּנוּ לִקְרוֹת שָׁלֹשׁ פָּרָשִׁיּוֹת, שֶׁהֵן: שְׁמַע,
וְהָיָה אִם שָׁמֹעַ, וַיֹּאמֶר; וּמַקְדִּימִין לִקְרוֹת פָּרָשַׁת "שְׁמַע", שֶׁיֵּשׁ בָּהּ צִוּוּי עַל
יִחוּד הַשֵּׁם (יִתְבָּרַךְ) וְאַהֲבָתוֹ וְתַלְמוּד תּוֹרָתוֹ, שֶׁהוּא הָעִקָּר הַגָּדוֹל שֶׁהַכֹּל תָּלוּי בּוֹ;
וְאַחֲרֶיהָ "וְהָיָה אִם שָׁמֹעַ", שֶׁיֵּשׁ בָּהּ צִוּוּי עַל שְׁאָר הַמִּצְוֹת כֻּלָּן, וְאַחֲרֶיהָ פָּרָשַׁת
צִיצִית, שֶׁגַּם הִיא יֵשׁ בָּהּ צִוּוּי עַל זְכִירַת כָּל הַמִּצְוֹת. וְאִם־כֵּן, בֶּאֱמֶת, בִּהְיוֹת

8. TB B'rachoth 9b; MT *hilchoth kri'ath sh'ma* i 13.

9. Expressions based on Jeremiah 32:19 and Job 31:4.

10. Our Talmud editions have Symmachos, but see *Dikduké Sof'rim*, note.

11. Because with that letter the word *'eḥad* ("one") becomes complete, and thus
the word is lengthened, and not a meaningless part of it (Rashi). In the time and
place of the Talmud the *da-leth* (without *dagésh*) was evidently sounded as a voiced
fricative, and so the sound could be sustained.

12. See our author's opening sentence and note 1. This is also the view of R.
Judah heḤassid, cited in *Tur 'Oraḥ Ḥayyim* §46, and of R. Aaron haLévi, in *P'kudath
haL'vi-im* (Mayence/Mainz 1874) p. 21, and as cited in *Béth Yoséf* to Tur ibid. s.v.
v'kathav haRe'ah. Rashba likewise gives this opinion in his novellae (*ḥiddushim*) to
TB B'rachoth (Jerusalem 1980) col. 66, and more explicitly in col. 68 (at note 13);
so too in his *Responsa*, I §320. Earlier in his novellae, however (*op. cit.* col. 6, at note
16), he states that the whole first section (Deuteronomy 6:4–9) needs to be recited
by Torah law, this being the view of his master teacher, R. Yonah Gerondi. (See R.
Ḥizkiah da Silva, *P'ri Ḥadash* on *Shulḥan 'Aruch 'Oraḥ Ḥayyim* §76, who discusses
fully which authorities hold these views, and which a third opinion, that the first

and His ability extend over all and everything, and he takes to heart [the concept] that His eyes are open over all his ways and He counts all his steps,[9] nothing of all his affairs being hidden from Him, and he cannot conceal from Him any one of his thoughts, then this conception of his and the acknowledgment of his mouth about this matter will serve as a protection for him that entire day; whereas the acknowledgment of this at night will equally serve as a protection the entire night.

Now, because the basis of the precept is what we have noted, the Sages of blessed memory obligated us to have the heart's attention focused on it; and they said that if one did not focus his heart (attention) on it, he did not acquit himself of his obligation. For a man does not remember anything unless he gives it his focused attention. This is why they (of blessed memory) said in the second chapter of the Talmud tractate *B'rachoth* (13b): Our Sages taught: *Hear, Israel: the Lord our God, the Lord is one* — till here the heart's attention is required. And they required us to be lengthy, drawn out in pronouncing the word *'ehad* (one), as it was taught there in a *baraitha*: Sephakos b. Joseph[10] said: Whoever lengthens the word *'ehad* (one), his days and years are lengthened for him. R. 'Aha b. Ya'akov added: [This means] at the letter *da-leth*.[11] Said R. 'Ashi: provided one does not rush through the *heth*. Then the Sages said there: To what extent should this lengthening [of the word] be? And the answer was: long enough for you to establish Him [in your mind] as Sovereign Ruler in heaven and on earth, and over the four directions of the world. In other words, that you should conceive His dominion extending over all and everything, so that nothing whatever is concealed from Him, and the existence of all things is by His desire.

Among the laws of the precept there is what the Sages of blessed memory taught: that the obligation about the first verse of the Scriptural section is by the law of the Torah, as we said,[12] but the Sages obligated us to recite the three sections, namely, *Sh'ma* (Deuteronomy 6:4–9), *And it shall be if you hearken* (ibid. 11:13–21), *And the Lord spoke to Moses* (Numbers 15:37–41). The section of *Sh'ma* is said first because it contains the instruction about the oneness of the Eternal Lord, about bearing Him love, and the study of His Torah, which is the great main principle on which everything depends. After that comes the section, *And it shall be if you hearken*, which contains a command about all the other *mitzvoth*; and afterward the section about

הָאָדָם זוֹכֵר אֵלֶּה בְּכָל יוֹם פַּעַם אַחַת וּבְכָל לַיְלָה פַּעַם אַחֶרֶת, בְּכַנָּנָה, יִנָּצֵל מִן הָעֲבֵרָה עַל־כָּל־פָּנִים, אִם יֵשׁ דַּעַת בּוֹ.

וְכֵן מֵעִנְיַן הַמִּצְוָה שֶׁחִיְּבוּנוּ שֶׁחִיְּבוּנוּ זִכְרוֹנָם לִבְרָכָה לְבָרֵךְ קֹדֶם הַקְּרִיאָה וְאַחֲרֶיהָ, בַּשַּׁחַר שְׁתַּיִם לְפָנֶיהָ: יוֹצֵר אוֹר וְאַהֲבַת עוֹלָם, וְאַחַת לְאַחֲרֶיהָ: אֱמֶת וְיַצִּיב; וּבָעֶרֶב שְׁתַּיִם לְפָנֶיהָ: מַעֲרִיב עֲרָבִים וְאַהֲבַת עוֹלָם, וּשְׁתַּיִם לְאַחֲרֶיהָ: אֱמֶת וֶאֱמוּנָה וְהַשְׁכִּיבֵנוּ; וְאֵין צֹרֶךְ לְהַאֲרִיךְ בָּהֶן, שֶׁיְּדִיעוֹת הֵן בְּכָל יִשְׂרָאֵל בְּפְתִיחָתָן וּבַחֲתִימָתָן וּבַנֶּפֶשׁ שֶׁלָּהֶן; וְעֶזְרָא וּבֵית־דִּינוֹ תִּקְּנוּם עִם שְׁאָר כָּל הַבְּרָכוֹת הָעֲרוּכוֹת בְּפִי כָל יִשְׂרָאֵל.

וְכֵן מֵעִנְיַן הַמִּצְוָה מַה שֶּׁאָמְרוּ שֶׁהַקּוֹרֵא אֶת "שְׁמַע" צָרִיךְ לְהַשְׁמִיעַ לְאָזְנוֹ, וְאִם לֹא הִשְׁמִיעַ אֲבָל מִכָּל־מָקוֹם קָרָא הַדְּבָרִים בִּשְׂפָתָיו, יָצָא דִּיעֲבַד; וְכֵן מַה שֶּׁאָמְרוּ שֶׁצָּרִיךְ לְדַקְדֵּק בְּאוֹתִיּוֹתֶיהָ, וְאִם לֹא דִּקְדֵּק בָּהֶן יָצָא. וְאָמְרוּ מִן הַמְפָרְשִׁים שֶׁאֵין הָעִנְיָן שֶׁלֹּא יַזְכִּיר הַתֵּבוֹת וְהָאוֹתִיּוֹת, שֶׁבָּזֶה וַדַּאי לֹא נֶאֱמַר שֶׁאִם לֹא דִּקְדֵּק יָצָא, שֶׁכָּל שֶׁלֹּא קָרָא קְרִיאַת שְׁמַע כֻּלּוֹ לֹא יָצָא יְדֵי חוֹבָתוֹ; אֲבָל עִנְיַן "לֹא דִּקְדֵּק" הוּא שֶׁלֹּא נָתַן רֶוַח בֵּין הַדְּבֵקִים, כְּגוֹן: בְּכָל לְבָבְךָ, (עֵשֶׂב בְּשָׂדְךָ,) וַאֲבַדְתֶּם מְהֵרָה, (בְּכָל לְבַבְכֶם,) הַכָּנָף פְּתִיל, וְכֵן שֶׁלֹּא הִתִּיז ז'

---

two sections of the *Sh'ma* must be recited by Torah law.) Our author's view is also held later by R. Shim'on b. Tzemaḥ Duran in his commentary (*pirush*) to TB B'rachoth (B'né B'rak 1971, p. 78a); and he adds, "and so wrote the commentators of blessed memory."

13. TB B'rachoth 13a and 12b; MT *hilchoth k'ri'ath sh'ma* i 2.

14. TB B'rachoth 11a.

15. Daily Prayer Book, ed. Birnbaum, pp. 71–75. ("With everlasting love" —'ahavath 'olam—is the version in *nusaḥ s'farad*, followed by Rambam and in the Spain of our author; in *nusaḥ 'ashkenaz* it begins, 'ahavah rabbah—"With a great love.")

16. *Ibid.* pp. 78 (bottom)–81.

17. *Ibid.* p. 191.

18. *Ibid.* pp. 195–97 (the third benediction, "Blessed is the Lord," is a later addition, to allow late-comers to catch up; it is omitted in the Land of Israel); MT *hilchoth k'ri'ath sh'ma* i 5–6.

19. Literally, that are arranged in the mouth. TB B'rachoth 33a.

20. TB B'rachoth 15a; MT *ibid.* ii 8.

21. This is the reading of the three oldest manuscripts. The first edition (printed from an unknown manuscript) adds *l'ozno*, "to his ear," in keeping with the sources in note 20. The last of the four manuscripts consulted, however, and later editions, add *lo' yatza'*, "he has not fulfilled the obligation"—which is a contradiction to what follows (see MY). Quite possibly *l'ozno* was added in the margin in an early copy, and a later copyist erroneously incorporated it into the text as *lo' yatza'*.

22. See TB *ibid.* 15b and MT *ibid.* 9.

tzitzith (ritual tassels; § 386), for that too contains a charge about remembering all the *mitzvoth*.[13] Hence, in truth, as a man remembers these once every day and once again every night, with focused attention, he will be kept safe from sin under all circumstances, if there is sense in him.

So is it also of the subject-matter of the precept that the Sages of blessed memory obligated us[14] to say benedictions before the recital [of the *Sh'ma*] and after it. In the morning, there are two benedictions before it — "who forms light" and "With everlasting love";[15] and one after — "True and certain."[16] In the evening there are two before it — "brings on the evenings" and "With everlasting love";[17] and two after — "True and trustworthy" and "Grant that we lie down."[18] There is no need to go on at length about them, since they are known throughout Jewry by their opening words and closing sentences, and by their texts. Ezra and his court of scholars formulated them along with all the other benedictions that are ready knowledge on the tongue[19] of every Jew.

There is likewise in the subject-matter of the precept what the Sages said:[20] that one who says the *Sh'ma* must make it audible to his ear; however, if he did not make it audible[21] but in any event he said the words with his lips, having done so he has fulfilled the obligation. There is, similarly, what the Sages said:[20] that a person needs to be precise about its letters; yet if one was not precise in their pronunciation, he has acquitted himself of the obligation. Now, some of the authorities[22] noted that the meaning [here] is not if one does not utter words or letters — for about that it was certainly not stated that if a person was not precise he yet fulfilled his obligation; for if anyone does not recite the entire *Sh'ma*, he does not acquit himself of his duty. The meaning of not having been precise is rather that a person did not leave a space (a pause) between two combining (identical) sounds, such as *b'chol l'vav'cha* (with all your heart: Deuteronomy 6:5), *ésev b'sad'cha* (grass in your field: *ibid.* 15), *va'avad'tem m'hérah* (and you will quickly perish: *ibid.* 11:17), *b'chol l'vav'chem* (with all your heart: *ibid.* 18), *ha-kanaf p'sil* (on the tassel of each corner: Numbers 15:38);[23] so too if one does not enunciate clearly the z-sound in *tiz-k'ru* (that you shall remember: *ibid.* 40), which needs to be articulated;[24] or if one was not long (drawn out) at

23. I.e. one should not let the final sound of the first word and the opening

דְּ"תִּזְכְּרוּ", שֶׁצָּרִיךְ לְהַתִּיזָהּ, אוֹ שֶׁלֹּא הֶאֱרִיךְ בְּדָל"ת — כְּפִי הָרָאוּי לְכַתְּחִלָּה לַעֲשׂוֹת הַכֹּל.

וְכֵן מֵעִנְיַן הַמִּצְוָה מַה שֶּׁאָמְרוּ שֶׁאָדָם שׁוֹאֵל בְּשָׁלוֹם מִי שֶׁהוּא חַיָּב לְכַבְּדוֹ וּמֵשִׁיב שָׁלוֹם לְכָל אָדָם בֵּין הַפְּרָקִים, וּבָאֶמְצָע שׁוֹאֵל מִפְּנֵי הַיִּרְאָה, כְּלוֹמַר לְמַלְכֵי הָאֻמּוֹת אוֹ לַשָּׂרִים הַגְּדוֹלִים, וּמֵשִׁיב מִפְּנֵי הַכָּבוֹד; וְזֶה כַּמָּה שֶׁלֹּא רָאִינוּ מִי שֶׁיַּקְפִּיד עַל חֲבֵרוֹ כְּלָל אִם לֹא יַפְסִיק לוֹ, וַאֲפִלּוּ בֵין הַפְּרָקִים. וְחֵזֶר רֻבֵּי דִּינֵי הַמִּצְוָה, וְכָל הָעִנְיָנִים שֶׁמְּבַטְּלִין בִּשְׁבִילָן קְרִיאַת שְׁמַע, יִתְבָּאֲרוּ בִּבְרָכוֹת בִּפְרָקִים רִאשׁוֹנִים.

וְנוֹהֶגֶת בְּכָל מָקוֹם וּבְכָל זְמַן, בַּזְּכָרִים אֲבָל לֹא בַנְּקֵבוֹת, לְפִי שֶׁהִיא מִכְּלַל מִצְוֹת עֲשֵׂה שֶׁהַזְּמַן גְּרָמָא, שֶׁהַנָּשִׁים פְּטוּרוֹת. וְעוֹבֵר עַל זֶה וְלֹא קָרָא קְרִיאַת שְׁמַע בְּכָל יוֹם וּבְכָל לַיְלָה בִּזְמַנָּהּ שֶׁקָּבְעוּ לָהּ חֲכָמִים, בִּטֵּל עֲשֵׂה זֶה. וְהָרַב רַבֵּנוּ מֹשֶׁה בֶּן נַחְמָן זִכְרוֹנוֹ לִבְרָכָה מָנָה בְּחֶשְׁבּוֹן הַמִּצְוֹת קְרִיאַת שְׁמַע בַּיּוֹם מִצְוָה אַחַת, וּבַלַּיְלָה מִצְוָה אַחֶרֶת, לְפִי שֶׁזְּמַנָּהּ שֶׁל זוֹ לֹא זְמַנָּהּ שֶׁל זוֹ, וְזוֹ אֵינָהּ מְעַכֶּבֶת זוֹ.

[מִצְוַת תְּפִלִּין שֶׁל יָד]

תכא לִקְשֹׁר תְּפִלִּין עַל הַיָּד, שֶׁנֶּאֱמַר "וּקְשַׁרְתָּם לְאוֹת עַל־יָדֶךָ", וּבָא הַפֵּרוּשׁ עַל זֶה הַמִּקְרָא שֶׁנִּקְשַׁר עַל יָדֵינוּ מִדִּבְרֵי תוֹרָה אַרְבַּע פָּרָשִׁיּוֹת, וְהֵן נִקְרָאוֹת תְּפִלִּין כְּשֶׁהֵן קְשׁוּרוֹת בִּרְצוּעוֹת, כְּמוֹ שֶׁבָּאָה הַקַּבָּלָה בָּהֶן. וְאֵלּוּ הֵן אַרְבַּע פָּרָשִׁיּוֹת אֵלּוּ: שְׁתַּיִם מֵהֶן בְּסוֹף סֵדֶר בֹּא אֶל פַּרְעֹה, וְהֵן פָּרָשַׁת "קַדֶּשׁ לִי כָל בְּכוֹר" עַד "וְשָׁמַרְתָּ אֶת הַחֻקָּה הַזֹּאת לְמוֹעֲדָהּ מִיָּמִים יָמִימָה", שֶׁהִיא פָּרָשָׁה אַחַת בְּכָל סֵפֶר מְדֻיָּק; וּמִ"וְהָיָה כִּי יְבִאֲךָ" עַד סוֹף הַסֵּדֶר שֶׁגּוֹמֵר "כִּי בְּחֹזֶק יָד הוֹצִיאָנוּ יי מִמִּצְרָיִם" פָּרָשָׁה שְׁנִיָּה; וּבְסוֹף סֵדֶר וָאֶתְחַנַּן בְּסֵפֶר אֵלֶּה הַדְּבָרִים,

sound of the second merge into one; a slight pause should separate each two words. The second and fourth of these examples are not in the oldest manuscripts, and thus seem later interpolations from the Talmud; they are equally absent in MT (note 19).

24. So TJ B'rachoth ii 4.

25. See three paragraphs above.

26. TB B'rachoth 13a.

27. Literally, one may inquire about the peace (welfare) of.

28. I.e. the three sections listed three paragraphs above, and the benedictions before the *Sh'ma* (MT *hilchoth k'ri'ath sh'ma* ii 17).

29. I.e. whose wrath he fears if he should fail to greet them; TB B'rachoth 13a.

30. I.e. to people whom he is obligated to honor; *ibid.* and MT *ibid.* 15–16.

31. I.e. they become obligatory at a specific time.

32. I.e. if one was recited but not the other; Ramban, commentary (*hassagoth*) to ShM, end section, s.v. *v'attah 'im tavin*.

the *da-leth* [in the word *'ehad*][25] as it is fitting initially to do [observe] all [these minutiae].

There is likewise within the subject-matter of the precept what the Sages said:[26] that a man may greet[27] a person whom he is duty-bound to honor, and return the greeting of every man, between the sections [of the *Sh'ma*];[28] in their middle he may give a greeting[27] on account of fear, i.e. to kings of the nations or to high officers,[29] and he may return a greeting for the sake of honor.[30] Yet in such a long time we have not seen anyone mind about his fellow-man at all if he should not interrupt for him [to give or return a greeting] even between the sections [of the *Sh'ma*]. The rest of the precept's many laws, and all the matters on whose account the recital of the *Sh'ma* is set aside, are clarified in the Talmud tractate *B'rachoth*, in the early chapters.

It is in force everywhere, at every time, for males but not for women, because it is in the category of positive precepts brought into effect by time,[31] of which women are free. If someone transgresses this and does not recite the *Sh'ma* every day and every night at its proper time that the Sages set for it, he disobeys this positive precept. R. Moses b. Naḥman, though, lists in his reckoning of the *mitzvoth* the recital of the *Sh'ma* by day as one precept, and at night as another precept—because the time for one is not the time for the other, and one does not prevent the other [from being acceptable].[32]

[THE PRECEPT OF THE T'FILLIN
OF THE HAND]

421 to bind *t'fillin* (a phylactery) on the hand, as it is written, *And you shall bind them for a sign upon your hand* (Deuteronomy 6:8); and the explanation of this verse was given [in the Oral Tradition][1] that we are to bind on our hand, by the law of the Torah, four sections of Scripture. These are called *t'fillin* when they are tied by straps, as the Oral Tradition was given about them. Now, these are the four sections of Scripture: two of them are at the end of *sidrah bo*, namely, *Sanctify to Me every firstborn* (Exodus 13:2) until, *You shall therefore keep this ordinance at its season from year to year* (ibid. 10), which is one section in every accurate Torah scroll or volume; then, from *And it shall be when the Lord shall bring you* (ibid.11) till the end of the *sidrah*, which concludes, *for by strength of hand the Lord brought us forth out of Egypt* (ibid. 16)—this is the second section. Toward the end of *sidrah va'eth-ḥanan* in the *Book of Deuteronomy*, the section of *Hear, Israel*

פָּרָשַׁת "שְׁמַע יִשְׂרָאֵל" עַד "וּבִשְׁעָרֶיךָ" פָּרָשָׁה שְׁלִישִׁית, וּבְסוֹף סֵדֶר וְהָיָה עֵקֶב, פָּרָשַׁת "וְהָיָה אִם שָׁמֹעַ תִּשְׁמְעוּ" עַד "(לָתֵת לָהֶם כִּימֵי הַשָּׁמַיִם) עַל הָאָרֶץ" פָּרָשָׁה רְבִיעִית.

אַרְבַּע פָּרָשִׁיּוֹת אֵלּוּ כּוֹתְבִין בִּקְלָף אֶחָד וְגוֹלְלוֹ כְּמִין סֵפֶר תּוֹרָה לִתְחִלָּתוֹ, וּמַנִּיחוֹ בְּבַיִת שֶׁל עוֹר, וּמַעֲבִיר בְּקָצֶה הָעוֹר רְצוּעָה אַחַת, וְקוֹשֵׁר אוֹתוֹ הָעוֹר שֶׁהַפָּרָשִׁיּוֹת בְּתוֹכוֹ עַל הַזְּרוֹעַ שְׂמֹאל, וְאַחַר שֶׁהֵן קְשׁוּרוֹת בַּזְּרוֹעַ הֵן שׁוֹכְבוֹת כְּנֶגֶד הַלֵּב, וְהֵן הַנִּקְרָאִין תְּפִלִּין שֶׁל יָד בְּכָל מָקוֹם.

מִשָּׁרְשֵׁי הַמִּצְוָה, לְפִי שֶׁהָאָדָם בִּהְיוֹתוֹ בַּעַל חֹמֶר יִמָּשֵׁךְ בְּהֶכְרֵחַ אַחַר הַתַּאֲווֹת, כִּי כֵן טֶבַע הַחֹמֶר לְבַקֵּשׁ כָּל הֲנָאוֹת אֵלָיו וְהָעֵרֶב, כְּסוּס כְּפֶרֶד אֵין הָבִין, אִם לֹא שֶׁהַנֶּפֶשׁ שֶׁחֲנָנוּ הָאֵל תִּמְנָעֵנוּ לְפִי כֹחָהּ מִן הַחֵטְא; וּמֵאֲשֶׁר תִּשְׁכֹּן בִּגְבוּלוֹ שֶׁהִיא הָאָרֶץ וּרְחוֹקָה מְאֹד מִגְּבוּלָהּ שֶׁהוּא הַשָּׁמַיִם, לֹא תוּכַל לוֹ, יִגְבַּר כֹּחוֹ עָלֶיהָ תָּמִיד, לָכֵן הִיא צְרִיכָה עַל־כָּל־פָּנִים לְהַרְבֵּה שׁוֹמְרִים לְשָׁמְרָהּ מִשְּׁכֵנָהּ הָרַע, פֶּן יָקוּם עָלֶיהָ וְיַהַרְגָהּ, אַחֲרֵי הֱיוֹתָהּ בִּגְבוּלוֹ וְתַחַת יָדוֹ.

וְרָצָה הַמָּקוֹם לְזַכּוֹתֵנוּ אֲנַחְנוּ עַם הַקֹּדֶשׁ, וְצִוָּנוּ לְהַעֲמִיד שׁוֹמְרִים גְּבּוֹרִים סָבִיב לָהּ, וְהֵם שֶׁנִּצְטַוֵּינוּ לְבַל נַפְסִיק דִּבְרֵי תוֹרָה מִפִּינוּ יוֹמָם וָלַיְלָה, וְשֶׁנִּתֵּן אַרְבַּע צִיצִיּוֹת בְּאַרְבַּע כַּנְפוֹת כְּסוּתֵנוּ וּמְזוּזָה בְּפִתְחֵנוּ וְהַתְּפִלִּין בְּיָדֵנוּ וּבְרֹאשֵׁנוּ, וְהַכֹּל לְהַזְכִּירֵנוּ לְמַעַן נֶחְדַּל מֵעֵשֶׂק יָדֵינוּ וְלֹא נָתוּר אַחֲרֵי עֵינֵינוּ וְאַחֲרֵי יֵצֶר מַחְשְׁבוֹת לִבֵּנוּ.

וּמִפְּנֵי־כֵן אָמְרוּ זִכְרוֹנָם לִבְרָכָה שֶׁהַכֹּהֲנִים וְהַלְוִיִּים בִּשְׁעַת עֲבוֹדָה פְּטוּרִין מֵהֶן. וּבִהְיוֹת מִיסוֹד הַתְּפִלִּין מַה שֶּׁזָּכַרְנוּ, נִצְטַוֵּינוּ עֲלֵיהֶם לְבַל נָסִיחַ מֵהֶן דַּעְתֵּנוּ. וְעַתָּה, בְּנִי, רְאֵה גַם רְאֵה כַּמָּה כֹחַ גּוּפֵנוּ גָדוֹל עַל נַפְשֵׁנוּ, כִּי עַל כָּל אֵלֶּה יַעֲלֶה

§421   1. Mechilta, *bo*, end.

2. TB M'naḥoth 34b.

3. Derived from *ibid.* 31b.

4. *Ibid.* 35a.

5. *Ibid.* 36b.

6. *Ibid.* 37b.

7. Literally, according to its strength.

8. TB Z'vaḥim 19a.

9. I.e. the obligation of wearing *t'fillin*, since the Divine service at the Temple is sufficient to keep them beyond the power of sin.

(Deuteronomy 6:4), till *and upon your gates* (*ibid.* 9), is the third section. And toward the end of *sidrah 'ékev*, the section, *And it shall be if you hearken* (*ibid.* 11:13), until the words, *as the.days of the heavens above the earth* (*ibid.* 21), is the fourth section.[1]

These four portions of Scripture are written on one sheet of parchment,[2] which is rolled in the form of a Torah scroll, from its end to its beginning.[3] It is then placed in a container of leather,[2] and at one edge of the leather [box] one strap extends.[4] This leather [box] in which the Scriptural sections lie is then bound to the left arm;[5] and after they are fastened to the arm, they lie against the heart.[6] These are called everywhere "the *t'fillin* of the hand."

At the root of the precept lies the reason that a man, being a creature of physical matter, would be drawn perforce after desires — for such is the nature of physical matter, to seek whatever is gratifying and pleasurable to it, *as a horse, as a mule, without understanding* (Psalms 32:9) — were it not that the spirit with which God graced him prevents him, as it is able to,[7] from sin. Yet since it [the spirit] dwells in its [physical matter's] region, which is the earth, and is far away from its own region, heaven, it cannot prevail against it [physical matter]; its power overcomes it constantly. It [the spirit] therefore needs, in any event, many guards to protect it from its evil neighbor, for it [physical matter] might rise up against it and kill it, since it [the spirit] is in its region and under its hand.

Yet the omnipresent God wished to make us, the people of holiness, virtuous; and so He commanded us to position mighty guards around it [the spirit]. This is why we were ordered not to let the words of Torah cease in our mouth day or night, and that we are to put four tassels *(tzitzith)* at the four corners of our garments (§ 386), a *m'zuzah* at our entrances (§ 423), and *t'fillin* on our hands and heads — all to keep us remembering, in order that we may stay our hand from wrongdoing, and shall not go straying after our eyes and after the inclination of our heart's thoughts.

For this reason the Sages of blessed memory taught[8] that *kohanim* and Levites, during the Temple service, are free of their obligation.[9] And since the fundamental reason for *t'fillin* (phylacteries) is what we have mentioned, we were commanded about them[5] that we are not to let our mind be diverted from them. Yet now see, my son, but see how much greater is the strength of our body than that of our spirit: for with all these it will rise up at times and break through our fences.

לִפְעָמִים וּפָרַץ גְּדֵרֵנוּ, הָאֵל בַּחֲסָדָיו יְהִי בְעֶזְרֵנוּ וְיִשְׁמְרֵנוּ מִמֶּנּוּ.

מִדִּינֵי הַמִּצְוָה, מַה שֶּׁאָמְרוּ זִכְרוֹנָם לִבְרָכָה שֶׁעֲשָׂרָה דְבָרִים יֵשׁ בַּתְּפִלִּין, בֵּין שֶׁל רֹאשׁ וְשֶׁל יָד, כֻּלָּן הֲלָכָה לְמֹשֶׁה מִסִּינַי, וְהַמְשַׁנֶּה בְּאַחַת מִכֻּלָּם הֲרֵי הַתְּפִלִּין פְּסוּלוֹת: שְׁנַיִם מֵהֶן בִּכְתִיבָתָן, וּשְׁמוֹנָה בַּחֲפוּיָן וּקְשִׁירַת רְצוּעוֹתֵיהֶן. וְאֵלּוּ הֵן הַשְּׁנַיִם שֶׁבִּכְתִיבָתָן: שֶׁכּוֹתְבִין אוֹתָם בִּדְיוֹ, וְשֶׁיִּהְיוּ נִכְתָּבוֹת עַל הַקְּלָף; וְאֵלּוּ הֵן הַשְּׁמוֹנָה שֶׁבַּחֲפוּיָן: א. שֶׁיִּהְיוּ מְרֻבָּעוֹת, וְכֵן תְּפִירָתָן בְּרִבּוּעַ וַאֲלַכְסוֹנָם בְּרִבּוּעַ, עַד שֶׁיִּהְיֶה לָהֶן אַרְבַּע זָוִיּוֹת שָׁווֹת; ב. וְשֶׁיִּהְיֶה בָּעוֹר שֶׁל רֹאשׁ צוּרַת שׁי"ן מִיָּמִין וּמִשְּׂמֹאל; ג. וְשֶׁיִּכְרֹךְ הַפָּרָשִׁיּוֹת בְּמַטְלִית; ד. וְשֶׁיִּכְרֹךְ אוֹתָן בִּשְׂעַר שֶׁל בְּהֵמָה אוֹ חַיָּה טְהוֹרָה וְאַחַר־כָּךְ מַכְנִיסָן בְּבָתֵּיהֶן שֶׁל עוֹר; ה. וְשֶׁיִּהְיוּ תוֹפְרִין אוֹתָן בְּגִידִין; ו. וְשֶׁעוֹשִׂין לָהֶן מַעֲבֹרֶת מֵעוֹר הַחִפּוּי שֶׁתִּכָּנֵס בָּהּ הָרְצוּעָה עַד שֶׁתְּהֵא עוֹבֶרֶת וְהוֹלֶכֶת בְּתוֹךְ תִּבָּה שֶׁלָּהּ; ז. וְשֶׁיִּהְיוּ הָרְצוּעוֹת שְׁחוֹרוֹת; ח. וְשֶׁיִּהְיֶה הַקֶּשֶׁר שֶׁלָּהֶן יָדוּעַ בְּצוּרַת דל"ת.

וּמַה שֶּׁאָמְרוּ שֶׁאֵין עוֹשִׂין הַתְּפִלִּין וּרְצוּעוֹתֵיהֶן אֶלָּא יִשְׂרָאֵל, וְאֹרֶךְ הָרְצוּעָה שֶׁל יָד כְּדֵי שֶׁתַּקִּיף הַזְּרוֹעַ בִּמְקוֹם הַנַּחְתָּן בּוֹ וְיִקְשֹׁר מִמֶּנָּה הַקֶּשֶׁר הַיָּדוּעַ שֶׁצָּרִיךְ לִהְיוֹת בְּצוּרַת יו"ד, וְתִמָּתַח עַד הָאֶצְבַּע הָאֶמְצָעִית וְיִכְרֹךְ מִמֶּנָּה עַל אֶצְבָּעוֹ שָׁלֹשׁ כְּרִיכוֹת וְיִקְשֹׁר; וְאִם הָיְתָה אֲרֻכָּה יוֹתֵר מִזֶּה, כְּשֵׁרָה.

וּבְאֵי זֶה מָקוֹם מִן הַזְּרוֹעַ קוֹשְׁרִין אוֹתָהּ — עַל הַקִּבֹּרֶת, וְהוּא הַבָּשָׂר הַתָּפוּחַ שֶׁבַּמַּרְפֵּק שֶׁבֵּין פֶּרֶק הַכָּתֵף וּפֶרֶק הַזְּרוֹעַ, שֶׁנִּמְצָא כְּשֶׁהוּא מְדַבֵּק מַרְפְּקוֹ לְצַלְעָיו יִהְיוּ הַתְּפִלִּין שׁוֹכְבִין כְּנֶגֶד לִבּוֹ, וְנִמְצָא מְקֻיָּם "וְהָיוּ הַדְּבָרִים הָאֵלֶּה... עַל לְבָבֶךָ".

וּמַה שֶּׁאָמְרוּ שֶׁתְּפִלָּה שֶׁל יָד אֵינָהּ מְעַכֶּבֶת שֶׁל רֹאשׁ וְשֶׁל רֹאשׁ אֵינָהּ מְעַכֶּבֶת

10. MT *hilchoth t'fillin* i 3, iii 1.

11. TB Shabbath 103b; TJ M'gillah i 9.

12. TB M'nahoth 32a.

13. Before being put into the leather box; TJ M'gillah i 9.

14. TB Shabbath 108a.

15. TB M'nahoth 35b; MT *hilchoth t'fillin* iii 1.

16. TB Gittin 45b.

17. MT *ibid.* 12, based on his understanding of TB M'nahoth 35b (*Kessef Mishneh*).

18. TB M'nahoth 38a.

19. I.e. if only one of the two could be put on, it is acceptable as the fulfillment of its precept.

May God in His mercies come to our aid and protect us from it.

Among the laws of the precept there is what the Sages of blessed memory taught:[10] that there are ten things [required] about t'fillin, both of the hand and of the head, all being law [given orally] to Moses at Sinai; and if a person alters any one of them all, the t'fillin are disqualified. Two of them concern their writing, and eight concern their enclosure and the tying of their straps. These are the two about their writing: that they [the Scriptural sections] are to be written with ink,[11] and are to be written on parchment.[12] And these are the eight about their enclosures: (1) that they should be square, and so should their stitching be in a square, with [equal] diagonals of a square, so that they should have four equal [right-angled] corners;[4] (2) on the leather [box] of the [t'fillin] of the head there should be the form of the letter *shin* at the right and left sides;[4] (3) the Scriptural sections should be wrapped in a strip of cloth;[13] (4) they should then be wrapped in the hair of a pure (kosher) domestic or wild animal— [put] over the strip of cloth—and then inserted in their leather container;[14] (5) the stitching should be done with sinews [of a kosher animal];[14] (6) a "passageway" (a folded border open at both ends) should be made next to them out of the leather of the enclosure, in which the strap is inserted, so that it can pass through its own box;[4] (7) the straps should be black;[4] (8) and their knot should be the one known as the form of the letter *da-leth.*[15]

Then there is what the Sages said:[16] that none but a Jew may make the t'fillin and their straps; the length of the strap [for the t'fillin] of the hand should be enough to go about the arm at the place where it is put on, and the known knot should be tied with it, which needs to be in the form of the letter *yod*; and then it should stretch till the middle finger, whereupon one should make three windings with it about his finger and fasten it. If it is longer than that, it is acceptable.[17]

At which place on the arm is it to be fastened?—at the biceps, which is the elevated flesh above the elbow, between the shoulder and arm joints; consequently, when one attaches his elbow to his ribs, the t'fillin will rest against his heart; and the result is that he fulfills [the Torah's instruction] *And these words...shall be upon your heart* (Deuteronomy 6:6).[6]

There is, too, what the Sages said:[18] that the t'fillin (phylactery) of the hand does not prevent that of the head [from being acceptable], nor does that of the head prevent the one of the hand[19]—because

שֶׁל יָד, מִפְּנֵי שֶׁהֵן שְׁתֵּי מִצְוֹות, וְעַל שֶׁל רֹאשׁ מְבָרֵךְ "עַל מִצְוַת תְּפִלִּין", וְעַל שֶׁל
יָד "לְהָנִיחַ תְּפִלִּין"; וּבַמֶּה דְבָרִים אֲמוּרִים, בְּשֶׁהִנִּיחַ אֶחָד מֵהֶן, אֲבָל אִם הִנִּיחַ
שְׁנֵיהֶן (יַחַד) מְבָרֵךְ בְּרָכָה אַחַת בִּלְבַד, וְהִיא "לְהָנִיחַ תְּפִלִּין", וּמֵנִיחַ תְּחִלָּה שֶׁל
יָד וְאַחַר־כָּךְ שֶׁל רֹאשׁ. וּכְשֶׁהוּא חוֹלְצָן חוֹלֵץ שֶׁל רֹאשׁ תְּחִלָּה.

וּמַה שֶּׁאָמְרוּ שֶׁזְּמַן הַנַּחַת תְּפִלִּין בַּיּוֹם, מִשֶּׁיִּרְאֶה חֲבֵרוֹ עַד שֶׁתִּשְׁקַע הַחַמָּה,
שֶׁנֶּאֱמַר "וְשָׁמַרְתָּ אֶת הַחֻקָּה הַזֹּאת...מִיָּמִים יָמִימָה", וְחֻקָּה זוֹ הִיא מִצְוַת תְּפִלִּין.
וְשַׁבָּת וְיוֹם־טוֹב, וְהוּא הַדִּין לְחֻלּוֹ שֶׁל מוֹעֵד, אֵינוֹ זְמַן הַנַּחַת תְּפִלִּין, שֶׁנֶּאֱמַר
עֲלֵיהֶם "וְהָיוּ לְאוֹת", וְשַׁבָּתוֹת וְיָמִים־טוֹבִים הֵן עַצְמָן אוֹת וְאֵין צְרִיכִין לְאוֹת
אַחֵר.

וּמַה שֶּׁאָמְרוּ שֶׁתְּפִלִּין צְרִיכִין גּוּף נָקִי, וְאָמְרוּ בַגְּמָרָא: מַאי גּוּף נָקִי, שֶׁיִּזָּהֵר
שֶׁלֹּא יָפִיחַ בָּהֶן; אֲבָל אֵין הָעִנְיָן לוֹמַר שֶׁצְּרִיכִין גּוּף נָקִי מֵעֲבֵרוֹת אוֹ מִטֻּמְאָה, כִּי
כָל אָדָם וַאֲפִלּוּ טָמֵא וּבַעַל עֲבֵרוֹת מְחֻיָּב בְּמִצְוַת תְּפִלִּין, וּבִלְבַד שֶׁיֵּדַע לְהִזָּהֵר
שֶׁלֹּא יָפִיחַ בָּהֶן; וְאוּלַי מִתּוֹךְ הַתְמָדָתוֹ בְּמִצְוַת הַתְּפִלִּין, שֶׁהֵן הַזִּכָּרוֹן גָּדוֹל לְאָדָם
בִּמְלֶאכֶת שָׁמַיִם, יָשׁוּב מִדַּרְכּוֹ הָרָעָה וְיִטַּהֵר מִכָּל גִּלּוּלָיו.

וַחֲכָמִים זִכְרוֹנָם לִבְרָכָה חִיְּבוּנוּ בְּמִצְוַת הַתְּפִלִּין לְחַנֵּךְ בָּהּ אֲפִלּוּ הַנְּעָרִים
הַקְּטַנִּים, כָּל זְמַן שֶׁהִגִּיעוּ לִכְלָל שֶׁיֵּדְעוּ לִשְׁמֹר אוֹתָן. וּמִזֶּה יֵשׁ לְהָבִין שֶׁדַּעַת
רַבּוֹתֵינוּ זִכְרוֹנָם לִבְרָכָה לִהְיוֹת כָּל אָדָם מַחֲזִיק בְּמִצְוָה זוֹ וְרָגִיל בָּהּ, כִּי הִיא עִקָּר

---

20. MT *hilchoth t'fillin* iv 4–5, based on TB M'naḥoth 36a. (Our practice, based on other authorities, differs.)

21. TB *ibid.*

22. TB B'rachoth 9b, M'naḥoth 36a; MT *ibid.* 10.

23. Literal translation.

24. So Mechilta on the verse.

25. Of the special relationship and bond between Jewry and the Almighty. On the Sabbath, Rashi (M'naḥoth 36b, s.v. *shehén*) cites Exodus 31:13, *for it is a sign between Me and you.* R. Yitzḥak of Vienna, *'Or Zaru'a* (I § 589) cites R. 'Elyakim as giving *ibid.* 17, *Between Me and the Israelites it is a sign forever.* As for the festivals, R. 'Elyakim continues that both they and the Sabbath are themselves signs because on these days both the river Sambatyon, and spirits of the dead that mediums (*'ovim*) raise by their masculinity, remain at rest. So too *Shittah M'kubetzeth* on TB M'naḥoth 36b. Alternatively, continues R. 'Elyakim, these days are themselves signs because work (labor) is forbidden then.

The elder R. Moshe of Trani (*Kiryath Séfer*, on MT *ibid.*) writes: The word *'oth* (sign) is written in regard to the Passover of Egypt [Exodus 12:13], and in *sidrah 'emor* (Leviticus 23) all the festivals are denoted as equal. Or else it is because the word *'oth* is written twice about the Sabbath (Exodus 31:13, 17): once for itself, and once to apply to the festival days; or alternatively, because it is written, *You shall but keep My Sabbaths [for it is a sign*, etc.] (Exodus 31:13): it can be applied to

they are two [separate] precepts. Over the phylactery of the head the benediction is said, "[Blessed art Thou, Lord our God, who hallowed us with His *mitzvoth* and commanded us] about the precept of *t'fillin*"; and over the one on the hand, "[and commanded us] to put on *t'fillin*." Now, where does this rule hold?—where a person puts on one of them; but if he puts on both [together, at one time], he is to say only one benediction, namely, "[and commanded us] to put on *t'fillin*,"[20] whereupon he puts on first the one on the hand, and then the one on the head;[21] and when he takes them off, he is to remove the one on the head first.[21]

There is, further, what the Sages taught:[22] that the time for putting on *t'fillin* is during the day, from the time one can see his fellow-man until the sun sets; for it stated, *You shall therefore keep this ordinance...from days to days*[23] (Exodus 13:10), and "this ordinance" means the precept of *t'fillin*.[24] The Sabbath and a festival day, though —and the same law applies to the non-holy (intermediate) days of a festival—are not a time for putting on *t'fillin*: for it is stated about them [*t'fillin*], *and it shall be for a sign* (ibid. 9), and the Sabbaths and festival days are themselves a sign,[25] thus needing no other token.[26]

Then there is what the Sages said:[27] that *t'fillin* require a clean body; and it was stated in the Talmud:[27] What does "a clean body" mean?—that one should take care not to emit flatulence while wearing them. The meaning, however, is not to convey that one needs a body clean of sins or ritual defilement. For every man, even if ritually unclean or sinful, is duty-bound by the precept of *t'fillin*, as long as he knows to take care not to pass flatulence while wearing them. And perhaps, through his steady observance of the precept of *t'fillin*, which are a great reminder for a man of the work of Heaven, he will turn back from his evil way and will become purified of all his foulnesses.

Now, the Sages of blessed memory obligated us about the precept of *t'fillin* to train even small boys in it, as long as they have reached the stage where they know to take care of them.[28] From this it can be understood that the view of our Sages of blessed memory is that every man should hold fast to this *mitzvah* and be accustomed to it. For it is

the festival days as well, since "Sabbaths" is in the plural.

26. Mechilta on the verse; TB 'Eruvin 96a, M'naḥoth 36b; MT *ibid.*
27. TB Shabbath 49a; MT *ibid.* iv 15.
28. TB Sukkah 42a (this is not the general practice today).

גָּדוֹל וּשְׁמִירָה רַבָּה מִן הָעֲבֵרוֹת וְסֻלָּם חָזָק לַעֲלוֹת עָמָּהּ לְהִכָּנֵס בַּעֲבוֹדַת הַבּוֹרֵא
בָּרוּךְ הוּא; וְהַמַּחְמִירִים בִּקְדֻשַּׁת הַמִּצְוָה וּמְנִיאִים לֵב הֲמוֹן בְּדִבְרֵיהֶם מְהִתְעַסֵּק
בָּהּ, אוּלֵי כַוָּנָתָם לְטוֹבָה, אֲבָל בֶּאֱמֶת יֵשׁ בָּזֶה מְנִיעָה לִבְנֵי־אָדָם בְּכַמָּה מִצְווֹת,
וְהִיא רָעָה רַבָּה.

וְאִם יָדַעְתִּי כִּי יִסְמְכוּ הַדּוֹרְשִׁים דְּרָשׁוֹת אֵלּוּ עַל מַעֲשֶׂה שֶׁנִּזְכַּר בִּירוּשַׁלְמִי
בְּחַד בַּר־נָשׁ דְּאַפְקִיד גַּבֵּי חַבְרֵהּ כָּסָא דְכַסְפָּא וְלַזְּמָן תַּבְעֵהּ נִיהֲלֵהּ וּכְפַר בֵּהּ,
וַאֲמַר לֵהּ בַּעַל הַכּוֹס "לָא לָךְ הַיְמִינִית אֶלָּא לְאָלֵין שֶׁבְּרֹאשֶׁךָ", וְכַוָּנָתָם לוֹמַר
שֶׁיֵּשׁ חִלּוּל הַשֵּׁם לְהִתְחַסֵּד בְּקְצָת מִצְווֹת וּלְהַרְשִׁיעַ בְּקְצָתָן, לֹא כֵן בֵּיתִי אָנִי עִם
הָאֵל, כִּי יָדַעְתִּי שֶׁאֵין צַדִּיק בָּאָרֶץ אֲשֶׁר יַעֲשֶׂה טוֹב וְלֹא יֶחֱטָא, וְעִם כָּל זֶה לֹא
נִמְנָעֵהוּ מֵהִתְעַסֵּק בַּמִּצְוָה בְּעֵת רוּחַ אֱלֹהִים טוֹבָה יִלְבָּשֵׁהוּ לַעֲשׂוֹת טוֹב, כִּי מִי
יוֹדֵעַ אִם אוּלֵי יִמְשֵׁךְ בְּדַרְכוֹ הַטּוֹבָה עַד עֵת מוֹתוֹ וְהַמָּוֶת פִּתְאֹם תָּבוֹא, וּכְבָר
לִמְּדוּנוּ זִכְרוֹנָם לִבְרָכָה שֶׁמִּצְוָה גּוֹרֶרֶת מִצְוָה, וְשֶׂכַר מִצְוָה מִצְוָה; בְּכָל אֵלֶּה
הַדְּבָרִים וּמוּסָרִים טוֹבִים קַדְמוּנוּ וְהוֹרוּנוּ זִכְרוֹנָם לִבְרָכָה; וְהַמִּתְחַכְּמִים לְהוֹסִיף
עַל דִּבְרֵיהֶם אוֹ לִגְרֹעַ, אֵינָהּ חָכְמָה.

וּמַה שֶּׁאָמְרוּ שֶׁסִּדּוּר הַפָּרְשִׁיּוֹת בִּקְלַף הַתְּפִלִּין כָּךְ הוּא: שֶׁכּוֹתְבִין תְּחִלָּה
פָּרָשַׁת "קַדֶּשׁ לִי", וְאַחַר־כָּךְ פָּרָשַׁת "וְהָיָה כִּי יְבִאֲךָ", וְאַחַר־כָּךְ פָּרָשַׁת "שְׁמַע
יִשְׂרָאֵל", וְאַחַר־כָּךְ פָּרָשַׁת "וְהָיָה אִם שָׁמֹעַ". וַאֲשֶׁר אָמְרוּ שֶׁכּוֹתְבִים הַיְנוֹת
בָּאֶמְצַע, כְּלוֹמַר פָּרָשַׁת "וְהָיָה כִּי יְבִאֲךָ" וּפָרָשַׁת "וְהָיָה אִם שָׁמֹעַ" בָּאֶמְצַע,
וּפָרָשַׁת "קַדֶּשׁ לִי" בָּרֹאשׁ וּפָרָשַׁת "שְׁמַע" בַּסּוֹף, לֹא כִּוְּנוּ הָעִנְיָן יָפֶה, וַהֲרֵי

29. Evidently by stressing the great condition of holiness, etc. that must be maintained while wearing t'fillin, they made great numbers reluctant or afraid to put them on. In *Séfer Mitzvoth Gadol* (positive precept §3) R. Moses of Coucy indicates that many Jews in his time neglected the precept of t'fillin; and he writes that in 1236 he succeeded in inspiring Spain's Jews to return to the faithful observance of the *mitzvoth* of t'fillin, m'zuzah (§ 423) and tzitzith (§ 386).

30. Evidently in the sense that putting on t'fillin and wearing them would induce people to pray the more, with greater intensity and concentration, study Torah the more, and in general become more observant of the *mitzvoth*. See the citation in the next paragraph that "one *mitzvah* draws another in its wake, and the reward of one *mitzvah* is another *mitzvah*."

31. TJ B'rachoth ii 3.

32. Expression based on II Samuel 23:5.

33. Mishnah, 'Avoth iv 2.

34. I.e. the desire, opportunity and merit of fulfilling another.

35. Mechilta, *bo*, to Exodus 13:16.

36. See e.g. Rabbénu Tam in *tosafoth* to TB M'naḥoth 34b, s.v. *v'ha-koré*. On the term הויות which follows, cf. the phrase סימן הויות להדדי in *loc cit.* etc.

a great matter of main importance, a major protection from sins, and a sturdy ladder by which to ascend to enter upon the service and worship of the Creator, blessed is He. As for those who are stringent about the holiness of the precept, and they dissuade the heart of the mass of people by their words, from occupying themselves with it[29] — perhaps their intention is for the good, but in truth this entails a restraint for people from many *mitzvoth*,[30] and it is a great ill.

Very well I know that those who expound these teachings base themselves perhaps on an incident mentioned in the Jerusalem Talmud,[31] about a certain man who left a silver cup with his fellow-man for safekeeping. After a time he claimed it from him, and the other denied the matter. Said the owner of the cup to him, "Not in you did I believe, but in those [*t'fillin*] on your head." Their meaning is thus to say that it is a desecration of the Divine name to act piously with some of the precepts and act wickedly about some of them. Not so is my own house [conception] established with God;[32] for I know that *there is no righteous man on earth who does good and does not sin* (Ecclesiastes 7:20); yet despite that, we should not restrain a person from occupying himself with a *mitzvah* when a good Divine spirit possesses him to do good. For who knows if he will [not] perhaps continue in his good path until the time of his death, as death can come suddenly. And long ago our Sages of blessed memory taught us[33] that one *mitzvah* (good religious deed) draws another in its wake, and the reward of one *mitzvah* is another *mitzvah*.[34] With all these words and good moral teachings, the Sages of blessed memory preceded us and instructed us. As for those who grow overly wise to add to their words or detract from their words — that is not wisdom.

There is, moreover, what the Sages said:[35] that the order of the Scriptural portions on the parchment of the *t'fillin* is this: First the section, *Sanctify to Me every firstborn* (Exodus 13:1–10) is written; then the section, *And it shall be when the Lord will bring you* (ibid. 11–16); then the portion, *Hear, Israel* (Deuteronomy 6:4–9); and afterward the section, *And it shall be if you hearken* (ibid. 11:13–21). As for those who said[36] that the parts beginning "And it shall be," are written in the middle — which means the portion, *And it shall be when the Lord will bring you*, and the section, *And it shall be if you hearken*, [are to be written] in the middle; the portion, *Sanctify to Me*, at the head; and the section of *Sh'ma [Hear, Israel]* at the end — they did not apprehend the matter well. For you see, Rashi, Rambam and R. Hai

רַשִׁ"י וְהָרַמְבַּ"ם וְרַבֵּנוּ הַאי גָאוֹן זִכְרוֹנָם לִבְרָכָה דַּעַת כֻּלָּם שֶׁלֹּא נִכְתָּב הַנָּיוֹת בָּאֶמְצַע אֶלָּא כְּסֵדֶר שֶׁהֵן כְּתוּבִין בַּתּוֹרָה.

וְהָרְאָיָה מִמַּה שֶׁנִּמְצָא בְּפֶרֶק הַקּוֹמֵץ בִּמְנָחוֹת גַּבֵּי סִדּוּר הַתְּפִלִּין, שֶׁאָמְרוּ שָׁם "וְהַקּוֹרֵא קוֹרֵא", כְּלוֹמַר כְּדֵי שֶׁיְּהֵא הַקּוֹרֵא קוֹרֵא כְּסֵדֶר הַתּוֹרָה; וְנֶסַח זֶה וַדַּאי לֹא מְצָאוּהוּ בְּסִפְרָם אוֹתָם בְּנֵי-אָדָם שֶׁהָיָה דַעְתָּם לוֹמַר דְּכַתְבִינָן הַנָּיוֹת בָּאֶמְצַע. וּמִכָּל-מָקוֹם כֵּן הַסְכִּימוּ מוֹרֵינוּ יִשְׁמְרֵם אֵל עַכְשָׁיו כְּמוֹ שֶׁכָּתַבְנוּ, שֶׁנִּכְתָּבֵם כְּסֵדֶר הַפָּרָשִׁיוֹת שֶׁכְּתוּבוֹת בַּתּוֹרָה.

וְדִין כְּתִיבָתָן, וְדִין הַתָּגִין שֶׁבָּהֶן, וְדִין הַכּוֹתֵב בָּהֶן אֶת הַשֵּׁם בֵּין הַשִּׁטִין אוֹ אוֹת אַחַת מֵהֶן, מַה דִּינוֹ; וְדִין עִבּוּד הָעוֹר, וּבְאֵי זֶה צַד מִן הָעוֹר הֵן נִכְתָּבִין, וְדִין אִם כְּתָבָן מִין אוֹ גוֹי, וְדִין שֶׁאֵין צְרִיכִין בְּדִיקָה — וַאֲפִלּוּ לְמֵאָה שָׁנָה — כְּמוֹ מְזוּזָה, וְדִין הַלּוֹקֵחַ תְּפִלִּין מִמִּי שֶׁאֵינוֹ מָמְחֶה, וְדִין תְּפִירָתָן בְּגִידִין שֶׁל בְּהֵמָה אוֹ חַיָּה טְהוֹרָה, וְדִין תְּפִלִּין שֶׁנִּפְסְקוּ הַתְּפִירוֹת שֶׁלָּהֶן אוֹ רְצוּעוֹתֵיהֶן, וְדִין מִי שֶׁתְּפִלִּין עָלָיו וְצָרִיךְ לֶאֱכֹל אוֹ לְהִכָּנֵס בְּבֵית הַכִּסֵּא קָבוּעַ אוֹ עֲרַאי, אוֹ שֶׁשָּׁכַח וְנִכְנַס בָּהֶן; וְדִין הַנִּכְנָס בָּהֶן לְבֵית הַמֶּרְחָץ; וְיֶתֶר פְּרָטֵי הַמִּצְוָה, מְבֹאָרִין בִּמְנָחוֹת פֶּרֶק רְבִיעִי.

וְנוֹהֶגֶת מִצְוָה זוֹ בְּכָל מָקוֹם וּבְכָל זְמָן, בִּזְכָרִים אֲבָל לֹא בִנְקֵבוֹת, לְפִי שֶׁהִיא מִצְוַת עֲשֵׂה שֶׁהַזְּמָן גְּרָמָא; וּמִכָּל-מָקוֹם אִם רָצוּ לְהַנִּיחַ אֵין מְמַחִין בְּיָדָם וְשָׂכָר

---

37. Rashi: in TB M'naḥoth 34b, s.v. *v'ha-koré*; Rambam: in MT *hilchoth t'fillin* iii 5–6. R. Hai Ga'on, however, according to the following sources (including Rashba; see note 38) holds the opposing view: *tosafoth* (note 35); R. Baruch of Worms, *Séfer haT'rumah, hilchoth t'fillin* §206 (ed. Warsaw 1897, p. 136a); R. Isaac of Vienna, *'Or Zaru'a, hilchoth t'fillin* §588 (ed. Zhitomir 1862, I p. 153b); *Maḥzor Vitry* §512 (p. 640); etc. Such works, though, as *Kol Bo (hilchoth t'fillin), Séfer haT'rumah (loc. cit.)* and R. Aaron of Lunel, *'Orḥoth Ḥayyim* (I, *hilchoth t'fillin* §26; ed. Jerusalem 1957, p. 19b) cite *Shimmusha Rabba* as a third authority agreeing with Rashi and Rambam; and this forms part of *Halachoth G'doloth* in ed. *M'kitzé Nirdamim* (Jerusalem 1971; pp. 488–96, and see Introduction p. 46). Perhaps our author similarly knew *Shimmusha Rabba* as part of the larger work and therefore wrote בה"ג = *ba'al* (author of) *Halachoth G'doloth*, and a scribal error changed it to רה"ג = R. Hai Ga'on.

38. Literally, should read [the sections], etc. I.e. what occurs earlier in the Torah is to be written earlier on the parchment for the *t'fillin.*

39. So Rashba (R. Sh'lomoh ibn 'Adreth), *Responsa ascribed to Ramban,* §234; see also his *Responsa,* I §639.

40. See the sixth paragraph, at notes 11–12, and MT *hilchoth t'fillin* ii.

41. Small grace-lines above the letters; TB M'naḥoth 29b.

42. TB M'naḥoth 30b; TJ M'gillah i 9; MT *ibid.* i 16.

43. TB Gittin 22a, M'naḥoth 32a; MT *ibid.* 6–8.

Ga'on of blessed memory are all of the view that the parts beginning
"And it shall be" are not to be written in the middle, but only in the
order in which they are written in the Torah.[37]

The proof lies in what we find in the third chapter of the Talmud
tractate *M'naḥoth* (34b) concerning the order in the *t'fillin*: For it was
stated there, "and a reader is to read"; in other words, [they should be
written] so that one who reads it should find [the sections] in the
order of the Torah:[38] Well, those people whose opinion is to say that
the parts beginning "And it shall be" should be written first certainly
did not find this text in their volume [of the Talmud]. In any event,
though, our master teachers (God protect them) thus agreed now, as
we have written, that we are to write them in the order that the
portions are written in the Torah.[39]

Then there is the law on writing them,[40] the law of the tittles[41] in
them; the law for one who writes the Divine name in them between
the lines, or one letter of them [thus], what the ruling for him should
be;[42] the law on treating (preparing) the leather (parchment), and on
which side of the leather they are written;[43] the law if a sectarian
heretic or a non-Jew wrote them;[44] and the law that they do not
require inspection even 100 years after,[45] as a *m'zuzah* (§ 423) [indeed
does]. Then we have the law if a person buys *t'fillin* from one who is
not a learned expert;[46] the law on sewing them with sinews of a pure
(kosher) domestic or wild animal;[14] the law on *t'fillin* whose stitches
or straps became severed;[47] the law if a person has *t'fillin* on him and
he needs to eat or enter a permanent or temporary place of easement,
or if he forgot and entered them;[48] and the law if a person wearing
them entered a bath-house.[49] The remaining details of the precept are
explained in the Talmud tractate *M'naḥoth*, chapter 4.

This precept is in force everywhere, at every time, for males but
not for women, since it is a positive precept which time brings on.[50]
Yet in any event, if they wish to put [*t'fillin*] on, they are not to be
prevented, and they have reward — but not like the reward of a man:

44. TB Gittin 45b; MT *ibid.* 13.
45. TJ 'Eruvin x 1, toward the end; MT *ibid.* ii 11.
46. TB 'Eruvin 97a.
47. TB M'naḥoth 45a–b; MT *ibid.* iii 18–19.
48. TB B'rachoth 23a–b, 25a; MT *ibid.* iv 16–18, 20.
49. TB Shabbath 10a; MT *ibid.* 22.
50. The obligation is at a specific time only — i.e. by day, but not at night.

יֵשׁ לָהֶן, אֲבָל לֹא כִשְׂכַר הָאִישׁ, שֶׁאֵינוֹ דוֹמֶה שְׂכַר הַמִּצְוָה וְעוֹשֶׂה כְּשָׂכָר שֶׁאֵינוֹ מְצֻוֶּה וְעוֹשֶׂה. וּבְמַסֶּכֶת עֵרוּבִין בְּרֵישׁ פֶּרֶק הַמּוֹצֵא תְּפִלִּין אָמְרוּ זִכְרוֹנָם לִבְרָכָה שֶׁמִּיכַל בַּת כּוּשִׁי הָיְתָה מַנַּחַת תְּפִלִּין וְלֹא מִחוּ בְיָדָהּ חֲכָמִים; וְשָׁם אָמְרוּ: אִשְׁתּוֹ שֶׁל יוֹנָה הָיְתָה עוֹלָה לָרֶגֶל וְלֹא מִחוּ בְיָדָהּ חֲכָמִים.

וְעוֹבֵר עַל זֶה וְאֵינוֹ מַנִּיחַ תְּפִלִּין שֶׁל יָד וְשֶׁל רֹאשׁ, בִּטֵּל שְׁמוֹנָה עֲשֵׂה, שֶׁהֲרֵי בְּאַרְבַּע פָּרָשִׁיּוֹת צִוָּה הַכָּתוּב עַל תְּפִלִּין שֶׁל יָד וְשֶׁל רֹאשׁ.

[מִצְוַת תְּפִלִּין שֶׁל רֹאשׁ]

תכב לְהָנִיחַ תְּפִלִּין עַל הָרֹאשׁ, שֶׁנֶּאֱמַר: וְהָיוּ לְטֹטָפֹת בֵּין עֵינֶיךָ. הִנֵּה כָּתַבְתִּי בַּמִּצְוָה הַקּוֹדֶמֶת מַהוּ עִנְיַן הַתְּפִלִּין, שֶׁהוּא אַרְבַּע פָּרָשִׁיּוֹת הַכְּתוּבוֹת בַּתּוֹרָה בְּסֵדֶר בֹּא אֶל פַּרְעֹה וּבְסֵדֶר וְאֶתְחַנַּן וְסֵדֶר וְהָיָה עֵקֶב. וְנִצְטַוֵּינוּ לִכְתֹּב אַרְבַּע פָּרָשִׁיּוֹת אֵלּוּ בִּקְלָף וּלְהַנִּיחָן עַל רֹאשֵׁנוּ בֵּין עֵינֵינוּ, וְעַל זְרוֹעֵנוּ כְּנֶגֶד הַלֵּב. וְהָעִנְיָן בְּאַרְבַּע פָּרָשִׁיּוֹת אֵלּוּ יוֹתֵר מִבִּשְׁאָר פָּרָשִׁיּוֹתֶיהָ שֶׁל תּוֹרָה, לְפִי שֶׁיֵּשׁ בְּאֵלּוּ קַבָּלַת מַלְכוּת שָׁמַיִם וְאַחְדוּת הַשֵּׁם, וְעִנְיַן יְצִיאַת מִצְרַיִם, שֶׁהוּא מַכְרִיחַ אֱמוּנַת חִדּוּשׁ הָעוֹלָם וְהַשְׁגָּחַת הַשֵּׁם בַּתַּחְתּוֹנִים, וְאֵלֶּה הֵם יְסוֹדוֹת דָּת יְהוּדִית.

וְלָכֵן נִצְטַוֵּינוּ לְהַנִּיחַ אֵלּוּ יְסוֹדוֹת כָּל הַיּוֹם בֵּין עֵינֵינוּ וְעַל לוּחַ לִבֵּנוּ, כִּי שְׁנֵי אֵלֶּה הָאֵבָרִים יֹאמְרוּ חַכְמֵי הַטֶּבַע שֶׁהֵן מִשְׁכַּן הַשֵּׂכֶל, וּבְהַנִּיחֵנוּ עֲלֵיהֶם דְּבָרִים אֵלֶּה לְזִכָּרוֹן נִתְחַזֵּק בָּהֶם וְנוֹסִיף זֵכֶר בְּדַרְכֵי הַשֵּׁם, וְנִזְכֶּה לְחַיֵּי עַד.

וּקְצָת דִּינֵי הַתְּפִלִּין כְּתוּבִין לְמַעְלָה בְּשֶׁל יָד. וְהִנְנִי אוֹדִיעֲךָ הַחִלּוּק שֶׁבֵּינֵיהֶם בְּעוֹרָן וּבִתְפִירָתָן: דַּע, שֶׁהַשִּׁעוּר שֶׁגּוֹנְזִין בְּתוֹכוֹ תְּפִלִּין שֶׁל יָד עוֹשִׂין אוֹתוֹ בַּיִת

---

51. The reward for obedience of a Divine precept is greater; TB Kiddushin 31a.

52. I.e. King Saul, so designated according to TB Mo'éd Katan 16b; our author's citation from the Talmud here is precisely as in MS Munich (*Dikduké Sof'rim*).

53. I.e. the four written for the *t'fillin*; see the first paragraph.

§422   1. See below, the fifth paragraph, toward the end, that this is not understood literally.

For the reward of a person who is commanded and observes is not to be compared to the reward of one who is not commanded and observes it.[51] Well, in the Talmud tractate *'Eruvin*, at the beginning of the tenth chapter (96a), the Sages of blessed memory related that Michal the daughter of the Cushite[52] used to put on *t'fillin*, and the Sages [of her time] did not prevent her. They said there, too, that [the prophet] Jonah's wife used to go up [to Jerusalem for the festivals] on pilgrimage, and the Sages did not prevent her.

If a person transgresses this and does not put on the *t'fillin* of the hand and of the head, he disobeys eight positive precepts: because in four sections of Scripture[53] the Writ has commanded about the *t'fillin* of the hand and that of the head.

[THE PRECEPT OF THE T'FILLIN OF THE HEAD]

422 to put *t'fillin* on the head, as it is stated, *and they shall be for frontlets between your eyes*[1] (Deuteronomy 6:8). Now, I have written here, in the previous precept, what *t'fillin* are in substance, i.e. four sections written in the Torah—in *sidrah bo, sidrah va'eth-ḥanan*, and *sidrah 'ékev*;[2] and we were commanded to write these four portions on parchment and place them on our head "between our eyes,"[1] and on our arm opposite the heart. The reason why these four parts [were chosen] above the other sections of the Torah is that these contain the acceptance of the kingship of Heaven and the oneness of the Eternal Lord, and the theme of the exodus from Egypt, which compels a belief in the creation of the world as a new entity, and the watchful care and regulation of the lower (earthly) realm by the Eternal Lord;[3] and these are the foundations of the Jewish religion. .

We were therefore commanded to set these foundations [of our faith] every day between our eyes[1] and on the tablet of our heart. For these two organs, say the learned scholars of nature, are the seat of the intelligence. And by setting these objects on them for a remembrance, we will be strengthened [in our faith] by them, and will augment our remembrance of the ways of the Eternal Lord, so meriting to achieve eternal life.

A few of the laws about *t'fillin* are written above, concerning that of the hand (§421). Now let me inform you of the difference between them [the *t'fillin* of the hand and of the head], in their leather [coverings] and in their stitching. Know that the leather in which the *t'fillin* of the hand is enclosed is made as one box, in which are placed

אַחַת, וּמַנִּיחִין שָׁם אַרְבַּע הַפָּרָשִׁיּוֹת שֶׁזָּכַרְנוּ, כְּתוּבוֹת בִּקְלָף אֶחָד; וְהָעוֹר שֶׁל
רֹאשׁ עוֹשִׂין אוֹתוֹ חָלוּק לְאַרְבָּעָה בָּתִּים, וּבְכָל אֶחָד מַנִּיחִין פָּרָשָׁה אַחַת מֵאַרְבַּע

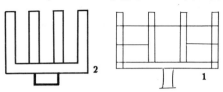

פָּרָשִׁיּוֹת אֵלּוּ, וְהוּא עָשׂוּי כְּגוֹן זֶה:
וְעוֹשִׂין מִן הָעוֹר בְּעוֹדֶנּוּ רָטֹב דְּמוּת
שִׁי״ן עִם שְׁלֹשָׁה רָאשִׁין מִימִין הַמַּנִּיחַ
הַתְּפִלִּין, וּדְמוּת שִׁי״ן עִם אַרְבַּע רָאשִׁין
מִשְּׂמֹאל הַמַּנִּיחַ.

וּמַכְנִיסִים רְצוּעַת הָרֹאשׁ בְּתוֹךְ אוֹתוֹ הָעוֹר הָעוֹדֵף בְּסוֹף הַבַּיִת, וְהוּא שֶׁקּוֹרִין
אוֹתוֹ חֲכָמִים "מַעֲבֹרֶת", כְּלוֹמַר שֶׁמַּעֲבִירִין בּוֹ הָרְצוּעָה, וְאַחַר־כָּךְ מַקִּיפִין מִן
הָרְצוּעָה כְּשִׁעוּר הָרֹאשׁ שֶׁל מַנִּיחַ, וְעוֹשִׂין בְּאוֹתוֹ מָקוֹם קֶשֶׁר אֶחָד הֶעָשׂוּי
בְּצוּרַת דל״ת; וְזֹאת הַצּוּרָה אִי־אֶפְשָׁר לְצַיְּרָהּ בְּמִכְתָּב, אֲבָל כָּל אֶחָד מְלַמְּדָהּ
לְתַלְמִידָיו, וִידוּעָה הִיא בֵּינֵינוּ עִם הַקָּדוֹשׁ. וְזֶהוּ קֶשֶׁר תְּפִלִּין שֶׁאָמְרוּ זִכְרוֹנָם
לִבְרָכָה שֶׁכָּל תַּלְמִיד־חָכָם צָרִיךְ לֵידַע אוֹתוֹ; וּמָנוּ אוֹתוֹ עִם שְׁאָר דְּבָרִים גַּם־כֵּן
שֶׁאָמְרוּ עֲלֵיהֶן שֶׁרָאוּי לֵידַע אוֹתָם עַל־כָּל־פָּנִים, וְהֵן כְּתָב וּשְׁחִיטָה וּמִילָה
וּבִרְכַּת חֲתָנִים וְצִיצִית.

וְאֹרֶךְ רְצוּעַת הָרֹאשׁ כְּדֵי שֶׁיַּקִּיף בָּהּ הָרֹאשׁ וְיִקְשֹׁר בָּהּ הַקֶּשֶׁר מֵאֲחוֹרָיו וְיִהְיֶה
בָּהּ כְּדֵי לְהִמָּתַח שְׁנֵי רָאשֵׁי הָרְצוּעָה עַד כְּנֶגֶד טַבּוּרוֹ, אוֹ לְכָל הַפָּחוֹת רֹאשָׁה
הָאֶחָד עַד כְּנֶגֶד הַלֵּב וְהָאַחֵר עַד כְּנֶגֶד הַטַּבּוּר. וּמְקוֹם הַנַּחַת תְּפִלִּין בָּרֹאשׁ,
כְּלוֹמַר קְצִיצַת הָעוֹר שֶׁהַפָּרָשִׁיּוֹת מֻנָּחוֹת בְּתוֹכָהּ, הוּא כְּנֶגֶד הַמֹּחַ, מָקוֹם שֶׁמֹּחוֹ
שֶׁל תִּינוֹק רוֹפֵס, וְזֶהוּ הַפֵּרוּשׁ הַמְקֻבָּל לָנוּ בְּ"וְהָיוּ לְטֹטָפֹת בֵּין עֵינֶיךָ", שֶׁזֶּהוּ
נִקְרָא בֵּין הָעֵינַיִם; וְהַמַּנִּיחָן בֵּין הָעֵינַיִם מַמָּשׁ, הֲרֵי זֶה מַכְחִישׁ דִּבְרֵי קַבָּלָה. וְיֶתֶר
פְּרָטֵי הַמִּצְוָה וְכָל עִנְיָנָהּ, כְּמוֹ בַּחֲבֶרְתָּהּ הַקּוֹדֶמֶת.

2. See § 421, first paragraph.

3. So Ramban on Exodus 20 : 1.

4. Two diagrams appear in the Hebrew text, based respectively on the drawings
in the first and second of the four manuscripts consulted; cf. the diagram in MT
hilchoth t'fillin iii 5, in ed. Mosad R. Kook. (This teaching is in TB M'nahoth 34b.)

5. TB M'nahoth 35a, and tosafoth there, s.v. shin.

6. I.e. a folded flap open at both ends; TB ibid.

7. TB Ḥullin 9a. (The paragraph is based on MT hilchoth t'fillin iii 13.)

8. MT ibid. 12.

9. So tosafoth, TB M'nahoth 38b, s.v. v'chamah.

the four sections of Scripture that we mentioned,[2] written on one piece of parchment. However, the leather [container] for that of the head is made divided into four compartments, and in each, one of these four portions of Scripture is placed; and it is made in this manner.[4] Out of the leather, while it is yet moist, the shape of the letter *shin* with three heads is formed [embossed] on the right side of the one who will wear the *t'fillin*; and the shape of a *shin* with four heads, at the left of the one who will wear it.[5]

The strap of the *t'fillin* of the head is then inserted within the leather [of the container] itself, which is left [folded] over at the end of the container. This is what the Sages call "the passageway,"[6] signifying that the strap is passed through it. Then enough of the strap is left to encircle the head of the wearer, and at that point [where the two parts of the strap will meet behind the wearer's head] one knot is made, formed in the shape of the letter *da-leth*. It is not possible to describe this shape in writing; but everyone teaches it to his students, and it is known among us, the holy people. This is the knot of *t'fillin* which the Sages of blessed memory said[7] every Torah scholar must know. They listed it with other things as well, about which they said that it is fitting to know them under all circumstances — these being writing, the ritual slaying [of a kosher animal], circumcision, the benediction over a bridegroom, and *tzitzith* (§ 386).

The length of the strap for [the *t'fillin* of] the head should be enough to encircle the head with it and tie the knot with it behind him [the wearer], and enough of it should then remain for the two ends of the strap to extend to the level of his navel,[8] or at least one end to the level of the heart and the other to that of the navel.[9] The place for setting the *t'fillin* of the head, meaning the leather box in which the Scriptural portions are put, is opposite the brain, at the place where an infant's brain pulsates. This is the traditional, accepted interpretaion that we have for the verse, *and they shall be for frontlets between your eyes* (Deuteronomy 6:8) — that this is what "between the eyes" means.[10] If someone places it actually, literally between the eyes, he denies the words (teachings) of the Oral Tradition. The remaining details of the precept and all its subject-matter are as for its preceding companion-precept (§ 421).

10. I.e. on the head, but neither right nor left of the midpoint between the eyes.

TB M'naḥoth 37b.

[מִצְוַת מְזוּזָה]

תכג לִקְבֹּעַ מְזוּזָה בִּמְזוּזַת בֵּיתֵנוּ, שֶׁנֶּאֱמַר, וּכְתַבְתָּם עַל מְזוּזוֹת בֵּיתֶךָ וּבִשְׁעָרֶיךָ. וְעִנְיַן הַמְּזוּזָה הוּא שֶׁכּוֹתְבִין שְׁתֵּי פָרָשִׁיּוֹת מִן הַתּוֹרָה בִּקְלָף אֶחָד, וְהֵן "שְׁמַע" עַד "וּבִשְׁעָרֶיךָ", "וְהָיָה אִם שָׁמֹעַ" עַד "עַל הָאָרֶץ", וְקוֹבְעִין אוֹתָן בִּמְזוּזַת פֶּתַח הַבַּיִת.

וּמִשָּׁרְשֵׁי הַמִּצְוָה, לִהְיוֹת זִכְרוֹן לָאָדָם בֶּאֱמוּנַת הַשֵּׁם בְּכָל עֵת בֹּאוֹ לְבֵיתוֹ וְצֵאתוֹ, וּכְמוֹ שֶׁכָּתַבְתִּי בְּעִנְיַן הַתְּפִלִּין, וּכְעִנְיָן שֶׁאָמְרוּ זִכְרוֹנָם לִבְרָכָה בְּמִצְוָה זוֹ: אָמַר רַבִּי זֵירָא אָמַר רַב מַתְנָא אָמַר רַב שְׁמוּאֵל: מִצְוָה לְהַנִּיחָהּ בִּתְחִלַּת שְׁלִישׁ הָעֶלְיוֹן; אָמַר רַבָּה: מִצְוָה לְהַנִּיחָהּ בַּטֶּפַח הַסָּמוּךְ לִרְשׁוּת הָרַבִּים; מַאי טַעְמָא — רַבָּנָן אָמְרִי: כִּי הֵיכִי דְתִפְגַּע בֵּיהּ מִצְוָה מִיָּד.

מִדִּינֵי הַמִּצְוָה, מַה שֶּׁאָמְרוּ זִכְרוֹנָם לִבְרָכָה שֶׁשְּׁתֵּי פָרָשִׁיּוֹת אֵלּוּ מְעַכְּבוֹת זוֹ אֶת זוֹ, וַאֲפִלּוּ כָּתַב אֶחָד מְעַכְּבָן, כְּלוֹמַר אֲפִלּוּ אוֹת אַחַת שֶׁאֵינָהּ עֲשׂוּיָה כַּהֹגֶן, כְּלוֹמַר שֶׁאֵין גַּוִּיל מַקִּיף אוֹתָהּ מֵאַרְבַּע רוּחוֹתֶיהָ, מְעַכֶּבֶת בִּמְזוּזָה. וּמַה שֶּׁאָמְרוּ שֶׁחִיּוּב הַמְּזוּזָה לְהַנִּיחָהּ בִּמְזוּזַת הַפֶּתַח מִיָּמִין, שֶׁנֶּאֱמַר "בֵּיתֶךָ", וּמְפָרְשֵׁי לָהּ רַבָּנָן: בִּיאָתְךָ, וְכִי עָקַר אִינִשׁ, רַגְלֵיהּ דִּימִינָא עָקַר בְּרֵישָׁא.

וּמַה שֶּׁאָמְרוּ זִכְרוֹנָם לִבְרָכָה: תָּנוּ רַבָּנָן: "וּבִשְׁעָרֶיךָ", אֶחָד שַׁעֲרֵי בָתִּים, חֲצֵרוֹת, מְדִינוֹת, עֲיָרוֹת, רֶפֶת, לוּלִין, מַתְבֵּן, אוֹצְרוֹת יַיִן וְאוֹצְרוֹת שֶׁמֶן, כֻּלָּן חַיָּבִין בִּמְזוּזָה; יָכוֹל שֶׁאֲנִי מַרְבֶּה בֵּית־שַׁעַר, אַכְסַדְרָה וּמִרְפֶּסֶת — תַּלְמוּד לוֹמַר "בַּיִת", מַה בַּיִת מְיֻחָד לְדִירָה אַף כָּל שֶׁמְּיֻחָדִין לְדִירָה, וְיָצְאוּ אֵלּוּ. יָכוֹל שֶׁאֲנִי

§423   1. Similarly Ramban on Exodus 13:16.
   2. TB M'naḥoth 33a–b.
   3. I.e. the *m'zuzah* will be seen immediately upon entering—a reminder of the Almighty, the focus of our faith.
   4. TB M'naḥoth 28a.
   5. If there is something wrong with one, the other is of no value either.
   6. *Ibid.* 32b.
   7. TB Yoma 11b, M'naḥoth 34a, Ḥullin 135b.
   8. TB Yoma 11a–b.
   9. A small structure (booth or hut) in front of the forecourt, through which all pass.

423 to fasten a *m'zuzah* on the doorpost of our house, as it is stated, *And you shall write them on the doorposts of your house, and on your gates* (Deuteronomy 6:9). The substance of the *m'zuzah* is that two sections of the Torah are written on a piece of parchment, these being from *Hear, Israel* till *and on your gates* (ibid. 4–9), and from *And it shall be if you hearken* till *upon the earth* (ibid. 11:13–21); and they are fastened on the doorpost of the entrance to the home.

At the root of the precept lies the purpose that it should remind a man about faith in the Eternal Lord every time he enters his home or leaves it[1] — as I wrote regarding *t'fillin*, and in keeping with what the Sages of blessed memory said about this precept:[2] R. Zéra quoted R. Matna in the name of Sh'mu'él: It is a religious duty to place it at the beginning of the upper third part [of the doorpost]. Said Rabbah: It is a religious duty to place it on the handbreadth [of the width of the doorpost] closest to the public domain. What is the reason? The Sages said: so that you will encounter a *mitzvah* (religious act) through it at once.[3]

Among the laws of the precept there is what the Sages of blessed memory said:[4] that these two Scriptural portions prevent one another [from being acceptable];[5] even one [unit of] writing can prevent them [from being acceptable] — which is to say, even one letter not made properly, i.e. without space surrounding it on all its four sides, prevents [acceptability] in a *m'zuzah*.

Then there is what the Sages said:[6] that the duty with a *m'zuzah* is to place it on the doorpost of the entrance at the right; for Scripture states *béthecha* (your house), which the Sages interpret[7] as *bi'ath'cha* (your coming in), and when a man picks up his feet [to walk], he lifts up the right foot first.

There is, further, what they (of blessed memory) said:[8] Our Sages taught: "and upon your gates" — whether they are the gates of houses, forecourts, provinces, villages, a shed, enclosed staircases, a shed for straw, storerooms for wine (wine-cellars), or storerooms for oil — all involve the obligation of a *m'zuzah*. I might think that I should add on [under this obligation] a small gate-house,[9] a covered entrance-area, and a balcony? — hence Scripture says "house"; just as a house is especially intended for dwelling, so all entities particularly intended for dwelling [are under this obligation] — thus excluding

⟨285⟩

מַרְבֶּה אַף בֵּית־הַכִּסֵּא וּבֵית־הַמֶּרְחָץ וּבֵית־הַטְּבִילָה — תַּלְמוּד לוֹמַר "בַּיִת", מַה בַּיִת הֶעָשׂוּי לְכָבוֹד, אַף כָּל הֶעָשׂוּי לְכָבוֹד, וְיָצְאוּ אֵלּוּ. יָכוֹל שֶׁאֲנִי מַרְבֶּה הָרְ־הַבַּיִת וְהַלְּשָׁכוֹת וְהָעֲזָרוֹת — תַּלְמוּד לוֹמַר "בַּיִת", מַה בַּיִת שֶׁהוּא חֹל אַף כָּל שֶׁהוּא חֹל, יָצְאוּ אֵלּוּ שֶׁהֵן קֹדֶשׁ; וּבֵית־הַכְּנֶסֶת בִּכְלָל בָּתֵּי קֹדֶשׁ הוּא כָּל זְמַן שֶׁאֵין בָּהּ דִּירָה, אֲבָל לֹא אִם יֵשׁ בָּהּ דִּירָה, כְּגוֹן בֵּית־כְּנֶסֶת דִּכְפָרִים דְּדָיְרֵי בָהּ אוֹרְחִים.

וּמַה שֶּׁאָמְרוּ שֶׁמְּזוּזַת יָחִיד נִבְדֶּקֶת פַּעֲמַיִם בַּשָּׁבוּעַ, וְשֶׁל רַבִּים פַּעֲמַיִם בַּיּוֹבֵל; וּמַה שֶּׁאָמְרוּ גַם־כֵּן בְּמִזוּזָה בְּעִנְיָן הַתָּגִין: אָמַר רַבָּה: שִׁבְעָה אוֹתִיּוֹת שֶׁבַּמְּזוּזָה צְרִיכִין שְׁלֹשָׁה שְׁלֹשָׁה זַיִּנִין, וְאֵלּוּ הֵן: שעטנז ג"ץ — כְּלוֹמַר כָּל אוֹת שֶׁבַּמְּזוּזָה מֵאֵלּוּ צְרִיכָה שְׁלֹשָׁה תָגִין.

וּמַה שֶּׁאָמְרוּ שֶׁהַשּׂוֹכֵר בַּיִת בְּחוּצָה לָאָרֶץ וְהַדָּר בְּפֻנְדָּק בְּאֶרֶץ־יִשְׂרָאֵל פָּטוּר מִן הַמְּזוּזָה שְׁלֹשִׁים יוֹם, אֲבָל הַשּׂוֹכֵר בַּיִת בְּאֶרֶץ־יִשְׂרָאֵל חַיָּב בִּמְזוּזָה מִיָּד; וְהַמַּשְׂכִּיר בַּיִת לַחֲבֵרוֹ, עַל הַשּׂוֹכֵר לְהָבִיא מְזוּזָה וְלִקְבֹּעַ אוֹתָהּ, דְּחוֹבַת הַדָּר הִיא; וּכְשֶׁהוּא יוֹצֵא לֹא יִטְּלֶנָּה בְּיָדוֹ, אֶלָּא־אִם־כֵּן הָיְתָה הַבַּיִת שֶׁל גּוֹי.

וַעֲשָׂרָה תְנָאִים צָרִיךְ בְּבַיִת שֶׁיִּתְחַיֵּב בִּמְזוּזָה, וְאֵלּוּ הֵן: א. שֶׁיִּהְיֶה כְדֵי לְרַבֵּעַ בּוֹ אַרְבַּע אַמּוֹת עַל אַרְבַּע אַמּוֹת, ב. וְיִהְיוּ לוֹ שְׁתֵּי מְזוּזוֹת, ג. וּמַשְׁקוֹף, ד. וְתִקְרָה, ה. וּדְלָתוֹת, ו. וְשֶׁיִּהְיֶה הַשַּׁעַר גָּבֹהַּ עֲשָׂרָה טְפָחִים אוֹ יוֹתֵר, ז. וְיִהְיֶה הַבַּיִת חֹל, ח. וְיִהְיֶה עָשׂוּי לְדִירַת אָדָם, ט. וְשֶׁיִּהְיֶה עָשׂוּי לְדִירַת כָּבוֹד, י. וְשֶׁיִּהְיֶה עָשׂוּי לְדִירַת קֶבַע.

בַּיִת שֶׁיֵּשׁ לוֹ פְּתָחִים הַרְבֵּה, חַיָּב לִקְבֹּעַ מְזוּזָה בְּכָל אֶחָד מֵהֶן, וְאַף־עַל־פִּי שֶׁאֵין רָגִיל לְהִכָּנֵס בְּהַתְמָדָה אֶלָּא בְּאֶחָד מֵהֶם; וּפֶתַח קָטָן שֶׁבֵּין בַּיִת וַעֲלִיָּה

10. The fourth manuscript and later editions after the first add שאינן מיוחדין לדירה "which are not specifically intended for dwelling."

11. TB M'naḥoth 29b.

12. So the oldest manuscripts; the editions, like the printed Talmud, have Rava; but see *Dikduké Sof'rim* XV 72 note 7, which also has the reading of *sh'loshah sh'loshah* (our printed Talmud has the word only once).

13. *Ibid.* 44a.

14. TB Bava M'tzi'a 102a.

15. TB Sukkah 3a.

16. TB 'Eruvin 11b.

17. TB Yoma 10a; MT *hilchoth m'zuzah* vi 1.

these.[10] I might think that I should include also a room of easement, a bath-house, and a structure for ritual immersion?—hence Scripture says "house"; just as a house was made for a purpose of dignity, so everything made for a purpose of dignity [is under this obligation]— excluding these. I might think I should add the Temple Mount and the Sanctuary chambers and forecourts?—Scripture says "house"; just as a house is non-holy, so is everything non-holy [under the obligation]—excluding these, which are hallowed. A synagogue is included among holy structures as long as there are no living quarters in it, but not if there are living quarters in it: for example, a village synagogue, where guests (visitors) lodge.[8]

There is; too, what the Sages said:[8] that the m'zuzah of an individual should be examined twice in a septennate (period of seven years); and a public one, twice in a jubilee period. There is likewise what was taught about a m'zuzah in regard to tittles [grace lines above the letters]:[11] Said Rabbah:[12] Seven letters in the m'zuzah require three tittles each, these being gimmel, za-yin, teth, nun, 'a-yin, tzadi, shin. In other words, every letter among these in the m'zuzah needs to have three grace-lines above it.

Then we have what the Sages said:[13] that a person who rents a house outside the land [of Israel] and one who lives at an inn in the land of Israel are free of the duty of a m'zuzah for thirty days. But if one rents a house in the land of Israel, he has the obligation of a m'zuzah at once. When a person rents a house to his fellow-man, it is for the tenant to provide a m'zuzah and affix it, since it is the obligation of the dweller. When he leaves, however, he should not take it [with him] in his hand, unless the house is that of a non-Jew.[14]

Now, a house must fulfill ten conditions before it bears the obligation of a m'zuzah, namely: (1) its area should be sufficient to make a square of four cubits by four cubits;[15] (2) it should have two doorposts, (3) a lintel, (4) a ceiling, (5) and doors;[2] (6) the gate [entrance] should be ten handbreadths high or more;[16] (7) the house should be non-holy;[8] (8) it should be made [intended] for human occupancy;[8] (9) it should be made for dignified occupancy;[8] (10) it should be made for permanent occupancy.[17]

If a house has many entrances, there is an obligation to affix a m'zuzah at each one of them, even if it is the custom to enter constantly through no more than one of them.[17] The small entrance between a house and an attic [or loft] that people sometimes make at

שֶׁעוֹשִׂין בְּנֵי־אָדָם לִפְעָמִים בְּרַגְלֵי סֻלָּם שֶׁעוֹלִין בּוֹ בְּנֵי־אָדָם לַעֲלִיָּה, חַיָּב בִּמְזוּזָה; וְחֶדֶר שֶׁבַּבַּיִת, אֲפִלּוּ חֶדֶר בְּחֶדֶר, חַיָּבִין בִּמְזוּזָה כֻּלָּן, שֶׁכֻּלָּן עֲשׂוּיִין לְדִירָה; וְיֶתֶר פְּרָטֵי הַמִּצְוָה, מְבֹאָרִין בְּמַסֶּכֶת מְנָחוֹת פֶּרֶק שְׁלִישִׁי.

וְנוֹהֶגֶת בְּכָל מָקוֹם וּבְכָל זְמַן, בִּזְכָרִים וּנְקֵבוֹת. וְעוֹבֵר עַל זֶה וּבָנָה בַיִת וְנָתַן עָלָיו תִּקְרָה וְלֹא הִנִּיחַ בָּהּ מְזוּזָה, אוֹ שֶׁשָּׂכַר בַּיִת בְּחוּצָה לָאָרֶץ אוֹ פָּנְדָּק בָּאָרֶץ וְעָבְרוּ עָלָיו יוֹתֵר מִשְּׁלֹשִׁים יוֹם וְלֹא הִנִּיחַ בָּהּ מְזוּזָה, אוֹ שֶׁשָּׂכַר בַּיִת בָּאָרֶץ וְלֹא הִנִּיחַ בָּהּ מְזוּזָה מִיָּד, בִּטֵּל עֲשֵׂה זֶה; וְאַף־עַל־פִּי־כֵן שֶׁעָבְרָה הַשָּׁעָה שֶׁהָיָה חַיָּב לְהַנִּיחָהּ, מֻזְהָר הוּא לְקָבְעָהּ לְעוֹלָם בְּכָל עֵת שֶׁיָּדוּר בַּבַּיִת.

[שֶׁלֹּא לְנַסּוֹת נְבִיא אֱמֶת יוֹתֵר מִדַּי]

תכד שֶׁנִּמְנַעְנוּ שֶׁלֹּא לְנַסּוֹת יוֹתֵר מִדַּאי הַנָּבִיא הַמִּיֻסָּר אֶת הָעָם וְהַמְלַמְּדָם דַּרְכֵי הַתְּשׁוּבָה, אַחַר שֶׁנֵּדַע אֲמִתַּת נְבוּאָתוֹ, וְעַל זֶה נֶאֱמַר "לֹא תְנַסּוּ אֶת יי אֱלֹהֵיכֶם כַּאֲשֶׁר נִסִּיתֶם בַּמַּסָּה", כְּלוֹמַר לֹא תְנַסּוּ גְמוּלֵי הַשֵּׁם וַעֲנָשָׁיו שֶׁהוֹדִיעַ לָכֶם עַל־יַד נְבִיאָיו, עַל צַד שֶׁתִּסְתַּפְּקוּ בָּהֶם.

מִשָּׁרְשֵׁי הַמִּצְוָה, לְפִי שֶׁבַּנִּסָּיוֹן הַיָּתֵר בַּנָּבִיא הָאֱמֶת יִמָּצֵא הֶפְסֵד, כִּי פְעָמִים יַחְלְקוּ עָלָיו מִתּוֹךְ כָּךְ בְּנֵי־אָדָם הַמִּתְקַנְּאִים בּוֹ וְהַכּוֹאֲבִים לְמַעֲלָתוֹ, וּדְבַר הַנְּבוּאָה אֵינֶנּוּ עִנְיָן תְּמִידִי לְכָל נָבִיא, כִּי פְעָמִים לֹא יִתְנַבֵּא כִּי־אִם מְעַט, וְאִם בְּכָל פַּעַם וּפַעַם נַטְרִידֵהוּ לָתֵת אוֹת וּמוֹפֵת נֶאֱמָן שֶׁהוּא נָבִיא, יִהְיֶה סִבָּה לָעָם שֶׁיִּמְרְדוּ בוֹ וְיָקֵלּוּ בִדְבָרָיו הַרְבֵּה פְעָמִים; וְעַל־כֵּן הִזְהִירָנוּ לְהַאֲמִין בּוֹ וְשֶׁלֹּא לְנַסּוֹתוֹ יוֹתֵר מִדַּאי, אַחַר שֶׁיִּהְיֶה מֻחְזָק עִמָּנוּ כְּטוֹב וְנֶאֱמָן לְנָבִיא.

וְהַדָּבָר הַזֶּה אֵרַע לִנְבִיאֵי הָאֱמֶת עִם נְבִיאֵי הַבַּעַל, שֶׁהָיוּ מַכְחִישִׁים נְבוּאָתָם

---

18. TB M'naḥoth 34a.

19. *Ibid.* 33b.

20. From the last semicolon to here is in the oldest manuscripts but missing in all the editions, by an oversight between identical phrases.

the foot of the ladder by which people go up to the attic, bears the obligation of a *m'zuzah*.[18] As for any room in a house, even one room within another, all entail the duty of a *m'zuzah*, since all were made for habitation.[19] Other details of the precept are clarified in the Talmud tractate *M'naḥoth*, chapter 3.

It is in force everywhere, at every time, for both man and woman. If a person transgresses this, building a house and putting a ceiling on it, and not placing a *m'zuzah* on it; or if he rents a house outside the land of Israel or a room at an inn within the land, and more than thirty days pass by and he does not put a *m'zuzah* on it; or if he rents a house in the land [of Israel] and does not put a *m'zuzah* on it[20] at once —he thus violates this positive precept. Yet even if the time has passed when he was obligated to place it, he is adjured [under a duty] forever to affix it, all the time that he dwells in the house.

[NOT TO TEST A TRUE PROPHET
TO AN UNDUE DEGREE]

424 that we were forbidden to test unduly a prophet who chastens the people and teaches them the ways of repentance, after we are certain of the truth of his prophecy. About this it was stated, *You shall not put the Lord your God to the test, as you tested Him at Massah* (Deuteronomy 7:16); in other words, you should not test the rewards of the Eternal Lord and His punishments, of which He told you through His prophets, in such a way that you cast doubt on them.

At the root of the precept lies the reason that from the excessive testing of a true prophet, damage will result. For at times, as a result of it, people who envy him and ache over his exalted status will quarrel with him. And the matter of prophecy is not something constant with every prophet: for at times he will prophesy to no more than a small extent; and if we will trouble and plague him every single time to give a trustworthy sign and wonder that he is [indeed] a prophet, it will be a cause for the people to rebel against him and treat his words at times with great disparagement. We were therefore adjured to believe in him and not test him overly much, after he has become firmly established among us as good and trustworthy as a prophet.

This thing happened to the true prophets [in their interaction] with the prophets of Baal. For they [the latter] would deny their

prophecy, harass them, and refute their words, so much so that one

וּמְחַטְּטִים אַחֲרֵיהֶם וּמַכְחִישִׁים דִּבְרֵיהֶם, עַד שֶׁלֹּא הָיָה מַסְפִּיק לָהֶם אוֹת אַחַר אוֹת וּמוֹפֵת אַחַר מוֹפֵת.

וּכְמוֹ־כֵן בִּכְלָל הָאַזְהָרָה שֶׁלֹּא לַעֲשׂוֹת מִצְווֹת הַשֵּׁם בָּרוּךְ הוּא עַל דֶּרֶךְ הַנִּסָּיוֹן, כְּלוֹמַר שֶׁיַּעֲשֶׂה אָדָם מִצְוָה לְנַסּוֹת אִם יִגְמְלֵהוּ הַשֵּׁם כְּצָדְקוֹ, לֹא לְאַהֲבַת הָאֵל וְיִרְאָתוֹ אוֹתוֹ. וְאַל יִקְשֶׁה עָלֶיךָ מַה שֶּׁאָמְרוּ זִכְרוֹנָם לִבְרָכָה בְּפֶרֶק קַמָּא דְמַסֶּכֶת תַּעֲנִית: "עַשֵּׂר תְּעַשֵּׂר", עַשֵּׂר בִּשְׁבִיל שֶׁתִּתְעַשֵּׁר — שֶׁכְּבָר תֵּרְצוּהָ שָׁם וְאָמְרוּ שֶׁבְּכָל הַמִּצְווֹת נֶאֱמַר "לֹא תְנַסּוּ", חוּץ מִזּוֹ דְמַעֲשֵׂר, שֶׁנֶּאֱמַר: הָבִיאוּ אֶת כָּל הַמַּעֲשֵׂר אֶל בֵּית הָאוֹצָר...וּבְחָנוּנִי נָא בָּזֹאת וְגוֹמֵר. וְהַטַּעַם בָּזוֹ כְּעִנְיָן שֶׁכָּתוּב: מַלְוֵה ה' חוֹנֵן דָּל, כְּלוֹמַר שֶׁהוֹדִיעָנוּ הָאֵל בָּרוּךְ הוּא כִּי בְּפַרְנָסֵנוּ מְשָׁרְתֵי בֵּיתוֹ בְּמַעֲשֵׂר נִמְצָא הַתּוֹעֶלֶת וְהַבְּרָכָה בְּמָמוֹנֵנוּ עַל־כָּל־פָּנִים, וְלֹא יְעַכֵּב זֶה שׁוּם דְּבַר חֵטְא וְעָוֹן.

וְטַעַם אִסּוּר הַנִּסָּיוֹן בְּמִצְווֹת, מִפְּנֵי שֶׁשְּׂכַר מִצְווֹת אֵינוֹ בָּעוֹלָם הַזֶּה, וּכְמוֹ שֶׁדָּרְשׁוּ זִכְרוֹנָם לִבְרָכָה בְּרֵישׁ מַסֶּכֶת עֲבוֹדָה זָרָה: "הַיּוֹם לַעֲשׂוֹתָם", וּלְמָחָר, כְּלוֹמַר לָעוֹלָם הַבָּא, לִטֹּל שְׂכָרָם. וְזֶה שֶׁאָמְרוּ זִכְרוֹנָם לִבְרָכָה: הָאוֹמֵר "סֶלַע זוֹ לִצְדָקָה בִּשְׁבִיל שֶׁיִּחְיֶה בְנִי", הֲרֵי זֶה צַדִּיק גָּמוּר — תֵּרְצוּהָ חֲכָמִים הַמְפָרְשִׁים: כְּשֶׁגּוֹמֵר הַנּוֹתֵן בְּלִבּוֹ לָתֵת אוֹתָהּ בֵּין שֶׁיִּחְיֶה אוֹ לֹא יִחְיֶה, שֶׁאֵין זֶה מְנַסֶּה אֶת הַשֵּׁם.

דִּינֵי הַמִּצְוָה, כְּגוֹן7 מַה שֶּׁאָמְרוּ שֶׁהוֹדִיעוּנוּ זִכְרוֹנָם לִבְרָכָה בַּמֶּה תִּתְאַמֵּת לָנוּ נְבוּאַת הַנָּבִיא עַד שֶׁלֹּא נִסְפֹּק בִּדְבָרָיו אַחַר כֵּן: הוּא שֶׁיֹּאמַר דְּבָרִים הָעֲתִידִים לִהְיוֹת בָּעוֹלָם, פְּעָמִים אוֹ שָׁלֹשׁ, וְיֵאָמְנוּ דְבָרָיו בְּכִוּוּן, וְלֹא נְחַיְּבֵהוּ לַעֲשׂוֹת אוֹת אוֹ מוֹפֵת בְּשִׁנּוּי הַטֶּבַע כְּמוֹ שֶׁעָשָׂה מֹשֶׁה אוֹ כְּאֵלִיָּהוּ וֶאֱלִישָׁע; וְגַם־כֵּן צָרִיךְ

§424   1. So too R. Moses of Couçy, *Séfer Mitzvoth Gadol*, negative precept § 4.
   2. I.e. Scripture specifically allows using this for a test or experiment, to verify if the Almighty will give His promised reward. Our author wrote similarly in § 395.
   3. Since, as it were, He thus repays a loan that was given Him.
   4. TB 'Arachin 22a, P'saḥim 8a, Rosh haShanah 4a, Bava Bathra 10b.
   5. A coin; see § 355, note 1. This question and answer are also given by R. Moses of Couçy (note 1).
   6. MT *hilchoth yesodé torah* x 1–2.

sign after another, one wonder after another was not enough for them.

It is likewise within the scope of the injunction not to observe the precepts of the Eternal Lord, blessed is He, in the way of a test: in other words, that a man should do a *mitzvah* to test if the Eternal Lord will reward him according to his righteousness, and not out of love for God or reverent fear of Him.[1] Now, let it not be a difficulty for you that the Sages of blessed memory taught in the first chapter of the Talmud tractate *Ta'anith* (9a): *assér t'assér* (tithe shall you tithe; Deuteronomy 14:22) — give the tithe in order that *tith'ashér*, you will become wealthy. For long ago this was explained there, as they said that regarding all the precepts it was stated, *You shall not put the Lord… to the test*, except about the *mitzvah* of the tithe — for it is stated, *Bring the whole tithe into the storehouse…and pray put Me to the test thereby*, etc. (Malachi 3:10).[2] The reason for this is in keeping with the verse, *He who is gracious to the poor lends to the Lord* (Proverbs 19:17); in other words, God, blessed is He, informed us that when we sustain the ministering servants of his Temple with the tithe, benefit and blessing will be present in our monetary welfare under all circumstances;[3] and no matter of sin or iniquity whatever will prevent this.

Now, the reason for the prohibition against making any tests with the precepts is that the reward for [observing] the precepts is not [given] in this world; as the Sages of blessed memory interpreted at the beginning of the Talmud tractate *'Avodah Zarah* (3a), *this day to do them* (Deuteronomy 7:11), but tomorrow — meaning in the world-to-come — to receive their reward. As for what the Sages of blessed memory taught:[4] If someone says, "This *sela*[5] is for charity in order that my son may live," he is a completely righteous (virtuous) person — the scholars of the commentaries explained it to mean when the donor decides in his heart to give it whether [his son] will live or not; for this is not testing the Eternal Lord.

The laws of the precept are, for example, what the Sages taught,[6] when they (of blessed memory) informed us how the oracular word of a prophet should be verified for us as true, so that we should have no doubts about his words afterward: if he relates things that are going to happen in the world, two or three times, and his words come true precisely; and we should not compel him to produce a sign or a wonder through a change in nature, as Moses did, or like Elijah and Elisha. So also, the man whom we would firmly hold to be a

הָאִישׁ שֶׁנַּחֲזִיק אוֹתוֹ בְּנָבִיא וְנַאֲמִין בּוֹ, לִהְיוֹת אִישׁ יָשָׁר תָּמִים הוֹלֵךְ, כִּי יָדוּעַ שֶׁאֵין הַנְּבוּאָה שׁוֹרָה כִּי־אִם עַל הַחֲסִידִים וְאַנְשֵׁי מַעֲשֶׂה.

וְנָבִיא שֶׁהִבְטִיחַ עַל רָעָה שֶׁתָּבוֹא, אַף־עַל־פִּי שֶׁלֹּא בָאת אֵין סְתִירָה בִּנְבוּאָתוֹ בְּכָךְ, כִּי הַשֵּׁם אֶרֶךְ אַפַּיִם וְרַב חֶסֶד וְנִחָם עַל הָרָעָה כְּשֶׁעוֹשִׂין בְּנֵי־אָדָם תְּשׁוּבָה, כְּמוֹ בְּאַנְשֵׁי נִינְוֵה, וּכְמוֹ בְּחִזְקִיָּהוּ שֶׁהוֹסִיפוּ מִן הַשָּׁמַיִם עַל יָמָיו אַחַר הַגְּזֵרָה שֶׁיָּמוּת. אֲבָל כָּל נָבִיא שֶׁהִבְטִיחַ עַל הַטּוֹבָה, אִם לֹא נִתְאַמְּתָה נְבוּאָתוֹ הִיא סְתִירָה בֶּאֱמֶת לִנְבוּאָתוֹ, שֶׁכָּל דָּבָר טוֹבָה שֶׁיִּגְזֹר הָאֵל עַל־יַד נָבִיא שָׁלוּחַ, אֲפִלּוּ עַל תְּנַאי, אֵינוֹ חוֹזֵר לְעוֹלָם, וְזֶה מֵרֹב טוּבוֹ וְחַסְדּוֹ הַגָּדוֹל; נִמְצָא שֶׁבְּדִבְרֵי הַטּוֹבָה יִבָּחֵן הַנָּבִיא. וְיֶתֶר פְּרָטֶיהָ, בִּמְקוֹמוֹת בַּתַּלְמוּד.

וְנוֹהֶגֶת מִצְוָה זוֹ בִּזְכָרִים וּנְקֵבוֹת, בְּכָל מָקוֹם וּבְכָל זְמַן שֶׁיָּקוּם נָבִיא לְיִשְׂרָאֵל. וְעוֹבֵר עַל זֶה וּמְנַסֶּה הַנָּבִיא יוֹתֵר מִדַּאי, עָבַר עַל לָאו זֶה, וְאֵין לוֹקִין עָלָיו, לְפִי שֶׁאֵין בּוֹ מַעֲשֶׂה.

[מִצְוַת הֲרִינַת שִׁבְעָה עֲמָמִין]

תכה לַהֲרֹג שִׁבְעָה עֲמָמִים הַמַּחֲזִיקִין בְּאַרְצֵנוּ טֶרֶם כָּבַשְׁנוּ אוֹתָהּ מֵהֶם, וְהֵם הַכְּנַעֲנִי וְהָאֱמֹרִי וְכוּלֵי, וּלְאַבְּדָם בְּכָל מָקוֹם שֶׁנִּמְצָאִם, שֶׁנֶּאֱמַר עֲלֵיהֶם: הַחֲרֵם תַּחֲרִים אֹתָם; וְנִכְפְּלָה הַמִּצְוָה בְּסֵדֶר שׁוֹפְטִים, שֶׁנֶּאֱמַר שָׁם: כִּי הַחֲרֵם תַּחֲרִימֵם הַחִתִּי וְהָאֱמֹרִי וְגוֹמֵר.

מִשָּׁרְשֵׁי הַמִּצְוָה, לְפִי שֶׁאֵלּוּ הַשִּׁבְעָה עֲמָמִים הֵם שֶׁהֶחֵלּוּ לַעֲשׂוֹת כָּל מִינֵי עֲבוֹדָה זָרָה וְכָל תּוֹעֲבוֹת הַשֵּׁם אֲשֶׁר שָׂנֵא, וְעַל־כֵּן בִּהְיוֹתָם עִקַּר עֲבוֹדָה זָרָה וִיסוֹדָהּ הָרִאשׁוֹן, נִצְטַוִּינוּ עֲלֵיהֶן לְמָחֳתָן וּלְאַבְּדָן מִתַּחַת הַשָּׁמַיִם, לֹא יִזָּכְרוּ וְלֹא

---

7. *Ibid.* 4.

§425   1. Expression based on Deuteronomy 12:31.   〈292〉

prophet and would believe in him, needs to be an upright man who walks a path of simple honesty; for it is known that [the spirit of] prophecy rests on none but those of kindly piety and men of conscientious observance.

If a prophet gave assurance that an evil event would occur, even if it did not come about there is no contradiction to his prophecy in this: for the Eternal Lord is forbearing and abounding in loving-kindness, and repents (retracts) about the evil when people turn penitent — as with the people of Nineveh (Jonah 3:10), and as with Hezekiah, to whose life Heaven added years after the [Divine] decree that he should die (II Kings 20:6). If, however, any prophet promised some good thing, if his prophecy did not come true, that is truly a contradiction of his prophecy. For any matter of good that God may decree through a delegated prophet, even conditionally, is never retracted — this out of the abundance of His goodness and His great loving-kindness.[7] Consequently, through words of a good occurrence a prophet can be tested. The rest of its details are in [various] places in the Talmud.

This precept applies to both man and woman, in every place and every time that a prophet arises for Israel (Jewry). If a person transgressed this and put a prophet to the test beyond the proper extent, he would violate this injunction; but whiplashes would not be suffered for it, since it entails no physical action.

[THE PRECEPT OF KILLING OUT
THE SEVEN NATIONS]

425 to put to death the seven nations that held our land before we captured it from them — these being the Canaanite, Amorite, Hittite, Hivite, Perizzite and Jebusite — and to eliminate them wherever we may find them: for it is stated about them, *you shall utterly destory them* (Deuteronomy 7:2); and the precept was reiterated in *sidrah shof'tim*, since it is stated there, *for you shall utterly destroy them — the Hittite and the Amorite*, etc. (*ibid.* 20:17).

At the root of the precept lies the reason that these seven nations are the ones that started to perform all kinds of idol-worship, and every abomination to the Lord, which He detests.[1] Therefore, since they were a main (root) element of idolatry and its first foundation, we were commanded about them to extirpate and eliminate them from under heaven, that they may not be remembered or recalled in

יִפָּקְדוּ בְּאֶרֶץ הַחַיִּים; וּבְמִצְוָתֵנוּ זֹאת עֲלֵיהֶם לְהַחֲרִימָם, יִמָּצֵא לָנוּ תוֹעֶלֶת שֶׁנְּאַבֵּד זִכְרָם מִן הָעוֹלָם, וְלֹא נִלְמַד מִמַּעֲשֵׂיהֶן. וְגַם יֵשׁ לָנוּ לְקַח מוּסָר בָּזֶה שֶׁלֹּא נִפְנֶה אַחַר עֲבוֹדָה זָרָה, כִּי בְּרָדְפֵנוּ אַחַר כָּל אִישׁ מֵהַמִּשְׁפָּחָה הָרָעָה הַזֹּאת לְהָרְגוֹ עַל הִתְעַסְּקָם בַּעֲבוֹדָה זָרָה, לֹא יַעֲלֶה עַל לֵב אִישׁ לַעֲשׂוֹת כְּמַעֲשֵׂיהֶם בְּשׁוּם פָּנִים.

וְאֵין לִשְׁאֹל כְּלָל לָמָּה נִבְרְאוּ הָאֻמּוֹת הָרָעוֹת אֵלּוּ, אַחַר שֶׁסּוֹפָן לְאַבֵּד לְנִגְמְרֵי מִן הָעוֹלָם — כִּי כְבָר יָדַעְנוּ שֶׁרְשׁוּת נְתוּנָה בְּיָדוֹ שֶׁל אָדָם לִהְיוֹת טוֹב אוֹ רַע, וְשֶׁלֹּא יַכְרִיחַ הַשֵּׁם אֶת הָאָדָם עַל אֶחָד מֵהֶן; וְאַחַר שֶׁכֵּן, נֹאמַר כִּי שִׁבְעָה עֲמָמִים אֵלּוּ קִלְקְלוּ מַעֲשֵׂיהֶן וְהִרְשִׁיעוּ עַד שֶׁנִּתְחַיְּבוּ כֻלָּן אֲבַדּוֹן נָמֵץ, וּבִתְחִלַּת הַבְּרִיאָה הָיוּ רְאוּיִין גַּם לְטוֹבָה; וְאֶל הַטַּעַם הַזֶּה נִסְמָךְ מִצְוַת כִּלְיוֹן עֲמָלֵק שֶׁבְּסֵדֶר כִּי תֵצֵא בְּסוֹף מִצְוֹת עֲשֵׂה שֶׁבַּסֵּדֶר [סִי' תרי"ד].

וְאִם נַחְפֹּץ נֹאמַר עוֹד כִּי אֶפְשָׁר שֶׁהָיָה לָהֶם בִּזְמַן מִן הַזְּמַנִּים שְׁעַת הַכֹּשֶׁר, וּמִפְּנֵי אוֹתָהּ הַשָּׁעָה זָכוּ לְהִבָּרְאוֹת; אוֹ אוּלַי נֹאמַר שֶׁיָּצָא מִבֵּין כֻּלָּם אָדָם אֶחָד הָגוּן, וּבִשְׁבִילוֹ זָכוּ כֻלָּן לְהִבָּרְאוֹת, וּכְעִנְיָן שֶׁמָּצִינוּ חָכָם אֶחָד שֶׁאָמְרוּ זִכְרוֹנָם לִבְרָכָה שֶׁהָיָה מִבְּנֵי בָנָיו שֶׁל עֲמָלֵק, וְהוּא אַנְטוֹנִינוֹס. וְאֵין מִן הַנִּמְנָע אֵצֶל הַבּוֹרֵא לִבְרֹאת כַּמָּה בְנֵי-אָדָם בִּשְׁבִיל אֶחָד, כִּי הוּא בָּרוּךְ הוּא לֹא יִרְאֶה עָמָל בְּכָל אֲשֶׁר יַחְפֹּץ עֲשׂוֹהוּ, כִּי בְהַנָּחַת חֶפְצוֹ יַעֲשֶׂה כָל אֲשֶׁר חָפֵץ, וְהוּא בָּרוּךְ הוּא הַמֵּבִין אֶל כָּל מַעֲשֵׂינוּ יוֹדֵע מַה צֹּרֶךְ לַאֲחֵרִים אֶל הָאֶחָד הַמְיֻחָד כִּי יִבָּרְאוּ כֻלָּם בִּשְׁבִילוֹ.

מִדִּינֵי הַמִּצְוָה, מַה שֶּׁאָמְרוּ זִכְרוֹנָם לִבְרָכָה שֶׁאֵין מֶלֶךְ יִשְׂרָאֵל נִלְחָם תְּחִלָּה אֶלָּא מִלְחֶמֶת מִצְוָה, שֶׁהִיא מִלְחֶמֶת שִׁבְעָה עֲמָמִין הַנִּזְכָּרִים, וּמִלְחֶמֶת עֲמָלֵק, וּמִלְחֶמֶת עֶזְרַת יִשְׂרָאֵל מִצָּר שֶׁבָּא עֲלֵיהֶם; וּבְמִלְחָמוֹת אֵלּוּ אֵינוֹ צָרִיךְ לִטֹּל רְשׁוּת מִבֵּית-דִּין; וְיֶתֶר פְּרָטֶיהָ מְבֹאָרִים.

---

2. Literally, that the right (or permission) is given into the hand of a man.

3. Mentioned in the Talmud as a Roman ruler and friend of R. Judah haNassi; according to TB 'Avodah Zarah 10b, he was descended from Esau, 'Amalek's grandfather.

4. Similarly Rambam, commentary to Mishnah, introduction. Cf. TB B'rachoth 6b.

5. MT *hilchoth m'lachim* v1–2, based on TB Sotah 44b, Sanhedrin 20b, 'Eruvin 45a.

6. I.e. before embarking on any voluntary battle of his own choosing.

the land of the living. And in this precept of ours about them, to destroy them, a benefit will result for us: we will eliminate their remembrance from the world, and [thus] we will not learn from their actions. It is, moreover, for us to learn a moral lesson from this—that we should not turn toward idol-worship: For when we pursue every man in this evil family [of nations] to kill him, because they occupied themselves with idolatry, the thought will not arise in the heart of any man to do acts like theirs under any circumstances.

Now, it should not be asked at all: Why were these evil nations created, since ultimately they were to be completely removed from the world? For we have previously known [learned] that the free choice is given to a man[2] to be good or evil, and the Eternal Lord will not impel a man toward either one of them. And since it is so, we have to say that these seven peoples corrupted their ways of action and turned wicked, until they all incurred the fate of elimination and death, although at the beginning of Creation they were fit also for goodness. Now, to this reason we would [also] ascribe the precept of extirpating 'Amalek, in *sidrah ki thétzé*, the last of the positive precepts in the *sidrah* (§ 604).

If we like, we could further say that perhaps they had at some certain time a brief period of worthiness, and because of that brief period they merited to be created. Or perhaps we could say that from among them all, one worthy person emerged; and for his sake they all merited to be created—in keeping with what we find that the Sages of blessed memory said, that there was one wise man among the descendants of 'Amalek, namely Antoninus.[3] It is not out of the question for the Creator to produce any number of persons for the sake of one: for He (blessed is He) experiences no wearisome effort in whatever He desires to do. As His desire is established, whatever He wishes is done; and He (blessed is He), who comprehends all our actions, knows what need there is for others because of the one particular person, so that all should be created for his sake.[4]

Among the laws of the precept there is what the Sages of blessed memory said:[5] that a king of Israel may wage first[6] nothing but a war of religious duty, which means a war against the seven nations mentioned [above], war with 'Amalek, and war to help the Israelites against an oppressor that attacks them; and for these campaigns he does not need to have permission from the *beth din* [the Sanhedrin, supreme court]. The rest of its details are clarified.

וְנוֹהֶגֶת מִצְוָה זוֹ בִּזְכָרִים וּנְקֵבוֹת, בְּכָל מָקוֹם וּבְכָל זְמַן שֶׁיֵּשׁ כֹּחַ בְּיָדֵינוּ לְהָרְגָם. וְכָתַב הָרַב מֹשֶׁה בֶּן מַיְמוֹן זִכְרוֹנוֹ לִבְרָכָה: אוּלַי חוֹשֵׁב יַחֲשֹׁב שֶׁזּוֹ מִצְוָה שֶׁאֵינָהּ נוֹהֶגֶת לְדוֹרוֹת, אַחַר שֶׁשִּׁבְעָה עֲמָמִין כְּבָר אָבְדוּ; וְזֶה אָמְנָם יַחְשְׁבֵהוּ מִי שֶׁלֹּא יָבִין עִנְיַן נוֹהֵג לְדוֹרוֹת וְאֵינוֹ נוֹהֵג לְדוֹרוֹת.

וּכְלַל דְּבָרָיו זִכְרוֹנוֹ לִבְרָכָה שֶׁיֵּשׁ לָדַעַת כִּי כָל מִצְוָה שֶׁלֹּא תִהְיֶה עֲשִׂיָּתָהּ נֶעְדֶּרֶת מֵחֲמַת שֶׁעָבַר זְמַנָּהּ, כְּגוֹן מִצְוֹת שֶׁהָיוּ בַּמִּדְבָּר וְלֹא אַחַר־כֵּן בָּאָרֶץ, וְכֵן מִצְוַת הֲסִבַּת נַחֲלָה, שֶׁלֹּא הָיְתָה אֶלָּא לְאוֹתוֹ הַדּוֹר שֶׁהָיוּ בְחִלּוּק הָאָרֶץ בִּכְנִיסָתָן לָאָרֶץ, כְּגוֹן אֵלּוּ הֵן שֶׁנִּקְרָאוֹת "אֵינָן נוֹהֲגוֹת לְדוֹרוֹת"; אֲבָל כָּל מִצְוָה שֶׁהִיא נֶעְדֶּרֶת מִמֶּנּוּ מֵחֲמַת שֶׁאֵינָהּ נִמְצֵאת לָנוּ שֶׁנּוּכַל לַעֲשׂוֹתָהּ, אֲבָל לֹא שֶׁהֶהָתוּב יִתְלֶה אוֹתָהּ בִּזְמַן מִן הַזְּמַנִּים, כְּגוֹן זוֹ שֶׁל (אבדן) אָבְדָן שִׁבְעָה עֲמָמִים וַעֲמָלֵק, שֶׁהַכָּתוּב צִוָּנוּ לִמְחוֹת שְׁמָם וּלְאַבְּדָם לְעוֹלָם בְּכָל דּוֹר וָדוֹר שֶׁנִּמְצָאִים; וְאַף כִּי כְּבָר עָשִׂינוּ בָּהֶם הַמְּחֻיָּב עַל יַד דָּוִד מַלְכֵּנוּ שֶׁהִשְׁחִיתָם וְכֻלָּם עַד שֶׁלֹּא נִשְׁאֲרוּ מֵהֶם רַק מְתֵי מִסְפָּר שֶׁנִּתְפַּזְּרוּ וְטָבְעוּ בֵּין הָאֻמּוֹת עַד שֶׁלֹּא נוֹדַע זִכְרָם, וְאֵין בְּיָדֵינוּ עַתָּה לִרְדֹּף אַחֲרֵיהֶם וּלְהָרְגָם, אַף־עַל־פִּי־כֵן לֹא תִקָּרֵא מִצְוָה זוֹ מִפְּנֵי זֶה "מִצְוָה שֶׁאֵינָהּ נוֹהֶגֶת", וְהָבֵן זֶה הָעִקָּר וְהַחֲזֵק בּוֹ.

וְעוֹבֵר עַל זֶה וּבָא לְיָדוֹ אֶחָד מֵהֶם וְיָכוֹל לְהָרְגוֹ מִבְּלִי שֶׁיִּסְתַּכֵּן בַּדָּבָר וְלֹא הֲרָגוֹ, בִּטֵּל עֲשֵׂה זֶה, מִלְּבַד שֶׁעָבַר עַל לָאו שֶׁנֶּאֱמַר עֲלֵיהֶם, "לֹא תְחַיֶּה כָּל נְשָׁמָה", כְּמוֹ שֶׁנִּכְתַּב בְּסוֹף סֵדֶר שׁוֹפְטִים בְּעֶזְרַת הַשֵּׁם בְּסִימָן (תקכ"ט) [תקכ"ח].

[שֶׁלֹּא לָחֹן עַל עוֹבְדֵי עֲבוֹדָה זָרָה]

תכו שֶׁלֹּא נַחְמֹל עַל עוֹבְדֵי עֲבוֹדָה זָרָה וְלֹא יִישַׁר בְּעֵינֵינוּ דָּבָר מֵהֶם, כְּלוֹמַר

7. ShM positive precept §187. What follows constitutes a problem that must be dealt with, because in ShM, root principle 3, Rambam sets down a basic rule that any precept or commandment in the Torah which applied only for a certain time and not for all generations, cannot be ranked as one of the 613 precepts. Hence, at first glance, it is difficult to see how this precept can be so listed.

8. E.g. to leave nothing for the next day from the daily portion of manna in the wilderness (Exodus 16:19).

9. I.e. if someone's daughter received a portion of the land of Israel as an inheritance, she was to marry only a person from her father's tribe, so that the estate would not be transferred to another tribe through her marriage (Numbers 36:8-9).

10. Literally, drowned.

11. For quite simply, should a tribe of Amalekites, for example, be discovered today, the precept would very much apply to them.

§426   1. Literally, that we should not have mercy on.

This precept is in effect for both man and woman everywhere and at every time that the power lies in our hands to put them to death. Now, R. Moses b. Maimon of blessed memory wrote:[7] One might think perhaps that this is a precept which is not in effect for all generations, since the seven nations perished in the past. In truth, though, only one who does not understand the concept of something being in force for all generations or not being thus in force, could think so.

The sum import of his words (be his memory for a blessing) is that this should be known: If there is any precept whose observance is not lacking, because its time has passed—for example, the precepts that existed in the wilderness but not afterward in the land [of Israel],[8] and so too the precept about diverting an inherited estate,[9] which was not [applicable] to any but that generation who were [involved] in the apportionment of the land, upon their entry into the land—the like of these are what we consider as not in effect for all generations. However, any precept that we are lacking because it is not available to us so that we should be able to observe it, but Scripture does not make it dependent on a particular period of time—for instance, this one, of eliminating the seven nations and 'Amalek, where the Writ commanded us to eradicate their name and destroy them from the world forever, in every generation where they are found—then even if we previously did with them what was obligatory, through our King David, who demolished them and destroyed them until none but a small number remained of them, who became scattered and disappeared[10] among the nations, until we could not find their traces, and now we have not the means to pursue them and kill them—this precept is nevertheless not called (considered) on that account a commandment not in effect [any longer].[11] Understand this main principle, and retain it firmly.

If someone transgresses it, when one of them comes into his hand and he is able to kill him without imperiling himself in the matter, and he does not take his life, he disobeys this positive precept, apart from violating the negative precept stated about them, *you shall save alive nothing that breathes* (Deuteronomy 20:16), as we will write toward the end of *sidrah shof'tim* (§ 528), with the Eternal Lord's help.

[TO SHOW NO MERCY TO IDOL-WORSHIPPERS]

⟨297⟩ **426** that we should have no kind feelings for[1] those who worship

שֶׁנַּרְחִיק מִמַּחֲשַׁבְתֵּנוּ וְלֹא יַעֲלֶה עַל פִּינוּ שֶׁיִּהְיֶה בְּמִי שֶׁהוּא עוֹבֵד עֲבוֹדָה זָרָה
דְּבַר תּוֹעֶלֶת, וְלֹא יְהִי מַעֲלֶה חֵן בְּעֵינֵינוּ בְּשׁוּם עִנְיָן, עַד שֶׁאָמְרוּ רַבּוֹתֵינוּ זִכְרוֹנָם
לִבְרָכָה שֶׁאָסוּר לוֹמַר "כַּמָּה נָאֶה גּוֹי זֶה" אוֹ "מַה נֶּחְמָד וְנָעִים הוּא"; וְעַל זֶה
נֶאֱמַר "וְלֹא תְחָנֵּם", וּבָא הַפֵּרוּשׁ עַל זֶה: לֹא תִתֵּן לָהֶם חֵן, בְּעִנְיָן שֶׁאָמַרְנוּ. וְיֵשׁ
מֵרַבּוֹתֵינוּ שֶׁלָּמְדוּ מִ"לֹא תְחָנֵּם": לֹא תִתֵּן לָהֶם מַתְּנוֹת חִנָּם; וְהַכֹּל שֹׁרֶשׁ אֶחָד.
וּבִירוּשַׁלְמִי דַעֲבוֹדָה זָרָה (אָמְרוּ):"לֹא תְחָנֵּם", לֹא תִתֵּן לָהֶם חֵן — בְּלֹא־תַעֲשֶׂה.

מִשָּׁרְשֵׁי הַמִּצְוָה, לְפִי שֶׁתְּחִלַּת כָּל מַעֲשֶׂה בְּנֵי־אָדָם הִיא קְבִיעוּת הַמַּחֲשָׁבָה
בְּמַעֲשִׂים וְהַעֲלוֹת הַדְּבָרִים עַל שְׂפַת לָשׁוֹן, וְאַחַר הַמַּחֲשָׁבָה וְהַדִּבּוּר בָּהּ תֵּעָשֶׂה
כָּל מְלָאכָה; וְעַל־כֵּן בְּהִמָּנְעֵנוּ בְּמַחֲשָׁבָה וּבְדִבּוּר מִמֹּצָא בְּעוֹבְדֵי עֲבוֹדָה זָרָה
תּוֹעֶלֶת וָחֵן, הִנְנוּ נִמְנָעִים בְּכָךְ מִלְּהִתְחַבֵּר עִמָּהֶם וּמִלִּרְדֹּף אַחַר אַהֲבָתָם וּמִלִּלְמֹד
דָּבָר מִכָּל מַעֲשֵׂיהֶם הָרָעִים.

מִדִּינֵי הַמִּצְוָה, מַה שֶׁאָמְרוּ זִכְרוֹנָם לִבְרָכָה בְּשֶׁאֵין נוֹתְנִין לָהֶם מַתְּנוֹת חִנָּם,
דְּדַוְקָא לְמִי שֶׁעוֹבֵד עֲבוֹדָה זָרָה, אֲבָל לֹא לְמִי שֶׁאֵינוֹ עוֹבֵד עֲבוֹדָה זָרָה, וְאַף־עַל־
פִּי שֶׁהוּא עוֹמֵד בְּגִיּוּתוֹ לֶאֱכֹל שְׁקָצִים וּרְמָשִׂים וּשְׁאָר כָּל הָעֲבֵרוֹת, כְּגוֹן גֵּר
תּוֹשָׁב, דְּמִכֵּינָן שֶׁקִּבֵּל עָלָיו שֶׁבַע מִצְווֹת, מְפַרְנְסִין אוֹתוֹ וְנוֹתְנִין לוֹ מַתְּנוֹת חִנָּם.
וְאָמְרוּ זִכְרוֹנָם לִבְרָכָה שֶׁאֵין מְקַבְּלִין גֵּר תּוֹשָׁב אֶלָּא בִּזְמַן שֶׁהַיּוֹבֵל נוֹהֵג. וְעוֹד
אָמְרוּ זִכְרוֹנָם לִבְרָכָה שֶׁמֻּתָּר לְפַרְנֵס עֲנִיֵּי גוֹיִם עִם עֲנִיֵּי יִשְׂרָאֵל, מִפְּנֵי דַרְכֵי
שָׁלוֹם. וְיֶתֶר פְּרָטֶיהָ, מְבֹאָרִים בְּמַסֶּכֶת עֲבוֹדָה זָרָה.

וְנוֹהֶגֶת בְּכָל מָקוֹם וּבְכָל זְמַן, בִּזְכָרִים וּנְקֵבוֹת. וְעוֹבֵר עַל זֶה וְשִׁבַּח עוֹבְדֵי

2. TB ʿAvodah Zarah 20a.

3. This is how the verse is obviously understood here; it is generally rendered,
and you shall show no mercy to them.

4. The verb *thʾhaném* (be gracious to them) is now linked to *hinnám*, free, gratuitous, without any consideration of benefit or reward; TB *ibid.* (and see Meʾiri on
this, p. 46 s.v. *kʾvar*, for an interesting reason for the ban).

5. Not to have any positive relationship with an idolater.

6. The paragraph is based on ShM negative precept §50.

7. TB ʿAvodah Zarah 64b–65a.

8. A heathen who settles in the Land of Israel, renouncing idolatry.

9. Which the Torah imposes on the descendants of Noaḥ, i.e. on all mankind;
listed in §26, note 32.

10. TB ʿArachin 29a.

11. TB Gittin 61a.

12. Literally, "on account of the ways of peace"; though ordinarily gratuitous
gifts, for no reason, for nothing gained in return, are not to be given to heathens
(see note 4), here it is permissible because something *is* gained in return: an atmosphere of peace and harmony.

idols, and nothing about them should be good or pleasing in our eyes; in other words, we should remove far from our mind, and it should not [ever] arise in our speech, that there could be anything of value in one who worships in idolatry, and he should find no grace or favor in our eyes—to such an extent that the Sages of blessed memory taught[2] that it is forbidden to say, "How handsome that heathen is," or "How charming and pleasant he is." About this it is stated, *and you shall not be gracious to them*[3] (Deuteronomy 7:2), for which the interpretation was given [in the Oral Tradition]: Do not ascribe grace or charm to them—in keeping with what we said. Now, there are some of our Sages who inferred from the verse, *you shall not be gracious to them,* that you shall not give them gratuitous gifts;[4] but it is all from one root [principle].[5] And in the tractate 'Avodah Zarah in the Jerusalem Talmud (i 9) it was stated: "you shall not be gracious to them"—it is a negative precept.[6]

At the root of the precept lies the reason that the beginning of every human activity is fixing one's thought on the acts and bringing the matters up on the speech of the tongue; after thinking and talking about it, every task is carried out. Therefore, by refraining in thought and speech from finding anything gainful or charming in those who worship in idolatry, we will thus refrain from joining them and striving after their affection, and from learning anything from all their evil deeds.

Among the laws of the precept there is what the Sages of blessed memory taught about not giving them gifts gratuitously:[7] that this applies specifically to one who worships in idolatry, but not to one who does not practice idol-worship, even if he stands firm in his non-Jewish ways, eating loathsome and swarming creatures and committing all the other iniquities — such as a *gér toshav*;[8] for since he undertook to observe the seven precepts,[9] he may be sustained and given gratuitous gifts.

Our Sages of blessed memory taught[10] that a *gér toshav* may be accepted at no other time but when the law of the jubilee is in effect. And they (of blessed memory) said[11] that it is permissible to sustain the poor of the non-Jews along with the Israelite poor, for the sake of peace.[12] The rest of its details are explained in the Talmud tractate *'Avodah Zarah.*

This is in effect in every place and time, for both man and woman. If someone transgressed this and praised idol-worshippers and their

עֲבוֹדָה זָרָה וּמַעֲשֵׂיהֶם, זוּלָתִי בְּעִנְיָן שֶׁיִּמָּצֵא שֶׁבַח יָתֵר מְאֹד לְאָמְתֵנוּ מִתּוֹךְ שִׂבְחָם, עָבַר עַל לָאו זֶה; וְאֵין בּוֹ מַלְקוֹת לְפִי שֶׁאֵין בּוֹ מַעֲשֶׂה, אֲבָל עָנְשׁוֹ גָּדוֹל מְאֹד, כִּי הוּא סִבָּה לְתַקָּלָה מְרֻבָּה שֶׁאֵין לָהּ תַּשְׁלוּמִין, כִּי הַדְּבָרִים יֵרְדוּ לִפְעָמִים בְּחַדְרֵי בֶטֶן הַשּׁוֹמְעִים, וְכָל יוֹדֵעַ דַּעַת יָבִין זֶה.

[שֶׁלֹּא לְהִתְחַתֵּן בְּעוֹבְדֵי עֲבוֹדָה זָרָה]

תכז שֶׁלֹּא נִתְחַתֵּן עִם הָאֻמּוֹת; וְכָתַב הָרַב רַבֵּנוּ מֹשֶׁה בֶּן מַיְמוֹן זִכְרוֹנוֹ לִבְרָכָה: לֹא עִם שִׁבְעָה עֲמָמִים וְלֹא עִם שְׁאָר הָאֻמּוֹת — שֶׁנֶּאֱמַר: וְלֹא תִתְחַתֵּן בָּם.

וְעִנְיַן הַחַתְנוּת הוּא שֶׁיִּתֵּן בִּתּוֹ לִבְנוֹ אוֹ בְנוֹ לְבִתּוֹ, וּכְמוֹ שֶׁבֵּאֵר הַכָּתוּב: בִּתְּךָ לֹא תִתֵּן לִבְנוֹ וּבִתּוֹ לֹא תִקַּח לִבְנֶךָ; וְכָל שֶׁכֵּן הַמִּזְדַּוֵּג עִמָּהֶם, שֶׁהוּא בְעַצְמוֹ בִּכְלַל הָאִסּוּר; וְאָמְרִינָן בְּמַסֶּכֶת עֲבוֹדָה זָרָה: דֶּרֶךְ חַתְנוּת אָסְרָה תוֹרָה.

וְאַף־עַל־פִּי שֶׁהַכָּתוּב הַזֶּה דְּ"לֹא תִתְחַתֵּן" בְּשִׁבְעָה עֲמָמִים הוּא דִכְתִיב, וּבְגֵרוּתָן דַּוְקָא, וְהָכִי מַשְׁמַע לְהוּ לְרַבָּנָן, שֶׁאָמְרוּ בַגְּמָרָא: בְּגֵרוּתָן אִית לְהוּ חַתְנוּת, בְּגֵיוּתָן לֵית לְהוּ חַתְנוּת — בְּמַה שֶׁחָזַר הַכָּתוּב "בִּתְּךָ לֹא תִתֵּן לִבְנוֹ וּבִתּוֹ לֹא תִקַּח לִבְנֶךָ" יַרְבֶּה שִׁבְעָה עֲמָמִים וְכָל שְׁאָר הָאֻמּוֹת בָּאִסּוּר אַף בְּגֵיוּתָן; אֲבָל שִׁבְעָה עֲמָמִין נֶאֶסְרוּ אַף בְּגֵרוּת, לְפִי שֶׁהָיוּ עִקַּר עֲבוֹדָה זָרָה וִיסוֹדָהּ הָרִאשׁוֹן, וּשְׁאָר עֲמָמִים מֻתָּרִין בְּגֵרוּת.

וְאִסּוּר זֶה יִהְיֶה דַּוְקָא כְּשֶׁהוּא מְיַחֲדָהּ לוֹ לְאִשָּׁה, אֲבָל הַבָּא עַל הַגּוֹיָה דֶּרֶךְ

§427   1. MT *hilchoth 'issuré bi'ah* xii 1 (following R. Shim'on b. Yoḥai's view in TB Kiddushin 68b and 'Avodah Zarah 46b).

2. See §425, beginning.

3. TB Yevamoth 76a.

4. A marital bond with a non-Jewish mate has no legal validity. Hence Scripture's prohibition against the seven nations must mean even if one among them converted to Judaism.

5. For on the level of the plain meaning, this part of the verse is patently superfluous; hence it is interpreted to extend the meaning or scope of the precept (and hence, our author implies, Rambam follows R. Shim'on b. Yoḥai rather than the Sages; see note 1 and MY).

6. I.e. they were the "founders" of idolatry in the world, who established it as a major force; see §425, second paragraph.

activities, other than in some matter where he would find much more to praise in our nation as a result of their praise, he would violate this negative precept. It entails no penalty of whiplashes, though, since it involves no physical action. Yet his punishment would be very great, since it is a cause of great misfortune for which there is no compensation: for the words may penetrate at times to the innermost depths of the listeners. Anyone who has sensible knowledge will understand this.

[TO FORM NO MARITAL BONDS WITH
IDOL-WORSHIPPERS]

427 that we should not intermarry with the nations; and R. Moses b. Maimon of blessed memory wrote:[1] neither with the seven nations [that we were commanded to exterminate][2] nor with the other nations—for it is stated, *neither shall you make marriages with them* (Deuteronomy 7:3).

Making marriages means in substance giving one's daughter to another's son or one's son to another's daughter [for a mate]—as the Writ explains, *your daughter you shall not give to his son, nor shall you take his daughter for your son (ibid)*; and all the more certainly if a person himself forms a marital union with one of them, for he is himself included under the prohibition. And it was taught in the tractate '*Avodah Zarah* (36b): The Torah prohibited [a bond with the nations] by way of marriage.

Now, actually, this verse, *neither shall you make marriages*, was written about the seven nations, and particularly in regard to their conversion to Judaism. For so the Sages understand it, since they said in the Talmud:[3] In their converted state, marriage with them could take effect; in their heathen state it could not.[4] Nevertheless, when Scripture reiterates, *your daughter you shall not give to his son, nor shall you take his daughter for your son,* it thus extends the application of the ban to the seven nations and all other nations as well, in their heathen state.[5] Thus the seven nations were banned even if converted to Judaism, because they were the core element in idol-worship, and its first foundation;[6] whereas other peoples are permissible through conversion.

Now, this prohibition applies when a person singles someone out specifically for a wife; but if a person is conjugally intimate with a

heathen woman casually, like a man who is thus intimate with his

מִקְרֶה כְּאָדָם הַבָּא עַל זוֹנָתוֹ שֶׁלֹּא בְּפַרְהֶסְיָא, אֵין בָּזֶה אֶלָּא אִסּוּר דִּבְרֵיהֶם, וְהוּא אָסוּר נשג״ז הַמֻּזְכָּר בַּעֲבוֹדָה זָרָה.

מִשָּׁרְשֵׁי הַמִּצְוָה, לְפִי שֶׁרֹב הֲמוֹן הָעָם, דֶּרֶךְ טִפְּשׁוּת, יִמָּשְׁכוּ אַחַר עֲצַת נְשׁוֹתֵיהֶם, וְאִם יִשָּׂא אָדָם בַּת אֵל נֵכָר תִּמְשְׁכֵהוּ לַעֲבוֹדַת עֲבוֹדָה זָרָה; וְעוֹד כִּי גַם בָּנֶיהָ מִמֶּנּוּ תְגַדֵּל לַעֲבוֹדָה זָרָה, וְאוֹי לוֹ לְפוֹסֵל אֶת זַרְעוֹ.

מִדִּינֵי הַמִּצְוָה, מַה שֶׁאָמְרוּ זִכְרוֹנָם לִבְרָכָה: הַבּוֹעֵל אֲרַמִּית בְּפַרְהֶסְיָא, כְּלוֹמַר לְעֵינֵי עֲשָׂרָה יִשְׂרָאֵל אוֹ יוֹתֵר, קַנָּאִין פּוֹגְעִין בּוֹ; וּרְאָיָה לַדָּבָר מַעֲשֵׂה פִּינְחָס וְזִמְרִי. וּמִכָּל־מָקוֹם אֵין הַקַּנָּאִי רַשַּׁאי לִפְגֹּעַ בּוֹ אֶלָּא בִּשְׁעַת מַעֲשֵׂה הַזִּמָּה, וּכְמַעֲשֵׂה שֶׁהָיָה, שֶׁנֶּאֱמַר "וְאֶת הָאִשָּׁה אֶל קֳבָתָהּ", אֲבָל אִם פֵּרַשׁ אֵין הוֹרְגִין אוֹתוֹ, אֲבָל מְבִיאִין אוֹתוֹ לְבֵית־דִּין וּמַלְקִין אוֹתוֹ, מִכֵּיוָן שֶׁעָשָׂה הַמַּעֲשֶׂה בְּפַרְהֶסְיָא. לֹא פָּגְעוּ בּוֹ קַנָּאִין וְלֹא הִלְקוּהוּ בֵּית־דִּין, יָדַעְנוּ מִדִּבְרֵי קַבָּלָה שֶׁהוּא בְּכָרֵת, דִּכְתִיב: וּבָעַל בַּת אֵל נֵכָר יַכְרֵת ה' לָאִישׁ אֲשֶׁר יַעֲשֶׂנָּה.

וְגוֹי הַבָּא עַל בַּת יִשְׂרָאֵל, אִם הִיא אֵשֶׁת אִישׁ נֶהֱרָג עָלֶיהָ, וְאִם לָאו אֵינוֹ נֶהֱרָג; אֲבָל יִשְׂרָאֵל הַבָּא עַל הַגּוֹיָה בְּזָדוֹן וַאֲפִלּוּ דֶּרֶךְ זְנוּת, הִיא תֵּהָרֵג מִכָּל־מָקוֹם, מִפְּנֵי שֶׁבָּא לְיִשְׂרָאֵל תַּקָּלָה עַל יָדָהּ, כְּדִין הַבְּהֵמָה. וְדָבָר זֶה מְפֹרָשׁ בַּתּוֹרָה, שֶׁנֶּאֱמַר "הֵן הֵנָּה הָיוּ לִבְנֵי יִשְׂרָאֵל" וְגוֹמֵר "וְכָל אִשָּׁה יֹדַעַת אִישׁ לְמִשְׁכַּב זָכָר הֲרֹגוּ". וְיֶתֶר פְּרָטֵי דְּבָרִים אֵלֶּה, מְבֹאָרִים בַּעֲבוֹדָה זָרָה וּבְסַנְהֶדְרִין וּבִיבָמוֹת וְקִדּוּשִׁין.

וְנוֹהֶגֶת בְּכָל מָקוֹם וּבְכָל זְמַן, בַּזְּכָרִים וּנְקֵבוֹת. וְעוֹבֵר עַל זֶה וְנִתְחַתֵּן עִם שִׁבְעָה עֲמָמִים בְּגֵרוּתָן, כְּלוֹמַר שֶׁיִּחַד לוֹ אִשָּׁה מֵהֶן וּבָא עָלֶיהָ, לוֹקֶה. וְהַמְּיַחֵד

---

7. I.e. the Sages decreed that conjugal intimacy with a non-Jewish woman should be the equivalent of immoral relations with all these four.

8. TB Sanhedrin 81b–82a.

9. So implied in MT *hilchoth 'issuré bi'ah* xii 2, 6.

10. MT *ibid.* 6.

11. TB Sanhedrin 57b; MT *hilchoth m'lachim* ix 7.

12. MT *hilchoth 'issuré bi'ah* xii 10 (see *Maggid Mishneh*).

mistress [or harlot], not openly, no more than a prohibition by the ruling of the Sages applies to it, this being the prohibition on a menstruant, a slave-woman, a non-Jewish woman, and a harlot, mentioned in the tractate 'Avodah Zarah (36b).[7]

At the root of the precept lies the reason that most of the mass of people are drawn by way of foolishness after the counsel of their wives; and if a man will marry a daughter of [a people under] a foreign god, she will lure him to idol-worship; moreover, she will also raise her sons by him to idol-worship; and woe to him who thus ruins his progeny.

Among the laws of the precept, there is what the Sages of blessed memory said:[8] If one is conjugally intimate with an Aramite (a non-Jewish) woman publicly, i.e. in the sight of ten Israelites or more, zealots may attack him. Proof of the matter is the incident of Pinḥas (Phinehas) and Zimri (Numbers 25:6–8, 14). However, a zealot has no right to attack him except during the act of immorality — as in the incident that happened: for it is stated, *and the woman through her belly* (*ibid.* 8). If he separated [from her] though, he may not be killed, but is to be brought to the *beth din* (court), where he is given whiplashes, because he committed the deed in public.[9] If zealots did not attack him and the *beth din* did not flog him, we know through the Oral Tradition that he will be punished by *kareth* [Divine severance of existence] for it is written, *and he has been as a husband with the daughter of a foreign god: the Lord will cut off* [impose kareth] *for the man who does this* (Malachi 2:11–12).[10]

If a heathen was conjugally intimate with an Israelite daughter, if she is a married woman, he is put to death for it; and if not, his life is not ended.[11] However, if an Israelite was thus intimate with a heathen woman deliberately, even if by way of immorality, she is to be put to death in any event,[12] since the Israelite came to grief through her — as the law is for an animal (§ 210). This matter is clearly expressed in the Torah, for it is stated, *Behold, these caused the Israelites... kill every woman that has known man by lying with him* (Numbers 31:16–17). Other details of these topics are explained in the tractates 'Avodah Zarah, Sanhedrin, Yevamoth and Kiddushin.

It is in effect everywhere, at every time, for both man and woman. If a person violated this and intermarried with the seven nations in their state of conversion to Judaism — in other words, he selected a wife for himself from among them, and was conjugally intimate with

אִשָּׁה מֵהֶן לִבְנוֹ, אוֹ שֶׁנָּתַן בִּתּוֹ לְאֶחָד מֵהֶן, הָאָב עָבַר עַל לָאו, אֲבָל אֵינוֹ לוֹקֶה
לְפִי שֶׁאֵין בּוֹ מַעֲשֶׂה, אֲבָל הַבֵּן שֶׁעָשָׂה מַעֲשֵׂה הַבִּיאָה לוֹקֶה. וּבִשְׁאָר עֲמָמִים וְכֵן
בְּשִׁבְעָה עֲמָמִים בְּגִיּוּתָן, הַמְיַחֵד לוֹ אִשָּׁה מֵהֶן לָבוֹא עָלֶיהָ תָּמִיד, לוֹקֶה
מִדְּאוֹרַיְתָא בְּבִיאָה רִאשׁוֹנָה מֵאַחַר שֶׁיְּחֲדָהּ, וְהִיא תֵהָרֵג; וְאִם לֹא יִחֲדָהּ אֶלָּא
שֶׁבָּא עָלֶיהָ פַּעַם אַחַת דֶּרֶךְ זְנוּת, מַכִּין אוֹתוֹ מַכַּת מַרְדּוּת מִדְּרַבָּנָן.

✡ וְהָיָה עֵקֶב

יֵשׁ בָּהּ שֵׁשׁ מִצְווֹת עֲשֵׂה וּשְׁתֵּי מִצְווֹת לֹא־תַעֲשֶׂה

[שֶׁלֹּא לֵהָנוֹת מִצִּפּוּיֵי עֲבוֹדָה זָרָה]

תכח שֶׁנִּמְנַעְנוּ שֶׁלֹּא לֵהָנוֹת מִצִּפּוּיֵי עֲבוֹדָה זָרָה, וְאַף־עַל־פִּי שֶׁהָעֲבוֹדָה זָרָה
עַצְמָהּ אֵינָהּ אֲסוּרָה בַּהֲנָאָה, כְּגוֹן הַמִּשְׁתַּחֲוֶה לְדָבָר שֶׁאֵין בּוֹ תְּפִיסַת יַד אָדָם,
כְּגוֹן הַר אוֹ בְהֵמָה אוֹ אִילָן, שֶׁאֵינָם נֶאֱסָרִין בַּהֲנָאָה, אֲבָל הַצִּפּוּי שֶׁעֲלֵיהֶם מִכָּל־
מָקוֹם אֲסוּרִים בַּהֲנָאָה, שֶׁהוּא בִּכְלַל מְשַׁמְּשֵׁי עֲבוֹדָה זָרָה שֶׁאֲסוּרִין, וְעַל זֶה
נֶאֱמַר: לֹא תַחְמֹד כֶּסֶף וְזָהָב עֲלֵיהֶם וְלָקַחְתָּ לָךְ; וְאַף־עַל־פִּי שֶׁנֶּאֱמַר בְּמָקוֹם אַחֵר
דֶּרֶךְ כְּלָל "וְלֹא יִדְבַּק בְּיָדְךָ" וְגוֹמֵר, נִתְיַחֵד לָאו בַּצִּפּוּי, לְפִי שֶׁיִּתְּנוּ עֵינֵיהֶם בּוֹ
הַפְּתָאִים.

מִשָּׁרְשֵׁי הַמִּצְוָה, כְּדֵי לְהַרְחִיק כָּל עִנְיַן עֲבוֹדָה זָרָה וְכָל הַנִּטְפָּל לָהּ. דִּינֵי
הַמִּצְוָה יִתְבָּאֲרוּ בְּפֶרֶק שְׁלִישִׁי מֵעֲבוֹדָה זָרָה. וְנוֹהֶגֶת בְּכָל מָקוֹם וּבְכָל זְמַן,

13. See §24, note 14.

1. So TB ʿAvodah Zarah 45a.

2. Literally, in which there is no hold of the hand of man; i.e. it was not formed by human hands.

3. I.e. they would strongly desire them; and they might think such things permissible, since they are only incidental additions to the entities actually worshipped.

her — he should be given whiplashes. If someone selected a wife from among them for his son, or if he gave his daughter to one of them [in marriage], the father would violate a negative precept, but would not receive whiplashes, since it involved no physical action [on his part]; however, the son, who performed the act of conjugal intimacy, would receive lashes. As to other peoples, and so too the seven nations in their heathen state, if someone selected a wife for himself from among them, to be conjugally intimate with her regularly, he would receive a whipping by Torah law upon the first act of conjugal intimacy, since he singled her out [for his mate], while she should be put to death. If, however, he did not choose her for his spouse but was rather intimate with her by way of immorality, he should be whipped with lashes of disobedience,[13] by the ruling of the Sages.

sidrah 'ékev
(Deuteronomy 7:12–11:25)

It contains six positive and two negative precepts.

[NOT TO DERIVE BENEFIT FROM ANY ORNAMENTATION OF AN IDOL]

428 that we were forbidden to have any benefit from the adornments of an idolatrously worshipped object, even if having benefit from the worshipped object itself is not forbidden[1] — for example, if one bows down in worship to something unconnected with human hands,[2] such as a mountain, an animal or a tree, from which all benefit does not become forbidden [thereby]; yet benefit from adornment on them becomes forbidden in any event, because that is included in the category of things that serve a worshipped object, which are forbidden. About this it is stated, *you shall not covet the silver or the gold that is on them, or take it for yourself* (Deuteronomy 7:25). Although it was stated elsewhere, as a general rule, *And none of the banned things shall cling to your hand* (ibid. 13:18), a particular negative precept was given about adornments, because fools would set their eyes on them.[3]

At the root of the precept lies the purpose to move the entire matter of idol-worship and everything connected with it far away. The laws of the precept are explained in the third chapter of the tractate *'Avodah Zarah*. It is in effect everywhere, at every time, for

בִּזְכָרִים וּנְקֵבוֹת; וְעוֹבֵר עַל זֶה וְנֶהֱנֶה בְּצִפּוּיָן, וַאֲפִלּוּ בְּכָל שֶׁהוּא, חַיָּב מַלְקוֹת.

[שֶׁלֹּא לְהַדְבִּיק שׁוּם דָּבָר מֵעֲבוֹדָה זָרָה עִם מָמוֹנֵנוּ וּבִרְשׁוּתֵנוּ לֵהָנוֹת בּוֹ]

תכט שֶׁלֹּא נַדְבִּיק שׁוּם דָּבָר מֵעֲבוֹדָה זָרָה עִם מָמוֹנֵנוּ וּבִרְשׁוּתֵנוּ לֵהָנוֹת בּוֹ,
וְעַל זֶה נֶאֱמַר "וְלֹא תָבִיא תוֹעֵבָה אֶל בֵּיתֶךָ" וְגוֹמֵר.

מִשָּׁרְשֵׁי הַמִּצְוָה, כְּדֵי לְהַרְחִיק כָּל עִנְיַן עֲבוֹדָה זָרָה הַנִּמְאָסֶת.

דִּינֵי מִצְוָה זוֹ גַּם־כֵּן בְּפֶרֶק שְׁלִישִׁי מִמַּסֶּכֶת עֲבוֹדָה זָרָה. וּבֵאֲרוּ זִכְרוֹנָם
לִבְרָכָה שֶׁהַמְּבַשֵּׁל בַּעֲצֵי אֲשֵׁרָה לוֹקֶה שְׁתַּיִם, מִשּׁוּם "וְלֹא תָבִיא תוֹעֵבָה" וּמִשּׁוּם
"וְלֹא יִדְבַּק בְּיָדְךָ מְאוּמָה", שֶׁשְּׁנֵי עִנְיָנִים הֵם, אֶחָד הַמַּכְנִיס דְּבַר עֲבוֹדָה זָרָה
לִרְשׁוּתוֹ כְּדֵי לֵהָנוֹת בּוֹ, וְאֶחָד הַנֶּהֱנֶה בּוֹ, שֶׁבִּשְׁנֵיהֶם מַרְאֶה הָאָדָם בְּנַפְשׁוֹ הַחֵפֶץ
אֵלֶיהָ; וְלוֹקֶה עַל שְׁנֵיהֶם, כְּמוֹ שֶׁכָּתַבְנוּ.

וְאַף־עַל־פִּי שֶׁשְּׁנֵיהֶם עִקָּר אֶחָד לָהֶם, וְהִיא הַהֲנָאָה, שֶׁהֲרֵי אֵינוֹ לוֹקֶה אֶלָּא
בִּשְׁבִיל הַהֲנָאָה, מִכָּל־מָקוֹם מִכֵּיוָן שֶׁיֵּהָנֶה יִלְקֶה שְׁתַּיִם, וּכְעִנְיָן שֶׁאָמַרְנוּ לְמַעְלָה
בְּסֵדֶר אֱמֹר לָאו (ח) [ט] בְּסִימָן (רצ"ד) [רע"ב], בְּכֹהֵן גָּדוֹל שֶׁבָּעַל אַלְמָנָה,
שֶׁלּוֹקֶה שְׁתַּיִם, וְאַף־עַל־פִּי שֶׁשְּׁנֵי הַלָּאוִין עִקָּר אֶחָד לָהֶן, כְּמוֹ שֶׁכָּתַבְנוּ שָׁם.

וּבִכְלָל אִסּוּר זֶה בֵּין עֲבוֹדָה זָרָה עַצְמָהּ בֵּין מְשַׁמְּשֶׁיהָ בֵּין תִּקְרֹבֶת שֶׁלָּהּ, וּבֵין
עֲבוֹדָה זָרָה שֶׁל יִשְׂרָאֵל אוֹ שֶׁל גּוֹי. וּמַה בֵּין זוֹ לָזוֹ: שֶׁל גּוֹי זוֹ אֲסוּרָה מִיָּד שֶׁנַּעֲשֵׂית,

§429   1. I.e. the very act of bringing such a thing into one's house, with the idea of benefiting from it, is forbidden, and is punishable once its benefit is enjoyed.

    2. I.e. like the laws of § 428.

    3. TB P'saḥim 48a.

    4. So MT hilchoth 'avodath kochavim vii 2, and ShM negative precept § 25.

    5. Vol. 3 pp. 212–13, first paragraph of § 274. There, as we find, the act of marrying a widow is by itself not punishable for a *kohen gadol*; once he consummates the marriage, however, the act of marriage becomes (retroactively) punishable, along with the act of consummation. Likewise here, merely taking an idolatrously worshipped object into one's possession is not by itself punishable. Once benefit is obtained from it, however, the taking of the object is seen in retrospect as a criminal act.

both man and woman. If someone violated it and had some benefit from their adornments or decorations, even in the slightest amount, he would be punishable by whiplashes.

[NOT TO TAKE ANY OBJECT FROM IDOLATRY
INTO OUR POSSESSION, TO DERIVE BENEFIT
FROM IT]

429 that we should not attach anything from an idolatrously worshipped object to our possessions or [bring it] into our domain in order to benefit from it; about this it is stated, *And you shall not bring an abomination into your house,* etc. (Deuteronomy 7:26).[1]

At the root of the precept lies the purpose to far remove the entire repugnant matter of idolatrous worship.

The laws of this precept are likewise[2] in the third chapter of the Talmud tractate *'Avodah Zarah.* Now, the Sages of blessed memory explained[3] that if someone cooks with logs from an 'Ashérah [an idolatrously worshipped tree, using them for fuel for the fire] he is to receive whiplashes twice: because of the injunction, *you shall not bring an abomination,* and because of the injunction, *none...shall cling to your hand* (Deuteronomy 13:18) — for they are two [separate] matters: One concerns a person who brings something from an idolatrously worshipped object into his domain in order to benefit from it; and one concerns a person who derives benefit from it. In both instances, though, the man shows his innate desire for it; hence he is given whiplashes for both, as we have written.

Now, even though there is one principle behind both of them, i.e. benefiting, since he is whipped on account of nothing else but the benefit [he would derive], nevertheless, once he does enjoy benefit, he is given a whipping of two sets of lashes.[4] It is akin to what we said above, in *sidrah 'emor,* the ninth negative precept (§ 274), regarding a *kohen gadol* who was conjugally intimate with a widow — that he would receive a flogging of two sets of lashes, even though the two negative precepts are based on one principle, as we wrote there.[5]

Included under this prohibition are both the worshipped object itself, things which serve it, and its offerings; and whether it is an idolatrously worshipped object of an Israelite or of a heathen. What is the difference [in law] however, between the one and the other? — That of a heathen becomes forbidden at once when it is made, for it is
stated, *The graven images of their gods* (Deuteronomy 7:25): from the

שֶׁנֶּאֱמַר "פְּסִילֵי אֱלֹהֵיהֶם", מִשֶּׁפְּסָלוֹ; וְשֶׁל יִשְׂרָאֵל אֵינָהּ אֲסוּרָה עַד שֶׁתֵּעָבֵד, שֶׁנֶּאֱמַר "וְשָׂם בַּסָּתֶר", עַד שֶׁיַּעֲשֶׂה לָהּ דְּבָרִים שֶׁבְּסָתֶר.

וּמִן הַנִּכְלָל בְּמִצְוָה זוֹ, שֶׁלֹּא יַדְבִּיק הָאָדָם אֶל מָמוֹנוֹ שֶׁחֲנָנוּ הָאֵל בְּצֶדֶק, מָמוֹן אַחֵר שֶׁהוּא שֶׁל גֵּזֶל אוֹ חָמָס אוֹ מַרְבִּית אוֹ מִכָּל דָּבָר מְכֹעָר, שֶׁכָּל זֶה בִּכְלַל מְשַׁמְּשֵׁי עֲבוֹדָה זָרָה הוּא, שֶׁיֵּצֶר לֵב הָאָדָם רַע חוֹמֵד אוֹתוֹ וּמְבִיאוֹ אֶל הַבַּיִת, וְהַיֵּצֶר הָרָע נִקְרָא בְּשֵׁם עֲבוֹדָה זָרָה, וּכְמוֹ שֶׁאָמְרוּ זִכְרוֹנָם לִבְרָכָה, שֶׁבּוֹ נֶאֱמַר "פֶּן יִהְיֶה דָבָר עִם לְבָבְךָ בְלִיַּעַל", וּכְתִיב בְּעִנְיַן עֲבוֹדָה זָרָה "יָצְאוּ אֲנָשִׁים בְּנֵי בְלִיַּעַל מִקִּרְבֶּךָ וַיַּדִּיחוּ" וְגוֹמֵר; וּבְמָמוֹנוֹת כָּאֵלּוּ שֶׁנְּזַכַּרְנוּ וּבִמְשַׁמְּשֵׁי עֲבוֹדָה זָרָה, עַל כֻּלָּן נֶאֱמַר "וְהָיִיתָ חֵרֶם כָּמֹהוּ", כְּלוֹמַר שֶׁכָּל הַנִּדְבָּק עִמּוֹ הוּא חֵרֶם, שֶׁאֵין בִּרְכַּת הָאֵל מְצוּיָה בּוֹ וְאָבֵד וְכָלֶה, וּכְעִנְיָן שֶׁאָמְרוּ זִכְרוֹנָם לִבְרָכָה שֶׁפְּרוּטָה שֶׁל רִבִּית מְכַלָּה כַּמָּה אוֹצָרוֹת שֶׁל מָמוֹן, שֶׁבָּא זֶה וּמְאַבֵּד אֶת זֶה.

וְנוֹהֵג אִסּוּר זֶה בְּכָל מָקוֹם וּבְכָל זְמַן, בִּזְכָרִים וּנְקֵבוֹת. וְעוֹבֵר עַל זֶה וְלָקַח שׁוּם דָּבָר מֵעֲבוֹדָה זָרָה וְהֱבִיאוֹ לִרְשׁוּתוֹ וְנֶהֱנָה בּוֹ, לוֹקֶה שְׁתַּיִם: מִשּׁוּם "וְלֹא תָבִיא תוֹעֵבָה" וְכוּלֵי, וּמִשּׁוּם "וְלֹא יִדְבַּק" וְכוּלֵי; כֵּן כָּתַב הָרַב מֹשֶׁה בֶּן מַיְמוֹן זִכְרוֹנוֹ לִבְרָכָה.

[מִצְוַת בִּרְכַּת הַמָּזוֹן]

תל לְבָרֵךְ אֶת הַשֵּׁם (יִתְבָּרַךְ) אַחַר שֶׁיֹּאכַל הָאָדָם וְיִשְׂבַּע מִלֶּחֶם אוֹ מִשִּׁבְעַת הַמִּינִין הַנִּזְכָּרִים בַּכָּתוּב, כְּשֶׁהוּא זָן מֵהֶם. וְלֶחֶם סְתָם נִקְרָא פַּת הֶעָשׂוּי מֵחִטָּה וּשְׂעוֹרָה, וּבִכְלַל הַחִטָּה הַכֻּסֶּמֶת, וּבִכְלַל הַשְּׂעוֹרָה שִׁבֹּלֶת שׁוּעָל וְשִׁיפוֹן. וְעַל כְּלַל שִׁבְעַת הַמִּינִין הַזָּנִין נֶאֱמַר: וְאָכַלְתָּ וְשָׂבָעְתָּ וּבֵרַכְתָּ אֶת יְיָ אֱלֹהֶיךָ עַל הָאָרֶץ הַטֹּבָה אֲשֶׁר נָתַן לָךְ.

---

6. So TB 'Avodah Zarah 51b–52a.

7. Implicit in TB K'thuboth 68a.

8. See the two Talmudic citations given in § 343 (vol. 3, pp. 442–43, top).

§430   1. Deuteronomy 8:8 — wheat, barley, grapes, figs, pomegranates, olives, dates (the origin of Scripture's term, honey).

2. Derived from TB M'nahoth 70a–b.

time they are graven [sculptured, formed]; that of an Israelite, though, does not become forbidden until it is worshipped, for it is stated, *and sets it up in secret* (*ibid.* 27:15): until he does secret, hidden things in relation to it.[6]

Included also in this prohibition is the rule that a man should not attach to the possessions which God has graciously given him in righteousness, other possessions acquired by robbery, forced purchase, interest charges, or by any ugly, repugnant business—for all this is included under things that serve in idolatry, which the evil inclination of a man's heart covets, and he thus brings them into his house. The evil inclination is called an idolatrously worshipped object, as the Sages of blessed memory said[7]—for about that it is stated, *lest there be a base thought* (b'li-ya'al) *in your heart* (Deuteronomy 15:9); and it is written regarding idolatry, *that certain base fellows* (b'li-ya'al) *have gone out from your midst and have drawn away*, etc. (*ibid.* 13:14). And regarding such goods and possessions that we mentioned, as well as things serving worshipped objects—about them all it is stated, *and you would be accursed like it* (*ibid.* 7:26). In other words, whatever [of such possessions] clings to him, is accursed; for God's blessing is not to be found in it, and it will be lost and gone—in keeping with what the Sages of blessed memory taught, that a *p'rutah* (penny) of interest destroys many accumulations of possessions; for the one comes and gets rid of the other.[8]

This prohibition is in force everywhere, at every time, for both man and woman. If a person transgressed this and took anything whatever from an object of idol-worship, brought it into his domain, and derived benefit from it, he would be flogged with two sets of whiplashes: on account of the injunction, *you shall not bring*, etc. and on account of the admonition, *none...shall cling*, etc. So wrote R. Moses b. Maimon of blessed memory.[4]

[THE PRECEPT OF BLESSING THE ALMIGHTY
FOR THE FOOD WE RECEIVE]

430 to bless the Eternal Lord after a man eats his fill of bread or of the seven species [of produce] mentioned in the Writ,[1] when he feeds on them. The general, unspecified term "bread" means a loaf made of wheat or barley; included in the category of wheat is spelt; and the category of barley includes oats and rye.[2] But about the seven nutritive species in general it is stated, *And you shall eat and be satisfied,*

וְזֹאת הַשְּׂבִיעָה אֵין לָהּ שִׁעוּר שָׁוֶה בְּכָל אָדָם, אֲבָל כָּל אֶחָד יוֹדֵעַ שְׂבִיעָתוֹ;
וְיָדַעְנוּ שִׁעוּר שְׂבִיעַת הַצַּדִּיק, שֶׁהוּא בְּאָכְלוֹ לְשֹׂבַע נַפְשׁוֹ, אֶרְצֶה לוֹמַר כְּדֵי
מִחְיָתוֹ לְבַד. וְהָרְאָיָה שֶׁאֵין חִיּוּב הַבְּרָכָה מִן הַתּוֹרָה רַק אַחַר שְׂבִיעָה, מַה
שֶּׁאָמְרוּ זִכְרוֹנָם לִבְרָכָה בְּפֶרֶק מִי שֶׁמֵּתוֹ בִּבְרָכוֹת: דָּרַשׁ רַב עֲוִירָא וְכוּלֵי, עַד
"אָמַר לָהֶם: לֹא אֶשָּׂא פָנִים לְיִשְׂרָאֵל—שֶׁאֲנִי כָּתַבְתִּי בְתוֹרָתִי: וְאָכַלְתָּ וְשָׂבָעְתָּ
וּבֵרַכְתָּ, וְהֵם דִּקְדְּקוּ עַל עַצְמָם עַד כְּזַיִת וְעַד כְּבֵיצָה"; וְעוֹד אַרְחִיב הַמַּאֲמָר
בְּפֵרוּשׁ הַכָּתוּב הַזֶּה וּבַדִּינִין הַיּוֹצְאִים מִמֶּנּוּ, בְּדִינֵי הַמִּצְוָה זוֹ, בְּעֶזְרַת הַשֵּׁם,
וְאוֹדִיעַ הַמַּחֲלֹקֶת שֶׁיֵּשׁ לְרַבּוֹתֵינוּ בְּמַשְׁמָעוּתוֹ.

מְשָׁרְשֵׁי הַמִּצְוָה הַקְּדָמָה, הַקְּדַּמְתִּי לְךָ, בְּנִי, בְּכַמָּה שְׁקָדַם, כִּי לַשֵּׁם בָּרוּךְ
הוּא כָּל הַכָּבוֹד וְהַהוֹד וְכָל הַטּוֹב וְכָל הַחָכְמָה וְכָל הַיְכֹלֶת וְכָל הַבְּרָכָה, וְדִבְרֵי בֶן־
אָדָם וְכָל מַעֲשֵׂהוּ, אִם טוֹב וְאִם רַע, לֹא יוֹסִיף וְלֹא יִגְרַע. עַל־כֵּן צָרִיךְ אַתָּה
לְהָבִין כִּי בְּאָמְרֵנוּ תָּמִיד בַּבְּרָכוֹת "בָּרוּךְ אַתָּה הַשֵּׁם" אוֹ "יִתְבָּרַךְ", אֵין
הַמַּשְׁמָעוּת לְפִי הַדּוֹמֶה לְהוֹסִיף בְּרָכָה בְּמִי שֶׁאֵינֶנּוּ צָרִיךְ לְשׁוּם תּוֹסֶפֶת חָלִילָה,
כִּי הוּא הָאָדוֹן עַל הַכֹּל וְעַל הַבְּרָכוֹת, הוּא מְחַדֵּשׁ אוֹתָן וּמַמְצִיאָן מֵאַיִן וּמַשְׁפִּיעַ
מֵהֶן שֶׁפַע רַב בַּאֲשֶׁר תִּהְיֶה שָׁם רְצוֹנוֹ הַטּוֹב; עַל־כֵּן צְרִיכִין אָנוּ לְחַפֵּשׂ כַּוָּנַת
הָעִנְיָן מַהוּ, וְלֹא נוֹצִיא זְמַנֵּנוּ בַּמֶּה שֶׁהָעֵסֶק בּוֹ תָּמִיד, מִבְּלִי הֲבָנָה בּוֹ כְּלָל.

וַאֲנִי הַמְעוֹרֵר, אֵין מַחֲשַׁבְתִּי שֶׁיַּשִּׂיג שִׂכְלִי אֲפִלּוּ כְּטִפָּה מִן הַיָּם בַּאֲמִתַּת
הָעִנְיָן, כִּי כְבָר הֻגַּד לִי וְשָׁמַעְתִּי מִפִּי חֲכָמִים כִּי יֵשׁ בַּדְּבָרִים אֵלֶּה יְסוֹדוֹת חֲזָקִים
וְסוֹדוֹת נִפְלָאִים, יוֹדְעִים חַכְמֵי הַתּוֹרָה לְתַלְמִידֵיהֶם כְּשֶׁהֵם נְבוֹנִים וּכְשֵׁרִים

3. This is the view of *Halachoth G'doloth* (ed. Warsaw 1874, fol. 10d, end; 1st ed.
Hildesheimer, pp. 60–61), noted in *Séfer Mitzvoth Gadol*, positive precept §27; as
well as Ramban, R. Yitzḥak of Vienna (*Séfer 'Or Zaru'a*), R. 'Asher, and Rashba
(the last two cited in *Béth Yosef* to Tur 'Oraḥ Ḥayyim, §209; see *Halachoth G'doloth*,
1st ed. Hildesheimer, *ibid.* note 86)—that by the Torah's law a benediction is
required after one has eaten his fill of any of the seven species for which the Land of
Israel is praised in Deuteronomy 8:8. It is stated more explicitly in paragraph 18
(but see paragraph 19, that Rambam differs).

4. So Proverbs 13:25, *The righteous eats to the satisfaction of his spirit.*

5. This is preceded by a question: Said the ministering angels before the Holy
One, blessed is He, "Master of the world, it is written in Thy Torah, *who shows no
favor and takes no bribe* (Deuteronomy 10:17); yet dost Thou not show favor to the
Israelites?—as it is written, *the Lord show His favor to you* (Numbers 6:26)."

6. According to R. Me'ir, we say the benediction (grace) after an olive's
amount; according to R. Judah, after the amount of an egg (Rashi, *ad loc.*). Thus
Jewry shows Him favor, as it were, observing the precept beyond the letter of the
law; and He must therefore repay in kind, so to speak.

7. Literally: Have I not told you, my son, in what has gone before.

8. Cf. Job 35:6–7.

and you shall bless the Lord your God for the good land He has given you
(Deuteronomy 8:10).³

Now, for this satiety (satisfaction or fullness in eating) there is no
[single] uniform measure for every person, but everyone knows his
own satiety; and we know the measure for the satisfaction of a
righteous person, which is when he eats to the satisfaction of his
spirit,⁴ by which I mean only enough for his sustenance. Well, the
proof that the duty of the blessing, by the law of the Torah, comes
only after satiety, lies in what the Sages of blessed memory said in the
third chapter of the tractate *B'rachoth* (20b): R. 'Avira expounded, and
so forth, until [we read that the Almighty] said to them, "Shall I then
not show favor to the Israelites?⁵ I wrote in My Torah, *And you shall
eat and be satisfied, and you shall bless*, and they became strict with
themselves [to say the blessing even] over the amount of an olive and
the amount of an egg."⁶ I will enlarge further on the interpretation of
this verse, and on the laws that ensue from it, in the laws of this
precept, with the Eternal Lord's help; and I will relate the
controversy among our Sages about its meaning.

As for the root reasons for the precept, [let me begin with] a
preface: I clearly told you, my son, in previous pages⁷ that the Eternal
Lord, blessed is He, possesses all glory and majesty, all goodness, all
wisdom, all ability and all blessing; and all the words of a human
being and all his activity, whether good or bad, will neither add [to
these attributes] nor detract anything.⁸ Therefore you must understand that when we say continually, "Blessed art Thou, Lord,"
or "be He blessed," the meaning is evidently not to add blessing to
One who has no need of any addition [to His attributes], perish the
thought. For He is the sovereign Master over everything and over
blessings. He creates them anew, producing them out of nothing, and
bestows a great beneficent flow from them where it is His good will
[to do so]. We therefore need to seek [to know] what the significance
of the matter is, and not expend our time on something with which
there is constant occupation⁹ without any understanding of it at all.

Now, when I take up this matter,¹⁰ it is not my thought that my
intelligence will grasp even as much as a drop in the ocean of the
truth of the subject. For it was previously told me, and I heard from
the mouths of the wise, that in these matters lie mighty fundamentals
and wondrous secrets, which the wise scholars of the Torah convey to
their disciples when they have understanding and are worthy, and in

וּבְכָל מַעֲשֵׂיהֶם נָאִים; אֲבָל רֹב חֶפְצִי לְהַשִּׂיג בָּזֶה קְצָת טַעַם יַשִּׂיאֵנִי לְדַבֵּר בּוֹ; וְאוּלַי הָיְתָה טוֹבָה הַשְּׁתִיקָה, אֲבָל הָאַהֲבָה תְקַלְקֵל הַשּׁוּרָה.

יָדוּעַ הַדָּבָר וּמְפֻרְסָם כִּי הַשֵּׁם בָּרוּךְ הוּא פּוֹעֵל כָּל הַנִּמְצָא, וּבָרָא הָאָדָם וְהִשְׁלִיטוֹ עַל הָאָרֶץ וְעַל כָּל אֲשֶׁר בָּהּ; וּמִמִּדּוֹתָיו בָּרוּךְ הוּא, שֶׁהוּא רַב חֶסֶד חָפֵץ בְּטוֹבַת בְּרִיּוֹתָיו וְרוֹצֶה לִהְיוֹתָן רְאוּיִין וְזַכָּאִין לְקַבֵּל טוֹבָה מֵאִתּוֹ; וְזֶה בֶאֱמֶת מִשְּׁלֵמוּתוֹ בָּרוּךְ הוּא, כִּי לֹא יִקָּרֵא שָׁלֵם בַּטּוֹבָה רַק מִי שֶׁהוּא מֵיטִיב לַאֲחֵרִים זוּלָתוֹ, אֵין סָפֵק בָּזֶה לְכָל בֶּן־דַּעַת.

וְאַחַר הַסְכָּמָה זוֹ שֶׁיְּדַעְנוּ בְחִיּוּב מֵרֹב שְׁלֵמוּת טוֹבוֹ שֶׁחֶפְצוֹ לְהָרִיק עָלֵינוּ מִבִּרְכָתוֹ, נֹאמַר שֶׁעִנְיַן הַבְּרָכָה שֶׁאָנוּ אוֹמְרִים לְפָנָיו אֵינֶנּוּ רַק הַזְכָּרָה לְעוֹרֵר נַפְשֵׁנוּ בְּדִבְרֵי פִינוּ, כִּי הוּא הַמְבֹרָךְ, וּמְבֹרָךְ יִכְלֹל כָּל הַטּוֹבוֹת; וּמִתּוֹךְ הַהִתְעוֹרְרוּת הַטּוֹב הַזֶּה בְנַפְשֵׁנוּ וְיִחוּד מַחֲשַׁבְתֵּנוּ לְהוֹדוֹת אֵלָיו, שֶׁכָּל הַטּוֹבוֹת כְּלוּלוֹת בּוֹ וְהוּא הַמֶּלֶךְ עֲלֵיהֶם לְשָׁלְחָם עַל כָּל אֲשֶׁר יַחְפֹּץ, אָנוּ זוֹכִים בַּמַּעֲשֶׂה הַטּוֹב הַזֶּה לְהַמְשִׁיךְ עָלֵינוּ מִבִּרְכָתוֹ.

וְאַחַר הַזְכָּרָה וְהַהוֹדָאָה זוֹ לְפָנָיו, אָנוּ מְבַקְשִׁים מִמֶּנּוּ מַה שֶּׁאָנוּ צְרִיכִים: דַּעַת אוֹ סְלִיחָה לַעֲווֹנוֹתֵינוּ אוֹ רְפוּאָה אוֹ עֹשֶׁר, וְכָל דָּבָר; וְכֵן אַחַר הַבַּקָּשָׁה מִמֶּנּוּ אָנוּ חוֹזְרִים וּמוֹדִים אֵלָיו בָּזֶה, לוֹמַר כִּי מִמֶּנּוּ יָבוֹא אֵלֵינוּ, וְזֶהוּ פְּתִיחָה וַחֲתִימָה שֶׁל בְּרָכוֹת, פֶּן נֵחָשֵׁב כְּעֶבֶד שֶׁנָּטַל פְּרָס מֵרַבּוֹ וְהוֹלֵךְ לוֹ בְּלֹא רְשׁוּת, כְּמִתְגַּנֵּב.

וְנִמְצָא לְפִי הַנַּחַת טַעַם זֶה שֶׁיִּהְיֶה "בָּרוּךְ" תֹּאַר, כְּלוֹמַר הוֹדָאָה אֵלָיו כִּי הוּא כָּלוּל כָּל הַבְּרָכוֹת. וּבִלְשׁוֹן "יִתְבָּרֵךְ" שֶׁאָנוּ מַזְכִּירִין תָּמִיד, שֶׁהוּא מֵהִתְפַּעֵל, נֹאמַר שֶׁהַכַּוָּנָה בּוֹ שֶׁאֲנַחְנוּ מִתְחַנְּנִים אֵלָיו שֶׁיִּהְיֶה רָצוֹן מִלְּפָנָיו לְסַבֵּב לֵב בְּרִיּוֹתָיו לִהְיוֹת נָכוֹן לְפָנָיו, שֶׁיּוֹדוּ הַכֹּל אֵלָיו וּבוֹ יִתְהַלָּלוּ.

---

9. I.e. the observant Jew constantly utters benedictions and blessings to the Almighty.

10. Literally: Now, I the arouser.

11. So B'réshith Rabbah 55, 8 (i.e. the love of attaining some understanding of the matter drives him to go beyond this line).

12. Our author echoes here the teaching in TB B'rachoth 34a: The final benedictions [in the *sh'moneh 'esréh*, the "Eighteen Benedictions," the central prayer of each daily service, said silently, standing] are like [the acknowledgment of] a servant who receives a ration of sustenance from his master, whereupon he takes his leave and goes his way. (In both this and the preceding paragraph, our author is patently referring or alluding only — or at least primarily — to the blessings and entreaties of the *sh'moneh 'esréh*; cf. *Daily Prayer Book*, ed. Birnbaum, pp. 81-93.) As regards our author's conception of the meaning and significance of a benediction, the sense in which a human can call the Almighty "blessed" in his prayer to Him, Rashba writes somewhat similarly in his *Responsa*, V §51.

13. Literally, to environ or envelop.

all their actions are becoming. Yet my abounding desire to attain some reason about this persuades me to speak of it. Perhaps silence were better, but love distorts the line of propriety.[11]

It is a matter of widespread knowledge that the Eternal Lord (blessed is He) produced all that exists; He created man and gave him dominion over the earth and everything in it. And among His qualities (blessed is He) is [the Divine characteristic] that He has abounding loving-kindness, desiring good for His human beings; He wishes them to be worthy and meritorious to receive good [reward] from Him. This, in truth, stems from His perfection: for none can be called perfect in goodness but one who does good to others than himself; of this there can be no doubt for any person with sensible knowledge.

Now, after this accepted premise, knowing that inevitably, in the great perfection of His goodness, it is His desire to impart to us generously of His blessing, we can say that the significance of the blessing which we recite before Him is nothing but a reminder, to arouse our spirit with the words of our mouth to know that He is the blessed One; and the blessed One thus contains all blessings. Out of this good arousal of our spirit and the focusing of our thought to gratefully acknowledge to Him that all good favors are contained in Him and He rules over them to send them wherever He wishes, we merit through this good deed to draw [down] of His blessing upon us.

After this remembrance and acknowledgment before Him, we entreat Him for what we need: knowledgeable understanding, forgiveness of our sins, healing, wealth, or anything [else]. Then likewise after this entreaty of Him, we again make a grateful avowal to Him, to say that from Him it will be imparted to us. This, then, is the opening and the close of the benedictions—lest we be considered as a servant who takes an allotment of support from his master and goes off without permission, as though sneaking away with a theft.[12]

Consequently, according to the premise of this reason, the term "Blessed" is an adjective—in other words, an avowal to Him that He contains all blessings. As to the term *yithbarach*, "be He blessed," which we mention continually, we would say its import is that we beseech Him that it may be His will to influence[13] the heart of His human beings to be rightly prepared before Him, so that all will acknowledge Him and grant Him their praise.

וְזֶהוּ פֵּרוּשׁ "יִתְבָּרַךְ", כְּלוֹמַר: יְהִי רָצוֹן מִלְּפָנֶיךָ שֶׁכָּל בְּנֵי הָעוֹלָם יִהְיוּ מְיַחֲסִים הַבְּרָכָה אֵלֶיךָ וּמוֹדִים כִּי מִמְּךָ תִּתְפַּשֵּׁט בַּכֹּל; וְעִם הוֹדָאַת הַכֹּל בָּזֶה תָּנוּחַ בְּרָכָתוֹ בָּעוֹלָם וְיֵשָׁלֵם חֶפְצוֹ שֶׁהוּא חָפֵץ לְהֵיטִיב כְּמוֹ שֶׁאָמַרְנוּ, וְתַשְׁלוּם הַחֵפֶץ תַּכְלִית כָּל הַמְבֻקָּשׁ. וְהִנֵּה מָצָאנוּ קְצָת טַעַם אַף בִּלְשׁוֹן "יִתְבָּרַךְ" הַמַּתְמִיהַּ.

וּמִן הַשֹּׁרֶשׁ הַזֶּה הוּא מַה שֶּׁאָמְרוּ זִכְרוֹנָם לִבְרָכָה שֶׁהַקָּדוֹשׁ בָּרוּךְ הוּא מִתְאַוֶּה לִתְפִלָּתָן שֶׁל צַדִּיקִים, לוֹמַר שֶׁחֶפְצוֹ שֶׁיַּעֲשׂוּ פְּעָלָם שֶׁיִּזְכּוּ בָהּ לְפָנָיו וְיַמְשִׁיכוּ עֲלֵיהֶם מְטוּבוֹ, כִּי חָפֵץ לַעֲשׂוֹת חֶסֶד הוּא, וְלָתֵת עֲלֵיהֶם מִבִּרְכָתוֹ מֵרֹב שְׁלֵמוּתוֹ, כְּמוֹ שֶׁכָּתַבְנוּ. וְזֶהוּ הַשֹּׁרֶשׁ הַגָּדוֹל לְכָל אֲשֶׁר יַעֲשֶׂה הָאָדָם טוֹב בָּעוֹלָם הַזֶּה, שֶׁזֶּהוּ שְׂכָרוֹ מֵאֵת הַשֵּׁם שֶׁמַּשְׁלִים חֶפְצוֹ בַּאֲשֶׁר הוּא רוֹצֶה בְּטוֹבָתָן שֶׁל בְּרִיּוֹת.

וּמִן הַשֹּׁרֶשׁ הַזֶּה שֶׁאָמַרְתִּי שֶׁהַזְכָּרַת "בָּרוּךְ" הוּא הוֹדָאָה לְפָנָיו עַל הַבְּרָכוֹת שֶׁהֵן לוֹ, וְשֶׁצָּרִיךְ לְהוֹדוֹת אֵלָיו בָּזֶה בִּתְחִלַּת הַשְּׁאֵלָה וּבְסוֹפָהּ, לְבַל יְהִי כְּעֶבֶד שֶׁנָּטַל פְּרָס מֵרַבּוֹ וְהָלַךְ בְּלֹא רְשׁוּת, יָצְאוּ לְפִי דַעְתִּי הַחִלּוּקִין שֶׁקָּבְעוּ לָנוּ חֲכָמֵינוּ זִכְרוֹנָם לִבְרָכָה בְּעִנְיַן הַבְּרָכוֹת, שֶׁיֵּשׁ מֵהֶן פּוֹתְחוֹת בְּ"בָּרוּךְ" וְחוֹתְמוֹת גַּם־כֵּן, וְיֵשׁ חוֹתְמוֹת וְלֹא פּוֹתְחוֹת, וְיֵשׁ פּוֹתְחוֹת וְלֹא חוֹתְמוֹת.

כֵּיצַד: כָּל בְּרָכָה בָּעוֹלָם שֶׁיֵּשׁ בָּהּ בַּקָּשַׁת דָּבָר מֵאֵת הַשֵּׁם אוֹ הַזְכָּרַת גֵּס, וְאֵינָהּ סְמוּכָה לִבְרָכָה אַחֶרֶת, פּוֹתַחַת בְּ"בָּרוּךְ" וְחוֹתֶמֶת בְּ"בָּרוּךְ" — כְּגוֹן "יוֹצֵר אוֹר" דְּשַׁחֲרִית וּ"מַעֲרִיב עֲרָבִים" דְּעַרְבִית, וְכַיּוֹצֵא בָּהֶן כַּמָּה — מִן הַטַּעַם הַנִּזְכָּר; וְכָל בְּרָכָה שֶׁסְּמוּכָה לִבְרָכָה חוֹתֶמֶת בְּ"בָּרוּךְ" אֲבָל אֵינָהּ פּוֹתַחַת, מִן הַטַּעַם הַזֶּה, שֶׁהֲרֵי מִכֵּיוָן שֶׁהוֹדָה וְנָתַן הַמֶּמְשָׁלָה לָאֵל בְּסוֹף הַבְּרָכָה הַסְּמוּכָה לְזוֹ, וְלֹא הִפְסִיק אַחַר הוֹדָאָה זוֹ בְּדָבָר קָטָן אוֹ גָּדוֹל, אֵין רָאוּי לִכְפֹּל הוֹדָאַת קַבָּלַת הָאַדְנוּת

---

14. TB Yevamoth 64a.
15. TB B'rachoth 46a.
16. Generally, "Blessed art Thou, Lord," etc.
17. *Daily Prayer Book*, ed. Birnbaum, respectively pp. 71–73 and p. 191.
18. See e.g. *ibid.* p. 85, last four paragraphs.

This, then, is the meaning of *yithbarach* [in the reflexive tense], i.e. "May it be Thy will that all mankind shall ascribe blessing to Thee, and avow that from Thee does it radiate to everything." With everyone's acknowledgment of this, His blessing will abide in the world, and His desire will be achieved—this being the desire to bestow good, as we stated—and this desire will fulfill the purpose of all that was besought. Thus we have found some slight meaning even in the puzzling expression *yithbarach*, "be He blessed."

Well, it is for this root reason that the Sages of blessed memory declared[14] that the Holy One, blessed is He, yearns for the prayer of the righteous. [It means] to say that His desire is for them to perform a task by which they will achieve merit before Him and will draw down of His good reward upon themselves. For He delights to act in loving-kindness, and to bestow of His blessing upon them, as we have written. This is the great root reason for all the good that a man is to do in this world—so that this will be his reward from the Eternal Lord, because he fulfills His desire, since He wishes for the good fortune of His human beings.

Now, from this root principle that I have stated, that the mention of "blessed is He" is an avowal before Him about blessings, that they belong to Him, and this needs to be acknowledged to Him before an entreaty and after at its end, so that one should not be as a servant who took his measure of sustenance from his master and went off without permission—there ensue, to my mind, the different forms that our Sages of blessed memory set down for us in the matter of benedictions;[15] that some of them open with "Blessed"[16] *(baruch)* and so likewise close, some close but do not open so, while some open thus but do not so close.

How is this?—Every benediction in the world which contains an entreaty for something from the Eternal Lord, or the mention of a miracle, and is not attached to [follow directly] another benediction, opens with "Blessed" and closes with "Blessed": for instance, "who forms light" in the morning prayer, and "brings on evenings" in the night prayer,[17] and so many others like them, for the reason mentioned. Every benediction that is close to another [following it directly] ends with "Blessed," but does not begin so,[18] for this reason: Since one has acknowledged and ascribed dominion to God at the close of the benediction near it [directly before it], and he has made no interruption, great or small, after this avowal, it would not be

פְּעָמִים בְּבַת אַחַת בִּשְׁבִיל חִלּוּק הַשְּׁאֵלוֹת שֶׁאֲנַחְנוּ שׁוֹאֲלִין לְפָנָיו; אֲבָל רָאוּי לִהְיוֹת חוֹתֶמֶת בְּ"בָּרוּךְ", כִּי אַחַר שֶׁהִפְסִיק בְּשְׁאֵלַת צְרָכָיו רָאוּי לוֹ לַחֲזֹר וּלְהַזְכִּיר וְלָתֵת אֶל לִבּוֹ פַּעַם אַחֶרֶת קַבָּלַת מַלְכוּתוֹ וְאַדְנוּתוֹ עָלָיו.

וְעַל הַדֶּרֶךְ הַזֶּה תִּמְצָא לְפִי דַעְתִּי טַעַם כֻּלָּן, אִם תַּחְשֹׁב בָּהֶן. וַאֲשֶׁר סְמוּכוֹת יוֹצְאוֹת מִגֶּדֶר זֶה, כְּגוֹן בִּרְכַּת חֲתָנִים וְקִדּוּשָׁא וְאַבְדְּלְתָּא וַאֲחֵרוֹת, כְּבָר תֵּרְצוּם לָנוּ כֻלָּן מוֹרֵינוּ יִשְׁמְרֵם אֵל. וְהַטַּעַם שֶׁלִּמְּדוּנוּ בִּקְצָתָם, לְפִי שֶׁפְּעָמִים נֶאֶמְרוֹת אוֹתָן הַבְּרָכוֹת שֶׁלֹּא בִסְמִיכוּת, וְרַבּוֹתֵינוּ לֹא רָצוּ לַחֲלֹק וְלוֹמַר כְּשֶׁתָּבוֹא בִסְמִיכוּת תֹּאמַר בָּעִנְיָן כֵּן וּבְשֶׁלֹּא בִסְמִיכוּת כֵּן, כִּי הֵם יִבְרְחוּ מִן הַחִלּוּקִין לְעוֹלָם בְּכָל מַה שֶּׁמָּסוּר בְּיַד הֶהָמוֹן, וְכֵן הַדַּעַת.

וְכָל בְּרָכָה בָּעוֹלָם שֶׁאֵין בָּהּ בַּקָּשַׁת דָּבָר מֵהָאֵל וְלֹא הַזְכָּרַת נֵס שֶׁל יִשְׂרָאֵל, כְּגוֹן הַבְּרָכוֹת שֶׁלִּפְנֵי מַאֲכָל וּמִשְׁתֶּה וְכָל הֲנָאוֹת הַגּוּף, וְכֵן בִּרְכַּת נֵס שֶׁל יָחִיד, שֶׁאֵין בְּאֵלּוּ הַבְּרָכוֹת לְעוֹלָם נֵס שֶׁל אָרֹךְ, יָדוּעַ הַדָּבָר לְכָל יוֹדֵעַ סֵפֶר שֶׁכֻּלָּן פּוֹתְחוֹת בְּ"בָּרוּךְ" וְלֹא חוֹתְמוֹת, מִן הַטַּעַם הַנִּזְכָּר: דְּמִכֵּיוָן שֶׁהַזְכִּיר מַלְכוּת הַשֵּׁם וְאַדְנוּתוֹ וּמִיָּד גָּמַר דְּבָרָיו, אֵינוֹ מִן הַחִיּוּב לַחֲזֹר פַּעַם שְׁנִית הַזְכָּרַת "בָּרוּךְ", שֶׁיִּדְמֶה כְּכֹפֵל דָּבָר בְּמַה שֶּׁאֵין צֹרֶךְ — דָּבָר בָּרוּר הוּא.

וְכָל הַבְּרָכוֹת שֶׁהֵן קְבוּעוֹת לְשֶׁבַח הַשֵּׁם לְבַד, כְּגוֹן הָרוֹאֶה הַיָּם הַגָּדוֹל וְאִילָנוֹת טוֹבוֹת וְכֵן שׁוֹמֵעַ קוֹל רְעָמִים, וְיֶתֶר הָעִנְיָנִים הַנִּזְכָּרִים בְּפֶרֶק הָרוֹאֶה, מֵהֶן פּוֹתְחוֹת בְּ"בָּרוּךְ" וְלֹא חוֹתְמוֹת, וּמֵהֶן חוֹתְמוֹת וְלֹא פּוֹתְחוֹת, וְהַכֹּל מִן הַטַּעַם הַנִּזְכָּר: כִּי הַמַּזְכִּיר שְׁבָחִים דַּי לוֹ לְפִי הַנִּרְאֶה בְּהַזְכָּרַת הָאַדְנוּת בַּתְּחִלָּה, אוֹ אֲפִלּוּ

19. When a groom weds his bride under the canopy, seven benedictions are said. The second, third, fourth and seventh begin with "Blessed art Thou," although preceded directly by others that begin thus.

20. "Sanctification," over a cup of wine, to usher in the Sabbath and festival days as times of holiness. After the first benediction, over the wine, the second one also begins "Blessed art Thou."

21. "Separation," to mark the end of a Sabbath or a festival and the beginning of an ordinary day. Here too, after a benediction over wine, other benedictions follow, each beginning "Blessed art Thou."

22. So Rashba.*hiddushim* toTB B'rachoth 11a. Cf.also his *Responsa*, I §§ 317, 318.

23. E.g. TB B'rachoth 59b.

proper to repeat the acknowledgment of the acceptance of [Divine] rule, twice at one time, on account of the division of the entreaties that we make before Him. But it is fitting that the close should start with "Blessed": for since one interrupted by beseeching his needs, it is proper for him to mention again and instill in his heart once more his acceptance of His kingship and sovereignty over him.

By this approach you will find, to my thinking, the reason for them all, if you will ponder them. As for those which are linked to others and yet go out of this category—for instance, the benediction over a bridegroom,[19] kiddush[20] and havdalah,[21] and certain others, our master instructors (God protect them) explained them all for us in the past.[22] The reason they gave us about some of them is that at times some of those benedictions are said without being linked to others; and our Sages did not wish to make a distinction and rule that when one of them occurs in connection with another it should be said in this form, and when not linked with another, in that way. For they would always flee from [fine] distinctions in whatever is given over into the hand of the masses; and so is it sensible.

Now, as to any benediction in the world which contains no entreaty for anything from God, nor the mention of a miracle for the Israelites—for example, benedictions before taking food and drink, or anything beneficial or pleasurable to the body; and so too a benediction over a miracle for an individual, in which blessings there is never a long text—the matter is known to everyone versed in the Torah that they all begin with "Blessed" but do not so close—for the reason mentioned: For since one has declared the kingship of the Eternal Lord and His sovereign mastery, and he has concluded his words at once, it could not be obligatory to return again, a second time, to the mention of "Blessed"; because it would seem like a repetition of an unnecessary element. This is something quite clear.

As for all benedictions formulated solely for the praise of the Eternal Lord—for instance, if a person sees the great [Mediterranean] ocean or goodly [blossoming] trees, and so if one hears the sound of thunder, and the other instances mentioned in the ninth chapter of the tractate B'rachoth[23]—some open with "Blessed" but do not close with it, while others close with it but do not so open. And it is all for the reason mentioned. For when a person declares [His] praises, it is apparently enough for him to mention the Divine sovereignty at the start or even at the end, since he entreats nothing

בַּסּוֹף, אַחַר שֶׁאֵינֶנּוּ מְבַקֵּשׁ דָּבָר לוֹ וְאֵינוֹ מְבָרֵךְ בִּשְׁבִיל הֲנָאָה שֶׁיִּרְצֶה לְקַבֵּל, שֶׁאִלּוּ הַמְבַקֵּשׁ דָּבָר אוֹ רוֹצֶה לְהָנוֹת, רָאוּי בֶּאֱמֶת לְהָאִיר פֶּתַח דְּבָרָיו וּלְהַתְחִיל בְּהַזְכָּרַת אֲדֹנוּתוֹ בָּרוּךְ הוּא. וְזֶהוּ שֶׁאָמַרְנוּ שֶׁהַבְּרָכוֹת שֶׁל נֶהֱנִין פּוֹתְחוֹת בְּ"בָרוּךְ", וְכֵן בִּרְכַּת הַמִּצְווֹת פּוֹתְחוֹת בְּ"בָרוּךְ", לְרֹב הַתּוֹעֶלֶת שֶׁהוֹעִילָנוּ הָאֵל בָּרוּךְ הוּא בָּהֶן.

דִּינֵי הַמִּצְוָה, כְּגוֹן מַה שֶׁאָמְרוּ זִכְרוֹנָם לִבְרָכָה שֶׁאַף־עַל־פִּי שֶׁהַתּוֹרָה לֹא תְחַיֵּב אוֹתָנוּ לְבָרֵךְ כִּי־אִם אַחַר שֶׁנִּשְׂבַּע בַּמָּזוֹן, חֲכָמִים זִכְרוֹנָם לִבְרָכָה חִיְּבוּנוּ לְבָרֵךְ גַּם־כֵּן אַחַר כָּל דָּבָר שֶׁיֵּהָנֶה אָדָם מִמֶּנּוּ, בֵּין שֶׁהוּא מִפֵּרוֹת שִׁבְעַת הַמִּינִין שֶׁנִּשְׁתַּבְּחָה בָהֶן הָאָרֶץ אוֹ מִכָּל שְׁאָר דְּבָרִים; וְלָמְדוּ הַדָּבָר בִּרְאוֹתָם שֶׁהַתּוֹרָה תְחַיֵּב הָאָדָם לְבָרֵךְ הָאֵל אַחַר שֶׁיִּשְׂבַּע מִן הַמָּזוֹן הַמְקַיֵּם גּוּפוֹ קִיּוּם חָזָק, וְהָלְכוּ הֵם אַחַר הַטַּעַם הַזֶּה, וְחִיְּבוּנוּ לְבָרֵךְ גַּם־כֵּן עַל כָּל אֲשֶׁר יֹאכַל הַגּוּף מִמֶּנּוּ, בֵּין שֶׁיִּהְיֶה מָזוֹן אוֹ שֶׁאֵינוֹ דָבָר הַזָּן, מִכֵּיוָן שֶׁיֵּהָנֶה הָאָדָם בּוֹ.

וּכְמוֹ־כֵן חִיְּבוּנוּ לִבְרָכָה לְבָרֵךְ לְבָרְכָה קֹדֶם אֲכִילָה, וְלָמְדוּ לוֹמַר כֵּן מִן הַסְּבָרָא שֶׁרָאוּי לוֹ לְאָדָם שֶׁלֹּא יֵהָנֶה מִן הָעוֹלָם הַזֶּה בְּלֹא בְרָכָה; עָשׂוּ הַבְּרָכָה עַל דֶּרֶךְ מָשָׁל כִּנְטִילַת רְשׁוּת מִבַּעַל הַבַּיִת לֶאֱכֹל מִן הַנִּמְצָא בְּבֵיתוֹ.

וְיֵשׁ מֵרַבּוֹתֵינוּ שֶׁדַּעְתָּן לוֹמַר כִּי הַתּוֹרָה תְּחַיְּבֵנוּ בְּרָכָה אַחַר כָּל שִׁבְעַת הַמִּינִין, כְּמוֹ שֶׁנִּתְחַיַּבְנוּ בֶּאֱמֶת לְבָרֵךְ אַחַר אוֹתָן מֵהֶן שֶׁנָּזוֹן, כְּמוֹ תְמָרִים וְיַיִן וּדְבֵלַת תְּאֵנִים, וְאָמְרוּ שֶׁעַל כֵּלָּן נֶאֱמַר "וְאָכַלְתָּ וְשָׂבָעְתָּ וּבֵרַכְתָּ"; וְאָמְרוּ גַּם־כֵּן שֶׁשְּׁבִיעָה דְאוֹרַיְתָא הִיא בִּכְבֵיצָה לְבַד, דִּבְהָכִי מִיַּתְבָא דַעְתֵּהּ דְּאִינִישׁ.

וְרוֹאֶה אֲנִי בָּזֶה רְאָיָה קְצָת לְדִבְרֵיהֶם מִמַּה שֶּׁאָמְרוּ בְּרֵישׁ פֶּרֶק כֵּיצַד בְּאוֹתָהּ שַׁקְלָא וְטַרְיָא שֶׁהִיא בַּגְּמָרָא, לִמְצֹא חִיּוּב בְּרָכָה דְאוֹרַיְתָא: אָמְרוּ שָׁם: מַה

---

24. MT *hilchoth b'rachoth* i 1–2.

25. Literally, when they saw; TB B'rachoth 35a.

26. *Ibid.* and MT *ibid.*

27. See note 3 ("those of them which provide sustenance" denotes wheat and barley, from which bread is made; "dates, wine and pressed figs" denotes the rest of the seven species for which the Land of Israel is praised in Deuteronomy 8:8).

28. So Rabad (R. David of Posquières) to MT *hilchoth b'rachoth* v 15, and the sages of Lunel, cited in *Kessef Mishneh, ibid.*

for himself and does not say the benediction because of a benefit or enjoyment that he wants to receive. For when one entreats for something or wishes to enjoy something, it is fitting in truth to illumine the opening of his words and begin by mentioning His sovereign mastery (blessed is He). This is why, as we have said, the benedictions over enjoyment begin with the word "Blessed"; and so do benedictions over *mitzvoth* open with "Blessed," on account of the great benefit that God (blessed is He) grants us through them.

The laws of the precept are, for example, what the Sages of blessed memory taught:[24] that although the Torah does not obligate us to say a benediction except when we are sated (satisfied) with food, the Sages of blessed memory obligated us to say a benediction likewise after everything from which a man has benefit and pleasure, whether it be of the seven kinds of produce for which the land [of Israel] was praised,[1] or of any other things. They inferred the matter by noting[25] that the Torah obligates a man to bless God after he has become satisfied by food that provides his body with a firm power of sustenance; and they followed this reason and obligated us to say a benediction likewise over anything by which the body is nourished, be it food or something not nutritive, as long as a man has benefit or enjoyment from it.

So too they (of blessed memory) gave us the duty to say a benediction before eating. They learned to rule so by reasoning that it is proper for a man not to derive benefit or enjoyment from the world without a benediction. They made the benediction, by way of analogy, like the taking of permission from a householder to eat of what there is in his house.[26]

Now, there are some of our master authorities whose thought is to say that the Torah gives us the duty of a blessing after any of the seven species of food, as we were obligated in truth to say blessing (grace) after those of them which provide sustenance — such as dates, wine, and pressed figs; so they ruled that about them all Scripture states, *and you shall eat and be satisfied, and you shall bless*.[27] And they said likewise that "satisfaction" by the law of the Torah is by the amount of an egg alone, for with this the mind of a man can be pacified.[28]

Now, in this regard, I see a slight proof for their words in what was stated at the beginning of the sixth chapter of the tractate *B'rachoth* (35a) in the discussion held in the *g'mara* to find an obligation for a benediction by the law of the Torah. It was stated

שִׁבְעַת הַמִּינִין דָּבָר שֶׁנְּהֶנֶה וְטָעוּן בְּרָכָה, אַף כֹּל שֶׁנֶּהֱנֶה טָעוּן בְּרָכָה. נִרְאֶה מִכָּאן
שֶׁאֵין חִלּוּק בְּשִׁבְעַת הַמִּינִין בֵּין אוֹתָן הַנָּנִים מֵהֶן לַאֲחֵרִים, שֶׁבְּכֻלָּן חַיָּב הַבְּרָכָה
מִן הַתּוֹרָה.

אֲבָל מִכָּל־מָקוֹם רָאִיתִי הָרַב רַבֵּנוּ מֹשֶׁה בֶּן מַיְמוֹן זִכְרוֹנוֹ לִבְרָכָה וַאֲחֵרִים
עִמּוֹ, שֶׁנִּרְאֶה לִי מִדִּבְרֵיהֶם לוֹמַר שֶׁאֵין עִקַּר בְּרָכָה חַיּוּב אֶלָּא דְאוֹרַיְתָא אֶלָּא עַל
אֲכִילַת שְׂבִיעַת מָזוֹן וְלֹא עַל שְׁאָר מִינִין, אַף־עַל־פִּי שֶׁהֵן מִשִּׁבְעַת מִינִין, כְּגוֹן
רִמּוֹנִים וַעֲנָבִים וּתְאֵנִים לַחִים וְזֵיתִים, מִכֵּיוָן דְּלָא זַיְנֵי, כִּי הַתּוֹרָה לֹא תְחַיֵּב אֶלָּא
עַל מָזוֹן; וּמִפְּנֵי־כֵן סָמַךְ אֶל הַבְּרָכָה, כְּמוֹ שֶׁכָּתוּב "תֹּאכַל בָּהּ לֶחֶם", וְהָדַר
"וְאָכַלְתָּ וְשָׂבָעְתָּ". וְאֶל הַגְּדוֹלִים שֶׁבְּדוֹרֵנוּ נִשְׁמַע בְּמִצְוַת הַתּוֹרָה.

וְאַחַר הַבְּרָכָה זוֹ, מִי שֶׁנִּסְתַּפֵּק לוֹ אִם בֵּרַךְ מֵעֵין (שֶׁבַע) [שָׁלֹשׁ] אַחַר כָּל
שִׁבְעָה מִינִין חַיָּב לְבָרֵךְ מִסָּפֵק, וְכֵן אִם נִסְתַּפֵּק בְּבִרְכַּת הַמָּזוֹן. וַאֲפִלּוּ כְשֶׁאָכַל
פָּחוֹת מִכְּדֵי שְׂבִיעָה חַיָּב לְבָרֵךְ, וּבִלְבַד שֶׁאָכַל כְּבֵיצָה; אֲבָל הָאוֹכֵל כְּזַיִת אוֹ יוֹתֵר
עַד כְּבֵיצָה, אִם נִסְתַּפֵּק אִם בֵּרַךְ אוֹ לֹא, מִן הַדּוֹמֶה שֶׁאֵינוֹ חַיָּב לְבָרֵךְ לְדִבְרֵי כֻלָּם,
שֶׁשִּׁעוּר זֶה דְרַבָּנָן הוּא.

וּלְפִי הַנִּרְאֶה לִי מִדִּבְרֵי הָרִאשׁוֹנִים, כָּל זְמַן שֶׁלֹּא שָׂבַע בַּמָּזוֹן לֹא יִתְחַיֵּב לַחֲזֹר
וּלְבָרֵךְ מִסָּפֵק. וְאוֹמֵר אֲנִי בְּאוּלַי כִּי מַה שֶׁנִּרְאֶה רַבִּים מֵהֲמוֹן הָעָם מְקִלִּין

29. See note 27.

30. MT *hilchoth b'rachoth* i 1 (literally, "I have seen R. Moses" etc.)

31. I.e. bread made from wheat or barley, etc. (see the first paragraph of this precept).

32. Apparently Ramban and perhaps some of the other *rishonim* listed in note 3 —that a benediction is required by Torah law after eating any of the seven species—in preference to the ruling of Rambam, who was of an earlier generation than our author.

33. I.e. the short grace (*b'rachah 'aharonah*) said after any food from the seven species (including wheat and barley, if they have been eaten in a form other than bread) which contains in brief, summary form the first three blessings of the grace after meals with bread (TB B'rachoth 37b, 44a). The manuscripts and the first edition read "the benediction embodying the seven," but this evident scribal error was emended in later editions; in the oldest manuscript, too, there is a correction in the margin by another hand.

34. It is a standard rule that in any doubt concerning a law of the Torah, we act stringently; but if the doubt concerns an enactment of the Sages, we act leniently (TB Bétzah 3b).

35. See three paragraphs above, end.

36. On the surface we have a contradiction here: One paragraph above, we read, "So likewise if one was uncertain about the grace after meals [if he said it], even if he ate less than enough to be satisfied he would be duty-bound to say the grace, provided he ate the amount of an egg." Now we find something quite

there: Just as the seven species are something that one enjoys, and they require a benediction, so does everything that one enjoys require a benediction. From this it would appear that there is no difference among the seven species[1] between those that provide sustenance and the others:[29] for all there is the duty of a benediction by the Torah's law.

Nevertheless, I have read R. Moses b. Maimon of blessed memory,[30] and others with him, whereupon it seems right to me from their words to conclude that the core obligation for a benediction by the Torah's law applies to nothing but the eating of satisfying nourishing food,[31] and not to other kinds of food, even if they are of the seven species, such as pomegranates, grapes, fresh figs and olives, since they are not mainly sustaining. For the Torah imposes the duty over nothing other than basic sustaining food;[31] and for this reason it linked bread with the benediction: as it is written, *wherein you shall eat bread* (Deuteronomy 8:9), and then, *And you shall eat and be satisfied* (*ibid.* 10). Well, we shall hearken to the great authorities of our generations[32] about the precepts of the Torah.

Now, following this decision, if someone is in doubt whether he said the benediction embodying the three[33] after any of the seven species, he is obligated to say the blessing on account of the doubt.[34] So likewise if one was uncertain about the grace after meals [if he said it], even if he ate less than enough to be satisfied he would be duty-bound to say the grace, provided he ate the amount of an egg.[35] However, if one ate an olive's amount or more, up to the bulk of an egg, if he was then in doubt whether he had said the grace or not, it would seem that he is not obligated to recite it, according to the rulings of all, because this amount [entails the obligation] by the decree of the Sages.[34]

Yet, as it seems to me from the words of the early authorities, as long as one has not eaten his fill of sustaining food, he would not be obligated to turn back and say the grace out of doubt.[36] And I would say that perhaps when we see great numbers of the mass of people

different: As long as one has not eaten enough to feel satisfied, he need not turn back and say the grace if he does not remember whether he said it.

As MY writes, to resolve the contradiction we must pay attention to the "early authorities" that our author cites. At the start of the paragraph above he writes, "Now, following this decision"—i.e. to accept contemporary authorities even

בְּבִרְכַּת מֵעֵין שָׁלֹשׁ וְאֵין אֶחָד אֲפִלּוּ עַם־הָאָרֶץ גָּמוּר מֵקֵל בְּבִרְכַּת הַמָּזוֹן, כִּי הוּא
מִיסוֹד הָרִאשׁוֹנִים שֶׁדַּעְתָּן לוֹמַר שֶׁעִקַּר צִוּוּי הַתּוֹרָה לֹא יָבוֹא כִּי־אִם עַל שְׂבִיעַת
מָזוֹן; וּמִפְּשׁוּטוֹ שֶׁל מִקְרָא כֵּן הָיָה נִרְאֶה.

נִמְצָא עִנְיָן הַבְּרָכוֹת כֵּן הוּא: שֶׁחִיּוּב מִצְוַת הַתּוֹרָה אֵינוֹ רַק לְבָרֵךְ אַחַר הַמָּזוֹן,
לֹא לְפָנָיו, וּבְדִבְרֵי הָאַחֲרוֹנִים אַף עַל שִׁבְעַת מִינִין הַנִּזְכָּרִים בַּתּוֹרָה; וְכָל שְׁאָר
הַבְּרָכוֹת כֻּלָּן הֵן מִדְּרַבָּנָן, חוּץ מֵאַחַת שֶׁהִיא מִן הַתּוֹרָה, וְכֵן הוּא מְפֹרָשׁ בַּגְּמָרָא
בִּבְרָכוֹת, וְהִיא בִּרְכַּת הַתּוֹרָה לְפָנֶיהָ; גַּם הָרַב רַבֵּנוּ מֹשֶׁה בֶּן נַחְמָן זִכְרוֹנוֹ לִבְרָכָה
יַחְשֹׁב אוֹתָהּ מִצְוַת עֲשֵׂה בִּפְנֵי עַצְמָהּ.

וְהָעִנְיָן הַזֶּה שֶׁחִיְּבָנוּ הָאֵל (בָּרוּךְ הוּא) בְּרָכָה בִּקְרִיאַת הַתּוֹרָה לְפָנֶיהָ וּבַמָּזוֹן
לְאַחֲרָיו, מִן הַדּוֹמֶה שֶׁהַטַּעַם לְפִי שֶׁהוּא בָּרוּךְ הוּא לֹא יִשְׁאַל מִן הַחָמֵר לְעָבְדוֹ
וּלְהוֹדוֹת בְּטוּבוֹ רַק אַחַר שֶׁיְּקַבֵּל פֶּרֶס מִמֶּנּוּ, כִּי הַחֵלֶק הַבַּהֲמִי לֹא תַכִּיר בַּטּוֹבָה
רַק אַחַר הַהֶרְגֵּשׁ; אֲבָל קְרִיאַת הַתּוֹרָה, שֶׁהוּא חֵלֶק הַשֵּׂכֶל, וְהַשֵּׂכֶל יוֹדֵעַ וּמַכִּיר
וְקֹדֶם קַבָּלַת הַתּוֹעֶלֶת יָבִין וְרָאוֹי אוֹתוֹ, עַל־כֵּן יְחַיְּבֵנוּ הָאֵל לְהוֹדוֹת לְפָנָיו קֹדֶם קְרִיאַת
הַתּוֹרָה. וּמוֹדֶה עַל הָאֱמֶת יִמְצָא טַעַם בִּדְבָרָי.

וְאַחֲרֵי זֹאת נַגִּיד דֶּרֶךְ כְּלָל חִיּוּב הַבְּרָכוֹת דְּרַבָּנָן, וְהֵם לְבָרֵךְ קֹדֶם אֲכִילָה
וּשְׁתִיָּה בְּכָל דָּבָר שֶׁיֵּשׁ בּוֹ טַעַם כְּלָל לַחֵךְ, וְאַחֲרָיו כְּמוֹ־כֵן; וְכֵן חִיְּבוּנוּ לְבָרֵךְ עַל
כָּל רֵיחַ טוֹב שֶׁנָּרִיחַ, קֹדֶם הָרֵיחַ אֲבָל לֹא אַחֲרָיו, וּכְלָלוֹ שֶׁל דָּבָר, עַל כָּל שֶׁהַגּוּף
נֶהֱנֶה בּוֹ קָבְעוּ בּוֹ בְּרָכָה.

וְכֵן חִיְּבוּנוּ לְבָרֵךְ הַשֵּׁם וּלְהוֹדוֹת לְפָנָיו עַל כָּל הַטּוֹבָה אֲשֶׁר גְּמָלָנוּ בַּעֲשׂוֹתֵנוּ
מִצְוֹתָיו הַיְקָרוֹת, וְאָמְרוּ שֶׁמְּבָרְכִין עֲלֵיהֶן עוֹבֵר לַעֲשִׂיָּתָן, וְהָעִנְיָן הוּא לְדַעְתִּי

---

when Rambam differs (see note 32). In this paragraph, however, he is following
"the words of the early authorities"; and for him "early authorities" does not mean
rishonim but *ge'onim*, still earlier scholars, before the time of R. Isaac 'Alfasi. At this
point our author has relinquished his statement in the previous paragraph,
preferring rather to follow the ruling we find in *Halachoth G'doloth* (as recorded in
note 3). It is likewise found in the name of R. Yehuda'i Ga'on (often regarded in
early sources as the author of *Halachoth G'doloth*) in *Séfer Tanya Rabbathi*, §26 (ed.
Warsaw 1879, fol. 32d); and R. 'Eli'ezer of Metz, *Séfer Yeré'im*, §253 [24] (ed.
Vilna 1892, p. 231). Inasmuch as this is a geonic ruling, our author now decides to
follow it, in preference to the views of both his contemporaries and Rambam.

   37. Ramban, *hassagoth* (commentary) to ShM, list of precepts at the end, positive
§15.

   38. Literally, will find.

   39. TB B'rachoth 44b; MT *hilchoth b'rachoth* i 2.

   40. TB P'saḥim 7b.

being quite lenient in their observance of the benediction embodying the three,[33] while no one, not even a total ignoramus, treats the grace after meals lightly, it is because it stems from a basic ruling of the early authorities, whose view it was to say that the core command of the Torah applies to nothing but being satisfied with sustaining food; and from the plain sense of the verse (Deuteronomy 8:10) it would seem so.

Consequently, the matter of the benedictions is so: the obligation of the Torah's precept is only to say the grace after the meal, but not a benediction before it; but according to the later authorities,[27] it applies also to the seven species mentioned in the Torah. And all the other benedictions are entirely by the ruling of the Sages—except for one, which is by Torah law; and so is it explained in the Talmud tractate *B'rachoth* (21a)—this being the blessing over the Torah, before its study. R. Moses b. Naḥman of blessed memory also reckons this as a positive precept by itself.[37]

Now, regarding this matter, that God (blessed is He) gave us the duty to say a blessing over the reading of the Torah before it, and with food after it—it would seem that the reason is that He (blessed is He) asks of [a creature of] physical matter to worship Him and acknowledge His goodness only after he receives a measure of sustenance from Him; for the animal element [in man] cannot appreciate a good favor [before but] only after the experience [of it]. As for reading the Torah, however, that is the porton of the intelligence, and the intelligence knows and recognizes [the matter]; and yet before receiving the benefit, it can understand it. Therefore God obligates a person to give thanks before Him before the reading of the Torah. Anyone who admits truth will appreciate[38] the reason in my words.

After this let us relate in a general way the duty of benedictions by the ruling of the Sages. It is to say a blessing before eating or drinking anything that has any taste whatever for the palate, then after it as well. So they also obligated us to say a blessing over every good fragrance before smelling it, but not after it.[39] The nub of the matter is that over anything that the body enjoys they set a benediction.

The Sages likewise obligated us to bless the Eternal Lord and give thanks before Him for all the good that He renders us upon our observing His precious *mitzvoth*; and they ruled[40] that one should recite the benedictions over them and go on directly to fulfill them.

כַּטַּעַם הַנִּזְכָּר סָמוּךְ בִּקְרִיאַת הַתּוֹרָה; וּכְמוֹ־כֵן חִיְּבוּנוּ לְבָרֵךְ בִּרְכוֹת בְּשֶׁבַח
הַבּוֹרֵא עַל עֹצֶם גְּבוּרוֹתָיו, כְּגוֹן הָרוֹאֶה הַיָּם לִפְרָקִים וְכַיּוֹצֵא בָּאֵלּוּ הָעִנְיָנִים, כְּמוֹ
שֶׁמְּזֻכָּר בְּפֶרֶק הָרוֹאֶה. וְנֻסַּח הַבְּרָכוֹת כֻּלָּן, עֶזְרָא וּבֵית־דִּינוֹ תִּקְּנוּם; וְאַף־עַל־פִּי
שֶׁאָמְרוּ זִכְרוֹנָם לִבְרָכָה: מֹשֶׁה תִּקֵּן בִּרְכַּת הַזָּן, יְהוֹשֻׁעַ בִּרְכַּת הָאָרֶץ, עַל עִקַּר
הָעִנְיָן אָמְרוּ כֵן, אֲבָל כָּל נֻסַּח הַבְּרָכוֹת, עֶזְרָא וּבֵית־דִּינוֹ תִּקְּנוּם, וְאֵין רָאוּי
לְהוֹסִיף אוֹ לִגְרֹעַ בְּנֻסַּח שֶׁלָּהֶן, וְכָל הַמְּשַׁנֶּה בָּהֶן אֵינוֹ אֶלָּא טוֹעֶה; וּמִכָּל־מָקוֹם
בְּדִיעֲבַד מִי שֶׁשִּׁנָּה אוֹ שֶׁשָּׁכַח קְצָת מִנֻּסַּח הַבְּרָכָה, כָּל זְמַן שֶׁהִזְכִּיר עִקַּר
מַשְׁמָעוּתָא וְאָמַר חֲתִימָתָא כְּתִקְנָהּ, אֵין מַחֲזִירִין אוֹתוֹ.

וְאָמְרוּ זִכְרוֹנָם לִבְרָכָה שֶׁהַבְּרָכוֹת נֶאֱמָרוֹת בְּכָל לָשׁוֹן, וּבִלְבַד בְּאַזְכָּרַת הַשֵּׁם
וּמַלְכוּת שָׁמַיִם. וְחִיְּבוּנוּ זִכְרוֹנָם לִבְרָכָה לְהַזְכִּיר בְּבִרְכַּת הַמָּזוֹן קְדֻשַּׁת הַיּוֹם,
כְּלוֹמַר עִנְיַן שַׁבָּת אוֹ יָמִים־טוֹבִים, כְּמוֹ שֶׁיָּדוּעַ; וְהַשּׁוֹכֵחַ וְלֹא זָכַר אוֹתָן בְּבִרְכָּה,
מַחֲזִירִין אוֹתוֹ בְּאוֹתָן הַיָּמִים שֶׁחַיָּב אָדָם לֶאֱכֹל עַל־כָּל־פָּנִים, וְהֵן שְׁתֵּי סְעֻדּוֹת
מְחֻיָּבוֹת, דְּהַיְנוּ לֵיל רִאשׁוֹן שֶׁל פֶּסַח וְלֵיל רִאשׁוֹן שֶׁל חַג הַסֻּכּוֹת. וּכְדַעַת קְצָת
הַמְּפָרְשִׁים, בְּכָל שַׁבָּת וּבְכָל יוֹם־טוֹב מַחֲזִירִין אוֹתוֹ גַם־כֵּן.

וְאֶכְתֹּב לְךָ, בְּנִי, עוֹד מְעַט בְּדִינֵי בִּרְכוֹת הַסְּעֻדָּה, וְאַף־עַל־פִּי שֶׁהַרְבֵּה הִרְוַחְנוּ
הַדִּבּוּר בְּזֹאת הַמִּצְוָה מֵחֶפְצִי בִּבְרָכָה, וְלֹא כֵן דַּרְכִּי בְּמָקוֹם אַחֵר בְּזֹאת הַמְּלָאכָה.
כָּל יִשְׂרָאֵל צָרִיךְ לִטֹּל יָדָיו קֹדֶם אֲכִילַת פַּת בְּמַיִם הָרְאוּיִין, כְּלוֹמַר שֶׁלֹּא נִפְסְלוּ
מִלִּשְׁתּוֹת לְכֶלֶב וְלֹא נַעֲשָׂה בָּהֶן מְלָאכָה; וְשִׁעוּרָן רְבִיעִית לֹג, שֶׁהוּא בֵּיצָה
וּמֶחֱצָה לִנְטִילָה אַחַת, וּלְכָל הַפָּחוֹת צָרִיךְ לִטֹּל לַאֲכִילַת פַּת עַד הַפֶּרֶק (שסוף)
[שֶׁל סוֹף] הָאֶצְבָּעוֹת, וּמְבָרֵךְ "בָּרוּךְ אַתָּה יי אֱלֹהֵינוּ מֶלֶךְ הָעוֹלָם אֲשֶׁר קִדְּשָׁנוּ

41. After an interval of at least thirty days.

42. So TB B'rachoth 33a and Rashi s.v. *k'va'uhah*, and Rambam in MT introduction.

43. TB B'rachoth 48b.

44. Of each of the two benedictions which are ascribed respectively to Moses and Joshua; i.e. they determined what the benedictions should concern, but not the exact wording.

45. So TB B'rachoth 40b.

46. TB Sotah 32a, B'rachoth 40b.

47. TB B'rachoth 49a.

48. So Rashba, commentary to *ibid*. See §§ 10, 325.

49. *Tosafoth* TB B'rachoth 49a, s.v. *'ee ba'ee*; MT *hilchoth b'rachoth* ii 12.

50. Or, in my desire for blessing.

51. Mishnah, Yadayim i 3.

52. *Ibid*. 1.

53. So Rashi, TB Ḥullin 106b, s.v. *u-sh'mu'él*; the standard practice today is to wash till the wrist, following R. Isaac 'Alfasi.

The reason, to my mind, is like the explanation noted shortly above, about the reading of the Torah. Quite similarly, too, the Sages required us to say blessings in praise of the Creator for the immensity of His manifestations of strength — for example, if a person sees the ocean at infrequent times,[41] and other such experiences, as recorded in the ninth chapter of the Talmud tractate *B'rachoth* (54a).

As to the text of all the benedictions, Ezra and his *beth din* (colleagues) established them.[42] Although the Sages of blessed memory said[43] that Moses formulated the first benediction in the grace after meals, and Joshua the second, they said this about the main theme;[44] but as to the entire text of the benedictions, Ezra and his *beth din* formulated them; and it is not proper to either add anything or subtract anything from their text. Whoever makes any change in them is nothing more than in error. Yet in any event, after the fact, if someone altered or forgot a bit from the text of a benediction, as long as he expressed its main meaning and said its closing part in its proper formulation, he is not to be made to repeat it.[45]

Further, our Sages of blessed memory said[46] that the benedictions may be recited in any language, provided there is the mention of the Eternal Lord and the kingship of Heaven. And they (of blessed memory) obligated us to mention the sanctity of the day in the grace after meals[47] — in other words, the theme of the Sabbath or the festivals [on those days], as it is known. If someone forgot and did not mention them in the proper benediction, he is made to repeat the grace on those days when a man is duty-bound to eat in any event, namely, the two obligatory meals: i.e. the first night of Passover and the first night of *Sukkoth*.[48] But by the view of some authorities,[49] on every Sabbath and festival day one is equally to be made to repeat it.

Now let me write you, my son, another little bit on the laws of benedictions at a meal, even though we have greatly broadened our discourse on this precept in my delight concerning blessing,[50] which is not my way elsewhere in this work. Every Jew needs to wash his hands before eating bread, with proper water — in other words, which did not become unfit for a dog to drink, and with which no labor or task was done.[51] Its minimal amount is a quarter of a *log*, which is [the volume of] one and a half eggs for one washing [of both hands].[52] But at the very least one needs to wash, for eating bread, till the joint of the end of the fingers.[53] He says the benediction, "Blessed art ⟨325⟩ Thou, Lord our God, King of the world, who hallowed us with His

בְּמִצְוֹתָיו וְצִוָּנוּ עַל נְטִילַת יָדַיִם", וּמְבָרֵךְ עַל אֲכִילַת הַפַּת בַּתְּחִלָּה "בָּרוּךְ אַתָּה
יי אֱלֹהֵינוּ מֶלֶךְ הָעוֹלָם הַמּוֹצִיא לֶחֶם מִן הָאָרֶץ", וְלַבְּסוֹף, אִם אָכַל מִמֶּנּוּ כְזַיִת,
מְבָרֵךְ אַרְבַּע בְּרָכוֹת הַיְדוּעוֹת: הַזָּן וּבִרְכַּת הָאָרֶץ וּבוֹנֶה יְרוּשָׁלַיִם, וְהַטּוֹב וְהַמֵּטִיב
שֶׁתִּקְּנוּ בְּיַבְנֶה.

וְכָל דָּבָר שֶׁבָּא בִסְעֻדָּה מִשֶּׁהִתְחִיל לְבָרֵךְ עַל הַפַּת, בֵּין דְּבָרִים הַבָּאִים, כְּגוֹן
תַּבְשִׁילִין הַרְבֵּה שֶׁעוֹשִׂין בְּנֵי-אָדָם מֵחֲמֵשֶׁת מִינֵי דָגָן, בֵּין כָּל שְׁאָר מִינֵי פֵרוֹת
שֶׁבָּעוֹלָם, כָּל שֶׁאוֹכֵל אוֹתוֹ אָדָם לְהַשְׂבִּיעַ בִּטְנוֹ לְמַלֵּא רְעָבוֹנוֹ, בֵּין שֶׁיֹּאכַל אוֹתָן
דְּבָרִים בְּאֶמְצַע סְעֻדָּתוֹ בֵּין אַחַר שֶׁגָּמַר מִלֶּאֱכֹל פִּתּוֹ, הַכֹּל בִּרְכַּת הַפַּת פּוֹטֶרֶת
לְפָנָיו וּלְאַחֲרָיו; וְכֵן הַדִּין אִם אֵינָן בָּאִין בָּאֵין דְּבָרִים אֵלוּ לְהַשְׂבִּיעַ אֶלָּא לְלַפֵּת הַפַּת,
שֶׁבִּרְכַּת הַפַּת פּוֹטַרְתָּן לִפְנֵיהֶם וּלְאַחֲרֵיהֶם.

וְאִם אֵינָן בָּאִין לֹא לְהַשְׂבִּיעַ וְלֹא לְלַפֵּת אֶלָּא לְתַעֲנוּג בְּעָלְמָא בְּתוֹךְ הַסְּעֻדָּה,
אִי מִידֵי דְזָיֵין הוּא, כְּגוֹן תַּבְשִׁיל מֵחֲמֵשֶׁת הַמִּינִין, פָּטוּר בְּבִרְכַּת הַפַּת בֵּין לְפָנָיו
בֵּין לְאַחֲרָיו; וְאִי מִידֵי דְלָא עָבְדֵי אֱנָשֵׁי לְמָזוֹן וּבָא לְתַעֲנוּג בְּתוֹךְ הַמָּזוֹן, כְּגוֹן
פֵּרוֹת שֶׁאוֹכְלִין בְּנֵי-אָדָם לְתַעֲנוּג בְּתוֹךְ הַמָּזוֹן, מְבָרֵךְ לִפְנֵיהֶן וְלֹא לְאַחֲרֵיהֶן,
דְּבִרְכַּת הַמָּזוֹן פּוֹטַרְתָּן.

וּבִכְלַל תַּעֲנוּג זֶה הוּא מִי שֶׁאוֹכֵל בְּתוֹךְ הַסְּעֻדָּה זַיִת מָלִיחַ וְכַיּוֹצֵא בוֹ, לִפְתֹּחַ
תַּאֲוַת הַמַּאֲכָל, וּלְפִיכָךְ מְבָרֵךְ לְפָנָיו וְלֹא לְאַחֲרָיו; תְּמָרִים, אַף-עַל-פִּי שֶׁהֵן
פֵּרוֹת, דִּין מָזוֹן יֵשׁ לָהֶן וּפְטוּרִין בְּבִרְכַּת הַפַּת לִפְנֵיהֶן וּלְאַחֲרֵיהֶן.

הֵבִיאוּ לְפָנָיו מִינֵי פֵרוֹת הַרְבֵּה, אִם בְּרְכוֹתֵיהֶן שָׁווֹת, כְּגוֹן שֶׁכֻּלָּן שֶׁל עֵץ,
מְבָרֵךְ עַל הָאֶחָד הֶחָבִיב לוֹ, וְאַחַר-כָּךְ אוֹכֵל כָּל הַשְּׁאָר בְּלֹא בְרָכָה; וְאִם אֵין אֶחָד
מֵהֶן חָבִיב לוֹ יוֹתֵר מִן הַשְּׁאָר, אִם יֵשׁ בֵּינֵיהֶם מִשִּׁבְעָה פֵרוֹת הַמְּנוּיִין בַּתּוֹרָה
לְשֶׁבַח אֶרֶץ-יִשְׂרָאֵל, מְבָרֵךְ תְּחִלָּה עַל הַקּוֹדֵם בַּפָּסוּק, וְכֻלָּן פְּטוּרִין מִבְּרָכָה.

54. TB *ibid.* calls it a *mitzvah* (religious duty) and three paragraphs above, our
author noted that before fulfilling a *mitzvah* a benediction should be said.

55. TB B'rachoth 35a.

56. *Daily Prayer Book*, ed. Birnbaum, pp. 759–65.

57. Listed in the first paragraph, second sentence.

58. I.e. there is no need for a separate benediction before or after these foods; the
blessing over the bread and the grace after meals are sufficient for everything; so
tosafoth, TB B'rachoth 41b, s.v. *hilch'tha*.

59. As a relish, spread, or side dish; TB B'rachoth 44a.

60. *Ibid.* 42b.

61. *Ibid.* 41b.

62. Derived perhaps from TB B'rachoth 12a (MY).

63. I.e. for refreshment, not during a meal.

64. TB B'rachoth 41a.

mitzvoth and commanded us about washing the hands."[54] Then he says the benediction over the eating of bread: before it, "Blessed art Thou, Lord our God, who dost bring forth bread from the earth";[55] and at the end, if he has eaten an olive's amount of it, he is to say the four known benedictions [of the grace]: "who sustains the whole world," the blessing for the land, "who rebuilds Jerusalem," and "who is good and does good"[56]—which was formulated at Yavneh.[43]

Now, everything that comes [is served] during the meal, from the time he has begun to say the benediction over the bread, whether it be nourishing items, such as the many cooked dishes that people make from the five species of grain,[57] or whether it be any other kind of produce in the world—whatever a man eats to satisfy his stomach, to sate his hunger, whether he eats these things in the middle of his meal or after he has finished eating his bread—the benediction over the bread acquits everything of the obligation, both before it and after it.[58] The law is the same, too, if these items came not to satiate but to accompany the bread:[59] the blessing over the bread clears them [of the obligation of a benediction] both before [eating] them and after.[59]

If they come neither to satiate nor to accompany [as a relish or spread etc.] but for mere pleasure during the meal—if it is something nourishing, such as a cooked dish from the five species [of grains], it is freed of the obligation by the blessing over the bread, both before and after.[60] If it is something which people do not make for nourishment, but is rather served to give pleasure amid the meal, such as fruit that people eat for enjoyment within the meal, he is to say a benediction before it, but not afterward,[61] for the grace after meals acquits it.

Now, it is in this category of pleasure [food] when someone eats a salted olive during the meal, or something similar, to develop the appetite for food. Therefore the benediction before it is said, but not the one after it. As for dates, even though they are a fruit, they are under the law of nutritive food, and are cleared of the obligation by the blessing over bread, both before and after.[62]

If many different kinds of produce were brought before a person,[63] if their benedictions are identical—for instance, if they are all tree fruits—he is to say the blessing over the one he likes the most, and then he may eat the rest without a benediction.[64] If there is none of them that he likes more than the rest, then if there are among them some of the seven kinds of produce listed in the Torah in praise of the land of Israel,[65] he is to say the blessing first over that [kind] which

וְאִם אֵין בְּרְכוֹתֵיהֶן שָׁווֹת, כְּגוֹן פְּרִי עֵץ וּפְרִי אֲדָמָה, מְבָרֵךְ עַל כָּל אֶחָד
וְאֶחָד, וּמַקְדִּים הֶחָבִיב לוֹ, כְּלוֹמַר אוֹתוֹ שֶׁרְצוֹנוֹ לֶאֱכֹל בַּתְּחִלָּה; וְאִם אֵין שָׁם
חָבִיב לוֹ יוֹתֵר מֵחֲבֵרוֹ, מַקְדִּים הֶחָשׁוּב בִּבְרָכָה, דְּהַיְנוּ פְּרִי עֵץ שֶׁהַבְּרָכָה מְיֻחֶדֶת
לוֹ, יוֹתֵר מִפְּרִי אֲדָמָה שֶׁכּוֹלֵל כָּל מַה שֶׁבָּאֲדָמָה.

יַיִן אֵינוֹ בִכְלַל פַּת כְּלָל וְאֵין בִּרְכַּת הַפַּת פּוֹטַרְתּוֹ, דְּעִנְיָן שְׁתִיָּה הוּא, וּמְבָרְכִין
עָלָיו אֲפִלּוּ בָא בְּתוֹךְ הַמָּזוֹן. וְעוֹד קָבְעוּ חֲכָמִים זִכְרוֹנָם לִבְרָכָה בְּרָכָה אַחֶרֶת עַל
הַיַּיִן, הֵיכָא שֶׁהֵבִיאוּ יַיִן שֵׁנִי בְּתוֹךְ הַסְּעֻדָּה אוֹ אַחַר סְעֻדָּה מִלְּבַד אוֹתוֹ שֶׁהֵבִיאוּ
תְּחִלָּה, וְהִיא הַטּוֹב וְהַמֵּטִיב; וְהוּא שֶׁיְהוּ הָאוֹכְלִים שְׁנַיִם אוֹ יוֹתֵר. וְיַיִן שֶׁלְּפָנֵי
הַמָּזוֹן פּוֹטֵר מִבְּרָכָה רִאשׁוֹנָה כָּל הַיַּיִן הַבָּא אַחֲרָיו, בֵּין בְּתוֹךְ הַסְּעֻדָּה בֵּין אַחֲרֶיהָ;
אֲבָל יַיִן שֶׁבְּתוֹךְ הַמָּזוֹן אֵינוֹ פּוֹטֵר אֶת שֶׁל אַחַר הַמָּזוֹן מִבְּרָכָה רִאשׁוֹנָה, אֲבָל
מִבְּרָכָה אַחֲרוֹנָה בִּרְכַּת הַמָּזוֹן פּוֹטֶרֶת הַכֹּל, דְּיַיִן בִּכְלַל מָזוֹן הוּא, דְּאִיהוּ נַמִּי זָיֵין
וִישַׂמַּח.

מַיִם אַחֲרוֹנִים חוֹבָה, וּצְרִיכִים לִהְיוֹת מַיִם קָרִים, וְשֶׁיִּפְּלוּ לִכְלִי אוֹ לְכָל דָּבָר
שֶׁחוֹצֵץ בֵּינֵיהֶן וְלַקַּרְקַע, כְּגוֹן קְסָמִין וְכַיּוֹצֵא בָהֶן. וּמִי שֶׁלֹּא אָכַל דָּבָר מְזֹהָם וְלֹא
טִלְטֵל מֶלַח בִּסְעֻדָּתוֹ אֵינוֹ צָרִיךְ לָהֶן.

65. Deuteronomy 8:8.

66. Derived from TB B'rachoth 40b.

67. See e.g. *Daily Prayer Book*, ed. Birnbaum, p. 773.

68. So *Halachoth G'doloth, hilchoth b'rachoth* vi (ed. Warsaw 1874, fol. 7d; 2nd ed. Hildesheimer, I p. 92), based on TB B'rachoth 39a.

69. Of a different kind.

70. However, the blessing over the first wine need not be repeated.

71. TB B'rachoth 59b.

72. Regarding wine after the meal: Mishnah, B'rachoth vi 5 (TB 42a); regarding wine during the meal: deduced from TB *ibid.* 42b, in *tosafoth* to *ibid.* s.v. *Rav Shésheth*; *Tosafoth R. Judah* to *op. cit.*, II p. 46; *Piské Rid* to *op. cit.*, col. 125; Me'iri (2nd ed. Dickman), p. 153a; Rashba to B'rachoth, ed. Kravitz, p. 204–05, citing "some of our rabbinic authorities."

While our author merely states this law on "wine after the meal" from the Mishnah, other medieval authorities considered it obsolete in their day. In Talmudic times, after a preliminary cup of wine (perhaps) and some *hors d'oeuvres*, the main meal would be served each diner on a small individual table, at the place where he reclined to take his food. When the table was eventually removed, before the grace after meals, it was then the time "after the meal" to which the Mishnah (likewise our author) refers. In later times, however, the use of such individual tables ceased (see *tosafoth* to TB P'sahim 100b, s.v. *lav*). Hence *tosafoth* to TB B'rachoth 42b, s.v. *v'Rav Shésheth*, states that "we, however, have no need for this law"; and similarly *Séfer Kol Bo* (ed. Fürth 1787, fol. 14c). On the other hand, R. Hanan'él (cited in *Séfer 'Or Zaru'a*, I §156, and *'Aruch*, 1st s.v. *baréch*) and MT *hilchoth b'rachoth* iv 12

⟨328⟩

occurs earliest in the Scriptural verse,[65] and all are then free of the obligation of a benediction.[66]

If their benedictions are not identical — for example, tree fruits with produce of the soil[67] — one says the benediction over each and every one, taking first what he is fond of, i.e. the one he wishes to eat first.[64] If there is nothing there which he likes more than something else, he is to give preference to what is more important in regard to the benediction, i.e. tree fruit, which has a specific blessing, rather than the soil's produce, whose benediction includes everything [that grows] from the earth.[68]

Wine is not included in the range of bread at all, and the benediction over bread does not acquit it of its obligation. For it is in the nature of a beverage, and a blessing is said over it even if it comes during a meal.[61] Furthermore, the Sages of blessed memory formulated a second benediction over wine where a second wine[69] is brought during the meal or after the meal, apart from the one brought served at first: namely, "who is good and does good"[70] — but this if two or more are dining.[71] Now, wine before the meal frees of the obligation of a first benediction all wine served afterward, whether during the meal or after it.[72] However, wine during the meal does not clear that after the meal from the duty of the first blessing.[73] As for the later benediction [after it], however, the grace after the meal frees everything of that obligation:[74] for wine is included under food, because it is nutritive also, and lifts the spirits.

The final water [for washing the fingers] is obligatory.[75] It needs to be cold water, and it is to fall into a vessel or onto anything that will keep it off the ground, such as wood chips or something similar.[75] But if a person ate nothing soiling [to the hands] and did not handle salt in his meal, he does not need it.[76]

cite the law as in effect on certain special days and occasions when it is a set custom to start the meal with a cup of wine; while Rabad and R. Z'raḥyah haLévi (cited in Rashba to B'rachoth, ed. Kravitz col. 203, bottom) hold that only in Talmudic times did this restriction apply, because wine was not generally available in any great quantity, but in later times, with wine in good supply, the law is always in effect. *Tur 'Oraḥ Ḥayyim* § 174 cites the law as in effect only at banquets, etc. but *Shulḥan 'Aruch ibid.* makes no mention of it; and in *ibid.* § 177, 2, laws relating to "after the meal" are declared to be no longer relevant; yet see *Bi'ur Halachah ad loc.* s.v. *she'én r'gilin.*

73. TB *ibid.*

74. *Halachoth G'doloth*, cited by Rashbam, TB P'saḥim 103b, s.v. *'asur.*

בְּשַׁבָּת וְיוֹם-טוֹב צָרִיךְ אָדָם לְהַזְכִּיר קְדֻשַּׁת הַיּוֹם בִּבְרָכָה שְׁלִישִׁית, כְּמוֹ
שֶׁאָמַרְנוּ, וְאִם לֹא הִזְכִּיר וּפָתַח בְּ"הַטּוֹב וְהַמֵּטִיב" חוֹזֵר לָרֹאשׁ; לֹא פָתַח בּוֹ
אֶלָּא שֶׁחָתַם בִּבְרָכָה שְׁלִישִׁית — אִם בְּשַׁבָּת, אוֹמְרִים נֻסָּח זֶה: "בָּרוּךְ אַתָּה יי
אֱלֹהֵינוּ מֶלֶךְ הָעוֹלָם אֲשֶׁר נָתַן שַׁבָּת מְנוּחָה לְעַמּוֹ יִשְׂרָאֵל לְאוֹת וְלִבְרִית; בָּרוּךְ
אַתָּה יי מְקַדֵּשׁ הַשַּׁבָּת"; וְאִם בְּיוֹם-טוֹב, אוֹמְרִים "בָּרוּךְ אַתָּה יי אֱלֹהֵינוּ מֶלֶךְ
הָעוֹלָם אֲשֶׁר נָתַן יָמִים-טוֹבִים לְעַמּוֹ יִשְׂרָאֵל לְשָׂשׂוֹן וּלְשִׂמְחָה; בָּרוּךְ אַתָּה יי
מְקַדֵּשׁ יִשְׂרָאֵל וְהַזְּמַנִּים".

וְכֵן רֹאשׁ חֹדֶשׁ וְחֻלּוֹ שֶׁל מוֹעֵד וַחֲנֻכָּה וּפוּרִים יֵשׁ לָהֶן הַזְכָּרָה בְּבִרְכַּת הַמָּזוֹן
בִּבְרָכָה שְׁלִישִׁית; אֲבָל שָׁכַח וְחָתַם הַבְּרָכָה, אֵין מַחֲזִירִין אוֹתוֹ וְאֵין מַזְכִּירָן כְּלָל.

כָּךְ מְקֻבָּל אֲנִי מֵרַבּוֹתַי יִשְׁמְרֵם אֵל, שֶׁכָּל הַזָּהִיר בְּבִרְכַּת הַמָּזוֹן, מְזוֹנוֹתָיו
מְצוּיִּין לוֹ בְכָבוֹד כָּל יָמָיו. וְיֶתֶר פְּרָטֵי הַמִּצְוָה, יִתְבָּאֲרוּ בְּמַסֶּכֶת בְּרָכוֹת.

וְנוֹהֶגֶת מִצְוָה זוֹ מִן הַתּוֹרָה בְּכָל מָקוֹם וּבְכָל זְמָן בַּזְּכָרִים; וּנְקֵבוֹת, הוּא סָפֵק
לְרַבּוֹתֵינוּ אִם חַיָּבוֹת בָּהּ מִן הַתּוֹרָה אִם לֹא. וְאִישׁ הָעוֹבֵר עַל זֶה וְאָכַל מָזוֹן וְלֹא
בֵרַךְ אַחֲרָיו, בִּטֵּל עֲשֵׂה זֶה; וְאִשָּׁה שֶׁעֶבְרָה וְלֹא בֵרְכָה, בִּטְּלָה מִצְוָה דְרַבָּנָן, וְאוּלַי
מִצְוָה דְאוֹרַיְתָא. וְכֵן כָּל שֶׁקּוֹרָא בַתּוֹרָה בְּשַׁחֲרִית קֹדֶם שֶׁיְּבָרֵךְ הַבְּרָכוֹת הַמְתֻקָּנוֹת
בַּתּוֹרָה אוֹ בִרְכַּת "אַהֲבַת עוֹלָם", בִּטֵּל מִצְוָה דְאוֹרַיְתָא; וּלְפִיכָךְ מִי שֶׁשָּׁכַח אִם
בֵּרַךְ בִּרְכַּת הַתּוֹרָה בְּשַׁחֲרִית אִם לֹא בֵרַךְ, חוֹזֵר וּמְבָרֵךְ.

וּמִי שֶׁעָבַר וְלֹא בֵרַךְ כָּל שְׁאָר הַבְּרָכוֹת שֶׁבָּעוֹלָם לְבַד אֵלּוּ שֶׁזָּכַרְנוּ, בִּטֵּל מִצְוַת
חֲכָמִים, וּפוֹרֵץ גָּדֵר יִשְׁכֶנּוּ נָחָשׁ, וְהַזָּהִיר בָּהֶן יִתְבָּרֵךְ מִדָּה כְּנֶגֶד מִדָּה.

---

75. I.e. after the meal, before grace is said; TB Ḥullin 105a.

76. So Rashba, commentary to *ibid.*

77. Nine paragraphs above.

78. TB B'rachoth 49b.

79. This is a loose general statement; more precisely, on *Ḥanukkah* and *Purim* an added part (beginning *'al ha-nissim*) is added in the second benediction; TB B'rachoth 49a, Shabbath 24a.

80. Cited in *'Atereth Z'kénim* to *Shulḥan 'Aruch 'Oraḥ Ḥayyim,* § 185, 1, as from both this text and *Séfer haGan.*

81. TB B'rachoth 20b.

82. Depending on how the unresolved question in *ibid.* is decided.

83. Which equally concerns the Torah, and thus serves the same purpose (TB B'rachoth 11b); see 17 paragraphs above, at note 37; and see §420, note 13. The morning blessing over the Torah can be found in *Daily Prayer Book,* ed. Birnbaum, p. 13.

84. Literally, all the other blessings in the world (i.e. any one of them).

85. In TB B'rachoth 4b we find in regard to a Rabbinic enactment, "The Sages made a barrier for their words...and whoever violates the words of the Sages

On a Sabbath and a festival day a man needs to mention the sanctity of the day in the third benediction [of the grace after meals], as we said.[77] If he did not mention it and began the [fourth] benediction, "who is good and does good," he is to return to the beginning.[78] If he did not begin it but ended the third benediction, if it is the Sabbath, this text is said: "Blessed art Thou, Lord our God, King of the world, who gave the Sabbath of rest to His people Israel for a sign and a covenant. Blessed art Thou, Lord, who dost sanctify the Sabbath." If it is a festival day, one says, "Blessed art Thou, Lord our God, who gave festival days to His people Israel for rejoicing and for happiness. Blessed art Thou, Lord, who dost sanctify Israel and the festive times."[47]

So too on *Rosh Ḥodesh* (the beginning of a month) and the non-holy (intermediate) days of a festival, and on *Ḥanukkah* and *Purim*, they are to be mentioned in the grace after meals, in the third benediction.[79] But if one forgot and closed the benediction, he is not made to repeat the grace, and they are then not mentioned at all.[78]

Thus I received the tradition from my master teachers, God protect them: that whoever is careful in [the observance of] the grace after meals, his provisions will be available to him in dignity all his days.[80] The remaining details of the precept are clarified in the Talmud tractate *B'rachoth*.

By the law of the Torah, this precept is in force everywhere, at every time, for males. As to women, our Sages are in doubt if they are obligated about it by the Torah's law, or not.[81] If a man violates this, eating sustaining food and saying no benediction after it, he disobeys this positive precept. If a woman transgresses and says no benediction, she disobeys a commandment of the Sages, and perhaps a precept of the Torah.[82] So too, if anyone reads [or studies] the Torah in the morning before saying the benedictions formulated for the Torah, or the blessing "With everlasting love,"[83] he disobeys a precept of the Torah. Therefore, if someone has forgotten whether he said the benediction over the Torah in the morning prayers or did not say it, he is to turn back and recite it.[34]

If someone transgresses and does not say any of the other blessings that exist,[84] apart from those we mentioned, he disobeys an enactment of the Sages; and *he who breaks through a fence, a serpent shall bite him* (Ecclesiastes 10:8). He (be He blessed) cautioned about them: "measure for measure."[85]

וְצָרִיךְ הָאָדָם לְהִזָּהֵר מְאֹד מֵהַזְכִּיר בְּרָכָה לְבַטָּלָה, שֶׁיֵּשׁ בַּדָּבָר עֹנֶשׁ חָמוּר, שֶׁמַּזְכִּיר שֵׁם שָׁמַיִם הַמְּקֻדָּשׁ שֶׁלֹּא לְצֹרֶךְ; וַחֲכָמִים סָמְכוּ הַדָּבָר לַלָּאו דְּ"לֹא תִשָּׂא אֶת שֵׁם יי אֱלֹהֶיךָ לַשָּׁוְא".

וּבוֹא וּרְאֵה כַּמָּה הָיוּ זְהִירִין בָּזֶה בַּדּוֹרוֹת הָרִאשׁוֹנִים, שֶׁהֲרֵי שִׁמְשׁוֹן נְזִיר אֱלֹהִים נָשָׂא אִשָּׁה מִפְּלִשְׁתִּים אֲשֶׁר אָהֵב בְּנַחַל שׂוֹרֵק, וְהָיָה נָזִיר כָּל־כָּךְ בְּהַזְכָּרַת הַשֵּׁם שֶׁלֹּא לְהַזְכִּירוֹ כְּלָל, בֵּין לְצֹרֶךְ אוֹ שֶׁלֹּא לְצֹרֶךְ, שֶׁדְּלִילָה הַפִּילָה כִּי הִגִּיד לָהּ אֶת כָּל לִבּוֹ בְּהַזְכִּירוֹ אֱלֹהִים בְּתוֹךְ דְּבָרָיו, בְּאָמְרוֹ אֵלֶיהָ "כִּי נְזִיר אֱלֹהִים אָנִי", וּכְמוֹ שֶׁכָּתוּב אַחֲרָיו: וַתֵּרֶא דְלִילָה כִּי הִגִּיד לָהּ אֶת כָּל לִבּוֹ — וְאָמְרוּ זִכְרוֹנָם לִבְרָכָה: מִנָּא יָדְעָה; וּמֵהֶן שֶׁאָמְרוּ: נִכָּרִין דִּבְרֵי אֱמֶת, וּמֵהֶם שֶׁאָמְרוּ: עַל שֶׁהִזְכִּיר שִׁמְשׁוֹן אֱלֹהִים בְּתוֹךְ דְּבָרָיו, וְאַף־עַל־פִּי שֶׁלֹּא אָמַר דֶּרֶךְ שְׁבוּעָה אֶלָּא דֶּרֶךְ סִפּוּר.

[מִצְוַת אַהֲבַת הַגֵּרִים]

תלא שֶׁנִּצְטַוֵּינוּ לֶאֱהֹב הַגֵּרִים, כְּלוֹמַר שֶׁנִּזָּהֵר שֶׁלֹּא לְצַעֵר אוֹתָם בְּשׁוּם דָּבָר אֲבָל נַעֲשֶׂה לָהֶם טוֹבָה וְנִגְמֹל אוֹתָם חֶסֶד כְּפִי הָרָאוּי וְהַיְכֹלֶת. וְהַגֵּרִים הֵם כָּל מִי שֶׁנִּתְחַבֵּר אֵלֵינוּ מִשְּׁאָר הָאֻמּוֹת, שֶׁהִנִּיחַ דָּתוֹ וְנִכְנַס בְּדָתֵנוּ; וַעֲלֵיהֶם נֶאֱמַר "וַאֲהַבְתֶּם אֶת הַגֵּר כִּי גֵרִים הֱיִיתֶם"; וְאַף־עַל־פִּי שֶׁיִּכְלָלֵהוּ כְּמוֹ־כֵן הַצִּוּוּי בְּיִשְׂרָאֵל, שֶׁנֶּאֱמַר עָלָיו "וְאָהַבְתָּ לְרֵעֶךָ", שֶׁהֲרֵי גֵר צֶדֶק בִּכְלַל רֵעֶךָ הוּא, הוֹסִיף לָנוּ הַשֵּׁם בּוֹ מִצְוָה מְיֻחֶדֶת לוֹ בְּאַהֲבָתוֹ.

וּכְמוֹ־כֵן הַדָּבָר בִּמְנִיעָה מִלְּדַמּוֹת אוֹתוֹ, שֶׁאַף־עַל־פִּי שֶׁהָיָה בִּכְלַל "וְלֹא תוֹנוּ אִישׁ אֶת עֲמִיתוֹ" הוֹסִיף לָנוּ הַכָּתוּב בּוֹ מְנִיעָה מְיֻחֶדֶת לוֹ בְּאָמְרוֹ "וְגֵר לֹא

incurs a penalty of death"; in TB Shabbath 110a (and see 'Avodah Zarah 27b) the above verse (Ecclesiastes 10:8) is applied to anyone who violates a Rabbinic law, and the Talmud speaks of his being "bitten by a snake of the Sages." Hence the concept of "measure for measure": If a person breaks through the fence they erected; he makes a break (as it were) in the fence that generally protects him from Divine punishment.

86. TB B'rachoth 33a (as understood by *tosafoth*, TB Rosh haShanah 33a, s.v. *ha*; MT *hilchoth t'fillah* i 15 differs).

87. TB Sotah 9b.

88. I.e. since he had lied to her previously (Rashi).

§431   1. The term *gér* literally means a sojourner (temporary resident), or a foreigner; but in the literature of the Sages it invariably denotes a convert to Judaism.

2. I.e. one who resolves to live fully as a Jew, observing all the 613 precepts — in contrast to a *gér toshav*, who undertakes to observe only the Divine ban on idolatry

Now, a man needs to beware greatly of uttering a benediction in vain [needlessly]: for the matter entails severe punishment, since he would thus mention the hallowed name of Heaven to no purpose. The Sages based the matter on the negative precept, *You shall not take the name of the Lord your God in vain* (Exodus 20:7).[86]

Come and see how careful the early generations were about this. Samson, a *nazir* [under vow] to God, took a wife from the Philistines, whom he loved, in the valley of Sorek. Yet he was so very careful about uttering the Divine name, not to mention it at all, whether for a need or without any necessity, that Delilah recognized that he had told her his entire heart when he mentioned God in the midst of his words, telling her, *for I am a* nazir *to God* (Judges 16:17). As it is written afterward, *Then Delilah saw that he had told her all his heart* (ibid. 18). Our Sages of blessed memory asked:[87] How did she know?[88] Some answered: words of truth can be recognized; and some answered: because Samson mentioned God amidst his words — even though he did not say it by way of an oath but only in the course of relating something.

[THE PRECEPT OF LOVE FOR CONVERTS TO JUDAISM]

431 that we were commanded to bear affection for converts (proselytes), not to make them suffer about anything whatever, but we should rather do good for them and treat them with loving-kindness, as it is fitting and according to one's ability. Now, "converts" means anyone out of the other nations who has joined us, having left his religion and entered ours. About them it is stated, *And you shall love the* gér *(alien sojourner),*[1] *for you were alien sojourners* (Deuteronomy 10:19). Even though he is included in the commandment about Israelites, regarding whom it is stated, *but you shall love your neighbor* (Leviticus 19:18), since a *gér tzedek* (righteous convert)[2] is clearly included in the category of "your neighbor," the Eternal Lord gave us an additional precept about him specifically in regard to affection for him.

The matter is the same in regard to the restraint against cheating him: Even though he is included in the scope of the admonition, *And you shall not wrong one another* (Leviticus 25:17), Scripture gave us another prohibition about it specifically concerning him, by stating, *And a gér you shall not wrong* (Exodus 22:20). It was then taught in the

תוֹנֶה", וְאָמְרוּ בַּגְּמָרָא שֶׁהַמְאַנֶּה הַגֵּר עוֹבֵר מִשּׁוּם "לֹא תוֹנוּ" וְגוֹמֵר, וּמִשּׁוּם "וְגֵר לֹא תוֹנֶה", וּכְמוֹ־כֵן מְבַטֵּל מִצְוַת "וְאָהַבְתָּ לְרֵעֶךָ", וּמִצְוַת "וַאֲהַבְתֶּם אֶת הַגֵּר".

מִשָּׁרְשֵׁי הַמִּצְוָה, כִּי הַשֵּׁם בָּחַר בְּיִשְׂרָאֵל לִהְיוֹת לוֹ לְעַם קָדוֹשׁ וְרָצָה לְזַכּוֹתָם, וְלָכֵן הִדְרִיכָם וְצִוָּם עַל דַּרְכֵי הַחֲנִינָה וְהַחֶמְלָה, וְהִזְהִירָם לְהִתְעַטֵּר בְּכָל מִדָּה חֲמוּדָה וִיקָרָה לִמְצֹא חֵן בְּעֵינֵי כָל רוֹאֵיהֶם, וְיֹאמְרוּ "עַם יי אֵלֶּה". וְכַמָּה הִיא דֶרֶךְ נְעִימוּת וַחֲמֵדָה לְהִתְחַסֵּד וְלִגְמֹל טוֹבָה לַאֲשֶׁר הִנִּיחַ אִמּוֹ וְכָל מִשְׁפַּחַת בֵּית אָבִיו וְאִמּוֹ, וַיָּבוֹא לַחֲסוֹת תַּחַת כַּנְפֵי אֻמָּה אַחֶרֶת בְּאַהֲבָתוֹ אוֹתָהּ וּבְבָחִירָתוֹ בָּאֱמֶת וְשִׂנְאַת הַשֶּׁקֶר; וּבִהְיוֹתֵנוּ זוֹכִים לְמִדּוֹת טוֹבוֹת הַלָּלוּ, תָּחוּל טוֹבַת הָאֵל עָלֵינוּ וְתִדְבַּק בָּנוּ, וְשׁוּם דָּבָר לֹא תִמְנָעֶה מִמֶּנּוּ, כִּי הַטּוֹבָה תִתְפַּשֵּׁט בַּטּוֹבִים וְהֶפְכָּהּ בָּרָעִים.

מִדִּינֵי הַמִּצְוָה, מַה שֶּׁאָמְרוּ זִכְרוֹנָם לִבְרָכָה שֶׁלֹּא יֹאמַר אָדָם לְגֵר "זְכֹר מַעֲשֶׂיךָ הָרִאשׁוֹנִים"; וּמַה שֶּׁאָמְרוּ: גִּיּוֹרָא עַד עֲשָׂרָה דָרֵי לָא תִּבְזֵי אֲרַמָּאָה בְּאַנְפֵּהּ — וְכָל זֶה שֶׁלֹּא לְצַעֲרוֹ בְּשׁוּם עִנְיָן; וְהַפְלָגַת הָאַהֲבָה שֶׁהִפְלִיגוּ בָּהֶם עַד שֶׁאָמְרוּ שֶׁהִשְׁנָה הַכָּתוּב אַהֲבָתָם לְאַהֲבַת הַמָּקוֹם, שֶׁבָּהֶם נֶאֱמַר "וַאֲהַבְתֶּם", וּבְאַהֲבַת הַמָּקוֹם "וְאָהַבְתָּ" וְגוֹמֵר, כְּמוֹ שֶׁכָּתַבְתִּי בְּסֵדֶר מִשְׁפָּטִים לֹא־תַעֲשֶׂה וּ [סִי' ס"ג]. וְיֶתֶר פְּרָטֶיהָ, בְּמִדְרָשׁוֹת וּבִמְקוֹמוֹת בַּגְּמָרָא.

וְנוֹהֶגֶת מִצְוָה זוֹ בְּכָל מָקוֹם וּבְכָל זְמַן, בַּזְּכָרִים וּבַנְּקֵבוֹת. וְעוֹבֵר עָלֶיהָ וּמְצַעֵר אוֹתָם אוֹ שֶׁמִּתְרַשֵּׁל בַּהַצָּלָתָם אוֹ בְּהַצָּלַת מָמוֹנָם, אוֹ שֶׁמְּקַל בִּכְבוֹדָם מִצַּד שֶׁהֵם גֵּרִים וְאֵין לָהֶם עוֹזֵר בָּאֻמָּה, בִּטֵּל עֲשֵׂה זֶה, וְעָנְשׁוֹ גָּדוֹל מְאֹד, שֶׁהֲרֵי בְּכַמָּה

(our author's view, §94) or, as others hold, all seven precepts imposed by the Torah on all mankind.

3. TB Bava M'tzi'a 59b.

4. The first two paragraphs are based on ShM positive precept §207.

5. Expression based on Ezekiel 36:20.

6. A phrase stemming from Ruth 2:12, generally used as a metaphor for conversion.

7. TB Bava M'tzi'a 58b.

8. I.e. before your conversion.

9. TB Sanhedrin 94a.

10. I.e. not in the presence of nine generations of the convert and his descendants, because the sensitivity over their origins yet remains.

Talmud[3] that a person who treats a convert ill transgresses both the injunction, "you shall not wrong," etc. and the admonition, "a *ger* you shall not wrong." Likewise, then [here] one would disobey the precept, "and you shall love your neighbor," and the precept, "you shall love the *gér*."[4]

At the root of the precept lies the reason that the Eternal Lord chose the Israelites to be a holy people to Him, and wished to make them meritorious. He therefore guided and ordered them onto the ways of kindly grace and compassion, and adjured them to adorn themselves with every desirable and precious trait of character, to find favor in the eyes of all who behold them, that they should say, "These are the people of the Lord."[5] Well, how much a way of gratification and delight it is to adopt loving-kindness and do good for a person who left his nation and the entire family of his father's and mother's house, and came to shelter under the wings[6] of another nation, in his affection for it, and in his preference for truth and hatred of falsehood. And as we attain these good traits of character, the good favor of God will be bestowed upon us and will cling to us; nothing whatever will bar it from us. For good will extend to good persons, and its opposite to evil ones.

Among the laws of the precept, there is what the Sages of blessed memory taught:[7] that a man should not tell a proselyte, "Remember your original activities."[8] Then there is what they taught:[9] With a convert, until ten generations you are not to despise an Aramean [a non-Jew] in his presence.[10] All this—so as not to cause him pain in any way. And the stress on affection which they emphasized about them [converts] is to such an extent that they taught that Scripture equated love for them with love for the omnipresent God: for it is stated about them, *And you shall love the* gér, and about love of the omnipresent One, *you shall love the Lord your God*, etc. (Deuteronomy 6:5)—as I wrote in *sidrah mishpatim*, in the sixth negative precept (§ 63). The rest of its details are in the Midrashim and in various places in the Talmud.

This precept is in force everywhere, at every time, for both man and woman. If a person transgresses it and causes them pain, or is negligent about rescuing them or rescuing their possesions, or is disparaging about their dignity, because they are converts·and have no one in the nation to aid them—he disobeys this positive precept,

מְקוֹמוֹת הֻזְהֲרָה תּוֹרָה עֲלֵיהֶם.

וְיֵשׁ לָנוּ לִלְמֹד מִן הַמִּצְוָה הַיְקָרָה הַזֹּאת לְרַחֵם עַל כָּל אָדָם שֶׁהוּא בְּעִיר שֶׁאֵינָה אֶרֶץ מוֹלַדְתּוֹ וּמְקוֹם מִשְׁפַּחַת אֲבוֹתָיו, וְלֹא נַעֲבִיר עָלָיו הַדֶּרֶךְ בְּמֹצְאֵנוּ אוֹתוֹ יְחִידִי וְרָחֲקוּ מֵעָלָיו עוֹזְרָיו: כְּמוֹ שֶׁאָנוּ רוֹאִים שֶׁהַתּוֹרָה תַּזְהִירֵנוּ לְרַחֵם עַל כָּל מִי שֶׁצָּרִיךְ עֵזֶר. וְעִם הַמִּדּוֹת הַלָּלוּ נִזְכֶּה לִהְיוֹת מְרֻחָמִים מֵהַשֵּׁם יִתְבָּרֵךְ, וּבִרְכוֹת שָׁמַיִם יָנוּחוּ עַל רָאשֵׁינוּ.

וְהַכָּתוּב רָמַז טַעַם הַצִּוּוּי|בְּאָמְרוֹ "כִּי גֵרִים הֱיִיתֶם בְּאֶרֶץ מִצְרָיִם": הִזְכִּיר לָנוּ שֶׁכְּבָר נִכְוֵינוּ בַּצַּעַר הַגָּדוֹל הַהוּא שֶׁיֵּשׁ לְכָל אִישׁ הָרוֹאֶה אֶת עַצְמוֹ בְּתוֹךְ אֲנָשִׁים זָרִים וּבְאֶרֶץ נָכְרִיָּה, וּבְזָכְרֵנוּ גֹּדֶל דַּאֲגַת הַלֵּב שֶׁיֵּשׁ בַּדָּבָר, וְכִי כְּבָר עָבַר עָלֵינוּ, וְהַשֵּׁם בַּחֲסָדָיו הוֹצִיאָנוּ מִשָּׁם, יִכְמְרוּ רַחֲמֵינוּ עַל כָּל אָדָם שֶׁהוּא כֵן.

[מִצְוַת יִרְאַת הַשֵּׁם]

תלב לִהְיוֹת יִרְאַת הַשֵּׁם עַל פָּנֵינוּ תָּמִיד לְבִלְתִּי נֶחֱטָא, כְּלוֹמַר שֶׁנִּירָא בִּיאַת עָנְשׁוֹ וְלֹא יִהְיֶה לְבָבֵנוּ בְּלִי מָגוֹר אֵלָיו כָּל הַיּוֹם; וְעַל זֶה נֶאֱמַר: אֶת יי אֱלֹהֶיךָ תִּירָא.

וְהָרְאָיָה שֶׁזֶּהוּ מִצְוָה עֲשֵׂה אַחַת מֵחֶשְׁבּוֹן תרי"ג מִצְווֹת שֶׁנִּצְטַוֵּינוּ, מַה שֶׁאָמְרוּ בְּסַנְהֶדְרִין עַל דֶּרֶךְ הַוִּכּוּחַ בְּפֵרוּשׁ "וְנֹקֵב שֵׁם יי" וְגוֹמֵר: וְאֵימָא פָּרוּשֵׁי דִּכְתִיב "אֲשֶׁר נִקְּבוּ בְּשֵׁמוֹת", וְאַזְהָרוֹתֵיהּ מִן "אֶת יי אֱלֹהֶיךָ תִּירָא" — יִרְצֶה לוֹמַר עַל דֶּרֶךְ הַוִּכּוּחַ (כִּי) אוּלַי נְפָרֵשׁ "וְנֹקֵב" בְּהַזְכָּרַת הַשֵּׁם לְבַד מִבְּלִי שֶׁיְּבָרֵךְ, וְהָעֹנֶשׁ שֶׁיִּהְיֶה בָּזֶה לְפִי שֶׁהִפְסִידוֹ הַיִּרְאָה, כִּי מִיִּרְאַת הַשֵּׁם שֶׁלֹּא יַזְכִּיר שְׁמוֹ

11. Literally, let us not make the road pass by him—apparently an idiomatic expression for maltreatment, quite possibly based on the implication of the literal sense; for if we were to make the road bypass someone, he would be left isolated and abandoned. As noted in vol. 1 p. 433, commentaries to TB Sanhedrin 31b and Midrash Sifre explain the expression as denoting maltreatment, grievous physical injury, or dealing unjustly, improperly with another person.

§432   1. I.e. in the forefront of our awareness.

and his punishment will be very great: for the Torah patently warned about them in so many places.

It is for us to learn from this precious *mitzvah* to take pity on any man who is in a town or city that is not his native ground and the site of the family of his fathers. Let us not maltreat him in any way,[11] finding him alone, with those who would aid him quite far from him—just as we see that the Torah adjures us to have compassion on anyone who needs help. With these qualities we will merit to be treated with compassion by the Eternal Lord, be He blessed, and the blessings of Heaven will abide about our heads.

Scripture alludes to the reason for the command by stating, *for you were* gérim *(alien sojourners) in the land of Egypt* (Deuteronomy 10:19). It thus reminds us that long ago we were scorched by that great pain that comes upon every man who sees himself among alien people, in a foreign land. Remembering, then, the great anxiety of the heart that the matter entails, which we experienced in the past, until the Eternal Lord in His loving-kindness took us out from there, we will be moved to compassion for every man who is so [situated].

[THE PRECEPT OF REVERENT AWE FOR THE
ETERNAL LORD]

432 that a reverent fear of the Lord should be on our visages[1] constantly, so that we should not sin; in other words, we should fear the advent of His punishment, and our heart should not be without apprehension toward Him the entire day. About this it was stated, *You shall fear the Lord your God* (Deuteronomy 10:20).

Now, the proof that this is one positive precept in the reckoning of the 613 *mitzvoth* that we were commanded, lies in what was stated in the Talmud tractate *Sanhedrin* (56a), in the course of a discussion of the meaning of the verse, *And he who blasphemes the name of the Lord,* etc. (Leviticus 24:16): But perhaps we could say the verb means uttering it distinctly, as it is written, *that were distinctly called by name* (Numbers 1:17), while its admonition derives from the verse, *You shall fear the Lord your God?* This means to say, by way of argument, that perhaps we should explain the verb *v'nokév* ("And he who blasphemes") to denote merely uttering the Divine name, without blaspheming; and the sin in this would be because it means a loss of reverent fear, since it is part of reverent fear of the Eternal Lord that His name should not be mentioned in vain [needlessly]. It was then

לְבַטָּלָה; וְהֵשִׁיבוּ שָׁם דְּלֵכָּא לְמֵימַר הָכִי, דְּשִׁתֵּי תְשׁוּבוֹת בַּדָּבָר: חֲדָא דְּבָעֵינָא שֵׁם בְּשֵׁם וְלֵכָּא, כְּלוֹמַר שֶׁיְּבָרֵךְ הַשֵּׁם בְּשֵׁם, כְּגוֹן יַכֶּה יַבֶּה יוֹסֵי אֶת יוֹסֵי, וְעוֹד אַזְהָרַת עֲשֵׂה הוּא, וְכָל אַזְהָרַת עֲשֵׂה לָאו שְׁמָהּ אַזְהָרָה — כְּלוֹמַר דִּקְרָא דְּ"אֶת יי אֱלֹהֶיךָ תִּירָא" מִצְוַת עֲשֵׂה הוּא.

שֹׁרֶשׁ הַמִּצְוָה בְּיִרְאַת הַשֵּׁם נִגְלֶה לְכָל רוֹאֵי הַשֶּׁמֶשׁ, כִּי הַשְּׁמִירָה הַגְּדוֹלָה מִן הַחֵטְא הוּא יִרְאַת עָנְשׁוֹ.

וְדִינֵי הַמִּצְוָה כְּלוּלִים בִּפְשַׁט הַכָּתוּב.

וְנוֹהֶגֶת בְּכָל מָקוֹם וּבְכָל זְמַן וּבְכָל מִין הָאָדָם. וְזֹאת אַחַת מִן הַמִּצְווֹת הַתְּמִידִיּוֹת עַל הָאָדָם, שֶׁלֹּא יִפְסֹק חִיּוּבָן מֵעַל הָאָדָם לְעוֹלָם אֲפִלּוּ רֶגַע; וּמִי שֶׁבָּא דְבַר עֲבֵרָה לְיָדוֹ, חַיָּב לְהָעִיר רוּחוֹ וְלָתֵת אֶל לִבּוֹ בְּאוֹתוֹ הַפֶּרֶק שֶׁהַשֵּׁם בָּרוּךְ הוּא מַשְׁגִּיחַ בְּכָל מַעֲשֵׂה בְנֵי־אָדָם, וְיָשִׁיב לָהֶם נָקָם כְּפִי רֹעַ הַמַּעֲשֶׂה.

וְעוֹבֵר עַל זֶה, וְלֹא שָׁת לִבּוֹ בְכָךְ בְּאוֹתָן שָׁעוֹת, בִּטֵּל עֲשֵׂה זֶה, שֶׁזּוּ הִיא שְׁעַת קִיּוּם עֲשֵׂה זֶה בְכִוּוּן. וְאוּלָם כָּל יְמֵי הָאָדָם וְכָל עִתּוֹתָיו בִּכְלָל הַמִּצְוָה לַעֲמֹד זָרִיז וְנִזְכָּר עָלֶיהָ.

[מִצְוַת תְּפִלָּה]

תלג לַעֲבֹד אֶת הַשֵּׁם, שֶׁנֶּאֱמַר "אֹתוֹ תַעֲבֹד"; וְנִכְפְּלָה זֹאת הַמִּצְוָה כַּמָּה פְעָמִים, שֶׁנֶּאֱמַר "וַעֲבַדְתֶּם אֵת יי אֱלֹהֵיכֶם", וּבְמָקוֹם אַחֵר (אוֹמֵר) "וְאֹתוֹ תַעֲבֹד", וּבְמָקוֹם אַחֵר "וּלְעָבְדוֹ בְּכָל לְבַבְכֶם".

וְכָתַב הָרַב רַבֵּנוּ מֹשֶׁה בֶּן מַיְמוֹן זִכְרוֹנוֹ לִבְרָכָה: אַף־עַל־פִּי שֶׁמִּצְוָה זוֹ הִיא מֵהַמִּצְווֹת הַכּוֹלְלוֹת, כְּלוֹמַר שֶׁכּוֹלְלוֹת כָּל הַתּוֹרָה, כִּי תִּכְלֹל כָּל הַמִּצְווֹת — יֵשׁ בָּזוֹ כְּמוֹ־כֵן פְּרָט, וְהוּא שֶׁיְּצַוֵּנוּ הָאֵל לְהִתְפַּלֵּל אֵלָיו, וּכְמוֹ שֶׁאָמְרוּ בְסִפְרֵי: "וּלְעָבְדוֹ בְּכָל לְבַבְכֶם", אֵי זוֹ הִיא עֲבוֹדָה שֶׁבַּלֵּב, זוֹ תְּפִלָּה;

2. Before a penalty of death can be given for the misdeed described in Leviticus 24 : 16.

3. "Yosé" being a euphemism for the Divine name.

4. The first two paragraphs are based on ShM positive precept §4.

5. This would seem to mean non-Jews as well — apparently in consonance with what our author wrote in §26 (vol. 1 pp. 146–47), that the precept to believe in no other Divine power but the Eternal Lord is one of the seven commandments that apply to all mankind. For patently belief in Him should require a concomitant reverent awe, which should act as a moral barrier.

6. The words *kiyyum 'aséh zeh* (fulfilling this positive precept) are absent in three of the oldest manuscripts, whereas MS Vatican has only קיו. Hence the correct reading might be *kiyyumo*, "its fulfillment," which is smoother.

§433   1. ShM positive precept §5; see §282, note 2.

answered there that this cannot be said, for there are two reasons against the matter: one, that one name by another name is required,[2] and it is thus lacking; in other words, that he should blaspheme (curse) one Divine name by another — for example, "May Yosé strike down Yosé";[3] and furthermore, it would then be an injunction by a positive command, and any caution given through a positive command is not considered an injunction. So this means that the verse, *You shall fear the Lord your God*, is a positive precept.[4]

The root reason for the precept of reverent fear for the Lord is obvious to all who can see the sun: For *the* great guard against sin is fear of its penalty. The laws of the precept are implicit in the plain meaning of the Writ.

It applies in every place and every time, and for every sort of human being.[5] It is one of the constant precepts, imposed continuously on a person, whose obligation is never lifted from a man for even an instant. If a sinful matter comes to someone's hand, he is duty-bound to arouse his spirit and reflect at that time that the Eternal Lord (blessed is He) watches every action of human beings, and He takes vengeance from them according to the evil of the act.

If a person violates this and gives this matter no heed at those times [when sin looms] he disobeys this positive precept: for that is particularly the time for fulfilling this positive precept.[6] However, all the days of a man and all his periods of time are included under the precept, for him to stand alert, bearing it in mind.

[THE PRECEPT OF PRAYER TO THE ALMIGHTY]

433 to serve (worship) the Eternal Lord, as it is stated, *Him shall you serve* (Deuteronomy 10:20); and this precept was reiterated several times, as it is stated, *And you shall serve the Lord your God* (Exodus 23:25); and elsewhere it says, *and Him shall you serve* (Deuteronomy 6:13); then elsewhere [we read] *and to serve Him with all your heart* (ibid. 11:13).

Now, R. Moses b. Maimon of blessed memory wrote:[1] Although this *mitzvah* is one of the all-inclusive precepts — in other words, those which include the entire Torah [in their scope], since the service of God includes all the *mitzvoth*[2] — it likewise contains a specific detail: namely, that God commanded us to pray to Him. As it was taught in the Midrash *Sifre*:[3] "and to serve Him with all your heart" (Deuteronomy 11:13) — what service is with the heart? — it is prayer.

וּבְמִשְׁנָתוֹ שֶׁל רַבִּי אֱלִיעֶזֶר בְּנוֹ שֶׁל רַבִּי יוֹסֵי הַגְּלִילִי אָמְרוּ: מִנַּיִן לְעַקֵּר תְּפִלָּה
בְּתוֹךְ הַמִּצְוֹות — מֶהָכָא: אֶת יי אֱלֹהֶיךָ תִּירָא אֹתוֹ תַעֲבֹד.

מִשָּׁרְשֵׁי הַמִּצְוָה, מַה שֶּׁהִקְדַּמְתִּי הַרְבֵּה פְּעָמִים, כִּי הַטּוֹבוֹת וְהַבְּרָכוֹת יָחוּלוּ
עַל בְּנֵי־אָדָם כְּפִי פְּעֻלָּתָם וְטוּב לְבָבָם וְכֹשֶׁר מַחְשְׁבוֹתָם; וַאֲדוֹן הַכֹּל שֶׁבְּרָאָם
חָפֵץ בְּטוֹבָתָם וְהִדְרִיכָם וְהִצְלִיחָם בְּמִצְוֹותָיו הַיְקָרוֹת שֶׁיִּזְכּוּ בָהֶן, וְהוֹדִיעָם גַּם־כֵּן
וּפָתַח לָהֶם פֶּתַח בַּאֲשֶׁר יַשִּׂיגוּ כָּל מִשְׁאֲלוֹתֵיהֶם לְטוֹב, וְהוּא שֶׁיְּבַקְשׁוּ מִמֶּנּוּ בָּרוּךְ
הוּא אֲשֶׁר בְּיָדוֹ הַהִסְתַּפְּקוּת וְהַיְכֹלֶת כָּל חֶסְרוֹנָן, כִּי הוּא יַעֲנֶה אֶת הַשָּׁמַיִם לְכָל
אֲשֶׁר יִקְרָאוּהוּ בֶּאֱמֶת.

וּמִלְּבַד הַהוֹדָעָה לָהֶם בְּזֹאת הַמִּדָּה, צִוָּם שֶׁיִּשְׁתַּמְּשׁוּ בָהּ וִיבַקְשׁוּ מִמֶּנּוּ תָּמִיד
כָּל צָרְכֵיהֶם וְכָל חֶפְצֵי לְבָּם; וּמִלְּבַד הַשָּׂגַת חֶפְצֵי לְבָּנוּ יֵשׁ לָנוּ זְכוּת בַּדָּבָר
בְּהִתְעוֹרֵר רוּחֵנוּ וְקָבְעֵנוּ כָּל מַחְשַׁבְתֵּנוּ כִּי הוּא הָאָדוֹן הַטּוֹב וְהַמֵּיטִיב לָנוּ, וְכִי
עֵינָיו פְּקוּחוֹת עַל כָּל דְּרָכֵינוּ, וּבְכָל עֵת, וּבְכָל רֶגַע יִשְׁמַע וַעֲקָתֵנוּ אֵלָיו, לֹא יָנוּם
וְלֹא יִישָׁן שׁוֹמֵר יִשְׂרָאֵל, וְהֶאֱמַנֵּנוּ בְּמַלְכוּתוֹ וִיכָלְתּוֹ וִיכַלְתּוֹ מִבְּלִי שׁוּם צַד פִּקְפּוּק, וְכִי
אֵין לְפָנָיו מוֹנֵעַ וּמְעַכֵּב בְּכָל אֲשֶׁר יַחְפֹּץ.

וְאוּלָם אֵין לָנוּ בַּתּוֹרָה בְּזֹאת הַמִּצְוָה זְמַן קָבוּעַ לַעֲשׂוֹתָהּ, וּמִפְּנֵי־כֵן מִסְפָּקִים
רַבּוֹתֵינוּ בָּעִנְיָן. הָרַב רַבֵּנוּ מֹשֶׁה בֶּן מַיְמוֹן זִכְרוֹנוֹ לִבְרָכָה כָּתַב בְּחִבּוּרוֹ הַגָּדוֹל
שֶׁהַמִּצְוָה הִיא לְהִתְפַּלֵּל בְּכָל יוֹם; וְהָרַב רַבֵּנוּ מֹשֶׁה בֶּן נַחְמָן זִכְרוֹנוֹ לִבְרָכָה תָּפַשׂ
עָלָיו וְאָמַר שֶׁהַתּוֹרָה לֹא צִוַּתְנוּ לְהִתְפַּלֵּל בְּכָל יוֹם וְגַם לֹא בְּכָל שָׁבוּעַ, וְלֹא תָּאַחַד
זְמַן בַּדָּבָר כְּלָל, וְתָמִיד יֹאמְרוּ זִכְרוֹנָם לִבְרָכָה "תְּפִלָּה — דְּרַבָּנָן"; וְהוּא כְּמִסְפָּק
יֹאמַר שֶׁהַמִּצְוָה הִיא לְהִתְפַּלֵּל וְלִזְעֹק לִפְנֵי הָאֵל בָּרוּךְ הוּא בְּעֵת הַצָּרָה.

2. And hence it ought not be reckoned as one of the 613 precepts.

3. Sifre, Deuteronomy §41; but what follows is the wording in TB Ta'anith 2a.
(On the citation below from the teachings of R. 'Eli'ezer b. R. Yosé the Galilean,
see *Mishnath R. 'Eli'ezer* p. 228, l. 15–16.

4. Expression based on Hosea 2:23; the translation follows Malbim, there.

5. Expression taken from Psalms 145:18.

6. The central point that prayer to Him induces and strengthens faith in Him is
intimated in the Targumim to Exodus 17:12. The Scriptural text reads literally, *and
his hands were faith*; in Targum Onkelos we find, "and his hands were spread in
prayer"; in Pseudo-Jonathan, "and his hands were spread in faith, in prayer and
fasting"; while the complete Targum Yerushalmi (Vatican MS) has the fullest
version, q.v.

7. MT *hilchoth t'fillah* i 1.

8. Ramban, commentary to ShM positive precept §5.

⟨340⟩

And in the collection of Oral Torah of R. 'Eli'ezer the son of R. Yosé the Galilean it was taught: Where do we learn the main principle of prayer amid the precepts?—from here: *You shall fear the Lord your God; Him shall you serve* (Deuteronomy 10:20).

At the root of the precept lies what I have written previously many times: that favors and blessings are bestowed on human beings in accord with their activity, the goodness of their heart and the worthiness of their thoughts. The sovereign Ruler of all, who created them, desires good for them, and He has [therefore] guided them and led them to succeed through His precious *mitzvoth*, that they might become virtuous by them. Then He likewise informed them and opened an entranceway for them by which they can attain all their wishes for good: namely, that they should entreat Him, blessed is He, in whose hand (power) lies all adequacy and ability, for all that they lack. For He will have the heavens respond[4] to all who will call to Him in truth.[5]

Apart from informing them of this method, He commanded them that they should use it, and they should continually entreat Him for all their needs and for their every heart's desire. Well, apart from attaining our heart's wishes, we earn merit by this method, when our spirit is stirred and we set our entire thought firmly that He is the sovereign Ruler who is good and does good for us; that His eyes are open watching all our ways; at every time and every instant He will hear our outcry to Him; *the Protector of Israel neither slumbers nor sleeps* (Psalms 121:4); and we are [thus] brought to have faith in His kingship and His capability without any element of misgivings, and [He gives us faith] that there is no bar or hindrance before Him to whatever He desires.[6]

In the Torah, however, we do not have a set time for this precept, to observe it; and for this reason our master scholars are in doubt on the subject. R. Moses b. Maimon of blessed memory wrote in his work[7] that it is a *mitzvah* (religious duty) to pray every day. However, R. Moses b. Naḥman of blessed memory refuted him,[8] saying that the Torah did not command us to pray every day, nor even every week, not assigning any particular time for it at all; and the Sages of blessed memory say constantly that prayer-service is by the enactment of the Sages. Hence he tentatively declares that the religious duty is to pray and cry out before God (blessed is He) at a time of trouble.

גַּם הָרַב רַבֵּנוּ מֹשֶׁה בֶּן מַיְמוֹן זִכְרוֹנוֹ לִבְרָכָה בְּעַצְמוֹ כָּתַב שֶׁאֵין מִנְיַן הַתְּפִלּוֹת וְלֹא מַטְבֵּעַ הַתְּפִלָּה מִן הַתּוֹרָה, וְאֵין לַתְּפִלָּה זְמַן קָבוּעַ בַּיּוֹם מִן הַתּוֹרָה, אֲבָל מִכָּל־מָקוֹם חִיּוּב הַתּוֹרָה הוּא לְהִתְחַנֵּן לָאֵל בְּכָל יוֹם וּלְהוֹדוֹת לְפָנָיו כִּי כָל הַמֶּמְשָׁלָה אֵלָיו וְהַיְכֹלֶת לְהַשְׁלִים כָּל בַּקָּשָׁה. עַד כָּאן.

וּמִן הַדּוֹמֶה כִּי בִהְיוֹת עִקַּר מִצְוַת הַתּוֹרָה בְּכָךְ וְלֹא יוֹתֵר, תִּקְּנוּ זִכְרוֹנָם לִבְרָכָה לְמִי שֶׁהוּא בְמָקוֹם סַכָּנָה וְאֵינוֹ יָכוֹל לַעֲמֹד וּלְכַוֵּן תְּפִלָּה, כְּדֵי לָצֵאת יְדֵי חוֹבָתוֹ בְּמִצְוַת הַתּוֹרָה, לוֹמַר "צָרְכֵי עַמְּךָ יִשְׂרָאֵל מְרֻבִּין" וְגוֹמֵר, כְּמוֹ שֶׁבָּא בְמַסֶּכֶת בְּרָכוֹת.

מִדִּינֵי הַמִּצְוָה, מַה שֶּׁאָמְרוּ זִכְרוֹנָם לִבְרָכָה שֶׁחַיָּב אָדָם לְהִתְפַּלֵּל שָׁלֹשׁ פְּעָמִים בַּיּוֹם: שַׁחֲרִית וּבֵין הָעַרְבַּיִם וּבַלַּיְלָה פַּעַם אֶחָת. וְאֵלּוּ הַשָּׁלֹשׁ תְּפִלּוֹת כְּנֶגֶד הַקָּרְבָּנוֹת תִּקְּנוּם, שֶׁבְּכָל יוֹם הָיוּ מַקְרִיבִים בַּמִּקְדָּשׁ תָּמִיד שֶׁל שַׁחַר וְתָמִיד שֶׁל בֵּין הָעַרְבַּיִם, וּתְפִלַּת הָעֶרֶב גַּם־כֵּן תִּקְּנוּ כְּנֶגֶד אֵבְרֵי הָעוֹלָה שֶׁל בֵּין הָעַרְבַּיִם שֶׁהָיוּ מִתְאַכְּלִין וְהוֹלְכִין כָּל הַלַּיְלָה.

וּמִפְּנֵי שֶׁזֹּאת הַתְּפִלָּה שֶׁל לַיְלָה הִיא כְּנֶגֶד עִנְיָן מֵהַקָּרְבָּנוֹת שֶׁאֵינוֹ חוֹבָה, שֶׁאִם נִתְאַכְּלָה מִבְּעוֹד יוֹם עוֹלַת הָעַרְבַּיִם לֹא הָיָה מִתְאַכֶּלֶת בַּלַּיְלָה, אָמְרוּ זִכְרוֹנָם לִבְרָכָה גַּם־כֵּן שֶׁתְּפִלַּת הָעֶרֶב רְשׁוּת הִיא: אִם יִהְיֶה פְנַאי לָאָדָם וְיִמְצָא בְעַצְמוֹ נַחַת לְהִתְפַּלֵּל יִתְפַּלֵּל, וְאִם לָאו לֹא יִתְפַּלֵּל, וְאֵין עָלָיו אָשָׁם בְּכָךְ; וְאַף־עַל־פִּי־כֵן נָהֲגוּ יִשְׂרָאֵל הַיּוֹם בְּכָל מָקוֹם לְהִתְפַּלֵּל תְּפִלַּת הָעֶרֶב בְּקֶבַע בְּכָל לַיְלָה, וְאַחַר שֶׁקִּבְּלוּהָ עֲלֵיהֶם דֶּרֶךְ חוֹבָה, חַיָּב כָּל אֶחָד מִיִּשְׂרָאֵל לְהִתְפַּלֵּל אוֹתָהּ עַל־כָּל־פָּנִים.

וּכְמוֹ־כֵן תִּקְּנוּ זִכְרוֹנָם לִבְרָכָה בְּשַׁבָּתוֹת וּבְמוֹעֲדִים תְּפִלָּה רְבִיעִית, וְהִיא הַנִּקְרֵאת תְּפִלַּת מוּסָף, וְהִיא כְּנֶגֶד הַקָּרְבָּן שֶׁהָיָה נוֹסָף בַּמִּקְדָּשׁ בִּזְמַן שֶׁהָיָה קַיָּם; וְעוֹד תִּקְּנוּ תְּפִלָּה חֲמִישִׁית בְּיוֹם הַכִּפּוּרִים לְבַד, לְרֹב קְדֻשַּׁת הַיּוֹם וּבַעֲבוּר הֱיוֹתוֹ

9. TB B'rachoth 31a.

10. *Ibid.* 26b.

11. *Ibid.* 27b; Rashi, TB Shabbath 9b, s.v. *l'man d'amar*; MT *hilchoth t'fillah* i 5–6.

12. So R. Isaac 'Alfasi, TB B'rachoth 27b; MT *ibid.* 6.

Well, even R. Moses b. Maimon (of blessed memory) himself wrote[7] that neither the number of prayer-services nor the set form of the prayer is by the law of the Torah, and neither does prayer have a fixed time of the day for it by the Torah; yet in any event, the obligation imposed by the Torah is to supplicate God every day, and to acknowledge before Him that all dominion is His, and the ability to fulfill every plea. Thus far [his words].

It would then seem that since the core precept of the Torah means this and no more, the Sages established that if a person is in a place of peril and he cannot stand and concentrate on prayer to fulfill his obligation under the precept of the Torah, he is to say, "The needs of Thy people Israel are numerous," etc. as it is set down in the Talmud tractate B'rachoth (29b).

Among the laws of the precept there is what the Sages of blessed memory said:[9] that a man is obligated to pray three times a day: in the morning and the afternoon, and once at night. These three prayer-services were instituted to correspond to the offerings; for every day they would offer up at the Sanctuary the daily sacrifice of the morning and the daily sacrifice of the afternoon (§401);[10] and the evening prayer they likewise instituted to correspond to the parts of the afternoon 'olah (burnt-offering) that would go on being burned [on the altar] the whole night.[11]

Now, because this prayer of the night corresponds to an aspect of the offerings that was not obligatory—for if the 'olah of the afternoon was consumed [in the altar fire] while it was yet day, it would not be burned at night—the Sages of blessed memory said equally that the evening prayer-service is voluntary: If a man has free time and finds himself the tranquillity to pray, let him worship; and if not, let him not pray, and he will bear no guilt for it. Nevertheless, the Jewish people have the accepted practice today, everywhere, to say the evening prayer-service regularly, invariably, every night. And since they took it upon themselves in the nature of a duty, everyone in Jewry is obligated to say the prayers in any event.[12]

So too, the Sages of blessed memory instituted, for the Sabbath and festival days, a fourth prayer-service, called the musaf ("additional") service, which correspond to the offering that was added [on such days] at the Sanctuary at the time it existed.[10] And they further instituted a fifth prayer-service on the Day of Atonement alone, on account of the great holiness of the day, and because it is a

יוֹם סְלִיחָה וְכַפָּרָה לַכֹּל, וְהִיא הַנִּקְרֵאת תְּפִלַת נְעִילָה.

וְכָל נֻסַח הַתְּפִלּוֹת, עֶזְרָא וּבֵית-דִּינוֹ תִּקְּנוּם; וּבִימֵי הַחֵל תִּקְּנוּ לְהִתְפַּלֵּל שְׁמוֹנֶה-עֶשְׂרֵה בְּרָכוֹת הַיְדוּעוֹת בְּכָל פְּנוֹת יִשְׂרָאֵל, מִלְּבַד בִּרְכַּת הַמִּינִין שֶׁתִּקֵּן שְׁמוּאֵל הַקָּטָן בְּהַסְכָּמַת רַבָּן גַּמְלִיאֵל וּבֵית-דִּינוֹ, כִּדְאִיתָא בִּמְגִלָּה.

וּמֵהֶן שְׁלֹשָׁה מְסַפְּרוֹת שֶׁבַח הַשֵׁם, וּשְׁלֹשָׁה הוֹדָאָה לְפָנָיו, וּשְׁנֵים-עֶשְׂרֵה שֶׁנִּכְלָל בָּהֶם שְׁאֵלַת צֹרֶךְ כָּל אִישׁ מִיִשְׂרָאֵל. וְהֵם זִכְרוֹנָם לִבְרָכָה סְדָרוּם כַּסֵּדֶר שֶׁהֵם סְדוּרוֹת הַיּוֹם בְּפִי כָל יִשְׂרָאֵל: הַשָׁלֹשׁ רִאשׁוֹנוֹת בְּשֶׁבַח הַשֵׁם, וְאֶמְצָעִיוֹת בְּבַקָּשַׁת צְרָכִים, וְאַחֲרוֹנוֹת בְּהוֹדָאַת הָאֵל עַל כָּל הַטּוֹבָה שֶׁעוֹשֶׂה עִמָּנוּ בָּרוּךְ הוּא; וְאַחַר-כָּךְ לִזְמָן רַב נִשְׁכַּח כִּוּוּן סְדוּרָם, וְשִׁמְעוֹן הַפָּקוּלִי יָדַע אוֹתָם וְהִסְדִּירָם עַל הַסֵּדֶר הַמְכֻנָּן כְּמוֹ שֶׁסְּדָרוּם עֶזְרָא וּבֵית-דִּינוֹ, לִשְׁאֹל תְּחִלָּה דַּעַת, כִּי הוּא רֹאשׁ וְאָב לְכָל הַקִּנְיָנִים, שֶׁאִם אֵין דַּעַת אֵין כְּלוּם, וְאַחַר-כָּךְ תְּשׁוּבָה וְכוּלֵי, כְּמוֹ שֶׁהֵם מְסֻדָּרוֹת.

וּבְשַׁבָּתוֹת וְיָמִים-טוֹבִים, כְּדֵי שֶׁלֹּא לְהַטְרִיחַ הַצִּבּוּר בְּיוֹם שִׂמְחָתָם, תִּקְּנוּ לְהִתְפַּלֵּל בָּהֶם שֶׁבַע בְּרָכוֹת לְבַד: שָׁלֹשׁ רִאשׁוֹנוֹת וְאַחֲרוֹנוֹת, וּבְרָכָה אַחַת בָּאֶמְצַע, שֶׁמַּזְכִּירִין בָּהּ עִנְיַן הַיּוֹם, כָּל מוֹעֵד וּמוֹעֵד וְשַׁבָּת כְּפִי עִנְיָנוֹ — זוּלָתִי בְּיוֹם-טוֹב שֶׁל רֹאשׁ הַשָּׁנָה, שֶׁיֵּשׁ בַּמּוּסָף שֶׁלּוֹ תֵּשַׁע בְּרָכוֹת: שָׁלֹשׁ רִאשׁוֹנוֹת וְשָׁלֹשׁ אַחֲרוֹנוֹת, וְשָׁלֹשׁ אֲחֵרוֹת, שֶׁהֵן מַלְכִיּוֹת זִכְרוֹנוֹת וְשׁוֹפָרוֹת, הַכֹּל כְּמוֹ שֶׁמְּקֻבָּל בְּפִי כָל יִשְׂרָאֵל, גַּם בְּפִי הַתִּינוֹקוֹת; אֵין צֹרֶךְ לַאֲרִיכוּת בַּדְּבָרִים אֵלּוּ.

וְאוּלָם יֵשׁ לְךָ לָדַעַת כִּי בִתְפִלַת מוּסַף רֹאשׁ הַשָּׁנָה יֵשׁ דִּין מְחַדֵּשׁ מִשְׁאָר תְּפִלּוֹת, שֶׁשְּׁלִיחַ-צִבּוּר מוֹצִיא בָּהֶן הַבָּקִי וְשֶׁאֵינוֹ בָקִי, וּבִשְׁאָר הַיָּמִים אֵינוֹ

---

13. See § 430, note 42.

14. The *sh'moneh 'esréh*, the central part of each daily service, recited silently, standing (*Daily Prayer Book*, ed. Birnbaum, pp. 81–97).

15. Added to the eighteen, within the *sh'moneh 'esréh* (ibid. p. 87); it was subsequently altered to refer to slanderers.

16. Of the eighteen benedictions in the *sh'moneh 'esréh*.

17. So TB B'rachoth 28b, M'gillah 17b.

18. See *Daily Prayer Book*, ed. Birnbaum, p. 85, middle.

19. In place of the *sh'moneh 'esréh*; TB B'rachoth 21a.

20. These six being the same as in the *sh'moneh 'esréh*, the weekday prayer.

21. Literally: called "sovereignties," "remembrances," and "shofars."

22. I.e. if they listen intently to the reader, responding to each benediction with *amén*, and intending that this should be in place of their own prayer, they need not say the *musaf* prayers themselves.

day of forgiveness and atonement for all. This is the one called the prayer of *ne'ilah* ("closing").

As to the entire text of the prayer, Ezra and his *beth din* (colleagues) formulated them.[13] In the weekdays they instituted the rule to say the prayer of the eighteen benedictions,[14] known in all corners of Jewry, and in addition, the benediction about sectarian heretics,[15] which Samuel the Younger instituted with the consent of Rabban Gamli'él and his *beth din* (supreme court), as we read in the tractate *M'gillah* (17b).

Three of them[16] relate the praise of the Eternal Lord, and three are acknowledgment and thanks before Him, while twelve contain the entreaty for the needs of every man in Jewry. The Sages of blessed memory arranged them in order as they are arranged today in the mouth of every Jew: the first three in praise of the Eternal Lord; the middle ones, with the entreaty for needs; and the final [three] in acknowledgment to God for all the good He did with us, blessed is He. Afterward, for a long time the exact way of their arrangement was forgotten; but Shim'on the cotton-dealer knew them, and he placed them in the correct order, as Ezra and his *beth din* had set them[17]—to pray first for knowledge, since that is first and foremost among all acquisitions, because if there is no knowledge, there is nothing. After that, [the benediction on] repentance, and so forth,[18] as they are arranged.

On the Sabbath and festival days, in order not to overburden the community on a day of its happiness, the sages instituted to say then a prayer of only seven benedictions:[19] three first ones, three last ones,[20] and one benediction in the middle, in which the theme of the day is mentioned—every single festival and the Sabbath, [each] according to its theme—except for the festival of *Rosh HaShanah*: In its *musaf* (additional) service there are nine benedictions: the three first ones and three last ones,[20] and three others, [centering respectively about Divine] sovereignty and remembrance, and the *shofar*[21] (§ 405)—all as traditionally received and accepted by every Jew, even by the children. There is no need to be lengthy about these matters.

However, you ought to know that for the *musaf* service of *Rosh haShanah* there is a new law which does not apply to other prayer-services: that [with his prayer] the reader of the congregation can acquit of their duty both someone versed [in the prayer] and someone unversed,[22] while on other days he cannot so acquit a person fluent [in

מוֹצִיא הַבָּקִי; כֵּן תִּמְצָא הָעִנְיָן אִם תִּזְכֶּה לִלְמֹד עַל דֶּרֶךְ הָאֱמֶת.
וְכֵן מֵעִנְיַן הַמִּצְוָה מַה שֶּׁהִזְהִירוּ אוֹתָנוּ בְּכַוָּנַת הַלֵּב הַרְבֵּה בַּתְּפִלָּה, וְיוֹתֵר
בִּבְרָכָה רִאשׁוֹנָה, שֶׁאָמְרוּ זִכְרוֹנָם לִבְרָכָה שֶׁמִּי שֶׁלֹּא כִוֵּן בָּהּ מַחֲזִירִין אוֹתוֹ. וְעִנְיַן
הַכַּוָּנָה זוֹ שֶׁחִיְּבוּ בִשְׁבִילָהּ חֲזָרָה, הִיא לְפִי הַדּוֹמֶה שֶׁיִּתֵּן הָאָדָם אֶל לִבּוֹ שֶׁלִּפְנֵי
הַשֵּׁם הוּא מִתְפַּלֵּל וְאֵלָיו הוּא קוֹרֵא, וְיַפְנֶה מַחֲשַׁבְתּוֹ מִכָּל שְׁאָר מַחְשֶׁבֶת הָעוֹלָם,
וִייַחֵד אוֹתָהּ עַל זֶה.

23. Since he can say it for himself; derived from TB Rosh haShanah 33b, 34b, 35a.

24. Derived from TB B'rachoth 30b, 34b (MY); MT hilchoth t'fillah x 1.

25. Similarly MT hilchoth t'fillah iv 16: What is the concentration?—that one should turn his heart away from all thoughts, and he should regard himself as though standing before the shechinah (Divine Presence).

Thus our author has followed here MT ibid. x 1 and iv 16. In the first of these sources Rambam writes, "If one has prayed [the sh'moneh 'esréh or t'fillath 'amidah] but did not focus his heart, he is to pray again, with concentration. But if he focused his heart in the first benediction [of the sh'moneh esréh or t'fillath 'amidah] he no longer needs [to repeat the prayer]." However, R. Ḥayyim of Brisk (Lithuania, 5613/1853–5678/1918) notes that in ibid. iv 1 Rambam lists the focus or concentration of the heart as one of five factors that prevent t'fillah (prayer) from being acceptable, if one of them is lacking; and in ibid. 15 Rambam writes further that "any t'fillah (prayer) which is without the focus of the heart is no prayer; and if one has prayed without concentration, he is to pray again, with concentration. If he finds his mind in disorder and his heart distressed, he is forbidden to pray until his mind settles." Hence R. Ḥayyim of Brisk finds a flat contradiction in MT hilchoth t'fillah: In iv 1 and 15 Rambam seems to rule that if heart and mind are not settled, focused and attuned for prayer, no part of the sh'moneh 'esréh or t'fillath 'amidah is acceptable; whereas in x 1 he writes that if there was proper concentration for the first benediction, there is no need to repeat the prayer (Maran Rabbénu Ḥayyim haLévi, Ḥiddushé...al haRambam, Brisk [Brest-Litovsk] 1936, fol. 1b–d).

Hence R. Ḥayyim of Brisk postulates two types of focus or concentration (kavvanah): (1) keeping one's mind on the meaning of the words spoken in prayer; (2) maintaining awareness that one is standing before the Eternal Lord in prayer, and there is no other reality. Without the second kind (continues R. Ḥayyim), one cannot be considered praying at all, but rather engaging in some idle mindless activity. Hence any prayer without this focused awareness is no prayer at all (MT iv 15). On the other hand (R. Ḥayyim argues) the first kind of kavvanah (concentration) is required only initially for all prayer; after the fact it is enough if the worshipper bore in mind the meaning of the words for the first benediction alone. If he failed to do so for any or all of the succeeding benedictions, there is no need to repeat the prayer (MT x 1).

If we accept this as Rambam's thesis, it places our author here clearly at variance   ⟨346⟩

the service] of his duty.²³ So you will find the matter if you merit to study in the way of the truth.

It is likewise of the subject-matter of the precept that the Sages cautioned us greatly about the concentration of the heart in the prayer, and especially so in the first benediction;¹⁶ for they (of blessed memory) ruled that if someone did not concentrate on it, he is to begin again.²⁴ The substance of this concentration, on account of which they required returning to the beginning, is, as it seems, that a man should realize in his heart that he is praying before the Lord and to Him he calls; he should turn his mind away from every other thought in the world and focus it on this.²⁵

with him: for our author states quite simply that the *kavvanah* needed during the first benediction of *sh'moneh 'esréh*, to free the worshipper from any obligation to repeat the prayer, is R. Ḥayyim's second type, not the first. In § 409, when MH believed that our author differed with Rambam, it was deemed a difficulty in *Séfer haḤinnuch*, a matter for query (see § 409 note 2). Hence, according to R. Ḥayyim's question and answer, this sentence in our text should likewise be considered a difficulty.

To my humble mind, however, the true answer to the problem lies in the precise meaning of the verb "pray" and the noun "prayer" as used in MT and the Talmudic passages on which Rambam's rulings are based. They clearly refer to the *sh'moneh 'esréh* or *t'fillath 'amidah* as a whole, in its entirety. This is patently evident from MT *hilchoth t'fillah* x 1: It states literally, "If one has prayed but did not focus his heart, he is to pray again, with concentration. But if he focused his heart in the first benediction, he no longer needs to [do so]." Indisputably Rambam refers here to the *sh'moneh 'esréh* (or *t'fillath 'amidah*) as an entity, in its entirety. Only this need not be repeated if the first benediction was said with *kavvanah*. Hence *ibid.* iv 1 must be similarly understood: The heart's focus is one of five factors which can prevent the prayer of *sh'moneh 'esréh* (etc.) from being acceptable — if this factor, *kavvanah*, was absent in the entire prayer, including the first benediction. Similarly *ibid.* x 15: "Any prayer [of *sh'moneh 'esréh*, etc.] which is [in entirety, including the first benediction] without the focus of the heart, is no prayer. And if one has prayed [said the *entire sh'moneh 'esréh*, etc.] without *kavvanah*, he is to pray [say it all] again, with *kavvanah*." (On the meaning of *t'fillah*, "prayer," in Talmudic usage, cf. the expression of "putting *ge'ulah* close to *t'fillah*," in TB B'rachoth 4b, 9b, etc. — which means saying the *sh'moneh 'esréh* or *t'fillath 'amidah* immediately, without interruption, after the benediction of *ge'ulah*, redemption: "Blessed art Thou, Lord, who redeemed the people Israel." Cf. too the way of *tosafoth* to TB B'rachoth 34b, s.v. *yechavén*, to resolve the apparently contradictory Talmudic passages on which Rambam's rulings are based.)

This approach would leave MT without contradictory rulings, and our author in complete harmony with MT. As regards R. Ḥayyim's postulate of two types of *kavvanah* in Rambam's thinking, it must be pointed out that in MT, Rambam writes

וּמַה שֶּׁאָמְרוּ שֶׁיֵּשׁ דְּבָרִים שֶׁהֵם מְעַכְּבִים הָאָדָם מֵהִתְפַּלֵּל אַף־עַל־פִּי שֶׁהִגִּיעַ זְמַן תְּפִלָּה, וּמֵהֶם טָהֳרַת הַיָּדַיִם וְכִסּוּי הָעֶרְוָה וְטָהֳרַת מְקוֹם הַתְּפִלָּה וּדְבָרִים הַחוֹפְזִין אוֹתוֹ, כְּגוֹן הַצָּרִיךְ לִנְקָבָיו.

וּמַה שֶּׁאָמְרוּ שֶׁיֵּשׁ דְּבָרִים שֶׁצָּרִיךְ הַמִּתְפַּלֵּל לְהִזָּהֵר בָּהֶן, אֲבָל אֵין מְעַכְּבִין הַתְּפִלָּה בִּשְׁבִילָם, וְאֵלּוּ הֵן: עֲמִידָה, וּלְכַוֵּן שֶׁיִּתְפַּלֵּל נֹכַח הַמִּקְדָּשׁ, וְשֶׁיְּתַקֵּן הַגּוּף כְּלוֹמַר שֶׁיַּעֲמֹד בְּיִרְאָה נָפֶּחַד, עֵינָיו לְמַטָּה וְלִבּוֹ לַשָּׁמַיִם וּמַנִּיחַ יָדָיו עַל לִבּוֹ כְּעֶבֶד הָעוֹמֵד לִפְנֵי רַבּוֹ, וְשֶׁיְּתַקֵּן מַלְבּוּשָׁיו וְלֹא יַעֲמֹד בְּלִבּוּשׁ דֶּרֶךְ הַהֶדְיוֹטוֹת, וְיַשְׁוֶה הַקּוֹל, לֹא גָּבוֹהַּ יוֹתֵר מִדַּי וְלֹא נָמוּךְ, וְיִכְרַע בַּבְּרָכוֹת הַיְּדוּעוֹת, וְאֵלּוּ הֵן: בְּאָבוֹת תְּחִלָּה וְסוֹף, וּבְהוֹדָאָה תְּחִלָּה וְסוֹף.

וּזְמַנֵּי הַתְּפִלּוֹת אֵלּוּ הֵן: תְּפִלַּת הַשַּׁחַר מֵהָנֵץ הַחַמָּה עַד סוֹף שָׁעָה רְבִיעִית, וּמִי שֶׁעָבַר וְהִתְפַּלֵּל אַחַר־כֵּן עַד חֲצוֹת יָצָא יְדֵי חוֹבַת תְּפִלָּה אֲבָל לֹא חוֹבַת תְּפִלָּה בִּזְמַנָּהּ; וּמִי שֶׁהִתְפַּלֵּל בִּשְׁעַת הַדֹּחַק, כְּגוֹן הָרוֹצֶה לְהַשְׁכִּים לַדֶּרֶךְ, תְּפִלַּת שַׁחֲרִית אַחַר שֶׁעָלָה עַמּוּד הַשַּׁחַר, יָצָא. וּתְפִלַּת הַמִּנְחָה מִשֵּׁשׁ שָׁעוֹת וּמֶחֱצָה בַּיּוֹם עַד הָעֶרֶב, וּתְפִלַּת הָעֶרֶב כָּל הַלַּיְלָה עַד שֶׁיַּעֲלֶה עַמּוּד הַשַּׁחַר. וְצָרִיךְ כָּל אָדָם לְהִזָּהֵר

only of R. Ḥayyim's second type (*ibid.* iv 16), and our author follows suit here. In *Guide* III 51, Rambam writes of saying words of prayer while thinking of business matters. There, however, both types of *kavvanah* postulated by R. Ḥayyim are lacking, and it cannot be adduced that Rambam considers R. Ḥayyim's first type as a separate form of required concentration. Only in *Séfer Mitzvoth Katan*, by the 13th-century R. Isaac of Corbeil, do we first find it: "What is the [proper, required] *kavvanah*?—that one should be mindful of the meaning of every word, and should take care not to skip any word, as though he were counting coins" (ed. Kapust 1830, §11; ed. Rosenberg, §12; cited in *Haggahoth Maimonioth* to MT *ibid.* iv 16). And in *Tur 'Oraḥ Ḥayyim*, §98 begins with both types, as R. Ḥayyim lists them.

It might be noted, however, that as early as the eighth century CE, R. Yehuda'i Ga'on expressed the view that the requirement of *kavvanah* applied only "in the early generations, for they could concentrate well when they prayed; but not in the present time" (*T'shuvoth haGe'onim* ed. Mussafia, §89; *T'shuvoth haGe'onim Sha'aré T'shuvah*, §89; cited verbatim in *Séfer ha'Eshkol*, ed. Auerbach, I p. 24; ed. Albeck, I p. 35). Similar views are given in *Haggahoth Maimonioth* to MT *hilchoth t'fillah* iv §20, citing *tosafoth*; in *Me'iri* to TB *B'rachoth*, 2nd ed. Dickman, p. 109b; and in *Tur 'Oraḥ Ḥayyim* §98, citing R. Meir of Rothenburg.

26. *Ibid.* i (sources given in *Kessef Mishneh*).

27. *Ibid.* v 1, explained there in the subsequent paragraphs.

28. I.e. when saying the *sh'moneh 'esréh*, or the shorter prayer in its place on the Sabbath and festivals.

29. The very first benediction (*Daily Prayer Book*, ed. Birnbaum, p. 81 bottom paragraph to p. 83, third Hebrew line). The knees are bent at the word "Blessed" in the phrase "Blessed art Thou," and the body bowed at "Thou."

There is, further, what the Sages said:[26] that there are matters which can prevent a man from praying even if the time for prayer has come: among them, the cleanness of the hands, the covering of exposed private parts of the body, the cleanness of the place of prayer, and matters which can confound one — for instance, if he needs to relieve himself.

Then there is what the Sages said:[27] that there are things about which the worshipper needs to be careful,[28] but prayer is not prevented on their account. These are: standing; to choose a direction so as to pray toward the Sanctuary; to prepare the body — in other words, that one should stand in fear and awe, his eyes down and his heart toward Heaven, and is to put his hands on his heart, like a servant standing before his master; he should set his clothing right, and not stand dressed in the way of undignified commoners; he should moderate his voice — not unduly high or low; and he should bend the knee at the known benedictions, these being the one about the Patriarchs,[29] at the beginning and at the end, and the one of acknowledgment,[30] at the beginning and at the end.

These are the times for the prayer-services: the morning prayer — from sunrise till the end of the fourth hour.[31] If someone passes [this time] and prays afterward, [in the period] till midday, he acquits himself of the duty of prayer, but not of the duty of prayer at its proper time.[32] If someone says [his] prayer under pressing circumstances — for example, one who wishes to rise early for a journey — [if he then says] the morning prayer after dawn has come up, he fulfills his obligation.[33] [The time for] minḥah, the afternoon prayer, is from six and a half hours in the day[34] till the evening.[35] [The time for] the evening prayer is the entire night, until dawn comes up;[35] but every man needs to be careful to say the prayer

30. Ibid. p. 91 middle to p. 93, next to last Hebrew line.

31. TB B'rachoth 9b, 26a, 27a. (As noted previously, an "hour" means one twelfth the period from the start to the end of the day; see § 420 note 6.)

32. MT hilchoth t'fillah iii 1.

33. TB B'rachoth 30a, and tosafoth there, s.v. 'avuha.

34. I.e. a half hour past midday, with midday reckoned as the midpoint between the start and end of the day; TB P'saḥim 58a. (Perhaps needless to say, the half hour too is reckoned on the basis indicated in § 420 note 6.)

35. TB B'rachoth 26a.

שֶׁיִּתְפַּלֵּל קֹדֶם שֶׁיִּתְעַסֵּק בִּמְלָאכוֹת אֲחֵרוֹת, כְּדֵי שֶׁלֹּא יִפְשַׁע.

וְדִין טָעָה וְלֹא הִתְפַּלֵּל תְּפִלָּה אַחַת, שֶׁמִּתְפַּלֵּל שְׁתַּיִם מִן הַסְּמוּכָה לָהּ; וְדִין הַמִּתְפַּלֵּל שֶׁלֹּא יַפְסִיק בִּשְׁבִיל כְּבוֹד שׁוּם אָדָם, וַאֲפִלּוּ מֶלֶךְ יִשְׂרָאֵל שׁוֹאֵל בִּשְׁלוֹמוֹ; וַאֲפִלּוּ נָחָשׁ כָּרוּךְ עַל עֲקֵבוֹ לֹא יַפְסִיק תְּפִלָּתוֹ, אִם יוֹדֵעַ וַדַּאי שֶׁהוּא מִן הַנְּחָשִׁים שֶׁאֵינָם מְמִיתִין. וְכֵן מֵעִנְיַן הַמִּצְוָה מַה שֶּׁאָמְרוּ שֶׁחַיָּב כָּל אָדָם לְחַזֵּר עַל כָּל־פָּנִים לִהְיוֹת מִתְפַּלֵּל עִם הַצִּבּוּר, שֶׁתְּפִלַּת הַצִּבּוּר נִשְׁמַעַת יוֹתֵר מִתְּפִלַּת יָחִיד. וְיֶתֶר פְּרָטֵי הַמִּצְוָה, מִתְבָּאֲרִים בְּמַסֶּכֶת בְּרָכוֹת בַּאֲרֻכָּה.

וְנוֹהֶגֶת מִצְוָה זוֹ בְּכָל מָקוֹם וּבְכָל זְמַן, בִּזְכָרִים וּנְקֵבוֹת. וְעוֹבֵר עַל זֶה וְעָמַד יוֹם וָלַיְלָה בְּלֹא תְּפִלָּה כְּלָל, בִּטֵּל עֲשֵׂה זֶה, כְּדַעַת מֹשֶׁה בֶּן מַיְמוֹן זִכְרוֹנוֹ לִבְרָכָה. וּמִי שֶׁצַּר לוֹ וְלֹא קָרָא אֶל הַשֵּׁם לְהוֹשִׁיעוֹ, בִּטֵּל עֲשֵׂה זֶה, כְּדַעַת הָרַב מֹשֶׁה בֶּן נַחְמָן זִכְרוֹנוֹ לִבְרָכָה; וְעָנְשׁוֹ גָּדוֹל, שֶׁהוּא כְּמֵסִיר הַשְׁגָּחַת הַשֵּׁם מֵעָלָיו.

[מִצְוַת הַחֶבְרָה וְהַדְּבִיקָה עִם חַכְמֵי הַתּוֹרָה]

תלד שֶׁנִּצְטַוֵּינוּ לְהִתְחַבֵּר וּלְהִתְדַּבֵּק עִם חַכְמֵי הַתּוֹרָה, כְּדֵי שֶׁנִּלְמַד עִמָּהֶם מִצְווֹתֶיהָ הַנִּכְבָּדוֹת וְיוֹרוּנוּ הַדֵּעוֹת הָאֲמִתִּיוֹת בָּהּ שֶׁהֵם מְקֻבָּלִים מֵהֶם, וְעַל זֶה נֶאֱמַר "וּבוֹ תִדְבָּק". וְנִכְפַּל הַצִּוּוּי בְּמָקוֹם אַחֵר, שֶׁנֶּאֱמַר "וּלְדָבְקָה בוֹ", וְאָמְרוּ זִכְרוֹנָם לִבְרָכָה: וְכִי אֶפְשָׁר לוֹ לְאָדָם לְהִדָּבֵק בַּשְּׁכִינָה, וְהָא כְתִיב: כִּי יי אֱלֹהֶיךָ אֵשׁ אֹכְלָה הוּא — אֶלָּא הִדָּבֵק לְתַלְמִידֵי־חֲכָמִים וּלְתַלְמִידֵיהֶם, כְּאִלּוּ נִדְבַּק בּוֹ בָּרוּךְ הוּא. וּמִזֶּה לָמְדוּ זִכְרוֹנָם לִבְרָכָה לוֹמַר שֶׁכָּל הַנּוֹשֵׂא בַּת תַּלְמִיד־חָכָם

36. *Ibid.* 14a.
37. Or the shorter prayer that replaces it on the Sabbath or a festival day.
38. Literally, asks after his welfare; TB B'rachoth 30b, 32b.
39. *Ibid.* 33a.
40. *Ibid.* 7b-8a.
41. See above, paragraph 5.

§434 1. This is the reading of the manuscripts and the first edition, עמהם, which is well borne out by ShM positive precept §6, the basis of this entire first paragraph. Later editions have מהם, "from them."
2. TB K'thuboth 111b.

before he occupies himelf with other tasks, so that he should not commit a wrong [by forgetting to pray].[36]

Then there is the law if someone erred and did not say one prayer-service, that he is to say the prayer [of sh'moneh esréh[37] in the service] directly after it, twice.[35] There is, too, the law about a person praying [the sh'moneh esréh][37] that he should not interrupt on account of the honor of any man, even if the king of Israel greets him;[38] and so even if a snake winds itself about his heels, he is not to interrupt his prayer [of sh'moneh esréh][37] if he knows for certain that it is one of the snakes that do not kill.[39] There is likewise in the subject-matter of the precept what the Sages said:[40] that every man is duty-bound to look about under all circumstances to pray with a congregation; for the prayer of a congregation is more heeded [in heaven] than the prayer of an individual. Other details of the precept are explained at length in the Talmud tractate B'rachoth.

This precept is in force everywhere, at every time, for both man and woman. If someone transgresses this and goes through a day and a night without any prayer at all, he disobeys this positive precept in the view of R. Moses b. Maimon of blessed memory.[41] If someone is in pressing trouble and he does not call to the Lord to rescue him, he disobeys this positive precept in the view of R. Moses b. Naḥman of blessed memory.[41] And his punishment will be great, because he is as one who removes the Eternal Lord's watchful care from him.

[THE MITZVAH OF ASSOCIATING WITH TORAH
SCHOLARS AND ADHERING TO THEM]

434 that we were commanded to join and cling to wise scholars of the Torah so that we may learn with them[1] its noble precepts and they may teach us the true concepts in it, which they received in the Oral Tradition. About this it is stated, *and to Him shall you cling* (Deuteronomy 10:20); the command was reiterated elsewhere, as it is stated, *and to cling to Him* (ibid. 11:22): but our Sages of blessed memory taught:[2] Is it then possible for a man to become attached to the *shechinah* (Divine Presence)? yet it is written, *for the Lord your God is a devouring fire* (ibid. 4:24)? It rather means that when one clings to Torah scholars and their disciples, it is as though he were bound to Him, blessed is He. From this our Sages of blessed memory inferred further to say[2] that whoever weds the daughter of a Torah scholar or gives his daughter to a Torah scholar in marriage, or has him benefit

וְהַמַּשִּׂיא בִּתּוֹ לְתַלְמִיד־חָכָם וּמְהַנֵּהוּ מִנְּכָסָיו, כְּאִלּוּ נִדְבָּק בַּשְּׁכִינָה. וְעוֹד דָּרְשׁוּ
בְּסִפְרִי: "וּלְדָבְקָה בּוֹ" — לְמַד דִּבְרֵי אַגָּדָה, שֶׁמִּתּוֹךְ כָּךְ אַתָּה מַכִּיר מִי שֶׁאָמַר
וְהָיָה הָעוֹלָם.

שֹׁרֶשׁ הַמִּצְוָה נִגְלֶה הוּא: כְּדֵי שֶׁנִּלְמַד לָדַעַת דַּרְכֵי הַשֵּׁם. וְדִינֵי הַמִּצְוָה, כְּבָר
זָכַרְתִּי קְצָתָן.

וְנוֹהֶגֶת מִצְוָה זוֹ בְּכָל מָקוֹם וּבְכָל זְמַן בִּזְכָרִים; וְגַם הַנְּקֵבוֹת מִצְוָה עֲלֵיהֶן גַּם־
כֵּן לִשְׁמֹעַ דִּבְרֵי חֲכָמִים, כְּדֵי שֶׁיִּלְמְדוּ לָדַעַת אֶת הַשֵּׁם. וְעוֹבֵר עַל זֶה וְאֵינוֹ
מִתְחַבֵּר עִמָּהֶם וְקוֹבֵעַ בְּלִבּוֹ אַהֲבָתָם וּמִשְׁתַּדֵּל בְּטוֹבָם וְתוֹעַלְתָּם בְּעֵצוֹת שֶׁיֵּשׁ
סָפֵק בְּיָדוֹ לַעֲשׂוֹת כֵּן, מְבַטֵּל עֲשֵׂה זֶה, וְעָנְשׁוֹ גָּדוֹל מְאֹד, כִּי הֵם קִיּוּם הַתּוֹרָה
וִיסוֹד חָזָק לִתְשׁוּעַת הַנְּפָשׁוֹת, שֶׁכָּל הָרָגִיל עִמָּהֶם לֹא בִמְהֵרָה הוּא חוֹטֵא. וְהַמֶּלֶךְ
שְׁלֹמֹה אָמַר "הוֹלֵךְ אֶת חֲכָמִים יֶחְכָּם", וְרַבּוֹתֵינוּ זִכְרוֹנָם לִבְרָכָה אָמְרוּ: הֱוֵי
מִתְאַבֵּק בַּעֲפַר רַגְלֵיהֶם.

וְהָרַב רַבֵּנוּ מֹשֶׁה בֶּן נַחְמָן זִכְרוֹנוֹ לִבְרָכָה כָּתַב כִּי עִקַּר מִצְוָה זוֹ הִיא לְהִשָּׁבַע
בִּשְׁמוֹ בָּרוּךְ הוּא לְקַיֵּם מִצְוָה, וְהָרְאָיָה מִמַּה שֶׁאָמְרוּ בַּתְּמוּרָה: מִנַּיִן שֶׁנִּשְׁבָּעִין
לְקַיֵּם הַמִּצְוָה — שֶׁנֶּאֱמַר "נִשְׁבַּעְתִּי וָאֲקַיֵּמָה לִשְׁמֹר מִשְׁפְּטֵי צִדְקֶךָ"; וְהֵשִׁיבוּ
שָׁם: הַהוּא מִ"וּבוֹ תִדְבָּק" נַפְקָא, וְכוּלֵי, כְּמוֹ שֶׁבָּא לְשָׁם.

[מִצְוָה עַל כָּל הַצָּרִיךְ לִשָּׁבַע שֶׁיִּשָּׁבַע בְּשֵׁם הַשֵּׁם]

תלה לְהִשָּׁבַע בִּשְׁמוֹ בָּרוּךְ הוּא בְּעֵת שֶׁנִּצְטָרֵךְ לְהַחֲזִיק וּלְקַיֵּם דָּבָר אוֹ
לְהַרְחִיקוֹ, לְפִי שֶׁיֵּשׁ בַּזֶּה גְּדֻלָּה בְּחֶקּוֹ וְהַגְּבוּרָה וְהָרוֹמְמוּת, וְעַל זֶה נֶאֱמַר: וּבִשְׁמוֹ
תִּשָּׁבֵעַ. וּבְבֵאוּר אָמְרוּ זִכְרוֹנָם לִבְרָכָה: אָמְרָה תּוֹרָה הִשָּׁבַע בִּשְׁמוֹ, וְאָמְרָה תּוֹרָה
אַל תִּשָּׁבַע — כְּלוֹמַר כִּי כְּמוֹ שֶׁהַשְּׁבוּעָה שֶׁאֵינָהּ צְרִיכָה הִיא נִמְנַעַת וְהִיא מִצְוַת

3. Sifre, Deuteronomy §49.
4. Literally, you will recognize.
5. Mishnah, 'Avoth i 4.
6. Ramban, commentary to ShM positive precept §7.
7. I.e. so to ensure that one will observe it.
8. I.e. in the version of the Talmud that Ramban had; our standard edition
differs somewhat.

§435   1. TB Sh'vu'oth 35b.
        2. Exodus 20:7.

from his wealth, it is as though he clings to the *shechinah*. They further interpreted in the Midrash *Sifre*:[3] "and to cling to Him" — learn the words of the homiletic, ethical teachings, for out of them you will come to know[4] the One who spoke, and the world came into existence.

The root purpose of the precept is obvious: it is in order that we may learn to know the ways of the Eternal Lord. As to the laws of the precept, I have previously mentioned some of them.

This precept is in effect everywhere, at every time, for men; and a religious duty lies on the women also to hear the words of Torah scholars, so that they will learn to know the Lord. If someone transgresses it and does not attach himself to them, setting an affection for them firmly in his heart, and striving for their good and their benefit at those times when he has the means to do so, he disobeys this positive precept, and his punishment will be very great: For they are the continuing maintenance of the Torah and a mighty foundation for the deliverance of the spirit. For whoever is familiar with them will not quickly sin. King Solomon said, *He who walks with wise men shall be wise* (Proverbs 13:20); and our Sages of blessed memory taught:[5] Wallow in the dust of their feet.

Now, R. Moses b. Naḥman of blessed memory wrote[6] that the main element of this precept is to swear by His name (blessed is He) to fulfill a *mitzvah* (religious duty);[7] and the proof lies in what the Sages said in the tractate *T'murah* (3b): Where do we learn that one should swear to fulfill a *mitzvah*? — because it is stated, *I have sworn and will fulfill it, to keep Thy righteous ordinances* (Psalms 119:106). But it was retorted there:[8] We derive that from the verse, *and to Him shall you cling*; and so forth, as we read there.

[THAT WHOEVER NEEDS TO TAKE AN OATH
SHOULD SWEAR BY THE NAME OF THE
ETERNAL LORD]

435 to swear by His name (blessed is He) at a time that we need to reinforce and confirm something, or to thrust it far away: for thus the greatness, power and exalted nobility of His law are manifested. About this it is stated, *and by His name shall you swear* (Deuteronomy 10:20); and in elucidation the Sages of blessed memory stated:[1] The Torah said, "Swear by His name," and the Torah [also] said, "Do not swear."[2] In other words, just as an unnecessary oath is prohibited, and

לֹא־תַעֲשֶׂה, כֵּן הַשְּׁבוּעָה בְּעֵת הַצֹּרֶךְ הִיא חוֹבָה וְהִיא מִצְוַת עֲשֵׂה.

וּלְפִיכָךְ אֵין נִשְׁבָּעִין לְעוֹלָם בְּשׁוּם דָּבָר מִכָּל הַנִּבְרָאִים; וְאָמְרוּ זִכְרוֹנָם לִבְרָכָה: כָּל הַמְשַׁתֵּף שֵׁם שָׁמַיִם וְדָבָר אַחֵר, נֶעֱקַר מִן הָעוֹלָם. וְאָמְנָם זֶה נֶאֱמַר בְּמִי שֶׁמְּכַוֵּן לְהַשְׁבִּיעַ בְּאוֹתוֹ דָּבָר מִן הַנִּבְרָאִין לְבַד, אֲבָל הַנִּשְׁבָּע בַּשָּׁמַיִם אוֹ בַּשֶּׁמֶשׁ וּבַיָּרֵחַ לְכַוָּנַת הָאָדוֹן שֶׁעֲלֵיהֶם שֶׁבְּרָאָם, זֶה אֵינוֹ בִּכְלַל הָאִסּוּר כְּלָל, וְתָמִיד נִרְאֶה שֶׁנִּשְׁבָּעִין כֵּן בְּכָל גְּבוּל יִשְׂרָאֵל.

מִשָּׁרְשֵׁי הַמִּצְוָה, כִּי בִּהְיוֹתֵנוּ מְקַיְּמִים דְּבָרֵינוּ בִּשְׁמוֹ הַגָּדוֹל, תִּתְחַזֵּק בְּלִבֵּנוּ הָאֱמוּנָה בּוֹ וְהַשְׁגָּחָתוֹ עָלֵינוּ וְעַל כָּל דְּבָרֵינוּ, וְזֶה דָּבָר בָּרוּר.

וּבְדִינֵי מִצְוַת הַשְּׁבוּעָה וְהַנְּדָרִים, הֶאֱרַכְתִּי בָּהֶם הַרְבֵּה בְּסֵדֶר וַיִּשְׁמַע יִתְרוֹ [סִי׳ ל׳].

וְנוֹהֶגֶת בְּכָל מָקוֹם וּבְכָל זְמַן, בִּזְכָרִים וּנְקֵבוֹת. וְעוֹבֵר עַל זֶה וְלֹא רָצָה לְהִשָּׁבַע בִּשְׁמוֹ לְעֵת הַצֹּרֶךְ, בִּטֵּל עֲשֵׂה זֶה לְדַעַת הָרַב רַבֵּנוּ מֹשֶׁה בֶּן מַיְמוֹן זִכְרוֹנוֹ לִבְרָכָה; אֲבָל הָרַב רַבֵּנוּ מֹשֶׁה בֶּן נַחְמָן זִכְרוֹנוֹ לִבְרָכָה כָּתַב שֶׁאֵין הַשְּׁבוּעָה בִּשְׁמוֹ גַּם בְּעֵת הַצֹּרֶךְ מִצְוַת עֲשֵׂה כְּלָל, כִּי־אִם רְשׁוּת גְּמוּרָה, שֶׁאִם נִרְצָה נִשָּׁבַע, וְאִם לֹא נִרְצָה לְהִשָּׁבַע לְעוֹלָם אֵין בְּכָךְ כְּלוּם; וְגַם כִּי יֵשׁ בְּמִנְיָנֵעָה מֵהַשְּׁבוּעָה מִצְוָה, וּכְעִנְיָן שֶׁאָמְרוּ בְּמִדְרַשׁ רַבִּי תַנְחוּמָא: אָמַר לָהֶם הַקָּדוֹשׁ בָּרוּךְ הוּא לְיִשְׂרָאֵל: לֹא תִהְיוּ סְבוּרִים שֶׁהֻתַּר לָכֶם לְהִשָּׁבַע בִּשְׁמִי אֲפִלּוּ בֶּאֱמֶת, אֶלָּא אִם־כֵּן יִהְיוּ בְךָ כָּל הַמִּדּוֹת הָאֵלֶה: "אֶת יְיָ אֱלֹהֶיךָ תִּירָא אֹתוֹ תַעֲבֹד וּבוֹ תִדְבָּק", וְאַחַר כָּךְ "וּבִשְׁמוֹ תִּשָּׁבֵעַ".

וְאִם נִרְצֶה, נוּכַל לוֹמַר שֶׁיָּבוֹא "וּבִשְׁמוֹ תִּשָּׁבֵעַ" לִתֵּן עֲשֵׂה וְלֹא־תַעֲשֵׂה לַנִּשְׁבָּע בְּשֵׁם עֲבוֹדָה זָרָה, כְּלוֹמַר בִּשְׁמוֹ תִּשָּׁבֵעַ וְלֹא בְּשֵׁם אֱלֹהִים אֲחֵרִים. וְעִנְיָן מַה שֶׁאָמְרוּ זִכְרוֹנָם לִבְרָכָה שֶׁנִּשְׁבָּעִין לְקַיֵּם הַמִּצְוָה, כְּבָר כָּתַב הָרַב זִכְרוֹנוֹ לִבְרָכָה כִּי מ"וּבוֹ תִדְבָּק" נַפְקָא לָן.

---

3. TB Sanhedrin 63a.

4. From the beginning to here is based on ShM positive precept §7.

5. Ramban, commentary to ShM *ibid.* (the source of Rambam's view).

6. Tanḥuma (and ed. Buber), *mattoth* 1.

7. So that in doing so he violates both.

it is a negative precept, so is an oath at a time of necessity and duty, and it is a positive precept.

For this reason, one may never swear by anything at all out of everything that was created; and the Sages of blessed memory said:[3] Whoever unites the [Divine] name of Heaven with something else [as deities] will be uprooted from the world.[4] In truth, though, this was said about a person who has the intention of swearing solely by that entity among all that was created; but if someone swears by heaven or the sun or the moon, meaning thus to signify the sovereign Ruler over them who created them, that is not included at all under this prohibition; and we always see that people swear so within every boundary of Jewry.

At the root of the precept lies the reason that when we affirm our [mundane] matters by His great name, in our heart will be strengthened [our] faith in Him and in His providential watch over us and over all our affairs. This is something clear and certain.

As to the laws of the precepts concerning oaths and vows, I wrote of them at abundant length in *sidrah yithro* (§ 30).

It is in effect everywhere, at every time, for both man and woman. If a person transgresses it and does not wish to swear by His name at a time of necessity, he disobeys this positive precept, in the view of R. Moses b. Maimon of blessed memory. However, R. Moses b. Naḥman of blessed memory wrote[5] that an oath by His name even at a time of necessity is not a positive precept at all, but only a completely voluntary matter: If he wishes, a person may take an oath; and if he never wishes to swear, it is no matter at all. Moreover, there is a *mitzvah* [religious way of behavior, observed] in refraining from oaths, in keeping with what was stated in the Midrash of R. Tanḥuma:[6] The Holy One, blessed is He, told the Israelites: Do not think it was permitted you to swear by My name even in truth, unless there are all these qualities in you: *You shall fear the Lord your God; Him shall you serve, and to Him shall you cling;* then, afterward, *and by His name shall you swear.*

Now, if we wish, we can say that the phrase "and by His name shall you swear" comes to apply both a positive and a negative precept to a person who swears by the name of an idol:[7] In other words, by His name shall you swears, and not by the name of other gods. As to what the Sages of blessed memory said, that one should take an oath to fulfill a *mitzvah,* the master scholar of blessed memory

רְאֵה אָנֹכִי ❧

יֵשׁ בָּהּ שְׁבַע־עֶשְׂרֵה מִצְוֹת עֲשֵׂה וּשְׁלֹשִׁים וּשְׁמוֹנֶה מִצְוֹת לֹא־תַעֲשֶׂה

[מִצְוָה לְאַבֵּד עֲבוֹדָה זָרָה וּמְשַׁמְּשֶׁיהָ]

תלו שֶׁנִּצְטַוִּינוּ לְאַבֵּד בָּתֵּי עֲבוֹדָה זָרָה כֻּלָּם בְּכָל מִינֵי אִבּוּד, בְּשַׁבָּרוֹן וּבִשְׂרֵפָה וּבַהֲרִיסָה וּבִכְרִיתָה, כָּל מִין בְּמַה שֶׁרָאוּי לוֹ, כְּלוֹמַר בְּמַה שֶׁיִּהְיֶה יוֹתֵר מַשְׁחִית וּמְמַהֵר בְּחֻרְבָּנוֹ, וְהַכַּוָּנָה שֶׁלֹּא נַנִּיחַ רֹשֶׁם לַעֲבוֹדָה זָרָה; וְעַל זֶה נֶאֱמַר "אַבֵּד תְּאַבְּדוּן אֶת כָּל הַמְּקֹמוֹת" וְגוֹמֵר, וְנֶאֱמַר גַּם־כֵּן "כִּי אִם כֹּה תַעֲשׂוּ לָהֶם מִזְבְּחֹתֵיהֶם תִּתֹּצוּ" וְכוּלֵּי, וְאָמַר עוֹד "וְנִתַּצְתֶּם אֶת מִזְבְּחֹתָם" וְגוֹמֵר.

וְהָרְאָיָה שֶׁזֶּה מִצְוַת עֲשֵׂה, מַה שֶּׁאָמְרוּ בְּסַנְהֶדְרִין: בַּעֲבוֹדָה זָרָה מַאי מִצְוַת עֲשֵׂה אִיכָּא, כְּלוֹמַר לְאַבְּדָהּ — תִּרְגְּמָהּ רַב חִסְדָּא "וְנִתַּצְתֶּם" וְגוֹמֵר; וּלְשׁוֹן סִפְרִי: מִנַּיִן אַתָּה אוֹמֵר שֶׁאִם קָצַץ אֲשֵׁרָה וְהֶחֱלִיפָה אֲפִלּוּ עֶשֶׂר פְּעָמִים, שֶׁחַיָּב אַתָּה לְקָצְצָהּ — תַּלְמוּד לוֹמַר "אַבֵּד תְּאַבְּדוּן" וְגוֹמֵר; וְנֶאֱמַר שָׁם עוֹד "וְאִבַּדְתֶּם אֶת שְׁמָם מִן הַמָּקוֹם הַהוּא": בְּאֶרֶץ־יִשְׂרָאֵל אַתָּה מְצֻוֶּה לִרְדֹּף אַחֲרֵיהֶם, וְאִי אַתָּה מְצֻוֶּה לִרְדֹּף אַחֲרֵיהֶם בְּחוּצָה לָאָרֶץ.

מִשָּׁרְשֵׁי הַמִּצְוָה, לִמְחוֹת שֵׁם עֲבוֹדָה זָרָה וְכָל זִכְרָהּ מִן הָעוֹלָם. וְדִינֶיהָ כְּלוּלִים בִּפְשָׁט הַכָּתוּב.

וְנוֹהֶגֶת בִּזְכָרִים וּנְקֵבוֹת בְּכָל מָקוֹם וּבְכָל זְמַן, שֶׁמִּצְוָה עָלֵינוּ לְאַבֵּד שֵׁם עֲבוֹדָה זָרָה אִם יֵשׁ כֹּחַ בְּיָדֵינוּ; אֲבָל אֵין אָנוּ חַיָּבִים לִרְדֹּף אַחֲרֵיהֶם לְאַבְּדָהּ אֶלָּא

---

8. See §434, last paragraph.

§436　　1. Sifre, Deuteronomy §60.
2. In the Hebrew the verb is repeated (literally, "Destroy shall you destroy"); hence it conveys a command to do so again and again if necessary.
3. *Ibid.* §61.
4. The first two paragraphs are based on ShM positive precept §185.

[Ramban] wrote previously that it is derived from the phrase, *to Him shall you cling* (Deuteronomy 10:20).[8]

sidrah re'éh

(Deuteronomy 11:26–16:17)
There are seventeen positive and thirty-eight negative precepts in it.

[THE PRECEPT TO DESTROY AN IDOL
AND ALL THAT SERVES IT]

436 that we were commanded to demolish the temples of idolatry, all of them, by every type of destruction: breakage, burning, smashing, chopping down — every kind by the way suited for it; in other words, by the way that will be most destructive and will hasten its demolition — the intention being that we should leave no trace of idolatry. About this it was stated, *You shall surely destroy all the places where the nations...served their gods*, etc. (Deuteronomy 12:2); it is stated likewise, *But thus shall you deal with them: you shall break down their altars*, etc. (ibid. 7:5); then it is stated further, *And you shall break down their altars*, etc. (ibid. 12:3).

Now, the proof that this is a positive precept lies in what was taught in the Talmud tractate *Sanhedrin* (90a): Regarding idol-worship, what positive precept is there — i.e. to destroy it? R. Ḥisda explained it: *And you shall break down their altars*, etc. In the language of the Midrash *Sifre:*[1] How would you learn to say that if someone cut down an 'Ashérah [an idolatrously worshipped tree] and it grew again, even ten times, you are duty-bound to cut it down? — Scripture states, *You shall surely destroy*, etc.[2] It was taught there further:[3] *and you shall destroy their name out of that place* (Deuteronomy 12:3) — in the land of Israel you are commanded to pursue them, but you are not commanded to pursue them outside the land.[4]

At the root of the precept lies the purpose of eradicating the name of idolatry and every memory of it from the world. Its laws are implicit in the plain meaning of the Writ.

It applies to both man and woman, in every place and every time; for it is a religious duty for us to destroy the name of an idol there, if it lies in our power. However, we are not obligated to go pursuing

בְּאֶרֶץ־יִשְׂרָאֵל בִּזְמַן שֶׁיָּדֵינוּ תַּקִּיפָה עַל עוֹבְדֶיהָ. וְעוֹבֵר עַל זֶה וְלֹא אִבְּדָהּ כָּל זְמַן שֶׁיֵּשׁ סְפֵק בְּיָדוֹ, בִּטֵּל עֲשֵׂה זֶה.

[שֶׁלֹּא לִמְחוֹת סִפְרֵי הַקֹּדֶשׁ וְהַשֵּׁמוֹת שֶׁל הַקָּדוֹשׁ בָּרוּךְ הוּא
הַכְּתוּבִים שָׁם וְכֵן בָּתֵּי עֲבוֹדַת הַקֹּדֶשׁ]

תל"ז שֶׁלֹּא נְאַבֵּד וְנִמְחֶה וְנַשְׁחִית הַדְּבָרִים שֶׁשֵּׁם הַקָּדוֹשׁ בָּרוּךְ הוּא נִקְרָא עֲלֵיהֶם, כְּגוֹן בֵּית־הַמִּקְדָּשׁ וְסִפְרֵי הַקֹּדֶשׁ וּשְׁמוֹתָיו הַיְקָרִים בָּרוּךְ הוּא; וְעַל כָּל זֶה נֶאֱמַר "לֹא תַעֲשׂוּן כֵּן לַיָי אֱלֹהֵיכֶם": אַחַר שֶׁקָּדַם הַמִּצְוָה לְאַבֵּד עֲבוֹדָה זָרָה וְלִמְחוֹת שְׁמָהּ וְלַהֲרֹס בָּתֶּיהָ וּמִזְבְּחוֹתֶיהָ כֻּלָּם, מָנַע וְאָמַר "לֹא תַעֲשׂוּן כֵּן לַיָי אֱלֹהֵיכֶם". וּבְסוֹף מַסֶּכֶת מַכּוֹת אָמְרוּ זִכְרוֹנָם לִבְרָכָה: מִי שֶׁשָּׂרַף עֲצֵי הֶקְדֵּשׁ לוֹקֶה, וְאַזְהָרָתֵיהּ מִ"וְאִבַּדְתֶּם אֶת שְׁמָם... לֹא תַעֲשׂוּן כֵּן" וְגוֹמֵר; וּכְמוֹ־כֵן אָמְרוּ שָׁם שֶׁהַמּוֹחֵק אֶת הַשֵּׁם לוֹקֶה, וְאַזְהָרָתֵיהּ מִזֶּה הַכָּתוּב בְּעַצְמוֹ.

שֹׁרֶשׁ הַמִּצְוָה נִגְלֶה, כִּי בְּגֶשֶׁת בְּנֵי־יִשְׂרָאֵל אֶל הַקֹּדֶשׁ בְּאֵימָה בְּרֶתֶת בְּזִיעַ, מִתּוֹךְ־כָּךְ יַכְנִיסוּ בִּלְבָבָם הַפַּחַד וְהַיִּרְאָה וְהַגְּדוֹלָה אֶל הַשֵּׁם בָּרוּךְ הוּא.

מִדִּינֵי הַמִּצְוָה, מַה שֶּׁאָמְרוּ זִכְרוֹנָם לִבְרָכָה שֶׁשִּׁבְעָה שֵׁמוֹת הֵם שֶׁהֵם בְּאִסּוּר לָאו זֶה, וְאֵלּוּ הֵם: שֵׁם שֶׁל יו"ד ה"א וא"ו ה"א, שֶׁיִּקְרָאוּ אוֹתוֹ חֲכָמִים שֵׁם הַמְפֹרָשׁ, וְכֵן הַשֵּׁם שֶׁנִּכְתָּב אל"ף דל"ת נו"ן יו"ד, וְאַל וֶאֱלוֹהַּ וֶאֱלֹהִים וְשַׁדַּי

§437 1. Literally, on which the Holy One, blessed is He, set His name.

2. I.e. if he burned for his own use logs intended (consecrated) for the altar fire.

3. The paragraph is based on ShM negative precept §65.

4. TB Sh'vu'oth 35a; MT *hilchoth yesodé torah* vi 2.

5. The most holy (ineffable) name, which since the destruction of the Sanctuary may not be pronounced as written, and is therefore read as the name spelled *'alef da-leth nun yod* ("Lord").

6. Rendered in English as "Lord."

7. All three are generally translated as *God*; the first, however, is understood by the early lexicographers to connote His might and power (R. Yonah ibn Janaḥ, and likewise R. David Kimḥi, *Séfer haShorashim*, s.v. *'a,y,l*; cf. Rashi to Psalms 36:7). For the Midrash, however, it denotes His aspect of mercy (apparently power used for compassion): Mechilta, *shirah* 3 (ed. Horovitz, p. 128) and MdRSbY (pp. 80 and 233) on Exodus 15:2 (cited by Ramban on the verse). Cf. on Numbers 13:12, Pseudo-Jonathan and the complete Targum Yerushalmi (from a MS Vatican), in *Torah Shelémah* vol. 38, p. 279b.

The second and third names are actually the same Divine appellation, in the singular and in the plural. They are understood by the Sages to denote His aspect of stern justice (Sifre, Deuteronomy §26 end, etc. and Midrashim cited above).

8. While this is generally translated as the Almighty, to the Sages and scholars of old it denotes the Divine Creator and Ruler who set boundaries and bounds to the

after them to eradicate it anywhere but in the land of Israel, at the time that our hand has power over its worshippers. If someone transgressed this and did not demolish it as long as he had the means, he would thus disobey this positive precept.

[NOT TO ERASE HOLY WRITINGS OR WRITTEN
NAMES OF THE HOLY ONE, NOR DESTROY
THE TEMPLES OF HOLY WORSHIP]

437 that we should not demolish or eradicate those entities with which the name of the Holy One, blessed is He, is linked[1]—for instance, the Sanctuary, sacred Torah scrolls and volumes, and His precious names (blessed is He). About all this it was stated, *You shall not do so to the Lord your God* (Deuteronomy 12:4). After the precept was previously given to demolish idol-worship and eradicate its name, and smash all its temples and altars, Scripture placed a restraint and said, "You shall not do so to the Lord your God." And toward the end of the Talmud tractate *Makkoth* (22a) the Sages of blessed memory taught: If someone burned hallowed logs,[2] he should receive whiplashes; the injunction is from the verses, *and you shall destroy their name... You shall not do so*, etc. (*ibid.* 3–4). So too, the Sages stated there that if someone erases the Divine name, he should receive lashes, and its injunction is from this very verse.[3]

The root reason for the precept is obvious: for when Israelites will approach [matters of] holiness in awe, trembling and quivering, as a result they will develop in their heart a great fear and reverence for the Eternal Lord, blessed is He.

Among the laws of the precept there is what the Sages of blessed memory taught:[4] that there are seven Divine names under the prohibition of this negative precept, these being: the name spelled *yod hé vav hé,* which the Sages call "the distinct Name" [the Tetragrammaton],[5] and likewise the name spelled *'alef da-leth nun yod,*[6] *'él, 'elo-ah, 'elo-him,*[7] *sha-dai,*[8] *'ehyeh 'asher 'ehyeh,* and *tz'va'oth.*[9]

elements of creation (B'réshith Rabbah 5, 4 and 46, 3), and whose Divinity suffices for the requirements of every creature (Rashi to Genesis 17:1; and see Rashi to Genesis 35:11).

9. Of these last two names, the first means "I shall be what (or who, or as) I shall be"; see Exodus 3:14. The second is generally translated "hosts" when it occurs as an ordinary word (e.g. in Deuteronomy 20:9). In *P'sikta Rabbathi* xxi (ed. Friedmann p. 104a) one Sage declares that this is the name of the Holy One, blessed

וְאֶהְיֶה אֲשֶׁר אֶהְיֶה, וּצְבָאוֹת. וְעוֹד אָמְרוּ זִכְרוֹנָם לִבְרָכָה שֶׁכָּל אוֹת שֶׁנִּטְפַּל לַשֵּׁם
מִלְּפָנָיו מֻתָּר לְמָחֳקָהּ, כְּגוֹן ל׳ מִ"לַיי", ב׳ מִ"בֵּאלֹהִים"; אֲבָל הַנִּטְפָּל לַשֵּׁם
מִלְּאַחֲרָיו, כְּגוֹן ךָ׳ שֶׁל אֱלֹהֶיךָ וְ"כֶם" שֶׁל אֱלֹהֵיכֶם וְכַיּוֹצֵא בָהֶם, אֵין נִמְחָקִים,
מִפְּנֵי שֶׁהַשֵּׁם מְקַדְּשָׁם.

וְהַכּוֹתֵב אֵל מֵאֱלֹהִים וְיָהּ מֵיָי, אֵינוֹ נִמְחָק, מִפְּנֵי שֶׁאֵלּוּ הֵן שֵׁמוֹת בִּפְנֵי עַצְמָן;
אֲבָל הַכּוֹתֵב שד מִשַּׁדַּי וְצב מִצְּבָאוֹת, הֲרֵי זֶה נִמְחָק. שְׁאָר הַכִּנּוּיִין שֶׁמְּשַׁבְּחִין
בָּהֶן הַשֵּׁם, כְּגוֹן רַחוּם וְחַנּוּן גָּדוֹל גִּבּוֹר נוֹרָא וְכַיּוֹצֵא בָהֶן, הֲרֵי הֵן כִּשְׁאָר כִּתְבֵי
הַקֹּדֶשׁ, שֶׁמֻּתָּר לְמָחֳקָן לְצֹרֶךְ שׁוּם דָּבָר.

וּמַה שֶּׁאָמְרוּ זִכְרוֹנָם לִבְרָכָה שֶׁכָּל כִּתְבֵי הַקֹּדֶשׁ וּפֵרוּשֵׁיהֶן בִּכְלַל אִסּוּר זֶה
מִדִּבְרֵי סוֹפְרִים, שֶׁאָסוּר לְאַבְּדָן וּלְשָׂרְפָן; וְכָל זֶה שֶׁאָמַרְנוּ, בִּשְׁכְּתָבָן יִשְׂרָאֵל,
אֲבָל כְּתָבָן מִין יִשְׂרָאֵל, שׂוֹרְפִין הַכֹּל, וּמֻתָּר וּמִצְוָה לְשָׂרְפָם, שֶׁלֹּא לְהַנִּיחַ שֵׁם
לַמִּינִין וּלְכָל מַעֲשֵׂיהֶם; אֲבָל גּוֹי שֶׁכָּתַב הַשֵּׁם, גּוֹנְזִין אוֹתוֹ.

וּמַה שֶּׁאָמְרוּ שֶׁכָּל הַשֵּׁמוֹת הָאֲמוּרִים בְּאַבְרָהָם בְּעִנְיַן הַמַּלְאָכִים שֶׁבָּאוּ אֵלָיו

is He; and another explains that "even one letter (*'oth*) of His name can form a host (*tzava'*, multitude, army), just like His entire name." This would seem to connect with the fact that in reference to Him, the word always follows another Divine name, and the two are then rendered "Lord of Hosts" or "God of Hosts." In *Mechilta*, *shirah* 1 (ed. Horovitz, p. 120) we find: "What is the sense of *tz'va'oth?* — He is the *'oth* (sign, ensign) amidst His *tzava'* (host, army)." Cf. the Sages' explanation of Hannah's use of the term in her prayer for a son, in I Samuel 1:11 (TB B'rachoth 31b; Midrash Sh'mu'él, ed. Buber, pp. 48–25a).

It should be noted that in the first edition, this last name is absent, while the name before last is found only in the first edition. It may be conjectured, however, that our author's original text was as given here, following MT *hilchoth yesodé haTorah* v 2 (evidently derived from TJ M'gillah i 11 [9], 71c; cf. *Halachoth G'doloth*, ed. Warsaw 1874 p. 281a, 1st ed. Hildesheimer p. 505), *its* correct text being as given in voweled ed. Mosad R. Kook (see note 2 there, and variorem ed. Mosad R. Kook, I p. 120, notes to lines 4–5). It may be suspected that, finding eight names here after our author prepared to list seven, some copyists omitted the last name, and some the penultimate one. The actual explanation for the eight instead of seven seems to lie in MT *ibid*. Instead of our author's "and likewise the named spelled *'alef da-leth*" etc. (after the first name), MT reads "or which is written *'alef da-leth*" etc. The second name is only a substitute for the first, and is not a separate, distinct appellation of the Creator (so explained in voweled ed. Mosad R. Kook, p. 31, note 1). Alternatively, confirming that in its correct reading MT does list our penultimate Divine name, R. David ibn Zimra explains that the eight are only seven because the fourth and fifth, as listed in our text, are (as remarked above in note 7) but the single and plural forms of the same Divine name (Radbaz, *Responsa*, V § 1407; reprinted in MT ed. Shulsinger, I, appendix: *liLshonoth haRambam*, 5).

　　10. TB Sh'vu'oth 35b; MT *ibid*. 3.

Our Sages of blessed memory taught further[10] that it is permissible to erase any letter attached to a Divine name before it [as a prefix]: for example, the *la-med* meaning "to" in the Hebrew word for "to the Lord," and the *beth* meaning "about" in the Hebrew word for "about God." But anything attached to a Divine name after it [as a suffix] — such as the final *chaf* (denoting "your") in the Hebrew word for "your God," and the final *chaf mem* (meaning "your" in the plural) in the Hebrew word "your God," and so forth — may not be erased, because the Divine name hallows them.[10]

If a person writes the letters *'alef la-med* of *'elo-him* or the letters *yod hé* of the Tetragrammaton,[11] that is not to be erased, since they are Divine names by themselves. But if someone writes the letters *shin da-leth* of *sha-dai*, or *tza-di béth* of *z'va'oth* ("Hosts"), that may be eradicated.[12] As to other, attributive names by which the Eternal Lord is extolled — such as Merciful One, gracious, great, mighty, awesome One, and so forth — they are like the rest of the sacred Writ, which it is permissible to erase for any particular purpose.[13]

Then there is what the Sages of blessed memory said:[14] that all Scripture and its commentaries are included under this prohibition by the decree of the Scribes, so that it is forbidden to destroy them or burn them. However, all this that we have said applies when an Israelite [a worthy Jew] wrote them; but if a Jewish sectarian heretic wrote them, all is to be burned. It is permissible — nay, a *mitzvah* (religious duty) — to burn them, not to leave a memorial for the sectarian heretics and any of their activities.[15] But if a heathen wrote the Divine name, it is to be hidden away.[16]

Then there is what the Sages said:[17] that all the names [of divinity] mentioned in connection with Abraham in the incident of the angels who came to him,[18] are sacred, while those occurring in connection

11. I.e. he intended to write a complete Divine name, but stopped after the first two letters (Rashi to TB *ibid.* s.v. *kathav*).

12. TB Sh'vu'oth 35b; MT *ibid.* 4.

13. TB *ibid.* MT *ibid.* 5.

14. TB Shabbath 115a (and see *tosafoth*, s.v. *'aliba*); tractate Sof'rim xvii 1; MT *ibid.* 8.

15. TB Shabbath 116a; MT *ibid.*

16. TB Gittin 45b; MT *ibid.*

17. TB Sh'vu'oth 35b; MT *hilchoth yesodé torah* vi 9.

18. Genesis 18; it specifically alludes to verse 3, where the name seems non-holy in the plain meaning.

קֹדֶשׁ, וְהָאֲמוּרִין בְּלוֹט חוֹל, חוּץ מֵאֶחָד: אַל נָא אֲדֹנָי הִנֵּה מָצָא עַבְדְּךָ חֵן בְּעֵינֶיךָ;
וְכָל הַשֵּׁמוֹת הָאֲמוּרִים בְּגִבְעַת בִּנְיָמִן קֹדֶשׁ, וְכָל הָאֲמוּרִים בְּמִיכָה (מֵהֶם) חוֹל,
(וּמֵהֶם קֹדֶשׁ: אֱל׳ חוֹל, יה׳ קֹדֶשׁ, חוּץ מֵאֶחָד שֶׁהוּא אֱל׳ וְהוּא קֹדֶשׁ: כָּל יְמֵי הֱיוֹת
בֵּית הָאֱלֹהִים בְּשִׁלֹה); וְכָל הָאֲמוּרִים בִּנְבוֹת קֹדֶשׁ; כָּל שְׁלֹמֹה הָאָמוּר בְּשִׁיר־
הַשִּׁירִים קֹדֶשׁ וְהוּא כִשְׁאָר הַכִּנּוּיִים, חוּץ מֵאֶחָד: הָאֶלֶף לְךָ שְׁלֹמֹה; כָּל מַלְכַּיָּא
הָאֲמוּרִין בְּדָנִיֵּאל חוֹל, חוּץ מֵאֶחָד: אַנְתְּ מַלְכָּא מֶלֶךְ מַלְכַיָּא—וַהֲרֵי הוּא כִשְׁאָר
הַכִּנּוּיִים; וְיֶתֶר פְּרָטֶיהָ, בְּמַסֶּכֶת שְׁבוּעוֹת.

וְנוֹהֵג אִסּוּר זֶה בְּכָל מָקוֹם וּבְכָל זְמַן, בַּזְּכָרִים וּנְקֵבוֹת. וְעוֹבֵר עַל זֶה וּמָחַק
אֲפִלּוּ אוֹת אַחַת מִשִּׁבְעָה הַשֵּׁמוֹת שֶׁזְּכַרְנוּ, חַיָּב מַלְקוֹת; וְאִם סָתַר אוֹת אַחַת מִן
הָאוֹתִיּוֹת הַנִּטְפָּלוֹת לְאַחֲרֵיהֶן, מַכִּין אוֹתוֹ מַכַּת מַרְדּוּת. וְכֵן הַסּוֹתֵר אֲפִלּוּ אֶבֶן
אַחַת דֶּרֶךְ הַשְׁחָתָה מִן הַמִּזְבֵּחַ אוֹ מִן הַהֵיכָל אוֹ מִשְּׁאָר הָעֲזָרָה, חַיָּב מַלְקוֹת.

[מִצְוָה לְהַקְרִיב כָּל הַקָּרְבָּנוֹת שֶׁיֵּשׁ עַל הָאָדָם בְּחוֹבָה אוֹ בִנְדָבָה]

בְּרֶגֶל רִאשׁוֹן שֶׁפּוֹגֵעַ בּוֹ]

תלח שֶׁכָּל מִי שֶׁנָּדַר אוֹ הִתְנַדֵּב שׁוּם קָרְבָּן לַמִּזְבֵּחַ אוֹ שׁוּם דָּבָר לְבֶדֶק הַבַּיִת
בְּתוֹךְ הַשָּׁנָה, שֶׁיָּבִיא אוֹתוֹ בָּרֶגֶל שֶׁפָּגַע רִאשׁוֹן אַחַר נִדְרוֹ, שֶׁנֶּאֱמַר: וּבָאתָ שָּׁמָּה
וַהֲבֵאתֶם שָׁמָּה עֹלֹתֵיכֶם וְגוֹמֵר; "וְנִדְרֵיכֶם" זֶה נֶדֶר, כְּלוֹמַר דַּאֲמַר "הֲרֵי עָלַי
קָרְבָּן", וּלְעוֹלָם חַיָּב בְּאַחֲרָיוּתוֹ עַד שֶׁיַּקְרִיב אוֹתוֹ; "וְנִדְבֹתֵיכֶם" זוֹ נְדָבָה, כְּגוֹן
דַּאֲמַר "הֲרֵי זוֹ עוֹלָה", וְאִם נֶאֶבְדָה אֵינוֹ חַיָּב בְּאַחֲרָיוּתָהּ.

19. Genesis 19.

20. Judges 20.

21. Judges 17–18.

22. This is the reading of the oldest manuscripts, in agreement with MT *hilchoth yesodé torah* vi 9, giving the first view in TB Sh'vu'oth 35b. The printed editions read: As for all those occurring about Micah, some are non-holy and some are sacred: *'alef la-med* [i.e. the Divine name beginning with these letters; see three paragraphs above] is non-holy, while *yod hé* [i.e. the Divine name that begins with these letters] is holy—except for one occurrence of *'alef la-med* which is sacred: *all the time that the house of God was at Shiloh* (Judges 18:31). This is the view of R. 'Eli'ezer in TB Sh'vu'oth 35b. See *Minhath Shai* to Judges 17.

23. I Kings 21.

24. Alluding to the Almighty as the Master of *shalom*, peace.

25. MT *hilchoth yesodé torah* vi 3; see § 24, note 14.

26. MT *ibid*. 7.

§438   1. The exact meaning is explained below.
        2. I.e. to fulfill his vow; if the animal he designates for his offering should die,

with Lot[19] are non-holy, except for one: *Not so, pray, my Lord; pray behold, Thy servant has found grace in Thy sight* (Genesis 19:18–19). All names of divinity mentioned in regard to Gebeah of Benjamin[20] are sacred;[17] all those occurring about Micah[21] are non-holy.[22] Now, all those mentioned in regard to Naboth[23] are sacred.[17] Every occurrence of the name Sh'lomoh (Solomon) in the *Song of Songs* is sacred,[24] being like other attributive Divine names—except for one: *you, O Solomon, shall have the thousand* (Song of Songs 8:12).[17] Every mention of "kings" in the Book of Daniel is non-holy, except for one: *Thou, O King, King of kings* (Daniel 2:37); that is like the other attributive Divine names.[17] The rest of its details are in the Talmud tractate *Sh'vu'oth.*

This precept is in force everywhere, at every time, for both man and woman. If someone transgresses it and erases even one letter of the seven Divine names that we mentioned, he is punishable by whiplashes. If he eradicates one of the letters attached to them as suffixes, he should be given lashes for disobedience.[25] So too if a person demolished, in a destructive way, even one stone of the altar, the *héchal* (Temple "palace"), or elsewhere in the Temple forecourt, he would be punishable by whiplashes.[26]

[TO BRING ALL OBLIGATORY OR VOLUNTARY
OFFERINGS AT THE FIRST PILGRIMAGE FESTIVAL
THAT COMES ALONG]

438 that whoever has vowed or volunteered any offering for the altar,[1] or anything toward maintaining the Temple in repair, during the year, he is to bring it at the pilgrimage festival that occurs first after his vow: for it is stated, *and thither you shall come; and thither you shall bring your 'olah (burnt) offerings…your votive offerings and your freewill offerings*, etc. (Deuteronomy 12:5–6). "Your votive offerings" means [by] a vow, i.e. if someone said, "The obligation of an offering hereby lies upon me"; he then bears responsiblity for it forever,[2] until he offers it up. "Your freewill offerings" denotes a voluntary gift: for example, if a person said, "This is hereby to be an 'olah (burnt-offering)"; if it was then lost, he bears no obligation of responsibility about it.[3]

etc. his obligation continues: he must designate another animal, and yet another if necessary, until the offering is sacrificed.

וְאָמְרוּ בְסִפְרִי: "וּבָאתָ שָׁמָּה וַהֲבֵאתֶם שָׁמָּה", לְקָבְעָם חוֹבָה לַהֲבִיאָם בָּרֶגֶל רִאשׁוֹן; וְכֵן מַשְׁמָעוּת הַכָּתוּב: מִיָּד שֶׁתָּבוֹא שָׁמָּה, דְּהַיְנוּ רֶגֶל רִאשׁוֹן, וְהֵבֵאתָ הַקָּרְבָּן.

מִשָּׁרְשֵׁי הַמִּצְוָה, לְפִי שֶׁאֵין רָאוּי לוֹ לְאָדָם שֶׁיִּתְעַצֵּל בְּמַה שֶׁנָּדַר לַעֲשׂוֹת מִצְוָה, כַּיָּדוּעַ בֵּין בְּנֵי־אָדָם שֶׁזְּהִירִים הַרְבֵּה בְּמַה שֶׁיֵּשׁ לָהֶם לַעֲשׂוֹת בְּמִצְוַת מַלְכֵי אֶרֶץ, כָּל־שֶׁכֵּן מִצְוַת מֶלֶךְ מַלְכֵי הַמְּלָכִים הַקָּדוֹשׁ בָּרוּךְ הוּא. וּמִכָּל־מָקוֹם לֹא תַטְרִיחֵנּוּ הַתּוֹרָה לַעֲלוֹת מִיָּד, פֶּן יִמָּנְעוּ בְנֵי־אָדָם מִנְּדָרִים וּנְדָבוֹת, אֲבָל בָּרֶגֶל שֶׁיֵּשׁ לָהֶם לַעֲלוֹת שָׁם יַזְהִירֵם לְשַׁלֵּם נִדְרָם. וּלְעִנְיָן לַעֲבֹר עֲלֵיהֶם בְּ"בַל תְּאַחֵר" אֵינוֹ אֶלָּא עַד שְׁלֹשָׁה רְגָלִים, וּכְמוֹ שֶׁנִּכְתֹּב בְּעֶזְרַת הַשֵּׁם בְּסֵדֶר כִּי־תֵצֵא בְּמִצְוָה ט"ו בְּסִימָן (תקמ"ו) [תקע"ה].

מִדִּינֵי הַמִּצְוָה, (כְּגוֹן) מַה שֶׁאָמְרוּ זִכְרוֹנָם לִבְרָכָה בְסִפְרֵי: "וּבָאתָ שָׁמָּה וַהֲבֵאתֶם שָׁמָּה", לֹא נֶאֱמַר אֶלָּא לְקָבְעָם חוֹבָה, שֶׁיּוּבְאוּ בָּרֶגֶל רִאשׁוֹן שֶׁפָּגַע בּוֹ. וְשָׁם אָמְרוּ: אֵינוֹ עוֹבֵר עָלָיו בְּבַל תְּאַחֵר עַד שֶׁיַּעַבְרוּ עָלָיו שָׁלֹשׁ רְגָלִים, אֲבָל מִכָּל־מָקוֹם, מִכֵּיוָן שֶׁעָבַר רֶגֶל אֶחָד וְלֹא הֵבִיא, עוֹבֵר בַּעֲשֵׂה; וְכֵן אָמַר רָבָא בַּגְּמָרָא דְּרֹאשׁ הַשָּׁנָה בְּפֵרוּשׁ. וְיֶתֶר פְּרָטֶיהָ, שָׁם בְּרֹאשׁ הַשָּׁנָה.

וְנוֹהֶגֶת מִצְוָה זוֹ בִּזְמַן הַבַּיִת, שֶׁאָז לָנוּ רְשׁוּת לַעֲשׂוֹת נְדָרִים וּנְדָבוֹת, וְהָיָה לָנוּ מָקוֹם לְהַקְרִיב; אֲבָל בַּזְּמַן הַזֶּה אָמְרוּ זִכְרוֹנָם לִבְרָכָה שֶׁאֵין מַקְדִּישִׁין, וּכְעִנְיָן שֶׁכָּתַבְתִּי בְּסֵדֶר אִם בְּחֻקֹּתַי עֲשֵׂה רִאשׁוֹן בְּסִימָן ש"נ. וַאֲפִלּוּ מִי שֶׁעָבַר וְהִקְדִּישׁ, אֵין סְפֵק בְּיָדוֹ הַיּוֹם לַהֲבִיאוֹ לַמִּקְדָּשׁ, לְפִי שֶׁהַבַּיִת חָרֵב בַּעֲוֹנוֹתֵינוּ.

3. Since his obligation, by his vow, extends no further than the animal he chose; Mishnah, Kinnim i 1.

4. Sifre, Deuteronomy §63.

5. TB Yoma 16a, etc.

Now, it was taught in the Midrash *Sifre*:[4] "and thither you shall come, and thither you shall bring" — this is to establish them as an obligation to bring them at the first pilgrimage festival. And this is indeed the plain sense of the verses: as soon as you come there, i.e. at the first pilgrimage festival, you shall bring the offering.

At the root of the precept lies the reason that it is not seemly for a man to be indolent about a religious duty that he vowed to do, as it is known among people: For they are greatly conscientious regarding something they have to do by the order of the kings of the earth; then all the more certainly [should it be] so about a commandment from the supreme King over kings, the Holy One, blessed is He. Yet, nevertheless, the Torah does not burden a person to go up at once, for then people might refrain from vowed and freewill offerings. At the pilgrimage festival, however, when they have to go up there (§ 489), He adjures them to fulfill their vows. Yet as regards their transgressing the injunction, *you shall not be slack to fulfill it* (Deuteronomy 23:22), that does not occur until [after] three pilgrimage festivals, as we will write, with the Eternal Lord's help, in the fifteenth [positive] precept of *sidrah ki thétzé* — § 575.

Among the laws of the precept there is, for example, what the Sages of blessed memory said in the Midrash *Sifre*:[4] "and thither you shall come, and thither you shall bring" — this was stated only to fix an obligation about them, that they are to be brought at the first pilgrimage festival that comes along. Then they said there:[4] One does not transgress over it the injunction, *you shall not be slack to fulfill it* (*ibid.*) until three pilgrimage festivals have passed by for him. Yet, nevertheless, once one pilgrimage festival has passed by and he still has not brought it, he has transgressed a positive precept; and so Rava said distinctly in the Talmud tractate *Rosh haShanah* (6a). The rest of its details are there, in the tractate *Rosh haShanah*.

This precept is in effect at the time that the Temple exists: for then we had the right to vow votive and freewill offerings, and we had the place to offer them up. At the present time, though, the Sages of blessed memory said[5] that nothing is to be consecrated — in keeping with what I wrote in the first positive precept in *sidrah b'ḥukothai* (§ 350). And even if someone should transgress and consecrate something, he does not have the ability today to bring it to the Sanctuary, since the Temple is destroyed, for our sins.

[שֶׁלֹּא לְהַעֲלוֹת קָדָשִׁים בַּחוּץ]

תלט שֶׁלֹּא לְהַקְרִיב שׁוּם דָּבָר מֵהַקָּרְבָּנוֹת חוּץ לָעֲזָרָה, וְזֶה יִקָּרֵא מַעֲלֶה בַּחוּץ, וְעַל זֶה נֶאֱמַר "הִשָּׁמֶר לְךָ פֶּן תַּעֲלֶה עֹלֹתֶיךָ בְּכָל מָקוֹם"; פֵּרוּשׁ עֲלִיָּה — שְׂרֵפָה.

וְאָמְרוּ בְּסִפְרֵי: אֵין לִי אֶלָּא עוֹלוֹת; שְׁאָר קָדָשִׁים מִנַּיִן — תַּלְמוּד לוֹמַר "וְשָׁם תַּעֲשֶׂה כֹל אֲשֶׁר אָנֹכִי מְצַוֶּךָ"; וַעֲדַיִן אֲנִי אוֹמֵר עוֹלָה בַּעֲשֵׂה, שֶׁהַכָּתוּב אוֹמֵר "שָׁם תַּעֲלֶה [עֹלֹתֶיךָ]", דְּמַשְׁמַע עוֹלָה לְבַד, וְכֵן הִיא גַּם־כֵּן בְּלֹא־תַעֲשֶׂה, שֶׁהַכָּתוּב אוֹמֵר "הִשָּׁמֶר לְךָ פֶּן תַּעֲלֶה [עֹלֹתֶיךָ]", דְּמַשְׁמַע עוֹלָה לְבַד; שְׁאָר קָדָשִׁים לֹא יְהוּ אֶלָּא בַּעֲשֵׂה, כְּלוֹמַר שֶׁהַמַּקְרִיב קָדָשִׁים בַּחוּץ לֹא יְהֵא עוֹבֵר אֶלָּא בַּעֲשֵׂה, שֶׁאָמַר הַכָּתוּב "וְשָׁם תַּעֲשֶׂה" וְגוֹמֵר, דְּמַשְׁמַע וְשָׁם תַּעֲשֶׂה וְלֹא בַחוּץ, וְלָאו הַבָּא מִכְּלַל עֲשֵׂה, עֲשֵׂה — תַּלְמוּד לוֹמַר: "שָׁם תַּעֲלֶה עֹלֹתֶיךָ"; עוֹלָה בַּכְּלָל הָיְתָה, וְלָמָּה יָצָאת — לְהַקִּישׁ אֵלֶיהָ וְלוֹמַר לְךָ: מָה עוֹלָה מְיֻחֶדֶת שֶׁהִיא בַּעֲשֵׂה וְלֹא־תַעֲשֶׂה, כָּךְ כָּל שֶׁהוּא בַּעֲשֵׂה הֲרֵי הוּא בְּלֹא־תַעֲשֶׂה.

כָּל עִנְיָנָהּ כְּמוֹ דִּזְבִיחָה בַּחוּץ, שֶׁכָּתַבְתִּי בְּאַחֲרֵי־מוֹת לָאו ב', בְּסִימָן (קפ"ז) [קפ"ו].

[מִצְוָה לְהַקְרִיב כָּל הַקָּרְבָּנוֹת בְּבֵית הַבְּחִירָה וְלֹא בַחוּץ]

תם שֶׁנִּצְטַוֵּינוּ לְהַקְרִיב כָּל קָרְבָּן בְּבֵית הַמִּקְדָּשׁ וְלֹא בַחוּץ, וְעַל זֶה נֶאֱמַר "כִּי אִם בַּמָּקוֹם אֲשֶׁר יִבְחַר יְיָ" וְגוֹמֵר "שָׁם תַּעֲלֶה עֹלֹתֶיךָ וְשָׁם תַּעֲשֶׂה כֹל אֲשֶׁר אָנֹכִי

§439   1. It is a Talmudic rule that every occurrence of "take heed," "lest" or "do not" indicates a negative precept; TB 'Eruvin 96a, Sh'vu'oth 7a.

2. Sifre, Deuteronomy §70.

3. Since only they are mentioned in the verse.

4. Indicating that the restriction to the Sanctuary applies to all offerings.

5. In verse 14, *and there you shall do all that I command you* — which includes the sacrifice of this offering too.

6. I.e. for a separate positive commandment in the same verse.

7. From the beginning to here is based on ShM negative precept §89.

439 not to offer up any of the offerings at all outside the Temple forecourt, this being called "sacrificing outside"; about this it is stated, *Take heed to yourself that you do not offer up your burnt-offerings at every place* (Deuteronomy 12:13)[1] — the meaning of "offering up" being burning.

Now, it was taught in the Midrash *Sifre*:[2] I thus know this about nothing but *'olah* (burnt) offerings;[3] how do I learn it about other offerings? — Scripture states, *and there you shall do all that I command you (ibid.* 14).[4] Yet I would still say that *'olah* (a burnt-offering) is under a positive precept, since Scripture states, *there you shall offer up your burnt-offerings (ibid.)*, which would apply only to the *'olah*, and so is it likewise under a negative precept, since Scripture states, *Take heed to yourself that you do not offer up your burnt-offerings*, which would apply only to the *'olah*; but other offerings should be under no more than a positive precept *(ibid.* 14)? In other words, a person who offers up holy sacrifices outside [the domain of the Sanctuary] shall have transgressed only a positive precept, because the Writ says, *and there you shall do*, etc. *(ibid.* 14), which means, there you shall do [the offering up] and not outside [the sacred precincts]; and an injunction derived from a positive precept is [has the force of] a positive precept. Hence Scripture states, *there you shall offer up your burnt-offerings*: the *'olah* (burnt-offering) was included in the general category [of offerings];[5] why was it then singled out?[6] — to equate [others] to it and to tell you: just as the particular law about the *'olah* is that it is under both a positive and a negative precept, so every [offering] that is under the positive precept is [also] under a negative one.[7]

Its entire subject-matter is like that of the injunction against the ritual slaying [of offerings] outside [the Temple precincts], of which I wrote in the second negative precept in *sidrah aḥaré moth* (§ 186).

[THE PRECEPT TO SACRIFICE ALL OFFERINGS
AT THE SANCTUARY, AND NOT ANYWHERE
OUTSIDE IT]

440 that we were commanded to present every offering at the Sanctuary and not outside it; about this it was stated, *but at the place which the Lord will choose...there you shall offer up your burnt-offerings, and*

מְצֻוֶּךְ"; וְכֵן הוּא בְּסִפְרִי: אֵין לִי אֶלָּא עוֹלוֹת, שְׁאָר קָדָשִׁים מִנַּיִן, תַּלְמוּד לוֹמַר
"וְשָׁם תַּעֲשֶׂה כֹּל" וְגוֹמֵר; וַעֲדַיִן אֲנִי אוֹמֵר עוֹלָה בַּעֲשֵׂה וְלֹא־תַעֲשֶׂה — פֵּרוּשׁ,
עֲשֵׂה זֶה שֶׁזָּכַרְנוּ, וְלָאו מִמַּה שֶּׁנֶּאֱמַר בַּפָּרָשָׁה "הִשָּׁמֶר לְךָ פֶּן תַּעֲלֶה עֹלֹתֶיךָ בְּכָל
מָקוֹם אֲשֶׁר תִּרְאֶה", שֶׁהִזְכִּיר "עֹלֹתֶיךָ" בְּפֵרוּשׁ, אֲבָל שְׁאָר קָדָשִׁים לֹא יְהוּ אֶלָּא
בַּעֲשֵׂה — תַּלְמוּד לוֹמַר "שָׁם תַּעֲלֶה" וְכוּלֵי, כְּמוֹ שֶׁבָּא לְשָׁם, וּכְמוֹ שֶׁנִּכְתְּבָה בְּסֵדֶר
זֶה בְּלָאו שֵׁנִי [סי׳ תל"ט] בְּעֶזְרַת הַשֵּׁם. וּכְלָל הָעִנְיָן, שֶׁאֲפִלּוּ בִּשְׁאָר קָדָשִׁים
הַמַּקְרִיבִין בַּחוּץ עוֹבֵר בַּעֲשֵׂה וְלֹא־תַעֲשֶׂה, וְחַיָּבִין עֲלֵיהֶן כָּרֵת.

מִשָּׁרְשֵׁי הַמִּצְוָה, כִּי בִּהְיוֹת מָקוֹם מְיֻחָד בָּעוֹלָם לְקָרְבָּנוֹת, וְהַהִתְמָדָה בּוֹ לְבַקֵּשׁ
מִשָּׁם אֶת הַשֵּׁם אֱלֹהֶיךָ, יִתְקַדֵּשׁ הַמָּקוֹם וְנָחָה עָלָיו רְצוֹן הָאֵל, וְשֶׁפַע בִּרְכָתוֹ
שׁוֹפֵעַ עָלָיו תָּמִיד, וְיִהְיוּ לְבָבוֹת בְּנֵי־אָדָם מִתְפַּחֲדִים וּמִתְרַכְּכִים לְזָכְרוֹ, וְיָשׁוּב כָּל
אִישׁ מִדַּרְכּוֹ הָרָעָה וּמִן הֶחָמָס אֲשֶׁר בְּכַפָּיו בִּרְאוֹתוֹ אוֹתוֹ. וְאִם כָּל הַמְּקוֹמוֹת
יִכְשְׁרוּ לְהַקְרָבָה, לֹא יִהְיֶה כֵן בְּכֻלָּן, יָדוּעַ הַדָּבָר. וְזֶה נֹאמַר אֶל הַיְלָדִים עַד אֲשֶׁר
יִגְדְּלוּ בְחָכְמָה וְיָבִינוּ בְּכָל דִּבְרֵי הַתּוֹרָה סוֹדוֹת נִפְלָאִים.

דִּינֵי הַמִּצְוָה, בְּלָאו שֵׁנִי שֶׁבְּסֵדֶר זֶה [סי׳ תל"ט] נִכְתַּב קְצָת מֵהֶם; וְיֶתֶר
פְּרָטֶיהָ, בְּסוֹף מַסֶּכֶת זְבָחִים.

וְנוֹהֶגֶת מִצְוָה זוֹ בִּזְכָרִים וּנְקֵבוֹת בְּכָל מָקוֹם וּבְכָל זְמַן; אֶרֶצָה לוֹמַר שֶׁהָעוֹבֵר
עַל זֶה אֲפִלּוּ בַזְּמַן הַזֶּה וְהִקְרִיב קָרְבָּן חוּץ לְבֵית הַבְּחִירָה, שֶׁהוּא מְבַטֵּל עֲשֵׂה,
וְעוֹבֵר עַל לָאו הַבָּא עַל זֶה, כְּמוֹ שֶׁנִּכְתַּב לְמַטָּה בְּסֵדֶר זֶה לָאו שֵׁנִי [סי׳ תל"ט];
אֲבָל אֵין הַכַּוָּנָה לוֹמַר שֶׁיִּהְיֶה עָלֵינוּ חִיּוּב לְהַקְרִיב קָרְבָּן בְּבֵית הַמִּקְדָּשׁ עַכְשָׁיו
שֶׁהוּא חָרֵב, זֶה דָּבָר בָּרוּר.

§440   1. Sifre, Deuteronomy §70; as our author writes below, this was quoted and explained in §439, q.v.

2. See §439, note 1.

3. From the beginning to here is somewhat based on ShM positive precept §84.

4. While in this edition, as in all editions after the third, the *mitzvoth* are arranged in the order of the verses of Scripture from which they are derived, the author wrote first on all the positive precepts in each *sidrah*, and then on the negative. Hence, in his original, this occurs below, while here it is found earlier.

5. This is the reading of the oldest manuscript and the first edition; in the three other manuscripts and all editions after the first, the last Hebrew word (= "your God") is lacking.

there you shall do all that I command you (Deuteronomy 12:14). And so we read in the Midrash *Sifre*:[1] I thus know it only about '*olah* (burnt) offerings; how do we learn it about other offerings?—Scripture states, "and there you shall do," etc. Yet I could still say that the '*olah* (burnt-offering) is thus under both a positive and a negative precept—i.e. this positive commandment that we mentioned, and the negative one, since it is stated in the section of Scripture, *Take heed to yourself that you do not offer up your burnt-offerings at every place that you see* (ibid. 13),[2] which mentions "your burnt-offerings" distinctly—but other holy offerings should be under no more than a positive precept? Hence Scripture states, *there you shall offer up*, etc.[3] as it is conveyed there, and as we will write in this *sidrah*, in the second negative precept (§ 439) with the help of the Lord.[4] The crux of the matter is that even if other holy offerings are sacrificed outside [the Temple grounds], both a positive and a negative precept are transgressed, and it is punishable by *karéth* [Divine severance of existence].

At the root of the precept lies the reason that when there was a particular place in the world for offerings, and constant activity there to *seek from there the Lord your God*[5] (Deuteronomy 4:29), the location was hallowed, the [benevolent] will of God rested upon it, and the flow of His blessing would pour down to it constantly. And thus the heart of people would be fearful and grow soft upon remembering it, and every man would return in repentance from his evil way and from the booty of violence in his possession, upon seeing it. But if all locations were made acceptable for presenting offerings, it would not be so with them all—this is something known (evident). This reason, though, we address to the children, until they mature in wisdom and will understand wondrous mysteries in all the words of the Torah.

As to the laws of the precept, in the second negative precept in this *sidrah* (§ 439) we will write a few of them.[4] The rest of its details are toward the end of the tractate *Z'vahim*.

This precept applies to both man and woman, in every place and time—by which I mean that if someone transgresses it even at the present time and sacrifices outside the chosen Temple, he disobeys this positive precept, and he violates the injunction that applies to it, as we will write below in this *sidrah*, in the second negative precept (§ 439).[4] But the intention is not to convey that an obligation lies upon us to present an offering at the Sanctuary now, when it is demolished. This

⟨369⟩ is something quite clear.

[מִצְוַת פְּדִיַּת קָדָשִׁים שֶׁנָּפַל בָּהֶם מוּם וְאַחַר־כָּךְ מַתִּרִים בַּאֲכִילָה]

תמא שֶׁנִּצְטַוֵּינוּ לִפְדּוֹת קָדָשִׁים שֶׁנָּפַל בָּהֶם מוּם, וְלוֹקְחִין בִּדְמֵיהֶן בְּהֵמָה אַחֶרֶת לְקָרְבָּן, וְאַחַר הַפִּדְיוֹן הֵם יוֹצְאִין לְחֻלִּין, וְזוֹבְחִים וְאוֹכְלִין אוֹתָן הַבְּעָלִים כְּחֻלִּין גְּמוּרִים; וְעַל זֶה נֶאֱמַר "רַק בְּכָל אַוַּת נַפְשְׁךָ תִּזְבַּח וְאָכַלְתָּ בָשָׂר" וְגוֹמֵר "הַטָּמֵא וְהַטָּהוֹר יֹאכְלֶנּוּ כַּצְּבִי וְכָאַיָּל": אַחַר שֶׁהִזְכִּירָה הַפָּרָשָׁה הַקָּרְבָּנוֹת הַתְּמִימִים, וְחִיְּבָה שֶׁלֹּא לְהַקְרִיבָם כִּי־אִם בַּמָּקוֹם אֲשֶׁר יִבְחַר יְיָ, נֶאֱמַר אַחֲרֵי־כֵן עַל הַקָּרְבָּנוֹת בְּעַצְמָם שֶׁאִם נָפַל בָּהֶם מוּם שֶׁנִּפְדָּם וְנֹאכְלֵם בְּכָל אַוַּת נַפְשֵׁנוּ, כְּלוֹמַר שֶׁנַּעֲשֶׂה בָהֶם כָּל חֶפְצֵנוּ כְּמוֹ בִצְבִי וְאַיָּל, שֶׁאֵין גּוּפָן קָדוֹשׁ לְעוֹלָם; וְכֵן בָּא אֵלֵינוּ הַפֵּרוּשׁ הַמְקֻבָּל שֶׁאֵינוֹ מְדַבֵּר זֶה הַפָּסוּק אֶלָּא בִּפְסוּלֵי הַמֻּקְדָּשִׁין שֶׁיִּפָּדוּ.

מִשָּׁרְשֵׁי הַמִּצְוָה, שֶׁהָיָה מֵחַסְדֵי הָאֵל עָלֵינוּ לְהַרְשׁוֹת אוֹתָנוּ לֵהָנוֹת מִבֶּהֱמוֹת הַקָּרְבָּן אַחַר שֶׁנָּפַל בָּהֶם מוּם; וְאַף־עַל־פִּי שֶׁכְּבָר נִפְרְשׁוּ לִהְיוֹת קֹדֶשׁ וְכָח שֵׁם שָׁמַיִם חָל עֲלֵיהֶם, צַדִּיק הוּא הַשֵּׁם וּצְדָקָה יַעֲשֶׂה עִם בְּרִיּוֹתָיו, וְשֵׁבֶט מַלְכוּתוֹ וְרוֹמְמוּתוֹ יָקַל מֵעֲלֵיהֶם, וְלֹא יְדַקְדֵּק עִמָּם לֵאמֹר "אַל תִּגְּעוּ בַּקֹּדֶשׁ מֵאַחַר שֶׁהָיָה לִי אֲפִלּוּ רֶגַע אֶחָד".

וְעוֹד הִפְלִיא חַסְדּוֹ עִמָּנוּ וְחִיְּבָנוּ בַּדָּבָר בְּמִצְוַת עֲשֵׂה, שֶׁאִלּוּ הִנִּיחַ הַדָּבָר בִּרְשׁוּתֵנוּ לְבַד, אוּלַי עֲדַיִן נָחוּשׁ מִדֶּרֶךְ חֲסִידוּת לִגַּע בָּהֶן, אֲבָל לְאַחַר שֶׁיֵּשׁ קִיּוּם מִצְוָה בַּדָּבָר לֹא יִשָּׁאֵר שׁוּם חֲשָׁשׁ בָּעִנְיָן; וּמִטַּעַם זֶה בֵּאֵר הַכָּתוּב בְּאוֹר רָחָב לֵאמֹר "הַטָּמֵא וְהַטָּהוֹר יֹאכְלֶנּוּ כַּצְּבִי וְכָאַיָּל", כְּלוֹמַר שֶׁאֵין קַדְשַׁת הַגּוּף חָלָה עֲלֵיהֶם לְעוֹלָם, כְּלוֹמַר אָכְלוּהוּ מִבְּלִי פִקְפּוּק כְּלָל.

דִּינֵי הַמִּצְוָה, כְּגוֹן מַה שֶׁאָמְרוּ זִכְרוֹנָם לִבְרָכָה שֶׁאִם מֵתָה הַבְּהֵמָה קֹדֶם

---

§441
1. I.e. exchange them for money, to free them of their consecration.

2. Sifre, Deuteronomy §71.

3. I.e. redeeming them is not something we may do, but rather something we are obligated to do.

4. TB T'murah 32a (and Rashi), etc.

441 that we were commanded to redeem [animals consecrated for] holy offerings which have acquired a blemishing defect,[1] and for their money another animal is bought for an offering; then after their redemption they emerge non-holy, and their owners may ritually slay and eat them as completely non-holy food. About this it was stated, *Only with all the desire of your soul may you slay and eat flesh…the unclean and the clean may eat it, like a gazelle and a hart* (Deuteronomy 12:15). After the Scriptural section mentions whole, unblemished offerings and imposes the duty to offer them nowhere *but at the place which the Lord shall choose* (*ibid.* 14), it is then stated about the offerings themselves that if they acquired a blemishing defect, we should redeem them and eat them "with all the desire of our soul"; in other words, we may do with them whatever we wish, as with a gazelle and a hart, whose bodies can never be holy. So the traditional interpretation came down to us,[2] that this verse speaks of nothing other than disqualified consecrated animals—that they are to be redeemed.

At the root of the precept lies the thought that it was of God's loving-kindness to permit us to benefit from animals for offerings after they became blemished. Although they were previously set apart to be holy, and the force of the name of Heaven became attached to them, the Eternal Lord is righteous, and He acts charitably with His human beings; He lightens for them the burden of His sovereignty and exalted nobility, and is not exacting with them, to say, "Do not touch the sacred thing, since it was Mine, if even for a moment."

Indeed, He extended His kindness with us further, and gave us the duty to fulfill a positive precept in the matter.[3] For had He left the matter to our free choice alone, we might perhaps have yet been reluctant, from the aspect of piety, to touch them. However, since there lies in the matter the fulfillment of a religious duty, no misgivings could remain for us about the question. For this reason Scripture gave a broad elucidation, saying, *the unclean and the clean shall eat it, like a gazelle and like a hart* — which is to say that a holiness of the body can never take effect on them. In other words, eat it without any qualms at all.

The laws of the precept are, for example, what the Sages of blessed memory said:[4] that if the animal died before it was redeemed,

שֶׁתִּפָּדֶה, תִּקָּבֵר, כְּדִין קָדָשִׁים הַתְּמִימִים שֶׁמֵּתִים, שֶׁהֵם נִקְבָּרִים, שֶׁלֹּא יֵהָנֶה אָדָם
בָּהֶם, שֶׁאִי אֶפְשָׁר לִפְדּוֹתָהּ אַחַר מִיתָה, שֶׁהַכָּתוּב הִצְרִיכָהּ הַעֲמָדָה וְהַעֲרָכָה, כְּמוֹ
שֶׁכָּתַבְתִּי בְּסֵדֶר אִם בְּחֻקֹּתַי עֲשֵׂה ג' בְּסִימָן (שנ"ב) [שנ"ג].

וְאִם יָלְדָה קֹדֶם פִּדְיוֹן, הַוָּלָד שֶׁהוּא תָמִים מַקְרִיבִין אוֹתוֹ; אֲבָל אִם נִתְעַבְּרָה
קֹדֶם שֶׁתִּפָּדֶה וְיָלְדָה אַחַר שֶׁנִּפְדֵּית, הַוָּלָד אָסוּר וְאֵינוֹ נִפְדֶּה; אֶלָּא כֵּיצַד יַעֲשֶׂה:
סָמוּךְ לְפִדְיוֹן אִמּוֹ, מַתְפִּיס וָלָד לְשֵׁם הַזֶּבַח שֶׁהִקְדִּישׁ אִמּוֹ, לְפִי שֶׁאֵינוֹ יָכוֹל
לְהַקְרִיבוֹ מִכֹּחַ אִמּוֹ, מִפְּנֵי שֶׁהִיא קָדְשָׁה דְחוּיָה מֵחֲמַת מוּמָהּ.

וְכָל פְּסוּלֵי הַמֻּקְדָּשִׁים כְּשֶׁיִּפָּדוּ מֻתָּר לִשְׁחֹט אוֹתָם בְּשׁוּק הַטַּבָּחִים וְלִמְכֹּר
אוֹתָם שָׁם וְלִשְׁקֹל בְּלִיטְרָא כִּשְׁאָר הַחֻלִּין, חוּץ מִן הַבְּכוֹר וּמִן הַמַּעֲשֵׂר, שֶׁאֵין
שׁוֹחֲטִין אוֹתָן שָׁם וְאֵין מוֹכְרִין אוֹתָם שָׁם; וְטַעַם הַדָּבָר, מִפְּנֵי שֶׁשְּׁאָר קָדָשִׁים
חוֹזְרִין דְּמֵיהֶם לַהֶקְדֵּשׁ, שֶׁחוֹזְרִין וְקוֹנִים בָּהֶם בְּהֵמָה אַחֶרֶת לְקָרְבָּן, וּלְפִיכָךְ,
שֶׁלֹּא לְמַעֵט בִּדְמֵיהֶן, מוֹכְרִין אוֹתָם בְּכָל מָקוֹם; אֲבָל הַבְּכוֹר וְהַמַּעֲשֵׂר שֶׁנֶּאֱכָלִין
בְּמוּמָן וְאֵין צָרֵךְ לִקְנוֹת בִּדְמֵיהֶם בְּהֵמָה אַחֶרֶת לְקָרְבָּן, אֵין שׁוֹחֲטִין וּמוֹכְרִין אוֹתָן
בְּשׁוּק שֶׁל טַבָּחִים. וּבְעִנְיַן הַמּוּמִין הַפּוֹסְלִין בְּקָרְבָּן כְּבָר דִּבַּרְתִּי בָּהֶן בְּסֵדֶר אֱמֹר
[סִי' רפ"ו]. וְיֶתֶר פְּרָטֵי הַמִּצְוָה, מְבֹאָרִים בְּמַסֶּכֶת בְּכוֹרוֹת וּבִתְמוּרָה וּבִמְקוֹמוֹת
מֵחֻלִּין וַעֲרָכִין וּמְעִילָה.

וְנוֹהֶגֶת מִצְוָה זוֹ בִּזְכָרִים וּנְקֵבוֹת בִּזְמַן הַבַּיִת; אֲבָל עַכְשָׁו בַּזְּמַן הַזֶּה, אָמְרוּ
זִכְרוֹנָם לִבְרָכָה שֶׁאֵין מַקְדִּישִׁין, וְהוּא הַדִּין שֶׁאֵין פּוֹדִין, וְכָל הָעִנְיָן כְּמוֹ שֶׁכָּתַבְתִּי
בְּסֵדֶר אִם בְּחֻקֹּתַי עֲשֵׂה ש"נ, בְּסִימָן א' בְּסִימָן ש"נ, קָחֶנּוּ מִשָּׁם. וְאַף־עַל־פִּי שֶׁכָּתַבְתִּי שָׁם
שֶׁמִּי שֶׁהִקְדִּישׁ אֲפִלּוּ בַּזְּמַן הַזֶּה שֶׁהֶקְדֵּשׁוֹ נִתְפָּס וְצָרִיךְ תַּקָּנָה לַדָּבָר, כְּמוֹ שֶׁכָּתוּב

5. Because the consecrated state of the dam applies to it too; TB B'choroth 15b.

6. It may not be offered up, since the dam's state of consecration was terminated; and not being consecrated, it cannot be redeemed; *ibid.*

7. *Ibid.*

8. Once a firstling or a tithe animal becomes blemished, it simply loses its holy
state; no obligation remains to offer it up, or any replacement for it. Hence there is
no need to sell it and buy another animal with the money; and thus the only
consideration that remains is to prevent ritually slaying it or selling it in the
butcher's market, so that the mistaken impression should not arise that unblemished
consecrated animals may be treated thus; TB B'choroth 31a–b.

it is to be buried, as the law is for whole, unblemished [animals consecrated for] holy offerings which died—that they are to be buried, so that no man can derive benefit from them—because it is not possible to redeem it after death, since the Writ requires having it stand and be appraised, as I wrote in the third positive precept in *sidrah b'ḥukothai* (§ 353).

If it gave birth before redemption, the young, being unblemished, is offered up.[5] If, however, it became pregnant before redemption and gave birth after it was redeemed, the young is forbidden and may not be redeemed.[6] Then what should one do instead? Shortly before the redemption of the dam (mother) he is to make the young consecrated for the sacrifice for which he had consecrated its dam. For he cannot offer it up on the strength of [the hallowed state of] the dam, since that is a consecration thrust aside on account of its defect.[7]

All disqualified consecrated animals, when they have been redeemed, are permitted to be ritually slain in the market of the butchers, and to be sold there, [the meat] weighed by the pound, like other non-holy meat—except a firstling and an animal of the tithe: They may not be ritually slain there and may not be sold there. The reason for that is that with other [animals intended for] holy offerings, the money for them is turned over to the treasury of consecration, since another animal is in turn bought for it, for an offering. Therefore, in order not to lessen their price, they may be sold anywhere. As to a firstling and an animal of the tithe, however, which may be eaten in their blemished state, and there is no need to buy another animal for an offering with their monetary value, they may not be ritually slain or sold in the butchers' market.[8] As to those defects which disqualify an animal as an offering, I spoke of them previously in *sidrah 'emor* (§ 286). The remaining details of the precept are clarified in the Talmud tractates *B'choroth* and *T'murah*, and in certain places in *Ḥullin*, *'Arachin* and *Me'ilah*.

This precept applies to both man and woman, at the time the Temple exists. As for now, however, at the present time, the Sages of blessed memory taught that nothing is to be consecrated, and so is it the law that nothing is to be redeemed. The entire subject is as I wrote in *sidrah b'ḥukothai*, in the first positive precept (§ 350); gather it from there. Now, although I wrote there that if a person consecrates something even at the present time, his act of consecration takes effect and a rectification for the matter is necessary, as noted there,

שָׁם, מִכָּל־מָקוֹם לְעִנְיַן הַפְּדִיָּה יֵשׁ לָנוּ לִכְתֹּב שֶׁאֵינָהּ נוֹהֶגֶת בַּזְּמַן הַזֶּה בְּשׁוּם צַד, וּכְעִנְיָן שֶׁכָּתַבְתִּי שָׁם בְּדִין עֶרְכֵּי בְהֵמָה בְּמִצְוָה ג' בְּסִימָן (שנ"ב) [שנ"ג], מִשָּׁם תִּרְאֶה הָעִנְיָן.

[שֶׁלֹּא לֶאֱכֹל מַעֲשֵׂר שֵׁנִי שֶׁל דָּגָן חוּץ לִירוּשָׁלַיִם]

תמב שֶׁלֹּא לֶאֱכֹל מַעֲשֵׂר שֵׁנִי שֶׁל דָּגָן חוּץ לִירוּשָׁלַיִם, וְעַל זֶה נֶאֱמַר "לֹא תוּכַל לֶאֱכֹל בִּשְׁעָרֶיךָ מַעְשַׂר דְּגָנְךָ", וְהַכָּתוּב הַבָּא אַחֲרָיו יוֹרֶה עָלָיו שֶׁבְּמַעֲשֵׂר שֵׁנִי הוּא מְדַבֵּר, שֶׁנֶּאֱמַר "כִּי אִם לִפְנֵי [יי אֱלֹהֶיךָ תֹּאכְלֶנּוּ] ... אַתָּה וּבִנְךָ וּבִתֶּךָ וְעַבְדְּךָ וַאֲמָתֶךָ", וְאִלּוּ שְׁאָר מַעַשְׂרוֹת לַלְוִיִּם אוֹ לָעֲנִיִּים הֵם. וְעִנְיַן מַעֲשֵׂר שֵׁנִי מַהוּ, כָּתַבְתִּי לְמַעְלָה בְּסֵדֶר זֶה עָשֹׂה י' [סי' תע"ג], וְטַעַם הֱיוֹתוֹ נֶאֱכָל בִּירוּשָׁלַיִם כָּתַבְתִּי בְּסֵדֶר אִם בְּחֻקֹּתַי בְּמִצְוַת מַעֲשֵׂר בְּהֵמָה עָשֹׂה ז', בְּסִימָן (שנ"ו) [ש"ס].

דִּינֵי הַמִּצְוָה, כְּגוֹן מַה שֶּׁאָמְרוּ זִכְרוֹנָם לִבְרָכָה, שֶׁאֵין חַיָּבִין מַלְקוּת עַל אֲכִילָתוֹ אֶלָּא־אִם־כֵּן יֹאכְלוּ אוֹתוֹ בְּלִי פִדְיוֹן אַחַר שֶׁרָאָה פְּנֵי הַבַּיִת; וְכֵן אָמְרוּ בְּסוֹף מַכּוֹת: מֵאֵימָתַי חַיָּבִין עָלָיו—מִשֶּׁיִּרְאֶה פְּנֵי הַבַּיִת. וּכְבָר הִרְחַבְתִּי דְּבָרַי בְּדִינֵי קְבִיעוּת פֵּרוֹת לְמַעֲשֵׂר בְּסֵדֶר וַיִּקַּח קֹרַח עָשֹׂה ד', בְּסִימָן (שצ"א) [שצ"ה], וְשָׁם תִּרְאֶנּוּ אִם תַּחְפֹּץ. וְיֶתֶר פְּרָטֵי הַמִּצְוָה, מְבֹאָרִים בְּמַסֶּכֶת מַעֲשֵׂר שֵׁנִי.

וְנוֹהֵג אִסּוּר זֶה בִּזְכָרִים וּנְקֵבוֹת, בִּזְמַן שֶׁחִיּוּב מַעֲשֵׂר שֵׁנִי נוֹהֵג, וּבְסֵדֶר שֹׁפְטִים עָשֹׂה ו' בְּסִימָן (תצ"ו) [תק"ז] נְבָאֵר בְּעֶזְרַת הַשֵּׁם הַזְּמַן וְהַמְּקוֹמוֹת שֶׁנּוֹהֵג שָׁם. וְעוֹבֵר עַל זֶה וְאָכַל כַּזַּיִת מִמֶּנּוּ חוּץ לִירוּשָׁלַיִם חַיָּב מַלְקוּת.

9. As MY clarifies it, in §353 our author deals with the use of a method of rectification·formulated by Sh'mu'él, to release a consecrated creature from its state of holiness — if, although forbidden to do so, a man has gone and declared an animal consecrated to the altar. That can be necessary in the present as well: see our author's penultimate sentence. The point of *this* precept, however, is to redeem a blemished consecrated animal in order to buy a replacement for it and offer that upon the altar; and this procedure cannot and must not be carried out at the present time.

§442
    1. Respectively, the first and the third.

    2. In his original our author wrote first on all the positive precepts in each *sidrah*, and then on the negative; hence he wrote this earlier. In this edition, as in most Hebrew editions, the precepts are arranged in the order of their sources in Scripture; hence this comes below.

    3. Literally, after it has seen the face of the Temple; i.e. after it has entered within the city walls.

nevertheless, as regards redemption we certainly have to write that it is not in effect at the present time in any way. It is in keeping with what I wrote there about the law of valuations of an animal, in the third positive precept (§ 353); from that you will see the substance of it.[9]

[THE PROHIBITION AGAINST EATING THE SECOND
TITHE OF GRAIN OUTSIDE JERUSALEM]

442 not to eat the Second Tithe of grain outside of Jerusalem; about this it is stated, *You may not eat within your gates the tithe of your grain* (Deuteronomy 12:17); and the verse which follows it shows about it that it speaks of the Second Tithe: for it is stated, *but you shall eat them before the Lord your God...you and your son and your daughter, and your manservant and your maidservant* (ibid. 18) — whereas the other tithes[1] are for the Levites and for the poor. Regarding the substance of the Second Tithe, what it is, I have written above in this *sidrah,* in the tenth positive precept (§ 473).[2] And the reason why it is to be eaten in Jerusalem, I wrote in *sidrah b'hukothai,* in the seventh positive precept, about the animal tithe (§ 360).

The laws of the precept are, for example, what the Sages of blessed memory taught: that a flogging of whiplashes is not incurred for eating it unless it is eaten without redemption after it has come within sight of the Temple.[3] And so it was taught toward the end of the Talmud tractate *Makkoth* (19b); From what time is the punishment incurred for it? — from when it comes within view of the Temple.[3] I previously elaborated my words about the laws of the stages of the produce when the obligation of the tithe takes effect — in *sidrah korah,* the fourth positive precept (§ 395); you can see it there if you wish. Further details of the precept are clarified in the Mishnah tractate *Ma'asér Shéni.*

This prohibiton applies to both man and woman at the time that the duty of the Second Tithe is in effect. In *sidrah shof'tim,* the sixth positive precept (§ 507), we will explain, with the Eternal Lord's help, the time and locations where it applies. If a person violated it and ate an olive's amount of it outside Jerusalem, he would be punishable by whiplashes.

[שֶׁלֹּא לֶאֱכֹל מַעֲשֵׂר שֵׁנִי שֶׁל תִּירוֹשׁ חוּץ לִירוּשָׁלַיִם]

תמג שֶׁלֹּא לֶאֱכֹל מַעֲשֵׂר שֵׁנִי שֶׁל תִּירוֹשׁ חוּץ לִירוּשָׁלַיִם, שֶׁנֶּאֱמַר "לֹא תוּכַל לֶאֱכֹל בִּשְׁעָרֶיךָ" וְגוֹמֵר "וְתִירֹשְׁךָ". כָּל עִנְיַן מִצְוַת אִסּוּר הַתִּירוֹשׁ כְּעִנְיַן מִצְוַת הַדָּגָן, אֵין צֹרֶךְ לְהַאֲרִיךְ בָּהּ הַדִּבּוּר.

[שֶׁלֹּא לֶאֱכֹל מַעֲשֵׂר שֵׁנִי שֶׁל יִצְהָר חוּץ לִירוּשָׁלַיִם]

תמד שֶׁלֹּא לֶאֱכֹל מַעֲשֵׂר שֵׁנִי שֶׁל יִצְהָר, פֵּרוּשׁ שֶׁמֶן, חוּץ לִירוּשָׁלַיִם, שֶׁנֶּאֱמַר "לֹא תוּכַל לֶאֱכֹל בִּשְׁעָרֶיךָ" וְכוּלֵּי "וְיִצְהָרֶךָ". כָּל עִנְיַן הַיִּצְהָר כְּעִנְיַן הַדָּגָן וְהַתִּירוֹשׁ.

וְשִׁעוּר אֲכִילַת הַשֶּׁמֶן לְחַיֵּב עָלָיו הוּא בִּכְזַיִת, לְפִי מַה שֶּׁשָּׁמַעְתִּי מִמּוֹרַי יִשְׁמְרֵם אֵל; וְאַף־עַל־פִּי שֶׁהוּא מַשְׁקֶה, לַאֲכִילָה הוּא עוֹמֵד לְכָל בְּנֵי־אָדָם; וְאִם יָדַעְנוּ כִּי מִקְצָת מִן הַיִּשְׁמְעֵאלִים יִשְׁתּוּהוּ, בָּטְלָה דַעְתָּם אֵצֶל כָּל בְּנֵי־אָדָם.

וְאַל תַּחְשֹׁב לוֹמַר שֶׁזֶּה הַלָּאו דְּ"לֹא תוּכַל" שֶׁיִּהְיֶה לָאו שֶׁבִּכְלָלוּת, שֶׁכָּל עִנְיַן וְעִנְיָן הוּא לָאו בִּפְנֵי עַצְמוֹ, וְכֵן הוּא מְפֹרָשׁ בְּמַסֶּכֶת (מכות) [כְּרֵתוֹת]: אֲבָל מַעֲשֵׂר דָּגָן וְתִירוֹשׁ וְיִצְהָר, חַיָּב עַל כָּל אֶחָד וְאֶחָד; וְקָא פָרִיךְ הָתָם: וְכִי לוֹקִין עַל לָאו שֶׁבִּכְלָלוּת —וּמְהַדֵּר לֵהּ: קְרָא יִתְרָא הוּא: מִכְּדִי כְּתִיב "וַאֲכַלְתָּ לִפְנֵי יי אֱלֹהֶיךָ... מַעֲשֵׂר דְּגָנְךָ תִּירֹשְׁךָ וְיִצְהָרֶךָ", [לָמָּה לִי לְמֶהְדַּר וּלְמִכְתְּבִינְהוּ לְכֻלְּהוּ —שְׁמַע מִנַּהּ לְחַלֵּק. וּבִגְמָרָא מַכּוֹת אָמְרוּ: מִכְּדִי כְּתִיב "וַאֲכַלְתָּ לִפְנֵי יי אֱלֹהֶיךָ... מַעֲשֵׂר דְּגָנְךָ תִּירֹשְׁךָ וְיִצְהָרֶךָ"], לִכְתֹּב רַחֲמָנָא "לֹא תוּכַל לֶאֱכֹל אוֹתָם

§444   1. Similarly, in MT *hilchoth ma'asér shéni* ii 5, Rambam writes of "Whoever eats an olive's amount of the Second Tithe."

2. So that the minimal amount for the law to apply should be a quarter (*r'vi'ith*) of a *log* (see § 31, note 2).

3. I.e. mixed with food that is eaten.

4. I.e. a single injunction covering several different matters—in this case, the tithe of grain, wine and oil; and there is a standard rule that for violating such a negative precept, no whiplashes should be given (TB K'réthoth 4b).

5. The original has *Makkoth*, but what follows is found in TB K'réthoth 4b, worded differently (in fact, what follows here rather seems a summary paraphrase; however, cf. MhG Deuteronomy 12:17, p. 258 l. 24ff.—which strongly suggests that Rambam had before him another version of the Talmudic passage). In ShM negative precept § 143, the source of this entire paragraph, we also find *Makkoth*, and there it is patently erroneous, since further on we read, "and in clarification they [the Sages] said in the tractate *Makkoth*"; hence this citation is clearly from a different source. In ShM root principle 3 (ed. Heller, p. 23a; voweled ed. Kafeḥ, p. 37) it is given explicitly as from TB K'réthoth.

6. From "why do I need" etc. to here is not in the original, neither in the manuscripts nor in the printed editions. It is present, however, in ShM negative

[THE PROHIBITION AGAINST CONSUMING THE
SECOND TITHE OF WINE OUTSIDE JERUSALEM]

443 not to consume the Second Tithe of wine outside Jerusalem: for it is stated, *You may not eat within your gates the tithe of your grain or your wine* (Deuteronomy 12:17). The entire subject-matter of the prohibition on wine is like that of the precept about grain (§ 442); there is no need to multiply words about it.

[THE PROHIBITION AGAINST CONSUMING
THE SECOND TITHE OF OIL OUTSIDE JERUSALEM]

444 not to consume the Second Tithe of oil outside Jerusalem: for it is stated, *You may not eat within your gates the tithe of your grain or your wine or your oil* (Deuteronomy 12:17). The entire subject-matter about oil is like those concerning grain (§ 442) and wine (§ 443).

Now, the minimal amount of oil to be consumed so that punishment for it is incurred, is the bulk of an olive, according to what I heard from my master teachers, God protect them.[1] Although it is a liquid,[2] it is used as a food by all human beings.[3] And even if we know that some of the Ishmaelites drink it, their view is considered nought in comparison with that of all human beings.

Nor should you think to say that this injunction, "You may not eat within your gates," is a composite, omnibus negative precept.[4] For each and every item is a negative precept by itself; and so it is made explicit in the Talmud tractate *K'réthoth*,[5] "If one ate the tithe of grain, wine and oil, he is punishable over each and every one." It is then asked there: Is one then given lashes of the whip over a general, omnibus injunction? And the reply is given: It is a verse with superfluous words: It is written in any case, *And you shall eat before the Lord your God...the tithe of your grain, your wine and your oil* (Deuteronomy 14:23); why do I need them all written yet again?— Learn from this to have separate [prohibitions for each item]. And in the Talmud tractate *Makkoth* (18a) they [the Sages] said: It is written in any case, *And you shall eat before the Lord your God...the tithe of your grain, your wine, and your oil;*[6] then let the merciful God write, "You may not eat them within your gates"; what need was there to list

precept § 143, the source of this entire paragraph; and as R. Chaim Heller points out in his edition (note 19), an early copyist evidently omitted it here by a jump of the eye between two identical series of words.

בִּשְׁעָרֶיךָ״, פָּרְשִׁינְהוּ כֻּלְּהוּ — שְׁמַע מִנַּהּ לְיִחוּדֵי לְהוּ לָאו לְכָל חַד נַחַד. וְזֶה הַכָּתוּב שֶׁל ״וְאָכַלְתָּ״ הוּא בְּסוֹף סֵדֶר זֶה.

(וּמַה שֶּׁהִזְכִּיר בְּמִקְרָא זֶה ״וּבְכֹרוֹת בְּקָרְךָ וְצֹאנֶךָ״, וְאַף־עַל־פִּי שֶׁהֵם לַכֹּהֲנִים, בְּסִפְרֵי נִדְרָשׁ כִּי בָא לְהַקִּישׁ מַעֲשֵׂר לִבְכוֹר וְגוֹמֵר.)

[שֶׁלֹּא לֶאֱכֹל בְּכוֹר תָּמִים חוּץ לִירוּשָׁלַיִם]

תמה שֶׁלֹּא יֹאכַל הַכֹּהֵן בְּכוֹר תָּמִים חוּץ לִירוּשָׁלַיִם, וּכְמוֹ־כֵן שֶׁלֹּא יֹאכַל זָר מִן הַבְּכוֹר בְּשׁוּם מָקוֹם, כִּי הַמִּצְוָה בּוֹ שֶׁיֹּאכְלוּהוּ הַכֹּהֲנִים מְשָׁרְתֵי הַשֵּׁם, מִן הַטַּעַם שֶׁכָּתַבְתִּי בְּסֵדֶר בֹּא אֶל פַּרְעֹה עָשָׂה ו', בְּסִימָן (ט') [י״ח]. וְעַל כָּל זֶה נֶאֱמַר ״לֹא תוּכַל לֶאֱכֹל בִּשְׁעָרֶיךָ״ וְגוֹמֵר ״וּבְכֹרֹת בְּקָרְךָ וְצֹאנֶךָ״.

וּלְשׁוֹן סִפְרֵי: ״וּבְכֹרֹת״, זֶה הַבְּכוֹר, וְלֹא בָא הַכָּתוּב אֶלָּא לְזָר שֶׁאָכַל בְּכוֹר, בֵּין לִפְנֵי זְרִיקַת דָּמִים בֵּין לְאַחַר זְרִיקָה, שֶׁעוֹבֵר בְּלֹא־תַעֲשֶׂה. וְאֵין הַכַּוָּנָה שֶׁלֹּא יְלַמֵּד הַכָּתוּב זוּלָתִי עִנְיָן זֶה, אֲבָל יֹאמַר שֶׁזֶּהוּ בִּכְלַל הַלָּאו הַזֶּה; וְנִמְצָא שֶׁכְּלוּלִים בּוֹ שְׁנֵי הָעִנְיָנִים שֶׁנִּזְכָּרוּ: מְנִיעַת הַזָּר מֵאֱכֹל בְּכוֹר תָּמִים בְּשׁוּם מָקוֹם, וּמְנִיעַת הַכֹּהֵן כְּמוֹ־כֵן מֵאֱכֹל אוֹתוֹ חוּץ לִירוּשָׁלַיִם; וּשְׁנֵי הָעִנְיָנִים תְּלוּיִין בִּבְכוֹר תָּמִים.

וְשָׁם בְּסֵדֶר בֹּא אֶל פַּרְעֹה כָּתַבְתִּי מִצְוַת הַבְּכוֹרוֹת, בְּאֵי זֶה זְמַן וּבְאֵי זֶה מָקוֹם נוֹהֶגֶת, וְחִלּוּק הַדֵּעוֹת לָרַבּוֹתֵי יִשְׁמְרֵם אֵל בְּעִנְיַן הַבְּכוֹר בַּזְּמַן הַזֶּה. וּבְטַעַם הֱיוֹתוֹ

---

7. Evidently our author anticipated that his young son *et al.* (for whom, by his own avowal, he wrote this work) might have trouble finding the verse, as the negative instruction, *You may not eat* etc. occurs considerably earlier.

Yet at first sight this might pose a difficulty: How can the Talmud argue that Scripture could have stated, more briefly, "You may not eat *them*" in Deuteronomy 12:17, if the meaning of "them" is to be found only some sixty-odd verses later? There is, however, the known rule of the Sages that the Written Torah is not to be regarded as in strict chronological order: we can always apply to an earlier passage what we learn from a later one. Moreover, as Rashi notes in TB Makkoth 14a, beginning, in Deuteronomy 12:6 we have the general term "your tithes," and the only passage that specifies which tithes is the much later verse, 14:23. (MY argues forcefully that this entire sentence is a printer's error; but it is found in all four early manuscripts.)

8. Then why are they listed in an injunction to Israelites not to eat them in their own locations? An ordinary Israelite might not eat them anywhere!

9. Sifre, Deuteronomy §106.

10. I.e. just as a firstborn animal might be eaten (by *kohanim*) only within the city walls of Jerusalem, so the contents of the Second Tithe by Israelites. This last paragraph is not in the oldest manuscripts, and would thus seem to be a later addition.

them all here explicitly? Hence we infer from it to assign a negative precept to each and every one.

That verse, "And you shall eat," occurs toward the end of this *sidrah*.[7]

(As to the fact that this verse lists *or the firstlings of your herd or your flock (ibid.)* although they are for the *kohanim*,[8] in the Midrash *Sifre* it is interpreted[9] that this was added to equate the contents of the tithe with a firstborn animal, etc.)[10]

[THE PROHIBITION AGAINST EATING
AN UNBLEMISHED FIRSTBORN ANIMAL
OUTSIDE JERUSALEM]

445 that a *kohen* should not eat an unblemished firstling outside of Jerusalem, and likewise that an outsider (non-*kohen*) is not to eat of a firstborn animal anywhere: because the religious duty about it is that the *kohanim*, the servitors of the Eternal Lord, should eat it, for the reason I wrote in *sidrah bo*, at the sixth positive precept (§ 18). Regarding all this it is stated, *You may not eat within your gates…the firstlings of your herd or your flock* (Deuteronomy 12:17).

In the language of the Midrash *Sifre*:[1] "or the firstlings"—this means a firstborn animal; and the verse applies to none but an outsider (non-*kohen*) who eats a firstling, whether before the sprinkling of the blood [on the altar] or after the sprinkling—that he violates a negative precept. Now, the meaning [of this] is not that the verse teaches nothing else but this point; it is rather to say that this is included in this negative precept.[2] Consequently, both rules that we mentioned are included in it: the restraint of a non-*kohen* from eating an unblemished firstling anywhere, and likewise the restraint of a *kohen* from eating it outside Jerusalem. And both rules relate only to[3] a whole, unblemished firstborn animal.[4]

There, in *sidrah bo* (§ 18), I wrote the precept of firstborn animals—at which time and in which location it is in force, and the difference of opinion among my master teachers, God protect them,

§445   1. Sifre, Deuteronomy § 72.

2. I.e. it is aside from the precept mentioned further on (and the expression in Sifre is idiomatic, not literal).

3. Literally, depend on.

⟨379⟩   4. The first two paragraphs are based on ShM negative precept § 144.

נֶאֱכָל בִּירוּשָׁלַיִם אֵין צֹרֶךְ לְהַאֲרִיךְ, כִּי הוּא מִכְּלַל הַקֳּדָשִׁים, וּכְמוֹ שֶׁבָּא בַּמִּשְׁנָה בְּזְבָחִים פֶּרֶק ה': הַבְּכוֹר וְהַמַּעֲשֵׂר וְהַפֶּסַח קֳדָשִׁים קַלִּים וְכוּלֵי; וּכְבָר הֶאֱרַכְתִּי דְבָרַי בְּכַמָּה מְקוֹמוֹת בְּטַעַם אֲכִילַת הַקֳּדָשִׁים בִּמְקוֹם הַקֹּדֶשׁ וַאֲכַל אוֹתָם מְשָׁרְתֵי הַשֵּׁם.

דִּינֵי הַמִּצְוָה, מִי הוּא הַזָּר אֵצֶל אֲכִילַת הַבְּכוֹר, וְהַמּוּמִין הַפּוֹסְלִין בּוֹ, וּזְמַן אֲכִילָתוֹ, הַכֹּל מְבֹאָר בְּמַסֶּכֶת בְּכוֹרוֹת; וּבִמְקוֹמוֹת אֲחֵרִים מִקֳּדָשִׁים, קְצָת מִדִּינִין אֵלּוּ. וְכֹהֵן הָעוֹבֵר עַל זֶה וְאָכַל כְּזַיִת מִבְּכוֹר תָּמִים חוּץ לִירוּשָׁלַיִם, וְכֵן יִשְׂרָאֵל בְּכָל מָקוֹם, חַיָּב מַלְקוֹת.

[שֶׁלֹּא לֶאֱכֹל בְּשַׂר חַטָּאת וְאָשָׁם חוּץ לַקְּלָעִים, וַאֲפִלּוּ הַכֹּהֲנִים]

תמו שֶׁלֹּא לֶאֱכֹל מִבְּשַׂר חַטָּאת וְאָשָׁם, וַאֲפִלּוּ הַכֹּהֲנִים, חוּץ לַקְּלָעִים; וּפֵרְשׁוּ בַּעֲלֵי הַקַּבָּלָה שֶׁאִסּוּר זֶה הוּא בִּכְלָל "לֹא תוּכַל לֶאֱכֹל בִּשְׁעָרֶיךָ וְגוֹמֵר, בְּקֹרֶךְ וְצֹאנֶךָ", שֶׁכֵּן אָמְרוּ זִכְרוֹנָם לִבְרָכָה: לֹא בָא הַכָּתוּב אֶלָּא לְאוֹכֵל חַטָּאת וְאָשָׁם חוּץ לַקְּלָעִים, שֶׁהוּא עוֹבֵר בְּלֹא-תַעֲשֶׂה. וּכְמוֹ-כֵן אוֹכֵל קֳדָשִׁים קַלִּים חוּץ לַחוֹמָה בִּכְלָל אִסּוּר זֶה, כְּמוֹ שֶׁבָּא בַּגְּמָרָא מַכּוֹת (שֶׁאָמְרוּ שָׁם) שֶׁכָּל הָאוֹכֵל דָּבָר חוּץ לִמְקוֹם אֲכִילָתוֹ, "לֹא תוּכַל לֶאֱכֹל בִּשְׁעָרֶיךָ" קָרִינָא בֵּהּ; וְאָמְרָם זִכְרוֹנָם לִבְרָכָה "לֹא בָא הַכָּתוּב אֶלָּא לָזֶה", הַכַּוָּנָה לוֹמַר שֶׁגַּם זֶה בַּכְּלָל.

5. See Volume 1, pp. 124–25, top.
6. TB B'choroth 37a–41a.
7. TB Z'vaḥim 56b–57a.

§446   1. I.e. the 'ezrath yisra'el, the court or area where an ordinary Israelite (a non-kohen) might go. The Hebrew means literally "outside the hangings (or curtains)": for in the wilderness, hangings formed the boundaries of the mishkan (the Tabernacle, temporary, portable Sanctuary); hence in the Talmud and halachic Midrash, the term "hangings" is used to denote the bounds of the corresponding area, the walls of the 'ezrath yisra'el, in the permanent Sanctuary of Jerusalem. However, ShM negative precept §145, the source or basis of this paragraph, has ḥutz la'azarah, "outside the Sanctuary grounds," which is patently clearer, and the translation here follows suit. (As our author evidently had a Hebrew rendering of a lost earlier version of ShM—see ed. Heller p. 8—likely that version had ḥutz la-k'la'im, which our author copied, and Rambam later altered it.)

See tosafoth to TB Yoma 25a, s.v. 'en yeshivah, that while ordinarily, none but kings descended from David might sit in the 'ezrath yisra'el, to eat the flesh of these offerings a kohen might equally be seated.

2. Sifre, Deuteronomy §73; TB Makkoth 17a.

3. See note 1. Here the translation is literal, as Rambam in ShM retains the phrase ḥutz la-k'la'im from the sources in note 2.

in regard to a firstling at the present time.[5] About the reason why it was to be eaten in Jerusalem, there is no need to be lengthy, since it is in the category of holy offerings, as we find in the Mishnah tractate *Z'vahim*, chapter 5 (v 8): The firstling, a tithe animal and the Passover offering are sacrifices of lesser holiness, etc. I have previously set forth my words in several places about the reason why holy offerings were eaten in the holy place, and why the ministering servants of the Eternal Lord ate them.

Some laws of the precept are: who is an outsider (non-*kohen*) in regard to eating a firstling; the blemishing defects that would disqualify it;[6] and the time for eating it.[7] All is explained in the Talmud tractate *B'choroth*, and some of these laws in other places in the Talmud order of *Kodashim*. If a *kohen* transgressed this and ate an olive's amount [of meat] from an unblemished firstling outside Jerusalem — and likewise an Israelite (non-*kohen*) anywhere — he would be punishable by whiplashes.

[NOT TO EAT OF A ḤATTATH OR AN 'ASHAM
OUTSIDE THE HOLY TEMPLE]

446 that the flesh of a *hattath* (sin-offering) or an *'asham* (guilt-offering) is not to be eaten even by the *kohanim* outside the *'azarah* (the Sanctuary grounds);[1] the masters of the Oral Tradition explained that this prohibition is contained in the verse, *You may not eat within your gates...of your herd or your flock* (Deuteronomy 12:17). For so the Sages of blessed memory said:[2] The verse refers to none but one who eats [the flesh of] a *hattath* or an *'asham* outside the hangings[3] (the boundary of the *'azarah*) — that he transgresses a negative precept. So too, a person who eats [the flesh of] offerings of lesser holiness outside the wall [of Jerusalem] is included under this prohibition — as we find in the Talmud tractate *Makkoth* (17a); for whoever eats anything[4] outside the proper place for eating it, to him we apply the verse, *You may not eat within your gates.* Now, when the Sages of blessed memory said, "The verse refers to none but this," the meaning is to convey that this too is included.[5]

4. The original reads, "for it was taught there that whoever eats," etc. But what follows is not found in the Talmud; hence MY suggests that the words "it was taught there that" should be ómitted as a scribal error — which would harmonize this with ShM negative precept §145, on which the paragraph is based. (On the

מִשָּׁרְשֵׁי הַמִּצְוָה, לֶאֱכֹל כָּל קָרְבָּן בְּמָקוֹם מְיֻחָד כְּדֵי שֶׁיְּכַוְּנוּ לָבָּם אוֹכְלָיו עַל הַכַּפָּרָה שֶׁנֶּאֶכָלִין בִּשְׁבִילָהּ, וּכְעִנְיָן שֶׁאָמְרוּ זִכְרוֹנָם לִבְרָכָה: כֹּהֲנִים אוֹכְלִים וּבְעָלִים מִתְכַּפְּרִים; וְאִלּוּ יֵאָכְלוּ בִּמְקוֹמוֹת אֲחֵרִים יַסִּיחוּ כַּוָּנָתָם מִן הָעִנְיָן, יָדוּעַ דָּבָר זֶה וּבָרוּר.

דִּינֵי הַמִּצְוָה בַּזְּבָחִים.

וְנוֹהֵג אִסּוּר זֶה בְּכָל מָקוֹם [וּבְכָל זְמַן], שֶׁאֲפִלּוּ הַמַּקְדִּישׁ הַיּוֹם חַטָּאת וְאָשָׁם, וְעָבְרוּ וְאָכְלוּ מֵהֶם, אֲפִלּוּ הַכֹּהֲנִים, כְּזַיִת, חַיָּבִין מַלְקוֹת מִזֶּה הַלָּאו, מִלְּבַד הָאִסּוּר שֶׁהוּא בְּנֶהֱנֶה מִן הַהֶקְדֵּשׁ.

[שֶׁלֹּא לֶאֱכֹל בְּשַׂר הָעוֹלָה]

תמז שֶׁלֹּא לֶאֱכֹל שׁוּם דָּבָר מִבְּשַׂר הָעוֹלָה, שֶׁנֶּאֱמַר "לֹא תוּכַל לֶאֱכֹל בִּשְׁעָרֶיךָ" וְגוֹמֵר "נְדָרֶיךָ אֲשֶׁר תִּדֹּר", וּפֵרוּשׁ הַכָּתוּב כְּאִלּוּ יֹאמַר: לֹא תוּכַל לֶאֱכֹל נְדָרֶיךָ אֲשֶׁר תִּדֹּר; וְאָמְרוּ רַבּוֹתֵינוּ בַּעֲלֵי הַקַּבָּלָה: "נְדָרֶיךָ", זוֹ עוֹלָה, וְלֹא בָא הַכָּתוּב אֶלָּא לְלַמֶּדְךָ לְאוֹכֵל עוֹלָה, בֵּין לִפְנֵי זְרִיקַת דָּמִים בֵּין לְאַחַר זְרִיקַת דָּמִים, בֵּין לִפְנִים מִן הַקְּלָעִים בֵּין חוּץ לַקְּלָעִים, שֶׁהוּא עוֹבֵר בְּלֹא תַעֲשֶׂה. גַּם אָמְרוּ זִכְרוֹנָם לִבְרָכָה שֶׁזֶּה הַלָּאו הוּא אַזְהָרָה לְכָל מוֹעֵל בְּקָדָשִׁים.

כְּבָר כָּתַבְתִּי בְּסֵדֶר וַיִּקְחוּ לִי תְרוּמָה [סִי' צ"ה] מַה שֶׁיָּדַעְתִּי עַל צַד הַפְּשָׁט בְּעִנְיַן הַקָּרְבָּן וְהַתּוֹעֶלֶת הַיּוֹצֵא לָנוּ בְּשָׁרְפֵנוּ בַּעֲלֵי הַחַיִּים בַּבַּיִת הַגָּדוֹל; וְהָאַזְהָרָה בָהֶם שֶׁלֹּא נֹאכַל מֵהֶם אֶלָּא שֶׁיִּשָּׂרֵף הַכֹּל, נִמְשָׁךְ אַחַר אוֹתוֹ הַטַּעַם, קֶשֶׁר אֶחָד

other hand, our author may have written this in the sense of the rule the Sages meant to teach us by their statements of law.)

5. See §445, at note 2.

6. TB P'saḥim 59b, etc.

§447   1. Sifre, Deuteronomy §74; TB Makkoth 17a. (For the plain meaning of a votive offering see §438, first paragraph.)

2. See §446, notes 1 and 3.

3. ShM negative precept §146 (the basis of this paragraph) reads, "and this negative precept [never to eat the flesh of an 'olah] is an injunction to anyone who would commit any breach of holiness." In MT hilchoth me'ilah i 3 Rambam writes, "And the injunction against a breach of holiness [derives] from Scripture's statement, *You may not eat within your gates the tithe of your grain . . . or any of your votive offerings.* By word of the Oral Tradition it was learned that this is an injunction to one who would eat of the 'olah, because it is all for the Eternal Lord; and the law is the same for every other holy entity which is [consecrated] for the Eternal Lord alone . . ." Hence, apparently, our author's phrase "our Sages of blessed memory taught"—for with Rambam he holds that it is a direct corollary of the teaching of

At the root of the precept lies the principle to eat every offering at the particular location alloted to it, so that those eating it should focus their heart [thoughts] on the atonement for whose sake it is eaten — in keeping with what the Sages of blessed memory said:[6] The *kohanim* eat, and the owner [of the offering] finds atonement. But if they should eat them in other locations, their attention would be diverted from the matter. This matter is known (evident) and clear.

The laws of the precept are in the tractate *Z'vahim*. This prohibition is in effect in every place and in every time: for even if someone consecrated [an animal] today for a *hattath* or an *'asham*, and others transgressed and ate of it — even *kohanim* — the amount of an olive, they would deserve whiplashes because of this negative precept, apart from the prohibition on deriving benefit from something consecrated.

[NOT TO EAT THE FLESH OF AN 'OLAH, A BURNT-OFFERING]

447 to eat nothing at all of the flesh of an *'olah* (burnt-offering): for it is stated, *You may not eat within your gates... any of your votive offerings that you vow* (Deuteronomy 12:17), and the meaning of the verse is as though it stated, "you may not eat your votive offerings that you vow." Now, our Sages, the masters of the Oral Tradition, taught:[1] "your votive offerings" means an *'olah*, and the verse comes only to teach you about one who eats [the flesh of] an *'olah*, whether before or after the sprinkling of the blood [on the altar], whether within or outside the hangings (the boundary of the *'azarah*, the Sanctuary grounds)[2] — that he violates a negative precept. Moreover, our Sages of blessed memory taught that this injunction serves as an admonition for anyone who would commit a breach of holiness with holy offerings.[3]

I wrote previously, in *sidrah t'rumah* (§ 95), what I knew, from the aspect of the plain meaning, about the theme of the offering and the useful benefit we obtain when we burn animals at the great Temple. Now, the injunction about these ['*olah* offerings], that we should not

the Talmudic Sages. However, Rashi to TB P'sahim 33a, s.v. *va-hachamim*, writes that the injunction lies in Leviticus 22:10, *And let no outsider [non-kohen] eat any holy food*; whereas Rabad to MT *ibid.* derives it more simply from Leviticus 22:12, in regard to the daughter of a *kohen* who marries an "outsider": *of the portion set apart*

הוּא. וְנִתְיַחֲדָה הָאַזְהָרָה בָּעוֹלָה, כִּי הִיא מִצְוָתָהּ לִהְיוֹתָהּ כָּלִיל; וּבִכְלַל הָאַזְהָרָה כָּל מוֹעֵל בְּקָדָשִׁים, כְּמוֹ שֶׁכָּתַבְתִּי.

דִּינֵי הַמִּצְוָה, בְּמַסֶּכֶת מְעִילָה וּבִמְקוֹמוֹת מִסֵּדֶר קָדָשִׁים.

וְנוֹהֵג אִסּוּר זֶה בְּכָל מָקוֹם וּבְכָל זְמָן, בִּזְכָרִים וּנְקֵבוֹת, שֶׁאֲפִלּוּ הַמַּקְדִּישׁ בְּהֶמְתּוֹ הַיּוֹם לְעוֹלָה אָסוּר לוֹ לֶאֱכֹל מִמֶּנָּה כְּלוּם. וְהָעוֹבֵר עַל זֶה וְאָכַל מִבְּשַׂר בֶּהֱמַת עוֹלָה, וְכֵן כָּל הָאוֹכֵל גַּם־כֵּן מִשְּׁאָר קָדָשִׁים, מָעַל, וְחַיָּב מַלְקוֹת בְּמֵזִיד כְּשֶׁיֵּשׁ עֵדִים וְהַתְרָאָה, כְּמוֹ שֶׁיָּדוּעַ בְּכָל מָקוֹם; וְאִם הוּא שׁוֹגֵג, יַקְרִיב קָרְבַּן מְעִילָה וְיַחֲזִיר מַה שֶּׁנֶּהֱנָה בְּתוֹסֶפֶת חֹמֶשׁ, כְּמוֹ שֶׁמְּבֹאָר בְּמַסֶּכֶת מְעִילָה. וּבְפֶרֶק תְּשִׁיעִי מִסַּנְהֶדְרִין אָמְרוּ זִכְרוֹנָם לִבְרָכָה: הַזִּיד בַּמְּעִילָה, רַבִּי אוֹמֵר בְּמִיתָה וַחֲכָמִים אוֹמְרִים בְּאַזְהָרָה. וְיֵשׁ לָדוּן גַּם־כֵּן שֶׁאָסוּר זֶה וְכָל כַּיּוֹצֵא בּוֹ אֵינוֹ נוֹהֵג אֶלָּא בִּזְמַן הַבַּיִת.

[שֶׁלֹּא לֶאֱכֹל בְּשַׂר קָדָשִׁים קַלִּים קֹדֶם זְרִיקַת דָּמִים]

תמח שֶׁלֹּא לֶאֱכֹל שׁוּם דָּבָר מִבְּשַׂר קָדָשִׁים קַלִּים קֹדֶם זְרִיקַת דָּמִים, וְקָדָשִׁים קַלִּים הֵן כְּמוֹ תּוֹדָה וּשְׁלָמִים וְכַיּוֹצֵא בָהֶן, הַשְּׁנוּיִין בְּמִשְׁנַת זְבָחִים פֶּרֶק ה'; וְעַל זֶה נֶאֱמַר "לֹא תוּכַל לֶאֱכֹל בִּשְׁעָרֶיךָ" וְגוֹמֵר "וּנְדָבֹתֶיךָ", שֶׁפֵּרוּשׁוֹ כְּאִלּוּ

from holy foods, she shall not eat. See *Kessef Mishneh* to MT *ad loc.* and the commentary of R. Joseph Corcos on this, in MT ed. Shulsinger, Vol. IV, appendices, p. 14a.

4. Literally, it is one knot.

5. Hence it may clearly and obviously not be eaten.

6. I.e. which he was forbidden to eat.

7. See §129.

8. From the paragraph's second sentence to here is based on ShM negative precept §146.

9. In this last sentence, no longer citing or borrowing from ShM negative precept §146, our author offers an alternative view, at variance with his statements here, in §446, and in §448. As MY well notes, our author may have based himself on a teaching in TB Makkoth 19b:

R. 'Assi taught in the name of R. Yoḥanan: From which time is one guilty over the Second Tithe [if he eats it beyond its permitted area, outside Jerusalem's city wall]? — from [the moment] it comes in sight of the [interior] wall. What is the reason? Scripture states, *before the Lord your God shall you eat it* (Deuteronomy 12:18) [so in TB MS Munich], and it is written too, *You may not eat within your gates [the tithe of your grain, etc.]* (ibid. 17). Where we can apply [the first text], *before the Lord your God* [etc.] there we apply [the second], *You may not eat within your gates* [etc.]; and where we cannot apply [the first text] we do not apply [the second].

Now Deuteronomy 12:17 is also the source for this precept §447, forbidding the flesh of an 'olah to be eaten; and from this, Rambam adduces further a general

eat of them but that the whole should rather be burned, follows in the wake of that reason; they are linked together.[4] The injunction was given particularly about the 'olah because it lies under a religious duty to be entirely burned;[5] but [actually] anyone who commits a breach of holiness with sacred offerings is included under the injunction, as I have written.

The laws of the precept are in the Talmud tractate *Me'ilah*, and in certain places in the Talmud order of *Kodashim*.

This prohibition is in effect everywhere, at every time, for both man and woman: because if a person consecrates his animal even today for an 'olah, he is forbidden to eat anything of it. If someone violated this and ate of the flesh of an animal that was an 'olah, and so likewise if anyone ate of any other holy offerings,[6] he would thus commit a breach of holiness, and would deserve whiplashes if it was deliberate, if there were witnesses and a [prior] warning, as [the rule] is known in every instance. If he acted unwittingly, he should bring a *me'ilah* (breach-of-holiness) offering,[7] and pay for the benefit he had, with the addition of a fifth—as explained in the Talmud tractate *Me'ilah*. In the ninth chapter of the tractate *Sanhedrin* (83a) the Sages of blessed memory taught: If one committed a breach of holiness deliberately, Rabbi [Judah haNassi] says it entails a punishment of death [by Divine hand]; the Sages say he violates an injunction.[8] Yet it can also be decided that this prohibition and any other like it are in effect only at the time the Temple stands.[9]

[NOT TO EAT OF OFFERINGS OF LESSER HOLINESS
BEFORE THEIR BLOOD IS SPRINKLED ON
THE ALTAR]

448 to eat nothing whatever of the flesh from offerings of lesser holiness before the sprinkling of the blood. Offerings of lesser holiness are e.g. a *todah* (thank-offering), *sh'lamim* (peace-offering), and so forth, that are listed in the Mishnah tractate *Z'vaḥim*, chapter 5 (v 6–8). About this it is stated, *You may not eat within your gates...your freewill offerings* (Deuteronomy 12:17), whose meaning is as though it

injunction against any breach of holiness. Hence it can well be our author's alternative present view that just as the ban on eating Second Tithe "out of bounds" can be violated only after it has been brought "before the Lord," which means in effect to Jerusalem when the Temple is extant, so likewise can the prohibition

אָמַר: לֹא תוּכַל לֶאֱכֹל נְדָבוֹתֶיךָ; וְאָמְרוּ בַּעֲלֵי הַקַּבָּלָה זִכְרוֹנָם לִבְרָכָה: לֹא בָא
הַכָּתוּב אֶלָּא לֶאֱכֹל תּוֹדָה וּשְׁלָמִים לִפְנֵי זְרִיקַת דָּמִים, שֶׁהוּא עוֹבֵר בְּלֹא־תַעֲשֶׂה.

מִשָּׁרְשֵׁי הַמִּצְוָה, לָתֵת אֶל לִבֵּנוּ שֶׁרָאוּי לָנוּ לְהַקְדִּים לְעוֹלָם תּוֹעֶלֶת נַפְשׁוֹתֵינוּ
לְתוֹעֶלֶת גּוּפֵנוּ בְּכָל דָּבָר בָּעוֹלָם; עַל־כֵּן אֵין רָאוּי שֶׁיֵּהָנֶה הַגּוּף בָּאֲכִילָה טֶרֶם
זְרִיקַת דָּמִים שֶׁבָּאִין לְכַפָּרָה עַל הַנֶּפֶשׁ.

דִּינֵי הַמִּצְוָה גַּם־כֵּן מְבֹאָרִים בִּמְעִילָה וּבִמְקוֹמוֹת מְקֻדָּשִׁים.

וְנוֹהֵג אִסּוּר זֶה בְּכָל מָקוֹם וּבְכָל זְמַן, בִּזְכָרִים וּנְקֵבוֹת, שֶׁאֲפִלּוּ הַמַּקְדִּישׁ
בְּהֶמְתּוֹ הַיּוֹם לְקָדָשִׁים קַלִּים וְעָבַר וְאָכַל מִמֶּנָּה אַחַר־כֵּן כַּזַּיִת, חַיָּב מַלְקוֹת.

[שֶׁלֹּא יֹאכְלוּ כֹהֲנִים בִּכּוּרִים קֹדֶם הַנָּחָתָם בָּעֲזָרָה]

תמט שֶׁנִּמְנַעְנוּ מִלֶּאֱכֹל בִּכּוּרִים, וְעַל זֶה נֶאֱמַר "לֹא תוּכַל לֶאֱכֹל" וְגוֹמֵר
"וּתְרוּמַת יָדֶךָ", וּפֵרְשׁוּ בַּעֲלֵי הַקַּבָּלָה: "וּתְרוּמַת יָדֶךָ" אֵלּוּ הַבִּכּוּרִים. וְנִתְבָּאֵר
בְּסוֹף מַסֶּכֶת מַכּוֹת שֶׁאֵין חַיָּבִין עֲלֵיהֶם אֶלָּא קֹדֶם שֶׁיֻּנְּחוּ בָּעֲזָרָה, אֲבָל מִשֶּׁיֻּנְּחוּ
בָּעֲזָרָה אָדָם פָּטוּר עֲלֵיהֶם.

וּלְשׁוֹן סִפְרֵי: לֹא בָא הַכָּתוּב אֶלָּא לֶאֱכֹל בִּכּוּרִים שֶׁלֹּא קָרָא עֲלֵיהֶן, שֶׁהוּא
עוֹבֵר בְּלֹא־תַעֲשֶׂה. וּפֵרוּשׁ הָעִנְיָן "מִפְּנֵי שֶׁלֹּא קָרָא עֲלֵיהֶן", מִפְּנֵי שֶׁלֹּא הֻנְּחוּ
בָּעֲזָרָה, אֲבָל אִם הֻנְּחוּ שָׁם, אַף־עַל־פִּי שֶׁלֹּא קָרָא עֲלֵיהֶם, אֵין בָּהֶן חִיּוּב מַלְקוֹת.

וּכְמוֹ־כֵן יֵשׁ בָּהֶן לְעִנְיַן חִיּוּב הַמַּלְקוֹת הַתְּנַאי שֶׁהוּא בְּמַעֲשֵׂר שֵׁנִי, שֶׁאֵין,

against eating the flesh of an 'olah, or committing a breach of holiness, be
transgressed only when the Temple is in existence.

§448   1. Sifre, Deuteronomy § 72; TB Makkoth 17a.
        2. See § 445, at note 2.
        3. Which makes it permissible to eat the offering.
        4. I.e. like those of § 447.

§449   1. Because it is written about bikkurim, "And the kohen shall take the basket from
        your hand" (Deuteronomy 26:4); Sifre, Deuteronomy § 72; TB Makkoth 17a, etc.
        2. In keeping with Deuteronomy 26:4, And the kohen shall take the basket from
        your hand, and set it down before the altar, etc.
        3. I.e. a kohen, as our author makes clear further on, since bikkurim were in any
        case given the kohanim to eat, being always forbidden to others.
        4. Sifre ibid.
        5. Deuteronomy 26:5–10.
        6. So TB Makkoth 19a.

read, "You may not eat your free-will offerings"; and the masters of the Oral Tradition (of blessed memory) taught:[1] The verse refers to none but[2] a person who eats [the flesh of] a *todah* or *sh'lamim* before the sprinkling of the blood [on the altar][3]—that he transgresses a negative precept.

At the root of the precept lies the purpose that we should consider in our heart that it is always worthwhile for us to give preference to the benefit of our spirit over the benefit of our physical body, in every matter in the world. It is therefore not right that the body should have the enjoyment of food before the sprinkling of the blood, which is done to bring atonement to the spirit.

The laws of the precept are likewise[4] explained in the Talmud tractate *Me'ilah*, and in certain places in the Talmud order of *Kodashim*.

This prohibition applies everywhere, at every time, for both man and woman: for even if someone consecrates his animal today for an offering of lesser holiness, and he transgresses and eats of it afterward an olive's amount, he deserves whiplashes.

[THAT THE KOHANIM SHOULD NOT EAT BIKKURIM
BEFORE THEY ARE SET DOWN IN THE 'AZARAH,
THE SANCTUARY GROUNDS]

449 that we are restricted from eating *bikkurim* (first-fruits); regarding this it is stated, *You may not eat...or the offering of your hand* (Deuteronomy 12:17), about which the masters of the Oral Tradition explained: "or the offering of your hands"—this means *bikkurim*.[1] It was explained toward the end of the Talmud tractate *Makkoth* (18b) that punishment is incurred over them only before they are set down in the 'azarah, the Temple grounds;[2] but from the time they are set down in the 'azarah, a man is free of guilt over them.[3]

In the language of the Midrash *Sifre*:[4] The verse applies to none but [a *kohen*] who eats *bikkurim* over which [the proper verses of Scripture][5] were not recited—that he transgresses a negative precept. Now, the meaning of the reason given, that [the Scriptural verses] were not recited over them, is that they were not set down in the Temple forecourt; but if they were set down there, even if the verses were not recited over them, they would entail no punishment of whiplashes.[6]

So too, in regard to the penalty of whiplashes, there is the same

חַיָּבִין עַל אֲכִילָתָן עַד שֶׁיֵּרָאוּ פְּנֵי הַבַּיִת תְּחִלָּה, וְאַחַר־כָּךְ שֶׁיֹּאכַל מֵהֶם קֹדֶם הַנָּחָה בָּעֲזָרָה: בְּעִנְיָן זֶה יֵשׁ בָּהֶן חִיּוּב מַלְקוֹת לַכֹּהֵן הָאוֹכֵל מֵהֶם; וְיִשְׂרָאֵל חַיָּב בָּהֶם מִיתָה בִּידֵי שָׁמַיִם כָּל זְמַן שֶׁאוֹכֵל מֵהֶם, וַאֲפִלּוּ אַחַר שֶׁקָּרָא עֲלֵיהֶם הַקְּרִיאָה הַיְדוּעָה, וְהִיא הַמְפֹרֶשֶׁת בְּסֵדֶר וְהָיָה כִּי תָבֹא.

וְכֵן אָמְרוּ זִכְרוֹנָם לִבְרָכָה: הַתְּרוּמָה וְהַבִּכּוּרִים חַיָּבִין עֲלֵיהֶן חֹמֶשׁ בְּשׁוֹגֵג וּמִיתָה בְּמֵזִיד; וְזֶהוּ כְּדִין הַתְּרוּמָה בְּשָׁוֶה, שֶׁאַחַר שֶׁקְּרָאָן הַכָּתוּב לַבִּכּוּרִים בְּשֵׁם תְּרוּמָה נִתְחַיְּבוּ בְּדִינֵי הַתְּרוּמָה.

וְהָבֵן, בְּנִי, זֶה הַחִלּוּק שֶׁיֵּשׁ בָּהֶן בֵּין יִשְׂרָאֵל לַכֹּהֵן, וּזְכֹר אוֹתוֹ: שֶׁהַכֹּהֵן כְּשֶׁיֹּאכַל בִּכּוּרִים מִשֶּׁיֵּרָאוּ פְּנֵי הַבַּיִת קֹדֶם הַנָּחָה בָּעֲזָרָה לוֹקֶה, וְאַזְהָרָתֵיהּ מִ"לֹּא תוּכַל" וְגוֹמֵר. וְאַל תִּתְמַהּ לוֹמַר אֵיךְ יִתְחַיֵּב מַלְקוֹת הַכֹּהֵן עֲלֵיהֶם, אַחַר שֶׁהוּא בְּעַצְמוֹ יֹאכְלֵם אַחַר הַנָּחָה בָּעֲזָרָה—שֶׁהֲרֵי כְּמוֹ כֵן בְּשָׁוֶה בְּמַעֲשֵׂר שֵׁנִי, שֶׁיִּתְחַיֵּב הַיִּשְׂרָאֵל עָלָיו מַלְקוֹת בְּאָכְלוֹ אוֹתוֹ חוּץ לִירוּשָׁלַיִם, וְאַף־עַל־פִּי שֶׁהוּא בְּעַצְמוֹ אוֹכֵל אוֹתוֹ בַּמָּקוֹם הָרָאוּי לוֹ. וְיִשְׂרָאֵל שֶׁיֹּאכַל בִּכּוּרִים, כָּל זְמַן שֶׁיֹּאכְלֵם חַיָּב מִיתָה בִּידֵי שָׁמַיִם, וְאַזְהָרָתֵיהּ מִ"וְכָל זָר לֹא יֹאכַל קֹדֶשׁ", וּכְמוֹ שֶׁכָּתַבְתִּי בְּסֵדֶר אֱמֹר אֶל הַכֹּהֲנִים לֹא־תַעֲשֶׂה ט"ו בְּסִימָן (ש"א) [ר"פ].

מִשָּׁרְשֵׁי עִנְיַן הֲבָאַת הַבִּכּוּרִים לְבֵית־הַמִּקְדָּשׁ שֶׁיֹּאכְלוּם מְשָׁרְתֵי הַשֵּׁם, כָּתַבְתִּי בְּדָבָר מַה שֶּׁיָּדַעְתִּי (בְּ"כֶסֶף תַּלְוֶה") בְּסוֹף מִצְוֹת עֲשֵׂה בְּסִימָן ע"ב [בְּמִשְׁפָּטִים סִי' צ"א]. וְטַעַם מִצְוָה זוֹ, שֶׁלֹּא יֹאכְלוּם הַכֹּהֲנִים קֹדֶם שֶׁיַּנִּיחוּ אוֹתָם בָּעֲזָרָה וְשֶׁלֹּא יֹאכַל מֵהֶם יִשְׂרָאֵל בְּשׁוּם עִנְיָן, נִמְשָׁךְ אַחַר אוֹתוֹ הַשֹּׁרֶשׁ הַכָּתוּב שָׁם; יִמְצָאֵהוּ מְבֹאָר נִגְלֶה כָּל שֶׁיֵּשׁ בּוֹ דֵּעָה לָדַעַת טוֹב וָרָע; וְלַהֲגוֹת הַרְבֵּה בַּמֶּה שֶׁאֵינוֹ צָרִיךְ, יְגִיעַת בָּשָׂר.

---

7. Before a person may be sentenced to flogging for eating them.

8. Literally, until they see the face of the Temple (i.e. until they enter within the city walls).

9. Mishnah, Bikkurim ii 1, etc.

10. I.e. at Heaven's hand, as our author writes in the next paragraph (see Mishnah, Ḥallah i 9, with commentaries of Rambam and R. Samson of Sens, and Bikkurim ii 1).

11. In Deuteronomy 12:17, quoted at the beginning; in it, t'rumah is rendered as ''the offering,'' as required by the context.

12. From the beginning to here is based on ShM negative precept §149.

13. Expression based on Ecclesiastes 12:12.

⟨388⟩

requirement about them[7] as for the Second Tithe (§ 442): that no penalty is incurred for eating them until they come within sight of the Temple[8] at first, and after that the person eats of them before they are set down in the Temple court. In this situation there would be a penalty of whiplashes for a *kohen* who eats of them; while an Israelite (non-*kohen*) would incur over them death at Heaven's hand, whenever he eats of them, even after he has recited the known text over them, which is the one given explicitly in *sidrah ki thavo*.[5]

And so the Sages of blessed memory said:[9] Over *t'rumah* [the *kohen*'s portion from all produce] and *bikkurim* (first-fruits) one incurs [the obligation to pay an additional] fifth if he acted unwittingly [in eating them], and death[10] if it was deliberate. This [*bikkurim*] has the same law as *t'rumah*: for since Scripture called *bikkurim* by the name of *t'rumah*,[11] they were made subject to the laws of *t'rumah*.

Understand then, my son, this difference that exists about them between an Israelite (non-*kohen*) and a *kohen*, and remember it: that when a *kohen* eats *bikkurim* from the time it comes in view of the Temple,[8] before it is set down in the Temple forecourt, he is to receive a flogging of lashes; and the admonition about it derives from the verse, *You may not eat*, etc. (Deuteronomy 12:17). Now, do not wonder and ask, "How could a *kohen* be punishable by whiplashes over them, when he himself was to eat them after they were set down in the Temple court?" For you see, the law is just the same about the Second Tithe: an Israelite incurs a whipping over it if he eats it outside Jerusalem, even though he himself is to eat it in its proper location. However, if an Israelite (non-*kohen*) eats *bikkurim*, whenever he eats them he incurs death at Heaven's hand; the admonition on this is from the verse, *And no outsider shall eat of a holy thing* (Lev. 22:10),[12] as I wrote in *sidrah 'emor*, in the fifteenth negative precept (§ 280).

As to the root reason for the matter of bringing *bikkurim* to the Sanctuary, so that the ministering servants of the Eternal Lord should eat them, I wrote what I knew of the matter in *sidrah mishpatim*, toward the end of precept § 91. The reason for this precept, that the *kohanim* should not eat them before they are set down in the Temple forecourt, and that an Israelite (non-*kohen*) should not eat of them under any circumstances, follows from that root reason written there. Whoever has the sense to know right and wrong can find it there explained and revealed; much teaching where it is not necessary is a weariness of the flesh.[13]

דִּינֵי הַמִּצְוָה מְבֹאָרִים בְּמַסֶּכֶת מַכּוֹת.

וְנוֹהֵג אִסּוּר זֶה בִּזְכָרִים וּנְקֵבוֹת, וְדַוְקָא בִּזְמַן הַבַּיִת, כִּי אָז הַחוֹבָה עָלֵינוּ בַּהֲבָאַת בִּכּוּרִים; וְהַחִיּוּב מִן הַתּוֹרָה דַּוְקָא בְּפֵרוֹת יְדוּעִים וּבִמְקוֹמוֹת יְדוּעִים, וּכְמוֹ שֶׁכָּתַבְתִּי שָׁם בְּ"כֶסֶף תַּלְוֶה" סוֹף מִצְוֹת עֲשֵׂה [מִשְׁפָּטִים סִי' צ"א]. וְאַף־עַל־פִּי שֶׁאָמַרְנוּ שָׁם שֶׁחִיּוּב מִצְוַת הֲבָאַת בִּכּוּרִים הוּא עַל הַזְּכָרִים לְבַד וְלֹא עַל הַנְּקֵבוֹת, בְּאִסּוּר אֲכִילָתָן בְּכָל מָקוֹם שָׁוָה אִשָּׁה לְאִישׁ, וּכְעִנְיָן שֶׁיֹּאמְרוּ זִכְרוֹנָם לִבְרָכָה בַּגְּמָרָא דֶרֶךְ כְּלָל בַּפָּסוּק "אִישׁ אוֹ אִשָּׁה כִּי יַעֲשׂוּ מִכָּל חַטֹּאת הָאָדָם": הִשְׁוָה הַכָּתוּב אִשָּׁה לְאִישׁ לְכָל עֳנָשִׁין שֶׁבַּתּוֹרָה.

וְכֹהֵן הָעוֹבֵר עַל זֶה וְאָכַל מִבִּכּוּרִים כְּזַיִת בָּעִנְיָן שֶׁאָמַרְנוּ, עָבַר עַל לָאו וְחַיָּב מַלְקוּת; וְכֵן יִשְׂרָאֵל שֶׁאָכַל מֵהֶם כְּזַיִת בְּשׁוּם צַד, כְּלוֹמַר בֵּין קֹדֶם שֶׁהֻנְּחוּ בָּעֲזָרָה אוֹ לְאַחַר מִכֵּן.

[שֶׁלֹּא לַעֲזֹב אֶת הַלְוִיִּים מִלָּתֵת לָהֶם מַתְּנוֹתֵיהֶם וּמִלְשַׂמְּחָם בָּרְגָלִים]

תן שֶׁהֻזְהַרְנוּ שֶׁלֹּא לַעֲזֹב הַלְוִיִּים וְלֹא נִתְרַשֵּׁל מֵהֲשִׁלִים לָהֶם חֻקָּם, כְּלוֹמַר שֶׁלֹּא נַשֶּׁה לָהֶם מַעְשְׂרוֹתָם, וְכָל־שֶׁכֵּן בָּרְגָלִים, שֶׁאָנוּ מֻזְהָרִין עֲלֵיהֶן בְּיוֹתֵר כְּדֵי לְשַׂמְּחָן בַּמּוֹעֵד; וְעַל זֶה נֶאֱמַר: הִשָּׁמֶר לְךָ פֶּן תַּעֲזֹב אֶת הַלֵּוִי כָּל יָמֶיךָ עַל אַדְמָתֶךָ.

מִשָּׁרְשֵׁי הַמִּצְוָה, לְפִי שֶׁהָאֵל בָּרוּךְ הוּא חָפֵץ בְּטוֹב עַמּוֹ יִשְׂרָאֵל אֲשֶׁר בָּחַר לוֹ לְעַם וְרָצָה לְזַכּוֹתָם וְלַעֲשׂוֹתָם סְגֻלָּה בְּעוֹלָמוֹ, עַם חָכָם וְנָבוֹן, לְמַעַן יַכִּירוּם כָּל רוֹאֵיהֶם כִּי הֵם זֶרַע בֵּרַךְ הַשֵּׁם, אַנְשֵׁי אֱמֶת אַנְשֵׁי שֵׁם; וּבִהְיוֹת רְצוֹנוֹ בָּרוּךְ הוּא בָּזֶה, הֵבִיא עֵצוֹת מֵרָחוֹק לְסַבֵּב דְּרָכִים לִהְיוֹת עִסְקָם בְּחָכְמָה וְתָמִיד כָּל הַיּוֹם

14. TB Sukkah 28b, etc.

15. I.e. between the time they were brought within the city walls of Jerusalem and the time they were set down in the Temple forecourt.

16. See sources in note 10.

1. See §439, note 1. (The First Tithe, a tenth of all the produce raised by every Israelite on his land, was to be given the Levites.)

The laws of the precept are explained in the Talmud tractate *Makkoth*.

This prohibition applies to both man and woman, but specifically at the time the Temple exists: for then the obligation lies upon us about bringing *bikkurim*. The obligation, by the law of the Torah, is only for certain, known produce, and in certain known locations, as I wrote there, in *sidrah mishpatim*, toward the end of the positive precept (§ 91). And although we said there that the duty of the precept of bringing *bikkurim* lies only on the men and not on the women, in regard to the prohibition against eating them man and woman are equal. It is in keeping with what the Sages of blessed memory said in the Talmud[14] as a general rule, about the verse, *When a man or woman shall commit anything out of all the sins of man* (Numbers 5:6): Scripture equated a man and a woman for all penalties in the Torah.

If a *kohen* transgressed this and ate an olive's amount of *bikkurim* under the circumstances that we stated,[15] he would violate a negative precept, and would deserve whiplashes; and so likewise an Israelite (non-*kohen*) who ate an olive's amount of them under any circumstances — in other words, whether before they were set down in the Temple forecourt or afterward — [incurs death at Heaven's hand].[16]

[NOT TO NEGLECT THE LEVITES BY FAILING
TO GIVE THEM THEIR GIFTS, ETC.]

450 that we were adjured not to forsake the Levites and not to neglect to give them their complete lawful ration; in other words, we should not delay giving them their tithes; and especially so at the pilgrimage festivals, when we are adjured about them yet more, so as to make them happy at the festive time. About this it was stated, *Take heed to yourself lest you forsake the Levite, all your days on your land* (Deuteronomy 12:19).[1]

At the root of the precept lies the reason that God, blessed is He, desires the good fortune of His Israelite people, whom He chose for Himself as a people, and He wished to make them meritorious, so to make them a treasured entity in His world — *a wise and understanding people* (Deuteronomy 3:6) — so that all who see them may recognize in them that they are a progeny blessed of the Eternal Lord, a people of truth and renown. This being His will (blessed is He), He brought plans to bear from afar, to arrange ways whereby their occupation would be with wisdom, to be intent upon it constantly, all the day.

יִהְיוּ עָלֶיהָ שׁוֹקְדִים, וְהַנְהִיג וְסַדֵּר אוֹתָם בְּמִנְהָגִים נְכוֹנִים וּנְעִימִים וּבְנִימוּסִים יְקָרִים וַחֲזָקִים, לְמַעַן יִלְמְדוּ לָדַעַת אֶת הַשֵּׁם מִקְּטַנָּם וְעַד גְּדוֹלָם, וְיַעֲמֹד זַרְעָם וְשִׁמָם קַיָּם לְעוֹלָם.

וּמִן הַחֲקִים הַמַּחֲזִיקִים וְהַמַּעֲמִידִים הַחַכְמָה בְתוֹכָם הָיָה לִהְיוֹת שֵׁבֶט אֶחָד כֻּלּוֹ בָהֶם מִבְּלִי חֵלֶק וְנַחֲלָה בְקַרְקָעוֹת, לֹא יֵצֵא הַשָּׂדֶה לַחֲרֹשׁ וְלִזְרֹעַ וְלַחְפֹּר בּוֹרוֹת לְהַשְׁקוֹת, וְכָל זֶה לִהְיוֹת סִבָּה אֵלָיו לְהוֹצִיא עִתּוֹתָיו עַל־כָּל־פָּנִים לִלְמֹד חַכְמוֹת וּלְהָבִין דַּרְכֵי הָאֵל הַיְשָׁרוֹת, וְהֵמָּה יוֹרוּ מִשְׁפָּטָיו לַאֲחֵיהֶם בְּכָל מְדִינָה וּמְדִינָה וּבְכָל הָעֲיָרוֹת.

וְעַל־כֵּן, בִּהְיוֹת הַשֵּׁבֶט הַזֶּה נִבְחָר הוּא וְזַרְעוֹ לְעוֹלָם אֶל עֵסֶק הַחַכְמָה וְהַתְּבוּנָה, וְכָל יִשְׂרָאֵל צְרִיכִין לְבַקֵּשׁ תּוֹרָה מִפִּיהֶם וּלְהַסְכִּים דַּעְתָּם וְלָלֶכֶת אַחַר עֲצָתָם כְּכֹל אֲשֶׁר יוֹרוּ אוֹתָם, הָיָה מֵרְצוֹנוֹ שֶׁיְּסַפְּקוּ לָהֶם אֲחֵיהֶם כָּל מִחְיָתָם, פֶּן תִּתְבַּלַּע חָכְמָתָם בְּחֶסְרוֹן חֻקָּם.

וּמִן הַיְסוֹד הַזֶּה בָּאָה עַל כָּל יִשְׂרָאֵל הָאַזְהָרָה כְּפוּלָה בְּזֶה הַכָּתוּב, בְּ"הִשָּׁמֶר" וּ"פֶן", לְבִלְתִּי עָזְבָם וּלְבִלְתִּי הִתְרַשֵּׁל כְּלָל בְּכָל עִנְיָנָם. וְהִזְכִּיר לָהֶם בָּאַזְהָרָה הָאֲדָמָה, שֶׁאָמַר "כָּל יָמֶיךָ עַל אַדְמָתֶךָ", לוֹמַר: הִנָּהֲרוּ מְאֹד בָּהֶם, כִּי לָכֶם נַחֲלַת הָאֲדָמָה, וְהַשֵּׁם שֶׁהוּא מַצְמִיחַ זַרְעֶיהָ הוּא נַחֲלָתוֹ, כְּלוֹמַר וְאַל תַּחְשְׁבוּ לְהִתְגָּאוֹת כְּנֶגְדּוֹ בִּשְׁבִיל נַחֲלַתְכֶם בָּאֲדָמָה, כִּי הוּא הַגְּבִיר.

אוֹ נֹאמַר שֶׁהַזְכָּרַת הָאֲדָמָה הוּא לוֹמַר כִּי צָרִיךְ הוּא אֵלֶיךָ עַל־כָּל־פָּנִים, שֶׁאַתָּה בַּעַל הַנַּחֲלָה וְהַכֹּל צְרִיכִין אֵלֶיהָ, שֶׁכָּל מִי שֶׁאֵין לוֹ קַרְקַע אֲפִלּוּ יֵשׁ לוֹ כַּמָּה כְּסָפִים צָרִיךְ הוּא רַחֲמִים, כִּי הַכֹּל הוּא מִן הַקַּרְקַע, וְאֵין כָּל דָּבָר קַיָּם לוֹ לְאָדָם שֶׁיִּהְיֶה לְבּוֹ סָמוּךְ עָלָיו כָּמוֹהוּ; וּבַעֲלֵי הַקַּרְקָעוֹת הֵם הַמְּגַדְּלִים עֶגְלֵי מַרְבֵּק וּבַרְבּוּרִים אֲבוּסִים, לָהֶם תַּרְנְגוֹלוֹת פְּטוּמוֹת וְיוֹנֵי שׁוֹבָךְ, גְּדָיִים וּטְלָאִים; וּכְדֶרֶךְ

---

2. Or their fixed, allotted rations; cf. Genesis 47:22, Leviticus 10:13, Proverbs 30:8. The Hebrew literally means "their wisdom might be swallowed up," etc. — i.e. their wisdom in Torah could not develop and endure properly amid the grinding need to earn a livelihood. Cf. Ralbag (R. Lévi b. Gershon), commentary on the Torah, *korah* (ed. Bomberg, Venice 1547, 190b): It was the Torah's intention by this that they [the *kohanim* and Levites] should not be troubled about their sustenance but should have free time to engage in Torah study and gain cognizance of their Creator. At the end of *korah* (*to'eleth* 18) he writes again: When the Torah arranged [regular] gifts for the *kohanim*, it was in order that they should have free time to engage in Torah study and fathom the secrets of existence as much as possible....

3. Here, palpably, our author was in mind of Deuteronomy 10:9: *Therefore Lévi* [the Levite] *has had neither portion nor inheritance with his brethren: the Eternal Lord is his inheritance*... Cf. in this regard the cogent words of Rambam in MT *hilchoth sh'mittah* xiii 12–13 (end).

He guided and set them in sound and pleasant customs, and in priceless, effective ways of conduct, that they might learn to know the Lord from their early years till their grown years, and their progeny might stand firm and their name endure forever.

One of the statutes that upheld and maintained wisdom among them was that one complete tribe among them should be without any share or inheritance of the landed properties. It was not to go out into the field to plow and sow, dig pits and irrigate the land—and all this should be the cause for it to spend its time, under all circumstances, to learn wisdom and understand the upright ways of integrity of God. Thus they were to teach His laws to their brethren in every region and in all the towns and villages.

Therefore, since this tribe was chosen—it and its descendants forever—for occupation with wisdom and understanding, and all Israelites would need to seek Torah from their mouth, to concur in their thinking and follow their counsel, all as they would instruct them—it was His will that their brethren should provide them their entire sustenance, for fear that their wisdom might disappear through the lack of their daily needs.[2]

For this basic reason all Israelites were given a double warning in this verse, by the terms, "Take heed" and "lest,"[1] that they should not forsake them and should not be negligent in any way about anything concerning them. In the admonition He also mentioned the land to them, as it stated, *all your days on your land*—as much as to say, "Take great care about them, for you have the inheritance of the land, yet the Eternal Lord, who makes its plantings sprout, is his [the Levite's] inheritance."[3] In other words, do not think to become overweeningly proud against him on account of your possession of the land: for he is the [true] man of wealth.

Or we might say that the mention of the land is to convey that he [the Levite] needs you in any event, since you are the owner of the inheritance [of the land], and all have need of it [are dependent on it]. For whoever has no land, even if he has any amount of money, he is in need of mercy:[4] because all comes from the land, and there is nothing that exists for a man on which his heart can rely [for security] as on that. It is the owners of land who raise calves in stalls and swans

4. Our author echoes here a Talmudic dictum: Any man who has no land is no man (TB Yevamoth 63a).

מַלְכֵי אֶרֶץ וְשָׂרֶיהָ, יָבִיאוּ לָהֶם עוֹבְדֵי הָאֲדָמָה מִכָּל אֵלֶּה בְּחַגִּים — הִזָּהֲרוּ בְּנֵי־
יִשְׂרָאֵל לַעֲשׂוֹת כְּמוֹ־כֵן לַלְוִיִּים. וְעַל זֶה נִכְפְּלוּ כַמָּה אַזְהָרוֹת בַּכָּתוּב בְּכַמָּה
מְקוֹמוֹת, בְּאָמְרוֹ: וְהַלֵּוִי אֲשֶׁר בִּשְׁעָרֶיךָ לֹא תַעַזְבֶנּוּ; וְעִנְיַן אָמְרוֹ "אֲשֶׁר
בִּשְׁעָרֶיךָ", אֵין הַכַּוָּנָה שֶׁיַּחְזְרוּ עַל הַפְּתָחִים חָלִילָה, רַק לוֹמַר שֶׁאֵין לוֹ נַחֲלַת
קַרְקָעוֹת כְּמוֹ לְיִשְׂרָאֵל.

דִּינֵי הַמִּצְוָה מְבֹאָרִים בַּכָּתוּב.

וְנוֹהֶגֶת מִצְוָה זוֹ בִּזְמַן שֶׁיִּשְׂרָאֵל שְׁרוּיִין עַל אַדְמָתָן. וְעוֹבֵר עַל זֶה וְעוֹזֵב אֶת
הַלֵּוִי מִלְּשַׂמְּחוֹ וּמַשֶּׁהֶא מִמֶּנּוּ מַעְשְׂרוֹתָיו בָּרְגָלִים, עָבַר עַל לָאו זֶה, אֲבָל אֵין בּוֹ
מַלְקוֹת, לְפִי שֶׁאֵין בּוֹ מַעֲשֶׂה.

וּבַמִּצְוָה הַזֹּאת יֵשׁ לִלְמֹד לְכָל מֵבִין, לִסְעֹד וּלְהֵטִיב אֶל כָּל הַמִּשְׁתַּדְּלִים תָּמִיד
בְּחָכְמַת הַתּוֹרָה, כִּי הֵם הַמַּעֲמִידִים דַּת הָאֱמֶת וּמְחַזְּקִים הָאֱמוּנָה, מַרְבִּים שָׁלוֹם
בָּעוֹלָם וְאוֹהֲבִים הַבְּרִיּוֹת וּשְׂמֵחִים בְּיִשּׁוּב הַמְּדִינָה, בְּצֶדֶק יֶחֱזוּ פָּנֵימוֹ כָּל הַצָּרִיךְ
חֲנִינָה: שֶׁאֵין לָהֶם פְּנַאי לְשׁוֹטֵט בַּחוּצוֹת אַחַר מִחְיָתָם הֵנָּה וָהֵנָּה; עַל־כֵּן
הַמְרַחֲמָם וּמְבַקֵּשׁ תּוֹעַלְתָּם יְרֻחַם מִן הַשָּׁמַיִם, וְחֵלֶק כְּחֵלֶק יֹאכַל עִמָּהֶם לָעוֹלָם
הַבָּא.

[מִצְוַת שְׁחִיטָה]

תנא שֶׁכָּל מִי שֶׁיִּרְצֶה לֶאֱכֹל בָּשָׂר בְּהֵמָה חַיָּה אוֹ עוֹף, שֶׁיִּשְׁחַט אוֹתָם תְּחִלָּה
כָּרָאוּי, וְלֹא יִהְיֶה לוֹ הֶתֵּר אֶלָּא בִּזְבִיחָה; וְעַל זֶה נֶאֱמַר: וְזָבַחְתָּ מִבְּקָרְךָ וּמִצֹּאנְךָ
כַּאֲשֶׁר צִוִּיתִךָ וְגוֹמֵר ...

וּלְשׁוֹן סִפְרִי: מַה מֻּקְדָּשִׁים בִּשְׁחִיטָה אַף חֻלִּין — "כַּאֲשֶׁר צִוִּיתִךָ" — מְלַמֵּד

5. I.e. that this is why they are (or should be) "within your gates."

6. I.e. with each of the twelve tribes on its territory, as our author wrote at the end of §335.

7. Our author echoes here the Talmudic teaching: Torah scholars increase peace in the world (TB B'rachoth 64a).

8. Literally, with righteousness (*tzedek*); but the Hebrew word is meant here in the sense of *tz'dakah*, charity—in keeping with the statement in the Talmud that "R.'El'azar would give a *p'rutah* [the equivalent of a penny] to a poor man, and then pray; said he: It is written, *As for me, with* tzedek *I shall behold Thy visage* (Psalms 17:15)"; and Rashi explains: I will deal with charity first, and afterward I shall behold Thy visage—in prayer (TB Bava Bathra 10a).

9. Literally, eat.

§451   1. Sifre, Deuteronomy §75.

2. Since it is written about them, *And he shall slay the bullock* (Leviticus 1:5), *And he shall slay it on the side of the altar* (ibid. 11), etc.

in sheds. They have fatted hens, pigeons in the dovecote, goats and sheep. And in the manner of [homage to] the kings of the land and its noblemen, those who work the land bring them of all these [as gifts] at the festive holidays. [Hence] the Israelites were adjured to do as much for the Levites. Many admonitions were reiterated about it in Scripture, in many places, where it is stated, "and the Levite who is within your gates, do not forsake him." Now, the reason for stating, "who is within your gates," is not to intend to convey that they should make the rounds [begging] at doorways,[5] perish the thought, but only to convey that he has no inheritance of landed property, as an Israelite has.

The laws of the precept are explained in the Writ.

This precept is in effect when the Israelites are settled on their land.[6] If a person transgressed this and forsook the Levite, not giving him cause for joy, holding back his tithes from him at the pilgrimage festivals, he would thus violate this negative precept. But it would not bring the penalty of whiplashes, since it involved no physical action.

Through this precept it is for every understanding person to learn to sustain and do good for all those who strive continually for the wisdom of the Torah. For they establish the religion of truth and uphold the faith, increasing peace in the world.[7] They bear the people affection and find happiness in the proper settlement of the country. Then let everyone who needs compassionate grace from God welcome their visages with charity.[8] For they do not have free time to roam about the streets after their livelihood, hither and thither. Therefore, when a person has compassion on them and seeks their benefit, there will be compassion from heaven for him, and he will enjoy[9] equal shares with them in the world-to-come.

[THE PRECEPT OF SHEḤITTAH, RITUAL SLAYING]

451 that when anyone wishes to eat the meat of a domestic or wild animal, or of fowl, he is to ritually slay them first, properly; and he has no permitted way [to eat them] but by ritual slaying. About this it is stated, *then you shall slay of your herd and of your flock...as I have commanded you*, etc. (Deuteronomy 12:21).

In the language of the Midrash *Sifre*:[1] Just as consecrated animals require ritual slaying *(sheḥittah)*,[2] so do non-holy animals; "as I have commanded you"—this teaches that Moses our master was

שֶׁנִּצְטַוָּה מֹשֶׁה רַבֵּנוּ עַל הַוֶּשֶׁט וְעַל הַגַּרְגֶּרֶת וְעַל רֹב אֶחָד בְּעוֹף וְעַל רֹב שְׁנַיִם בִּבְהֵמָה; פֵּרוּשׁ, לֹא שֶׁיִּהְיֶה כֵן כְּמַשְׁמַע הַכָּתוּב, אֶלָּא שֶׁהַצִּוּוּי הַזֶּה בָּאָה הַקַּבָּלָה עָלָיו שֶׁהָיָה כֵן, שֶׁנִּצְטַוָּה בְּכָל עִנְיַן הַשְּׁחִיטָה, כְּמוֹ שֶׁיָּדוּעַ לָנוּ, בְּסַכִּין וְשָׁעוּר מְקוֹם הַשְּׁחִיטָה בַּוֶּשֶׁט וּבַקָּנֶה וּשְׁאָר הָעִנְיָנִים.

וְאַף־עַל־פִּי שֶׁלֹּא הִזְכִּיר הַכָּתוּב רַק בָּקָר וָצֹאן, יָדַעְנוּ שֶׁהַחַיָּה בִּכְלַל בְּהֵמָה, שֶׁהַכָּתוּב הִקִּישָׁן, דִּכְתִיב בִּפְסוּלֵי הַמֻּקְדָּשִׁין: אַךְ כַּאֲשֶׁר יֵאָכֵל אֶת הַצְּבִי וְאֶת הָאַיָּל כֵּן תֹּאכְלֶנּוּ; וְהָעוֹף גַּם־כֵּן צָרִיךְ שְׁחִיטָה, דְּאִתְקַשׁ לִבְהֵמָה, דִּכְתִיב "זֹאת תּוֹרַת הַבְּהֵמָה וְהָעוֹף", אֶלָּא שֶׁחֲכָמִים דְּקְדְּקוּ, וְהַקַּבָּלָה שֶׁמְּסַיַּעַת, וּמְכֵּינָן שֶׁהִטִּילוֹ הַכָּתוּב לָעוֹף בֵּין בְּהֵמָה שֶׁצְּרִיכָה שְׁחִיטָה לְדָגִים שֶׁאֵין בָּהֶם שְׁחִיטָה, דִּכְתִיב "זֹאת תּוֹרַת הַבְּהֵמָה וְהָעוֹף וְכֹל נֶפֶשׁ הַחַיָּה הָרֹמֶשֶׂת בַּמָּיִם", שֶׁבַּשְּׁחִיטַת סִימָן אֶחָד דֵּי לוֹ.

וּמֵהֵיכָן לָמְדוּ לוֹמַר שֶׁאֵין שְׁחִיטָה בְּדָגִים — דִּכְתִיב בְּהוּ "אִם אֶת כָּל דְּגֵי הַיָּם יֵאָסֵף לָהֶם", בַּאֲסִיפָה בְּעָלְמָא, בֵּין שֶׁהֵם נֶאֱסָפִים חַיִּים אוֹ אֲפִלּוּ מֵתִים. וְכֵן כָּל מִין חָגָב אֵין לוֹ שְׁחִיטָה, שֶׁבָּהֶן כָּתוּב גַּם־כֵּן לְשׁוֹן אֲסִיפָה כְּמוֹ בְּדָגִים, דִּכְתִיב "אָסַף הֶחָסִיל"; וְעוֹד דְּבָתַר דָּגִים אַדְּרִינְהוּ קְרָא בְּסוֹף סֵדֶר בַּיּוֹם הַשְּׁמִינִי, שֶׁנֶּאֱמַר "זֹאת תּוֹרַת הַבְּהֵמָה וְהָעוֹף וְכֹל נֶפֶשׁ הַחַיָּה הָרֹמֶשֶׂת [בַּמָּיִם]", אֵלּוּ דָגִים, "וּלְכָל נֶפֶשׁ הַשֹּׁרֶצֶת [עַל הָאָרֶץ]", אֵלּוּ חֲגָבִים; וְעוֹד דְּקַשְׂקַשִׂין אִית לְהוּ בְּגוּפָן כְּדָגִים.

כְּבָר כָּתַבְתִּי בְּסוֹף סֵדֶר צַו בְּאִסּוּר דָּם בְּסִימָן קמ"ח, וּבְרֹאשׁ אַחֲרֵי־מוֹת עָשָׂה דְכִסּוּי הַדָּם בְּסִימָן (קפ"ה) [קפ"ז], בְּעִנְיַן הַהַרְחָקָה שֶׁהִרְחִיקָה מִמֶּנּוּ הַתּוֹרָה דָם

---

3. So TB Ḥullin 27b.

commanded about the gullet and the trachea (windpipe), regarding the greater part of one of these in fowl, and the greater part of the two in an animal [that these are to be cut in ritual slaying]. In other words, this is not in the meaning of the verse, but an Oral Tradition was rather given about this order that it was so: that he was commanded about the entire subject of *shehittah* (ritual slaying) as it is known to us—with a knife, and within the range of the place for cutting in the gullet and trachea, and so the other details of the subject.

Now, although the Writ mentions only a herd (cattle) and a flock (sheep), we know that wild animals are included in the category of domestic ones, because Scripture equates them: for it is written in regard to consecrated animals that were disqualified, *Only, as the gazelle and the hart are eaten, so shall you eat it* (Deuteronomy 12:22). And fowl likewise require *shehittah*, since they are likened to animals: for it is written, *This is the law of the beast and the fowl* (Leviticus 11:46).[3] However, the Sages made a distinction,[3] which the Oral Tradition supports, that since Scripture set fowl between animals, which require *shehittah*, and fish, which have no requirement of *shehittah*—for it is written, *This is the law of the beast and the fowl and every living creature that moves in the water (ibid.)*—the cutting of one organ [either the gullet or the windpipe] is enough for it.

Now, how did the Sages learn to rule that there is no *shehittah* [required] for fish?[3]—because it is written about them, *or if all the fish of the sea be gathered for them* (Numbers 11:22): [they became permissible] merely by being gathered, whether they are gathered alive or even dead. Likewise, any kind of locust has no *shehittah* [required] for it: for the expression of gathering is also written about them, as about fish—since it is written, *as the gathering of the locust* (Isaiah 33:4). Moreover, the Writ mentions them after fish, toward the end of *sidrah sh'mini*: for it is stated, *This is the law of the beast and the fowl and every living creature that moves in the water*—these being fish—*and of every creature that swarms on the earth* (Leviticus 11:46)—these being locusts. Furthermore, they have scales on their bodies like fish.[3]

Previously, toward the end of *sidrah tzav*, regarding the prohibition on blood (§ 148), and near the beginning of *sidrah aharé moth* in the positive precept of covering the blood [of a ritually slain animal] (§ 187), I wrote what I knew about the distancing, [the fact]

⟨397⟩

כָּל בָּשָׂר, מַה שֶּׁיָּדַעְתִּי; וְאוֹמַר גַּם־כֵּן עַל צַד הַפְּשָׁט כִּי מִצְוַת הַשְּׁחִיטָה הִיא מֵאוֹתוֹ הַטַּעַם, לְפִי שֶׁיָּדוּעַ כִּי מִן הַצַּוָּאר יֵצֵא דָם מִבְּשָׁאַר מְקוֹמוֹת הַגּוּף, וְלָכֵן נִצְטַוִּינוּ לְשָׁחֳטוֹ מִשָּׁם טֶרֶם שֶׁנֹּאכְלֵהוּ, כִּי מִשָּׁם יֵצֵא כָל דָּמוֹ, וְלֹא נֹאכַל הַנֶּפֶשׁ עִם הַבָּשָׂר.

וְעוֹד נֹאמַר בְּטַעַם הַשְּׁחִיטָה מִן הַצַּוָּאר וּבְסַכִּין בָּדוּק, כְּדֵי שֶׁלֹּא נְצַעֵר בַּעֲלֵי־ הַחַיִּים יוֹתֵר מִדַּאי, כִּי הַתּוֹרָה הִתִּירָן לָאָדָם לְמַעֲלָתוֹ לָזוּן מֵהֶם וּלְכָל צְרָכָיו, לֹא לְצַעֲרָן חִנָּם; וּכְבָר דִּבְּרוּ חֲכָמִים הַרְבֵּה בְּאִסּוּר צַעַר בַּעֲלֵי־חַיִּים בְּבָבָא מְצִיעָא וּבְשַׁבָּת, אִם הוּא אָסוּר דְּאוֹרַיְתָא, וְהֵלְלוּ לְפִי הַדּוֹמֶה שֶׁאָסוּר דְּאוֹרַיְתָא.

מִדִּינֵי הַמִּצְוָה, מַה שֶּׁאָמְרוּ זִכְרוֹנָם לִבְרָכָה שֶׁחֲמִשָּׁה דְבָרִים הֵם שֶׁמַּפְסִידִין הַשְּׁחִיטָה אִם אֵרַע אַחַת מֵהֶן בַּשְּׁחִיטָה, וְאֵלּוּ הֵן: שְׁהִיָּה, דְּרָסָה, חֲלָדָה, הַגְרָמָה; וְעִקּוּר. עִנְיַן הַשְּׁהִיָּה הוּא כְּגוֹן אַחַר שֶׁהִתְחִיל לִשְׁחֹט הַגֵּשֶׁ וְקֹדֶם שֶׁשָּׁחַט רֻבּוֹ, פָּסַק מִלִּשְׁחֹט: אִם שָׁהָה בְּהַפְסָקָה זוֹ כְּשִׁעוּר שְׁחִיטָה אַחֶרֶת, שְׁחִיטָתוֹ פְּסוּלָה — פֵּרוּשׁ, כְּדֵי שְׁחִיטַת הָעוֹר וְהַסִּימָנִין שֶׁל בְּהֵמָה אַחֶרֶת כְּמוֹתָהּ, וּכְדֵי שְׁחִיטַת בְּהֵמָה דַקָּה לְעוֹף. וְיֵשׁ מַחְמִירִין שֶׁאֵין הַשִּׁעוּר אֶלָּא כְּדֵי שְׁחִיטַת רֹב הַסִּימָנִין בִּבְהֵמָה וְרֹב אֶחָד בְּעוֹף.

אֲבָל הַשּׁוֹחֵט בְּסַכִּין רָעָה, אֲפִלּוּ הוֹלִיךְ וְהֵבִיא כָּל הַיּוֹם כֻּלּוֹ שְׁחִיטָתוֹ כְשֵׁרָה, זוּלָתִי אִם הוֹלִיךְ וְהֵבִיא אוֹתוֹ אַחַר שֶׁשָּׁחַט בִּבְהֵמָה רֹב סִימָן אֶחָד לְבַד, שֶׁאִם בְּאוֹתוֹ הַמְעוּט הַנִּשְׁאָר מִמֶּנּוּ הוֹלִיךְ וְהֵבִיא סַכִּין רָעָה כְּשִׁעוּר שְׁהִיָּה, שְׁחִיטָתוֹ פְּסוּלָה.

וְעִנְיַן הַדְּרָסָה הוּא מִי שֶׁדָּרַס הַסַּכִּין בְּעֵת הַשְּׁחִיטָה כְּמוֹ שֶׁחוֹתְכִין הַצָּנוֹן,

---

4. Similarly Rambam, *Guide* III 48.

5. TB Ḥullin 9b.

6. *Ibid.* 32a.

7. So R. Isaac 'Alfasi, following Sh'mu'él in *ibid.*

8. So Rashi, *ibid.* s.v. *dakkah l'dakkah.*

9. Because cutting the remaining part is not necessary in the ritual slaying; once the greater part is cut through, it is as though the entire organ is severed; hence the time spent cutting the remaining part constitutes a needless interruption; and when the cutting is done too slowly and that takes too long, it disqualifies the *sheḥittah.*

〈398〉

that the Torah removed the blood of every [creature of] flesh far from us. I would likewise say, by way of the plain meaning, that the precept of *shehittah* is for the same reason. For it is known that the blood of a body will issue out of the neck [throat] more so than from any other place in the body. We were therefore commanded to perform the *shehittah* there before we eat it, because from there all its blood will come out, and we will not eat the life-spirit with the flesh.

We would say furthermore about the reason for *shehittah* being done at the throat and with an inspected knife, that it is in order not to cause living creatures undue sufferng.[4] For the Torah permitted them to a man, in his superior state, to use them for food and for all his needs, [but] not to cause them needless pain. Long ago the Sages greatly discussed the prohibition against pain for living creatures, in the tractates *Bava M'tzi'a* (32b) and *Shabbath* (128b), whether it is forbidden by the law of the Torah; and they concluded, as it seems, that it is prohibited by Torah law.

Among the laws of the precept there is what the Sages of blessed memory taught:[5] that there are five things which can spoil *shehittah*, if any one of them occurred during ritual slaying. These are: pausing, pressing down, incising underneath, swerving and tearing. Pausing means in substance if, for example, after beginning to cut the gullet, before he cut through the greater part of it, one interrupted the *shehittah*. If he paused in this interruption long enough for another ritual slaying, his *shehittah* is disqualified.[6] This means the time needed to cut through the skin and organs [gullet and trachea] of another animal like it; and for a fowl, long enough to ritually slay a small domestic animal.[7] Some rule stringently, though, that the minimal amount of time [for a disqualifying pause] is no more than the duration needed to sever most of the organs for a domestic animal, and most of one [the gullet or the trachea] for a fowl.[8]

If, however, someone does *shehittah* with a bad [dull] knife, even if he moves it back and forth the entire day, his *shehittah* is acceptable[6] — unless he thus moved it back and forth after severing the greater part of only one organ in an animal. If in the remaining small part of it he moved a bad [dull] knife back and forth for the duration of a [disqualifying] pause, his *shehittah* is disqualified.[9]

"Pressing down" occurs when someone forces the knife downward during the ritual slaying, as in cutting a radish; in other words,

כְּלוֹמַר שֶׁלֹּא הוֹלִיךְ וְהֵבִיא הַסַּכִּין; בְּעִנְיָן זֶה שְׁחִיטָתוֹ פְסוּלָה.

וְעִנְיַן חֲלָדָה הוּא שֶׁקִּבַּלְנוּ שֶׁבְּשָׁעָה שֶׁשּׁוֹחֲטִין צָרִיךְ לַעֲמֹד הַסַּכִּין מְגֻלֶּה, וּמִפְּנֵי־כֵן אָמְרוּ זִכְרוֹנָם לִבְרָכָה שֶׁאִם הִטְמִין הַסַּכִּין תַּחַת סִימָן הָאֶחָד וְשָׁחַט הַשֵּׁנִי, אוֹ אֲפִלּוּ אִם טָמַן אוֹתוֹ תַּחַת הָעוֹר וְשָׁחַט הַסִּימָנִין, אוֹ אֲפִלּוּ תַּחַת הַצֶּמֶר הַמְסֻבָּךְ אוֹ אֲפִלּוּ תַּחַת מַטְלִית דְּבוּקָה הַרְבֵּה בַּצַּוָּאר, הַשְּׁחִיטָה פְסוּלָה; אֲבָל אִם אֵינָהּ דְּבוּקָה הַרְבֵּה אֵינָהּ נִפְסֶלֶת בְּכָךְ.

וְעִנְיַן הַגְרָמָה הוּא שֶׁקִּבַּלְנוּ שֶׁאַף־עַל־פִּי שֶׁהַשְּׁחִיטָה הִיא מִן הַצַּוָּאר, גְּבוּלִים יְדוּעִים הֵם בַּצַּוָּאר שֶׁהַשְּׁחִיטָה כְשֵׁרָה בָּהֶן, וְלֹא לְמַטָּה מֵאוֹתוֹ גְבוּל וְלֹא לְמַעְלָה; וּגְבוּל מְקוֹם הַשְּׁחִיטָה בַּקָּנֶה מִשִּׁפּוּי כּוֹבַע וּלְמַטָּה עַד רֹאשׁ הַכְּנָפַיִם הַקְּטַנִּים שֶׁל רֵאָה, לֹא עַד עִקָּרָן שֶׁל כְּנָפַיִם שֶׁמְּחֻבָּרִים בָּרֵאָה אֶלָּא עַד רֹאשָׁן; וְשִׁעוּר זֶה הוּא כָּל מָקוֹם מִן הַצַּוָּאר שֶׁהַבְּהֵמָה פּוֹשֶׁטֶת אוֹתוֹ בְּשָׁעָה שֶׁהִיא רוֹעָה כְדַרְכָּהּ בְּלֹא אֹנֶס; וּבְשֶׁט מַנִּיחַ לְמַעְלָה כְּדֵי תְפִיסַת יָד, וּלְמַטָּה שִׁעוּרוֹ עַד הַמָּקוֹם שֶׁהַבְּשֶׁט מַשְׂעִיר, כְּלוֹמַר שֶׁעוֹמֵד שָׁם פְּרָצוֹת פְּרָצוֹת כִּדְמוּת הַכֶּרֶס.

וּפֵרוּשׁ תְּפִיסַת הַיָּד יֵשׁ אוֹמְרִים שֶׁהוּא כְדֵי שְׁלֹשָׁה אֶצְבָּעוֹת, וְיֵשׁ אוֹמְרִים כְּדֵי שֶׁיִּתְפֹּס בִּשְׁתֵּי אֶצְבָּעוֹת מִשְּׁנֵי צִדֵּי הַצַּוָּאר, וְזֶהוּ שִׁעוּר רֹחַב אֶצְבַּע; וְזֶה בַּבְּהֵמָה וְחַיָּה, אֲבָל בְּעוֹף הַכֹּל לְפִי גָדְלוֹ וְקָטְנוֹ.

וְאָמְרוּ בַגְּמָרָא שֶׁמִּי שֶׁהִתְחִיל לִשְׁחֹט בְּמָקוֹם שְׁחִיטָה בַּקָּנֶה וְשָׁחַט שְׁלִישׁ, וְאַחַר־כָּךְ הוֹצִיא הַסַּכִּין מִמְּקוֹם הַשְּׁחִיטָה, דְּהַיְנוּ לְמַעְלָה מִשִּׁפּוּי כּוֹבַע, וְחָתַךְ בּוֹ שְׁלִישׁ, וְאַחַר־כֵּן חָזַר הַסַּכִּין בִּמְקוֹם הַשְּׁחִיטָה וְשָׁחַט בּוֹ שְׁלִישׁ, שֶׁזּוֹ הַשְּׁחִיטָה פְסוּלָה, דִּלְעוֹלָם בָּעִנְיָן בְּדִין זֶה שֶׁל הַגְרָמָה שֶׁיְּהֵא רֹב מִיתַת הַבְּהֵמָה בַּשְּׁחִיטָה, וּבְשָׁעַת יְצִיאַת הַחַיּוּת מִמֶּנָּה, דְּהַיְנוּ שְׁלִישׁ אֶמְצָעִי, שֶׁיִּהְיֶה אָז רֻבּוֹ בַּשְּׁחִיטָה: כָּל שֶׁהִיא כֵן כְּשֵׁרָה, בְּעִנְיָן אַחֵר פְּסוּלָה.

10. TB Ḥullin 30b (and Rashi).

11. The ruling about the strip of cloth is that of *Halachoth G'doloth* (see ed. Warsaw 1874, fol. 125d, bottom; 1st ed. Hildesheimer, p. 511 and note 83), cited by Rashba, commentary to Ḥullin *ibid*. MT *hilchoth shehittah* iii 10 differs.

12. TB Ḥullin 19a, 45a.

13. *Ibid.* 44a.

14. Rashi *ibid.* s.v. *ad k'dé*, citing his aged master teacher.

15. *Halachoth G'doloth*, cited in *tosafoth* to *ibid.*, s.v. *k'dé*.

16. TB Ḥullin 19a.

he does not move the knife [swiftly] back and forth. In this way, his *shehittah* is disqualified.[10]

The requirement about "incising underneath" is what we learned by the Oral Tradition: that at the time of the *shehittah*, the knife must remain exposed. For this reason the Sages of blessed memory said that if one hid the knife under one organ [gullet or windpipe] and cut the other, or even if he hid it under the skin and cut the organs, or even [if he thus hid it] under the thick, curly wool,[10] or even under a strip of cloth strongly attached to the throat, the *shehittah* is unacceptable; but if it was not very strongly attached, it would not be thus disqualified.[11]

The meaning of "swerving" is what we received in the Oral Tradition: that although *shehittah* is [to be done] at the throat, there are certain known limits at the throat within which the *shehittah* is valid, but not either below or above those limits. The delimitation of the area for cutting the trachea is from the thyroid cartilage down to the beginning of the small laps (extreme ends) of the lungs — not to the main part of the laps, where they are attached to the lungs, but to their tops.[12] This measure is the full length of the throat that the animal stretches out when it grazes in its natural way, without duress.[12] With the gullet, enough is to be left at the top for the hand to grasp; while below, its limit is at the place where the gullet becomes hairy, i.e. where there are many openings, as in the form of the stomach.[13]

As to the meaning of "enough for the hand to grasp," some say[14] it is the width of three fingers, while others say[15] it means enough [of the gullet] to seize with two fingers from both sides of the neck, which is the measure of the width of a finger. This [length] is for a domestic or wild animal; but with a fowl, it is all according to how large or small it is.

Now, it was stated in the Talmud[16] that if a person began to cut at the proper place of *shehittah* in the windpipe, and he thus cut through a third, then he moved the knife away from the place of *shehittah*,[17] i.e. above the thyroid cartilage, and he cut through one third, and then brought the knife back to the proper place of *shehittah* and cut [the final] third — this ritual slaying is not acceptable. For it is always required, by this law about "swerving," that most of the slaying of the animal should occur by [proper] *shehittah*; hence when its life leaves it, i.e. at [the cutting of] the middle third, when the larger part

וְעִנְיָן זֶה שֶׁל הַגְרָמָה אֵינוֹ נִמְצָא כִּי־אִם בַּקָּנֶה וּלְמַעְלָה סָמוּךְ לִשְׁפּוּי כּוֹבַע,
דְּאִלּוּ לְמַטָּה סָמוּךְ לְכַנְפֵי רֵאָה, נְקוּבָתָהּ שָׁם בְּמַשֶּׁהוּ, וְלֹא שַׁיָּךְ בָּהּ הַגְרָמִים שְׁלִישׁ
כְּלָל; וְכֵן בַּוֵּשֶׁט בֵּין לְמַעְלָה וּלְמַטָּה נְקוּבָתוֹ בְּמַשֶּׁהוּ, וְלֹא שַׁיָּךְ בֵּהּ דִּין הַגְרָמִים
שְׁלִישׁ כְּלָל.

כָּל מִי שֶׁאֵינוֹ בָּקִי בְּאַרְבָּעָה דְּבָרִים אֵלֶּה שֶׁהֵן פּוֹסְלִין הַשְּׁחִיטָה, אֵינוֹ רַשַּׁאי
לִשְׁחֹט, וְאִם שָׁחַט אָסוּר לֶאֱכֹל מִשְּׁחִיטָתוֹ; וַאֲפִלּוּ אִם אַחַר שֶׁשָּׁחַט שָׁאֲלוּ אוֹתוֹ
אִם נִזְהַר בָּהֶן וְאָמַר "הֵן הֵן", אֵין מַמָּשׁ בִּדְבָרָיו, דְּמַכִּינָן שֶׁלֹּא יָדַע אוֹתָן
מִתְּחִלָּה, שֶׁמָּא פָּשַׁע בָּהֶן וְאֵינוֹ זָכוּר כְּלָל.

וּמִלְבַד אַרְבָּעָה דְּבָרִים אֵלּוּ שֶׁזְּכַרְנוּ שֶׁצָּרִיךְ כָּל שׁוֹחֵט לָדַעַת, חִיְּבוּהוּ חֲכָמִים
עוֹד לָדַעַת דָּבָר חֲמִישִׁי, וְאַף־עַל־פִּי שֶׁאֵינוֹ מֵהִלְכוֹת שְׁחִיטָה, מִפְּנֵי שֶׁעִנְיָן זֶה
תָּמִיד יָבוֹא בִּשְׁעַת שְׁחִיטָה וְהַבְּהֵמָה נַעֲשֵׂית נְבֵלָה בַּדָּבָר, וְאִם לֹא יֵדַע אוֹתוֹ
הַשּׁוֹחֵט, יַאֲכִיל נְבֵלוֹת לַכֹּל; וּלְפִיכָךְ אָמְרוּ גַם־כֵּן בָּזֶה שֶׁכָּל טַבָּח שֶׁאֵינוֹ יוֹדֵעַ
אוֹתוֹ, אָסוּר לֶאֱכֹל מִשְּׁחִיטָתוֹ.

וְהוּא הָאִסּוּר הַנִּקְרָא עִקּוּר, וְעִנְיָנוֹ הוּא שֶׁנֶּעֶקְרוּ הַקָּנֶה וְהַוֵּשֶׁט, שְׁנֵיהֶם אוֹ
אֶחָד מֵהֶם, מִמְּקוֹם חִבּוּרָן שֶׁהֵן מְחֻבָּרִין בַּלֶּחִי וּבַבָּשָׂר שֶׁעָלָיו, וְנֶעֶקְרוּ מִשָּׁם
לְגַמְרֵי, אוֹ אֲפִלּוּ לֹא נֶעֶקְרוּ לְגַמְרֵי אֶלָּא שֶׁנֻּדַּלְדְּלוּ רֻבָּם, הֲרֵי זוֹ אֲסוּרָה; וְהוּא
דְּאִפָּרוּק אִיפָּרוּקֵי, כְּלוֹמַר כְּשֶׁאָנוּ אוֹסְרִין אוֹתָהּ בְּשֶׁנֻּדַּלְדְּלוּ רֻבָּן, כְּלוֹמַר שֶׁיִּהְיֶה
הַדִּלְדּוּל כָּאן וְכָאן, דְּכָל שֶׁהוּא כְעִנְיָן זֶה אֲפִלּוּ מַה שֶּׁמְּחֻבָּר מֵהֶן אֵינוֹ חִבּוּר יָפֶה,
וַהֲרֵי הֵן נֶחְשָׁבִין כַּעֲקוּרִים לְגַמְרֵי.

אֲבָל אִם נִדַּלְדְּל הַסִּימָן בְּצַד אֶחָד, כְּלוֹמַר שֶׁנֻּפְסַק וְנֶעֱקַר מִן הַלֶּחִי בְּמָקוֹם

17. E.g. by cutting at a slant.

18. Hence, once the knife makes the slightest cut there, the animal can no longer
be made legally fit to eat; TB Ḥullin 45a.

19. *Ibid.* 9a.

20. This is what any animal is called if it died without *shehittah* that made it
permissible for food.

21. I.e. of their cross-sectional area.

[of the organ] is [thus severed] in the ritual slaying, whatever is so done, is acceptable; in any other manner, it is disqualified.

This matter of "swerving" can occur nowhere but in the trachea (windpipe), at the upper part, near the thyroid cartilage. For below, near the extreme ends of the lungs, its perforation [that disqualifies it immediately] is any amount at all;[18] then the question of swerving and cutting a third [beyond the limit] cannot be considered at all. So too with the gullet, both above and below, a disqualifying perforation may be in any amount whatever; and the law about swerving and cutting a third has no relevance at all.

Anyone who is not expert in these four things which disqualify shehittah, is not permitted to do ritual slaying; and if he did, it is forbidden to eat of his shehittah.[19] Even if after he did the ritual slaying he was asked whether he had been careful in regard to them, and he said, Yes, yes, his words are of no matter. For since he did not know them at the start, perhaps he did wrong in regard to them, and does not remember it at all.

Now, apart from these four things that we mentioned, that every shohêt (ritual slayer) needs to know, the Sages obligated him further to know a fifth thing. Although it is not among the laws of shehittah, because this matter can occur constantly during ritual slaying and the animal becomes thereby n'vélah[20] [like a carcass], if the shohêt is not familiar with it he will [unwittingly] give everyone n'vélah [non-kosher meat] to eat. Therefore the Sages said about this too that if any butcher does not know it, it is forbidden to eat of his shehittah.

This is the prohibition called "tearing." In substance it means that the trachea and gullet — either the two of them or one of them — were torn or uprooted from their place of connection, where they were attached to the jaw and to the flesh on it, becoming detached completely. Even if they did not become completely detached, but the greater part of them [21] tore loose, [the animal] is forbidden — but this if they are well separated: In other words, when we forbid it because they became mostly torn loose, it means that the detachment occurs here and there, all in such a way that even the part of them that is attached is not bound well, so that they can be reckoned as completely torn away.[13]

However, if the organ [the gullet or trachea] became detached at one side — in other words, it became separated and torn away from the jaw at one place alone — then even if the greater part of it[21] tore

אֶחָד לְבַד, אֲפִלּוּ נֶעֱקַר מִמֶּנּוּ רֻבּוֹ, כָּל שֶׁהָעֲקוּר אֵינוֹ אֶלָּא בְּמָקוֹם אֶחָד, אַף־עַל־
פִּי שֶׁהוּא בְּרֹב הַסִּימָן וְלֹא נִשְׁאַר מִמֶּנּוּ אֶלָּא הַמְּעוּט מְחֻבָּר, אוֹתוֹ מְעוּט מַצִּיל
וּכְשֵׁרָה; וְכָל־שֶׁכֵּן שֶׁנַּכְשִׁיר אוֹתוֹ הֵיכָא שֶׁהַסִּימָן כֻּלּוֹ מְחֻבָּר אֶל הַבָּשָׂר שֶׁלְּמַטָּה,
וְאַף־עַל־פִּי שֶׁנִּגְמַם הַלֶּחִי וְנִטַּל לְגַמְרֵי מִמְּקוֹם חִבּוּרוֹ בָּרֹאשׁ, חִבּוּר הַבָּשָׂר עִם
הַסִּימָן מַצִּיל. נִמְצָא שֶׁהָעֲקוּר הוּא הָאוֹסֵר הוּא כְּשֶׁנֶּעֶקְרוּ הַסִּימָנִין בְּהַרְבֵּה מְקוֹמוֹת
הֵנָּה וָהֵנָּה בְּרֻבָּן, אֲבָל בְּכָל עִנְיָן אַחֵר אֵין הָעָקוּר אוֹסֵר.

וְעִקּוּר זֶה שֶׁאָמַרְנוּ אֵינוֹ עוֹשֶׂה הַבְּהֵמָה טְרֵפָה, אֲבָל כָּךְ לָמַדְנוּ מִפִּי שְׁמוּעָה,
שֶׁסִּימָנִין עֲקוּרִין אֵינָם בְּנֵי שְׁחִיטָה, כְּלוֹמַר שֶׁמִּצְוַת הַשְּׁחִיטָה לֹא הָיְתָה בְּסִימָנִין
שֶׁהֵן עֲקוּרִין; וּלְפִיכָךְ הַשּׁוֹחֵט בְּסִימָנִין עֲקוּרִין הֲרֵי הוּא כְּאִלּוּ לֹא שָׁחַט, (וכמי)
[וּכְאִלּוּ] שֶׁמֵּתָה הַבְּהֵמָה מֵאֵלֶיהָ, שֶׁהִיא נְבֵלָה.

וְעוֹף, אַף־עַל־פִּי שֶׁהֻכְשַׁר בְּסִימָן אֶחָד, כְּמוֹ שֶׁאָמַרְנוּ, כָּל זְמַן שֶׁנֶּעֱקַר הָאֶחָד
קֹדֶם שֶׁשָּׁחַט הָאַחֵר אֵין הַשְּׁחִיטָה מַתִּיר אוֹתוֹ, וְאָסוּר; כָּךְ לָמַדְנוּ מִפִּי הַשְּׁמוּעָה.

אֵלּוּ חֲמִשָּׁה הַהֲלָכוֹת שֶׁזָּכַרְתִּי, שֶׁהֵן שְׁהִיָּה, דְּרָסָה, חֲלָדָה, הַגְרָמָה וְעִקּוּר,
צָרִיךְ כָּל אֶחָד מִיִּשְׂרָאֵל לֵידַע אוֹתָם וְלִהְיוֹת בָּקִי בָּהֶן קֹדֶם שֶׁיִּשְׁחַט, וְכָל שֶׁאֵינוֹ
בָּקִי בָּהֶם וְשָׁחַט, אָסוּר לֶאֱכֹל מִשְּׁחִיטָתוֹ; וַאֲפִלּוּ נִשְׁאַל אַחֲרֵי־כֵן וְאָמַר "בָּרִיא
לִי שֶׁשְּׁחַטְתִּי כָּרָאוּי", אֵין שׁוֹמְעִין לוֹ כְּלָל.

וְגַם־כֵּן צָרִיךְ לָדַעַת כָּל הָרוֹצֶה לִשְׁחֹט עִנְיַן בְּדִיקַת סַכִּין, שֶׁהִצְרִיכוּ חֲכָמִים
לִבְדֹּק אוֹתוֹ עִם הַצִּפֹּרֶן וְעִם הַבָּשָׂר וּבִשְׁלֹשׁ רוּחוֹתֶיהָ שֶׁל סַכִּין, וְאִם נַרְגִּישׁ בּוֹ
פְּגִימָה אֲפִלּוּ כָל־שֶׁהִיא, הַשְּׁחִיטָה אֲסוּרָה; וּמֻתָּר לִשְׁחֹט בְּכָל דָּבָר שֶׁחוֹתֵךְ יָפֶה
וְאֵין בּוֹ פְּגִימָה כְּלָל; וְאִם נִמְצֵאת הַסַּכִּין פְּגוּמָה אַחַר שְׁחִיטָה, נֹאמַר שֶׁבְּעֵצֶם
נִפְגְּמָה וְהַסִּימָנִין נִשְׁחֲטוּ בְּסַכִּין פָּגוּם; וְזֶה נֹאמַר הֵיכָא שֶׁלֹּא נִשְׁבְּרוּ עֲצָמוֹת

22. View of *Halachoth G'doloth* (ed. Warsaw 1874, fol. 126b; 1st ed. Hildesheimer, p. 512), cited in *tosafoth* to TB Ḥullin 9a, s.v. *kulhu*.

23. I.e. the surface of the keen edge, and its either side; along these a fingernail and the flesh of a finger are very lightly passed, to detect any imperfections (nicks), etc. TB Ḥullin 17b.

24. TB Ḥullin 15b, 17a.

away, as long as the uprooting is only at one place, even if it is so for the greater part of the organ and no more than the smaller part remains attached, that lesser part can save [the animal from becoming disqualified as *n'vélah* and it is thus kosher (acceptable). And all the more certainly we would declare it kosher when the organ is entirely attached to the flesh of the jaw; even if the jaw is damaged and completely dislocated from its place of attachment to the head, the union of the flesh with the organ saves it. Consequently, the detachment that makes an animal forbidden is when the organs were torn away in many places, here and there, for their greater part. But in any other circumstances, the "tearing" [separation] does not make it forbidden.[13]

Now, this detachment does not make the animal *t'réfah* [fatally injured]. Yet so we learned in the Oral Torah:[22] that detached organs are not fit for *shehittah*; in other words, the precept of *shehittah* does not hold for organs [trachea and gullet] that are torn away. Therefore, if someone cut through detached organs, it is as though he did no ritual slaying, and [thus] as though the animal died of itself, so that it is *n'vélah* (a carcass). As for fowl, even though it is made permissible [as food] by [the cutting of] one organ, as we said, as long as one became torn away before the other was cut, the ritual slaying does not make it permitted, and it is forbidden.[22] So we learned through the Oral Tradition.

These five laws that I mentioned — pausing, pressing down, incising underneath, swerving, and tearing away — every Jew needs to know and be expert in them before he does ritual slaying. If anyone was not expertly versed in them and he did ritual slaying, it is forbidden to eat of his *shehittah*. Even if he was asked afterward and he said, "I am certain that I did the *shehittah* properly," he is not heeded at all.[16]

So likewise, whoever wishes to do ritual slaying needs to know the subject of the knife's inspection; For the Sages made it a requirement to inspect it with the fingernail and with the flesh, and along the three sides of the knife;[23] and if we detect even the slightest defect in it, anything ritually slain with it is forbidden. It is permitted to do *shehittah* with anything that cuts well and has no defect at all.[24] If the knife is found to have a defect after a ritual slaying, we assume that it was damaged by the skin, and the organs were thus cut by a defective knife. But this applies where no bones were broken by the knife after

בְּאוֹתוֹ סַכִּין אַחַר שְׁחִיטָה, כְּלוֹמַר שֶׁלֹּא נָגַע הַסַּכִּין בְּדָבָר שֶׁאֶפְשָׁר לוֹ שֶׁיִּפָּגֵם בּוֹ,
אֲבָל אִם יָדַעְנוּ בְּוַדַּאי שֶׁנָּגַע הַסַּכִּין אַחַר שְׁחִיטָה בְּדָבָר שֶׁאֶפְשָׁר לוֹ לְהִפָּגֵם בּוֹ,
תָּלִינַן פְּגִימָתוֹ בְּאוֹתוֹ דָבָר; וְכָל זְמַן שֶׁיִּסְתַּפֵּק לָנוּ אִם נָגַע בְּדָבָר הַפּוֹגֵם אוֹתוֹ אִם
לֹא, תָּלִינַן בְּעוֹר; זֶהוּ הַנִּרְאֶה יָפֶה בַּפְּלֻגְתָּא דְרַב הוּנָא וְרַב חִסְדָּא בְּעִנְיָן זֶה בְּרֵישׁ
פֶּרֶק קַמָּא דְחֻלִּין.

וְדִין מַה שֶּׁאָמְרוּ זִכְרוֹנָם לִבְרָכָה שֶׁכָּל הַמָּצוּי אֵצֶל הַשְּׁחִיטָה מַחֲזִיקִין אוֹתוֹ
שֶׁהוּא מֻמְחֶה, וַאֲפִלּוּ הוּא בְּפָנֵינוּ אֵין אָנוּ צְרִיכִין לְבָדְקוֹ, דְּסַמְכִינַן אַחֶזְקָתֵהּ;
וּמִן הַמְּפָרְשִׁים שֶׁאָמְרוּ שֶׁאִם יֶשְׁנוֹ בְּפָנֵינוּ, בּוֹדְקִין אוֹתוֹ; וְיֶתֶר פְּרָטֵי הַמִּצְוָה,
מְבֹאָרִים בְּמַסֶּכֶת חֻלִּין בִּשְׁנֵי פְּרָקִים רִאשׁוֹנִים.

וְנוֹהֶגֶת מִצְוָה זוֹ בְּכָל מָקוֹם וּבְכָל זְמַן, בִּזְכָרִים וּנְקֵבוֹת, שֶׁאַף הַנְּקֵבוֹת
מֻזְהָרוֹת שֶׁלֹּא לֶאֱכֹל מִבְּהֵמָה חַיָּה וָעוֹף אֶלָּא לְאַחַר שְׁחִיטָה הָרְאוּיָה; וּרְשׁוּת יֵשׁ
לָהֶן לִשְׁחֹט, וּשְׁחִיטָתָן כְּשֵׁרָה לְכָל אָדָם, אִם יוֹדְעוֹת הִלְכוֹת שְׁחִיטָה וּבְקִיאוֹת
בָּהֶם. וַאֲפִלּוּ שְׁחִיטַת הַקְּטַנִּים אָמְרוּ חֲכָמִים שֶׁכְּשֶׁרָה כָּל זְמַן שֶׁאָדָם גָּדוֹל וּבָקִי
בְּהִלְכוֹת שְׁחִיטָה רוֹאֶה אוֹתָן שׁוֹחֲטִין כָּרָאוּי; אֲבָל הִזְהִירוּנוּ חֲכָמִים שֶׁלֹּא נִמְסֹר
לָהֶם לִשְׁחֹט לְכַתְּחִלָּה, לְפִי שֶׁהֵם מוּעָדִים לְקַלְקֵל מִפְּנֵי מְעוּט דַּעְתָּם, וְיִמָּצֵא
הֶפְסֵד בַּדָּבָר.

וְעוֹבֵר עַל זֶה וְלֹא נִזְהַר מִלֶּאֱכֹל בְּשַׂר בְּהֵמָה אוֹ חַיָּה אוֹ עוֹף שֶׁאֵרַע בָּהֶן אֶחָד
מִן הַחֲמִשָּׁה פְּסוּלִין שֶׁזָּכַרְנוּ, אוֹ שֶׁנִּשְׁחֲטָה גַם-כֵּן בְּסַכִּין שֶׁאֵינוֹ בָדוּק, בִּטֵּל עֲשֵׂה
זֶה, מִלְּבַד שֶׁעָבַר עַל לַאו דְּלֹא תֹאכְלוּ כָל נְבֵלָה, וְלוֹקֶה בַּאֲכִילַת כְּזַיִת מֵהֶן, וּכְמוֹ
שֶׁנִּכְתֹּב בְּסֵדֶר זֶה [סִי' תע"ב] בְּעֶזְרַת הַשֵּׁם.

וְכֵן אָמְרוּ זִכְרוֹנָם לִבְרָכָה בְּפֶרֶק שֵׁנִי דְחֻלִּין: כָּל שֶׁנִּפְסְלָה בִּשְׁחִיטָתָהּ — נְבֵלָה,
כְּלוֹמַר כָּל זְמַן שֶׁנִּפְסְלָה הַבְּהֵמָה בִּמְקוֹם שְׁחִיטָתָהּ, דְּהַיְנוּ הַסִּימָנִין, כְּגוֹן שֶׁאֵרַע

25. *Ibid.* 3b.

26. So R. Yeruḥam, *Tol'doth 'Adam v'Ḥavvah,* xv 1.

27. A *ga'on* cited in Rashba, commentary to TB Ḥullin 3a, s.v. *'amar 'abbaye.* So also Rashba, *Torath haBa-yith,* I 1.

28. So *tosafoth,* TB Ḥullin 2a, s.v. *ha-kol.*

29. TB *ibid.*

30. TB Ḥullin 12b.

the *shehittah*; in other words, the knife touched nothing by which it could have been damaged. If we know for certain, however, that the knife touched something after the *shehittah* by which it could have been damaged, we attribute its defect to that thing. But as long as we are in doubt if it did or did not touch something that could have harmed it, we attribute it to the skin. This is what appears right and clear in the difference of opinion between R. Huna and R. Hisda in this subject, near the beginning of the first chapter of the Talmud tractate *Hullin* (10a-b).

Then there is the law that the Sages of blessed memory taught:[25] that if anyone is generally occupied with *shehittah*, we assume him to be an expert; and even if he is before us, we have no need to examine him, since we rely on his presumptive status.[26] Yet there are some authorities[27] who said that if he is before us, he is to be examined. The remaining details of the precept are explained in the tractate *Hullin*, in the first two chapters.

This precept is in force everywhere, at every time, for both man and woman: because women are also adjured not to eat of any domestic or wild animal, or fowl, except after proper *shehittah*. They have the right to do ritual slaying, and their *shehittah* is acceptable for everyone if they know the laws of *shehittah* and are well versed in them.[28] Even ritual slaying by children, the Sages said is acceptable, as long as a grown man expert in the laws of *shehittah* watches them doing the ritual slaying properly.[29] But the Sages cautioned us[30] not to assign them to do ritual slaying initially, because they are prone to spoil it on account of their paucity of intelligence, and the result of the matter will be a loss.

If a person transgresses this and does not take care to avoid eating the flesh of a domestic or wild animal or a fowl with which there occurred one of the five causes of disqualification that we mentioned; or equally, if it was ritually slain with an uninspected knife—he disobeys this positive precept, apart from violating the injunction, *You shall not eat any* n'vélah (*carcass*; Deuteronomy 14:21); and he should be given whiplashes upon eating an olive's amount from them, as we will write in this *sidrah* (§472), with the Eternal Lord's help.

And so the Sages of blessed memory said in the second chapter of *Hullin* (32a-b): Whatever became disqualified at its *shehittah*, is *n'vélah*. In other words, as long as something disqualifying happened to the animal at the place of its *shehittah*, i.e. the organs [gullet and

בָּהֵן אֶחָד מִן הַחֲמִשָּׁה פְּסוּלִין שֶׁזָּכַרְנוּ, אוֹ שֶׁשְּׁחָטָן בְּסַכִּין שֶׁאֵינוֹ בָדוּק, הֲרֵי זוֹ נִקְרֵאת נְבֵלָה; וְכָל שֶׁשְּׁחִיטָתָהּ כָּרָאוּי וְדָבָר אַחֵר גּוֹרֵם לָהּ לְהִפָּסֵל — טְרֵפָה, כְּלוֹמַר אִם לֹא אֵרַע שׁוּם פְּסוּל בְּעִנְיַן הַשְּׁחִיטָה בִּבְדִיקַת הַסַּכִּין וּבְסִימָנִין, אֶלָּא שֶׁדָּבָר אַחֵר גּוֹרֵם לָהּ לְהִפָּסֵל, כְּגוֹן שֶׁנִּטְרְפָה בְּאֶחָד מִשְׁמוֹנֶה-עֶשְׂרֵה טְרֵפוֹת הַיְּדוּעִים שֶׁזָּכַרְתִּי לְמַעְלָה בְּ"כֶסֶף תִּלְוֶה" [מִשְׁפָּטִים (ע"ט)] בְּסִימָן (ע"ט) [ע"ג], הֲרֵי זוֹ נִקְרֵאת טְרֵפָה, וְלוֹקִין עַל כְּלוֹמַר זוֹ מִשּׁוּם טְרֵפָה; וְאַף-עַל-פִּי שֶׁבִּשְׁנֵיהֶם מַלְקוּת אַבָּא, נַפְקָא לָן מִנֵּיהּ לְעִנְיַן הַתְרָאָה.

וְזֶה שֶּׁשָּׁנִינוּ, כָּל שֶׁנִּפְסְלָה בִשְׁחִיטָתָהּ — נְבֵלָה, אֵין הָעִנְיָן שֶׁעִקַּר הַנְּבֵלָה הַנִּזְכֶּרֶת בַּכָּתוּב תִּהְיֶה הַמִּתְנַבֶּלֶת בַּשְּׁחִיטָה, דְּוַדַּאי נְבֵלָה סְתָם תִּקָּרֵא בְּהֵמָה שֶׁמֵּתָה מֵאֵלֶיהָ מֵחֲמַת חֹלִי אוֹ בְּאֵי זֶה עִנְיָן שֶׁתָּמוּת, אֲבָל בַּעַל הַמִּשְׁנָה בָּא לְלַמֵּד שֶׁכָּל שֶׁלֹּא נִשְׁחֲטָה כָּרָאוּי, כְּמֵתָה מֵאֵלֶיהָ הִיא חֲשׁוּבָה.

[שֶׁלֹּא לֶאֱכֹל אֵבֶר מִן הַחַי]

תנב שֶׁנִּמְנַעְנוּ שֶׁלֹּא לֶאֱכֹל אֵבֶר מִן הַחַי, כְּלוֹמַר אֵבֶר שֶׁנֶּחְתַּךְ מִבַּעַל-חַיִּים בְּעוֹדֶנּוּ חַי, וְעַל זֶה נֶאֱמַר "וְלֹא תֹאכַל הַנֶּפֶשׁ עִם הַבָּשָׂר" —זֶה אֵבֶר מִן הַחַי. וְאָמְרִינַן בְּמַסֶּכֶת חֻלִּין: אָכַל אֵבֶר מִן הַחַי וּבָשָׂר מִן הַחַי, לוֹקֶה שְׁתַּיִם, לְפִי שֶׁיֵּשׁ עַל זֶה שְׁנֵי לָאוִין, הָאֶחָד זֶה שֶׁזָּכַרְנוּ, וְהַשֵּׁנִי "וּבָשָׂר בַּשָּׂדֶה טְרֵפָה [לֹא תֹאכֵלוּ]" שֶׁהוּא לֹא-תַעֲשֶׂה בְּאוֹכֵל בָּשָׂר מִן הַחַי, כְּמוֹ שֶׁכָּתַבְתִּי (בְּ"כֶסֶף תִּלְוֶה") לָאו ז' בְּסִימָן ע"ט) [בְּפָרָשַׁת מִשְׁפָּטִים סִי' ע"ג]. וְנִכְפְּלָה הָאַזְהָרָה בְּאֵבֶר מִן הַחַי בְּמָקוֹם אַחֵר בַּתּוֹרָה, בְּפָרָשַׁת נֹחַ, שֶׁנֶּאֱמַר: אַךְ בָּשָׂר בְּנַפְשׁוֹ דָמוֹ לֹא תֹאכֵלוּ.

מִשָּׁרְשֵׁי הַמִּצְוָה, כְּדֵי שֶׁלֹּא נִלְמַד נַפְשֵׁנוּ בְּמִדַּת הָאַכְזָרִיּוּת, שֶׁהִיא מִדָּה מְגֻנָּה

31. For a man to be given lashes of the whip for eating such meat, he must be observed by witnesses, who testify afterward in court; and they must first warn him. In the warning they must state exactly why the meat is forbidden, hence whether it is *n'vélah* or *t'réfah*.

§452   1. The paragraph is based on ShM negative precept §182.

windpipe] — for instance, if one of the five causes of disqualification that we mentioned occurred to them, or if they were ritually slain with a knife that was not inspected — this is called *n'vélah* (a carcass). Whatever had a proper *shehittah*, but something else caused it to become disqualified, is *t'réfah*. In other words, if no disqualifying factor occurred in regard to the ritual slaying, either through the inspection of the knife or with the organs, but something else made it unacceptable — for example, if it became fatally wounded through one of the eighteen known mortal injuries that I mentioned above, in *sidrah mishpatim* (§ 73) — it is called *t'réfah*. This is to say that one is given whiplashes over it because it is *t'réfah*. And although both entail a penalty of lashes, there is a difference for us between them, in regard to the warning.[31]

As to what we learned, "whatever became disqualified in its ritual slaying is *n'vélah*," the meaning is not that the main definition of *n'vélah* mentioned in Scripture is one that became spoiled at the ritual slaying. For certainly the general term *n'vélah* applies to an animal that died of itself on account of illness, or for any reason that it died. The Sage in the Mishnah rather wishes to teach that whatever was not ritually slain properly is considered as though it died of itself.

[NOT TO EAT A LIMB OR PART TAKEN
FROM A LIVING ANIMAL]

452 that we were restricted not to eat a limb from a living creature — in other words, an organ or limb that was cut from an animal while it was yet alive. About this it is stated, *and you shall not eat the life-spirit with the flesh* (Deuteronomy 12:23), which means an organ from a living creature. It was taught in the tractate *Hullin* (102b): If one ate a limb from a living creature and flesh from a living creature, he is to be flogged with two sets of whiplashes — because there are two injunctions about it: the one that we mentioned, and the second, *therefore you shall not eat any flesh in the field that is torn of beasts* (Exodus 22:30), which is a negative precept about eating flesh from a living animal, as I wrote in *sidrah mishpatim* (§ 73). The ban on a part from a living creature was reiterated elswhere in the Torah, in *sidrah noah*, where it is stated, *Only, flesh with its life, its blood, you shall not eat* (Genesis 9:4).[1]

At the root of the precept lies the reason that we should not train our spirit in the quality of cruelty, which is a most reprehensible trait

בְּיוֹתֵר; וּבֶאֱמֶת שֶׁאֵין אַכְזָרִיּוּת גָּדוֹל מִמִּי מֵי שֶׁיַּחְתֹּךְ אֵבֶר אוֹ בָּשָׂר מִבַּעַל־
חַיִּים בְּעוֹדֶנּוּ חַי לְפָנָיו וְיֹאכְלֶנּוּ; וּכְבָר כָּתַבְתִּי כַּמָּה פְּעָמִים הַתּוֹעֶלֶת הַגְּדוֹלָה לָנוּ
בְּקִנוֹתֵנוּ הַמִּדּוֹת הַטּוֹבוֹת וְנִתְרַחֵק מִן הָרָעוֹת, כִּי הַטּוֹב יִדְבַּק בַּטּוֹב, וְהָאֵל הַטּוֹב
חָפֵץ לְהֵטִיב, וְלָכֵן יְצַוֶּה עַמּוֹ לִבְחֹר בַּטּוֹב. זֶהוּ דַרְכִּי בְּרֹב הַמִּצְווֹת עַל צַד הַפְּשָׁט.

מִדִּינֵי הַמִּצְוָה, מַה שֶׁאָמְרוּ זִכְרוֹנָם לִבְרָכָה שֶׁאִסּוּר אֵבֶר מִן הַחַי נוֹהֵג בִּבְהֵמָה
חַיָּה וָעוֹף בַּטְּהוֹרִים, אֲבָל לֹא בַּטְּמֵאִים. וּמַה שֶׁאָמְרוּ שֶׁאֶחָד שֶׁיֵּשׁ בּוֹ בָּשָׂר
וְגִידִים וַעֲצָמוֹת, כְּגוֹן הַיָּד וְהָרֶגֶל, וְאֶחָד אֵבֶר שֶׁאֵין בּוֹ עֶצֶם, כְּגוֹן הַלָּשׁוֹן וְהַבֵּיצִים
וְהַטְּחוֹל וְהַכְּלָיוֹת וְהַלֵּב וְכַיּוֹצֵא בָהֶן, בְּאִסּוּר זֶה —— אֶלָּא שֶׁהָאֵבֶר שֶׁאֵין בּוֹ עֶצֶם,
בֵּין שֶׁחֲתָכוֹ כֻּלּוֹ בֵּין שֶׁחָתַךְ מִקְצָתוֹ הֲרֵי זֶה אָסוּר מִשּׁוּם אֵבֶר מִן הַחַי; וְהָאֵבֶר
שֶׁיֵּשׁ בּוֹ עֶצֶם, אֵינוֹ חַיָּב מִשּׁוּם אֵבֶר מִן הַחַי עַד שֶׁיִּפְרֹשׁ כִּבְרִיָּתוֹ בָּשָׂר וְגִידִים
וַעֲצָמוֹת; אֲבָל אִם פֵּרַשׁ מִן הַחַי הַבָּשָׂר בִּלְבַד, חַיָּב מִשּׁוּם טְרֵפָה, כְּמוֹ שֶׁבֵּאַרְנוּ,
וְלֹא מִשּׁוּם אֵבֶר מִן הַחַי.

הָאוֹכֵל מֵאֵבֶר מִן הַחַי כְּזַיִת לוֹקֶה עָלָיו; וַאֲפִלּוּ אָכַל אֵבֶר שָׁלֵם, אִם יֵשׁ בּוֹ
כְּזַיִת חַיָּב, פָּחוֹת מִכְּזַיִת פָּטוּר. חֲתַךְ מִן הָאֵבֶר כִּבְרִיָּתוֹ בָּשָׂר וְגִידִים וַעֲצָמוֹת כְּזַיִת
וַאֲכָלוֹ, לוֹקֶה, אַף־עַל־פִּי שֶׁאֵין בּוֹ בָּשָׂר אֶלָּא כָּל־שֶׁהוּא; אֲבָל אִם הִפְרִיד הָאֵבֶר
אַחַר שֶׁתְּלָשׁוֹ מִן הַחַי וְהִפְרִישׁ הַבָּשָׂר מִן הַגִּידִין וּמִן הָעֲצָמוֹת אֵינוֹ לוֹקֶה, עַד
שֶׁיֹּאכַל כְּזַיִת מִן הַבָּשָׂר לְבַדּוֹ, וְאֵין הָעֲצָמוֹת וְהַגִּידִין מִצְטָרְפִין בּוֹ לִכְזַיִת, מֵאַחַר
שֶׁשִּׁנָּה בְרִיָּתוֹ. חִלְּקוֹ לְאֵבֶר זֶה וַאֲכָלוֹ מְעַט מְעַט, אִם יֵשׁ בְּמַה שֶׁאָכַל כְּזַיִת בָּשָׂר
חַיָּב, וְאִם לָאו פָּטוּר. לָקַח כְּזַיִת מִן הָאֵבֶר כִּבְרִיָּתוֹ, בָּשָׂר גִּידִין וַעֲצָמוֹת, וַאֲכָלוֹ,
אַף־עַל־פִּי שֶׁנֶּחֱלַק בְּפִיו בִּפְנִים קֹדֶם שֶׁבְּלָעוֹ, חַיָּב (לְפִי שֶׁכֵּן דֶּרֶךְ אֲכִילָה).

2. I.e. a limb from a non-kosher animal is forbidden only because it is not
kosher, but this prohibition is not violated, in addition, if it is eaten; TB Ḥullin 101b.

3. MT *hilchoth ma'achaloth 'asuroth* v 2.

4. I.e. on "flesh that is torn of beasts"; see the first paragraph.

5. TB Ḥullin 102a.

6. MT *ibid.* 3, based on TB Ḥullin 103b.

of character. In truth, there is no greater cruelty in the world than when one cuts a limb or flesh from an animal while it is yet alive before him, and he eats it. And I have previously written many times the great benefit we have when we attain the good qualities and move far away from the evil ones: For good will cling to the good, and the good God desires to do good. Therefore He commands His people to choose the good. This is my approach about most of the precepts, by way of the plain meaning.

Among the laws of the precept there is what the Sages of blessed memory taught: that the ban on a limb from a living creature applies to pure (kosher) domestic and wild animals and fowl, but not to the impure (non-kosher) ones.[2] Then there is what they said:[3] that both a limb with flesh, sinews and bones, such as a foreleg or hind leg, as well as an organ that has no bone, such as the tongue, testes, spleen, kidneys, heart, and so forth, are under this prohibition. Only, when it is an organ that has no bone, whether one cut it out entirely or cut part of it out, it is forbidden as a part from a living creature. An organ or limb that has a bone, however, does not bring guilt as a part from a living creature until it is separated in its whole state—flesh, sinews and bones. But if one separated from a living creature the flesh alone, he is punishable for it on account of [the ban on] *t'réfah*,[4] as we explained, but not because it is a part of a living creature.

If someone eats an olive's amount out of a part from a living creature, he should be given whiplashes for it. Even if he ate a whole limb or organ, if it contained an olive's amount, he is punishable; if less than an olive's amount, he is free of penalty.[5] If someone cut from a limb or organ in its whole state, flesh, sinews and bones in the amount of an olive, and ate that, he should be given whiplashes, even if it contained no more than the slightest amount of flesh. But if he took the organ or limb apart after detaching it from the living creature, and separated the flesh from the sinews and bones, he is to receive no whipping until he eats an olive's amount of the flesh alone, the bones and sinews not being reckoned together with it, since he changed it from its natural state.[6] If he divided this organ or limb into pieces and ate it bit by bit, if what he ate contained an olive's amount of flesh, he is punishable; and if not, he is free of penalty. If, however, he took an olive's amount from the organ or limb in its natural state—flesh, sinews and bones—and ate it, then even if it became

⟨411⟩ divided [into its components] inside his mouth before he swallowed

תָּלַשׁ אֵבֶר מִן הַחַי וְנִטְרְפָה בִּנְטִילָתוֹ וַאֲכָלוֹ, חַיָּב שְׁתַּיִם, מִשּׁוּם אֵבֶר מִן הַחַי וּמִשּׁוּם טְרֵפָה, שֶׁהֲרֵי שְׁנֵי הָאִסּוּרִין בָּאִין כְּאֶחָד. וְכֵן הַתּוֹלֵשׁ חֵלֶב מִן הַחַי וַאֲכָלוֹ לוֹקֶה שְׁתַּיִם, מִשּׁוּם אֵבֶר מִן הַחַי וּמִשּׁוּם חֵלֶב. תָּלַשׁ חֵלֶב מִן הַטְּרֵפָה וַאֲכָלוֹ, לוֹקֶה שָׁלֹשׁ.

בָּשָׂר הַמְּדֻלְדָּל בִּבְהֵמָה וְאֵבֶר הַמְּדֻלְדָּל בָּהּ, אִם אֵינוֹ יָכוֹל לַחֲזוֹר וְלִחְיוֹת, אַף־עַל־פִּי שֶׁלֹּא פֵרַשׁ אֶלָּא שֶׁנִּשְׁחֲטָה, אָסוּר, וְאֵין לוֹקִין עָלָיו; וְאִם מֵתָה הַבְּהֵמָה, רוֹאִין אוֹתוֹ כְּאִלּוּ נָפַל מֵחַיִּים; לְפִיכָךְ לוֹקִין עָלָיו מִשּׁוּם אֵבֶר מִן הַחַי; אֲבָל הַיָּכוֹל לַחֲזוֹר וְלִחְיוֹת, אִם נִשְׁחֲטָה הַבְּהֵמָה הֲרֵי זֶה מֻתָּר.

אִם נִשְׁמַט אֵבֶר מִן הַחַי, אוֹ מְעָכוֹ אוֹ דָכוֹ, כְּגוֹן הַבֵּיצִים שֶׁמְּעָכָן אוֹ נְתָקָן אוֹ נְתָקָן, הֲרֵי זֶה אֵינוֹ אָסוּר מִן הַתּוֹרָה, שֶׁהֲרֵי יֵשׁ בּוֹ מִקְצָת חַיִּים, וּלְפִיכָךְ אֵין מַסְרִיחַ; וְאַף־עַל־פִּי־כֵן אָסוּר לְאָכְלוֹ, מִמִּנְהָג שֶׁנָּהֲגוּ יִשְׂרָאֵל מִקֶּדֶם, שֶׁהֲרֵי הוּא דּוֹמֶה לְאֵבֶר מִן הַחַי.

עֶצֶם שֶׁנִּשְׁבַּר, אִם הָיָה הַבָּשָׂר חוֹפֶה רֹב עָבְיוֹ שֶׁל עֶצֶם הַנִּשְׁבָּר וְרֹב הֶקֵּף הַשֶּׁבֶר, הֲרֵי זֶה מֻתָּר; וְאִם יָצָא הָעֶצֶם לַחוּץ, הֲרֵי הָאֵבֶר אָסוּר, וּכְשֶׁיִּשְׁחַט הַבְּהֵמָה אוֹ הָעוֹף יַחְתֹּךְ הָאֵבֶר וּמִמְּקוֹם הַשֶּׁבֶר מְעַט וְיַשְׁלִיכֶנּוּ, וְהַשְּׁאָר מֻתָּר. נִשְׁבַּר הָעֶצֶם וְהָיָה הַבָּשָׂר חוֹפֶה אֶת רֻבּוֹ, אִם הָיָה אוֹתוֹ בָּשָׂר מְרֻסָּס, אוֹ שֶׁנִּתְאַכֵּל כְּבָשָׂר שֶׁהָרוֹפֵא גוֹרְרוֹ, אוֹ שֶׁהָיָה הַבָּשָׂר שֶׁעָלָיו נְקָבִים נְקָבִים, אוֹ שֶׁנִּסְדַּק הַבָּשָׂר, אוֹ שֶׁנִּקְדַּר כְּמִין טַבַּעַת, אוֹ שֶׁנִּגְרַר הַבָּשָׂר מִלְמַעְלָה עַד שֶׁלֹּא נִשְׁאַר עַל הַבָּשָׂר אֶלָּא כִּקְלִפָּה, אוֹ שֶׁנִּתְאַכֵּל הַבָּשָׂר מִלְמַטָּה מִכָּל הָעֶצֶם שֶׁנִּשְׁבַּר עַד שֶׁנִּמְצָא הַבָּשָׂר הַחוֹפֶה אֵינוֹ נוֹגֵעַ בָּעֶצֶם—בְּכָל אֵלּוּ מוֹרִין לְאִסּוּר עַד שֶׁיִּתְרַפֵּא הַבָּשָׂר; וְאִם אָכַל מִכָּל אֵלּוּ, מַכִּין אוֹתוֹ מַכַּת מַרְדּוּת.

7. MT *ibid.* 4, based on TB *ibid.* The phrase in parentheses is not in the oldest manuscripts, and thus seems to be a later interpolation. It is likewise absent in MT.

8. TB Ḥullin 103a; MT *ibid.* 5.

9. *Ibid.* 73b; MT *ibid.* 6.

10. MT *ibid.*

11. I.e. within the sac, without separating them from the body.

12. MT *hilchoth ma'achaloth 'asuroth* v 7, based on TB Ḥullin 93b.

it, he is punishable (because it was in the natural way of eating).[7]

If someone detached an organ or limb from a living animal and it became *t'réfah* (fatally injured) by his taking it, and he ate it, he is punishable by two sets of whiplashes: because it is a limb from a living creature, and because it is *t'réfah*, since the two prohibitions took effect as one [together]. So also if someone detached forbidden fat from a living animal and ate it, he should be flogged with two sets of whiplashes: because it is a part from a living creature, and because it is forbidden fat. If one detached forbidden fat from a *t'réfah* (fatally injured) animal and ate it, he is to be whipped three times.[8]

As to flesh that hung loose, partly detached in an animal, or an organ or limb that hung partly detached, if it cannot return to its healthy, living state, then even if it was not entirely separated and the animal was ritually slain, it is forbidden, but whiplashes are not suffered over it. If the animal died, however, we regard it as though it had fallen off while the animal was alive; therefore lashes are suffered over it, as over a part from a living creature.[9] But as for a part that could return to its healthy state, if the animal was ritually slain, it is permissible.[10]

If an organ or limb in a living animal became dislocated, or if it was smashed or crushed—for example, if one smashed the testes or severed them[11]—it is not forbidden by the law of the Torah, since it yet possesses some life, and it therefore does not putrefy. Nevertheless, it is for forbidden to eat it, on account of a practice that the Israelites adopted in days of yore, since it resembles an organ from a living creature.[12]

If a bone broke, if the flesh covered most of the thickness of the broken bone and most of the area of the fracture, it is permissible. But if the bone protruded to the outside [of the body], that limb is forbidden; and when the animal or the fowl is ritually slain, that limb and a bit around the place of the fracture are to be cut off and thrown away, and the rest is permissible. If a bone broke and flesh covered most of it, if that flesh was ground away, or it became worn down like flesh that a physician scrapes; or if the flesh over it became full of holes, or the flesh became cracked, or cut away in the shape of a ring; or if the flesh wore away from above until nothing but a thin layer of the flesh remained; or if the flesh below eroded away from the entire broken bone, until as a result the covering flesh did not touch the bone—in all these instances the ruling is that it is forbidden, until the

הַמּוֹשִׁיט יָדוֹ לִמְעֵי הַבְּהֵמָה וְחָתַךְ מִן הַטְּחוֹל וּמִן הַכְּלָיוֹת וְכַיּוֹצֵא בָּהֶן וְהִנִּיחַ
הַחֲתִיכוֹת תּוֹךְ מֵעֶיהָ וְאַחַר־כָּךְ שְׁחָטָהּ, הֲרֵי אוֹתָן הַחֲתִיכוֹת אֲסוּרוֹת מִשּׁוּם אֵבֶר
מִן הַחַי, וְאַף־עַל־פִּי שֶׁהוּא בְּתוֹךְ מֵעֶיהָ; אֲבָל אִם חָתַךְ מִן הָעֻבָּר שֶׁבְּמֵעֶיהָ וְלֹא
הוֹצִיאוֹ, וְאַחַר־כָּךְ שְׁחָטָהּ, הֲרֵי חֲתִיכוֹת הָעֻבָּר מֻתָּרוֹת, הוֹאִיל וְלֹא יָצָא.

וְנוֹהֵג אִסּוּר זֶה בְּכָל מָקוֹם וּבְכָל זְמַן, בַּזְּכָרִים וּנְקֵבוֹת. וְעוֹבֵר עַל זֶה וְאָכַל
אֵבֶר מִן הַחַי אוֹ כַּזַּיִת מִמֶּנּוּ בְּעִנְיָן שֶׁזָּכַרְנוּ, חַיָּב מַלְקוֹת. וְזֹאת אַחַת מִן הַשֶּׁבַע
מִצְוֹת שֶׁהֵן עַל כָּל בְּנֵי הָעוֹלָם בִּכְלָל; אֲבָל מִכָּל־מָקוֹם יֵשׁ חִלּוּק בִּפְרָטֵי הַמִּצְוָה
בֵּין יִשְׂרָאֵל לִשְׁאָר הָאֻמּוֹת, וְהַכֹּל כְּמוֹ שֶׁכָּתַבְתִּי בְּנִיְשְׁמַע יִתְרוֹ, סִימָן (כ״ח)
[כ״ו]. וּמִן הַדּוֹמֶה שֶׁהַחִיּוּב לִשְׁאָר הָאֻמּוֹת בְּאֵבֶר מִן הַחַי בֵּין בִּטְהוֹרִים בֵּין
בִּטְמֵאִים; וְכֵן הוֹרָה זָקֵן.

[מִצְוָה לְהִטַּפֵּל בַּהֲבָאַת הַקָּרְבָּן לָאָרֶץ לְבֵית הַבְּחִירָה]

תנג לְהָבִיא אֶל בֵּית הַבְּחִירָה וּלְהַקְרִיב שָׁם מַה שֶּׁנִּתְחַיֵּב נַפְשֵׁנוּ בְּחַטָּאת וְאָשָׁם
וְעוֹלָה וּשְׁלָמִים, וְאַף־עַל־פִּי שֶׁהַבְּהֵמוֹת הָהֵן בְּחוּצָה לָאָרֶץ, חוֹבָה עָלֵינוּ לַהֲבִיאָם
אֶל הַמָּקוֹם הַנִּבְחָר; וְעַל זֶה נֶאֱמַר: רַק קָדָשֶׁיךָ אֲשֶׁר יִהְיוּ לְךָ וּנְדָרֶיךָ תִּשָּׂא וּבָאתָ.
וְאַף־עַל־פִּי שֶׁבֵּאַתְנוּ מִצְוָה לְהַקְרִיב כָּל קָרְבָּן בְּבֵית הַבְּחִירָה, כְּמוֹ שֶׁכָּתַבְתִּי
בְּסֵדֶר זֶה [סִי׳ ת״מ], אַף־עַל־פִּי־כֵן בָּאָה לָנוּ מִצְוָה מְיֻחֶדֶת עַל קָרְבָּנוֹת חוּצָה
לָאָרֶץ.

וְכֵן הוּא בְּסִפְרִי: "רַק קָדָשֶׁיךָ", אֵינוֹ מְדַבֵּר אֶלָּא בְּקָדְשֵׁי חוּצָה לָאָרֶץ; "תִּשָּׂא
וּבָאתָ", מְלַמֵּד שֶׁחַיָּב בְּטִפּוּל הֲבָאָתָם עַד שֶׁיְּבִיאֵם לְבֵית הַבְּחִירָה. וְשָׁם אָמְרוּ
שֶׁזֶּה הַחִיּוּב הוּא בְּחַטָּאת וְאָשָׁם וְעוֹלָה וּשְׁלָמִים.

13. MT *ibid.* 8 (sources in *Maggid Mishneh*).

14. MT *ibid.* 9 (sources in *Maggid Mishneh*). (The injury to the spleen or kidneys would not make the animal *t'réfah*: Rashi, TB Ḥullin 68a, s.v. *'asur*.)

15. MT *hilchoth m'lachim* ix 13.

§453 1. Sifre, Deuteronomy §77.

2. From the beginning to here is based on ShM positive precept §85.

flesh is healed. If a person ate any of all these, he is to be punished with whiplashes of disobedience.[13]

If someone thrust his hand into an animal's innards and cut off part of the spleen or kidneys, and so forth, and he left the pieces in its viscera, after which he ritually slew it, those pieces are forbidden as parts from a living creature, even though they were in its viscera. However, if he cut off part of an embryo in its womb and did not remove the piece, and afterward he ritually slew it, such pieces of the embryo are permissible, since they were not [previously] removed.[14]

This prohibition is in force everywhere, at every time, for both man and woman. If a person transgresses it and eats an organ or limb from a living animal, or the amount of an olive from it, under the conditions we mentioned, he deserves whiplashes. This is one of the seven precepts imposed on the population of the world generally. Yet in any event, there is a difference in details of the precept between the Israelites and the other nations—all as I wrote in *sidrah yithro*, in the eighth negative precept (§ 26). And as it would seem, punishment is incurred among the other nations over a part from a living creature whether it is of the pure [kosher] kinds or of the impure [non-kosher]; and so the elder [Rambam] ruled.[15]

[TO ATTEND TO BRINGING AN ANIMAL OFFERING
FROM ANOTHER LAND TO THE SANCTUARY]

453 to bring to the chosen Temple and offer up there what we have become obligated [to bring] as *ḥattath* (sin-offering), *'asham* (guilt-offering), *'olah* (burnt-offering) and *sh'lamim* (peace-offering). Even if those animals are outside the land [of Israel], a duty lies on us to bring them to the chosen place. About this it is stated, *Only, your holy things that you have, and your votive offerings, you shall take, and you shall come* (Deuteronomy 12:26). Even though we received a precept to present every offering at the chosen Temple, as I wrote in this *sidrah* (§ 440), a particular precept was nevertheless given us about offerings from outside the land.

So we find in the Midrash *Sifre*:[1] "Only your holy things"—this pertains to nothing other than holy offerings from outside the land; "you shall take, and you shall come"—this teaches that there is an obligation to attend to their transportation until they are brought to the chosen Temple. It was then stated there that the obligation applies to a *ḥattath*, *'asham*, *'olah* and *sh'lamim*.[2]

וְאֶפְשָׁר שֶׁנֹּאמַר שֶׁנִּתְיַחֲדָה לָנוּ מִצְוָה בְּקָדְשֵׁי חוּצָה לָאָרֶץ לְהַזְהִירֵנוּ עֲלֵיהֶן,
מִפְּנֵי שֶׁהַטֹּרַח בָּהֶן מְרֻבֶּה מִבְּקָדְשֵׁי הָאָרֶץ, שֶׁהֵן קְרוֹבִים אֶל הַבַּיִת יוֹתֵר.

אֲבָל הָרַב רַבֵּנוּ מֹשֶׁה בֶּן נַחְמָן זִכְרוֹנוֹ לִבְרָכָה כָּתַב שֶׁבְּכָל הַקֳּדָשִׁים, בֵּין
בְּקָדְשֵׁי הָאָרֶץ אוֹ שֶׁל חוּצָה לָאָרֶץ, הַכֹּל מִצְוָה אַחַת הִיא, וְלֹא נַעֲשָׂם שְׁתֵּי
מִצְוֹת; וְאַף-עַל-פִּי שֶׁהָאֱמֶת כִּי בְּסִפְרֵי נִדְרַשׁ לְקָדְשֵׁי חוּצָה לָאָרֶץ, אֵין זֶה בֶּאֱמֶת
רְאָיָה לַעֲשׂוֹתָן שְׁתֵּי מִצְוֹת. וּבְמַסֶּכֶת תְּמוּרָה בְּפֶרֶק שְׁלִישִׁי דְּרָשׁוּהוּ זִכְרוֹנָם
לִבְרָכָה בְּעִנְיָן אַחֵר, שֶׁאָמְרוּ שָׁם: "רַק קָדָשֶׁיךָ" אֵלּוּ הַתְּמוּרוֹת, "אֲשֶׁר יִהְיוּ לְךָ"
אֵלּוּ הַוְּלָדוֹת, "וּנְדָרֶיךָ" זֶה נֶדֶר, "תִּשָּׂא וּבָאתָ": יָכוֹל יַכְנִיסֵם לְבֵית הַבְּחִירָה
וְיִמְנַע מֵהֶם מַיִם וּמָזוֹן כְּדֵי שֶׁיָּמוּתוּ, תַּלְמוּד לוֹמַר "וְעָשִׂיתָ עֹלֹתֶיךָ הַבָּשָׂר
וְהַדָּם": כְּדֶרֶךְ שֶׁאַתָּה נוֹהֵג בְּעוֹלָה כָּךְ אַתָּה נוֹהֵג בִּתְמוּרָתָהּ, וּכְדֶרֶךְ שֶׁאַתָּה נוֹהֵג
בִּשְׁלָמִים כָּךְ אַתָּה נוֹהֵג בְּוַלְדֵי שְׁלָמִים וּבִתְמוּרָתָן.

כָּל עִנְיַן מִצְוָה זוֹ כְּעִנְיַן מִצְוָה ג' שֶׁבְּסֵדֶר זֶה [סִי׳ ת״מ] וְשֹׁרֶשׁ אֶחָד לִשְׁתֵּיהֶן,
אֵין צֹרֶךְ לְהַאֲרִיךְ בָּהּ הַדִּבּוּר.

[שֶׁלֹּא לְהוֹסִיף עַל מִצְוֹת הַתּוֹרָה]

תנד שֶׁנִּמְנַעְנוּ שֶׁלֹּא נוֹסִיף בַּתּוֹרָה שֶׁבִּכְתָב וְלֹא בַתּוֹרָה שֶׁבְּעַל-פֶּה, וְעַל זֶה
נֶאֱמַר "לֹא תֹסֵף עָלָיו"; וְכֵיצַד יִהְיֶה הַתּוֹסֶפֶת — כָּתַב הָרַב רַבֵּנוּ מֹשֶׁה בֶּן מַיְמוֹן
זִכְרוֹנוֹ לִבְרָכָה: כְּגוֹן חָכָם הַמּוֹרֶה שֶׁבְּשַׂר עוֹף בְּחָלָב אָסוּר מִן הַתּוֹרָה — וְזֶה
מוֹסִיף עַל דְּבַר הַקַּבָּלָה, שֶׁכָּךְ קִבַּלְנוּ בְּפֵרוּשׁ: "לֹא תְבַשֵּׁל גְּדִי" וְגוֹמֵר, שֶׁבְּשַׂר
בְּהֵמָה וְחַיָּה נֶאֶסְרוּ לְבַשֵּׁל בְּחָלָב, אֲבָל לֹא בְשַׂר עוֹף. וְכֵן אִם הוֹרָה שֶׁבְּשַׂר הַחַיָּה

---

3. Ramban, commentary to ShM *ibid.*

4. I.e. after consecrating an animal for an offering, the owner decides to replace
it with another; both are then sanctified and must be offered up (§ 352).

Now, we might possibly say that a particular precept was given us about holy offerings from outside the land to adjure us about them because the trouble they involve is much greater than the burden with holy offerings in the land, which are nearer the Temple.

However, R. Moses b. Naḥman of blessed memory wrote[3] that all holy offerings, both those in the land and those from abroad, are all under one precept, and we are not to make two precepts of them. And although it is true that in the Midrash *Sifre* [this verse] is interpreted to refer to holy offerings from outside the land, in truth this is no proof that they are to be taken as two precepts. In the Talmud tractate *T'murah*, chapter 3 (17b), the Sages of blessed memory interpreted it [the verse] in a different regard. For they said there: "Only your holy things"—this means animals exchanged for offerings;[4] "that you have"—this denotes the young [born to consecrated animals]; "and your votive offerings"—what was vowed [as an offering]; "you shall take, and you shall come"—I might think one may bring them into the Sanctuary, then withhold water and food from them so that they should die? Hence Scripture states, *and you shall do [the duty of] your burnt-offerings, the flesh and the blood* (Deuteronomy 12:27); in the way that you deal with an *'olah* (burnt-offering), so are you to deal with its exchange-animal; and in the way that you deal with *sh'lamim* (peace-offerings), so are you to deal with their young and their exchange-animals.

The entire subject-matter of this precept is like that of the third positive precept in this *sidrah* (§ 440), and there is one root-reason for the both. There is no need to lengthen the discourse about it.

[THE PROHIBITION AGAINST ADDING TO THE
PRECEPTS OF THE TORAH]

454 that we were restricted not to add anything to the Written or Oral Torah; about this it was stated, *you shall not add to it* (Deuteronomy 13:1). Now, how might this addition be made? R. Moses b. Maimon of blessed memory wrote:[1] For instance, if a scholar rules that the flesh of fowl in milk is forbidden by the law of the Torah. He thus adds to something in the Oral Tradition; for so we received the tradition distinctly: "you shall not boil a goat," etc. (Exodus 23:19)—it was made forbidden to boil meat from a domestic or wild animal in milk, but not the meat of fowl. So too if one ruled that animal meat is permitted in milk, he transgresses

מֻתָּר בְּחָלָב, עוֹבֵר מִשּׁוּם "לֹא תִגְרַע", לְפִי שֶׁזֶּה גּוֹרֵעַ הוּא, שֶׁכָּךְ קַבַּלְנוּ שֶׁבְּשַׂר בְּהֵמָה וְחַיָּה בִּכְלַל הָאִסּוּר. עַד כָּאן.

וְרַבֵּי הַמְּפָרְשִׁים יֹאמְרוּ דְלָא שַׁיָּךְ לֹא תוֹסִיף כְּלָל אֶלָּא בְמִצְוַת עֲשֵׂה; וְהָעִנְיָן הוּא, לְפִי שֶׁשָּׁמַעְתִּי אֲנִי מִפִּי מוֹרִי יִשְׁמְרֵם אֵל, כְּגוֹן מִי שֶׁמַּנִּיחַ שְׁנֵי תְפִלִּין כְּשֵׁרִין בְּרֹאשׁוֹ אוֹ בְיָדוֹ, וְכֵן הָעוֹשֶׂה חָמֵשׁ טוֹטָפוֹת בִּתְפִלִּין, וּכְמוֹ־כֵן הַנּוֹטֵל שְׁנֵי לוּלָבִין כְּשֵׁרִין בְּיָדוֹ, וְכָל כַּיּוֹצֵא בָזֶה, וְכֵן הַיּוֹשֵׁב בַּסֻּכָּה אַחַר הֶחָג בְּכַוָּנָה לַעֲשׂוֹת מִצְוַת סֻכָּה, אַף־עַל־פִּי שֶׁיּוֹדֵעַ שֶׁעָבַר זְמַנָּהּ, שֶׁאֵין עוֹבְרִין מִשּׁוּם בַּל תּוֹסִיף אֶלָּא בִמְכַוֵּן לַעֲשׂוֹת הַמִּצְוָה, וְכֵן הַנּוֹטֵל לוּלָב אַחַר הֶחָג וּמְכַוֵּן בּוֹ הַמִּצְוָה עִם הֱיוֹתוֹ יוֹדֵעַ שֶׁעָבַר הֶחָג.

וְכֵן הוּא בַגְּמָרָא בְּרֹאשׁ הַשָּׁנָה פֶּרֶק רָאוּהוּ בֵית־דִּין, דְּמַסִּיק הָתָם: אֶלָּא אָמַר רָבָא: לָצֵאת — לָא בָעֵי כַוָּנָה, כְּלוֹמַר שֶׁמִּצְוֹת אֵין צְרִיכוֹת כַּוָּנָה; לַעֲבֹר — בִּזְמַנּוֹ לָא בָעֵי כַוָּנָה, שֶׁלֹּא בִזְמַנּוֹ בָּעֵי כַוָּנָה.

אֲבָל הַנּוֹטֵל לוּלָב בֶּחָג אֲפִלּוּ מֵאָה פְעָמִים בַּיּוֹם עַל דַּעַת לָצֵאת בְּכָל פַּעַם וּפַעַם, אֵין כָּאן בַּל תּוֹסִיף; וְכֵן הַתּוֹקֵעַ שׁוֹפָר בְּיוֹם רֹאשׁ־הַשָּׁנָה כַּמָּה פְעָמִים, וְכֵן כָּל כַּיּוֹצֵא בָזֶה; וְאֵין צָרִיךְ לוֹמַר שֶׁהַנּוֹטֵל לוּלָב פָּסוּל, וְכֵן אִם אֲגָד עִמּוֹ מִין פָּסוּל, אַלְבָּא דְהִלְכְתָא דְּקַיְמָא לָן אֵין צָרִיךְ אֶגֶד, שֶׁאֵין כָּאן מִשּׁוּם בַּל תּוֹסִיף. זֶהוּ כְּלָל הַדְּבָרִים בְּעִנְיָן זֶה שֶׁהֶעֱלוּ מוֹרַי יִשְׁמְרֵם אֵל מִדִּבְרֵי הַגְּמָרָא אַחַר יְגִיעָה רַבָּה. וְעַתָּה, בְּנִי, אִם תִּזְכֶּה וְתֹאכַל יַגִּיעַ כַּפֶּיךָ גַּם אַתָּה, אַשְׁרֶיךָ וְטוֹב לָךְ.

2. E.g. Rabad to *ibid.*

3. I.e. compartments for sections of Scripture in the *t'fillin* of the head (MT *ibid.* iv 3); see §422.

4. See §324.

5. It is enough to do (perform) the required deeds; one need not be aware of, or intent upon, observing the *mitzvah* thereby.

6. I.e. the intention to observe the precept, beyond the Torah's requirement.

7. Hence tying something unacceptable to the *lulav* has no relevance to its precept.

8. So Rashba, commentary to TB Rosh haShanah 16b, as well as *tosafoth, ibid.* s.v. *v'tok'im.*

9. I.e. to reach a firm conclusion of your own by studying the Talmud.

because of the order, *nor shall you diminish from it* (*ibid.*): because this detracts [from the Torah], since we received the tradition so, that the meat of a domestic or wild animal is included under this prohibition. Thus far [his words].

Most authorities say, however,[2] that "you shall not add" does not at all relate to anything but a positive precept. The meaning, according to what I heard from my master teachers, God protect them, is, for example, if a person puts on two kosher (acceptable) *t'fillin* (phylacteries) on his head or on his hand; so too if a person makes five frontlets in *t'fillin*;[3] likewise, if someone takes two *lulavim* (palm-branches) in his hand,[4] and thus anything similar. Thus too if someone sits in a *sukkah* (booth) after the festival, with the intention to fulfill the precept of *sukkah* (§ 325), although he knows that the proper time for it has gone. For there is no transgression on account of the injunction, *you shall not add*, unless there is an intention to fulfill a precept. So too if someone took up a *lulav* after the festival [of *Sukkoth*] intending to fulfill the precept (§ 324) with it, despite his knowing that the festival was over.

Thus it is also [conveyed] in the Talmud tractate *Rosh haShanah*, in the third chapter (28b). For it is concluded there: Finally Rava said: To acquit oneself [of the obligation of a precept], intention is not needed; in other words, *mitzvoth* (religious duties) do not require the intention [to fulfill them];[5] to transgress during [a religious duty's] proper time, the intention is not needed; if not during its proper time, the intention is necessary.[6]

If, however, someone takes up a *lulav* during the festival [of *Sukkoth*] even a hundred times a day with the thought in mind of fulfilling the obligation every single time, the injunction, *you shall not add*, does not apply here. So too if someone sounded the *shofar* on a day of *Rosh haShanah* many times; and thus anything similar. And there is no need to say that if someone took a disqualified, unacceptable *lulav* (palm branch), and likewise if he bound to it one of the other species that was unacceptable, according to the standing ruling we have that the binding of the species is not necessary[7]—the injunction, *you shall not add*, does not apply here. This is the rule regarding this prohibition at which my master teachers, God protect them, arrived from the words of the Talmud after great toil.[8] And now, my son, if you too will merit to *eat the fruit of the labor of your hands*,[9] *happy shall you be, and it will be well with you* (Psalms 128:2).

מִשָּׁרְשֵׁי הַמִּצְוָה, כִּי הָאָדוֹן הַמְצַוֶּה אוֹתָנוּ עַל הַתּוֹרָה, בָּרוּךְ הוּא, בְּתַכְלִית
הַשְּׁלֵמוּת, וְכָל מַעֲשָׂיו וְכָל צִוּוּיָיו הֵם שְׁלֵמִים וְטוֹבִים, וְהַתּוֹסֶפֶת בָּהֶם חִסָּרוֹן
וְכָל־שֶׁכֵּן הַגֵּרָעוֹן; זֶה דָּבָר בָּרוּר הוּא.

דִּינֵי הַמִּצְוָה בְּמַסֶּכֶת סַנְהֶדְרִין, וּכְמוֹ־כֵן בְּמַסֶּכֶת רֹאשׁ־הַשָּׁנָה פֶּרֶק רָאוּהוּ
בֵית־דִּין, וְגַם בְּעֵרוּבִין דִּבְּרוּ בָעִנְיָן פֶּרֶק הַמּוֹצֵא תְּפִלִּין.

וְנוֹהֵג אִסּוּר זֶה בְּכָל מָקוֹם וּבְכָל זְמַן, בַּזְּכָרִים וּנְקֵבוֹת. וְעוֹבֵר עַל זֶה וְהוֹסִיף
בַּמִּצְווֹת, כְּגוֹן שֶׁמֵּנִיחַ חָמֵשׁ טוֹטָפוֹת בַּתְּפִלִּין אוֹ מֵנִיחַ שְׁנֵי תְּפִלִּין כְּשֵׁרִין עֲשׂוּיִין
כְּתִקְּנָן בְּרֹאשׁוֹ, וְכֵן הַנּוֹטֵל שְׁנֵי לוּלָבִין בְּיָדוֹ, וְכָל כַּיּוֹצֵא בָזֶה, וְכֵן הַיּוֹשֵׁב בַּסֻּכָּה
אַחַר הֶחָג אוֹ הַנּוֹטֵל לוּלָב בְּכַוָּנָה לַעֲשׂוֹת הַמִּצְוָה, וְאַף־עַל־פִּי שֶׁיּוֹדֵעַ שֶׁעָבַר
זְמַנָּהּ, עָבַר עַל לָאו זֶה וְחַיָּב מַלְקוֹת וּבְעֵדִים וְהַתְרָאָה, כְּמוֹ שֶׁיָּדוּעַ בְּכָל מָקוֹם.

[שֶׁלֹּא לִגְרֹעַ מִמִּצְווֹת הַתּוֹרָה]

תנה שֶׁנִּמְנַעְנוּ שֶׁלֹּא לִגְרֹעַ דָּבָר מִמַּה שֶּׁחִיְּבַתְנוּ תוֹרָתֵנוּ הַשְּׁלֵמָה, וְעַל זֶה
נֶאֱמַר: וְלֹא תִגְרַע מִמֶּנּוּ.

וְכֵיצַד יִהְיֶה זֶה הָאִסּוּר: כְּגוֹן מַה שֶּׁאָמְרוּ זִכְרוֹנָם לִבְרָכָה בְּפֶרֶק ג׳ מֵרֹאשׁ
הַשָּׁנָה, שֶׁאִם נִתְעָרֵב דָּם הַנִּתָּן בְּמַתָּנָה אַחַת עִם דָּם הַנִּתָּן בְּמַתַּן אַרְבַּע, רַבִּי
אֱלִיעֶזֶר אוֹמֵר: יִנָּתְנוּ בְּמַתַּן אַרְבַּע; רַבִּי יְהוֹשֻׁעַ אוֹמֵר: יִנָּתְנוּ בְּמַתָּנָה אַחַת, שֶׁאִם
אַתָּה נוֹתֵן בְּמַתַּן אַרְבַּע, [אַתָּה] עוֹבֵר עַל בַּל תּוֹסִיף וְעוֹשֶׂה מַעֲשֶׂה; וּכְשֶׁאַתָּה
נוֹתֵן בְּמַתָּנָה אַחַת, אַף־עַל־פִּי שֶׁאַתָּה עוֹבֵר עַל בַּל תִּגְרַע, אִי אַתָּה עוֹשֶׂה מַעֲשֶׂה.
עַד כָּאן. יָדַעְנוּ מִזֶּה שֶׁבְּדֶרֶךְ זוֹ וְכָל כַּיּוֹצֵא בָהּ הוּא לָאו דְּ״לֹא תִגְרַע״.

מִשָּׁרְשֵׁי הַמִּצְוָה, כְּעִנְיָן שֶׁאָמַרְנוּ בְּמִצְוַת בַּל תּוֹסִיף הַקּוֹדֶמֶת לָהּ; וְיֶתֶר כָּל
עִנְיָנֶיהָ כְּמוֹתָהּ.

---

10. I.e. either for sitting in a *sukkah* or for taking up the *lulav*.
11. I.e. these conditions must obtain for whiplashes to be given.

§455   1. Derived from ShM negative precept § 314.
2. Cf. TB Rosh haShanah 28b, standard editions, and *Dikduké Sof'rim ad loc.* note 80.   〈420〉

At the root of the precept lies the reason that the sovereign Master who commands us about the Torah is the very ultimate of perfection; all His works and all His commands are wholly perfect and good. Any addition to them is thus a defect, and all the more certainly so anything diminished. This is a clear matter.

The laws of the precept are in the Talmud tractate *Sanhedrin* (28b), and so too in the third chapter of tractate *Rosh haShanah*; and the subject is also discussed in the tenth chapter of *'Eruvin* (100a).

This prohibition applies everywhere, at every time, for both man and woman. If someone transgressed it and added something to the precepts—for instance, if he placed five frontlets in *t'fillin*, or he put on two kosher (acceptable) *t'fillin*, properly made, on his head; and so if one took two *lulavim* (palm branches) in his hand, or anything similar; and likewise if one sat in a *sukkah* after the festival, or took up a *lulav* [then] with the intention of observing the precept, although he knew the time for it[10] had passed—he would violate this negative precept, and would deserve whiplashes if there were witnesses and a [prior] warning, as is known in every instance.[11]

[NOT TO DIMINISH THE PRECEPTS OF
THE TORAH IN ANY WAY]

455 that we were restricted not to detract anything from what our whole, perfect Torah obligated us [to do]; about this it was stated, *nor shall you take anything away from it* (Deuteronomy 13:1).[1]

Now, how could this prohibited act be done?—for example, as the Sages of blessed memory said in chapter 3 of the tractate *Rosh haShanah* (28b): that if blood [of an offering] with which one splash is to be made became mixed with blood requiring four splashes,[2] R. 'Eli'ezer says four splashes are to be made with it; R. Joshua says one splash is to be made with it: for if you make four splashes with it, you transgress the injunction, *you shall not add to it* (Deuteronomy 13:1), by doing a deed; but when you make one splash, even though you transgress the injunction, *nor shall you take anything away*, you do no action. Thus far [the Talmud]. So we know from this that in this way or any similar way, the negative precept to detract nothing [from the Torah is impinged].

The root reason for the precept is like the point we stated about the precept to add nothing, which precedes this. And in all the rest of its subject-matter it is similar to that.

[שֶׁלֹּא לִשְׁמֹעַ מִמִּתְנַבֵּא בְּשֵׁם עֲבוֹדָה זָרָה]

תנו שֶׁלֹּא נִשְׁמַע נְבוּאַת מִתְנַבֵּא בְּשֵׁם עֲבוֹדָה זָרָה, כְּלוֹמַר שֶׁלֹּא נִשְׁאָלֵהוּ וְנַחְקְרֵהוּ עַל אוֹת אוֹ מוֹפֵת שֶׁיִּתֵּן עַל נְבוּאָתוֹ כְּמוֹ שֶׁאָנוּ עוֹשִׂים בְּמִתְנַבֵּא בְּשֵׁם הַשֵּׁם, אֲבָל נִמְנָעֵהוּ מִן הַדָּבָר כְּמוֹ שֶׁרָאוּי בְּכָל פּוֹשֵׁעַ וְאָשֵׁם; וְאִם יַחֲזִיק בְּדַעְתּוֹ נְקַיֵּם בּוֹ הָעֹנֶשׁ הַיָּדוּעַ שֶׁחִיַּבְתּוּ הַתּוֹרָה, וְהוּא לַהֲמִיתוֹ בְּחֶנֶק; וְעַל זֶה נֶאֱמַר: לֹא תִשְׁמַע אֶל דִּבְרֵי הַנָּבִיא הַהוּא.

מִשָּׁרְשֵׁי הַמִּצְוָה, לְפִי שֶׁהַטָּעוּת נִמְצָא אֵצֶל בְּנֵי־אָדָם תָּמִיד וְשִׂכְלָם אֵינֶנּוּ בָּרִיא לָבוֹא עַד תַּכְלִית הָאֱמֶת בַּדְּבָרִים, וְתָחוּשׁ הַתּוֹרָה כִּי אוּלַי מִתּוֹךְ הַטָּעֲנוֹת הַמַּכְזִיבוֹת וַאֲרִיכוּת הַדִּבּוּר וְהַוִּכּוּחַ עִם הַנָּר דוֹבֵר שְׁקָרִים הַמִּתְנַבֵּא בְּשֵׁם עֲבוֹדָה זָרָה, יִתְפַּתֶּה הָאָדָם לִדְבָרָיו; וְאַף כִּי לֹא יִתְפַּתֶּה אֵלָיו, אוּלַי יְפַקְפֵּק בְּלִבָּבוֹ אֲפִלּוּ שָׁעָה אַחַת לִהְיוֹת שׁוּם סֶרֶךְ בִּכְזָבָיו; וְאַף־עַל־פִּי שֶׁיְּדַעְנוּ שֶׁאֵין תְּקוּמָה לִדְבָרָיו רַק לְשָׁעָה, כִּי הָאֱמֶת יוֹרָה דַרְכּוֹ וְיָעִיד עַל דִּבְרֵי הַנָּבִיא הַהוּא כִּי שֶׁקֶר בְּפִיו, אַף־עַל־פִּי־כֵן חָסָה הַתּוֹרָה עָלֵינוּ לְבַל נְאַבֵּד אֲפִלּוּ שָׁעָה אַחַת מִכָּל יָמֵינוּ בְּפִקְפּוּק הַמַּחֲשָׁבָה הָרָעָה הַהִיא.

וְדִינֵי הַמִּצְוָה, בְּפֶרֶק י״א מִסַּנְהֶדְרִין. וְנוֹהֶגֶת בְּכָל מָקוֹם וּבְכָל זְמַן, בִּזְכָרִים וּנְקֵבוֹת. וְעוֹבֵר עַל זֶה וְשָׁמַע אֶל הַנָּבִיא הַמִּתְנַבֵּא בְּשֵׁם עֲבוֹדָה זָרָה, כְּגוֹן שֶׁהֶאֱרִיךְ עִמּוֹ בִּדְבָרִים אוֹ שֶׁשָּׁאַל מִמֶּנּוּ אוֹת אוֹ מוֹפֵת, עָבַר עַל לָאו זֶה; אֲבָל אֵין לוֹקִין עָלָיו, לְפִי שֶׁאֵין בּוֹ מַעֲשֶׂה.

[שֶׁלֹּא לֶאֱהֹב הַמֵּסִית]

תנז שֶׁנִּמְנַעְנוּ כְּמוֹ־כֵן שֶׁלֹּא לְהַטּוֹת אֹזֶן לְדִבְרֵי מֵסִית וְלֹא לְחַבֵּב אוֹתוֹ בְּשׁוּם דָּבָר; וְעִנְיַן מֵסִית הוּא מִי שֶׁמֵּסִית אֶחָד מִבְּנֵי־יִשְׂרָאֵל לָלֶכֶת לַעֲבֹד עֲבוֹדָה זָרָה,

---

§456   1. To prove that his prophecy is true.
2. The paragraph is based on ShM negative precept §28.

456 that we should not give heed to the prophecy of one who speaks oracularly in the name of an idol; in other words, we should not ask and probe him about a sign or token that he should give for his prophecy,[1] as we do with one who prophesies in the name of the Eternal Lord (§ 416). We should rather prevent him from the matter, as it is proper [to do] with every wrongdoer and guilty person. And if he persists in his concepts, we are to carry out with him the known punishment that the Torah imposed for him, which is to end his life by strangulation. About this it is stated, *you shall not hearken to the words of that prophet* (Deuteronomy 13:4).[2]

At the root of the precept lies the reason that error is found among people constantly, and their intelligence is not clear enough to arrive at the ultimate truth about things. Now, the Torah was apprehensive that perhaps as a result of lying arguments and long discussion and debate with a falsehood-speaking stranger who prophesies in the name of an idol, a man might be persuaded by his words. And even if he is not persuaded by him, he may perhaps have some doubt in his heart for even one brief while that there might be some substance in the other's lies. And though we know the other's words cannot stand firm for more than some brief time, since the truth will show its way and attest about that prophet that there was falsehood in his mouth, nevertheless the Torah was concerned for us that we should not lose even one small while out of all our days in uncertainty about that evil thought.

The laws of the precept are in chapter 11 of the tractate *Sanhedrin*. It applies in every place and time, for both man and woman. If a person transgressed this and paid heed to a prophet speaking oracularly in the name of an idol — for example, if he spoke with him at length or asked him for a sign or a wonder[1] — he would violate this negative precept. But no flogging of whiplashes is received for it, since it involves no physical action.

457 that we were likewise restricted not to give ear to the words of an enticer, and not to like him in any respect. In substance, an enticer is one who lures someone among the Israelites to go and

כְּגוֹן שֶׁיְּשַׁבַּח לוֹ פְּעֻלַּת עֲבוֹדָה זָרָה וִישַׁבְּחֶנָּה לוֹ כְּדֵי שֶׁיֵּלֵךְ אַחֲרֶיהָ וְיַעֲבְדָהּ וְיֵצֵא מִתַּחַת כַּנְפֵי הַשְּׁכִינָה; וְעַל זֶה נֶאֱמַר: לֹא תֹאבֶה לוֹ.

מִשָּׁרְשֵׁי הַמִּצְוָה, כָּעִנְיָן הַכָּתוּב בַּמִּצְוָה הַקּוֹדֶמֶת לָהּ; וְדִינֶיהָ וְהַנִּהְנָתָהּ, בְּכָל תַּגִּיד עָלֶיהָ חֲבֶרְתָּהּ.

[שֶׁלֹּא לַעֲזֹב הַשִּׂנְאָה מִן הַמֵּסִית]

תנח שֶׁתִּהְיֶה שִׂנְאַת הַמֵּסִית קְבוּעָה בִּלְבָבֵנוּ, כְּלוֹמַר שֶׁלֹּא נָקֵל בִּנְטִירַת הַנְּקָמָה מִמֶּנּוּ עַל כָּל הָרָעָה אֲשֶׁר חָשַׁב לַעֲשׂוֹת; וְעַל זֶה נֶאֱמַר "וְלֹא תִשְׁמַע אֵלָיו", כְּלוֹמַר אַל תְּהִי נִשְׁמָע אֵלָיו לְהַעֲבִיר מִלִּבְּךָ נְטִירַת נִקְמָתְךָ מִמֶּנּוּ. וְכֵן אָמְרוּ זִכְרוֹנָם לִבְרָכָה בְּפֵרוּשׁ זֶה הַכָּתוּב: מִכְּלַל שֶׁנֶּאֱמַר בְּיִשְׂרָאֵל "עָזֹב תַּעֲזֹב עִמּוֹ", וְתִרְגֵּם אוּנְקְלוֹס "מִשְׁבָּק תִּשְׁבּוֹק מָה דְּבִלִּיבָּךְ עֲלוֹהִי", יָכוֹל אַתָּה עוֹזֵב לְזֶה הַמֵּסִית גַּם־כֵּן—תַּלְמוּד לוֹמַר: וְלֹא תִשְׁמַע אֵלָיו.

מִשָּׁרְשֵׁי הַמִּצְוָה, כָּעִנְיָן שֶׁתֵּי הַמִּצְווֹת הַקּוֹדְמוֹת, שֶׁהַכֹּל לְהַרְחִיק כָּל עִנְיַן עֲבוֹדָה זָרָה, לְבִלְתִּי הִכָּשֵׁל בָּהּ בְּשׁוּם עִנְיָן. וְדִינֶיהָ בְּסַנְהֶדְרִין, וּשְׁאָר כָּל עִנְיָנָהּ כְּמוֹתָן.

[שֶׁלֹּא לְהַצִּיל הַמֵּסִית]

תנט שֶׁנִּמְנַע הַמּוּסָת מִלְּהַצִּיל הַמֵּסִית כְּשֶׁיִּרְאֵהוּ בְּסַכָּנַת מָוֶת וְאָבוֹד, וְעַל זֶה נֶאֱמַר: וְלֹא תָחוֹס עֵינְךָ עָלָיו; וְכֵן אָמְרוּ זִכְרוֹנָם לִבְרָכָה: מִכְּלַל שֶׁנֶּאֱמַר "לֹא תַעֲמֹד עַל דַּם רֵעֶךָ", יָכוֹל אִי אַתָּה עוֹמֵד עַל דָּמוֹ שֶׁל זֶה—תַּלְמוּד לוֹמַר: וְלֹא תָחֹס עֵינְךָ עָלָיו.

שֹׁרֶשׁ הַמִּצְוָה כָּתוּב בַּקּוֹדְמוֹת הַבָּאוֹת עַל מֵסִית, וְכָל עִנְיָנָהּ כְּמוֹתָן.

§458   1. Sifre, Deuteronomy §89.

§459   1. Sifre, Deuteronomy §89.

worship an idol: for instance, if he praises to him the achievement of the idol, and extols it to him, so that he should follow it and worship, leaving the shelter of the wings of the *shechinah* (Divine Presence). About this it is stated, *you shall not yield to him* (Deuteronomy 13:9).

At the root of the precept lies a reason similar to the one written about the precept that precedes it (§ 456). As to its laws and its application, about all that its companion-precept (§ 456) relates.

[NOT TO RELINQUISH HATRED FOR AN ENTICER TO IDOLATRY]

458 that hatred of an enticer should be set firmly in our heart; in other words, we should not [ever] lessen our vengeful resentment toward him for all the evil he thought to do. About this it is stated, *nor shall you hearken to him* (Deuteronomy 13:9); in other words, do not accede (yield) to him, to remove from your heart your strong determination on vengeance upon him. And so our Sages of blessed memory said in explaining this verse:[1] Since the rule was stated about an Israelite, *you shall surely release it with him* (Exodus 23:5)—which Onkelos renders as, "you shall surely abandon what is in your heart about him"—I might think you should abandon it equally about this enticer? Hence Scripture states, *nor shall you hearken to him.*

At the root of the precept lies a reason like that of the two previous precepts. For it is all to move far away every matter of idolatry, that no one should come to grief through it in any way. Its laws are in the Talmud tractate *Sanhedrin*; and all the rest of its subject-matter is like that of the others (§§ 456, 457).

[NOT TO RESCUE FROM DEATH AN ENTICER TO IDOL-WORSHIP]

459 that an enticed person is forbidden to rescue the enticer [to idolatry] when he sees him in danger of death and perdition; for it is stated about this, *neither shall your eye pity him* (Deuteronomy 13:9). And so the Sages of blessed memory said:[1] Since the rule was stated, *you shall not stand idly by the blood of your neighbor* (Leviticus 19:16), I might think you are not to stand idly by [the shedding of] this one's blood? Hence Scripture states, *neither shall your eye pity him.*

The root reason for the precept is written in the previous ones that relate to an enticer (§§ 456–58), and all its subject-matter is like theirs.

[שֶׁלֹּא יְלַמֵּד הַמּוּסָת זְכוּת עַל הַמֵּסִית]

ת ס שֶׁנִּמְנַע הַמּוּסָת שֶׁלֹּא לִטְעֹן דָּבָר שֶׁל זְכוּת בְּעַד הַמֵּסִית וַאֲפִלּוּ יוֹדֵעַ לוֹ זְכוּת, וְלֹא יְלַמְּדֵהוּ וְלֹא יִזְכְּרֵהוּ עָלָיו, וְעַל זֶה נֶאֱמַר "וְלֹא תַחְמֹל"; וְכֵן אָמְרוּ זִכְרוֹנָם לִבְרָכָה: לֹא תְלַמֵּד עָלָיו זְכוּת. וְעִנְיָנָהּ כְּמוֹ הָאֲחֵרוֹת שֶׁזָּכַרְנוּ סָמוּךְ.

[שֶׁלֹּא יִשְׁתֹּק הַמּוּסָת מִלְּלַמֵּד חוֹבָה עַל הַמֵּסִית]

ת ס א שֶׁלֹּא יַחֲרִישׁ הַמּוּסָת מִלְּלַמֵּד חוֹבָה עַל הַמֵּסִית, אֲבָל יְלַמְּדָהּ עָלָיו, וְעַל זֶה נֶאֱמַר "וְלֹא תְכַסֶּה עָלָיו"; וְאָמְרוּ זִכְרוֹנָם לִבְרָכָה בְּפֵרוּשׁ "לֹא תְכַסֶּה": אִם אַתָּה יוֹדֵעַ לוֹ חוֹבָה, אִי אַתָּה רַשַּׁאי לִשְׁתֹּק.

כָּל עִנְיָנָהּ כְּמוֹ בְּחַבְרוֹתֶיהָ הַסְּמוּכוֹת לָהּ.

וּמֵרֹב אַזְהָרוֹת אֵלֶּה עַל הַמֵּסִית יֵשׁ לִי לְהָבִין שֶׁמַּתָּר וְגַם מִצְוָה עָלֵינוּ לִשְׂנֹאת גַּם־כֵּן אֲפִלּוּ, הָרְשָׁעִים בִּשְׁאָר עֲבֵרוֹת, אַחַר רְאוֹתֵנוּ שֶׁהִשְׁחִיתוּ וְהִתְעִיבוּ מַעֲשֵׂיהֶם עַד שֶׁאֵין תִּקְנָה בָּהֶם, וְלֹא יִשְׁמְעוּ לְקוֹל מוֹרִים אֲבָל יָבוּזוּ דִבְרֵיהֶם וְלִמְלַמְּדָם לֹא יַטּוּ אֹזֶן, אֲבָל לְהַזִּיקָם מְגַמַּת פְּנֵיהֶם, הִנֵּה אֵלֶּה רְשָׁעִים שֶׁהָיָה דָּוִד אוֹמֵר עֲלֵיהֶם: הֲלוֹא מְשַׂנְאֶיךָ יְיָ אֶשְׂנָא וּבִתְקוֹמְמֶיךָ אֶתְקוֹטָט.

[שֶׁלֹּא לְהָסִית אֶחָד מִיִּשְׂרָאֵל אַחַר עֲבוֹדָה זָרָה]

ת ס ב שֶׁלֹּא נָסִית אֶחָד מִיִּשְׂרָאֵל לַעֲבוֹדַת עֲבוֹדָה זָרָה, וְהָעוֹשֶׂה כֵן נִקְרָא מֵסִית, וְעַל זֶה נֶאֱמַר בְּסוֹף הַפָּרָשָׁה שֶׁל מֵסִית: וְלֹא יוֹסִפוּ לַעֲשׂוֹת כַּדָּבָר הָרָע הַזֶּה בְּקִרְבֶּךָ.

---

§460   1. Sifre, Deuteronomy § 89.

§461   1. Literally, should not keep silent.
         2. Sifre, Deuteronomy § 89.
         3. Literally, the direction of their faces being.
         4. I.e. to harm those who would try to improve them.

[THAT SOMEONE ENTICED TO IDOLATRY
SHOULD NOT SPEAK IN FAVOR OF THE ENTICER]

460 that an enticed person is forbidden to argue anything in favor of the innocence of the enticer; even if he knows something in favor of his acquittal, he is not to expound it and not to bring it to mind about him. About this it is stated, *nor shall you spare [him]* (Deuteronomy 13:9). And so the Sages of blessed memory taught:[1] You shall demonstrate nothing in his favor, for his acquittal. Its subject-matter is like that of the others that we recorded directly above (§§ 456–59).

[THAT A PERSON ENTICED TO IDOL-WORSHIP
SHOULD NOT REFRAIN FROM SPEAKING OUT
AGAINST THE ENTICER]

461 that an enticed person should not hold back[1] from demonstrating something detrimental about the enticer [showing his guilt], but should convey it about him. About this it is stated, *nor shall you conceal about him* (Deuteronomy 13:9); and the Sages of blessed memory said in interpreting "nor shall you conceal":[2] If you know something pointing to his guilt, you do not have the right to keep quiet.

Its entire subject-matter is like that of its companion-precepts directly above it (§§ 456–60).

Now, from the great number of these injunctions about an enticer, I can understand that it is permitted — nay, it is even a religious duty — for us to hate likewise even those who are wicked with other transgressions, after we see that they have corrupted and befouled their ways of action until there is no hope for them, and they will not listen to the voice of instructors but rather scorn their words, giving no heed to anyone who would teach them, their way being rather set[3] to harm them.[4] These are clearly the wicked about whom David would say, *Do I not hate them that hate Thee, O Lord? and do I not contend with those that rise up against Thee?* (Psalms 138:21).

[NOT TO ENTICE AN ISRAELITE TOWARD
IDOL-WORSHIP]

462 that we should not lure anyone in Israel (Jewry) to idol-worship: and whoever does so is called an enticer. About this it is stated at the end of the Scriptural section regarding an enticer, *and*

שֹׁרֶשׁ הַמִּצְוָה נִגְלֶה לַכֹּל. דִּינֵי הַמִּצְוָה, כְּגוֹן מַה שֶּׁאָמְרוּ זִכְרוֹנָם לִבְרָכָה: כֵּיצַד
הוּא עִנְיַן הַהֲסָתָה שֶׁל מֵסִית—כְּגוֹן הָאוֹמֵר לַחֲבֵרוֹ "נֵלֵךְ וְנַעֲבֹד עֲבוֹדָה זָרָה
פְּלוֹנִית", אוֹ "נֵלֵךְ וְנִזְבַּח" אוֹ "נֵלֵךְ וּנְקַטֵּר" אוֹ "נֵלֵךְ וּנְנַסֵּךְ" אוֹ "נֵלֵךְ
וְנִשְׁתַּחֲוֶה"; אוֹ שֶׁאָמַר לַחֲבֵרוֹ בִּלְשׁוֹן יָחִיד: אֵלֵךְ אֶעֱבֹד, אֵלֵךְ אֶזְבַּח, אוֹ אֲקַטֵּר,
אֲנַסֵּךְ, אֶשְׁתַּחֲוֶה—בֵּין בִּלְשׁוֹן יָחִיד בֵּין בִּלְשׁוֹן רַבִּים, הֲרֵי זֶה נִקְרָא מֵסִית; וְאַף־
עַל־פִּי שֶׁלֹּא נַעֲשָׂה הַמַּעֲשֶׂה, שֶׁלֹּא עָבַד הָעֲבוֹדָה זָרָה לֹא הַמֵּסִית וְלֹא הַמּוּסָת,
אַף־עַל־כֵּן דִּינוֹ כְּדִין מֵסִית מִפְּנֵי הַדִּבּוּר לְבָד.

וּמַה שֶּׁאָמְרוּ שֶׁהַמֵּסִית לִשְׁנַיִם, הֵן הֵן עֵדָיו, וְהֵן מְבִיאִין אוֹתוֹ לְבֵית־דִּין,
וְסוֹקְלִין אוֹתוֹ עַל פִּיהֶם; וּמַה שֶּׁאָמְרוּ שֶׁמֵּסִית אֵינוֹ צָרִיךְ הַתְרָאָה, מִפְּנֵי חֹמֶר
עִנְיָנוֹ, שֶׁהוּא עִנְיָן רָע; וּכְמוֹ כֵן אָמְרוּ זִכְרוֹנָם לִבְרָכָה בְּעֵדִים זוֹמְמִין שֶׁאֵינָן
צְרִיכִין הַתְרָאָה, לְרֹב רָעָתָם, וּכְמוֹ שֶׁנִּכְתֹּב בְּעֶזְרַת הַשֵּׁם בְּסֵדֶר שׁוֹפְטִים עָשָׂה
י"א בְּסִימָן (תק"א) [תקכ"ד].

וּמַה שֶּׁאָמְרוּ שֶׁהַמֵּסִית לְאָדָם אֶחָד, שֶׁחַיָּב הַמּוּסָת לֵאמֹר אֵלָיו "יֵשׁ לִי חֲבֵרִים
שֶׁרוֹצִים בְּכָךְ; אָמַר לָהֶם גַּם־כֵּן"—וְזֶה יַעֲשֶׂה כְּדֵי שֶׁיָּעִידוּ עָלָיו שְׁנַיִם וִיהֵא נָדוֹן
עַל־פִּי בֵית־דִּין. וְעוֹד אָמְרוּ זִכְרוֹנָם לִבְרָכָה שֶׁאִם לֹא רָצָה לְהָסִית לִשְׁנַיִם,
שֶׁמִּצְוָה לְהַכְמִין לוֹ עֵדִים: וְהָעִנְיָן הוּא שֶׁמַּסְתִּיר עֵדִים בְּמָקוֹם שֶׁיִּרְאוּ הֵם הַמֵּסִית
וְהוּא לֹא יִרְאֵם, וְנִכְנָס עִמּוֹ בְּאוֹתָן דְּבָרִים שֶׁאָמַר לוֹ בְּיִחוּד, וְהַמּוּסָת מְשִׁיבוֹ
"הֵאֵיךְ נַנִּיחַ אֱלֹהֵינוּ שֶׁבַּשָּׁמַיִם וְנַעֲבֹד הָעֵצִים וְהָאֲבָנִים"; וְאִם חָזַר בּוֹ מֵסִית אוֹ
שָׁתַק, פָּטוּר; וְאִם אָמַר לוֹ "כָּךְ רָאוּי לַעֲשׂוֹת וְכֵן יָפֶה לָנוּ", מְבִיאִין אוֹתוֹ הָעֵדִים
לְבֵית־דִּין לָדוּן.

§462
    1. TB Sanhedrin 67a.
    2. MT *hilchoth 'avodath kochavim* v 1, based on *ibid.*
    3. MT *ibid.* 3, based on TB *ibid.*
    4. TB K'thuboth 33a.

they shall do no more any such wickedness as this in your midst (Deuter-onomy 13:12).

The root reason for the precept is obvious to all. The laws of the precept are, for example, what the Sages of blessed memory said:[1] How is the matter of persuasion [done] by an enticer?—for instance, if one says to his neighbor, "Let us go and worship that certain idol," or "Let us go and sacrifice [an offering to it]," or "Let us go and burn incense," "Let us go and pour a drink-offering," or "Let us go and bow down to the ground [before it]"; or if one spoke to his fellow-man in the singular: "I am going to worship," "I am going to sacrifice [an offering]," "I will burn incense," "I will pour a drink-offering," or "I will bow down to the ground"—whether [he spoke] in the singular or the plural, he is called an enticer. Even if the act was not done, as neither the enticer nor the lured man worshipped the idol, nevertheless the law for an enticer applies to him, on account of the utterance alone.[2]

Then there is what the Sages said:[1] that if someone entices two people, they become the witnesses about him; they bring him to the *beth din* (court), and he is stoned to death by their word. There is, further, what they said:[3] that an enticer needs no [prior] warning [to be liable to a death sentence], because of the seriousness of his course of action, which is an evil matter. The Sages of blessed memory likewise taught about scheming witnesses[4] that they need no [prior] warning [to be punishable], because of their great wickedness, as we will write, with the Eternal Lord's help, in the eleventh positive precept of *sidrah shof'tim* (§ 524).

There is, too, what the Sages said:[1] that if someone entices one person, the lured man has the duty to tell him, "I have friends who desire this. Speak to them as well." He is to do this so that two can testify about him [the enticer], and he can be sentenced by the *beth din*. The Sages of blessed memory taught further[1] that if the man did not wish to entice two, it is a religious duty to conceal witnesses for him. The meaning is that witnesses are hidden in a place where they can see the enticer but he does not see them. Then he engages him in conversation about those things that he told him in private. The lured man is to answer him, "How can we leave our God in heaven and worship wood and stone?" If the enticer retracts or keeps silent, he
⟨429⟩ goes free of penalty; but if he tells him, "It is right to do so, and so it

וְכָל חַיְּבֵי מִיתוֹת שֶׁבַּתּוֹרָה אֵין מַכְמִינִין לָהֶם עֵדִים חוּץ מִזֶּה, וְכָל עִנְיָן זֶה לְהַרְחָקַת עֲבוֹדָה זָרָה.

וְאָמְרוּ זִכְרוֹנָם לִבְרָכָה שֶׁמִּצְוָה הוּא בְּיַד הַמּוּסָת בְּעַצְמוֹ לְהָרְגוֹ אַחַר שֶׁדָּנוּהוּ בֵית־דִּין, וְעַל זֶה נֶאֱמַר "יָדְךָ תִּהְיֶה בּוֹ בָרִאשׁוֹנָה לַהֲמִיתוֹ"; וְזֹאת הַמִּצְוָה לְהָרְגוֹ, חֵלֶק מִצְוָה הִיא, וְאֵין לָנוּ לַחֲשֹׁב אוֹתָהּ לְמִצְוָה בִּפְנֵי עַצְמָהּ. וְיֶתֶר פְּרָטֶיהָ, בְּמַסֶּכֶת סַנְהֶדְרִין.

וְנוֹהֵג אִסּוּר זֶה בְּכָל מָקוֹם וּבְכָל זְמַן, בִּזְכָרִים וּנְקֵבוֹת. וְכָל הָעוֹבֵר עַל זֶה, בֵּין שֶׁהוּא הֶדְיוֹט אוֹ חָכָם וְנָבִיא, וְהֵסִית אֶחָד מִיִּשְׂרָאֵל, בֵּין אִישׁ אוֹ אִשָּׁה, בְּעִנְיָן שֶׁאָמַרְנוּ, חַיָּב סְקִילָה.

[מִצְוַת חֲקִירַת הָעֵדִים הֵיטֵב]

תסג לַחֲקֹר עֵדוּת חֲקִירָה גְדוֹלָה וְלִדְרֹשׁ אוֹתָהּ הֵיטֵב בְּכָל כֹּחֵנוּ, כְּדֵי לָדַעַת שֹׁרֶשׁ הַדָּבָר וַאֲמִתּוֹ עַל הַכִּוּוּן הַגָּמוּר; וּמִיּסוֹד עִנְיָן זֶה אָמְרוּ זִכְרוֹנָם לִבְרָכָה: הֱווּ מְתוּנִים בַּדִּין; וְהַכֹּל לְמַעַן נִתְיַשֵּׁב עַל הַדָּבָר וְנֵדַע בּוֹ כָּל הָאֱמֶת וְלֹא נִהְיֶה נִמְהָרִין בַּדִּין, פֶּן נָמִית הַזַּכַּאי אוֹ נַפְסִיד מָמוֹנוֹ בְּהַעֲלָמַת הָאֱמֶת; וְעַל זֶה נֶאֱמַר: וְדָרַשְׁתָּ וְחָקַרְתָּ וְשָׁאַלְתָּ הֵיטֵב וְהִנֵּה אֱמֶת נָכוֹן הַדָּבָר.

כָּל אֲשֶׁר עֵינָיו בְּרֹאשׁוֹ יַבִּיט וְיִרְאֶה כִּי רֹבֵּי הָאַזְהָרוֹת וְכֹפֶל הָעִנְיָן בְּמִלּוֹת שׁוֹנוֹת שֶׁתִּכְפֹּל הַתּוֹרָה בְּדָבָר זֶה, הוּא לְהַזְהִירֵנוּ יָפֶה בָּעִנְיָן, כִּי דָבָר גָּדוֹל הוּא וְעַמּוּד חָזָק שֶׁדַּם נֶפֶשׁ הַבְּרִיּוֹת מֻנָּח עָלָיו; וְאֵין לְהַאֲרִיךְ בְּשֹׁרֶשׁ הַמִּצְוָה, כִּי נִגְלֶה הוּא.

מִדִּינֵי הַמִּצְוָה, מַה שֶּׁאָמְרוּ זִכְרוֹנָם לִבְרָכָה שֶׁבְּשֶׁבַע חֲקִירוֹת בּוֹדְקִין כָּל עֵד, וְאֵלּוּ הֵן: בְּאֵי זוֹ שְׁמִטָּה מִשֶּׁבַע שְׁמִטּוֹת שֶׁבַּיּוֹבֵל אֵרַע הַמַּעֲשֶׂה שֶׁהוּא מֵעִיד עָלָיו,

---

5. Sifre, Deuteronomy §89; MT *ibid.* 4.

§463   1. Literally, the root.
2. Mishnah, 'Avoth i 1.
3. TB Sanhedrin 40a (Mishnah v 1).

will be fine for us," the witnesses are to bring him to the *beth din* (court) to be judged.[3]

For all those in the Torah punishable by death, witnesses are not concealed, except for him[1] — this entire matter being in order to keep idolatry far removed.

The Sages of blessed memory taught, too,[5] that it is a religious duty for the hand of the lured man himself to put him to death after the *beth din* has judged him, as it is stated about this, *your hand shall be first against him, to put him to death* (Deuteronomy 13:10). But this duty to execute him is part of the precept, and we are not to reckon it as a precept by itself. The rest of its details are in the Talmud tractate *Sanhedrin*.

This precept applies everywhere, in every time, for both man and woman. Whoever transgresses it, whether he is an ordinary, common man or a learned scholar and prophet, if he entices any Israelite, man or woman, in the manner we stated, he deserves death by stoning.

[THE PRECEPT OF EXAMINING WITNESSES THOROUGHLY]

463 to examine testimony very searchingly and query it well, with all our ability, in order to know the heart[1] of the matter and its truth with complete precision. On the basis of this rule the Sages of blessed memory said:[2] Be deliberate [patient, careful] in judgment — all in order that we may consider and reflect on the matter and know all the truth about it, and we should not be hasty in judgment, for we may put an innocent man to death or make him lose his property by leaving the truth concealed. About this it was stated, *then you shall inquire and search and ask diligently; and behold, if it be true and the matter certain* (Deuteronomy 13:15).

Whoever has eyes in his head can look and see that the multiplication of admonitions and the reiteration of the idea in different words, which the Torah restates in this subject, is in order to caution us strongly about the matter. For it is a great thing and a mighty pillar [of justice] on which the lifeblood of human beings depends. There is no need to go on at length about the root reason for the precept, since it is obvious.

Among the laws of the precept there is what the Sages of blessed memory taught:[3] that by seven questions every witness is to be examined, these being, (1) In which septennate (seven-year cycle) of

וּבְאֵי זוֹ שָׁנָה מִשְּׁבַע שָׁנִים שֶׁבַּשְּׁמִטָּה, וּבְאֵי זֶה חֹדֶשׁ מִן הַשָּׁנָה, וּבְכַמָּה יָמִים בַּחֹדֶשׁ, וּבְאֵי זֶה יוֹם מִשֵּׁשֶׁת יְמֵי הַשָּׁבוּעַ, וּבְכַמָּה שָׁעוֹת בַּיּוֹם, וּבְאֵי זֶה מָקוֹם; וַאֲפִלּוּ אָמַר הַיּוֹם הֲרָגוֹ, אוֹ אֶמֶשׁ, שׁוֹאֲלִין אוֹתוֹ כָּל זֶה.

וּמִלְּבַד שֶׁבַע הַחֲקִירוֹת אֵלּוּ, שֶׁשּׁוֹאֲלִין בְּכָל עֵדוּת, יֵשׁ בִּכְלַל מִצְוַת הַחֲקִירָה לִשְׁאֹל אוֹתוֹ, אִם הֵעִיד עָלָיו שֶׁעָבַד עֲבוֹדָה זָרָה, אִי זוֹ עֲבוֹדָה זָרָה עָבַד וּבְאֵי זוֹ עֲבוֹדָה; וְאִם הֵעִיד שֶׁחִלֵּל שַׁבָּת, אוֹמְרִים לוֹ בְּאֵיזוֹ מְלָאכָה חִלְּלוֹ וְהֵיאַךְ עָשָׂה הַמְּלָאכָה; וְאִם הֵעִיד שֶׁאָכַל בְּיוֹם הַכִּפּוּרִים, אוֹמְרִים לוֹ אֵיזֶה מַאֲכָל אָכַל וְכַמָּה אָכַל; וְכֵן כָּל כַּיּוֹצֵא בָזֶה.

וּמִלְּבַד כָּל זֶה שֶׁזָּכַרְנוּ, שֶׁהֵן נִקְרָאוֹת חֲקִירוֹת וּדְרִישׁוֹת, שֶׁהֵן עִקָּר הָעֵדוּת וְעִמָּהֶן יִתְחַיֵּב אוֹ יִפָּטֵר הַנִּדּוֹן וּבָהֶן יָזֵמּוּ הָעֵדִים, עוֹד מַרְבִּין הַבֵּית־דִּין לִבְדֹּק הָעֵדִים בְּעִנְיָנִים אֲחֵרִים שֶׁאֵינָם עִקָּר גָּדוֹל בָּעֵדוּת, וְעַל שֶׁאֵינָן עִקָּר יִקְרְאוּ אוֹתָם זִכְרוֹנָם לִבְרָכָה בְּדִיקוֹת, וַעֲלֵיהֶן אָמְרוּ: כָּל הַמַּרְבֶּה בִּבְדִיקוֹת, מְשֻׁבָּח.

וּמַהוּ זֶה שֶׁנִּקְרָא בְדִיקוֹת: כְּגוֹן מַה הָיָה לָבוּשׁ הַנֶּהֱרָג אוֹ הַהוֹרֵג, וּכְמוֹ־כֵן שׁוֹאֲלִין אוֹתוֹ: עֲפַר הָאָרֶץ שֶׁנֶּהֱרַג עָלֶיהָ הָיָה לָבָן אוֹ אָדֹם, וְכַיּוֹצֵא בְעִנְיָנִים אֵלֶּה. וְאָמְרוּ זִכְרוֹנָם לִבְרָכָה שֶׁבַּחֲקִירוֹת, אִם כִּוֵּן הָעֵד הָאֶחָד עֵדוּתוֹ וְהַשֵּׁנִי אֵינִי יוֹדֵעַ, עֵדוּתָן בְּטֵלָה; אֲבָל בִּבְדִיקוֹת, אֲפִלּוּ שְׁנֵיהֶם אוֹמְרִים אֵין אָנוּ יוֹדְעִין, עֵדוּתָן קַיֶּמֶת, וְכָל־שֶׁכֵּן אִם אָמַר הָאֶחָד לְבַד אֵינִי יוֹדֵעַ. וּבַמֶּה דְבָרִים אֲמוּרִים, בְּשֶׁלֹּא הִכְחִישׁוּ זֶה אֶת זֶה; אֲבָל הִכְחִישׁוּ זֶה אֶת זֶה, אֲפִלּוּ בִּבְדִיקוֹת, עֵדוּתָן בְּטֵלָה.

וְאֶחָד דִּינֵי נְפָשׁוֹת אוֹ דִינֵי מָמוֹנוֹת בִּכְלַל מִצְוָה זוֹ, שֶׁנֶּאֱמַר ”מִשְׁפָּט אֶחָד יִהְיֶה לָכֶם”, אֲבָל אָמְרוּ חֲכָמִים כְּדֵי שֶׁלֹּא לִנְעֹל דֶּלֶת בִּפְנֵי לוֹוִין, שֶׁלֹּא נַצְרִיךְ

---

4. In his explanatory expansion of the brief language of the Mishnah, our author's expression here is somewhat puzzling: for as R. Isaiah Pik notes in his glosses, the event under question might have taken place on the Sabbath. The Mishnah merely reads, "On which day?" and MT *hilchoth 'eduth* i 6 rephrases it, "On which day of the days of the week?" (Perhaps, though, our author wished to intimate that a criminal or "uncivil" act on the Sabbath should be unthinkable.)

5. MT *hilchoth 'eduth* i 4, based on *ibid.*

6. MT *ibid.* 6, based on TB *ibid.*

7. TB Sanhedrin 32a, etc.

the seven cycles in the jubilee period did the event occur about which he testifies? (2) In which year of the seven in the septennate? (3) In which month of the year? (4) On which day of the month? (5) On which day of the six days of the week?[4] (6) At which hour of the day? (7) At which place? Even if he said, "Today he killed him" or "Yesterday," he is asked all this.

Apart from these seven questions, which are the same for every testimony, the precept of examination includes the duty to ask him [the witness], if he testified about someone that he committed idol-worship, which idol he worshipped, and by which method of worship. If he testified that someone violated the Sabbath, he is asked by which labor the other violated it, and how he did the labor. If he testified that someone ate on the Day of Atonement, he is asked what food the other ate, and how much of it he ate; and so everything like this.[5]

Now, except for all that we have mentioned, called "examinations and queries," which are the main part of [taking] testimony, and by which the person on trial is declared either guilty or innocent, and the witnesses may be proven to be scheming and lying, the *beth din* further examines the witnesses at great length in other matters, which are not an important main part of taking testimony; and because they are not a main element, the Sages of blessed memory called them investigations, stating about them:[3] Whoever enlarges the investigations, is praiseworthy.

Now, what is this that was named investigations?—for instance, "What was the murdered man wearing?" or, "the murderer?" He is likewise questioned about the soil of the ground on which the man was killed: was it white or reddish? and so forth, along these lines.[6] And the Sages of blessed memory said[3] that in the [formal] examination, if one witness was precise in his testimony, whereas the second one said, "I do not know," their testimony is null and void. But in the investigation, even if both say, "We do not know," their testimony is valid; and all the more certainly so if only one said, "I do not know." Yet where does this rule hold?—where they did not contradict one another; but if they contradicted one another even in the investigation, their testimony is null and void.[3]

Both capital and civil cases are equally included in this precept, for it is stated, *You shall have one manner of law* (Leviticus 24:22). The Sages ruled, however,[7] in order not to lock the door in the face of

בַּעֲדֵי מָמוֹן דְּרִישָׁה וַחֲקִירָה. כֵּיצַד: אָמְרוּ הָעֵדִים "בְּפָנֵינוּ הִלְוָה זֶה אֶת זֶה מָנֶה בְּשָׁנָה פְּלוֹנִית", אַף־עַל־פִּי שֶׁלֹּא כִוְּנוּ אֶת הַחֹדֶשׁ וְאֶת הַמָּקוֹם שֶׁהִלְוָה בּוֹ, וְלֹא אֶת הַמָּנֶה מֵאֵי זֶה מַטְבֵּעַ, אֲבָל עֵדוּת שְׁנֵיהֶם שָׁוָה בְּשִׁוּוּי הַמָּנֶה, עֵדוּתָן קַיֶּמֶת בְּכָךְ. וּבַמֶּה דְּבָרִים אֲמוּרִים, בְּהוֹדָאוֹת וְהַלְוָאוֹת וּמַתָּנוֹת וּמְכִירוֹת וְכַיּוֹצֵא בָהֶן, אֲבָל בְּדִינֵי קְנָסוֹת צְרִיכִין דְּרִישָׁה וַחֲקִירָה, וְאֵין צָרִיךְ לוֹמַר בְּמַלְקוֹת (וּבְגָלוּת).

וּכְמוֹ־כֵן אָמְרוּ זִכְרוֹנָם לִבְרָכָה שֶׁאִם רָאָה הַדַּיָּן אֲפִלּוּ בְּדִינֵי הוֹדָאוֹת וְהַלְוָאוֹת שֶׁהַדִּין מִרְמָה, שֶׁצָּרִיךְ לַעֲשׂוֹת בָּהֶן דְּרִישָׁה וַחֲקִירָה; וְאִם הִכְחִישׁוּ זֶה אֶת זֶה בַּחֲקִירוֹת וּדְרִישׁוֹת, עֵדוּתָן בְּטֵלָה, אֲבָל אִם הִכְחִישׁוּ זֶה אֶת זֶה בִּבְדִיקוֹת, עֵדוּתָן קַיֶּמֶת; כֵּיצַד: אִם אָמַר הָאֶחָד בְּנִיסָן לָוָה, וְהָאַחֵר אָמַר לֹא כִי אֶלָּא בְאִיָּר, אוֹ שֶׁאָמַר הָאֶחָד בִּירוּשָׁלַיִם, וְהָאַחֵר אָמַר לֹא כִי אֶלָּא בְלוֹד, וְכֵן שֶׁאָמַר הָאֶחָד חָבִית יַיִן לָוָה, וְהָאַחֵר אָמַר לֹא כִי אֶלָּא חָבִית שֶׁל שֶׁמֶן, זֶהוּ חֲקִירָה וּדְרִישָׁה וְעֵדוּתָן בְּטֵלָה; אֲבָל אִם אָמַר הָאֶחָד מָנֶה שָׁחוֹר לָוָה, וְהַשֵּׁנִי אוֹמֵר מָנֶה לָבָן, וְעֶרֶךְ שְׁנֵיהֶם שָׁוֶה, אוֹ שֶׁהָאֶחָד אוֹמֵר בַּדְּיוֹטָא הָעֶלְיוֹנָה הָיוּ כְּשֶׁהִלְוָהוּ, וְהַשֵּׁנִי אוֹמֵר בַּדְּיוֹטָא הַתַּחְתּוֹנָה, זֶהוּ בְּדִיקוֹת וְעֵדוּתָן קַיֶּמֶת; וְיֶתֶר פְּרָטֶיהָ, בְּמַסֶּכֶת סַנְהֶדְרִין.

וְנוֹהֶגֶת מִצְוָה זוֹ לְעִנְיַן מָמוֹן בְּכָל מָקוֹם וּבְכָל זְמַן, בַּזְּכָרִים, כִּי לָהֶם לַעֲשׂוֹת מִשְׁפָּט, וְלֹא לְנָשִׁים; וּלְעִנְיַן נְפָשׁוֹת וּמַלְקִיּוֹת וּקְנָסִין נוֹהֶגֶת בָּאָרֶץ בִּזְמַן שֶׁהַסַּנְהֶדְרִין יוֹשֶׁבֶת בִּמְקוֹמוֹ, כְּמוֹ שֶׁכָּתַבְתִּי בְּסֵדֶר מִשְׁפָּטִים [סִי' מ"ז].

וְעוֹבֵר עַל זֶה וְלֹא חָקַר הָעֵדִים כָּרָאוּי, בִּטֵּל עֲשֵׂה זֶה וְעָנְשׁוֹ גָּדוֹל מְאֹד, מִפְּנֵי שֶׁהוּא סִבָּה לְחַיֵּב נְפָשׁוֹת וּלְהַפְסִיד מָמוֹן שֶׁלֹּא כַדִּין, וְהוּא רָשָׁע וּמַחֲטִיא הָרַבִּים

---

8. I.e. people would refuse to lend anyone money, for fear that if they should have to go to court to collect (e.g. if the borrower denies the loan) the witnesses might not remember details accurately, and they would never recover their money.

9. MT *hilchoth 'eduth* iii 1.

10. I.e. where witnesses testify that one person admitted owing another money, in their presence.

11. MT *ibid.* 2, based on TB Sanhedrin 32b. "Or exile" is not in the oldest manuscripts, but is present in MT.

12. TB *ibid.*

13. MT *ibid.* 3, based on TB Sanhedrin 30b.

14. MT *ibid.* based on TB Sanhedrin 40a, 31a.

15. E.g. the coin or coins were blackened through use.

borrowers, that we should not require the [formal] querying and examination of witnesses in civil cases.[8] How so? If witnesses said, "In our presence this man lent that one a *maneh* [a sum of money] in this-and-this year," even if they were not exact about the month, the place where the man lent it, or what coins comprised the *maneh*, but the testimony of both agreed on the amount of the *maneh*, their testimony is thereby effective.[9] Where does this rule hold, though? —in regard to admissions,[10] loans, gifts, sales, and so forth. In cases involving fines, however, querying and examination are necessary, and needless to say, [so too] in cases involving a penalty of whiplashes or exile (§ 409).[11]

Our Sages of blessed memory taught likewise[12] that if a judge sees even in cases of admissions and loans that a [particular] case is fraudulent, he must subject them [the witnesses] to querying and examination; and if they contradict one another in the examination and querying, their testimony is null and void.[13] However, if they contradict each other in the investigation, their testimony stands.[13] How so? If one said, "In the month of Nissan he took the loan," and the other said, "No, it was only in Iyar"; or if one said, "It was in Jerusalem," and the other said, "No, it was rather in Lod"; and so too if one said, "He borrowed a cask of wine," and the other said, "No, it was nothing other than a cask of oil"—this is examination and querying; and their testimony is null and void.[14] But if one said, "He borrowed a black *maneh*,"[15] and the second one said, "a white *maneh*," but the value [in the testimony] of both was the same; or if one said, "They were on the upper floor when he gave him the loan," and the second said, "on the lower floor"—this relates to investigation, and their testimony is valid.[14] The rest of its details are in the Talmud tractate *Sanhedrin*.

In regard to property (civil cases) this precept is in effect everywhere, at every time, for men, since it is for them to carry out justice, and not for women. As regards cases involving capital punishment, a flogging of whiplashes, or fines, it is in effect in the land [of Israel] at the time that the *Sanhedrin* (supreme court) meets in session at its place, as I wrote in *sidrah mishpatim* (§ 47).

If someone violated this and did not examine witnesses properly, he would disobey this precept, and his punishment would be very great, since this could be the cause of condemning lives [to be ended] and having property lost unjustly. He is thus a wicked person, who

לְהַאֲכִילָם מָמוֹן שֶׁל אֲחֵרִים. וּמִי שֶׁדָּן דִּין אֱמֶת לַאֲמִתּוֹ, אָמְרוּ זִכְרוֹנָם לִבְרָכָה שֶׁזְּכוּתוֹ גְּדוֹלָה, וְדִמּוּ אוֹתוֹ עַל דֶּרֶךְ מָשָׁל כְּאִלּוּ נַעֲשָׂה שֻׁתָּף לְהַקָּדוֹשׁ בָּרוּךְ הוּא בְּמַעֲשֵׂה בְרֵאשִׁית, כְּלוֹמַר שֶׁיֵּשׁ בָּעִנְיָן קִיּוּם הָעוֹלָם וְיִשּׁוּבוֹ.

[מִצְוַת שְׂרֵפַת עִיר הַנִּדַּחַת וְכָל אֲשֶׁר בָּהּ]

תסד לִשְׂרֹף עִיר הַנִּדַּחַת וְכָל אֲשֶׁר בָּהּ, וְעִיר הַנִּדַּחַת נִקְרֵאת עִיר מִיִּשְׂרָאֵל שֶׁנִּדְּחוּ עַל־יְדֵי אֲנָשִׁים בְּנֵי בְלִיַּעַל לָצֵאת מִתַּחַת כַּנְפֵי הַשְּׁכִינָה, וַיֵּלְכוּ אַחֲרֵי שְׁרִירוּת לִבָּם הָרַע לַעֲבֹד עֲבוֹדָה זָרָה; וְעַל זֶה נֶאֱמַר: וְשָׂרַפְתָּ בָאֵשׁ אֶת הָעִיר, וְאֶת כָּל אֲשֶׁר בָּהּ, וְאֶת כָּל שְׁלָלָהּ.

שֹׁרֶשׁ מִצְוָה זוֹ יָדוּעַ הוּא, שֶׁאֲנָשִׁים רָעִים וְחַטָּאִים כָּאֵלֶּה שֶׁהִסְכִּימוּ יַחַד הַסְכָּמָה רָעָה וְנִמְאֶסֶת כָּזוֹ, רָאוּי לִמְחוֹת שָׁמָם וּלְאַבֵּד זִכְרָם מִן הָעוֹלָם, וְלֹא יִשָּׁאֵר בָּעוֹלָם מָקוֹם זֵכֶר לָהֶם כְּלָל; וְאֵין לָהֶם כִּלָּיוֹן חָרוּץ יוֹתֵר מִן הַשְּׂרֵפָה.

מִדִּינֵי הַמִּצְוָה, מַה שֶּׁאָמְרוּ זִכְרוֹנָם לִבְרָכָה שֶׁאֵין הָעִיר נַעֲשֵׂית עִיר הַנִּדַּחַת, כְּלוֹמַר לָדוּן אוֹתָם בְּדִין עִיר הַנִּדַּחַת שֶׁאֲנָשֶׁיהָ נֶהֱרָגִין בְּסַיִף וּמָמוֹנָם נִשְׂרָף עִם הָעִיר, עַד שֶׁיִּהְיוּ מַדִּיחֶיהָ שְׁנַיִם אוֹ יוֹתֵר עַל שְׁנַיִם, שֶׁנֶּאֱמַר "יָצְאוּ אֲנָשִׁים" וְגוֹמֵר; וְיִהְיוּ מַדִּיחֶיהָ מֵאוֹתוֹ הַשֵּׁבֶט וּמֵאוֹתָהּ הָעִיר, שֶׁנֶּאֱמַר "מִקִּרְבְּךָ" וּמַדִּיחֵי; וְעַד שֶׁיַּדִּיחוּ רֻבָּהּ וְיִהְיוּ הַמֻּדָּחִים מִמֵּאָה וְעַד חֶצְיוֹ שֶׁל שֵׁבֶט, אֲבָל אִם הֻדַּח רֻבּוֹ שֶׁל שֵׁבֶט אֵינָם נִדּוֹנִין בְּדִין עִיר הַנִּדַּחַת אֶלָּא כִּיחִידִים, שֶׁהֵם נִסְקָלִים וּמָמוֹנָם לְיוֹרְשֵׁיהֶם: שֶׁנֶּאֱמַר "יֹשְׁבֵי הָעִיר" וְלֹא כְפַר קָטָן וְלֹא כְרַךְ גָּדוֹל, וּפָחוֹת מִמֵּאָה

16. TB Shabbath 10a, etc.

§464   1. TB Sanhedrin 111b.

2. In keeping with Deuteronomy 13:16–17.

3. I.e. "fellows" is plural, and the minimum plural is two.

4. TB Sanhedrin 15b. While this is the reading of the oldest manuscripts, the printed editions have "up to the majority of the tribe," as TB (and MT—note 6). But it is clear from what follows that the Talmud's wording is understood as exclusive, while our text is meant inclusively; hence both mean the same thing.

5. This again is the reading of the oldest manuscripts, while the printed editions have "was *not* led astray"! MH justly declares this a scribal error, to be corrected, just as *Kessef Mishneh* writes of the same erroneous reading in MT (note 6); but in old manuscripts of MT the word "not" (*lo*) is equally absent (MT variorem ed. Mosad haRav Kook, I).

brings others to sin by having them enjoy the benefit of others' property. On the other hand, if a person judged a case correctly, with a true verdict, the Sages of blessed memory said[16] that his merit would be very great; and they ranked him, by way of simile, as though he had become a partner of the Holy One, blessed is He, in the act of Creation. In other words, in this matter lies the maintenance of the world and its settlement.

[THE PRECEPT OF BURNING A CITY
GONE ASTRAY INTO IDOLATRY]

464 to burn a misled city and everything in it, a misled city being what a city in Israel is called that was led astray by base, conscienceless people to leave the shelter of the wings of the *shechinah* (Divine Presence), so that they [its inhabitants] followed the imperious rule of their evil heart to engage in idol-worship. About this it is stated, *and you shall burn with fire the city and all its spoil, wholly to the Lord your God* (Deuteronomy 13:17).

The root reason for this precept is known (evident). For if such wicked, sinful people as these agreed to such an evil, repugnant decision as this, it is right to eradicate their name and eliminate their memory from the world, so that no place of commemoration whatever should remain for them in the world. And there is no more effective way of extirpation than burning.

Among the laws of the precept there is what the Sages of blessed memory said:[1] that a city does not become a "misled city"—in other words, to have them [its inhabitants] sentenced with the verdict for a misled city, that its people should be killed by the sword and their property burned together with the city[2]—unless those leading it astray were two or more than two; for it is stated, *Certain base fellows have gone out*, etc. (Deuteronomy 13:14);[3] and those leading it astray must be of the same tribe and of the same town: for it is stated, *from the midst of you (ibid.)*;[1] and so not unless the greater part of it [the population] was led astray,[1] those misled numbering from a hundred up to half of the tribe.[4] But if the majority of the tribe was led astray,[5] they are not judged by the law of the misled city, but rather as individuals: they are stoned to death, and their property goes to their heirs; for it is stated, the *inhabitants of that city (ibid. 16)*, hence neither a small village nor a great metropolis; fewer than a hundred constitute a

כְּרַךְ קָטָן, וְרֻבּוֹ שֶׁל שֵׁבֶט כְּרַךְ גָּדוֹל.

וְדִין עָרֵי מִקְלָט, וְכֵן יְרוּשָׁלַיִם, שֶׁאֵין נַעֲשִׂין עִיר הַנִּדַּחַת, וְכֵן עִיר שֶׁהִיא בַּסְּפָר אֵינָהּ נַעֲשֵׂית עִיר הַנִּדַּחַת; וְדִין הֵיאַךְ עוֹשִׂין אוֹתָהּ עִיר הַנִּדַּחַת, וְהַהַתְרָאוֹת שֶׁשּׁוֹלְחִין לָהּ עַל־יְדֵי שְׁנֵי תַלְמִידֵי־חֲכָמִים; וּמַה שֶּׁאָמְרוּ בְּעִנְיַן רְחוֹבָהּ, וּמַה שֶּׁאָמְרוּ בְּנִכְסֵי צַדִּיקִים שֶׁבְּתוֹכָהּ, שֶׁלֹּא הָדִּחוּ עִמָּהּ; וְדִין הַקֳּדָשׁוֹת שֶׁבְּתוֹכָהּ, וְדִין פֵּרוֹת דְּקָלִים שֶׁבְּתוֹכָהּ, וְדִין נִכְסֵי אַנְשֵׁי עִיר אַחֶרֶת שֶׁבְּתוֹכָהּ, אוֹ נִכְסֵי אַנְשֵׁי עִיר הַנִּדַּחַת שֶׁבְּמָקוֹם אַחֵר; וְיֶתֶר פְּרָטֶיהָ, בְּמַסֶּכֶת סַנְהֶדְרִין.

וְנוֹהֶגֶת מִצְוָה זוֹ בִּזְכָרִים כִּי לָהֶם הַמִּשְׁפָּט, וּבִזְמַן שֶׁיִּשְׂרָאֵל עַל אַדְמָתָן, וּבֵית־דִּין הַגָּדוֹל שֶׁל שִׁבְעִים וְאֶחָד בִּמְקוֹמוֹ, שֶׁאֵין דָּנִין עִיר הַנִּדַּחַת אֶלָּא בְּבֵית־דִּין הַגָּדוֹל. וְזֹאת מִן הַמִּצְווֹת הַמֻּטָּלוֹת עַל הַצִּבּוּר, וְיוֹתֵר עַל הַסַּנְהֶדְרִין. וְאִם עָבְרוּ עַל זֶה, כְּגוֹן שֶׁיָּדְעוּ עַל אַחַת מֵעָרֵי יִשְׂרָאֵל שֶׁרְאוּיָה לְהֵעָשׂוֹת עִיר הַנִּדַּחַת וְלֹא עָשׂוּ בָהּ דִּין, בִּטְּלוּ עֲשֵׂה זֶה, וְעָנְשָׁן גָּדוֹל מְאֹד, פֶּן תִּתְפַּשֵּׁט רָעָתָהּ בַּעֲיָרוֹת אֲחֵרוֹת.

[שֶׁלֹּא לִבְנוֹת עִיר הַנִּדַּחַת לִכְמוֹת שֶׁהָיְתָה]

תסה שֶׁלֹּא לִבְנוֹת עִיר הַנִּדַּחַת לְעוֹלָם, וְעַל זֶה נֶאֱמַר: וְהָיְתָה תֵּל עוֹלָם, לֹא תִבָּנֶה עוֹד.

שֹׁרֶשׁ הַמִּצְוָה, כְּעִנְיַן מַה שֶּׁכָּתַבְתִּי בְּסֵדֶר זֶה בִּשְׂרֵפַת עִיר הַנִּדַּחַת עֲשֵׂה ח' [סִי' תס"ד].

דִּינֵי הַמִּצְוָה, כְּגוֹן מַה שֶּׁאָמְרוּ זִכְרוֹנָם לִבְרָכָה בְּפֵרוּשׁ "לֹא תִבָּנֶה", שֶׁאֵין בּוֹנִין אוֹתָהּ לַעֲשׂוֹתָהּ מְדִינָה, דְּהַיְנוּ בָּתִּים כְּמוֹ שֶׁהָיְתָה, אֲבָל מֻתָּר לַעֲשׂוֹתָהּ גַּנּוֹת וּפַרְדֵּסִים; וְיֶתֶר פְּרָטֶיהָ, מְבֹאָרִין בְּפֶרֶק עֲשִׂירִי מִסַּנְהֶדְרִין.

6. MT *hilchoth 'avodath kochavim* iv 2.
7. MT *ibid.* 4, based on TB *Bava Kamma* 82b (MY).
8. TB *Sanhedrin* 2a, 16b; MT *ibid.*
9. MT *ibid.* 6.
10. TB *Sanhedrin* 111b–112a.
11. *Ibid.* 113a.
12. TB *Sanhedrin* 2a.

§465   1. TB *Sanhedrin* 111b.

small village-town, while the majority of a tribe would mean a major metropolis.[6]

Then there is the law on cities of refuge (§ 408), and so too Jerusalem, that they cannot be declared misled cities.[7] So also a city on the border may not be declared a misled city.[8] There is, further, the law on how it [a place led astray] is declared a misled city, and the warnings sent it by two Torah scholars.[9] And there is what the Sages said regarding its open square;[1] and what they said about the property of righteous people within it, who were not led astray along with it.[10] We have, further, the law on consecrated things within it;[1] the law on the fruit of palm-trees within it;[11] and the law about the property of people of another city within it, or the property of people in a misled city that is in another location.[10] [These] and the rest of its details are in the Talmud tractate *Sanhedrin*.

This precept applies to the men, since justice is for them [to carry out], and at the time that the Israelites are on their land, the great *beth din* (supreme court) of seventy-one being in its place; for a misled city is to be judged nowhere but at the great *beth din*.[12] This is among the precepts imposed on the community [as a whole to observe], but more so on the *Sanhedrin* (supreme court). If they [the justices] transgressed this — for example, if they knew about one of the cities in Israel that it was fit to be declared a misled city, and they did not bring it to judgment — they would thus disobey this positive precept, and their punishment would be very great, for its evil might perhaps spread to other towns.

[NOT TO REBUILD TO ITS FORMER CONDITION
A CITY GONE ASTRAY INTO IDOLATRY]

465 not to rebuild a misled city ever, as it is stated about this, *and it shall be a heap for ever; it shall not be built again* (Deuteronomy 13:17).

The root reason for the precept is akin to what I wrote in this *sidrah*, in the eighth positive precept (§ 464), on the burning of a misled city.

The laws of the precept are, for example, what the Sages of blessed memory said in interpretation of "it shall not be built":[1] that it is not to be built up to make it a large town, i.e. with houses, as it was; but it is permissible to convert it into gardens and orchards. The rest of its details are explained in chapter 10 of the tractate *Sanhedrin*.

This prohibition applies to both man and woman, at the time that

וְאִסּוּר זֶה נוֹהֵג בִּזְכָרִים וּנְקֵבוֹת, בִּזְמַן שֶׁדִּין עִיר הַנִּדַּחַת נוֹהֵג, וְהוּא בִּזְמַן
שֶׁיִּשְׂרָאֵל עַל אַדְמָתָן וְסַנְהֶדְרִין יוֹשְׁבִין בִּמְקוֹמָן, כְּמוֹ שֶׁכָּתַבְתִּי לְמַעְלָה [סִי׳
תס"ד].

[שֶׁלֹּא לֵהָנוֹת בְּמָמוֹן עִיר הַנִּדַּחַת]

תסו שֶׁנִּמְנַעְנוּ מִלֵּהָנוֹת וְלָקַחַת דָּבָר מִמָּמוֹן עִיר הַנִּדַּחַת, וְעַל זֶה נֶאֱמַר "וְלֹא
יִדְבַּק בְּיָדְךָ מְאוּמָה מִן הַחֵרֶם"; וְגַם בִּכְלָל הַלָּאו הַזֶּה גַּם־כֵּן כָּל דְּבַר עֲבוֹדָה זָרָה,
כְּמוֹ שֶׁכָּתַבְתִּי לְמַעְלָה בְּסֵדֶר וְהָיָה עֵקֶב, בָּאַזְהָרָה אַחֲרוֹנָה שֶׁבַּסֵּדֶר, בְּסִימָן
(תל"ה) [תכ"ט]; וּבָהּ כָּתוּב מִשָּׁרְשֵׁי מִצְוָה זוֹ, וְכָל עִנְיָנָם שָׁוֶה.

[שֶׁלֹּא לְהִתְגּוֹדֵד כְּמוֹ עוֹבְדֵי עֲבוֹדָה זָרָה]

תסז שֶׁלֹּא לְהִתְגּוֹדֵד גּוּפֵנוּ כְּמוֹ שֶׁיַּעֲשׂוּ עוֹבְדֵי עֲבוֹדָה זָרָה, וְעַל זֶה נֶאֱמַר "לֹא
תִתְגֹּדְדוּ"; וְנִכְפַּל לָאו זֶה בְּמִלָּה אַחֶרֶת, שֶׁנֶּאֱמַר "וְשֶׂרֶט לָנֶפֶשׁ לֹא תִתְּנוּ
בִּבְשַׂרְכֶם" וְגוֹמֵר.

וּבְמַסֶּכֶת יְבָמוֹת אָמְרוּ זִכְרוֹנָם לִבְרָכָה: "לֹא תִתְגֹּדְדוּ" — לֹא תַעֲשׂוּ חֲבוּרָה;
וְשָׁם נֶאֱמַר עוֹד: "לֹא תִתְגֹּדְדוּ" מִבָּעֵי לֵהּ לְגוּפֵהּ, דַּאֲמַר רַחֲמָנָא: לֹא תַעֲשׂוּ
חֲבוּרָה עַל מֵת; וּבְמַסֶּכֶת מַכּוֹת אָמְרוּ זִכְרוֹנָם לִבְרָכָה וּגְרִידָה שֶׁשָּׂרִיטָה וּגְרִידָה דָּבָר אֶחָד
הוּא; וְשָׁם נֶאֱמַר שֶׁהַשּׂוֹרֵט עַל הַמֵּת, בֵּין בְּיָד בֵּין בִּכְלִי, חַיָּב; וְעַל עֲבוֹדָה זָרָה,
בִּכְלִי חַיָּב, בְּיָד פָּטוּר — שֶׁכֵּן הָיָה מִנְהָגָם לְהִתְגּוֹדֵד לִפְנֵי עֲבוֹדָה זָרָה בִּכְלִי,
וּכְעִנְיָן שֶׁכָּתוּב: וַיִּתְגֹּדְדוּ כְּמִשְׁפָּטָם בַּחֲרָבוֹת וּבָרְמָחִים.

וּמִכָּל־מָקוֹם, לְפִי הַנִּרְאֶה מִדִּבְרֵי רַבּוֹתֵינוּ זִכְרוֹנָם לִבְרָכָה, שֶׁאֵין חִיּוּב הַלָּאו
רַק בְּמִתְגּוֹדֵד עַל מֵת אוֹ עַל עֲבוֹדָה זָרָה, אֲבָל הַמִּתְגּוֹדֵד בְּלֹא טַעֲנָה אוֹ מִתּוֹךְ כַּעַס
עַל בֵּיתוֹ שֶׁנָּפַל אוֹ סְפִינָתוֹ שֶׁטָּבְעָה, אַף־עַל־פִּי שֶׁהוּא דָּבָר נִמְאָס בְּיוֹתֵר וּמְכֹעָר
וְאָסוּר, אֵין חִיּוּב הַלָּאו עַל זֶה.

§467   1. In place of the manuscripts' version לא תעשו חבורה על מת the editions (including the first) read מת לא תתגודדו על מת לא תעשו חבורה ושם נאמר עוד; evidently by a scribal
error a phrase from a previous line was repeated.

the law of the misled city is in effect, which is the time when the Israelites are on their land and the *Sanhedrin* (supreme court justices) meet regularly in session at their proper location, as I have written above (§ 464).

[TO DERIVE NO BENEFIT FROM THE WEALTH
OF A CITY GONE ASTRAY INTO IDOLATRY]

466 that we were prohibited from benefiting or taking anything from the property of a misled city, as it was stated about this, *And none of the proscribed matter shall cling to your hand* (Deuteronomy 13:18). Included also in the scope of this injunction is anything from idol-worship, as I wrote above, in *sidrah 'ékev*, in the last injunction in the *sidrah* (§ 429). There it is written about the root reason for this precept; and their entire subject-matter is the same.

[THE PROHIBITION AGAINST GASHING ONESELF
AS IDOL-WORSHIPPERS DO]

467 not to gash our bodies as idol-worshippers do, for it is stated about this, *you shall not cut yourselves* (Deuteronomy 14:1); and this injunction was reiterated in other words, as it is stated, *You shall not make any slashing in your flesh for the dead*, etc. (Leviticus 19:28).

Now, in the Talmud tractate *Yevamoth* (13b) the Sages of blessed memory taught: "you shall not cut yourselves"—do not make a wound. It was further stated there: "you shall not cut yourselves" — this is needed for its own meaning, for the merciful God [thus] said, "Do not make any wound [in yourselves] over the dead.[1] In tractate *Makkoth* (21a) the Sages of blessed memory said "slashing" and "cutting" are one thing; and it was stated there that if someone slashes himself [in grief] over a dead person, whether with the hand or with an instrument, he is punishable; but over an idol, if with an instrument, he is punishable, whereas by hand, he is free of penalty. For so was it their [the heathens'] practice, to slash themselves before an idol with an instrument, in accord with the verse, *and they cut themselves after their custom with swords and lances* (I Kings 18:28).

In any event, though, as it appears from the words of our Sages of blessed memory, punishment through the negative precept is incurred only when one cuts himself on account of the dead or an idol. But if a person cuts himself for no reason, or in anger over his house that collapsed or his ship that sank, even though it is a most vile and

מִשָּׁרְשֵׁי הַמִּצְוָה, כְּדֵי שֶׁלֹּא נַעֲשֶׂה בָּנוּ שׁוּם עִנְיָן דּוֹמֶה בָּעוֹלָם לְעוֹבְדֵי עֲבוֹדָה זָרָה, וּכְעִנְיָן שֶׁכָּתַבְתִּי בְּלָאו דְהַקָּפַת הָרֹאשׁ, בְּסֵדֶר "קְדֹשִׁים תִּהְיוּ" לֹא-תַעֲשֶׂה ל"א בְּסִימָן (רנ"ה) [רנ"א]; וְנִמְנַעְנוּ מִן הַגְּדִידָה עַל מֵת כִּי לֹא יָאוֹת לְעָם הַנִּבְחָר, בַּעֲלֵי חָכְמַת הַתּוֹרָה הַיְקָרָה, לְהִצְטַעֵר בְּדָבָר מִמַּעֲשֵׂה הָאֵל, רַק עַל הָעִנְיָן שֶׁצִּוָּנוּ בָרוּךְ הוּא לְהִצְטַעֵר בּוֹ, וּמִן הַטַּעַם שֶׁכָּתַבְתִּי בְּסֵדֶר "אֱמֹר אֶל הַכֹּהֲנִים" בְּמִצְוָה [מִצְוַת עֲשֵׂה] רִאשׁוֹנָה [סִי' רס"ד]; אֲבָל שֶׁנַּשְׁחִית גּוּפֵנוּ וּנְקַלְקֵל עַצְמֵנוּ כְּשׁוֹטִים, לֹא טוֹב לָנוּ וְלֹא דֶרֶךְ חֲכָמִים וְאַנְשֵׁי בִינָה הִיא, רַק מַעֲשֵׂה הֲמוֹן הַנָּשִׁים הַפְּחוּתוֹת וַחֲסֵרֵי הַדַּעַת, שֶׁלֹּא הֵבִינוּ דָבָר בְּמַעֲשֵׂה הָאֵל וְנִפְלְאוֹתָיו.

וְהָרַב רַבֵּנוּ מֹשֶׁה בֶּן נַחְמָן זִכְרוֹנוֹ לִבְרָכָה כָּתַב: מִכַּאן סֶמֶךְ לְרַבּוֹתֵינוּ זִכְרוֹנָם לִבְרָכָה בְּאָסְרָם לְהִתְאַבֵּל עַל הַמֵּת יוֹתֵר מִדַּי.

מִדִּינֵי הַמִּצְוָה, מַה שֶּׁאָמְרוּ זִכְרוֹנָם לִבְרָכָה שֶׁהַשּׂוֹרֵט עַל הַמֵּת חַיָּב עַל כָּל שְׂרִיטָה וּשְׂרִיטָה מַלְקוּת אַחַת, וְהוּא שֶׁהִתְרוּ בוֹ עַל כָּל אַחַת וְאַחַת; וְהַשּׂוֹרֵט שְׂרִיטָה אַחַת עַל חֲמִשָּׁה מֵתִים חַיָּב חָמֵשׁ מַלְקִיּוֹת, וְיֶתֶר פְּרָטֶיהָ, בְּסוֹף מַסֶּכֶת מַכּוֹת.

וְכָתַב הָרַב רַבֵּנוּ מֹשֶׁה בֶּן מַיְמוֹן זִכְרוֹנוֹ לִבְרָכָה כִּי עוֹד דָּרְשׁוּ זִכְרוֹנָם לִבְרָכָה בִּכְלָל אַזְהָרָה זוֹ שֶׁלֹּא יְהוּ שְׁנֵי בָתֵּי דִינִין בְּעִיר אַחַת זֶה נוֹהֵג בְּמִנְהָג אֶחָד וְזֶה נוֹהֵג בְּמִנְהָג אַחֵר, שֶׁדָּבָר זֶה גּוֹרֵם לְמַחֲלֹקֶת, וּלְשׁוֹן "לֹא תִתְגֹּדְדוּ" כְּלוֹמַר לֹא תַעֲשׂוּ אֲגֻדּוֹת אֲגֻדּוֹת, כְּלוֹמַר שֶׁתִּהְיוּ חֲלוּקִין אֵלּוּ עַל אֵלּוּ.

וּמִמּוֹרַי יִשְׁמְרֵם אֵל לָמַדְתִּי שֶׁאֵין אִסּוּר זֶה אֶלָּא זֶה בַּחֲבוּרָה אַחַת שֶׁחוֹלְקִין קְצָתָן עַל קְצָתָן וְהֵן שָׁוִין בְּחָכְמָה, שֶׁאָסוּר לַעֲשׂוֹת כָּל כַּת מֵהֶן כְּדִבְרָיו, שֶׁזֶּה

2. The first three paragraphs are based on ShM negative precept § 45.

3. Ramban, commentary, Deuteronomy 14 : 1.

4. TB Moʿéd Katan 27b.

5. TB Makkoth 20b.

6. In contrast to the usual וממורי י"א the third of the four early manuscripts has וממוריי י"א which seems to indicate the plural. Text and translation have been rendered accordingly.

7. ShM negative precept § 45; MT *hilchoth ʾavodath kochavim* xii 14.

heinous deed, and it is forbidden, punishment on account of this negative precept is not incurred for it.[2]

At the root of the precept lies the purpose that we should do to ourselves nothing whatever in the world in resemblance to idol-worshippers—in keeping with what I wrote of the injunction against trimming the corners of the head, in *sidrah k'doshim*, the thirty-first negative precept (§ 251). Then we were restricted from inflicting gashes [on ourselves] over the dead, because it is not becoming for the chosen people, possessed of the precious wisdom of the Torah, to suffer anguish over some incident of God's doing, except in an instance where He (blessed is He) commanded us to grieve over it—this for the reason I wrote in *sidrah 'emor*, at the first positive precept (§ 264). But that we should be destructive to our body and injure ourselves like witless fools—this is not good for us, and is not the way of the wise and the people of understanding. It is solely the activity of the mass of low, inferior women lacking in sense, who have understood nothing of God's handiwork and His wonders.

Now, R. Moses b. Naḥman of blessed memory wrote:[3] From here we have a basis of support for our Sages of blessed memory, regarding their ban on grieving over the dead excessively.[4]

Among the laws of the precept there is what the Sages of blessed memory taught:[5] that a person who slashes himself [in grief] over the dead is punishable for every single incision by a flogging of one set of whiplashes—but this if he was cautioned over each and every one. But if someone inflicts one gash on himself over five dead persons, he incurs five sets of whiplashes. The rest of its details are in the Talmud tractate *Makkoth*.

Well, R. Moses b. Maimon of blessed memory wrote[6] that our Sages of blessed memory taught within the scope of this injunction that two courts of Jewish law in one city should not [conduct themselves at variance with one another], one *beth din* following one practice, and the other *beth din* another practice; for this matter will cause dissension. The expression *lo thithgo-d'du* (you shall not cut yourselves) is understood as, "you shall not form *'agudoth*, separate groups," i.e. by which you will be divided among yourselves.

However, from my master instructors, God protect them,[7] I learned that this prohibition applies to none but one group, some of whose members differ with others, [all] being equal in wisdom—that ⟨443⟩ it is forbidden for each subgroup among them to act according to its

גּוֹרֵם מַחֲלֹקֶת בֵּינֵיהֶן; אֶלָּא יִשָּׂאוּ וְיִתְּנוּ בַּדָּבָר הַרְבֵּה עַד שֶׁיַּסְכִּימוּ כֻלָּם לְדֵעָה אַחַת; וְאִם אִי־אֶפְשָׁר בְּכָךְ, יַעֲשׂוּ הַכֹּל כְּדִבְרֵי הַמַּחְמִירִין אִם הַמַּחֲלֹקֶת הוּא עַל דָּבָר שֶׁהוּא מִן הַתּוֹרָה; אֲבָל בִּשְׁנֵי דִינֵי חֲלוּקִין וְהֵן שָׁוִין בְּחָכְמָה, לֹא נֶאֱמַר עַל זֶה "לֹא תִתְגֹּדְדוּ"; וְהֵבִיאוּ רְאָיָה מִמַּעֲשֶׂה דְמַסֶּכֶת חֻלִּין, שֶׁאָמְרוּ שָׁם: נַפְקֵי שׁפּוּרֵי דְרַב וְאַסְרֵי, וְנַפְקֵי שׁפּוּרֵי דִשְׁמוּאֵל וּשְׁרוֹ.

וְנֹהֵג אִסּוּר זֶה בְּכָל מָקוֹם וּבְכָל זְמַן, בִּזְכָרִים וּנְקֵבוֹת. וְעוֹבֵר עַל זֶה וְשָׂרַט שְׂרִיטָה אַחַת בְּכָל מָקוֹם שֶׁבְּגוּפוֹ עַל מֵת אוֹ לְשֵׁם עֲבוֹדָה זָרָה, חַיָּב מַלְקוּת.

[שֶׁלֹּא לַעֲשׂוֹת קָרְחָה עַל מֵת]

תסח שֶׁלֹּא לִקְרֹחַ שְׂעַר הָרֹאשׁ עַל הַמֵּתִים כְּמוֹ שֶׁיַּעֲשׂוּ חַסְרֵי הַדַּעַת, וְעַל זֶה נֶאֱמַר "וְלֹא תָשִׂימוּ קָרְחָה בֵּין עֵינֵיכֶם לָמֵת"; וְנִכְפַּל לָאו זֶה בְּכֹהֲנִים, שֶׁנֶּאֱמַר עֲלֵיהֶם "לֹא יִקְרְחוּ קָרְחָה בְּרֹאשָׁם", וְלָמַדְנוּ מִשָּׁם לְחַיֵּב עַל כָּל הָרֹאשׁ כְּמוֹ כְּבֵין הָעֵינַיִם, כְּמוֹ שֶׁבָּא בְּמַסֶּכֶת מַכּוֹת.

וּמִן הַכָּתוּב הַזֶּה לָמְדוּ גַם־כֵּן שֶׁאֵין הַחִיּוּב בְּקָרְחָה כִּי־אִם הַקּוֹרֵחַ עַל מֵת דַּוְקָא. וְנִמְצָא עִם שְׁנֵי הַכְּתוּבִים תַּשְׁלוּם הַמִּצְוָה וּבֵאוּרָהּ בֵּין בְּיִשְׂרָאֵל בֵּין בַּכֹּהֲנִים, שֶׁהַכֹּל מִתְחַיְּבִין עַל כָּל הָרֹאשׁ כְּבֵין הָעֵינַיִם. וְאֵין לְךָ לִשְׁאֹל בְּמָקוֹם זֶה וּבְכָל כַּיּוֹצֵא בוֹ: לָמָּה לֹא בָא בֵּאוּר הַכָּתוּב כֻּלּוֹ בְּמָקוֹם אֶחָד; עִם הַהַקְדָּמָה שֶׁכָּתַבְתִּי לְךָ בְּרֹאשׁ סֵפֶר זֶה שֶׁל אֵלֶּה הַדְּבָרִים, הֲלֹא הִיא תָנִיחַ דַּעְתְּךָ בְּעִנְיָנִים אֵלֶּה בִּמְקוֹמוֹת רַבִּים.

שָׁרְשֵׁי הַמִּצְוָה, כָּתוּב בַּמִּצְוָה הַקּוֹדֶמֶת.

מִדִּינֵי הַמִּצְוָה, מַה שֶּׁאָמְרוּ זִכְרוֹנָם לִבְרָכָה שֶׁהַקּוֹרֵחַ קָרְחָה אַחַת עַל חָמֵשׁ

<hr>

8. This follows Rava in TB Yevamoth 14a.

9. Since it is a standing rule that matters of doubt involving a law of the Torah should be decided stringently (TB Bétzah 3b).

10. In our editions of the Talmud this is found not in Ḥullin but in TB 'Avodah Zarah 40a, with the Sages named differently, though.

§468   1. From the beginning to here is based on ShM negative precept §171.

2. Tosefta, Makkoth iii 7; cf. §467, paragraph 6.

words, since this will cause dissension among them.[8] They should rather discuss and debate the matter greatly, until they all agree to one view. If this is impossible, all should act according to the words of those who think stringently, if the difference of opinion concerns a matter of Torah law.[9] But if two courts of Jewish law differ and they are equal in wisdom, *lo thithgo-d'du* does not apply to this. And he brought proof from an incident in the Talmud tractate *Ḥullin*, where it was stated:[10] The announcements of Rav went forth and proclaimed it forbidden, and the announcements of Sh'mu'él went forth and proclaimed it permitted.

This prohibition is in force everywhere, at every time, for both man and woman. If a person transgressed this and made one gash anywhere on his body [in grief] over a dead person or for the sake of idolatry, he would deserve whiplashes.

[NOT TO CAUSE BALDNESS, TEARING THE HAIR
IN GRIEF OVER THE DEAD]

468 not to uproot hair of the head [in grief] over the dead, as those lacking in sense do: as it is stated about this, *nor shall you make any baldness between your eyes for the dead* (Deuteronomy 14:1). This injunction was reiterated for the *kohanim*, as it was stated about them, *They shall not make baldness on their head* (Leviticus 21:5); and from that we learn to impose punishment for anywhere on the head as for [the area directly above] between the eyes, as we read in the tractate *Makkoth* (21a).

From this verse it was also learned that there is no punishment for baldness unless one causes it specifically over the dead. Thus with the two verses we find the entirety of the precept and its clarification, [that it applies to] both Israelites (non-*kohanim*) and *kohanim* — all are punishable for anywhere on the head as for [directly above] between the eyes.[1] And you need not ask at this instance or anywhere similar, why the elucidation of Scripture was not given all at one place — in view of the preface I wrote for you at the head of this Book of Deuteronomy. That will surely set your mind at rest about these matters in many instances.

Regarding root reasons for the precept, I wrote in the precept before this.

Among the laws of the precept there is what the Sages of blessed memory taught:[2] that if someone made one area of baldness over five

מֵתִים, לוֹקֶה חָמֵשׁ; וְהַקּוֹרֵחַ חָמֵשׁ קָרְחוֹת עַל מֵת אֶחָד, לוֹקֶה חָמֵשׁ, כְּשֶׁהִתְרוּ בוֹ
עַל כָּל אַחַת וְאַחַת. הַקּוֹרֵחַ בְּיָד אוֹ בְּסַם, חַיָּב; וַאֲפִלּוּ הִטְבִּיל אֶצְבְּעוֹתָיו בְּסַם
וְהִנִּיחָן בְּחָמֵשׁ מְקוֹמוֹת בְּרֹאשׁוֹ בְּבַת-אַחַת, הוֹאִיל וְקָרַח חָמֵשׁ קָרְחוֹת לוֹקֶה
חָמֵשׁ, וְאַף-עַל-פִּי שֶׁהִיא הַתְרָאָה אַחַת, הוֹאִיל וְכֻלָּן בָּאִין כְּאַחַת. וְיֶתֶר פְּרָטֵי
הַמִּצְוָה, בְּסוֹף מַכּוֹת. וְכָל עִנְיָנֶיהָ כְּדִין חֲבֶרְתָּהּ הַקּוֹדֶמֶת בְּשָׁוֶה.

[שֶׁלֹּא לֶאֱכֹל פְּסוּלֵי הַמֻּקְדָּשִׁין]

תסט שֶׁלֹּא נֹאכַל פְּסוּלֵי הַמֻּקְדָּשִׁין: וְהַלָּאו הַזֶּה בִּפְסוּלֵי הַמֻּקְדָּשִׁין פֵּרְשׁוּ
זִכְרוֹנָם לִבְרָכָה בְּמַסֶּכֶת בְּכוֹרוֹת שֶׁהוּא דַּוְקָא כְּשֶׁנַּעֲשָׂה אֲנַחְנוּ הַמּוּם בַּמֻּקְדָּשִׁין
שֶׁיִּפָּסְלוּ עַל יָדֵינוּ, וְאַחַר-כָּךְ אִם נֹאכַל מֵהֶן, אָז יִהְיֶה בַּאֲכִילָתָן לָאו; וּכְמוֹ-כֵן אִם
יִפָּסֵל הַקָּרְבָּן בְּשׁוּם צַד אַחַר זְבִיחָתוֹ, בָּזֶה גַּם-כֵּן יֵשׁ בּוֹ לָאו; וְעַל כָּל זֶה נֶאֱמַר:
לֹא תֹאכַל כָּל תּוֹעֵבָה.

וְכֵן הוּא בְּסִפְרִי: "לֹא תֹאכַל כָּל תּוֹעֵבָה"—בִּפְסוּלֵי הַמֻּקְדָּשִׁין הַכָּתוּב
מְדַבֵּר; וְשָׁם נֶאֱמַר עוֹד: רַבִּי אֱלִיעֶזֶר בֶּן יַעֲקֹב אוֹמֵר: מִנַּיִן לְצוֹרֵם אֹזֶן הַבְּכוֹר
וְאָכַל מִמֶּנּוּ שֶׁעוֹבֵר בְּלֹא-תַעֲשֶׂה—שֶׁנֶּאֱמַר "לֹא תֹאכַל כָּל תּוֹעֵבָה"; וְעוֹד אָמְרוּ
זִכְרוֹנָם לִבְרָכָה שֶׁיֵּשׁ בִּכְלָל זֶה הַלָּאו אַזְהָרָה שֶׁלֹּא לֶאֱכֹל פִּגּוּל וְנוֹתָר—וּכְבָר
כָּתַבְתִּי עִנְיָנָם בְּסֵדֶר צַו [סִי׳ קמ״ג, קמ״ד]; וְכֵן כָּל אִסּוּרֵי מַאֲכָלוֹת, וּכְעִנְיָנָן

---

3. TB Makkoth 21a; MT *hilchoth 'avodath kochavim* xii 15.
4. *Ibid.* 21b; MT *ibid.*

§469

1. Sifre, Deuteronomy §99.

2. Because a firstborn animal is automatically consecrated from birth, to be brought as an offering at the Sanctuary, and then eaten by *kohanim*; but if it developed a blemishing defect, it became permissible for its owner to eat it after ordinary *shehittah* (ritual slaying). The Hebrew verb *tzaram* is explained in the *'Aruch* as "split, or crushed leaving a permanent effect." Other meanings: in the commentary ascribed to Rashi, Mo'éd Katan 13a, "cut off a bit" (of the ear), and so too R. Jonathan in *Shittah M'kubetzeth* to TB Bava Kamma 90a; in *ibid.* to TB *ibid.* 98a, a geonic view: "scratched"; Rashi, Bava Kamma 90a end: "pulled"; *idem*, TB B'choroth 34a: "blemished."

The citation of R. 'Eli'ezer b. Ya'akov's ruling from Sifre is somewhat difficult, since it is not accepted in *halachah*. Actually, the difficulty lies with Rambam, for in citing it our author merely follows ShM negative precept §140; whereas in MT *hilchoth b'choroth* ii 7 Rambam gives the superseding view of the Sages in Mishnah, B'choroth v 3 (TB 34a) that only Rabbinic law forbids the man from ritually slaying the blemished firstborn animal. See the relevant gloss of R. Isaiah Pik on the

dead persons, he should be given five sets of whiplashes; and if someone makes five areas of baldness over one dead person, he [too] is to receive five sets of whiplashes, if he was cautioned about each and every one.³ Whether one makes the baldness by hand or with a drug (depilatory), he is punishable.⁴ Even if he dipped his [five] fingers in the drug and put them on five places on his head at once, since he made five bald spots, he is to receive five sets of lashes — even if there was one caution [given him about it], since they all came at once.⁴ Other details of the precept are [to be found] toward the end of the tractate *Makkoth*. In its entire subject-matter it is like its companion-precept that precedes it, being quite the same.

[NOT TO EAT HOLY ANIMAL OFFERINGS
THAT BECAME DISQUALIFIED]

469 that we should not eat disqualified consecrated animals; but this negative precept about disqualified hallowed animals, our Sages of blessed memory explained in the tractate *B'choroth* (34a), applies specifically when we make a blemishing defect in the consecrated animals so that they should become disqualified [as offerings] through our deed; after that, if we eat them, their consumption then entails the violation of a negative precept. So too, if an offering becomes disqualified in any way after it is ritually slain, to this also the negative precept applies. About all this it is stated, *You shall not eat any abominable thing* (Deuteronomy 14:3).

And so it is [taught] in the Midrash *Sifre:*¹ "You shall not eat any abominable thing" — the verse relates to disqualified consecrated animals. It was then stated there, further: R. 'Eli'ezer b. Ya'akov said: How do we know that if someone seriously damaged the ear of a firstborn animal² and ate of it, he transgressed a negative precept? — because it is stated, *You shall not eat any abominable thing.* In addition, the Sages of blessed memory said that within the meaning of this negative precept lies an injunction not to eat *piggul* (§ 144) or *nothar* (§ 143); I wrote their subject-matter previously, in *sidrah tzav*; and so all forbidden foods — in keeping with the interpretation that the Sages of blessed memory gave:³ "You shall not eat any abominable

Ḥinnuch, ad loc.; MH and MY (which goes into the question at great length); and note 477 to ShM *loc. cit.* in ed. Mosad R. Kook.

〈447〉 3. TB 'Avodah Zarah 66a, Ḥullin 114b.

שֶׁדָּרְשׁוּ זִכְרוֹנָם לִבְרָכָה: "לֹא תֹאכַל כָּל תּוֹעֵבָה" — כָּל שֶׁתִּעַבְתִּי לְךָ הֲרֵי הוּא בְּבַל תֹּאכַל.

וּמִכָּל־מָקוֹם אֵינֶנּוּ נִקְרָא לָאו שֶׁבִּכְלָלוֹת, לְפִי שֶׁעֲקָרוֹ לֹא בָא אֶלָּא עַל פְּסוּלֵי הַמֻּקְדָּשִׁין, וּשְׁאָר הָאֲסוּרִין יוֹצְאִין מִכְּלָלָן, כְּלוֹמַר מִמַּה שֶׁהוֹצִיא הַכָּתוּב אַזְהָרָה זוֹ בְּלָשׁוֹן כְּלָל, שֶׁאָמַר "כָּל תּוֹעֵבָה" וְלֹא אָמַר "לֹא תֹאכַל פְּסוּלֵי הַמֻּקְדָּשִׁין" בְּפֵרוּשׁ; וּמִפְּנֵי־כֵן נַחְשְׁבֵהוּ לָאו מְיֻחָד לְעָקְרוֹ וְנִלְמַד מִמֶּנּוּ אַזְהָרָה לִשְׁאָר הָעִנְיָנִים; וְקַבֵּל הָאֱמֶת מִמִּי שֶׁאֲמָרוֹ.

כְּבָר כָּתַבְתִּי כַּמָּה פְעָמִים כִּי מִשָּׁרְשֵׁי הַמִּצְווֹת שֶׁתִּמְנָעֵנוּ הַתּוֹרָה מֵהִתְקָרֵב אֶל הַקֹּדֶשׁ וּמִנְּגֹעַ בְּקָצֵהוּ, הוּא כְּדֵי לָתֵת מוֹרָאַת הָעִנְיָנִים הָאֵלֶּה אֶל לִבֵּנוּ וּלְיַקְּרָם בְּעֵינֵינוּ, לְמַעַן יִתְעוֹרֵר רוּחֵנוּ וְיֶהֱמוּ רַעְיוֹנֵינוּ וְיֵרַךְ לְבָבֵנוּ, וְיִתְחַדֵּשׁ בָּנוּ רוּחַ נָכוֹן בְּבוֹאֵנוּ לְבַקֵּשׁ סְלִיחָה עַל עֲווֹנוֹתֵינוּ; וּמִתּוֹךְ כָּךְ יֵעָתֵר לָנוּ הָאֵל בָּרוּךְ הוּא וְיוֹשִׁיעֵנוּ מִכָּל צָרוֹתֵינוּ, וְנִהְיֶה טוֹבִים; וְאַף גַּם זֹאת לְטוֹבָה זוֹ נִפְרַשׁ שָׁרְשָׁהּ.

וְדִינֵי הַמִּצְוָה בְּמַסֶּכֶת בְּכוֹרוֹת.

וְנוֹהֵג אִסּוּר זֶה בַּזְּכָרִים וּנְקֵבוֹת, בְּכָל מָקוֹם וּבְכָל זְמַן: שֶׁאַף־עַל־פִּי שֶׁאָמְרוּ זִכְרוֹנָם לִבְרָכָה שֶׁבַּזְּמַן הַזֶּה אֵין מַקְדִּישִׁין, כְּמוֹ שֶׁכָּתַבְתִּי בְּרֹאשׁ סֵדֶר אִם בְּחֻקֹּתַי [סִי׳ שׁ״ן], מִכָּל־מָקוֹם מִי שֶׁהִקְדִּישׁ בְּהֵמָה לַקָּרְבָּן, קְדֻשָּׁה חָלָה עָלָיו וְדִין קָדָשִׁים יֵשׁ לָהּ, וּמִי שֶׁהִטִּיל בָּהּ מוּם וְאָכַל מִמֶּנָּה, עוֹבֵר עַל לָאו זֶה וְחַיָּב מַלְקוֹת מִשּׁוּם זֶה, וּכְשֶׁאָכַל מִמֶּנָּה כְּזַיִת וְיֵשׁ עֵדִים וְהַתְרָאָה.

[מִצְוַת בְּדִיקַת סִימָנֵי הָעוֹף]

תע לִבְדֹּק בְּסִימָנֵי הָעוֹף, וְעַל זֶה נֶאֱמַר: כָּל צִפּוֹר טְהֹרָה תֹּאכֵלוּ; וְכֵן אָמְרוּ

---

4. I.e. one negative precept covering several unrelated things; for violating such a precept, no flogging of whiplashes is given (TB K'réthoth 4b).

5. So *tosafoth*, TB 'Avodah Zarah 66a, s.v. *kol*.

6. TB Yoma 66a; TJ Sh'kalim, toward the end.

thing"—all that I [God] declared as abominable for you, is under the injunction not to eat it.

It is nevertheless not called a general, omnibus injunction,[4] because essentially, in the main, it applies to nothing else but disqualified consecrated animals, and the other prohibitions are derived from their general rule—in other words, from the fact that Scripture expressed this injunction by a general term, stating, "any abominable thing," and not, "You shall not eat disqualified consecrated animals"— explicitly. For this reason we reckon it as a negative precept particularly about its main subject, and from that we derive an injunction about the other topics.[5] Accept the truth from the one who speaks it.

I have previously written many times that one of the root reasons for the precepts whereby the Torah restricts us from getting close to the sacred and touching even its furthest part, is in order to instill a reverent fear of these matters in our heart and make them treasured in our eyes, so that our spirit may be stirred, our perception stimulated, and our heart softened [made receptive], and a new steadfast spirit may arise in us when we come to implore forgiveness for our sins. As a result, God, blessed is He, will accept our entreaty and rescue us from all our troubles, that all may be well for us. Then regarding this [precept] too, we would explain its root reason as for this good purpose.

Now, the laws of the precept are in the Talmud tractate *B'choroth*. This prohibition applies to both man and woman, in every place and every time. For even though the Sages of blessed memory said[6] that at the present time nothing should be consecrated, as I wrote near the beginning of *sidrah b'ḥukothai* (§ 350), nevertheless, if someone consecrated an animal for an offering, it assumes a state of sanctity, and is subject to the law for consecrated animals; and if anyone inflicted a blemishing injury on it and ate of it, he would transgress this negative precept, and would be punishable by whiplashes on account of it, if he ate an olive's amount of it and there were witnesses and a [prior] warning.

[THE RELIGIOUS DUTY OF EXAMINING THE
MARKS OF A FOWL, IF IT MAY BE EATEN]

470

to examine the distinguishing signs of fowl [to determine if
they are of a kosher, permissible species], as it is stated about this,

בְּסִפְרִי: "כָּל צִפּוֹר טְהֹרָה תֹּאכֵלוּ" — זוֹ מִצְוַת עֲשֵׂה.

כָּל עִנְיַן מִצְוָה זוֹ, שָׁרָשֶׁיהָ וְדִינֶיהָ, וּבְאֵי זֶה מָקוֹם נוֹהֶגֶת וּבְאֵי זֶה זְמַן, הַכֹּל כָּתַבְתִּי בְּרֹאשׁ סֵדֶר וַיְהִי בַּיּוֹם הַשְּׁמִינִי בְּעִנְיַן בְּדִיקַת סִימָנֵי בְּהֵמָה וְחַיָּה דָגִים וַחֲגָבִים [סִי' קנ"ג], שֶׁדִּין כֻּלָּם שָׁוֶה]. וְגַם שָׁם כָּתוּב שֶׁהָרַב רַבֵּנוּ מֹשֶׁה בֶּן נַחְמָן זִכְרוֹנוֹ לִבְרָכָה יַחֲלֹק עִם הָרַב רַבֵּנוּ מֹשֶׁה בֶּן מַיְמוֹן זִכְרוֹנוֹ לִבְרָכָה בְּחָשְׁבוֹ הַבְּדִיקָה בַּבְּהֵמָה וּבִשְׁאָר הַמִּינִין מִצְוַת עֲשֵׂה, וְהוּא סוֹבֵר שֶׁלֹּא בָא אֶלָּא לִתֵּן עֲשֵׂה וְלֹא-תַעֲשֶׂה לֶאֱכֹל מִן הַטָּמֵא. וְשָׁם בְּאוֹתוֹ סֵדֶר בְּלֹא-תַעֲשֶׂה ז' בְּסִימָן (קס"א) [קנ"ז] כָּתַבְתִּי בְּסִימָנֵי הָעוֹף קְצָת מִמַּה שֶּׁשָּׁמַעְתִּי בָהֶן מֵרַבּוֹתַי יִשְׁמְרֵם אֵל, וְקָחֶנּוּ מִשָּׁם.

[שֶׁלֹּא לֶאֱכֹל חָגָב טָמֵא וְכֵן כָּל שֶׁרֶץ הָעוֹף]

תעא שֶׁלֹּא לֶאֱכֹל שֶׁרֶץ הָעוֹף, כְּגוֹן הַזְּבוּבִים וְהַדְּבוֹרִים וְהַצְּרָעוֹת וְזוּלָתָן מִמִּינִין אֵלּוּ, וְעַל זֶה נֶאֱמַר "וְכָל שֶׁרֶץ הָעוֹף טָמֵא הוּא לָכֶם לֹא יֵאָכֵלוּ"; וּלְשׁוֹן סִפְרִי: "וְכָל שֶׁרֶץ הָעוֹף" וְכוּלֵי — מִצְוַת לֹא-תַעֲשֶׂה.

וְדַע כִּי מִפְּנֵי שֶׁאָסְרָה הַתּוֹרָה הָעוֹפוֹת הַטְּמֵאִים וְהִזְכִּירָן בְּפֵרוּשׁ, לְפִי שֶׁהֵן מוּעָטִין, וּכְמוֹ שֶׁכָּתַבְתִּי בָּאֲרֻכָּה בְּסֵדֶר זֶה בַּיּוֹם הַשְּׁמִינִי בְּלֹא-תַעֲשֶׂה ז' בְּסִימָן (קס"א) [קנ"ז], וְנִשְׁאֲרוּ כָל שְׁאָר הָעוֹפוֹת בְּחֶזְקַת הֶתֵּר — הֻצְרַךְ הַכָּתוּב לֶאֱסֹר שֶׁרֶץ הָעוֹף, לְהוֹדִיעֵנוּ שֶׁאֵינוֹ מִכְּלַל הַמֻּתָּרִין, וְאַף-עַל-פִּי שֶׁהַסִּימָנִין שֶׁל טְהוֹרִין מְקֻבָּלִים וִידוּעִים הֵם לָנוּ. אוֹ נֹאמַר כִּי מֵהֱיוֹת שֶׁרֶץ הָעוֹף מִין בִּפְנֵי עַצְמוֹ, הֻצְרַךְ לְאָסְרָן בְּפֵרוּשׁ. וְהִנֵּה בְּסֵדֶר בַּיּוֹם הַשְּׁמִינִי אָמַר "וְאֶת אֵלֶּה תְּשַׁקְּצוּ מִן הָעוֹף", וְכָאן אָמַר "וְכָל שֶׁרֶץ הָעוֹף", נִתְיַחֵד בָּהֶן לָאו, כִּי עוֹף וְשֶׁרֶץ הָעוֹף שְׁנֵי עִנְיָנִים חֲלוּקִין הֵם לְגַמְרֵי.

---

§470   1. Sifre, Deuteronomy § 103.

2. I.e. to make certain it is "clean" (a kosher species).

3. I.e. that if anyone does so, he violates both precepts (this one and § 157).

§471   1. Sifre, Deuteronomy § 103.

2. Hence we would know that flying insects are forbidden, since they lack the required signs; nevertheless, Scripture made the matter explicit, past any shred of doubt.

3. Although Scripture uses the same Hebrew word, *'of* (bird, winged creature), about both fowl and flying insects.

Every clean bird you may eat (Deuteronomy 14:11). And so it was taught in the Midrash *Sifre:*[1] "Every clean bird you may eat" — this is a positive precept.[2]

The entire subject-matter of this precept, its root reason and its laws, in which location it is in effect, and at which time — all this I wrote around the beginning of *sidrah sh'mini* (§ 153), in regard to examining the distinguishing signs of domestic and wild animals, fish and locusts — for the law is the same for them all. It was also written there that R. Moses b. Naḥman of blessed memory differs with R. Moses b. Maimon of blessed memory in his reckoning the examination of domestic animals and other species of creatures as a positive precept. He holds that this was set down only to impose a positive and a negative precept in regard to eating from an impure [non-kosher] animal creature.[3] There, in that *sidrah*, in the seventh negative precept (§ 157), I wrote regarding the distinguishing signs of fowl a bit of what I heard about them from my master teachers, God protect them. Then gather it from there.

[TO EAT NO UNCLEAN, NON-KOSHER LOCUSTS,
NOR ANY WINGED INSECTS]

471 not to eat any winged swarming creatures, such as flies, bees, wasps, and others of these kinds. About this it is stated, *And all winged insects are unclean for you; they shall not be eaten* (Deuteronomy 14:19); in the language of the Midrash *Sifre:*[1] "And all winged insects," etc. — it is a negative precept.

Now, know that because the Torah forbade unclean [non-kosher] fowl, and listed them explicitly since they are few [in kind] — as I wrote at length in *sidrah sh'mini*, in the seventh negative precept (§ 157) — all other winged creatures remained under an assumption of permissibility. It was therefore necessary for Scripture to forbid the winged insects, to let us know they are not included in the category of permitted species — this even though the distinguishing signs of the clean [kosher] ones are learned by the Oral Tradition and are known to us.[2] Or we might say that since winged insects are separate species,[3] it was necessary to forbid them explicitly. Hence, in *sidrah sh'mini* it is stated, *And these you shall hold in repugnance among the birds* (Leviticus 11:13); while here it is stated, *And all winged insects*, etc. A particular negative precept was given about them, because birds and winged insects are two entirely different matters.

מִשָּׁרְשֵׁי הַמִּצְווֹת הַבָּאוֹת בְּאִסּוּר הַמַּאֲכָלוֹת, כָּתַבְתִּי מַה שֶּׁעָלָה בְּמַחֲשַׁבְתִּי בְּסֵדֶר (אִם כֶּסֶף תַּלְוֶה) [מִשְׁפָּטִים] בְּאִסּוּר טְרֵפָה בְּסִימָן (ע״ג) [ע״ט], וְקָחֶנּוּ מִשָּׁם.

דִּינֵי הַמִּצְוָה, בְּמַסֶּכֶת חֻלִּין.

וְנוֹהֵג אִסּוּר זֶה בְּכָל מָקוֹם וּבְכָל זְמַן, בִּזְכָרִים וּנְקֵבוֹת. וְעוֹבֵר עַל זֶה וְאָכַל כְּזַיִת מִשִּׁרְצֵי הָעוֹף אוֹ שֶׁאָכַל שֶׁרֶץ אֶחָד מִן הָעוֹף כֻּלּוֹ וְאַף־עַל־פִּי שֶׁאֵין בּוֹ כְּזַיִת, מִכֵּיוָן שֶׁאֲכָלוֹ כֻּלּוֹ וַאֲפִלּוּ הוּא כַּעֲדָשָׁה, אוֹ שֶׁאָכַל מִמֶּנּוּ כְּזַיִת וַאֲפִלּוּ גָּדוֹל, חַיָּב מַלְקוֹת. וּכְבָר הֶאֱרַכְתִּי בְּבֵאוּר אִסּוּר שְׁרָצִים וְחֹמֶר אִסּוּר בְּרִיָּה, בְּסֵדֶר בַּיּוֹם הַשְּׁמִינִי בְּלֹא־תַעֲשֶׂה ח׳ ט׳ י׳, סִימָן קס״ב.

[שֶׁלֹּא לֶאֱכֹל מִבְּשַׂר בְּהֵמָה וְחַיָּה וָעוֹף שֶׁמֵּתוּ מֵאֲלֵיהֶם]

תעב שֶׁלֹּא לֶאֱכֹל מִבְּשַׂר בְּהֵמָה חַיָּה וָעוֹף שֶׁמֵּתוּ מֵאֲלֵיהֶן, וְעַל זֶה נֶאֱמַר: לֹא תֹאכְלוּ כָל נְבֵלָה, לַגֵּר אֲשֶׁר בִּשְׁעָרֶיךָ תִּתְּנֶנָּה וַאֲכָלָהּ אוֹ מָכֹר לְנָכְרִי. וּכְבָר כָּתַבְתִּי לְמַעְלָה בְּסֵדֶר זֶה בְּמִצְוַת שְׁחִיטָה [סִי׳ תנ״א] הַכְּלָל שֶׁאָמְרוּ זִכְרוֹנָם לִבְרָכָה, דְּכָל שֶׁנִּפְסְלָה בִּשְׁחִיטָתָהּ תִּקָּרֵא גַם־כֵּן נְבֵלָה; וְעִנְיַן טֻמְאָתָהּ כָּתוּב בְּסֵדֶר בַּיּוֹם הַשְּׁמִינִי עֲשֵׂה ו׳ בְּסִימָן (ק״ס) [קס״א], וְהִיא מִצְוָה בִּפְנֵי עַצְמָהּ.

מִשָּׁרְשֵׁי הַמִּצְוָה, מַה שֶּׁכָּתַבְתִּי בְּאִסּוּר טְרֵפָה (בְּכֶסֶף תַּלְוֶה) [בְּמִשְׁפָּטִים] בְּסִימָן (ע״ט) [ע״ג].

מִדִּינֵי הַמִּצְוָה, מַה שֶּׁאָמְרוּ זִכְרוֹנָם לִבְרָכָה שֶׁנְּבֵלָה הָרְאוּיָה לַגֵּר הִיא קְרוּיָה נְבֵלָה, וְיֵשׁ חִיּוּב בַּאֲכִילָתָהּ, אֲבָל נְבֵלָה שֶׁאֵינָהּ רְאוּיָה לַגֵּר, כְּלוֹמַר נְבֵלָה מַסְרַחַת, אֵין חִיּוּב בַּאֲכִילָתָהּ; וּמִפְּנֵי זֶה הֶאֱרִיךְ הַכָּתוּב לוֹמַר ״לַגֵּר תִּתְּנֶנָּה״, לְלַמֵּד זֶה, שֶׁאִם לֹא כֵן אֵין צֹרֶךְ לְלַמְּדֵנוּ לְמִי נִתֵּן מַה שֶּׁיֵּשׁ לָנוּ. וְאֵין לוֹמַר שֶׁבָּא לְהַתִּירָהּ

§472   1. TB Ḥullin 32a.
2. I.e. the term applies to any healthy, kosher kind of animal that died for any reason without proper *sheḥittah* (ritual slaying) to make it permitted to be eaten.
3. TB ʿAvodah Zarah 67b.

About root reasons for the precepts given on the prohibition of [certain] foods, I wrote what came to my mind in *sidrah mishpatim*, at the prohibition of *t'réfah* (a fatally injured animal; § 73). Gather it from there.

The laws of the precept are in the Talmud tractate *Ḥullin*. This prohibition is in force everywhere, at every time, for both man and woman. If someone violated it and ate an olive's amount of flying insects; or if he ate one winged insect entirely, even if it did not contain an olive's bulk, as long as he ate it all, even if it was the size of a lentil; or [alternatively] if he ate an olive's amount of it even if it was larger—he deserves whiplashes. I previously wrote at length in elucidation of the ban on swarming creatures and the severity of the prohibition on any whole creature—in *sidrah sh'mini*, in the eighth, ninth and tenth negative precepts (§§ 162–64).

[NOT TO EAT THE FLESH OF ANY KOSHER ANIMAL THAT DIED OF ITSELF]

472 not to eat of the flesh of a domestic or wild animal, or a fowl, that died of itself, as it is stated about this, *You shall not eat* n'vélah, *anything that dies of itself; to the alien who is within your gates you may give it, that he may eat it, or you may sell it to a foreigner* (Deuteronomy 14:21). I have already written, above, in this *sidrah*, in the precept of ritual slaying (§ 451), the general rule that the Sages of blessed memory gave:[1] that whatever becomes disqualified (unacceptable) by its *shehittah* (ritual slaying) is likewise called n'vélah, "something that died of itself."[2] The subject of its ritual uncleanness has been written of in *sidrah sh'mini*, in the sixth positive precept (§ 161), as it is a precept by itself.

At the root of the precept lies the reason I wrote about the prohibition on the *t'réfah* (fatally injured creature) in *sidrah mishpatim* (§ 73).

Among the laws of the precept there is what the Sages of blessed memory taught:[3] that a carcass suitable for an alien [to eat] is called n'vélah, and there is a punishable guilt for eating it; but with a carcass unfit for an alien, i.e. a malodorous (putrefying) carcass, there is no punishable guilt for eating it. For this reason the Writ elaborated, saying, "to the alien you may give it"—to teach this; for otherwise, there is no need to instruct us to whom we should give what we own.

⟨453⟩ Nor can it be said that this is meant to permit having benefit from it,

בַּהֲנָאָה, שֶׁכְּבָר כָּתוּב בְּמָקוֹם אַחֵר: וְחֵלֶב נְבֵלָה וְחֵלֶב טְרֵפָה יֵעָשֶׂה לְכָל מְלָאכָה.

וּמִכָּאן לָמְדוּ זִכְרוֹנָם לִבְרָכָה לוֹמַר נוֹתֵן טַעַם לִפְגָם מֻתָּר, שֶׁיְּדָעֻנוּ בָזֶה
שֶׁהַתּוֹרָה לֹא תֶאֱסֹר וּתְחַיֵּב כִּי־אִם עַל אֲכִילַת הַדְּבָרִים שֶׁרְאוּיִים לַאֲכִילַת בְּנֵי־
אָדָם, לֹא עַל דָּבָר שֶׁנַּפְשׁוֹ שֶׁל אָדָם קָצָה בּוֹ, דִּכְעָפָר בְּעָלְמָא הוּא חָשִׁיב; וְזֶהוּ
הַהֶתֵּר הַנִּזְכָּר בַּגְּמָרָא בְּחָמֵץ אָסוּר שֶׁנָּפַל לְתוֹךְ גְּרִיסִין, מִפְּנֵי שֶׁפּוֹגֵם בָּהֶן.

וּמִן הַיְסוֹד הַזֶּה נָהֲגֻנוּ לְהַגְעִיל הַכֵּלִים שֶׁאֵינָם בְּנֵי יוֹמָן בְּמַיִם רוֹתְחִין, וְאַף־
עַל־פִּי שֶׁאֵין בַּמַּיִם שִׁשִּׁים חֲלָקִים כְּנֶגֶד הַכֵּלִי, מִפְּנֵי שֶׁהַבָּלַע הַיּוֹצֵא מֵהֶן כְּשֶׁאֵינָן
בְּנֵי יוֹמָן הוּא פָגוּם, וּמִכֵּיוָן שֶׁיָּצָא הַבָּלַע מִן הַכֵּלִי בְּכֹחַ הַמַּיִם, שֶׁטִּבְעָן לְמָרֵק
וּלְהוֹצִיא כָל הַבָּלַע שֶׁבַּכֵּלִי, אַף־עַל־פִּי שֶׁהַכֵּלִי עוֹמֵד אַחַר־כֵּן עִם בְּלִיעוֹ שֶׁהֶקִיא
בְּתוֹךְ הַמַּיִם רוֹתְחִין בְּפָחוֹת מִשִּׁשִּׁים וְחוֹזֵר וּבוֹלֵעַ מִמֶּנּוּ, אֵינוֹ נֶאֱסָר בְּכָךְ, לְפִי
שֶׁהוּא כִנְבֵלָה מְסָרַחַת, שֶׁהַתִּירָה הַתּוֹרָה, כְּמוֹ שֶׁאָמַרְנוּ.

וְאוּלַי תֹּאמַר: וְאֵיךְ אָנוּ מַתִּירִין אֲפִלּוּ בִנְבֵלָה מְסָרַחַת לְאָכְלָהּ לְכַתְּחִלָּה, הָא
אִכָּא בָהּ מִשּׁוּם "בַּל תְּשַׁקְּצוּ"—הַתְּשׁוּבָה בָּזֶה דְכָל שֶׁהוּא דָבָר מוּעָט כָּזֶה וְעוֹד
שֶׁנִּבְלַע בַּכֵּלִי וְנִפְגַּם בְּתוֹכוֹ וְנֶחֱלַשׁ כֹּחוֹ, בִּכְעִנְיָן זֶה וַדַּאי לֵכָּא מִשּׁוּם "בַּל
תְּשַׁקְּצוּ", וּמֻתָּר לְכַתְּחִלָּה.

וְאֵין לְךָ לְהַקְשׁוֹת כְּלָל וְלוֹמַר, אִם־כֵּן כְּלֵי מִדְיָן אֵיךְ הִתִּירָה אוֹתָן הַתּוֹרָה
בְּהַגְעָלָה, וַהֲלֹא לֹא הָיָה הַבָּלַע פָּגוּם, לְפִי מַה שֶּׁאָמְרוּ בַּגְּמָרָא דְלֹא אָסְרָה תוֹרָה
אֶלָּא קְדֵרָה בַת יוֹמָא—שֶׁיֵּשׁ לִי לוֹמַר לְךָ שֶׁהִגְעִילוּ אוֹתָן כֵּלִים בְּמַיִם רַבִּים
שֶׁהָיָה בָּהֶן שִׁשִּׁים כְּנֶגֶד הַכֵּלִים.

---

4. *Ibid.* 65b, etc.

5. I.e. they had been used previously to cook forbidden food, some of which thus became absorbed into the metal of the vessel. Hence the need to cleanse it (to "kasher" it), to render it fit for use in preparing kosher food.

6. As a rule, almost anything mixed or blended into sixty times it own amount is considered to be thus rendered null and void (too insignificant to matter).

7. I.e. by the next day, anything the vessel absorbed which could impart its flavor to food cooked in it later, would tend only to spoil the food, not improve it.

8. I.e. by eating anything disgusting or abominable; cf. Rashi on the verse.

9. Numbers 31:23. (The question and answer are found also in Rashba, *Torath haBa-yith*, IV 4.)

10. Since the Written Torah gives instructions here for cleansing utensils taken from the Midianites as booty, they evidently needed cleansing because they had been used the same day. The Torah would not give instructions for something required only by the far later decree of the Sages.

since it is already written elsewhere, *And the fat of* n'vélah *(what dies of itself) and the fat of* t'réfah *(what is torn of beasts) may be put to any other use* (Leviticus 7:24).

From this the Sages of blessed memory learned to state [the rule that anything forbidden which] gives an impairing (detrimental) flavor is permissible.[4] For through this we know that the Torah forbids and imposes punishment over nothing but eating things that are fit for human consumption, not over something that would disgust a man's spirit; for that is ranked as mere plain dust. This is [the reason for] the permissibility mentioned in the Talmud[4] where forbidden vinegar spills into pounded beans: because it spoils them.

From this basic tenet we have also derived the practice to cleanse with boiling water vessels that were not used the same day,[5] even if the water is not sixty times the amount of the vessel:[6] because the absorbed matter which emerges from them [the vessels] when they were not used the same day, is spoiled;[7] and since the absorbed matter has emerged from [the material of] the vessel through the force of the water, whose nature it is to cleanse and draw out all the absorbed substance in the vessel, even if the vessel should stand afterward with its absorbed matter that it emitted into the boiling water, which is less than sixty times its amount, and it absorbs some of this again, it does not become forbidden by this—because it is like a putrefying carcass, which the Torah permitted, as we said.

Now, you might ask perhaps, "But how can we permit even a putrefying carcass to be eaten from the start? It surely involves the injunction, *You shall not befoul your selves disgustingly*[8] (Leviticus 11:43)?" The answer to this is that whatever is a small thing or amount, like this, and moreover, it is absorbed into [the material of] the vessel and becomes impaired [lessened in intensity] there, its strength thus being weakened, in such a situation the injunction not to make oneself detestable is certainly not applicable, and it is permissible right from the start.

Nor should you pose this difficulty at all, to ask, "If so, how did the Torah permit the vessels of the Midianites [to be used] by cleansing them?[9] Surely the absorbed matter was not spoiled, in keeping with what was stated in the Talmud,[3] that the Torah forbade nothing but a pot that had been used the same day?"[10] For I can answer you that they cleansed those vessels with a great quantity of water that was sixty times the measure of the vessels.[6]

וּמִזֶּה יֵשׁ לָנוּ לִלְמֹד גַּם־כֵּן שֶׁאִם נָפַל אֶחָד מִן הַשְּׁרָצִים הַמְּאוּסִים שֶׁבָּעוֹלָם בְּקֵדֵרָה, אַף־עַל־פִּי שֶׁאֵין אֹכֶל בַּקְּדֵרָה שִׁשִּׁים כְּנֶגֶד אוֹתוֹ הַשֶּׁרֶץ, שֶׁהַכֹּל מֻתָּר אַחַר שֶׁנּוֹצִיא מִן הַקְּדֵרָה גּוּפוֹ שֶׁל שֶׁרֶץ, וְלֹא נָחוּשׁ לִפְלֵיטָתוֹ כְּלָל, הוֹאִיל וְהוּא מִן הַמְּאוּסִים וּפוֹגֵם טַעַם הַקְּדֵרָה: שֶׁהֲרֵי זֶה דּוֹמֶה לִנְבֵלָה מַסְרַחַת, שֶׁאֵין בָּהּ אִסּוּר, כְּמוֹ שֶׁאָמַרְנוּ; וּמִכָּל־מָקוֹם צָרִיךְ שֶׁיִּהְיֶה מַה שֶּׁבַּקְּדֵרָה שְׁנֵי חֲלָקִים כְּנֶגֶד גּוּפוֹ שֶׁל שֶׁרֶץ, כְּדֵי שֶׁיִּבָּטֵל בָּרֹב: שֶׁאִם לֹא כֵן, יִהְיֶה נָדוֹן הָאֹכֶל כְּגוּפוֹ שֶׁל שֶׁרֶץ מַמָּשׁ, וְגוּפוֹ אַף־עַל־פִּי שֶׁהוּא מָאוּס הַתּוֹרָה אֲסָרַתּוּ.

וְיֶתֶר רַבֵּי עִנְיָנִים אֵלֶּה יִתְבָּאֲרוּ בְּמַסֶּכֶת חֻלִּין עִם סִפְרֵי הַמְּפָרְשִׁים הַטּוֹבִים. וְהַמְּעַט הַזֶּה שֶׁכָּתַבְתִּי לְךָ, בְּנִי, כָּאן, אֵינוֹ כְּנֶגֶד רֹב הַדִּינִין שֶׁנֶּאֱמַר בְּעִנְיָן זֶה כִּנְקֻדָּה דַקָּה בְּשֶׁטַח הָאָרֶץ; וּכְבָר הוֹדַעְתִּיךָ בְּכַמָּה מְקוֹמוֹת שֶׁאֵין כַּוָּנָתִי רַק לְהָעִיר רוּחֲךָ בָּעִנְיָנִים, וּמַרְאֶה מָקוֹם אֲנִי לָךְ. וְאִם תִּזְכֶּה וְתוֹרָה תְהֵא אֻמָּנוּתְךָ, תָּבִין כָּל הַדְּבָרִים וְתִשְׂמַח בָּהֶם.

וְנוֹהֵג אִסּוּר זֶה בְּכָל מָקוֹם וּבְכָל זְמַן, בִּזְכָרִים וּנְקֵבוֹת. וְעוֹבֵר עַל זֶה וְאָכַל כַּזַּיִת מִנְּבֵלָה, חַיָּב מַלְקוֹת.

[מִצְוַת מַעֲשֵׂר שֵׁנִי]

תעג לְהוֹצִיא מַעֲשֵׂר שֵׁנִי מִן הַתְּבוּאָה בְּאַרְבַּע שְׁנֵי הַשְּׁמִטָּה, כְּלוֹמַר אַחַר שֶׁנַּפְרִישׁ מַעֲשֵׂר רִאשׁוֹן, הַנִּתָּן לַלְוִיִּם, שֶׁנַּפְרִישׁ עוֹד מַעֲשֵׂר אַחֵר, וְעַל־כֵּן הוּא נִקְרָא שֵׁנִי; וְזֶה הַמַּעֲשֵׂר הָיָה דִינוֹ שֶׁיֵּאָכֵל בִּירוּשָׁלַיִם; וְעַל זֶה נֶאֱמַר "עַשֵּׂר תְּעַשֵּׂר אֵת כָּל תְּבוּאַת זַרְעֶךָ". וּבֵאֵר הַכָּתוּב שֶׁאִם יִרְחַק מִמֶּנּוּ הַמָּקוֹם וְלֹא נוּכַל שְׂאֵתוֹ שָׁם רַק בְּטֹרַח גָּדוֹל וּבְהוֹצָאָה מְרֻבָּה, שֶׁנִּפְדֶּה אוֹתוֹ וְנַעֲלֶה דָמָיו לִירוּשָׁלַיִם, וְנוֹצִיאֵם שָׁם בְּצָרְכֵי אֲכִילָה וּשְׁתִיָּה לְבָד.

וּבֵאֵר הַכָּתוּב כְּמוֹ־כֵן שֶׁהַפּוֹדֶה מַעֲשֵׂר שֵׁנִי שֶׁלּוֹ שֶׁצָּרִיךְ לְהוֹסִיף חֹמֶשׁ

11. Hence anything it emitted cannot make the food forbidden.

12. I.e. by a specific precept about swarming creatures (§§ 162–65).

13. Literally, and I show the place (or, I am a "place-shower") for you.

§473   1. I.e. the first and second, fourth and fifth.

2. And the next verse adds that it is to be eaten "in the place which He will choose, to make His name dwell there."

3. Deuteronomy 14:24–26.

4. The Hebrew, *liYrushalayim*, is the reading of the third of the four early manuscripts; the other three, and all the editions, have *biYrushalayim*, "in Jerusalem."

From this we can learn too that if any one of all the repugnant swarming creatures in the world fell into a pot, even if the food in the pot is not sixty times the size of that swarming creature, it is all permissible after we remove from the pot the body of the creature; and we need not be concerned at all about anything it emitted, since it is one of the loathsome entities and it can but impair the flavor of the dish.[11] For it is clearly like a putrefying carcass, which involves no prohibition, as we stated. Yet in any event, it is necessary that in the contents of the pot there should be [at least] twice the quantity of the swarming creature's body, so that it should be [legally] nullified by a majority; for if not, the food must be considered legally like the actual body of the creature — and although its body is loathsome, the Torah forbade it.[12]

The remainder of the multitude of these topics are elucidated in the Talmud tractate *Hullin*, along with the volumes of the good commentaries. This little bit that I wrote for you, my son, is no more, in comparison with the multitude of laws taught in this subject, than as a small point on the surface of the earth. But I have previously informed you in several instances that it is my intention to do no more than arouse your interest in the topics, and I serve as a guide for you.[13] If you merit that the Torah should be your occupation, you will understand all the matters, and will be gladdened by them.

This prohibition is in effect everywhere, at every time, for both man and woman. If someone transgresses this and eats an olive's amount of *n'vélah*, he deserves lashes of the whip.

[THE PRECEPT OF THE SECOND TITHE]

473 to separate the Second Tithe from produce in four years of the septennate (seven-year cycle);[1] in other words, after we set apart the First Tithe, which is given to the Levites, we are to separate another tithe (tenth); and it is therefore called the Second. For this tithe the law was that it should be eaten in Jerusalem, as it is stated about it, *You shall surely tithe all the yield of your seed*, etc. (Deuteronomy 14:22).[2] Scripture then explains[3] that if the location [Jerusalem] is too far from us, and we cannot carry it there except with great toil and at considerable expense, we may redeem it and take the money for it up to Jerusalem,[4] and we are to spend it there solely for the needs of food and drink.

Scripture likewise explains that a person who redeems his tithe

בְּדָמִים, כְּלוֹמַר שֶׁאִם הוּא שָׁוֶה אַרְבָּעָה דִינָרִים שֶׁיֹּאכַל בִּמְקוֹמוֹ חֲמִשָּׁה דִינָרִים
בִּירוּשָׁלַיִם, וְעַל זֶה נֶאֱמַר "וְאִם גָּאֹל יִגְאַל אִישׁ מִמַּעַשְׂרוֹ חֲמִשִׁיתוֹ יֹסֵף עָלָיו";
וְדִקְדְקוּ זִכְרוֹנָם לִבְרָכָה: "מִמַּעַשְׂרוֹ" וְלֹא מִמַּעְשַׂר חֲבֵרוֹ, "אִישׁ מִמַּעַשְׂרוֹ" וְלֹא
אִשָּׁה.

מִשָּׁרְשֵׁי הַמִּצְוָה, כָּתַבְתִּי בְּמִצְוַת מַעֲשֵׂר בְּהֵמוֹת בְּסֵדֶר אִם בְּחֻקֹּתַי עֲשֵׂה ז'
בְּסִימָן (שנ"ו) [ש"ס], וְאַף־עַל־פִּי שֶׁהָעִנְיָן מְבֹאָר טַעֲמוֹ בַּכָּתוּב, שֶׁהוּא: לְמַעַן
תִּלְמַד לְיִרְאָה אֶת יְיָ אֱלֹהֶיךָ כָּל הַיָּמִים.

מִדִּינֵי הַמִּצְוָה, מַה שֶּׁאָמְרוּ זִכְרוֹנָם לִבְרָכָה שֶׁאֵין מְעַשְּׂרִין מַעֲשֵׂר שֵׁנִי מִשָּׁנָה
לַחֲבֶרְתָּהּ, וְכֵן הוּא בְּסִפְרִי: "שָׁנָה שָׁנָה", מְלַמֵּד שֶׁאֵין מְעַשְּׂרִין אוֹתוֹ מִשָּׁנָה
לַחֲבֶרְתָּהּ; אֵין לִי אֶלָּא מַעֲשֵׂר שֵׁנִי, שֶׁבּוֹ דִּבֵּר הַכָּתוּב; מִנַּיִן לְרַבּוֹת שְׁאָר
מַעַשְׂרוֹת—תַּלְמוּד לוֹמַר: עַשֵּׂר תְּעַשֵּׂר.

וְאָמְרוּ זִכְרוֹנָם לִבְרָכָה שֶׁיּוֹם חֲמִשָּׁה־עָשָׂר בִּשְׁבָט הוּא רֹאשׁ הַשָּׁנָה לְמַעֲשַׂר
הָאִילָנוֹת, כְּלוֹמַר שֶׁכָּל אִילָן שֶׁהִגִּיעַ לְעוֹנַת הַמַּעַשְׂרוֹת קֹדֶם חֲמִשָּׁה־עָשָׂר בִּשְׁבָט,
מִתְעַשֵּׂר בְּמַעֲשֵׂר שֶׁל אוֹתָהּ שָׁנָה, שֶׁאִם הִיא שְׁנַת מַעֲשֵׂר שֵׁנִי מַפְרִישִׁין מִמֶּנּוּ
מַעֲשֵׂר שֵׁנִי, וְאִם הִיא שְׁנַת מַעֲשֵׂר עָנִי מַפְרִישִׁין מִמֶּנּוּ מַעֲשַׂר עָנִי.

וּכְבָר כָּתַבְתִּי לְמַעְלָה בְּסֵדֶר בְּמִצְוַת מַעֲשֵׂר רִאשׁוֹן, עֲשֵׂה רְבִיעִי,
בְּסִימָן (שצ"א) [שצ"ה], עוֹנַת הַמַּעֲשֵׂר בְּמִקְצָת מִן הָאִילָנוֹת, וְשָׁם כָּתוּב שֶׁעִקָּר
חִיּוּב מַעֲשֵׂר מִדְּאוֹרַיְתָא אֵינוֹ אֶלָּא בְּדָגָן תִּירוֹשׁ וְיִצְהָר, וְכָל הַשְּׁאָר דְּרַבָּנָן. וְיֶתֶר
רֻבֵּי דִינֵי מַעֲשֵׂר שֵׁנִי, כֻּלָּם מְבֹאָרִים בְּמַסֶּכְתָּא הַבְּנוּיָה עַל זֶה, וְהִיא מַסֶּכֶת מַעֲשֵׂר
שֵׁנִי.

וּמִצְוָה זוֹ אֵינָהּ נוֹהֶגֶת בְּכָל מָקוֹם אֶלָּא בִּזְמַן שֶׁיִּשְׂרָאֵל שְׁרוּיִין עַל אַדְמָתָם
וִירוּשָׁלַיִם בְּיִשּׁוּבָהּ, נִזְכֶּה וְתֶחֱזֶינָה עֵינֵינוּ בְּטוֹבָה. וּבְסֵדֶר שׁוֹפְטִים בְּמִצְוַת
תְּרוּמָה עֲשֵׂה ו' בְּסִימָן (תצ"ו) [תק"ז] אֶכְתֹּב בְּעֶזְרַת הַשֵּׁם הַמְּקוֹמוֹת שֶׁנּוֹהֵג שָׁם
מַעֲשֵׂר רִאשׁוֹן וְשֵׁנִי וּתְרוּמָה.

5. I.e. the amount he adds should form a fifth of the new total, after the addition; hence it is a fourth of the original (TB Bava M'tzi'a 54a).

6. Mishnah, Ma'asér Shéni iv 3.

7. TB Kiddushin 24a, version of R. Tam in tosafoth, s.v. 'e-la.

8. TB B'choroth 53b, etc.

9. Sifre, Deuteronomy § 105.

10. In the Hebrew the verb is repeated (literally: Tithe shall you tithe); since the first verb is apparently superfluous, it is understood to extend the precept to all the tithes.

11. TB Rosh haShanah 2a.

needs to add a fifth of its monetary value. In other words, if it is worth four *denarii*, he is to eat in place of it the value of five *denarii* in Jerusalem.[5] About this it is stated, *And if a man will redeem any of his tithe, he shall add to it a fifth of it* (Leviticus 27:31) — from which the Sages of blessed memory inferred: "any of his tithe," but not of his neighbor's tithe;[6] "a man...of his tithe," and not a woman.[7]

Regarding the root purpose of the precept, I wrote in the *mitzvah* of the animal tithe, the seventh positive precept in *sidrah b'ḥukothai* (§ 360) — although the reason for the matter is explained in the Writ: *that you may learn to fear the Lord your God always* (Deuteronomy 14:23).

Among the laws of the precept there is what the Sages of blessed memory said:[8] that the Second Tithe is not to be taken from [the produce of] one year for [that of] another; and so we find in the Midrash *Sifre*:[9] "[You shall surely tithe all the yield...from the field] year by year" (Deuteronomy 14:22) — this teaches that it is not to be tithed from one year for another. Thus I know it only about the Second Tithe, since the verse speaks of that; how do I learn to include other tithes? — Scripture states, *You shall surely tithe.*[10]

The Sages of blessed memory said too[11] that the fifteenth day of Sh'vat is the beginning of the year for the tithe of trees. In other words, if any tree reached the period for tithing before the fifteenth of Sh'vat, the tenth part of its fruit is to be taken in the tithe of that year — so that if it is a year of the Second Tithe, the Second Tithe is to be separated from it, and if it is a year of the tithe for the poor, the tithe for the poor is to be separated from it.

I wrote previously, above in *sidrah koraḥ*, at the fourth positive precept, of the First Tithe (§ 395), the period of tithing for some of the trees. It was also written there that the core obligation of the tithe, by the law of the Torah, applies to nothing other than grain, wine and oil, all the rest being by the decree of the Sages. The rest of the numerous laws of the Second Tithe are all clarified in the tractate composed about it, namely, the Mishnah tractate *Ma'asér Shéni*.

This precept is not in effect anywhere but at the time that the Israelites are settled on their land and Jerusalem is in its settled, inhabited state — may we merit that our eyes see it in its good fortune. In *sidrah shof'tim*, at the sixth positive precept, of *t'rumah* (the *kohen's* portion; § 507), I will write, with the Eternal Lord's help, those

⟨459⟩ locations where the First and Second Tithe and *t'rumah* are in effect.

[מִצְוַת מַעְשַׂר עָנִי תַּחַת מַעֲשֵׂר שֵׁנִי בְּשָׁנָה שְׁלִישִׁית]

תעד לְהוֹצִיא מַעְשַׂר עָנִי בְּשָׁנָה שְׁלִישִׁית וְשִׁשִּׁית מִן הַשְּׁמִטָּה, וְעַל זֶה נֶאֱמַר "מִקְצֵה שָׁלֹשׁ שָׁנִים תּוֹצִיא אֶת כָּל מַעְשַׂר תְּבוּאָתְךָ" וְגוֹמֵר "וְהִנַּחְתָּ בִּשְׁעָרֶיךָ", וּבַשָּׁנָה הַזֹּאת הָיוּ מַפְרִישִׁין מַעְשַׂר עָנִי בִּמְקוֹם מַעֲשֵׂר שֵׁנִי שֶׁל שְׁאָר שָׁנִים, וְאֵין מַפְרִישִׁין מַעֲשֵׂר שֵׁנִי כְּלָל.

מִשָּׁרְשֵׁי הַמִּצְוָה, כְּעִנְיָן מַה שֶּׁכָּתַבְתִּי בְּמִצְוַת הַלְוָאָה לֶעָנִי (בְּכֶסֶף תַּלְוֶה עֲשֵׂה א') [בְּמִשְׁפָּטִים] בְּסִימָן ס"ו.

דִּינֵי הַמִּצְוָה, כְּגוֹן מַה שֶּׁאָמְרוּ זִכְרוֹנָם לִבְרָכָה שֶׁבַּעַל הַשָּׂדֶה שֶׁעָבְרוּ עָלָיו עֲנִיִּים, נוֹתֵן לְכָל אֶחָד מֵהֶם מִן הַמַּעֲשֵׂר כְּדֵי שָׂבְעוֹ, שֶׁנֶּאֱמַר: וְאָכְלוּ בִשְׁעָרֶיךָ וְשָׂבֵעוּ; וְכַמָּה כְּדֵי שָׂבְעוֹ — מִן הַחִטִּים לֹא יִפְחַת מֵחֲצִי קַב, מִשְׁעוֹרִים לֹא יִפְחַת מִקַּב, כֻּסְּמִין לֹא יִפְחַת מִקַּב וָחֵצִי, דְּבֵלָה לֹא יִפְחַת מִמִּשְׁקַל חָמֵשׁ וְעֶשְׂרִים סֶלַע, יַיִן לֹא יִפְחַת מֵחֲצִי לֹג, שֶׁמֶן מֵרְבִיעִית לֹג, אֹרֶז רֹבַע קַב, יָרָק מִשְׁקַל לִטְרָא, חָרוּבִין שְׁלֹשָׁה קַבִּין, אֱגוֹזִים עֲשָׂרָה, אֲפַרְסְקִים חֲמִשָּׁה, רִמּוֹנִים שְׁתַּיִם, אֶתְרֹג אֶחָד. הָיָה לוֹ דָּבָר מְעַט וְהָעֲנִיִּים מְרֻבִּים, מַנִּיחַ לִפְנֵיהֶם וְהֵם מְחַלְּקִין בֵּינֵיהֶם. וּמַעְשַׂר עָנִי הַמִּתְחַלֵּק בַּגֹּרֶן, אֵין בּוֹ טוֹבַת הֲנָאָה לַבְּעָלִים; וְאִישׁ וְאִשָּׁה שֶׁבָּאוּ לִטֹּל, נוֹתְנִין תְּחִלָּה לָאִשָּׁה וְאַחַר־כָּךְ לָאִישׁ; וְיֶתֶר פְּרָטֵי הַמִּצְוָה, מְתֹבָאָרִים בְּמַסֶּכְתּוֹת פֵּאָה וּמַעְשָׂרוֹת וּדְמַאי, וּבִמְקוֹמוֹת מִזְרָעִים וּמַכְשִׁירִים וְיָדַיִם. וּכְסֵדֶר שׁוֹפְטִים בִּגְזֵרַת הַשֵּׁם עֲשֵׂה ו' [סִי' תק"ז] אֶכְתֹּב בְּאֵי זֶה מָקוֹם נוֹהֶגֶת וּבְאֵי זֶה זְמָן.

§474 1. I.e. every last year of a group of three in the seven-year cycle or period; hence the third and sixth years. The seventh year is *sh'mittah* ("release"; §§ 84, 326–29), when the land is left fallow, its produce free to all, and no tithes are given.

2. So TB Rosh haShanah 12b.

3. Sifre, Deuteronomy § 110.

4. Mishnah, Pé'ah viii 5. The *kav* is equivalent to four *log* (see Rambam, Commentary to Mishnah, *ibid*); and a *log* is reckoned as slightly less than 300 grams, or 297.5 cubic centimeters (see Y. G. Weiss, *Middoth uMishkaloth shel Torah*, p. 381 paragraph 2). Hence a *kav* would be about 1196 grams, or 1190 cubic centimeters.

5. *Ibid.* The *sela* of the Talmud is reckoned as about 17 grams (see Y. G. Weiss, *loc. cit.* paragraph 1); 25 *s'la'im* would thus be approximately 425 grams.

6. See note 4 about the *log*.

7. TJ Pé'ah viii 4.

8. Rambam (MT *hilchoth mat'noth 'aniyyim* vi 8) adds that this is the weight of 35 *dinar*. Taking the *dinar* as approximately 17 grams in weight (Weiss, *loc. cit.*) gives a total of about 595 grams.

[THE PRECEPT OF THE TITHE FOR THE POOR,
IN PLACE OF THE SECOND TITHE
IN THE THIRD YEAR]

474 to set apart the tithe for the poor in the third and sixth years
of the septennate (seven-year cycle), as it is stated about this, *At the
end of every three years you shall bring forth all the tithe of your produce*, etc.
and you shall set it down within your gates (Deuteronomy 14:28); in that
[third] year[1] they would set apart the tithe for the poor in place of the
Second Tithe, and would not set apart the Second Tithe at all.[2]

As to some root reason for the precept, it is akin to what I wrote in
the precept of lending to the poor, in *sidrah mishpatim* (§ 66).

The laws of the precept are, for example, what the Sages of
blessed memory said:[3] that when poor people pass by the owner of a
field, he is to give each one of them enough from the tithe to satisfy
his hunger: for it is stated, *that they may eat within your gates and be
satisfied* (Deuteronomy 26:12). Now, how much is enough to satisfy
one? — of wheat he should give not less than half a *kav*; of barley, not
less than a *kav*; spelt, not less than a *kav* and a half;[4] of pressed figs he
should give not less than the weight of twenty-five *s'la'im*;[5] wine, not
less than half a *log*;[6] oil, at least a fourth of a *log*;[4] rice, a quarter of a
kav;[7] green vegetables, the weight of a *litra*;[8] carob, three *kav*;
nuts — ten; peaches — five; pomegranates — two; *'ethrog* (citron) —
one.[7] If he has a small quantity and the poor are many, he is to set it
down before them, and they divide it among themselves.[9]

When tithe of the poor is given out in the granary, the owner may
not have the privilege of benefiting [any particular poor].[10] If a man
and a woman came to take [of the tithe], the woman is to be given
first, and then the man.[11] Other details of the precept are explained in
the Mishnah tractates *Pé'ah, Ma'as'roth, D'mai*, and in various places in
the Mishnah order *Z'ra'im* and the tractates *Mach-shirin* and *Yadayim*.
In the sixth positive precept of *sidrah shof'tim* (§ 507), as the Eternal
Lord ordains, I will write in which area it is in force, and in which
time.

9. Mishnah, Pé'ah viii 6; MT *hilchoth mat'noth 'aniyyim* vi 7–9.

10. I.e. he may not choose to which poor to give, for his own advantage or
reasons; TB Ḥullin 131a, and *tosafoth* there, s.v. *ma'asér 'ani*.

11. TB Yevamoth 100a; MT *ibid.* 10, 13.

[שֶׁלֹּא לִתְבֹּעַ הַהַלְוָאָה שֶׁעָבַר עָלֶיהָ שְׁבִיעִית]

תעה שֶׁלֹּא לִתְבֹּעַ הַחוֹב בִּשְׁנַת הַשְּׁמִטָּה אֲבָל יְהִי נִשְׁמָט וְלֹא נִתְבָּעֶנּוּ עוֹד,

וְעַל זֶה נֶאֱמַר "לֹא יִגֹּשׂ אֶת רֵעֵהוּ וְאֶת אָחִיו" וְכוּלֵי.

מִשָּׁרְשֵׁי מִצְוָה זוֹ וְכָל עִנְיָנֶיהָ, כְּמִנְהָגִי, כָּתַבְתִּי בְּמִצְוַת עֲשֵׂה י"ג שֶׁבְּסֵדֶר זֶה [סִי' תע"ז]. וְעוֹבֵר עַל זֶה וְתָבַע הַלְוָאָתוֹ אַחַר שְׁנַת הַשְּׁמִטָּה בִּזְמַן הַבַּיִת, עָבַר עַל לָאו זֶה, אֲבָל אֵין בּוֹ מַלְקוֹת, לְפִי שֶׁאֵין בּוֹ מַעֲשֶׂה.

[מִצְוָה לִנְגֹּשׂ אֶת הַנָּכְרִי]

תעו לִנְגֹּשׂ הַנָּכְרִי (עוֹבֵד עֲבוֹדָה זָרָה) שֶׁיִּפְרַע מַה שֶּׁהוּא חַיָּב לָנוּ וְלֹא נַחְמֹל

וּנְרַחֵם עָלָיו לְהַאֲרִיךְ לוֹ הַמִּלְוֶה, וְעַל זֶה נֶאֱמַר: אֶת הַנָּכְרִי תִּגֹּשׂ; וְכֵן אָמְרוּ בְּסִפְרֵי: "אֶת הַנָּכְרִי תִּגֹּשׂ", זוֹ מִצְוַת עֲשֵׂה.

וּמִשָּׁרְשֵׁי הַמִּצְוָה שֶׁלֹּא נִלְמַד נַפְשׁוֹתֵינוּ לַחֲמֹל וּלְרַחֵם עֲלֵיהֶם, לְמַעַן לֹא נִמָּשֵׁךְ אַחַר מַעֲשֵׂיהֶם וְאַחַר עֲצָתָם בְּשׁוּם דָּבָר.

וְהָרַב רַבֵּנוּ מֹשֶׁה בֶּן נַחְמָן זִכְרוֹנוֹ לִבְרָכָה כָּתַב שֶׁאֵין זֶה מִצְוַת עֲשֵׂה כְּלָל, אֲבָל עִנְיַן הַכָּתוּב לְהַזְהִיר עַל הַחֶמְלָה בְּיִשְׂרָאֵל בַּעֲשֵׂה וְלֹא־תַעֲשֶׂה, וְאָמַר "אֶת הַנָּכְרִי תִּגֹּשׂ" וְלֹא אָחִיךָ, וְהוּא לָאו הַבָּא מִכְּלַל עֲשֵׂה, דְּקַיְמָא לָן שֶׁהוּא כְּמוֹ עֲשֵׂה, וְהַלָּאו הַמְבֹאָר בּוֹ כְּמוֹ־כֵן "וּלְאָחִיךָ לֹא תִגֹּשׂ"; וְכֵן הָעִנְיָן מַמָּשׁ בְּאִסּוּר רִבִּית, כְּמוֹ שֶׁנִּכְתּוֹב בְּסֵדֶר כִּי תֵצֵא [סִי'תקע"ג] בְּעֶזְרַת הַשֵּׁם.

דִּינֵי הַמִּצְוָה כְּלוּלִים בְּבֵאוּר בַּכָּתוּב, לְפִי דַעְתִּי.

---

§475   1. I.e. the last year of every septennate (seven-year cycle), when the land must be left fallow, unworked (§§ 84, 326).

2. As our author wrote first, in each *sidrah*, on all its positive precepts, in his original version this occurs earlier; in this edition, as in virtually all others, the precepts are arranged in the order of their verses in Scripture, and hence this comes below.

§476   1. Sifre, Deuteronomy § 113.

2. Ramban, commentary (*hassagoth*) to ShM root principle 6 (ed. Chavel, p. 81).

3. The Hebrew can mean either "you shall" or "you may"; it is generally rendered so.

4. I.e. we observe the positive precept by obeying this inference from it. (It should be noted that this refers to a loan made to a fellow-Jew, "your brother," after which a *sh'mittah*, sabbatical, year has gone by.)

[NOT TO DEMAND PAYMENT FOR A LOAN OVER
WHICH THE SEVENTH YEAR, SH'MITTAH,
HAS PASSED]

475 not to demand payment of a debt at a year of *sh'mittah* (release),[1] but it should rather be abandoned and be claimed no more, as it is stated about this, *he shall not exact it of his neighbor or of his brother*, etc. (Deuteronomy 15:2).

About the root reason for this precept, and its entire subject-matter, according to my custom, I have written in the thirteenth positive precept in this *sidrah* (§ 477).[2] If someone transgressed this and demanded payment of his loan after the year of *sh'mittah* (release) at the time of the Temple, he would violate this negative precept; but it would not mean a flogging of whiplashes, since it involved no physical action.

[THE PRECEPT OF EXACTING A LOAN RIGOROUSLY
FROM A HEATHEN]

476 to press a non-Jewish idol-worshipper that he should pay what he owes us, and we should have no compassion or mercy on him to extend the loan for him, as it is stated about this, *Of a foreigner you shall exact it* (Deuteronomy 15:3); and so it was taught in the Midrash *Sifre*:[1] "Of a foreigner you shall exact it"—this is a positive precept.

At the root of the precept lies the purpose that we should not teach ourselves to have pity and compassion on them, in order that we should not be drawn after their activities or after their counsel in anything.

Now, R. Moses b. Naḥman of blessed memory wrote[2] that this is not a positive precept at all, the purpose of the verse being rather to adjure about compassion for an Israelite with both a positive and a negative precept; and it thus means, "Of a foreigner you may exact it,[3] but not of your brother." It is then an injunction derived from a positive precept, which we have a standing rule is as a positive precept; and the injunction which is thus made clear by it is, "but of your brother you may not exact it."[4] There is the very same situation about the ban on usury, as we will write in *sidrah ki thétzé* (§ 573), with the Eternal Lord's help.

The laws of the precept are implicit in the explanation in the Writ, to my mind.

וְנוֹהֶגֶת מִצְוָה זוֹ בְּכָל מָקוֹם וּבְכָל זְמַן, בִּזְכָרִים וּנְקֵבוֹת. וְעוֹבֵר עָלֶיהָ וְהֶאֱרִיךְ
זְמַן פִּרְעוֹנוֹ מִן הַנָּכְרִי עַל צַד הַחֶמְלָה עָלָיו לְבַד, לֹא מִצַּד הַיִּרְאָה לָלֹוֶה אוֹ
לְהֶפְסֵד חוֹבוֹ אוֹ לְשׁוּם תּוֹעֶלֶת אַחֵר, בִּטֵּל עֲשֵׂה זֶה, לְדַעַת הָרַב רַבֵּנוּ מֹשֶׁה בֶּן
מַיְמוֹן זִכְרוֹנוֹ לִבְרָכָה; וּלְדַעַת הָרַב רַבֵּנוּ מֹשֶׁה בֶּן נַחְמָן זִכְרוֹנוֹ לִבְרָכָה, הַנּוֹגֵשׂ
יִשְׂרָאֵל בְּחוֹבוֹ בִּטֵּל עֲשֵׂה זֶה, מִלְּבַד שֶׁעָבַר עַל לָאו, אֲבָל אֲרִיכוּת חוֹב לְנָכְרִי לֹא
מַעֲלֶה וְלֹא מוֹרִיד.

[מִצְוַת הַשְׁמָטַת כְּסָפִים בְּשָׁנָה שְׁבִיעִית]

תעז לַעֲזֹב הַחוֹבוֹת בִּשְׁנַת הַשְׁמָטָה, וְעַל זֶה נֶאֱמַר "וַאֲשֶׁר יִהְיֶה לְךָ אֶת אָחִיךָ
תַּשְׁמֵט יָדֶךָ"; וְנִכְפְּלָה הָאַזְהָרָה בְּזֹאת הַמִּצְוָה, שֶׁנֶּאֱמַר "וְזֶה דְּבַר הַשְׁמִטָּה שָׁמוֹט
כָּל בַּעַל מַשֵּׁה יָדוֹ"—וְאָמְרוּ בְּתוֹסֶפְתָּא: בִּשְׁתֵּי שְׁמִטּוֹת הַכָּתוּב מְדַבֵּר: אַחַת שְׁמִטַּת
קַרְקַע וְאַחַת שְׁמִטַּת כְּסָפִים.

כְּבָר כָּתַבְתִּי (בְּכֶסֶף תָּלְוֶה) [בְּמִשְׁפָּטִים] בְּמִצְוַת שְׁבִיעִית (עֲשֵׂה ד') בְּסִימָן
(ס"ט) [פ"ד] מַה שֶׁיָּדַעְתִּי בְּשֹׁרֶשׁ הַמִּצְוָה, וּשְׁמִטַּת כְּסָפִים גַּם-כֵּן אַחַר אוֹתוֹ
הַטַּעַם נִמְשָׁךְ, לְלַמֵּד נַפְשֵׁנוּ בַּמִּדּוֹת הַמַּעֲלוֹת, מִדַּת הַנְּדִיבוּת וְעַיִן טוֹב, וְנִקְבַּע
בִּלְבָבֵנוּ הַבִּטָּחוֹן הַגָּדוֹל בַּשֵּׁם בָּרוּךְ הוּא, וְאָז תִּכְשַׁר נַפְשֵׁנוּ לְקַבֵּל טוֹב מֵאֵת אֲדוֹן
הַכֹּל, כָּלוּל הַבְּרָכָה וְהָרַחֲמִים; וְגַם נִמְצָא מִזֶּה גָּדֵר חָזָק וּמְחִיצָה שֶׁל בַּרְזֶל
לְהִתְרַחֵק מְאֹד מִן הַגֵּזֶל וּמִן הַחַמְדָה בְּכָל אֲשֶׁר לְרֵעֵנוּ, כִּי נִשָּׂא קַל וָחֹמֶר בְּנַפְשֵׁנוּ
לֵאמֹר: אֲפִלּוּ הַלְוִיתִיו מָמוֹנִי וְהִגִּיעַ שְׁנַת הַשְׁמָטָה, אָמְרָה תּוֹרָה לְהַשְׁמִיט בְּיָדוֹ

5. ShM positive precept § 142; MT *hilchoth malveh* i 2.

6. I.e. in violation of what follows in our source-text of Deuteronomy 15:3; see two paragraphs above, and note 4.

§477   1. See § 475, note 1.

2. A *baraitha* found in TB Mo'éd Katan 2b, Gittin 36a, and Kiddushin 38b. In ShM positive precept § 141, the source of this paragraph, the citation is likewise given as from a Tosefta; but as Lieberman notes in his *Tashlum Tosefta* (Preface to Tosefta ed. Zuckermandl, Jerusalem 1970: p. 7, par. 2, end), this is one of many instances in which *rishonim* (Early Scholars) thus referred to a *baraitha* in the Talmud (a tannaitic teaching not found in the Mishnah), although it is not in the Tosefta as we have it. (See MY for a different explanation.)

3. In the Scriptural text we have "*ha-sh'mittah* (the release) *shamot* (relinquish)": The two forms in succession of the same root word are taken to denote "two kinds of release" (or relinquishment). In *tosafoth* to TB Gittin 36a, s.v. *bizman*, R. Tam concludes that "release of land" refers not to letting one's field lie fallow during a *sh'mittah* (sabbatical) year, but to returning to its original owner, in a jubilee year, land bought from someone's inherited estate (for as in relinquishing a debt, one thus

This precept is in force everywhere, at every time, for both man and woman. If someone violates it and extends the time for payment [of a loan] by a heathen solely out of compassion for him, not on account of fear of the borrower or of losing his debt, or for any other advantage, he thus disobeys this positive precept, in the view of R. Moses b. Maimon of blessed memory.[5] In the opinion of R. Moses b. Naḥman of blessed memory, if someone presses an Israelite for his debt [after a sabbatical year — *sh'mittah*][6] he disobeys this positive precept, apart from violating a negative precept; but lengthening [the time of payment on] a loan to a heathen is of no consequence one way or another.

[THE PRECEPT OF RELINQUISHING MONEY OWED IN THE SEVENTH YEAR]

477 to relinquish debts in a year of *sh'mittah* (release),[1] as it is stated about it, *but whatever of yours is with your brother, your hand shall release* (Deuteronomy 15:3). The injunction about this precept was reiterated; as it is stated, *And this is the manner of the release: every creditor shall relinquish the claim of his hand* (ibid. 2); and it was taught in the Tosefta:[2] Scripture speaks of two kinds of release: one is the release of land, and one is the relinquishing of money.[3]

I wrote previously, in *sidrah mishpatim*, about the religious duty of the seventh year (§ 84), what I knew of a root reason for that precept. Now, the relinquishment of money follows too in the wake of that reason — to inculcate in our spirit among noble, exalted traits of character, the quality of generosity and magnanimity, and that we should implant in our heart a great trust in the Eternal Lord, blessed is He. Then our spirit will become worthy and ready to receive goodness from the sovereign Master of all, embodying blessing and compassion. Through this we will also find a strong boundary wall and an iron partition to keep well away from robbery and craving for anything that belongs to our neighbor. For we will apply a *kal va-ḥomer* for ourselves, reasoning from the less to the more, saying, "Even if I had lent him money and the year of *sh'mittah* (release)

gives up what has hitherto been his). That this is correct is evident from the version of this teaching in TJ Gittin iv 3 (45d), near the end; and from there, MT *hilchoth sh'mittah* ix 2 (and cf. Me'iri to TB Kiddushin 38b, p.197).

הַמַּלְוֶה; שֶׁלֹּא לִגְזֹל וְשֶׁלֹּא לַחֲמֹס מָשְׁלוֹ לֹא כָל־שֶׁכֵּן שֶׁרָאוּי לִי לְהִתְרַחֵק עַד הַקָּצֶה הָאַחֲרוֹן.

מִדִּינֵי הַמִּצְוָה, מַה שֶׁאָמְרוּ זִכְרוֹנָם לִבְרָכָה שֶׁאֵין הַשְּׁבִיעִית מְשַׁמֶּטֶת אֶלָּא בְּסוֹפָהּ, כְּשֶׁתִּשְׁקַע חַמָּה בְּעֶרֶב רֹאשׁ הַשָּׁנָה שֶׁל מוֹצָאֵי שְׁבִיעִית, שֶׁנֶּאֱמַר: מִקֵּץ שֶׁבַע שָׁנִים; וּמְשַׁמֶּטֶת אֲפִלּוּ מִלְוֶה שֶׁבִּשְׁטָר שֶׁיֵּשׁ בּוֹ אַחֲרָיוּת נְכָסִים, וְאִם סִיֵּם לוֹ שָׂדֶה בְּהַלְוָאָתוֹ אֵינוֹ מְשַׁמֵּט — כֵּן כָּתַב הָרַב מֹשֶׁה בֶּן מַיְמוֹן זִכְרוֹנוֹ לִבְרָכָה, וְתֻמַּהּ הוּא, דְּרַבִּי יוֹחָנָן דָּחֵי לַהּ בְּפֶרֶק הַשּׁוֹלֵחַ.

הַקָּפַת חֲנוּת וּשְׂכַר שָׂכִיר אֵינוֹ נִשְׁמָט, וְאִם זָקְפוּ אוֹתָם בְּמִלְוֶה נִשְׁמָט, וְכֵן הַדִּין בִּקְנָסוֹת. הַמְגָרֵשׁ אִשְׁתּוֹ קֹדֶם שְׁמִטָּה, אֵין כְּתֻבָּתָהּ נִשְׁמֶטֶת, אֶלָּא־אִם־כֵּן פְּגָמָהּ אוֹ זְקָפָתָהּ עָלָיו בְּמִלְוֶה; וְהַמַּלְוֶה עַל הַמַּשְׁכּוֹן אֵינוֹ מְשַׁמֵּט, וְהוּא שֶׁיִּהְיֶה הַחוֹב כְּנֶגֶד הַמַּשְׁכּוֹן — כֵּן כָּתַב הָרַב רַבֵּנוּ מֹשֶׁה בֶּן מַיְמוֹן זִכְרוֹנוֹ לִבְרָכָה; וּבְפֶרֶק הַזָּהָב אָמְרִינַן דְּאַף־עַל־פִּי שֶׁאֵינוֹ שָׁוֶה אֶלָּא פְּלַג חוֹבוֹ.

וְהַנֵּי מִלֵּי, בְּמַשְׁכּוֹן שֶׁל מִטַּלְטְלִין, אֲבָל בְּמַשְׁכּוֹן שֶׁל קַרְקַע בְּאַתְרָא דְמַסַּלְקֵי, שְׁבִיעִית מְשַׁמֶּטֶת, וּבְכוֹר אֵינוֹ נוֹטֵל בָּהּ פִּי שְׁנַיִם, לְפִי שֶׁהוּא כְּחוֹב גָּמוּר; אֲבָל

---

4. TB 'Arachin 28b, etc.

5. MT *hilchoth sh'mittah* ix 6.

6. In our editions of the Talmud, R. Yoḥanan rejects only a ruling that if a promissory note offers the borrower's property in general as collateral, the year of *sh'mittah* does not void it; hence Rambam could well decide that where a specific field is allocated as collateral, the loan is not voided, because it is as if that field became the creditor's property to ensure his repayment of the loan, so that the debt is regarded as having been paid in a sense. Ramban, however, in his commentary to TB Gittin 36b, s.v. *v'ha*, specifically makes no distinction whether the debtor's property in general or one particular field was named as collateral; it is his view that our author follows here.

7. Mishnah, Sh'vi'ith x 1. These are originally not loans because there is no firm demand or obligation for payment of a specific amount at a specific time; it is such a claim or demand which "converts them into a loan" (R. 'Asher, note to commentary of R. Samson of Sens, *ad loc.*; and commentary to TB Gittin, iv §17). (See also TB Gittin 18a, that other obligations are converted into loans due by being turned over to a *beth din* for collection.)

8. TB Gittin 18a.

9. In which the husband obligated himself to pay her a certain sum should he divorce her (and so must his heirs if he should die).

10. So that the balance remains a general obligation, not that of the *k'thubah*, and hence akin to a loan.

11. Because the pledge becomes the property of the creditor to guarantee him recompense, until the debt is paid; hence in a sense the debt was already collected (TB Bava M'tzi'a 82a).

arrived, the Torah says to give up and leave the loan in his hand; then in order not to rob him or take anything of his by force, is it not all the more certainly right for me to keep far away from that, to the utmost degree?"

Among the laws of the precept there is what the Sages of blessed memory taught:[4] that the seventh year brings the release at no other time but its end, when the sun sets on the day before *Rosh haShanah* [the beginning of the new year] at the close of the seventh year: for it is stated, *At the end of every seven years* (Deuteronomy 15:1). It releases even a loan [recorded] in a document [promissory note] pledging property as collateral. But if he [the borrower] assigned him [the creditor, a particular] field for his debt, this is not released; so wrote R. Moses b. Maimon of blessed memory;[5] yet it is puzzling, since R. Yoḥanan rejected this [law] in the fourth chapter of the Talmud tractate *Gittin* (37a).[6]

Credit at a shop or store, and the wages of a hired man, are not released; but if they were converted into the form of a loan, they are released;[7] and the law is the same for fines.[8] If someone divorces his wife before *sh'mittah*, her *k'thubah* (marriage contract)[9] is not voided, unless it was impaired [by partial payment][10] or she converted it into a loan for him.[8] If someone lends money for a pledge (a pawned object), it is not voided,[11] provided the loan corresponds to the pledge [in value]; so wrote R. Moses b. Maimon of blessed memory.[12] But in the fourth chapter of the tractate *Bava M'tzi'a* (48a) it was taught that [the law applies] even if it is not equal [in value] but worth only half his debt.

When does this hold true, however?—when the pledge is of movable goods; but with a pledge of landed property, in a region where [the creditor] may be removed [from the property],[13] the seventh year voids it [the loan], and a firstborn son [of the creditor] does not take two shares of it [the property, in his inheritance], because it is like a pure debt.[14] However, in a region where they do

---

12. MT *hilchoth sh'mittah* ix 13–14.

13. I.e. the common rule there, if no other terms were specified, is that the borrower regains possession of the pledged field at any time that he can repay the lender, although the lender has the produce of the field until then; but there is no minimal period in which the field must remain in his possession, for him to have its produce (see Rashi, TB Bava M'tzi'a 67a).

14. The pledged field never becomes the lender's property in any sense; TB

בְּאַתְרָא דְּלָא מְסַלְּקֵי, אֵין שְׁבִיעִית מְשַׁמַּטְתּוֹ; וְהַשְׁתָּא דְּקַיְמָא לָן סְתַם מַשְׁכַּנְתָּא שַׁתָּא, דְּהָכִי אַסִּיקְנָא בַּגְּמָרָא, לִמְדוּנוּ מוֹרֵינוּ יִשְׁמְרֵם אֵל: כָּל הַמַּשְׁכּוֹנוֹת כְּאַתְרָא דְּלָא מְסַלְּקֵי דַּיְנִינַן לְהוּ, וְאֵין שְׁבִיעִית מְשַׁמֶּטֶת מַשְׁכּוֹנָא, וּבְכוֹר נוֹטֵל פִּי שְׁנַיִם, וּבַעַל חוֹב דְּיתוֹמִים גּוֹבֶה מִמֶּנּוּ, דְּכַקַּרְקַע שֶׁלָּהֶם הוּא.

וְהַמּוֹסֵר שְׁטָרוֹתָיו לְבֵית־דִּין וְאָמַר לָהֶם ״אַתֶּם גְּבוּ לִי חוֹב זֶה״, אֵינוֹ מְשַׁמֵּט, שֶׁנֶּאֱמַר ״וַאֲשֶׁר יִהְיֶה לְךָ אֶת אָחִיךָ״, וְזֶה כְּבָר נִתְּנוּ בְּיַד בֵּית־דִּין. וּמִזֶּה הַטַּעַם אָמְרוּ זִכְרוֹנָם לִבְרָכָה שֶׁחוֹב שֶׁיֵּשׁ לִיתוֹמִים עַל אֲחֵרִים, אֵין שְׁבִיעִית מְשַׁמַּטְתּוֹ, דְּרַבָּן גַּמְלִיאֵל וּבֵית־דִּינוֹ אֲבִיהֶן שֶׁל יְתוֹמִים, וְאַחֲרֵיהֶם כָּל בֵּית־דִּין שֶׁבְּכָל דּוֹר וָדוֹר, וּכְאִלּוּ מָסְרוּ שְׁטָרוֹתֵיהֶם בְּיַד בֵּית־דִּין דָּמֵי.

וְכֵן מֵעִנְיָן הַמִּצְוָה מַה שֶּׁאָמְרוּ שֶׁהַמַּלְוֶה אֶת חֲבֵרוֹ לְעֶשֶׂר שָׁנִים, אֵין שְׁבִיעִית מְשַׁמַּטְתּוֹ, דְּכִי אָמַר רַחֲמָנָא ״לֹא יִגֹּשׂ״, בְּחוֹב הָרָאוּי לִנְגֹּשׂ, וְזֶה לֹא הִגִּיעַ זְמַנּוֹ לִנְגֹּשׂ עֲדַיִן. וּמַה שֶּׁאָמְרוּ שֶׁהַמַּתְנֶה עִם חֲבֵרוֹ בְּחוֹבוֹ עַל־מְנָת שֶׁלֹּא תַשְׁמִיטֶנּוּ שְׁבִיעִית, הֲרֵי זֶה מְשַׁמֵּט, לְפִי שֶׁהוּא כְּמַתְנֶה עַל מַה שֶּׁכָּתוּב בַּתּוֹרָה; אֲבָל אָמַר לוֹ ״עַל־מְנָת שֶׁלֹּא תַשְׁמִיט חוֹב זֶה וַאֲפִלּוּ בַּשְּׁבִיעִית״, כְּלוֹמַר אַף־עַל־פִּי שֶׁדִּין שְׁבִיעִית לְהַשְׁמִיט, אִם מַתְנֶה עִמְּךָ שֶׁלֹּא תַשְׁמִיט חוֹב זֶה אֵין שְׁבִיעִית מְשַׁמַּטְתּוֹ בְּעִנְיָנֵן זֶה, שֶׁכָּל תְּנַאי שֶׁבְּמָמוֹן קַיָּם, כְּמוֹ שֶׁכָּתַבְתִּי בְּסֵדֶר בְּהַר סִינַי לֹא־תַעֲשֶׂה י״ב [סִי׳ שמ״ג]. וְיֶתֶר פְּרָטֶיהָ, בְּמַסֶּכֶת שְׁבִיעִית.

וְנוֹהֶגֶת מִצְוָה זוֹ מִדְּאוֹרַיְתָא בְּאֶרֶץ־יִשְׂרָאֵל וּבְכָל מָקוֹם, בִּזְמַן שֶׁהַיּוֹבֵל נוֹהֵג, בִּזְכָרִים וּנְקֵבוֹת; וּכְבָר כָּתַבְתִּי לְמַעְלָה בְּסֵדֶר בְּהַר סִינַי [סִי׳ של״ב, של״ה] בְּאֵי

Bava M'tzi'a 67b. See §400, that a firstborn son does not take a double share of a debt uncollected at his father's death.

15. I.e. for a certain fixed minimal period, even if the borrower is able to repay the loan.

16. For much the same reason as in note 11; *ibid.*

17. I.e. during this period the land cannot be taken from the creditor, even if the borrower is able to repay him.

18. TB Bava M'tzi'a 68a.

19. I.e. the orphans of the lender who received the field in pledge, and died.

20. Mishnah, Sh'vi'ith x 2 (and see *tosafoth*, TB Makkoth 3b, s.v. *ha-mosér*).

21. Or rather: but whatever is due you from your brother; cf. Sifre, Deuteronomy §113.

22. TB Gittin 37a.

23. TB Makkoth 3b.

24. His words can have no validity where the Torah decrees otherwise.

25. I.e. the duty of payment should remain as a personal obligation, regardless of the abolition of the loan.

not remove [the creditor from the mortgaged property],[15] the seventh year does not void it.[16] Now, though, when we have a standing rule that any general, unspecified pledge of landed property is [given] for a year[17]—for this is the conclusion reached in the Talmud,[18] as our master teachers instructed us—all instances of pledged land are judged as though in a region where [the creditor] is not removed [from it]. Hence the seventh year does not void the pledge; a firstborn son takes two shares [of it in inheritance]; and a creditor of the orphans[19] may collect [his debt] from it, for it is as their debt.

If a person gives his documents [promissory notes] over to the *beth din* (court) and says to them [the justices], "You collect this debt for me," it is not released:[20] for it is stated, *but whatever of yours is with your brother*[21] (Deuteronomy 15:3), and this he already transferred to the hand [power] of the *beth din*. For this reason the Sages of blessed memory said[22] that if orphans have a debt to collect from others, the seventh year does not release it: for Rabban Gamli'él and his *beth din* were the "father" [acting guardians] of orphans, and after them every *beth din* in every generation; hence it is as though they had given their promissory notes over to the hand of the *beth din*.

In the subject-matter of the precept there is likewise what the Sages said:[23] that if someone gives his fellow-man a loan for ten years, the seventh year does not release it: for when the merciful God said, "he shall not exact it," it referred to a loan due to be claimed, and for this the time did not yet come to press for it. There is, further, what the Sages said,[23] that if someone stipulates to his fellow-man about his loan, "on condition that the seventh year should not release it," it does release it—for he is as a person who makes a condition against something written in the Torah.[24] If he told him, however, "on condition that you do not cancel this debt even in the seventh year"— in other words, even though the law of the seventh year is to void it, if he made the condition "with you that you should not nullify this debt"[25]—the seventh year does not release it under these circumstances: for every condition [stipulated] about monetary matters holds firm, as I wrote in *sidrah b'har*, in the twelfth negative precept (§ 343). The rest of its details are in the Mishnah tractate *Sh'vi'ith*.

This precept in effect, by the law of the Torah, in the land of Israel and everywhere, at the time that the law of the jubilee is observed—for both man and woman. I wrote previously, above, in

זֶה זְמַן הַיּוֹבֵל נוֹהֵג; אֲבָל בִּזְמַן שֶׁאֵין הַיּוֹבֵל נוֹהֵג, אֵין שְׁמִטַּת קַרְקָעוֹת וּכְסָפִים נוֹהֶגֶת מִדְּאוֹרַיְתָא. אֲבָל מִדִּבְרֵי סוֹפְרִים נוֹהֶגֶת שְׁמִטַּת כְּסָפִים אֲפִלּוּ בַּזְּמַן הַזֶּה וַאֲפִלּוּ בְּכָל מָקוֹם, כְּדֵי שֶׁלֹּא תִשְׁתַּכַּח תּוֹרַת הַשְׁמָטַת כְּסָפִים מִיִּשְׂרָאֵל. וּכְבָר כָּתַבְתִּי לְמַעְלָה בְּסֵדֶר בְּהַר סִינַי בְּסוֹף מִצְוָה רִאשׁוֹנָה [סִי׳ ש״ל] אֵי זוֹ הִיא שְׁנַת הַשְּׁמִטָּה לָדַעַת הַמְפָרְשִׁים הַגְּדוֹלִים הַיּוֹדְעִים דַּרְכֵי הַתַּלְמוּד.

וְעוֹבֵר עַל זֶה וְתָבַע אֶת חֲבֵרוֹ עַל חוֹב שֶׁעָבְרָה עָלָיו שָׁנָה שְׁבִיעִית בִּזְמַן הַבַּיִת, בִּטֵּל עֲשֵׂה זֶה, מִלְּבַד שֶׁהוּא עוֹבֵר עַל לָאו, כְּמוֹ שֶׁנִּכְתֹּב בְּסֵדֶר זֶה בְּעֶזְרַת הַשֵּׁם [סִי׳ תע״ה]; וּבַזְּמַן הַזֶּה קָא עָבִיד אִסּוּרָא דְרַבָּנָן. וְאִם יָדְעוּ הַבֵּית־דִּין שֶׁשְּׁבִיעִית עָבְרָה עָלָיו, אֵין נִזְקָקִין לִנְגֹּשׁ אוֹתוֹ כְּלָל, וַאֲפִלּוּ בַּזְּמַן הַזֶּה; וְאַף־עַל־פִּי שֶׁהַשְׁמָטַת כְּסָפִים עַכְשָׁו דְּרַבָּנָן וְקַיְמָא לָן שֶׁעֲבוּדָא דְאוֹרַיְתָא, הָא אִפְסִיקָא הִלְכְתָא, דְּבְכָל דָּבָר שֶׁבְּמָמוֹן יֵשׁ כֹּחַ בְּיַד חֲכָמִים לִדְחוֹת דְּבַר תּוֹרָה, מִטַּעַם דְּהֶפְקֵר בֵּית־דִּין הֶפְקֵר.

[שֶׁלֹּא לִמְנֹעַ מִלְּהַחֲיוֹת הֶעָנִי וּמִלְּתֵּן לוֹ מַה שֶּׁהוּא צָרִיךְ]

תעח שֶׁלֹּא נִמְנַע הַחֶסֶד וְהַצְּדָקָה מֵאַחֵינוּ בְּנֵי־יִשְׂרָאֵל, וְכָל־שֶׁכֵּן מִן הַקְּרוֹבִים, בְּדַעְתֵּנוּ חֻלְשַׁת עִנְיָנָם וְיֵשׁ בָּנוּ יְכֹלֶת לְסַעֲדָם, וְעַל זֶה נֶאֱמַר ״לֹא תְאַמֵּץ אֶת לְבָבְךָ וְלֹא תִקְפֹּץ אֶת יָדְךָ מֵאָחִיךָ הָאֶבְיוֹן״, כְּלוֹמַר אַל תַּשְׁלִיט עָלֶיךָ מִדַּת הַכִּילוּת וְהַנִּבְזָה, אֲבָל הָכֵן לְבָבְךָ עַל־כָּל־פָּנִים בְּמִדַּת הַנְּדִיבוּת וְהַחֶמְלָה, וְאַל תַּחְשֹׁב שֶׁיִּהְיֶה לְךָ בַּדָּבָר חֶסְרוֹן מָמוֹנֶךָ, כִּי בִגְלַל הַדָּבָר הַהוּא יְבָרֶכְךָ הַשֵּׁם; וְיָפָה לְךָ בִּרְכָתוֹ רֶגַע קָטָן מִכַּמָּה אוֹצָרוֹת שֶׁל זָהָב וָכָסֶף.

26. The teaching of the Sages at the end of the first paragraph (see note 2) continues: "At a time that you release land, you relinquish money; at a time that you do not release land, you are not to relinquish money." See note 3, that "releasing land" in this passage refers to a jubilee year; hence the present rule. (It should be noted, though, that "the release of land" here, in this sentence, refers to letting one's field lie fallow during a year of sh'mittah: i.e. this too is not required by Torah law in a period when the rule of the jubilee is not in effect.)

27. In his original, the author dealt with all the negative precepts in a *sidrah* after the positive ones; hence, in his draft, it occurs below (as §481).

28. Since a properly constituted *beth din* is empowered to transfer one man's possessions to another, its decree regarding the release of debts has the validity of Torah law; TB Yevamoth 89b.

§478   1. So TB Bava M'tzi'a 71a (and Rashi, s.v. 'aniyecha), that poor relatives should take precedence.

sidrah b'har (§§ 332, 335), at which time the law of the jubilee is in effect. However, when the jubilee's law is not in force, the release of land and money is not in effect by the law of the Torah.[26] By the decree of the Sages, though, the release of money is in force even at the present time, and indeed everywhere, so that the law of the relinquishment of money should not be forgotten by Jewry. I wrote previously, above in *sidrah b'har*, at the end of the first positive precept (§ 330), which is a [calendar] year of *sh'mittah* (release) in the view of the great authorities who know the ways of the Talmud.

If a person transgressed this and demanded payment from his fellow-man for a debt which passed the seventh year, at the time of the Temple, he would disobey this positive precept, apart from violating a negative precept, as we will write in this *sidrah*, with the Eternal Lord's help (§ 475).[27] At the present time he would commit a deed forbidden by the Sages. If the *beth din* (court) justices know that a seventh year has passed by it [a debt], they are not compelled at all to demand its payment, even at the present time. Even though the release of money now is by the decree of the Sages, and the standing rule we have is that a creditor's right to a debtor's property is by the law of the Torah, the definitive ruling was decided that in any matter regarding goods and possessions, the Sages have the power to set aside the word of the Torah, by virtue of the rule that what a *beth din* declares ownerless is ownerless.[28]

[NOT TO REFRAIN FROM SUSTAINING A POOR MAN AND GIVING HIM WHAT HE NEEDS]

478 that we should not withhold kindness and charity from our Jewish brethren, and all the more certainly not from relatives,[1] when we know the sorry state of their situation and we have the ability to aid them. About this it is stated, *you shall not harden your heart or shut your hand against your needy brother* (Deuteronomy 15:7); in other words, do not let the quality of miserliness and meanness rule you,[2] but rather train your heart, under all circumstances, in the quality of generosity and compassion, and do not reckon that the matter will mean a lack in your personal wealth, *because for the sake of this thing, the Lord...will bless you* (ibid. 10), and His blessing for a brief instant is better for you than any number of treasures of gold and silver.

2. From the beginning to here is based on ShM negative precept § 232.

מִשָּׁרָשֵׁי מִצְוַת הַצְּדָקָה כָּתַבְתִּי (בְּכֶסֶף תַּלְוֶה, מִצְוָה רִאשׁוֹנָה) [בְּמִשְׁפָּטִים] בְּסִימָן ס"ו, וּקְצָת דִּינֶיהָ וְעִנְיָנָהּ כְּמִנְהָגִי.

[מִצְוַת צְדָקָה]

תעט לַעֲשׂוֹת צְדָקָה עִם הַצָּרִיךְ אֵלֶיהָ, בְּשִׂמְחָה וּבְטוּב לֵבָב, כְּלוֹמַר שֶׁנִּתֵּן מִמָּמוֹנֵנוּ לְמִי שֶׁיֶּחְסַר לוֹ וּלְחַזֵּק הֶעָנִי בְּכָל מַה שֶּׁצָּרִיךְ לְמִחְיָתוֹ בְּכָל יְכָלְתֵּנוּ; וְעַל זֶה נֶאֱמַר "פָּתֹחַ תִּפְתַּח אֶת יָדְךָ לוֹ"; וְדָרְשׁוּ זִכְרוֹנָם לִבְרָכָה: "פָּתֹחַ תִּפְתָּח", וַאֲפִלּוּ כַּמָּה פְּעָמִים; וְעוֹד נֶאֱמַר "וְהֶחֱזַקְתָּ בּוֹ גֵּר וְתוֹשָׁב וָחַי עִמָּךְ", וְאָמַר עוֹד: וְחֵי אָחִיךָ עִמָּךְ.

מִשָּׁרָשֵׁי הַמִּצְוָה כָּתַבְתִּי (בְּכֶסֶף תַּלְוֶה מִצְוָה א') [בְּמִשְׁפָּטִים] בְּסִימָן ס"ו מַה שֶּׁיָּדַעְתִּי.

דִּינֵי הַמִּצְוָה, כְּגוֹן מַה שֶּׁאָמְרוּ זִכְרוֹנָם לִבְרָכָה שֶׁעִקָּר מִצְוָה זוֹ לִתֵּן הַצְּדָקָה לְיַד גַּבַּאי, שֶׁיִּתְּנֶנָּה לְמִי שֶׁצָּרִיךְ לָהּ, כְּדֵי שֶׁלֹּא יִתְבַּיֵּשׁ הַמְקַבֵּל כְּשֶׁהוּא מְקַבְּלָהּ מִיַּד הַנּוֹתְנָהּ בְּכָל עֵת שֶׁיִּרְאֶנּוּ, וְגַם הַנּוֹתֵן לֹא יָבִיּשֵׁנּוּ עָלֶיהָ לְעוֹלָם — שֶׁזֶּה אֵינוֹ יוֹדֵעַ לְמִי נוֹתְנָהּ וְזֶה אֵינוֹ יוֹדֵעַ מִמִּי נוֹטְלָהּ.

וְאַתָּה בְּנִי, אַל תַּחְשֹׁב שֶׁעִנְיַן מִצְוַת הַצְּדָקָה לֹא יִהְיֶה רַק בְּעָנִי אֲשֶׁר אֵין לֶחֶם וְשִׂמְלָה, כִּי אַף בַּעֲשִׁירִים גְּדוֹלִים גַּם־כֵּן תִּתְכַּיֵּם מִצְוַת הַצְּדָקָה לִפְעָמִים, כְּגוֹן עָשִׁיר שֶׁהוּא בְּמָקוֹם שֶׁאֵין מַכִּירִין אוֹתוֹ וְצָרִיךְ לִלְווֹת, וַאֲפִלּוּ בְּעָשִׁיר שֶׁהוּא בְּעִירוֹ וּבִמְקוֹם מַכָּרָיו, פְּעָמִים שֶׁיִּצְטָרֵךְ מִפְּנֵי חֳלִי אוֹ מִפְּנֵי שׁוּם מִקְרֶה אַחֵר לְדָבָר אֶחָד שֶׁהוּא בְּיָדְךָ וְלֹא יִמָּצֵא מִמֶּנּוּ בְּמָקוֹם אַחֵר.

גַּם זֶה בִּכְלַל מִצְוַת הַצְּדָקָה הוּא בְּלִי סָפֵק, כִּי הַתּוֹרָה תִּבְחַר לְעוֹלָם בִּגְמִילוּת חֲסָדִים, וּתְצַוֶּה אוֹתָנוּ לְהַשְׁלִים רְצוֹן הַנִּבְרָאִים, בְּנֵי־בְּרִית, כַּאֲשֶׁר תַּשִּׂיג יָדֵנוּ. וּכְלַל הָעִנְיָן שֶׁכָּל הַמְהַנֶּה אֶת חֲבֵרוֹ, בֵּין בְּמָמוֹן בֵּין בְּמַאֲכָל אוֹ בִשְׁאָר צְרָכָיו, אוֹ

§479   1. In the Hebrew the verb is doubled (literally, "open shall you open"); hence it connotes a command to do so over and over, as often as necessary; Sifre, Deuteronomy §116; cf. TB Bava M'tzi'a 31b. (This paragraph is based on MT *hilchoth mat'noth 'aniyyim* vii 1.)

2. TB Bava Bathra 10b.

3. Since the donor and the recipient never come to know one another, as each sees only the treasurer or manager of the charity, who acts as collector and distributor.

4. Cf. MT *hilchoth mat'noth 'aniyyim* x 8.

5. I.e. the covenant of the Torah and its *mitzvoth*.

Regarding root reasons for the precept of charity, I wrote in *sidrah mishpatim* (§ 66), along with a bit of its laws and its subject-matter, as is my custom.

[THE MITZVAH OF CHARITY]

479 to act with charity toward a person who needs it, with gladness and a good heart; in other words, that we should give of our personal wealth to anyone in need, and support the poor man with whatever he requires for his sustenance, with all our ability. About this it is stated, *you shall surely open your hand to him* (Deuteronomy 15:8); and the Sages of blessed memory interpreted, "you shall surely open"—even a hundred times.[1] It is also stated, *then you shall uphold him; as a stranger and a settler shall he live with you* (Leviticus 25:35); and further *that your brother may live, along with you* (ibid. 6).

Concerning root reasons for the precept, I have written in *sidrah mishpatim* (§ 66) what I knew. The laws of the precept are, for example, what the Sages of blessed memory taught:[2] that the main way [to fulfill] this *mitzvah* is to give charity into the hand of a treasurer or manager, that he should give it to anyone who needs it, so that the recipient should not feel ashamed when he receives it from the hand that gives it to him every time he sees him.[3] Moreover, the donor will never embarrass him by it: for this one does not know to whom he gave it, and that one does not know from whom he received it.[4]

Now you, my son, are not to think that the subject of the precept of charity applies to none but a poor man who has neither bread nor clothing. For with men of great wealth, too, the precept of charity can be fulfilled at times: for example, if a wealthy man is in a place where he is not recognized, and he needs to borrow money. Even for a wealthy man in his own town, among those who know him, there can be times when, on account of illness or some other event, he needs one thing that is in your possession, and he will not find any of it anywhere else.

This too is included in the scope of the precept of charity, without any doubt. For the Torah always prefers deeds of kindness, and it commands us to fulfill the wishes of those human beings who are members of the covenant,[5] insofar as we are able. The nub of the matter is that whoever benefits his fellow-man, whether with goods, food, or any other needs of his, or even with good words, words of

אֲפִלּוּ בִדְבָרִים טוֹבִים, דְּבָרִים נְחוּמִים — בִּכְלַל מִצְוַת הַצְּדָקָה הִיא וּשְׂכָרוֹ הַרְבֵּה מְאֹד. וְיִכָּנְסוּ דְבָרֶיךָ בְּאָזְנֶיךָ, כִּי טוֹבִים הֵמָּה בְּאֹזֶן תִּבְחַן מִלִּים.

וְאָמְרוּ זִכְרוֹנָם לִבְרָכָה שֶׁעָנִי שֶׁאֵינוֹ רוֹצֶה לָקַח, מַעֲרִימִין עָלָיו וְנוֹתְנִין לוֹ לְשֵׁם הַלְוָאָה, וְאַחַר־כָּךְ אֵין שׁוֹאֲלִין אוֹתָהּ מִמֶּנּוּ; אֲבָל עָשִׁיר הַמַּסְגֵּף עַצְמוֹ וְעֵינוֹ צָרָה בְמָמוֹנוֹ, אֵין מַשְׁגִּיחִין בּוֹ; וְאָמְרוּ זִכְרוֹנָם לִבְרָכָה: "דֵּי מַחְסֹרוֹ", אַתָּה מְצֻוֶּה לְהַשְׁלִים חֶסְרוֹנוֹ אֲבָל אֵין אַתָּה מְצֻוֶּה לְעַשְּׁרוֹ.

וְכָתַב הָרַב רַבֵּנוּ מֹשֶׁה בֶּן מַיְמוֹן זִכְרוֹנוֹ לִבְרָכָה כִּי מֵעוֹלָם לֹא רָאָה וְלֹא שָׁמַע עִיר שֶׁיִּהְיוּ בָהּ עֲשָׂרָה מִיִּשְׂרָאֵל שֶׁלֹּא יִהְיֶה לָהֶם קֻפָּה שֶׁל צְדָקָה.

וְאָמְרוּ זִכְרוֹנָם לִבְרָכָה שֶׁאֲפִלּוּ עָנִי הַמִּתְפַּרְנֵס מִן הַצְּדָקָה חַיָּב לַעֲשׂוֹת צְדָקָה אִם יִמְצָא לְמַטָּה מִמֶּנּוּ שֶׁצָּרִיךְ לָהּ. וְאָמְרוּ זִכְרוֹנָם לִבְרָכָה שֶׁאֵין אָדָם שׁוּם בָּא לַעֲנִיּוּת לְעוֹלָם בִּשְׁבִיל רִבּוּי צְדָקָה שֶׁיַּעֲשֶׂה, שֶׁנֶּאֱמַר "וְהָיָה מַעֲשֵׂה הַצְּדָקָה שָׁלוֹם", וְאֵין יִשְׂרָאֵל נִגְאָלִין אֶלָּא בִזְכוּת הַצְּדָקָה, שֶׁנֶּאֱמַר: צִיּוֹן בְּמִשְׁפָּט תִּפָּדֶה וְשָׁבֶיהָ בִּצְדָקָה. וְיֶתֶר פְּרָטֶיהָ, בִּמְקוֹמוֹת בַּתַּלְמוּד בְּפִזּוּר, וְרֻבָּם בְּמַסֶּכֶת כְּתֻבּוֹת וּבָבָא בַתְרָא.

וְנוֹהֶגֶת בְּכָל מָקוֹם וּבְכָל זְמַן, בַּזְּכָרִים וּנְקֵבוֹת. וְעוֹבֵר עַל זֶה וְלֹא עָשָׂה צְדָקָה בְּעֵת שֶׁנִּשְׁאַל עָלֶיהָ, אוֹ רָאָה שֶׁצָּרִיךְ הַדָּבָר וְיֵשׁ יְכֹלֶת בְּיָדוֹ לַעֲשׂוֹתָהּ, בִּטֵּל עֲשֵׂה זֶה.

[שֶׁלֹּא נִמָּנַע מִלְּהַלְווֹת לֶעָנִי מִפְּנֵי הַשְּׁמִטָּה]

תפ שֶׁלֹּא לְהִמָּנַע מֵהַלְווֹת אֶל הַצְּרִיכִים מִפְּנֵי פַּחַד הַשְּׁמִטָּה שֶׁלֹּא תַפְקִיעַ הַחוֹב, וְעַל זֶה נֶאֱמַר "הִשָּׁמֶר לְךָ פֶּן יִהְיֶה דָבָר עִם לְבָבְךָ בְלִיַּעַל לֵאמֹר קָרְבָה שְׁנַת הַשֶּׁבַע" וְגוֹמֵר; וּלְשׁוֹן סִפְרִי: "הִשָּׁמֶר" בְּלֹא־תַעֲשֶׂה, "פֶּן יִהְיֶה" בְּלֹא־

---

6. Expression based on Job 12:11.

7. TB K'thuboth 67b.

8. He is not to be helped in his self-imposed, gratuitous "poverty"; *ibid.*

9. MT *hilchoth mat'noth 'aniyyim* ix 3.

10. TB Gittin 7b.

11. MT *ibid.* x 2, based perhaps on Mishnath R.'Eli'ezer, 76 l.4–6 (Yalkut Shim'oni, Psalms § 711).

12. TB Shabbath 139a; MT *ibid.* 1.

§480   1. See § 475, note 1.

2. Sifre, Deuteronomy § 117.

3. See § 439, note 1.

comfort — it is [all] within the meaning of the precept of charity, and his reward will be very great. Let my words enter your ears, for they are good in an ear that assays words.[6]

Our Sages of blessed memory said too[7] that if a poor man does not wish to accept, guile is used upon him and he is given it under the name of a loan; and afterward it is not requested of him. However, if a rich man mortifies himself [by poverty], being miserly toward his own wealth, no attention is paid him.[8] Our Sages taught further:[7] "sufficient for his need" (Deuteronomy 15:8) — you are commanded to supply what he lacks, but you are not commanded to enrich him.

Well, R. Moses b. Maimon of blessed memory wrote[9] that never did he see or hear of a town containing ten Jews that did not have a charity fund.

Our Sages of blessed memory taught further[10] that even a poor man who is maintained by charity is obligated to practice charity if he finds someone below him [in financial status] who needs it. They (of blessed memory) also taught[11] that no man whatever will ever be reduced to poverty on account of the great amount of charity he gives: for it is stated, *And the work of charity shall be peace* (Isaiah 32:17); and Jewry will be redeemed in nothing other than the merit of charity: for it is stated, *Zion shall be redeemed by justice, and those of her who return, by charity* (ibid. 1:27).[12] The rest of its details are in various places in the Talmud, scattered, but mostly in the tractates *K'thuboth* and *Bava Bathra*.

It applies in every place and time, for both man and woman. If a person violates this and does not practice charity at a time that he is asked for it, or when he sees the matter is needed and he has the ability to do it, he disobeys this positive precept.

[THAT WE SHOULD NOT AVOID LENDING MONEY
TO THE POOR BECAUSE OF SH'MITTAH]

480 not to refrain from lending to those in need, on account of fear of *sh'mittah* [the year of release],[1] that the debt may be cancelled: as it is stated about this, *Take heed of yourself lest there be a base thought in your heart, to say: The seventh year, the year of release is near,* etc. (Deuteronomy 15:9). In the language of the Midrash *Sifre*:[2] "Take heed" — it is [thus] under a negative precept; "lest there be" — it is [thus again] under a negative precept.[3] In other words, these two

תַעֲשֶׂה: כְּלוֹמַר שֶׁאֵלּוּ שְׁנֵי לָאוִין בָּאוּ בָּזֶה הָעִנְיָן, זֶה אַחַר זֶה, לְחִזּוּק.

מִשָּׁרְשֵׁי הַמִּצְוָה, לְחַזֵּק וְלִקְבֹּעַ בְּלִבְבֵנוּ מִדַּת הַנְּדִיבוּת וּלְהַרְחִיק תַּכְלִית הַרְחָקָה מִדַּת הַכִּילוּת; וְאֵין נָדִיב בָּעוֹלָם כְּמַלְּוֶה מְעוֹתָיו עִם הֱיוֹתוֹ יוֹדֵעַ שֶׁהַזְּמַן קָרֵב לְהַשְׁמִיט הַלְוָאָתוֹ וּלְהַפְסִידָהּ מִמֶּנּוּ אוּלַי אִם יֶאֱרַע בּוֹ אֹנֶס אוֹ שׁוּם מִקְרֶה שֶׁלֹּא יוּכַל לִתְבֹּעַ הַלְוָאָתוֹ קֹדֶם שְׁנַת הַשְּׁמִטָּה. וְכָל מֵבִין דַּרְכֵי הַתּוֹרָה וּמַשִּׂיג לָדַעַת אֲפִלּוּ מְעַט מְעַט בְּחִין עֶרְכָּהּ יֵדַע בְּבֵרוּר כִּי הַמְּפַזֵּר מָמוֹנוּ אֶל הַצְּרִיכִים—נוֹסָף עוֹד, וְחוֹשֵׂךְ מִיֹּשֶׁר אַךְ לְמַחְסֹר: כִּי הַשֵּׁם יָדִין אֶת הָאָדָם לְפִי מַעֲשָׂיו וִיעַנְּיֵקְהוּ מִבִּרְכָתוֹ כְּפִי הִתְקָרְבוֹ אֵלֶיהָ, וּמִדַּת הַכִּילוּת מְחִצָּה שֶׁל בַּרְזֶל בֵּינוֹ וְהַבְּרָכָה, וְהַנְּדִיבוּת חֵלֶק מֵחֶלְקֵי הַבְּרָכָה, וְנִמְצָא הַמִּתְנַהֵג בּוֹ שֶׁהוּא בְתוֹכָהּ; יִשְׁמַע חָכָם וְיוֹסֵף לָקַח.

דִּינֵי הַמִּצְוָה קְצָרִים, כְּלוּלִים בִּפְשַׁט הַכָּתוּב לְפִי דַעְתִּי.

וְנוֹהֵג אִסּוּר זֶה בַּזְּכָרִים וּנְקֵבוֹת, בְּכָל מָקוֹם וּבְכָל זְמַן: שֶׁאַף בַּזְּמַן הַזֶּה שֶׁאֵין שְׁמִטַּת כְּסָפִים נוֹהֶגֶת מִדְּאוֹרַיְתָא אֶלָּא מִדְּרַבָּנָן, מִכָּל־מָקוֹם אָנוּ מֻזְהָרִים גַּם־כֵּן שֶׁלֹּא נִמָּנַע מִלְּהַלְווֹת אֶל הַצָּרִיךְ מִפְּנֵי פַחַד שְׁנַת הַשְּׁמִטָּה, שֶׁמְּשַׁמֶּטֶת מִדְּרַבָּנָן בַּזְּמַן הַזֶּה, וּמִן הַתּוֹרָה בִּזְמַן הַבַּיִת.

וְעוֹבֵר עַל זֶה וְנִמְנַע מִלְּהַלְווֹת אֶל הַצָּרִיךְ מִפְּנֵי זֶה, עָבַר עַל לָאו, אֲבָל אֵין בּוֹ מַלְקוֹת, לְפִי שֶׁאֵין בּוֹ מַעֲשֶׂה. וְאוּלַי יַעֲלֶה בְמַחֲשַׁבְתְּךָ, בְּנִי, לֵאמֹר: וְאֵיךְ יִמָּנַע אָדָם מֵהַלְוָאָה לְעוֹלָם מִפְּנֵי זֶה, וְלָמָּה נִכְתַּב עַל זֶה לָאו, וַהֲלֹא בְיָדוֹ לְהַתְנוֹת עִמּוֹ עַל מְנָת שֶׁלֹּא תַשְׁמִיטֶנּוּ בַּשְּׁבִיעִית, וּכְדֶרֶךְ שֶׁאָנוּ עוֹשִׂין תָּמִיד בִּשְׁטָרוֹתֵינוּ—אַל

---

4. Hebrew, *karév*; but the manuscripts read *'arév*, which might mean "is interven-ing" (linked with *hith'arév*).

5. This is the reading of the four early manuscripts. In the editions it has evidently been "emended" to ויוסף לקח "and let him increase [his] learning" or "learned awareness"—in keeping with Proverbs 1:5.

6. See §477, paragraph 7, at note 24.

injunctions were applied to this subject, one after the other, to reinforce the point.

At the root of the precept lies the purpose to strengthen and set firmly in our heart the quality of generosity, and to remove utterly far the quality of miserliness. There is no one in the world so generous as a person who lends his money although he knows that the time is drawing near[4] that will release his loan and make it lost to him, if any accident whatever should happen to him, or any chance occurrence, so that he will be unable to demand payment of his loan before the year of sh'mittah (release). Whoever understands the ways of the Torah and attains to know even a bit of its great, gracious worth, will know clearly that whoever distributes his money generously among those in need, yet more will be given him, while *he who holds back from a just, decent way of giving will find only lack* (Proverbs 11:24). For the Eternal Lord judges a man according to his deeds, and He bestows of His blessing amply upon him to the extent that he draws close to it. The quality of miserliness, on the other hand, is a partition of iron between him and blessing, while generosity is one of the elements of blessing. Consequently, a person who behaves with this [quality] is within it [blessing]. Let the wise hear, and give ever more.[5]

The laws of the precept are brief, implicit in the plain meaning of the verse, in my view.

This prohibition applies to both man and woman, everywhere, at every time. For at the present time too, when the release of money is not in effect by the law of the Torah, but only by the decree of the Sages, we are equally adjured, in any event, that we should not hold back from lending to one who needs it out of fear of the year of sh'mittah, which releases [debts] by the enactment of the Sages at the present time, and by the Torah's law at the time the Temple stands.

If a person transgresses this and refuses to lend money to someone in need for this reason, he violates a negative precept; but it brings no punishment of whiplashes, since it involves no physical action. But perhaps it might come to your mind, my son, to ask, "Yet why should a man ever refrain from granting a loan on account of this, and why was a negative precept written about it [in Scripture]? Surely it is in our power to stipulate to him [the borrower, that it is] 'on condition that you do not abolish it in the seventh year,'[6] in the way that we do it continually in our promissory notes." Let this matter not

יַבְהִילְךָ דָּבָר זֶה, כִּי הַתּוֹרָה תַּזְהִירֵנוּ בִּדְבָרִים וְאַף־עַל־פִּי שֶׁאֶפְשָׁר בְּתַקָּנוֹת וּתְנָאִים.

[שֶׁלֹּא לְשַׁלֵּחַ עֶבֶד עִבְרִי רֵיקָם כְּשֶׁיֵּצֵא חָפְשִׁי]

תפא שֶׁלֹּא נוֹצִיא עֶבֶד עִבְרִי בְּיָדַיִם רֵיקָנִיּוֹת מֵעֲבוֹדָתֵנוּ כְּשֶׁיֵּצֵא בֶן־חוֹרִין לְסוֹף שֵׁשׁ שָׁנִים, אֲבָל נַעֲנִיקֵהוּ מֵהוֹגְנֵנוּ עַל־כָּל־פָּנִים, וְעַל זֶה נֶאֱמַר: וְכִי תְשַׁלְּחֶנּוּ חָפְשִׁי מֵעִמָּךְ לֹא תְשַׁלְּחֶנּוּ רֵיקָם.

מִשָּׁרְשֵׁי מִצְוָה זוֹ וְכָל עִנְיָנָהּ, וּמָקוֹם בְּאֻרֶהָ, כָּתוּב בְּמִצְוַת עֲשֵׂה דְּהַעֲנָקָה שֶׁבְּסֵדֶר זֶה [סִי' תפ"ב].

[מִצְוַת הַעֲנֵק עֶבֶד עִבְרִי]

תפב לָתֵת מִמַּה שֶּׁיֵּשׁ לָנוּ לְעֶבֶד עִבְרִי בִּזְמַן שֶׁיֵּצֵא מִתַּחַת יָדֵינוּ לְחֵרוּת, וְלֹא נְשַׁלְּחֶנּוּ בְּיָדַיִם רֵיקָנִיּוֹת; וְעַל זֶה נֶאֱמַר: הַעֲנֵיק תַּעֲנִיק לוֹ מִצֹּאנְךָ וּמִגָּרְנְךָ וּמִיִּקְבֶךָ, אֲשֶׁר בֵּרַכְךָ יְיָ אֱלֹהֶיךָ תִּתֶּן לוֹ.

מִשָּׁרְשֵׁי הַמִּצְוָה, לְמַעַן נִקְנֶה בְּנַפְשֵׁנוּ מִדּוֹת מְעֻלּוֹת יְקָרוֹת נַחֲמָדוֹת, וְעִם הַנֶּפֶשׁ הַיְקָרָה וְהַמְּעֻלָּה נִזְכֶּה לְטוֹב, וְהָאֵל הַטּוֹב חָפֵץ לְהֵיטִיב לְעַמּוֹ, וְהוֹדִיעָנוּ וַחֲדָרֵנוּ הוּא שֶׁנְּרַחֵם עַל מִי שֶׁעָבַד אוֹתָנוּ וְנִתֶּן לוֹ מִשֶּׁלָּנוּ בְּתוֹרַת חֶסֶד מִלְּבַד מַה שֶּׁהִתְנֵינוּ עִמּוֹ לָתֵת לוֹ בִּשְׂכָרוֹ; וְדָבָר מֻשְׂכָּל הוּא, אֵין צֹרֶךְ לְהַאֲרִיךְ בּוֹ.

מִדִּינֵי הַמִּצְוָה, מַה שֶּׁאָמְרוּ זִכְרוֹנָם לִבְרָכָה שֶׁאֶחָד עֶבֶד עִבְרִי הַיּוֹצֵא בְּסוֹף שֵׁשׁ אוֹ בְּיוֹבֵל אוֹ בְּמִיתַת אָדוֹן, וְכֵן אָמָה שֶׁיָּצָאת בְּאֶחָד מִכָּל אֵלּוּ אוֹ בְּסִימָנִין, הֲרֵי אֵלּוּ מַעֲנִיקִין לָהֶם; אֲבָל הַיּוֹצְאִין בְּגִרְעוֹן כֶּסֶף אֵין מַעֲנִיקִין לָהֶם, שֶׁנֶּאֱמַר "וְכִי

§481   1. The period for which a Hebrew might go into servitude: Exodus 21:2.

2. In his original, evidently under the influence of Rambam's ShM, our author dealt first, in each *sidrah*, with all its positive precepts, and afterward with all the negative. Hence, in his original Hebrew text, our §482 "is [already] written" before our §481.

§482   1. This last sentence is not in the manuscripts, but it seems an authentic part of the original.

2. TB Kiddushin 16b.

3. When all Hebrew bondservants go free (§332), even in the middle of a six-year period.

4. I.e. signs of puberty; she then goes free of the servitude into which her father sold her (TB Kiddushin 16a).

5. E.g. if the master paid 600 *denarii* for the Hebrew servant's labor, after two years the servant may pay the master 400 *denarii* and go free; for the 600 was in payment for six years of labor, and two years of service were given.

⟨478⟩

bewilder you; for the Torah adjures us about matters even where amendments and stipulated conditions are possible.

[NOT TO SEND AWAY A HEBREW MANSERVANT
EMPTY-HANDED WHEN HE GOES FREE]

481 that we should not discharge a Hebrew servant empty-handed from our service when he goes out a free man at the end of six years,[1] but we should rather supply him liberally from our personal wealth, in any event: as it is stated about it, *And when you let him go free from you, you shall not let him go empty-handed* (Deuteronomy 15:13).

About the root reason for this precept, all its subject-matter, and the place where it is clarified, [all this] is [already] written in the positive precept of supplying him liberally, in this *sidrah* (§482).[2]

[THE PRECEPT OF GIVING A BONUS TO
A HEBREW MANSERVANT AT HIS DISCHARGE]

482 to give of what we have to a Hebrew servant at the time he goes out from under our hand (mastery), and we should not send him off empty-handed. About this it is stated, *you shall supply him liberally out of your flock and out of your threshing-floor and out of your wine press; with what the Lord your God has blessed you, [of that] you shall give him* (Deuteronomy 15:14).

At the root of the precept lies the purpose that we should acquire in ourselves noble, precious, cherished traits of character; and with a precious, noble spirit we will merit to attain good reward, as the beneficent God desires to do good for His people. It is our splendor and glory that we should have compassion on a person who served us, and we should give him of what we own as an act of loving-kindness, apart from what we stipulated with him to give him as his wages. It is something understandable by the intelligence; there is no need to continue at length about it.[1]

Among the laws of the precept there is what the Sages of blessed memory said:[2] that it is all one whether a servant leaves at the end of six years, in the jubilee year,[3] or upon the death of the master; and so too when a maidservant leaves in one of these ways or upon acquiring signs of maturity[4] — these are to be given the liberal bonus. But those who leave by deducting money [from their price of servitude and refunding the balance][5] are not supplied liberally with the bonus: for it is stated, *And when you send him off free* (Deuteronomy 15:13), and

תְּשַׁלְּחֶנּוּ חָפְשִׁי״, וְזֶה לֹא שִׁלּוּחוֹ הוּא אֶלָּא הָעֲבֵד הוּא שֶׁגֵּרַם בִּנְתִינַת הַכֶּסֶף לָצֵאת מִתַּחַת יָדוֹ.

וְכֵן מַה שֶּׁדָּרְשׁוּ זִכְרוֹנָם לִבְרָכָה בְּמַה שֶׁהִזְכִּיר הַכָּתוּב צֹאן וְגֹרֶן וְיֶקֶב, שֶׁבִּדְבָרִים שֶׁיֵּשׁ בָּהֶן בְּרָכָה מֵחֲמַת עַצְמָם הוּא שֶׁחַיָּב לְהַעֲנִיקָם, אֲבָל לֹא כְּסָפִים וּבְגָדִים. וּמַה שֶּׁאָמְרוּ זִכְרוֹנָם לִבְרָכָה שֶׁאֵין פּוֹחֲתִין לוֹ מִשְּׁלֹשִׁים סֶלַע; וּבֵין נִתְבָּרֵךְ בַּעַל הַבַּיִת לְרַגְלוֹ אוֹ לֹא נִתְבָּרֵךְ, חַיָּב לְהַעֲנִיק לוֹ; וְעֶנֶק הָעֶבֶד לְעַצְמוֹ וְאֵין בַּעַל חוֹבוֹ גוֹבֶה הֵימֶנּוּ; וְיֶתֶר פְּרָטֶיהָ, מְבֹאָרִים בְּפֶרֶק רִאשׁוֹן מִקִּדּוּשִׁין.

וְנוֹהֶגֶת מִצְוָה זוֹ בִּזְכָרִים וּנְקֵבוֹת בִּזְמַן הַבַּיִת, שֶׁאֵין דִּינֵי עֶבֶד עִבְרִי נוֹהֵג אֶלָּא בִּזְמַן שֶׁהַיּוֹבֵל נוֹהֵג, כְּמוֹ שֶׁכָּתַבְתִּי בְּמָה שֶׁקָּדַם; וּמִכָּל־מָקוֹם אַף בַּזְּמַן הַזֶּה יִשְׁמַע חָכָם וְיוֹסֵף לֶקַח, שֶׁאִם שָׂכַר שָׂכָר אֶחָד מִיִּשְׂרָאֵל וַעֲבָדוֹ זְמַן מְרֻבֶּה, אוֹ אֲפִלּוּ מוּעָט, שֶׁיַּעֲנִיק לוֹ בְּצֵאתוֹ מֵעִמּוֹ מֵאֲשֶׁר בֵּרְכוֹ הַשֵּׁם.

[שֶׁלֹּא לַעֲבֹד בְּקֳדָשִׁים]

תפג שֶׁלֹּא נַעֲבֹד עֲבוֹדָה בְּבַהֲמוֹת הַקֳּדָשִׁים, וְעַל זֶה נֶאֱמַר ״לֹא תַעֲבֹד בִּבְכֹר שׁוֹרֶךְ״ וּשְׁאָר הַקֳּדָשִׁים נִלְמָדִים מִן הַבְּכוֹר, כְּמוֹ שֶׁבָּא בִּבְכוֹרוֹת.

מִשָּׁרְשֵׁי הַמִּצְוָה, לְהַרְחִיקֵנוּ מֵהִתְקָרֵב אֶל הַקֳּדָשִׁים וּמִנְּגֹעַ בָּהֶן, כָּתַבְתִּי בְּסֵדֶר זֶה בְּלָאו דְּאִסּוּר פְּסוּלֵי הַמֻּקְדָּשִׁין כ״ו [סִי׳ תס״ט] וּבְכַמָּה מְקוֹמוֹת.

מִדִּינֵי הַמִּצְוָה, מַה שֶּׁאָמְרוּ זִכְרוֹנָם לִבְרָכָה: כָּל קָדְשֵׁי מִזְבֵּחַ בֵּין קָדְשֵׁי קָדָשִׁים בֵּין קָדָשִׁים קַלִּים אֲסוּרִים בְּגִזָּה וַעֲבוֹדָה; וְאָסוּר לְהֶדְיוֹט לֵהָנוֹת לְהַקְדֵּשֵׁי הַשֵּׁם,

6. MT *hilchoth 'avadim* iii 14.
7. TB Kiddushin 17a–b; MT *ibid.*
8. I.e. they grow and multiply of themselves.
9. TB Kiddushin 16b; MT *ibid.* 15.

§483 1. So also Sifre, Deuteronomy § 124.
2. TB B'choroth 25a, etc. Sifre *ibid.*

this man he [the master] did not send off, but it was rather the servant who brought it about by giving money so as to leave his mastery.[6]

There is likewise what the Sages of blessed memory interpreted from the fact that Scripture mentions the flock, the threshing-floor, and the wine press:[7] that of those things endowed with blessing by their own nature,[8] a man is obligated to give them a liberal bonus, but not money and clothing. There is, too, what the Sages of blessed memory said:[7] that he is not to be given less than [the value of] thirty *s'la'im*; whether the householder [the owner] was blessed because of him or was not blessed, he is duty-bound to give him a liberal bonus;[7] the bonus of a servant is for himself [alone]: a creditor of his may not collect from it.[9] The rest of its details are explained in the first chapter of the tractate *Kiddushin*.

This precept applies to both man and woman, at the time the Temple is extant: for the law of a Hebrew servant is in effect only at the time that the law of the jubilee is observed, as I wrote earlier (§ 42). Yet in any event, even today, *let the wise man hear and gain in learning* (Proverbs 1:5) — that if he hired one of the Israelites and the man served him a long time, or even a short time, he is to give him a liberal bonus when he leaves him — as the Lord has blessed him.

[TO DO NO WORK WITH ANIMALS
CONSECRATED FOR OFFERINGS]

483 that we should not do any work with animals consecrated for offerings, as it was stated about this, *you shall do no work with the firstling of your ox* (Deuteronomy 15:19); and for [animals consecrated for] other holy offerings we derive the law from the instance of the firstling, as we find in the Talmud tractate *B'choroth* (25a).[1]

At the root of the precept lies the purpose to keep us away from any closeness to holy offerings and from touching them, which I wrote in this *sidrah*, in the twenty-sixth negative precept, about the prohibition of disqualified consecrated animals (§ 469), and in several other instances.

Among the laws of the precept there is what the Sages of blessed memory said:[2] Regarding all animals consecrated for holy offerings on the altar, whether most-holy offerings or those of lesser holiness, it is forbidden to shear them or work with them. It is forbidden for an ordinary human being to have any benefit from anything consecrated to the Eternal Lord — whether entities that will be offered up on the

בֵּין מִדְּבָרִים הַקְּרֵבִים עַל־גַּבֵּי הַמִּזְבֵּחַ בֵּין מִקְדְּשֵׁי בֶדֶק הַבַּיִת, וְכָל הַנֶּהֱנֶה בְּשָׁוֶה פְרוּטָה מִקְדְּשֵׁי הַשֵּׁם, מָעַל. דְּבָרִים שֶׁהִתְּרוּ בַאֲכִילָה מִן הַקָּרְבָּנוֹת, כְּגוֹן בְּשַׂר חַטָּאת וְאָשָׁם אַחַר זְרִיקַת דָּמָן, אוֹ שְׁתֵּי הַלֶּחֶם אַחַר זְרִיקַת דַּם שְׁנֵי הַכְּבָשִׂים, אֵין בָּהֶן מְעִילָה, אֲפִלּוּ אָכַל הֶדְיוֹט מֵאֵלּוּ וְכַיּוֹצֵא בָהֶן: הוֹאִיל וְהֵן מֻתָּרִין לְמִקְצָת בְּנֵי־ אָדָם לֵהָנוֹת בָּהֶן, כָּל הַנֶּהֱנֶה מֵהֶן לֹא מָעַל; וַאֲפִלּוּ נִפְסְלוּ וְנֶאֶסְרוּ בַאֲכִילָה, הוֹאִיל וְהָיְתָה לָהֶן שָׁעַת הֶתֵּר אֵין חַיָּבִין עֲלֵיהֶן מְעִילָה.

כָּל הַמּוֹעֵל בְּזָדוֹן לוֹקֶה וּמְשַׁלֵּם מַה שֶּׁפָּגַם מִן הַקֹּדֶשׁ בְּרֹאשׁוֹ; וְאַזְהָרָה שֶׁל מְעִילָה מִזֶּה שֶׁנֶּאֱמַר "לֹא תוּכַל לֶאֱכֹל בִּשְׁעָרֶיךָ" וְגוֹמֵר "(וַנְדָּרֶיךָ) [וְכָל נְדָרֶיךָ]"; מִפִּי הַשְּׁמוּעָה לָמַדְנוּ שֶׁזּוֹ אַזְהָרָה לְאוֹכֵל בְּשַׂר עוֹלָה, כְּמוֹ שֶׁאָמַרְנוּ לְמַעְלָה [סִי׳ תמ״ז], הוֹאִיל וְכֻלָּה לַשֵּׁם; וְהוּא הַדִּין לִשְׁאָר כָּל קֹדֶשׁ שֶׁהוּא לַשֵּׁם לְבַדּוֹ, בֵּין מִקְדְּשֵׁי מִזְבֵּחַ בֵּין מִקְדְּשֵׁי בֶדֶק הַבַּיִת, אִם נֶהֱנָה מֵהֶן בְּשָׁוֶה פְרוּטָה, לוֹקֶה.

מָעַל בִּשְׁגָגָה, מְשַׁלֵּם מַה שֶּׁנֶּהֱנָה וְתוֹסֶפֶת חֹמֶשׁ, וּמֵבִיא אַיִל בִּשְׁתֵּי סְלָעִים וּמַקְרִיבוֹ אָשָׁם וּמִתְכַּפֵּר לוֹ, וְזֶהוּ הַנִּקְרָא אֲשַׁם מְעִילוֹת: שֶׁנֶּאֱמַר "בִּשְׁגָגָה

3. TB Me'ilah 15a. It should be noted that our author writes here with pre-cision: Working with an animal consecrated for the altar is forbidden by Torah law, and so too shearing its wool (§484)—even if no benefit is derived from it. If benefit is derived, another law of the Torah, against breach of holiness, is also violated; and this applies as well to an animal consecrated for the Temple treasury, so that it can be sold and the money used for Temple repairs. (As to working with an animal consecrated to the Temple treasury, or shearing its wool, while Torah law does not forbid it, a decree of the Sages does: TB B'choroth 25a.)

4. The Mishnah (Kiddushin i 1) evaluates a p'rutah as one eighth of an Italian 'issar, and this is discussed further in TB Kiddushin 12a. To this valuation Halachoth G'doloth adds: which is one part in 192 (one one hundred and ninety-second part) of a zuza of shashdang (ed. Warsaw 1874, p. 161b; 1st ed. Hildesheimer, p. 340). R. Isaac 'Alfasi records this verbatim, and adds: this [zuza of shashdang] being the gold dinar of the Arabs (Hilchoth R. 'Alfas, ed. Mosad R. Kook, II, p. 136b). Earlier, we find R. Sa'adyah Ga'on valuing the p'rutah as "one part in 192 of the Arabian dinar" (T'shuvoth haGe'onim ed. Harkavy, §386, p. 200; thence in 'Otzar haGe'onim IX pp. 19–20). See the thorough study by Y. G. Weiss, Middoth uMishkaloth shel Torah (Jerusalem 1985), who concludes (p. 381) that the "gold dinar of the Arabs" is the most stable, reliable monetary unit to be found in our Torah literature, and is to be evaluated at a weight of four and a quarter grams. Taking the p'rutah as one one hundred and ninety-second part of it, we get a value of about one forty-fifth part of a gram. This is the determination of weight; however, all monetary value in the Torah's laws, beginning with the shekel, is reckoned in silver (see Exodus 21:32, Leviticus 5:15, 27:3, 6, 16, Numbers 18:16). Early sources equally evaluate the p'rutah as half the weight of a kernel of barley (ge'onim cited in Rashba, Responsa, I §1011, and in R. 'Asher to TB B'choroth viii §9; R. Ḥanan'él to TB Sh'vu'oth 38b, 39b, 40a; R. Isaac 'Alfasi, loc. cit.; Rambam, Commentary to Mishnah, Kiddushin

altar or things consecrated toward maintaining the Temple in repair.[3] Whoever benefits by the worth of a *p'rutah*[4] from things consecrated to the Eternal Lord, commits a breach of holiness.[5] However, with those things that were permitted to be eaten among the offerings, such as the flesh of the *ḥattath* (sin-offering) and the *'asham* (guilt-offering) after the sprinkling of their blood, or the two loaves (§ 307) after the sprinkling of the blood of the two lambs, there is no breach of holiness.[6] Even if an outsider (non-*kohen*) ate of these or of similar things, since they were permitted to some people[7] to derive benefit from them, whoever benefits from them commits no breach of holiness.[6] And even if they became disqualified and forbidden to be eaten, because they had a period of permissibility there is no penalty for breach of holiness with them.[8]

Whoever commits a breach of holiness deliberately is to receive whiplashes and is to restore in full what he took away from the consecrated entity.[9] The admonition against a breach of holiness is derived from the verse, *You may not eat within your gates...your votive offerings* (Deuteronomy 12:17). By the Oral Tradition we learned that this is an injunction against eating the flesh of an *'olah*, as we stated above (§ 447), since it is entirely for the Lord. And the same law holds for any other consecrated entity which is for the Lord alone, whether consecrated for the altar or for the fund for Temple repairs: If one benefits from them to the extent of a *prutah*'s worth, he is to receive whiplashes.[10]

If someone commits a breach of holiness inadvertently, he is to pay for as much as he benefited, with the addition of a fifth, and is to bring a ram for two *s'la'im*,[11] which he offers up as an *'asham*, and he thus finds atonement. This is called *'asham me'iloth* (a guilt-offering for

i 1, and MT *hilchoth sh'kalim* i 3); and contemporary rabbinic authorities reckon this as a fortieth of a gram of silver.

5. TB Me'ilah 18a.

6. *Ibid.* 2a (although they are forbidden to an ordinary Israelite by other prohibitions of the Torah).

7. I.e. the *kohanim*.

8. Although (as remarked in note 6) other prohibitions still make them impermissible. *Ibid.* and MT *hilchoth me'ilah* 1–2.

9. TB Sanhedrin 83a; MT *ibid.* 3.

10. MT *ibid.*

⟨483⟩ 11. See § 355, note 1. In Leviticus 5:15 we read, *according to the valuation in silver*

מִקָּדְשֵׁי יי וְהֵבִיא אֶת אֲשָׁמוֹ לַיי״ וְגוֹמֵר ״וְאֵת אֲשֶׁר חָטָא מִן הַקֹּדֶשׁ יְשַׁלֵּם וְאֶת
חֲמִישִׁתוֹ יוֹסֵף עָלָיו״; וְשִׁלּוּם הַקֶּרֶן עִם תּוֹסֶפֶת חֹמֶשׁ וַהֲבָאַת הַקָּרְבָּן מִצְוַת עֲשֵׂה.
תַּשְׁלוּם הַקֶּרֶן וַהֲבָאַת הָאָשָׁם מְעַכְּבִין אֶת הַכַּפָּרָה, וְאֵין הַחֹמֶשׁ מְעַכֵּב, שֶׁנֶּאֱמַר
״בְּאֵיל הָאָשָׁם וְנִסְלַח לוֹ״: אַיִל וְאָשָׁם מְעַכְּבִין וְאֵין הַחֹמֶשׁ מְעַכֵּב.

הֵבִיא מְעִילָתוֹ עַד שֶׁלֹּא הֵבִיא אֲשָׁמוֹ, לֹא יָצָא. נִסְתַּפֵּק לוֹ אִם מָעַל אִם לֹא
מָעַל, פָּטוּר מִן הַתַּשְׁלוּמִין וּמִן הַקָּרְבָּן. וְהַחֹמֶשׁ הֲרֵי הוּא כִּתְחִלַּת הַהֶקְדֵּשׁ, וְאִם
נֶהֱנָה בּוֹ מוֹסִיף חֹמֶשׁ עַל חֹמֶשׁ; וּכְבָר בֵּאַרְנוּ כַּמָּה פְּעָמִים שֶׁהַחֹמֶשׁ אֶחָד
מֵאַרְבָּעָה עַל הַקֶּרֶן, עַד שֶׁיִּהְיֶה הוּא וְחֻמְשׁוֹ חֲמִשָׁה.

וְיֵשׁ דְּבָרִים שֶׁאֵין חַיָּבִין עֲלֵיהֶן מְעִילָה מִדִּבְרֵי תוֹרָה אֲבָל אָסוּר לֵהָנוֹת בָּהֶן
מִדִּבְרֵי סוֹפְרִים, וְהַנֶּהֱנֶה מֵהֶם מְשַׁלֵּם קֶרֶן לְבַד וְאֵינוֹ מוֹסִיף חֹמֶשׁ, וְאֵינוֹ מֵבִיא
אָשָׁם, כְּמוֹ שֶׁמְּבֹאָר בְּמַסֶּכֶת מְעִילָה.

וְכָל קָדְשֵׁי מִזְבֵּחַ, בֵּין קָדְשֵׁי קָדָשִׁים בֵּין קָדָשִׁים קַלִּים, אֲסוּרִין בְּגִזָּה וַעֲבוֹדָה,
שֶׁנֶּאֱמַר ״לֹא תַעֲבֹד בִּבְכֹר שׁוֹרֶךָ וְלֹא תָגֹז בְּכוֹר צֹאנֶךָ״, וְהוּא הַדִּין לִשְׁאָר
קָדָשִׁים; וְהַגּוֹזֵז אֶת הַשּׁוֹר אוֹ הָעוֹבֵד בּוֹ לוֹקֶה מִן הַתּוֹרָה, וְתוֹלֵשׁ אֵינוֹ כְּגוֹזֵז.
וְכָתַב הָרַב רַבֵּנוּ מֹשֶׁה בֶּן מַיְמוֹן זִכְרוֹנוֹ לִבְרָכָה: יֵרָאֶה לִי שֶׁאֵינוֹ לוֹקֶה עַד שֶׁיִּגְזֹז
כְּדֵי רֹחַב הַסִּיט כָּפוּל; לֹא יִהְיֶה זֶה חָמוּר מִשַּׁבָּת.

סְפֵק קָדָשִׁים, כְּגוֹן בְּהֵמָה שֶׁהִיא סְפֵק בְּכוֹר וְכַיּוֹצֵא בָהּ, הֲרֵי הֵן אֲסוּרִין בְּגִזָּה

---

by *shekels*; and the minimum possible number of "shekels" (plural, = s'la'im) is two (Sifra on the verse).

12. The Hebrew reads "of the 'asham," which is generally translated "of the guilt-offering," but this is evidently how the term is understood here.

13. TB Bava Kamma 110a, 111a; MT *hilchoth me'ilah* i 3–4.

14. TB Bava Kamma 111a.

15. TB K'rithoth 22a.

16. TB Bava M'tzi'a 54b.

17. *Ibid.* 54a; MT *ibid.* 5.

18. MT *ibid.* 6; see TB Me'ilah 10b–13b.

19. TB B'choroth 25a; MT *ibid.* 7.

20. MT *ibid.*

21. TB Shabbath 105b teaches that if at least this amount of wool is washed white, hackled, dyed or spun on the Sabbath, it is a violation of the Sabbath.

a breach of holiness). For it is stated, *and he sins unwittingly in any of the holy things of the Lord, then he shall bring his guilt-offering to the Lord... And he shall make restitution for what he has done amiss in the holy thing, and shall add its fifth part to it* (Leviticus 5:15–16). Paying the principal with the addition of the fifth, and bringing the offering, are a positive precept. The payment of the principal and the bringing of the *'asham* prevent atonement [if not done], but the [additional] fifth does not so prevent it [if it is unpaid]; for it is stated, *with the ram of the guilt-payment,*[12] *and it shall be forgiven him* (ibid. 16): the ram and the guilt-payment can prevent it, but the fifth does not.[13]

If a person brought his *'asham* for the breach before he brought his guilt-payment, he would not acquit himself [of the requirement for atonement].[14] If one is in doubt if he did or did not commit a breach of holiness, he is free of the duty of the restitution and the offering.[15] The fifth is as something itself originally consecrated; hence if a person benefits from it, he is to add a fifth part to the fifth.[16] We have previously explained several times that the fifth part is [actually] one fourth of the principal, so that it and the fifth constitute five parts.[17]

Now, there are things over which there is no guilt for breach of holiness by the law of the Torah, yet it is forbidden to derive benefit from them, by the decree of the Scribes [the Sages]. If someone has benefit from them, he is to pay the principal alone, and does not add on a fifth; nor does he bring an *'asham* (guilt-offering) — as explained in the Talmud tractate *Me'ilah* (10b).[18]

As for all animals consecrated for the altar, whether for most-holy offerings or for offerings of lesser holiness, it is forbidden to shear them or work with them: for it is stated, *you shall do no work with the firstling of your ox, nor shear the firstling of your flock* (Deuteronomy 15:19), and the law is the same for other consecrated animals.[2] If someone shears an ox or works with it, he is to be given lashes (a whipping) by the law of the Torah. Plucking, however, is not equivalent to shearing.[19] And R. Moses b. Maimon of blessed memory wrote:[20] It seems to me that one should not receive whiplashes until he shears enough [wool] for a length of thread that is twice the spread between thumb and forefinger; this should not be more stringent than in regard to the Sabbath.[21]

If there is a doubt whether certain animals are consecrated for offerings — for instance, if there is a doubt whether an animal is a firstling, and so forth — it is forbidden to shear them or work with

וּבַעֲבוֹדָה, וְהַגּוֹזֵז אוֹ הָעוֹבֵד בָּהֶן אֵינוֹ לוֹקֶה. בְּהֶמַת הַקֹּדֶשׁ שֶׁנָּפַל בָּהּ מוּם וְנִפְדֵּת כְּמוֹ שֶׁבֵּאַרְנוּ, אֵינָהּ מֻתֶּרֶת בְּגִזָּה וַעֲבוֹדָה, וַהֲרֵי הִיא בְּאִסּוּרָהּ עַד שֶׁתִּשָּׁחֵט; נִשְׁחֲטָה אַחַר פְּדִיּוֹנָהּ, הֻתְּרָה בַּאֲכִילָה.

בַּמֶּה דְּבָרִים אֲמוּרִים, בְּשֶׁקָּדַם הֶקְדֵּשָׁן אֶת מוּמָן אוֹ קָדַם מוּם עוֹבֵר לְהֶקְדֵּשָׁן; אֲבָל הַמַּקְדִּישׁ בַּעֲלַת מוּם קָבוּעַ לַמִּקְדָּשׁ, אֵינָהּ אֲסוּרָה בְּגִזָּה וַעֲבוֹדָה אֶלָּא מִדִּבְרֵיהֶם; נִפְדֵּת, הֲרֵי הִיא כְחֻלִּין לְכָל דָּבָר וְתֵצֵא לְחֻלִּין לְהִגָּזֵז וּלְהֵעָבֵד — חוּץ מִן הַבְּכוֹר וְהַמַּעֲשֵׂר, שֶׁהֶקְדֵּשָׁהּ חָלָה עַל גּוּפָן אַף־עַל־פִּי שֶׁהֵן בַּעֲלֵי מוּמִין קְבוּעִין מִתְּחִלָּה, וְאֵינָן יוֹצְאִין לְחֻלִּין לְגַזֵּז וְלַעֲבֹד לְעוֹלָם.

וְאָסוּר לְהַרְבִּיעַ בִּבְכוֹר אוֹ בִּפְסוּלֵי הַמֻּקְדָּשִׁין; וּמֻתָּר לִתְלֹשׁ אֶת הַשֵּׂעָר לְכַתְּחִלָּה מִן הַקֳּדָשִׁים כְּדֵי לְהַרְאוֹת הַמּוּם לְמֻמְחֶה, וְאוֹתוֹ הַשֵּׂעָר שֶׁתָּלַשׁ אוֹ שֶׁנִּשְׁאַר מִן הַבְּהֵמָה אוֹ מִן הַבְּכוֹר אוֹ מִן הַמַּעֲשֵׂר, הֲרֵי זֶה אָסוּר בַּהֲנָאָה אֲפִלּוּ לְאַחַר שֶׁיִּשָּׁחֲטוּ מִפְּנֵי מוּמָן, גְּזֵרָה שֶׁמָּא יַשְׁהֶא אוֹתָן הוֹאִיל וְאֵינָן בְּנֵי כַפָּרָה; אֲבָל צֶמֶר הַנּוֹשֵׁר מִן הַחַטָּאת וְהָאָשָׁם מֻתָּר בַּהֲנָאָה לְאַחַר שְׁחִיטָתָן מִפְּנֵי מוּמָן: הוֹאִיל וּלְכַפָּרָה הֵן בָּאִין אֵינוֹ מַשְׁהֵא אוֹתָן; וְאִם נִתְלַשׁ מִן הָעוֹלָה, הֲרֵי זֶה סָפֵק.

וְכָל שֶׁנִּתְלַשׁ מִן הַקֳּדָשִׁים אַחַר שֶׁנָּפַל בָּהֶן מוּם, הֲרֵי זֶה מֻתָּר בַּהֲנָאָה מִכֵּינָן שֶׁלֹּא תָלַשׁ בְּיָדוֹ, חוּץ מִן הַבְּכוֹר, שֶׁאַף הַנִּתְלָשׁ מִמֶּנּוּ אַחַר שֶׁנָּפַל בּוֹ מוּם אָסוּר בַּהֲנָאָה; הַשּׁוֹחֵט בְּכוֹר אוֹ שְׁאָר הַמֻּקְדָּשִׁין, תּוֹלֵשׁ הַשֵּׂעָר מִכַּאן וּמִכַּאן לַעֲשׂוֹת מָקוֹם לַסַּכִּין, וּבִלְבַד שֶׁלֹּא יְזִיזֶנּוּ מִמְּקוֹמוֹ.

קָדְשֵׁי בֶדֶק הַבַּיִת, אֲפִלּוּ בְּגִזָּה וַעֲבוֹדָה אֲסוּרִין מִדִּבְרֵי סוֹפְרִים, אֲבָל מִן

22. TB N'darim 19a.
23. Since it is a matter of doubt.
24. TB B'choroth 14a; MT *hilchoth me'ilah* 8–9.
25. I.e. for the altar, to be brought as an offering; very possibly למקדש is an early scribal error for למזבח ("for the altar"), the reading of MT *hilchoth me'ilah* i 9; for if an animal is consecrated for the Temple treasury (as a source of money for repairs), even if it has no defect only a Rabbinic decree forbids working with it or shearing its wool (see note 3).
26. Since human assistance in mounting is required, and this is regarded as a form of doing work with the animal; TB Mo'ed Katan 12a (and Rashi); MT *ibid.* 9.
27. TB B'choroth 24b, 26a.
28. I.e. to let the wool grow thick, whereupon the wool may inadvertently be shorn, or the animal may be used for work (Rashi, TB B'choroth 25b top, s.v. *va-hachamim 'os'rin*).
29. TB B'choroth 25a, 26a.
30. *Ibid.* 26a; MT *hilchoth me'ilah* i 10.
31. MT *ibid.*
32. I.e. he should leave it attached to (tangled with) the remaining wool on

them;²² but if someone shears them or works with them, he is not given whiplashes.²³ If a consecrated animal acquired a blemishing defect and was redeemed, as we explained (§ 441), it is not permitted for shearing or work, and it thus remains under its ban until it is ritually slain. If it is ritually slain after its redemption, it becomes permissible to be eaten.²⁴

Now, where does this rule hold?—where their consecration preceded their blemishing defect, or where a temporary blemish occurred before their hallowing. But if someone consecrates an animal with a permanent defect for the Sanctuary,²⁵ it becomes forbidden for shearing or work only by the decree of the Sages. If it is redeemed, it becomes as a non-holy animal in every respect, and goes out for non-holy use, for shearing and work—except for a firstling and an animal of the tithe: because sanctity takes effect on their bodies even if they were permanently blemished from the start; and they never go out to non-holy use, for shearing or work.²⁴

It is forbidden to couple a firstling or a disqualified consecrated animal with a mate.²⁶ It is permissible initially (from the start) to pluck the hair from a consecrated animal in order to show a blemishing defect to an expert.²⁷ Yet from that hair which was plucked, or that remains on the animal, or on a firstling or a tithe animal, it is forbidden to have any benefit, even after they are ritually slain on account of their defect: it is a protective decree for fear that they might be kept back, postponed,²⁸ since they do not bring atonement. However, from any wool that falls loose from a *ḥattath* or an *'asham*, it is permitted to benefit after they are ritually slain on account of a blemishing defect of theirs. Since they are to bring atonement, they would not be kept back.²⁹ If hair was plucked from an *'olah* (a burnt-offering), the decision is doubtful.³⁰

Whatever [wool] becomes loosened from consecrated animals after they acquire a blemishing defect, it is permitted to benefit from it, since it was not plucked loose by hand—except with a firstling: even of what becomes torn loose from it after it has acquired a defect, benefit is forbidden.³¹ When someone is to ritually slay a firstling or any other consecrated animal he should pluck out the hair on either side to make room for the knife; only, he should not remove it [the hair] from its place.³²

As to animals consecrated for the fund for Temple repairs, it is
forbidden even to shear them or work with them, by the decree of the

הַתּוֹרָה אֵינָן אֲסוּרִין; לְפִיכָךְ הַגּוֹזֵז אוֹתָן אוֹ הָעוֹבֵד בָּהֶן אֵינוֹ לוֹקֶה, אֲבָל מַכִּין
אוֹתוֹ מַכַּת מַרְדּוּת; הַמַּקְדִּישׁ עֵבֶר לַמִּזְבֵּחַ, אִמּוֹ אֲסוּרָה בַּעֲבוֹדָה מִדִּבְרֵי סוֹפְרִים,
אֲבָל מִן הַתּוֹרָה אֵינָהּ אֲסוּרָה; אֲבָל לְגָזוֹ אוֹתָהּ מֻתָּר: מִפְּנֵי שֶׁעֲבוֹדָתָהּ מַכְחֶשֶׁת
אֶת הָעֻבָּר גָּזְרוּ בָהּ, וַהֲרֵי הִיא מֻתֶּרֶת בְּגִזָּה לְפִי שֶׁאֵין בָּהּ הֶפְסֵד לַוָּלָד. הִקְדִּישׁ
אֵבֶר אֶחָד מִן הַבְּהֵמָה, בֵּין לְבֶדֶק הַבַּיִת בֵּין לַמִּזְבֵּחַ, הֲרֵי הַדָּבָר סָפֵק אִם אֲסוּרָה
כֻּלָּהּ בְּגִזָּה וַעֲבוֹדָה אוֹ אֵינָהּ אֲסוּרָה; לְפִיכָךְ אֵין לוֹקִין עָלֶיהָ; וְיֶתֶר פְּרָטֶיהָ,
בְּמַסֶּכֶת בְּכוֹרוֹת.

וְנוֹהֵג אִסּוּר זֶה בְּכָל זְמַן וּבְכָל מָקוֹם, בִּזְכָרִים וּנְקֵבוֹת, שֶׁאַף-עַל-פִּי שֶׁאָמְרוּ
זִכְרוֹנָם לִבְרָכָה שֶׁאֵין מַקְדִּישִׁין בְּהֵמָה לַקָּרְבָּן וְלֹא לְבֶדֶק הַבַּיִת בַּזְּמַן הַזֶּה, כְּמוֹ
שֶׁכָּתַבְתִּי הַרְבֵּה פְּעָמִים, מִכָּל-מָקוֹם מִי שֶׁהִקְדִּישׁ, הֶקְדֵּשׁוֹ הֶקְדֵּשׁ. וְעוֹבֵר עַל זֶה
וְעָבַד בְּבֶהֱמַת קָדָשִׁים כָּעִנְיָן שֶׁאָמַרְנוּ, חַיָּב מַלְקוֹת.

[שֶׁלֹּא לִגְזֹז אֶת הַקֳּדָשִׁים]

תפד שֶׁלֹּא נָגֹז הַצֶּמֶר מִבֶּהֱמַת הַקֳּדָשִׁים, וְעַל זֶה נֶאֱמַר "וְלֹא תָגֹז בְּכוֹר
צֹאנֶךָ", וְכָל שְׁאָר הַקֳּדָשִׁים נִלְמָדִים מִן הַבְּכוֹר בְּאִסּוּר זֶה. וְכָל עִנְיַן הַגִּזָּה
כְּאִסּוּר הָעֲבוֹדָה, אֵין רָאוּי לְהַאֲרִיךְ בּוֹ עוֹד. הִנֵּה כָּתַבְתִּי קְצָת דִּינֵי הַגִּזָּה לְמַעְלָה
עִם דִּינֵי הָעֲבוֹדָה.

[שֶׁלֹּא לֶאֱכֹל חָמֵץ אַחַר חֲצוֹת]

תפה שֶׁלֹּא נֹאכַל חָמֵץ אַחַר חֲצוֹת בְּיוֹם אַרְבָּעָה-עָשָׂר בְּנִיסָן, וְעַל זֶה נֶאֱמַר
"לֹא תֹאכַל עָלָיו חָמֵץ". כָּתַב הָרַב רַבֵּנוּ מֹשֶׁה בֶּן מַיְמוֹן זִכְרוֹנוֹ לִבְרָכָה: מִלַּת

either side, so that it cannot be mistakenly thought that some kind of shearing has
been done on an animal consecrated for an offering (Rashi, s.v. *v'tolésh*): Mishnah,
B'choroth iii 3 (TB 24b); MT *ibid.* 11.

33. *Ibid.* 25a; MT *ibid.* 12 (See §24, note 14.)

34. TB T'murah 11b; MT *ibid.* 13.

35. TB Yoma 66a.

§485   1. Literal translation; "upon it" (the usual translation is "with it") is here
understood in the sense of "upon its (the Passover sacrifice's) being offered up on
the altar''; cf. Ibn 'Ezra: "no leavened food is to be found at the time of the ritual
slaying of the Passover offering."

Scribes [the Sages]; but by the law of the Torah it is not prohibited. Therefore, if someone shears them or works with them, he does not receive the standard whipping of lashes, but he is to be smitten with lashes of disobedience.[33] If someone consecrates an embryo to the altar, it is forbidden to work with its dam (mother) by decree of the Sages; but by the Torah's law it is not forbidden. To shear it, however, is permissible: Because its work would enfeeble the embryo, they decreed it forbidden; hence shearing it is permissible, since that has no adverse effect on the embryo.[34] If a person consecrated one organ or limb of an animal, either to the fund for Temple repairs or to the altar, it is a matter of doubt whether all of it is forbidden for shearing or work, or is not forbidden.[34] Therefore whiplashes are not suffered for it. More of its details are in the Talmud tractate *B'choroth*.

This prohibition applies in every time and place, for both man and woman. For although the Sages of blessed memory ruled[35] that no animal is to be consecrated at the present time for an offering or for the fund for Temple repairs, as I have written many times, nevertheless, if someone made a consecration, the sanctity takes effect. If a person violated this and worked with a consecrated animal in the circumstances we mentioned, he would deserve a flogging of whiplashes.

[NOT TO SHEAR ANIMALS CONSECRATED
FOR OFFERINGS]

484 that we should not shear the wool from consecrated sheep, as it is stated about this, *nor shall you shear the firstling of your flock* (Deuteronomy 15:19), and about all other consecrated animals we learn from the firstling in regard to this prohibition. The entire subject-matter of the ban on cutting the wool is like that of the ban on work (§ 483); there is no need to continue further at length. I have written, too, some laws about shearing, above, with the laws concerning work.

[NOT TO EAT ḤAMÉTZ AFTER NOON ON
THE DAY BEFORE PASSOVER]

485 that we shall not eat *ḥamétz* (leavened food) after midday on the fourteenth day of Nissan, as it is stated about this, *You shall eat no leavened food upon it*[1] (Deuteronomy 16:3). R. Moses b. Maimon of

"עָלָיו" שָׁבָה עַל כֶּבֶשׂ הַפֶּסַח, שֶׁהַחוֹבָה בִּזְבִיחָתוֹ בֵּין הָעַרְבַּיִם בְּיוֹם אַרְבָּעָה־
עָשָׂר, וְאָמְרוּ: מֵעֵת שֶׁיַּגִּיעַ זְמַן זְבִיחָתוֹ לֹא תֹאכַל חָמֵץ; וּבִפְסָחִים אָמְרוּ זִכְרוֹנָם
לִבְרָכָה: מִנַּיִן לְאוֹכֵל חָמֵץ מִשֵּׁשׁ שָׁעוֹת וּלְמַעְלָה שֶׁהוּא בְלֹא־תַעֲשֶׂה—שֶׁנֶּאֱמַר
"לֹא תֹאכַל עָלָיו חָמֵץ"; וְשָׁם נֶאֱמַר: לְכוּלֵּי עָלְמָא מִיחַת חָמֵץ מִשֵּׁשׁ שָׁעוֹת
וּלְמַעְלָה דְּאוֹרַיְתָא; כָּךְ מָצָאנוּ לְשׁוֹן כָּל הַנֻּסְחָאוֹת הַמְדֻיָּקוֹת שֶׁנִּקְרְאוּ עַל זִקְנֵי
הַתַּלְמוּד; וְשָׁם נֶאֱמַר בְּטַעַם אִסּוּר הֶחָמֵץ בְּשָׁעָה שִׁשִּׁית: עָבְדוּ רַבָּנָן הַרְחָקָה כִּי
הֵיכִי דְּלָא לִגַּע בְּאִסּוּרָא דְּאוֹרַיְתָא. וּמִי שֶׁיַּעֲבֹר וְיֹאכַל חָמֵץ אַחַר חֲצוֹת לוֹקֶה.
עַד כָּאן.

מִשָּׁרְשֵׁי הַמִּצְוָה, לְפִי שֶׁעִנְיַן אִסּוּר חָמֵץ בְּפֶסַח הוּא אִסּוּר חָמוּר בְּיוֹתֵר, מִצַּד
שֶׁעִנְיָן זֶה יְסוֹד גָּדוֹל בְּדָתֵנוּ: כִּי יְצִיאַת מִצְרַיִם הוּא אוֹת וּמוֹפֵת מְכֻרָח בְּחִדּוּשׁ
הָעוֹלָם, שֶׁהוּא הָעַמּוּד הַגָּדוֹל שֶׁאוּלְמֵי הַתּוֹרָה נִסְמָכִים בּוֹ, כְּמוֹ שֶׁכָּתַבְתִּי כַּמָּה
פְעָמִים; וְעַל־כֵּן כָּל מִצְוָה שֶׁהִיא לְזֵכֶר יְצִיאַת מִצְרַיִם חֲמוּרָה עָלֵינוּ וַחֲבִיבָה
הַרְבֵּה. עַל־כֵּן, מִצַּד הֶחָמֵר הַגָּדוֹל שֶׁבָּהּ, תַּזְהִירֵנוּ הַתּוֹרָה לְהַתְחִיל בָּהּ שֵׁשׁ שָׁעוֹת
קֹדֶם זְמַן הַגִּיעַ זְמַן הַנּוֹעֵד לְאוֹתוֹ הַנֵּס, שֶׁהוּא הַתְחָלַת יוֹם חֲמִשָּׁה־עָשָׂר. וְכָל זֶה לְמַעַן
נִתֵּן אֶל לִבֵּנוּ חֹמֶר הַמִּצְוָה וְגֹדֶל עִנְיָנָהּ, בִּרְאוֹתֵנוּ כִּי הַתּוֹרָה תַּעֲשֶׂה לָנוּ גֶּדֶר סָבִיב
לָהּ.

מִדִּינֵי הַמִּצְוָה, מַה שֶּׁאָמְרוּ זִכְרוֹנָם לִבְרָכָה שֶׁאוֹכְלִין חָמֵץ כָּל אַרְבַּע שָׁעוֹת
מִיּוֹם זֶה, וְתוֹלִין כָּל חָמֵשׁ—כְּלוֹמַר לֹא אוֹכְלִין, גְּזֵרָה מִשּׁוּם יוֹם הַמְעֻנָּן, וְלֹא
שׂוֹרְפִין, אֶלָּא נֶהֱנִין לְהַאֲכִילוֹ לְכָל בְּרִיָּה אוֹ לְמָכְרוֹ לְכָל אָדָם—וְשׂוֹרְפִין אוֹתוֹ
בִּתְחִלַּת שָׁעָה שִׁשִּׁית; וְזוֹ הִיא תַּקָּנַת חֲכָמִים בַּמִּצְוָה, כְּדֵי לְהַרְחִיק אָדָם מִן

<hr/>

2. ShM negative precept §199; see §282, note 2, which applies here. (In Ramban's citation *ad loc.* —ed. Chavel, pp. 340–41—there are points of similarity to our author's version.)

3. See §5, note 1.

4. Which, in Jewish reckoning, begins at nightfall after the fourteenth day.

5. TB P'saḥim 11b.

6. (More literally, on account of a cloudy day.) When the time was ascertained by the sun, on a cloudy day the end of the fifth hour would be uncertain, and if *ḥamétz* were not prohibited in that hour as a general rule, the Torah's law might be transgressed; *ibid.* 12b.

blessed memory wrote:[2] The word *'alav* ("upon it") refers to the lamb of the Passover offering, for which the duty of its ritual slaying is in effect in the afternoon[3] of the fourteenth day. It is thus stated that from the time the period for its ritual slaying arrives, you are not to eat *hamétz*. In the tractate *P'sahim* (4b) the Sages of blessed memory taught: How do we know that if a person eats *hamétz* from six hours on, he transgresses a negative precept?—because it is stated, *You shall eat no leavened food upon it*. It was stated there too: According to all, however, *hamétz* from six hours onward is forbidden by the law of the Torah. So we find the wording in all the accurate texts that were read by the elder scholars of the Talmud. It was then stated there, as a reason for the prohibition on *hamétz* [even] during the sixth hour: The Sages enacted an extra measure of safe distance, so that a prohibition by the Torah should not be touched. Hence, if someone transgresses and eats *hamétz* after midday, he should receive a whipping (lashes). Thus far [his words].

At the root of the precept lies the reason that the matter of *hamétz* during Passover is under an extremely severe prohibition, in view of the fact that this subject is a great fundamental in our religion. For the exodus from Egypt is an indisputable sign and wonder demonstrating the creation of the world as a new entity without pre-existence, which is the mighty pillar that supports the halls of the Torah—as I have written many times. Therefore, any precept that is in commemoration of the exodus from Egypt is very serious for us, and is greatly cherished. Hence, in view of the great seriousness in it, the Torah adjures us to begin six hours before the time comes that was set for that miracle, which is the beginning of the fifteenth day.[4] All this is in order that we may ponder in our heart the seriousness of the precept and the importance of its theme, as we see that the Torah has made for us a protective fence about it.

Among the laws of the precept, there is what the Sages of blessed memory taught:[5] that *hamétz* may be eaten all [the first] four hours of this day, and the entire fifth hangs in abeyance. In other words, it is not to be eaten [then] as a protective measure taking into account a cloudy day,[6] nor is it to be burned; rather, one may derive benefit from it by giving it to any creature to eat or by selling it to any man. And it is burned up at the beginning of the sixth hour. This is the amendment of the Sages in the precept, in order to keep a man far from sin, so that he should not come to grief by eating it at the

הָעֲבֵרָה, שֶׁלֹּא יִכָּשֵׁל לְאָכְלוֹ בִּתְחִלַּת שָׁעָה שְׁבִיעִית, שֶׁהוּא אָסוּר מִן הַתּוֹרָה, כְּמוֹ שֶׁאָמַרְנוּ.

וּכְמוֹ שֶׁדָּרְשׁוּ זִכְרוֹנָם לִבְרָכָה גַּם־כֵּן מִכָּתוּב אַחֵר—שֶׁאָמְרוּ שָׁם בִּפְסָחִים: כָּתִיב "שִׁבְעַת יָמִים שְׂאֹר לֹא יִמָּצֵא בְּבָתֵּיכֶם" וּכְתִיב "אַךְ בַּיּוֹם הָרִאשׁוֹן תַּשְׁבִּיתוּ שְּׂאֹר מִבָּתֵּיכֶם"; הָא כֵּיצַד—לְרַבּוֹת אַרְבָּעָה־עָשָׂר לַבִּעוּר, וְיִהְיֶה פֵּרוּשׁ "רִאשׁוֹן" כְּמוֹ "הֲרִאשׁוֹן אָדָם תִּוָּלֵד", שֶׁפֵּרוּשׁוֹ: קֹדֶם. וּמִמַּה שֶׁחִיֵּב הַכָּתוּב לְהַשְׁבִּיתוֹ בְּאוֹתוֹ יוֹם, יָדַעְנוּ שֶׁמִּקְצָת הַיּוֹם הוּא מֻתָּר בַּהֶכְרֵחַ, שֶׁאִי־אֶפְשָׁר לְכַוֵּן רֶגַע הָרִאשׁוֹן שֶׁל יוֹם וּלְהַשְׁבִּיתוֹ בוֹ; וְאַחַר שֶׁכֵּן, שֶׁמִּקְצָתוֹ שֶׁל יוֹם מֻתָּר, וְלֹא בֵּאֵר לָנוּ הַכָּתוּב אֵי זֶה חֵלֶק מִמֶּנּוּ הוּא שֶׁמֻּתָּר, נְחַלְּקֵהוּ אֲנַחְנוּ בְּשָׁוֶה מִן הַסְּבָרָה הָאֲמִתִּית, שֶׁאִם תְּחַלְּקֵהוּ בְּעִנְיָן אַחֵר, לֹא יִהְיֶה שֹׁרֶשׁ לַדָּבָר כְּלָל; וְזֶהוּ אָמְרָם שָׁם: "אַךְ" חֵלֶק. וְהַמְפָרְשִׁים כִּי מִלַּת "אַךְ" בְּאַלְפָא בֵּיתָא "חֵץ", לֹא יָבִינוּ דִּבְרֵי חֲכָמִים. וְיֶתֶר פְּרָטֵי הַמִּצְוָה, בְּמַסֶּכֶת פְּסָחִים פֶּרֶק רִאשׁוֹן.

וְנוֹהֶגֶת בִּזְכָרִים וּנְקֵבוֹת, בְּכָל מָקוֹם וּבְכָל זְמַן, וַאֲפִלּוּ בַּזְּמַן הַזֶּה שֶׁאֵין לָנוּ קָרְבַּן פֶּסַח. וְעוֹבֵר עַל זֶה וְאָכַל כְּזַיִת חָמֵץ אַחַר חֲצוֹת, חַיָּב מַלְקוֹת לְדַעַת הָרַב רַבֵּנוּ מֹשֶׁה בֶּן מַיְמוֹן זִכְרוֹנוֹ לִבְרָכָה, כִּי הוּא סוֹבֵר שֶׁהֲלָכָה כְּרַבִּי יְהוּדָה, דְּאָמַר דְּחָמֵץ לִפְנֵי זְמַנּוֹ, אֶרְצֶה לוֹמַר בְּיוֹם אַרְבָּעָה־עָשָׂר בְּנִיסָן מֵחֲצוֹת הַיּוֹם וּלְמַעְלָה, עוֹבֵר עָלָיו הָאוֹכְלוֹ בְּלָאו זֶה שֶׁזְּכַרְנוּ.

אֲבָל הָרַב רַבֵּנוּ מֹשֶׁה בֶּן נַחְמָן זִכְרוֹנוֹ לִבְרָכָה חוֹלֵק עָלָיו, וּלְדַעְתּוֹ אֵין בָּזֶה לָאו, שֶׁהֲלָכָה כְּרַבִּי שִׁמְעוֹן, דְּפָלִיג עָלֵיהּ דְּרַבִּי יְהוּדָה וְאָמַר דְּבֵין לִפְנֵי זְמַנּוֹ בֵּין לְאַחַר זְמַנּוֹ, אֵינוֹ עוֹבֵר בְּלֹא כְלוּם; וְדָרִישׁ מִלְּתֵיהּ מִדִּכְתִיב "לֹא תֹאכַל עָלָיו

7. Thus R. Sa'adyah Ga'on renders the verse: Were you born before the first of humans? (*Job with R. Sa'adyah Ga'on's translation and commentary*, ed. Kafeḥ, Jerusalem 1973, p. 98).

8. TB P'saḥim 5a; so also Mechilta on the verse.

9. The cipher arranges 21 of the 22 characters in the Hebrew alphabet (omitting the last) in three groups, with seven letters in each. The first letter of the first group then becomes interchangeable with that of the second and that of the third group; and so their respective second letters, the third letters, etc. Thus 'alef becomes interchangeable with ḥeth and samech; béth with teth and 'a-yin; etc. The word ḥétz is linked with ḥatzi, "half," perhaps because a well-aimed arrow would split something in half. This interpretation of 'ach is found in *Lekaḥ Tov* on the verse, and is given by Rashi (TB P'saḥim 5a, s.v. ḥalak) as what "some explain."

10. ShM negative precept § 199; MT *hilchoth ḥametz u-matzah* i 8.

11. TB P'saḥim 28b.

12. Ramban, commentary to ShM negative precept § 199.

beginning of the seventh hour, when it is forbidden by the Torah, as we stated.[5]

And so the Sages of blessed memory likewise interpreted from another verse; for they taught there in the tractate *P'sahim* (4b): It is written, *Seven days, no leaven shall be found in your houses* (Exodus 12:19), and it is written, *only, on the first* (ha-rishon) *day you shall put away leaven out of your houses* (ibid. 16). How can this be [reconciled? It is meant] to add the fourteenth day [of Nissan as the time] for clearing out [the *hamétz*]. The meaning of *ha-rishon* ("the first": *ibid.* 15) would then be as in the verse, *Were you* ha-rishon *(the first) man to be born?* (Job 15:7), where it has the sense of "earlier, before all."[7] Now, from the fact that Scripture made it a duty to remove it on that day, we know that some part of the day, it is necessarily permissible: because it is impossible to find precisely the first instant of the day and to remove it then. Since for some part of the day it is consequently permissible, and the Writ did not clarify for us in which portion of the day it is permitted, we divide it into equal parts, by true reasoning: For if you divide it in any other manner, there can be no root reason whatever for that. This is why it was stated there:[8] *'ach,* "only" (Exodus 12:15)—this divides it equally. However, those who explain that the word *'ach* ("only") really denotes *hétz* ("arrow") by an alphabetic cipher,[9] do not understand the words of the Sages. Further details of the precept are in the first chapter of the Talmud tractate *P'sahim.*

It applies to both man and woman, in every place and time—even at the present time, when we have no Passover offering. If a person transgresses this and eats an olive's amount of *hamétz* after midday, he is punishable by whiplashes, in the view of R. Moses b. Maimon of blessed memory.[10] For he holds that the definitive law follows R. Judah, who said[11] that regarding *hamétz* before its time [of forbiddance], which is to say, on the fourteenth day of Nissan, from midday onward, whoever eats it transgresses this negative precept that we mentioned.

However, R. Moses b. Nahman of blessed memory disagrees with him.[12] In his view, there is no negative precept on this, because the definitive law follows R. Shim'on, who differs with R. Judah, and rules that before and after its time, one transgresses nothing.[11] He derives his teaching from the verse, *You shall eat no leavened food upon it; seven days you shall eat unleavened food in conjunction with it*

חָמֵץ שִׁבְעַת יָמִים תֹּאכַל עָלָיו מַצּוֹת": בְּשָׁעָה שֶׁיֶּשְׁנוֹ הָאָדָם בְּקוּם אֱכֹל מַצָּה
יֶשְׁנוֹ בְּבַל תֹּאכַל חָמֵץ; בְּשָׁעָה שֶׁאֵינוֹ בְּקוּם אֱכֹל מַצָּה, דְּהַיְנוּ בֵּין לִפְנֵי זְמַן הַפֶּסַח
בֵּין לְאַחֲרָיו, אֵינוֹ בְּאַזְהָרַת בַּל תֹּאכַל חָמֵץ. וּלְדַעַת רַבִּי שִׁמְעוֹן מִלַּת "עָלָיו"
תָּשׁוּב עַל אֲכִילָתוֹ שֶׁל פֶּסַח שֶׁהָיָה נֶאֱכָל לָעֶרֶב; וְכֵן הוּא מְפֹרָשׁ בִּירוּשַׁלְמִי,
שֶׁלְּדִבְרֵי רַבִּי יְהוּדָה מִלַּת "עָלָיו" שָׁבָה עַל שְׁחִיטָתוֹ, וְלִדְבְרֵי רַבִּי שִׁמְעוֹן עַל
אֲכִילָתוֹ, שֶׁהָיָה נֶאֱכָל לָעֶרֶב.

וְזֶה שֶׁבָּא בַּגְּמָרָא "לְכֻלֵּי עָלְמָא חָמֵץ מִשֵּׁשׁ שָׁעוֹת וּלְמַעְלָה אָסוּר", וְכֵן מַה
שֶּׁאָמְרוּ "עֲבַדוּ רַבָּנָן הַרְחָקָה יְתֵרָא דְּלָא לִגַּע לִידֵי אִסּוּרָא דְאוֹרַיְתָא", כָּל זֶה
אֱמֶת, שֶׁיֵּשׁ אִסּוּר דְּאוֹרַיְתָא בַּהֲנָאָה מִן הֶחָמֵץ אַחַר חֲצוֹת; וְאָמְנָם הָאִסּוּר הוּא
דְּקָאִי עֲלֵיהּ בְּמִצְוַת הַשַּׁבָּתָה מִדְּאוֹרַיְתָא, מִשֵּׁשׁ שָׁעוֹת וּלְמַעְלָה, אֲבָל וַדַּאי אֵין בּוֹ
אִסּוּר לָאו כְּלָל, כְּרַבִּי שִׁמְעוֹן, דְּקַיְמָא לָן כְּוָתֵהּ.

וְכֵן הוּא מְפֹרָשׁ הָעִנְיָן שָׁם בַּגְּמָרָא: שֶׁאָמְרוּ, דְּכֻלֵּי עָלְמָא מֵיחַת חָמֵץ מִשֵּׁשׁ
שָׁעוֹת וּלְמַעְלָה דְּאוֹרַיְתָא, מְנָא לָן — אָמַר אַבַּיֵּי: תְּרֵי קְרָאֵי כְּתִיבֵי, וְכוּלֵּי, וְסִיּוּם
דְּבָרָיו שָׁם: הָא כֵּיצַד — לְרַבּוֹת אַרְבָּעָה-עָשָׂר לַבִּעוּר. הִנֵּה זֶה מְבֹאָר שֶׁאֵין
הָאִסּוּר בּוֹ אַחַר חֲצוֹת אַלָּבָא דְּהִלְכְתָא, זוּלָתִי מִצְוַת הַשַּׁבָּתָה.

הִנֵּה לְדַעְתּוֹ זִכְרוֹנוֹ לִבְרָכָה אֵין זֶה וְלֹא זֶה דְּלָא תֹאכַל בַּכְּלָל מִנְיַן הַמִּצְוֹת. הַט
אָזְנְךָ וּשְׁמַע דִּבְרֵי חֲכָמִים, אֵלּוּ וָאֵלּוּ דִּבְרֵי אֱלֹהִים (חַיִּים הֵם וְכֻלָּם גֵּר), וְדַע כִּי
יֵשׁ בַּתּוֹרָה שִׁבְעִים פָּנִים וְכֻלָּם נְכוֹחִים.

[שֶׁלֹּא לְהוֹתִיר מִבְּשַׂר קָרְבַּן הַחֲגִיגָה שֶׁנַּקְרִיב בְּיוֹם י"ד בְּנִיסָן
עַד יוֹם הַשְּׁלִישִׁי]

תפו שֶׁלֹּא לְהוֹתִיר דָּבָר מִבְּשַׂר חֲגִיגַת אַרְבָּעָה-עָשָׂר עַד יוֹם הַשְּׁלִישִׁי, וְהוּא

---

13. Since the two are linked in the verse.

14. TJ P'saḥim i 4 (which, however, has R. Me'ir instead of R. Shim'on).

15. TB P'saḥim 4b.

16. I.e. even though (following R. Shim'on's view) there is no negative precept on it.

17. The ban on benefiting from it is understood from the positive precept to have it cleared away and gone by then.

18. As in the third paragraph.

19. A Talmudic expression, used about the controversies between the Schools of Hillel and Shammai; TB 'Eruvin 13b, etc.

20. This metaphor would seem to be based on Proverbs 6:23, *For a mitzvah is a lamp, and Torah is light.* Since their difference of opinion is about this *mitzvah* (precept) their words are as a lamp, providing the light of Torah. But the words in parentheses are not in the oldest manuscripts, and thus are evidently a later addition.

(Deuteronomy 16:3): When a person is under the obligation to arise and eat *matzah* (unleavened bread) he is under the injunction not to eat *hamétz*; but when a person is not under the command to arise and eat *matzah*, which means both before the time of Passover and after it, he is not under the injunction to eat no *hamétz*.[13] In the view of R. Shim'on, the word *'alav* ("with it") refers to the eating of the Passover offering, which was done in the evening. And so it is explained in the Jerusalem Talmud,[14] that according to R. Judah, the word *'alav* refers to its ritual slaying, and according to R. Shim'on, to its eating, which took place in the evening.

As to the statement in the Talmud[15] that in the view of everyone, from six hours onward *hamétz* is forbidden, and so too the statement[15] that the Sages enacted an extra measure of distance so that one should not impinge on a prohibition of the Torah—that is all true,[16] since there *is* a prohibition by the law of the Torah on benefiting from *hamétz* after midday. However, the prohibition applies to it by virtue of the precept of clearing it away, by the law of the Torah—from six hours and onward;[17] but there is certainly no prohibition on it by any negative precept, according to R. Shim'on, whose view we accept as the standard ruling.

And so the subject is explained there in the Talmud.[15] For it was asked: According to everyone, in any event, how do we derive the law about *hamétz* from six hours onward by the ruling of the Torah? Said Abbaye: Two verses are written, etc.[18] And the conclusion of his words is: Then how [can they be reconciled?—It is meant] to add the fourteenth [of Nissan as the time] for clearing it away. It is thus made clear that the prohibition on it, according to the definitive ruling, is only by the precept of removing it, under the law of the Torah.

Hence in his [Ramban's] view (of blessed memory), this injunction, "You shall not eat," is not included in the listing of the *mitzvoth*. Incline your ear and hear the words of the wise scholars. Both these and those are words of (the living) God,[19] (and they are all a lamp).[20] Know too that there are seventy facets [of meaning] to the Torah, and all are right.

[NOT TO LEAVE OVER TILL THE THIRD DAY ANY
FLESH OF THE FESTIVAL OFFERING AT PASSOVER]

486 not to leave anything over until the third day from the flesh of the festival offering (*hagigah*) of the fourteenth [of Nissan], this

‏הַקָּרְבָּן הַבָּא עִם הַפֶּסַח לְהַגְדִּיל הַשִּׂמְחָה, אֶלָּא יֵאָכֵל כֻּלּוֹ בְּתוֹךְ שְׁנֵי הַיָּמִים, שֶׁהֵם‏
‏אַרְבָּעָה-עָשָׂר וַחֲמִשָּׁה-עָשָׂר; וְעַל זֶה נֶאֱמַר "וְלֹא יָלִין מִן הַבָּשָׂר אֲשֶׁר תִּזְבַּח‏
‏בָּעֶרֶב בַּיּוֹם הָרִאשׁוֹן לַבֹּקֶר", וּבָא הַפֵּרוּשׁ הַמְקֻבָּל עַל זֶה שֶׁבַּחֲגִיגָה הַבָּאָה עִם‏
‏הַפֶּסַח הַכָּתוּב מְדַבֵּר, שֶׁזְּמַן אֲכִילָתוֹ עַד שְׁנֵי יָמִים; וְעַל זֹאת הַחֲגִיגָה אָמַר הַכָּתוּב‏
‏"וְזָבַחְתָּ פֶּסַח לַיי אֱלֹהֶיךָ צֹאן וּבָקָר", כְּלוֹמַר שֶׁיָּבִיא עִם הַפֶּסַח קָרְבָּן אַחֵר‏
‏לַחֲגִיגָה, כְּלוֹמַר לְהַרְבּוֹת הַשִּׂמְחָה.‏

‏וּמִשָּׁרְשֵׁי הַמִּצְוָה, הַיְסוֹד הַקָּבוּעַ לָנוּ בְּמִצְוַת עִנְיַן הַפֶּסַח, שֶׁהִיא מִצְוָה וִיסוֹד‏
‏חָזָק בְּתוֹרָתֵנוּ; עַל-כֵּן נִצְטַוִּינוּ לַעֲשׂוֹת יוֹם שְׁחִיטָתוֹ יוֹם שִׂמְחָה, וְאֵין שִׂמְחָה‏
‏שְׁלֵמָה לִבְנֵי-אָדָם רַק בְּרִבּוּי בָּשָׂר; וְזֶהוּ שֶׁנִּצְטַוִּינוּ שֶׁלֹּא לְהוֹתִיר כְּלָל מִכָּל בָּשָׂר‏
‏הַנִּשְׁחָט לִכְבוֹד שִׂמְחַת הַפֶּסַח עַד יוֹם הַשְּׁלִישִׁי אֶלָּא יֵאָכֵל כֻּלּוֹ בְּיוֹמוֹ, לְהַרְבּוֹת בּוֹ‏
‏גִילָה וְשֹׂבַע שְׂמָחוֹת. וְזֶה נֹאמַר בְּכָאן מִלְּבַד הַטַּעַם הַכָּתוּב בְּנוֹתָר בְּסֵדֶר צַו עֲשֵׂה‏
‏ח' בְּסִימָן (קל"ח) [קמ"ג], טַעַם לְשֶׁבַח בְּכָל אִסּוּר הַנּוֹתָרוֹת.‏

‏מִדִּינֵי הַמִּצְוָה, מַה שֶּׁאָמְרוּ זִכְרוֹנָם לִבְרָכָה שֶׁחֲגִיגַת אַרְבָּעָה-עָשָׂר אֵין אָדָם‏
‏יוֹצֵא בָהּ יְדֵי חוֹבָתוֹ מֵחִיּוּב חֲגִיגַת הַמּוֹעֵד, שֶׁהִיא מִצְוַת עֲשֵׂה, כְּמוֹ שֶׁכָּתַבְתִּי‏
‏(ב"כֶסֶף תְּלְוֶה" עֲשֵׂה ו' בְּסִימָן ע"א) [בְּמִשְׁפָּטִים סִי' פ"ח], אֲבָל יוֹצֵא בָהּ יְדֵי‏
‏חוֹבָתוֹ מֵחִיּוּב שִׂמְחַת הַמּוֹעֵד, שֶׁהוּא מִצְוַת עֲשֵׂה גַּם-כֵּן, כְּמוֹ שֶׁכְּתַבְנוּ בְּסֵדֶר‏
‏זֶה—לְפִי שֶׁעִנְיַן הַשִּׂמְחָה חִיּוּב אֵינוֹ אֶלָּא לְהַרְבּוֹת בָּשָׂר כְּדֵי לִשְׂמֹחַ, וַהֲרֵי יֵשׁ‏
‏בָּשָׂר.‏

‏וּמִזֶּה הַטַּעַם אָמְרוּ זִכְרוֹנָם לִבְרָכָה שֶׁיּוֹצְאִין יְדֵי שַׁלְמֵי שִׂמְחָה אֲפִלּוּ בְּנֶדֶר אוֹ‏
‏נְדָבָה שֶׁל שְׁלָמִים, וְאַף-עַל-פִּי שֶׁשְּׁחָטָן קֹדֶם הָרֶגֶל, וּבִלְבַד שֶׁיֹּאכַל מֵהֶם בָּרֶגֶל,‏

§486   1. TB P'saḥim 71a.

2. Since the Passover offering was a lamb ("sheep"), this is the meaning inferred from the extra words, "and cattle"; Sifre, Deuteronomy §129.

3. The paragraph is based on ShM negative precept §118.

4. So TB P'saḥim 109a.

5. Ibid. 70a; MT hilchoth ḥagigah ii 10.

6. As this is a positive precept, our author wrote of it earlier, for in his draft he dealt first, in each sidrah, with all the positive precepts. With the precepts rearranged here (as in virtually all editions) according to their sources (verses) in Scripture, it occurs below.

7. MT ibid. derived from TB Ḥagigah 7b.

8. These offerings are explained in §438, first paragraph.

being the offering brought with the Passover offering to increase the rejoicing; it must rather be eaten entirely within the two days, namely, the fourteenth and fifteenth [of Nissan]. About this it is stated, *nor shall any of the flesh which you sacrifice on the eve of the first day remain all night until morning* (Deuteronomy 16:4); and the traditional interpretation was given on it[1] that the verse refers to the *ḥagigah* (festival offering) brought with the Passover offering — that the time for eating it is until [the end of] two days. About this festival offering Scripture states, *And you shall sacrifice the passover offering to the Lord your God, sheep and cattle* (*ibid.* 2): in other words, one should bring with the Passover offering another offering,[2] for the festive celebration, which is to say, to increase the rejoicing.[3]

At the root of the precept lies the fundamental principle firmly established for us about the *mitzvah* concerning the Passover offering, that it is a commandment and a mighty foundation in our Torah. We were therefore ordered to make the day of its *sheḥittah* (ritual slaying) a day of rejoicing; and there is no complete rejoicing for human beings other than with an abundance of meat.[4] Then this is why we were commanded not to let anything whatever remain until the third day of all the flesh that is ritually slain in honor of the Passover rejoicing, but it should rather all be eaten on its own day, to increase gaiety then, with a full satisfaction of joys. This is what we would say here, apart from the reason written about *nothar*, the eighth positive precept in *sidrah tzav* (§ 143), which gives an explanation of praise for every prohibition on leftover meat of offerings.

Among the laws of the precept there is what the Sages of blessed memory said:[5] that with the *ḥagigah* (festival offering) of the fourteenth [of Nissan] a man does not acquit himself of the obligation of the festival offering for the holy season, which is a positive precept, as I wrote in *sidrah mishpatim* (§ 88); but he does fulfill with it the requirement of rejoicing at the holy season, which is equally a positive precept, as we have written in this *sidrah* (§ 488).[6] For the substance of the obligation of rejoicing (*simḥah*) is nothing other than to have an increased, abundant supply of meat in order to enjoy happiness, and here there is meat.

For this reason, too, the Sages of blessed memory said[7] that the obligation of a *sh'lamim* (peace-offering) for rejoicing *(shalmé simḥah)* can be fulfilled even with a votive or freewill offering of *sh'lamim*,[8] and this even if they are ritually slain before the festival, provided one

שֶׁשַּׁלְמֵי שִׂמְחָה אֵין צָרִיךְ לְשָׁחֲטָן בִּשְׁעַת שִׂמְחָה; וְגַם־כֵּן אֵין אָדָם צָרִיךְ לְשָׁחֲטָן לְשֵׁם שַׁלְמֵי שִׂמְחָה, שֶׁאֵין עִקַּר הַמַּחֲשָׁבָה רַק לְהַרְבּוֹת הַשִּׂמְחָה בְּבָשָׂר, כְּמוֹ שֶׁאָמַרְנוּ. וְיֶתֶר פְּרָטֵי הַמִּצְוָה, מְבֹאָרִין בְּמַסֶּכֶת חֲגִיגָה וּבִמְקוֹמוֹת מִמַּסֶּכֶת פְּסָחִים.

וְנוֹהֶגֶת מִצְוָה זוֹ בִּזְמַן הַבַּיִת, בִּזְכָרִים וּנְקֵבוֹת—שֶׁאֲפִלּוּ הַנָּשִׁים חַיָּבוֹת בְּשַׁלְמֵי שִׂמְחָה, אַף־עַל־פִּי שֶׁהַזְּמַן גְּרָמָא, כְּמוֹ שֶׁהֵן חַיָּבוֹת בִּשְׂבִיעָתָה בּוֹ. וְעוֹבֵר עַל זֶה וְהוֹתִיר כְּלוּם מֵחֲגִיגָה זוֹ לַיּוֹם הַשְּׁלִישִׁי, חַיָּב לִשְׂרֹף אוֹתוֹ בָאֵשׁ, כְּמוֹ שֶׁהַדִּין בְּנוֹתָר; וּלְפִיכָךְ אֵין חִיּוּב מַלְקוֹת בְּלָאו זֶה, אַחַר שֶׁהוּא נִתָּק לַעֲשֵׂה, מִן הַכְּלָל הַיָּדוּעַ לָנוּ בָּזֶה.

[שֶׁלֹּא לְהַקְרִיב קָרְבַּן פֶּסַח בְּבָמַת יָחִיד]

תפז שֶׁנִּמְנַעְנוּ מֵהַקְרִיב שֶׂה הַפֶּסַח בְּבָמַת יָחִיד, וַאֲפִלּוּ בִּשְׁעַת הֶתֵּר בָּמוֹת; וְעִנְיַן הַבָּמוֹת הוּא שֶׁהָיָה כָּל יָחִיד וְיָחִיד מִיִּשְׂרָאֵל שֶׁרְצוֹנוֹ לְהַקְרִיב קָרְבָּן, בּוֹנֶה בִּנְיָן בְּכָל מָקוֹם שֶׁיִּרְצֶה וּמַקְרִיב שָׁם קָרְבְּנוֹתָיו לַשֵּׁם, קֹדֶם בִּנְיַן בֵּית הַבְּחִירָה; וַאֲפִלּוּ בַּזְּמַן הַהוּא, שֶׁהָיָה מֻתָּר לָהֶם לַעֲשׂוֹת כֵּן, דַּוְקָא בִּשְׁאָר הַקָּרְבָּנוֹת, אֲבָל קָרְבַּן פֶּסַח אֵין מַקְרִיבִין אוֹתוֹ לְעוֹלָם אֶלָּא בְּבָמָה רַבִּים, וְהוּא הַמָּקוֹם שֶׁהָיָה הַמִּשְׁכָּן שָׁם; וְעַל זֶה נֶאֱמַר "לֹא תוּכַל לִזְבֹּחַ אֶת הַפֶּסַח בְּאַחַד שְׁעָרֶיךָ"; וְכֵן אָמְרוּ זִכְרוֹנָם לִבְרָכָה בְּסוֹף פֶּרֶק רִאשׁוֹן מִמַּסֶּכֶת מְגִלָּה: אֵין בֵּין בָּמָה גְדוֹלָה לְבָמָה קְטַנָּה אֶלָּא פְּסָחִים.

9. MT *ibid.* 12.

10. So TB Ḥagigah 6b, etc.

11. I.e. it is a positive precept to be observed at a specific time only; and from such precepts women are generally exempt.

12. I.e. where the violation of a negative precept can be rectified by observing a positive precept, no whiplashes are given for it; TB Ḥullin 141a.

§487   1. Literally, when *bamoth* (singular, *bamah*) were permitted; the term denotes originally any high point or structure used for offering up sacrifices. By association or later development it signifies anything like an altar, natural or man-made, which serves this purpose. As recorded in the Oral Torah, such places for private individual worship were permissible at first, until the *mishkan* (Tabernacle) was erected by Moses in the wilderness (Mishnah, *Z'vaḥim* xiv 4). When Joshua led the Israelites across the Jordan into the promised Land, the *mishkan* was erected and left at Gilgal, for the seven years of conquest and seven years of settlement (TB Z'vaḥim 118b); in these fourteen years, individual *bamoth* were again permitted (Mishnah, *ibid.* 5). With the relocation of the *mishkan* at Shiloh (Joshua 18:1), individual *bamoth* became forbidden once more (Mishnah, *ibid.* 6), to become permitted again only after the *mishkan* was destroyed at Shiloh and the *aron* (the holy ark) was taken to Nob and afterward to Gibeon, where it remained, at both sites, a total of fifty-

eats of them on the festival. For *sh'lamim* (peace-offerings) of rejoicing do not need to be ritually slain at the time of the rejoicing.[9] It is likewise not necessary for a man to ritually slay them for the purpose of *sh'lamim* of rejoicing.[7] For the main, core purpose is nothing but to increase the rejoicing by meat, as we said. Further details of the precept are explained in the Talmud tractate *Hagigah*, and in certain places in the tractate *P'sahim*.

This precept is in effect at the time the Temple is extant, for both man and woman: for even women have the obligation of *sh'lamim* of rejoicing,[10] despite the fact that it is caused [brought on] by time,[11] just as they have the obligation of resting from work then [during the festival]. If a person transgressed this and left over anything of this festival offering for the third day, he would be duty-bound to burn it in fire, as the law is for *nothar* (§§ 142–43). For this reason no punishment of whiplashes is incurred over this negative precept, since it is given over to a positive precept for rectification, following the general rule known to us about this.[12]

[NOT TO OFFER UP THE PASSOVER OFFERING
ON AN INDIVIDUAL'S PROVISIONAL ALTAR]

487 that we were forbidden to offer up the Passover lamb on an individual's provisional altar, even at the time when such altars were permitted.[1] In substance, the meaning of the provisional altars is that every individual Israelite whose desire it was to present an offering, would build a structure[2] anywhere he wished, and would present there his offerings to the Eternal Lord, before the construction of the chosen Sanctuary. Yet even at that time, when it was permitted them to do this, [that meant] specifically with other offerings; as to the Passover offering, however, it was never to be offered up anywhere but on the community altar, this being [at] the place where the *mishkan* [Tabernacle] was. About this it is stated, *You may not sacrifice the passover offering within any one of your gates* (Deuteronomy 16:5). And so the Sages of blessed memory said toward the end of the first chapter of the Talmud tractate *M'gillah* (9b): There was no matter of

seven years (TB *ibid.*). With the construction of the Sanctuary in Jerusalem by Solomon, *bamoth* were no longer permitted, ever (Mishnah *ibid.* 8).

2. I.e. a platform shaped like an altar.

מִשָּׁרְשֵׁי הַמִּצְוָה, לִקְבֹּעַ בְּנַפְשֵׁנוּ גֹדֶל עִנְיַן הַפֶּסַח וִיֹקֶר הַמִּצְוָה, מִן הַטַּעַם
שֶׁכָּתַבְתִּי בּוֹ כַּמָּה פְעָמִים; וּבֶאֱמֶת כִּי כְבוֹד הַמִּצְוָה וּפִרְסוּמָהּ יוֹתֵר כְּשֶׁיַּעֲשׂוּהָ
בְּמָקוֹם מְסֻיָּם הַכֹּל יַחַד, וְלֹא כָל יָחִיד וְיָחִיד בִּמְחוֹז חֶפְצוֹ.
דִּינֵי הַמִּצְוָה, בִּמְגִלָּה פֶּרֶק רִאשׁוֹן.

וְנוֹהֵג אִסּוּר זֶה בִּזְמַן הַבַּיִת, כִּי אָז מַקְרִיב קָרְבָּן הַפֶּסַח, בִּזְכָרִים וּנְקֵבוֹת—שֶׁאַף
הֵן חַיָּבוֹת בְּקָרְבַּן הַפֶּסַח, וּכְמוֹ שֶׁכָּתַבְתִּי בְּמִצְוַת הַפֶּסַח ב' בְּסֵדֶר בֹּא בְּסִימָן ה'.
וְאֶפְשָׁר לוֹמַר שֶׁאַף בַּזְּמַן הַזֶּה, הָעוֹבֵר וְהִקְדִּישׁ שֶׂה לְפֶסַח וְהִקְרִיבוֹ בְּבָמַת יָחִיד,
עָבַר עַל לָאו זֶה וְחַיָּב מַלְקוֹת.

3. This precept, given as one of the 613 permanent *mitzvoth* of the Torah, is patently baffling. In his glosses to *Séfer haḤinnuch*, R. Judah Rosanes (author of *Mishneh l'Melech* on MT) writes: "Among those who made listings of the *mitzvoth*, I have seen not one count this among the negative precepts, for this prohibition [was given] specifically during the time when *bamoth* (individual provisional altars) were permissible: Although it was [then] permitted to offer up [sacrifices] on an individual's *bamah*, the Passover offering was admissible nowhere but on the large [communal] *bamah*. After the Sanctuary was built, however, there was no difference between the Passover and other offerings: whoever might offer up any sacrifice whatever outside the Sanctuary, even at the present time, would incur *karéth* (Divine severance of existence)....I have noticed, moreover, the negative precept which he [our author] omitted from Rambam's listing in place of this injunction, namely, *but an outsider shall not eat [of them] for they are holy* (Exodus 29:33), stated in *sidrah tetzaveh*, which is a caution to a *zar* (a non-*kohen*) who would eat of the most-holy offerings; and Rambam included it in his listing of the negative precepts as § (147) [148—in ed. Kafeḥ, 149; see ed. Heller, note 16].... It is a puzzlement how the author, of blessed memory, could omit it."

The answer to the puzzlement lies in the fact that our author patently had a Hebrew translation of a *first version* of ShM, which (like the second version) Rambam wrote in Arabic (it is mentioned by R. Sh'mu'él ibn Tibbon in his introduction to his translation of the second version; and see ShM ed. Heller, pp. 7-8). What we have here is evidently a fairly faithful rendering of what Rambam originally wrote, and later replaced by the negative precept derived from Exodus 29:33—quite certainly on account of the very objection that R. Judah Rosanes raised against this precept in the Ḥinnuch.

Yet in writing this about *bamoth* in his first version of ShM, let it be noted that Rambam was merely following his predecessors: In *Halachoth G'doloth* (8th century CE) there is a preface giving all the Scriptural passages regarded as sources of the 613 *mitzvoth*; and among them is Deuteronomy 16:5 (ed. Warsaw 1874, p. 5b). Some two centuries later, for recital in the *musaf* (additional prayer service) on *Shavu'oth*, R. Sa'adyah Ga'on composed a *piyyut* (liturgical poem) presenting in brief rhymed form all the 613 *mitzvoth*; and this is included as the 174th negative precept (*Kovetz*

difference between the large altar and a small provisional one other than the Passover offerings.³

At the root of the precept lies the purpose to impress firmly on our spirit the greatness of the Passover offering's significance and the immeasurable value of the precept, for the reason that I wrote about it many times. And in truth, the prestige of the precept and its renown would be the greater when it would be sacrificed at a specific place, with everyone together, and not by each and every individual in the haven of his desire.

The laws of the precept are in the tractate *M'gillah*, chapter 1. This prohibition is in effect at the time the Temple stands, for then we will present the Passover offering; [and it applies] to both man and woman, since they [women] too have the obligation of a Passover offering, as I wrote in the precept of this offering in *sidrah bo* (§5). Yet it can be said that at the present time too, if someone transgresses and consecrates a lamb for a Passover offering, and then offers it up on an

Ma'asé Yedé Ge'onim Kadmonim, Berlin 1856, part 2 p. 34, verse 4; *Siddur R. Sa'adyah Ga'on*, Jerusalem 1941, p. 170 line 141, and see note). In about the middle of the 11th century CE the precept was included in other *piyyutim* of this kind: [1] by R. Elijah the Elder (a brother-in-law of R. Hai Ga'on: see *Kovetz, op. cit.* p. 98; *'Otzar haSifruth* III, Cracow 1889–90, p. 128 note 1); [2] by R. Solomon ibn Gabirol ([1]: *Kovetz, op. cit.* p. 65 line 31; [2]: *Minhath Bikkurim*, Livorno 1837 and 1856, p. 40 line 4). Somewhat later it was similarly included by R. Yitzhak b. Re'uven alBargeloni (*Minhath Bikkurim*, p. 24 line 12).

Interestingly enough, in 4973 (1213) Rambam's son, R. Abraham, put into writing (in Arabic) a series of sharp queries and objections to ShM by R. Daniel haBavli, a contemporary Talmudic scholar of Baghdad and Damascus; and to these R. Abraham added his rejoinders (published with a Hebrew translation by R. Ber Goldberg, as *Ma'aséh Nissim*, Paris 1867). In his second query (p. 11) R. Daniel objects to this very precept, precisely on the grounds that it was in effect only at certain times in the far past; and Rambam's son replies (p. 15), "I have no need to respond to your amazing words, other than [to say] that he, of blessed memory, did not list this in the reckoning of the *mitzvoth*, and never thus considered it: neither in ShM nor [in MT] at the beginning of the Book of Knowledge, nor in *hilchoth korban pesah* nor in any of his essays...."

It can hardly be doubted that R. Daniel haBavli was querying negative precept §148 (or 149) in Rambam's first version of ShM, written about 4928 (1168) or soon after (see R. Yosef Kafeh, foreword to voweled ed. ShM, p. 11; to bilingual ed. *Moreh N'vuchim*, pp. 12–13). Having been born in 4946 (1186), Rambam's son was evidently all unaware of this first draft; while in far-off Baghdad or Damascus, R. Daniel—like our author in Barcelona—knew nothing of the second (final) version, in which this precept was gone.

[מִצְוָה לִשְׂמֹחַ בָּרְגָלִים]

תפח לִשְׂמֹחַ בָּרְגָלִים, שֶׁנֶּאֱמַר "וְשָׂמַחְתָּ בְּחַגֶּךָ"; וְהָעִנְיָן הָרִאשׁוֹן הָרָמוּז
בְּשִׂמְחָה זוֹ הוּא שֶׁנַּקְרִיב שְׁלָמִים עַל-כָּל-פָּנִים בְּבֵית הַבְּחִירָה, וּכְעִנְיָן שֶׁכָּתוּב
"וְזָבַחְתָּ שְׁלָמִים", וְהָדָר "וְשָׂמַחְתָּ (בחגך) [לִפְנֵי יְיָ]".

וּבִשְׁבִיל הַקְרָבַת הַשְּׁלָמִים אָמְרוּ זִכְרוֹנָם לִבְרָכָה: נָשִׁים חַיָּבוֹת בְּשִׂמְחָה—לוֹמַר
שֶׁאַף הֵן חַיָּבוֹת לְהָבִיא שַׁלְמֵי שִׂמְחָה; וְעוֹד אָמְרוּ זִכְרוֹנָם לִבְרָכָה: שָׂמַח בְּכָל
מִינֵי שִׂמְחָה, וּבִכְלָל זֶה הוּא אֲכִילַת הַבָּשָׂר וּשְׁתִיַּת הַיַּיִן וְלִלְבֹּשׁ בְּגָדִים חֲדָשִׁים
וְחִלּוּק פֵּרוֹת וּמִינֵי מְתִיקָה לַנְּעָרִים וְלַנָּשִׁים, וְלִשְׂחֹק בִּכְלֵי שִׁיר בַּמִּקְדָּשׁ לְבַד, וְזוֹ
הִיא שִׂמְחַת בֵּית-הַשּׁוֹאֵבָה הַנִּזְכֶּרֶת בַּגְּמָרָא; כָּל זֶה שֶׁזָּכַרְתִּי בִּכְלָל "וְשָׂמַחְתָּ
בְּחַגֶּךָ".

וְאָמְרוּ זִכְרוֹנָם לִבְרָכָה בְּמַסֶּכֶת פְּסָחִים: חַיָּב אָדָם לְשַׂמֵּחַ בָּנָיו וּבְנֵי-בֵיתוֹ
בָּרֶגֶל; וְשָׁם נֶאֱמַר: תַּנְיָא, רַבִּי יְהוּדָה בֶּן בְּתֵירָה אוֹמֵר: בִּזְמַן שֶׁבֵּית-הַמִּקְדָּשׁ קַיָּם
אֵין שִׂמְחָה אֶלָּא בְּבָשָׂר, שֶׁנֶּאֱמַר "וְזָבַחְתָּ שְׁלָמִים" וְגוֹמֵר; עַכְשָׁיו אֵין שִׂמְחָה

4. In MT *hilchoth korban pesaḥ* i 3, Rambam writes, "The Passover offering is not
to be ritually slain anywhere but in the *'azarah* (the general grounds for Israelites at
the Sanctuary). Even at the time *bamoth* were permitted, the Passover [sacrifice]
would not be offered up on an individual's *bamah*; and whoever might offer up the
Passover [sacrifice] on the *bamah* of an individual would receive whiplashes: for it is
stated, *You may not sacrifice the Passover offering within any of your gates*, [and] by word
of the Oral Tradition it was learned that this is a forbiddance to one who would
ritually slay [this offering] at an individual's *bamah* even when *bamoth* were
permissible."

This evidently refers only to the time in the far past when *bamoth* might be used
for other offerings (and so R. Shim‘on b. Tzemaḥ Duran flatly states in his responsa,
Séfer Tashbétz, III § 120). As R. Judah Rosanes writes in his gloss on this precept in
the *Hinnuch*, Rambam made this point about whiplashes "only to emphasize the
law" that the Passover sacrifice must be offered up nowhere but at the Sanctuary.
Our author, however, seeks to justify the presence of this precept among the 613
(which, by Rambam's third root principle in ShM, must have force for all time).
Hence he makes it apply today too, to impose whiplashes for its violation; and as R.
Judah Rosanes points out, it would mean in addition to the penalty of *karéth* (Divine
severance of existence), incurred for the sacrifice of any offering, at any time,
anywhere but at the Sanctuary. Yet there would seem to be no basis for this
postulate by our author.

§488   1. The original reads, "and then it continues *and you shall rejoice on your
festival*"—which would make it an amalgamation of Deuteronomy 27:7 and 16:14.
As MH notes, this is patently an oversight or scribal error, and it has consequently
been emended in accordance with ShM positive precept §54, the evident source of

individual provisional altar, he violates this negative precept, and deserves a punishment of whiplashes.[4]

[THE PRECEPT OF BEING HAPPY
ON THE PILGRIMAGE FESTIVALS]

488 to rejoice on the pilgrimage festivals, as it is stated, *and you shall rejoice on your festival* (Deuteronomy 16:14). Now, the first matter implied by rejoicing is that we should offer up a *sh'lamim* (peace-offering), under all circumstances, at the chosen Sanctuary, in accord with the verse, *And you shall sacrifice peace-offerings and shall eat there,* and then [it continues] *and you shall rejoice before the Lord* (Deuteronomy 27:7).[1]

Now, on account of the offering of *sh'lamim*, the Sages of blessed memory said[2] that women have the obligation of rejoicing, meaning that they too are duty-bound to bring *sh'lamim* of rejoicing. They (of blessed memory) taught further:[3] Rejoice with all kinds of gladness. Included in this is the eating of meat and the drinking of wine, wearing new clothes, distributing fruit and sweet confections to the young and the women, and playing on musical instruments, [this last] in the Sanctuary alone, [done at] the festivity of water-drawing, that is mentioned in the Talmud.[4] All this that I have mentioned is included under the rule that "you shall rejoice on your festival."

The Sages of blessed memory taught further in the tractate *P'sahim* (109a): A man has the duty to make his children and household members happy on a pilgrimage festival. It was stated there, too: We learned in a *baraitha*: R. Judah b. Bathyrah said: At the time that the Sanctuary existed, there was no rejoicing with anything but meat; for it is stated, *And you shall sacrifice peace-offerings*, etc.[5] Now there is no rejoicing with anything other than wine, as it is stated, *and wine*

the first three paragraphs here. Actually, Deuteronomy 27:7 refers not to any festival but to the arrival of the Israelites at Mount Ebal (in the far past) after crossing the Jordan; yet R. Judah b. Bathyrah so cites the verse originally in the Talmud (see paragraph 3, below): for as *tosafoth* explains (TB P'sahim 109a, s.v. *v'zavahta*), this verse specifically links rejoicing with bringing an offering that will provide meat for it.

2. TB Hagigah 6b.

3. Midrash haGadol, Deuteronomy 16:14 (362); Sifre, Deuteronomy § 141.

4. TB Sukkah 51a.

5. See first paragraph, end.

אֶלָּא בְּיַיִן, שֶׁנֶּאֱמַר: וְיַיִן יְשַׂמַּח לְבַב אֱנוֹשׁ; וְאָמְרוּ עוֹד: בַּמֶּה מְשַׂמְּחִים — אֲנָשִׁים בְּרָאוּי לָהֶם, בְּיַיִן, וְנָשִׁים בָּרָאוּי לָהֶן, בִּבְגָדִים נָאִים. וְהִזְהִירַתְנוּ הַתּוֹרָה כְּמוֹ־כֵן לְהַכְנִיס בִּכְלַל הַשִּׂמְחָה הַחֲלוּשִׁים וְהָעֲנִיִּים וְהַגֵּרִים, שֶׁנֶּאֱמַר: אַתָּה ... וְהַלֵּוִי וְהַגֵּר וְהַיָּתוֹם וְהָאַלְמָנָה.

מִשָּׁרְשֵׁי הַמִּצְוָה, לְפִי שֶׁהָאָדָם נָכוֹן עַל עִנְיָן שֶׁיִּצְטָרֵךְ טִבְעוֹ לִשְׂמֹחַ לִפְרָקִים כְּמוֹ שֶׁהוּא צָרִיךְ אֶל הַמָּזוֹן עַל־כָּל־פָּנִים וְאֶל הַמְּנוּחָה וְאֶל הַשֵּׁנָה; וְרָצָה הָאֵל לְזַכּוֹתֵנוּ אֲנַחְנוּ עַמּוֹ וְצֹאן מַרְעִיתוֹ, וְצִוָּנוּ לַעֲשׂוֹת הַשִּׂמְחָה לִשְׁמוֹ לְמַעַן נִזְכֶּה לְפָנָיו בְּכָל מַעֲשֵׂינוּ; וְהִנֵּה קָבַע לָנוּ זְמַנִּים בַּשָּׁנָה לְמוֹעֲדִים, לִזְכֹּר בָּהֶם הַנִּסִּים וְהַטּוֹבוֹת אֲשֶׁר גְּמָלָנוּ, וְאָז בָּעִתִּים הָהֵם צִוָּנוּ לְכַלְכֵּל הַחֹמֶר בְּדָבָר הַשִּׂמְחָה הַצְּרִיכָה אֵלָיו; וְיִמָּצֵא לָנוּ תְרוּפָה גְדוֹלָה בִּהְיוֹת שֶׁבַע הַשְּׂמָחוֹת לִשְׁמוֹ וּלְזִכְרוֹ, כִּי הַמַּחֲשָׁבָה הַזֹּאת תִּהְיֶה לָנוּ גֶדֶר לְבַל נֵצֵא מִדֶּרֶךְ הַיָּשָׁר יוֹתֵר מִדַּאי. וַאֲשֶׁר עִמּוֹ הִתְבּוֹנְנוּת מִבְּלִי הַחֵפֶץ בְּקִטְרוּג יִמְצָא טַעַם בִּדְבָרַי.

מִדִּינֵי הַמִּצְוָה כָּתַבְתִּי קְצָת לְמַעֲלָה; וְיֶתֶר פְּרָטֶיהָ, בְּמַסֶּכֶת חֲגִיגָה וּבִמְקוֹמוֹת מִן הַתַּלְמוּד בְּפִזּוּר.

וְנוֹהֶגֶת מִצְוָה זוֹ לְעִנְיַן הַשִּׂמְחָה, אֲבָל לֹא לְעִנְיַן הַקָּרְבָּן, בְּכָל מָקוֹם וּבְכָל זְמָן, בִּזְכָרִים וּנְקֵבוֹת. וְעוֹבֵר עַל זֶה וְאֵינוֹ מְשַׂמֵּחַ עַצְמוֹ וּבְנֵי־בֵיתוֹ וְהָעֲנִיִּים כְּפִי יְכָלְתּוֹ לְשֵׁם מִצְוַת הָרֶגֶל, בִּטֵּל עֲשֵׂה זֶה; וְעַל הַדֶּרֶךְ הַזֶּה שֶׁזָּכַרְנוּ יֹאמְרוּ זִכְרוֹנָם לִבְרָכָה: וְכָל מַעֲשֶׂיךָ יִהְיוּ לְשֵׁם שָׁמַיִם.

[מִצְוָה לְהֵרָאוֹת בָּרְגָלִים בְּבֵית־הַמִּקְדָּשׁ]
תפט שֶׁנִּצְטַוֵּינוּ לְהֵרָאוֹת כָּל זָכָר בִּירוּשָׁלַיִם בְּבֵית הַבְּחִירָה שָׁלֹשׁ פְּעָמִים

6. TB P'saḥim 109a.
7. The first three paragraphs are based on ShM positive precept §54.
8. In the first three paragraphs.
9. Two paragraphs above.
10. Mishnah, 'Avoth ii 12.

gladdens the heart of man (Psalms 104:15). The Sages taught as well:[6] How is joy given?—for men, with what is suitable for them: with wine; for women, with what is suitable for them: with beautiful clothes. And the Torah likewise adjured us to include in the range of rejoicing the powerless, the poor, and the strangers (converts): as it is stated, *you . . . and the Levite and the stranger and the orphan and the widow* (Deuteronomy 16:14).[7]

At the root of the precept lies the reason that man was constructed in such a manner that his nature needs to rejoice at times, just as he needs food under all circumstances, and rest, and sleep. Now, God wished to make us meritorious—us, *His people, and the flock of His pasture* (Psalms 10:3); and He commanded us to make the rejoicing for His sake, that we might earn merit before Him with all our actions. He set certain times of the year as holy seasons, [for us] to remember during them the miracles and kindnesses that He did for us. Then at those times He commanded us to provide the physical self with the materials for rejoicing that it needs; and the result would be a great healing medicine for us, as the full satisfaction of joys is for His sake and His remembrance. For this thought serves as a bounding fence for us, that we should not swerve from the just and proper path unduly. Whoever possesses the capacity to reflect and understand, without any wish for contentiousness, will find meaningful reason in my words.

As to the laws of the precept, I have written a few above.[8] The rest of its details are in the Talmud tractate *Ḥagigah* and in various places in the Talmud, scattered about.

In regard to rejoicing but not in respect of the animal offering, this precept is in effect everywhere, in every time, for both man and woman. If a person transgresses this and does not bring joy to himself, his household, and the poor, according to his ability, for the sake of the commandment of the pilgrimage festival, he disobeys this positive precept. But regarding this approach that we noted,[9] the Sages of blessed memory would say,[10] Let all your deeds be for the sake of Heaven.

[THE PRECEPT TO APPEAR ON THE PILGRIMAGE
FESTIVALS AT THE SANCTUARY]

489 that we were commanded that every male is to appear in Jerusalem, at the chosen Sanctuary, three set times in the year,

קְבוּעִים בַּשָּׁנָה, וְהֵן פֶּסַח וְשָׁבוּעוֹת וְסֻכּוֹת; וְעַל זֶה נֶאֱמַר: שָׁלוֹשׁ פְּעָמִים בַּשָּׁנָה יֵרָאֶה כָל זְכוּרְךָ אֶת פְּנֵי יי אֱלֹהֶיךָ.

וְעִנְיַן הַמִּצְוָה שֶׁיַּעֲלֶה כָל אָדָם עִם כָּל בֵּן זָכָר שֶׁיֵּשׁ לוֹ שֶׁיּוּכַל לָלֶכֶת לְבַדּוֹ בְּרַגְלָיו לַמִּקְדָּשׁ וְיִתְרָאֶה לְשָׁם; וּמֵחִיּוּב רְאִיָּה זוֹ שֶׁיַּקְרִיב שָׁם קָרְבַּן עוֹלָה, וְזֶה הַקָּרְבָּן נִקְרָא עוֹלַת רְאִיָּה; וְאֵין לְקָרְבָּן זֶה שְׁעוּר, אֲפִלּוּ תוֹר אֶחָד אוֹ גוֹזָל פּוֹטֵר. וּכְבָר כָּתַבְתִּי (בְּכֶסֶף תִּלְוֶה, עֲשֵׂה שִׁשִּׁי) [בְּמִשְׁפָּטִים סי' פ"ח] מַה שֶּׁאָמְרוּ זִכְרוֹנָם לִבְרָכָה: שָׁלֹשׁ מִצְווֹת נִצְטַוּוּ יִשְׂרָאֵל בָּרֶגֶל: חֲגִיגָה, רְאִיָּה, שִׂמְחָה; וְעַל כָּל אַחַת מִשָּׁלֹשׁ מִצְווֹת אֵלּוּ הָיוּ מְבִיאִין קָרְבָּן, וְנִקְרָאִין קָרְבַּן חֲגִיגָה, שַׁלְמֵי שִׂמְחָה, עוֹלַת רְאִיָּה.

מִשָּׁרְשֵׁי הַמִּצְוָה, לְמַעַן יִרְאוּ כָל יִשְׂרָאֵל וְיִתְּנוּ אֶל לִבָּם בִּפְעֻלַּת הַקָּרְבָּן הַמְעוֹרֵר הַלְּבָבוֹת, כִּי כֻלָּם מִקְּטַנָּם וְעַד גְּדוֹלָם חֵלֶק הַשֵּׁם וְנַחֲלָתוֹ, עַם קָדוֹשׁ וְנִבְחָר, נוֹצְרֵי עֵדוּתוֹ, סְגֻלַּת כָּל הָעַמִּים אֲשֶׁר תַּחַת כָּל הַשָּׁמַיִם, לִשְׁמֹר חֻקָּיו וּלְקַיֵּם דָּתוֹ. עַל־כֵּן יוּבְאוּ שָׁלֹשׁ פְּעָמִים בַּשָּׁנָה בֵּית־הַשֵּׁם; וְהוּא כְאָמְרָם עַל דֶּרֶךְ מָשָׁל: הִנְנוּ לָאֵל לַעֲבָדִים, נִכְנָסִים וּבָאִים בְּצֵל קוֹרָתוֹ, וּבְחֶזְקָתוֹ סְמוּכִים לָעַד לְעוֹלָם בְּאַהֲבָתוֹ וּבְיִרְאָתוֹ, זָר לֹא יָבוֹא בְּתוֹכֵנוּ כִּי אֲנַחְנוּ לְבַדֵּנוּ בְנֵי־בֵיתוֹ; וְעִם הַמַּעֲשֶׂה הַזֶּה יִתְעוֹרֵר דַּעְתֵּנוּ וְנַכְנִיס בְּלִבֵּנוּ מוֹרָאוֹ, וְנִקְבַּע בְּרַעְיוֹנֵנוּ אַהֲבָתוֹ, וְנִזְכֶּה לְקַבֵּל חַסְדּוֹ וּבִרְכָתוֹ.

וּבָא עָלֵינוּ הַחִיּוּב הַחִיּוּב בַּזְּכָרִים לְבַד, כִּי הֵם עִקַּר הַבַּיִת, וְהַטַּף וְהַנָּשִׁים טְפֵלָה לָהֶם, וְעִם הַחֲזָקָה בָּהֶם לַעֲבָדִים נַעֲשֵׂית הַחֲזָקָה בְּכָל שֶׁהוּא תַּחַת יָדָם.

וּמִזֶּה הַיְסוֹד נִתְיַחֲדָה לָנוּ מִצְוָה בְּמוֹעֵד שְׁנַת הַשְּׁמִטָּה בְּחַג הַסֻּכּוֹת, לְהַקְהִיל

§489   1. So TB Ḥagigah 2a.
        2. Implied in MT hilchoth ḥagigah i 1.
        3. The first two paragraphs are based on ShM positive precept § 53.

⟨506⟩

namely: Passover, *Shavu'oth* and *Sukkoth*. About this it was stated, *Three times in a year shall all your males appear before the Lord your God* (Deuteronomy 16:16).

The substance of the precept is that every man is to go up, with every son he has who is able to walk alone [unaided] on his feet,[1] to the Sanctuary, and he is to appear there. Part of this obligation of appearing is that he should bring there an *'olah* (burnt) offering, this offering being called "the *'olah* of appearance." There is no minimal requirement for this offering; even one turtledove or fledgling dove acquits a person of the obligation.[2] I wrote previously, in *sidrah mishpatim* (§ 88), that the Sages of blessed memory taught: The Israelites were commanded three precepts at the pilgrimage festival: festive celebration (§ 88), appearance, rejoicing (§ 488); and over each of these three precepts they would bring an offering, called respectively the festival offering, the *sh'lamim* of rejoicing, [and] the *'olah* of appearance.[3]

At the root of the precept lies the reason that all Israelites should see and set their heart to meditate on the execution of the offering, which bestirs the heart. For all of them, from their smallest to their eldest, are the portion of the Lord and His allotment, the holy, chosen people who keep His testimony—the treasure selected from all the peoples under heaven to keep His statutes and maintain His religion. Therefore they were to be brought three times a year to the Temple of the Eternal Lord. It is as though they thus said, by way of simile, "Here we are, to be servants to God, entering and coming under the protective shadow of His roof, relying on His might for ever and ever, in love and fear of Him. Let no stranger enter our midst, for we alone are the members of His household." With this act our mind will be inspired, and we will instill in our heart a reverent fear of Him, and set firmly in our concepts a love of Him, thus meriting to receive His loving-kindness and His blessing.

Now, the obligation was given us for the males alone, since they are the main element of the household, the women and children being supplementary to them; and with confirmation-possession of them [the males, by their obligatory appearance at the Sanctuary,] in the status of [Divine] servants, the confirmation-possession becomes [of firm effect in turn] on whoever is under their hand [their authority].

And so, for this fundamental reason, we were given a particular *mitzvah* at the set holy season of the year of *sh'mittah* (release), at the

שָׁם הָאֲנָשִׁים וְהַנָּשִׁים וְהַטַּף וְהַגֵּרִים, לְפִי שֶׁאוֹתָהּ הַשָּׁנָה מְשֻׁחְרֶרֶת הַכֹּל וּמֻפְקַעַת הַשִּׁעְבּוּד מִכָּל הַחַי מִכָּל בָּשָׂר, לְהָשִׁיב הַכֹּל תַּחַת יַד הָאָדוֹן יי צְבָאוֹת, וְאָז בְּאוֹתָהּ הַשָּׁנָה לֹא תּוֹעִיל חֶזְקָתָם לַאֲשֶׁר תַּחְתֵּיהֶם, שֶׁאֵין שָׁם אֲדָנוּת בָּאָרֶץ בָּעֵת הַהִיא. וְעוֹד יֵשׁ עִמָּנוּ טַעַם אַחֵר בְּמִצְוַת הַקְהֵל, נִכְתַּב אוֹתוֹ בִּמְקוֹמוֹ בְּסֵדֶר (אתם נצבים) [וַיֵּלֶךְ מֹשֶׁה, סִי׳ תקי״ב] בְּעֶזְרַת הַשֵּׁם.

מִדִּינֵי הַמִּצְוָה, מַה שֶּׁאָמְרוּ זִכְרוֹנָם לִבְרָכָה שֶׁעוֹלַת רְאִיָּה וְשַׁלְמֵי (שמחה) [חֲגִיגָה] אֵין דּוֹחִין לֹא שַׁבָּת וְלֹא טֻמְאָה, אֲבָל דּוֹחִין יוֹם־טוֹב, אַף־עַל־פִּי שֶׁאֵין מַקְרִיבִין בְּיוֹם־טוֹב נְדָרִים וּנְדָבוֹת. וְעוֹד כָּתַבְתִּי קְצָת מִדִּינֶיהָ בְּסֵדֶר (אם כֶּסֶף תַּלְוֶה) [מִשְׁפָּטִים] בְּמִצְוַת חֲגִיגָה (עֲשֵׂה ו׳) בְּסִימָן (ע״א) [פ״ח], וְשָׁם כָּתוּב בְּמִי נוֹהֶגֶת וּבְמִי אֵינָהּ נוֹהֶגֶת וְכָל עִנְיָנֶיהָ, כְּמִנְהַג הַסֵּפֶר.

[שֶׁלֹּא לַעֲלוֹת לָרֶגֶל בְּלֹא קָרְבָּן שֶׁיִּהְיֶה עִמָּנוּ, שֶׁנַּקְרִיבוּ שָׁם]

תצ שֶׁלֹּא נַעֲלֶה לְבֵית הַבְּחִירָה בָּרֶגֶל בְּלֹא קָרְבָּן שֶׁנַּקְרִיב שָׁם, וְהוּא הַקָּרְבָּן

4. The expression *b'mo'éd sh'nath ha-sh'mittah* is from Deuteronomy 31:10, which refers to the season of festivals that *follows* a year of *sh'mittah* (the last year of a septennate, a seven-year-cycle, when the fields must lie fallow). Hence this means the *Sukkoth* festival that comes *after* this sabbatical year. Cf. the complete Targum Yerushalmi (Vatican MS) and Pseudo-Jonathan to Deuteronomy 31:10, which render *mo'éd* as *'ishon* (*'ishoné*) or *'ishun* (*'ishuné*), which denotes a set, focused time for a special, particular event (see *'Aruch haShalém*, I p. 319b; J. Levy, *Chaldäisches Wörterbuch über die Targumim*, I p. 72b–73a). In his commentary, R. M'yuhas b. Eliyah understands *b'mo'éd* in the sense of *b'motza'é*, "after the conclusion of."

5. I.e. with the fields lying fallow, humans and farm animals are freed from laboring on the land; and all human beings as well as animals, domestic or not, are free to eat of the produce of the fields (per Leviticus 25:6–7; see Rashi). Thus restraints are lifted.

6. I.e. since the head of the household is not master of his land in the seventh (sabbatical) year, and the wife and children (and bondservants) cannot be required to help with the farming, if such was the usual routine, one can expect a general sense of release from his customary authority and discipline. In the year-long bucolic atmosphere of freedom, there is bound to be a relaxation of the sense of authority associated with the head of the house in matters of religious observance. Hence the need to have his wife and children accompany him to the assembly in Jerusalem, so that religious awe and restraint can be imposed on all, to continue afterward under his authority.

7. In place of this phrase in the Hebrew, *b'ezrath haShem*, the oldest manuscript and the first edition have *bigzérath haShem*, "by the decree of the Eternal Lord" (as He ordains or wills it). This variant occurs in these two early sources in many other

festival of *Sukkoth*,[4] to assemble there the men, women and children, and the strangers (converts). For that year liberates everything and removes the servitude from every living creature, from every being of flesh,[5] to return all and everything under the hand of the sovereign Master, the Lord of Hosts. Then in that year, their [the men's] firm status will not be effective for those beneath [subservient to] them, since there is no name of mastery there, [prevailing] in the land at that time.[6] We have, moreover, another reason for the precept of the assembly; that we will write in its proper place, in *sidrah va-yélech* (§ 512), with the Eternal Lord's help.[7]

Among the laws of the precept, there is what the Sages of blessed memory taught:[8] that the *'olah* of appearance and the *sh'lamim* of festive celebration (*hagigah*) do not thrust aside the Sabbath[9] or ritual uncleanness;[10] but they do thrust aside [the law of] the festival,[11] even though votive and freewill offerings[12] are not offered up on a festival day.[13] In addition, I wrote some of its laws in *sidrah mishpatim* in the precept of the festival offering (§ 88). And it is written there to whom it applies and to whom it does not, along with all its subject-matter, following the custom of the work.

[NOT TO GO UP TO JERUSALEM
FOR A PILGRIMAGE FESTIVAL
WITHOUT AN ANIMAL OFFERING]

490 that we should not go up to the chosen Sanctuary at a pilgrimage festival without an offering that we will present there. This is

instances, in place of the more familiar *b'ezrath haShem*; as a rule, however, it has not been recorded in the notes.

8. MT *hilchoth hagigah* i 8. (The original text that follows reads, "and the *sh'lamim* of *simhah*, rejoicing"; this has been emended in accordance with MT *ibid.*, following MY, which explains well why this original reading must be considered an early copyist's error.)

9. Since the *sh'lamim* of *hagigah* may be brought on other days if for some valid reason it cannot be brought on its proper day, with the Passover sacrifice (TB P'sahim 86b); and the *'olah* of appearance may equally be brought on other days if a good reason exists to block it on its original day (Mishnah, Hagigah i 6; TB 9a).

10. If the entire Jewish populace, or the greater part of it, is in a state of *tum'ah* (defilement), the Passover sacrifice is nevertheless to be offered up; the preventative factor of *tum'ah*, which would force a ritually unclean individual to defer his Passover offering for a month (§ 380), is thrust aside (Mishnah, P'sahim vii 6; TB

שֶׁפֵּרַשְׁנוּ לְמַעְלָה בְּסֵדֶר זֶה, עָשָׂה אַחֲרוֹן [סִי׳ תפ״ט], שֶׁנִּקְרָא עוֹלַת רְאִיָּה; וְעַל
זֶה נֶאֱמַר ״וְלֹא (יראו פני) [יֵרָאֶה אֶת פְּנֵי יי] רֵיקָם״ — פֵּרוּשׁ ״פְּנֵי״ כְּמוֹ לְפָנָי.
וְשָׁם כָּתַבְתִּי מִשָּׁרְשֵׁי הַמִּצְוָה וְכָל עִנְיָנָהּ. וְזֹאת הָאַזְהָרָה אֵינָהּ נוֹהֶגֶת בִּנְקֵבוֹת,
כְּמוֹ שֶׁאֵין מִצְוַת הָעֲשֵׂה הַבָּאָה עַל זֶה נוֹהֶגֶת בָּהֶן.

79a). For the *sh'lamim* of *ḥagigah* (rejoicing), however, the block of *tum'ah* is not thrust aside (Mishnah *ibid.* vi 3; TB 69b), since it can be brought on another day as well, if necessary (TB *ibid.* 76b); and the same applies to the *'olah* of appearance (see note 9).

11. That work not needed for the preparation of human food is forbidden then.

12. Explained in §438, note 1.

13. So TB Bétzah 19a.

§490   1. By an apparent oversight the original has the similar verse of Exodus 23:15, rather than this passage in *sidrah re'éh*.

2. For our proof-text states earlier, *Three times in the year shall all your males appear*, etc.